Fodor's 2012

HAWAI'I

D1021008

Fodor's Travel Publications New York Toronto London Sydney Auckland
www.fodors.com

Eugene Fodor: The Spy Who Loved Travel

As Fodor's celebrates our 75th anniversary, we are honoring the colorful and adventurous life of Eugene Fodor, who revolutionized guidebook publishing in 1936 with his first book, *On the Continent, The Entertaining Travel Annual.*

Eugene Fodor's life seemed to leap off the pages of a great spy novel. Born in Hungary, he spoke six languages and graduated from the Sorbonne and the London School of Economics. During World War II he joined the Office of Strategic Services, the budding spy agency for the United States. He commanded the team that went behind enemy lines to liberate Prague, and recommended to Generals Eisenhower, Bradley, and Patton that Allied troops move to the capital city. After the war, Fodor worked as a spy in Austria, posing as a U.S. diplomat.

In 1949 Eugene Fodor—with the help of the CIA—established Fodor's Modern Guides. He was passionate about travel and wanted to bring his insider's knowledge of Europe to a new generation of sophisticated Americans who wanted to explore and seek out experiences beyond their borders. Among his innovations were annual updates, consulting local experts, and including cultural and historical perspectives and an emphasis on people—not just sites. As Fodor described it, "The main interest and enjoyment of foreign travel lies not only in 'the sites,' . . . but in contact with people whose customs, habits, and general outlook are different from your own."

Eugene Fodor died in 1991, but his legacy, Fodor's Travel, continues. It is now one of the world's largest and most trusted brands in travel information, covering more than 600 destinations worldwide in guidebooks, on Fodors.com, and in ebooks and iPhone apps. Technology and the accessibility of travel may be changing, but Eugene Fodor's unique storytelling skills and reporting style are behind every word of today's Fodor's guides.

Our editors and writers continue to embrace Eugene Fodor's vision of building personal relationships through travel. We invite you to join the Fodor's community at fodors.com/community and share your experiences with like-minded travelers. Tell us when we're right. Tell us when we're wrong. And share fantastic travel secrets that aren't yet in Fodor's. Together, we will continue to deepen our understanding of our world.

Happy 75th Anniversary, Fodor's! Here's to many more.

Tim Jarrell, Publisher

FODOR'S HAWAI'I 2012

Editors: Jess Moss, Linda Cabasin, Erica Duecy, Carolyn Galgano
Writers: Melissa Chang, Nathan Eagle, Eliza Escaño-Vasquez, Bonnie Friedman, Trina Kudlacek, Michael Levine, Chad Pata, Heidi Pool, Charles E. Roessler, Joana Varawa, Katie Young Yamanaka

Production Editor: Evangelos Vasilakis
Maps & Illustrations: David Lindroth and Mark Stroud, *cartographers;* Bob Blake, Rebecca Baer, *map editors;* William Wu, *information graphics*
Design: Fabrizio La Rocca, *creative director;* Guido Caroti, Siobhan O'Hare, *art directors;* Tina Malaney, Nora Rosansky, Chie Ushio, *designers;* Melanie Marin, *senior picture editor*
Cover Photo: (Bird of Paradise, Big Island) Wasmac/eStock Photo
Production Manager: Angela L. McLean

COPYRIGHT

ISBN 978-0-679-00927-6

ISSN 0071-6421

SPECIAL SALES

This book is available at special discounts for bulk purchases for sales promotions or premiums. Special editions, including personalized covers, excerpts of existing books, and corporate imprints, can be created in large quantities for special needs. For more information, write to Special Markets/Premium Sales, 1745 Broadway, MD 6-2, New York, NY 10019, or e-mail specialmarkets@randomhouse.com.

AN IMPORTANT TIP & AN INVITATION

Although all prices, opening times, and other details in this book are based on information supplied to us at press time, changes occur all the time in the travel world, and Fodor's cannot accept responsibility for facts that become outdated or for inadvertent errors or omissions. So **always confirm information when it matters**, especially if you're making a detour to visit a specific place. Your experiences—positive and negative—matter to us. If we have missed or misstated something, **please write to us**. Share your opinion instantly through our online feedback center at fodors.com/contact-us.

PRINTED IN CHINA

10 9 8 7 6 5 4 3 2 1

CONTENTS

Fodor's Features

ABOUT
THIS BOOK

Our Ratings

At Fodor's, we spend considerable time choosing the best places in a destination so you don't have to. By default, anything we recommend in this book is worth visiting. But some sights, properties, and experiences are so great that we've recognized them with additional accolades. Orange **Fodor's Choice** stars indicate our top recommendations; black stars highlight places we deem **Highly Recommended**; and **Best Bets** call attention to top properties in various categories. Disagree with any of our choices? Care to nominate a new place? Visit our feedback center at www.fodors.com/feedback.

TripAdvisor ◎◎

Fodor's partnership with TripAdvisor helps to ensure that our hotel selections are timely and relevant, taking into account the latest customer feedback about each property. Our team of expert writers selects what we believe will be the top choices for lodging in a destination. Then, those choices are reinforced by TripAdvisor reviews, so only the best properties make the cut.

Hotels

Hotels have private bath, phone, TV, and air-conditioning, and do not offer meals unless we specify that in the review. We always list facilities but not whether you'll be charged an extra fee to use them.

Restaurants

Unless we state otherwise, restaurants are open for lunch and dinner daily. We mention dress only when there's a specific requirement and reservations only when they're essential or not accepted—it's always best to book ahead.

Credit Cards

We assume that restaurants and hotels accept credit cards. If not, we'll note it in the review.

Budget Well

Hotel and restaurant price categories from ¢ to $$$$ are defined in the opening pages of the respective chapters. For attractions, we always give standard adult admission fees; reductions are usually available for children, students, and senior citizens.

Listings
- ★ Fodor's Choice
- ★ Highly recommended
- ⊠ Physical address
- ✦ Directions or Map coordinates
- ⌂ Mailing address
- ☎ Telephone
- 🖷 Fax
- ⊕ On the Web
- ✎ E-mail
- ☜ Admission fee
- ⊙ Open/closed times
- Ⓜ Metro stations
- ▭ No credit cards

Hotels & Restaurants
- 🏨 Hotel
- ⇷ Number of rooms
- ⚇ Facilities
- ⏐○⏐ Meal plans
- ✕ Restaurant
- ⚇ Reservations
- 🏛 Dress code
- ⤬ Smoking

Outdoors
- 🏌 Golf
- ⚑ Camping

Other
- ☪ Family-friendly
- ⇨ See also
- ⊠ Branch address
- ☞ Take note

Experience
Hawai'i

WHAT'S WHERE

Numbers correspond to chapters.

2 O'ahu. Honolulu and Waikīkī are here—and it's a great big lū'au. It's got hot restaurants and lively nightlife as well as gorgeous white-sand beaches, knife-edged mountain ranges, and cultural sites including Pearl Harbor.

3 Maui. The phrase "Maui nō ka 'oi" means Maui is the best, the most, the tops. There's good reason for the superlatives. It's the most diversified Hawaiian island, perfect for families with divergent interests.

4 Big Island of Hawai'i. It has two faces, watched over by snowcapped Mauna Kea and steaming Mauna Loa. The Kona side has parched, lava-strewn lowlands, and eastern Hilo is characterized by lush flower farms and waterfalls.

5 Kaua'i. This is the "Garden Isle," and it's where you'll find the lush, green folding sea cliffs of Nāpali Coast, the colorful and awesome Waimea Canyon, and more beaches per mile of coastline than any other Hawaiian island.

6 Moloka'i. It's the least changed, most laid-back of the Islands. Come here to experience riding a mule down a cliff to Kalaupapa Peninsula; the Kamakou Preserve, a 2,774-acre wildlife refuge; and plenty of peace and quiet.

7 Lāna'i. For years there was nothing here except for pineapples and red-dirt roads. Today it attracts the well-heeled in search of privacy, with a few upscale resorts, archery and shooting, four-wheel-drive excursions, and superb scuba diving.

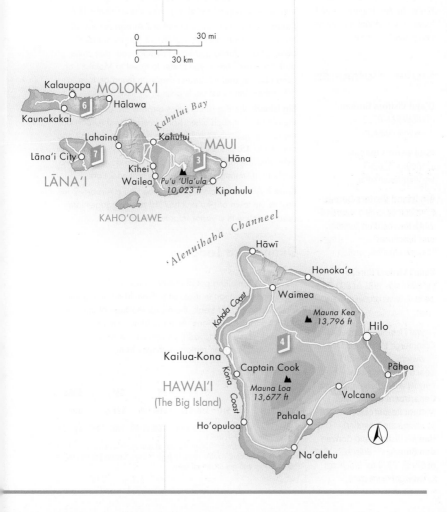

0   30 mi

0   30 km

Kalaupapa

MOLOKA'I

6

Hālawa

Kaunakakai

Kahului Bay

Lahaina

Kahului

MAUI

Lāna'i City

7

Kīhei

3

Hāna

LĀNA'I

Wailea

Pu'u 'Ula'ula
10,023 ft

Kipahulu

KAHO'OLAWE

'Alenuihaha Channeel

Hāwī

Honoka'a

Waimea

Kohala Coast

Mauna Kea
13,796 ft

Hilo

Kailua-Kona

4

Pāhoa

Captain Cook

Kona Coast

HAWAI'I
(The Big Island)

Mauna Loa
13,677 ft

Volcano

Pahala

Ho'opuloa

Na'alehu

HAWAI'I PLANNER

When You Arrive

Honolulu's International Airport is the main stopover for most domestic and international flights, but all Hawai'i's major Islands have their own airports. Flights to the Neighbor Islands leave from Honolulu almost every half hour daily.

Visitor Information

O'ahu Visitors Bureau (☎ 808/524–0722 www.visit-oahu.com).

Maui Visitors Bureau (☎ 800/525–6284 www.visitmaui.com).

Big Island Visitors Bureau (☎ 808/961–5797, 800/648–2441 for vacation planner and brochures ⊕ www.bigisland.org).

Kaua'i Visitors Bureau (☎ 808/245–3971 or 800/262–1400 ⊕ www.kauaidiscovery.com).

Hawai'i Island Chamber of Commerce (☎ 808/935–7178 ⊕ www.hicc.biz). **Hawai'i Beach Safety** (⊕ www.hawaiibeachsafety.org). **Hawai'i Department of Land and Natural Resources** (⊕ www.state.hi.us/dlnr). **Hawai'i Visitors and Convention Bureau** (☎ 808/923–1811, 800/464–2924 for brochures ⊕ www.gohawaii.com).

Getting Here

O'ahu: Honolulu International Airport is 20 minutes (40 during rush hour) from Waikīkī. Car rental is across the street from baggage claim. An inefficient airport taxi system requires you to line up to a taxi wrangler who radios for cars (about $30 to Waikīkī). Other options: TheBus ($2, one lap-size bag allowed) or public airport shuttle ($9).

Maui: Most visitors arrive at Kahului Airport in Central Maui. For trips to Moloka'i or Lāna'i, ferries are available to both islands and have room for your golf clubs and mountain bike. If you prefer to travel to Moloka'i or Lāna'i by air, and you're not averse to flying on four- to 12-seaters, your best bet is a small air taxi.

Big Island: The Big Island's two airports are directly across the island from each other. Kona International Airport on the west side is about a 10-minute drive from Kailua-Kona and 30 to 45 minutes from the Kohala Coast. On the east side, Hilo International Airport, 2 mi from downtown Hilo, is about 40 minutes from Volcanoes National Park.

Kaua'i: All commercial flights use the Līhu'e Airport, 2 mi east of the town of Līhu'e. It has just two baggage-claim areas, each with a visitor information center.

Dining and Lodging

Hawai'i is a melting pot of cultures, and nowhere is this more apparent than in its cuisine. From lū'au and "plate lunch" to sushi and steak, there's no shortage of interesting flavors and presentations. As for lodging, there are several top-notch resorts in Hawai'i, as well as a wide variety of condos and vacation rentals to choose from.

WHAT IT COSTS					
	¢	$	$$	$$$	$$$$
Restaurants	under $10	$10–$17	$18–$26	$27–$35	over $35
Hotels		under $100	$100–$180	$181–$260	$261–$340	over $340

Restaurant prices are for a main course at dinner. Hotel prices are for two people in a standard double room in high season. Condo price categories reflect studio and one-bedroom rates.

Getting Around

O'ahu: If you plan on getting outside Waikīkī and Honolulu, renting a car is a must. Heavy traffic toward downtown Honolulu begins as early as 6:30 am and lasts until 9 am. In the afternoon, expect traffic departing downtown to back up beginning around 3 pm until approximately 7 pm.

Maui: Driving from one point on Maui to another can take longer than the mileage indicates. It's 52 mi from Kahului Airport to Hāna, but the drive will take you about three hours. As for driving to Haleakalā, the 38-mi drive from sea level to the summit will take you about two hours. Traffic on Maui's roads can be heavy, especially during the rush hours of 6 am to 8:30 am and 3:30 pm to 6:30 pm.

Big Island: It's a good idea to rent a car with four-wheel drive, such as a Jeep, on the Big Island. Some of the island's best sights (and most beautiful beaches) are at the end of rough or unpaved roads. Most agencies make you sign an agreement that you won't drive on the path to Mauna Kea and its observatories. Keep in mind that, while a good portion of the Saddle Road is smoothly paved, it is also remote, winding, and bumpy in certain areas, unlighted, and bereft of gas stations.

Kaua'i: A rental car is the best way to get to your hotel, though taxis and some hotel shuttles are available. From the airport it will take you about 15 to 25 minutes to drive to Wailua or Kapa'a, 30 to 40 minutes to reach Po'ipū, and 45 minutes to an hour to get to Princeville or Hanalei. Kaua'i roads are subject to some pretty heavy traffic, especially going through Kapa'a and Līhu'e.

Island Driving Times

O'ahu: Waikīkī to Downtown Honolulu	4 mi/10 min
O'ahu: Waikīkī to Hololulu Int'l Airport	12 mi/25 min
O'ahu: Waikīkī to Hale'iwa	34 mi/45 min
Maui: Kahului to Wailea	17 mi/30 min
Maui: Kahului to Kā'anapali	25 mi/45 min
Maui: Kahului to Kapalua	36 mi/1 hr 15 min
Big Island: Kailua-Kona to Kohala Coast	32 mi/50 min
Big Island: Kailua-Kona to Hilo	86 mi/2.5 hr
Kaua'i: Hanalei to Līhu'e	32 mi/1 hr 5 min
Kaua'i: Līhu'e to Po'ipū	13 mi/25 min

Hawai'i's Best Festivals and Events

February: Chinese New Year; Lahania, Maui, and in Chinatown on O'ahu. Waimea Town Celebration, Waimea, Kaua'i.

March: Kona Chocolate Festival, Kona, Big Island. Prince Kuhio Day Celebration, Līhu'e, Kaua'i.

April: Merrie Monarch Hula Festival, Hilo, Big Island.

May: World Fire-Knife Dance Championships & Samoa Festival, Polynesian Cultural Center, Laie, O'ahu.

June: Hawaiian Slack-Key Guitar Festival, Kahului, Maui. King Kamehameha Hula Competition, Honolulu, O'ahu; Flavors of Honolulu, Honolulu, O'ahu.

July: Fourth of July celebrations off Magic Island, Kailua Beach, and at Pearl Harbor's Schofield Barracks, O'ahu. In Honolulu, displays light up the skies.

September: A Taste of Lahaina, Lahaina, Maui.

October: Ironman Triathalon World Championship, Kailua-Kona, Big Island. Halloween Festivities in Lahaina, Maui and Chinatown and Waikīkī on O'ahu.

November: Kona Coffee Cultural Festival, Kona, Big Island. Triple Crown of Surfing, North Shore, O'ahu.

HAWAI'I TODAY

Hawaiian culture and tradition here have experienced a renaissance over the last few decades. There's a real effort to revive traditions and to respect history as the Islands go through major changes. New developments often have a Hawaiian cultural expert on staff to ensure cultural sensitivity and to educate newcomers.

Nonetheless, development remains a huge issue for all Islanders—land prices are skyrocketing, putting many areas out of reach for the native population. Traffic is becoming a problem on roads that were not designed to accommodate all the new drivers, and the Islands' limited natural resources are being seriously tapped. The government, though sluggish to respond at first, is trying to make development in Hawai'i as sustainable as possible.

Sustainability

Although sustainability is an effective buzzword and authentic direction for the Islands' dining establishments, 90% of Hawai'i's food and energy is imported.

Most of the land was used for monocropping of pineapple or sugarcane, both of which have all but vanished. Sugarcane is now produced in only two plants on Kaua'i and Maui, while pineapple production has dropped precipitously. Dole, once the largest pineapple company in Hawai'i, closed its plants in 1991, and after 90 years, Del Monte stopped pineapple production in 2008. The next year, Maui Land and Pineapple Company also ceased its Maui Gold pineapple operation, although in early 2010 a group of executives took over one third of the land and created a new company. Low cost of labor and transportation from Latin American and Southeast Asian pineapple producers are factors contributing to the industry's demise in Hawai'i. Although

this proves daunting, it also sets the stage for great agricultural change to be explored.

Back-to-Basics Agriculture

Emulating how the Hawaiian ancestors lived and returning to their simple ways of growing and sharing a variety of foods has become a statewide initiative. Hawai'i has the natural conditions and talent to produce far more diversity in agriculture than it currently does.

The seed of this movement thrives through various farmers' markets and partnerships between restaurants and local farmers. Localized efforts such as the Hawai'i Farm Bureau Federation are collectively leading the organic and sustainable agricultural renaissance. From home-cooked meals to casual plate lunches to fine-dining cuisine, these sustainable trailblazers enrich the culinary tapestry of Hawai'i and uplift the Islands' overall quality of life.

Tourism and the Economy

The over-$10 billion tourism industry represents a third of Hawai'i's state income. Naturally, this dependency causes economic hardship as the financial meltdown of recent years affects tourists' ability to visit and spend.

One way the industry has changed has been to adopt more eco-conscious practices, as many Hawaiians feel that development shouldn't happen without regard for impact to local communities and their natural environment.

Belief that an industry based on the Hawaiians' *aloha* should protect, promote, and empower local culture and provide more entrepreneurial opportunities for local people has become more important to tourism businesses. More companies are incorporating authentic

Hawaiiana in their programs and aim not only to provide a commercially viable tour but also to ensure that the visitor leaves feeling connected to his or her host.

The concept of *kuleana*, a word for both privilege and responsibility, is upheld. Having the privilege to live in such a sublime place comes with the responsibility to protect it.

Sovereignty

Political issues of sovereignty continue to divide Native Hawaiians, who have formed myriad organizations, each operating with a separate agenda and lacking one collectively defined goal. Ranging from achieving complete independence to solidifying a nation within a nation, existing sovereignty models remain fractured and their future unresolved.

The introduction of the Native Hawaiian Government Reorganization Act of 2009 attempts to set up a legal framework in which Native Hawaiians can attain federal recognition and coexist as a self-governed entity. Also known as the Akaka Bill after Senator Daniel Akaka of Hawai'i, this pending bill has been presented before Congress and is still awaiting a vote at the time of this writing.

Rise of Hawaiian Pride

After Hawai'i received statehood in 1959, a process of Americanization transpired. Traditions were duly silenced in the name of citizenship. Teaching Hawaiian language was banned from schools and children were distanced from their local customs.

But Hawaiians are resilient people, and with the rise of the civil rights movement they began to reflect on their own national identity, bringing an astonishing renaissance of the Hawaiian culture to fruition.

The people rediscovered language, the hula, the chant or *mele*, and even the traditional Polynesian art of canoe building and wayfinding (navigation by the stars without use of instruments). This cultural resurrection is now firmly established in today's Hawaiian culture, with a palpable pride that exudes from Hawaiians young and old.

The election of President Barack Obama has definitely done its share of fueling not only Hawaiian pride but also ubiquitous hope for a better future. The president's strong connection and commitment to Hawaiian values of diversity, spirituality, family, and conservation have restored confidence that Hawai'i can inspire a more peaceful, tolerant, and environmentally conscious world.

HAWAI'I TOP EXPERIENCES

Hike Maui's Haleakalā

(A) Trek down into Maui's Haleakalā National Park's massive bowl and see proof, at this dormant volcano, of how very powerful the earth's exhalations can be. You won't see landscape like this anywhere, outside of visiting the moon. The barren terrain is deceptive, however—many of the world's rarest plants, birds, and insects live here.

Surf at Waikīkī Beach on O'ahu

(B) Waikīkī, with its well-shaped but diminutive waves, remains the perfect spot for grommets (surfing newbies), though surf schools operate at beaches (and many hotels) around the island. Most companies guarantee at least one standing ride in the course of a lesson. And catching your first wave? We guarantee you'll never forget it.

Visit O'ahu's Pearl Harbor

(C) This top Honolulu site is not to be missed—spend the better part of a day touring the *Missouri*, the *Arizona* Memorial, and, if you have time, the *Bowfin*.

Hit the Road to Hāna on Maui

(D) Spectacular views of waterfalls, lush forests, and the sparkling ocean are part of the pleasure of the twisting drive along the North Shore to tiny, timeless Hāna in East Maui. The journey is the destination, but once you arrive, kick back and relax.

Enjoy O'ahu After Hours

(E) Yes, you can have an umbrella drink at sunset. But in the multicultural metropolis of Honolulu, there's so much more to it than that. Sip a glass of wine and listen to jazz at The Dragon Upstairs in Chinatown, join the beach-and-beer gang at Duke's Canoe Club, or head to Zanzabar, where DJs spin hip-hop and techno.

Whale-watch in Maui

(F) Maui is the cradle for hundreds of humpback whales that return every year to frolic in the warm waters and give birth. Watch a mama whale teach her one-ton calf how to tail-wave. You can eavesdrop on them, too: book a tour boat with a hydrophone or just plunk your head underwater to hear the strange squeaks, groans, and chortles of the cetaceans.

See a Lava Show on the Big Island

(G) At Hawai'i Volcanoes National Park, watch as fiery red lava pours, steaming, into the ocean; stare in awe at nighttime lava fireworks; and hike across the floor of a crater.

Watch a Lū'au

(H) There are lū'au that are spectacle performances and those that lean toward the more authentic. Both have their merits, depending on the experience you're after. Two that are worthy of mention are Old Lahaina's in Maui and at the Polynesian Cultural Center on O'ahu.

Catch the Views at Kaua'i's Waimea Canyon

(I) From its start in the west Kaua'i town of Waimea to the road's end some 20 uphill miles later at Pu'u O Kila Lookout, you'll pass through several microclimates—from hot, desertlike conditions at sea level to the cool, deciduous forest of Kōke'ē—and navigate through the traditional Hawaiian system of land division called *ahupua'a*.

Explore Kaua'i's Nāpali Coast

(J) Experiencing Kaua'i's emerald green Nāpali Coast is a must-do. You can see these awesome cliffs on the northwest side of the island by boat, helicopter, or by hiking the Kalalau Trail. Whichever you pick, chances are you won't be disappointed.

THE HAWAIIAN ISLANDS

O'ahu. The state's capital, Honolulu, is on O'ahu; this is the center of Hawai'i's economy and by far the most populated island in the chain—907,000 residents adds up to 71% of the state's population. At 597 square mi O'ahu is the third largest island in the chain; the majority of residents live in or around Honolulu, so the rest of the island still fits neatly into the tropical, untouched vision of Hawai'i. Situated southeast of Kaua'i and northwest of Maui, O'ahu is a central location for island hopping. Pearl Harbor, iconic Waikīkī Beach, and surfing contests on the legendary North Shore are all here.

Maui. The second largest island in the chain, Maui is northwest of the Big Island and close enough to be visible from its beaches on a clear day. The island's 729 square mi are home to only 145,000 people but host nearly 2 million tourists every year. With its restaurants and lively nightlife, Maui is the only island that competes with O'ahu in terms of entertainment; its charm lies in the fact that although entertainment is available, Maui's towns still feel like island villages compared to the heaving modern city of Honolulu.

Hawai'i (The Big Island). The Big Island has the second largest population of the Islands (177,000) but feels sparsely settled due to its size. It's 4,038 square mi and growing—all the other Islands could fit onto the Big Island and there would still be room left over. The southernmost island in the chain (slightly southeast of Maui), the Big Island is home to Kīlauea, the most active volcano on the planet. It percolates within Volcanoes National Park, which draws nearly 3 million visitors every year.

Kaua'i. The northernmost island in the chain (northwest of O'ahu), Kaua'i is, at approximately 622 square mi, the fourth largest of all the Islands and the least populated of the larger Islands, with just under 64,000 residents. Known as the Garden Isle, this island is home to lush botanical gardens as well as the stunning Nāpali Coast and Waimea Canyon. The island is a favorite with honeymooners and others wanting to get away from it all—lush and peaceful, it's the perfect escape from the modern world.

Moloka'i. North of Lāna'i and Maui, and east of O'ahu, Moloka'i is Hawai'i's fifth-largest island, encompassing 260 square mi. On a clear night, the lights of Honolulu are visible from Moloka'i's western shore. Moloka'i is sparsely populated, with just under 7,400 residents, the majority of whom are Native Hawaiians. Most of the island's 85,000 annual visitors travel from Maui or O'ahu to spend the day exploring its beaches, cliffs, and former leper colony on Kalaupapa Peninsula.

Lāna'i. Lying just off Maui's western coast, Lāna'i looks nothing like its sister Islands, with pine trees and deserts in place of palm trees and beaches. Still, the tiny 140-square-mi island is home to nearly 3,000 residents and draws an average of 90,000 visitors each year to two resorts (one in the mountains and one at the shore), both operated by Four Seasons.

Hawai'i's Geology

The Hawaiian Islands comprise more than just the islands inhabited and visited by humans. A total of 19 islands and atolls constitute the State of Hawai'i, with a total landmass of 6,423.4 square mi.

The Islands are actually exposed peaks of a submersed mountain range called the Hawaiian Ridge-Emperor Seamounts chain. The range was formed as the Pacific plate moves very slowly (around 32 mi

every million years—or about as much as your fingernails grow in one year) over a hot spot in the Earth's mantle. Because the plate moves northwestwardly, the Islands in the northwest portion of the archipelago (chain) are older, which is also why they're smaller—they have been eroding longer and have actually sunk back into the sea floor.

The Big Island is the youngest, and thus the largest, island in the chain. It is built from five different volcanoes, including Mauna Loa, which is the largest mountain on the planet (when measured from the bottom of the sea floor). Mauna Loa and Kīlauea are the only Hawaiian volcanoes still erupting with any sort of frequency. Mauna Loa last erupted in 1984. Kīlauea has been continuously erupting since 1983.

Mauna Kea (Big Island), Hualālai (Big Island), and Haleakalā (Maui) are all in what's called the post-shield-building stage of volcanic development—eruptions decrease steadily for up to a million years before ceasing entirely. Kohala (Big Island), Lāna'i (Lāna'i), and Wai'anae (O'ahu) are considered extinct volcanoes, in the erosional stage of development; Ko'olau (O'ahu) and West Maui (Maui) volcanoes are extinct volcanoes in the rejuvenation stage—after lying dormant for hundreds of thousands of years, they began erupting again, but only once every several thousand years.

There is currently an active undersea volcano to the south and east of the Big Island called Lo'ihi that has been erupting regularly. If it continues its current pattern, it should breach the ocean's surface in tens of thousands of years.

Hawai'i's Flora and Fauna

More than 90% of native Hawaiian flora and fauna are endemic (they evolved into unique species here), like the koa tree and the yellow hibiscus. Long-dormant volcanic craters are perfect hiding places for rare native plants. The silversword, a rare cousin of the sunflower, grows on Hawai'i's three tallest peaks: Haleakalā, Mauna Kea, and Mauna Loa, and nowhere else on Earth. 'Ōhi'a trees—thought to be the favorite of Pele, the volcano goddess—bury their roots in fields of once-molten lava and sprout ruby pom-pom-like lehua blossoms. The deep yellow petals of 'ilima (once reserved for royalty) are tiny discs, which make the most elegant lei.

But most of the plants you see while walking around, however, aren't Hawaiian at all and came from Tahitian, Samoan, or European visitors. Plumeria is ubiquitous; alien orchids run rampant on the Big Island; bright orange relatives of the 'ilima light up the mountains of O'ahu. Though these flowers are not native, they give the Hawaiian lei their color and fragrance.

Hawai'i's state bird, the nēnē goose, is making a comeback from its former endangered status. It roams freely in parts of Maui, Kaua'i, and the Big Island. Rare Hawaiian monk seals breed in the northwestern Islands. With only 1,500 left in the wild, you probably won't catch many lounging on the beaches, though they have been spotted on the shores of Kaua'i in recent years. Spinner dolphins and sea turtles can be found off the coast of all the Islands; and every year from November to April, the humpback whales migrate past Hawai'i in droves.

CHOOSING YOUR ISLANDS

You've decided to go to Hawaii, but should you stay put and relax on one island or try sampling more than one? If all you have is a week, it is probably best to stick to just one island. You traveled all this way, why spend your precious vacation time at car rental counters, hotel check-in desks and airports? But, with seven or more nights, a little island hopping is a great way to experience the diversity of sights and experiences that are packed into this small state. Here are five of our favorite island-pairing itineraries for every type of trip.

Family Travel: O'ahu and Maui

If you're traveling with children, O'ahu and Maui have the most options.

Why O'ahu: O'ahu is by far the most kid-friendly island. For sea life, visit the Wakīkī Aquarium and Sea Life Park or let the little ones get up close and personal with fish at Hanauma Bay. At Pearl Harbor you can visit an aircraft carrier or, if the kids are at least four, a World War II submarine. Then there's the Honolulu Zoo and a slippery slide–filled water park, not to mention some very family-friendly and safe beaches. *Plan to spend 4 nights.*

Why Maui: Whales! Though you can see whales from any island between November and April, there's no better place than Maui. If your visit doesn't fall during peak whale-watching season, visit the Whalers Village Museum, the Hawaiian Islands Humpback Whale National Marine Sanctuary or the Maui Ocean Center (to get an up close look at some of Hawai'i's smaller sea creatures). Away from the water, there's the Sugar Cane Train. *Plan to spend at least 3 nights.*

Romance: Maui and Kaua'i

If you're getting away for seclusion, romantic walks along the beach, and the pampering at world-class spas, consider Maui and Kaua'i.

Why Maui: You'll find waterfalls, salt-and-pepper sand beaches, and incredible views as you follow the twisting turning Road to Hāna. The luxury resorts in Wailea or Kā'anapali provide lots of fine dining and spa treatment options. And for those who want to start their day early, there's the drive up to Haleakalā to see the sun rise—or for couples who prefer to sleep in there's the arguably even more spectacular sunset from the summit. *Plan to spend 4 nights.*

Why Kaua'i: The north shore communities of Hanalei and Princeville provide the opportunity to get away from crowds and indulge in some spectacular beaches, hiking, and helicopter rides. At Princeville you can experience views straight out of *South Pacific* as well as excellent dining and spas at the St. Regis Hotel, while a drive to Kē'ē Beach at the end of the road provides innumerable options for pulling over and grabbing a beach, all for just the two of you. *Plan to spend at least 3 nights.*

Golf, Shopping, and Luxury: Maui and the Big Island

For luxurious travel, great shopping, restaurants, and accommodations you can't beat Maui and the Big Island.

Why Maui: The resorts at Wailea and Kā'anapali have endless options for dining, shopping, and spa treatments. And, the golf on Maui can't be beat with Kapalua, the Dunes at Maui Lani, and Mākena Resort topping the list of spectacular courses. *Plan to spend 4 nights.*

Why the Big Island: In addition to having incredible natural scenery, the Big Island

offers world-class resorts and golfing along the Kohala Coast. The Mauna Kea and Hapuna golf courses rank among the top in state while the courses at Mauna Lani Resort and Waikoloa Village allow the unusual experience of playing in and around lava flows. Gourmet dining and spa treatments are readily available at the top resorts and you'll find shopping opportunities at King's Shops at Waikoloa Village as well as within many of the resorts themselves. Or, travel to Hāwī or Waimea (Kamuela) for original island boutiques. *Plan to spend at least 3 nights.*

Natural Beauty and Pristine Beaches: The Big Island and Kaua'i

Really want to get away and experience nature at its most primal? The Big Island is the place to start, followed by a trip to Kaua'i.

Why the Big Island: Home to 11 different climate zones, the Big Island is large enough to contain all the other Hawaiian Islands inside it. There are countless options for those who want to get off the beaten track and get their hands (and feet) dirty—or sandy as the case may be. See lava flowing or steam rising from Kīlauea. Visit beaches in your choice of gold, white, green, or black sand. Snorkel or dive just offshore from an ancient Hawaiian settlement. Or, hike through rain forests to hidden waterfalls. The choices are endless on this island. *Plan to spend at least 4 nights.*

Why Kaua'i: The Nāpali Coast is the main draw for those seeking secluded beaches and incredible scenery. If you're interested in hiking to otherwise inaccessible beaches along sheer sea cliffs, this is as good as it gets. Or, head up to Waimea Canyon to see the "Grand Canyon of the Pacific." Want waterfalls? 'Ōpaeka'a Falls outside Līhu'e is one of the state's most breathtaking. And there's no better place for bird-watching than Kīlauea Point National Wildlife Refuge. *Plan to spend at least 3 nights.*

Volcanic Views: The Big Island and Maui

For those coming to Hawai'i for the volcanoes, there are really only two options: The Big Island and Maui.

Why the Big Island: Start by flying into Hilo and head straight to Hawai'i Volcanoes National Park and Kīlauea Volcano. Plan to spend at least two days at Kīlauea—you'll need time to really explore the caldera, drive to the end of Chain of Craters Road, and have some time for hiking in and around this active volcano. While eruptions are unpredictable, helicopter companies can get you views of otherwise inaccessible lava flows. You can also make a visit up to the summit of Mauna Kea with a tour company. From here you'll see views not only of the observatories (Mauna Kea is one of the best places in the world for astronomy), but also Kīlauea and Haleakalā volcanoes, which loom in the distance. *Plan to spend at least 4 nights.*

Why Maui: Though all the islands in Hawai'i were built from the same hot spot in the earth's crust, the only other island to have had volcanic activity in recorded history was Maui, at Haleakalā. The House of the Sun (as Haleakalā is known) has great hiking and camping opportunities. *Plan to spend 3 nights.*

ISLAND-FINDER CHART

Not sure which Hawaiian island is your kind of paradise? Any island would make a memorable vacation, but not every one has that particular mix of attributes that makes it perfect for you. Use this chart to compare how each island measures up to your vacation dreams.

Looking for great nightlife and world-class surfing? O'ahu would fit the bill. Hate crowds but love scuba? Lāna'i is your place. You can also consult What's Where to learn more about the specific attractions of each island.

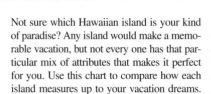

	O'AHU	MAUI	BIG ISLAND	KAUA'I	MOLOKA'I	LĀNA'I
Beaches						
Activities & Sports	◐	●	●	◐	◐	◐
Deserted	◐	◐	◐	●	●	◐
Party Scene	●	◐	◐	○	○	○
City Life						
Crowds	●	◐	◐	◐	○	○
Urban Development	●	◐	◐	◐	○	○
Entertainment						
Hawaiian Cultural Events	◐	◐	●	◐	○	○
Museums	●	◐	◐	◐	○	○
Nightlife	●	◐	○	○	○	○
Performing Arts	●	◐	○	○	○	○
Shopping	●	◐	◐	○	○	○
Lodging						
B&Bs	◐	◐	●	●	○	○
Condos	●	●	●	●	○	○
Hotels & Resorts	●	●	●	◐	○	●
Vacation Rentals	◐	◐	◐	◐	◐	○
Nature						
Rainforest Sights	◐	◐	◐	●	◐	○
Volcanic Sights	○	◐	●	○	○	○
Wildlife	○	◐	●	●	◐	◐
Sports						
Golf	◐	◐	●	◐	○	●
Hiking	◐	●	●	●	◐	◐
Scuba	◐	●	●	◐	○	●
Snorkeling	◐	●	●	◐	◐	◐
Surfing	●	◐	◐	◐	◐	○
Windsurfing	◐	●	◐	◐	◐	○

KEY: ● Noteworthy ◐ Some ○ Little or None

WHEN TO GO

Long days of sunshine and fairly mild year-round temperatures make Hawai'i an all-season destination. Most resort areas are at sea level, with average afternoon temperatures of 75°F to 80°F during the coldest months of December and January; during the hottest months of August and September the temperature often reaches 90°F. Only at high elevations does the temperature drop into the colder realms, and only at mountain summits does it reach freezing.

Most travelers head to the Islands in winter. From mid-December through mid-April, visitors find Hawai'i's sun-splashed beaches and balmy trade winds appealing. This high season means that fewer travel bargains are available; room rates average 10% to 15% higher during this season than the rest of the year. The highest rates you're likely to pay are between Christmas and New Year. Spring break (the month of March) and even summer can be pricey. A general rule of thumb: When kids are on recess from school, it's high season in Hawai'i.

Rainfall can be high in winter, particularly on the north and east shores of each island. Generally speaking, you're guaranteed sun and warm temperatures on the west and south shores no matter what time of year.

Only-in-Hawai'i Holidays

If you happen to be in the Islands on March 26 or June 11, you'll notice light traffic and busy beaches—these are state holidays not celebrated anywhere else. March 26 recognizes the birthday of Prince Jonah Kūhio Kalaniana'ole, a member of the royal line who served as a delegate to Congress and spearheaded the effort to set aside homelands for Hawaiian people. June 11 honors the first islandwide monarch, Kamehameha I; locals drape his statues with lei and stage elaborate parades.

May 1 isn't an official holiday, but it's the day when schools and civic groups celebrate the quintessential Islands gift, the flower lei, with lei-making contests and pageants.

Statehood Day is celebrated on the third Friday in August (Admission Day was August 21, 1959).

Another holiday much celebrated is Chinese New Year, in part because many Hawaiians married Chinese immigrants. Homes and businesses sprout bright red good-luck mottoes, lions dance in the streets, and everybody eats *gau* (steamed pudding) and *jai* (vegetarian stew).

The state also celebrates Good Friday as a spring holiday.

Climate

Moist trade winds drop their precipitation on the north and east sides of the Islands, creating tropical climates, while the south and west sides remain hot and dry with desertlike conditions. Higher "Upcountry" elevations typically have cooler, and often misty conditions.

Average maximum and minimum temperatures for Honolulu are listed here; temperatures throughout the Hawaiian Islands are similar.

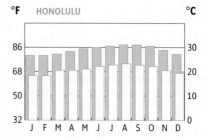

HAWAIIAN PEOPLE AND THEIR CULTURE

By October 2010, Hawai'i's population was more than 1.3 million with the majority of residents living on O'ahu. Nine percent are Hawaiian or other Pacific Islander, almost 40% are Asian American, 9% are Latino, and about 25% Caucasian. Nearly a fifth of the population list two or more races, making Hawai'i the most diverse state in the United States.

Among individuals 18 and older, about 84% finished high school, half attained some college, and 26% completed a bachelor's degree or higher.

The Role of Tradition

The kingdom of Hawai'i was ruled by a spiritual class system. Although the *ali'i*, or chief, was believed to be the direct descendent of a deity or god, high priests, known as *kahuna*, presided over every imaginable aspect of life and *kapu* (taboos) that strictly governed the commoners.

Each part of nature and ritual was connected to a deity—Kane was the highest of all deities, symbolizing sunlight and creation; Ku was the god of war; Lono represented fertility, rainfall, music, and peace; Kanaloa was the god of the underworld or darker spirits; and there is Pele, the goddess of fire.

The kapu not only provided social order, they also swayed the people to act with reverence for the environment. Any abuse was met with extreme punishment, often death, as it put the land and people's *mana*, or spiritual power, in peril.

Ancient deities play a huge role in Hawaiian life today—not just in daily rituals, but in the Hawaiians' reverence for their land. Gods and goddesses tend to be associated with particular parts of the land, and most of them are connected with many places, thanks to the body of stories built up around each.

One of the most important ways the ancient Hawaiians showed respect for their gods and goddesses was through the hula. Various forms of the hula were performed as prayers to the gods and as praise to the chiefs. Performances were taken very seriously, as a mistake was thought to invalidate the prayer, or even to offend the god or chief in question. Hula is still performed both as entertainment and as prayer; it is not uncommon for a hula performance to be included in an official government ceremony.

Who Are the Hawaiians Today?

To define the Hawaiians in a page, let alone a paragraph, is nearly impossible. First, there are Hawaiians by residence, similar to Californians, New Yorkers, or Texans. Those considered to be indigenous Hawaiians are descendents of the ancient Polynesians who crossed the vast ocean and settled Hawai'i. According to the government, there are Native Hawaiians or native Hawaiians (note the change in capitalization) depending on their blood makeup.

Federal and state agencies apply different methods to determine Hawaiian lineage, from measuring blood percentage to mapping genealogy. This has caused turmoil within the community because it excludes many who claim Hawaiian heritage. It almost guarantees that, as races intermingle, even those considered Native Hawaiian now will eventually disappear on paper, displacing generations to come.

Modern Hawaiian Culture

Perfect weather aside, Hawai'i might be the warmest place anyone can visit. The Hawai'i experience begins and ends with *aloha*, a word that envelops love, affection, and mercy, and has become a salutation for hello and good-bye. Broken

down, *alo* means "presence" and *ha* means "breath"—the presence of breath. It's to live with love and respect for self and others with every breath. Past the manicured resorts and tour buses, aloha is a spirit and moral compass that binds all of Hawai'i's people.

Hawaiians have been blessed with some of the most unspoiled natural wonders, and aloha extends to the land, or *'aina*. Hawaiians are raised outdoors and have strong ties to nature. They realize as children that the ocean and land are the delicate source of all life. Even ancient gods were embodied by nature, and this reverence has been passed down to present generations who believe in *kuleana*, their privilege and responsibility.

Hawaiians' diverse cultures unfold in a beautiful montage of customs and arts—from music, to dance, to food. Musical genres range from slack key to *Jawaiian* (Hawaiian reggae) to *hapa-haole* (Hawaiian music with English words). From George Kahumoku's Grammy-worthy laid-back strumming, to the late Iz Kamakawiwo'ole's "Somewhere over the Rainbow," to Jack Johnson's more mainstream tunes, contemporary Hawaiian music has definitely carved its ever-evolving niche.

The Merrie Monarch Festival is celebrating almost 50 years of worldwide hula competition and education. The fine-dining culinary scene, especially in Honolulu, has a rich tapestry of ethnic influences and talent. But the real gems are the humble hole-in-the-wall eateries that serve authentic cuisines of many ethnic origins in one plate, a deliciously mixed plate indeed.

And perhaps, the most striking quality in today's Hawaiian culture is the sense of family, or *ohana*. Sooner or later, almost everyone you meet becomes an uncle or auntie, and it is not uncommon for near strangers to be welcomed into a home as a member of the family.

Until the last century, the practice of *hanai*, in which a family essentially adopts a child, usually a grandchild, without formalities, was still prevalent. While still practiced to a somewhat lesser degree, the *hanai*, which means to feed or nourish, still resonates within most families and communities.

How to Act Like a Local

Adopting local customs is a firsthand introduction to the Islands' unique culture. So live in T-shirts and shorts. Wear cheap rubber flip-flops, but call them slippers. Wave people into your lane on the highway, and, when someone lets you in, give them a wave of thanks in return. Never, ever blow your horn, even when the pickup truck in front of you is stopped for a long session of "talk story" right in the middle of the road.

Holoholo means to go out for the fun of it—an aimless stroll, ride, or drive. "Wheah you goin', braddah?" "Oh, holoholo." It's local speak for Sunday drive, no plan, it's not the destination but the journey. Try setting out without an itinerary. Learn to *shaka*: pinky and thumb extended, middle fingers curled in, waggle sideways. Eat white rice with everything. When someone says, "Aloha!" answer, "Aloha nō!" ("And a real big aloha back to you"). And, as the locals say, "No make big body" ("Try not to act like you own the place").

THE HISTORY OF HAWAI'I

Hawaiian history is long and complex; a brief survey can put into context the ongoing renaissance of native arts and culture.

The Polynesians

Long before both Christopher Columbus and the Vikings, Polynesian seafarers set out to explore the vast stretches of the open ocean in double-hulled canoes. From western Polynesia, they traveled back and forth between Samoa, Fiji, Tahiti, the Marquesas, and the Society Isles, settling on the outer reaches of the Pacific, Hawai'i, and Easter Island, as early as AD 300. The golden era of Polynesian voyaging peaked around AD 1200, after which the distant Hawaiian Islands were left to develop their own unique cultural practices and subsistence in relative isolation.

The Islands' symbiotic society was deeply intertwined with religion, mythology, science, and artistry. Ruled by an *ali'i*, or chief, each settlement was nestled in an *ahupua'a*, a pie-shaped land division from the uplands where the ali'i lived, through the valleys and down to the shores where the commoners resided. Everyone contributed, whether it was by building canoes, catching fish, making tools, or farming land.

A United Kingdom

When the British explorer Captain James Cook arrived in 1778, he was revered as a god upon his arrival and later killed over a stolen boat. With guns and ammunition purchased from Cook, the Big Island chief, Kamehameha, gained a significant advantage over the other ali'i. He united Hawai'i into one kingdom in 1810, bringing an end to the frequent interisland battles that dominated Hawaiian life.

Tragically, the new kingdom was beset with troubles. Native religion was abandoned, and *kapu* (laws and regulations) were eventually abolished. The European explorers brought foreign diseases with them, and within a few short decades the Hawaiian population was cut in half.

New laws regarding land ownership and religious practices eroded the underpinnings of precontact Hawai'i. Each successor to the Hawaiian throne sacrificed more control over the Island kingdom. As Westerners permeated Hawaiian culture, Hawai'i became more riddled with layers of racial issues, injustice, and social unrest.

Modern Hawai'i

Finally in 1893, the last Hawaiian monarch, Queen Lili'uokalani, was overthrown by a group of Americans and European businessmen and government officials, aided by an armed militia. This led to the creation of the Republic of Hawai'i, and it became a U.S. territory for the next 60 years. The loss of Hawaiian sovereignty and the conditions of annexation have haunted the Hawaiian people since the monarchy was deposed.

Pearl Harbor was attacked in 1941, which engaged the United States immediately into World War II. Tourism, from its beginnings in the early 1900s, flourished after the war and naturally inspired rapid real estate development in Waikīkī. In 1959, Hawai'i officially became the 50th state. Statehood paved the way for Hawaiians and Hawai'i's immigrants to participate in the American democratic process. With the rise of the civil rights movement in the 1960s, Hawaiians began to reclaim their own identity, from language to hula. Political activism, too, has increased over the decades, though there's a wide spectrum of opinion.

HAWAI'I AND THE ENVIRONMENT

Sustainability. It's a word rolling off everyone's tongues these days. In a place known as the most remote island chain in the world (check your globe), Hawai'i relies heavily on the outside world for food and material goods—estimates put the percentage of food arriving on container ships as high as 90. Like many places, though, efforts are afoot to change that. And you can help.

Shop Local Farms and Markets

From O'ahu to Maui, farmers' markets are cropping up, providing a place for growers to sell fresh fruits and vegetables. There is no reason to buy imported mangoes, papayas, avocadoes, and bananas at grocery stores, when the ones you'll find at farmers' markets are not only fresher and bigger but tastier, too. Some markets allow the sale of fresh-packaged foods—salsa, say, or smoothies—and the on-site preparation of food—like pork *laulau* (pork, beef and fish or chicken with taro, or lū'au, leaves wrapped and steamed in *tī* leaves) or roasted corn on the cob—so you can make your run to the market a dining experience.

Not only is the locavore movement vibrantly alive at farmers' markets, but Hawai'i's top chefs are sourcing more of their produce—and fish, beef, chicken, and cheese—from local providers as well. You'll notice this movement on restaurant menus, featuring Kī'lauea greens or Hāmākua tomatoes or locally caught mahimahi.

And while most people are familiar with Kona coffee farm tours on Big Island, if you're interested in the growing slow-food movement in Hawai'i, you'll be heartened to know many farmers are opening up their operations for tours—as well as sumptuous meals.

Support Hawai'i's Merchants

Food isn't the only sustainable effort in Hawai'i. Buying local goods like art and jewelry, Hawaiian heritage products, crafts, music, and apparel is another way to "green up" the local economy. The County of Kaua'i helps make it easy with their **Kaua'i Made** program (⊕ *www.kauaimade.net*), which showcases products made on Kaua'i, by Kaua'i people, using Kaua'i materials. The Maui Chamber of Commerce does something similar with its **Made in Maui** program (⊕ *www.madeinmaui.com*). Think of both as the Good Housekeeping Seal of Approval for locally made goods.

Then there are the crafty entrepreneurs who are diverting items from the trash heap by repurposing garbage. Take **Muumuu Heaven** (⊕ *www.muumuuheaven.com*) on O'ahu. They got their start by reincarnating vintage aloha apparel into hip new fashions. **Kini Beach** (⊕ *www.kinibeach.com*) collects discarded grass mats and plastic inflatables from Waikīkī hotels and uses them to make pricey bags and totes.

Choose Green Tour Operators

Conscious decisions when it comes to Island activities go a long way to protecting Hawai'i's natural world. The **Hawai'i Ecotourism Association** (⊕ *www.hawaiiecotourism.org*) recognizes tour operators for, among other things, their environmental stewardship. The **Hawai'i Tourism Authority** (⊕ *www.hawaiitourismauthority.org*) recognizes outfitters for their cultural sensitivity. Winners of these awards are good choices when it comes to guided tours and activities. You can even rent a car that runs on biodiesel, a fuel made from used cooking oil.

TOP 10 HAWAIIAN FOODS TO TRY

Food in Hawai'i is a reflection of the state's diverse cultural makeup and tropical location. Fresh seafood, organic fruits and vegetables, free-range beef, and locally grown products are the hallmarks of Hawai'i regional cuisine. Its preparations are drawn from across the Pacific Rim, including Japan, the Philippines, Korea, and Thailand—and now, "local food" is a cuisine in its own right. Don't miss Hawaiian-grown coffee, either, whether it's smooth Kona from the Big Island or coffee grown on other islands.

Saimin

The ultimate hangover cure and the perfect comfort food during Hawai'i's mild winters, saimin ranks at the top of the list of local favorites. In fact, it's one of the few dishes deemed truly local, having been highlighted in cookbooks since the 1930s. Saimin is an Asian-style noodle soup so ubiquitous, it's even on McDonald's menus statewide. In mom-and-pop shops, a large melamine bowl is filled with homemade dashi, or chicken broth, and wheat-flour noodles and then topped off with strips of omelet, green onions, bright pink fish cake and char siu (Chinese roast pork) and/or canned luncheon meat, such as SPAM. Add shoyu and chili pepper water, lift your chopsticks and slurp away.

SPAM

Speaking of SPAM, Hawai'i's most prevalent grab-and-go snack is SPAM musubi. Often displayed next to cash registers at groceries and convenience stores, the glorified rice ball is rectangluar, topped with a slice of fried SPAM and wrapped in nori (seaweed). Musubi is a minimeal in itself. But just like sushi, the rice part hardens when refrigerated. So it's best to gobble it up, right after purchase.

Hormel Company's SPAM actually deserves its own recognition—way beyond as a mere musubi topping. About 5 million cans are sold per year in Hawai'i and the Aloha State even hosts a festival in its honor. It's inexpensive protein and goes a long way when mixed with rice, scrambled eggs, noodles or, well, anything. The spiced luncheon meat gained popularity in World War II days, when fish was rationed. Gourmets and those with aversions to salt, high cholesterol, or high blood pressure may cringe at the thought of eating it, but SPAM in Hawai'i is here to stay.

Manapua

Another savory snack is manapua, fist-sized dough balls fashioned after Chinese bao (a traditional Chinese bun) and stuffed with fillings such as char siu (Chinese barbeque) pork and then steamed. Many mom-and-pop stores sell them in commercial steamer display cases along with pork hash and other dim sum. Modern-day fillings include curry chicken.

Fresh 'Ahi or Tako Poke

There's nothing like fresh 'ahi or tako (octopus) poke to break the ice at a backyard party, except, of course, the cold beer handed to you from the cooler. The perfect pūpū, poke (pronounced poh-kay) is basically raw seafood cut into bite-sized chunks and mixed with everything from green onions to roasted and ground kukui nuts. Other variations include mixing the fish with chopped round onion, sesame oil, seaweed, and chili pepper water. Shoyu is the constant. These days, grocery stores sell a rainbow of varieties such as kimchi crab and anything goes, from adding mayonnaise to tobiko caviar. Fish lovers who want to take it to the next level order

sashimi, the best cuts of 'ahi sliced and dipped in a mixture of shoyu and wasabi.

Tropical Fruits

Tropical fruits such as apple banana and strawberry papaya are plucked from trees in Island neighborhoods and eaten for breakfast—plain or with a squeeze of fresh lime. Give them a try; the banana tastes like an apple and the papaya's rosy flesh explains its name. Locals also love to add their own creative touches to exotic fruits. Green mangoes are pickled with Chinese five spice, and Maui Gold pineapples are topped with li hing mui powder (heck, even margarita glasses are rimmed with it). Green papaya is tossed in a Vietnamese salad with fish paste and fresh prawns.

Plate Lunch

It would be remiss not to mention the plate lunch as one of the most beloved dishes in Hawai'i. It generally includes two scoops of sticky white rice, a scoop of macaroni and/or macaroni-potato salad, heavy on the mayo, and perhaps kimchi or *koko* (salted cabbage). There are countless choices of main protein such as chicken *katsu* (fried cutlet), fried mahimahi and beef tomato. The king of all plate lunches is the Hawaiian plate. The main item is laulau or kālua pig and cabbage along with poi, *lomilomi* salmon, chicken long rice, and sticky white rice.

Bento Box

The bento box gained popularity back in the plantation days, when workers toiled in the sugarcane fields. No one brought sandwiches to work then. Instead it was a lunch box with the ever-present steamed white rice, pickled *ume* (plum) to preserve the rice, and main meats such as fried chicken or fish. Today, many stores sell prepackaged bentos or you may go to an

okazuya (Japanese deli) with a hot buffet counter and create your own.

Malasadas

The Portuguese have contributed much to Hawai'i cuisine in the form of sausage, soup, and sweetbread. But their most revered food is *malasadas*, hot, deep-fried doughnuts rolled in sugar. Malasadas are crowd-pleasers. Buy them by the dozen, hot from the fryer, placed in brown paper bags to absorb the grease. Or bite into gourmet malasadas at restaurants, filled with vanilla or chocolate cream.

Shave Ice

Much more than just a snow cone, shave ice is what locals crave after a blazing day at the beach or a hot-as-Hades game of soccer. If you're lucky, you'll find a neighborhood store that hand-shaves the ice, but it's rare. Either way, the counter person will ask you first if you'd like ice cream and/or adzuki beans scooped into the bottom of the cone or cup. Then they shape the ice to a giant mound and add colorful fruit syrups. First-timers should order the Rainbow, of course.

Crack Seed

There are dozens of varieties of crack seed in dwindling specialty shops and at the drug stores. Chinese call the preserved fruits and nuts *see mui* but somehow the pidgin English version is what Hawaiians prefer. Those who like hard candy and salty foods will love li hing mangoes and rock salt plums, and those with an itchy throat will feel relief from the lemon strips. Peruse large glass jars of crack seed sold in bulk or smaller hanging bags—the latter make good gifts to give to friends back home.

BEST FARMERS' MARKETS

O'ahu

Although there are exceptions, the **People's Open Market** dominates farmers' markets on O'ahu. Others include the **Saturday Farmers' Market** at Kapiolani Community College on Diamond Head Road in Honolulu, **Thursday Kailua Farmers' Market** at Kailua Square Shopping Center, **Restaurant Row Farmers' Market** right on Ala Moana Boulevard in Honolulu (buy produce after you eat a restaurant meal!), **Waikīkī Farmer Market** at the Waikīkī Community Center, and the **North Shore Country Market** at Sunset in Hale'iwa. The Hawai'i Farm Bureau (⊕ *whfbf.org/markets*) has information and weekly tip sheets about farmers' markets on O'ahu.

Maui

Exotic oddities and fresh organic produce are wowing attendees of the **Ono Organic Farms** farmers' market near Hasegawa General store in Hāna, where you can taste from durian to star apple to egg fruit. **Maui Swap Meet** on Kahului Beach Road at Maui Community College is a great way to spend your Saturday. Peruse coconuts sliced open for you by a machete-wielding Tongan, banana bread just out of the oven, and much more. There are plenty of crafts as well. **Eddie Tam Community Center** in Makawao serves up tastes of paniolo country.

Those just heading back to the condo from the beach on Saturday morning will want to make leisurely pit stops at Maui farmers' markets in **Kīhei** (on Lipoa Street) and **Honokōwai** (at Hawaiian Motors parking lot).

Big Island

Each Hawaiian Island has its own flavor when it comes to farmers' markets. Because of its vast size, the Big Island even boasts specialties from its various regions.

For instance, those who shop at **Ka'ū Farmers' Market** in front of Ace Hardware at South Point, will find the best local Ka'u oranges.

Head to **Hilo Farmers' Market** on the corner of Kamehemeha Avenue and Mamo Street along with Keaau Village Farmers' Market on Old Volcano Road and you'll get the ripest and most colorful papaya displayed at the state's lowest prices, along with jams, salsas, and an incredible variety of Asian street-food treats.

Kona Farmers' Market in front of Kmart in Kailua-Kona entices with its distinct flavors, including some of the world's best coffees. For a taste of things "hippie" and "New Age," **Akebono Farmers' Market** in eccentric Pahoa can't be beat. Those staying in hotels and condos on the Kohala Coast will find **Waikoloa Village Farmers' Market** convenient. On Saturday morning **The Hawaiian Homestead Farmers' Market** is a lively stop if you're in Waimea (Kamuela).

Kaua'i

Sunshine Markets almost has a monopoly on Kaua'i with weekly displays all over the island. Luckily, the selection is good and the produce is quality. **Kekaha Neighborhood Center** on Elepaio Road in Kekaha is just one of seven produced by Sunshine Markets. Others include **Hanapēpē Park** in old Hanapēpē Town, **Kalaheo Neighborhood Center** on Papalina Road off Kaumualii in Kalaheo, **Kapa'a New Town Park** on Kahau Road in Kapa'a, **Kīlauea Neighborhood Center** off Lighthouse Road in Kīlauea, **Koloa Ball Park** on Maluhia Road and **Vidinha Stadium** in Līhu'e.

The independent **Kaua'i Community Market** thrives on the campus of the local community college across from Grove Farm.

KIDS AND FAMILIES

With dozens of adventures, discoveries, and fun-filled beach days, Hawai'i is a blast with kids. Even better, the things to do here do not appeal only to small fry. The entire family, parents included, will enjoy surfing, discovering a waterfall in the rain forest, and snorkeling with sea turtles. And there are plenty of organized activities for kids that will free parents' time for a few romantic beach strolls.

Choosing a Place to Stay

Resorts: All the big resorts make kids' programs a priority, and it shows. When you are booking your room, ask about "kids eat free" deals and the number of kids' pools at the resort. Also check out the size of the groups in the children's programs, and find out whether the cost of the programs includes lunch, equipment, and activities.

Condos: Condo and vacation rentals are a fantastic value for families vacationing in Hawai'i. You can cook your own food, which is cheaper than eating out and sometimes easier (especially if you have a finicky eater in your group), and you'll get twice the space of a hotel room for about a quarter of the price. If you decide to go the condo route, be sure to ask about the size of the complex's pool (some try to pawn a tiny soaking tub off as a pool) and whether barbecues are available.

Ocean Activities

Hawai'i is all about getting your kids outside—away from TV and video games. And who could resist the turquoise water, the promise of spotting dolphins or whales, and the fun of boogie boarding or surfing?

On the Beach: Most people like being in the water, but toddlers and school-age kids tend to be especially enamored of it. The swimming pool at your condo or hotel is always an option, but don't be afraid to hit the beach with a little one in tow. There are several beaches in Hawai'i that are nearly as safe as a pool—completely protected bays with pleasant white-sand beaches. As always, use your judgment, and heed all posted signs and lifeguard warnings.

On the Waves: Surf lessons are a great idea for older kids, especially if mom and dad want a little quiet time. Beginner lessons are always on safe and easy waves and last anywhere from two to four hours.

The Underwater World: If your kids are ready to try snorkeling, Hawai'i is a great place to introduce them to the underwater world. Even without the mask and snorkel, they'll be able to see colorful fish darting this way and that, and they may also spot turtles and dolphins at many of the island beaches.

Land Activities

In addition to beach experiences, Hawai'i has rain forests, botanical gardens, aquariums (O'ahu and Maui), and even petting zoos and hands-on children's museums that will keep your kids entertained and out of the sun for a day.

After Dark

At night, younger kids get a kick out of lū'au, and many of the shows incorporate young audience members, adding to the fun. The older kids might find it all a bit lame, but there are a handful of new shows in the Islands that are more modern, incorporating acrobatics, lively music, and fire dancers. If you're planning on hitting a lū'au with a teen in tow, we highly recommend going the modern route.

ONLY IN HAWAI'I

Traveling to Hawai'i is as close as an American can get to visiting another country while staying within the United States. There's much to learn and understand about the state's indigenous culture, the hundred years of immigration that resulted in today's blended society, and the tradition of aloha that has welcomed millions of visitors over the years.

Aloha Shirt

To go to Hawai'i without taking an aloha shirt home is almost sacrilege. The first aloha shirts from the 1920s and 1930s—called "silkies"—were classic canvases of art and tailored for the tourists. Popular culture caught on in the 1950s, and they became a fashion craze. With the 1960s' more subdued designs, the Aloha Friday was born, and the shirt became appropriate clothing for work, play, and formal occasions. Because of its soaring popularity, cheaper and mass-produced versions became available.

Hawaiian Quilt

Although ancient Hawaiians were already known to produce fine *kapa* (bark) cloth, the actual art of quilting originated from the missionaries. Hawaiians have created designs to reflect their own aesthetic, and bold patterns evolved over time. They can be pricey because the quilts are intricately made by hand and can take years to finish. These masterpieces are considered precious heirlooms that reflect the history and beauty of Hawai'i.

Popular Souvenirs

Souvenir shopping can be intimidating. There's a sea of Island-inspired and often kitschy merchandise, so we'd like to give you a breakdown of popular and fun gifts that you might encounter and consider bringing home. If authenticity is important to you, be sure to check labels and ask shopkeepers. Museum shops are good places for authentic, Hawaiian-made souvenirs.

Hula doll. The hula dancer has been immortalized and commodified in many ways, from the classic dashboard bobble hip to the newer hula girl desktop duster.

Grass skirts and coconut bras. Sometimes bought as a set and sometimes as separates, either way this costume will definitely elicit a smile or 10 at a lū'au.

Home accessories. Relive your spa treatment at home with Hawaiian bath and body products, or deck out the kitchen in festive lū'au style with bottle openers, pineapple mugs, tiki glasses, shot glasses, slipper and surfboard magnets, and salt-and-pepper shakers.

Lei and shell necklaces. From silk or polyester flower lei to kukui or puka shell necklaces, lei have been traditionally used as a welcome offering to guests (although the artificial ones are more for fun, as real flowers are always preferable).

Lauhala products. *Lauhala* weaving is a traditional Hawaiian art. The leaves come from the hala, or pandanus, tree and are hand-woven to create lovely gift boxes, baskets, bags, and picture frames.

Vintage Hawai'i. You can find vintage photos, reproductions of vintage postcards or paintings, heirloom jewelry, and vintage aloha wear in many specialty stores.

Warrior helmets. Traditionally called *makaki'i* or *makini* after ancient Hawaiian warriors, these helmets are miniature masks adorned with feathers. They're popular among a younger crowd and hung on the car's rearview mirror or doorway for protection.

Lū'au

The lū'au's origin, which was a celebratory feast, can be traced back to the earliest Hawaiian civilizations. In the traditional lū'au, the taboo or *kapu* laws were very strict, requiring men and women to eat separately. However, in 1819 King Kamehameha II broke the great taboo and shared a feast with women and commoners ushering in the modern-era lū'au. Today, traditional lū'au usually commemorate a child's first birthday, graduation, wedding, or other family occasion. They also are a Hawaiian experience that most visitors enjoy, and resorts and other companies have incorporated the fire-knife dance and other Polynesian dances into their elaborate presentations.

Nose flutes

The nose flute is an instrument used in ancient times to serenade a lover. For the Hawaiians, the nose is romantic, sacred and pure. The Hawaiian word for kiss is *honi*. Similar to an Eskimo's kiss, the noses touch on each side sharing one's spiritual energy or breath. The Hawaiian term, *'ohe hano ihu*, simply translated to "bamboo," with which the instrument is made; "breathe," because one has to gently breathe through it to make soothing music; and "nose," as it is made for the nose and not the mouth.

Slack-Key Guitar and the Paniolos

Kiho'alu, or slack-key music, evolved in the early 1800s when King Kamehameha III brought in Mexican and Spanish vaqueros to manage the overpopulated cattle that had run wild on the Islands. The vaqueros brought their guitars and would play music around the campfire after work. When they left, supposedly leaving their guitars to their new friends, the Hawaiian *paniolos,* or cowboys, began to infuse what they learned from the vaqueros with their native music and chants, and so the art of slack-key music was born.

Today, the paniolo culture thrives where ranchers have settled.

'Ukulele

The word *'ukulele* or *'uke* literally translates to the "the jumping flea" and came to Hawai'i in the 1880s by way of the Portuguese and Spanish. Once a fading art form, today it brings international kudos as a solo instrument, thanks to tireless musicians and teachers who have worked hard to keep it by our fingertips.

One such teacher is Roy Sakuma. Founder of four 'ukulele schools and a legend in his own right, Sakuma and his wife Kathy produced O'ahu's first 'Ukulele Festival in 1971. Since then, they've brought the tradition to the Big Island, Kaua'i, and Maui. The free event annually draws thousands of artists and fans from all over the globe.

Hula

"Hula is the language of the heart, therefore the heartbeat of the Hawaiian people." —Kalākaua I, the Merrie Monarch. Thousands—from tots to seniors—devote hours each week to hula classes. All these dancers need some place to show off their stuff. The result is a network of hula competitions (generally free or very inexpensive) and free performances in malls and other public spaces. Many resorts offer hula instruction or "hula-cise."

BEST BEACHES

No one ever gets as much beach time in Hawai'i as they planned to, it seems, but it's a problem of time, not beaches. Beaches of every size, color (even green), and description line the state's many shorelines.

They have different strengths: some are great for sitting but not so great for swimming; some offer beach-park amenities like lifeguards and showers, whereas others are more private and isolated. Read up before you head out.

O'ahu

Makapu'u Beach. Quite possibly O'ahu's most breathtaking scenic view—with a hiking trail to a historic lighthouse, offshore views of two rocky islets, home to thousands of nesting seabirds, and hang gliders launching off nearby cliffs.

While the white-sand beach and surroundings adorn many postcards, the treacherous ocean's currents invite experienced body boarders only.

Kailua Beach Park. This is a true family beach, offering something for everyone: A long stretch of sand for walking, turquoise seas set against cobalt skies for impressive photographs, a sandy-bottom shoreline for ocean swimming, and grassy expanses underneath shade trees for picnics.

You can even rent a kayak and make the short paddle to Popia (Flat) Island. This is Windward O'ahu, so expect wind. All the better if you're an avid windsurfer or kiteboarder.

Waimea Bay. This is the beach that makes Hawai'i famous every winter when monster waves and the world's best surfers roll in.

Show up to watch, not partake. If the rest of us want to get in the water here, we have to wait until summer when the safe, onshore break is great for novice bodysurfers.

White Plains. This beach is equal parts Kailua Beach Park with its facilities and tree-covered barbecue areas and Waikīkī with its numerous surf breaks—minus the crowds and high-rises.

Pack for the day—cooler with food and drink, snorkel gear, inflatables and body board—as this destination is 35 minutes from downtown Honolulu.

Maui

Nāpili Beach. There is much to love about this intimate, crescent-shaped beach. Sunbathing, snorkeling, swimming, bodysurfing, and—after a full day of beach fun—startling sunsets. Bring the kids; they'll love the turtles that nosh on the *limu* (seaweed) growing on the lava rocks.

Mākena (Big Beach). Don't forget the camera for this one. A bit remote and tricky to find, the effort is worth it—a long, wide stretch of golden sand and translucent offshore water. It's beautiful, yes, but the icing on the cake is this beach is never crowded. Use caution for swimming because the steep, onshore break can get big.

Wai'ānapanapa State Park. The rustic beauty will capture your heart here—a black-sand beach framed by lava cliffs and backed by bright green *naupaka* bushes. Ocean currents can be strong, so cool off in one of two freshwater pools.

Get an early start, because your day's destination is just shy of Hāna and requires a short, quarter-mile walk.

Big Island

Hāpuna Beach State Recreation Area. It's hard to know where to start with this beach—the long, perfect crescent-shaped beach. The calm, turquoise waters. Rocky

points for snorkeling. Even surf in winter. Just about everyone can find something to love here. With its west-facing views, this is a good spot for sunsets.

Kauna'oa Beach (Mauna Kea Beach). This is like the big brother, more advanced version of Hāpuna Beach with snorkeling, body-, and board surfing but trickier currents, so be careful. Still, it's worth it. Try them both and let us know which you prefer. For most, it's a toss-up.

Papakōlea Beach (Green Sand Beach). Papakōlea makes our list, because, really, how often do you run across a green-sand beach? That's right, green. The greenish tint here is caused by an accumulation of olivine crystals that formed in volcanic eruptions.

This isn't the most swimmable of beaches, but the sand, sculpted cliffs and dry, barren landscape make it quite memorable. A steep, 2-mi hike is required to access the beach.

Punalu'u Beach Park (Black Sand Beach). This might as well be called Turtle Beach. Both the endangered Hawaiian green sea turtle and hawksbill turtle bask on the rocky, black-sand beach here.

We prefer to stay dry at this beach—due to strong rip currents—and snap pictures of the turtles and picnic under one of the many pavilions.

Kaua'i

Hā'ena Beach Park (Tunnels Beach). Even if all you do is sit on the beach, you'll leave here happy. The scenic beauty is unsurpassed, with verdant mountains serving as a backdrop to the turquoise ocean.

Snorkeling is the best on the island during the calm, summer months. When the winter's waves arrive, surfers line up on the outside break.

Hanalei Bay Beach Park. When you dream of Hawai'i, this is what comes to mind: A vast bay rimmed by a wide beach and waterfalls draping distant mountains. Everyone finds something to do here—surf, kayak, swim, sail, sunbathe, walk and celebrity-watch.

Like most north shore beaches in Hawai'i, Hanalei switches from calm in summer to big waves in winter.

Po'ipū Beach Park. The *keiki* (child's) swimming hole makes Po'ipū a great family beach, but it's also popular with snorkelers and moderate to experienced surfers. And while Po'ipū is considered a tourist destination, the Kaua'i residents come out on the weekends, adding a local flavor.

Watch out for the endangered Hawaiian monk seals; they like it here, too.

Polihale State Park. If you're looking for remote, if you're looking for guaranteed sun, if you're thinking of camping on the beach, drive the 5-mi-long cane-haul road to the westernmost point of Kaua'i. Be sure to stay for the sunset.

Unless you're an experienced water person, we advise staying out of the water due to a steep, onshore break. You can walk for miles along this beach, the longest in Hawai'i.

BEST OUTDOOR ADVENTURES

In a place surrounded by the ocean, water sports abound. Surfing. Snorkeling. Scuba diving. Hawai'i has it all—and more. But that's just the sea. Interior mountains and valleys offer a never-ending stream of other outdoor adventures. Here are our picks for the best water and land adventures around the state.

O'ahu

Dive and snorkel at Shark's Cove. Some of the best things in life require a wait. That's the case with Shark's Cove—you have to wait for summer until it's safe to enter the water and swim with an amazing array of marine life thanks to the large boulders and coral heads dotting the sea floor and forming small caves and ledges. This is both a spectacular shore dive and snorkeling destination in one—perfect for the diver-snorkeler couple.

Bike the 'Aiea Loop Trail. This 4.5-mile, single-track, loop trail offers some of the most fun mountain biking in central O'ahu. Although it's listed as an intermediate trail, some sections are a bit technical with steep drop-offs. We recommend it for the weekend warrior who has a bit more experience. Caution: Do not attempt in wet weather.

Golf at Luana Hills Country Club. Carved out of the middle of a tropical rain forest, this peaceful setting offers an antidote to the hustle and bustle of Waikīkī. Bring your "A" game and a full bag, because club selection is key here. You'll want to hit each and every fairway.

Learn to surf at Waikīkī Beach. You've heard the age-old saying that goes, "When in Rome, do as the Romans do." Well, when in Hawai'i, surf. The sport that was once reserved for *ali'i*, royalty, knows no class barrier these days. And there is no better place to learn than Waikīkī, with its long and gentle rolling swells.

Hike to Ka'ena Point. For a raw and rugged look at O'ahu's coastline, head to hot, dry Ka'ena Point. Head out early in the morning as Ka'ena Point is situated at the northwestern tip of the island (about 45 min from Waikīkī). The 5-mi round-trip hike—rather, walk—ends at the westernmost tip of the island.

Maui

Explore Molokini Crater. Snorkeling here is like swimming in a tropical-fish aquarium. Molokini is a crescent-shaped crater that barely peeks its ridged spine above the ocean's surface, and the reef fish love it. If you're not comfortable leaping off the side of a boat into the open ocean, you may not go for this. Go early before the winds pick up.

Golf at Kapalua Resort. Geoff Ogilvy and Rory Sabbatini know a thing or two about the Plantation Course at Kapalua, the site of the PGA Tour's first event each January. You can take them on—sort of—by playing in their footsteps. Sabbatini owned the course on his fourth round in 2010, shooting a 63. Slope and wind will challenge the best of golfers here.

Hike in Haleakalā Crater. How about hiking on black sand on the top of a mountain? There aren't many places you can do that. Thirty miles of trails await here—everything from day hikes to multiday pack trips. At 10,000 feet and summit temperatures ranging from 40 to 60 degrees, you'll forget you're in Hawai'i.

Snorkel at Black Rock. We like Keka'a Point for its big marine life: a turtle the size of a small car, eagle rays with three-foot wingspans, and all kinds of Hawai'i's colorful endemic fish. But keep an eye out above, too, because this is a popular cliff-diving spot.

Big Island

Bike Kulani Trails. Stands of 80-foot eucalyptus. Giant tree ferns. The sweet song of honeycreepers overhead. Add single-track of rock and root—no dirt here—and we're talking a technically difficult ride. Did we mention this is a rain forest? That explains the perennial slick coat of slime on every possible surface. Advanced cyclists only.

Snorkel at Kealakekua Bay. Yes, the snorkeling here is tops for Big Island but, to be real, the draw here are the Hawaiian spinner dolphins that rest in the bay during the daytime. While it's enticing to swim with wild dolphins, doing so can disrupt their sleep patterns and make them susceptible to predators—aka sharks—so stick to an early morning or late afternoon schedule and give the dolphins their space between 9 and 3.

Search for lava at Volcanoes National Park. It isn't too often that you can witness the creation of rock in action. That's just what happens at Volcanoes National Park. The most dramatic example occurs where lava enters the sea. While Mother Nature rarely gives her itinerary in advance, if you're lucky, a hike or boat ride may pay off with spectacular views of nature's wonder. Sunrise and sunset makes for the best viewing opportunities.

Go horseback riding in Waipi'o Valley. The Valley of the Kings owes its relative isolation and off-the-grid status to the two-thousand-foot cliffs book-ending the valley. Really, the only way to explore this sacred place is on two legs—or four. We're partial to the horseback rides that wend deep into the rain forest to a series of waterfalls and pools—the setting for a perfect romantic getaway.

Kaua'i

Tour Nāpali Coast by boat. Every one of the Hawaiian Islands possesses something spectacularly unique to it, and this stretch of folding cliffs is it for Kaua'i. To see it, though, you'll want to hop aboard a boat. You may opt for the leisurely ride aboard a catamaran or the more adventurous inflatable raft. You can even stop for snorkeling or a walk through an ancient fishing village. Whatever you do, don't forget your camera.

Kayak the Wailua River. The largest river in all Hawai'i, the Wailua River's source is the center of the island—a place known as Mt. Wai'ale'ale—the wettest spot on earth. And yet it's no Mighty Mississippi. There are no rapids to run. And that makes it a great waterway on which to learn to kayak. Guided tours will take you to a remote waterfall. Bring the whole family on this one.

Hike the Kalalau Trail. The Sierra Club allegedly rates this famous, cliff-side trail a difficulty level of 9 out of 10. But don't let that stop you. You don't have to hike the entire 11 miles. A mile hike will reward you with scenic ocean views—where in winter you might see breaching whales—sights of soaring seabirds and tropical plant life dotting the trail sides. Wear sturdy shoes, pack your camera, and be prepared to ooh and aah.

Enjoy a Helicopter Ride. If you drive from Kē'ē Beach to Polihale, you may think you've seen all of Kaua'i, but we're here to tell you there's more scenic beauty awaiting you. Lots more. Save up for this one. It's not cheap, but a helicopter ride over the Garden Island will make you think you're watching a movie with 3-D glasses.

TOP SCENIC SPOTS

O'ahu

Nu'uanu Pali Lookout. With sweeping views of the verdant Ko'olau mountains and Kāne'ohe Bay, the point where Kamehameha I forced enemy warriors over the cliff is a must-stop on any tour around the island.

Waikīkī Beach at sunset. This is quintessential O'ahu: sailboats and catamarans cruise offshore, Diamondhead glows magenta in the last rays of sunlight while the turquoise Pacific washes gently up to pristine beaches.

Bellows Beach Park. With sugary coral sand and jade green waters this giant arc of a beach is why people come to Hawaii. While the colors of the sea and sand and few crowds are its best features, the jagged Ko'olau Mountains provide a backdrop for this idyllic tropical spot.

Maui

The Road to Hāna. Calling the Road to Hāna a "scenic spot" may be a bit of a stretch. With innumerable waterfalls, black-sand beaches, views over taro patches, and the sheer engineering involved in the narrow bridges and switchback curves, this stretch of highway in a tropical paradise provides scenic views around every corner.

Haleakalā. Most known for its views at sunrise, the summit of Haleakalā volcano is equally spectacular at sunset. On clear days the Big Island, Moloka'i, Lana'i, Kaho'olawe and Molokini Crater are visible.

Mākena Beach. Rolling waves, views of Kaho'olawe and golden sand make this wide beach a weekend favorite for locals.

The Big Island

Top of Mauna Kea at sunset. At almost 14,000 feet, a view from this cinder-covered summit at sunset provides an opportunity not only to see the sun slip into the Pacific through the pristine alpine atmosphere but also fabulous views of Maui's Haleakalā.

Waipi'o Valley Overlook. The road along the Hāmākua Coast ends with a view into one of the Big Island's most remote areas. From this point, view sheer black cliffs and the wide green valley that was once home to between 4,000 to 20,000 Hawaiians.

Hawai'i Tropical Botanical Garden. Drive past waterfalls, ponds, orchids and lush green vegetation on one of the Big Island's most scenic roads.

Kaua'i

Waimea Canyon. The oft-used term *breathtaking* does not do justice to your first view of Waimea Canyon (otherwise known as the Grand Canyon of the Pacific). Narrow waterfalls tumble thousands of feet to streams that cut through the rust-colored volcanic soil. Continue on to the end of the road for a view through the clouds of otherworldly Kalalau Valley.

Hanalei Valley Lookout. On the way to Hanalei (just past the Princeville shops), this pull-out provides views of Hanalei River winding its way through wet *lo'i* (taro patches) framed by jagged green mountains.

Kē'ē Beach. At the end of the road on the North Shore, Kē'ē Beach is as far as you can drive and as close as you can get to the fabled cliffs of Bali Hai. Surrounded by palm and almond trees, this stretch of white-sand beach is a great spot for viewing sunsets or even the occasional sea lion.

ULTIMATE HAWAIIAN INDULGENCES

Many indulgences in Hawai'i don't require reservations, appointments, or making a serious dent in your credit card. They can be as simple as lingering a bit longer in a botanical garden, smelling the plumeria or ginger flowers, or stealing a bit of time away for yourself and a book under an umbrella at one of countless secluded beaches. However, because of Hawai'i's world-class spas, chefs, and scenery, extravagant indulgences for the hedonist or gastronome abound.

O'ahu

SpaHalekulani at the Halekulani Hotel in Waikīkī offers a truly indulgent experience for two. Its Romance Remembered package is a six-hour experience which features massage, steam shower, a champagne lunch in a terrace setting, and concludes with a manicure and pedicure in the salon. For individuals, the four-hour Heavenly Journey offers a scrub and wrap, a soak in a deep Japanese soaking tub, a light lunch on their terrace, and a facial.

Looking for a gastronomic experience? **La Mer** in Waikīkī offers a gourmet menu degustation including cherrywood-smoked foie gras and sweet potato gnocchi with duck jus.

Maui

The traditional lomilomi massage at the **Spa at the Four Seasons Resort Wailea** is given in their Hawaiian Hale (a small replica of an authentic ancient Hawaiian home) overlooking Wailea Bay. The pair of therapists work in unison as they chant and dance while providing a restorative treatment which seeks to unite both mind and body.

Or, have your own personal chef prepare the decadent chocolate and berries dessert to cap off your meal in the private Il Teatro dining room at **Capische at the Hotel Wailea** in Wailea.

For those with a bit less time and money, the decadent mango margarita at **Polli's Mexican Restaurant** in Makawao is a frozen tropical twist on a traditional favorite. Stop in on your way to or from your trip to Haleakalā.

Big Island

Mauna Lani Spa has a unique Lava Watsu treatment that features pressure point techniques and stretching, but the treatment itself is only the beginning. Built inside a natural lava tube, this salt water Watsu pool is heated to body temperature. Clients float weightlessly throughout a treatment experience that is enhanced by a waterfall and underwater music.

Kaua'i

Kaua'i's natural wonders are a perfect opportunity to indulge in a helicopter ride. **Jack Harter Helicopters** offers an aerial tour of dramatic waterfalls and the spectacular Nāpali coastline—to avoid reflections in your photos, opt for a doors-off trip.

For those who prefer a more soothing experience; relax in your own private *hale* (cabana) in a tropical garden setting of orchids, ti, and other tropical greenery, as you experience the Kaua'i Clay detoxifying facial treatment at **ANARA Spa**. This treatment features a kava root scrub and mask made from local clays of Kaua'i.

WEDDINGS AND HONEYMOONS

There's no question that Hawai'i is one of the country's foremost honeymoon destinations. Romance is in the air here, and the white, sandy beaches, turquoise water, swaying palm trees, balmy tropical breezes, and perpetual sunshine put people in the mood for love. It's easy to understand why Hawai'i is fast becoming a popular wedding destination as well, especially as the cost of airfare is often discounted, and new resorts and hotels entice visitors. A destination wedding is no longer exclusive to celebrities and the superrich. You can plan a traditional ceremony in a place of worship followed by a reception at an elegant resort, or you can go barefoot on the beach and celebrate at a lū'au. There are almost as many wedding planners in the Islands as real estate agents, which makes it oh-so-easy to wed in paradise, and then, once the knot is tied, stay and honeymoon as well.

The Big Day

Choosing the Perfect Place. When choosing a location, remember that you really have two choices to make: the ceremony location and where to have the reception, if you're having one. For the former, there are beaches, bluffs overlooking beaches, gardens, private residences, resort lawns, and, of course, places of worship. As for the reception, there are these same choices, as well as restaurants and even lū'au. If you decide to go outdoors, remember the seasons—yes, Hawai'i has seasons. If you're planning a winter wedding outdoors, be sure you have a backup plan (such as a tent), in case it rains. Also, if you're planning an outdoor wedding at sunset—which is very popular—be sure you match the time of your ceremony to the time the sun sets at that time of year. If you choose an indoor spot, be sure to ask for pictures of the location when you're

planning. You don't want to plan a pink wedding, say, and wind up in a room that's predominantly red. Or maybe you do. The point is, it should be your choice.

Finding a Wedding Planner. If you're planning to invite more than a minister and your loved one to your wedding ceremony, seriously consider an on-island wedding planner who can help select a location, help design the floral scheme and recommend a florist as well as a photographer, help plan the menu and choose a restaurant, caterer, or resort, and suggest any Hawaiian traditions to incorporate into your ceremony. And more: Will you need tents, a cake, music? Maybe transportation and lodging? Many planners have relationships with vendors, providing packages—which mean savings.

If you're planning a resort wedding, most have on-site wedding coordinators; however, there are many independents around the Islands and even those who specialize in certain types of ceremonies—by locale, size, religious affiliation, and so on. A simple "Hawai'i weddings" Google search will reveal dozens. What's important is that you feel comfortable with your coordinator. Ask for references—and call them. Share your budget. Get a proposal—in writing. Ask how long they've been in business, how much they charge, how often you'll meet with them, and how they select vendors. Request a detailed list of the exact services they'll provide. If your idea of your wedding doesn't match their services, try someone else. If you can afford it, you might want to meet the planner in person.

Getting Your License. The good news about marrying in Hawai'i is that no waiting period, no residency or citizenship requirements, and no blood tests or shots

are required. However, both the bride and groom must appear together in person before a marriage-license agent to apply for a marriage license. You'll need proof of age—the legal age to marry is 18. (If you're 19 or older, a valid driver's license will suffice; if you're 18, a certified birth certificate is required.) Upon approval, a marriage license is immediately issued and costs $60, cash only. After the ceremony, your officiant will mail the marriage license to the state. Approximately four months later, you will receive a copy in the mail. (For $10 extra, you can expedite this process. Ask your marriage-license agent when you apply.) For more detailed information, visit ⊕ *www.ehawaii.gov.*

Also—this is important—the person performing your wedding must be licensed by the Hawai'i Department of Health, even if he or she is a licensed minister. Be sure to ask.

Wedding Attire. In Hawai'i, basically anything goes, from long, formal dresses with trains to white bikinis. Floral sundresses are fine, too. For the men, tuxedos are not the norm; a pair of solid-colored slacks with a nice aloha shirt is. In fact, tradition in Hawai'i for the groom is a plain white aloha shirt (they do exist) with slacks or long shorts and a colored sash around the waist. If you're planning a wedding on the beach, barefoot is the way to go.

If you decide to marry in a formal dress and tuxedo, you're better off making your selections on the mainland and hand-carrying them aboard the plane. Yes, it can be a pain, but ask your wedding-gown retailer to provide a special carrying bag. After all, you don't want to chance losing your wedding dress in a wayward piece of luggage. And when it comes to fittings,

again, that's something to take care of before you arrive in Hawai'i.

Local customs. The most obvious traditional Hawaiian wedding custom is the lei exchange in which the bride and groom take turns placing a lei around the neck of the other—with a kiss. Bridal lei are usually floral, whereas the groom's is typically made of *maile*, a green leafy garland that drapes around the neck and is open at the ends. Brides often also wear a *haku lei*—a circular floral headpiece. Other Hawaiian customs include the blowing of the conch shell, hula, chanting, and Hawaiian music.

The Honeymoon

Do you want champagne and strawberries delivered to your room each morning? A breathtaking swimming pool in which to float? A five-star restaurant in which to dine? Then a resort is the way to go. If, however, you prefer the comforts of a home, try a bed-and-breakfast. A small inn is also good if you're on a tight budget or don't plan to spend much time in your room. On the other hand, maybe you want your own private home in which to romp naked—or just laze around recovering from the wedding planning. Maybe you want your own kitchen so you can whip up a gourmet meal for your loved one. In that case, a private vacation-rental home is the answer. Or maybe a condominium resort. That's another beautiful thing about Hawai'i: the lodging accommodations are almost as plentiful as the beaches, and there's one that will perfectly match your tastes and your budget.

CRUISING THE HAWAIIAN ISLANDS

Cruising has become extremely popular in Hawai'i. For first-time visitors, it's an excellent way to get a taste of all the Islands; and if you fall in love with one or even two Islands, you know how to plan your next trip. It's also a comparatively inexpensive way to see Hawai'i.

The limited amount of time in each port can be an argument against cruising—there's enough to do on any island to keep you busy for a week, so some folks feel shortchanged by cruise itineraries.

Cruising to Hawai'i

Carnival Cruises. They call them "fun ships" for a reason—Carnival is all about keeping you busy and showing you a good time, both onboard and onshore. Great for families, Carnival always plans plenty of kid-friendly activities, and their children's program rates high with the little critics. Carnival offers 12-day itineraries starting in Ensenada and ending in Honolulu or departing from Honolulu and ending in Vancouver. Their ships stop on Maui (Kahului and Lahaina), the Big Island (Kailua-Kona and Hilo), O'ahu, and Kaua'i. ☎ 888/227–6482 ⊕ www.carnival.com.

Holland America. The grande dame of cruise lines, Holland America has a reputation for service and elegance. Holland America's 14-day Hawai'i cruises leave and return to San Diego, California, with a brief stop at Ensenada. In Hawai'i, the ship ties up at port in Maui (Lahaina), the Big Island (Hilo), O'ahu, and for half a day on Kaua'i. ☎ 877/932–4259 ⊕ www.hollandamerica.com.

Princess Cruises. Princess strives to offer affordable luxury. Their prices start out a little higher, but you get more bells and whistles (more affordable balcony rooms, nice decor, more restaurants to choose from, personalized service). They're not fantastic for kids, but they do a great job of keeping teenagers occupied. Princess's Hawaiian cruise on the *Golden Princess* is 14 days. They also have a round-trip from Los Angeles that stops on O'ahu, Maui, Kaua'i, and the Big Island with a service call in Ensenada. ☎ 800/774–6237 ⊕ www.princess.com.

Cruising within Hawai'i

American Safari Cruises. At this writing the *Safari Explorer* was preparing to launch a round-trip, eight-day, seven-night cruise from Lahaina, Maui starting in October 2011. The ship accomodates only 36 passengers; its smaller size allows it to dock at Moloka'i and Lāna'i in addition to a stop on the Big Island. The cruise is billed as "all inclusive"—and they mean it. Your passage includes shore excursions, water activities, and a massage. ☎ 888/862–8881 ⊕ www.americansafaricruises.com.

Hawai'i Nautical. Offering a completely different sort of experience, Hawai'i Nautical provides private multiple-day inter-island cruises on their catamarans, yachts, and sailboats. Prices are higher, but service is completely personal, right down to the itinerary. ☎ 808/234–7245 ⊕ www.hawaiinautical.com.

Norwegian Cruise Lines. Several of Norwegian's ships cruise the Islands. The main one is *Pride of America* (Vintage Americana theme, very new, big family focus with lots of connecting staterooms and suites), which offers seven-day or longer itineraries within the Islands, stopping on Maui, O'ahu, the Big Island, and overnighting on Kaua'i. ☎ 800/327–7030 ⊕ www.ncl.com.

O'ahu

WORD OF MOUTH

"O'ahu is really the best of all worlds as you can leave town to cavort in nature during the day and then return to eat at some amazing restaurants in the evening. You can also throw some historical/educational sights in along the way . . . [such as] Pearl Harbor and 'Iolani Palace."

—khor

WELCOME TO O'AHU

TOP REASONS TO GO

★ **Waves:** Boogie board or surf some of the best breaks on the planet.

★ **Pearl Harbor:** Remember Pearl Harbor with a visit to the *Arizona* Memorial.

★ **Diamond Head:** Scale the crater whose iconic profile looms over Waikīkī.

★ **Nightlife:** Raise your glass to the best party scene in Hawai'i.

★ **The North Shore:** See O'ahu's countryside—check out the famous beaches from Sunset to Waimea Bay and hike to the remote tip of the island.

1 Downtown Honolulu and Chinatown. The capital city of Honolulu holds the nation's only royal palace, free concerts under the tamarind trees in the financial district, and the galleries and open markets of Nu'uanu and Chinatown.

2 Waikīkī. This city is the dream that sells Hawai'i as the place to surf, swim, and sail by day and dine, dance, and party by night.

3 **Greater Honolulu and Pearl Harbor.** Aside from the most popular site to see on the island, there is much exploring to do, including taking a trip to the Bishop Museum, another attraction not to be missed.

4 **Southeast O'ahu.** Honolulu's main bedroom communities crawl up the steep-sided valleys. Also here is snorkelers' favorite Hanauma Bay and a string of wild and often hidden beaches.

5 **Windward O'ahu.** The offshore islands and remnants of ancient fishponds here are where the beach lovers live, along with many Native Hawaiians.

6 **The North Shore.** A melange of farmers and surfers call this part of the island home, where vacation rentals and plantation villages culminate in a tumble of black rocks at Ka'ena Point.

7 **Central and West (Leeward) O'ahu.** This part of the island includes Central O'ahu highlands, the Leeward coast, and the Hawaiian communities of Nānākuli and Wai'anae. It's finding a new identity as a "second city" of suburban homes and tech firms, coexisting with agriculture and traditional lifestyles.

GETTING ORIENTED

O'ahu, the third largest of the Hawaiian Islands, is not just Honolulu and Waikīkī. It's looping mountain trails on the western Wai'anae and eastern Ko'olau ranges. It's monster waves breaking on the golden beaches of the North Shore. It's country stores and beaches where turtles are your swimming companions.

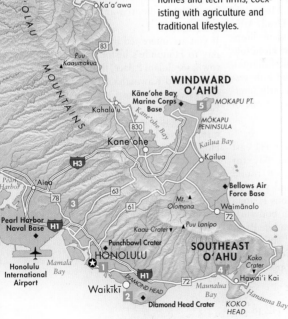

GREAT ITINERARIES

To experience even a fraction of O'ahu's charms, you need a minimum of four days and a bus pass. Five days and a car is better: Waikīkī is at least a day, Honolulu and Chinatown another, Pearl Harbor the better part of another. Each of the rural sections can swallow a day each, just for driving, sightseeing, and stopping to eat. And that's before you've taken a surf lesson, hung from a parasail, hiked a loop trail, or visited a botanical garden. The following itineraries will take you to our favorite spots on the island.

First Day in Waikīkī

You'll be up at dawn due to the time change and dead on your feet by afternoon due to jet lag. Have a dawn swim, change into walking gear, and head east along Kalākaua Avenue to Monsarrat Avenue, and climb Diamond Head. After lunch, nap in the shade, do some shopping, or visit the nearby East Honolulu neighborhoods of Mō'ili'ili and Kaimukī, rife with small shops and good little restaurants. End the day with an early, interesting, and inexpensive dinner at one of these neighborhood spots.

Southeast and Windward Exploring

For sand, sun, and surf, follow H1 east to keyhole-shaped Hanauma Bay for picture-perfect snorkeling, then round the southeast tip of the island with its windswept cliffs and the famous Hālona Blowhole. Fly a kite or watch bodysurfers at Sandy Beach. Take in Sea Life Park. In Waimānalo, stop for local-style plate lunch, or punch on through to Kailua, where there's intriguing shopping and good eating.

The North Shore

Hit H1 westbound and then H2 to get to the North Shore. You'll pass through pineapple country, then drop down a scenic winding road to Waialua and Hale'iwa. Stop in Hale'iwa town to shop, to experience shave ice, and to pick up a guided dive or snorkel trip. On winding Kamehameha Highway, stop at famous big-wave beaches, take a dip in a cove with a turtle, and buy fresh Island fruit at roadside stands.

Pearl Harbor

Pearl Harbor is almost an all-day investment. Be on the grounds by 7:30 am to line up for *Arizona* Memorial tickets. Clamber all over the USS *Bowfin* submarine. Finally, take the free trolley to see the "Mighty Mo" battleship. If it's Wednesday or Saturday, make the five-minute drive *mauka* (toward the mountains) for bargain-basement shopping at the sprawling Aloha Stadium Swap Meet.

Town Time

If you are interested in history, devote a day to Honolulu's historic sites. Downtown, see 'Iolani Palace, the Kamehameha Statue, and Kawaiaha'o Church. A few blocks east, explore Chinatown, gilded Kuan Yin Temple, and artsy Nu'uanu with its galleries. On the water is the informative Hawai'i Maritime Center. Hop west on H1 to the Bishop Museum, the state's anthropological and archaeological center. And 1 mi up Pali Highway is Queen Emma Summer Palace, whose shady grounds were a royal retreat. Worth a visit for plant lovers: Foster Botanical Garden.

2

Updated by
Chad Pata
and Melissa
Chang

O'ahu is one-stop Hawai'i—all the allure of the Islands in a chop-suey mix that has you kayaking around offshore islets by day and sitting in a jazz club 'round midnight, all without ever having to take another flight or repack your suitcase. It offers both the buzz of modern living in jam-packed Honolulu (the state's capital) and the allure of slow-paced island life on its northern and eastern shores. It is, in many ways, the center of the Hawaiian universe.

There are more museums, staffed historic sites, and walking tours here than you'll find on any other island. And only here do a wealth of renovated buildings and well-preserved neighborhoods so clearly spin the story of Hawai'i history. It's the only place to experience Island-style urbanity, since there are no other true cities in the state. And yet you can get as lost in the rural landscape and be as laid-back as you wish.

O'ahu is home to Waikīkī, the most famous Hawaiian beach with some of the world's most famous surf on the North Shore, and the Islands' best known historical site, Pearl Harbor. If it's isolation, peace, and quiet you want, O'ahu is probably not for you, but if you'd like a bit of spice with your piece of paradise, this island provides it.

GEOLOGY

Encompassing 597 square mi, O'ahu is the third-largest island in the Hawaiian chain. Scientists believe the island was formed about 4 million years ago by two volcanoes: Wai'anae and Ko'olau. Wai'anae, the older of the two, makes up the western side of the island, while Ko'olau shapes the eastern side. Central O'ahu is an elevated plateau bordered by the two mountain ranges, with Pearl Harbor to the south. Several of O'ahu's most famous natural landmarks, including Diamond Head and Hanauma Bay, are tuff rings and cinder cones formed during a renewed volcanic stage (roughly 1 million years ago).

Koko Head in Hawai'i Kai is a volcanic cinder cone near Hanauma Bay.

FLORA AND FAUNA

Due to its elevation, the eastern (Ko'olau) side of O'ahu is much cooler and wetter than the western side of the island, which tends to be dry and arid. The island's official flower, the little orange *ilima*, grows predominantly in the east, but lei throughout the island incorporate *ilima*. Numerous tropical fish call the reef at Hanauma Bay home, migrating humpback whales can be spotted off the coast past Waikīkī and Diamond Head from December through April, spinner dolphins pop in and out of the island's bays, and dozens of islets off O'ahu's eastern coast provide refuge for endangered seabirds.

HISTORY

O'ahu is the most populated island because early tourism to Hawai'i started here. Although Kīlauea volcano on Hawai'i was a tourist attraction in the late 1800s, it was the building of the Moana Hotel on Waikīkī Beach in 1901 and subsequent advertising of Hawai'i to wealthy San Franciscans that really fueled tourism in the Islands. O'ahu was drawing tens of thousands of guests yearly when, on December 7, 1941, Japanese Zeros appeared at dawn to bomb Pearl Harbor. Though tourism understandably dipped during the war (Waikīkī Beach was fenced with barbed wire), the subsequent memorial only seemed to attract more visitors, and O'ahu remains hugely popular with tourists to this day.

Seeing Pearl Harbor

Pearl Harbor is a must-see for many, but there are things to know before you go. Consider whether you want to see only the *Arizona* Memorial, or the USS *Bowfin* and USS *Missouri* as well. Allow approximately and hour and 15 minutes for the USS *Arizona* tour.

Plan to arrive early—tickets for the *Arizona* Memorial (free) are given out on a first-come, first-served basis and can disappear within an hour. There are restrictions on what you can bring with you, including purses, backpacks, and camera cases (although cameras are allowed). Baggage lockers are available for a small fee. Also, don't forget ID.

Note that children under four are not allowed on the *Bowfin* and may not enjoy the crowds and waiting in line at other sights. Older kids are likely to find the more experiential, hands-on history of the USS *Bowfin* and USS *Missouri* memorable.

The USS *Arizona* Memorial visitor's center, which recently reopened after a $58 million renovation, is open from 7:30 am to 5 pm. For more information, visit ⊕ *www.nps.gov/valr/index. htm.*

PLANNING

GETTING HERE AND AROUND
AIR TRAVEL
Honolulu International Airport is 20 minutes (40 during rush hour) from Waikīkī. Car rental is across the street from baggage claim.

GROUND TRANSPOR-TATION A cumbersome and inefficient airport taxi system requires you to line up to a taxi wrangler who radios for cars (about $25 to Waikīkī). Other options: TheBus ($2, one lap-size bag allowed) or public airport shuttle ($8). Ask the driver to take H1, not Nimitz Highway, at least as far as downtown, or your introduction to paradise will be Honolulu's industrial backside.

CAR TRAVEL
If you plan on getting outside of Waikīkī and Honolulu, renting a car is a must. But renting a Mustang convertible is a sure sign that you're a tourist and practically begs, "Come burglarize me." A good rule of thumb: When the car is out of your sight even for a moment, it should be empty of anything you care about. But there are other added bonuses of opting out of your Hawai'i dream machine—you'll save some money and won't be hassled by constantly having to put the top down during one of the island's intermittent rain showers.

Reserve your vehicle in advance, especially during the Christmas holidays. This will not only ensure that you get a car but also that you get the best rates.

See "Travel Smart Hawai'i" for more information on renting a car and driving.

ISLAND DRIVING TIMES It might not seem as if driving from your hotel in Waikīkī to the North Shore, say, would take very much time. But it will take longer than you'd think from glancing at a map, and roads are subject to some pretty heavy traffic.

Be aware that areas around Honolulu can have traffic jams that would rival Southern California, so plan your movements accordingly. Heavy traffic toward downtown Honolulu begins as early as 6:30 am and lasts until 9 am. In the afternoon, expect traffic departing downtown to back up beginning around 3 pm until approximately 7 pm.

Here are average driving times—without traffic—that will help you plan your excursions accordingly.

DRIVING TIMES	
Waikīkī to Kō'Ōlina	28 mi/40 mins
Waikīkī to Hale'iwa	33 mi/45 mins
Waikīkī to Kailua	15 mi/30 mins
Waikīkī to Downtown Honolulu	4 mi/10 mins
Waikīkī to Honolulu Int. Airport	12 mi/25 mins

RESTAURANTS

Honolulu is home to some of the world's most famous chefs, from Sam Choy and his down-home cooking to the artistic Roy Yamaguchi. While there are plenty of glitzy and recognizable names, some of the best cuisine is off Waikīkī's beaten path. Look to Kapahulu and Waialae Avenues for fantastic hole-in-the-wall sushi joints and local favorites. Chinatown is the spot for not just dim sum, but the best of Italian, French, and Cuban dishes.

HOTELS

Most of O'ahu's lodging options are located in Waikīkī. While the Royal Hawaiians and Hilton Hawaiian Villages get most of the airtime when TV shows try to capture this resort area, most of us stay at places that are a bit less flashy but still have their charms. Aqua Hotels have recently taken over several properties that create that boutique feel without the price tag, while the Outrigger chain carries broad appeal for those traveling with kids.

WHAT IT COSTS					
	¢	$	$$	$$$	$$$$
Restaurants	under $10	$10–$17	$18–$26	$27–$35	over $35
Hotels	under $100	$100–$180	$181–$260	$261–$340	over $340

Restaurant prices are for a main course at dinner. Hotel prices are for two people in a standard double room in high season. Condo price categories reflect studio and one-bedroom rates.

VISITOR INFORMATION

Before you go, contact the O'ahu Visitors Bureau (OVB). For general information on all the Islands, contact the Hawai'i Visitors & Convention Bureau. The HVCB Web site has a calendar section that shows what local events will be taking place during your stay.

Contacts **Hawai'i Visitors & Convention Bureau** (✉ 2270 Kalākaua Ave., Suite 801, Honolulu ☎ 808/923–1811, 800/464–2924 for brochures ⊕ www. gohawaii.com). **O'ahu Visitors Bureau** (✉ 733 Bishop St., Suite 1520, Honolulu ☎ 808/524–0722 ⊕ www.visit-oahu.com).

EXPLORING

O'ahu, the third largest of the Hawaiian Islands, is not just Honolulu and Waikīkī. It's looping mountain trails on the western Wai'anae and eastern Ko'olau ranges. It's monster waves breaking on the golden beaches of the North Shore. It's country stores and beaches where turtles are your swimming companions.

DOWNTOWN HONOLULU AND CHINATOWN

Here is Hawai'i's only true metropolis, its seat of government, center of commerce and shipping, entertainment and recreation mecca, a historic site and an evolving urban area.

Honolulu's past and present play a delightful counterpoint throughout the downtown sector. Postmodern glass-and-steel office buildings look down on the Aloha Tower, built in 1926 and, until the early 1960s, the tallest structure in Honolulu. Hawai'i's history is told in the architecture of these few blocks: the cut-stone turn-of-the-20th-century storefronts of Merchant Street, the gracious white-columned American-Georgian manor that was the home of the Islands' last queen, the jewel-box palace occupied by the monarchy before it was overthrown, the Spanish-inspired stucco and tile-roofed Territorial Era government buildings, and the 21st-century glass pyramid of the First Hawaiian Bank Building.

Chinatown's original business district was made up of dry goods and produce merchants, tailors and dressmakers, barbers, herbalists, and dozens of restaurants. The meat, fish, and produce stalls remain but the mix is heavier now on gift and curio stores, lei stands, jewelry shops and bakeries, with a smattering of noodle makers, travel agents, Asian-language video stores, and dozens of restaurants.

The name Chinatown here has always been a misnomer. Though three-quarters of O'ahu's Chinese lived closely packed in these 25 acres in the late 1800s, even then the neighborhood was half Japanese. Today, you hear Vietnamese and Tagalog as often as Mandarin and Cantonese, and there are touches of Japan, Singapore, Malaysia, Korea, Thailand, Samoa, and the Marshall Islands, as well.

Though much happened to Chinatown in the 20th century—beginning in January 1900, when almost the entire neighborhood was burned to the ground to halt the spread of bubonic plague—it remains a bustling, crowded, noisy, and odiferous place bent primarily on buying and selling, and sublimely oblivious to its status as a National Historic District or the encroaching gentrification on nearby Nu'uanu Avenue.

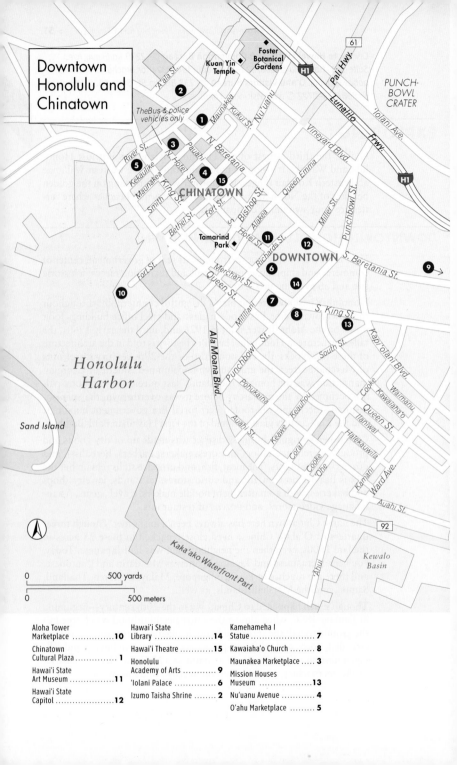

Downtown Honolulu and Chinatown

PUNCH-BOWL CRATER

Foster Botanical Gardens

Kuan Yin Temple

2 Izumo Taisha Shrine

'A'ala St.

TheBus & police vehicles only

Maunakea St.

Kukui St.

Nu'uanu Ave.

1

Pali Hwy.

61

H1

'Iolani Ave.

Lunalilo Hwy.

River St.

3

N. Beretania

N. Hotel St.

Pauahi

Vineyard Blvd.

Queen Emma

Kekaulike

5

Maunakea

King St.

4

15

Smith

CHINATOWN

Bishop St.

Fort St.

S.

Bethel St.

Miller St.

Punchbowl St.

H1

9

Fort St.

Tamarind Park

Alakea

Hotel St.

11

Richards St.

12

DOWNTOWN

S. Beretania St.

6

Merchant St.

Queen St.

14

Mililani

7

8

S. King St.

13

Kapi'olani Blvd.

South St.

Waimanu

Cooke

Honolulu Harbor

10

Ala Moana Blvd.

Punchbowl St.

Pohukaina

Kawaiaha'o

Queen St.

Kawaiaha'o

Iliani

Sand Island

Auahi St.

Keawe

Keauhou

Coral

Cooke

'Ohe

Hotel

Halekauwila

Kamani

Ward Ave.

Auahi St.

92

Kaka'ako Waterfront Park

Ahui

Kewalo Basin

0   500 yards

0   500 meters

GETTING HERE AND AROUND

To reach downtown Honolulu from Waikīkī by car, take Ala Moana Boulevard to Alakea Street and turn right; three blocks up on the right, between South King and Hotel; there's a municipal parking lot in Ali'i Place on the right. There are also public parking lots (75¢ per half hour for the first two hours) in buildings along Alakea, Smith, Beretania, and Bethel streets (Gateway Plaza on Bethel Street is a good choice). The best parking downtown, however, is street parking along Punchbowl Street—when you can find it.

Another option is to take route 19 or 20 of highly popular and convenient TheBus to the Aloha Tower Marketplace, or take a trolley from Waikīkī.

> **MONEY-SAVING TIPS**
>
> ■ Pick up free publications at the airport and at racks all over the island; many of them are filled with money-saving coupons.
>
> ■ Access to beaches and most hiking trails on the island is free to the public.
>
> ■ Grocery stores and Wal-Mart generally stock postcards and souvenirs; they can be less expensive here than at hotel gift shops.
>
> ■ For inexpensive fresh fruit and produce, check out farmers' markets and farm stands along the road—they'll often let you try before you buy.

Chinatown occupies 15 blocks immediately north of downtown Honolulu—it's flat, compact, and very walkable.

TIMING

Plan a couple of hours for exploring downtown's historic buildings, more if you're taking a guided tour or walk. The best time to visit is in the cool and relative quiet of morning or on the weekends when downtown is all but deserted except for the historic sites.

Chinatown can easily be explored in half a day. The best time to visit is morning, when the *popos* (grandmas) shop—it's cool out, and you can enjoy a cheap dim-sum breakfast. Chinatown is a seven-days-a-week operation. Sundays are especially busy with families sharing dim sum in raucous dining hall–size restaurants.

If you're here between January 20 and February 20, check local newspapers for Chinese New Year activities. Bakeries stock special sweets, stores and homes sprout bright red scrolls, and lion dancers cavort through the streets feeding on *li-see* (money envelopes). The Narcissus Queen is chosen, and an evening street fair draws crowds.

TOP ATTRACTIONS

Fodor'sChoice ★ **'Iolani Palace.** America's only royal residence was built in 1882 on the site of an earlier palace, and it contains the thrones of King Kalākaua and his successor (and sister) Queen Lili'uokalani. Bucking the stereotype of the primitive Islander, the palace had electricity and telephone lines installed even before the White House. Downstairs galleries showcase the royal jewelry, and kitchen and offices of the monarchy. The palace is open for guided or self-guided audio tours, and reservations are essential. ■ TIP➔ If you're set on taking a guided tour, call for reservations a few days in advance. The gift shop was formerly the 'Iolani Barracks, built to house the Royal Guard. ✉ *King and Richards Sts., Downtown Honolulu* ☎ *808/522–0832* 🌐 *www.iolanipalace.org* ✉ *$20 guided tour, $12 audio tour, $6 downstairs galleries only* ☉ *Tues.– Sat. 9–2, guided tours every 15 min 9–11:15, self-guided audio tours 11:45–3:30.*

WORD OF MOUTH

"Everyone should at least see the view of Diamond Head curving around from the beach. To me, that IS Hawaii, and I've been more than once to the four major Islands." —carolyn

Kamehameha I Statue. Paying tribute to the Big Island chieftain who united all the warring Hawaiian Islands into one kingdom at the turn of the 18th century, this statue, which stands with one arm outstretched in welcome, is one of three originally cast in Paris, France, by American sculptor T. R. Gould. The original statue, lost at sea and replaced by this one, was eventually salvaged and is now in Kapa'au, on the Big Island, near the king's birthplace. Each year on the king's birthday, June 11, the more famous copy is draped in fresh lei that reach lengths of 18 feet and longer. A parade proceeds past the statue, and Hawaiian civic clubs, the women in hats and impressive long *holokū* dresses and the men in sashes and cummerbunds, pay honor to the leader whose name means "The Lonely One." ✉ *417 S. King St., outside Ali'iōlani Hale, Downtown Honolulu.*

Kawaiaha'o Church. Fancifully called Hawai'i's Westminster Abbey, this 14,000-coral-block house of worship witnessed the coronations, weddings, and funerals of generations of Hawaiian royalty. Each of the building's coral blocks was quarried from reefs offshore at depths of more than 20 feet and transported to this site. Interior woodwork was created from the forests of the Ko'olau Mountains. The upper gallery has an exhibit of paintings of the royal families. The graves of missionaries and of King Lunalilo are adjacent. Services in English and Hawaiian are held each Sunday, and the church members are exceptionally welcoming, greeting newcomers with lei; their affiliation is United Church of Christ. Although there are no guided tours, you can look around the church at no cost. ✉ *957 Punchbowl St., at King St., Downtown Honolulu* ☎ *808/522–1333* ✉ *Free* ☉ *Service in English and Hawaiian Sun. at 9 am.*

Kuan Yin Temple. A couple of blocks *mauka* (toward the mountains) from Chinatown is the oldest Buddhist temple in the Islands. Mistakenly called a goddess by some, Kuan Yin, also known as Kannon, is a *bodhisattva*—one who chose to remain on earth doing good even after achieving enlightenment. Transformed from a male into a female figure centuries ago, she is credited with a particular sympathy for women. You will see representations of her all over the Islands: holding a lotus flower (beauty from the mud of human frailty), as at the temple; pouring out a pitcher of oil (like mercy flowing); or as a sort of Madonna with a child. Visitors are permitted but be aware this is a practicing place of worship. ✉ *170 N. Vineyard, Downtown* ☎ *No phone.*

★ **O'ahu Marketplace.** Here is a taste of old-style Chinatown, where you're likely to be hustled aside as a whole pig (dead, of course) is wrestled

SHOPPING IN CHINATOWN

You'll find ridiculously inexpensive gifts in Chinatown: folding fans for $1 and coconut purses for $5 at **Maunakea Marketplace,** for example. Curio shops sell everything from porcelain statues to woks, ginseng to Mao shoes. If you like to sew, or have a yen for a brocade cheongsam, visit the Hong Kong Supermarket in the Wo Fat Chop Sui building (at the corner of N. Hotel and Maunakea) for fresh fruit, crack seed (Chinese dried fruit popular for snacking), and row upon row of boxed, tinned delicacies with indecipherable names. Narrow, dim, and dusty **Bo Wah Trading Co.** (✉ *1037 Maunakea*) is full of cooking utensils, some quite decorative. **Chinatown Cultural Plaza** offers fine-quality jade. And Chinatown is Honolulu's lei center, with shops strung along Beretania and Maunakea. In spring look for gardenia nosegays wrapped in tī leaves.

through the crowd and where glassy-eyed fish of every size and hue lie stacked forlornly on ice. Try the bubble tea (juices and flavored teas with tapioca bubbles inside) or pick up a bizarre magenta dragonfruit for breakfast. ✉ *N. King St. at Kekaulike, Chinatown.*

WORTH NOTING

Aloha Tower Marketplace. In two stories of shops and kiosks you can find Island-inspired clothing, jewelry, art, and home furnishings. The Marketplace also has indoor and outdoor restaurants and live entertainment. For a bird's-eye view of this working harbor, take a free ride up to the observation deck of Aloha Tower. Cruise ships dock at piers 9 and 10 alongside the Marketplace and are often greeted and sent out to sea with music and hula dancing at the piers' end. ✉ *1 Aloha Tower Dr., at Piers 10 and 11, Downtown Honolulu* ☎ *808/528–5700 entertainment info* ⊕ *www.alohatower.com* ☉ *Mon.–Sat. 9–9, Sun. 9–6; restaurants open later.*

Chinatown Cultural Plaza. This sprawling multistory shopping square surrounds a courtyard with an incense-wreathed shrine and Moongate stage for holiday performances. The Chee Kung Tong Society has a beautifully decorated meeting hall here; a number of such *tongs* (meeting places) are hidden on upper floors in Chinatown. Outside, near the canal, local members of the community play cards and mah-jongg. ✉ *100 N. Beretania, Chinatown.*

Hawai'i State Art Museum. Hawai'i was one of the first states in the nation to legislate that a portion of the taxes paid on commercial building projects be set aside for the purchase of artwork. A few years ago, the state purchased an ornate period-style building (built to house the headquarters of a prominent developer) and dedicated 12,000 feet on the second floor to the art of Hawai'i in all its ethnic diversity. The **Diamond Head Gallery** features new acquisitions and thematic shows from the State Art Collection and the State Foundation on Culture and the Arts. The **'Ewa Gallery** houses more than 150 works documenting Hawai'i's visual-arts history since becoming a state in 1959. Also included are a sculpture gallery as well as a café, a gift shop, and educational meeting rooms.

✉ *250 S. Hotel St., 2nd fl., Downtown Honolulu* ☎ *808/586–0900 museum, 808/536–5900 restaurant* ⊕ *www.hawaii.gov/sfca* 🔲 *Free* ⊙ *Tues.–Sat. 10–4.*

Hawai'i State Capitol. The capitol's architecture is richly symbolic: the columns resemble palm trees, the legislative chambers are shaped like volcanic cinder cones, and the central court is open to the sky, representing Hawai'i's open society. Replicas of the Hawai'i state seal, each weighing 7,500 pounds, hang above both its entrances. The building, which in 1969 replaced 'Iolani Palace as the seat of government, is surrounded by reflecting pools, just as the Islands are embraced by water. A pair of statues, often draped in lei, flank the building: one of the beloved queen Lili'uokalani and the other of the sainted Father Damien de Veuster. ✉ *215 S. Beretania St., Downtown Honolulu* ☎ *808/586–0178* 🔲 *Free* ⊙ *Guided tours Mon., Wed., Fri. 1:30.*

Hawai'i State Library. This beautifully renovated main library was built in 1913. Its Samuel M. Kamakau Reading Room, on the first floor in the Mauka (Hawaiian for "mountain") Courtyard, houses an extensive Hawai'i and Pacific book collection and pays tribute to Kamakau, a missionary student whose 19th-century writings in English offer rare and vital insight into traditional Hawaiian culture. ✉ *478 King St., Downtown Honolulu* ☎ *808/586–3500* 🔲 *Free* ⊙ *Mon. and Wed. 10–5, Tues., Fri., and Sat. 9–5, Thurs. 9–8.*

Hawai'i Theatre. Opened in 1922, this theater earned rave reviews for its neoclassical design, with Corinthian columns, marble statues, and plush carpeting and drapery. Nicknamed the "Pride of the Pacific," the facility was rescued from demolition in the early 1980s and underwent a $30 million renovation. Listed on both the State and National Register of Historic Places, it has become the centerpiece of revitalization efforts of Honolulu's downtown area. The 1,200-seat venue hosts concerts, theatrical productions, dance performances, and film screenings. ✉ *1130 Bethel St., Chinatown* ☎ *808/528–0506* 🔲 *$5* ⊙ *1-hr guided tours Tues. at 11.*

Honolulu Academy of Arts. Originally built around the collection of a Honolulu matron who donated much of her estate to the museum, the academy is housed in a maze of courtyards, cloistered walkways, and quiet low-ceilinged spaces. There's an impressive permanent collection that includes Hiroshige's *ukiyo-e* Japanese prints, donated by James Michener; Italian Renaissance paintings; and American and European art. The newer Luce Pavilion complex, nicely incorporated into the more traditional architecture of the place, has a traveling-exhibit gallery, a Hawaiian gallery, an excellent café, and a gift shop. The Academy Theatre screens art films. This is also the jumping-off place for tours of Doris Duke's estate, Shangri-La. Call or check the Web site for special exhibits, concerts, and films. ✉ *900 S. Beretania St., Downtown Honolulu* ☎ *808/532–8700* ⊕ *www.honoluluacademy.org* 🔲 *$10 Academy, free 1st Wed. and 3rd Sun. of month* ⊙ *Tues.–Sat. 10–4:30, Sun. 1–5.*

Izumo Taisha Shrine. From Chinatown Cultural Plaza, cross a stone bridge to visit Okuninushi No Mikoto, a *kami* (god) who is believed in

Shinto tradition to bring good fortune if properly courted (and thanked afterward). ⊠ *N. Kukui and Canal, Chinatown* ☎ *No phone.*

Maunakea Marketplace. On the corner of Maunakea and Hotel streets is this plaza surrounded by shops, an indoor market, and a food court. ■ TIP➔ **If you appreciate fine tea, visit the Tea Hut, an unpretentious counter inside a curio shop.**

Within the Marketplace, the **Hawaiian Chinese Cultural Museum and Archives** (⊡ *$2* ⊙ *Mon.–Sat. 10–2*) displays historic photographs and artifacts. ⊠ *1120 Maunakea St., Chinatown* ☎ *808/524–3409.*

Mission Houses Museum. The determined Hawai'i missionaries arrived in 1820, gaining royal favor and influencing every aspect of island life. Their descendants became leaders in government and business. You can walk through their original dwellings, including Hawai'i's oldest wooden structure, a white-frame house that was prefabricated in New England and shipped around the Horn. Certain areas of the museum may be seen only on a one-hour guided tour. Costumed docents give an excellent picture of what mission life was like. Rotating displays showcase such arts as Hawaiian quilting, portraits, even toys. ⊠ *553 S. King St., Downtown Honolulu* ☎ *808/531–0481* ⊕ *www.missionhouses.org* ⊡ *$10* ⊙ *Tues.–Sat. 10–4; guided tours at 11 and 2:45.*

Nu'uanu Avenue. Here on Chinatown's southern border and on Bethel Street, which runs parallel, are clustered art galleries, restaurants, a wine shop, an antiques auctioneer, a dress shop or two, one tiny theater space (the Arts at Mark's Garage), and one historic stage (the Hawai'i Theatre). **First Friday** art nights, when galleries stay open until 9 pm, draw crowds. If you like art and people-watching and are fortunate enough to be on O'ahu the first Friday of the month, this event shouldn't be missed. ⊠ *Nu'uanu Ave., Chinatown.*

WAIKĪKĪ AND DIAMOND HEAD

A short drive from downtown Honolulu, Waikīkī is O'ahu's primary resort area. A mix of historic and modern hotels and condos front the sunny 2 ½ mi stretch of beach, and many have clear views of Diamond Head to the east. The area is home to much of the island's dining, nightlife, and shopping scene—from posh boutiques to hole-in-the-wall eateries to craft booths at the International Marketplace.

Waikīkī was once a favorite retreat for Hawaiian royalty. In 1901 the Moana Hotel debuted, introducing Waikīkī as an international travel destination. The region's fame continued to grow when Duke Kahanamoku helped popularize the sport of surfing, offering lessons to visitors at Waikīkī. You can see Duke immortalized in a bronze statue, with a surfboard, on Kūhiō Beach. Today, there is a decidedly "urban resort" vibe here; streets are clean, gardens are manicured, and the sand feels softer than at beaches farther down the coast. There isn't much of a local culture—it's mainly tourist crowds—but you'll still find the relaxed surfy vibe that has drawn people here for centuries.

Diamond Head Crater is perhaps Hawai'i's most recognizable natural landmark. It got its name from sailors who thought they had found precious gems on its slopes; these later proved to be calcite crystals, or fool's gold. Hawaiians saw a resemblance in the sharp angle of the crater's seaward slope to the oddly shaped head of the 'ahi fish and so called it Lē'ahi, though later they Hawaiianized the English name to Kaimana Hila. It is commemorated in a widely known hula—*"A 'ike i ka nani o Kaimana Hila, Kaimana Hila, kau mai i luna"* ("We saw the beauty of Diamond Head, Diamond Head set high above").

Kapi'olani Park lies in the shadow of the crater. King David Kalākaua established the park in 1887, named it after his queen, and dedicated it "to the use and enjoyment of the people." Kapi'olani Park is a 500-acre expanse where you can play all sorts of field sports, enjoy a picnic, see wild animals at the Honolulu Zoo, or hear live music at the Waikīkī Shell or the Kapi'olani Bandstand.

GETTING HERE AND AROUND

Bounded by the Ala Wai Canal on the north and west, the beach on the south, and the Honolulu Zoo to the east, Waikīkī is compact and easy to walk around. TheBus runs multiple routes here from the airport and downtown Honolulu. By car, finding Waikīkī from H1 can be tricky; look for the Punahou exit for western Waikīkī, and the King Street exit for eastern Waikīkī.

TOP ATTRACTIONS

Diamond Head State Monument and Park. Panoramas from this 760-foot extinct volcanic peak, once used as a military fortification, extend from Waikīkī and Honolulu in one direction and out to Koko Head in the other, with surfers and windsurfers scattered like confetti on the cresting waves below. This 360-degree perspective is a great orientation for first-time visitors. On a clear day, look to your left past Koko Head to glimpse the outlines of the Islands of Maui and Moloka'i. To enter the park from Waikīkī, take Kalākaua Avenue east, turn left at Monsarrat Avenue, head a mile up the hill, and look for a sign on the right. Drive through the tunnel to the inside of the crater. The ¾-mi trail to the top begins at the parking lot. New lighting inside the summit tunnel and a spiral staircase eases the way, but be aware that the hike to the crater is a strenuous upward climb; if you aren't in the habit of getting much exercise, this might not be for you. Take bottled water with you to ensure that you stay hydrated under the tropical sun. ■ TIP→ To beat the heat and the crowds, rise early and make the hike before 8 am. As you walk, note the color of the vegetation; if the mountain is brown, Honolulu has been without significant rain for a while; but if the trees and undergrowth glow green, you'll know it's the wet season (winter) without looking at a calendar. This is when rare Hawaiian marsh plants revive on the floor of the crater. Keep an eye on your watch if you're there at day's end, because the gates close promptly at 6. ⊠ *Diamond Head Rd. at 18th Ave., Waikīkī* ☎ *808/587–0300* ⊕ *www.hawaiistateparks.org/parks/oahu* ⊠ *$1 per person, $5 per vehicle* ☉ *Daily 6–6.*

Ⓒ **Waikīkī Aquarium.** This amazing little attraction harbors more than 3,000 organisms and 500 species of Hawaiian and South Pacific marine life, endangered Hawaiian monk seals, sharks, and the only chambered nautilus living in captivity. The Edge of the Reef exhibit showcases

Continued on page 65

INS & OUTS OF WAIKĪKĪ

Waikīkī is all that is wonderful about a resort area, and all that is regrettable. On the wonderful side: swimming, surfing, parasailing, and catamaran-riding steps from the street; the best nightlife in Hawai'i;

shopping from designer to dime stores; and experiences to remember: the heart-lifting rush the first time you stand up on a surfboard, watching the old men play cutthroat checkers in the beach pavilions, eating fresh grilled snapper as the sun slips into the sea. As to the regrettable: clogged streets, body-lined beaches, $5 cups of coffee, tacky T-shirts, $20 parking stalls, schlocky artwork, the same street performers you saw in Atlantic City, drunks, ceaseless construction—all rather brush the bloom from the plumeria.

Modern Waikīkī is nothing like its original self, a network of streams, marshes, and islands that drained the inland valleys. The Ala Wai Canal took

care of that in the 1920s. More recently, new landscaping, walkways, and a general attention to infrastructure have brightened a façade that had begun distinctly to fade.

But throughout its history, Waikīkī has retained its essential character: an enchantment that cannot be fully explained and one that, though diminished by high-rises, traffic, and noise, has not yet disappeared. Hawaiian royalty came here, and visitors continue to follow, falling in love with sharp-prowed Diamond Head, the sensuous curve of shoreline with its baby-safe waves, and the strong-footed surfers like moving statues in the golden light.

WAIKĪKĪ WEST

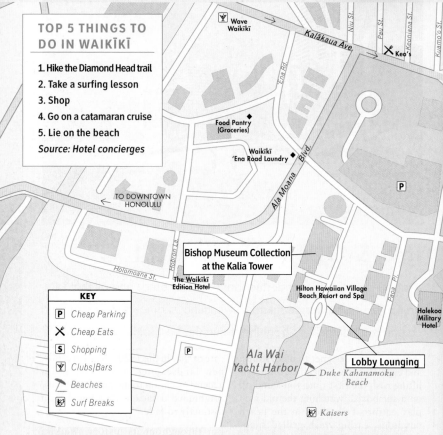

TOP 5 THINGS TO DO IN WAIKĪKĪ

1. Hike the Diamond Head trail
2. Take a surfing lesson
3. Shop
4. Go on a catamaran cruise
5. Lie on the beach

Source: Hotel concierges

KEY

P	*Cheap Parking*
✕	*Cheap Eats*
S	*Shopping*
▼	*Clubs/Bars*
	Beaches
	Surf Breaks

Wave Waikīkī

Kalākaua Ave.

Niu St.

Pau St.

Keoniana St.

Kuamo'o St.

Keo's

Ena Rd.

Food Pantry (Groceries)

Waikīkī 'Ena Road Laundry

Ala Moana Blvd.

TO DOWNTOWN HONOLULU

P

Bishop Museum Collection at the Kalia Tower

Holomoana St.

Hobron La.

The Waikīkī Edition Hotel

Hilton Hawaiian Village Beach Resort and Spa

Paoa Pl.

Halekoa Military Hotel

P

Ala Wai Yacht Harbor

Duke Kahanamoku Beach

Lobby Lounging

Kaisers

CHEAP EATS

Keo's, 2028 Kūhiō: Breakfast.

Pho Old Saigon, 2270 Kūhiō: Vietnamese.

Japanese noodle shops: Try Menchanko-Tei, Waikīkī Trade Center; Ezogiku, 2164 Kalākaua.

■ TIP➜ Thanks to the many Japanese nationals who stay here, Waikīkī is blessed with lots of cheap, authentic Japanese food, particularly noodles. Plastic representations of food in the window are an indicator of authenticity and a help in ordering.

SHOP, SHOP, SHOP/PARTY, PARTY, PARTY

2100 Kalākaua: Select high-end European boutiques (Chanel, Gucci, Yves Saint Laurent).

Waikīkī Beach Walk: Dine and shop for gifts and apparel from locally-owned stores. 227 Lewers St. 808/931-3591.

Zanzabar: Upscale Zanzabar is a different club every night—Latin, global, over 30, under 18. Waikīkī Trade Center, 2255 Kūhiō Ave. 808/924-3939.

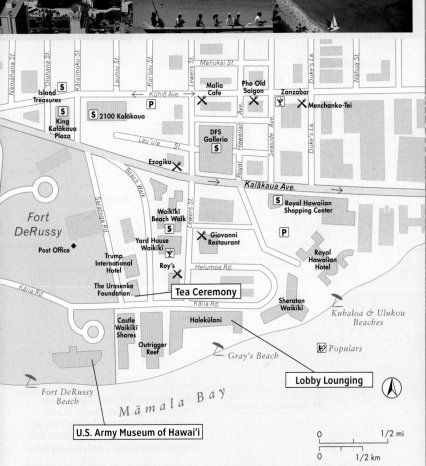

Manukai St.

Nāmahana St. Olohana St. Kalaimoku St. Launiu St. Kaʻiolu St. Lewers St.

[S] Island Treasures

[S] King Kalākaua Plaza

[S] 2100 Kalākaua

[P]

← Kūhiō Ave. →

Malia Cafe ✕

Pho Old Saigon ✕

Zanzabar ⌖

✕ Menchanko-Tei

Duke's La. Seaside Ave. Royal Hawaiian Ave. Nāhua St.

Lauʻula St.

DFS Galleria [S]

Ezogiku ✕

Kalākaua Ave. →

Beach Walk Saratoga Rd.

Fort DeRussy

Post Office ◆

Waikīkī Beach Walk [S]

Yard House Waikīkī ⌖

Giovanni ✕ Restaurant

[S] Royal Hawaiian Shopping Center

[P]

Trump International Hotel

Roy's ✕

Helumoa Rd.

Royal Hawaiian Hotel

The Urasenke Foundation

Tea Ceremony

Kālia Rd. Kālia Rd.

Sheraton Waikīkī ☂

Kuhaloa & Ulukou Beaches

Castle Waikīkī Shores

Halekūlani

Outrigger Reef ☂

Gray's Beach

🏖 *Populars*

Lobby Lounging

☂ Fort DeRussy Beach

U.S. Army Museum of Hawai'i

Mā mala Bay

0 ——— 1/2 mi
0 ——— 1/2 km

RAINY DAY IDEAS

Lobby Lounging: Among Waikīkī's great gathering spots are Halekūlani's tranquil courtyards with gorgeous flower arrangements and glimpses of the famous and the Hilton Hawaiian Village's flagged pathways with koi ponds, squawking parrots, and great shops.

Bishop Museum Collection at the Kalia Tower, Hilton Hawaiian Village: 8,000-square-foot branch of Hawai'i's premier cultural archive illuminates life in Waikīkī through the years and the history of the Hawaiian people. 2005 Kalia Rd. 808/947-2458. $7. Daily 10–5.

Tea Ceremony, Urasenke Foundation: Japan's mysterious tea ceremony is demonstrated. 245 Saratoga Rd. 808/923-3059. $3 donation. Wed., Fri. 10–11 am.

U.S. Army Museum of Hawai'i: Exhibits, including photographs and military equipment, trace the history of Army in the Islands. Battery Randolph, Kalia Rd., Fort DeRussy. 808/955-9552. Free. Tues.–Sst. 9–5.

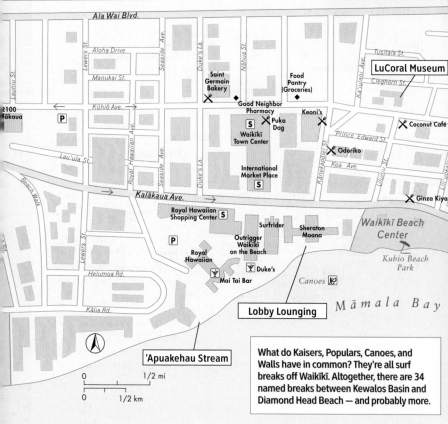

Ala Wai Blvd.

Aloha Drive

Manukai St.

Kūhiō Ave.

Lau'ula St.

Kalākaua Ave.

Helumoa Rd.

Kālia Rd.

Laumiu St.

Lewers St.

Seaside Ave.

Royal Hawaiian Ave.

Duke's La.

Nāhua St.

Kāne'kapōlei St.

Koa Ave.

Prince Edward St.

Kaiulani Ave.

Kuhio Ave.

Tusitala St.

Cleghorn St.

'Uluniu Ave.

Liliuokalani Ave.

Saint Germain Bakery

Good Neighbor Pharmacy

Food Pantry (Groceries)

LuCoral Museum

Keoni's

Coconut Café

Puka Dog

Odoriko

Waikīkī Town Center

International Market Place

Ginza Kiya

Royal Hawaiian Shopping Center

Surfrider

Sheraton Moana

Waikīkī Beach Center

Outrigger Waikīkī on the Beach

Kuhio Beach Park

Royal Hawaiian

Duke's

Mai Tai Bar

Canoes

Lobby Lounging

Māmala Bay

'Apuakehau Stream

0 ———— 1/2 mi
0 ———— 1/2 km

> What do Kaisers, Populars, Canoes, and Walls have in common? They're all surf breaks off Waikīkī. Altogether, there are 34 named breaks between Kewalos Basin and Diamond Head Beach — and probably more.

CHEAP EATS

Coconut Café, 2441 Kūhiō: Burgers, sandwiches under $5; fresh fruit smoothies.

Ginza Kiya, 2464 Kalākaua: Japanese noodle shop.

Keoni's, Outrigger East Hotel, 150 Kaiulani Ave.: Breakfasts at rock-bottom prices.

Odoriko, King's Village, 131 Kāiulani Ave.: Japanese noodle shop.

Puka Dog, 2301 Kūhiō #334: Delicious hot dogs baked into their buns.

■ TIP→ To save money, go inland. Kūhiō, one block toward the mountains from the main drag of Kalākaua, is lined with less expensive restaurants, hotels, and shops.

SHOP, SHOP, SHOP/PARTY, PARTY, PARTY

Sheraton Moana Surfrider: Pick up a present at Noeha Gallery or Sand People. Then relax with a drink at the venerable Banyan Veranda. The radio program *Hawai'i Calls* first broadcast to a mainland audience from here in 1935.

Duke's Canoe Club, Outrigger Waikīkī: Beach party central.

Mai Tai Bar at the Royal Hawaiian: Birthplace of the Mai Tai.

KEY

P   *Cheap Parking*

✕   *Cheap Eats*

S   *Shopping*

𝐘   *Clubs/Bars*

🏖   *Beaches*

🏄   *Surf Breaks*

Ala Wai Blvd.

Liliuokalani Garden

Wainani Way

Pualani Way

Kaneloa

Kūhiō Ave.

Cartwright Rd.

Lemon Rd.

Kapahulu Ave.

'Ohua Ave.

Paokalani Ave.

Kalākaua Ave.

Honolulu Zoo

TO DIAMOND HEAD →

TO WAIKĪKĪ AQUARIUM ↘

🏄 *Walls*

Queen's Surf

Sans Souci

WHAT THE LOCALS LOVE

Paid-parking–phobic Islanders usually avoid Waikīkī, but these attractions are juicy enough to lure locals:

■ **Royal Hawaiian Park Band**, free concerts every Sundays at the Kapiolani Bandstand.

■ **Pan-Pacific Festival-Matsuri in Hawaii**, a summer cultural festival that's as good as a trip to Japan.

■ **Aloha Festivals in September**, the legendary floral parade and evening show of contemporary Hawaiian music.

■ **The Wildest Show in Town**, $1 summer concerts at the Honolulu Zoo.

■ **Sunset on the Beach**, free films projected on an outdoor screen at Queen's Beach, with food and entertainment.

'APUAKEHAU STREAM

Wade out just in front of the Outrigger Waikīkī on the Beach and feel a current of chilly water curling around your ankles. This is the last remnant of three streams that once drained the inland valleys behind you, making of Waikīkī a place of swamps, marshes, taro and rice paddies, and giving it the name "spouting water." High-ranking chiefs surfed in a legendary break gouged out by the draining freshwater and rinsed off afterward in the stream whose name means "basket of dew." The Ala Wai Canal, completed in the late 1920s, drained the land, reducing proud 'Apuakehau Stream to a determined phantom passing beneath Waikīkī's streets.

RAINY DAY IDEAS

Lobby lounging: Check out the century-old, period-furnished lobby and veranda of the Sheraton Moana Surfrider Hotel on Kalākaua.

LuCoral Museum: Exhibit and shop explores the world of coral and other semi-precious stones; wander about or take $2 guided tour and participate in jewelry-making activity. 2414 Kūhiō.

WHAT'S NEW & CHANGING

Waikīkī, which was looking a bit shopworn, is in the midst of many makeovers. Ask about noise, disruption, and construction when booking.

In addition to fresh landscaping and period light fixtures along Kalākaua and a pathway that encircles Ala Wai Canal, expect:

BEACH WALK: After ten years of planning, the Waikīkī Beach Walk—a pedestrian walkway lined with restaurants and shops—opened in 2007 to rave reviews. It was a massive project

for the city, costing about $535 million and taking up nearly 8 acres of land. It's a great place to spend the afternoon, but be warned: this place gets packed on weekends.

ROYAL HAWAIIAN SHOPPING CENTER: The fortress-like Royal Hawaiian Shopping Center in the center of Kalākaua Avenue is an open, inviting space with a palm grove and a mix of shops and restaurants.

GETTING THERE

It can seem impossible to figure out how to get to Waikīkī from H-1. The exit is far inland, and even when you follow the signs, the route jigs and jogs; it sometimes seems a wonder that more tourists aren't found starving in Kaimuki.

FROM EASTBOUND H-1 (COMING FROM THE AIRPORT):
1. To western Waikīkī (Ft. DeRussy and most hotels): Take the Punahou exit from H-1, turn right on Punahou and get in the center lane. Go right on Beretania and almost immediately left onto Kalākaua, which takes you into Waikīkī.

2. To eastern Waikīkī (Kapiʻolani Park): Take the King Street exit, and stay on King for two blocks. Go right on Kapahulu, which takes you to Kalākaua.

FROM WESTBOUND H-1:
Take the Kapiʻolani Boulevard exit. Follow Kapiʻolani to McCully, and go left on McCully. Follow McCully to Kalākaua, and you're in Waikīkī.

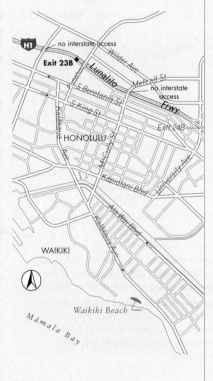

five different types of reef environments found along Hawai'i's shorelines. Check out the Northwestern Hawaiian Islands exhibit (scheduled at this writing to open summer 2011), the Ocean Drifters jellyfish exhibit, outdoor touch pool, and the self-guided audio tour, which is included with admission. The aquarium offers programs of interest to adults and children alike, including the Aquarium After Dark when visitors grab a flashlight and view fish going about their rarely observable nocturnal activities. Plan to spend at least an hour at the aquarium, including 10 minutes for a film in the Sea Visions Theater.

WAIKĪKĪ'S BEST FREE ENTERTAINMENT

Waikīkī's entertainment scene isn't just dinner shows and lounge acts. There are plenty of free or nearly free things to do right on the beach and at Kapi'olani Park. Queen's Surf Beach hosts the popular Sunset on the Beach, which brings big-screen showings of recent Hollywood blockbusters to the great outdoors. Also, during the summer months, the Honolulu Zoo has weekly concerts, and admission is just $1.

✉ *2777 Kalākaua Ave., Waikīkī* ☎ *808/923–9741* ⊕ *www.waquarium. org* ⌂ *$9* ⊙ *Daily 9–4:30.*

WORTH NOTING

🔄 **Honolulu Zoo.** To get a glimpse of the endangered *nēnē*, the Hawai'i state bird, check out the zoo's Kipuka Nēnē Sanctuary. Though many animals prefer to remain invisible, the monkeys appear to enjoy being seen and are a hoot to watch. It's best to get to the zoo right when it opens, since the animals are livelier in the cool of the morning. There are bigger and better zoos, but this one, though showing signs of neglect due to budget constraints, is a lush garden and has some great programs. The Wildest Show in Town, a series of concerts ($2 donation), takes place on Wednesday evenings in summer. You can have a family sleepover inside the zoo during Snooze in the Zoo on a Friday or Saturday night every month. Or just head for the petting zoo, where kids can make friends with a llama or stand in the middle of a koi pond. There's an exceptionally good gift shop. On weekends, the Zoo Fence Art Mart, on Monsarrat Avenue on the Diamond Head side outside the zoo, has affordable artwork by contemporary artists. Metered parking is available all along the *makai* (ocean) side of the park and in the lot next to the zoo. TheBus, O'ahu's only form of public transportation, makes stops here along the way to and from Ala Moana Center and Sea Life Park (routes 22 and 58). ✉ *151 Kapahulu Ave., Waikīkī* ☎ *808/971– 7171* ⊕ *www.honoluluzoo.org* ⌂ *$12* ⊙ *Daily 9–4:30.*

Kapi'olani Bandstand. Victorian-style Kapi'olani Bandstand, which was originally built in the late 1890s, is Kapi'olani Park's stage for community entertainment and concerts. The nation's only city-sponsored band, the Royal Hawaiian Band, performs free concerts on Sunday afternoon. Local newspapers list event information. ✉ *2805 Monsarrat Ave., Waikīkī.*

Waikīkī Shell. Locals bring picnics and grab one of the 6,000 "grass seats" (lawn seating) for music under the stars (there are actual seats, as well). Concerts are held May 1 to Labor Day, with a few winter dates, weather permitting. Check newspaper Friday entertainment sections to see who is performing. ✉ *2805 Monsarrat Ave., Waikīkī* ☎ *808/924–8934* ⊕ *www.blaisdellcenter.com.*

Waikīkī War Memorial Natatorium. This 1927 World War I monument, dedicated to the 102 Hawaiian servicemen who lost their lives in battle, stands proudly—its 20-foot archway, which was completely restored in 2002, is floodlighted at night. Despite a face-lift in 2000, the 100-meter saltwater swimming pool, the training spot for Olympians Johnny Weissmuller and Buster Crabbe and the U.S. Army during World War II, is closed as the pool needs repair. The city has commissioned a study of the natatorium's future while a nonprofit group fights to save the facility. ✉ *2777 Kalākaua Ave., Waikīkī.*

GREATER HONOLULU AND PEARL HARBOR

Downtown Honolulu and Chinatown can easily swallow up a day's walking, sightseeing, and shopping. Another day's worth of attractions surrounds the city's core. To the north, just off H1 in the tightly packed neighborhood of Kalihi, explore a museum gifted to the Islands in memory of a princess. Immediately *mauka* (toward the mountain), off Pali Highway, are a renowned resting place and a carefully preserved home where royal families retreated during the doldrums of summer.

Just west of the Pali is the heart of the Pacific fleet in its home at Pearl Harbor. Visitors can witness not just historic vessels but also spy top military flight instruments that are in use today.

GETTING HERE AND AROUND

Bus routes criss-cross this region with complimentary transfers, making this an area you can explore thoroughly by public transport. If you're coming via car, avoid the typical rush hour times in the morning heading east and in the afternoon heading west.

EXPLORING

★ **Bishop Museum.** Founded in 1889 by Charles R. Bishop as a memorial to his wife, Princess Bernice Pauahi Bishop, the museum began as a repository for the royal possessions of this last direct descendant of King Kamehameha the Great. Today it's the Hawai'i State Museum of Natural and Cultural History. Its five exhibit halls house almost 25 million items that tell the history of the Hawaiian Islands and their Pacific neighbors. The latest addition to the complex is a 16,500 square-foot natural-science wing with a three-story simulated volcano at its center. The recently renovated Hawaiian Hall, with state-of-the art and often interactive displays, teaches about the Hawaiian culture. Hawaiian artifacts—lustrous feather capes, bone fish hooks, the skeleton of a giant sperm whale, photography and crafts displays, and an authentic, well-preserved grass house—are displayed inside a three-story 19th-century Victorian-style gallery. Also check out the planetarium, daily tours, hula and science demonstrations, special exhibits, and the Shop Pacifica. The building alone, with its huge Victorian turrets and immense stone walls, is worth seeing. ✉ *1525 Bernice St., Kalihi* ☎ *808/847–3511* ⊕ *www.bishopmuseum.org* 💲*$15.95* ⊙ *Daily 9–5.*

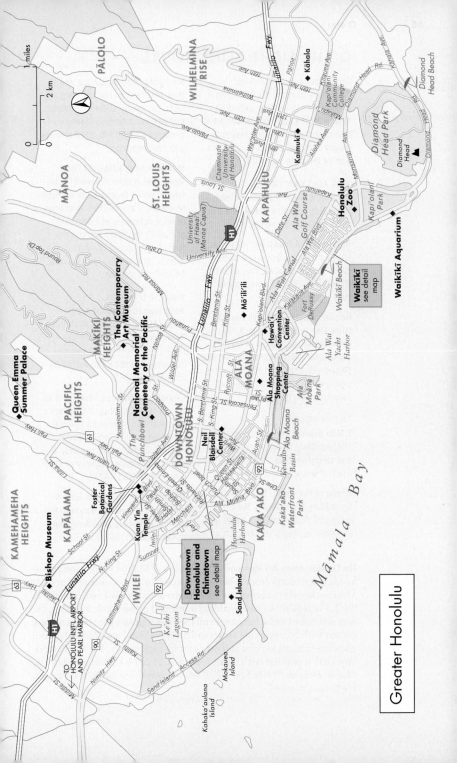

Greater Honolulu

1 miles

0

2 km

0

PĀLOLO

WILHELMINA RISE

MĀNOA

ST. LOUIS HEIGHTS

Chaminade University of Honolulu

University of Hawaii (Manoa Campus)

University Ave.

MAKIKI HEIGHTS

The Contemporary Art Museum

Kāhala

Kaimukī

KAPAHULU

Kapi'olani Community College

Diamond Head Park

Diamond Head Beach

Diamond Head

Honolulu Zoo

Kapi'olani Park

Waikīkī Aquarium

National Memorial Cemetery of the Pacific

Waikīkī Beach

Waikīkī see detail map

Ala Wai Golf Course

Ala Wai Canal

Mō'ili'ili

Hawai'i Convention Center

Fort DeRussy

Queen Emma Summer Palace

PACIFIC HEIGHTS

The Punchbowl

61

Pali Hwy.

Nu'uanu Ave.

KAMEHAMEHA HEIGHTS

KAPĀLAMA

Bishop Museum

Foster Botanical Gardens

Kuan Yin Temple

DOWNTOWN HONOLULU

Neil Blaisdell Center

ALA MOANA

Ala Moana Shopping Center

Ala Moana Park

Ala Moana Beach

Ala Wai Yacht Harbor

92

KAKA'AKO

Kaka'ako Waterfront Park

Kewalo Basin

Honolulu Harbor

Downtown Honolulu and Chinatown see detail map

Sand Island

IWILEI

63

Lunalilo Frwy.

Dillingham Blvd.

90

TO HONOLULU INT'L AIRPORT AND PEARL HARBOR

Nimitz Hwy.

Middle St.

Ke'ehi Lagoon

Sand Island Access Rd.

Mokauea Island

Kahaka'aulana Island

Māmala Bay

O'AHU SIGHTSEEING TOURS

Guided tours are convenient; you don't have to worry about finding a parking spot or getting admission tickets. Most of the tour guides have taken special Hawaiiana classes in history and lore, and many are certified by the state of Hawai'i.

BUS AND VAN TOURS

Ask exactly what the tour includes in the way of actual get-off-the-bus stops and window sights.

Polynesian Adventure. They lead tours of Pearl Harbor and a circle island tour. Best of all, kids are free. ☎ 808/833–3000 ⊕ www.polyad. com.

Roberts Hawai'i. Choose from a large selection of tours including downtown Honolulu ghost tours, underwater submarine tours, and the more traditional Pearl Harbor excursions. ☎ 808/539–9400 ⊕ www. robertshawaii.com.

THEME TOURS

E Noa Tours. Certified tour guides conduct Circle Island, Pearl Harbor, and shopping tours. ☎ 808/591–2561 ⊕ www.enoa.com.

Home of the Brave Tours. Perfect for military-history buffs. Narrated tours visit O'ahu's military bases and the National Memorial Cemetery of the Pacific. Also includes a visit to their private museum including artifacts and memorabilia from World War II. Day or evening itineraries available. ☎ 808/396–8112 ⊕ www. pearlharborhq.com.

Matthew Gray's Hawai'i Food Tours. Get a taste of Hawai'i's culture by going on one of three restaurant tours. Each includes samplings of local delicacies and discussion of Hawai'i foodways and the history of the culinary diversity of the Islands. ☎ 808/926–3663 ⊕ www. hawaiifoodtours.com.

WALKING TOURS

American Institute of Architects (AIA) Downtown Walking Tour. See downtown Honolulu from an architectural perspective. ✉ American Institute of Architects ☎ 808/545–4242.

Chinatown Walking Tour. Meet at the Chinese Chamber of Commerce for a fascinating peek into herbal shops, an acupuncturist's office, open-air markets, and specialty stores. ✉ Chinese Chamber of Commerce ☎ 808/533–3181.

Hawai'i Geographic Society. A number of downtown Honolulu temple and archaeology walking tours are available. ☎ 808/538–3952.

The Contemporary Art Museum. In the exclusive Makīkī Heights neighborhood, just minutes from downtown Honolulu, The Contemporary Art Museum houses collections of modern art dating from 1940. Situated in the 3.5-acre Alice Cooke Spalding home and estate (built in 1925), the museum boasts ever-changing exhibitions as well as a peaceful sculpture garden with breathtaking views of Diamond Head and Waikīkī. A fun gift shop features jewelry and other art by local artists. The Contemporary Café is popular with locals for lunch. ✉ 2411 Makīkī Heights Dr., Makīkī Heights ☎ 808/526–1322 ⊕ www.tcmhi.org ☜ $8 ☉ Tues.–Sat. 10–4, Sun. noon–4.

Continued on page 75

USS *West Virginia* (BB48), 7 December 1941

PEARL HARBOR

December 7, 1941. Every American then alive recalls exactly what he or she was doing when the news broke that the Japanese had bombed Pearl Harbor, the catalyst that brought the United States into World War II.

Although it was clear by late 1941 that war with Japan was inevitable, no one in authority seems to have expected the attack to come in just this way, at just this time. So when the Japanese bombers swept through a gap in Oʻahu's Koʻolau Mountains in the hazy light of morning, they found the bulk of America's Pacific fleet right where they hoped it would be: docked like giant stepping stones across the calm waters of the bay named for the pearl oysters that once prospered there. More than 2,000 people died that day, including 49 civilians. A dozen ships were sunk. And on the nearby air bases, virtually every American military aircraft was destroyed or damaged. The attack was a stunning success, but it lit a fire under America, which went to war with "Remember Pearl Harbor" as its battle cry. Here, in what is still a key Pacific naval base, the attack is remembered every day by thousands of visitors, including many curious Japanese, who for years heard little World War II history in their own country. In recent years, the memorial has been the site of reconciliation ceremonies involving Pearl Harbor veterans from both sides.

GETTING AROUND

Pearl Harbor is both a working military base and the most-visited O'ahu attraction. Four distinct destinations share a parking lot and are linked by footpath, shuttle, and ferry.

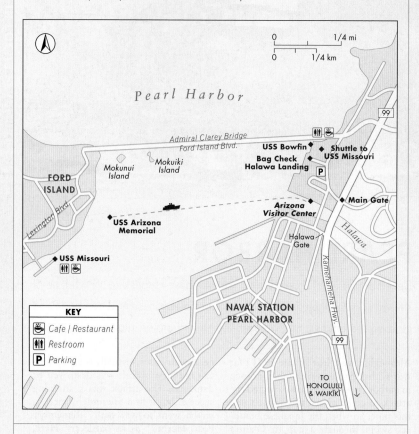

The USS *Arizona* visitor center is accessible from the parking lot. The *Arizona* Memorial itself is in the middle of the harbor; get tickets for the ferry ride at the visitor center. The USS *Bowfin* is also reachable from the parking lot.

The USS *Missouri* is docked at Ford Island, a restricted area of the naval base. Vehicular access is prohibited. To get there, take a shuttle bus from the station near the *Bowfin*.

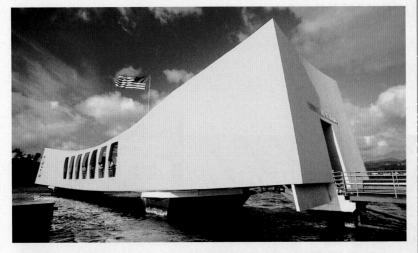

ARIZONA MEMORIAL

Snugged up tight in a row of seven battleships off Ford Island, the USS *Arizona* took a direct hit that December morning, exploded, and rests still on the shallow bottom where she settled.

The swooping, stark-white memorial, which straddles the wreck of the USS *Arizona*, was designed to represent both the depths of the low-spirited, early days of the war, and the uplift of victory.

A visit here begins at the USS *Arizona* Memorial Visitor Center, which recently underwent a $58 million renovation. High definition projectors and interactive exhibits were installed, and the building was modernized. From the visitor center, a ferry takes you to the memorial itself, and a new shuttle hub now gives access to sites that were previously inaccessible, like the USS *Utah* and USS *Oklahoma*.

A somber, contemplative mood descends upon visitors during the ferry ride to the *Arizona*; this is a place where 1,177 crewmen lost their lives. Gaze at the names of the dead carved into the wall of white marble. Scatter flowers (but no lei—the string is bad for the fish). Salute the flag. Remember Pearl Harbor.

☎ *808/422–0561*
⊕ *www.nps.gov/usar*

USS *MISSOURI* (BB63)

Together with the *Arizona* Memorial, the *Missouri's* presence in Pearl Harbor perfectly bookends America's WWII experience that began December 7, 1941, and ended on the "Mighty Mo's" starboard deck with the signing of the Terms of Surrender.

Surrender of Japan, USS 2 September 1945

In the parking area behind the USS *Bow-fin* Museum, board a jitney for a breezy, eight-minute ride to Ford Island and the teak decks and towering superstructure of the *Missouri*, docked for good in the very harbor from which she first went to war on January 2, 1945. The last battleship ever built, the *Missouri* famously hosted the final act of WWII, the signing of the Terms of Surrender. The commission that governs this floating museum has surrounded her with buildings tricked out in WWII style—a canteen that serves as an orientation space for tours, a WACs and WAVEs lounge with a flight simulator the kids will love ($5 for one person, $18 for four), Truman's Line restaurant serving Navy-style meals, and a Victory Store housing a souvenir shop and covered with period mottos ("Don't be a blabateur").
■TIP→ Definitely hook up with a tour guide (additional charge) or purchase an audio tour ($2)—these add a great deal to the experience.

The *Missouri* is all about numbers: 209 feet tall, six 239,000-pound guns, capable of firing up to 23 mi away. Absorb these during the tour, then stop to take advantage of the view from the decks. The Mo is a work in progress, with only a handful of her hundreds of spaces open to view.

☎808/423–2263 or ☎888/877–6477
⊕ *www.ussmissouri.org*

USS *BOWFIN* (SS287)

SUBMARINE MUSEUM & PARK

Launched one year to the day after the Pearl Harbor attack, the USS *Bowfin* sank 44 enemy ships during WWII and now serves as the centerpiece of a museum honoring all submariners.

 Although the *Bowfin* no less than the *Arizona* Memorial commemorates the lost, the mood here is lighter. Perhaps it's the childlike scale of the boat, a metal tube just 16 feet in diameter, packed with ladders, hatches, and other obstacles, like the naval version of a jungle gym. Perhaps it's the World War II-era music that plays in the covered patio. Or it might be the museum's touching displays—the penciled sailor's journal, the Vargas girlie posters. Aboard the boat nicknamed "Pearl Harbor Avenger," compartments are fitted out as though "Sparky" was away from the radio room just for a moment, and "Cooky" might be right back to his pots and pans. The museum includes many artifacts to spark family conversations, among them a vintage dive suit that looks too big for Shaquille

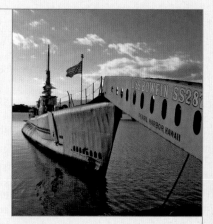

O'Neal. A caution: The *Bowfin* could be hazardous for very young children; no one under four allowed.

☏ *808/423–1341*
⊕ *www.bowfin.org*

THE PACIFIC AVIATION MUSEUM

This museum opened on December 7, 2006, as phase one of a four-phase tribute to the air wars of the Pacific. Located on Ford Island in Hangar 37, an actual seaplan hangar that survived the Pearl Harbor attack, the museum is made up of a theater where a short film on Pearl Harbor kicks off the tour, an education center, a shop, and a restaurant. Exhibits—many of which are interactive and involve sound effects—include an authentic Japanese Zero in a diorama setting a chance to don a flight suit and play the role of a World War II pilot using one of six flight simulators. Various aircrafts are employed to narrate the great battles: the Doolittle Raid on Japan, the Battle of Midway, Guadalcanal, and so on. The actual Stearman N2S-3 in which President George H. W. Bush soloed is another exhibit. ☏ *808/441–1000* ⊕ www.pacificaviationmuseum.org 🎫 $20.

PLAN YOUR PEARL HARBOR DAY
LIKE A MILITARY CAMPAIGN

DIRECTIONS

Take H–1 west from Waikīkī to Exit 15A and follow signs. Or take TheBus route 20 or 47 from Waikīkī. Beware high-priced private shuttles. It's a 30-minute drive from Waikīkī.

WHAT TO BRING

Picture ID is required during periods of high alert; bring it just in case.

You'll be standing, walking, and climbing all day. Wear something with lots of pockets and a pair of good walking shoes. Carry a light jacket, sunglasses, hat, and sunscreen.

No purses, packs, or bags are allowed. Take only what fits in your pockets. Cameras are okay but without the bags. A private bag storage booth is located in the parking lot near the visitors' center. Leave nothing in your car; theft is a problem despite bicycle security patrols.

HOURS

Hours are 8 AM to 5 PM for all attractions. However, the *Arizona* Memorial starts giving out tickets on a first-come, first-served basis at 7:30 AM; the last tickets are given out at 3 PM. Spring break, summer, and holidays are busiest, and tickets sometimes run out by noon.

TICKETS

Arizona: Free. Add $5 for museum audio tours.

Aviation: $20 adults, $10 children. Add $10 for aviator's guided tour.

Missouri: $20 adults, $10 children. Add $6 for chief's guided tour or audio tour; add $33 for in-depth, behind-the-scenes tours.

Bowfin: $10 adults, $4 children. Add $2 for audio tours. Children under 4 may go into the museum but not aboard the *Bowfin*.

KIDS

This might be the day to enroll younger kids in the hotel children's program. Preschoolers chafe at long waits, and attractions involve some hazards for toddlers. Older kids enjoy the *Bowfin* and *Missouri*, especially.

MAKING THE MOST OF YOUR TIME

Expect to spend at least half a day; a whole day is better.

At the *Arizona* Memorial, you'll get a ticket, be given a tour time, and then have to wait anywhere from 15 minutes to 3 hours. You must pick up your own ticket so you can't hold places. If the wait is long, skip over to the *Bowfin* to fill the time.

SUGGESTED READING

Pearl Harbor and the USS Arizona Memorial, by Richard Wisniewski. $5.95. 64-page magazine-size quick history.

Bowfin, by Edwin P. Hoyt. $14.95. Dramatic story of undersea adventure.

The Last Battleship, by Scott C. S. Stone. $11.95. Story of the Mighty Mo.

National Memorial Cemetery of the Pacific. Nestled in the bowl of Puowaina, or Punchbowl Crater, this 112-acre cemetery is the final resting place for more than 50,000 U.S. war veterans and family members. Among those buried here is Ernie Pyle, the famed World War II correspondent who was killed by a Japanese sniper on Ie Shima, an island off the northwest coast

of Okinawa. Puowaina, formed 75,000–100,000 years ago during a period of secondary volcanic activity, translates as "Hill of Sacrifice." Historians believe this site once served as an altar where ancient Hawaiians offered sacrifices to their gods. ■TIP→ The entrance to the cemetery has unfettered views of Waikīkī and Honolulu—perhaps the finest on Oʻahu. ⊠ *2177 Puowaina Dr., Nuʻuanu* ☎ *808/532–3720* ⊕ *www.cem. va.gov/cem/cems/nchp/nmcp.asp* ☒ *Free* ☉ *Mar.–Sept., daily 8–6:30; Oct.–Feb., daily 8–5:30.*

 Fodorʼs Choice ★

★ **Pearl Harbor.** *See highlighted feature in this chapter.*

Queen Emma Summer Palace. Queen Emma and her family used this stately white home, built in 1848, as a retreat from the rigors of court life in hot and dusty Honolulu during the mid-1800s. It has an eclectic mix of European, Victorian, and Hawaiian furnishings and has excellent examples of Hawaiian quilts and koa-wood furniture. ⊠ *2913 Pali Hwy.* ☎ *808/595–3167* ⊕ *www.queenemmasummerpalace.org* ☒ *$6* ☉ *Self-guided or guided tours daily 9–4.*

SOUTHEAST OʻAHU

Driving southeast from Waikīkī on busy four-lane Kalanianaʻole Highway, you'll pass a dozen bedroom communities tucked into the valleys at the foot of the Koʻolau Range, with just fleeting glimpses of the ocean from a couple of pocket parks. Suddenly, civilization falls away, the road narrows to two lanes, and you enter the rugged coastline of Koko Head and Ka Iwi.

This is a cruel coastline: dry, windswept, and rocky shores, with untamed waves that are notoriously treacherous. While walking its beaches, do not turn your back on the ocean, don't venture close to wet areas where high waves occasionally reach, and heed warning signs.

At this point, you're passing through Koko Head Regional Park. On your right is the bulging remnant of a pair of volcanic craters that the Hawaiians called Kawaihoa, known today as Koko Head. To the left is Koko Crater and the area of the park that includes a hiking trail, a dryland botanical garden, a firing range, and a riding stable. Ahead is a sinuous shoreline with scenic pullouts and beaches to explore. Named the Ka Iwi Coast (*iwi,* "ee-vee," are bones—sacred to Hawaiians and full of symbolism) for the channel just offshore, this area was once home to a ranch and small fishing enclave that were destroyed by a tidal wave in the 1940s.

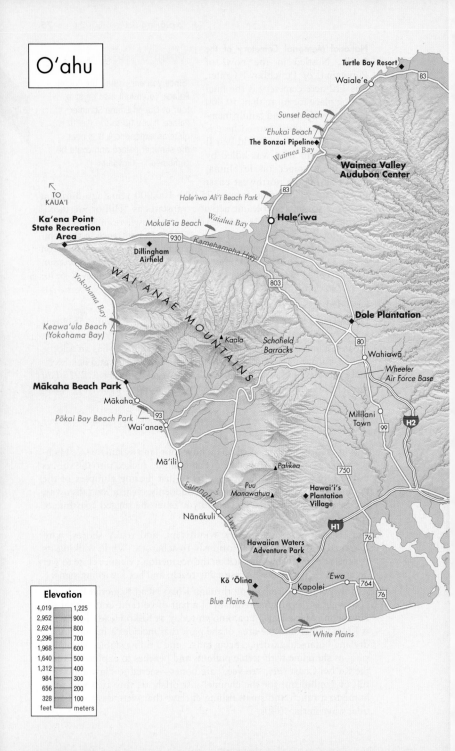

O'ahu

Turtle Bay Resort
Waiale'e
Sunset Beach
'Ehukai Beach
The Bonzai Pipeline
Waimea Bay
Waimea Valley Audubon Center

Hale'iwa Ali'i Beach Park
Hale'iwa

→ TO KAUA'I

Ka'ena Point State Recreation Area

Mokulē'ia Beach
Waialua Bay
Kamehameha Hwy

Dillingham Airfield

Yokohama Bay

WAI'ANAE MOUNTAINS

Keawa'ula Beach (Yokohama Bay)

Kaala
Schofield Barracks

803

Dole Plantation

80

Wahiawā
Wheeler Air Force Base

Mākaha Beach Park
Mākaha
Pōkai Bay Beach Park
Wai'anae
93

Mililani Town
99
H2

Mā'ili

Palikea
Puu Manawahua

750

Farrington Hwy

Nānākuli

Hawai'i's Plantation Village

H1

Hawaiian Waters Adventure Park

76

Kō 'Ōlina
Blue Plains
Kapolei
'Ewa
764
76

White Plains

Elevation

feet	meters
4,019	1,225
2,952	900
2,624	800
2,296	700
1,968	600
1,640	500
1,312	400
984	300
656	200
328	100
feet	meters

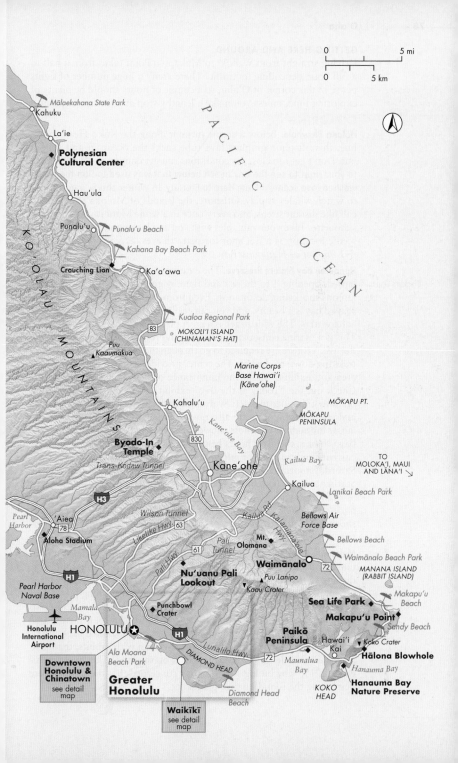

PACIFIC OCEAN

0   5 mi

0   5 km

Mālaekahana State Park

Kahuku

La'ie

Polynesian Cultural Center

Hau'ula

Punalu'u

Punalu'u Beach

Kahana Bay Beach Park

Crouching Lion

Ka'a'awa

KO'OLAU   MOUNTAINS

Kualoa Regional Park

83

MOKOLI'I ISLAND (CHINAMAN'S HAT)

Puu Kaaumakua

Marine Corps Base Hawai'i (Kāne'ohe)

MŌKAPU PT.

Kahalu'u

MŌKAPU PENINSULA

Kane'ohe Bay

Byodo-In Temple

830

Kailua Bay

Kane'ohe

TO MOLOKA'I, MAUI AND LĀNA'I

Kailua

Lanikai Beach Park

Trans-Kodaw Tunnel

H3

Wilson Tunnel

'Aiea

78

Pearl Harbor

Aloha Stadium

Likelike Hwy.   63

Pali Tunnel

Kailua Rd.

Bellows Air Force Base

Bellows Beach

Mt. Olomana

Pali Hwy.

61

Kalanianaole Hwy.

Waimānalo

72

Waimānalo Beach Park

MANANA ISLAND (RABBIT ISLAND)

H1

Pearl Harbor Naval Base

Puu Lanipo

Kaau Crater

Nu'uanu Pali Lookout

Sea Life Park

Makapu'u Point

Makapu'u Beach

Mamala Bay

Punchbowl Crater

Honolulu International Airport

HONOLULU

H1

Paikō Peninsula

Hawai'i Kai

Koko Crater

Sandy Beach

Ala Moana Beach Park

DIAMOND HEAD

Lunalilo Hwy.

72

Hālona Blowhole

Maunalua Bay

Downtown Honolulu & Chinatown see detail map

Greater Honolulu

Diamond Head Beach

Waikīkī see detail map

KOKO HEAD

Hanauma Bay

Hanauma Bay Nature Preserve

GETTING HERE AND AROUND

Driving straight from Waikīkī to Makapuʻu Point takes from a half to a full hour, depending on traffic. There aren't a huge number of sights per se in this corner of Oʻahu, so a couple of hours should be plenty of exploring time, unless you make a lengthy stop at a particular point.

EXPLORING

Hālona Blowhole. Below a scenic turnout along the Koko Head shoreline, this oft-photographed lava tube sucks the ocean in and spits it out. Don't get too close, as conditions can get dangerous. ■TIP➔ **Look to your right to see the tiny beach below that was used to film the wave-washed love scene in From Here to Eternity.** In winter this is a good spot to watch whales at play. Offshore, the Islands of Molokaʻi and Lānaʻi call like distant sirens, and every once in a while Maui is visible in blue silhouette. Take your valuables with you and lock your car, because this scenic location is a hot spot for petty thieves. ⊠ *Kalanianaʻole Hwy.* ✚ *1 mi east of Hanauma Bay.*

ⓒ
Fodor's Choice
★

Hanauma Bay Nature Preserve. The exterior wall of a volcanic crater collapsed, opening it to the sea and thereby giving birth to Oʻahu's most famous snorkeling destination. Even from the overlook, the horseshoe-shaped bay is a beauty, and you can easily see the reefs through the clear aqua waters. The wide beach is a great place for sunbathing and picnics. This is a marine conservation district, and regulations prohibit feeding the fish. Visitors are required to go through the Education Center before trekking down to the bay. The center provides a cultural history of the area and exhibits about the importance of protecting its marine life. Check out the "Today at the Bay" exhibit for up-to-date information on daily tides, ocean safety warnings, and activities. Food concessions and equipment rentals are also on-site. ■TIP➔ **Come early to get parking, as the number of visitors allowed per day is limited.** Also note that the bay is best in the early hours before the waters are churned up. Call for current conditions or for information about Thursday evening lectures, Saturday morning field trips, and Saturday night Hanauma Bay by Starlight events (extending opening hours to 10 pm) are held weekly. ⊠ *7455 Kalanianaʻole Hwy.* ☎ *808/396–4229* ⊕ *www.honolulu.gov/ parks/facility/hanaumabay* ⌨ *Nonresident fee $5; parking $1; mask, snorkel, and fins rental $6; tram from parking lot to beach $1.50 round-trip* ⊘ *Wed.–Mon. 6–6.*

Makapuʻu Point. This spot has breathtaking views of the ocean, mountains, and the Windward Islands. The point of land jutting out in the distance is **Mōkapu Peninsula,** site of a U.S. Marine base. The spired mountain peak is **Mt. Olomana.** In front of you on the long pier is part of the **Makai Undersea Test Range,** a research facility that's closed to the public. Offshore is **Manana Island (Rabbit Island),** a picturesque cay said to resemble a swimming bunny with its ears pulled back. Ironically enough, Manana Island was once overrun with rabbits, thanks to a rancher who let a few hares run wild on the land. They were eradicated in 1994 by biologists who grew concerned that the rabbits were destroying the island's native plants.

Nestled in the cliff face is the **Makapu'u Lighthouse,** which became operational in 1909 and has the largest lighthouse lens in America. The lighthouse is closed to the public, but near the Makapu'u Point turnout you can find the start of a mile-long paved road (closed to traffic). Hike up to the top of the 647-foot bluff for a closer view of the lighthouse and, in winter, a great whale-watching vantage point. ⌧ *Kalaniana'ole Hwy.* ✥ *Turnout above Makapu'u Beach.*

Paikō Peninsula. Secluded within the confines of the bay, private and quiet, this slim spit of land is a lovely place to spend a morning or afternoon swimming, snorkeling, reading, and dozing. The peninsula is reached by a narrow residential road that dead-ends at the Paikō Lagoon State Reserve. The reserve is off-limits to the public, but all beaches in Hawai'i are public to the high-water line, and there is a beach-access pathway a few houses before the road's end. Turn left when you get to the beach and find your spot near where the houses end. ⌧ *Kalaniana'ole Hwy.* ✥ *Just past Niu Valley, on right, on Paikō Dr.*

WINDWARD O'AHU

Looking at Honolulu's topsy-turvy urban sprawl, you would never suspect the Windward side existed. It's a secret Oahuans like to keep, so they can watch the awe on the faces of their guests when the car emerges from the tunnels through the mountains and they gaze for the first time on the panorama of turquoise bays and emerald valleys watched over by the knife-edged Ko'olau ridges. Jaws literally drop. Every time. And this just a 15-minute drive from downtown.

It is on this side of the island that many Native Hawaiians live. Evidence of traditional lifestyles is abundant in crumbling fishponds, rock platforms that once were altars, taro patches still being worked, and throw-net fishermen posed stock-still above the water (though today, they're invariably wearing polarized sunglasses, the better to spot the fish).

Here, the pace is slower, more oriented toward nature. Beachgoing, hiking, diving, surfing, and boating are the draws, along with a visit to the Polynesian Cultural Center, and poking through little shops and wayside stores.

GETTING HERE AND AROUND

For a driving experience you won't soon forget, take the H3 freeway from the Leeward side (the side including Waikīkī and Honolulu) over to the Windward side. As you pass through the tunnels, be prepared for one of the most breathtaking stretches of road anywhere.

You can easily spend an entire day exploring Windward O'ahu, or you can just breeze on through, nodding at the sights on your way to the North Shore. Waikīkī to Windward is a drive of less than half an hour; to the North Shore via Kamehameha Highway along the Windward Coast is one hour minimum.

TOP ATTRACTIONS

Byodo-In Temple. Tucked away in the back of the Valley of the Temples cemetery is a replica of the 11th-century Temple at Uji in Japan. A 2-ton carved wooden statue of the Buddha presides inside the main temple

The Byodo-In Temple on the Windward side of O'ahu is a replica of an 11th-century temple in Japan.

building. Next to the temple building are a meditation pavilion and gardens set dramatically against the sheer, green cliffs of the Ko'olau Mountains. You can ring the 5-foot, 3-ton brass bell for good luck and feed some of the hundreds of carp that inhabit the garden's 2-acre pond. ⊠ 47-200 Kahekili Hwy., Kāne'ohe ☎ 808/239–8811 ☜ $2 ⊘ Daily 8–5.

NEED A BREAK? Generations of children have purchased their beach snacks and sodas at **Kalapawai Market** (⊠ *306 S. Kalāheo Ave.*), near Kailua Beach. A Windward landmark since 1932, the green-and-white market has distinctive charm. You'll see slipper-clad locals sitting in front sharing a cup of coffee and talking story at picnic tables or in front of the market. It's a good source for your carryout lunch, since there's no concession stand at the beach. With one of the better selections of wine on the island, the market is also a great place to pick up a bottle.

Nu'uanu Pali Lookout. This panoramic perch looks out to Windward O'ahu. It was in this region that King Kamehameha I drove defending forces over the edges of the 1,000-foot-high cliffs, thus winning the decisive battle for control of O'ahu. ■ TIP → From here you can see views that stretch from Kāne'ohe Bay to Mokoli'i (little lizard), a small island off the coast, and beyond. Temperatures at the summit are several degrees cooler than in warm Waikīkī, so bring a jacket along. And hang on tight to any loose possessions; it gets extremely windy at the lookout. Lock your car; break-ins have occurred here. ⊠ Top of Pali Hwy. ⊘ Daily 9–4.

**EN
ROUTE**

As you drive the Windward and North shores along Kamehameha Highway, you'll note a number of interesting geological features. At Kualoa look to the ocean and gaze at the uniquely shaped little island of **Mokoli'i** (little lizard), a 206-foot-high sea stack also known as China-man's Hat. According to Hawaiian legend, the goddess Hi'iaka, sister of Pele, slew the dragon Mokoli'i and flung its tail into the sea, forming the distinct islet. Other dragon body parts—in the form of rocks, of course—were scattered along the base of nearby Kualoa Ridge. ■TIP➔ In Lā'ie, if you turn right on Anemoku Street, and right again on Naupaka, you come to a scenic lookout where you can see a group of islets, dramatically washed by the waves.

Polynesian Cultural Center. Re-created individual villages showcase the lifestyles and traditions of Hawai'i, Tahiti, Samoa, Fiji, the Marquesas Islands, New Zealand, and Tonga. Focusing on individual Islands within its 42-acre center, 35 mi from Waikīkī, the Polynesian Cultural Center was founded in 1963 by the Church of Jesus Christ of Latter-day Saints. It houses restaurants, hosts lū'aus, and demonstrates cultural traditions such as tribal tattooing, fire dancing, and ancient customs and ceremonies. The expansive open-air shopping village carries Polynesian handicrafts. ■TIP➔ If you're staying in Honolulu, see the center as part of a van tour so you won't have to drive home late at night after the two-hour evening show. Various packages are available, from basic admission to an all-inclusive deal. Every May, the PCC hosts the World Fire-Knife Dance Competition, an event that draws the top fire-knife dance performers from around the world. ✉ *55-370 Kamehameha Hwy., Lā'ie* ☎ *808/293–3333 or 800/367–7060* ⊕ *www.polynesia.com* ✉ *$45–$225* ⊙ *Mon.–Sat. noon–9:30. Islands close at 6.*

Windward Villages. Tiny villages—generally consisting of a sign, store, a beach park, possibly a post office, and not much more—are strung along Kamehameha Highway on the Windward side. Each has something to offer. In **Waiahole**, look for fruit stands and an ancient grocery store. In **Ka'a'awa**, there's a lunch spot and convenience store/gas station. In **Punalu'u**, stop at the gallery of fanciful landscape artist Lance Fairly and the woodworking shop, Kahaunani Woods & Crafts, plus venerable Ching General Store or the Shrimp Shack. Kim Taylor Reece's photo studio, featuring haunting portraits of hula dancers, is between Punalu'u and Hau'ula. Hau'ula has Hau'ula Gift Shop and Art Gallery, formerly yet another Ching Store, now a clothing shop where sarongs wave like banners and, at Ha'ula Kai Shopping Center, Tamura Market, with excellent seafood and the last liquor before Mormon-dominated **Lā'ie.**

WORTH NOTING

Sea Life Park. Dolphins leap and spin, penguins frolic, and a killer whale performs impressive tricks at this marine-life attraction 15 mi from Waikīkī at scenic Makapu'u Point. The park has a 300,000-gallon Hawaiian reef aquarium, the Hawaiian Monk Seal Care Center, and a breeding sanctuary for Hawai'i's endangered *honu* sea turtle. Join the Stingray or Dolphin Encounter and get up close and personal in the water with these sea creatures (don't worry, the rays' stingers have been removed) or go on an underwater photo safari. ✉ *41-202*

Kalaniana'ole Hwy., Waimānalo ☎ *808/259–2500 or 866/365-7446*
⊕ *www.sealifeparkhawaii.com* ⚌ *$31* ☉ *Daily 10:30–5.*

Waimānalo. This modest little seaside town flanked by chiseled cliffs is
worth a visit. Its biggest draws are its beautiful beaches, offering glorious views to the Windward side. **Bellows Beach** is great for swimming
and bodysurfing, and **Waimānalo Beach Park** is also safe for swimming.
Down the side roads, as you head *mauka* (toward the mountains), are
little farms that grow a variety of fruits and flowers. Toward the back
of the valley are small ranches with grazing horses. ■TIP➜ If you see
any trucks selling corn and you're staying at a place where you can cook it,
be sure to get some in Waimānalo. It may be the sweetest you'll ever eat,
and the price is the lowest on O'ahu. ⊠ *Kalaniana'ole Hwy.*

THE NORTH SHORE

An hour from town and a world away in atmosphere, O'ahu's North
Shore, roughly from Kahuku Point to Ka'ena Point, is about small farms
and big waves, tourist traps and otherworldly landscapes. Parks and
beaches, roadside fruit stands and shrimp shacks, a bird sanctuary, and
a valley preserve offer a dozen reasons to stop between the one-time
plantation town of Kahuku and the surf mecca of Hale'iwa.

Hale'iwa has had many lives, from resort getaway in the 1900s to
plantation town through the 20th century to its life today as a surf and
tourist magnet. Beyond Hale'iwa is the tiny village of Waialua, a string
of beach parks, an airfield where gliders, hang gliders, and parachutists
play, and, at the end of the road, Ka'ena Point State Recreation Area,
which offers a brisk hike, striking views, and whale-watching in season.

Pack wisely for a day's North Shore excursion: swim and snorkel gear,
light jacket and hat (the weather is mercurial, especially in winter),
sunscreen and sunglasses, bottled water and snacks, towels and a picnic blanket, and both sandals and closed-toe shoes for hiking. A small
cooler is nice; you may want to pick up some fruit or fresh corn. As
always, leave valuables in the hotel safe and lock the car whenever
you park.

GETTING HERE AND AROUND
From Waikīkī, the quickest route to the North Shore is H1 east to
H2 north and then the Kamehameha Highway past Wahiawā; you'll
hit Hale'iwa in less than an hour. The Windward route (H1 east, H3
through the mountains, and Kamehameha Highway north) takes at
least 90 minutes to Hale'iwa.

EXPLORING
Hale'iwa. During the 1920s this seaside hamlet boasted a posh hotel
at the end of a railroad line (both long gone). During the 1960s, hippies gathered here, followed by surfers from around the world. Today
Hale'iwa is a fun mix, with old general stores and contemporary boutiques, galleries, and eateries. Be sure to stop in at **Lili'uokalani Protestant Church,** founded by missionaries in the 1830s. It's fronted by a
large, stone archway built in 1910 and covered with night-blooming
cereus. ✣ *Follow H1 west from Honolulu to H2 north, exit at Wahiawā,*

follow Kamehameha Hwy. 6 mi, turn left at signaled intersection, then right into Hale'iwa.

NEED A BREAK?

For a real slice of Hale'iwa life, stop at **Matsumoto's** (✉ 66-087 Kamehameha Hwy. ⊕ www.matsumotoshaveice.com), a family-run business in a building dating from 1910, for shave ice in every flavor imaginable. For something different, order a shave ice with adzuki beans—the red beans are boiled until soft, mixed with sugar, and then placed in the cone with the ice on top.

WORD OF MOUTH

"I'd definitely plan a drive to the North Shore (famous beaches, Banzai Pipeline, the town of Haleiwa—get shave ice at Matsumoto or Aoki's), drive across the island (on Hwy. H3, spectacular), [and] a visit to Kailua/Lanikai."
—sf7307

Ka'ena Point State Recreation Area. The name means "the heat" and, indeed, this windy barren coast lacks both shade and fresh water (or any man-made amenities). Pack water, wear sturdy closed-toe shoes, don sunscreen and a hat, and lock the car. The hike is along a rutted dirt road, mostly flat and 3 mi long, ending in a rocky, sandy headland. It is here that Hawaiians believed the souls of the dead met with their family gods, and, if judged worthy to enter the afterlife, leaped off into eternal darkness at Leinaaka'uane, just south of the point. In summer and at low tide, the small coves offer bountiful shelling; in winter, don't venture near the water. Rare native plants dot the landscape. November through March, watch for humpbacks, spouting and breaching. Binoculars and a camera are highly recommended. ✉ *North end of Kamehameha Hwy.*

Pu'uomahuka Heiau. Worth a stop for its spectacular views from a bluff high above the ocean overlooking Waimea Bay, this sacred spot was once the site of human sacrifices. It's now on the National Register of Historic Places. ✉ *Pūpūkea Rd.* ✛ *½ mi north of Waimea Bay, from Rte. 83 turn right on Pūpūkea Rd. and drive 1 mi uphill.*

 ★ **Waimea Valley Park.** Waimea may get lots of press for the giant winter waves in the bay, but the valley itself is a newsmaker and an ecological treasure in its own right. The Office of Hawaiian Affairs is working to conserve and restore the natural habitat. Follow the Kamananui Stream up the valley through the 1,800 acres of gardens. The botanical collections here include more than 5,000 species of tropical flora, including a superb gathering of Polynesian plants. It's the best place on the island to see native species, such as the endangered Hawaiian moorhen. You can also see the remains of the Hale O Lono *heiau* (temple) along with other ancient archaeological sites; evidence suggests that the area was an important spiritual center. Daily activities between 10 and 2 include hula lessons, native plant walks, lei-making lessons, kapa cloth-making demonstrations. At the back of the valley, **Waihī Falls** plunges 45 feet into a swimming pond. ■TIP➔ Bring your suit—a swim is the perfect way to end your hike. Be sure to bring mosquito repellent, too; it gets buggy.

See colorful wildlife at the Waimea Valley Audubon Center on Oʻahu's North Shore.

✉ *59-864 Kamehameha Hwy., Haleʻiwa* ☎ *808/638–7766* ⊕ *www.audubon.org* ✉ *$13*, ☺ *Daily 9–5.*

QUICK BITES

The chocolate *haupia* (coconut) pie at **Ted's Bakery** (✉ *59-024 Kamehameha Hwy., near Sunset Beach* ☎ *808/638–8207*) is legendary. Stop in for a take-out pie or for a quick plate lunch or sandwich.

CENTRAL AND WEST (LEEWARD) OʻAHU

Oʻahu's central plain is a patchwork of old towns and new residential developments, military bases, farms, ranches, and shopping malls, with a few visit-worthy attractions and historic sites scattered about. Central Oʻahu encompasses the Moanalua Valley, residential Pearl City, and the old plantation town of Wahiawā, on the uplands halfway to the North Shore.

West (or Leeward) Oʻahu has the island's fledgling "second city"— the planned community of Kapolei, where the government hopes to attract enough jobs to lighten inbound traffic to downtown Honolulu— then continues on past a far-flung resort to the Hawaiian communities of Nānākuli and Waiʻanae, to the beach and the end of the road at Keaweʻula, aka Yokohama Bay.

A couple of cautions as you head to the Leeward side: Highway 93 is a narrow, winding two-lane road notorious for accidents. There's an abrupt transition from freeway to highway at Kapolei, and by the time you reach Nānākuli, it's a country road, so slow down. ⚠ Car break-ins and beach thefts are common here.

GETTING HERE AND AROUND

For central Oahu, all sights are most easily reached by either the H1 or H2 freeway. West O'ahu begins at folksy Waipahu and continues past Makakilo and Kapolei on H1 and Highway 93, Farrington Highway.

EXPLORING

Dole Plantation. Celebrate Hawai'i's famous golden fruit at this promotional center with exhibits, a huge gift shop, a snack concession, educational displays, and the world's largest maze. Take the self-guided Garden Tour, plant your own pineapple, or hop aboard the *Pineapple Express* for a 20-minute train tour to learn a bit about life on a pineapple plantation. Kids love the more than 3-acre Pineapple Garden Maze, made up of 14,000 tropical plants and trees. This is about a 40-minute drive from Waikīkī, a suitable stop on the way to or from the North Shore. ⊠ *64-1550 Kamehameha Hwy., Wahiawā* 🕾 *808/621–8408* ⊕ *www.dole-plantation.com* 🖀 *Pavilion free, maze $6, train $8, garden tour $5* ☉ *Daily 9–5; train, maze, and garden close at 5.*

Mākaha Beach Park. Famous as a surfing-and-boogie-boarding park, Mākaha hosts an annual surf meet and draws many scuba divers in summer, when the waves are calm, to explore underwater caverns and ledges. It's popular with families year-round but, in winter, watch for riptides and currents; *Mākaha* means "fierce," and there's a reason for that. ⊠ *84-369 Farrington Hwy., Wai'anae.*

BEACHES

Tropical sun mixed with cooling trade winds and pristine waters make O'ahu's shores a literal heaven on Earth. But contrary to many assumptions, the island is not one big beach. There are miles and miles of coastline without a grain of sand, so you need to know where you are going to fully enjoy the Hawaiian experience.

Much of the island's southern and eastern coast is protected by inner reefs. The reefs provide still coastline water but not much as far as sand is concerned. However, where there are beaches on the south and east shores, they are mind-blowing. In West O'ahu and on the North Shore you can find the wide expanses of sand you would expect for enjoying the sunset. Sandy bottoms and protective reefs make the water an adventure in the winter months. Most visitors assume the seasons don't change a thing in the Islands, and they would be right—except for the waves, which are big on the South Shore in summer and placid in winter. It's exactly the opposite on the north side where winter storms bring in huge waves, but the ocean goes to glass come May and June.

HONOLULU

The city of Honolulu only has one beach, the monstrous Ala Moana. It hosts everything from Dragon Boat competitions to the Aloha State Games.

☾ **Ala Moana Beach Park.** Ala Moana has a protective reef, which makes it essentially a ½-mi-wide saltwater swimming pool. After Waikīkī,

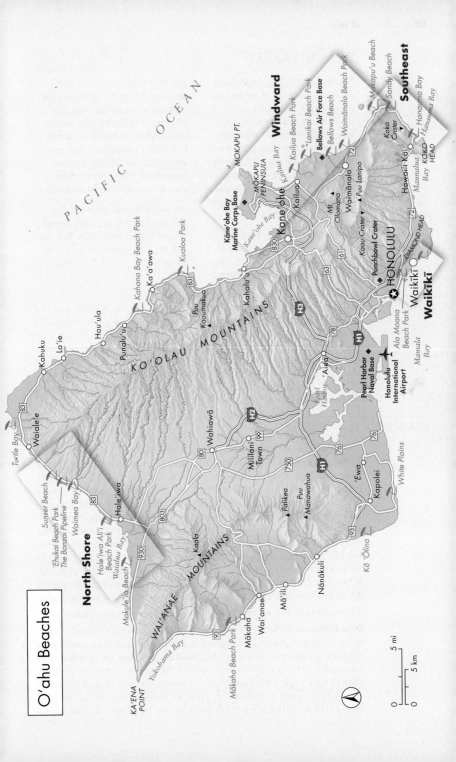

BEACH SAFETY

Yes, the beaches are beautiful, but always be cognizant of the fact you are on a little rock in the middle of the Pacific Ocean. The current and waves will be stronger and bigger than any you may have experienced. Riptides can take you on a ride they call the "Moloka'i Express"—only problem is that it doesn't take you to the island of Moloka'i but rather out into the South Pacific.

Never swim alone. It is hard for even the most attentive lifeguards to keep their eyes on everyone at once, but a partner can gain their attention if you should run into trouble. There are many safe spots, but always pay attention to the posted signs. The lifeguards change the signs daily, so the warnings are always applicable to the day's conditions. If you have any doubts, ask a lifeguard for an assessment. They're professionals and can give you competent advice.

Use sunblock early and often. The SPF you choose is up to you, but we suggest nothing lower than 30 if you plan to spend more than an hour in the sun.

this is the most popular beach among visitors. To the Waikīkī side is a peninsula called Magic Island, with shady trees and paved sidewalks ideal for jogging. Ala Moana also has playing fields, tennis courts, and a couple of small ponds for sailing toy boats. This beach is for everyone, but only in the daytime. It's a high-crime area after dark. **Amenities:** Lifeguard, food concession, grills, parking lot, picnic tables, showers, toilets. ⊠ *Ala Moana Blvd.* ✢ *From Waikīkī take Bus 8 to Ala Moana Shopping Center and cross Ala Moana Blvd.*

WAIKĪKĪ

The 2½-mi strand called Waikīkī Beach extends from Hilton Hawaiian Village on one end to Kapi'olani Park and Diamond Head on the other. Although it's one continuous piece of beach, it's as varied as the people who inhabit the Islands. Whether you're an old-timer looking to enjoy the action from the shade or a sports nut wanting to do it all, you can find every beach activity here without ever jumping in the rental car. ■ TIP➔ If you're staying outside the area, our best advice is to park at either end of the beach and walk in. Plentiful parking exists on the west end at the Ala Wai Marina, where there are myriad free spots on the beach as well as metered stalls around the harbor. For parking on the east end, Kapi'olani Park and the Honolulu Zoo both have metered parking for $1 an hour—more affordable than the $10 per hour the resorts want.

The beaches in this section are listed in order from west to east.

☺ **Duke Kahanamoku Beach.** Named for Hawai'i's famous Olympic swimming champion, Duke Kahanamoku, this is a hard-packed beach with the only shade trees on the sand in Waikīkī. It's great for families with young children because of the shade and the calmest waters in Waikīkī, thanks to a rock wall that creates a semiprotected cove. The ocean clarity here is not as brilliant as most of Waikīkī because of the stillness of the surf, but it's a small price to pay for peace of mind about

youngsters. **Amenities:** Food concession, showers, toilets. ⊠ *2005 Kalia Rd.* ✥ *In front of Hilton Hawaiian Village Beach Resort and Spa.*

🕑 **Fort DeRussy Beach Park.** Even before you take the two newly refurbished beach parks into account, this is one of the finest beaches on the south side of Oʻahu. Wide, soft, ultrawhite beaches with gently lapping waves make it a family favorite for running/jumping/frolicking fun (this also happens to be where the NFL holds their rookie sand football game every year). Add to that the new, heavily shaded grass grilling area, sand volleyball courts, and aquatic rentals, making this a must for the active visitor. **Amenities:** Lifeguard, food concession, grills, picnic tables, playground, showers, toilets. ⊠ *Kalia Rd.* ✥ *In front of Fort DeRussy and Hale Koa Hotel.*

Kahaloa and Ulukou Beaches. The beach widens back out here, creating the "it" spot for the bikini crowd. Beautiful bodies abound. This is where you find most of the sailing catamaran charters for a spectacular sail out to Diamond Head or surfboard and outrigger canoe rentals for a ride on the rolling waves of the Canoe surf break. Great music and outdoor dancing beckon the sand-bound visitor to Duke's Canoe Club where shirt and shoes not only aren't required, they're discouraged. **Amenities:** Lifeguard, food concession, showers, toilets. *Kalakaua Ave.* ✥ *In front of Royal Hawaiian Hotel and Moana Surfrider.*

🕑 **Kūhiō Beach Park.** This beach has experienced a renaissance after a recent face-lift. Now bordered by a landscaped boardwalk, it's great for romantic walks any time of day. Check out the Kūhiō Beach hula mound Tuesday to Sunday at 6:30 for free hula and Hawaiian-music performances and a torch-lighting ceremony at sunset. Surf lessons for beginners are available from the beach center every half hour. **Amenities:** Lifeguard, food concession, showers, toilets. ⊠ *Kapahulu Ave.* ✥ *Past Moana Surfrider Hotel to Kapahulu Ave. pier.*

🕑 **Queen's Surf.** So named as it was once the site of Queen Liliʻuokalani's beach house, this beach draws a mix of families and gay couples—and it seems as if someone is always playing a steel drum. Many weekends, movie screens are set up on the sand, and major motion pictures are shown after the sun sets (⊕ *www.sunsetonthebeach.net*). In the daytime, there are banyan trees for shade and volleyball nets for pros and amateurs alike (this is where Misty May and Kerri Walsh play while in town). The water fronting Queen's Surf is an aquatic preserve,

providing the best snorkeling in Waikīkī. **Amenities:** Lifeguard, grills, picnic tables, showers, toilets. ⊠ *Kalakaua Ave.* ⊕ *Across from entrance to Honolulu Zoo.*

Ⓒ **Sans Souci.** Nicknamed Dig-Me Beach because of its outlandish display of skimpy bathing suits, this small rectangle of sand is nonetheless a good sunning spot for all ages. Children enjoy its shallow, safe waters that are protected by the walls of the historic natatorium, an Olympic-size saltwater swimming arena. Serious swimmers and triathletes also swim in the channel here, beyond the reef. Sans Souci is favored by locals wanting to avoid the crowds while still enjoying the convenience of Waikīkī. **Amenities:** Lifeguard, picnic tables, showers, toilets. ⊠ *Kalakaua Ave* ⊕ *Across from Kapi'olani Park, between New Otani Kaimana Beach Hotel and Waikīkī War Memorial Natatorium.*

SOUTHEAST O'AHU

Much of Southeast O'ahu is surrounded by reef, making most of the coast uninviting to swimmers, but the spots where the reef opens up are true gems. The drive along this side of the island is amazing with its sheer lava-rock walls on one side and deep-blue ocean on the other. There are plenty of restaurants in the suburb of Hawai'i Kai, so you can make a day of it, knowing that food isn't far away.

The beaches in this section are listed in order from west to east.

Ⓒ **Hanauma Bay Nature Preserve.** Picture this as the world's biggest open-air aquarium. You go here to see fish, and fish you'll see. Due to their exposure to thousands of visitors every week, these fish are more like family pets than the skittish marine life you might expect. An old volcanic crater has created a haven from the waves where the coral has thrived. There's an educational center where you must watch a nine-minute video about the nature preserve before being allowed down to the bay. ■ TIP→ **The bay is best early in the morning (around 7), before the crowds arrive; it can be difficult to park later in the day.** There's a $7.50 entry fee for nonresidents. Smoking is not allowed, and the beach is closed on Tuesday. Wednesday to Monday, the beach is open from 6 am to 7 pm. Parking costs $1 and there's a tram from the parking lot to the beach ($1.50 round-trip). **Amenities:** Lifeguard, food concession, parking lot, picnic tables, showers, toilets.

DID YOU KNOW?

O'ahu has more than 100 miles of shoreline and countless beaches where you can surf, sunbathe, or simply stroll.

For a hopping scene with everything from surfing to volleyball, head to Waikīkī Beach.

Hanauma Bay Dive Tours (☎ 808/256–8956) runs snorkeling, snuba, and scuba tours to Hanauma Bay with transportation from Waikīkī hotels on Monday, Wednesday, Thursday, and Friday only. ✉ *7455 Kalanianaʻole Hwy.* ☎ *808/396–4229* ⊕ *www.honolulu.gov/parks/facility/hanaumabay.*

★ **Sandy Beach.** Probably the most popular beach with locals on this side of Oʻahu, the broad, sloping beach is covered with sunbathers there to watch the "Show" and soak up rays. The Show is a shore break that's like no other in the Islands. Monster ocean swells rolling into the beach combined with the sudden rise in the ocean floor causes waves to jack up and crash magnificently on the shore. Expert surfers and body boarders young and old brave this danger to get some of the biggest barrels you can find for bodysurfing. ⚠ But keep in mind that the beach is nicknamed "Break-Neck Beach" for a reason: many neck and back injuries are sustained here each year. Use extreme caution when swimming here, or just kick back and watch the drama unfold from the comfort of your beach chair. **Amenities:** Lifeguard, picnic tables, showers, toilets. ✉ *Kalanianaʻole Hwy.* ✛ *Makai of Kalanianaʻole Hwy., 2 mi east of Hanauma Bay.*

WINDWARD OʻAHU

The Windward side lives up to its name with ideal spots for windsurfing and kiteboarding, or for the more intrepid, hang gliding. For the most part the waves are mellow, and the bottoms are all sand—making for nice spots to visit with younger kids. The only drawback is that this

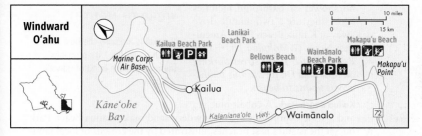

side does tend to get more rain. But, as beautiful as the vistas are, a little sprinkling of pineapple juice shouldn't dampen your experience; plus it turns on the waterfalls that cascade down the Ko'olau.

Beaches in this section are listed from south to north.

Fodor'sChoice ★ **Makapu'u Beach.** A magnificent beach protected by Makapu'u Point welcomes you to the Windward side. Hang gliders circle above the beach, and the water is filled with body boarders. Just off the coast you can see Bird Island, a sanctuary for aquatic fowl, jutting out of the blue. The currents can be heavy, so check with a lifeguard if you're unsure of safety. Before you leave, take the prettiest (and coldest) outdoor shower available on the island. Being surrounded by tropical flowers and foliage while you rinse off that sand will be a memory you will cherish from this side of the rock. **Amenities:** Lifeguard, grills, picnic tables, showers, toilets. ⊠ *Kalaniana'ole Hwy.* ⊹ *Across from Sea Life Park, 2 mi south of Waimānalo.*

ℭ **Waimānalo Beach Park.** One of the most beautiful beaches on the island, Waimānalo is a local beach, busy with picnicking families and active sports fields. Expect a wide stretch of sand; turquoise, emerald, and deep blue seas; and gentle shore-breaking waves that are fun for all ages. Theft is an occasional problem, so lock your car. **Amenities:** Lifeguard, parking lot, picnic tables, showers, toilets. ⊠ *Kalaniana'ole Hwy.* ⊹ *South of Waimānalo town.*

Bellows Beach. Bellows is the same beach as Waimānalo, but it's under the auspices of the military, making it more friendly for visitors. The park area is excellent for camping, and ironwood trees provide plenty of shade. ■**TIP**➜ **The beach is best before 2 pm. After 2 the trade winds bring clouds that get hung up on steep mountains nearby, causing overcast skies until midafternoon.** There are no food concessions, but McDonald's and other takeout fare, including *huli huli* (rotisserie) chicken on weekends, are right outside the entrance gate. **Amenities:** Lifeguard, parking lot, grills, picnic tables, showers, toilets. ⊠ *Entrance on Kalaniana'ole Hwy.* ⊹ *Near Waimānalo town center.*

★ **Lanikai Beach Park.** Think of the beaches you see in commercials: peaceful jade green waters, powder-soft white sand, families and dogs frolicking mindlessly, offshore Islands in the distance. It's an ideal spot for camping out with a book. Though the beach hides behind multimillion-dollar houses, by state law there is public access every 400 yards. ■**TIP**➜ **Look for walled or fenced pathways every 400 yards, leading to the beach. Be sure not to park in the marked bike/jogging lane.** There are no shower or bathroom facilities here—they are a two-minute drive away at Kailua Beach Park. **Amenities:** None. ✉ *Mokulua Dr.* ✛ *Past Kailua Beach Park; street parking on Mokulua Dr. for various public-access points to beach.*

🄲 **Kailua Beach Park.** A cobalt blue sea

FodorśChoice and a wide continuous arc of powdery sand make Kailua Beach Park
★ one of the island's best beaches, illustrated by the crowds of local families that spend their weekend days here. This is like a big Lanikai Beach, but a little windier and a little wider, and a better spot for spending a full day. Kailua Beach has calm water, a line of palms and ironwoods that provide shade on the sand, and a huge park with picnic pavilions where you can escape the heat. This is the "it" spot if you're looking to try your hand at wind- or kiteboarding. **Amenities:** Lifeguard, grills, parking lot, picnic tables, playground, showers, toilets.

You can rent kayaks nearby at **Kailua Sailboards and Kayaks** (✉ *130 Kailua Rd.* ☎ *808/262–2555*) and take them to the Mokulua Islands for the day. ✉ *Kailua Rd.* ✛ *Near Kailua town, turn right on Kailua Rd. at market, cross bridge, then turn left into beach parking lot.*

Kualoa Park. Grassy expanses border a long, narrow stretch of beach with spectacular views of Kāne'ohe Bay and the Ko'olau Mountains, making Kualoa one of the island's most beautiful picnic, camping, and beach areas. Dominating the view is an islet called Mokoli'i, better known as Chinaman's Hat, which rises 206 feet above the water. You can swim in the shallow areas year-round. The one drawback is that it's usually windy, but the wide-open spaces are ideal for kite flying. **Amenities:** Lifeguard, grills, picnic tables, showers, toilets. ✉ *Kamehameha Hwy.* ✛ *North of Waiāhole.*

🄲 **Kahana Bay Beach Park.** Local parents often bring their children here to wade in safety in the very shallow, protected waters. This pretty beach cove, surrounded by mountains, has a long arc of strip that is great for walking and a cool, shady grove of tall ironwood and pandanus trees that is ideal for a picnic. An ancient Hawaiian fishpond, which was in use until the 1920s, is visible nearby. The water here is not generally a clear blue due to the runoff from heavy rains in the valley. **Amenities:** Lifeguard, picnic tables, showers, toilets. ✉ *Kamehameha Hwy.* ✛ *North of Kualoa Park.*

THE NORTH SHORE

"North Shore, where the waves are mean, just like a washing machine," sing the Ka'au Crater Boys about this legendary side of the island. And in winter they are absolutely right. At times the waves overtake the road, stranding tourists and locals alike. When the surf is up, there are signs on the beach telling you how far to stay back so that you aren't swept out to sea. The most prestigious big-wave contest in the world, the Eddie Aikau, is held at Waimea Bay on waves the size of a six-story

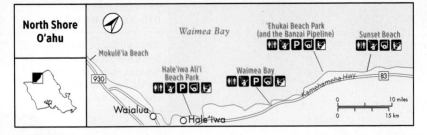

building. The Triple Crown of Surfing roams across three beaches in the winter months.

All this changes come summer when this tiger turns into a kitten, with water smooth enough to water-ski on and ideal for snorkeling. The fierce Banzai Pipeline surf break becomes a great dive area, allowing you to explore the coral heads that, in winter, have claimed so many lives on the ultrashallow but big, hollow tubes created here. Even with the monster surf subsided, this is still a time for caution: Lifeguards are scarcer, and currents don't subside just because the waves do.

That said, it's a place like no other on earth and must be explored. From the turtles at Mokulē'ia to the tunnels at Shark's Cove, you could spend your whole trip on this side and not be disappointed.

Beaches in this section are listed from north to south.

Turtle Bay. Now known more for its resort than its magnificent beach, Turtle Bay is mostly passed over on the way to the better-known beaches of Sunset and Waimea. But for the average visitor with the average swimming capabilities, this is the place to be on the North Shore. The crescent-shaped beach is protected by a huge sea wall. You can see and hear the fury of the northern swell, while blissfully floating in cool, calm waters. The convenience of this spot is also hard to pass up—there is a concession selling sandwiches and sunblock right on the beach. The resort has free parking for beach guests. **Amenities:** Food concessions, picnic tables, showers, toilets. ⊠ *Kamehameha Hwy. ✛ 4 mi north of Kahuku. Turn into resort and let guard know where you are going; they offer free parking to beach guests.*

★ **Sunset Beach.** The beach is broad, the sand is soft, the summer waves are gentle, making for good snorkeling, and the winter surf is crashing. Many love searching this shore for the puka shells that adorn the necklaces you see everywhere. Carryout truck stands selling shave ice, plate lunches, and sodas usually line the adjacent highway. **Amenities:** Lifeguard, picnic tables, showers, toilets. ⊠ *Kamehameha Hwy. ✛ 1 mi north of 'Ehukai Beach Park.*

'Ehukai Beach Park. What sets 'Ehukai apart is the view of the famous **Banzai Pipeline**, where the winter waves curl into magnificent tubes, making it an experienced wave-rider's dream. It's also an inexperienced swimmer's nightmare, though spring and summer waves are more accommodating to the average swimmer, and there's good snorkeling. Except when the surf contests are going on, there's no reason to stay on the central strip. Travel in either direction from the center, and the conditions remain the same but the population thins out, leaving you with a magnificent stretch of sand all to yourself. **Amenities:** Lifeguard, parking lot, showers, toilets. ⊠ *Kamehameha Hwy.* ♱ *Small parking lot borders Kamehameha Hwy., 1 mi north of Foodland at Pūpūkea.*

Fodor'sChoice **Waimea Bay.** Made popular in that old Beach Boys song "Surfin'
★ U.S.A.," Waimea Bay is a slice of big-wave heaven, home to king-size 25- to 30-foot winter waves. Summer is the time to swim and snorkel in the calm waters. The shore break is great for novice bodysurfers. Due to its popularity, the postage-stamp parking lot is quickly filled, but everyone parks along the side of the road and walks in. **Amenities:** Lifeguard, parking lot, picnic tables, showers, toilets. ⊠ *Kamehameha Hwy.* ♱ *Across from Waimea Valley, 3 mi north of Hale'iwa.*

Hale'iwa Ali'i Beach Park. The winter waves are impressive here, but in summer the ocean is like a lake, ideal for family swimming. The beach itself is big and often full of locals. Its broad lawn off the highway invites volleyball and Frisbee games and groups of barbecuers. This is also the opening break for the Triple Crown of Surfing, and the grass is often filled with art festivals or carnivals. **Amenities:** Lifeguard, parking lot, picnic tables, showers, toilets. ⊠ *Kamehameha Hwy.* ♱ *North of Hale'iwa town center and past harbor.*

Mokulē'ia Beach Park. There is a reason why the producers of the TV show *Lost* chose this beach for their set. On the remote northwest point of the island, it is about 10 mi from the closest store or public restroom; you could spend a day here and not see another living soul. And that is precisely its beauty—all the joy of being stranded on a deserted island without the trauma of the plane crash. The beach is wide and white, the waters bright blue (but a little choppy) and full of sea turtles and other marine life. Mokulē'ia is a great secret find, just remember to pack supplies and use caution, as there are no lifeguards. **Amenities:** None. ♱ *East of Hale'iwa town center, across from Dillingham Airfield.*

WEST (LEEWARD) O'AHU

The North Shore may be known as "Country," but the West side is truly the rural area on O'ahu. There are commuters from this side to Honolulu, but many are born, live, and die on this side with scarcely a trip to town. For the most part, there's less hostility and more curiousity toward outsiders. Occasional problems have flared up, mostly due to drug abuse that has ravaged the fringes of the island. But the problems have generally been car break-ins, not violence. So, in short, lock your car, don't bring valuables, and enjoy the amazing beaches.

The beaches on the west side are expansive and empty. Most O'ahu residents and tourists don't make it to this side simply because of the drive; in traffic it can take almost 90 minutes to make it to Ka'ena Point from downtown Honolulu. But you'll be hard-pressed to find a better sunset anywhere.

Beaches are listed here in a south to north direction, starting from just west of Honolulu.

Fodor's Choice
★
White Plains. Concealed from the public eye for many years as part of the Barbers Point Naval Air Station, this beach is reminiscent of Waikīkī but without the condos and the crowds. It is a long, sloping beach with numerous surf breaks, but it is also mild enough at shore for older children to play freely. It has views of Pearl Harbor and, over that, Diamond Head. Although the sand lives up to its name, the real joy of this beach comes from its history as part of a military property for the better part of a century. Expansive parking, great restroom facilities, and numerous tree-covered barbecue areas make it a great day-trip spot. As a bonus, a Hawaiian monk seal takes up residence here several months out of the year (seals are rare in the Islands). **Amenities:** Lifeguard, picnic tables, showers, toilets. ⊠ *Off H1 West* ✛ *Take Makakilo exit off H1 West, turn left. Follow it into base gates, make a left. Blue signs lead to beach.*

☺
★
Kō 'Olina. This is the best spot on the island if you have small kids. The resort commissioned a series of four man-made lagoons, but, as they have to provide public beach access, you are the winner. Huge rock walls protect the lagoons, making them into perfect spots for the kids to get their first taste of the ocean without getting bowled over. The large expanses of seashore grass and hala trees that surround the semi-circle beaches are made-to-order for naptime. A 1½-mi jogging track connects the lagoons. Due to its appeal for *keiki* (children), Kō 'Olina is popular and the parking lot fills up quickly when school is out and on weekends, so try to get there before 10 am. The biggest parking lot is at the farthest lagoon from the entrance. **Amenities:** Food concession, showers, toilet. ⊠ *92 Aliinui Dr.* ✛ *23 mi west of Honolulu. Take Kō 'Olina exit off H1 West and proceed to guard shack.*

Mākaha Beach Park. This beach provides a slice of local life most visitors don't see. Families string up tarps for the day, fire up hibachis, set up lawn chairs, get out the fishing gear, and strum 'ukulele while they "talk story" (chat). Legendary waterman Buffalo Kaeulana can be found in the shade of the palms playing with his grandkids and spinning yarns of yesteryear. In these waters Buffalo not only invented some of the most outrageous methods of surfing, but also raised his world-champion son Rusty. He also made Mākaha the home of the world's first international surf meet in 1954 and still hosts his Big Board Surfing Classic. The swimming is generally decent in summer, but avoid the big winter waves. With its long, slow-building waves, it's a great spot to try out longboarding. The swimming is generally decent in summer, but avoid the big winter waves. **Amenities:** Lifeguards, grills, picnic tables, showers, toilets. ⊠ *Farrington Hwy. 32 miles west of Honolulu on H1 Hwy., then Farrington Hwy. Beach will be on your left.*

WATER SPORTS AND TOURS

There's more to the beach than just lying on it. O'ahu is rife with every type of activity you can imagine. Most of the activities are offered in Waikīkī, right off the beach.

On the sand in front of your hotel, the sights and sounds of what is available will overwhelm you. Rainbow-color parachutes dot the

Continued on page 104

Imagine picking your seat for free at the Super Bowl or wandering the grounds of Augusta National at no cost during The Masters, and you glimpse the opportunity you have when attending the Vans Triple Crown of Surfing on the North Shore.

NORTH SHORE SURFING & THE TRIPLE CROWN

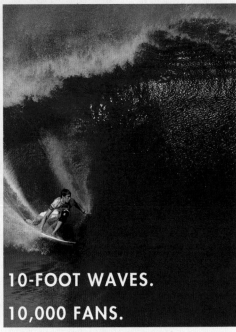

10-FOOT WAVES.

10,000 FANS.

TOP 50 SURFERS.

Long considered the best stretch of surf breaks on Earth, the North Shore surf area encompasses 6 mi of coastline on the northwestern tip of O'ahu from Hale'iwa to Sunset Beach. There are over 20 major breaks within these 6 mi. Winter storms in the North Pacific send huge swells southward which don't break for thousands of miles until they hit the shallow reef of O'ahu's remote North Shore. This creates optimum surfing all winter long and was the inspiration for having surf competitions here each holiday season.

Every November and December the top 50 surfers in world rankings descend on "The Country" to decide who is the best all-around surfer in the world. Each of the three invitation-only contests that make up the Triple Crown has its own winner; competitors also win points based on the final standings. The surfer who excels in all three contests, racking up the most points overall, wins the Vans Triple Crown title. The first contest is held at **Hale'iwa Beach,** the second at **Sunset Beach.** The season reaches its crescendo at the most famous surf break in the world, the **Banzai Pipeline.**

The best part is the cost to attend the events—nothing; your seat for the show—wherever you set down your beach towel. Just park your car, grab your stuff, and watch the best surfers in the world tame the best waves in the world.

The only surfing I understand involves a mouse.

The contests were created not only to fashion an overall champion, but to attract the casual fan to the sport. Announcers explain each ride over the loudspeakers, discussing the nuances and values being weighed by the judges. A scoreboard displays points and standings during the four days of each event.

If this still seems incomprehensible to you, the action on the beach can also be exciting as some of the most beautiful people in the world are attracted to these contests.

For more information, see www.triplecrownofsurfing.com

What should I bring?

Pack for a day at the Triple Crown the way you would for any day at the beach—sun block, beach towel, bottled water, and if you want something other than snacks, food.

These contests are held in rural neighborhoods (read: few stores), so pack anything you might need during the day. Also, binoculars are suggested, especially for the contest at Sunset. The pros will be riding huge outside ocean swells, and it can be hard to follow from the beach without binoculars. Hale'iwa's breaks and Pipeline are considerably closer to shore, but binoculars will let you see the intensity on the contestants' faces.

Hale'iwa Ali'i Beach Park
Vans Triple Crown Contest #1: OP Pro Hawaii

The Triple Crown gets underway with high-performance waves (and the know-how to ride them) at Hale'iwa. Though lesser known than the other two breaks of the Triple Crown, it is the perfect wave for showing off: the contest here is full of sharp cutbacks (twisting the board dramatically off the top or bottom of the wave), occasional barrel rides, and a crescendo of floaters (balancing the board on the top of the cresting wave) before the wave is destroyed on the shallow tabletop reef called the Toilet Bowl. The rider who can pull off the most tricks will win this leg, evening the playing field for the other two contests, where knowledge of the break is the key. Also, the beach park is walking distance from historic Hale'iwa town, a mecca to surfers worldwide who make their pilgrimage here every winter to ride the waves. Even if you are not a fan, immersing yourself in their culture will make you one by nightfall.

Sunset Beach
Vans Triple Crown Contest #2: O'Neill World Cup of Surfing

At Sunset, the most guts and bravado win the day. The competition is held when the swell is at 8 to 12 feet and from the northwest. Sunset gets the heaviest surf because it is the exposed point on the northern tip of O'ahu. Surfers describe the waves here as "moving mountains." The choice of waves is the key to this contest as only the perfect one will give the competitor a ride through the jigsaw-puzzle outer reef, which can kill a perfect wave instantly, all the way into the inner reef. Big bottom turns (riding all the way down the face of the wave before turning dramatically back onto the wave) and slipping into a super thick tube (slowing down to let the wave catch you and riding inside its vortex) are considered necessary to carry the day.

2

IN FOCUS NORTH SHORE SURFING & THE TRIPLE CROWN

Banzai Pipeline
Vans Triple Crown Contest #3: Rip Curl Pipeline Masters

Surfing competitions are generally judged on the top three waves ridden by the competitors. In the Pipeline Masters, however, instead of accruing points through tricks and jumps, the surfers score high by dropping in the deepest and staying inside the tube the longest. The best trick at Pipeline is surviving this incredibly hollow and heavy wave, no other artistry is necessary.

How does the wave become hollow in the first place? When the deep ocean floor ascends steeply to the shore, the waves that meet it will pitch over themselves sharply, rather than rolling. This pitching causes a tube to form, and in most places in the world that tube is a mere couple of feet in diameter. In the case of Pipeline, however, its unique, extremely shallow reef causes the swells to open into 10-foot-high moving hallways that surfers can pass through. Only problem: a single slip puts them right into the raggedly sharp coral heads that caused the wave to pitch in the first place. Broken arms and boards are the rule rather than the exception for those who dare to ride and fail.

■ TIP➔ The Banzai Pipeline is a surf break, not a beach. The best place to catch a glimpse of the break is from 'Ehukai Beach.

When Are the Contests?

The first contests at Haleʻiwa begin the second week of November, and the Triple Crown finishes up right before Christmas.

Surfing, more so than any other sport, relies on Mother Nature to allow competition. Each contest in the Triple Crown requires only four days of competition, but each is given a window of twelve days. Contest officials decide by 7 AM of each day whether the contest will be held or not, and they release the information to radio stations and via a hotline (whose number changes each year, unfortunately). By 7:15, you will know if it is on or not. Consult the local paper's sports section for the hotline number or listen to the radio announcement. The contests run from 8:30 to 4:30, featuring half-hour heats with four to six surfers each.

If big crowds bother you, go early on in the contests, within the first two days of each one. While the finale of the Pipeline Masters may draw about 10,000 fans, the earlier days have the same world class surfers with less than a thousand fans.

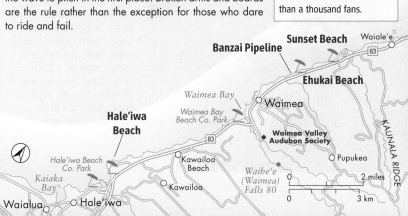

How Do I Get There?

If you hate dealing with parking and traffic, take TheBus. It will transport you from Waikīkī to the contest sites in an hour for two bucks and no hassle.

If you must drive, watch the news the night before. If they are expecting big waves that night, there is a very good chance the contest will be on in the morning. Leave by 6 AM to beat the crowd. When everybody else gets the news at 7:15 AM that the show is on, you will be parking your car and taking a snooze on the beach waiting for the surfing to commence.

Parking is limited so be prepared to park alongside Kamehameha Highway and trek it in.

But I'm not coming until Valentine's Day.

There doesn't need to be a contest underway for you to enjoy these spots from a spectator's perspective. The North Shore surf season begins in October and concludes at the end of March. Only the best can survive the wave at Pipeline. You may not be watching Kelly Slater or Andy Irons ripping, but, if the waves are up, you will still see surfing that will blow your mind. Also, there are surf contests year-round on all shores of O'ahu, so check the papers to see what is going on during your stay. A few other events to be on the lookout for:

Buffalo's Annual Big Board Surfing Classic
Generally held in March at legendary waterman "Buffalo" Keaulana's home beach of Mākaha, this is the Harlem Globetrotters of surfing contests. You'll see tandem riding, headstands, and outrigger canoe surfing. The contest is more about making the crowds cheer than beating your competitors, which makes it very accessible for the casual fan.

Converse Hawaiian Open
During the summer months, the waves switch to the south shore, where there are surf contests of one type or another each week. The Open is one of the biggest and is a part of the US Professional Longboard Surfing Championships. The best shoot it out every August on the waves Duke Kahanamoku made famous at Queen's Beach in Waikīkī.

Quiksilver in Memory of Eddie Aikau Big Wave Invitational
The granddaddy of them all is a one-day, winner-take-all contest in 25-foot surf at Waimea Bay. Because of the need for huge waves, it can be held only when there's a perfect storm. That could be at any time in the winter months, and there have even been a few years when it didn't happen at all. When Mother Nature does comply, however, it is not to be missed. You can hear the waves from the road, even before you can see the beach or the break.

BOARD SHAPES

Longboard: Lengthier (about 2.5–3 m/9–10.5 feet), wider, thicker, and more buoyant than the often-miniscule shortboards. Offers more flotation and speedier paddling, which makes it easier to get into waves. Great for beginners and those with relaxed surf styles. Skill level; Beginner to Intermediate.

Funboard: A little shorter than the longboard with a slightly more acute nose and blunt tail, the Funboard combines the best attributes of the longboards with some similar characteristics of the shorter boards. Good for beginners or surfers looking for a board more maneuverable and faster than a longboard. Skill level; Beginner to Intermediate.

Fishboard: A stumpy, blunt-nosed, twin-finned board that features a "V" tail (giving it a "fish" like look, hence the name) and is fast and maneuverable. Good for catching small, steep slow waves and pulling tricks. At one point this was the world's best-selling surfboard. Skill level; Intermediate to Expert.

Shortboard: Shortboards came on the scene in 1967-70 when the average board length dropped from 9'6" to 6'6" (2.9m to 2m) and changed the wave riding styles in the surf world forever. This board is a short, light, high-performance stick that is designed for carving the wave with a high amount of maneuverability. These boards need a fast steep wave, completely different than a longboard break, which tends to be slower with shallower wave faces. Skill level; Expert.

Beginner   **Expert**

Funboards
Fish
Longboards
Shortboards

Shallow wave faces, easiest surfing   Steeper wave faces, difficult surfing

horizon as parasailers improve their vantage point on paradise. The blowing of conch shells announces the arrival of the beach catamarans that sail around Diamond Head Crater. Meanwhile, the white caps of Waikīkī are being sliced by all manner of craft, from brilliant red outrigger canoes to darting white surfboards. Enjoy observing the flurry of activity for a moment, then jump right in.

As with all sports, listen to the outfitter's advice—they're not just saying it for fun. Caution is always the best bet when dealing with "mother" ocean. She plays for keeps and forgives no indiscretions. That being said, she offers more entertainment than you can fit into a lifetime, much less a vacation. So try something new and enjoy.

A rule of thumb is that the ocean is much more wily and unpredictable on the north- and west-facing shores, but that's also why those sides have the most famous waves on Earth. So plan your activity side according to your skill level.

BOAT TOURS AND CHARTERS

Boat tours can cover the gambit from weddings to funerals, and being on the water is the best way to enjoy the Islands. Whether you want to see the fish in action or experience how they taste, there is a tour for you.

For a sailing experience in O'ahu, you need go no farther than the beach in front of your hotel in Waikīkī. Strung along the sand are seven beach catamarans that will provide you with one-hour rides during the day and 90-minute sunset sails. Look for $23 to $25 for day sails and $30 to $34 for sunset rides. ■TIP➡ They all have their little perks and they're known for bargaining, so feel free to haggle, especially with the smaller boats. Some provide drinks for free, some charge for them, and some let you pack your own, so keep that in mind when pricing the ride.

Hawai'i Nautical. It's a little out of the way, but the experiences with this local company are worth the drive. Catamaran cruises lead to snorkeling with dolphins, gourmet-dinner cruises head out of beautiful Kalaeloa harbor, and sailing lessons are available on a 20-foot sailboat and a 50-foot cat. If you're driving out from Waikīkī, you may want to make a day of it, with sailing in the morning then 18 holes on one of the five courses in the area in the afternoon. Three-hour cruise rates with snacks and two drinks begin at $110 per person. ⊠ *91-550 Malakole St., Kapolei* ☎ *808/234–7245.*

Mai'Tai Catamaran. Taking off from in front of the Sheraton Hotel, this cat is the fastest and sleekest on the beach. If you have a need for speed and enjoy a little more upscale experience, this is the boat for you. ☎ *808/922–5665.*

Na Hoku II Catamaran. The diametric opposite of *Mai'Tai*, this is the Animal House of catamarans with reggae music and free booze. Their motto is "Free drinks, Easy Crew." They're beached right out in front of Duke's Barefoot Bar at the Outrigger Waikīkī Hotel and sail five times daily. ☎ *No phone* ⊕ *www.nahokuii.com.*

2

Paradise Cruises. This is one-stop shopping for specialty cruises. Offerings run the gamut from day cruises around Diamond Head with snorkeling, kayaking, and windsurfing to fine-dining night cruises with lobster and live entertainment to winter whale-watching cruises. You can learn lei making or coconut-frond weaving, or you can take a 'ukulele or hula lesson. They also offer seminars on Hawaiian

WORD OF MOUTH

"Whale-watching should be good in March—try to book a cruise. They also have glass-bottom boat rides, which I enjoyed. Parasailing, stand-up paddling, snorkeling at Hanauma Bay are all fun activities and can be arranged at your hotel or in advance." —Himom

history and culture, and there are artifact displays on board the boat. Two-hour dinner-cruise rates begin at $77 per person. ⊠ *Pier 5, Honolulu Harbor, Honolulu* ☎ *808/983–7700* ⊕ *www.starofhonolulu.com.*

Sashimi Fun Fishing. A combination trip suits those who aren't quite ready to troll for big game in the open-ocean swells. Sashimi Fun Fishing runs a dinner cruise with fishing and music. They keep close enough to shore that you can still see O'ahu while jigging for a variety of reef fish. The cruise includes a local barbecue dinner, and you can also cook what you catch. The four-hour fishing cruises rates with hotel transportation begin at $63 per person. ☎ *808/955–3474* ⊕ *www.808955fish.com.*

Tradewind Charters. Tradewind specializes in everything from weddings to funerals. They offer half-day private-charter tours for groups ranging from 2 to 110 people featuring sailing, snorkeling, and whale watching. Traveling on these luxury yachts not only gets you away from the crowds but also gives you the opportunity to "take the helm" if you wish. The cruise includes snorkeling at an exclusive anchorage as well as hands-on snorkeling and sailing instruction. Charter prices are approximately $495 for up to six passengers. ⊠ *796 Kalanipuu St., Honolulu* ☎ *808/973–0311* ⊕ *www.tradewindcharters.com.*

BODY BOARDING AND BODYSURFING

Body Boarding (also known as boogie boarding or sponging) has become a popular alternative to surfing for a couple of reasons. First, the start-up cost is much less—a usable board can be purchased for $30 to $40 or can be rented on the beach for $5 an hour. Second, it's a whole lot easier to ride a boogie board than to tame a surfboard. For beginner boogie boarding all you must do is paddle out to the waves, turn toward the beach, and kick like crazy when the wave comes.

Most grocery and convenience stores sell boogie boards. Though the boards do not rival what the pros use, you won't notice a difference in their handling on smaller waves. ■TIP→ **Another small investment you'll want to make is surf fins.** These smaller, sturdier versions of dive fins sell for $25–$35 at surf and dive stores, sporting-goods stores, or even Wal-Mart. Most beach stands do not rent fins with the boards. Though they are not necessary for boogie boarding, fins do give you a tremendous advantage when you are paddling into waves. If you plan to go out in bigger surf, we would also advise you to get fin leashes

A top choice among boogie boarders and bodysurfers is Sandy Beach, for its big surf.

to prevent loss. For bodysurfing, you definitely want to invest in fins. Check out the same spots for boogie boarding.

If the direction of the current or dangers of the break are not readily apparent to you, don't hesitate to ask a lifeguard for advice.

BEST SPOTS

Boogie boarding and bodysurfing can be done anywhere there are waves, but, due to a paddling advantage surfers have over spongers, it's usually more fun to go to exclusively boogie-boarding spots.

Kūhiō Beach Park (⊠ *Waikīkī* ⊹ *Past Moana Surfrider Hotel to Kapahulu Ave. pier*) is an easy spot for the first-timer to check out the action. Try **The Wall**, a break so named for the break wall in front of the beach. It's a little crowded with kids, but it's close enough to shore to keep you at ease. There are dozens of breaks in Waikīkī, but the Wall is the only one solely occupied by spongers. Start out here to get the hang of it before venturing out to **Canoes** or **Kaiser Bowl's**.

The best spot on the island for advanced boogie boarding is **Sandy Beach** (⊠ *Kalaniana'ole Hwy.* ⊹ *2 mi east of Hanauma Bay*) on the Windward side. It's a short wave that goes right and left, but the barrels here are unparalleled for pure sponging. The ride is intense and breaks so sharply that you actually see the wave suck the bottom dry before it crashes on to it. That's the reason it's also called "Break Neck Beach." It's awesome for the advanced, but know its danger before enjoying the ride.

Makapu'u Beach (⊠ *Kalaniana'ole Hwy.* ⊹ *Across from Sea Life Park, 2 mi south of Waimānalo*) on the Windward side is a sponger's dream beach with its extended waves and isolation from surfers. If you're a little more timid, go to the far end of the beach to **Keiki's,** where the waves are mellowed by Makapu'u Point, for an easier, if less thrilling, ride. Although the main break at Makapu'u is much less dangerous than Sandy's, check out the ocean floor—the sands are always shifting, sometimes exposing coral heads and rocks. Also always check the currents: they can get strong. But for the most part, this is the ideal beach for both boogie boarding and bodysurfing.

EQUIPMENT

There are more than 30 rental spots on Waikīkī Beach, all offering basically the same prices. But if you plan to do it for more than just an hour, we would suggest buying a board for $20 to $30 at an ABC convenience store and giving it to a kid when you're preparing to end your vacation. It will be more cost-effective for you and will imbue you with the Aloha spirit while making a kid's day.

DEEP-SEA FISHING

The joy of fishing in Hawai'i is that there isn't really a season; it's good year-round. Sure, the bigger yellowfin tuna ('*ahi*) are generally caught in summer, and the coveted spearfish are more frequent in winter, but you can still catch them any day of the year. You can also find dolphin fish (*mahimahi*), wahoo (*ono*), skipjacks, and the king—Pacific blue marlin—ripe for the picking on any given day.

When choosing a fishing boat in the Islands, look for the older, grizzled captains who have been trolling these waters for half a century. All the fancy gizmos in the world can't match an old tar's knowledge of the waters.

The general rule for the catch is an even split with the crew. Unfortunately, there are no freeze-and-ship providers in the state, so unless you plan to eat the fish while you're here, you'll probably want to leave it with the boat. Most boats do offer mounting services for trophy fish; ask your captain.

Besides the gift of fish, a gratuity of 10% to 20% is standard but use your own discretion depending on how you felt about the overall experience.

BOATS AND CHARTERS

Hawai'i Fishing Adventures. Based out of Kō 'Olina resort, Captain Jim and his crew try to bring the full Hawaiian experience to their fishing trips. While most fishing boats head straight out to the open ocean, Captain Jim trolls along the Leeward coast giving visitors a nice sense of the island while stalking the fish. They also offer an overnighter to Molokai's Penguin Banks, reputed to be some of Hawai'i's best fishing grounds. The six-hour tour runs $725 with the overnighter booking at $2,500. ☎ 808/520–4852 ⊕ *www.hawaiifishingcharters.net.*

Inter-Island Sportfishing. The oldest-running sportfishing company on O'ahu also boasts the largest landed blue marlin—more than 1,200 pounds. With two smaller boats and the 53-foot *Maggie Joe* (which can hold up to 25), they can manage any small party with air-conditioned cabins and cutting-edge fishing equipment. They also work with Grey's

Taxidermy, the world's largest marine taxidermist, to mount the monster you reel in. Half-day exclusive charter rates for groups of six begin at $700. ☎ *808/591–8888* ⊕ *www.maggiejoe.com.*

Magic Sportfishing. The awards Magic has garnered are too many to mention here, but we can tell you their magnificent 50-foot *Pacifica* fishing yacht is built for comfort, whether you're fishing or not. Unfortunately, Magic can accommodate only up to six. Full-day exclusive charter rates begin at $975. ☎ *808/596–2998* ⊕ *www.magicsportfishing.com.*

KAYAKING

Kayaking is quickly becoming a top choice for visitors to the Islands. Kayaking alone or with a partner on the open ocean provides a vantage point not afforded by swimming and surfing. Even amateurs can travel long distances and keep a lookout on what's going on around them.

This ability to travel long distances can also get you into trouble. ■ TIP→ **Experts agree that rookies should stay on the Windward side.** Their reasoning is simple: if you tire, break or lose an oar, or just plain pass out, the onshore winds will eventually blow you back to the beach. The same cannot be said for the offshore breezes of the North Shore and West O'ahu.

Kayaks are specialized: some are better suited for riding waves while others are designed for traveling long distances. Your outfitter can address your needs depending on your activities. Sharing your plans with your outfitter can lead to a more enjoyable experience.

BEST SPOTS

The hands-down winner for kayaking is **Lanikai Beach** (⊠ *Mokulua Drive* ⊹ *Past Kailua Beach Park; street parking on Mokulua Drive for various public-access points to beach*) on the Windward side. This is perfect amateur territory with its still waters and onshore winds. If you're feeling more adventurous, it's a short paddle out to the "Mokes." This pair of Islands off the coast has beaches, surf breaks on the reef, and great picnicking areas. Due to the distance from shore (about a mile), the Mokes usually afford privacy from all but other intrepid kayakers. Lanikai is great year-round, and most kayak-rental companies have a store right up the street in Kailua.

For something a little different, try **Kahana River** (⊹ *This stream empties into Kahana Bay, 8 mi east of Kāne'ohe*), also on the Windward side. The river may not have the blue water of the ocean, but the Ko'olau Mountains, with waterfalls aplenty when it's raining, are magnificent in the background. It's a short jaunt, about 2 mi round-trip, but it's packed with rain-forest foliage and the other rain-forest denizens, mosquitos. Bring some repellent and enjoy this light workout.

EQUIPMENT, LESSONS, AND TOURS

Go Bananas. Staffers make sure that you rent the appropriate kayak for your abilities, and they also outfit the rental car with soft racks to transport the boat to the beach. The store also carries clothing and kayaking accessories. Full-day rates begin at $30 for single kayaks, and $45 for doubles. ⊠ *799 Kapahulu Ave., Honolulu* ☎ *808/737–9514.*

Twogood Kayaks Hawai'i. The one-stop shopping outfitter for kayaks on the Windward side offers rentals, lessons, guided kayak tours, and even weeklong camps if you want to immerse yourself in the sport. Guides are trained in history, geology, and birdlife of the area. Kayak a full day with a guide for $125; this includes lunch, snorkeling gear, and transportation from Waikīkī. Although their rental prices are about $10 more than average, they do deliver the boats to the water for you and give you a crash course in ocean safety. It's a small price to pay for the convenience and for peace of mind when entering new waters. Full-day rates begin at $55 for single kayaks, and $65 for doubles. ⊠ *345 Hahani St., Kailua* ☎ *808/262–5656* ⊕ *www.twogoodkayaks.com.*

SCUBA DIVING

All the great stuff to do atop the water sometimes leads us to forget the real beauty beneath the surface. Although snorkeling and snuba (swimming with an air hose attached to an airtank on the surface) do give you access to this world, nothing gives you the freedom of scuba.

The diving on O'ahu is comparable with any you might do in the tropics, but its uniqueness comes from the isolated environment of the Islands. There are literally hundreds of species of fish and marine life that you can only find in this chain. Adding to the singularity of diving off O'ahu is the human history of the region. Military activities and tragedies of the 20th century filled the waters surrounding O'ahu with wreckage that the ocean creatures have since turned into their homes.

Although instructors certified to license you in scuba are plentiful in the Islands, we suggest that you get your PADI certification before coming, as a week of classes may be a bit of a commitment on a short vacation. ■ TIP→ **You can go on introductory dives without the certification, but the best dives require it.**

BEST SPOTS

Hanauma Bay (⊠ *7455 Kalaniana'ole Hwy.*) is an underwater state park and a popular dive site in Southeast O'ahu. The shallow inner reef of this volcanic crater bay is filled with snorkelers, but its floor gradually drops from 10 to 70 feet at the outer reef where the big fish prefer the lighter traffic. It's quite a trek down into the crater and out to the water, so you may want to consider a dive-tour company to do your heavy lifting. Expect to see butterfly fish, goatfish, parrot fish, surgeonfish, and sea turtles.

The *Mahi Wai'anae,* a 165-foot minesweeper, was sunk in 1982 in the waters just south of Wai'anae on O'ahu's Leeward coast to create an artificial reef. It's intact and penetrable, but you'll need a boat to access it. In the front resides an ancient moray eel who is so mellowed that you can pet his barnacled head without fearing for your hand's safety. Goatfish, tame lemon-butterfly fish, and blue-striped snapper hang out here, but the real stars are the patrols of spotted eagle rays that are always cruising by. It can be a longer dive as it's only 90 feet to the hull.

Fodor'sChoice
★   The best shore dive on O'ahu is **Shark's Cove** (⊠ *Kamehameha Hwy.* ✛ *Across from Foodland in Pūpūkea*) on the North Shore, but

unfortunately it's only accessible during the summer months. Novices can drift along the outer wall, watching everything from turtles to eels. Veterans can explore the numerous lava tubes and tunnels where diffused sunlight from above creates a dreamlike effect in spacious caverns. It's 10- to 45-feet deep, ready-made for shore diving with a parking lot right next to the dive spot. Increase your caution the later in the year you come to this spot; the waves pick up strength in fall, and the reef can be turned into a washboard for you and your gear.

Three Tables is just west of Shark's Cove, enabling you to have a second dive without moving your car. Follow the three perpendicular rocks that break the surface out to this dive site, where you can find a variety of parrot fish and octopus, plus occasional shark and ray sightings at depths of 30 to 50 feet. It's not as exciting as Shark's Cove, but it's more accessible for the novice diver.

EQUIPMENT, LESSONS, AND TOURS

Captain Bruce's Hawai'i. Captain Bruce's focuses on the west and east shores, covering the *Mahi* and the *Corsair*. This full-service company has refresher and introductory dives as well as more advanced drift and night dives. No equipment is needed; they provide it all. Most important, this is the only boat on O'ahu that offers hot showers on board. Two-tank boat-dive rates begin at $115 per person. ☎ 808/373–3590 or 800/535–2487 ⊕ www.captainbruce.com.

Reeftrekkers. The owners of the slickest dive Web site in Hawai'i are also the *Scuba Diving* Reader's Choice winners for the past four years. Using the dive descriptions and price quotes on their Web site, you can plan your excursions before ever setting foot on the island. Two-tank boat dive rates begin at $115 per person. ☎ 808/943–0588 ⊕ www.reeftrekkers.com.

Surf-N-Sea. The North Shore headquarters for all things water-related is great for diving that side as well. There is one interesting perk—the cameraman can shoot a video of you diving. It's hard to see facial expressions under the water, but it still might be fun for those who need documentation of all they do. Two-tank boat dive rates begin at $140 per person. ☎ 808/637–3337 ⊕ www.surfnsea.com.

SNORKELING

One advantage that snorkeling has over scuba is that you never run out of air. That and the fact that anyone who can swim can also snorkel without any formal training. A favorite pastime in Hawai'i, snorkeling can be done anywhere there's enough water to stick your face in it. Each spot will have its great days depending on the weather and time of year, so consult with the purveyor of your gear for tips on where the best viewing is that day. Keep in mind that the North Shore should only be attempted when the waves are calm, namely in the summertime.

■ TIP→ Think of buying a mask and snorkel as a prerequisite for your trip—they make any beach experience better. Just make sure you put plenty of sunblock on your back because once you start gazing below, your head may not come back up for hours.

O'ahu's North Shore has the island's biggest waves as well as some of the best snorkeling.

BEST SPOTS

As Waimea Bay is to surfing, **Hanauma Bay** (⊠ *7455 Kalaniana'ole Hwy.*) in Southeast O'ahu is to snorkeling. By midday it can look like the mall at Christmas with all the bodies, but with over a half-million fish to observe, there's plenty to go around. Due to the protection of the narrow mouth of the cove and the prodigious reef, you will be hard-pressed to find a place you will feel safer while snorkeling.

Directly across from the electric plant outside of Kō 'Olina resort, **Electric Beach** (⊠ *Farrington Hwy.* ⊹ *1 mi west of Kō'Ōlina*) in West O'ahu has become a haven for tropical fish. The expulsion of hot water from the plant warms the ocean water, attracting all kinds of wildlife. Although the visibility is not always the best, the crowds are thin, and the fish are guaranteed. Just park next to the old train tracks and enjoy this secret spot.

Fodor's Choice
★ Great shallows right off the shore with huge reef protection make **Shark's Cove** (⊠ *Kamehameha Hwy.* ⊹ *Across from Foodland in Pūpūkea*) on the North Shore a great spot for youngsters in the summertime. You can find a plethora of critters from crabs to octopus, in waist-deep or shallower water. The only caveat is that once the winter swell comes, this becomes a human pinball game rather than a peaceful observation spot. Summer only.

EQUIPMENT AND TOURS

Kō 'Olina Kat. The dock in Kō 'Olina harbor is a little more out of the way, but this is a much more luxurious option than the town snorkel cruises. Two-hour morning and afternoon tours of the west side of O'ahu are punctuated with stops for observing dolphins from the boat and a snorkel spot well populated with fish. All gear, snacks, sandwiches, and two alcoholic beverages make for a more complete experience, but also a pricier one (starting at $110 per person). ☏ *808/234–7245* ⊕ *www.hawaiinautical.com.*

Snorkel Bob's. We suggest buying your gear, unless it's going to be a one-day affair. Either way, Snorkel Bob's has all the stuff you'll need (and a bunch of stuff you don't) to make your water adventures enjoyable. Also feel free to ask the staff about the good spots at the moment, as the best spots can vary with weather and seasons. ⊠ *702 Kapahulu Ave.* ☏ *808/735–7944.*

SURFING

Perhaps no word is more associated with Hawai'i than *surfing*. Every year the best of the best gather here to have their Super Bowl: Vans Triple Crown of Surfing. The pros dominate the waves for a month, but the rest of the year belongs to people like us, just trying to have fun and get a little exercise.

O'ahu is unique because it has so many famous spots: Banzai Pipeline, Waimea Bay, Kaiser Bowls, and Sunset Beach resonate in young surfers' hearts the world over. The renown of these spots comes with a price: competition for those waves. The aloha spirit lives in many places but not on premium waves. If you're coming to visit and want to surf these world-famous breaks, you need to go out with a healthy dose of respect and patience. As long as you follow the rules of the road and concede waves to local riders, you should not have problems. Just remember that locals view these waves as their property, and everything should be all right.

If you're nervous and don't want to run the risk of a confrontation, try some of the alternate spots listed below. They may not have the name recognition, but the waves can be just as great.

BEST SPOTS

If you like to ride waves in all kinds of craft, try **Mākaha Beach** (⊠ *Farrington Hwy.* ✛ *32 miles west of Honolulu on H1 and Farrington Hwy.*). It has interminable rights that allow riders to perform all manner of stunts: from six-man canoes with everyone doing headstands to bully boards (oversize boogie boards) with dad's whole family riding with him. Mainly known as a longboarding spot, it's predominantly local but not overly aggressive to the respectful outsider. The only downside is that it's way out on the west shore. Use caution in the wintertime, as the surf can get huge.

In Waikīkī, try getting out to **Populars,** a break at **Ulukou Beach** (⊠ *Waikīkī, in front of the Sheraton Waikīkī hotel*). Nice and easy, Populars never breaks too hard and is friendly to both the rookie and the veteran. The only downside here is the ½-mi paddle out to the

> **WORD OF MOUTH**
>
> "Depending on the time of the year, you can watch world-class bodysurfing at Sandy Beach and Makapu'u Beach." —Lubon66

Stand-up paddling has become one of Hawai'i's most popular water activities.

break, but no one ever said it was going to be easy. Plus the long pull keeps it from getting overcrowded.

White Plains Beach (⊠ *Off H1 West* ✛ *Take Makakilo exit off H1 West, turn left. Follow it into base gates, make a left. Blue signs lead to beach*) is a spot where trouble will not find you. Known among locals as "mini-Waikīkī," it breaks in numerous spots, preventing the logjam that happens with many of O'ahu's more popular breaks. As part of a military base in West O'ahu, the beach was closed to the public until a couple of years ago. It's now occupied by mostly novice to intermediate surfers, so egos are at a minimum, though you do have to keep a lookout for loose boards.

EQUIPMENT AND LESSONS

C&K Beach Service. To rent a board in Waikīkī, visit the beach fronting the Hilton Hawaiian Village. Rentals cost $12 to $15 per hour, depending on the size of the board, and $18 for two hours. Small group lessons are $50 per hour with board, and trainers promise to have you riding the waves by lesson's end. ☎ *No phone.*

🕭 **Hawaiian Fire, Inc.** Off-duty Honolulu firefighters—and some of Hawai'i's most knowledgeable water-safety experts—man the boards at one of Hawai'i's hottest new surfing schools. Lessons include equipment, safety and surfing instruction, and two hours of surfing time (with lunch break) at a secluded beach near Barbers Point. Transportation is available from Waikīkī. Two-hour group lesson rates begin at $109 per person, $189 per person for a private lesson. ☎ *808/737–3473* ⊕ *www. hawaiianfire.com.*

North Shore Eco-Surf Tours. The only prerequisites here are "the ability to swim and the desire to surf." North Shore Eco-Surf has a more relaxed view of lessons, saying that the instruction will last somewhere between 90 minutes and four hours. The group rate begins at $78 per person, $135 for a private lesson. ☎ 808/638–9503 ⊕ www.ecosurf-hawaii.com.

★ **Surf 'N Sea.** This is the Wal-Mart of water for the North Shore. Rent a shortboard for $5 an hour or a longboard for $7 an hour ($24 and $30 for full-day rentals). Lessons cost $85 for three hours. Depending on how you want to attack your waves, you can also rent boogie boards or kayaks. ⊠ 62-595 Kamehameha Hwy. ☎ 808/637–9887 ⊕ www.surfnsea.com.

WHALE-WATCHING

November is marked by the arrival of snow in most of America, but in Hawai'i it marks the return of the humpback whale. These migrating behemoths move south from their North Pacific homes during the winter months for courtship and calving, and they put on quite a show. Watching males and females alike throwing themselves out of the ocean and into the sunset awes even the saltiest of sailors. Newborn calves riding gently next to their two-ton mothers will stir you to your core. These gentle giants can be seen from the shore as they make quite a splash, but there is nothing like having your boat rocking beneath you in the wake of a whale's breach.

★ **Wild Side Specialty Tours.** Boasting a marine-biologist crew, this west-side tour boat takes you to undisturbed snorkeling areas. Along the way you can view dolphins, turtles, and, in winter, whales. The tours leave early (7 am) to catch the wildlife still active, so it's important to plan ahead as they're an hour outside Honolulu. Four-hour whale-watching cruise rates with Continental breakfast start at $115. ⊠ Wai'anae Boat Harbor, Slip A11 ☎ 808/306–7273 ⊕ www.sailhawaii.com.

WINDSURFING AND KITEBOARDING

Those who call windsurfing and kiteboarding cheating because they require no paddling have never tried hanging on to a sail or kite. It will turn your arms to spaghetti quicker than paddling ever could, and the speeds you generate . . . well, there's a reason why these are considered extreme sports.

Windsurfing was born here in the Islands. For amateurs, the Windward side is best because the onshore breezes will bring you back to land even if you don't know what you're doing. The new sport of kiteboarding is tougher but more exhilarating as the kite will sometimes take you in the air for hundreds of feet. We suggest only those in top shape try the kites, but windsurfing is fun for all ages.

EQUIPMENT AND LESSONS

Kailua Sailboard and Kayaks Company. The appeal here is that they offer both beginner and high-performance gear. They also give lessons, either at $129 for a four-hour group lesson or $109 for a one-hour individual

2

lesson. ■TIP→ Since both options are around the same price, we suggest the one-hour individual lesson; then you have the rest of the day to practice what they preach. Half-day rentals for the more experienced run from $59 for the standard board to $79 for a high-performance board. ⊠ *130 Kailua Rd., Kailua* ☎ *808/262–2555* ⊕ *www.kailuasailboards.com.*

Naish Hawai'i. If you like to learn from the best, try out world-champion Robby Naish and his family services. Not only do they build and sell boards, rent equipment, and provide accommodation referrals, but they also offer their windsurfing and kiteboarding expertise. A three-hour package, including 90 minutes of instruction and a three-hour board rental, costs $100. ⊠ *155A Hāmākua Dr., Kailua* ☎ *808/261–6067* ⊕ *www.naish.com.*

GOLF, HIKING, AND OUTDOOR ACTIVITIES

Although much is written about the water surrounding this little rock known as O'ahu, there is as much to be said for the rock itself. It's a wonder of nature, thrust from the ocean floor a hundred millennia ago by a volcanic hot spot that is still spitting out islands today. This is the most remote island chain on earth, and there are creatures and plants that can be seen here and nowhere else. And there are dozens of ways for you to check it all out.

AERIAL TOURS

An aerial tour of the Islands opens up a world of perspective. Looking down from the sky at the outline of the USS *Arizona* where it lays in its final resting place below the waters of Pearl Harbor or getting a glimpse of how Mother Nature carved a vast expanse of volcanic crater are the kinds of views only seen by an "eye in the sky." If you go, don't forget your camera.

★ **Island Seaplane Service.** Harking back to the days of the earliest air visitors to Hawai'i, the seaplane has always had a special spot in island lore. The only seaplane service still operating in Hawai'i takes off from Ke'ehi Lagoon. Flight options are either a half-hour south and eastern O'ahu shoreline tour or an hour island circle tour. The *Pan Am Clipper* may be gone, but you can revisit the experience for $135 to $250. ⊠ *85 Lagoon Dr., Honolulu* ☎ *808/836–6273* ⊕ *www.islandseaplane.com.*

Makani Kai Helicopters. This may be the best way to see the infamous and now closed Sacred Falls park, where a rock slide killed 20 people and injured dozens more; Makani Kai dips their helicopter down to show you one of Hawai'i's former favorite hikes. Half-hour tour rates begin at $155 per person, and customized private charters are available starting at $1,750 per hour. ⊠ *130 Iolana Pl., Honolulu* ☎ *808/834–5813* ⊕ *www.makanikai.com.*

★ **The Original Glider Rides.** "Mr. Bill" has been offering piloted glider (sailplane) rides over the northwest end of O'ahu's North Shore since 1970. These are piloted scenic rides for one or two passengers in sleek, bubble-top, motorless aircraft. You'll get aerial views of mountains, shoreline, coral pools, windsurfing sails, and, in winter, humpback whales. Reservations are recommended; 10-, 15-, 20-, and 30-minute flights leave every 20 minutes daily 10–5. The charge for one passenger is $79–$145, depending on the length of the flight; two people fly for $170–$260. ⊠ *Dillingham Airfield, Mokulē'ia* ☎ *808/677–3404* ⊕ *www.honolulusoaring.com.*

BIKING

O'ahu's coastal roads are flat and well paved, and unfortunately, awash in vehicular traffic. Frankly, biking is no fun in either Waikīkī or Honolulu, but things are a bit better outside the city.

Honolulu City and County Bike Coordinator (☎ *808/768–8335*) can answer all your biking questions concerning trails, permits, and state laws.

BEST SPOTS

Fodor's Choice ★

Our favorite ride is in central O'ahu on the **'Aiea Loop Trail** (⊠ *End of 'Aiea Heights Dr.* ⊹ *Just past Kea'iwa Heiau State Park*). There's a little bit of everything you expect to find in Hawai'i—wild pigs crossing your path, an ancient Hawaiian *heiau* (holy ground), and the remains of a World War II crashed airplane. Campsites and picnic tables are available along the way and, if you need a snack, strawberry guava trees abound. Enjoy the foliage change from bamboo to Norfolk pine in your climb along this 4½-mi track.

EQUIPMENT AND TOURS

Blue Sky Rentals & Sports Center. Known more for motorcycles than for man-powered bikes, Blue Sky does have bicycles for $20 for eight hours, $25 for a day, and $75 per week—no deposit is required. The prices include a bike, a helmet, and a lock. ⊠ *1920 Ala Moana Blvd.* ⊹ *Across from Hilton Hawaiian Village, Waikīkī, Honolulu* ☎ *808/947–0101.*

Boca Hawai'i LLC. This is your first stop if you want to do intense riding. The triathlon shop, owned and operated by top athletes, has full-suspension Trek 1200s for mountain bikes or Trek 1000 for street bikes, both for $40 a day and $175 a week. Call ahead and reserve a bike, as supplies are limited. ⊠ *330 Cooke St.* ⊹ *Next to Bike Factory, Kaka'ako, Honolulu* ☎ *808/591–9839* ⊕ *www.bocahawaii.com.*

CAMPING

Camping has always been the choice of cost-conscious travelers who want to be vacationing for a while without spending a lot of money. But now, with the growth of ecotourism and the skyrocketing cost of gas, it has become more popular than ever. Whatever your reasons for getting back to nature, O'ahu has plenty to offer year-round. ■TIP➔ **Camping here is not as highly organized as it is on the mainland: expect few marked sites, scarce electrical outlets, and nary a ranger station.** What you find instead are unblemished spots in the woods and on the beach. With price tags ranging from free to $18, it's hard to complain about the lack of amenities.

A good way to explore O'ahu's North Shore is to get off the road and hop on a bike or ATV.

STATE PARKS

There are four state recreation areas at which you can camp, one in the mountains and three on the beach. All state parks' campsites can now be reserved up to a year in advance online. The fee is $18 a night per campsite for up to six people. To obtain a camping permit in person stop by the office (✉ 1151 Punchbowl St., Room 310), or to receive their rules and regulations for state parks, write to the **Department of Land and Natural Services, State Parks Division** (📫 Box 621 Honolulu 96809 ☎ 808/587–0300 ⊕ www.hawaiistateparks.org).

Keaīwa Heiau State Recreation Area (✉ End of 'Aiea Heights Rd. ☎ 808/ 483–2511), the mountain option, consists of nearly 400 acres of forests and hiking trails in the foothills of the Ko'olau. The park is centered on an ancient Hawaiian holy site, known as a *heiau*, that is believed to be the site of many healings. Proper respect is asked of campers in the area.

Of the beach sites, **Kahana Valley State Park** (✉ Kamehameha Hwy. ✛ Near Kahana Bay) is the choice for a true Hawaiian experience. You camp alongside a beautiful Windward bay, a short walk away from the Huilua Fishpond, a national historic landmark. There are rain-forest hikes chock-full of local fruit trees, a public hunting area for pigs, and a coconut grove for picnicking. The water is suitable for swimming and bodysurfing, though it's a little cloudy for snorkeling. Camping here gives you a true taste of old Hawai'i, as they lived it.

COUNTY CAMPSITES

As for the county spots, there are 15 currently available and they all do require a permit. The good news is that the permits are free and are easy to obtain. Contact the **Department of Parks and Recreation** (✉ *650 S. King St., Honolulu* ☎ *808/768-3440*), or any of the satellite city halls (Ala Moana Mall, Fort St. Mall, and Kapolei Hale), for permits and rules and regulations.

Fodor's Choice For beach camping we suggest Bellows and Kualoa. **Bellows Field Beach**
★ **Park** (✉ *220 Tinker Rd.* ☎ *808/259-8080*) has the superior beach as well as excellent cover in the grove of ironwood trees. The Windward beach is over 3 mi long, and both pole fishing and campfires in designated areas are allowed here. You can feel secure with the kids as there are lifeguards and public phones. The only downside is that camping is only permitted on the weekends.

The beach at **Kualoa Regional Park** (✉ *49-479 Kamehameha Hwy.* ☎ *808/237-8525*) isn't the magnificent giant that Bellows is, but the vistas are both magnificent and historic. Near Chinaman's Hat (Mokoli'i Island) at the northern end of Kāne'ohe Bay, the park is listed on the National Registry of Historic Places due to its significance to the Hawaiians. The park is expansive, with large grassy areas, picnic tables, and comfort stations. Although the beach is just a bit of a sandy strip, the swimming and snorkeling are excellent.

Nestled in the foothills of the Ko'olau is the serene **Hoomaluhia Botanical Garden** (✉ *End of Luluku Rd. in Kāne'ohe* ☎ *808/233-7323*). The 400-acre preserve has catch-and-release fishing, extensive hiking trails, and a large selection of tropical shrubs and trees. There are five fire circles. Though it is a beautiful area, they do caution campers to be prepared for rain, mud, and mosquitoes.

GOLF

Unlike those of the Neighbor Islands, the majority of O'ahu's golf courses are not associated with hotels and resorts. In fact, of the island's three-dozen-plus courses, only five are tied to lodging and none of them are in the tourist hub of Waikīkī.

Greens fees listed here are the highest course rates per round for U.S. residents. (Some courses charge non–U.S. residents higher prices.) Discounts are often available for resort guests and for those who book tee times on the Web. Twilight fees are usually offered; call individual courses for information.

WAIKĪKĪ

Ala Wai Municipal Golf Course. Just across the Ala Wai Canal from Waikīkī, Ala Wai is said to host more rounds than any other U.S. course. Not that it's a great course, just really convenient, being Honolulu's only public "city course." Although residents can obtain a city golf card that allows automated tee-time reservation over the phone, the best bet for a visitor is to show up and expect to wait at least an hour. The course itself is flat. Robin Nelson did some redesign work in the 1990s, adding mounding, trees, and a lake. The Ala Wai Canal comes into play on several holes on the back nine, including the treacherous 18th. ✉ *404 Kapahulu Ave., Waikīkī, Honolulu* ☎ *808/733–7387, 808/739–1900 golf shop* ⊕ *www.co.honolulu.hi.us/des/golf/alawai.htm* 🚶 *18 holes. 5861 yds. Par 70. Greens fee: $46* ☞ *Facilities: Driving range, putting green, golf carts, pull carts, rental clubs, pro shop, lessons, restaurant, bar.*

SOUTHEAST O'AHU

Hawai'i Kai Golf Course. The Championship Golf Course (William F. Bell, 1973) winds through a Honolulu suburb at the foot of Koko Crater. Homes (and the liability of a broken window) come into play on many holes, but they are offset by views of the nearby Pacific and a crafty routing of holes. With several lakes, lots of trees, and bunkers in all the wrong places, Hawai'i Kai really is a "championship" golf course, especially when the trade winds howl. The **Executive Course** (1962), a par-55 track, is the first of only three courses in Hawai'i built by Robert Trent Jones Sr. Although a few changes have been made to his original design, you can find the usual Jones attributes, including raised greens and lots of risk-reward options. ✉ *8902 Kalaniana'ole Hwy., Hawai'i Kai* ☎ *808/395–2358* ⊕ *www.hawaiikaigolf.com* 🚶 *Championship Course: 18 holes. 6222 yds. Par 72. Greens fee: $100. Executive Course: 18 holes. 2223 yds. Par 55. Green fee: $37* ☞ *Facilities: Driving range, putting green, golf carts, pull carts, rental clubs, pro shop, lessons, restaurant, bar.*

WINDWARD O'AHU

Ko'olau Golf Club. Ko'olau Golf Club is marketed as the toughest golf course in Hawai'i and one of the most challenging in the country. Dick Nugent and Jack Tuthill (1992) routed 10 holes over jungle ravines that require at least a 110-yard carry. The par-4 18th may be the most difficult closing hole in golf. The tee shot from the regular tees must carry 200 yards of ravine, 250 from the blue tees. The approach shot is back across the ravine, 200 yards to a well-bunkered green. Set at the Windward base of the Ko'olau Mountains, the course is as much beauty as beast. Kāne'ohe Bay is visible from most holes, orchids and yellow ginger bloom, the shama thrush (Hawai'i's best singer since Don Ho) chirrups, and waterfalls flute down the sheer, green mountains above. ✉ *45-550 Kionaole Rd., Kāne'ohe* ☎ *808/236–4653* ⊕ *www.koolaugolfclub.com* 🚶 *18 holes. 7310 yds. Par 72. Greens fee: $130* ☞ *Facilities: Driving range, putting green, golf carts, rental clubs, pro shop, golf academy, restaurant, bar.*

Fodor'sChoice ★ **Luana Hills Country Club.** In the cool, lush Maunawili Valley, Pete and Perry Dye created what can only be called target jungle golf. In other words, the rough is usually dense jungle, and you may not hit a driver on three of the four par-5s, or several par-4s, including the perilous 18th that plays off a cliff to a narrow green protected by a creek. Mt. Olomana's twin peaks tower over Luana Hills. ■**TIP→** The back nine wanders deep into the valley, and includes an island green (par-3 11th) and perhaps the loveliest inland hole in Hawai'i (par-4 12th). ✉ *770 Auloa Rd., Kailua* ☎ *808/262–2139* ⊕ *www.luanahills.com* 🚶 *18 holes. 6164 yds.*

Par 72. Greens fee: $125 ☞ *Facilities: Driving range, putting green, golf carts, rental clubs, pro shop, restaurant, bar.*

★ **Olomana Golf Links.** Bob and Robert L. Baldock are the architects of record for this layout, but so much has changed since it opened in 1969 that they would recognize little of it. A turf specialist was brought in to improve fairways and greens, tees were rebuilt, new bunkers added, and mangroves cut back to make better use of natural wetlands. But what really puts Olomana on the map is that this is where wunderkind Michelle Wie learned the game. ✉ *41-1801 Kalanianasole Hwy., Waimānalo* ☎ *808/259–7926* ⊕ *www.olomanagolflinks.com* ⚲ *18 holes. 6326 yds. Par 72. Greens fee: $95* ☞ *Facilities: Driving range, putting green, golf carts, pull carts, rental clubs, pro shop, lessons, restaurant, bar.*

NORTH SHORE

Turtle Bay Resort & Spa. When the Lazarus of golf courses, the **Fazio Course** at Turtle Bay (George Fazio, 1971), rose from the dead in 2002, Turtle Bay on O'ahu's rugged North Shore became a premier golf destination. Two holes had been plowed under when the **Palmer Course** at Turtle Bay (Arnold Palmer and Ed Seay, 1992) was built, while the other seven lay fallow, and the front nine remained open. Then new owners came along and re-created holes 13 and 14 using Fazio's original plans, and the Fazio became whole again. It's a terrific track with 90 bunkers. The gem at Turtle Bay, though, is the Palmer Course. The front nine is mostly open as it skirts Punaho'olapa Marsh, a nature sanctuary, while the back nine plunges into the wetlands and winds along the coast. The short par-4 17th runs along the rocky shore, with a diabolical string of bunkers cutting diagonally across the fairway from tee to green. ✉ *57-049 Kuilima Dr., Kahuku* ☎ *808/293–8574* ⊕ *www.turtlebaygolf.com* ⚲ *Fazio Course: 18 holes. 6535 yds. Par 72. Greens fee: $125. Palmer Course: 18 holes. 7199 yds. Par 72. Green fee: $175* ☞ *Facilities: Driving range, putting green, golf carts, rental clubs, pro shop, lessons, restaurant, bar.*

CENTRAL AND WEST (LEEWARD) O'AHU

★ **Coral Creek Golf Course.** On the 'Ewa Plain, 4 mi inland, Coral Creek is cut from ancient coral—left from when this area was still under water. Robin Nelson (1999) does some of his best work in making use of the coral, and of some dynamite, blasting out portions to create dramatic lakes and tee and green sites. They could just as easily call it Coral Cliffs, because of the 30- to 40-foot cliffs Nelson created. They include the par-3 10th green's grotto and waterfall, and the vertical drop-off on the right side of the par-4 18th green. An ancient creek meanders across the course, but there's not much water, just enough to be a babbling nuisance. ✉ *91-1111 Geiger Rd., 'Ewa Beach* ☎ *808/441–4653* ⊕ *www.coralcreekgolfhawaii.com* ⚲ *18 holes. 6818 yds. Par 72. Greens fee: $130* ☞ *Facilities: Driving range, putting green, golf carts, rental clubs, pro shop, lessons, restaurant, bar.*

Kō 'Olina Golf Club. Hawai'i's golden age of golf-course architecture came to O'ahu when Kō 'Olina Golf Club opened in 1989. Ted Robinson, king of the water features, went splash-happy here, creating nine lakes that come into play on eight holes, including the par-3 12th, where you reach the tee by driving behind a Disney-like waterfall. Tactically, though, the most dramatic is the par-4 18th, where the approach is a minimum 120 yards across a lake to a two-tiered green guarded on the left by a cascading waterfall. Today, Kō 'Olina, affiliated with the adjacent 'Ihilani Resort and Spa (guests receive discounted

rates), has matured into one of Hawai'i's top courses. You can niggle about routing issues—the first three holes play into the trade winds (and the morning sun), and two consecutive par-5s on the back nine play into the trades—but Robinson does enough solid design to make those of passing concern. ⊠ *92-1220 Ali'inui Dr., Kapolei* ☎ *808/676–5300* ⊕ *www.koolinagolf.com* ⅃ *18 holes. 6867 yds. Par 72. Greens fee: $179* ⌂ *Facilities: Driving range, putting green, golf carts, rental clubs, pro shop, golf academy, restaurant, bar.*

Royal Kunia Country Club. At one time the PGA Tour considered buying Royal Kunia Country Club and hosting the Sony Open there. It's that good. ■ TIP➔ **Every hole offers fabulous views from Diamond Head to Pearl Harbor to the nearby Wai'anae Mountains.** Robin Nelson's eye for natural sight lines and dexterity with water features adds to the visual pleasure. ⊠ *94-1509 Anonui St., Waipahu* ☎ *808/688–9222* ⊕ *www.royalkuniacc.com* ⅃ *18 holes. 7007 yds. Par 72. Greens fee: $140* ⌂ *Facilities: Driving range, putting green, golf carts, rental clubs, pro shop, restaurant.*

Waikele Golf Course. Outlet stores are not the only bargain at Waikele. The adjacent golf course is a daily-fee course that offers a private club-like atmosphere and a terrific Ted Robinson (1992) layout. The target off the tee is Diamond Head, with Pearl Harbor to the right. Robinson's water features are less distinctive here, but define the short par-4 fourth hole, with a lake running down the left side of the fairway and guarding the green; and the par-3 17th, which plays across a lake. The par-4 18th is a terrific closing hole, with a lake lurking on the right side of the green. ⊠ *94-200 Paioa Pl., Waipahu* ☎ *808/676–9000* ⊕ *www.golfwaikele.com* ⅃ *18 holes. 6261 yds. Par 72. Greens fee: $130* ⌂ *Facilities: Driving range, putting green, golf carts, rental clubs, pro shop, lessons, restaurant, bar.*

HIKING

The trails of O'ahu cover a full spectrum of environments: desert walks through cactus, slippery paths through bamboo-filled rain forest, and scrambling rock climbs up ancient volcanic calderas. The only thing you won't find is an overnighter, as even the longest of hikes won't take you more than half a day. In addition to being short in length, many of the prime hikes are located within 10 minutes of downtown

2

Waikīkī, meaning that you won't have to spend your whole day getting back to nature.

BEST SPOTS

Every vacation has requirements that must be fulfilled so that when your neighbors ask, you can say, "Yeah, did it." **Diamond Head Crater** is high on that list of things to do on O'ahu. It's a moderate hike, due in part to the many stairs along the way; be sure to bring a water bottle because it's hot and dry. Only a mile up, a clearly marked trail with handrails scales the inside of this extinct volcano. At the top, the fabled 99 steps take you up to the pillbox overlooking the Pacific Ocean and Honolulu. It's a breathtaking view and a lot cheaper than taking a helicopter ride for the same photo op. ⊠ *Diamond Head Rd. at 18th Ave.* ✛ *Enter on east of crater; there's limited parking inside, most park on street and walk in.*

Fodor's Choice
★

Travel up into the valley beyond Honolulu to make the **Mānoa Falls** hike. Though only a mile long, this path passes through so many different ecosystems that you feel as if you're in an arboretum. Walk among the elephant ear ape plants, ruddy fir trees, and a bamboo forest straight out of China. At the top is a 150-foot falls with a small pool not quite suited for swimming but good for wading. This hike is more about the journey than the destination; make sure you bring some mosquito repellent because they grow 'em big up here. ⊠ *West Mānoa Rd.* ✛ *Behind Mānoa Valley in Paradise Park. Take West Mānoa Rd. to end, park on side of road, and follow trail signs in.*

For the less adventurous hiker and anyone looking for a great view, there is the **Makapu'u Lighthouse Trail.** The paved trail runs up the side of Makapu'u Point in southeast O'ahu. Early on, the trail is surrounded by lava rock but, as you ascend, foliage—the tiny white *koa haole* flower and the cream-tinged spikes of the *kiawe*—begins taking over the barren rock. Once atop the point, you begin to understand how alone these Islands are in the Pacific. The easternmost tip of O'ahu, this is where the island divides the sea, giving you a spectacular view of the cobalt ocean meeting the land in a cacophony of white caps. To the south are several tide pools and the lighthouse, while the eastern view looks down upon Rabbit and Kāohikaipu Islands, two bird sanctuaries just off the coast. The 2-mi round-trip hike is a great break on a circle-island trip. ⊠ *Kalaniana'ole Hwy.* ✛ *Take Kalaniana'ole Hwy. to base of Makapu'u Point. Look for asphalt strip snaking up mountain.*

GOING WITH A GUIDE

Hawai'i Nature Center. A good choice for families, the center in upper Makīkī Valley conducts a number of programs for both adults and children. There are guided hikes into tropical settings that reveal hidden waterfalls and protected forest reserves. They don't run tours every day so it is good to get advance reservations. ⊠ *2131 Makīkī Heights Dr., Makīkī Heights* ☎ *808/955–0100* ⊕ *www.hawaiinaturecenter.org.*

O'ahu Nature Tours. Guides explain the native flora and fauna that are your companions on glorious sunrise, hidden-waterfall, mountain-forest, rain-forest, and volcanic walking tours. ☎ *808/924–2473* ⊕ *www. oahunaturetours.com.*

HORSEBACK RIDING

A great way to see the island is atop a horse, leaving the direction to the pack while you drink in the views of mountains or the ocean. It may seem cliché, but there really is nothing like riding a horse down a stretch of beach to put you in a romantic state of mind.

★ **Happy Trails Hawai'i.** Take a guided horseback ride through the verdant Waimea Valley on the North Shore along trails that offer panoramic views from Ka'ena Point to the famous surfing spots. Rates for a 90-minute trail ride begin at $72. ☒ *Pupakea Rd ⊹ 1 mi mauka up Pupakea Rd. on right, Pupakea* ☎ *808/638–7433.*

Kualoa Ranch. This ranch across from Kualoa Beach Park on the Windward side leads trail rides in the Ka'a'awa Valley. Rates for a one-hour trail ride begin at $63. Kualoa has other activities such as bus and Jeep tours, all-terrain-vehicle trail rides, and children's activities, which may be combined for half- or full-day package rates. ☒ *49-560 Kamehameha Hwy., Ka'a'awa* ☎ *808/237–8515* ⊕ *www.kualoa.com.*

Turtle Bay Stables. This is the only spot on the island where you can take the horses on the beach. The stables here are part of the North Shore resort, but can be utilized by nonguests. The sunset ride is a definite must if you are a friend of our four-legged friends. Rates for a 45-minute trail ride begin at $65. ⊹ *4 mi north of Kahuku in Turtle Bay Resort* ☎ *808/293–8811* ⊕ *www.turtlebayresort.com/activities/horseback.asp.*

SHOPPING

Eastern and Western traditions meet on O'ahu, where savvy shoppers find luxury goods at high-end malls and scout tiny boutiques and galleries filled with pottery, blown glass, woodwork, and Hawaiian print clothing by local artists. ■TIP→ **Exploring downtown Honolulu, Kailua on the Windward side, and the North Shore often yields the most original merchandise.** Some of these small stores also carry a myriad of imported clothes and gifts from around the world—a reminder that, on this island halfway between Asia and North America, shopping is a multicultural experience.

DOWNTOWN HONOLULU AND CHINATOWN

SHOPPING CENTERS

Getting to the Ala Moana and downtown Honolulu shopping centers from Waikīkī is quick and inexpensive thanks to **TheBus** and the **Waikiki Trolley.**

Ala Moana Shopping Center. One of the nation's largest open-air malls is five minutes from Waikīkī by bus. More than 240 stores and 60 restaurants make up this 50-acre complex, which is a unique mix of national and international chains as well as smaller, locally owned shops and eateries—and everything in between. Designer shops in residence include Gucci, Louis Vuitton, Christian Dior, and Emporio Armani. All of Hawai'i's major department stores are here, including Neiman Marcus, Nordstrom, Sears, and Macy's. To get to the mall from Waikīkī, catch TheBus line 8, 19, or 20; a one-way ride is $2. Or hop aboard the Waikiki Trolley's Pink Line, which comes through the area every half hour. ⊠ *1450 Ala Moana Blvd., Ala Moana* ☎ *808/955–9517* ⊕ *www. alamoanacenter.com.*

Aloha Tower Marketplace. Billing itself as a festival marketplace, Aloha Tower cozies up to Honolulu Harbor. Along with restaurants and entertainment venues, it has about two-dozen shops and kiosks selling mostly visitor-oriented merchandise, from sunglasses to exceptional local artwork to souvenir refrigerator magnets. You can also find a nice selection of locally crafted 'ukuleles at The Hawaiian Ukulele Company, or music CDs if you prefer to just listen. To get there from Waikīkī take the E-Transit Bus, which goes along TheBus routes every 15 minutes. ⊠ *1 Aloha Tower Dr., at Piers 8, 9, and 10, Downtown Honolulu* ☎ *808/566–2337* ⊕ *www.alohatower.com.*

Ward Centers. Heading west from Waikīkī toward downtown Honolulu, you'll run into a section of town with five distinct shopping-complex areas; there are more than 125 specialty shops and 22 restaurants here. The Ward Entertainment Center features 16 movie theaters, including a brand new, state-of-the-art 3-D big-screen auditorium. For distinctive Hawaiian gift stores, visit Nohea Gallery, Martin & MacArthur, and Native Books/Na Mea Hawaii, carrying quality work from Hawai'i artists, including mu'umu'u, koa wood products, and unparalleled Ni'ihau shell necklaces. Island Soap and Candle Works (☎ *808/591–0533*) makes all of its candles and soaps on-site with Hawaiian flower scents. There is free parking in the area and a valet service. Take TheBus routes 19 or 20; fare is $2 one-way. Or follow the Waikiki Trolley Yellow Line, which comes through the area every 45 minutes. ⊠ *1050–1200 Ala Moana Blvd., Ala Moana* ☎ *808/591–8411.*

BOOKS

Borders Books. Borders stocks more than 200 books in its Hawaiian section; learn about Hawaiian plants, hula, or surfing. This two-story location has books, music, movies, and a café. ⊠ *Ward Centre, 1200 Ala Moana Blvd.* ☎ *808/591–8995.* ⊠ *Royal Hawaiian Center, 2201 Kalakaua Ave.* ☎ *808/922–4154.*

★ **Native Books/Na Mea Hawai'i.** In addition to clothing for adults and children and unusual artwork such as Ni'ihau shell necklaces, this boutique's book selection covers Hawaiian history and language, and offers children's books set in the Islands. ⊠ *Ward Warehouse, 1050 Ala Moana Blvd.* ☎ *808/596–8885.*

CLOTHING

Anne Namba Designs. Anne Namba brings the beauty of classic kimonos to contemporary fashions. In addition to women's apparel, she's also designed a men's line and a wedding couture line. ⊠ *324 Kamani St., Downtown Honolulu* ☎ *808/589–1135.*

Hilo Hattie. Busloads of visitors pour in through the front doors of the world's largest manufacturer of Hawaiian and tropical aloha wear. Once shunned by Honolulu residents for its three-shades-too-bright tourist wear, it has become a favorite source for Island gifts, macadamia nut and chocolate packages, and clothing for elegant Island functions.

Free shuttle service is available from Waikīkī. ⊠ *700 N. Nimitz Hwy., Iwilei* ☎ *808/535–6500.*

Reyn's. Reyn's is a good place to buy the aloha print fashions residents wear. Look for the limited-edition Christmas shirt, a collector's item manufactured each holiday season. Reyn's has 13 locations statewide and offers styles for men, women, and children. ⊠ *Ala Moana Shopping Center, 1450 Ala Moana Blvd., Ala Moana* ☎ *808/949–5929* ⊠ *Sheraton Waikīkī, 2255 Kalākaua Ave., Waikīkī* ☎ *808/923–0331* ⊠ *Kāhala Mall, 4211 Wai'alae Ave., Kāhala* ☎ *808/737–8313.*

★ **Shanghai Tang.** First opened in Hong Kong, Shanghai Tang now has its 11th branch at Ala Moana. An emphasis on workmanship and the luxury of fine fabrics upholds the tradition of old-Shanghai tailoring. They do custom work for men, women, and children. ⊠ *Ala Moana Shopping Center, Ala Moana* ☎ *808/942–9800.*

FOOD SPECIALTIES

Honolulu Chocolate Company. To really impress those back home, pick up a box of gourmet chocolates here. They dip the flavors of Hawai'i, from Kona coffee to macadamia nuts, in fine chocolate. ⊠ *Ward Centre, 1200 Ala Moana Blvd., Ala Moana* ☎ *808/591–2997.*

Longs Drugs. For gift items in bulk, try one of the many outposts of Longs, the perfect place to stock up on chocolate-covered macadamia nuts—at reasonable prices—to carry home. ⊠ *Ala Moana Shopping Center, 1450 Ala Moana Blvd., 2nd level, Ala Moana* ☎ *808/941–4433* ⊠ *Kāhala Mall, 4211 Wai'alae Ave., Kāhala* ☎ *808/732–0784.*

GALLERIES

Jeff Chang Pottery & Fine Crafts. With locations around the island, Jeff Chang has become synonymous with excellent craftsmanship and originality in Raku pottery, blown glass, and koa wood. Gift ideas include petroglyph stoneware coasters, ceramic and glass jewelry, blown-glass penholders and business-card holders, and Japanese Aeto chimes. The owners choose work from 300 different local and national artists. ⊠ *Ward Center 1200 Ala Moana Blvd., Honolulu* ☎ *808/262–4060.*

Louis Pohl Gallery. Modern works from some of Hawai'i's finest artists. ⊠ *1111 Nu'uanu Ave., Honolulu* ☎ *808/521–1812.*

Nohea Gallery. These shops are really galleries representing more than 450 artists who specialize in koa furniture, bowls, and boxes, as well as art glass and ceramics. Original paintings and prints—all with an Island theme—add to the selection. They also carry unique handmade Hawaiian jewelry with tī leaf, maile, and coconut-weave designs. ■ TIP➜ The koa photo albums in these stores are easy to carry home and make wonderful gifts. ⊠ *Ward Warehouse, 1050 Ala Moana Blvd., Ala Moana* ☎ *808/596–0074.*

GIFTS

Blue Hawaii Lifestyle. The Ala Moana store carries a large selection of locally made products, including soaps, honey, tea, salt, chocolates, art, and CDs. Every item, in fact, is carefully selected from various Hawai'i companies, artisans, and farms, from the salt fields of Molokai to the lavender farms on Maui to the single-estate chocolate on O'ahu's

North Shore. ⊠ *Ala Moana Center 1450 Ala Moana Blvd., Honolulu* ☏ *808/262–4060* ⊕ *www.bluehawaiilifestyle.com.*

HAWAIIAN ARTS AND CRAFTS

Hawaiian Quilt Collection. Traditional island comforters, wall hangings, pillows, and other Hawaiian-print quilt items are the specialty here. ⊠ *Ala Moana Center, 1450 Ala Moana Blvd., Ala Moana* ☏ *808/ 946–2233.*

Na Hoku. If you look at the wrists of *kamaʻāina* (local) women, you are apt to see Hawaiian heirloom bracelets fashioned in either gold or silver in a number of Island-inspired designs. Na Hoku sells jewelry in designs that capture the heart of the Hawaiian lifestyle in all its elegant diversity. ⊠ *Ala Moana Center, 1450 Ala Moana Blvd., Ala Moana* ☏ *808/946–2100.*

WAIKĪKĪ

SHOPPING CENTERS

2100 Kalākaua. Tenants of this elegant, town house–style center include Chanel, Coach, Tiffany & Co., Yves Saint Laurent, Gucci, and Tod's. ⊠ *2100 Kalākaua Ave., Waikīkī* ☏ *808/550–4449* ⊕ *www. 2100kalakaua.com.*

DFS Galleria Waikīkī. Hermès, Cartier, Michael Kors and Marc Jacobs are among the shops on the Waikīkī Luxury Walk in this enclosed mall, as well as Hawaiʻi's largest beauty and cosmetic store. The third floor caters to duty-free shoppers only and features an exclusive Watch Shop. The Kālia Grill and Starbucks offer a respite for weary shoppers. ⊠ *Kalākaua and Royal Hawaiian Aves., Waikīkī* ☏ *808/931–2655.*

Royal Hawaiian Center. An open and inviting façade has made this three-block-long center a Hawaiian shopping garden. There are more than 110 stores and restaurants, including Hawaiian Heirloom Jewelry Collection by Phillip Rickard, which also has a museum with Victorian pieces. Bike buffs can check out the Harley-Davidson Motor Clothes and Collectibles Boutique, and Bob's Ukulele may inspire musicians to learn a new instrument. There are restaurants and even a post office. ⊠ *2201 Kalākaua Ave., Waikīkī* ☏ *808/922–0588* ⊕ *www.shopwaikiki. com.*

Waikīkī Beach Walk. This open-air shopping center greets visitors at the west end of Waikiki's Kalakaua Avenue with 70 locally owned stores and restaurants. Get reasonably priced, fashionable resort wear for yourself at Mahina or for your pet at Planet U2; find unique pieces by local artists at Under the Koa Tree. Learn about Hawaiʻi's culture and take free hula, ʻukulele, or Hawaiian language lessons at Mana Hawaiʻi, as well. ⊠ *226 Lewers St., Waikīkī* ☏ *808/931–3591* ⊕ *www. waikikibeachwalk.com.*

CLOTHING

Moonbow Tropics. An elegant selection of silk Tommy Bahama Aloha shirts, as well as tropical styles for women. ⊠ *Moana Surfrider, 2365 Kalākaua Ave., Waikīkī* ☏ *808/924–1496* ⊕ *www.moonbowtropics. com.*

GALLERIES

Gallery Tokusa. A *netsuke* is a toggle used to fasten small containers to obi belts on a kimono. Gallery Tokusa specializes in intricately carved netsuke, both antique and contemporary, and one-of-a-kind necklaces. ⊠ *Halekulani, 2199 Kālia Rd., Waikīkī* ☎ *808/923–2311.*

Diamond Head Gallery. For something different, this gallery features the work of several of Hawai'i's most cutting edge artists. Browse works by North Shore-based Mark Swanson, who is known for his kitschy, retro pop art of beach culture and tikis; or Dennis Mathewson, one of the pioneers of airbrushing and a technique called Kustom painting. ⊠ *Waikiki Beach Walk, 226 Lewers St., Waikīkī* ☎ *808/971–4866.*

GIFTS

★ **Sand People.** This little shop stocks easy-to-carry gifts, such as fish-shaped Christmas ornaments, Hawaiian-style notepads, charms in the shape of flip-flops (known locally as "slippers"), soaps, and ceramic clocks. Also located in Kailua. ⊠ *Moana Surfrider, 2369 Kalākaua, Waikīkī* ☎ *808/924–6773.*

JEWELRY

Philip Rickard. The heirloom design collection of this famed jeweler features custom Hawaiian wedding jewelry, sought by various celebrities. ⊠ *Royal Hawaiian Shopping Center, 2201 Kalākaua Ave., Waikīkī* ☎ *808/924–7972.*

GREATER HONOLULU

Kapahulu begins at the Diamond Head end of Waikīkī and continues up to the H1 freeway. Shops and restaurants are located primarily on Kapahulu Avenue, which like many older neighborhoods should not be judged at first glance. It is full of variety.

KAPAHULU

Bailey's Antiques & Aloha Shirts. Vintage aloha shirts are the specialty at this kitschy store. Prices can start at $3.99 for the 10,000 shirts in stock, and the tight space and musty smell are part of the thrift-shop atmosphere. ■TIP→ Antiques hunters can also buy old-fashioned postcards, authentic military clothing, funky hats, and denim jeans from the 1950s. ⊠ *517 Kapahulu Ave., Kapahulu* ☎ *808/734–7628.*

KĀHALA AND HAWAI'I KAI

Island Treasures. Local residents come here to shop for gifts that are both unique and within reach of almost every budget, ranging in price from $1 to $5,000. Next to Zippy's and overlooking the ocean, the store has handbags, toys, jewelry, home accessories, soaps and lotions, and locally made original artwork. Certainly the most interesting shop in Hawai'i Kai's suburban-mall atmosphere, this store is also a good place to purchase CDs of some of the best Hawaiian music. ⊠ *Koko Marina Center, 7192 Kalaniana'ole Hwy., Hawai'i Kai* ☎ *808/396–8827.*

Kāhala Mall. The upscale residential neighborhood of Kāhala, near the slopes of Diamond Head, is 10 minutes by car from Waikīkī. The only shopping of note in the area is located at the indoor mall, which has

90 stores and restaurants, including Macy's, Gap, Reyn's Aloha Wear, and Barnes & Noble.

Don't miss fashionable boutiques such as **Ohelo Road** (☎ *808/735–5525*), where contemporary clothing for all occasions fills the racks. You can also browse local foods and products at Whole Foods.

Eight **movie theaters** (☎ *800/326–3264 express code 2712*) provide post-shopping entertainment.

✉ *4211 Wai'alae Ave., Kāhala* ☎ *808/732–7736* ⊕ *www.kahalamall-center.com.*

WINDWARD O'AHU

Bookends. The perfect place to shop for gifts, or just take a break with the family, this bookstore feels more like a small-town library, welcoming browsers to linger for hours. The large children's section is filled with toys and books to read. ✉ *600 Kailua Rd., Kailua* ☎ *808/261–1996.*

Fodor's Choice ★ **Global Village.** Tucked into a tiny strip mall near Maui Tacos, this boutique features contemporary apparel for women, Hawaiian-style children's clothing, and unusual jewelry and gifts from all over the world. Look for Kula Cushions eye pillows (made with lavender grown on Maui), coasters in the shape of flip-flops, a wooden key holder shaped like a surfboard, and placemats made from lauhala and other natural fibers, plus accessories you won't find anywhere else. ✉ *Kailua Village Shops, 539 Kailua Rd., Kailua* ☎ *808/262–8183* ⊕ *www. globalvillagehawaii.com.*

Fodor's Choice ★ **Under a Hula Moon.** Exclusive tabletop items and Pacific home decor, such as shell wreaths, shell night-lights, Hawaiian print kitchen towels, and Asian silk clothing, define this eclectic shop. ✉ *Kailua Shopping Center, 600 Kailua Rd., Kailua* ☎ *808/261–4252.*

NORTH SHORE

★ **The Growing Keiki.** Frequent visitors return to this store year after year for a fresh supply of original, hand-picked, Hawaiian-style clothing for youngsters. ✉ *66-051 Kamehameha Hwy., Hale'iwa* ☎ *808/637–4544* ⊕ *www.thegrowingkeiki.com.*

Fodor's Choice ★ **Silver Moon Emporium.** This small boutique carries everything from Brighton accessories and fashionable T-shirts to Betsy Johnson formal wear, and provides attentive yet casual personalized service. Its stock changes frequently, and there's always something wonderful on sale. No matter what your taste, you'll find something for everyday wear or special occasions. ✉ *North Shore Marketplace, 66-250 Kamehameha Hwy., Hale'iwa* ☎ *808/637–7710.*

WEST O'AHU

Aloha Stadium Swap Meet. This thrice-weekly outdoor bazaar attracts hundreds of vendors and even more bargain hunters. Every Hawaiian souvenir imaginable can be found here, from coral shell necklaces to bikinis, as well as a variety of ethnic wares, from Chinese brocade dresses to Japanese pottery. There are also ethnic foods, silk flowers, and luggage in aloha floral prints. Shoppers must wade through the typical sprinkling of used and stolen goods to find value. Wear comfortable shoes, use sunscreen, and bring bottled water. The flea market takes place in the Aloha Stadium parking lot Wednesday and Saturday from 8 to 3; Sunday from 6:30 to 3. Admission is $1 per person ages 12 and up. Several shuttle companies serve Aloha Stadium for the swap meet, including **VIP Shuttle** (☎ 808/839–0911), **Reliable Shuttle** (☎ 808/924–9292), and **Hawaii Supertransit** (☎ 808/841–2928). The average cost is $12 per person, round-trip. For a cheaper but slower ride, take **TheBus** (⊕ www.thebus.org). ✉ 99-500 Salt Lake Blvd., 'Aiea ☎ 808/486–6704.

Waikele Premium Outlets. Anne Klein Factory, Donna Karan Company Store, Kenneth Cole, and Saks Fifth Avenue Outlet anchor this discount destination. You can take a shuttle to the outlets, but the companies do change over frequently. One to try: **P.G. Plover** (☎ 808/744–2836); $10 round-trip. ✉ H1 Hwy., 30 min west of Downtown Honolulu, Waikele ☎ 808/676–5656.

SPAS

The majority of spas on O'ahu are located in the major hotels, but there are a few smaller ones well worth trying. Day spas provide additional options to the self-indulgent services offered in almost every major hotel on the island.

★ **Ampy's European Facials and Body Spa.** This 30-year-old spa has kept its prices reasonable over the years thanks to their "no frills" way of doing business. All of Ampy's facials are 75 minutes (except for teens), and the spa has become famous for custom aromatherapy treatments. Call at least a week in advance because the appointment book fills up quickly here. It's in the Ala Moana Building, adjacent to the Ala Moana Shopping Center. ✉ 1441 Kapi'olani Blvd., Suite 377, Ala Moana ☎ 808/946–3838 ✂ $90, 60-min lomilomi massage. Sauna. Services: body treatments, facials, hand and foot care, massage.

Hoala Salon and Spa. This Aveda concept spa has everything from Vichy showers to hydrotherapy rooms to customized aromatherapy. Ladies, they'll even touch up your makeup for free before you leave. ✉ Ala Moana Shopping Center, 3rd fl., 1450 Ala Moana Blvd., Ala Moana ☎ 808/947–6141 ⊕ www.hoalasalonspa.com ✂ $160, 75-min lomilomi massage. Hair salon, eucalyptus steam room. Services: body treatments, facials, massage, nail care, waxing.

Fodor's Choice ★ **JW Marriott 'Ihilani Resort & Spa.** Soak in warm seawater among velvety orchid blossoms at this unique Hawaiian hydrotherapy spa. Thalassotherapy treatments combine underwater jet massage with color therapy and essential oils. Specially designed treatment rooms have

2

a hydrotherapy tub, a Vichy-style shower, and a needle shower with 12 heads. The spa's Ohi'a A'i Mountain Apple line of natural aromatherapy products, which uses the essence of the mountain apple fruit in lotions, bath salts, shampoos and conditioners. ⊠ *92-1001 'Ōlani St., Kapolei* ☎ *808/679–0079* ⊕ *www.ihilani.com* ☞ *$145, 50-min lomilomi massage. Hair salon, hot tubs (indoor and outdoor), sauna, steam room. Gym with: cardiovascular machines, free weights, weight-training equipment. Services: aromatherapy, body wraps and scrubs, facials, massage, thalassotherapy. Classes and programs: aerobics, body sculpting, dance classes, fitness analysis, guided walks, personal training, Pilates, tai chi, yoga.*

Mandara Spa at the Hilton Hawaiian Village Beach Resort & Spa. From its perch in the Kālia Tower, Mandara Spa, an outpost of the chain that originated in Bali, overlooks the mountains, ocean, and downtown Honolulu. Fresh Hawaiian ingredients and traditional techniques headline an array of treatments. Try an exotic upgrade, such as reflexology or an eye treatment using Asian silk protein. The delicately scented, candlelit foyer can fill up quickly with robe-clad conventioneers, so be sure to make a reservation. There are spa suites for couples, a private infinity pool, and a café. ⊠ *Hilton Hawaiian Village Beach Resort and Spa, 2005 Kālia Rd., Waikīkī* ☎ *808/949–4321* ⊕ *www. hiltonhawaiianvillage.com* ☞ *$130, 50-min lomilomi massage. Hair salon, hot tubs (indoor and outdoor), sauna, steam room. Gym with: cardiovascular machines, free weights, weight-training equipment. Services: aromatherapy, body wraps and scrubs, facials, massages.*

Nā Hō'ola at the Hyatt Regency Waikīkī Resort & Spa. Nā Hō'ola is the largest spa in Waikīkī, sprawling across the fifth and sixth floors of the Hyatt, with 19 treatment rooms, jet baths, and Vichy showers. Arrive early for your treatment to enjoy the postcard views of Waikīkī Beach. Four packages identified by Hawai'i's native healing plants—noni, kukui, awa, and kalo—combine various body, face, and hair treatments and span 2½ to 4 hours. The Champagne of the Sea body treatment employs a self-heating mud wrap to release tension and stress. The small exercise room is for use by hotel guests only. ⊠ *Hyatt Regency Waikīkī Resort and Spa, 2424 Kalākaua Ave., Waikīkī* ☎ *808/921–6097* ⊕ *www.waikiki.hyatt.com* ☞ *$145, 50-min lomilomi massage. Sauna. Gym with: cardiovascular machines. Services: aromatherapy, body scrubs and wraps, facials, hydrotherapy, massages.*

Fodor's Choice
★

SpaHalekulani. SpaHalekulani mines the traditions and cultures of the Pacific Islands with massages, body, and facial therapies. Try the Polynesian Nonu, which uses warm stones and healing nonu gel. The exclusive line of bath and body products is scented by maile, lavender orchid, hibiscus, coconut passion, or Mānoa mint. ⊠ *Halekūlani Hotel, 2199 Kālia Rd., Waikīkī* ☎ *808/931–5322* ⊕ *www.halekulani.com* ☞ *$180, 75-min lomilomi massage. Use of facilities is specific to treatment but may include Japanese furo bath, steam shower or whirlpool tub. Services: body treatments, facials, hair salon, massages, nail care.*

The Spa Luana at Turtle Bay Resort. Luxuriate at the ocean's edge in this serene spa. Don't miss the tropical Pineapple Pedicure ($85), administered outdoors overlooking the North Shore. Tired feet soak in a bamboo bowl filled with coconut milk before the pampering really begins with Hawaiian algae salt, island bee honey, kukui nut oil, and crushed pineapple. There are private spa suites, an outdoor treatment cabana that overlooks the surf, an outdoor exercise studio, and a lounge area and juice bar. ✉ *Turtle Bay Resort, 57-091 Kamehameha Hwy., North Shore* ☎ *808/447–6868* ⊕ *www.turtlebayresort. com* ☞ *$140, 50-min lomilomi massage. Hair salon, outdoor hot tub, steam room. Gym with: cardiovascular machines, free weights, weight-training equipment. Services: body treatments, facials, massages, waxing. Classes and programs: aerobics, Pilates, yoga.*

The Spa at Trump Waikīkī. One of the newest in Waikīkī, The Spa at Trump offers private changing and showering areas for each room, creating an environment of uninterrupted relaxation. No matter what treatment you choose, it is inspired by "personal intention," such as purify, balance, heal, revitalize, or calm, to elevate the senses throughout your time there. Don't miss the signature gemstone treatments, which feature products by Shiffa; or treat yourself to a Kate Somerville facial to emerge with younger-looking skin. The Hawaiian pineapple lime exfoliation massage is the most popular, as it is exclusive to this spa. ✉ *Trump International Hotel Waikīkī, 223 Saratoga Rd., Waikīkī* ☎ *808/683–7466* ⊕ *www.trumpwaikikihotel.com* ☞ *$165, 50-min lomilomi massage. Services: aromatherapy, body scrubs and wraps, facials, hydrotherapy, lash extensions, massages, nail care, waxing.*

ENTERTAINMENT AND NIGHTLIFE

Many first-time visitors arrive in the Islands expecting to see scenic beauty and sandy beaches but not much at night. That might be true on some of the other Islands, but not in O'ahu. Honolulu sunsets herald the onset of the best nightlife scene in the Islands.

Local artists perform every night of the week along Waikīkī's Kalākaua and Kūhiō avenues and in downtown Honolulu; the clubs dance to every beat from Top 40 to alternative to '80s.

The arts also thrive alongside the tourist industry. O'ahu has an established symphony, a thriving opera company, chamber music groups, and community theaters. Major Broadway shows, dance companies, and rock stars also make their way to Honolulu. Check the local newspapers—*MidWeek*, the *Honolulu Star-Advertiser*, or the *Honolulu Weekly*; or online sites like ⊕ *www.nonstophonolulu.com*—for the latest events.

Whether you make it an early night or stay up to watch that spectacular tropical sunrise, there's lots to do in paradise.

DINNER CRUISES AND SHOWS

Dinner cruises depart either from the piers adjacent to the Aloha Tower Marketplace in downtown Honolulu or from Kewalo Basin, near Ala Moana Beach Park, and head along the coast toward Diamond Head. There's usually dinner, dancing, drinks, and a sensational sunset. Except as noted, dinner cruises cost approximately $40 to $110, cocktail

cruises $25 to $40. Most major credit cards are accepted. In all cases, reservations are essential.

***Ali'i Kai* Catamaran.** Patterned after an ancient Polynesian vessel, this huge catamaran casts off from Aloha Tower with 1,000 passengers. The deluxe dinner cruise has two bars, a huge dinner, and an authentic Polynesian show with colorful hula music. The food is good, the after-dinner show loud and fun, and everyone dances on the way back to shore. Rates begin at $74 and include round-trip transportation, the dinner buffet, and one drink. Vegetarian meals are available. ⊠ *Pier 5, street level, Honolulu* ☎ *808/539–9400 Ext. 5.*

★ **Atlantis Cruises.** The sleekly high-tech *Navatek,* a revolutionary craft designed to sail smoothly in rough waters, powers farther along Waikīkī's coastline than its competitors, sailing past Diamond Head. Enjoy sunset dinners or moonlight cruises aboard the 300-passenger boat where you can feast on beef tenderloin and whole lobster or opt for the downstairs buffet. There's also the option of humpback whale–watching cruises December to mid-April. Tours leave from Pier 6, next to Aloha Tower Marketplace. Rates begin at $89 for the buffet, including one drink; the five-course dinner, which includes three drinks, starts at $130. ⊠ *Honolulu Harbor* ☎ *808/973–1311* ⊕ *www. atlantisadventures.com.*

Creation: A Polynesian Journey. A daring Samoan fire-knife dancer is the highlight of this show that traces Hawai'i's culture and history, from its origins of discovery to statehood. The buffet dinner is priced at $95; a sit-down dinner with steak and lobster is $145. You can also choose to see the show without dinner for $55. ⊠ *'Ainahau Showroom, Sheraton Princess Ka'iulani Hotel, 120 Ka'iulani Ave., Waikīkī* ☎ *808/931–4660* ⊙ *Dinner shows Tues.–Sun. at 6; closed Mon. and Wed.*

★ **Magic of Polynesia.** Hawai'i's top illusionist, John Hirokawa, displays mystifying sleight of hand in this highly entertaining show, which incorporates contemporary hula and Island music into its acts. Reservations are required for dinner and the show, which is priced at $85, but walk-ups are permitted if you just want the entertainment for $52. ⊠ *Ohana Beachcomber Hotel, 2300 Kalākaua Ave., Waikīkī* ☎ *808/971–4321* ⊙ *Nightly at 8.*

Ⓒ **Polynesian Cultural Center.** Easily one of the best on the Islands, this
★ show has soaring moments and an "erupting volcano." The performers are students from Brigham University's Hawai'i campus. ⊠ *55-370 Kamehameha Hwy., Lā'ie* ☎ *808/293–3333 or 800/367–7060* ⊕ *www. polynesia.com* ⊙ *Mon.–Sat. 12:30–9:30.*

***Star of Honolulu* Cruises.** The award-winning 1,500-passenger *Star of Honolulu* boasts four sunset dinner cruise packages, from a roast beef buffet with Polynesian show for $79 to a romantic seven-course fine dining excursion with live jazz for $175. The company also runs whale- and dolphin-watching lunch cruises. ⊠ *1540 S. King St., Honolulu* ☎ *808/983–7827* ⊕ *www.starofhonolulu.com.*

Society of Seven. This lively, popular septet has great staying power and, after more than 30 years, continues to put on one of the best shows in Waikīkī. They sing, dance, do impersonations, play instruments, and, above all, entertain with their contemporary sound. ✉ *Outrigger Waikīkī on the Beach, 2335 Kalākaua Ave., Waikīkī* ☎ *808/922–6408* ⊕ *www.outrigger.com* ⊙ *Tues.–Sat. at 8:30.*

LŪʻAU

The lūʻau is an experience that everyone, both local and tourist, should have. Today's lūʻau still adhere to traditional foods and entertainment, but there's also a fun, contemporary flair. With most, you can even watch the roasted pig being carried out of its ʻimu, a hole in the ground used for cooking meat with heated stones.

Lūʻau cost anywhere from $56 to $195. Most that are held outside of Waikīkī offer shuttle service so you don't have to drive. Reservations are essential.

Fia Fia at the ʻIhilani. Whereas most lūʻau are based culturally on Hawaiian traditions and journey around Polynesia via song and dance, Fia Fia (which means "celebration" in Samoan) is based on Samoan culture, thanks to Chief Sielu Avea, the creator and host of the show. Every night's show is different and unscripted, but always a good look at Polynesian culture. It's the only show with eight fire-knife dancers in a blazing finale. Admission includes buffet and Polynesian show. ☎ *808/949–6626 or 800/367–5655* ✉ *$90* ⊙ *Thurs. at 4:30.*

Germaine's Lūʻau. Widely regarded as the most folksy and local, this lūʻau is held in Kalaeloa in Leeward Oʻahu. The food is the usual multicourse, all-you-can-eat buffet, but it's very tasty. It's a good lūʻau for first-timers and at a reasonable price. Expect a lively crowd on the 35-minute bus ride from Waikīkī. Admission includes buffet, three drinks, Polynesian show, and shuttle transport from Waikīkī. ☎ *808/949–6626 or 800/367–5655* ⊕ *www.germainesluau.com* ✉ *$72* ⊙ *Daily at 6. Closed Mon. in winter.*

★ **Paradise Cove Lūʻau.** The scenery is the best here—the sunsets are unbelievable. Watch Mother Nature's special-effects show in Kapolei/Kō ʻOlina Resort in Leeward Oʻahu, a good 27 mi from the bustle of Waikīkī. The party-hearty atmosphere is kid-friendly with Hawaiian games, canoe rides in the cove, and lots of predinner activities. The stage show includes a fire-knife dancer, singing emcee, and both traditional and contemporary hula and other Polynesian dances. Basic admission includes buffet, activities and the show, and shuttle transport from Waikīkī. You pay extra for table service and box seating. ☎ *808/842–5911* ⊕ *www.paradisecove.com* ✉ *$80–$137* ⊙ *Daily at 5:30, doors open at 5.*

FodorsChoice **Polynesian Cultural Center Aliʻi Lūʻau.** This elaborate lūʻau has the sharpest production values but no booze (it's a Mormon-owned facility). ★ It's held amid the seven re-created villages at the Polynesian Cultural Center in the North Shore town of Lāʻie, about an hour's drive from Honolulu. The lūʻau includes tours of the park with shows and activities, including the "Ha Breath of Life" show that has been popular with both residents and visitors. Package rates vary depending on activities and amenities (personalized tours, reserved seats, buffet vs. dinner service, backstage tour, etc.). Waikīkī transport is available; call for prices. ☎ *808/293–3333 or 800/367–7060* ⊕ *www.polynesia.com* ✉ *$88–$225* ⊙ *Mon.–Sat. center opens at noon; lū'au starts at 5.*

FILM

Hawai'i International Film Festival. It may not be Cannes, but this festival is unique and exciting. During the weeklong event in the middle of October, top films from all over the world, as well as some local film-makers, are screened day and night at the Dole Cannery theaters to packed crowds. It's a must-see for film adventurers. ☎ *808/792–1577* ⊕ *www.hiff.org.*

★ **Sunset on the Beach.** It's like watching a movie at the drive-in, minus the car and the impossible speaker box. Think romantic and cozy; bring a blanket and find a spot on the sand to enjoy live entertainment, food from top local restaurants, and a movie feature on a 40-foot screen. Held twice a month on Waikīkī's Queens Surf Beach across from the Honolulu Zoo, Sunset on the Beach is a favorite event for both locals and tourists. If the weather is blustery, beware of flying sand. ☎ *808/923–1094* ⊕ *www.sunsetonthebeach.net.*

MUSIC

First Friday. Rain or shine, on the first Friday of every month, the entire downtown Honolulu and Chinatown district comes alive after dark with a street party. All the art galleries open their doors to the public not just to display their works, but to showcase local musicians from all disciplines, including jazz, rock, new age, and world. ■ **TIP→** **Admission is free.** Be sure to check the Web site beforehand to get up-to-date information on the artists and musicians being featured. ⊠ *Downtown Honolulu* ☎ *808/739–9797* ⊕ *www.firstfridayhawaii.com* ✉ *Free* ⊙ *Venues open at 5.*

Hawai'i Opera Theater. Better known as "HOT," the Hawai'i Opera Theater has been known to turn the opera-challenged into opera lovers. All operas are sung in their original language with projected English translation. Tickets range from $29 to $120. ⊠ *Neil Blaisdell Center Concert Hall, Ward Ave. and King St., Downtown Honolulu* ☎ *808/596–7858* ⊕ *www.hawaiiopera.org.*

Honolulu Zoo Concerts. For almost two decades, the Honolulu Zoo Society has sponsored Wednesday evening concerts from June to August on the zoo's stage lawn. Listen to local legends play everything from Hawaiian to jazz to Latin music. ■ **TIP→** **At just $3 admission, this is one of the best deals in town.** Take a brisk walk through the zoo exhibits before they close at 5:30 pm or join in the family activities; bring your own picnic for the concert, which starts at 6 pm. It's an alcohol-free event, and there's a food concession for those who come unprepared. ⊠ *151 Kapahulu Ave., Waikīkī* ☎ *808/926–3191* ⊕ *www.honoluluzoo. org* ✉ *$1* ⊙ *Gates open at 4:30.*

Waikīkī Aquarium Concerts. In June and July, the Waikīkī Aquarium holds an ocean-side concert series every other Thursday. You can listen to the Islands' top performers under the stars while enjoying food from local restaurants. The aquarium and its exhibits stay open throughout the night to allow you to see the marine life in a new light. Bring your own

Experience one of Hawai'i's most spectacular lū'aus at the Polynesian Cultural Center.

mats or beach chairs. ✉ *2777 Kalakaua Ave., Waikīkī* ☎ *808/923-9741* ⊕ *www.waquarium.org* 🎫 *$30 per adult* ☉ *Gates open at 5:30.*

NIGHTLIFE

O'ahu is the best of all the Islands for nightlife. The locals call it *pau hana* but you might call it "off the clock and ready for a cocktail." The literal translation of the Hawaiian phrase means "done with work."

You can find a bar in just about any area on O'ahu. Most of the clubs, however, are in Waikīkī, Ala Moana, and downtown Honolulu. The drinking age is 21 on O'ahu and throughout Hawai'i. Many bars will admit younger people but will not serve them alcohol. By law, all establishments that serve alcoholic beverages must close by 2 am. The only exceptions are those with a cabaret license, which have a 4 am curfew. ■TIP→ Most clubs have a cover charge of $5 to $10, but with some establishments, getting there early means you don't have to pay.

HONOLULU

BARS

Fodor's Choice
★ **Mai Tai Bar at Ala Moana Center.** After a long day of shopping, the Mai Tai Bar on the third floor of Ala Moana Center is a perfect spot to relax. There's live entertainment and two nightly happy hours: one for food items and another strictly for specialty drinks. There's never a cover charge and no dress code, but to avoid waiting in line, get there before 9 pm. ✉ *1450 Ala Moana Blvd., Ala Moana* ☎ *808/947-2900.*

Murphy's Bar & Grill. On the edge of Chinatown, this 120-year-old bar has been serving drinks to visitors and *kama'aina* alike dating back to

Hawai'i's days as a territory. Voted the best bar in Hawai'i for the past several years, Murphy's is a great oasis from all the tropical drinks and thatched roofs. Once inside you would swear you were in an Irish pub back in Boston—it's definitely the place to be on St. Patrick's Day. ⊠ *2 Merchant St., Downtown Honolulu* ☎ *808/531–0422* ⊕ *www. murphyshawaii.com.*

thirtyninehotel. This loft and art gallery is on the cutting edge of what's hot downtown. Every three months it gets a new "art installation" where a local artist repaints and reconfigures the entire space. The bartenders and their "market-fresh" cocktails have become the stuff of local legend, using Hawaiian produce to recreate classic turn-of-the-century libations. Entertainment varies from jazz groups to DJs depending on the night. Come any night of the week for happy hour from 4–8 pm, when specialty cocktails are half off. ⊠ *39 N. Hotel St., Downtown* ☎ *808/599–2552.*

CLUBS

The Dragon Upstairs. This cool club in the heart of Chinatown serves up classic cocktails along with live jazz Wednesday through Sunday nights. You'll hear local jazz vocalists as well as small jazz combos in this unique venue that's upstairs, of course, from Hank's Restaurant. ⊠ *1038 Nu'uanu Ave., Chinatown* ☎ *808/526–1411.*

Pearl Ultralounge. The young, hip, after-work crowd tends to flock here on weekdays to unwind or to get ready for the weekend with special events. The weekends are packed with the see-and-be-seen set. ⊠ *Ala Moana Center, 1450 Ala Moana Blvd., Ala Moana* ☎ *808/944-8000* ⊕ *www.pearlhawaii.com.*

WAIKĪKĪ

BARS

Banyan Veranda. The Banyan Veranda is steeped in history. From this location the radio program *Hawai'i Calls* first broadcast the sounds of Hawaiian music and the rolling surf to a U.S. mainland audience in 1935. Today, a variety of Hawaiian entertainment continues to provide the perfect accompaniment to the sounds of the waves. ⊠ *Moana Surfrider, 2365 Kalākaua Ave., Waikīkī* ☎ *808/922–3111.*

★ **Duke's Canoe Club.** Making the most of its oceanfront spot on Waikīkī Beach, Duke's presents "Concerts on the Beach" every Friday, Saturday, and Sunday with contemporary Hawaiian musicians like Henry Kapono. National musicians like Jimmy Buffett have also performed here. At Duke's Barefoot Bar, solo Hawaiian musicians take the stage nightly, and it's not unusual for surfers to leave their boards outside to step in for a casual drink after a long day on the waves. ⊠ *Outrigger Waikīkī, 2335 Kalākaua Ave., Waikīkī* ☎ *808/922–2268.*

Lulu's Waikīkī. Even if you're not a surfer, you'll love the retro surf ambience and the unobstructed second-floor view of Waikīkī Beach. The open-air setting, casual dining menu, and tropical drinks are all you need to help you settle into your Island vacation. The venue transforms from a nice spot for lunch or dinner to a bustling, high-energy club in the late hours. They've also got live music, which really keeps the place jumping. ⊠ *Park Shore Waikīkī Hotel, 2586 Kalākaua Ave., Waikīkī* ☎ *808/926–5222* ⊕ *www.luluswaikiki.com.*

★ **Mai Tai Bar at the Royal Hawaiian.** The bartenders sure know how to make a killer mai tai—just one could do the trick. This is, after all, the establishment that came up with the famous drink in the first place. The pink, umbrella-covered tables at the outdoor bar are front-row seating for Waikīkī sunsets and an unobstructed view of Diamond Head. Contemporary Hawaiian music is usually on stage, and the staff is extremely friendly. ⊠ *Royal Hawaiian Hotel, 2259 Kalākaua Ave., Waikīkī* ☎ *808/923–7311.*

Fodor'sChoice **Moana Terrace.** Three floors up from Waikīkī Beach, this open-air terrace is the home of The Keawe Ohana, a family comprised of some of Hawai'i's finest musicians ⊠ *Waikīkī Beach Marriott Resort, 2552 Kalākaua Ave., Waikīkī* ☎ *808/922–6611.*

Rumfire. Locals and visitors like to come here for the food, the million-dollar ground floor view, and the ambience. Come early to get a seat for happy hour, which is daily from 4 to 6 pm and 9:30 to 11:15 pm. They also feature live music by local artists daily. ⊠ *Sheraton Waikīkī, 2255 Kalākaua Ave., Waikīkī* ☎ *808/922-4422* ⊕ *www.rumfirewaikiki.com.*

Tiki's Grill and Bar. Get in touch with your primal side at this restaurant–bar overlooking Kūhiō Beach. Tiki torches, tiki statues, and other South Pacific art set the mood. A twentysomething mix of locals and tourists comes on the weekends to get their fill of kitschy cool. There's nightly entertainment featuring contemporary Hawaiian musicians. Don't leave without sipping on a "lava flow." It's served in a whole coconut, which is yours to keep at the end of the night. ⊠ *Aston Waikīkī Beach Hotel, 2570 Kalākaua Ave., Waikīkī* ☎ *808/923–8454.*

CLUBS
Apartment 3. Tucked away on the third floor of an office/condo building on the edge of Waikīkī, this contempo-cool club is a favorite among cosmopolitan locals and the occasional celebrity—Johnny Depp has been spotted here. There's something going on every night, except Sunday (when it's closed), to cater to the stylish set. ⊠ *Century Center, 1750 Kalakaua Ave., Waikīkī* ☎ *808/955–9300* ⊕ *www.apartmentthree.com.*

Hula's Bar and Lei Stand. Hawai'i's oldest and best-known gay-friendly nightspot offers calming panoramic outdoor views of Diamond Head and the Pacific Ocean by day and a high-energy club scene by night. Check out the soundproof, glassed-in dance floor. ⊠ *Waikīkī Grand Hotel, 134 Kapahulu Ave., 2nd fl., Waikīkī* ☎ *808/923–0669.*

Nashville Waikīkī. Country music in the tropics? You bet! Put on your *paniolo* (Hawaiian cowboy) duds and mosey on out to the giant dance floor. There are pool tables, dartboards, line dancing, and free dance lessons (Wednesday at 6:30 pm) to boot. Look for wall-to-wall crowds on the weekend. ⊠ *Ohana Waikīkī West Hotel, 2330 Kūhiō Ave., Waikīkī* ☎ *808/926–7911.*

Zanzabar. Traverse a winding staircase and make an entrance at Zanzabar where DJs spin top hits, from hip-hop to soul and techno to trance. It's easy to find a drink at this high-energy nightspot with its three bars.

If it's nightlife you're after, there's no better place in Hawai'i than Waikīkī Beach.

Not exactly sure how to get your groove on? Zanzabar offers free Latin dance lessons every Tuesday at 8 pm. Most nights are 21 and over; Sunday, Tuesday, Wednesday, and Thursday allow 18 and over in for $15. ⊠ *Waikīkī Trade Center, 2255 Kūhiō Ave., Waikīkī* ☏ *808/924–3939.*

SOUTHEAST O'AHU

The Shack. This sports bar and restaurant is about the only late-night spot you can find in Southeast O'ahu. After a day of snorkeling at Hanauma Bay, stop by to kick back, have a beer, eat a burger, watch some sports, or play a game of pool. ⊠ *Hawai'i Kai Shopping Center, 377 Keahole St., Hawai'i Kai* ☏ *808/396–1919* ☾ *Nightly until 2 am.*

WINDWARD O'AHU

Boardrider's Bar & Grill. Tucked away in Kailua Town, this spot has long been the venue for local bands to strut their stuff. Renovations have spruced up the space, which now includes pool tables, dartboards, foosball, and eight TVs for sports viewing with the local and military crowd. Look for live entertainment—reggae to alternative rock to good old-fashioned rock and roll—Wednesday through Saturday from 10:30 pm to 1:30 am. Cover ranges from $3 to $10. ⊠ *201-A Hāmākua Dr., Kailua* ☏ *808/261–4600.*

THE NORTH SHORE

★ **Breaker's Restaurant.** Just about every surf contest post-party is celebrated at this family-owned establishment, as the owner's son, Benji Weatherly, is a pro surfer himself. Surfing memorabilia, including surfboards hanging from the ceiling, fill the space. The restaurant/bar is open from 11 am to 9:30 pm with a late-night menu until midnight. But things start to happen around 9 pm on Thursday for the 18-and-over crowd, who cruise while the DJ spins, and there's live music on Saturday. The party goes until 2 am. ⊠ *Marketplace Shopping Center, 66-250 Kamehameha Hwy., Haleʻiwa* ☎ *808/637–9898.*

WHERE TO EAT

Oʻahu, where the majority of the Islands' 2,000-plus restaurants are located, offers the best of all worlds: it's got the foreignness and excitement of Asia and Polynesia, but when the kids need McDonald's, or when you just have to have a Starbucks latte, they're here, too.

Budget for a pricey dining experience at the very top of the restaurant food chain, where chefs Alan Wong, Roy Yamaguchi, George Mavrothalassitis, and others you've read about in *Bon Appetit* put a sophisticated and unforgettable spin on local foods and flavors. Savor seared ʻahi tuna in sea urchin beurre blanc or steak marinated in Korean kimchi sauce.

Spend the rest of your food dollars where budget-conscious locals do: in plate-lunch places and small ethnic eateries, at roadside stands and lunch wagons, or at window-in-the-wall delis. Munch a *musubi* rice ball (rice wrapped with seaweed and often topped with Spam), slurp shave ice with red bean paste, order up Filipino pork adobo with two scoops of rice and macaroni salad.

In Waikīkī, where most visitors stay, you can find choices from gracious rooms with a view to surprisingly authentic Japanese noodle shops. But hop in the car, or on the trolley or bus, and travel just a few miles in any direction, and you can save your money and get in touch with the real food of Hawaiʻi.

Kaimukī's Waiʻalae Avenue, for example, offers one of the city's best espresso bars, a hugely popular Chinese bakery, a highly recommended patisserie, an exceptional Italian bistro, a dim sum restaurant, Mexican food (rare here), and a Hawaiʻi regional cuisine standout, 3660 on the Rise—all in three blocks and 10 minutes from Waikīkī. Chinatown, 10 minutes in the other direction and easily reached by the Waikiki Trolley, is another dining (and shopping) treasure, not only for Chinese but also Vietnamese, Filipino, Malaysian, Indian, and Eurasian food, and even a chic little tea shop.

WHAT IT COSTS					
	¢	$	$$	$$$	$$$$
Restaurants	under $10	$10–$17	$18–$26	$27–$35	over $35

Restaurant prices are for one main course at dinner.

DOWNTOWN HONOLULU AND CHINATOWN

$–$$ ✕ **Akasaka.** Step inside this tiny sushi bar tucked behind the Ala Moana
JAPANESE Hotel, and you'll swear you're in an out-of-the-way Edo neighborhood in some indeterminate time. Greeted with a cheerful *"Iraishaimasu!"*

BEST BETS FOR O'AHU DINING

Fodor's Choice★

Alan Wong's, $$$-$$$$, p. 152

Buzz's Original Steakhouse, $-$$, p. 157

Chef Mavro, $$$$, p. 153

Little Village Noodle House, ¢-$, p. 146

Ola at Turtle Bay Resort, $$-$$$, p. 158

By Price

¢-$

Bac Nam, p. 142

Kaka'ako Kitchen, p. 146

'Ono Hawaiian Foods, p. 154

Wailana Coffee House, p. 152

$$

Keo's in Waikīkī, p. 149

Roy's, p. 156

Sam Choy's Breakfast Lunch & Crab and Big Aloha Brewery, p. 147

$$$–$$$$

3660 on the Rise, p. 152

Nobu, p. 149

By Cuisine

HAWAIIAN

Alan Wong's, $$$-$$$$, p. 152

Chef Mavro, $$$$, p. 153

Roy's, $$-$$$, p. 156

SUSHI

Nobu, $$$-$$$$, p. 149

Sansei Seafood Restaurant & Sushi Bar, $$-$$$, p. 151

Sushi Sasabune, $$-$$$, p. 156

Yanagi Sushi, $, p. 148

By Experience

MOST ROMANTIC

Hau Tree Lānai, $$-$$$, p. 149

Hoku's at the Kāhala, $$$$, p. 154

La Mer, $$$$, p. 149

Michel's at the Colony Surf, $$$-$$$$, p. 154

BEST VIEW

John Dominis, $$$-$$$$, p. 145

La Mer, $$$$, p. 149

Orchids, $$$-$$$$, p. 149

(Welcome!), sink down at a diminutive table or perch at the handful of seats at the sushi bar. It's safe to let the sushi chefs here decide (*omakase*-style) or you can go for the delicious grilled specialties, such as scallop *battayaki* (grilled in butter). Reservations accepted for groups only. ⊠ *1646 B Kona St., Ala Moana* ☎ *808/942–4466* ▤ *AE, D, DC, MC, V* ⊗ *No lunch Sun.*

$$$
PACIFIC RIM
✕ **Alan Wong's Pineapple Room.** This is not your grandmother's department store restaurant. It's überchef Alan Wong's more casual second spot, where the chef de cuisine plays intriguing riffs on local food themes. Warning: the spicy chili-fried soybeans are addicting. Their house burger, made with locally raised grass-fed beef, bacon, cheddar cheese, hoisin-mayonnaise spread, and avocado, won a local tasting hands-down. Pleasant surroundings and service is very professional. Reservations recommended. ⊠ *Macy's, Ala Moana Center, 1450 Ala Moana Blvd., Ala Moana* ☎ *808/945–6573* ▤ *AE, D, DC, MC, V.*

¢-$
VIETNAMESE
✕ **Bac Nam.** Tam and Kimmy Huynh's menu is much more extensive than most, ranging far beyond the usual *pho* (beef noodle soup) and *bun* (cold noodle dishes). Coconut milk curries, an extraordinary crab noodle soup, and other dishes hail from both North and South Vietnam. The atmosphere is welcoming and relaxed, and they'll work with you to make choices. Reservations are not accepted for groups fewer

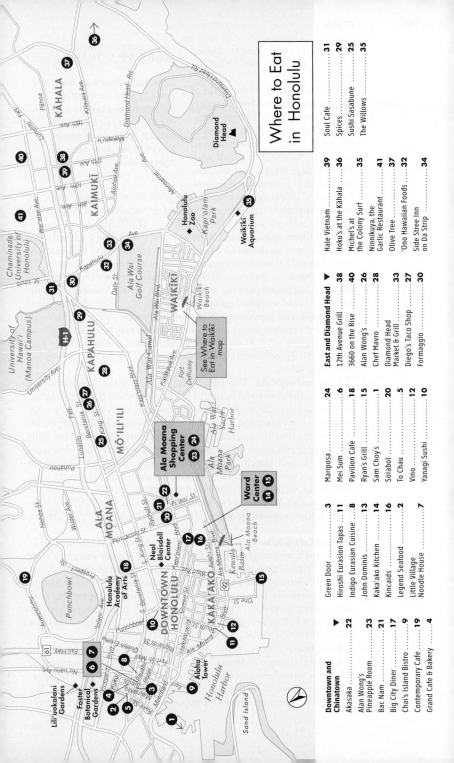

Where to Eat in Honolulu

than six. ✉ *1117 S. King St., Downtown Honolulu* ☎ *808/597–8201* ▬ *MC, V.*

$ ✕ **Big City Diner.** Part of a chain of
AMERICAN unfussy retro diners, Big City offers
☺ a short course in local-style breakfasts—rice instead of potatoes, fish or Portuguese sausage instead of bacon, steaming bowls of noodles—with generous portions, low prices, and pronounced flavors. Lunch and dinner focus on local-style comfort food—baby back ribs, kimchi fried rice—and burgers. ✉ *Ward Entertainment Center, 1060 'Auahi St., Ala Moana* ☎ *808/591–8891* ▬ *AE, D, MC, V.*

$$$ ✕ **Chai's Island Bistro.** Chai Chaowasaree's stylish, light-bathed, and
ECLECTIC orchid-draped lunch and dinner restaurant expresses the sophisticated side of this Thai-born immigrant. He plays East against West on the plate in signature dishes such as *kataifi* (baked and shredded phyllo), macadamia-crusted prawns, 'ahi *katsu* (tuna steaks dredged with crisp Japanese bread crumbs and quickly deep-fried), crispy duck confetti spring rolls, and Japanese eggplant zucchini soufflé. Some of Hawai'i's best-known contemporary Hawaiian musicians play brief dinner shows here every night. ✉ *Aloha Tower Marketplace, 1 Aloha Tower Dr., Downtown Honolulu* ☎ *808/585–0011* ▬ *AE, D, DC, MC, V* ☯ *No lunch Sat.–Mon.*

¢–$ ✕ **Contemporary Cafe.** This tasteful lunch spot in the Contemporary
AMERICAN Museum offers light and healthful food from a short but well-selected menu of housemade soups, crostini of the day, innovative sandwiches garnished with fruit, and a hummus plate with fresh pita. In the exclusive Makīkī Heights neighborhood above the city, the restaurant spills out of the ground floor of the museum onto the lawn. They now have a "Lauhala and Lunch" picnic lunch for two, priced at $30, which includes a choice of sandwich or salad for each person, dessert bars, and choice of beverages all packed in a pretty picnic basket. ✉ *The Contemporary Museum, 2411 Makīkī Heights Dr., Makīkī* ☎ *808/523–3362* ⟁ *Reservations not accepted* ▬ *AE, D, DC, MC, V* ☯ *No dinner; closed Mon.*

¢–$ ✕ **Grand Café & Bakery.** This well-scrubbed, pleasantly furnished break-
ECLECTIC fast, brunch, and lunch spot is ideal for taking a break before or after
☺ a trek around Chinatown. Its period feel comes from the fact that chef Anthony Vierra's great-grandfather had a restaurant of this name in Chinatown nearly 100 years ago. The delicious and well-presented food ranges from retro diner dishes (chicken potpie) to contemporary creations such as beet-and-goat-cheese-salad. ✉ *31 N. Pauahi, Chinatown* ☎ *808/531–0001* ▬ *MC, V.*

$ ✕ **Green Door.** Closet-size and fronted by a green door and a row of
ASIAN welcoming Chinese lanterns, this Chinatown café has introduced Honolulu to budget- and taste bud–friendly Malaysian and Singaporean foods, redolent of spices and crunchy with fresh vegetables. The restaurant's owner gets mixed reviews, as she may be rude to customers

Authentic Asian food can be found all over Hawai'i, and some of the best is in Chinatown in downtown Honolulu.

who question her cooking. Just order from the flavorful menu of fewer than 10 dishes, and you'll do fine. ⊠ *1110 Nu'uanu Ave., Chinatown* ☎ *808/533–0606* ▭ *No credit cards* ⚏ *Reservations not accepted* ⊗ *Closed Mon.*

$$–$$$
ASIAN

✕ **Hiroshi Eurasion Tapas.** Built around chef Hiroshi Fukui's signature style of "West & Japan" cuisine, this sleek dinner house focuses on small plates to share (enough for two servings each), with an exceptional choice of hard-to-find wines by the glass and in flights. Do not miss Hiroshi's braised veal cheeks (he was doing them before everyone else), the locally raised *kampachi* fish carpaccio, or the best *misoyaki* (marinated in a rich miso-soy blend, then grilled) butterfish ever. ⊠ *Restaurant Row 500 Ala Moana Blvd., Ala Moana* ☎ *808/533–4476* ⊕ *www.hiroshihawaii.com* ▭ *AE, D, MC, V* ⊗ *No lunch.*

$$–$$$
ECLECTIC

✕ **Indigo Eurasian Cuisine.** Indigo sets the right mood for an evening out on the town: the walls are redbrick, the ceilings are high, and from the restaurant's lounge next door comes the sultry sound of late-night jazz. Take a bite of goat cheese wontons with four-fruit sauce followed by rich Mongolian lamb chops. After dinner, duck into the hip Green Room lounge for a nightcap. If you're touring downtown at lunchtime, the Eurasian buffet with trio of dim sum is an especially good deal at around $16 per person. ⊠ *1121 Nu'uanu Ave., Downtown Honolulu* ☎ *808/521–2900* ▭ *AE, D, DC, MC, V.*

$$$–$$$$
SEAFOOD

✕ **John Dominis.** "Legendary" is the word for the Sunday brunch buffet at this long-established restaurant, named for a Hawaiian kingdom chamberlain who became the consort of the last queen, Lili'uokalani. With a network of koi ponds running through the multilevel restaurant, a view of Diamond Head and a favorite surfing area, and over-the-top seafood specials, it's the choice of Oahuans with something to celebrate. An appetizer-and-small-plates menu is available in the bar. ☒ *580 Nimitz Hwy., Downtown Honolulu* ☎ *808/523–0955* ☐ *AE, D, DC, MC, V.*

¢–$
MODERN
HAWAIIAN
☺

✕ **Kaka'ako Kitchen.** Russell Siu was the first of the local-boy fine dining chefs to open a place of the sort he enjoys when he's off-duty, serving high-quality plate lunches (house-made sauce instead of from-a-mix brown gravy, for example). Here you can get your two scoops of either brown or white rice, green salad instead of the usual macaroni salad, grilled fresh fish specials, and vegetarian fare. Breakfast is especially good, with combos like corned-beef hash and eggs, and exceptional baked goods. ☒ *Ward Centre, 1200 Ala Moana Blvd., Kaka'ako* ☎ *808/596–7488* ☆ *Reservations not accepted* ☐ *MC, V.*

$$$
SEAFOOD
☺

✕ **Kincaid's Fish, Chop & Steak House**. Known for Copper River salmon in season, consistently well-made salads and seafood specials, efficient service, and appropriate pricing, Kincaid's is business-lunch central. But, with its window-fronted room overlooking Kewalo Basin harbor, it's also a relaxing place for a postshopping drink or intimate dinner. ☒ *Ward Warehouse, 2nd level, 1050 Ala Moana Blvd., Kaka'ako* ☎ *808/591–2005* ☐ *AE, D, DC, MC, V.*

¢–$
CHINESE

✕ **Legend Seafood Restaurant.** Do as the locals do: start your visit to Chinatown with breakfast dim sum at Legend. If you want to be able to hear yourself think, get there before 9 am, especially on weekends. And don't be shy: use your best cab-hailing technique and sign language to make the cart ladies stop at your table and show you their wares. The pork-filled steamed buns, hearty spare ribs, prawn dumplings, and still-warm custard tarts are excellent preshopping fortification. ☒ *Chinese Cultural Plaza, 100 N. Beretania St., Chinatown* ☎ *808/532–1868* ☐ *AE, D, DC, MC, V.*

¢–$
CHINESE
Fodor's Choice
★

✕ **Little Village Noodle House.** Unassuming and budget-friendly, Little Village sets a standard of friendly and attentive service to which every Chinese restaurant should aspire. We have roamed the large, pan-China menu and found a new favorite in everything we've tried: shredded beef, spinach with garlic, Shanghai noodles, honey-walnut shrimp, orange chicken, dried green beans. Two words: go there. Reservations are accepted for parties of five or more. ■ TIP➔ **Two hours of free parking is available next door.** ☒ *1113 Smith St., Chinatown* ☎ *808/545–3008* ☐ *AE, D, MC, V.*

$$
PACIFIC RIM

✕ **Mariposa.** Yes, the popovers and the wee little cups of bouillon are there at lunch, but in every other regard, this Neiman Marcus restaurant menu departs from the classic model, incorporating a clear sense of Pacific place. The veranda, open to the breezes and view of Ala Moana Park, twirling ceiling fans, and life-size hula-girl murals say Hawai'i. The popovers at lunch come with a butter-pineapple-papaya spread; the oxtail osso buco is inspired, and local fish are featured nightly in luxuriant specials. ☒ *Neiman Marcus, Ala Moana Center, 1450 Ala Moana, Ala Moana* ☎ *808/951–3420* ☆ *Reservations essential* ☐ *AE, D, DC, MC, V.*

¢–$
CHINESE

✕ **Mei Sum Chinese Dim Sum Restaurant.** In contrast to the sprawling and noisy halls in which dim sum is generally served, Mei Sum is compact and shiny bright. It's open daily, serving nothing but small plates from 7:45 am to 8:45 pm. Be ready to guess and point at the color photos of dim sum favorites as not much English is spoken, but the delicate buns and tasty bits are exceptionally well prepared and worth the charades. ⊠ *1170 Nu'uanu Ave., Chinatown* ☎ *808/531–3268* ⊟ *No credit cards.*

$ ✕ **Pavilion Cafe.** The cool courtyards and varied galleries of the Hono-
AMERICAN lulu Academy of Arts are well worth a visit and, afterward, so is Mike Nevin's popular lunch restaurant. The café overflows onto a lānai from which you can ponder Asian statuary and a burbling water feature while you wait for your salade niçoise or signature Piadina Sandwich (fresh-baked flatbread rounds stuffed with arugula, tomatoes, basil, and cheese). ⊠ *Honolulu Academy of Arts, 900 S. Beretania St., Downtown Honolulu* ☎ *808/532–8734* ⊟ *AE, D, DC, MC, V* ☉ *Closed Sun. and Mon. No dinner.*

$–$$ ✕ **Ryan's Grill.** An all-purpose food and drink emporium, lively and
AMERICAN popular Ryan's has an exceptionally well-stocked bar, with 20 beers on tap, an outdoor deck, and TVs broadcasting sports. Lunch, dinner, and small plates are served from 11 am to 2 am. The eclectic menu ranges from an addictive hot crab-and-artichoke dip with focaccia bread to grilled fresh fish, pasta, salads, and sophisticated versions of local favor-ites, such as the Kobe beef hamburger steak. ⊠ *Ward Centre, 1200 Ala Moana Blvd., Kaka'ako* ☎ *808/591–9132* ⊟ *AE, D, DC, MC, V.*

$$–$$$ ✕ **Sam Choy's Breakfast, Lunch & Crab and Big Aloha Brewery.** In this casual,
SEAFOOD family-friendly setting, diners can down crab and lobster—but since
☺ these come from elsewhere, we recommend the catch of the day, the *char siu* (Chinese barbecue), baby back ribs, Sam's special fried *poke* (flash-fried tuna), or Papa Choy's beef stew omelet. This eatery's ware-house size sets the tone for its *bambucha* (huge) portions. An on-site microbrewery brews five varieties of Big Aloha beer. Sam Choy's is in Iwilei past downtown Honolulu on the highway heading to Honolulu International Airport. ⊠ *580 Nimitz Hwy., Iwilei* ☎ *808/545–7979* ⊟ *AE, D, DC, MC, V.*

$ ✕ **Sorabol.** The largest Korean restaurant in the city, this 24-hour eatery,
KOREAN with its impossibly tiny parking lot and maze of booths and private rooms, offers a vast menu encompassing the entirety of day-to-day Korean cuisine, plus sushi. English menu translations are cryptic at best. Still, it's great for wee hour "grinds" (local slang for food): *bi bim bap* (veggies, meats, and eggs on steamed rice), *kal bi* and *bulgogi* (barbecued meats), meat or fish *jun* (thin fillets fried in batter), and kimchi pancakes. ⊠ *805 Ke'eaumoku St., Ala Moana* ☎ *808/947–3113* ⊟ *AE, DC, MC, V.*

¢ ✕ **To Chau.** If you need proof that To Chau is highly regarded for its
VIETNAMESE authentic *pho* (Vietnamese beef noodle soup), just check the lines that form in front every morning of the week. It's said that the broth is the key, and it won't break the bank for you to find out, as the average check is less than $10. Open only until 12:30 pm. ⊠ *1007 River St., Chinatown* ☎ *808/533–4549* ⊟ *No credit cards* ☉ *No dinner.*

$$–$$$ ✕ **Vino.** Small plates of Italian-inspired appetizers, a wine list selected
ITALIAN by the state's first Master Sommelier, a relaxed atmosphere, and peri-odic special tastings are the formula for success at this wine bar.

■ TIP→ Vino is well situated for stopping off between downtown sightseeing and a return to your Waikīkī hotel. ⊠ *Restaurant Row, 500 Ala Moana Blvd., Downtown Honolulu* ☎ 808/524–8466 ⊟ *AE, D, DC, MC, V* ⊗ *Closed Sun.–Tues.*

$ ✕ **Yanagi Sushi.** One of relatively few
JAPANESE   restaurants to serve the complete menu until 2 am (Sunday only until 10 pm), Yanagi is a full-service Japanese restaurant offering not only sushi and sashimi around a small bar, but also *taishoku* (combination menus), tempura, stews, and grill-it-yourself shabu-shabu. The fish here can be depended on for freshness and variety. ⊠ *762 Kapi'olani Blvd., Downtown Honolulu* ☎ 808/597–1525 ⊟ *AE, D, DC, MC, V.*

> **PŪPŪ**
>
> Entertaining Hawaiian style means having a lot of *pūpū*—the local term for appetizers or hors d'oeuvres. Locals eat these small portions of food mostly as they wind down from their workday, relax, and enjoy a couple of beers. Popular pūpū include sushi, tempura, teriyaki chicken skewers, barbecue meat, and our favorite: *poke* (pronounced "po-keh"), or raw fish, seasoned with seaweed, shoyu, and other flavorings. We call them "local kine grinds."

WAIKĪKĪ

$$$ ✕ **dk Steakhouse.** Around the country, the steak house has returned to
STEAKHOUSE   prominence as chefs rediscover the art of dry-aging beef and of preparing the perfect béarnaise sauce. D. K. Kodama's chic second-floor restaurant characterizes this trend with such presentations as a 22-ounce "Paniolo" (cowboy) rib-eye steak, dry-aged 30 days on the bone with house-made rub, grilled local onions, and creamed corn. The restaurant shares space, but not a menu, with Kodama's Sansei Seafood Restaurant & Sushi Bar; sit at the bar perched between the two and you can order from either menu. ⊠ *Waikīkī Beach Marriott Resort and Spa, 2552 Kalākaua Ave., Waikīkī* ☎ 808/931–6280 ⊟ *AE, D, MC, V* ⊗ *No lunch.*

$$-$$$ ✕ **Duke's Canoe Club.** Named for the father of modern surfing, and out-
AMERICAN   fitted with much Duke Kahanamoku memorabilia, Duke's is both an open-air bar and a very popular steak-and-seafood grill. It's known for its Big Island pork ribs, *huli huli* (rotisserie) chicken, and grilled catch of the day, as well as for a simple and economical Sunday brunch. A drawback is that it's often loud and crowded, and the live contemporary Hawaiian music often stymies conversation. ⊠ *Outrigger Waikīkī on the Beach, 2335 Kalākaua Ave., Waikīkī* ☎ 808/922–2268 ⊕ *www. dukeswaikiki.com* ⌕ *Reservations essential* ⊟ *AE, DC, MC, V.*

$ ✕ **Eggs 'n Things.** This perennially popular breakfast spot has moved
AMERICAN   from its original location in the Hawaiian Monarch Hotel to a side
⊙   street on Waikīkī's west end. The second floor perch gives diners the option of balcony seating so they can watch the world go by as they eat. The menu isn't fancy, but it is good, solid food that will satisfy your grumbling stomach morning or night, as they are now open for breakfast, lunch, and dinner. Prepare to wait about 45 minutes for breakfast seating; longer on weekends. ⊠ *343 Saratoga Rd., Waikīkī* ☎ 808/923–3447 ⊕ *www.eggsnthings.com* ⊟ *MC, V* ⊗ *6 am–2 pm and 5–10 pm.*

$$–$$$ ✕**Hau Tree Lānai.** The vinelike *hau* tree is ideal for sitting under, and it's
ECLECTIC said that the one that spreads itself over this beachside courtyard is the
very one that shaded Robert Louis Stevenson as he mused and wrote
about Hawai'i. In any case, diners are still enjoying the shade, though
the view has changed—the gay-friendly beach over the low wall is paved
with hunky sunbathers. The food is unremarkable Island casual, but
we like the place for late-afternoon or early-evening drinks, pūpū, and
people-watching. ⊠ *New Otani Kaimana Beach Hotel, 2863 Kalākaua
Ave., Waikīkī* ☎ *808/921–7066* ⊕ *www.kaimana.com* ⊛ *Reservations
essential* ⊟ *AE, D, DC, MC, V.*

$$–$$$ ✕**Keo's in Waikīkī.** Many Islanders—and many Hollywood stars—got
THAI their first taste of pad thai noodles, lemongrass, and coconut milk curry
at one of Keo Sananikone's restaurants. This one, perched right at the
entrance to Waikīkī, characterizes his formula: a bright, clean space
awash in flowers with intriguing menu titles and reasonable prices. Evil
Jungle Prince, a stir-fry redolent of Thai basil, flecked with chilis and
rich with coconut milk, is a classic; also try the apple bananas (smaller,
sweeter variety of banana) in coconut milk. The Eastern and Western
breakfasts are popular. ⊠ *2028 Kūhiō Ave., Waikīkī* ☎ *808/951–9355*
⊟ *AE, D, DC, MC, V.*

$$$$ ✕**La Mer.** Like the hotel in which it's housed (Halekūlani, "House Befit-
FRENCH ting Heaven"), La Mer is pretty much heavenly: a softly lighted, low-
ceiling room has its windows open to the breeze, a perfectly framed
vista of Diamond Head, and the faint sound of music from a courtyard
below. The food captures the rich and yet sunny flavors of the south
of France in one tiny, exquisite course after another. We recommend
the degustation menu; place yourself in the sommelier's hands for wine
choices from the hotel's exceptional cellar. ⊠ *Halekūlani, 2199 Kālia
Rd., Waikīkī* ☎ *808/923–2311* ⊛ *Reservations essential; jacket required*
⊟ *AE, DC, MC, V* ☯ *No lunch.*

$$$$ ✕**Morimoto.** The long-awaited Iron Chef Morimoto of Food Network
JAPANESE fame has finally hit the scene in Honolulu. If you're adventurous, try
the *omakase* (chef's choice) menu, which changes daily. You can choose
to sit at the sushi bar, the regular bar, or at a table, but try to get a seat
outside, as the room gets pretty noisy. ⊠ *The Waikīkī Edition Hotel,
1775 Ala Moana Blvd., Waikīkī* ☎ *808/943–5900* ⊕ *morimotowaikiki.
com* ⊟ *AE, MC, V.*

$$$–$$$$ ✕**Nobu.** Famed chef Nobu Matsuhisa is the master of innovative Japa-
JAPANESE nese cuisine, and his Hawaiian outpost is definitely a Waikīkī hot spot.
Fish is the obvious centerpiece, with entrees such as Tasmanian ocean
trout with crispy spinach and yuzu soy, seafood harumaki with caviar
and Maui onion salsa, and even Nobu's version of fish-and-chips. Cold
dishes include tuna *tataki* (seared raw fish slices) with ponzu, yellow-
tail sashimi with jalapeño, and whitefish sashimi with dried miso. The
warm decor and sexy lighting means there isn't a bad seat in the house.
⊠ *Waikīkī Parc Hotel, 2233 Helumoa Rd., Waikīkī* ☎ *808/237–6999*
⊟ *AE, MC, V.*

$$$–$$$$ ✕**Orchids.** Perched along the seawall at historic Gray's Beach, Orchids
SEAFOOD is beloved by power breakfasters, ladies who lunch, and family groups
celebrating at the elaborate Sunday brunch. La Mer, upstairs, is better

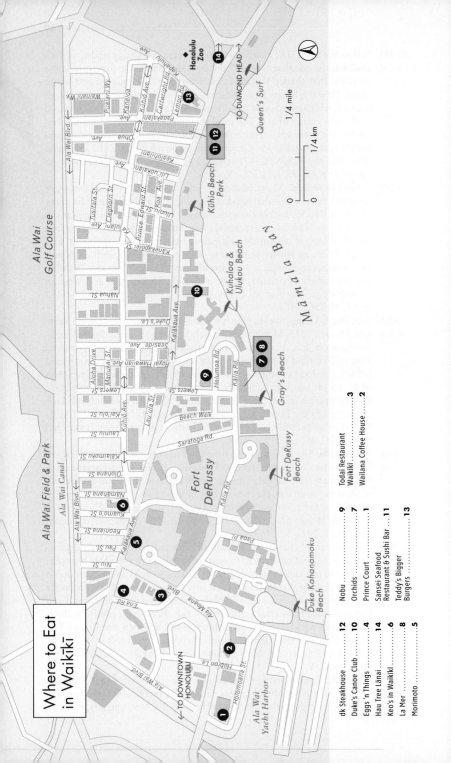

Where to Eat in Waikīkī

dk Steakhouse 12
Duke's Canoe Club 10
Eggs 'n Things 4
Hau Tree Lānai 14
Keo's in Waikīkī 6
La Mer 8
Morimoto 5

Nobu 9
Orchids 7
Prince Court 1
Sansei Seafood
Restaurant & Sushi Bar ... 11
Teddy's Bigger
Burgers 13

Todai Restaurant
Waikīkī 3
Wailana Coffee House 2

Honolulu Zoo

TO DIAMOND HEAD →

Queen's Surf

Ala Wai
Golf Course

Ala Wai Field & Park

Ala Wai Canal

Ala Wai Blvd.

Fort
DeRussy

Fort DeRussy
Beach

Gray's Beach

Kuhaloa &
Ulukou Beach

Kūhio Beach
Park

M ā m a l a   B a y

Duke Kahanamoku
Beach

Ala Wai Yacht Harbor

TO DOWNTOWN HONOLULU

TO DOWNTOWN
HONOLULU

1/4 mile
1/4 km

0

Kapahulu Ave.
Kanekoa Ave.
Pualani Wy.
Wainani Wy.
Kūhiō Ave.
Cartwright Rd.
Lemon Rd.
Paoakalani Rd.
'Ōhua Ave.
Kealohilani Ave.
Liliʻuokalani Ave.
Koa Ave.
Tusitala St.
Cleghorn St.
Kaʻiulani Ave.
Prince Edward St.
Uluniu St.
Kanekapolei St.
Nahua St.
Duke's La.
Seaside Ave.
Kalākaua Ave.
Royal Hawaiian Ave.
Manuka St.
Aloha Drive
Lewers St.
Kaiʻolu Ave.
Lauʻula St.
Lauʻula St.
Beach Walk
Launiu St.
Kalaimoku St.
Saratoga Rd.
ʻŌlohana St.
Nāmāhana St.
Keoniana St.
Kalākaua Ave.
Paʻu St.
Niu St.
Ena Rd.
Ala Moana Blvd.
Holomoana St.
Hobron La.
Kālia Rd.
Kālia Rd.
Helumoa Rd.
Paoa Pl.

A typical Hawaiian "plate lunch" usually includes meat along with one scoop of rice and another of macaroni salad.

known for the evening, but we have found dinner at Orchids equally enjoyable. The louvered walls are open to the breezes, the orchids add splashes of color, the seafood is perfectly prepared, and the wine list is intriguing. Plus, it is more casual and a bit less expensive than La Mer. Whatever meal you have here, finish with the hotel's signature coconut layer cake. ⊠ *Halekūlani, 2199 Kālia Rd., Waikīkī* ☎ *808/923–2311* ⏣ *Reservations essential* ▭ *AE, D, DC, MC, V.*

$$$
ECLECTIC
✕ **Prince Court.** This restaurant overlooking Ala Wai Yacht Harbor is a multifaceted success, with exceptional high-end lunches and dinners, daily breakfast buffets, weekly dinner seafood buffets, and sold-out weekend brunches. With a truly global mix of offerings, the overall style is Eurasian. Their ever-changing prix-fixe menu includes offerings such as Australian rack of lamb, Kahuku prawns, and medallions of New York Angus. ⊠ *Hawai'i Prince Hotel, 100 Holomoana St., Waikīkī* ☎ *808/944–4494* ⏣ *Reservations essential* ▭ *AE, D, DC, MC, V.*

$$–$$$
JAPANESE
✕ **Sansei Seafood Restaurant & Sushi Bar.** D. K. Kodama's Japanese-based Pacific Rim cuisine is an experience not to be missed, from early-bird dinners (from 5:30 pm) to late-night appetizers and sushi (until 1 am Fri. and Sat., with karaoke). The specialty sushi here—mango-crab roll, foie gras nigiri with eel sauce, and more—leaves California rolls far behind. We fantasize about the signature ramen with crabmeat and truffle butter. Cleverly named and beautifully prepared dishes come in big and small plates or in a multicourse tasting menu. Finish with tempura-fried ice cream or Mama Kodama's brownies. ⊠ *Waikīkī Beach Marriott Resort and Spa, 2552 Kalākaua Ave., Waikīkī* ☎ *808/931–6286* ▭ *AE, D, MC, V.*

¢   ✕ **Teddy's Bigger Burgers.** Though the focus at Teddy's is on the burgers,
AMERICAN   fries, and shakes, their success has inspired them to add a chicken, veggie, and fish sandwich to their menu. But, for those who like a classic,
the burgers are beefy, the fries crisply perfect, the shakes rich and sweet.
The original location in Waikīkī combines burger-shack simplicity with
surf-boy cool—there's even a place to store your surfboard while you
have your burger. This popular location has given birth to three others
in Honolulu, Kailua, and Hawai'i Kai. ⊠ *134 Kapahulu Ave., Waikīkī*
☎ *808/926–3444* ▭ *No credit cards.*

$$–$$$ ✕ **Todai Restaurant Waikīkī.** Bountiful buffets and menus that feature
SEAFOOD   seafood are popular with Islanders, so this Japan-based restaurant is a
local favorite. It's popular with budget-conscious travelers as well, for
the wide range of hot dishes, sushi, and the 160-foot seafood spread.
The emphasis here is more on quantity than quality. ⊠ *1910 Ala Moana
Blvd., Waikīkī* ☎ *808/947–1000* ⌁ *Reservations essential* ▭ *AE, D,
DC, MC, V.*

$ ✕ **Wailana Coffee House.** Despite the notoriously inattentive waitstaff,
AMERICAN   budget-conscious snowbirds, night owls with a yen for karaoke, all-day
drinkers of both coffee and the stronger stuff, hearty eaters, and lovers
of local-style plate lunches contentedly rub shoulders at this venerable
diner and cocktail lounge at the edge of Waikīkī. Most checks are under
$9; there's a $1.95 children's menu. It's open 24 hours a day, seven days
a week, 365 days a year but the place fills up and a line forms around
the corner at breakfast time, so arrive early or late. ⊠ *Wailana Condominium, ground floor, 1860 Ala Moana Blvd., corner of 'Ena Rd. and
Ala Moana, Waikīkī* ☎ *808/955–1674* ⌁ *Reservations not accepted*
▭ *AE, D, DC, MC, V.*

GREATER HONOLULU

$–$$ ✕ **12th Avenue Grill.** At this clean, well-lighted place on a back street, chef
MODERN   Bob McGee dishes up diner chic, including macaroni-and-cheese glazed
HAWAIIAN   with house-smoked Parmesan and topped with savory breadcrumbs.
The kimchi steak, a sort of teriyaki with kick, is a winner. Go early
(5 pm) or late (8:30 pm). Enjoy wonderful, homey desserts. There's
a small, reasonably priced wine list. ⊠ *1145C 12th Ave., Kaimukī*
☎ *808/732–9469* ⌑ *BYOB* ▭ *MC, V* ⊘ *Closed Sun. No lunch.*

$$$ ✕ **3660 on the Rise.** This casually stylish eatery is a 10-minute drive from
MODERN   Waikīkī in the culinary mecca of Kaimukī. Sample Chef Russell Siu's
HAWAIIAN   New York Steak Ala'e (steak grilled with Hawaiian clay salt), the crab
cakes, or the signature 'ahi katsu wrapped in nori and deep-fried with
a wasabi-ginger butter sauce. Siu combines a deep understanding of
local flavors with a sophisticated palate, making this place especially
popular with homegrown gourmands. The dining room can feel a bit
snug when it's full (as it usually is); go early or later. ⊠ *3660 Wai'alae
Ave., Kaimukī* ☎ *808/737–1177* ▭ *AE, DC, MC, V.*

$$$–$$$$ ✕ **Alan Wong's.** This not-to-be-missed restaurant is like that very rare shell
MODERN   you stumble upon on a perfect day at the beach—well polished and with-
HAWAIIAN   out a flaw. We've never had a bad experience here, and we've never heard
Fodor'sChoice   of anyone else having one either. The "Wong Way," as it's not-so-jokingly
★   called by his staff, includes an ingrained understanding of the aloha spirit,

evident in the skilled but unstarched service, and creative and playful interpretations of Island cuisine. Try Da Bag (seafood steamed in an aluminum pouch), Chinatown Roast Duck Nachos, and ginger crusted *onaga* (snapper). With a view of the Ko'olau Mountains, warm tones of koa wood, and *lauhala* grass weaving, you forget you're on the third floor of an office building. ✉ *McCully Court, 1857 S. King St., 3rd fl., Mōʻiliʻili* ☎ *808/949–2526* 🌐 *www.alanwongs.com* 💳 *AE, MC, V* ⏲ *No lunch.*

BEST BREAKFAST

Big City Diner (Ala Moana and Kailua). Start the day like a local: rice instead of toast, fish, or Portuguese sauce instead of bacon, even noodles.

Cinnamon's Restaurant (Kailua). Voted best for breakfast in a local newspaper poll, Cinnamon's does all the breakfast standards.

Duke's Canoe Club (Waikīkī). Duke's has an $11.95 buffet at breakfast.

$$$$ MODERN HAWAIIAN Fodor's Choice ★ ✕ **Chef Mavro.** George Mavrothalassitis, who took two hotel restaurants to the top of the ranks before founding this James Beard Award–winning restaurant, admits he's crazy. Crazy because of the care he takes to draw out the truest and most concentrated flavors, to track down the freshest fish, to create one-of-a-kind wine pairings that might strike others as mad. But for this passionate Provençal transplant, there's no other way. The menu changes quarterly, every dish (including dessert) matched with a select wine. We recommend the multicourse tasting menus (beginning at $69 for four courses without wine, up to $225 for 11 courses with wine). Etched-glass windows screen the busy street-corner scene and all within is mellow and serene with starched white tablecloths, fresh flowers, wood floors, and contemporary Island art. ✉ *1969 S. King St., Mōʻiliʻili* ☎ *808/944–4714* 🌐 *www.chefmavro.com* ✍ *Reservations essential* 💳 *AE, DC, MC, V* ⏲ *No lunch.*

¢–$ AMERICAN ✕ **Diamond Head Market & Grill.** Kelvin Ro's one-stop spot is a plate-lunch place, a gourmet market, a deli and bakery and espresso bar, too—and it's a five-minute hop from Waikīkī hotels. A take-out window offers grilled sandwiches or plates ranging from teriyaki beef to portobello mushrooms. The market's deli case is stocked with a range of heat-and-eat entrées from risotto cakes to lamb stew; specials change daily. There are packaged Japanese bento lunchboxes, giant scones, enticing desserts, and even a small wine selection. ✉ *3158 Monsarrat Ave., Diamond Head* ☎ *808/732–0077* ✍ *Reservations not accepted* 💳 *AE, D, MC, V.*

¢ MEXICAN ✕ **Diego's Taco Shop.** Diego's is a no-frills, simple joint where the smell of masa cooking permeates the air, salsa comes in mini plastic containers, and the food is filling and reasonable. The ambience, if you can call it that, is laid-back with college students shuffling in after the beach and "grinding" (eating) at the drive-in style tables. Carne asada is the top pick for taco and burrito filling and the flavor is San Diego Mexican. ✉ *2239 S. King St., McCully* ☎ *808/944–2942* 💳 *MC, V.*

¢–$ ITALIAN ✕ **Formaggio.** All but invisible on the backside of a strip mall, this wine bar seeks to communicate the feel of a catacomb in Italy and largely succeeds, with dim lighting and soft, warm tones. Choose a small sip or an entire bottle from the many wines they offer, enjoy the music, then ponder the small-dish menu of pizzas, panini, and hot and cold specialties such as eggplant Napoleon and melting short ribs in red wine. ✉ *Market City Shopping Center, rear, lower level, 2919 Kapi'olani Blvd., Kaimukī* 🕾 *808/739–7719* ⌖ *Reservations not accepted* ▭ *AE, MC, V* ✆ *Closed Sun. No lunch.*

$
ASIAN
✕ **Hale Vietnam.** One of O'ahu's first Vietnamese restaurants, this popular neighborhood spot expresses its friendly character with its name: *hale* (hah-lay) is the Hawaiian word for house or home. If you're not sure what to order, just ask. The staff is known for their willingness to help those who don't know much about Vietnamese food. Be sure to try the piquant and crunchy green-papaya salad. Reservations are taken for groups only. ✉ *1140 12th Ave., Kaimukī* 🕾 *808/735–7581* ▭ *AE, MC, V.*

$$$$
MODERN
HAWAIIAN
✕ **Hoku's at the Kāhala.** Everything about this room speaks of quality and sophistication: the wall of windows with their beach views, the avant-garde cutlery and dinnerware, the solicitous staff, and border-busting Pacific Rim cuisine. The menu constantly changes, but you can count on Chef Wayne Hirabayashi to use fresh, local ingredients when possible in his innovative fusion flair. An excellent choice for special occasions. The dress code is collared shirts, no beachwear. ✉ *The Kāhala Hotel & Resort, 5000 Kāhala Ave., Kāhala* 🕾 *808/739–8888* ▭ *AE, D, MC, V* ✆ *No lunch Sat.*

$$$–$$$$
FRENCH
✕ **Michel's at the Colony Surf.** With its wide-open windows so close to the water that you literally feel the soft mist at high tide, this is arguably the most romantic spot in Waikīkī for a sunset dinner for two. Venerable Michel's is synonymous with fine dining in the minds of Oahuans who have been coming here for more than 40 years. The menu is très, très French with both classic choices (escargot, foie gras) and contemporary items (Hardy's Hawaiian Bouillabaisse—named after the chef who created a Hawaiian twist on a French classic). There's dinner nightly and Sunday brunch. ✉ *Colony Surf, 2895 Kalākaua Ave., Waikīkī* 🕾 *808/923–6552* ⌖ *Reservations essential* ▭ *AE, D, DC, MC, V* ✆ *No lunch.*

$$–$$$
JAPANESE
✕ **Ninnikuya, the Garlic Restaurant.** Chef-owner Endo Eiyuki picked a powerful focus for his charming restaurant in a converted Kaimukī bungalow: garlic. He calls the menu Euro-Asian but the spicing and approach—except for the prevalence of garlic—are distinctly Japanese. Don't miss the Black Angus steak served on a sizzling stone. ✉ *3196 Waīalae Ave., Kaimukī* 🕾 *808/735–0784* ⌖ *Reservations essential* ▭ *AE, D, DC, MC, V* ✆ *Closed Sun. No lunch.*

¢–$
MEDITERRANEAN
✕ **Olive Tree.** Mediterranean food is scarce in the Islands, so Olive Tree keeps insanely busy; expect a wait for your hummus, fish souvlaki, Greek egg-and-lemon soup, and other specialties at this small spot behind Kāhala Mall. It's worth the wait, especially if you're looking to get your Greek-tooth on. ✉ *4614 Kīlauea Ave., Kāhala* 🕾 *808/737–0303* ⌖ *Reservations not accepted* ▭ *No credit cards* ✆ *No lunch.*

¢–$
HAWAIIAN
✕ **'Ono Hawaiian Foods.** The adventurous in search of a real local food experience should head to this no-frills hangout. You know it has to be good if residents are waiting in line to get in. Here you can sample *poi*

CLOSE UP

Musubi

Musubi needs translation. Here are balls of steamed rice, sometimes shaped like thick decks of cards and topped with luncheon meat, and bound with a strip of black, like a paper band around a stack of new bills. Swathed in plastic, they sit on the counter of every mom-and-pop store and plate-lunch place in Hawai'i, selling for $1.50 to $2.50. Everyone from T-shirted surfers with sandy feet, girls in pareus, and *tutus* (grandmas) in *mu'umu'u* are munching these oddities with apparent delight.

"Huh?" says the visitor.

So, a quick dictionary moment: *musubi* (*moo*-sue-bee), a ball of steamed Japanese-style rice topped with some sweet-salty morsel and held together with *nori* (*no*-ree; seaweed). Most common form in Hawai'i: Spam musubi, popularized in the early 1980s by vendor Mitsuko Kaneshiro.

Kaneshiro turned her children's favorite snack into a classic—Spam slices simmered in a sugar-soy mixture atop rectangular rice cakes, with nori for crisp contrast. The flavor is surprisingly pleasant and satisfying, like a portable rice bowl.

Musubi has its roots in Japan, where rice balls are standard festival, funeral, and family fare. But Islanders carried the tradition far afield, topping rice with slices of teriyaki chicken, putting baked salmon in the middle, or dressing the rice in piquant slivers of scarlet pickled plum, toasted sesame, and strips of seaweed.

These ubiquitous tidbits are Hawai'i's go-food, like hot dogs or pretzels on a New York street. Quality varies, but if you visit a craft fair or stumble on a school sale and see homemade musubi—grab one and snack like a local.

(a paste made from pounded taro root), *lomilomi* salmon (salmon massaged until tender and served with minced onions and tomatoes), laulau, *kālua* pork (roasted in an underground oven), and *haupia* (a light, gelatinlike dessert made from coconut milk). Appropriately enough, the Hawaiian word *'ono* means "delicious." ✉ *726 Kapahulu Ave., Kapahulu* ☎ *808/737–2275* ♲ *Reservations not accepted* ▭ *No credit cards* ✿ *Closed Sun.*

$ ✕ **Side Street Inn on Da Strip.** Famous as the place where celebrity chefs
HAWAIIAN gather after hours, local boy Colin Nishida's second pub is on the bustling Kapahulu Avenue, closer to Waikīkī. Local-style bar food comes in huge, share-plate portions, and Nishida's famous pork chops, fried rice, and lilikoi ribs make it worth the trip. This is a place to dress any way you like, nosh all night, and watch sports on TV. Pūpū (in portions so large as to be dinner) are served from 4 pm to 12:30 am daily. ✉ *614 Kapahulu Ave., Waikīkī* ☎ *808/591–0253* ♲ *Reservations essential* ▭ *AE, D, DC, MC, V* ✿ *No lunch weekends.*

$ ✕ **Soul Cafe.** If you have a hankering for down-home southern fare with
SOUTHERN a gourmet twist and Pacific flair, chef Sean Priester has it all. Must-tries include shrimp and cheesy grits with bacon gravy, crab cake on spring greens with an Asian black bean dressing, and the best fried chicken in town. Be prepared to order extra cornbread. It's that good. ✉ *3040 Waialae Ave., Kaimuki* ☎ *808/947–3113* ▭ *MC, V.*

$ ✕ **Spices.** Created by a trio of well-traveled friends who enjoy the foods
THAI   of Southeast Asia, Spices is alluringly decorated in spicelike oranges and
reds and offers a lunch and dinner menu far from the beaten path, even
in a city rich in the cuisine of this region. Leave room for dessert, as their
exotic ice cream is to die for. They claim inspiration but not authenticity and use Island ingredients to everyone's advantage. The menu
is vegetarian-friendly. ✉ *2671 S. King St., Mōʻiliʻili* ☎ *808/949–2679*
⌂ *Reservations essential* ▭ *MC, V* ⊘ *Closed Mon.*

$$–$$$ ✕ **Sushi Sasabune.** Meals here are unforgettable, though you may find
JAPANESE   the restaurant's approach exasperating and a little condescending. It's
possible to order from the menu, but you're strongly encouraged to
order *omakase*-style (oh-*mah*-ka-*say,* roughly, "trust me"), letting the
chef send out his choices for the night. The waiters keep up a steady
mantra to instruct patrons in the proper way to eat their delicacies:
"Please, no shoyu on this one." "One piece, one bite." But any trace of
annoyance vanishes with the first bite of California baby squid stuffed
with Louisiana crab, or unctuous *toro* ('ahi belly) smeared with a light
soy reduction, washed down with a glass of the smoothest sake you've
ever tasted. A caution: the courses come very rapidly—ask the server to
slow down the pace a bit. An even bigger caution: the courses, generally
two pieces of sushi or six to eight slices of sashimi, add up fast. ✉ *1419
S. King St., Mōʻiliʻili* ☎ *808/947–3800* ⌂ *Reservations essential* ▭ *AE,
D, DC, MC, V* ⊘ *Closed Sun. No lunch Sat. and Mon.*

$$–$$$ ✕ **The Willows.** An island dream, this buffet restaurant is made up of
HAWAIIAN   pavilions overlooking a network of ponds (once natural streams flowing from mountain to sea). The Island-style comfort food includes the
trademark Willows curry along with Hawaiian dishes such as *laulau* (a
steamed bundle of tī leaves containing pork, butterfish, and taro tops)
and local favorites such as Korean barbecue ribs. ✉ *901 Hausten St.,
Mōʻiliʻili* ☎ *808/952–9200* ⌂ *Reservations essential* ▭ *AE, D, MC, V.*

SOUTHEAST O'AHU

$$–$$$ ✕ **BluWater Grill.** Time your drive along Honolulu's South Shore to allow
ASIAN   for a stop at this relaxed restaurant on Kuapa Pond. The savvy chef-
manager team left a popular chain restaurant to found this "American eclectic" eatery, serving wok-seared moi fish, mango and guava
ribs, and lots of other interesting small dishes for $5 to $10. They're
open until 11 pm Monday through Thursday and on Sunday, and until
midnight Friday and Saturday. ✉ *Hawaiʻi Kai Shopping Center, 377
Keahole St., Hawaiʻi Kai* ☎ *808/395–6224* ▭ *AE, DC, MC, V.*

$$–$$$ ✕ **Roy's.** Roy Yamaguchi's flagship restaurant across the highway from
ASIAN   Maunalua Bay attracts food-savvy visitors as the North Shore attracts
surfers. But it also has a strong following among well-heeled Oahuans
from surrounding neighborhoods, who consider the place an extension
of their homes and Roy's team their personal chefs. For this reason, Roy's
is always busy and sometimes overly noisy. It's best to visit later in the
evening if you're sensitive to pressure to turn the table, or very early to
catch the sunset. The wide-ranging and ever-interesting Hawaiian fusion
menu changes daily except for signature dishes like Szechuan spiced barbecue baby back ribs, Roy's Original blackened 'ahi with soy mustard

butter sauce, and a legendary meat loaf. There's an exceptional wine list. ⊠ *Hawaiʻi Kai Corporate Plaza, 6600 Kalanianaʻole Hwy., Hawaiʻi Kai* ☎ *808/396–7697* ⌑ *Reservations essential* ▭ *AE, D, DC, MC, V.*

WINDWARD OʻAHU

$–$$
AMERICAN
Fodor'sChoice
★

✕ Buzz's Original Steakhouse. Virtually unchanged since it opened in 1967, this cozy maze of rooms opposite Kailua Beach Park is filled with the enticing aroma of grilling steaks. It doesn't matter if you're a bit sandy (but bare feet are not allowed). Stop at the salad bar, order up a steak, a burger, teri chicken, or the fresh fish special. If you sit at the bar, expect to make friends. ⊠ *413 Kawailoa Rd., Kailua* ☎ *808/261–4661* ▭ *No credit cards.*

¢–$
AMERICAN

✕ Cinnamon's Restaurant. Known for uncommon variations on common breakfast themes (pancakes, eggs Benedict, French toast, home fries, and eggs), this neighborhood favorite is tucked into a hard-to-find Kailua office park; call for directions. Lunch and dinner feature local-style plate lunch and a diner-style menu (meat loaf, baked beans) which are good, but the main attraction is breakfast. Don't miss the guava chiffon pancakes. ⊠ *315 Uluniu, Kailua* ☎ *808/261–8724* ▭ *D, DC, MC, V* ⊘ *No dinner Sun.–Wed.*

¢
FAST FOOD

✕ Keneke's BBQ. When you're sightseeing between Hanauma Bay and Makapuʻu, the food pickings are slim. But every day, 365 days a year, there's Keneke's in Waimāaalo town. It's the home of inexpensive plate lunches, shave ice, and Scriptural graffiti on the walls (Keith "Keneke"Ward, the burly, weight-lifting, second-generation owner of the place, is a born-again Christian). The food is diet busting, piled high, and mostly pretty good, particularly the Asian-style barbecue (including teriyaki chicken or beef and Korean *kal bi* (barbecue), and Filipino *guisantes* (pork and peas in tomato gravy) and adobo (piquant pork stew). If you want a treat, try the shave ice with ice cream. ⊠ *41-855 Kalanianaʻole Hwy., Waimānalo* ☎ *808/259–9800* ▭ *No credit cards.*

$$
AMERICAN

✕ Lucy's Grill and Bar. This Windward eatery offers outdoor lānai seating and an open-air bar that shakes up a mean martini to go with its eclectic and innovative menu. The indoor seating, though attractive, gets very noisy. Begin with the deep-fried *kālua* pig (pork roasted in an underground oven) pastry triangles with a mandarin orange–plum dipping sauce. Seafood offerings include daily fish specials with your choice of preparations. For meat lovers, there are Indonesian lamb chops or rib-eye steak. Brunch is served on Sunday. ⊠ *33 Aulike St., Kailua* ☎ *808/230–8188* ▭ *MC, V* ⊘ *No lunch weekends.*

$–$$
CHINESE

✕ Pah Ke's Chinese Restaurant. Chinese restaurants tend to be interchangeable, but this one—named for the local pidgin term for Chinese (literally translated this is Chinese's Chinese Restaurant)—is worth the drive from Honolulu for its focus on healthier cooking techniques and use of local ingredients, its seasonal specials such as cold soups and salads made from locally raised produce, and its exceptional East–West desserts. The menu offers all the usual suspects, but ask the owner and chef Raymond Siu, a former hotel pastry chef, if he's got anything different and interesting in the kitchen, or call ahead to ask for a special menu. ⊠ *46-018 Kamehameha Hwy., Kāneʻohe* ☎ *808/235–4505* ▭ *AE, MC, V.*

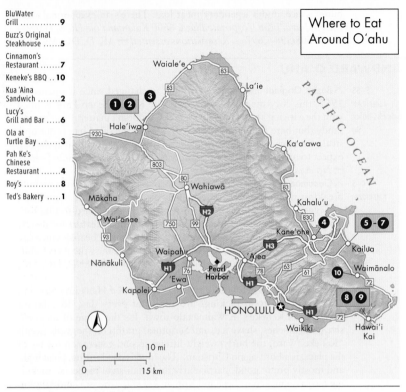

Where to Eat
Around O'ahu

THE NORTH SHORE

¢ | AMERICAN — ✕ **Kua 'Aina Sandwich.** A must-stop spot during a drive around the island, this North Shore eatery specializes in large, hand-formed burgers heaped with bacon, cheese, salsa, and pineapple; or try the grilled mahimahi sandwich. The crispy shoestring fries alone are worth the trip. Kua 'Aina also has a south-shore location across from the Ward Centre in Honolulu. ✉ *66-160 Kamehameha Hwy., Hale'iwa* ☎ *808/637–6067* ⌦ *Reservations not accepted* ☰ *No credit cards.*

$$–$$$ | MODERN HAWAIIAN | Fodor's Choice ★ — ✕ **Ola at Turtle Bay Resort.** In a pavilion literally on the sand, this casual but refined restaurant wowed critics from the moment it opened, both with its idyllic location on Kuilima Cove and with chef Fred DeAngelo's reliably wonderful food. Ola means "life, living, healthy," an apt name for a place that combines a commitment to freshness and wholesomeness with a discriminating and innovative palate in such dishes as a vegan risotto made with local mushrooms and orzo pasta, slow-poached salmon with caramelized cane sugar and Okinawan sweet potatoes. It is absolutely worth the drive. ✉ *57-091 Kamehameha Hwy., Kahuku* ☎ *808/293–0801* ☰ *DC, MC, V.*

¢ | AMERICAN — ✕ **Ted's Bakery.** Across from Sunset Beach and famous for its chocolate *haupia* pie (layered coconut and chocolate puddings topped with whipped cream), Ted's Bakery is also favored by surfers and area residents for quick breakfasts, sandwiches, or plate lunches, to-go or eaten at the handful of umbrella-shaded tables outside. ⊠ *59-024 Kamehameha Hwy., Haleʻiwa* ☎ *808/638–8207* ⚓ *Reservations not accepted* ▭ *DC, MC, V.*

2

WHERE TO STAY

The 2½-mi stretch of sand known as Waikīkī Beach is a 24-hour playground and the heartbeat of Hawaiʻi's tourist industry. Waikīkī has a lot to offer—namely, the beach, shopping, restaurants, and nightlife, all within walking distance of your hotel.

Business travelers stay on the western edge, near the Hawaiʻi Convention Center, Ala Moana, and downtown Honolulu. As you head east, Ala Moana Boulevard turns into Kalākaua Avenue, Waikīkī's main drag. This is hotel row (mid-Waikīkī), with historic boutique hotels, newer high-rises, and megaresorts. Bigger chains like Sheraton, Outrigger, ResortQuest, and Ohana have multiple properties along the strip, which can be confusing. Surrounding the hotels and filling their lower levels is a flurry of shopping centers, restaurants, bars, and clubs. As you get closer to Diamond Head Crater, the strip opens up again, with the Honolulu Zoo and Kapiʻolani Park providing green spaces. This end has a handful of smaller hotels and condos for those who like their Waikīkī with a "side of quiet."

Waikīkī is still the resort capital of this island and the lodging landscape is constantly changing. The Waikīkī Beach Walk opened in 2007 on 8 acres within the confines of Beach Walk, Lewers and Saratoga streets, and Kālia Road. It comprises a multitiered entertainment complex, cultural center, hotels, and vacation-ownership properties, all accented by lush tropical landscaping. Ko ʻOlina Resort and Marina, about 15 minutes from the airport in West Oʻahu, looms large on the horizon—this ongoing development already contains the JW Marriott ʻIhilani Resort, Marriott Ko ʻOlina Beach Club, and some outstanding golf courses, but it is slated, over the coming decade, to see the construction of an extensive planned resort community and marina, an aquarium, dozens of restaurants and shops, more hotels, and yet more vacation-ownership rentals.

Casual Windward and North Shore digs are shorter on amenities but have laid-back charms all their own. Oʻahu offers a more limited list of bed-and-breakfasts than other Islands because the state stopped licensing them here in the 1980s; many of those operating here now do so under the radar. If you can't find your match below, contact a reservation service to make reservations at one of Oʻahu's reputable bed-and-breakfasts. Legislators on Oʻahu are taking another look at this industry, and it's possible that bed-and-breakfasts will flourish here again in the next decade.

WHAT IT COSTS					
	¢	$	$$	$$$	$$$$
Hotels	under $100	$100–$180	$181–$260	$261–$340	over $340

Hotel prices are for two people in a standard double room in high season. Condo price categories reflect studio and one-bedroom rates. Prices exclude 13.96% tax.

HONOLULU

$$
HOTEL

Ala Moana Hotel. Shoppers might wear out their Manolos here; this renovated condo-hotel is connected to O'ahu's biggest mall, the Ala Moana Shopping Center, by a pedestrian ramp, and it's a four-block stroll away from the Victoria Ward Centers. Business travelers can walk one block in the opposite direction to the Hawai'i Convention Center. Swimmers, surfers, and beachgoers make the two-minute walk to Ala Moana Beach Park across the street. Rooms are like small, comfortable apartments, with cherrywood furnishings, kitchenettes, flat-screen TVs, and balconies with outdoor seating. The recreation deck features a pool with cabanas and a bar, outdoor yoga and Pilates studios, and a fitness center. The hotel recently underwent a multimillion-dollar renovation, updating the rooms and relaxing the feel of the lobby. **Pros:** adjacent to Ala Moana shopping center; rooms nicely appointed. **Cons:** outside the heartbeat of Waikīkī, can feel a bit distant from the action. **TripAdvisor:** "staff was courteous," "no room service," "good value for price." ⊠ 410 Atkinson Dr., Ala Moana ☎ 808/955–4811 or 888/367–4811 ⊕ www.alamoanahotel.com ↪ 1,150 studios, 67 suites ♨ In-room: a/c, safe, refrigerator, Internet, Wi-Fi. In-hotel: 4 restaurants, room service, bars, pool, gym, parking (paid) ⊟ AE, DC, MC, V.

$$$$
HOTEL
Fodor's Choice
★

The Kāhala. Hidden away in the wealthy residential neighborhood of Kāhala (on the other side of Diamond Head from Waikīkī), this elegant oceanfront hotel has played host to both presidents and princesses as one of Hawai'i's very first luxury resorts. The Kāhala is flanked by the exclusive Wai'alae Golf Links and the Pacific Ocean—surrounding it in a natural tranquillity. Pathways meander out along a walkway with benches tucked into oceanfront nooks for lazy viewing, offering an "outer Island" experience only 10 minutes from Waikīkī and Honolulu. The expansive oceanfront Chi Health Energy Fitness Center offers outdoor yoga and Pilates. Fine dining is available at Hokus, or the poolside bar and grill will serve at your lounge chair on the beach. The reef not far from shore makes the waters here calm enough for young kids. You can also sign up for dolphin interactions in the 26,000-square-foot lagoon. The rooms, decorated in an understated Island style with mahogany furniture, are spacious (550 square feet), with bathrooms with two vanities, and lānai big enough for a lounge chair. If you're a golf-lover visiting the second week of January, ask for a room overlooking the course for a bird's-eye view of the PGA Sony Open from your lānai. **Pros:** away from hectic Waikīkī; beautiful rooms and public spaces; heavenly spa. **Cons:** Waikīkī is a drive away. **TripAdvisor:** "quick and friendly service," "rooms were lovely," "we ate very well at

BEST BETS FOR O'AHU LODGING

Fodor'sChoice★

Halekūlani, $$$$, p. 168
The Kāhala, $$$$, p. 160
The Turtle Bay Resort, $$$-$$$$, p. 179

By Price

¢–$

Backpackers Vacation Inn, p. 177
The Breakers, p. 165
Royal Grove Hotel, p. 174

$$

Ala Moana Hotel, p. 160
The Equus, p. 168

$$$

Embassy Suites Hotel— Waikīkī Beach Walk, p. 166

Hilton Hawaiian Village Beach Resort and Spa, p. 170
Outrigger Reef on the Beach, p. 173
Waikīkī Parc, p. 176

$$$$

JW Marriott 'Ihilani Resort & Spa, p. 180
Marriott Ko 'Olina Beach Club, p. 180
Moana Surfrider, p. 172
The Royal Hawaiian Hotel, p. 174

By Experience

BEST FOR ROMANCE

Halekūlani, $$$$, p. 168
JW Marriott 'Ihilani Resort & Spa, $$$-$$$$, p. 180

The Kāhala, $$$$, p. 160
Moana Surfrider, $$$$, p. 172
The Royal Hawaiian Hotel, $$$$, p. 174

BEST BEACH

JW Marriott 'Ihilani Resort and Spa, $$$-$$$$, p. 180
The Kāhala, $$$$, p. 160
Marriott Ko 'Olina Beach Club, $$$-$$$$, p. 180
Moana Surfrider, $$$$, p. 172
The Turtle Bay Resort, $$$-$$$$, p. 179

2

the resort." ⊠ *5000 Kāhala Ave., Kāhala* ☎ *808/739–8888 or 800/367–25285* ⊕ *www.kahalaresort.com* ⌨ *345 rooms, 33 suites* ⌂ *In-room: a/c, safe, refrigerator, Internet, Wi-Fi. In-hotel: 5 restaurants, room service, bars, pool, gym, spa, beachfront, bicycles, children's programs (ages 5–12), parking (paid)* ⊟ *AE, D, DC, MC, V.*

WAIKĪKĪ

$

RENTAL

☺

Aston at the Waīkīki Banyan. The recreation deck at this family-oriented property has outdoor grills, a heated swimming pool, two hot tubs, a children's playground, a mini putting green, and volleyball, basketball, and tennis courts. The welcoming lobby is decorated in warm tropical woods with plenty of seating to enjoy the trade winds. There is also a koi pond and mini waterfall. One-bedroom suites contain Island-inspired decor and have complete kitchens and lānai that offer Diamond Head or ocean views. **Pros:** many rooms have great views. **Cons:** trekking to the beach with all your gear. **TripAdvisor:** "housekeeping staff seemed efficient," "toilet/tub area was small," "check-in was fast." ⊠ *201 Ohua Ave., Waikīkī* ☎ *808/922–0555 or 866/774–2924* ⊕ *www.astonhotels.com* ⌨ *876 units* ⌂ *In-room: a/c, kitchen,*

WHERE TO STAY IN WAIKĪKĪ AND O'AHU

Hotels and Resorts

	Property Name	Worth Noting	Cost $	Pools	Beach	Golf Course	Tennis Courts	Gym	Spa	Children's Programs	Rooms	Restaurants	Other	Location
29	Ala Moana Hotel	Ala Moana shopping	$$	1				yes			1,217	4		Honolulu
35	Aulani	Brand-new Disney resort	$$$$	4	yes			yes	yes	2-18	841	4		West O'ahu
4	Doubletree Alana Waikīkī	Near convention center	$$$-$$$$	1				yes			702	1		Waikīkī
11	Embassy Suites Hotel— Waikīkī Beach Walk	Near Beach Walk	$$$	1							421	4		Waikīkī
2	The Equus	Good value	$-$$	1							70		laundry	Waikīkī
13	Halekūlani	Great restaurants	$$$$	1	yes			yes	yes		454	3	shops	Waikīkī
1	Hawai'i Prince Hotel	Ala Moana shopping	$$$-$$$$	1		yes		yes	yes		578	3	shops	Waikīkī
5	Hilton Hawaiian Village	Bishop Museum, fireworks	$$$	5	yes			yes	yes	5-12	4,061	20	shops	Waikīkī
26	Hilton Waikīkī Beach Hotel	2 blocks to beach	$$$	1				yes			601	1		Waikīkī
17	Holiday Inn Waikīkī Beachcomber	1 block to beach, shows	$$-$$$	1						5-12	507	1	shops	Waikīkī
22	Hyatt Regency Waikīkī	Across from beach	$$$	1				yes	yes	5-12	1,248	3	shops	Waikīkī
34	JW Marriott 'Ihilani	Ko'Olina Resort, spa	$$$-$$$$	2	yes	yes	6	yes	yes	5-12	423	4	shops	West O'ahu
30	The Kāhala	Oceanfront views	$$$$	1	yes			yes	yes	5-12	378	5	shops	East Honolulu
33	Marriot Ko'Olina Beach Club	Sandy-bottom pool	$$$-$$$$	2	yes	yes	6	yes		5-12	200	2	kitchen	West O'ahu
21	Moana Surfrider	Landmark historic wing	$$$$	1	yes				yes		839	1	shops	Waikīkī
19	Ohana East	2 blocks to beach	$-$$	1				yes			440	3	kitchen	Waikīkī

#	Name	Features	Cost							Rooms			Location
8	Outrigger Reef on the Beach	Good value	$$-$$$	1	yes		yes	yes		675	2	laundry	Waikīkī
16	Outrigger Waikīkī on the Beach	Outrigger Waikīkī on the Beach	$$-$$$	1	yes		yes	yes	5–13	554	3	kitchen	Waikīkī
24	Royal Grove Hotel	Good value	¢	1						85	2	kitchen	Waikīkī
15	Royal Hawaiian Hotel	Iconic pink hotel	$$$-$$$$	1	yes		yes	yes		581	1	shops	Waikīkī
20	Sheraton Princess Kaiulani	1 block to beach	$$$-$$$$	1			yes			1,156	1		Waikīkī
14	Sheraton Waikīkī	Beachside Rum Fire	$$$$	2	yes		yes	yes	5–12	1,823	5	shops	Waikīkī
9	Trump International Hotel	Sunsets from the lobby	$$$$	1	yes		yes	yes		1,462	2	kitchen	Waikīkī
31	The Turtle Bay Resort	Beach cottages, trails	$$$-$$$$	2	yes	10	yes	yes	5–12	511	4	shops	North Shore
28	Waikīkī Beach Marriott	Great sushi, spa	$$$$	2	yes		yes	yes		1,323	6		Waikīkī
3	Waikīkī Edition	Modern chic	$$$$	2	yes		yes			353	2	laundry	Waikīkī
12	Waikīkī Parc	1 block to beach	$$$-$$$$	1	yes		yes			297	1		Waikīkī
23	Waikīkī Sand Villa	3 blocks to beach	¢-$	1						214	1		Waikīkī
Condos and Rentals													
25	Aston Waikīkī Beach Tower	Across from beach	$$$$	1		1				140		kitchen	Waikīkī
27	Aston at the Waikīkī Banyan	1 block to beach	$	1		1				876		kitchen	Waikīkī
10	The Breakers	½ block to beach	$	1						64	1	kitchen	Waikīkī
7	Castle Waikīkī Shore	Great location	$$$$		yes					168		kitchen	Waikīkī
18	'Ilima Hotel	2 blocks to beach	$$-$$$	1			yes			99		kitchen	Waikīkī
6	Outrigger Luana	2 blocks to beach	$$-$$$	1			yes			218		kitchen	Waikīkī
B&Bs and Inns													
32	Backpackers Vacation Inn	Near Waimea Bay	¢-$							25		no a/c	North Shore

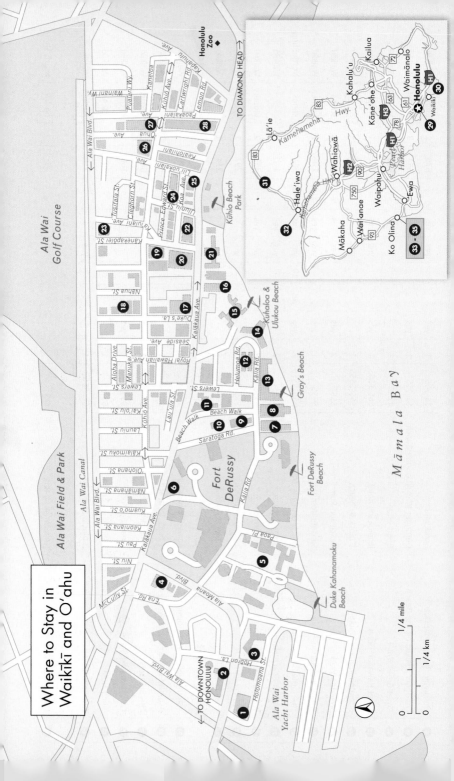

Where to Stay in Waikīkī and Oʻahu

Ala Wai Golf Course

Ala Wai Field & Park

Honolulu Zoo

TO DIAMOND HEAD

Kūhiō Beach Park

Fort DeRussy

Fort DeRussy Beach

Gray's Beach

Kūhaloa & Ulukou Beach

Māmala Bay

Duke Kahanamoku Beach

Ala Wai Yacht Harbor

TO DOWNTOWN HONOLULU

1/4 mile
1/4 km

Kāneʻohe
Kahaluʻu
Kailua
Waimānalo
Honolulu
Waikīkī
Lāʻie
Kamehameha Hwy.
Wahiawā
Haleʻiwa
Waipahu
Pearl Harbor
Ewa
Ko Olina
Waiʻanae
Mākaha
Kaneohe
Kahalu'u

WHERE TO STAY ON OʻAHU

	LOCAL VIBE	PROS	CONS
Honolulu	Lodging options are limited in downtown Honolulu, but if you want an urban feel or to be near Chinatown, look no farther.	Access to a wide selection of art galleries, boutiques, and new restaurants as well as Chinatown.	No beaches within walking distance. If you are looking to get away from it all, this is not the place.
Waikīkī	Lodgings abound in Waikīkī, from youth hostels to five-star accommodations. The area is always abuzz with activity and anything you desire is within walking distance.	You can surf in front of the hotels, wander miles of beach, and explore hundreds of restaurants and bars.	This is tourist central. Prices are high and you are not going to get the true Hawaiian experience.
North Shore	This is true country living, with one luxurious resort exception. It is bustling in the winter (when the surf is up) but pretty open in the summer.	Amazing surf and long stretches of sand truly epitomize the beach culture in Hawaiʻi. Historic Haleʻiwa has enough stores to keep shopaholics busy.	There is no middle ground for accommodations; you are either in backpacker cabanas or $300-a-night suites. There is also zero nightlife.
West (Leeward) Oʻahu	This is the resort side of the rock with the modern Kō ʻOlina and the aged Makaha. There is little outside of the resorts, but plenty on the grounds to keep you occupied for a week.	Kō ʻOlina's lagoons offer the most kid-friendly swimming on the island and the golf courses on this side are magnificent. Rare is the rainy day out here.	You are isolated from the rest of Oʻahu, with little in the way of shopping or jungle hikes.

Internet. In-hotel: tennis court, pool, laundry facilities, parking (paid) ⊟ *AE, D, DC, MC, V.*

$$$$ 🏨 **Aston Waikīkī Beach Tower.** You'll find the elegance of a luxury all-
RENTAL suites condominium combined with the intimacy and service of a boutique hotel at this Kalākaua Avenue address. Facing Kūhiō Beach, this 40-story resort offers spacious (1,100–1,400 square feet) one- and two-bedroom suites with gourmet kitchens and windows that open to views of Waikīkī and the Pacific Ocean. Amenities include twice-daily maid service, washer-dryers, and spacious private lānai. **Pros:** *very* large rooms—big enough to move into. **Cons:** no on-site restaurants; you must cross a busy street to the beach. **TripAdvisor:** "staff made us feel like royalty," "twice daily maid service," "was easy to find." ⊠ *2470 Kalākaua Ave., Waikīkī* ☎ *808/926–6400 or 866/774–2924* ⊕ *www. astonhotels.com* ➾ *140 units* ⌂ *In-room: a/c, safe, kitchen, DVD, Internet. In-hotel: room service, pool, tennis court, laundry facilities, parking (free)* ⊟ *AE, D, DC, MC, V.*

$ 🏨 **The Breakers.** Despite an explosion of high-rise construction all around
RENTAL it, the low-rise Breakers continues to offer a taste of '60s Hawaiʻi in this small complex a mere half block from Waikīkī Beach. The Breakers' six two-story buildings surround its pool and overlook gardens

filled with tropical flowers. Guest rooms have Japanese-style shoji doors that open to the lānai, kitchenettes, and bathrooms with showers only. Units 130, 132, and 134 have views of the Urasenke Teahouse. The Breakers enjoys enviable proximity to the new Waikīkī Beach Walk entertainment, dining, and retail complex. The resort is very popular thanks to its reasonable prices and great location. **Pros:** intimate atmosphere; great location. **Cons:** parking space is limited. **TripAdvisor:** "rooms have some Japanese styling," "wonderful garden," "short walk to the beach." ✉ *250 Beach Walk, Waikīkī* ☎ *808/923–3181 or 800/426–0494* ⊕ *www.breakers-hawaii.com* ↘ *64 units* ♨ *In-room: a/c, kitchen. In-hotel: restaurant, bar, pool, Internet terminal, parking (paid)* ⊟ *AE, DC, MC, V.*

$$$$
RENTAL
⛩ **Castle Waikīkī Shore.** Nestled between Fort DeRussy Beach Park and the Outrigger Reef on the Beach, this is the only condo right on Waikīkī Beach. Units include studios and one- and two-bedroom suites, each with private lānai and panoramic views of the Pacific Ocean. All units have washers and dryers, and many have full kitchens, but some only have kitchenettes, so be sure to inquire when booking. Families love this place for its spaciousness, while others love it for its quiet location on the ʻewa end of Waikīkī. **Pros:** great security; great views; great management. **Cons:** beach out front is kind of thin. **TripAdvisor:** "beds were comfortable," "rooms are very clean," "don't expect high end luxury." ✉ *2161 Kālia Rd., Waikīkī* ☎ *808/952–4500 or 800/367–2353* ⊕ *www.castleresorts.com* ↘ *168 units* ♨ *In-room: a/c, safe, kitchen, Internet. In-hotel: beachfront, laundry facilities, parking (paid)* ⊟ *AE, D, DC, MC, V.*

$$$–$$$$
HOTEL
�
⛩ **Doubletree Alana Waikīkī.** The location (a 10-minute walk from the Hawai'i Convention Center), three phones in each room, and the 24-hour business center and gym meet the requirements of the Doubletree's global business clientele, but the smallness of the property, the staff's attention to detail, and the signature Doubletree chocolate chip cookies upon arrival resonate with vacationers. All rooms in the 19-story high-rise have lānai, but they overlook the city and busy Ala Moana Boulevard across from Fort DeRussy. To get to the beach, you cross Fort DeRussy or head through the Hilton Hawaiian Village. **Pros:** professional staff; pleasant public spaces. **Cons:** beach is a bit of a walk. **TripAdvisor:** "staff was very friendly and helpful," "hotel is fairly clean," "shower area is so small." ✉ *1956 Ala Moana Blvd., Waikīkī* ☎ *808/941–7275 or 800/222–8733* ⊕ *www.alana-doubletree. com* ↘ *317 rooms, 385 suites* ♨ *In-room: a/c, safe, Internet. In-hotel: restaurant, room service, bar, pool, gym, Internet terminal, parking (paid)* ⊟ *AE, D, MC, V.*

$$$
HOTEL
☏
⛩ **Embassy Suites Hotel–Waikīkī Beach Walk.** In a place where space is at a premium, the only all-suites resort in Hawai'i offers families and groups traveling together a bit more room to move about, with two 21-story towers housing one- and two-bedroom suites. All rooms have at least two balconies, some with ocean views; most overlooking the 1,965-square-foot Grand Lanai with its pool, bar, restaurant, and meeting areas. The experience begins with a sit-down check-in and a manager's reception with free appetizers and drinks and ends with an aloha

The Kāhala

lei ceremony. Rooms, with Tommy Bahama–meets–Island beach home style (carved-wood tables, pineapple-print upholstery, hula-dancer artwork), have relaxing earth tones, with amenities like pull-out beds and wet bars with microwaves and mini refrigerators inviting longer stays. Developed by locally based Outrigger Enterprises, the hotel is steeped in Hawaiiana, with tapa-pattern murals adorning the exterior and cultural programs for adults and youth. **Pros:** great location next to Waikīkī Beach Walk; great vibe; nice pool deck. **Cons:** no direct beach access. **TripAdvisor:** "staff was friendly and helpful," "grounds are well maintained," "great location for shopping and beach." ☒ *201 Beachwalk St., Waikīkī* ☎ *800/362–2779* ⊕ *www.embassysuiteswaikikibeachwalk. com* ⟿ *353 1-bedroom suites, 68 2-bedroom suites* ⚴ *In-room: a/c, safe, refrigerator, Wi-Fi. In-hotel: 4 restaurants, room service, bar, pool* ☰ *AE, D, MC, V.*

$–$$
HOTEL

🖼 **The Equus.** Formerly the Hawaii Polo Inn, this small hotel has been completely renovated with a Hawaiian country theme that pays tribute to Hawai'i's polo-playing history. It fronts busy Ala Moana Boulevard, on the 'ewa (west) end of Waikīkī, and is one block from both Ala Moana shopping center and Ala Moana Beach Park. All rooms are equipped with refrigerators and microwaves; some have balconies and partial ocean views; daily Continental breakfast is included. The front desk staff are happy to assist with driving directions to the polo playing fields at Mokulē'ia and Waimānalo, where guests receive free tickets in season—pack a picnic if you go. **Pros:** casual; fun atmosphere; attentive staff; nicely furnished rooms. **Cons:** on a very busy road you must cross to get to the beach. **TripAdvisor:** "parking in the area is expensive," "location is awesome," "perfect Hawaiian hospitality." ☒ *1696 Ala Moana Blvd., Waikīkī* ☎ *808/949–0061 or 800/535–0085* ⊕ *www.equushotel.com* ⟿ *70 rooms* ⚴ *In-room: a/c, safe, refrigerator, Internet. In-hotel: pool, laundry facilities, Wi-Fi hotspot, parking (paid)* ☰ *AE, DC, MC, V.*

$$$$
RESORT
Fodor's Choice
★

🖼 **Halekūlani.** Honeymooners and others seeking seclusion amid the frenetic activity of the Waikīkī scene find it here. Halekūlani exemplifies the translation of its name—the "house befitting heaven." From the moment you step inside the lobby, the attention to detail and service wraps you in luxury. It begins with private registration in your guest room and extends to the tiniest of details, such as complimentary tickets to the Honolulu Symphony, Contemporary Art Museum, and Honolulu Academy of Arts. Spacious guest rooms, artfully appointed in marble and wood, have ocean views and extra large lānai. If you want to honeymoon in the ultimate style, we recommend the 2,125-square-foot Vera Wang Suite, created by the noted wedding-dress designer herself. For a day of divine pampering, check into the Halekūlani Spa. Outside, the resort's freshwater pool has an orchid design created from more than 1.5 million glass mosaic tiles. Gray's Beach, which fronts the hotel just beyond the pool, is small and has been known to disappear at high tide. At this writing the hotel was planning to renovate rooms and other features. The hotel will remain open during the project, which was expected to be complete in June 2012. **Pros:** heavenly interior spaces and wonderful dining opportunities in house. **Cons:** might feel a bit

Halekūlani

formal for Waikīkī. **TripAdvisor:** "fantastic view of the ocean," "amazing pool," "great location for off-site restaurants." ✉ *2199 Kālia Rd., Waikīkī* ☎ *808/923–2311 or 800/367–2343* ⊕ *www.halekulani.com* ⇶ *412 rooms, 43 suites* ⚿ *In-room: a/c, safe, DVD, Internet, Wi-Fi. In-hotel: 3 restaurants, room service, bars, pool, gym, spa, beachfront, laundry service, Internet terminal, parking (paid)* ▤ *AE, DC, MC, V.*

$$$–$$$$
HOTEL

🏨 **Hawai'i Prince Hotel & Golf Club Waikīkī.** This slim high-rise fronts Ala Wai Yacht Harbor at the *'ewa* edge of Waikīkī, close to Honolulu's downtown business districts, the convention center, and Ala Moana's outdoor mall. There's no beach here, but Ala Moana Beach Park is a 10-minute stroll away along the harbor, and the hotel also offers complimentary shuttle service around Waikīkī and its surrounding beaches. It's the only resort in Waikīkī with a golf course—the 27-hole Arnold Palmer–designed golf course is in 'Ewa Beach, about a 45-minute ride from the hotel. The sleek, modern Prince looks to Asia both in its high-style decor and such pampering touches as the traditional *oshiburi* (chilled hand towel) for refreshment upon check-in. Floor-to-ceiling windows overlooking the harbor—ideal for sunsets—make up for the lack of lānai. **Pros:** fantastic views; all very elegant; easy exit from complicated-to-maneuver Waikīkī. **Cons:** can feel a bit stuffy as it caters more to business travelers. **TripAdvisor:** "all rooms have an ocean view," "just a bit outdated," "walking distance to everything." ✉ *100 Holomoana St., Waikīkī* ☎ *808/956–1111 or 866/774–6236* ⊕ *www.hawaiiprincehotel.com* ⇶ *521 rooms, 57 suites* ⚿ *In room: a/c, safe, refrigerator. In-hotel: 3 restaurants, room service, bar, golf course, pool, gym, spa, Internet terminal, parking (paid)* ▤ *AE, DC, MC, V.*

$$$
RESORT

🏨 **Hilton Hawaiian Village Beach Resort and Spa.** Location, location, location: this megaresort and convention destination sprawls over 22 acres on Waikīkī's widest stretch of beach, with the green lawns of neighboring Fort DeRussy creating a buffer zone to the high-rise lineup of central Waikīkī. The Hilton makes the most of its prime real estate—surrounding the five hotel towers with lavish gardens, an aquatic playground of pools, a 5-acre lagoon for kayaking, cascading waterfalls, koi ponds, penguins, and pink flamingos. Rainbow Tower, with its landmark 31-story mural, has knockout views of Diamond Head. Rooms in all towers have lānai offering ocean, city, or Waikīkī beach views. More of a city than a village, the HHV has an ABC sundries store, a bookstore, Louis Vuitton, and a post office. Culture comes in the form of an outpost of the Bishop Museum and the contemporary Hawaiian art gracing the public spaces. It even has its own pier, docking point for the *Atlantis* submarine. The sheer volume of options, including free stuff (lei making, 'ukelele lessons, and fireworks), makes the HHV a good choice for families. **Pros:** activities and amenities can keep you busy for weeks; big-resort perks like check-in kiosks (complete with room keys) in the baggage-claim area at the airport. **Cons:** temptation to stay on-site, missing out on the "real" Hawai'i; frequent renovations and construction; size of property can be overwhelming. **TripAdvisor:** "recommend this hotel for families," "pools and waterslides were very nice," "busy resort." ✉ *2005 Kālia Rd., Waikīkī* ☎ *808/949–4321 or 800/221–2424* ⊕ *www.hiltonhawaiianvillage.com* ⇶ *3,432 rooms, 365*

suites, 264 condominiums ♿ *In-room: a/c, safe, refrigerator, Internet.*
In-hotel: 20 restaurants, room service, bars, pools, gym, spa, beach-
front, children's programs (ages 5–12), laundry service, Wi-Fi hotspot,
parking (paid) ▬ *AE, D, DC, MC, V.*

$$$ 📺 **Hilton Waikīkī Beach Hotel.** You enter through a lobby of rich wood
HOTEL detailing, contemporary fabrics, and magnificent tropical floral displays
whose colors match the hibiscus reds of the carpeting. Two blocks from
Kūhiō Beach, this 37-story high-rise is on the Diamond Head end of
Waikīkī. The Lobby Bar mixes up tropical cocktails and an Island-style
pūpū menu and has wireless access and a wide-screen plasma TV for
sports fans and news junkies, while their restaurant MAC 24-7 offers
their version of modern comfort food 24 hours a day, seven days a
week. If marriage is on your mind, note the wedding gazebo anchoring
the hotel gardens. Book on an upper floor for an ocean view from your
lānai. **Pros:** good value; central location; pleasant, comfortable public
spaces. **Cons:** a bit of a distance to the beach; very few rooms with
views. **TripAdvisor:** "hotel is clean and modern," "a block from the
beach," "ocean-view rooms face busy Kuhio Ave." ✉ *2500 Kūhiō Ave.,*
Waikīkī ☏ *808/922–0811 or 800/333–3333* ⊕ *www.hilton.com* ☞ *601*
rooms ♿ *In-room: a/c, safe, Internet. In-hotel: restaurant, room service,*
bar, pool, gym, Wi-Fi hotspot, parking (paid) ▬ *AE, D, DC, MC, V.*

$$–$$$ 📺 **Holiday Inn Waikīkī Beachcomber Hotel.** Early check-in guests at this
HOTEL hotel can leave their bags, pick up a pager, and hit the beach; they'll be
alerted when their rooms are ready. The property hosts the popular Blue
Hawai'i show and is almost directly across from the Royal Hawaiian
Shopping Center and next door to the International Marketplace. The
third-floor pool deck is front-row seating for any of Waikīkī's year-
round parades or Ho'olaulea street-party festivals that happen year-
round. It's a family-friendly place, with cultural activities that include
'ukulele and hula lessons as well as arts and crafts. On the hotel's
ground level is an entrance to Macy's, and across the street is a public
access-way that opens up to the beach fronting the Royal Hawaiian
hotel. **Pros:** lots of freebies; in the thick of Waikīkī action. **Cons:** very
busy area; no direct beach access. **TripAdvisor:** "would definitely stay
there again," "reasonably priced," "very comfortable hotel." ✉ *2300*
Kalākaua Ave., Waikīkī ☏ *808/922–4646 or 800/462-6262* ⊕ *www.*
waikikibeachcomber.com ☞ *500 rooms, 7 suites* ♿ *In-room: a/c, refrig-*
erator, Internet. In-hotel: restaurant, room service, bar, pool, children's
programs (ages 5–12), laundry facilities, Wi-Fi hotspot, parking (paid)
▬ *AE, DC, MC, V.*

$$$ 📺 **Hyatt Regency Waikīkī Resort and Spa.** Though it's across the street
RESORT from the Kūhiō Beach section of Waikīkī, the Hyatt is actually on the
oceanfront, as there's no resort between it and the Pacific Ocean. A
pool-deck staircase leads directly to street level, for easy beach access.
An open-air atrium with three levels of shopping, a two-story waterfall, and free nightly live entertainment make this one of the liveliest
lobbies anywhere. An activity center offers kids' programs, including
lei-making lessons, 'ukulele lessons, and field trips to the aquarium and
zoo. **Pros:** public spaces are airy and waterfall is spectacular. **Cons:** in
a very busy and crowded part of Waikīkī. **TripAdvisor:** "service in the

hotel is outstanding," "sandy bottomed water," "hotel is beautiful." ✉ *2424 Kalākaua Ave., Waikīkī* 🕿 *808/923–1234 or 800/633–7313* ⊕ *www.waikiki.hyatt.com* 📞 *1,230 rooms, 18 suites* ⚲ *In-room: a/c, safe, refrigerator, Internet, Wi-Fi. In-hotel: 3 restaurants, room service, bars, pool, gym, spa, children's programs (ages 5–12), parking (paid)* ▭ *AE, D, DC, MC, V.*

$$–$$$
RENTAL
🏨 **'Ilima Hotel.** Tucked away on a residential side street near Waikīkī's Ala Wai Canal, this locally owned 17-story condominium-style hotel is a gem. The glass-wall lobby with koa-wood furnishings, original Hawaiian artwork, and friendly staff create a Hawaiian home-away-from-home. Rates are decent for the spacious studios with kitchenettes and the one- and two-bedroom suites with full kitchens, Jacuzzi baths, cable TV with free HBO and Disney channels, multiple phones, and spacious lānai. It's a two-block walk to Waikīkī Beach, shopping, and Kalākaua Avenue restaurants. The parking is free but limited. When the spots are full, you park on the street. **Pros:** big rooms are great for families. **Cons:** limited hotel parking and street parking can be difficult to find. **TripAdvisor:** "parking is limited," "rooms are large," "staff provided very good service." ✉ *445 Nohonani St., Waikīkī* 🕿 *808/923–1877 or 800/801–9366* ⊕ *www.ilima.com* 📞 *99 units* ⚲ *In-room: a/c, safe, kitchen, Internet. In-hotel: pool, gym, laundry facilities, Wi-Fi hotspot, parking (free)* ▭ *AE, DC, MC, V.*

$$$$
HOTEL
🏨 **Moana Surfrider.** Outrageous rates of $1.50 per night were the talk of the town when the "First Lady of Waikīkī" opened her doors in 1901. The *Hawai'i Calls* radio program was broadcast from the veranda during the 1940s and '50s. Today this historic beauty is still a wedding and honeymoon favorite with a sweeping main staircase and period furnishings in its historic main wing, the Moana. In the late 1950s, the hotel's Diamond Head Tower was built. In the '70s, the Surfrider hotel went up next door; all three merged into one hotel in the 1980s. The newly refurbished Surfrider has oceanfront suites with two separate lānai, one for sunrise and one for sunset viewing. Relax on the private beach or in a cabana by the pool. Enjoy live music and hula at The Banyan Court each evening or dine at the Beach House restaurant. **Pros:** elegant; historic property; best place on Waikīkī Beach to watch hula and have a drink. **Cons:** you might feel you have to tiptoe around formal public spaces. **TripAdvisor:** "shopping and restaurants all around," "like you are stepping back in time," "could improve the service." ✉ *2365 Kalākaua Ave., Waikīkī* 🕿 *808/922–3111, 888/488–3535, or 866/500–8313* ⊕ *www.moana-surfrider.com* 📞 *793 rooms, 46 suites* ⚲ *In-room: a/c, safe, Internet, Wi-Fi. In-hotel: restaurant, room service, bars, pool, beachfront, spa, laundry service, parking (paid)* ▭ *AE, DC, MC, V.*

$–$$
HOTEL
🏨 **Ohana East.** If you want to be in central Waikīkī and don't want to pay beachfront lodging prices, consider the flagship property for Ohana Hotels in Waikīkī. Next to the Sheraton Princess Kaiulani on the corner of Kaiulani and Kūhiō avenues, it's a mere two blocks from the beach and within walking distance of shopping, restaurants, and nightlife. Its location and reasonable rates tend to attract plenty of group travelers. Don't expect any fancy lobbies or outdoor gardens here. Certain rooms on lower floors have no lānai, and some rooms

have showers only. Suites have kitchenettes. **Pros:** close to the beach and reasonable rates. **Cons:** no lānai and very basic public spaces. **TripAdvisor:** "good value for the price," "four minute walk to the beach," "hotel is very basic." ✉ *150 Kaiulani Ave., Waikīkī* ☎ *808/922–5353 or 800/462–6262* ⊕ *www.ohanahotels.com* ↪ *420 rooms, 20 suites* ⚒ *In-room: a/c, safe, kitchen (some), refrigerator, Internet. In-hotel: 3 restaurants, room service, bar, pool, gym, laundry facilities, parking (paid)* ▭ *AE, D, DC, MC, V.*

$$–$$$
RENTAL
▦ **Outrigger Luana.** At the entrance to Waikīkī near Fort DeRussy is this welcoming hotel offering both rooms and condominium units. Luana's two-story lobby is appointed in rich, Hawaiian-wood furnishings with Island-inspired fabrics, along with a mezzanine lounge as comfortable as any living room back home. Units are furnished with the same mix of rich woods with etched accents of pineapples and palm trees. At bedside, hula-dancer and beach-boy lamps add another Hawaiian residential touch. The recreational deck features a fitness center, pool, and barbecue area with tables that can be enclosed cabana-style for privacy when dining outdoors. One-bedroom suites each have two lānai. If you like Hawaiiana and appreciate a bit of kitsch, this is a great option. **Pros:** two lānai in suites; barbecue area (rare for Waikīkī). **Cons:** no direct beach access. **TripAdvisor:** "clean and modern," "very clean, very friendly," "great staff." ✉ *2045 Kalākaua Ave., Waikīkī* ☎ *808/955–6000 or 800/688–7444* ⊕ *www.outrigger.com* ↪ *218 units* ⚒ *In-room: a/c, safe, kitchen (some), Internet. In-hotel: pool, gym, laundry facilities, Wi-Fi hotspot, parking (paid)* ▭ *AE, D, DC, MC, V.*

$$–$$$
HOTEL
▦ **Outrigger Reef on the Beach.** Recent renovations have drastically updated this beachfront property. Improvements include a new entrance that incorporates a Hawaiian voyaging design theme; expanded guest rooms; larger and more contemporary bathrooms, including full-size bathtubs in what was previously an all-shower hotel; and a new signature restaurant, though the Shore Bird and Ocean House remain. What had been a plain but pleasant oceanfront bargain now offers polished elegance in keeping with its prime location. Though the inland Pacific Tower has been renovated more recently, it's worthwhile to go for an ocean view or oceanfront accommodation in the Ocean Tower; other rooms have less enchanting views. New features include smoke-free rooms, flat-screen TVs, and free long distance to the U.S. mainland and Canada. **Pros:** on beach; direct access to Waikīkī Beach Walk. **Cons:** views from non-oceanfront rooms are uninspiring. **TripAdvisor:** "hospitality was exemplary," "food was really good," "large, clean, comfortable beds." ✉ *2169 Kālia Rd., Waikīkī* ☎ *808/923–3111 or 800/688–7444* ⊕ *www.outrigger.com* ↪ *631 rooms, 44 suites* ⚒ *In-room: a/c, refrigerator, Internet. In-hotel: 2 restaurants, bar, pool, gym, spa, beachfront, laundry facilities, Internet terminal, Wi-Fi hotspot, parking (paid)* ▭ *AE, D, DC, MC, V.*

$$–$$$
HOTEL
▦ **Outrigger Waikīkī on the Beach.** This star jewel of Outrigger Hotels & Resorts sits on one of the finest strands of Waikīkī Beach. The guest rooms in the 16-story no-smoking resort have rich dark-wood furnishings, Hawaiian art, and lānai that offer either ocean or Waikīkī-skyline views. The popular Duke's Canoe Club has beachfront concerts under

the stars. Waikīkī Plantation Spa offers Hawaiian seaweed wraps, hot-stone massages, and wedding packages. **Pros:** the best bar on the beach is downstairs; free Wi-Fi in lobby. **Cons:** the lobby feels a bit like an airport with so many people using it as a throughway to the beach. **TripAdvisor:** "staff cannot be equalled," "large room," "great place to gather in Duke's." ⊠ *2335 Kalākaua Ave., Waikīkī* ☎ *808/923–0711 or 800/688–7444* ⊕ *www.outrigger.com* ⤷ *524 rooms, 30 suites* ⚲ *In-room: a/c, safe, kitchen (some), refrigerator, Internet. In-hotel: 3 restaurants, room service, bars, pool, gym, spa, beachfront, children's programs (ages 5–13), laundry service, laundry facilities, Wi-Fi hotspot, parking (paid)* ⊟ *AE, D, DC, MC, V.*

¢   **Royal Grove Hotel.** Two generations of the Fong family have put their
HOTEL   heart and soul into the operation of this tiny (by Waikīkī standards), six-story hotel that feels like a throwback to the days of boarding houses, where rooms were outfitted for function, not style, and served up with a wealth of home-style hospitality at a price that didn't break the bank. During the hot summer months, seriously consider splurging on the highest-end accommodations, which feature air-conditioning, lānai, and small kitchens. The hotel's pool is its social center in the evenings, where you can usually find at least one or more members of the Fong family strumming a 'ukulele, dancing hula, and singing songs in the old Hawaiian style. On special occasions, the Fongs host a potluck dinner by the pool. Little touches that mean a lot include free use of boogie boards, surfboards, beach mats, and beach towels. The hotel is two blocks from Waikīkī's Kūhiō Beach. On property are a tiny sushi bar, a natural foods deli, and an authentic Korean barbecue plate-lunch place. For extra value, inquire about the Grove's weekly and monthly rates. Parking is available in a public lot down the street. **Pros:** very economical Waikīkī option; lots of character. **Cons:** no a/c in some rooms. **TripAdvisor:** "nice lanai," "it's a bargain," "a little dated." ⊠ *151 Uluniu Ave., Waikīkī* ☎ *808/923–7691* ⊕ *www.royalgrovehotel. com* ⤷ *78 rooms, 7 suites* ⚲ *In-room: a/c (some), kitchen. In-hotel: 2 restaurants, pool* ⊟ *AE, D, DC, MC, V.*

$$$–$$$$ **The Royal Hawaiian Hotel.** Fresh off its $85-million makeover, the Pink
HOTEL   Palace of the Pacific is young again. The newly designed entrance is airy and welcoming and the outdoor Mai Tai bar is reopened with its world-famous concoction. Originally built for luxury-cruise passengers, this icon on Waikīkī Beach is now outfitted with modern comfort in historical elegance. A modern tower has since been added, but we're partial to the romance and architectural detailing of the historic wing, with its canopy beds, Queen Anne–style desks, and color motifs that range from soft mauve to soothing sea foam. If you want a lānai for sunset viewing, rooms in the oceanfront tower are your best bet. **Pros:** can't be beat for history; mai tais and sunsets are amazing. **Cons:** history is not cheap. **TripAdvisor:** "bathrooms are beautifully appointed," "service was top notch," "great beach." ⊠ *2259 Kalākaua Ave., Waikīkī* ☎ *888/488–3535, 808/923–7311, or 866/500–8313* ⊕ *www.royal-hawaiian.com* ⤷ *528 rooms, 53 suites* ⚲ *In-room: a/c, refrigerator, Internet. In-hotel: restaurant, room service, pool, gym, spa, beachfront, bar, Internet terminal, parking (paid)* ⊟ *AE, DC, MC, V.*

$$$–$$$$ ⌂ **Sheraton Princess Kaiulani.** This hotel sits across the street from its
HOTEL   sister property, the Moana Surfrider. You can sleep at the Princess Kai-
ulani, taking advantage of the lower rates of a non-beachfront hotel,
oversee the bustle of Waikīkī from your private lānai, and dine at any of
the more-pricey oceanfront Sheratons, charging everything back to your
room at the Princess Kaiulani. Rooms are in two towers—some peer
at the ocean over the Moana's low-rise historic wing. It's a two-minute
stroll to the beach. The hotel's pool is street-side, facing Kalākaua Ave-
nue. **Pros:** in the heart of everything in Waikīkī. **Cons:** no direct beach
access; kids' activities off-site. **TripAdvisor:** "don't go for the cheaper
rooms," "price is very reasonable," "some street noise." ✉ *120 Kai-
ulani Ave., Waikīkī* ☎ *808/922–5811, 888/488–3535, or 866/500–8313*
⊕ *www.princesskaiulani.com* ⇗ *1,142 rooms, 14 suites* ⌂ *In-room: a/c,
Internet. In-hotel: 1 restaurant, room service, bars, pool, gym* ⊟ *AE,
D, DC, MC, V.*

$$$$ ⌂ **Sheraton Waikīkī.** Towering over its neighbors on the prow of
HOTEL   Waikīkī's famous sands, the Sheraton is center stage on Waikīkī Beach.
Designed for the convention crowd, it's big and busy; the ballroom,
one of O'ahu's largest, hosts convention expos, concerts, and box-
ing matches. A glass-wall elevator, with magnificent views of Waikīkī,
ascends 30 stories to the Hano Hano Room with its skyline view, or
hang beachside at Rum Fire with their selection of vintage rums and
ornate fire pits. The resort's best beach is on its Diamond Head side,
fronting the Royal Hawaiian Hotel. Lānai afford views of the ocean,
Waikīkī, or mountains. If you don't shy away from crowds, this could
be the place for you. The advantage here is that you have at your vaca-
tion fingertips a variety of amenities, venues, and programs, as well
as a location smack-dab in the middle of Waikīkī. **Pros:** location in
the heart of everything. **Cons:** busy atmosphere clashes with laid-back
Hawaiian style. **TripAdvisor:** "customer service is #1 here," "rooms
were clean but a bit small," "along the beach." ✉ *2255 Kalākaua
Ave., Waikīkī* ☎ *888/488–3535, 808/922–4422, or 866/500–8313*
⊕ *www.sheratonwaikiki.com* ⇗ *1,695 rooms, 128 suites* ⌂ *In-room:
a/c, refrigerator, Internet. In-hotel: 5 restaurants, room service, bars,
pools, beachfront, gym, children's programs (ages 5–12), laundry ser-
vice, Wi-Fi hotspot, parking (paid)* ⊟ *AE, DC, MC, V.*

$$$$ ⌂ **Trump International Hotel.** This new edition to Waikīkī has been draw-
HOTEL   ing rave reviews since its opening in November 2009. The innovative
sixth-floor lobby allows guests to see over the tree line at Fort DeRussy
to enjoy views of the Pacific while checking in. The rooms are pure
Trump luxury with SubZero fridges, Wolf ranges, and Trump's sig-
nature pillowtop mattresses. The attaché desk will do your grocery
and supply shopping for you at no charge and despite being across
the street from the beach they do have a designated stretch of sand for
guests with umbrellas—they even send you out with a beach bag full
of water, fresh fruit, and a towel. **Pros:** beautifully appointed rooms;
on the edge of Waikīkī so a bit quieter; great views of Friday fireworks.
Cons: must cross street to reach the beach. **TripAdvisor:** "room service
menu is delicious," "modern (top notch appliances)," "pure elegance
all the way." ✉ *223 Saratoga Rd., Waikīkī* ☎ *808/683–7777* ⊕ *www.*

trumpwaikikihotel.com ➴ *1,462 rooms* ⚬ *In-room: a/c, refrigerator, Internet, Wi-Fi. In-hotel: 2 restaurants, room service, bars, gym, spa, pools, laundry service, parking (paid)* ▱ *AE, DC, MC, V.*

$$$$ | **Waikīkī Beach Marriott Resort & Spa.** On the eastern edge of Waikīkī, this
RESORT flagship Marriott sits across from Kūhiō Beach and close to Kapi'olani Park, the zoo, and the aquarium. Deep Hawaiian woods and bold tropical colors fill the hotel's two towers, which have ample courtyards and public areas open to ocean breezes and sunlight. Rooms in the Kealohilani Tower are some of the largest in Waikīkī, and the Paoakalani Tower's Diamond Head–side rooms offer breathtaking views of the crater and Kapi'olani Park. All rooms have private lānai. The hotel's Spa Olakino, owned by Honolulu celebrity stylist Paul Brown, is one of the largest in Waikīkī and specializes in use of Hawai'i-based materials and treatments. Daily activities are offered for children and adults alike. **Pros:** stunning views of Waikīkī; professional service; airy tropical public spaces. **Cons:** noise from Kalākaua Avenue can drown out surf below. **TripAdvisor:** "oceanfront room views are breathtaking," "room for improvement," "great location." ✉ *2552 Kalākaua Ave., Waikīkī* ☎ *808/922–6611 or 800/367–5370* ⊕ *www.marriottwaikiki. com* ➴ *1,310 rooms, 13 suites* ⚬ *In-room: a/c, Internet, Wi-Fi. In-hotel: 6 restaurants, room service, bars, pools, gym, spa, parking (paid)* ▱ *AE, D, MC, V.*

$$$$ | **The Waikiki Edition.** Formerly an annex of the iconic Ilikai Hotel,
HOTEL this first incarnation of the Marriott International boutique chain is a delight. The lobby has the feel of an upscale jazz club, with recessed lighting and bookcases. This vibe continues into the rooms, which while austere are elegant. There are two new pools: one with teak decking, and the other surrounded by 100 tons of sand, creating a beach feel. There are four bars on the premises, each with their own signature cocktails. To attract the younger, hipper set Edition also boasts a nightclub, Crazybox, which is open until 3 am, and room service 24 hours a day. They even boast an outdoor movie theater so guests can enjoy a film under the stars of Waikīkī. This is perhaps the best pick for urbanites who like the feel of a hip, big-city hotel. **Pros:** newly refurbished; great bars and restaurants. **Cons:** not kid-friendly; on the outer edge of Waikīkī. **TripAdvisor:** "nice lobby and nightclub," "great for business travel," "noise from the adjacent main street." ✉ *1775 Ala Moana Blvd., Waikīkī* ☎ *808/943–5800* ⊕ *www.editionhotels.com* ➴ *353 rooms* ⚬ *In-room: a/c, safe, refrigerator. In-hotel: 2 restaurants, bars, room service, bars, pools, gym, spa, laundry services, Wi-Fi hotspot, parking (paid)* ▱ *AE, D, MC, V.*

$$$–$$$$ | **Waikīkī Parc.** Contrasting the stately vintage-Hawaiian elegance of
HOTEL her sister hotel, the Halekūlani, the Waikīkī Parc makes a chic and contemporary statement to its Gen-X clientele, offering the same attention to detail in service and architectural design but lacking the beachfront location and higher prices. The guest rooms in this high-rise complex have modern minimalist furnishings but give a nod to the tropics by keeping plantation-style shutters that open out to the lānai. A complimentary evening manager's reception features wine specially made for the hotel. Its heated pool and sundeck are eight floors up, affording a

bit more privacy and peace for sun-bathers, and guests can take advantage of the spa at the Halekūlani across the street. Nobu Waikīkī, of the world-renowned Nobu restaurant family, opened here in 2007, serving Japanese food with a South American accent. **Pros:** stunningly modern; high-design rooms; great access to Waikīkī Beach Walk. **Cons:** no direct beach access. **TripAdvisor:** "room is a little small," "reasonably priced," "pool was quite small." ⊠ 2233 Helumoa Rd., Waikīkī ☎ 808/921–7272 or 800/422–0450 ⊕ www.waikikiparc.com ⤴ 297 rooms ☖ In-room: a/c, safe, Internet. In-hotel: restaurant, room service, pool, gym, Wi-Fi hotspot, parking (paid) ⊟ AE, D, DC, MC, V.

LĀNAI

Islanders love their porches, balconies, and verandas—all wrapped up in the single Hawaiian word, *lānai*. When booking, ask about the lānai and be sure to specify the view (understanding that top views command top dollars). Also, check that the lānai is not merely a step-out or Juliet balcony, with just enough room to lean against a railing—you want a lānai that is big enough for patio seating.

¢–$
HOTEL
🖼 **Waikīkī Sand Villa.** Families and others looking for an economical rate without sacrificing proximity to Waikīkī's beaches, dining, and shopping return to the Waikīkī Sand Villa year after year. It's on the corner of Kaiulani Avenue and Ala Wai Boulevard, a three-block walk to restaurants and the beach. There's a high-rise tower and a three-story walkup building of studio accommodations with kitchenettes. Rooms are small but well planned. Corner deluxe units with lānai overlook Ala Wai Canal and the golf course. There's a fitness center with 24-hour access. Complimentary Continental breakfast is served poolside beneath shady coconut trees, and the hotel's Sand Bar comes alive at happy hour with a great mix of hotel guests and locals who like to hang out and "talk story." The Sand Bar also has computers and Web cams, so that you cannot only keep in touch with family by email, you can also taunt them with your developing tan. **Pros:** fun bar; economical choice. **Cons:** the noise from the bar might annoy some; 10-minute walk to the beach. **TripAdvisor:** "hard, old mattress covered in plastic," "pool area is just magic," "grill in the bar has great food." ⊠ 2375 Ala Wai Blvd., Waikīkī ☎ 808/922–4744 or 800/247–1903 ⊕ www.sandvillahotel.com ⤴ 214 rooms ☖ In-room: a/c, safe, refrigerator, Internet, Wi-Fi. In-hotel: restaurant, bar, pool, parking (paid) ⊟ AE, D, DC, MC, V.

NORTH SHORE

¢–$
B&B/INN
🖼 **Backpackers Vacation Inn and Plantation Village.** Laid-back Hale'iwa surfer chic at its best, Backpackers is spartan in furnishings, rustic in amenities, and definitely very casual in spirit. At Pūpūkea Beach Marine Sanctuary, otherwise known as Three Tables Beach, it's a short stroll to Waimea Bay. This is the place to catch z's between wave sets. Accommodations in this property's 10 buildings include hostel-type dorm rooms, double rooms (some with a double bed, others with two single beds), studios, and cabins. Some have kitchenettes while others have full kitchens. TVs are available in every building and pay

Turtle Bay Resort

phones and barbecues are on the property. It's a three-minute walk to the supermarket. **Pros:** friendly, laid-back staff; prices you won't find anywhere else. **Cons:** many rooms are plainly furnished. **Trip-Advisor:** "perfect if you wanna get away," "don't expect luxury," "2 minute walk from great beaches." ⊠ *59-788 Kamehameha Hwy., Hale'iwa* ☎ *808/638–7838* ⊕ *www.backpackers-hawaii.com* ⮐ *25 rooms* ⚭ *In-room: no a/c, no phone (some), kitchen (some), no TV (some). In-hotel: laundry facilities* ▭ *MC, V.*

$$$–$$$$
RESORT
Fodor'sChoice
★

The Turtle Bay Resort. Some 880 acres of raw natural Hawai'i landscape are your playground at this glamorous resort on O'ahu's scenic North Shore. On the edge of Kuilima Point, the Turtle Bay has spacious guest rooms averaging nearly 500 square feet, with lānai that showcase stunning peninsula views. In winter, when the big waves roll ashore, you get a front-row seat for the powerful surf. The sumptuous oceanfront beach cottages have Brazilian-walnut floors, teak rockers on the lānai, and beds you can sink right into while listening to the sounds of the ocean. Turtle Bay has a Hans Heidemann Surf School, horse stables, a spa, and the only 36-hole golf facility on O'ahu to keep you busy. There are two swimming pools, one with an 80-foot waterslide. While out exploring Turtle Bay's 12 mi of nature trails, don't be surprised if you suddenly find yourself "*Lost.*" The hit television series often used the resort's beaches, coves, and natural forests for location filming. **Pros:** great open, public spaces in a secluded area of O'ahu. **Cons:** very far from anything else—even Hale'iwa is a 20-minute drive. **TripAdvisor:** "good base for exploring," "beach is really calm," "rooms are showing their age." ⊠ *57-091 Kamehameha Hwy., Box 187, Kahuku* ☎ *808/293–8811 or 800/203–3650* ⊕ *www.turtlebayresort.com* ⮐ *373 rooms, 40 suites, 42 beach cottages, 56 ocean villas* ⚭ *In-room: a/c, refrigerator, Wi-Fi. In-hotel: 4 restaurants, room service, bars, golf courses, tennis courts, pools, gym, spa, beachfront, children's programs (ages 5–12)* ▭ *AE, D, DC, MC, V.*

> ## CONDO COMFORTS
>
> **Foodland.** The local chain has two locations near Waikīkī: Market City (⊠ *2839 Harding Ave., near intersection with Kapahulu Ave. and highway overpass, Kaimukī* ☎ *808/734–6303*) and **Ala Moana Center** (⊠ *1450 Ala Moana Blvd., ground level, Ala Moana* ☎ *808/949–5044*).
> **Food Pantry** sells apparel, beach stuff, and tourist-oriented items (⊠ *2370 Kūhiō Ave., across from Miramar hotel, Waikīkī* ☎ *808/923–9831*). For video and DVD rentals, try **Blockbuster Video** (⊠ *Ala Moana Shopping Center, 451 Piikoi St., Ala Moana* ☎ *808/593–2595*).

WEST (LEEWARD) O'AHU

$$$$
RESORT
☪

Aulani. At this writing, Hawai'i's new Disney Resort and Spa was slated to open in September 2011 on the West side of O'ahu. The 21-acre resort aims to capture the spirit of Hawai'i with a Disney flair and offers a wide range of activities for all ages. Arts and crafts programs, a man-made snorkeling lagoon, and a variety of pools, slides, and a lazy river promise to keep the kids occupied, while the 18,000-square-foot spa, four restaurants, and two lounges will help mom and dad cool their jets. Check the resort's Web site for updates. **Pros:** tons to do on premise; very kid-friendly **Cons:** a long way from Waikīkī. ⊠ *92-1185 Ali'inui Dr., Kō'Ōlina* ☎ *714/520–7001* ⊕ *resorts.disney.go.com/aulani-hawaii-resort* ⤳ *360 rooms, 481 villas* ⚄ *In-room: a/c, safe, kitchen (some), refrigerator, DVD, Internet, Wi-Fi (some). In-hotel: 4 restaurants, room service, bars, pools, gym, spa, beachfront, water sports, children's programs (ages 2–18), laundry facilities, laundry service, Internet terminal, Wi-Fi hotspot, parking (paid)* ☰ *AE, D, DC, MC, V.*

$$$–$$$$
RESORT
♻

🏨 **J W Marriott 'Ihilani Resort & Spa.** Forty-five minutes and a world away from the bustle of Waikīkī, this sleek, 17-story resort anchors the still-developing Ko 'Olina Resort and Marina on O'ahu's Leeward coastline. Honeymooners, NFL Pro Bowlers, and even local residents looking for a Neighbor Island experience without the hassle of catching a flight come to 'Ihilani for first-class R&R. The resort sits on one of Ko 'Olina's seven lagoons and features a lū'au cove, tennis garden, wedding chapel, yacht marina, and a Ted Robinson–designed 18-hole championship golf facility. The 650-square-foot rooms here are luxurious, with lulling color schemes; marble bathrooms with deep soaking tubs; spacious private lānai with teak furnishings; and high-tech control systems for lighting and temperature. Most have ocean views. A rental car is pretty much a necessity here. Most rooms have views. **Pros:** beautiful property; impeccable service; pool is stunning at night. **Cons:** a bit of a drive from Honolulu; rental car a necessity. **TripAdvisor:** "golf course was beautiful," "area is peaceful," "lagoon is a nice addition." ⊠ *92-1001 'Ōlani St., Kapolei* ☎ *808/679–0079 or 800/626–4446* ⊕ *www.ihilani.com* ⤳ *387 rooms, 36 suites* ⚄ *In-room: a/c, refrigerator. In-hotel: 4 restaurants, room service, golf course, tennis courts, pools, spa, beachfront, children's programs (ages 5–12)* ☰ *AE, DC, MC, V.*

$$$–$$$$
HOTEL
♻

🏨 **Marriott Ko 'Olina Beach Vacation Club.** If you have your heart set on getting away to O'ahu's western shores, check out the Marriott, which is primarily a vacation-ownership property. This property does offer nightly rental rates for its rooms, which range from hotel-style standard guest rooms to expansive and elegantly appointed one- or two-bedroom guest villa apartments. Interior decor soothes in rich reds, greens, and creamy soft yellows, with furnishings made of rare Hawaiian koa wood. The larger villas (1,240 square feet) have three TVs, full kitchens, and separate living and dining areas. Situated on 30 acres of Ko 'Olina, fronting a lagoon, this resort has two pools (one with sandy-beach bottom), a fitness center, and four outdoor hot tubs, including one overlooking the ocean that's ideal for sunset soaks. Guests can choose from two restaurants on the property or purchase groceries at The Market, on-site. **Pros:** suites are beautifully decorated and ample for families; nice views. **Cons:** 40-minute drive to Honolulu; ongoing construction at other properties nearby. **TripAdvisor:** "customer service is exceptional," "relaxing getaway for a week or more," "beach is great but is man-made." ⊠ *92-161 Waipahe Pl., Kapolei* ☎ *808/679–4900 or 877/229–4484* ⊕ *www.marriottvacationclub.com* ⤳ *200 units* ⚄ *In-room: a/c, safe, kitchen, DVD, Wi-Fi. In-hotel: 2 restaurants, bar, golf course, tennis courts, pools, gym, beachfront, children's programs (ages 5–12), parking (paid)* ☰ *AE, DC, MC, V.*

Maui

WORD OF MOUTH

"Take a day trip to Pā'ia on Maui's North Shore for lunch (lots of cute restaurants). Some fun shops, and you can take a drive to see the surfers in the big surf partway to Hāna. Drive to the top of Haleakalā and hike partway into the crater (wear layers!). It has odd and majestic scenery you can't see anywhere else."

—BlueSwimmer

WELCOME TO MAUI

TOP REASONS TO GO

★ **The Road to Hāna:** Each curve of this legendary cliff-side road pulls you deeper into the lush green rain forest of Maui's eastern shore.

★ **Haleakalā National Park:** Explore the lava bombs, cinder cones, and silverswords at the gasp-inducing, volcanic summit of Haleakalā, the House of the Sun.

★ **Ho'okipa Beach:** On Maui's North Shore, the world's top windsurfers will dazzle you as they maneuver above the waves like butterflies shot from cannons.

★ **Wai'ānapanapa State Park:** Head to East Maui and take a dip at the stunning black-sand beach or in the cave pool where an ancient princess once hid.

★ **Resorts, Resorts, Resorts:** Opulent gardens, pools, restaurants, and golf courses make Maui's resorts some of the best in the Islands.

1 West Maui. This leeward, sunny area is ringed by resorts and condominiums in areas such as Kā'anapali and Kapalua. Also on the coast is the busy, tourist-oriented town of Lahaina, a former whaling center.

2 South Shore. The leeward side of Maui's eastern half is what most people mean when they say South Shore. This popular area is sunny and warm year-round and is home to Wailea, an upscale resort area.

Honolua
Kapalua
Honokohau
Kahakuloa
Kahana
340
Honokōwai
30
Kā'anapali
WEST MAUI
WEST MAUI MOUNTAINS
Honoapi'ilani Hwy
Kahekili Hwy
Pā'ia
Kahului Bay
Kahului
Wailuku
32
37
TO MOLOKA'I
Lahaina
Waikapu
30
CENTRAL MAUI
311
380
N. Kihei Rd.
Mokulele Hwy
TO LĀNA'I
Honoapi'ilani Hwy
30
Mā'alaea
Mā'alaea Bay
Kīhei
SOUTH SHORE
0   5 mi
0   5 km
Wailea
S. Kihei Rd.
Keawakapu
31
'Ulupalakua
Mākena
Molokini Crater
La Pérouse Bay

3 Central Maui. Between Maui's two mountain areas is Central Maui, the location of the county seat of Wailuku and the commercial center of Kahului. Kahului Airport is here.

4 Upcountry. Island residents affectionately call the regions climbing up the slope of Haleakalā Crater Upcountry. This is farm and ranch country.

5 North Shore. The North Shore has no large resorts, just plenty of picturesque small towns like Pā'ia and Ha'ikū—and great surfing action at Ho'okipa Beach.

6 East Maui and Hāna. The island's northeastern, windward side is largely one great rain forest, traversed by the stunning Road to Hāna. The town of Hāna preserves the slow pace of the past.

GETTING ORIENTED

Maui, the second-largest island in the Hawaiian chain, is made up of two distinct circular landmasses. The smaller, on the western part of the island, consists of 5,788-foot Pu'u Kukui and the rain-chiseled West Maui Mountains. The large landmass composing the eastern half of Maui is Haleakalā, with its cloud-wreathed volcanic peak. Maui has very different areas, from the resorts of sunny West Maui and the South Shore to the ranches of Upcountry and the remote village of Hāna in unspoiled East Maui.

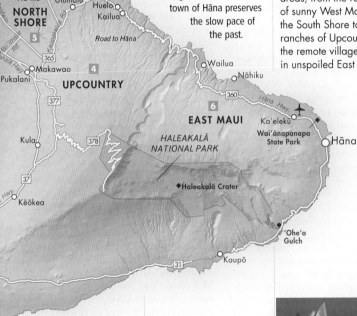

GREAT ITINERARIES

Maui's landscape is incredibly diverse, offering everything from underwater encounters with eagle rays to treks across moonlike terrain. Although daydreaming at the pool or on the beach may fulfill your initial island fantasy, Maui has much more to offer. The following one-day itineraries will take you to our favorite spots on the island.

Beach Day in West Maui

West Maui has some of the island's most beautiful beaches, though many of them are hidden by megaresorts. If you get an early start, you can begin your day snorkeling at Slaughterhouse Beach (in winter, D.T. Fleming Beach is a better option as it's less rough). Then spend the day beach hopping through Kapalua, Nāpili, and Kāʻanapali as you make your way south. You'll want to get to Lahaina before dark so you can spend some time exploring the historic whaling town before choosing a restaurant for a sunset dinner.

Focus on Marine Life on the South Shore

Start your South Shore trip early in the morning, and head out past Mākena into the rough lava fields of rugged La Pérouse Bay. At the road's end, there are areas of the ʻĀhihi-Kīnaʻu Marine Preserve (some are closed at this writing but are due to reopen in August 2012) open to the public that offer good snorkeling. If that's a bit too far afield for you, there's excellent snorkeling at Polo Beach. Head to the right (your right while facing the ocean) for plenty of fish and beautiful coral. Head back north to Kīhei for lunch, and then enjoy the afternoon learning more about Maui's marine life at the outstanding Maui Ocean Center at Māʻalaea.

The Road to Hāna

This cliff-side driving tour through rainforest canopy reveals Maui's most lush and tropical terrain. It will take a full day, especially if you plan to make it all the way to ʻOheo Gulch. You'll pass through communities where old Hawaiʻi still thrives, and where the forest runs unchecked from the sea to the summit. You'll want to make frequent exploratory stops. To really soak in the magic of this place, consider staying overnight in Hāna town. That way you can spend a full day winding toward Hāna, hiking and exploring along the way, and the next day traveling leisurely back to civilization.

Haleakalā National Park, Upcountry, and the North Shore

If you don't plan to spend an entire day hiking in the crater at Haleakalā National Park, this itinerary will at least allow you to take a peek at it. Get up early and head straight for the summit of Haleakalā (if you're jet-lagged and waking up in the middle of the night, you may want to get there in time for sunrise). Bring water, sunscreen, and warm clothing; it's freezing at sunrise. Plan to spend a couple of hours exploring the various lookout points in the park. On your way down the mountain, turn right on Makawao Avenue, and head into the little town of Makawao. You can have lunch here, or make a left on Baldwin Avenue and head downhill to the town of Pāʻia where there are a number of great lunch spots and shops to explore. Spend the rest of your afternoon at Pāʻia's main strip of sand, Hoʻokipa Beach.

3

"Maui nō ka 'oi" is what locals say—it's the best, the most, the top of the heap. To those who know Maui well, there's good reason for the superlatives. The island's miles of perfect-tan beaches, lush green valleys, historic villages, top-notch windsurfing and diving, stellar restaurants and high-end hotels, and variety of art and cultural activities have made it an international favorite.

At 729 square miles, Maui is the second-largest Hawaiian Island, but offers more miles of swimmable beaches than any of the other Islands. The island draws more than 2.5 million visitors each year, and some decide to return for good. Despite growth over the past few decades, the local population is still fairly small, totaling only 119,000.

GEOLOGY

Maui is made up of two volcanoes, one now extinct and the other dormant, that erupted long ago and joined into one island. The resulting depression between the two is what gives the island its nickname, the Valley Isle. West Maui's 5,788-foot Pu'u Kukui was the first volcano to form, a distinction that gives that area's mountainous topography a more weathered look. Rainbows seem to grow wild over this terrain as gentle mists fill the deeply eroded canyons. The Valley Isle's second volcano is the 10,023-foot Haleakalā, where desertlike terrain butts up against tropical forests.

FLORA AND FAUNA

Haleakalā is one of few homes to the rare 'ahinahina (silversword plant). The plant's brilliant silver leaves are stunning against the red lava rock that blankets the walls of Haleakalā's caldera—particularly during blooming season from July to September. A distant cousin of the sunflower, the silversword blooms just once before it dies—producing a single towering stalk awash in tiny fragrant blossoms. Also calling Haleakalā home are a few hundred nēnē—the Hawaiian state bird (related to the Canada goose), currently fighting its way back from near extinction. Maui is one of the better Islands for whale watching, and migrating humpbacks can be seen off the island's coast from December to April, and sometimes into May.

HISTORY

Maui's history is full of firsts—Lahaina was the first capital of Hawai'i and the first destination of the whaling industry (early 1800s), which explains why the town still has that fishing-village vibe; Lahaina was also the first stop for missionaries (1823). Although they suppressed aspects of Hawaiian culture, the missionaries did help invent the Hawaiian alphabet and built a printing press in Lahaina (the first west of the Rockies), which rolled out the news in Hawaiian. Maui also boasts the first sugar plantation in Hawai'i (1849) and the first Hawaiian luxury resort (Hotel Hāna-Maui, 1946).

ON MAUI TODAY

In the mid-1970s, savvy marketers saw a way to improve Maui's economy by promoting the Valley Isle to golfers and luxury travelers. The ploy worked all too well; Maui's visitor count continues to swell. Impatient traffic now threatens to overtake the ubiquitous aloha spirit, development encroaches on agricultural lands, and county planners struggle to meet the needs of a burgeoning population. But Maui is still carpeted with an eyeful of green, and for every tailgater, there's a carefree local on "Maui time" who stops for each pedestrian, whale spout, and sunset.

PLANNING

GETTING HERE AND AROUND

AIR TRAVEL

Most visitors arrive at Kahului Airport in Central Maui. A rental car is the best way to get from the airport to your destination. The major car-rental companies have desks at the airport and can provide a map and directions to your hotel. ■TIP➡ Flights in Maui tend to land around the same time, leading to long lines at car-rental windows. If possible, send one person to pick up the car while the others wait for the baggage.

CAR TRAVEL

A rental car is a must on Maui. It's also one of your biggest trip expenses, especially given the price of gasoline—higher on Maui than on O'ahu or the mainland. If you need to ask for directions, try your best to pronounce the multivowel road names. Locals don't use (or know) highway route numbers and will respond with looks as lost as yours. Also, they will give you directions by the time it takes to get somewhere instead of by the mileage.

Kahului is the transportation hub—the main airport and largest harbor are here. Traffic on Maui's roads can be heavy, especially during the rush hours of 6 am to 8:30 am and 3:30 pm to 6:30 pm.

See Travel Smart Hawai'i for more information on renting a car and driving.

ISLAND
DRIVING TIMES
Driving from one point on Maui to another can take longer than the mileage indicates. It's 52 mi from Kahului Airport to Hāna, but the drive will take you about three hours. As for driving to Haleakalā, the 38-mi

drive from sea level to the summit will take you about two hours. The roads are narrow and winding; you must go at a slow pace. Here are average driving times.

DRIVING TIMES	
Kahului to Wailea	17 mi/30 mins
Kahului to Kā'anapali	25 mi/45 mins
Kahului to Kapalua	36 mi/1 hr, 15 mins
Kahului to Makawao	13 mi/25 mins
Kapalua to Haleakalā	73 mi/3 hrs
Kā'anapali to Haleakalā	62 mi/2 hrs, 30 mins
Wailea to Haleakalā	54 mi/2 hrs, 30 mins
Kapalua to Hāna	88 mi/5 hrs
Kā'anapali to Hāna	77 mi/5 hrs
Wailea to Hāna	69 mi/4 hrs, 30 mins
Wailea to Lahaina	20 mi/45 mins
Kā'anapali to Lahaina	4 mi/15 mins
Kapalua to Lahaina	12 mi/25 mins

RESTAURANTS

There's a lot going on for a place the size of Maui, from ethnic holes-in-the-wall to fancy oceanfront fish houses. Much of it is excellent, but some of it is overpriced and touristy. Choose menu items made with products that are abundant on the island, including local fish. Local cuisine is a mix of foods brought by ethnic groups since the late 1700s, blended with the foods Native Hawaiians have enjoyed for centuries. For a food adventure, take a drive into Central Maui and eat at one of the "local" spots recommended here.

HOTELS

Maui is well known for its lovely resorts, some of them very luxurious; many cater to families. But there are other options, including abundant and convenient apartment and condo rentals for all budgets. The resorts and rentals cluster largely on Maui's sunny coasts, in West Maui and the South Shore. For a different, more local experience, you might spend part of your time at a small bed-and-breakfast. Check Internet sites and ask about discounts and packages.

WHAT IT COSTS					
	¢	$	$$	$$$	$$$$
Restaurants	under $10	$10–$17	$18–$26	$27–$35	over $35
Hotels	under $100	$100–$180	$181–$260	$261–$340	over $340

Restaurant prices are for a main course at dinner. Hotel prices are for two people in a standard double room in high season. Condo price categories reflect studio and one-bedroom rates.

VISITOR INFORMATION

The Hawai'i Visitors & Convention Bureau (HVCB) has plenty general and vacation-planning information for Maui and all the Islands, and offers a free official vacation planner. The Maui Visitors Bureau Web site includes information on accommodations, sights, events, and suggested itineraries for some of the most popular destinations and activities.

Information Hawai'i Visitors & Convention Bureau (⊠ *2270 Kalakaua Ave., Suite 801, Honolulu* ☎ *808/923–1811, 800/464–2924 to order free visitor guide* ⊕ *www.gohawaii.com*). **Maui Visitors Bureau** (⊕ *www.visitmaui.com*).

EXPLORING

Updated by Bonnie Friedman

Maui is more than a sandy beach with palm trees. The natural bounty of this place is impressive. Pu'u Kukui, the 5,788-foot interior of the West Maui Mountains, is one of the earth's wettest spots—annual rainfall of 400 inches has sculpted the land into impassable gorges and razor-sharp ridges. On the opposite side of the island, the blistering lava fields at 'Āhihi-Kīna'u receive scant rain. And just above this desert, *paniolo* (Hawaiian cowboys) herd cattle on rolling, fertile ranchlands reminiscent of northern California. On the island's rugged east side is the lush, tropical Hawai'i of travel posters.

But nature isn't all Maui has to offer—it's also home to a rich and vivid culture. In small towns like Pā'ia and Hāna you can see remnants of the past mingling with modern-day life. Ancient *heiau* (Hawaiian stone platforms once used as places of worship) line busy roadways. Old coral and brick missionary homes now house broadcasting networks. The antique smokestacks of sugar mills tower above communities where the children blend English, Hawaiian, Japanese, Chinese, Portuguese, Filipino, and more into one colorful language. Hawai'i is a melting pot like no other. Visiting an eclectic mom-and-pop shop (like Komoda Store & Bakery) can feel like stepping into another country, or back in time. The more you look here, the more you will find.

WEST MAUI

Separated from the remainder of the island by steep *pali* (cliffs), West Maui has a reputation for attitude and action. Once upon a time, this was the haunt of whalers, missionaries, and the kings and queens of Hawai'i; now it's one of Maui's main resort areas. Lahaina Town was not only once the kingdom's capital but also the *ali'i's* (royalty's) playground. Today the main drag, Front Street, is crowded with T-shirt and trinket shops, art exhibits, and restaurants. Farther north is Kā'anapali, Maui's first planned resort area. Its first hotel, the Sheraton, was opened in 1963. Since then, resorts, luxury condominiums, and a shopping center have sprung up along the white-sand beaches, with championship golf courses across the road. A few miles farther up the coast is the ultimate in West Maui luxury, the resort area of Kapalua. In between, dozens of condominiums and strip malls line both the *makai* (toward

Old Lahaina Lū'au: "A beautiful picture while waiting for the best lū'au in Hawai'i." –Tammy Davis, Fodors.com photo contest participant.

the sea) and *mauka* (toward the mountains) sides of the highway. There are gems here, too, like Nāpili Bay and its crescent of sand.

LAHAINA

27 mi west of Kahului; 4 mi south of Kā'anapali.

Today Lahaina may best be described as either charming or tacky, depending on your point of view—and opinions do differ. Too many T-shirt shops have supplanted ethnic mom-and-pops, but there are some excellent restaurants and interesting galleries. Sunset cruises and other excursions depart from Lahaina Harbor. Happily, at the far south end of town an important ancient site—Moku'ula—is being excavated and restored. ■TIP➔ If you arrange to spend a Friday afternoon exploring Front Street, you can dine in town and hang around for Art Night, when the galleries stay open into the evening and entertainment fills the streets.

GETTING HERE AND AROUND

It's about a 45-minute drive from Kahului Airport to Lahaina (take Route 380 to Route 30) depending on the traffic on this heavily traveled route. Traffic can be slow around Lahaina, especially between 4 and 6 pm. Shuttles and taxis are available from Kahului Airport. The Maui Bus Lahaina Islander route runs from Queen Ka'ahumanu Center in Kahului to the Wharf Cinema Center on Front Street, Lahaina's main thoroughfare.

TOP ATTRACTIONS

★ **Baldwin Home Museum.** Start at this informative museum if you want some insight into 19th-century Hawai'i. Begun in 1834 and completed the following year, the coral and stone house was originally home to missionary Dr. Dwight Baldwin and his family. The building has been

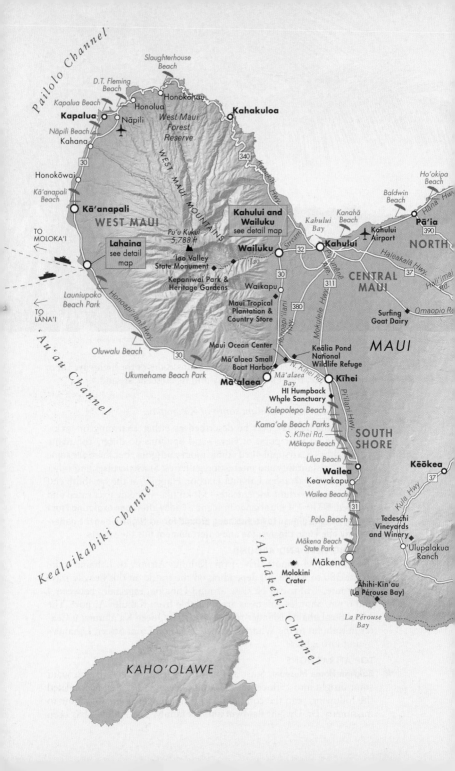

Maui

PACIFIC OCEAN

36

Haʻikū

365   Ulumalu

Twin Falls

Kailua   Huelo

Waikamoi
Nature Trail

Kaupakalua Rd.

SHORE

Baldwin Ave.

Hui Noʻeau Visual
Arts Center

Makawao

365

Pukalani

377

UPCOUNTRY

Kaumahina State
Wayside Park

Puahokamoa Stream

Honomanū Bay

Keʻanae Arboretum

Keʻanae
Overlook   Wailua

Wailua Overlook

Nāhiku

Road to Hāna
see detail map

Kula
Hwy.

Haleakalā
Hwy.

Haleakalā
Crater Rd.

Kula

378

Aliʻi Kula
Lavender

Puʻu ʻUlaʻula
10,023 ft

Puʻu ʻUlaʻula
Overlook

Polipoli Spring
State Recreation
Area

Haleakalā
National Park
Headquarters/
Visitor Center

Lēleiwi Overlook

Kalahaku
Overlook

Haleakalā Visitor
Center

Nuaailua Stream

Waikāni
Falls

Kōolau
Forest
Reserve

360

Hāna Lava Tube

Haleakalā
see detail map

Haleakalā
National
Park

Kahikinui
Forest Reserve

Hāna
Airport

Piʻilanihale
Heiau

EAST MAUI
Hāna Forest Reserve

KĪPAHULU VALLEY

Kīpahulu

Kaupō

31

Piʻilani   Hwy.

KANAIO   King's Trail

Waiʻānapanapa
State Park

Hāna Hwy.

Piʻilani Hwy.

Hāna

Red
Sand
Beach

Kōkī
Beach

Hāmoa
Beach

Oheʻo Gulch

Grave of
Charles Lindbergh

ʻAlenuihāhā Channel

N

0   5 mi

0   5 km

TO
THE BIG ISLAND OF HAWAIʻI →

Elevation

feet	meters
10,023	3,055
6,890	2,100
5,910	1,800
4,920	1,500
3,940	1,200
3,280	1,000
2,620	800
1,970	600
1,640	500
1,300	400
990	300
660	200
330	100
feet	meters

carefully restored to reflect the period; many of the original furnishings remain. You can view the family's grand piano, the carved four-poster bed, and most interestingly, Dr. Baldwin's dispensary. During a brief tour conducted by Lahaina Restoration Foundation volunteers, you'll be shown the "thunderpot" and told how the doctor single-handedly inoculated 10,000 Maui residents for smallpox. ⊠ *696 Front St., Lahaina* ☎ *808/661–3262* ⊕ *www.lahainarestoration.org* ✉ *$3 per person, $5 per couple; $4 per person, $6 per couple for candlelight tours* ⊙ *Daily 10–4; also Fri. 6–8:30 candlelight tours.*

Banyan Tree. Planted in 1873, this massive tree is the largest of its kind in the state and provides a welcome retreat for weary locals and visitors who come to sit under its awesome branches. ■TIP➔ **The Banyan Tree is a popular and hard-to-miss meeting place if your party splits up for independent exploring.** It's also a terrific spot to be when the sun sets—mynah birds settle in here for a screeching symphony, which can be an event in itself. ⊠ *Front St. between Hotel and Canal Sts., Lahaina.*

WALKING TOURS

Lahaina's fascinating side streets are best explored on foot. Both the Baldwin Home and the Lahaina Court House offer free self-guided walking-tour brochures and maps. The Court House booklet is often recommended and includes more than 50 sites. The Baldwin Home brochure is less well known but, in our opinion, easier to follow. It details a short but enjoyable loop tour of the town.

Hale Pa'ahao (Old Prison). Lahaina's jailhouse dates to rowdy whaling days. Its name literally means "stuck-in-irons house," referring to the wall shackles and ball-and-chain restraints. The compound was built in the 1850s by convict laborers out of blocks of coral that had been salvaged from the demolished waterfront fort. Most prisoners were sent here for desertion, drunkenness, or reckless horse riding. Today, a wax figure representing an imprisoned old sailor tells his recorded tale of woe. ⊠ *Waine'e and Prison Sts., Lahaina* ✉ *Free* ⊙ *Weekdays 10–4.*

Lahaina Courthouse. The Lahaina Town Action Committee and Lahaina Heritage Museum occupy this charming old government building in the center of town. Pump the knowledgeable staff for interesting trivia and ask for their walking-tour brochure, a comprehensive map to historic Lahaina sites. Erected in 1859 and restored in 1999, the building has served as a customs and courthouse, governor's office, post office, vault and collector's office, and police court. On August 12, 1898, its postmaster witnessed the lowering of the Hawaiian flag when Hawai'i became a U.S. territory. The flag now hangs above the stairway. You'll find terrific museum displays, the active Lahaina Arts Society, and an art gallery. ■TIP➔ **There's also a public restroom.** ⊠ *649 Wharf St., Lahaina* ☎ *808/661–0111 for the Arts Society; 808/667–9175 for the Lahaina Town Action Committee* ⊕ *www.lahaina-arts.com* ✉ *Free* ⊙ *Daily 9–5.*

Fodor'sChoice   **Waiola Church and Waine'e Cemetery.** Better known as Waine'e Church
★   and immortalized in James Michener's *Hawai'i,* the original building

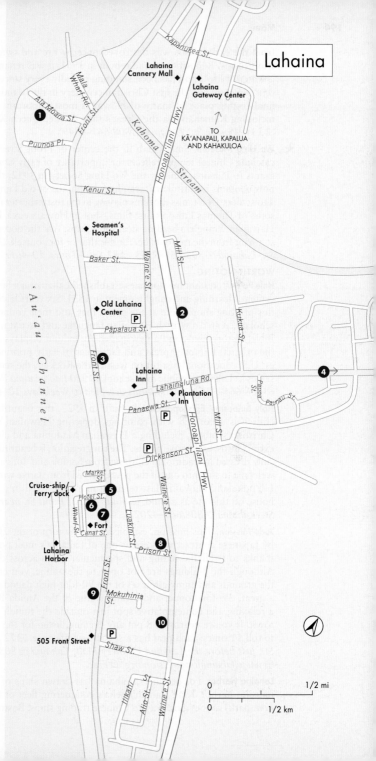

Lahaina

Kapanukea St.

Lahaina
Cannery Mall

Lahaina
Gateway Center

Mala
Wharf Rd.

Front St.

Ala Moana St.

1

Puunoa Pl.

Kahoma Stream

Honoapi'ilani Hwy.

TO
KĀ'ANAPALI, KAPALUA
AND KAHAKULOA

Kenui St.

Seamen's
Hospital

Baker St.

Waine'e St.

Mill St.

Kukua St.

'Au'au

Channel

Old Lahaina
Center

P

Pāpalaua St.

2

3

Front St.

Lahaina
Inn

Lahainaluna Rd

4

Pauoa St.

Paunau St.

Plantation
Inn

Panaewa St.

P

Honoapi'ilani Hwy.

Mill St.

P

Dickenson St.

Market
St.

Cruise-ship/
Ferry dock

5

Hotel St.

6

7

◆ Fort

Wharf St.

Canal St.

Luakini St.

Waine'e St.

8

Prison St.

Lahaina
Harbor

9

Mokuhinia
St.

10

Front St.

P

505 Front Street

Shaw St.

Tikahi
St.

Alio St.

Waine'e St.

0   1/2 mi

0   1/2 km

from the early 1800s was destroyed once by fire and twice by fierce windstorms. Repositioned and rebuilt in 1951, it was renamed Waiola ("water of life") and has been standing proudly every since. The adjacent cemetery was the first Christian cemetery in the Islands and is the final resting place of many of Hawai'i's most important monarchs, including Kamehameha the Great's sacred wife, Queen Keōpūolani. ⊠ *535 Waine'e St., Lahaina* ☎ *808/661–4349.*

★ **Wo Hing Museum.** Smack-dab in the center of Front Street, this eye-catching Chinese temple reflects the importance of early Chinese immigrants to Lahaina. Built by the Wo Hing Society in 1912, the museum now contains beautiful artifacts, historic photos of old Lahaina, and a Taoist altar. Don't miss the films playing in the rustic theater next door—some of Thomas Edison's first films, shot in Hawai'i circa 1898, show Hawaiian wranglers herding steer onto ships. Ask the docent for some star fruit from the tree outside, for the altar or for yourself. ⊠ *858 Front St., Lahaina* ☎ *808/661–5553* ☜ *$2 Sat. –Thurs. 10–4; Fr. 1–8 pm.*

WORTH NOTING

Hale Pa'i. Protestant missionaries established Lahainaluna Seminary as a center of learning and enlightenment in 1831. Six years later, they built this printing shop. Here at the press, they and their young Hawaiian scholars created a written Hawaiian language and used it to produce a Bible, history texts, and a newspaper. An exhibit displays a replica of the original Rampage press and facsimiles of early printing. The oldest U.S. educational institution west of the Rockies, the seminary now serves as Lahaina's public high school. ⊠ *980 Lahainaluna Rd., Lahaina* ☎ *808/661–3262* ☜ *Donations accepted* ۞ *Weekdays 10–4.*

Holy Innocents' Episcopal Church. Built in 1927, this beautiful open-air church is decorated with paintings depicting Hawaiian versions of Christian symbols, including a Hawaiian Madonna and child, rare or extinct birds, and native plants. The congregation is beautiful also, typically dressed in traditional clothing from Samoa and Tonga. Anyone is welcome to slip into one of the pews, carved from native woods. Queen Lili'uokalani, Hawai'i's last reigning monarch, lived in a large grass house on this site as a child. ⊠ *South end of Front St. near Mokuhina St., Lahaina* ☎ *808/661–4202.*

Jodo Mission. This mission, established at the turn of the 20th century by Japanese contract workers, is one of Lahaina's most popular sites, thanks to its idyllic setting and spectacular views across the channel. Although the buildings are not open to the public, you can stroll all the grounds and enjoy glimpses of the 90-foot-high pagoda, as well as a great, 3½-ton copper-and-bronze statue of the Amida Buddha. It's a relaxing and contemplative spot just outside the tumult of Lahaina town. If you're nearby at 8 pm any evening, listen for the temple bell to toll 11 times; each peal has a specific significance. ⊠ *12 Ala Moana St., just before the Lahaina Cannery Mall, Lahaina* ☎ *808/661–4304* ⊕ *www.lahainajodomission.org* ☜ *Free.*

Lahaina Harbor. For centuries, Lahaina has drawn ships of all sizes to its calm harbor. King Kamehameha's conquering fleet of 800 carved *koa* (bark) canoes gave way to Chinese trading ships, Boston Whalers,

U.S. Navy frigates, and finally, a slew of cruise ships, catamarans, and deep-sea fishing operators. During WWII, "a white tide" of navy seamen flooded the town. Stroll past the various tour boats, to see who's had the best luck fishing. If they're filleting their catch, you might glimpse eagle rays underwater snapping up the trimmings. ⊠ *Wharf St., Lahaina* 🖙 *Free.*

☙ **Lahaina–Kāʻanapali & Pacific Railroad.** Affectionately called the Sugarcane Train, Maui's only passenger train is an 1890s-vintage railway that once shuttled sugar but now moves sightseers between Kāʻanapali and Lahaina. This quaint little attraction with its singing conductor is a big deal for Hawaiʻi but probably not much of a thrill for those more accustomed to trains (though children like it no matter where they grew

ISLAND HOPPING

If you have a week or more on Maui, consider taking a day or two for a trip to Molokaʻi or Lānaʻi. Tour operators such as Trilogy offer day-trip packages to Lānaʻi that include snorkeling and a van tour. Ferries to both Islands have room for your golf clubs and mountain bike. (Avoid ferry travel on a blustery day.) If you prefer to travel to Molokaʻi or Lānaʻi by air and don't mind 4- to 12-seaters, you can take a small air taxi. Book with Pacific Wings *(see Air Travel in "Travel Smart Hawaiʻi")*. See Chapters 6 and 7 for more information.

up). ⊠ *1½ blocks north of Lahainaluna Rd. stoplight, at Hinau St., on Honoapiʻilani Hwy., Lahaina* 🕾 *808/661–0080* ⊕ *www.sugarcanetrain. com* 🖙 *Round-trip $22.50 adult; $15.50 child 3–12* ☉ *Daily 10:15–4.*

KĀʻANAPALI AND VICINITY
Kāʻanapali is 4 mi north of Lahaina.

As you drive north from Lahaina, the first resort community you come to is Kāʻanapali, a substantial cluster of high-rise hotels framing a beautiful white-sand beach. This is part of West Maui's famous resort strip. A little farther up the road lie the condo-filled beach towns of Honokōwai, Kahana, and Nāpili, followed by Kapalua.

GETTING HERE AND AROUND
Shuttles and taxis are available from Kahului and West Maui airports. Resorts offer free shuttles between properties and some hotels also provide free shuttles into Lahaina. In the Maui Bus system, the Nāpili Islander begins and ends at Whalers Village in Kāʻanapali and stops at most condos along the coastal road as far north as Nāpili Bay.

EXPLORING
Kāʻanapali. The theatrical look of Hawaiʻi tourism—planned resort communities where luxury homes mix with high-rise hotels, fantasy swimming pools, and a theme-park landscape—all began right here in the 1960s, when clever marketers built this sunny shoreline into a playground for the world's vacationers. Three miles of uninterrupted white-sand beach and placid water form the front yard for this artificial utopia, with its 40 tennis courts and two championship golf courses. The six major hotels here are all worth visiting, if only for a look around, especially the Hyatt Regency Maui, which has a multimillion-dollar art collection and plenty of exotic birds in the lobby. In ancient

MAUI SIGHTSEEING TOURS

Maui is really too big to see all in one day, so tour companies offer specialized tours, visiting either Haleakalā or Hāna and its environs. A tour of Haleakalā and Upcountry is usually a half-day excursion and is offered in several versions by different companies for about $60 and up. The trip often includes stops at a protea farm and at Tedeschi Vineyards, Maui's only winery.

A Haleakalā sunrise tour starts before dawn so that you can get to the top of the dormant volcano before the sun peeks over the horizon. Because they offer islandwide hotel pickup, many sunrise trips leave around 2:30 am.

A tour of Hāna is almost always done in a van, since the winding Road to Hāna just isn't built for bigger buses. Guides decide where you stop for photos. Tours run from $80 to $120.

The key is to ask how many stops you get and how many other passengers will be on board—otherwise you could end up on a packed bus, sightseeing through a window.

Most of the tour guides have been in the business for years and some have taken special classes to learn more about the culture and lore. They expect a tip ($1 per person at least), but they're just as cordial without one.

Polynesian Adventure Tours. This company uses large buses with floor-to-ceiling windows. The drivers are fun and, because they have extensive training, really know the island. Some Haleakalā tours also include visits to ʻīao Valley and Lahaina. ☎ 808/877-4242 or 800/622-3011 ⊕ www.polyad.com.

Roberts Hawaiʻi Tours. This is one of the state's largest tour companies, and its staff can arrange tours with bilingual guides if asked ahead of time. Eleven-hour trips venture out to Kaupo, the wild area past Hāna. ☎ 808/871-6226 or 866/898-2519 ⊕ www.robertshawaii.com.

Temptation Tours. Temptation Tours has targeted members of the affluent older crowd. Tours in plush eight-passenger limo-vans explore Haleakalā and Hāna, and range from $210 to $360 per person. The "Hāna Sky-Trek" includes a return trip via helicopter. ☎ 808/877-8888 or 800/817-1234 ⊕ www.temptationtours.com.

Tour da Food Maui. Maui resident Bonnie Friedman (a Fodor's contributor) guides small, customized food tours that include a couple of holes-in-the-wall some locals don't even know about. Tours leave Tuesday, Wednesday, and Thursday mornings and cost from $145–$180 per person. ⊠ Wailuku ☎ 808/242-8383 ⊕ www.tourdafoodmaui.com.

times, this area was known for its bountiful fishing (especially lobster) and its seaside cliffs. Puʻu Kekaʻa, today incorrectly referred to as "Black Rock," was a *lele*, a place in ancient Hawaiʻi from which souls leaped into the afterlife. (Today this site is near the Sheraton Maui.) But times changed and the sleepy fishing village was washed away by the wave of Hawaiʻi's new economy: tourism. ⊠ 2435 Kāʻanapali Pkwy., Kāʻanapali.

Whalers Village. While the kids hit Honolua Surf Company, mom can peruse Louis Vuitton, Coach, and several fine jewelry stores at this casual, classy mall fronting Kā'anapali Beach. Pizza and Häagen-Dazs ice cream are available in the center courtyard. At the beach entrance, you'll find a wonderful restaurant, Hula Grill. ⊠ *2435 Kā'anapali Pkwy.* ☎ *808/661–4567* ⊕ *www.whalersvillage.com.*

KAPALUA AND KAHAKULOA

Kapalua is 10 mi north of Kā'anapali and 36 mi west of Kahului.

Upscale Kapalua is north of the Kā'anapali resorts, past Nāpili. At the end of the Honoapi'ilani Highway, you'll find the remote village of Kahakuloa—quite a contrast to Kapalua.

GETTING HERE AND AROUND

Shuttles and taxis are available from Kahului and West Maui airports. The Ritz-Carlton, Kapaua has a resort shuttle within the Kapalua Resort.

EXPLORING

Kahakuloa. The wild side of West Maui and untouched by progress, this tiny village at the north end of Honoapi'ilani Highway is a relic of pre–jet travel Maui. Remote villages similar to Kahakuloa were once tucked away in several valleys of this area. Many residents still grow taro and live in the old Hawaiian way. Driving this route is not for the faint of heart. The unimproved road weaves along coastal cliffs, and there are lots of blind curves; it's not wide enough for two cars to pass in places. Watch out for stray cattle, roosters, and falling rocks. True adventurers will find terrific snorkeling and swimming along this drive, as well as some good hiking trails. ⊠ *North end of Honoapi'ilani Hwy.*

Kapalua. Beautiful and secluded, Kapalua is West Maui's northernmost, most exclusive resort community. First developed in the late 1970s when the luxurious Kapalua Bay Hotel was built, the resort now includes the Ritz-Carlton, posh residential complexes, two golf courses, and the surrounding fields of pineapple. (That first hotel has been razed and replaced with new upscale residences with a spa and a golf club.) The area's distinctive shops and freestanding restaurants cater to dedicated golfers, celebrities who want to be left alone, and some of the world's richest folks. In addition to golf, recreational activities include hiking and snorkeling. Mists regularly envelop the landscape of tall Cook pines and rolling fairways in Kapalua, which is cooler and quieter than its southern neighbors. The beaches here, including Kapalua and D.T. Fleming, are among Maui's finest. ⊠ *Bay Dr., Kapalua.*

NEED A BREAK?

In contrast to Kapalua's high-end glitz, the old **Honolua Store**, just above the Ritz-Carlton, still plies the groceries, fishnets, and household wares it did in plantation times. Hefty plates of 'ono (delicious) local foods are served at the deli until 8 pm. The plate lunches are the quintessential local meal and are popular. ⊠ *504 Office Rd., Kapalua* ☎ *808/669–6128* ☉ *Daily 6 am–8 pm.*

Ideal for snorkeling and swimming, sheltered Kapalua Bay Beach borders the luxurious Kapalua Resort.

THE SOUTH SHORE

Blessed by more than its fair share of sun, the southern shore of Haleakalā was an undeveloped wilderness until the 1970s. Then the sun worshippers found it; now restaurants, condos, and luxury resorts line the coast from the world-class aquarium at Māʻalaea Harbor, through working-class Kīhei, to lovely Wailea, a resort community rivaling those on West Maui. Farther south, the road disappears and unspoiled wilderness still has its way.

Because the South Shore includes so many fine beach choices, a trip here (if you're staying elsewhere on the island) is an all-day excursion—especially if you include a visit to the aquarium. Get active in the morning with exploring and snorkeling, then shower in a beach park, dress up a little, and enjoy the cool luxury of the Wailea resorts. At sunset, settle in for dinner at one of the area's many fine restaurants.

MĀʻALAEA
13 mi south of Kahului; 6 mi west of Kīhei; 14 mi southeast of Lahaina.

Māʻalaea, pronounced Mah-*ah*-lye-*ah,* is not much more than a few condos, an aquarium, and a wind-blasted harbor—but that's more than enough for some visitors. Humpback whales seem to think Māʻalaea is tops for meeting mates. Green sea turtles treat it like their own personal spa, regularly seeking appointments with cleaner wrasses in the harbor. Surfers revere this spot for "Freight Train," reportedly the world's fastest wave.

GETTING HERE AND AROUND

To reach Mā'alaea from Kahului Airport, take Route 380 to Route 30. The town is also a transfer point for many Maui Bus routes.

EXPLORING

Mā'alaea Small Boat Harbor. With only 89 slips and so many good reasons to take people out on the water, this active little harbor needs to be expanded. The Army Corps of Engineers has a plan to do so, but harbor users are fighting it—particularly the surfers, who say the plan would destroy their surf breaks. In fact, the surf here is world-renowned. The elusive spot to the left of the harbor called "freight train" rarely breaks, but when it does, it's said to be the fastest anywhere. ⊠ *Off Honoapi'ilani Hwy., Rte. 30.*

Ⓒ **Maui Ocean Center.** You'll feel as though you're walking from the sea-shore down to the bottom of the reef, and then through an acrylic tunnel in the middle of the sea at this aquarium, which focuses on Hawai'i and the Pacific. Special tanks get you up close with turtles, rays, sharks, and the unusual creatures of the tide pools; allow two hours or so to explore it all. It's not an enormous facility, but it does provide an excellent (though pricey) introduction to the sea life that makes Hawai'i special. The center is part of a complex of retail shops and restaurants overlooking the harbor. Enter from Honoapi'ilani Highway (Route 30) as it curves past Mā'alaea Harbor. ⊠ *192 Ma'alaea Rd., Mā'alaea* ☎ *808/270–7000* ⊕ *www.mauioceancenter.com* ⊠ *$25.50* ☉ *Sept.– June, daily 9–5; July and Aug., daily 9–6.*

Fodor's Choice
★

KĪHEI

9 mi south of Kahului; 20 mi east of Lahaina.

Traffic lights and minimalls may not fit your notion of paradise, but Kīhei offers dependably warm sun, excellent beaches, and a front-row seat to marine life of all sorts. Besides all the sun and sand, the town's relatively inexpensive condos and excellent restaurants make this a home base for many Maui visitors. Years ago, Kīhei was a dusty, dry nondestination. Now about one-third of the Maui population lives here in one of the fastest-growing towns in America. Development is still under way, from a greenway for bikers and pedestrians (under construction) to new homes.

GETTING HERE AND AROUND

Kīhei is a 20-minute ride from Kahului once you're past the heavy traffic on Dairy Road and get on the four-lane Mokulele Highway (Route 311).

EXPLORING

Ⓒ **Hawaiian Islands Humpback Whale National Marine Sanctuary.** Whether the whales are here or not, the sanctuary's Education Center is a great stop for youngsters curious to know how things work underwater. The sanctuary itself includes virtually all the waters surrounding the archipelago; the center is beside a restored ancient Hawaiian fishpond, in prime humpback-viewing territory. Interactive displays and informative naturalists will explain it all. Throughout the year, the center hosts intriguing activities, ranging from moonlight tidal-pool explorations to "Forty-Five-Ton Talks." ⊠ *726 S. Kīhei Rd., Kīhei* ☎ *808/879–2818*

★

MAUI'S BEST FARMERS' MARKETS

Join the locals seeking out Maui-grown fresh produce and flowers.

Farmers' Market of Maui–Honokōwai. From pineapples to corn, the produce at this West Maui open-air market is local and flavorful. Prices are good, too. Colorful tropical flowers and handcrafted items are also available. ⊠ *Lower Honoapi'ilani Hwy., parking lot across from Honokōwai Park, Honokōwai* ☎ *808/669–7004* ⊙ *Mon., Wed., and Fri. 7 am–11 am.*

Farmers' Market of Maui–Kīhei. Tropical produce and flowers along with locally made preserves, baked goods, and crafts are among the bargains. The South Shore location, known as the Suda Store parking lot, is at the west end of Kīhei, next to the ABC Store. ⊠ *61 S. Kīhei Rd., Kīhei* ☎ *808/875–0949* ⊙ *Weekdays 8 am–4 pm.*

Green Dragon Farmers' Market. Maui's only indoor farmer's market, in Central Maui, not only offers fresh flowers, local and organic produce, and Hawaiian arts and crafts but has live entertainment, too. Food vendors sell baked goods, coffee, and more. ⊠ *Kahului Shopping Center, 65 W. Ka'ahumanu Ave., Kahului* ☎ *808/333–2478* ⊙ *7 am–5 pm.*

Maui's Fresh Produce Farmers' Market. Local purveyors showcase their fruits, vegetables, orchids, and crafts in the center courtyard at Queen Ka'ahumanu Shopping Center. ⊠ *Ka'ahmanu Ave., Kahului* ☎ *808/877–4325* ⊙ *Tues., Wed., Fri. 7 am–4 pm.*

Maui Swap Meet. Even locals get up early and go to the Swap Meet for fresh produce and flower bouquets, and hundreds of stalls sell everything from art to didgeridoos. Enter the parking lot from the traffic light at Kahului Beach Road. ⊠ *University of Hawai'i Maui College, Kahului Beach Rd., Kahului* ☎ *808/244–3100* ⊕ *www.mauiexposition.com* ⊙ *Sat. 7 am–1 pm.*

Ono Organic Farms Farmers' Market. The family-owned Ono Farms offers certified organic produce at their roadside market held at the old gas station near Hasegawa General Store. You may find unusual produce including *rambutan* (somewhat like a grape), jackfruit (taste like bananas), and *liliko'i* (passion fruit). ⊠ *Hāna Hwy., Hāna* ☎ *808/248–7779* ⊕ *www.onofarms.com* ⊙ *Sun., Wed., and Thurs. 10–6.*

Upcountry Farmers' Market. Most of Maui's produce is grown Upcountry, so it's all fresh at this market in Kulamalu Town Center at the football field parking lot up from Longs on Route 37 (follow the signs). Farmers offer fruits, flowers, and vegetables, as well as jellies and breads. Go early; everything sells out. ⊠ *Rte. 37, Kula* ⊙ *Sat. 7 am–noon.*

---

or 800/831–4888 ⊕ *www.hawaiihumpbackwhale.noaa.gov* ▱ *Free* ⊙ *Weekdays 10–3.*

☾ ★ **Keālia Pond National Wildlife Reserve.** Natural wetlands have become rare in the Islands, and the 700 acres of this reserve attract migratory birds and other wildlife. Long-legged stilts casually dip their beaks in the shallow waters as traffic shuttles by. If you read the interpretive signs on the boardwalk, you can learn that endangered hawksbill turtles return to the sandy dunes here year after year. Sharp-eyed birders may catch sight of migratory visitors such as an osprey. The boardwalk stretches along the coast by North Kīhei Road; the main entrance to the reserve is on Highway 311 (Mokulele Highway). A new visitor center with the reserve headquarters and exhibits is scheduled to open at the main entrance in mid-2011. ⊠ *N. Kīhei Rd., Kīhei* ☎ *808/875–1582* ⊕ *www. fws.gov/kealiapond* 🖼 *Free* ⊙ *Weekdays 7:30–4.*

WAILEA AND FARTHER SOUTH
15 mi south of Kahului; at the southern border of Kīhei.

Wailea, the South Shore's resort community, is slightly quieter and drier than its West Maui sister, Kāʻanapali. Many visitors cannot pick a favorite, so they stay at both. The luxury of the resorts (edging on the excessive) and the simple grandeur of the coastal views make the otherwise stark landscape an outstanding destination; take time to stroll the coastal beach path. A handful of perfect little beaches, all with public access, front the resorts.

The first two resorts were built here in the late 1970s. Soon a cluster of upscale properties sprung up, including the Four Seasons and the Fairmont Kea Lani. Check out the Grand Wailea Resort's chapel, which tells a Hawaiian love story in stained glass.

GETTING HERE AND AROUND
From Kahului Airport, take Route 311 (Mokulele Highway) to Route 31 (Piʻilani Highway) until it ends in Wailea. Shuttles and taxis are available at the airport. By bus, transfer at Māʻalaea to the Kīhei Islander route of the Maui Bus to reach the Shops at Wailea. There's a resort shuttle, and a paved shore path goes between the hotels.

EXPLORING
ʻAhihi-Kīnaʻu (La Pérouse Bay). South of Mākena Beach, the road fades away into a vast territory of black-lava flows, the result of Haleakalā's last eruption and now a place for aquatic and hiking explorations. Also known as La Pérouse Bay, this is where Maui received its first official visit by a European explorer—the French admiral Jean-François de Galaup, Comte de La Pérouse, in 1786. Before it ends, the road passes through the ʻAhihi-Kīnaʻu Marine Preserve, an excellent place for morning snorkel adventures *(see Chapter 4, Water Sports and Tours).* However, visitors should note that some areas were closed to the public to help protect natural features including unofficial trails to Kalua o Lapa, Kalaeloa (popularly known as "the Aquarium"), and Mokuha (also known as "the Fishbowl"). These areas were due to reopen on August 1, 2012. Some open areas are Waiala Cove and the coastal area along ʻAhihi Bay, including the "Dumps" surf break. This area is also the start of the Hoapili Trail, or "the King's Trail," where you can hike through the remains of one of Maui's ancient villages. ■ TIP➔ Bring water and a hat, as there are no public facilities and little shade, and tread carefully over this culturally important landscape. ⊠ *Just before end of Mākena Alanui Rd., follow marked trails through trees* ⊕ *hawaii.gov/dlnr.*

★ **Coastal Nature Trail.** A 1.5-mile-long paved beach walk allows you to stroll among Wailea's prettiest properties, restaurants, and rocky coves. The trail teems with joggers in the morning hours. The *makai,* or ocean, side is landscaped with exceptionally rare native plants. Look for the silvery *hinahina*, named after the Hawaiian moon goddess because of its color. In winter this is a great place to watch whales. ⊠ *Accessible from Polo or Wailea Beach parks.*

Fodor's Choice
★

Mākena Beach State Park. Although it's commonly known as "Big Beach," its correct name is Oneloa ("long sand"), and that's exactly what it is—a huge stretch of heavenly golden sand without a house or hotel in sight. More than a decade ago, Maui citizens campaigned successfully to preserve this beloved beach from development. It's still wild, lacking in modern amenities (such as plumbing) but frequented by dolphins and turtles; sunsets are glorious. At the end of the beach farthest from Wailea, skimboarders catch air. On the opposite end rises the beautiful hill called Puʻu Ōlaʻi, a perfect cinder cone. A climb over the steep rocks at this end leads to "Little Beach," which, although technically it's illegal, is clothing-optional. On Sunday, it's a mecca for drummers and island gypsies. On any day of the week watch out for the mean shore break—those crisp, aquamarine waves are responsible for more than one broken arm. ⊠ *Off Wailea Alanui Dr.* ⊕ *www.hawaiistateparks. org* ⚑ *Free* ☉ *Weekdays 6–6.*

The Shops at Wailea. Louis Vuitton, Tiffany & Co., and the sumptuous Cos Bar lure shoppers to this elegant mall. Honolulu Coffee brews perfect shots of espresso to fuel those "shop-'til-you-drop" types. The kids can buy logo shirts in Pacific Sun while mom and dad ponder vacation ownership upstairs. Tommy Bahama's, Ruth's Chris, and Longhi's are all good dining options. ⊠ *3750 Wailea Alanui Dr.* ☎ *808/891–6770* ⊕ *www.shopsatwailea.com.*

CENTRAL MAUI

Kahului, where you most likely landed when you arrived on Maui, is the industrial and commercial center of the island. West of Kahului is Wailuku, the county seat since 1950. It's the most charming town in Central Maui, with some good, inexpensive restaurants. Outside of these towns are attractions from museums and historic sites to gardens.

You can combine sightseeing in Central Maui with some shopping at the Queen Kaʻahumanu Center, Maui Mall, and Maui Marketplace. This is one of the best areas on the island to stock up on groceries and supplies, thanks to major retailers including Walmart, Kmart, and Costco. Grocery prices are much higher than on the mainland.

KAHULUI AND WAILUKU

3 mi west of Kahului Airport; 9 mi north of Kīhei; 31 mi east of Kāʻanapali; 51 mi west of Hāna.

The area around Kahului, now Maui's commercial hub, was developed in the early 1950s to meet the housing needs of the large sugarcane interests here, specifically those of Alexander & Baldwin. The company was tired of playing landlord to its many plantation workers and sold land to a developer who promised to create affordable housing. The scheme worked, and "Dream City," the first planned city in Hawaiʻi, was born.

Wailuku is peaceful now—though it wasn't always so. Its name means "Water of Destruction," after the fateful battle in 'Īao Valley that pitted King Kamehameha the Great against Maui warriors. Wailuku was a politically important town until the sugar industry began to decline in the 1960s and tourism took hold. Businesses left the cradle of the West Maui Mountains and followed the new market (and tourists) to the shore. Wailuku houses the county government but has the feel of a town that's been asleep for several decades. The shops and offices now inhabiting Main Street's plantation-style buildings serve as reminders of a bygone era, and continued attempts at "gentrification," at the very least, open the way for unique eateries, shops, and galleries.

GETTING HERE AND AROUND
Heading to Wailuku from the airport, Hāna Highway turns into Ka'ahumanu Avenue, the main thoroughfare between Kahului and Wailuku. Maui Bus system's free Kahului and Wailuku Loops stop at shopping centers, medical facilities, and other points throughout Central Maui.

TOP ATTRACTIONS

★ **Alexander & Baldwin Sugar Museum.** "A&B," Maui's largest landowner, was one of the "Big Five" companies that spearheaded the planting, harvesting, and processing of sugarcane. At this museum, historic photos, artifacts, and documents explain the introduction of sugarcane to Hawai'i and how plantation managers brought in laborers from other countries, changing the Islands' ethnic mix. Exhibits also describe the sugar-making process. Although Hawaiian cane sugar is now being supplanted by cheaper foreign versions—as well as by sugar derived from inexpensive sugar beets—the crop was for many years the mainstay of the Hawaiian economy. You can find the museum in a small, restored plantation manager's house across the street from the post office and the still-operating sugar refinery (smoke billows up when cane is burning). ⊠ *3957 Hansen Rd., Pu'unēnē* ☎ *808/871–8058* ⊕ *www.sugarmuseum. com* 🖃 *$7* ⊗ *Mon.–Sat. 9:30–4:30; last admission at 4.*

Fodor's Choice **Bailey House.** This repository of the largest and best collection of Hawaiian artifacts on Maui—including objects from the sacred island of
★ Kaho'olawe—was first the Wailuku Seminary for Girls and then the home of missionary teachers Edward and Caroline Bailey. Built in 1833 on the site of the compound of Kahekili (the last ruling chief of Maui), the building was occupied by the Bailey family until 1888. Edward Bailey was something of a renaissance man: beyond being a missionary, he was also a surveyor, a naturalist, and an excellent artist. In addition to the fantastic Hawaiian collection, the museum displays a number of Bailey's landscape paintings, which provide a snapshot of the island during his time. There is missionary-period furniture, and the grounds include gardens with native Hawaiian plants and a fine example of a traditional canoe. ⊠ *2375A Main St., Wailuku* ☎ *808/244–3326* ⊕ *www. mauimuseum.org* 🖃 *$7* ⊗ *Mon.–Sat. 10–4.*

Fodor's Choice **'Īao Valley State Monument.** When Mark Twain saw this park, he dubbed
★ it the Yosemite of the Pacific. Yosemite it's not, but it is a lovely deep valley with the curious **'Īao Needle,** a spire that rises more than 2,000

feet from the valley floor. You can take an easy walk from the parking lot across 'Iao Stream and explore the thick, junglelike topography. This park has some lovely short strolls on paved paths, where you can stop and meditate by the edge of a stream or marvel at the native plants and flowers. Locals come to jump from the rocks or bridge into the stream—this isn't recommended. Mist often rises if there has been a rain, which makes being here even more magical. ⊠ *Western end of Rte. 32 ('Iao Valley Rd.)* 🖼 *Free; parking $5 per car (honor system)* ⊗ *Daily 7–7.*

⟳ **Kepaniwai Park & Heritage Gardens.** Picnic facilities and ethnic displays dot the landscape of this county park, a memorial to Maui's cultural roots. Among the displays are an early-Hawaiian *hale* (house), a New England–style saltbox, a Portuguese-style villa with gardens, and dwellings from such other cultures as China and the Philippines. Next door, the **Hawai'i Nature Center** has excellent interactive exhibits and hikes easy enough for children.

The peacefulness here belies the history of the area. During his quest for domination, King Kamehameha the Great brought his troops from the Island of Hawai'i to the Valley Isle in 1790 and waged a successful and particularly bloody battle against the son of Maui's chief, Kahekili, near Kepaniwai Park. An earlier battle at the site had pitted Kahekili himself against an older Hawai'i Island chief, Kalani'ōpu'u. Kahekili prevailed, but the carnage was so great that the nearby stream became known as Wailuku (water of destruction), and the place where fallen warriors choked the stream's flow was called Kepaniwai (damming of the waters). ⊠ *870 'Iao Valley Rd., Wailuku* 🖼 *Free* ⊗ *Daily 7–7.*

Market Street. An idiosyncratic assortment of shops makes Wailuku's Market Street a delightful place for a stroll. Brown-Kobayashi and the Bird of Paradise Unique Antiques are the best shops for interesting collectibles and furnishings. Wailuku Coffee Company started out as a great espresso spot and occasionally offers live entertainment in the evening. On the first Friday of every month Market Street closes to traffic from 6 to 8 for Wailuku's First Friday celebration. The fun includes street vendors, live entertainment, and food. ⊠ *Wailuku.*

★ **Maui Arts & Cultural Center.** You can hear all kinds of music at the MACC (as it's called): the multitiered Castle Theater seats 1,200 people on orchestra, mezzanine, and balcony levels; rock stars play the A&B Amphitheater. But a major draw is the Schaeffer International Gallery, which houses superb rotating art exhibits. The MACC also includes a small black-box theater, an art gallery with interesting exhibits, and classrooms. The building itself is worth a visit: It incorporates work by Maui artists, and its signature lava-rock wall pays tribute to the skills of the Hawaiians. ⊠ *One Cameron Way, above harbor on Kahului Beach Rd., Kahului* ☎ *808/242–2787, 808/242–7469 box office* ⊕ *www.mauiarts.org* ⊗ *Weekdays 9–5.*

WORTH NOTING

Haleki'i-Pihana Heiau State Monument. Stand here at either of the two *heiau* and imagine the king of Maui surveying his domain. That's what Kahekili, Maui's last fierce king, did, and so did Kamehameha the Great after he defeated Kahekili's soldiers. Today the view is most instructive.

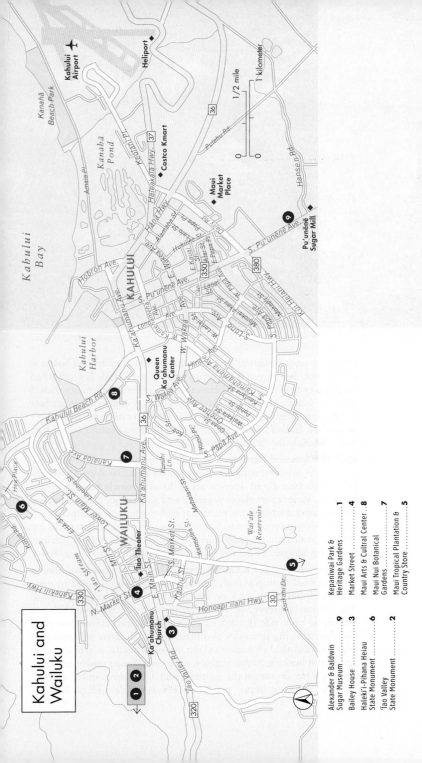

Kahului and Wailuku

Kanahā Beach Park

Kahului Airport

Heliport

Kanahā Pond

Costco Kmart

Maui Market Place

Kahului Bay

Hobron Ave.

KAHULUI

Pu'unēnē Sugar Mill

Queen Ka'ahumanu Center

Kahului Harbor

Kahului Beach Rd.

Hest Place

WAILUKU

'Iao Theater

Ka'ahumanu Church

Wai'ale Reservoirs

Honoapi'ilani Hwy.

1/2 mile

1 kilometer

Puʻunēnē Ave.

S. Puʻunēnē Ave.

S. Wakea Ave.

Kuihelani Hwy.

Kaahumanu Ave.

'Iao Valley Rd.

Kahekili Hwy.

'Iao Stream

Hawaiian Aquarium at the Maui Ocean Center: "We sat and just watched this sight. It was so calming."
–Kevin J. Klitzke, Fodors.com photo contest participant.

Below, the once-powerful 'Īao Stream has been sucked dry and boxed in by concrete. Before you is the urban heart of the island. The suburban community behind you is all Hawaiian Homelands—property owned solely by Native Hawaiians. Currently, access is in dispute, so it's best to call Hawai'i State Parks (☎ 808/984–8109) to make sure you can get to this site. ⊠ *End of Hea Pl., off Kuhio Pl. from Waiehu Beach Rd., Rte. 340, Kahului* ⌷ *Free* ☉ *Daily 7–7.*

Maui Nui Botanical Gardens. The fascinating plants grown on these seven acres are representative of precontact Hawai'i. Both native and Polynesian-introduced species are cultivated—including ice-cream bananas, varieties of sweet potatoes and sugarcane, native poppies, hibiscus, and *anapanapa,* a plant that makes a natural shampoo when rubbed between your hands. Ethnobotany tours and presentations are offered on occasion. ⊠ *150 Kanaloa Ave.* ☎ *808/249–2798* ⊕ *www. mnbg.org* ⌷ *Free; $4 for self-guided tour booklet* ☉ *Mon.–Sat. 8–4.*

Maui Tropical Plantation & Country Store. When Maui's once-paramount crop declined in importance, a group of visionaries decided to open an agricultural theme park on the site of this former sugarcane field. The 60-acre preserve, on Route 30 just outside Wailuku, offers a 30-minute tram ride through its fields with an informative narration covering growing processes and plant types. Children will probably enjoy the historical-characters exhibit as well as hands-on activities such as coconut husking, not to mention some entertaining spider monkeys. There's a restaurant on the property and a "country store" special- izing in "Made in Maui" products. ⊠ *Honoapi'ilani Hwy., Rte. 30,*

Waikapu ☎ 808/244–7643 🖂 *Free;*
$14 for a tram ride with narrated
tour ☉ *Daily 9–4.*

UPCOUNTRY MAUI

WORD OF MOUTH

"If you truly get a day that is wet
all over the island, there are some
small museums in Central Maui
that are interesting. My favorites
are the Bailey House in Wailuku
and the Alexander & Bladwin
Sugar Museum just outside Kahului." –Barbara5353

The west-facing upper slopes
of Haleakalā are locally called
"Upcountry." This region is
responsible for much of Hawai'i's
produce—lettuce, tomatoes, strawberries, sweet Maui onions, and
much, much more. You'll notice
cactus thickets mingled with purple jacaranda, wild hibiscus, and towering eucalyptus trees. Keep an eye out for *pueo*, Hawai'i's native owl,
which hunts these fields during daylight hours.

Upcountry is also fertile ranch land; cowboys still work the fields of the
historic 20,000-acre 'Ulupalakua Ranch and the 32,000-acre Haleakalā
Ranch. ■ TIP➔ This is a great area in which to take an agricultural tour and
learn more about the island's bounty. Lavender, vegetables, cheese, and
wine are among your choices.

A drive to Upcountry Maui from Wailea (South Shore) or Kā'anapali
(West Maui) can be an all-day outing if you take the time to visit Tedeschi Vineyards and the tiny but entertaining town of Makawao. You
may want to cut these side trips short and combine your Upcountry tour
with a visit to Haleakalā National Park. It's a Maui must-see. If you
leave early enough to catch the sunrise from the summit of Haleakalā,
you'll have plenty of time to explore the mountain, have lunch in Kula
or at 'Ulupalakua Ranch, and end your day with dinner in Makawao.

THE KULA HIGHWAY
15 mi east of Kahului; 44 mi east of Kā'anapali; 28 mi east of Wailea.

"Kula . . . " most Mauians say it with a hint of a sigh. Why? It's just
that much closer to heaven. On the broad shoulder of Haleakalā, this
is blessed country. From the Kula Highway most of Central Maui is visible—from the lava-scarred plains of Kenaio to the cruise-ship-lighted
waters of Kahului Harbor. Beyond the central valley's sugarcane fields,
the plunging profile of the West Maui Mountains can be seen in its
entirety, wreathed in ethereal mist. If this sounds too dramatic a description, you haven't been here yet.

GETTING HERE AND AROUND
From Kahului, take Route 37 (Haleakalā Highway), which runs into
Route 377 (Kula Highway). Upper and Lower Kula Highways are both
numbered 377 but join each other at two points.

EXPLORING
★ **Ali'i Kula Lavender.** Reserve a spot for tea or lunch at this lavender farm
with a falcon's view: It's *the* relaxing remedy for those suffering from
too much sun, shopping, or golf. Knowledgeable guides lead tours
through winding paths of therapeutic lavender varieties, proteas, suc-
culents, and rare Maui wormwood. Often, owner Ali'i Chang takes

visitors on a motorized cart tour. The gift shop abounds with many locally made, innovative, lavender-inspired products such as brownies, moisturizing body butters, and fragrant sachets. ✉ *1100 Waipoli Rd., Kula* ☎ *808/878–3004* ⊕ *www.aliikulalavender.com* ✍ *$12 for walking tours; combine with a lunch basket for $37 per person* ⚠ *Reservations essential for group tours* ☉ *Daily 9–4, walking tours leave 5 times a day.*

Fodor's Choice   **Haleakalā National Park.** *See the Golf, Hiking, and Outdoor Activities*
★   *section later in this chapter for information about this park, one of Maui's top attractions.*

Kēōkea. More of a friendly gesture than a town, this tiny outpost is the last bit of civilization before Kula Highway becomes the winding backside road, heading east around to Hāna. A coffee tree pushes through the sunny deck at Grandma's Coffee Shop, the morning watering hole for Maui's cowboys who work at 'Ulupalakua or Kaupō ranch. Kēōkea Gallery next door sells some of the most original artwork on the island. ■TIP→ The only restroom for miles is across the street at the public park, and the view makes stretching your legs worth it.

ↄ   **Surfing Goat Dairy.** It takes goats to make goat cheese, and they've got plenty of both at this 42-acre farm. Tours range from "casual" to "grand" and particularly delight children. If you have the time, both the two-hour grand tour (twice a month) and the "Evening Chores & Milking Tour" are educational and fun. The owners make more than two-dozen kinds of goat cheese, from the plain, creamy "Udderly Delicious" to more-exotic cheeses that include other, sometimes tropical, ingredients. All varieties are available for purchase in the dairy store, along with gift baskets and even goat milk soaps. ✉ *3651 Ōmaopio Rd., Kula* ☎ *808/878–2870* ⊕ *www.surfinggoatdairy.com* ✍ *$7–$25* ☉ *Mon.–Sat. 10–5, Sun. 10–2; check ahead for tour schedule.*

Tedeschi Vineyards and Winery. You can tour the winery and its historic grounds, the former Rose Ranch, and sample the island's only wines: a pleasant Maui Blush, Maui Champagne, and Tedeschi's annual Maui Nouveau. The top-seller, naturally, is the pineapple wine. The tasting room is a cottage built in the late 1800s for the frequent visits of King Kalākaua. The cottage also contains the **'Ulupalakua Ranch History Room,** which tells colorful stories of the ranch's owners, the *paniolo* (Hawaiian cowboy) tradition that developed here, and Maui's polo teams. The old General Store may look like a museum, but in fact it's an excellent pit stop. ✉ *Kula Hwy., 'Ulupalakua Ranch* ☎ *808/878–6058* ⊕ *www.mauiwine.com* ✍ *Free* ☉ *Daily 9–5; tours at 10:30, 1:30, and 3.*

MAKAWAO
10 mi east of Kahului; 7 mi southeast of Pa'ia.

At the intersection of Baldwin and Makawao avenues, this once-tiny town has managed to hang on to its country charm (and eccentricity) as it has grown in popularity. Its good selection of specialized shops makes it a fun place to spend some time.

The district was originally settled by Portuguese and Japanese immigrants who came to Maui to work the sugar plantations and then moved to Upcountry to establish small farms, ranches, and stores. Descendants now work the neighboring Haleakalā and 'Ulupalakua ranches.

Every July 4 the *paniolo* (Hawaiian cowboy) set comes out in force for the Makawao Rodeo. The crossroads of town—lined with shops and down-home eateries—reflects a growing population of people who came here just because they liked it. For those seeking greenery rather than beachside accommodations, there are secluded bed-and-breakfasts around the town.

GETTING HERE AND AROUND

To get to Makawao by car, take Route 37 (Haleakalā Highway) to Pukalanai, then turn left on Makawao Avenue. You can also take Route 36 (Hāna Highway) to Pā'ia and make a right onto Baldwin Avenue. Either way, you'll arrive in the heart of Makawao.

EXPLORING

Hui No'eau Visual Arts Center. "The Hui" is the grande dame of Maui's visual arts scene, and its exhibits are always satisfying. It also offers classes and maintains artists' studios. The lovely grounds might as well be a botanical garden, and the main building, just outside the town of Makawao on the old Baldwin estate, is an elegant two-story Mediterranean-style villa designed in the 1920s by the defining Hawai'i architect C. W. Dickey. ☒ *2841 Baldwin Ave., Makawao* ☎ *808/572–6560* ⊕ *www.huinoeau.com* ☒ *Free* ☺ *Mon.–Sat. 10–4.*

QUICK
BITES

One of Makawao's most famous landmarks is **Komoda Store & Bakery** (☒ *3674 Baldwin Ave.* ☎ *808/572–7261*), a classic mom-and-pop store that has changed little in three-quarters of a century, where you can get a delicious cream puff if you arrive early enough. They make hundreds but sell out each day.

THE NORTH SHORE

Blasted by winter swells and wind, Maui's North Shore draws watersports thrill seekers from around the world. But there's much more to this area of Maui than coastline. Inland, a lush, waterfall-fed Garden of Eden beckons. In forested pockets, wealthy hermits have carved out a little piece of paradise for themselves.

North Shore action centers around the colorful town of Pā'ia and the windsurfing mecca, Ho'okipa Beach. It's a far cry from the more developed resort areas of West Maui and the South Shore. Pā'ia is also a starting point for one of the most popular excursions in Maui, the Road to Hāna *(see Road to Hāna feature in this chapter)*. Waterfalls, phenomenal views of the coast and ocean, and lush rain forest are all part of the spectacular 55-mi drive into East Maui.

PĀ'IA

9 mi east of Kahului; 4 mi west of Ha'ikū.

★ This little town on Maui's North Shore was once a sugarcane enclave, with a mill, plantation camps, and shops. The town boomed during World War II when the marines set up camp in nearby Ha'ikū. The old HC&S sugar mill finally closed and no sign of the military remains, but the town continues to thrive. In the 1970s, Pā'ia became a hippie town as dropouts headed for Maui to open boutiques, galleries, and unusual eateries. In the 1980s windsurfers—many of them European—discovered nearby Hoʻokipa Beach and brought an international flavor to Pāʻia.

GETTING HERE AND AROUND

Route 36 (Hāna Highway) runs directly though Pāʻia; 4 mi later follow the sign to Haʻikū, a short detour off the highway. You can take the Maui Bus from the airport and Queen Kaʻahumanu Shopping Center in Kahului to Pāʻia and on to Haʻikū.

EXPLORING

Fodor'sChoice ★ **Hoʻokipa Beach.** There's no better place on this or any other island to watch the world's finest windsurfers in action. The surfers know the five different surf breaks here by name. Unless it's a rare day without wind or waves, you're sure to get a show. ■ TIP→ **It's not safe to park on the shoulder. Use the ample parking lot at the county park entrance.** ⊠ *2 mi past Pāʻia on Rte. 36.*

QUICK BITES

Charley's Restaurant (⊠ *142 Hāna Hwy.* ☎ *808/579–9453*) is an easygoing saloon-type hangout with pool tables. Breakfasts are big and delicious. **Mana Foods** (⊠ *49 Baldwin Ave.* ☎ *808/579–8078*), the North Shore's natural-foods store, has an inspired deli with wholesome hot and cold items. The long line at **Pāʻia Fishmarket Restaurant** (⊠ *2A Baldwin Ave.* ☎ *808/579–8030*) attests to the popularity of the tasty mahimahi sandwiches.

HAʻIKŪ

13 mi east of Kahului; 4 mi east of Paʻia.

At one time this area vibrated around a couple of enormous pineapple canneries. Both have been transformed into rustic warehouse malls. Because of the post office next door, Old Haʻikū Cannery earned the title of town center. Here you can snack on pizza at Colleen's or get massaged by the students at Spa Luna. Follow windy Haʻikū Road to Pauwela Cannery, the other defunct factory-turned-hangout. Don't fret if you get lost. This jungle hillside is a maze of flower-decked roads that seem to double back upon themselves. Up Kokomo Road is a large *puʻu* (volcanic cinder cone) capped with a grove of columnar pines, and the 4th Marine Division Memorial Park. During World War II, American GIs trained here for battles on Iwo Jima and Saipan.

GETTING HERE AND AROUND

Haʻikū is a short detour off Hāna Highway (Route 36) just past Hoʻokipa Beach Park on the way to Hāna. Haʻikū Road turns into Kokomo Road at the post office.

Continued on page 220

ROAD TO HĀNA

As you round the impossibly tight turn, a one-lane bridge comes into view. Beneath its worn surface, a lush forested gulch plummets toward the coast. The sound of rushing water fills the air, compelling you to search the overgrown hillside for waterfalls. This is the Road to Hāna, a 55-mi journey into the unspoiled heart of Maui. Tracing a centuries-old path, the road begins as a well-paved highway in Kahului and ends in the tiny town of Hāna on the island's rain-gouged windward side.

★ **Fodor's Choice** Despite the twists and turns, the road to Hāna is not as frightening as it may sound. You're bound to be a little nervous approaching it the first time; but afterwards you'll wonder if somebody out there is making it sound tough just to keep out the hordes. The challenging part of the road takes only an hour and a half, but you'll want to stop often and let the driver enjoy the view, too. Don't expect a booming city when you get to Hāna. Its lure is its quiet timelessness. As the adage says, the journey *is* the destination.

During high season, the road to Hāna tends to clog—well, not clog exactly, but develop little choo-choo trains of cars, with everyone in a line of six or a dozen driving as slowly as the first car. The solution: leave early (dawn) and return late (dusk). And if you find yourself playing the role of locomotive, pull over and let the other drivers pass. You can also let someone else take the turns for you—several companies offer van tours, which make stops all along the way (*see Maui Sightseeing Tours box in this chapter*).

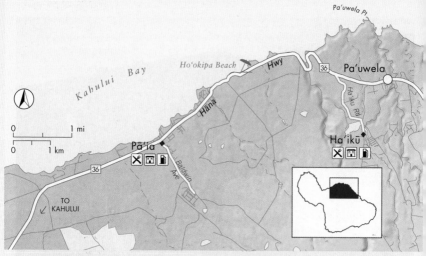

DRIVING THE ROAD TO HĀNA

Begin your journey in Pāʻia, the little town on Maui's North Shore. Be sure to fill up your gas tank here. There are no gas stations along Hāna Highway, and the station in Hāna closes by 6 PM. You should also pick up a picnic lunch. Lunch and snack choices along the way are limited to rustic fruit stands.

About 10 mi past Pāʻia, at the bottom of Kaupakalua Road, the roadside mileposts begin measuring the 36 mi to Hāna town. The road's trademark noodling starts about 3 mi after that. Once the road gets twisty, remember that many residents make this trip frequently. You'll recognize them because they're the ones zipping around every curve. They've seen this so many times before they don't care to linger. Pull over to let them pass.

All along this stretch of road, waterfalls are abundant. Roll down your windows. Breathe in the scent of guava and ginger. You can almost hear the bamboo growing. There are plenty of places to pull completely off the road and park safely. Do this often, since the road's curves make driving without a break difficult. ■ TIP→ If you're prone to carsickness, be sure to take medication before you start this drive. You may also want to stop periodicially.

❶ Twin Falls. Keep an eye out for the fruit stand just after mile marker 2. Stop here and treat yourself to some fresh sugarcane juice. If you're feeling adventurous, follow the path beyond the stand to the paradisiacal waterfalls known as Twin Falls. Once a rough trail plastered with "no trespassing" signs, this treasured spot is now easily accessible. In fact, there's usually a mass of cars surrounding the fruit stand at the trail head. Several deep, emerald pools sparkle beneath waterfalls and offer excellent swimming and photo opportunities.

While this is still private property, the "no trespassing" signs have been replaced by colorfully painted arrows pointing away from residences and toward the falls. ■ TIP→ Bring water shoes for crossing streams along the way. Swim at your own risk and beware: flash floods here and in all East Maui stream areas can be sudden and deadly. Check the weather before you go.

❷ Huelo and Kailua. Dry off and drive on past the sleepy country villages of Huelo (near mile marker 5) and Kailua (near mile marker 6). The little farm town of Huelo has two quaint churches. If you linger awhile, you could meet local residents and learn about a rural lifestyle you might not expect to find on the Islands.

The same can be said for nearby Kailua, home to Alexander & Baldwin's irrigation employees.

❸ Waikamoi Nature Trail. Between mile markers 9 and 10, the Waikamoi Nature Trail sign beckons you to stretch your car-weary limbs. A short (if muddy) trail leads through tall eucalyptus trees to a coastal vantage point with a picnic table and barbecue. Signage reminds visitors QUIET, TREES AT WORK and BAMBOO PICKING PERMIT REQUIRED. Awapuhi, or Hawaiian shampoo ginger, sends up fragrant shoots along the trail.

❹ Puohokamoa Stream. About a mile farther, near mile marker 11, you can stop at the bridge over Puohokamoa Stream. This is one of many bridges you cross en route from Pā'ia to Hāna. It spans pools and waterfalls. Picnic tables are available, but there are no restrooms.

❺ Kaumahina State Wayside Park. If you'd rather stretch your legs and use a flush toilet, continue another mile to Kaumahina State Wayside Park (at mile marker 12). The park has a picnic area, restrooms, and a lovely overlook to the Ke'anae Peninsula. The park is open from 6 AM to 6 PM and admission is free. ☎ 808/984–8109.

⏱ TIMING TIPS

With short stops, the drive from Pā'ia to Hāna should take you between two and three hours one-way. Lunching in Hāna, hiking, and swimming can easily turn the round-trip into a full-day outing, especially if you continue past Hāna to the seven pools and Kīpahulu. If you go that far, you might consider continuing around the "back side" for the return trip. The scenery is completely different and you'll end up in beautiful Upcountry Maui. Since there's so much scenery to take in, we recommend staying overnight in Hāna. It's worth taking time to enjoy the waterfalls and beaches without being in a hurry. Try to plan your trip for a day that promises fair, sunny weather—though the drive can be even more beautiful when it's raining.

Ke'anae Peninsula

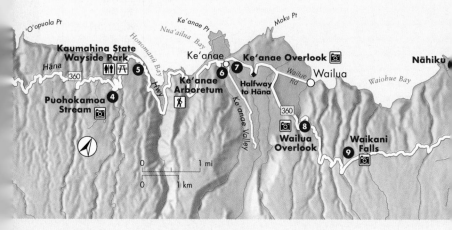

Near mile marker 14, before Keʻanae, you find yourself driving along a cliff side down into deep, lush Honomanū Bay, an enormous valley, with a rocky black-sand beach.

The Honomanū Valley was carved by erosion during Haleakalā's first dormant period. At the canyon's head there are 3,000-foot cliffs and a 1,000-foot waterfall, but don't try to reach them. There's not much of a trail, and what does exist is practically impassable.

❻ Keʻanae Arboretum. Another 4 mi brings you to mile marker 17 and the Keʻanae Arboretum where you can add to your botanical education or enjoy a challenging hike into a forest. Signs help you learn the names of the many plants and trees now considered native to Hawaiʻi. The meandering Piʻinaʻau Stream adds a graceful touch to the arboretum and provides a swimming pond.

You can take a fairly rigorous hike from the arboretum if you can find the trail at one side of the large taro patch. Be careful not to lose the trail once you're on it. A lovely forest waits at the end of the 25-minute hike. Access to the arboretum is free.

You can explore the lovely Keʻanae Peninsula by driving on the unmarked road shortly past the arboretum. It will take you to a small settlement that is a piece of traditional Hawaiʻi, and beyond that to a beach park with crashing surf.

❼ Keʻanae Overlook. A half mile farther down Hāna Highway you can stop at the Keʻanae Overlook. From this observation point, you can take in the quilt-like effect the taro patches create below. The people of Keʻanae are working hard to revive this Hawaiian agricultural art and the traditional cultural values that the crop represents. The ocean provides a dramatic backdrop for the patches. In the other direction there are awesome views of Haleakalā through the foliage.

■TIP→ **Coming up is the halfway mark to Hāna. If you've had enough scenery, this is as good a time as any to turn around and head back to civilization.**

Taro patch viewed from Hāna Highway

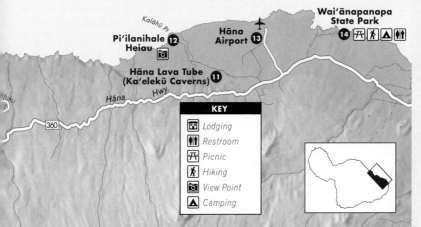

Wai'ānapanapa State Park

Pi'ilanihale Heiau ⑫
Kalāhū Pt.
Hāna Airport ⑬
Hāna Lava Tube (Ka'elekū Caverns) ⑪
Hāna Hwy.
360

KEY

🏨 Lodging
🚻 Restroom
⛲ Picnic
🚶 Hiking
📷 View Point
⛺ Camping

❽ Wailua Overlook. Shortly before mile marker 19, on the mountain side, you find Wailua Overlook. From the parking lot you can see Wailua Canyon, but you have to walk up steps to get a view of Wailua Village. The landmark in Wailua Village is a church made of coral, built in 1860. Once called St. Gabriel's Catholic Church, the current Our Lady of Fatima Shrine has an interesting legend surrounding it. As the story goes, a storm washed enough coral up onto shore to build the church and then took any extra coral back to sea.

Just after mile marker 19, there is another overlook on the ocean side.

❾ Waikani Falls. Past mile marker 21, you hit the best falls on the entire drive to Hāna, Waikani Falls. Though not necessarily bigger or taller than the other falls, these are the most dramatic falls you'll find in East Maui. That's partly because the water is not diverted for sugar irrigation; the taro farmers in Wailua need all the runoff. This is a particularly good spot for photos.

❿ Nāhiku. At about mile marker 25 you see a road that heads down toward the ocean and the village of Nāhiku. In ancient times this was a busy settlement with hundreds of residents. Now only about 80 people live in Nāhiku, mostly native Hawaiians

and some back-to-the-land types. A rubber grower planted trees here in the early 1900s, but the experiment didn't work out, and Nāhiku was essentially abandoned. The road ends at the sea in a pretty landing. This is the rainiest, densest part of the East Maui rain forest.

Coffee Break. Back on the Hāna Highway, about 10 minutes before Hāna town, you can stop for—of all things—espresso. The tiny, colorful **Nāhiku Ti Gallery and Coffee Shop** (between mile markers 27 and 28) sells local coffee, dried fruits and candies, and delicious (if pricey) banana bread. Sometimes the barbecue is fired up and you can try fish skewers or baked breadfruit (an island favorite nearly impossible to find elsewhere). The Ti Gallery sells Hawaiian crafts.

⓫ Hana Lava Tube (Ka'elekū Caverns). If you're interested in exploring underground, turn left onto 'Ula'ino Road, just after mile marker 31, and follow the signs to the Hana Lava Tube. Visitors get a brief orientation before heading into Maui's largest lava tube, which is accentuated with colorful underworld formations.

You can take a self-guided, 30- to 40-minute tour daily, from 10:30 to 4 PM, for $11.95 per person. LED flashlights are provided. Children under five are free with a paid adult. ☎ 808/248–7308 ⊕ *www.mauicave.com*

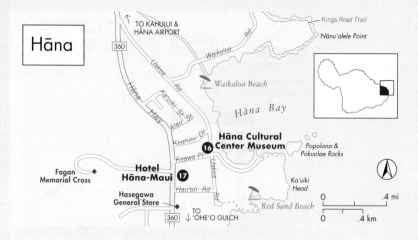

Hāna

TO KAHULUI &
HĀNA AIRPORT
360
Uakea Rd
Waikoloa Rd
Kings Road Trail
Nānu'alele Point
Waikaloa Beach
Hāna Hwy
Ka'uiki St
Hāna Bay
Alau St
Keanini Dr
Hāna Cultural
Center Museum 16
Popolana &
Pokuolae Rocks
Keawa Pl
Fagan
Memorial Cross
Hotel
Hāna-Maui 17
Uakea Rd
Ka'uiki
Head
Hasegawa
General Store
Hau'oli Rd
Red Sand Beach
360
TO
↓ 'OHE'O GULCH
0   .4 mi
0   .4 km

★ 12 Pi'ilanihale Heiau. Continue on 'Ula'ino
Road, which doubles back for a mile, loses its
pavement, and even crosses a stream before
reaching Kahanu Garden and Pi'ilanihale
Heiau, the largest pre-contact monument
in Hawai'i. This temple platform was built
for a great 16th-century Maui king named
Pi'ilani and his heirs. This king also supervised the construction of a 10-foot-wide
road that completely encircled the island.
(That's why his name is part of most of
Maui's highway titles.)

Hawaiian families continue to maintain
and protect this sacred site as they have for
centuries, and they have not been eager to
turn it into a tourist attraction. However,
they now offer a brochure so you can tour
the property yourself for $10 per person.
Tours include the 122-acre Kahanu Garden,
a federally funded research center focusing
on the ethno-botany of the Pacific (best
for those seriously interested in plants).
The heiau and garden are open weekdays
from 10 AM to 2 PM. For a guided tour on
Saturday, reserve through www.ntbg.org.
☎ 808/248–8912

13 Hāna Airport. Back on the Hāna Highway, and less than ½ mi farther, is the
turnoff for the Hāna Airport. Think of
Amelia Earhart. Think of Waldo Pepper.

If these picket-fence runways don't turn
your thoughts to the derring-do of barn-
storming pilots, you haven't seen enough
old movies. Only the smallest planes can
land and depart here, and when none of
them happens to be around, the lonely
wind sock is the only evidence that this is
a working airfield. ☎ 808/248–8471

★ 14 Wai'ānapanapa State Park. Just beyond
mile marker 32 you reach Wai'ānapanapa
State Park, home to one of Maui's only
volcanic-sand beaches and some freshwater caves for adventurous swimmers to
explore. The park is right on the ocean,
and it's a lovely spot in which to picnic,
camp, hike, or swim. To the left you'll
find the black-sand beach, picnic tables,
and cave pools. To the right you'll find
cabins and an ancient trail which snakes
along the ocean past blowholes, sea arches,
and archaeological sites.

The tide pools here turn red several times
a year. Scientists say it's explained by the
arrival of small shrimp, but legend claims
the color represents the blood of Popo'alaea,
a princess said to have been murdered
in one of the caves by her husband, Chief
Ka'akea. Whichever you choose to believe,
the drama of the landscape itself—black

sand, green beach vines, azure water—is bound to leave a lasting impression.

With a permit you can stay in state-run cabins here for less than $45 a night—the price varies depending on the number of people—but reserve early online. They often book up a year in advance. ☎ *808/984–8109* ⊕ *www.hawaiistateparks.org*

⑮ Hāna. By now the relaxed pace of life that Hāna residents enjoy should have you in its grasp, so you won't be discouraged to learn that "town" is little more than a gas station, a post office, a grocery, and the Hasegawa General Store (stuffed with all kinds of oddities and practical items).

Hāna, in many ways, is the heart of Maui. It's one of the few places where the slow pulse of island life is still strong. The town centers on its lovely circular bay, dominated on the right-hand shore by a pu'u called Ka'uiki. A short trail here leads to a cave, the birthplace of Queen Ka'ahumanu. This area is rich in Hawaiian history and legend. Two miles beyond town another pu'u presides over a loop road that passes two of Hāna's best beaches—Kōkī and Hāmoa. The hill is called Ka Iwi O Pele (Pele's Bone). Offshore here, at tiny 'Ālau Island, the demigod Maui supposedly fished up the Hawaiian islands.

Sugar was once the mainstay of Hāna's economy; the last plantation shut down in the '40s. In 1946 rancher Paul Fagan built the **Hotel Hāna-Maui** and stocked the surrounding pastureland with cattle. The cross you see on the hill above the hotel was put there in memory of Fagan. Now it's the ranch and hotel that put food on most tables, though many families still farm, fish, and hunt as in the old days. Houses around town are decorated with glass balls and nets, which indicate a fisherman's lodging.

⑯ Hāna Cultural Center Museum. If you're determined to spend some time and money in Hāna after the long drive, a single turn off the highway onto Uakea Street, in the center of town, will take you to the Hāna Cultural Center Museum. Besides operating a well-stocked gift shop, it displays artifacts, quilts, a replica of an authentic *kauhale* (an ancient Hawaiian living complex, with thatch huts and food gardens), and other Hawaiiana. The knowledgeable staff can explain it all to you. The center is open weekdays 10 to 4. ✉ *4974 Uakea Rd.* ☎ *808/248–8622* ⊕ *www. hanaculturalcenter.org*

⑰ Hotel Hāna-Maui. With its surrounding ranch, the upscale hotel is the mainstay around this beautifully rustic property. The library houses interesting, authentic local Hawaiian artifacts. In the evening, while local musicians play in the lobby bar their friends jump up to dance hula. The Sea Ranch cottages

Hala Trees, Wai'ānapanapa State Park

Hāna

across the road, built to look like authentic plantation housing from the outside, are also part of the hotel. *See Where to Stay for more information.*

Don't be suprised if the mile markers suddenly start descending as you head past Hāna. Technically, Hāna Highway (Route 360) ends at the Hāna Bay. The road that continues south is Pi'ilani Highway (Route 31)—though everyone still refers to it as the Hāna Highway.

18 Hāmoa Beach. Just outside Hāna, take a left on Haneo'o Loop to explore lovely Hāmoa. Indulge in swimming or body-surfing at this beautiful salt-and-pepper beach. Picnic tables, restrooms, and showers beneath the idyllic shade of coconut trees offer a more than comfortable rest stop.

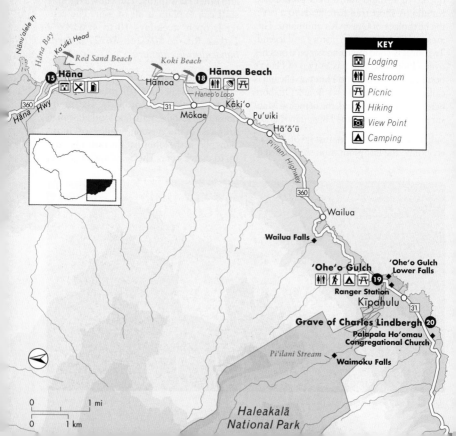

The road leading to Hāmoa also takes you to **Koki Beach**, where you can watch the Hāna surfers mastering the swells and strong currents, and the seabirds darting over 'Ālau, the palm-fringed islet off the coast. The swimming is safer at Hāmoa.

★ ⑲ **'Ohe'o Gulch.** Ten miles past town, at mile marker 42, you'll find the pools at 'Ohe'o Gulch. One branch of Haleakalā National Park runs down the mountain from the crater and reaches the sea here, where a basalt-lined stream cascades from one pool to the next. Some tour guides still call this area Seven Sacred Pools, but in truth there are more than seven, and they've never been considered sacred. You can park here—for a $10 fee—and walk to the lowest pools for a cool swim. The place gets crowded, since most people who drive the Hāna Highway make this their last stop.

If you enjoy hiking, go up the stream on the 2-mi hike to **Waimoku Falls.** The trail crosses a spectacular gorge, then turns into a boardwalk that takes you through an amazing bamboo forest. You can pitch a tent in the grassy campground down by the sea. *See Hiking in Golf, Hiking & Outdoor Activities.*

⑳ **Grave of Charles Lindbergh.** Many people travel the mile past 'Ohe'o Gulch to see the Grave of Charles Lindbergh. You see a ruined sugar mill with a big chimney on the right side of the road and then, on the left, a rutted track leading to Palapala Ho'omau Congregational Church. The simple one-room church sits on a bluff over the sea, with the small graveyard on the ocean side. The world-renowned aviator chose to be buried here because he and his wife, writer Anne Morrow Lindbergh, spent a lot of time living in the area. He was buried here in 1974. Since this is a churchyard, be considerate and leave everything exactly as you found it. Next to the churchyard on the ocean side is a small county park, good for a picnic.

Kaupō Road. The road to Hāna continues all the way around Haleakalā's "back side" through 'Ulupalakua Ranch and into

TROPICAL DELIGHTS

The drive to Hāna wouldn't be as enchanting without a stop or two at one of the countless fruit (and banana bread) and flower stands by the highway. Every 1/2 mi or so a thatched hut tempts passersby with apple bananas (a smaller firmer variety), liliko'i (passion fruit), avocados, or starfruit just plucked from the tree. Leave a few dollars in the can for the folks who live off the land. Huge bouquets of tropical flowers are available for a handful of change, and some farms will ship.

Kula. The desert-like topography, with its grand vistas, is unlike anything else on the island, but the road itself is bad, sometimes impassable in winter, and parts of it are unpaved. Car-rental agencies call it off-limits to their passenger cars and there is no emergency assistance available. The danger and dust from increasing numbers of speeding jeep drivers are making life tough for the residents, especially in Kaupō, with its 4 mi of unpaved road. The small communities around East Maui cling tenuously to the old ways. Please keep that in mind if you do pass this way. If you can't resist the adventure, try to make the drive just before sunset. The light slanting across the mountain is incredible. At night, giant potholes, owls, and loose cattle can make for some difficult driving.

The bridge that was damaged in a 2006 earthquake has been repaired, allowing visitors to once again drive all the way around East Maui. Please note, however, that the road remains rough.

BEACHES

Updated
by Bonnie
Friedman

Of all the beaches in the Hawaiian Islands, Maui's are some of the most diverse. You can find the pristine, palm-lined shores you expect with waters as clear and inviting as sea green glass, but you'll also discover rich red- and black-sand beaches, craggy cliffs with surging whitecaps, and year-round sunsets that quiet the soul. As on the other Islands, all Maui's beaches are public—but that doesn't mean it's not possible to find a secluded cove where you can truly get away from the world.

The island's leeward shores (the South Shore and West Maui) have the calmest, sunniest beaches. Hit the beach early, when the aquamarine waters are as accommodating as bathwater. In summer, afternoon winds can be a sandblasting force, which can chase even the most dedicated sun worshippers away. From November through May, the South and West beaches are also great spots to watch the parade of whales that spend the winter and early spring in Maui's waters.

Windward shores (the North Shore and East Maui) are for the more adventurous. Beaches face the open ocean (rather than other Islands) and tend to be rockier and more prone to powerful swells. This is particularly true in winter, when the North Shore becomes a playground for experienced big-wave riders and windsurfers. Don't let this keep you away completely, however. Some of the island's best beaches are those remote slivers of volcanic sand found on the wild windward shore.

WEST MAUI

West Maui beaches are legendary for their glittering aquamarine waters banked by long stretches of golden sand. Reef fronts much of the western shore, making the underwater panorama something to behold. Parking can be challenging in resort areas. Look for the blue "Shoreline Access" signs to find limited parking and a public path to the beach. Watch out for kiawe thorns when you park off-road: they can puncture tires—and feet.

There are a dozen roadside beaches to choose from on Route 30; these are the ones we like best.

The beaches listed here start in the north at Kapalua and head south past Kāʻanapali and Lahaina.

"Slaughterhouse" (Mokulēʻia) Beach. The island's northernmost beach is part of the Honolua-Mokulēʻia Marine Life Conservation District. "Slaughterhouse" is the surfers' nickname for what is officially Mokuleia. When the weather permits, this is a great place for bodysurfing and sunbathing. Concrete steps and a green railing help you get down the sheer cliff to the sand. The next bay over, Honolua, has no beach but offers one of the best surf breaks in Hawaiʻi. Competitions are often held there; telltale signs are cars pulled off the road and parked in the pineapple field. **Amenities:** None. ⊠ *Mile marker 32 on Rte. 30 past Kapalua*

D.T. Fleming Beach. Because the current can be quite strong, this charming, mile-long sandy cove is better for sunbathing than for swimming or

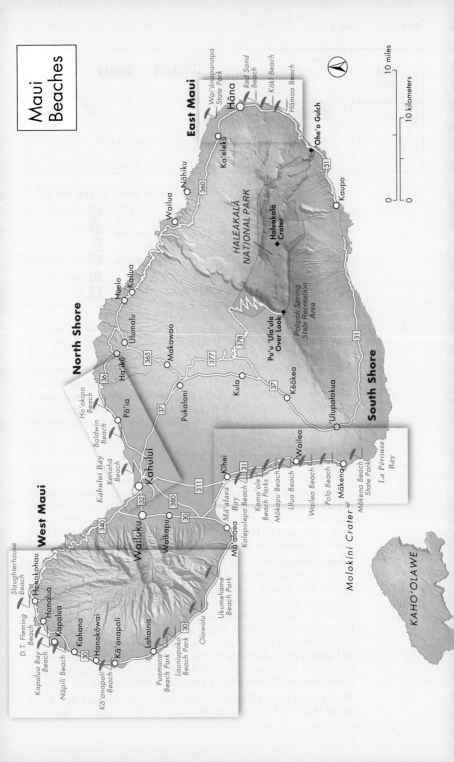

Maui
Beaches

West Maui

North Shore

East Maui

South Shore

Slaughterhouse Beach
D.T. Fleming Beach
Kapalua Bay Beach
Honokohau
Honolua
Nāpili Beach
Kapalua
Kahana
Kāʻanapali Beach
Honokōwai
Kāʻanapali
Lahaina
Puamana Beach Park
Launiupoko Beach Park
Ukumehame Beach Park
Olowalu

340
30
30

Wailuku
Waikapu
Waiʻehu
Kahului
Waiheʻe

32
380
30
311

Kahului Bay
Kanahā Beach
Baldwin Beach
Hoʻokipa Beach
Pāʻia
Haʻikū
Ulumalu
Huelo
Kailua

36
365
37

Makawao
Pukalani

378
377

Kula
Kēōkea

37

Ulupalakua

31

Molokini Crater

Māʻalaea
Māʻalaea Bay
Kalepolepo Beach
Kīhei
Kama ʻole Beach Parks
Mōkapu Beach
Ulua Beach
Wailea
Wailea Beach
Polo Beach
Mākena
Mākena Beach State Park
La Pérouse Bay

31

Wailua
Nāhiku
Keʻanae

360

Kaʻeleku
Hāna
Waiʻānapanapa State Park
Red Sand Beach
Kōkī Beach
Hāmoa Beach

HALEAKALĀ
NATIONAL PARK

Haleakalā Crater

Puʻu ʻUlaʻula Over Look

Polipoli Spring State Recreation Area

 Oheʻo Gulch

Kaupō

31

KAHOʻOLAWE

10 miles

10 kilometers

0

0

water sports. Still, it's one of the island's most popular beaches. It's a perfect place to watch the spectacular Maui sunsets. Part of the beach runs along the front of the Ritz-Carlton Hotel—a good place to grab a cocktail and enjoy the view. **Amenities:** Lifeguard, toilets, showers, picnic tables, grills/firepits, parking lot. ⊠ *Rte. 30, 1 mi north of Kapalua.*

BEACHES KEY	
🚹🚺	*Restroom*
🚿	*Showers*
🏄	*Surfing*
🤿	*Snorkel/Scuba*
🚸	*Good for kids*
🅿	*Parking*

Kapalua Bay Beach. Over the years Kapalua has been recognized by many major travel magazines as one of the world's best beaches. Walk through the tunnel at the end of Kapalua Place and you can see why—the beach fronts a pristine bay good for snorkeling, swimming, and general lazing. Just north of Nāpili Bay, this lovely, sheltered shore often remains calm late into the afternoon, although currents may be strong offshore. Snorkeling is easy here and there are lots of colorful reef fish. This area is quite popular and is bordered by the Kapalua Resort, so don't expect to have the beach to yourself. Walk through the tunnel from the parking lot to get here. **Amenities:** Toilets, showers, parking lot. ⊠ *From Rte. 30, turn onto Kapalua Pl.*

⟳ **Nāpili Beach.** Surrounded by sleepy condos, this round bay is a turtle-
Fodor's Choice filled pool lined with a sparkling white crescent of sand. Sunbathers
★ love this beach, which is also a terrific sunset spot. The shore break is steep but gentle and it's easy to keep an eye on kids here as the entire bay is visible from any point in the water. The beach is right outside the Nāpili Kai Beach Resort, a popular little resort for honeymooners, only a few miles south of Kapalua. **Amenities:** Showers, parking lot. ⊠ *5900 Lower Honoapi'ilani Hwy., look for Nāpili Pl. or Hui Dr.*

⟳ **Kā'anapali Beach.** Stretching from the Sheraton Maui at its northernmost
★ end to the Hyatt Regency Maui at its southern tip, Kā'anapali Beach is lined with resorts, condominiums, restaurants, and shops. If you're looking for quiet and seclusion, this is not the beach for you. But if you want lots of action, spread out your towel here. The center section in front of Whalers Village is also called "Dig Me Beach" and it is one of Maui's best people-watching spots: Folks in catamarans, windsurfers, and stand-up paddleboarders head out from here while the beautiful people take in the scenery. A cement pathway weaves along the length of this 3-mi-long beach, leading from one astounding resort to the next.

The drop-off from Kā'anapali's soft, sugary sand is steep, but waves hit the shore with barely a rippling slap. The area at the northernmost

The sandy crescent of Nāpili Beach on West Maui is a lovely place to wait for sunset.

end (in front of the Sheraton Maui), known as Kekaʻa, was, in ancient Hawaiʻi, a *lele,* or jumping-off place for spirits. It's easy to get into the water from the beach to enjoy the prime snorkeling among the lava rock outcroppings.

Throughout the resort, blue "Shoreline Access" signs point the way to a few free parking stalls and public right-of-way to the beach. Kāʻanapali Resort public beach parking can be found between the Hyatt and the Marriott, between the Marriott and the Kāʻanapali Aliʻi, next to Whalers Village, and at the Sheraton. You can park for a fee at most of the large hotels and at Whalers Village. The merchants in the shopping village will validate your parking ticket if you make a purchase. **Amenities:** Toilets, showers, parking lot. ✉ *Honoapiʻilani Hwy.; follow any of 3 Kāʻanapali exits.*

Launiupoko Beach Park. Launiupoko is the beach park of all beach parks. Both a surf break and a beach, it offers a little something for everyone with its inviting stretch of lawn, soft white sand, and gentle waves. The shoreline reef creates a protected wading pool, perfect for small children. Outside the reef, beginner surfers will find good longboard rides. From the long

DON'T FORGET

All the island's beaches are free and open to the public—even those that grace the front yards of fancy hotels—so you can make yourself at home on any one of them. Some of the prettiest beaches are often hidden by buildings; look for the blue Beach Access signs that indicate public rights-of-way through condominiums, resorts, and other private properties.

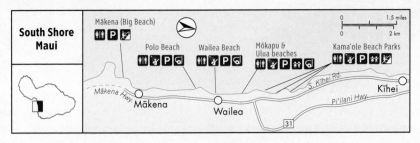

South Shore Maui

Mākena (Big Beach)

Polo Beach   Wailea Beach   Mōkapu & Ulua beaches   Kama'ole Beach Parks

Mākena Hwy   Mākena   Wailea   S. Kīhei Rd.   Kīhei   Pi'ilani Hwy.

31

sliver of beach (good for walking), you can enjoy superb views of the Neighbor Islands, and, landside, of deep valleys cutting through the West Maui Mountains. Because of its endless sunshine and serenity—not to mention its many amenities—Launiupoko draws a crowd on the weekends, but there's space for everyone (and overflow parking across the street). **Amenities:** Toilets, showers, picnic tables, grills/firepits, parking lot. ⊠ *Rte. 30, just south of Lahaina at mile marker 18.*

Olowalu. Olowalu is more an offshore snorkel spot than a beach, but it's a great place to watch for turtles and whales in season. The beach is literally a pullover from the road, which can make for some unwelcome noise if you're looking for quiet. The entrance can be rocky (reef shoes help), but if you've got your snorkel gear it's a 200-yard swim to an extensive and diverse reef. Shoreline visibility can vary depending on the swell and time of day; late morning is best. Except for during a south swell, the waters are usually calm. A half mile north of mile marker 14 you can find the rocky surf break, also called Olowalu. Snorkeling here is along pathways that wind among coral heads. Note: This is a local hangout and can be unfriendly at times. **Amenities:** None. ⊠ *Rte. 30, south of Olowalu General Store at mile marker 14.*

THE SOUTH SHORE

Sandy beach fronts nearly the entire southern coastline of Maui, from Kīhei at the northern end to Mākena at the southern tip. The farther south you go, the better the beaches get. Kīhei has excellent beach parks right in town, with white sand, showers, restrooms, picnic tables, and barbecues. Good snorkeling can be found along the beaches' rocky borders. As good as Kīhei is, Wailea is even better. Wailea's beaches are cleaner, facilities tidier, and views even more impressive. You can take a mile-long walk on a shore path from Ulua to near Polo Beach. Look for blue "Public Shoreline Access" signs for parking along the main thoroughfare, Wailea Alanui. Break-ins have been reported at many beach lots, so don't take valuables. As you head to Mākena, the terrain gets wilder; bring lunch, water, and sunscreen.

The following South Shore beaches are listed from North Kīhei southeast to Mākena.

☺ **Kama'ole I, II, and III.** Three steps from South Kīhei Road are three golden stretches of sand separated by outcroppings of dark, jagged lava rocks. You can walk the length of all three beaches if you're willing to get your feet wet. The northernmost of the trio, Kama'ole I (across from the ABC

Store, in case you forget your sunscreen), offers perfect swimming with a sandy bottom a long way out and an active volleyball court. If you're one of those people who like your beach sans sand, there's also a great lawn for you to spread out on at the south end of the beach. Kamaʻole II is nearly identical, minus the lawn. The last beach, the one with all the people on it, is Kamaʻole III, perfect for throwing a disk or throwing down a blanket. This is a great family beach, complete with a playground, volleyball net, barbecues, kite flying, and, frequently, rented inflatable castles—a must at birthday parties for cool kids.

Locally—and quite disrespectfully, according to Native Hawaiians—known as "Kam" I, II, and III, all three beaches have great swimming and lifeguards. In the morning the water can be as still as a lap pool. Kamaʻole III offers terrific breaks for beginning bodysurfers. ∎TIP➔ The public restrooms have seen better days; decent facilities are found at convenience stores and eateries across the street. **Amenities:** Lifeguard, toilets, showers, picnic tables, grills/firepits, playground, parking lot. ⊠ *S. Kīhei Rd. between Ke Aliʻi Alanui and Keonekai Rds.*

Keawakapu Beach. Who wouldn't love Keawakapu with its long stretch of golden sand, near-perfect swimming, and views of the crater and Kahoʻolawe? It's great fun to walk or jog this beach south into Wailea as the path is lined with over-the-top residences. It's best here in the morning as the winds pick up in the afternoon (beware of sandstorms). Keawakapu has two entrances: one at the Mana Kai Maui Resort (look for the blue "Shoreline Access" sign and the parking at Kilohana Street), and the second at the dead end of Kīhei Road. Toilets are portable. **Amenities:** Toilets, showers, parking lot. ⊠ *S. Kīhei Rd. at Kilohana St.*

☾ **Mōkapu and Ulua.** Look for a little road and public parking lot next to the Wailea Marriott if you are heading to Mōkapu and Ulua beaches. Though there are no lifeguards, families love this place. Reef formations create tons of tide pools for kids to explore and the beaches are protected from major swells. Snorkeling is excellent at Ulua, the beach to the left of the entrance. Mōkapu, to the right, tends to be less crowded. The Renaissance Wailea fronting this beach is closed, and construction of a new resort property is planned for some time in the future. **Amenities:** Toilets, showers, parking lot. ⊠ *Wailea Alanui Dr. north of Wailea Marriott resort.*

Wailea Beach. A road just after the Grand Wailea Resort takes you to Wailea Beach, a wide, sandy stretch with snorkeling, swimming, and, if you're a guest of the Four Seasons Resort, Evian spritzes. If you're not a guest at the Grand Wailea or Four Seasons, the private cabanas and chaise longues can be a little annoying, but any complaint is more than made up for by the calm, unclouded waters and soft, white sand. **Amenities:** Toilets, showers, parking lot. ⊠ *Wailea Alanui Dr. south of Grand Wailea Resort entrance.*

Polo Beach. From Wailea Beach you can walk to this small, secluded crescent fronting the Fairmont Kea Lani resort. Swimming and snorkeling are great here, and it's a good place to whale-watch. As at Wailea Beach, private cabanas occupy prime sandy real estate, but there's plenty of room for you and your towel, and even a nice grass picnic

BEST BEACHES

Maui has miles and miles of great beaches, so how do you choose where to park your towel? Here are some that are sure to satisfy.

BEST FOR FAMILIES

Baldwin Beach, the North Shore. The long, shallow, calm end closest to Kahului is safe even for toddlers—with adult supervision, of course.

Kama'ole III, the South Shore. There's sand, gentle surf, a playground, volleyball net, and barbecues—what more could a family want?

BEST OFFSHORE SNORKELING

Olowalu, West Maui. The beach remains shallow far offshore and there's plenty to see.

Ulua, the South Shore. It's beautiful and the kids can enjoy the tide pools while the adults experience the excellent snorkeling.

BEST SURFING

Ho'okipa, the North Shore. This is a great surfing spot, and one of the best windsurfing beaches in the world, though it's not for beginners.

Honolua Bay, West Maui. One bay over from Slaughterhouse (Mokulē'ia) Beach north of Kapalua, you can find one of the best surf breaks in Hawai'i.

BEST SUNSETS

Kapalua Bay, West Maui. The ambience here is as stunning as the sunset.

Keawakapu, the South Shore. Since most active beachgoers enjoy this gorgeous spot before midafternoon when the wind picks up, it's never crowded at sunset. ■TIP→ Bring a picnic.

BEST FOR SEEING AND BEING SEEN

Kā'anapali Beach, West Maui. The portion of this popular beach that fronts Whalers Village is called "Dig Me"—need we say more?

Wailea Beach, the South Shore. At this beach fronting the ultraluxurious Four Seasons and Grand Wailea resorts, you never know who might be "hiding" in that private cabana!

area. The pathway connecting the two beaches is a great spot to jog or leisurely take in awesome views of nearby Molokini and Kaho'olawe. Rare native plants grow along the ocean, or *makai*, side of the path; the honey-sweet-smelling one is *naio*, or false sandalwood. **Amenities:** Toilets, showers, picnic tables, grills/firepits, parking lot. ⊠ *Wailea Alanui Dr. south of Fairmont Kea Lani resort entrance.*

Fodor's Choice ★ **Mākena (Big Beach).** Locals successfully fought to give Mākena—one of Hawai'i's most breathtaking beaches—state-park protection. It's often mistakenly referred to as "Big Beach," but natives prefer its Hawaiian name, Oneloa. This stretch of deep-golden sand abutting sparkling aqua water is 3,000 feet long and 100 feet wide. It's never crowded, no matter how many cars cram into the lots. The water is fine for swimming, but use caution. ⚠ **The shore drop-off is steep, and swells can get deceptively big.** Despite the infamous "Mākena cloud," a blanket that rolls in during the early afternoon and obscures the sun, it rarely rains here. For a dramatic view of the beach, climb Pu'u Ōla'i, the steep cinder cone

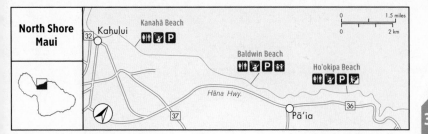

near the first entrance you pass if you're driving south. Continue over the cinder cone's side to discover "Little Beach"—clothing optional by popular practice, although this is technically illegal. On Sunday, free spirits of all kinds crowd Little Beach's tiny shoreline for a drumming circle and bonfire. Little Beach has the island's best bodysurfing (no pun intended). Skim boarders catch air at Mākena's third entrance. Each of the three paved entrances has portable toilets. **Amenities:** Lifeguard, toilets, parking lot. ⊠ *Off Wailea Alanui Dr.*

THE NORTH SHORE

Many of the folks you see jaywalking in Pā'ia sold everything they owned to come to Maui and live a beach bum's life. Beach culture abounds on the North Shore. But these folks aren't sunbathers; they're big-wave riders, windsurfers, or kiteboarders. The North Shore is their challenging sports arena. Beaches here face the open ocean and tend to be rougher and windier than beaches elsewhere on Maui—but don't let that scare you off. On calm days, the reef-speckled waters are truly beautiful and offer a quieter and less commercial beachgoing experience than the leeward shore.

Beaches below are listed from Kahului (near the airport) eastward to Ho'okipa.

Kanahā Beach. Windsurfers, kiteboarders, joggers, and picnicking families like this long, golden strip of sand bordered by a wide grassy area with lots of shade. The winds pick up in the early afternoon, making for the best kiteboarding and windsurfing conditions—if you know what you're doing, that is. The best spot for watching kiteboarders is at the far left end of the beach. Drive through airport and make a right onto the car-rental road (Koeheke); turn right onto Amala Place and take any left (there are three entrances) into Kanahā. **Amenities:** Lifeguard, toilets, showers, picnic tables, grills/firepits, parking lot. ⊠ *Amala Pl.*

🌀 **Baldwin Beach.** A local favorite, right off the highway and just west of
★ Pā'ia town, Baldwin Beach is a big stretch of comfortable white sand. It's a good place to stretch out, jog, or swim, though the waves can sometimes be choppy and the undertow strong. Don't be afraid of those big brown blobs floating beneath the surface; they're just pieces of seaweed awash in the surf. You can find shade along the beach beneath the ironwood trees, or in the large pavilion, a spot regularly used for local parties and community events.

DID YOU KNOW?

Maui's beaches are famous for their variety. Those on the North Shore are generally rockier and get larger swells than beaches in other areas, making them great for wind-surfing. When the water is calm, the reef-dotted waters are lovely. Beachgoing is often quieter here than in the busy resort areas.

The long, shallow pool at the Kahului end of the beach is known as "Baby Beach." Separated from the surf by a flat reef wall, this is where ocean-loving families bring their kids (and sometimes puppies) to practice a few laps. Take a relaxing stroll along the water's edge from the one end of Baldwin Beach to Baby Beach and enjoy the scenery. The view of the West Maui Mountains is hauntingly beautiful from here. **Amenities:** Lifeguard, toilets, showers, picnic tables, grills/firepits, parking lot. ⊠ *Hāna Hwy., 1 mi west of Baldwin Ave.*

★ **Ho'okipa Beach.** If you want to see some of the world's finest windsurfers in action, hit this beach along the Hāna Highway. The sport was largely developed right at Ho'okipa and has become an art to many and a career to some. This beach is also one of Maui's hottest surfing spots, with waves that can be as high as 20 feet. Ho'okipa is not a good swimming beach, nor the place to learn windsurfing, but it's great for hanging out and watching the pros. Bust out your telephoto lens at the cliff-side lookout to capture the aerial acrobatics of board sailors and kiteboarders. **Amenities:** Lifeguard, toilets, showers, picnic tables, grills/firepits, parking lot. ⊠ *Rte. 36, 2 mi east of Pā'ia.*

EAST MAUI AND HĀNA

Hāna's beaches will literally stop you in your tracks—they're that beautiful. Black and red sands stand out against pewter skies and lush tropical foliage creating picture-perfect scenes, which seem too breathtaking to be real. Rough conditions often preclude swimming, but that doesn't mean you can't explore the shoreline.

Beaches below are listed in order from the west end of Hāna town eastward.

Fodor's Choice ★ **Wai'ānapanapa State Park.** Small but rarely crowded, this beach will remain in your memory long after visiting. Fingers of white foam rush onto a black volcanic-pebble beach fringed with green beach vines and palms. Swimming here is both relaxing and invigorating: Strong currents bump smooth stones up against your ankles while seabirds flit above a black, jagged sea arch draped with vines. At the edge of the parking lot, a sign tells you the sad story of a doomed Hawaiian princess. Stairs lead through a tunnel of interlocking Polynesian *hau* (a native tree) branches to an icy cave pool—the secret hiding place of the ancient princess. ⚠ You can swim in this pool, but be wary of mosquitoes! In the other direction, a dramatic 3-mi coastal path continues beyond the campground, past sea arches, blowholes, and cultural sites all the way to Hāna town. Grassy tent sites and rustic cabins that accommodate up to six people are available by reservation only; call ahead for information. **Amenities:** Toilets, showers, picnic tables, grills/firepits, parking lot. ⊠ *Hāna Hwy. near mile marker 32* ☎ *808/984–8109.*

★ **Red Sand Beach (Kaihalulu Beach).** Kaihalulu Beach, better known as Red Sand Beach, is unmatched in its raw and remote beauty. It's not simple to find, but when you round the last corner of the trail and are confronted with the sight of it, your jaw is bound to drop. Earthy-red cliffs tower above the deep maroon–sand beach, and swimmers bob about in a turquoise blue lagoon formed by volcanic boulders just offshore. The

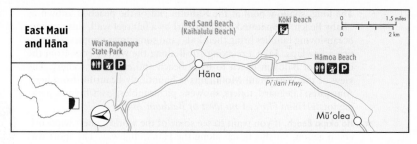

East Maui and Hāna

Wai'ānapanapa State Park

Red Sand Beach (Kaihalulu Beach)

Kōkī Beach

Hāmoa Beach

Hāna

Pi'ilani Hwy.

Mū'olea

0   1.5 miles
0   2 km

experience is like floating in a giant natural bathtub. It's worth spending a night in Hāna to make sure you can get here early and have time to enjoy it before anyone else shows up.

Keep in mind that getting here is not easy, and you have to pass through private property along the way—do so at your own risk. You need to tread carefully up and around Ka'uiki (the red-cinder hill); the cliff-side cinder path is slippery and constantly eroding. Hiking is not recommended in shoes without traction, or in bad weather. By popular practice, clothing on the beach is optional. The beach is at the end of Uakea Road past the baseball field. Park near the community center and walk through the grass lot to the trail below cemetery. **Amenities:** None. ⊠ *Uakea Rd.*

Kōkī Beach. You can tell from the trucks parked alongside the road that this is a favorite local surf spot. ■ TIP→ Watch conditions before swimming or bodysurfing; riptides can be mean. Look for awesome views of the rugged coastline and a sea arch on the left end. *Iwa,* or white-throated frigate birds, dart like pterodactyls over 'Alau islet offshore. **Amenities:** None. ⊠ *Haneo'o Loop Rd., 2 mi south of Hāna town.*

Hāmoa Beach. Why did James Michener describe this stretch of salt-and-pepper sand as the most "South Pacific" beach he'd come across, even though it's in the North Pacific? Maybe it was the perfect half-moon shape, speckled with the shade of palm trees. Perhaps he was intrigued by the jutting black coastline, often outlined by rain showers out at sea, or the pervasive lack of hurry he felt once settled in here. Whatever it was, many still feel the lure. The beach can be crowded but nonetheless relaxing. Expect to see a few chaise longues and a guest-only picnic area set up by the Hotel Hāna-Maui. Early mornings and late afternoons are best for swimming. At times, the churning surf might intimidate beginning swimmers, but bodysurfing can be great here. Hāmoa is half a mile past Kōkī Beach on Haneo'o Loop Road., 2 mi south of Hāna town. **Amenities:** Toilets, showers, picnic tables, parking lot. ⊠ *Haneo'o Loop Rd.*

WATER SPORTS AND TOURS

Updated by Eliza Escaño-Vasquez

Getting into (or onto) the water will be the highlight of your Maui trip. At Lahaina and Mā'alaea harbors, you can board boats for snorkeling, scuba diving, deep-sea fishing, parasailing, and sunset cocktail adventures. You can learn to surf, catch a ferry to Lāna'i, or grab a seat on a fast inflatable raft. From December into May, whale-watching adventures become a top attraction as humpbacks escaping Alaska's frigid winter arrive in Maui's warm waters to frolic, mate, and birth. Along the leeward coastline, from Kā'anapali on the West Shore all the way down to Waiala Cove on the South Shore, you can discover great snorkeling and swimming. If you're a thrill seeker, head out to the North Shore and Ho'okipa, where surfers, kiteboarders, and windsurfers catch big waves and big air.

BODY BOARDING AND BODYSURFING

Bodysurfing and "sponging" (as body boarding is called by the regulars; boogie boarding is another variation) are great ways to catch some waves without having to master surfing—and there's no balance or coordination required. A boogie board (or "sponge") is softer than a hard, fiberglass surfboard, which means you can ride safely in the rough-and-tumble surf zone. If you get tossed around (which is half the fun), you don't have a heavy surfboard nearby to bang your head on, but you do have something to hang onto. Serious spongers invest in a single short-clipped fin to help propel them into the wave.

BEST SPOTS

D.T. Fleming Beach (⊠ *Honoapi'ilani Hwy., below the Ritz-Carlton, Kapalua,* in West Maui, offers great surf almost daily along with some nice amenities: ample parking, restrooms, a shower, grills, picnic tables, and a daily lifeguard. However, caution is advised, especially during winter months when the current and undertow can get rough.

Kama'ole III (⊠ *S. Kīhei Rd.*), between Kīhei and Wailea on the South Shore, is another good spot for bodysurfing and boogie boarding. It has a sandy floor, with 1- to 3-foot waves breaking not too far out. It's often crowded late into the day, especially on weekends when local kids are out of school. Don't let that chase you away—the waves are wide enough for everyone.

On the North Shore, **Pā'ia Bay** (⊠ *Just before Pā'ia town, beyond large community building and grass field*) has waves suitable for spongers and bodysurfers. ■TIP➔ Park in the public lot across the street and leave your valuables at home, as this beach is known for break-ins.

EQUIPMENT

Most condos and hotels have boogie boards available to guests—some in better condition than others (but beat-up boogies work just as well for beginners). You can also pick up a boogie board from any discount shop, such as Kmart or Longs Drugs, for upward of $30.

Auntie Snorkel. You can rent decent boogie boards here for $5 a day, or $15 a week. ⊠ *2439 S. Kīhei Rd., Kīhei* ☎ *808/879–6263.*

West Maui Sports and Fishing Supply. This old country store has been around for more than 20 years and has possibly the best prices on the west side. Body boards go for $2.50 a day or $15 a week. ⊠ *1287 Front St., Lahaina* ☎ *808/661–6252* ⊕ *www.westmauisports.com.*

DEEP-SEA FISHING

If fishing is your sport, Maui is your island. In these waters you'll find 'ahi, *aku* (skipjack tuna), barracuda, bonefish, *kawakawa* (bonito), mahimahi, Pacific blue marlin, ono, and *ulua* (jack crevalle). You can fish year-round and you don't need a license. ■TIP→ **Because boats fill up fast during busy seasons (Christmas, spring break, tournament weeks), consider making reservations before coming to Maui.**

Plenty of fishing boats run out of Lahaina and Māʻalaea harbors. If you charter a private boat, expect to spend in the neighborhood of $700 to $1,000 for a thrilling half day in the swivel seat. You can share a boat for much less if you don't mind close quarters with a stranger who may get seasick, drunk, or worse—lucky! Before you sign up, you should know that some boats keep the catch. They will, however, fillet a nice piece for you to take home. And if you catch a real beauty, you might even be able to have it professionally mounted.

OUTRIGGER-CANOE RACES

Polynesians first traveled to Hawaiʻi by outrigger canoe, and racing the traditional craft is a favorite pastime on the Islands. Canoes were revered in old Hawaiʻi, and no voyage could begin without a blessing, ceremonial chanting, and a hula performance to ensure a safe journey. In Lahaina in mid-May, the two-week **Festival of Canoes** (☏ *808/667–9193* ⊕ *www.visitlahaina.com*) includes arts-and-crafts demonstrations, a chance for international canoe enthusiasts to mingle and observe how Polynesian vessels are rigged, and the launching of a "Parade of Canoes."

You're expected to bring your own lunch and nonglass beverages. (Shop the night before; it's hard to find snacks at 6 am.) Boats supply coolers, ice, and bait. 10% to 20% tips are suggested.

BOATS AND CHARTERS

★ *Finest Kind Inc.* A record 1,118-pound blue marlin was reeled in by the crew aboard *Finest Kind*, a lovely 37-foot Merritt kept so clean you'd never guess the action it's seen. Captain Dave has been around these waters long enough to befriend other expert fishers. This family-run company operates four boats and specializes in live bait. Shared charters start at $150 for four hours and go up to $195 for a full day. All-day private trips go from $800 to $1,100. Add 7% for tax and harbor fees. Check for any specials before booking and no bananas on board please; the captain thinks they're bad luck for fishing. ✉ *Lahaina Harbor, Slip 7* ☏ *808/661–0338* ⊕ *www.finestkindsportfishing.com.*

Kai Palena Sportfishing. Captain Fuzzy Alboro runs a serious and highly recommended operation on the 32-foot *Die Hard*. Check-in is at 2:45 am, and he takes a maximum of six people per trip. The cost is from $200 for a shared boat to $1,100 for a private charter; add 7% tax. ✉ *511 Pikanele St., Lahaina Harbor, Slip 10* ☏ *808/878–2362.*

Strike Zone. This is one of the few charters to offer morning bottom-fishing trips (for smaller fish such as snapper), as well as deep-sea trips (for the big ones—ono, 'ahi, mahimahi, and marlin). *Strike Zone* is a 43-foot Delta that offers plenty of room (16-person max). Lunch and soft drinks are included. The catch is shared with the entire boat. The cost is $168 per adult and $148 per child for a pole; spectators can ride for $78, plus 7% tax. The four- and six-hour bottom-fishing trips run Monday, Wednesday, Friday, and Saturday; the six-hour deep-sea trips run Tuesday, Thursday, and Sunday, all weather-permitting. All trips leave at 6:30 am. ⊠ *Mā'alaea Harbor, Slip 64, Mā'alaea* ☎ *808/879–4485.*

KAYAKING

Kayaking is a fantastic and eco-friendly way to experience Maui's coast up close. Floating aboard a "plastic popsicle stick" is easier than you might think, and allows you to cruise out to vibrant, living coral reefs and waters where dolphins and even whales roam. Kayaking can be a leisurely paddle or a challenge of heroic proportion, depending on your ability, the location, and the weather. ■ TIP➔ **Though you can rent kayaks independently, we recommend taking a guide.** An apparently calm surface can hide extremely strong ocean currents—and you don't *really* want to take an unplanned trip to Tahiti! Most guides are naturalists who will steer you away from surging surf, lead you to pristine reefs, and point out camouflaged fish, like the stalking hawkfish. Not having to schlep your gear on top of your rental car is a bonus. A half-day tour runs around $75. Custom tours can be arranged.

If you decide to strike out on your own, tour companies will rent kayaks for the day with paddles, life vests, and roof racks, and many will meet you near your chosen location. Ask for a map of good entries and plan to avoid paddling back to shore against the wind (schedule extra time for the return trip regardless). For beginners, get there early before the trade wind kicks in, and try sticking close to the shore. When you're ready to snorkel, secure your belongings in a dry pack on board and drag your boat by its bowline behind you. (This isn't as bad as it sounds).

BEST SPOTS

In West Maui, past the steep cliffs on the Honoapi'ilani Highway and before you hit Lahaina, there's a long stretch of inviting coastline, including **Ukumehame** and **Olowalu** (⊠ *Between mile markers 12 and 14 on Rte. 30*) beaches. This is a good spot for beginners; entry is easy and there's much to see in every direction. If you want to snorkel, the best visibility is farther out at Olowalu, at about 25 feet depth. ■ TIP➔ **Watch for sharp kiawe thorns buried in the sand on the way into the water.**

Mākena Landing (⊠ *Off Mākena Rd.*) is an excellent taking-off point for a South Maui adventure. Enter from the paved parking lot or the small sandy beach a little south. The bay itself is virtually empty, but the right edge is flanked with brilliant coral heads and juvenile turtles. If you round the point on the right, you come across **Five Caves,** a system of enticing underwater arches. In the morning you may see dolphins, and the arches are havens for lobsters, eels, and spectacularly hued butterfly fish. Check out the million-dollar mansions lining the shoreline and guess which celebrity lives where.

■TIP→ Most of the 'Āhihi-Kīna'u Natural Area Reserve, at the southernmost point of South Maui, was closed to all activities in 2008, to allow the area's coral reef system to recover from overuse. At the time of this writing, the ban was scheduled to end as of August 1, 2012. Small areas open in the northern part of the reserve include Waiala Cove and the coastal area of 'Āhihi Bay near the "Dumps" surf break.

EQUIPMENT AND TOURS

Kelii's Kayak Tours. One of the highest-rated kayak outfitters on the island, Kelii's offers kayaking trips as well as combo adventures where you can kayak and also paddle, surf, snorkel, or hike to a waterfall. They can take up to eight people per guide. Trips are available on the island's North, South, and West shores, and range from $54 to $155, plus 4.4% tax. ⊠ *Kīhei* ☎ *888/874–7652 or 808/874–7652* ⊕ *www.keliiskayak.com.*

Fodor'sChoice
★
South Pacific Kayaks. These guys pioneered recreational kayaking on Maui—they know their stuff. Guides are friendly, informative, and eager to help you get the most out of your experience; we're talking true, fun-loving, kayak geeks. Some activity companies show a strange lack of care for the marine environment; South Pacific stands out as adventurous *and* responsible. They offer a variety of trips leaving from both West Maui and South Shore locations, including an advanced four-hour "Molokini Challenge." Trips range from $54 to $99. ☎ *800/776–2326 or 808/875–4848* ⊕ *www.southpacifickayaks.com.*

KITEBOARDING

Catapulting up to 40 feet in the air above the breaking surf, kiteboarders hardly seem of this world. Silken kites hold the athletes aloft for precious seconds—long enough for the execution of mind-boggling tricks—then deposit them back in the sea. This new sport is not for the weak-kneed. No matter what people might tell you, it's harder to learn than windsurfing. The unskilled (or unlucky) can be caught in an upwind and carried far out in the ocean, or worse—dropped smack on the shore. Because of insurance (or the lack thereof), companies are not allowed to rent equipment. Beginners must take lessons, and then purchase their own gear. Devotees swear that after your first few lessons, committing to buying your kite is easy.

LESSONS

Aqua Sports Maui. "To air is human," or so they say at Aqua Sports, which calls itself the local favorite of kiteboarding schools. They've got a great location right near Kite Beach, at the west (left) end of Kanahā Beach, and offer basic through advanced kiteboarding lessons. Rates start at $210 for a three-hour basics course taught by certified instructors. ⊠ *90 Amala Pl., near Kite Beach, Kahului* ☎ *808/242–8015* ⊕ *www.mauikiteboardinglessons.com.*

Hawaiian Sailboarding Techniques. Pro kiteboarder and legendary windsurfer Alan Cadiz will have you safely ripping in no time at lower Kanahā Beach Park. A "Learn to Kitesurf" package starts at $225 or $599 for nine hours, equipment included. As opposed to observing from the shore, instructors paddle after students on a chaseboard to give immediate feedback. HST is in the Hi Tech Surf & Sports store, located in the Triangle Square shopping center. ⊠ *425 Koloa St., Kahului* ☎ *808/871–5423 or 800/968–5423* ⊕ *www.hstwindsurfing.com.*

PARASAILING

Parasailing is an easy, exhilarating way to earn your wings: just strap on a harness attached to a parachute, and a powerboat pulls you up and over the ocean from a launching dock or a boat's platform. ■ TIP→ Keep in mind, parasailing is limited to West Maui, and "thrill craft"—including parasails—are prohibited in Maui waters during humpback whale–calving season, December 15 to May 15.

LESSONS AND TOURS

West Maui Parasail. Launch 400 feet above the ocean for a bird's-eye view of Lahaina, or be daring at 800 feet for smoother rides and better views. The captain will be glad to let you experience a "toe dip" or "free fall" if you request it. For safety reasons, passengers weighing less than 100 pounds must be strapped together in tandem. Hour-long trips departing from Lahaina Harbor, Slip 15, and Kā'anapali Beach include eight- to 10-minute flights and run from $65 for the 400-foot ride to $75 for the 800-foot ride. Observers must pay $35 each. ☎ *808/661–4060* ⊕ *www. westmauiparasail.com.*

RAFTING

The high-speed, inflatable rafts you find on Maui are nothing like the raft that Huck Finn used to drift down the Mississippi. While passengers grip straps, these rafts fly, skimming and bouncing across the sea. Because they're so maneuverable, they go where the big boats can't— secret coves, sea caves, and remote beaches. Two-hour trips run around $50, half-day trips upward of $100. ■ TIP→ Although safe, these trips are not for the faint of heart. If you have back or neck problems or are pregnant, you should reconsider this activity.

TOURS

Blue Water Rafting. One of the only ways to get to the stunning Kanaio Coast (the roadless southern coastline beyond 'Āhihi-Kīna'u), this rafting tour begins trips conveniently at the Kīhei boat ramp. Dolphins, turtles, and other marine life are the highlight of this adventure, along with sea caves, lava arches, and views of Haleakalā. Two-hour trips to Molokini start at $50 plus tax; longer trips cost $100 to $125 and include a deli lunch. ⊠ *2777 South Kīhei Rd., Kīhei* ☎ *808/879–7238* ⊕ *www.bluewaterrafting.com.*

Ocean Riders. Start the day bright and early with a spectacular view of the sun rising above the West Maui mountains, then cross the 'Au'Au Channel to Lāna'i's Shipwreck Beach. From there, this tour circles the island of Lāna'i, allowing you to view 70 mi of remote coast. The "back side" of Lāna'i is one of Hawai'i's unsung marvels and you can expect to stop at three protected coves for snorkeling; you might chance upon sea turtles, monk seals, and a friendly reef shark. Guides slow down long enough for you to marvel at sacred burial caves and interesting rock formations and to take a short swim at a secluded beach. Tours—$129 plus tax per person—depart from Mala Wharf, at the northern end of Front Street and include snorkel gear, a fruit breakfast, and a deli lunch. ⊠ *Lahaina* ☎ *808/661–3586* ⊕ *www.mauioceanriders.com.*

SAILING

With the Islands of Moloka'i, Lāna'i, Kaho'olawe, and Molokini a stone's throw away, Maui waters offer visually arresting backdrops for sailing adventures. Sailing conditions can be fickle, so some operations throw in snorkeling or whale-watching, and others offer sunset cruises. Winds are consistent in summer, but variable in winter, and afternoons are generally windier all throughout the year. Prices range from around $40 for two-hour trips to $80 for half-day excursions. ■TIP➔ You won't be sheltered from the elements on the trim racing boats, so be sure to bring a hat (one that won't blow away), a light jacket or cover-up, sunglasses, and extra sunscreen.

BOATS AND CHARTERS

America II. This onetime America's Cup contender offers an exciting, intimate alternative to crowded catamarans. For fast action, try a morning trade-wind sail. All sails are two hours and cost $44.95 plus tax. Plan to bring a change of clothes, because you will get wet. Snack and beverages are provided. No one under five years old is permitted. ⊠ *Lahaina Harbor, Slip 6* ☎ *808/667–2195* ⊕ *www.sailingonmaui.com.*

Paragon. If you want to snorkel and sail, this is your boat. Many snorkel cruises claim to sail but actually motor most of the way; *Paragon* is an exception. Both *Paragon* vessels (one catamaran in Lahaina, the other in Mā'alaea) are ship-shape, and crews are competent and friendly. Their mooring in Molokini Crater is particularly good, and they often stay after the masses have left. The Lāna'i trip includes a picnic lunch on the beach, snorkeling, and an afternoon blue-water swim. Extras on their trips to Lāna'i include mai tais and sodas, hot and cold *pūpū* (Hawaiian tapas), and champagne. A similar spread comes with the sunset sail, which departs from Lahaina Harbor every Monday, Wednesday, and Friday. ⊠ *Lahaina and Mā'alaea Harbors* ☎ *808/244–2087 or 800/441–2087* ⊕ *www.sailmaui.com.*

Trilogy Excursions. With more than 35 years of sailing tradition, not to mention a commitment to Hawaiiana and the ecosystem, Trilogy remains a favorite of locals and visitors alike. It is one of only two companies that sail to Molokini. A two-hour sail starts at $59. Their sunset sail leaves in front of Kā'anapali Beach Hotel in West Maui and includes appetizers, beer, wine, and mai tais. Boarding the catamaran right off the shore can be tricky—timing is everything and getting wet is inevitable, but after that it's smooth sailing. Book online for a 10% discount. ⊠ *Mā'alaea Harbor, Slip 99, Lahaina Harbor, or by the Kā'anapali Beach Hotel* ☎ *808/661–4743 or 888/225–6284* ⊕ *www. sailtrilogy.com.*

SCUBA DIVING

Maui, just as scenic underwater as it is on dry land, has been rated one of the top 10 dive spots in the United States and the Caribbean. It's common to see huge sea turtles, eagle rays, and small reef sharks, not to mention many varieties of angelfish, parrot fish, eels, and octopi. Unlike other popular dive destinations, most of the species are unique to this area. For example, of Maui's 450 species of reef fish, 25% are endemic to the island. Dives are best in the morning, when visibility can hold a steady 100 feet. If you're a certified diver, you can rent gear at any Maui dive shop simply by showing your PADI or NAUI card. Unless you're familiar with the area, however, it's probably best to hook up with a dive shop for an underwater tour. Tours include tanks and weights and start around $130. Wet suits and BCs (buoyancy compensators) are rented separately, for an additional $15 to $30. Shops also offer introductory dives ($100 to $160) for those who aren't certified. ■TIP➔ Before signing on with any of these outfitters, it's a good idea to ask a few pointed questions about your guide's experience, the weather outlook, and the condition of the equipment.

BEST SPOTS

Honolua Bay (⊠ *Between mile markers 32 and 33 on Rte. 30, look for narrow dirt road to left*) has beach entry. This West Maui marine preserve is alive with many varieties of coral and tame tropical fish, including large *ulua* (jack crevalle), *kāhala*, barracuda, and manta rays. With depths of 20 to 50 feet, this is a popular summer dive spot, good for all levels. ■TIP➔ High surf often prohibits winter dives.

Three miles offshore from Wailea on the South Shore, **Molokini Crater** is world renowned for its deep, crystal clear, fish-filled waters. A crescent-shaped islet formed by the eroding top of a volcano, the crater is a marine preserve ranging 10 to 80 feet in depth. The numerous tame fish and brilliant coral dwelling within the crater make it a popular introductory dive site. On calm days, exploring the back side of Molokini (called Back Wall) can be a dramatic sight for advanced divers—giving them visibility of up to 150 feet. The enormous drop-off into the 'Alalākeiki Channel (to 350 feet) offers awesome seascapes, black coral, and chance sightings of larger pelagic fish and sharks.

On the South Shore, a popular dive spot is **Mākena Landing,** also called **Five Graves** or **Five Caves.** About 0.2 mi down Mākena Road, you'll feast on underwater delights—caves, ledges, coral heads, and an outer reef home to a large green sea-turtle colony (called "Turtle Town"). ⚠ Entry is rocky lava, so be careful where you step. This area is for the more experienced diver. Rookies can enter farther down Mākena Road at Mākena Landing, and dive to the right.

South of Mākena Landing, the best diving by far is at 'Āhihi Bay and La Pérouse Bay, both South Maui marine preserves; the former is about a 10-minute drive south of the landing. 'Āhihi Bay is part of the **'Āhihi-Kīna'u Natural Area Reserve,** most of which closed to foot traffic in August 2008; at the time of this writing it was scheduled to reopen on August 1, 2012 (for updates, visit ⊕ *hawaii.gov/dlnr*). The reserve is best known for its "Fishbowl," a small cove right beside the road, next

DIVING 101

If you've always wanted gills, Hawai'i is a good place to get them. Although the bulky, heavy equipment seems freakish onshore, underwater it allows you to move about freely, almost weightlessly. As you descend into another world, you slowly grow used to the sound of your own breathing and the strangeness of being able to do so 30-plus feet down.

Most resorts offer introductory dive lessons in their pools, which allow you to acclimate to the awkward breathing apparatus before venturing out into the great blue. If you aren't starting from a resort pool, no worries. Most intro dives take off from calm, sandy beaches, such as Ulua or Kā'anapali. If you're bitten by the deep-sea bug and want to continue diving, you should get certified. Only

certified divers can rent equipment or go on more adventurous dives, such as night dives, open-ocean dives, and cave dives.

There are several certification companies, including PADI, NAUI, and SSI. PADI, the largest, is the most comprehensive. Once you begin your certification process, stick with the same company. The dives you log will not apply to another company's certification. (Dives with a PADI instructor, for instance, will not count toward SSI certification). Remember that you will not be able to fly or go to the airy summit of Haleakalā within 24 hours of diving. Open-water certification will take three to four days and cost around $350. From that point on, the sky's—or rather, the sea's—the limit!

to a hexagonal house. Here you can find excellent underwater scenery, with many types of fish and coral. ⚠ **Be careful of the rocky bottom entry (wear reef shoes if you have them).** It can get crowded, especially in high season. If you want to steer clear of the crowds, look for a second entry ½ mi farther down the road—a gravel parking lot at the surf spot called Dumps. Entry into the bay here is trickier, as the coastline is all lava. ✉ *Mākena Rd.*

EQUIPMENT, LESSONS, AND TOURS

★ **Ed Robinson's Diving Adventures.** Ed wrote the book, literally, on Molokini. Because he knows so much, he includes a "Biology 101" talk with every dive. An expert marine photographer, he offers diving instruction and boat charters to South Maui, the backside of Molokini, and Lāna'i. Weekly night dives are available, and there's a 10% discount if you book three or more days. Check out the Web site for good info and links on scuba sites, weather, and sea conditions. Dives start at $129.95 plus fees and $20 for the gear. ✉ *50 Koki St., Kīhei* ☎ *808/879–3584 or 800/635–1273* ⊕ *www.mauiscuba.com.*

Maui Dive Shop. With eight locations islandwide, the well-regarded Maui Dive Shop offers scuba charters, diving instruction, and equipment rental. Excursions that offer awe-inspiring beach and boat dives go to Coral Gardens, Shipwreck Beach on Lāna'i, and more. Night dives and customized trips are available, as are full SSI and PADI certificate programs. ✉ *1455 S. Kīhei Rd., Kīhei* ☎ *808/879–3388 or 800/542–3483* ⊕ *www.mauidiveshop.com.*

Shaka Divers. Shaka provides personalized dives including a great four-hour intro dive ($89), a refresher course ($89), scuba certification ($395), and shore dives ($59) to Ulua, Turtle Town, Bubble Cave, and more. Typical dives last about an hour, with 30 to 100 feet visibility. Dives can be booked on short notice, with afternoon tours available (hard to find on Maui). Shaka also offers night dives and torpedo scooter dives. The twilight two-tank dive is nice for day divers who want to ease into night diving. ⊠ *24 Hakoi Pl., Kīhei* ☎ *808/250–1234* ⊕ *www.shakadivers.com.*

SNORKELING

No one should leave Maui without ducking underwater to meet a sea turtle, moray eel, or *humuhumunukunukuāpua'a*—the state fish. ■ TIP→ Visibility is best in the morning, before the wind picks up.

There are two ways to approach snorkeling—by land or by sea. Daily around 7 am, a parade of boats heads out to Lāna'i or Molokini Crater, that ancient cone of volcanic cinder off the coast of Wailea. Boat trips offer some advantages—deeper water, seasonal whale-watching, crew assistance, lunch, and gear. But you don't need a boat; much of Maui's best snorkeling is found just steps from the road. Nearly the entire leeward coastline from Kapalua south to 'Āhihi-Kīna'u offers prime opportunities to ogle fish and turtles. If you're patient and sharp-eyed, you may glimpse eels, octopuses, lobsters, eagle rays, and even a rare shark or monk seal.

BEST SPOTS
Snorkel sites here are listed from north to south, starting at the northwest corner of the island.

Fodor's Choice ★ On the west side of the island, just north of Kapalua, **Honolua Bay** (⊠ *Between mile markers 32 and 33 on Rte. 30, dirt road to left*), Marine Life Conservation District has a superb reef for snorkeling. When conditions are calm, it's one of the island's best spots with tons of fish and colorful corals to observe. ■ TIP→ Make sure to bring a fish key with you, as you're sure to see many species of triggerfish, filefish, and wrasses. The coral formations on the right side of the bay are particularly dramatic and feature pink, aqua, and orange varieties. Take care entering the water, there's no beach and the rocks and concrete ramp can be slippery.

The northeast corner of this windward-facing bay periodically gets hammered by big waves in winter and high-profile surf contests are held here. Avoid the bay then, and after a heavy rain (you'll know because Honolua stream will be running across the access path).

Just minutes south of Honolua, dependable **Kapalua Bay** (✦ *From Rte. 30, turn onto Kapalua Pl., and walk through tunnel*) beckons. As beautiful above the water as it is below, Kapalua is exceptionally calm, even when other spots get testy. Needle and butterfly fish dart just past the sandy beach, which is why it's sometimes crowded. ■ TIP→ Sand can be particularly hot here, watch your toes!

★ We think **Black Rock** (⊠ *In front of Kā'anapali Sheraton Maui, Kā'anapali Pkwy.*), at the northernmost tip of Kā'anapali Beach, is tops for

Snorkelers can see adorable green sea turtles around Maui.

snorkelers of any skill level. The entry couldn't be easier—dump your towel on the sand in front of the Sheraton Maui resort and in you go. Beginners can stick close to shore and still see lots of action. Advanced snorkelers can swim beyond the sand to the tip of Black Rock, or Keka'a Point, to see larger fish and eagle rays. One of the underwater residents, a turtle named "Volkswagen" for its hefty size, can be found here. He sits very still; you must look closely. Equipment can be rented on-site. Parking, in a small lot adjoining the hotel, is the only hassle.

Along Honoapi'ilani Highway (Route 30) there are several favorite snorkel sites including the area just out from the cemetery at **Hanakao'o Beach Park** (⊠ *Near mile marker 23 on Rte. 30*). At depths of 5 and 10 feet, you can see a variety of corals, especially as you head south toward **Waihikuli Wayside Park. Olowalu** (⊠ *South of Olowalu General Store on Rte. 30, at mile marker 14*) is good for a quick underwater tour, though the best spot is a ways out, at depths of 25 feet or more. Closer to shore, the visibility can be hit or miss, but if you're willing to venture out about 50 yards, you'll have easy access to an expansive coral reef with abundant fish life—no boat required. Swim offshore toward the pole sticking out of the reef. Except for during a south swell, this area is calm and good for families with small children; turtles are plentiful. Boats sometimes stop nearby (they refer to this site as "Coral Gardens") on their return trip from Molokini or when conditions in Honolua Bay are not ideal.

Excellent snorkeling is found down the coastline between Kīhei and Mākena. ■ TIP→ The best spots are along the rocky fringes of Wailea's beaches, Mōkapu, Ulua, Wailea, and Polo, off Wailea Alanui Drive. Find one of the public parking lots sandwiched between Wailea's luxury resorts, and enjoy these beaches' sandy entries, calm waters with relatively good visibility, and variety of fish species. Of the four beaches, Ulua has the best reef. You can glimpse a box-shaped puffer fish here, and listen to snapping shrimp and parrot fish nibbling on coral.

★ Between Maui and neighboring Kahoʻolawe, 3 mi offshore from Wailea, is the world-famous **Molokini Crater**. Its crescent-shaped rim provides a sanctuary for birds and marine life and draws masses of snorkel and dive tours year-round. Most snorkeling tour operators offer a Molokini trip. The journey to this sunken crater takes more than 90 minutes from Lahaina, an hour from Māʻalaea, and half an hour from the South Shore.

At the southernmost tip of paved road in South Maui lies **ʻĀhihi-Kīnaʻu Natural Area Reserve** (⊠ *Mākena Rd.*), also referred to as La Pérouse Bay. The reserve is just before the end of the road; follow marked trails through trees. Despite its lava-scorched landscape, the area gained such popularity with adventurers and activity purveyors that it had to be closed to commercial traffic and temporarily closed to all foot traffic (at this writing it was scheduled to reopen on August 1, 2012). If you're visiting Maui after the reopening, it's a must-visit. A ranger is stationed at the parking lot to assist visitors. It's difficult terrain and sometimes crowded, but if you make use of the rangers' suggestions (stay on marked paths, wear sturdy shoes to hike in and out), you can experience some of the reserve's outstanding treasures, such as the sheltered cove known as the "Aquarium" or "Fish Bowl." ■ TIP→ Be sure to bring water: this is a hot and unforgiving wilderness.

EQUIPMENT

Most hotels and vacation rentals offer free use of snorkel gear. Beachside stands fronting the major resort areas rent equipment by the hour or day. ■ TIP→ Don't shy away from asking for instructions—a snug fit makes all the difference in the world. A mask fits if it sticks to your face when you inhale deeply through your nose. Fins should cover your entire foot (unlike diving fins, which strap around your heel). If you're squeamish about using someone else's gear (or need a prescription lens), pick up your own at any discount shop. Costco and Longs Drugs have better prices than ABC stores; dive shops have superior equipment.

Maui Dive Shop. You can rent pro gear (including optical masks, boogie boards, and wet suits) from six locations islandwide. Pump these guys for weather info before heading out, they'll know better than last night's news forecaster, and they'll give you the real deal on conditions. ⊠ *1455 S. Kīhei Rd., Kīhei* ☎ *808/873–3388* ⊕ *www.mauidiveshop.com.*

Snorkel Bob's. If you need gear, Snorkel Bob's will rent you a mask, fins, and a snorkel, and throw in a carrying bag, map, and snorkel tips for as little as $9 per week. Avoid the circle masks and go for the split-level ($26 per week), it's worth the extra cash. ⊠ *Nāpili Village Hotel, 5425 Lower Honoapiʻilani Hwy., Nāpili* ☎ *808/669–9603* ⊠ *1217 Front St., Lahaina* ☎ *808/661–4421* ⊠ *1279 S. Kīhei Rd., #310, Kīhei* ☎ *808/875–6188* ⊠ *Kamaole Beach Center, 2411 S. Kīhei Rd., Kīhei* ☎ *808/879–7449* ⊕ *www.snorkelbob.com.*

TOURS

Molokini Crater, a crescent about 3 mi off the shore of Wailea, is the most popular snorkel cruise destination. You can spend half a day floating above the fish-filled crater for about $80. Some say it's not as good as it's made out to be, and that it's too crowded, but others consider it to be one of the best spots in Hawai'i. Visibility is generally outstanding and fish are incredibly tame. Your second stop will be somewhere along the leeward coast, either Turtle Town near Mākena or Coral Gardens toward Lahaina. ■TIP➔ On blustery mornings, there's a good chance the waters will be too rough to moor in Molokini and you'll end up snorkeling some place off the shore, which you could have driven to for free. For the safety of everyone on the boat, it's the captain's prerogative to choose the best spot for the day.

Snorkel cruises vary slightly—some serve mai tais and steaks whereas others offer beer and cold cuts. You might prefer a large ferryboat to a smaller sailboat, or vice versa. Whatever trip you choose, be sure you know where to go to board your vessel; getting lost in the harbor at 6 am is a lousy start to a good day. ■TIP➔ Bring sunscreen, an underwater camera (they're double the price on board), a towel, and a cover-up for the windy return trip. Even tropical waters get chilly after hours of swimming, so consider wearing a rash guard. Wet suits can usually be rented for a fee. Hats without straps will blow away, and valuables should be left at home.

★ **Ali'i Nui Maui.** This 65-foot luxury catamaran that takes 60 people maximum is a favorite recommendation among the island's upscale resorts. Come as you are (with a bathing suit of course); towels, sun block, and gear are provided. The boat is nicely appointed with eight tables, a heated freshwater shower, and trampolines. A morning snorkel sail (includes a diving option, too) heads to Turtle Town or Molokini and includes a Continental breakfast, lunch, and post-snorkel alcoholic drinks. The trip is $129 per adult, $89 per teen and $79 per child 3–12. Complimentary hotel transportation is offered and videography is available for a fee. ✉ *Mā'alaea Harbor, Slip 56, Mā'alaea* ☎ *800/542–3483 or 808/875–0333* ⊕ *www.aliinuimaui.com.*

Gemini Sailing Charters. Great value for the money is one draw of this snorkel sail charter. Check-in is vacation-friendly at 10:30 am, too. Although the primary destination is Honolua Bay, Lāna'i and Olowalu are possible options in case of choppy, murky waters. A quality, hot buffet lunch of lemon sautéed mahimahi, tender chicken teriyaki, and pasta and potato salad is catered by the Westin Maui hotel. The company's snorkel equipment is tops, and a videographer is on board for those who want to document their underwater adventure. The trip costs $110 plus tax. You can find Gemini on Kā'anapali Beach near the Westin Maui resort's American Express activity desk. ✉ *Westin Maui Resort & Spa, 2365 Kā'anapali Pkwy.* ☎ *800/820–7245 or 808/669–0508* ⊕ *www. geminicharters.com.*

♻ **Maui Classic Charters.** Leaving from the South Shore, this company offers two snorkel trips at a good value. Hop aboard the *Four Winds II*, a 55-foot, glass-bottom catamaran, for one of the most dependable snorkel trips around. You'll spend more time than the other charter boats do at Molokini and enjoy turtle-watching on the way home. The trip includes optional snuba ($49 extra), Continental breakfast, and a barbecue lunch, beer, wine, and soda. The price is $89 per adult and $59 per child 3–12. Or try the *Maui Magic*, Mā'alaea's fastest PowerCat. This boat takes fewer people (45 max) than some of the larger vessels, offers snuba, and plays Hawaiian music on the ride. This one's good for kids. Trips range from $92 to $112. Booking a trip online at least seven days in advance may save you up to $10. ⊠ *Ma'alaea Harbor, Slips 55 and 80* ☎ *808/879–8188 or 800/736–5740* ⊕ *www.mauicharters.com.*

☺ **Trilogy Excursions.** The longest-running operation on Maui is run by the
★ Coon family, and many people consider a Trilogy excursion the highlight of their trip. In terms of comprehensive offerings, this company's got it: six beautiful multihull 50- to 64-foot sailing vessels (though they usually sail only for a brief portion of the trip) at three departure sites. All excursions are manned by energetic crews who will keep you well fed and entertained with stories of the Islands and corny jokes. A full-day catamaran cruise to Lāna'i includes Continental breakfast and barbecue lunch on board, a guided van tour of the island, a "Snorkeling 101" class, and time to snorkel in the waters of Lāna'i's Hulopo'e Marine Preserve (Trilogy has exclusive commercial access). There is a barbecue dinner on Lāna'i and an optional dolphin safari. The company also offers a Molokini and Honolua Bay snorkel cruise that is top-notch. ⊠ *Ma'alaea Harbor, Slip 99; Lahaina Harbor; or by Kā'anapali Beach Hotel* ☎ *808/874–5649 or 888/225–6284* ⊕ *www.sailtrilogy.com.*

STAND-UP PADDLING

Stand-up paddling (also called stand-up paddle surfing or paddleboarding), where you stand on a longboard and paddle out with a canoe oar, is the new "comeback kid" of surf sports. While paddleboarding requires even more balance and coordination than regular surfing, it is still accessible to just about every skill level and most surf schools now offer stand-up paddle lessons. There used to be a lone paddler amid a pack of surfers, but the sport has gained such popularity in recent years that stand-up paddlers seem to have proliferated in the water (sometimes to the dismay of avid surfers). The fun thing about stand-up paddleboarding is that you can enjoy it whether the surf is good or the water is flat. ■TIP➔ Because of the size and speed of a longboard, stand-up paddling can be dangerous to you and those around you, so lessons are highly recommended.

LESSONS

Stand-Up Paddle Surf School. Maui's first school devoted solely to stand-up paddleboarding was founded by the legendary Maria Souza, the first woman to tow in and surf the treacherous waves of "Jaws" on Maui's North Shore. The class includes a proper warm-up with a hula-hoop and balance Bosu ball and a cool-down with a bit of yoga. The cost is $159 with a maximum of four paddlers, and $179 for a private session. Locations vary depending on conditions. ☎ *808/579–9231* ⊕ *www. standuppaddlesurfschool.com.*

SURFING

Maui's coastline has surf for every level of waterman or -woman. Waves on leeward-facing shores (West and South Maui) tend to break in gentle sets all summer long. Surf instructors in Kīhei and Lahaina can rent you boards, give you onshore instruction, and then lead you out through the channel, where it's safe to enter the surf. They'll shout encouragement while you paddle like mad for the thrill of standing on water—some will even give you a helpful shove. These areas are great for beginners, the only danger is whacking a stranger with your board or stubbing your toe against the reef.

The North Shore is another story. Winter waves pound the windward coast, attracting water champions from every corner of the world. Adrenaline addicts are towed in by Jet Ski to a legendary, deep-sea break called "Jaws." Waves here periodically tower upward of 40 feet, dwarfing the helicopters seeking to capture unbelievable photos. The only spot for viewing this phenomenon (which happens just a few times a year) is on private property. So, if you hear the surfers next to you crowing about Jaws "going off," cozy up and get them to take you with them.

Whatever your skill, there's a board, a break, and even a surf guru to accommodate you. A two-hour lesson is a good intro to surf culture.

You can get the wave report each day by checking page two of the *Maui News,* logging onto the Glenn James weather site at ⊕ *www.hawaiiweathertoday.com,* or calling ☎ *808/871–5054* (for the weather forecast) or ☎ *808/877–3611* (for the surf report).

BEST SPOTS

Beginners can hang 10 at Kīhei's **Cove Park** (⊠ *S. Kīhei Rd., Kīhei*), a sometimes crowded but reliable 1- to 2-foot break. Boards can easily be rented across the street, or in neighboring Kalama Park parking lot. The only bummer is having to balance the 9-plus-foot board on your head while crossing busy South Kīhei Road. But hey, that wouldn't stop world-famous longboarder Eddie Aikau, now would it?

Long- or shortboarders can paddle out anywhere along Lahaina's coastline. One option is at **Launiupoko State Wayside** (⊠ *Honoapi'ilani Hwy. near mile marker 18*). The east end of the park has an easy break, good for beginners. Even better is **Ukumehame** (⊠ *Honoapi'ilani Hwy. near mile marker 12*), also called "Thousand Peaks." You'll soon see how the spot got its name; the waves here break again and again in wide and consistent rows, giving lots of room for beginning and intermediate surfers.

Other **good surf spots** in West Maui include "Grandma's" at **Papalaua Park,** just after the *pali* (cliff)—where waves are so easy a grandma could ride 'em; **Puamana Beach Park** for a mellow longboard day; and **Lahaina Harbor,** which offers an excellent inside wave for beginners (called "Breakwall"), as well as the more-advanced outside (a great lift if there's a big south swell). Near-perfect waves can also be seen at **Honolua Bay,** on the northern tip of West Maui, 2 mi north of D.T. Fleming Park.

For advanced wave riders, **Ho'okipa Beach Park** (⌧ *2 mi past Pā'ia on Hāna Hwy.*) boasts several well-loved breaks, including "Pavilions," "Lanes," "the Point," and "Middles." Surfers have priority until 11 am, when windsurfers move in on the action. ■ TIP→ Competition is stiff here, and the attitudes can be "agro." If you don't know what you're doing, consider watching from the shore.

EQUIPMENT AND LESSONS

Surf camps are becoming increasingly popular, especially with women. One- or two-week camps offer a terrific way to build muscle and self-esteem simultaneously. **Maui Surfer Girls** (⊕ *www.mauisurfergirls.com*) immerses adventurous young ladies in wave-riding wisdom during overnight, one-, and two-week camps.

Big Kahuna Adventures. Rent surfboards (soft-top longboards) here for $20 for two hours, or $30 for the day. The shop also offers surf lessons, and rents kayaks and snorkel gear. Located across from Cove Park. ⌧ *1913–C S. Kīhei Rd., Kīhei* ☎ *808/875–6395* ⊕ *www. bigkahunaadventures.com.*

★ **Goofy Foot.** Surfing "goofy foot" means putting your right foot forward. They might be goofy, but we like the right-footed gurus here. Their safari shop is just plain cool and only steps away from "Breakwall," a great beginner's spot in Lahaina. Two-hour classes with five or fewer students are $65, and six-hour classes with lunch and an ocean-safety course are $300. ⌧ *505 Front St., Ste. 123, Lahaina* ☎ *808/244–9283* ⊕ *www.goofyfootsurfschool.com.*

Hi-Tech Surf Sports. Locals hold Hi-Tech in the highest regard. They have some of the best boards, advice, and attitudes around. Rent surfboards for $20 per day; $112 for the week. They rent even their best models—choose from longboards, shortboards, and hybrids. All rentals come with board bags, roof rags, and oh yeah, wax. ⌧ *425 Koloa St., Kahului* ☎ *808/877–2111* ⊕ *www.htmaui.com.*

★ **Nancy Emerson School of Surfing.** Nancy's motto is "If my dog can surf, so can you." Instructors here will get even the shakiest novice riding with their "Learn to Surf in One Lesson" program. A two-hour group lesson (six students max) is $78. Nancy currently lives in Australia, but private lessons with her equally qualified instructors are $165 for two hours. Semiprivate lessons with two people are $130 per person. Multiple-day sessions start at $350. They provide the boards and rash guards. ⌧ *505 Front St., Ste. 224B, Lahaina* ☎ *808/244–7873* ⊕ *www. mauisurfclinics.com.*

WHALE-WATCHING

From December through May, whale-watching becomes one of the most popular activities on Maui. During the season, all outfitters offer whale-watching in addition to their regular activities, and most do an excellent job. Boats leave the wharves at Lahaina and Mā'alaea in search of humpbacks, allowing you to enjoy the awe-inspiring size of these creatures in closer proximity.

Humpback whale calves are plentiful in winter; this one is breaching off West Maui.

As it's almost impossible *not* to see whales in winter on Maui, you'll want to prioritize: is adventure or comfort your aim? If close encounters with the giants of the deep are your desire, pick a smaller boat that promises sightings. Those who think "green" usually prefer the smaller, quieter vessels that produce the least amount of negative impact to the whales' natural environment. If an impromptu marine-biology lesson sounds fun, go with the Pacific Whale Foundation. For those wanting to sip mai tais as whales cruise calmly by, stick with a sunset cruise on a boat with an open bar and pūpū ($40 and up). ■TIP→ **Afternoon trips are generally rougher because the wind picks up, but some say this is when the most surface action occurs.**

Every captain aims to please during whale season, getting as close as legally possible (100 yards). Crew members know when a whale is about to dive (after several waves of its heart-shaped tail) but rarely can predict breaches (when the whale hurls itself up and almost entirely out of the water). Prime-viewing space (on the upper and lower decks, around the railings) is limited, so boats can feel crowded even when half full. If you don't want to squeeze in beside strangers, opt for a smaller boat with fewer bookings. Don't forget to bring sunscreen, sunglasses, light long sleeves, and a hat you can secure. Winter weather is less predictable and at times can be extreme, especially as the wind picks up. Arrive early to find parking.

BEST SPOTS

From December 15 to May 1 the Pacific Whale Foundation has naturalists stationed in two places—on the rooftop of their headquarters and at the scenic viewpoint at **Papawai Point Lookout** (✉ *Rte. 30, 3 mi west*

CLOSE UP

The Humpback's Winter Home

The humpback whales' attraction to Maui is legendary, and seeing them between December and May is a highlight for many visitors. More than half the Pacific's humpback population winters in Hawai'i, especially in the waters around the Valley Isle, where mothers can be seen just a few hundred feet offshore training their young calves in the fine points of whale etiquette. Watching from shore it's easy to catch sight of whales spouting, or even breaching—when they leap almost entirely out of the sea, slapping back onto the water with a huge splash.

At one time there were thousands of the huge mammals, but a history of overhunting and marine pollution dwindled the world population to about 1,500. In 1966 humpbacks were put on the endangered-species list. Hunting or harassing whales is illegal in the waters of most nations, and in the United States boats and airplanes are restricted from getting too close. The word is still out, however, on the effects military sonar testing has on the marine mammals.

Marine biologists believe the humpbacks (much like the humans) keep returning to Hawai'i because of its warmth. Having fattened themselves in subarctic waters all summer, the whales migrate south in the winter to breed, and a rebounding population of thousands cruise Maui waters. Winter is calving time, and the young whales probably couldn't survive in the frigid Alaskan waters. No one has ever seen a whale give birth here, but experts know that calving is their main winter activity, since the 1- and 2-ton youngsters suddenly appear while the whales are in residence.

The first sighting of a humpback-whale spout each season is exciting for locals on Maui. A collective sigh of relief can be heard, "Ah, they've returned." In the not-so-far distance, flukes and flippers can be seen rising above the ocean's surface. It's hard not to anthropomorphize the tail waving; it looks like such an amiable gesture. Each fluke is uniquely patterned, like a human's fingerprint, and is used to identify the giants as they travel halfway around the globe and back.

of Mā'alaea Harbor). Just like the commuting traffic, whales cruise along the *pali*, or cliff side, of West Maui's Honoapi'ilani highway all day long. ■TIP→ Make sure to park safely before craning your neck out to see them.

The northern end of **Keawakapu Beach** (⊠ *S. Kīhei Rd. near Kilohana Dr.*) seems to be a whale magnet. Situate yourself on the sand or at the nearby restaurant, and you're bound to see a mama whale patiently teaching her calf the exact technique of flipper waving.

BOATS AND CHARTERS

☺ **Pacific Whale Foundation.** This nonprofit organization pioneered whale-
★ watching back in 1979 and now runs four boats, with 15 trips daily. As the most recognizable name in whale-watching, the crew (with a certified marine biologist on board) offers insights into whale behavior (do they *really* know what those tail flicks mean?) and suggests ways for you to help save marine life worldwide. The best part about these trips

is the underwater hydrophone that allows you to actually listen to the whales sing. Trips meet at the foundation's store, where you can buy whale paraphernalia, snacks, and coffee—a real bonus for 8 am trips. Passengers are then herded much like migrating whales down to the harbor. These trips are more affordable than others, but you'll be sharing the boat with about 100 people in stadium seating. Once you catch sight of the wildlife up close, however, you can't help but be thrilled. ✉ *Māʻalaea and Lahaina harbors* ☎ *800/942–5311 or 808/249–8811* ⊕ *www.pacificwhale.org.*

★ **Trilogy Excursions.** Trilogy whale-watching trips consist of smaller crowds of about 20 to 30 passengers, and include beverages and snacks, an onboard marine naturalist, and hydrophones (microphones that detect underwater sound waves). Trips are $39 plus tax. Book online for a discount. ✉ *Loading at the Kāʻanapali Beach Hotel* ☎ *808/661–4743 or 888/225–6284* ⊕ *www. sailtrilogy.com.*

> ## ON THE SIDELINES
>
> Few places lay claim to as many windsurfing tournaments as Maui. In March the **PWA Hawaiian Pro-Am Windsurfing** competition gets under way at Hoʻokipa Beach. In June the **Da Kine Windsurfing Classic** lures top windsurfers to Kanahā Beach, and in November the **Aloha Classic World Wave Sailing Championships** take place at Hoʻokipa. For competitions featuring amateurs as well as professionals, check out the **Maui Race Series** (☎ *808/877–2111*), six events held at Kanahā Beach in Kahului in summer.

WINDSURFING

Something about Maui's wind and water stirs the spirit of innovation. Windsurfing, invented in the 1950s, found its true home at Hoʻokipa in 1980. Seemingly overnight, windsurfing pros from around the world flooded Maui's North Shore. Equipment evolved, amazing film footage was captured, and a new sport was born.

If you're new to the action, you can get lessons from the experts island-wide. For a beginner, the best thing about windsurfing is (unlike surfing) you don't have to paddle. Instead, you have to hold on like heck to a flapping sail, as it whisks you into the wind. Needless to say, you're going to need a little coordination and balance to pull this off. Instructors start you on a beach at Kanahā, where the big boys go. Lessons range from two-hour introductory classes to five-day advanced "flight school." If you're an old salt, pick up tips and equipment from the companies below.

BEST SPOTS

After **Hoʻokipa Bay** (✉ *2 mi past Pāʻia on Hāna Hwy.*) was discovered by windsurfers three decades ago, this windy beach 10 mi east of Kahului gained an international reputation. The spot is blessed with optimal wave-sailing wind and sea conditions, and can offer the ultimate aerial experience.

In summer the windsurfing crowd heads south to **Kalepolepo Beach** (✉ *S. Kīhei Rd. near Ohukai St.*). Trade winds build in strength and by

The world's best windsurfers love the action on Maui; it's fun to watch, too.

afternoon a swarm of dragonfly sails can be seen skimming the white-caps, with the West Maui Mountains as a backdrop.

A great site for speed, **Kanahā Beach Park** (⊠ *Behind Kahului Airport*) is dedicated to beginners in the morning hours, before the waves and wind really get roaring. After 11 am, the professionals choose from their quiver of sails the size and shape best suited for the day's demands. This beach tends to have smaller waves and forceful winds—sometimes sending sailors flying at 40 knots. ■TIP➜ **If you aren't ready to go pro, this is a great place for a picnic while you watch from the beach.**

EQUIPMENT AND LESSONS

Action Sports Maui. The quirky, friendly professionals here will meet you at Kanahā on the North Shore, outfit you with your sail and board, and guide you through your first "jibe" or turn. They promise your learning time will be cut in half. Don't be afraid to ask lots of questions. Lessons are held at 9 am every day except Sunday at Kanahā and start at $89 for a 2½-hour class. Three- and five-day courses cost $240 and $395. ⊠ *6 E. Waipuilani Rd., Kīhei* ☎ *808/871–5857* ⊕ *www. actionsportsmaui.com.*

Hi-Tech Surf & Sports. Known locally as Maui's finest windsurfing school, Hawaiian Sailboarding Techniques (HST, located in Hi-Tech) brings you quality instruction by skilled sailors. Founded by Alan Cadiz, an accomplished World Cup Pro, the school sets high standards for a safe, quality windsurfing experience. Intro classes start at $79 for 2½ hours, gear included. Hi-Tech itself offers excellent equipment rentals; $50 gets you a board, two sails, a mast, and roof racks for 24 hours. ⊠ *425 Koloa St., Kahului* ☎ *808/877–2111* ⊕ *www.htmaui.com.*

Second Wind. Located in Kahului, this company rents boards with two sails for $49 per day. Additional sails are $5 each. Intro classes start at $79. ⊠ *111 Hāna Hwy., Kahului* ☎ *808/877–7467* ⊕ *www. secondwindmaui.com.*

GOLF, HIKING, AND OUTDOOR ACTIVITIES

Updated by
Heidi Pool

You may come to Maui to sprawl out on the sand, but you'll soon realize there's much more here than the beach. For a relatively small island, Maui's interior landscapes vary wildly, from the moonlike surface of Haleakalā Crater to the green rain forest of 'Iao Valley State Monument. Whether you're exploring waterfalls on a day hike, riding horseback through ranchlands, soaring on a zipline, taking an exhilarating bicycle ride down Haleakalā, or teeing off on a world-class golf course, Maui has plenty to keep you busy. Some activities are free, while organized activities vary widely in price; but there's something for every outdoor enthusiast, regardless of age, interest, or fitness level.

AERIAL TOURS

Helicopter flight-seeing excursions can take you over the West Maui Mountains, Hāna, Haleakalā Crater, even the Big Island lava flow, or the Islands of Lāna'i and Moloka'i. This is a beautiful, exciting way to see the island, and the only way to see some of its most dramatic areas and waterfalls. Tour prices usually include a DVD of your trip so you can relive the experience at home. Prices run from about $150 for a half-hour rain-forest tour to more than $400 for a 90-minute mega-experience that includes a champagne toast on landing. Generally the 45- to 50-minute flights are the best value, discounts may be available online or, if you're willing to chance it, by calling at the last minute.

Blue Hawaiian Helicopters. Since 1985 this company has provided aerial adventures in Hawai'i and has been integral in some of the filming Hollywood has done on Maui. Its A-Star and Eco-Star helicopters are air-conditioned and have Bose noise-blocking headsets for all passengers. Flights are 30 to 120 minutes and cost $160 to $530, with considerable discounts on the Web site. Charter flights are also available. ⊠ *Kahului Heliport, Hangar 105, Kahului* ☎ *808/871–8844 or 800/745–2583* ⊕ *www.bluehawaiian.com.*

Sunshine Helicopters. Sunshine offers tours of Maui and Moloka'i in its *Black Beauty* FXStar or WhisperStar aircraft. A pilot-narrated DVD of your actual flight is available for purchase. Prices start at $185 for 30 to 65 minutes, with discounts available on the Web site. First-class seating is available for an additional fee. Charter flights can be arranged. ⊠ *Kahului Heliport, Hangar 107, Kahului* ☎ *808/270–3999 or 866/501–7738* ⊕ *www.sunshinehelicopters.com.*

BIKING

Maui County biking is safer and more convenient than in the past, but long distances and mountainous terrain keep it from being a practical mode of travel. Still, painted bike lanes enable cyclists to travel all the way from Mākena to Kapalua, and you'll see hardy souls battling the trade winds under the hot Maui sun.

Several companies offer guided downhill bike tours down Haleakalā. This activity is a great way to see the summit of the world's largest dormant volcano and enjoy an easy, gravity-induced bike ride, but isn't for those not confident in their ability to handle a bike. The ride is inherently dangerous due to the slope, sharp turns, and the fact that you're riding down an actual road with cars on it. That said, the guided-tour bike companies do take every safety precaution. A few companies are now offering unguided (or as they like to say "self-guided") tours where they provide you with the bike and transportation to the top and then you're free to descend at your own pace. Sunrise is downright brisk at the summit, so dress in layers.

■TIP→ Haleakalā National Park no longer allows commercial downhill bicycle rides within the park's boundaries. As a result, tour amenities and routes vary by company. Be sure to ask about sunrise viewing from the Haleakalā summit, if this is an important feature for you.

BEST SPOTS

At present there are few truly good spots to ride on Maui, though this is changing. Street bikers will want to head out to scenic **Thompson Road** (⊠ *Off Rte. 37, Kula Hwy., Keokea*). It's quiet, gently curvy, and flanked by gorgeous views on both sides. Plus, because it's at a higher elevation, the air temperature is cooler and the wind lighter. The coast back down toward Kahului is worth the ride up.

EQUIPMENT AND TOURS

Cruiser Phil's Volcano Riders. Owner Phil Feliciano ("Cruiser Phil") has been in the downhill bicycle industry since 1983. He offers sunrise tours ($150) and morning tours ($135) that include hotel pickup and drop-off, Continental breakfast at the company's base in Kahului, a van tour of the summit, and a guided 28-mi ride down the mountain. Riders will make a no-host meal stop in either Kula or Pā'ia. Participants should be at least 15 and under 65 years old; be at least 5 feet tall and weigh no more than 275 pounds; and have ridden a bicycle in the past 12 months. ⊠ *58-A Amala Pl., Kahului* 🕾 *808/893–2332 or 877/764–2453* ⊕ *www.cruiserphil.com.*

Haleakalā Bike Company. If you're thinking about an unguided Haleakalā bike trip, consider one of the trips offered by this company. Meet at the Old Ha'ikū Cannery and take their van shuttle to the summit. Along the way you can learn about the history of the island, the volcano, and other Hawaiiana. Food is not included, but there are several spots along the way down to stop, rest, and eat. The simple, mostly downhill route takes you right back to the cannery where you started. HBC also offers bike sales, rentals, and services, as well as van tours (no biking). Tour prices range from $70 to $115, with discounts available for online bookings. ✉ *810 Haʻikū Rd., Suite 120, Haʻikū* ☎ *808/575–9575 or 888/922–2453* ⊕ *www.bikemaui.com.*

Island Biker. Maui's premier bike shop for rentals, sales, and service offers Specialized standard front-shock bikes, road bikes, and full-suspension mountain bikes. Daily rental rates range from $50 to $75 and weekly rates are $150 to $200; the price includes a helmet, pump, water bottle, cages, flat-repair kit, and spare tube. Car racks are $5 per day or are free with weekly rentals. The shop can suggest routes appropriate for mountain or road biking. Call for information on scheduled group rides. ✉ *415 Dairy Rd., Kahului* ☎ *808/877–7744* ⊕ *www. islandbikermaui.com.*

West Maui Cycles. Servicing the west side of the island, WMC offers an assortment of cycles including cruisers for $15 per day ($60 per week); hybrids for $30 per day ($120 per week); and Cannondale road bikes and front-suspension Giant bikes for $50 per day ($200 per week). Tandems start at $30 per day ($120 per week). They also have baby joggers and car racks for rent. Sales and service are available. ✉ *1087 Limahana Pl., No. 6, Lahaina* ☎ *808/661–9005* ⊕ *www.westmauicycles.com.*

GOLF

Maui's natural beauty and surroundings offer some of the most jaw-dropping vistas imaginable on a golf course. Holes run across small bays, past craggy lava outcrops, and up into cool, forested mountains. Most courses feature mesmerizing ocean views, some close enough to feel the salt in the air. And although many of the courses are affiliated with resorts (and therefore a little pricier), the public courses are no less impressive. Greens fees listed here are the highest course rates per round on weekdays and weekends for U.S. residents. (Some courses charge non–U.S. residents higher prices.) Discounts are often available for resort guests and for those who book tee times on the Web. Rental clubs may or may not be included with greens fees. ■TIP➔ Cheaper twilight fees are usually offered; call individual courses for information.

Fodor's Choice **The Dunes at Maui Lani.** Here Robin Nelson (1999) is at his minimalist ★ best, creating a bit of British links in the middle of the Pacific. Holes run through ancient, lightly wooded sand dunes, 5 mi inland from Kahului Harbor. Thanks to the natural humps and slopes of the dunes, Nelson had to move very little dirt and created a natural beauty. During the design phase he visited Ireland, and not so coincidentally the par-3 3rd looks a lot like the Dell at Lahinch: a white dune on the right sloping down into a deep bunker and partially obscuring the right side of the green—just one of several blind to semiblind shots here. Popular with residents, this course has won several awards including "Five Best Kept Secret Golf Courses in America" by *Golf Digest*. ✉ *1333 Maui Lani Pkwy., Kahului* ☎ *808/873–0422* ⊕ *www.dunesatmauilani.com* ⚐ *18 holes. 6841 yds. Par 72. Slope 136. Greens Fee: $125* ☞ *Facilities: Driving range, putting green, golf carts, rental clubs, pro shop, golf academy/lessons, restaurant, bar.*

★ **Kāʻanapali Golf Resort.** The Royal Kāʻanapali (North) Course (1962) is one of three in Hawaiʻi designed by Robert Trent Jones Sr., the

Sunset views are lovely from many hotel rooms near West Maui's Kā'anapali Beach.

godfather of modern golf architecture. The greens average a whopping 10,000 square feet, necessary because of the often-severe undulation. The par-4 18th hole (into the prevailing trade breezes, with out-of-bounds on the left, and a lake on the right) is notoriously tough. The Kā'anapali Kai (South) Course (Arthur Jack Snyder, 1976) shares similar seaside-into-the-hills terrain but is rated a couple of strokes easier, mostly because putts are less treacherous. ⊠ *2290 Kā'anapali Pkwy., Lahaina* ☎ *808/661–3691* ⊕ *www.kaanapali-golf.com* ⚑ *North Course: 18 holes. 6,500 yds. Par 71. Slope 126. Greens Fee: $235. South Course: 18 holes. 6400 yds. Par 70. Slope 124. Greens Fee: $195* ☞ *Facilities: Driving range, putting green, rental clubs, golf carts, lessons, restaurant, bar.*

Kapalua Resort. Perhaps Hawai'i's best-known golf resort and the crown jewel of golf on Maui, Kapalua hosts the PGA Tour's first event each January: the Hyundai Tournament of Champions at the Plantation Course at Kapalua. Ben Crenshaw and Bill Coore (1991) tried to incorporate traditional shot values in a nontraditional site, taking into account slope, gravity, and the prevailing trade winds. The par-5 18th, for instance, plays 663 yards from the back tees (600 yards from the resort tees). The hole drops 170 feet in elevation, narrowing as it goes to a partially guarded green, and plays downwind and down-grain. Despite the longer-than-usual distance, the slope is great enough and the wind at your back usually brisk enough to reach the green with two well-struck shots—a truly unbelievable finish to a course that will challenge, frustrate, and reward the patient golfer.

BEFORE YOU HIT THE FIRST TEE . . .

Golf is golf, and Hawai'i is part of the United States, but island golf nevertheless has its own quirks. Here are a few tips to make your golf experience in the Islands more pleasant.

■ All resort courses and many daily fee courses provide rental clubs. In many cases, they're the latest lines from top manufacturers. This is true for both men and women, as well as left-handers, which means you don't have to schlep clubs across the Pacific.

■ Come spikeless—very few Hawai'i courses still permit metal spikes. And most of the resort courses require a collared shirt.

■ Maui is notorious for its trade winds. Consider playing early if you want to avoid the wind, and remember that while it'll frustrate you at times and make club selection difficult, you may very well see some of your longest drives ever.

■ In theory you can play golf in Hawai'i 365 days a year, but there's a reason the Hawaiian Islands are so green. An umbrella and light jacket can come in handy.

■ Unless you play a muni or certain daily fee courses, plan on taking a cart. Riding carts are mandatory at most courses and are included in the greens fees.

The Bay Course (Arnold Palmer and Francis Duane, 1975) is the more traditional of Kapalua's courses, with gentle rolling fairways and generous greens. The most memorable hole is the par-3 fifth, with a tee shot that must carry a turquoise finger of Onelua Bay. **The Kapalua Golf Academy** (⊠ *1000 Office Rd., Kapalua* ☎ *808/665–5455 or 877/527–2582*) offers 23 acres of practice turf and 11 teeing areas, an 18-hole putting course and 3-hole walking course, and an instructional bay with video analysis. Each of the courses has a separate clubhouse. **The Bay Course** ⊠ *300 Kapalua Dr., Kapalua* ☎ *808/669–8044 or 877/527–2582* ⊕ *www.kapalua.com/hawaii-golf* ⚑ *18 holes. 6600 yds. Par 72. Slope 133. Greens Fee: $208* ⚐ *Facilities: Driving range, putting green, rental clubs, pro shop, lessons, restaurant, bar.* **The Plantation Course** ⊠ *2000 Plantation Club Dr., Kapalua* ☎ *808/669–8044 or 877/527–2582* ⊕ *www.kapalua.com/hawaii-golf* ⚑ *18 holes. 7411 yds. Par 73. Slope 135. Greens Fee: $268* ⚐ *Facilities: Driving range, putting green, golf carts, pull carts, rental clubs, pro shop, golf academy/lessons, restaurant, bar.*

Fodor'sChoice ★ **Mākena Beach & Golf Resort.** Robert Trent Jones Jr. and Don Knotts (not the actor) built the first course at Mākena in 1981. A decade later Jones was asked to create 18 totally new holes and blend them with the existing course to form the North and South courses, which opened in 1994. Both courses—sculpted from the lava flows on the western flank of Haleakalā—offer quick greens with lots of breaks and plenty of scenic distractions. On the North Course, the fourth is one of the most picturesque inland par 3s in Hawai'i, with the green guarded on the right by a pond. The sixth is an excellent example of option golf: The fairway is sliced up the middle by a gaping ravine, which must sooner or later be crossed to reach the green. Although trees frame most holes on the North Course, the South Course is more open. This means it plays somewhat easier off the tee, but the greens are trickier. The view from the elevated tee of the par-5 10th is lovely with the lake in the foreground mirroring the ocean in the distance. The par-4 16th is another sight to see, with the Pacific running along the left side. Note: At the time of this writing, the South Course was closed for maintenance; nine holes may reopen in late 2011. Call to confirm. ⊠ *5415 Mākena Alanui, Mākena* 🕾 *808/891–4000* ⊕ *www.makenagolf.com* 🏌 *North Course: 18 holes. 6567 yds. Par 72. Slope 135. Greens Fee: $129. South Course: 18 holes. 6630 yds. Par 72. Slope 133. Greens Fee: $200* ☞ *Facilities: Driving range, putting green, golf carts, rental clubs, pro shop, golf academy/lessons, restaurant, bar.*

Pukalani Golf Course. At 1,110 feet above sea level, Pukalani (Bob E. Baldock and Robert L. Baldock, 1970) provides one of the finest vistas in all Hawai'i. Holes run up, down, and across the slopes of Haleakalā. The trade winds tend to come up in the late morning and afternoon. This, combined with frequent elevation change, makes club selection a test. The fairways tend to be wide, but greens are undulating and quick. ⊠ *360 Pukalani St., Pukalani* 🕾 *808/572–1314* ⊕ *www.pukalanigolf. com* 🏌 *18 holes. 6962 yds. Par 72. Slope 127. Greens Fee: $87* ☞ *Facilities: Driving range, putting green, golf carts, rental clubs, pro shop, restaurant, bar.*

Fodor'sChoice
★

Wailea. Wailea is the only Hawai'i resort to offer three different courses: Gold, Emerald, and Old Blue. Designed by Robert Trent Jones Jr., these courses share similar terrain, carved into the leeward slopes of Haleakalā. Although the ocean does not come into play, its beauty is visible on almost every hole. ■TIP➔ Remember, putts break dramatically toward the ocean.

Jones refers to the Gold Course at Wailea (1993) as the "masculine" course. Host to the Championship Senior Skins Game in January, it's all trees and lava and regarded as the hardest of the three courses. The trick here is to note even subtle changes in elevation. The par-3 eighth, for example, plays from an elevated tee across a lava ravine to a large, well-bunkered green framed by palm trees, the blue sea, and tiny Molokini. The course has been labeled a "thinking player's" course because it demands strategy and careful club selection. The Emerald Course at Wailea (1994) is the "feminine" layout with lots of flowers and bunkering away from greens. Although this may seem to render the bunker benign, the opposite is true. A bunker well in front of a green disguises the distance to the hole. Likewise, the Emerald's extensive flower beds are designed to be dangerous distractions because of their beauty. The Gold and Emerald share a clubhouse, practice facility, and 19th hole (watering hole and restaurant). Judging elevation change is also key at Wailea's first course, the Old Blue Course (Arthur Jack Snyder, 1971). Fairways and greens tend to be wider and more forgiving than on the Gold or Emerald, and run through colorful flora that includes hibiscus, wiliwili, bougainvillea, and plumeria. Old Blue Course: ⊠ *120 Kaukahi St., Wailea* 🕾 *808/875–7450 or 888/328–6284* ⊕ *www.waileagolf.com* 🏌 *18 holes. 6765 yds. Par 72. Slope 129. Greens fee: $190* ☞ *Facilities: Driving range, putting green, golf carts, rental clubs, pro shop, golf* *academy/lessons, restaurant, bar.* Gold and Emerald Courses: ⊠ *100 Wailea Golf Club Dr., Wailea* ☎ *808/875–7450 or 888/328–6284* ⊕ *www.waileagolf.com* ⚲ *Gold Course: 18 holes. 6653 yds. Par 72. Slope 132. Greens fee: $225. Emerald Course: 18 holes. 6407 yds. Par 72. Slope 130. Greens fee: $225* ☞ *Facilities: Driving range, putting green, golf carts, rental clubs, pro shop, golf academy/lessons, restaurant, bar.*

HANG GLIDING AND PARAGLIDING

If you've always wanted to know what it feels like to fly, hang gliding or paragliding might be your perfect Maui adventure. You'll get open-air, bird's-eye views of the Valley Isle that you'll likely never forget. And you don't need to be a daredevil to participate.

LESSONS AND TOURS

Hang Gliding Maui. Armin Engert will take you on an instructional powered hang-gliding trip out of Hāna Airport in East Maui. With more than 13,000 hours in flight and a perfect safety record, Armin flies you 1,000 feet over Maui's most beautiful coast. A 30-minute flight lesson costs $150, a 45-minute lesson costs $200, and a 60-minute lesson is $250. This is easily one of the coolest things you can do in Hāna. Snapshots of your flight from a wing-mounted camera cost an additional $30, and a 34-minute DVD of the flight is available for $70. Reservations are required. ⊠ *Hāna Airport, Hāna* ☎ *808/572–6557* ⊕ *www. hanaglidingmaui.com.*

Proflyght Paragliding. Proflyght is the only paragliding outfit on Maui to offer solo, tandem, and instruction at Polipoli Spring State Recreation Area. The leeward slope of Haleakalā lends itself to paragliding with breathtaking scenery and Upcountry air currents that increase and rise during the day. Polipoli creates tremendous thermals that allow you to peacefully descend 3,000 feet to land. Prices start at $95, with full certification available. ⊠ *Polipoli Spring State Recreation Area, Kula* ☎ *808/874–5433* ⊕ *www.paraglidehawaii.com.*

HIKING

Hikes on Maui range from coastal seashore to verdant rain forest to alpine desert. Orchids, hibiscus, ginger, heliconia, and anthuriums grow wild on many trails, and exotic fruits like mountain apple, *lilikoi* (passion fruit), thimbleberry, and strawberry guava provide refreshing snacks for hikers. Ironically, much of what you see in lower altitude forests is alien, brought to Hawai'i at one time or another by someone hoping to improve upon nature. Plants like strawberry guava and ginger may be tasty, but they grow over native forest plants and have become serious, problematic weeds.

The best hikes get you out of the imported landscaping and into the truly exotic wilderness. Hawai'i possesses some of the world's rarest plants, insects, and birds. Pocket field guides are available at most grocery or drug stores and can really illuminate your walk. Before you know it, you'll be nudging your companion and pointing out trees that look like something out of a Dr. Suess book. If you watch the right branches quietly you can spot the same honeycreepers or happy-face spiders scientists have spent their lives studying.

BEST SPOTS

Fodor's Choice ★   Undoubtedly the best hiking on the island is at **Haleakalā Crater**, with 30 mi of trails, two camping areas, and three cabins. If you're in shape, do a day hike descending from the summit along Keonehe'ehe'e Trail (also known as Sliding Sands Trail) to the crater floor. If you're in shape and have time, consider spending several days here amid the cinder cones, lava flows, and all that loud silence. Going into the crater is like going to a different planet. In the early 1960s NASA actually brought moon-suited astronauts here to practice what it would be like to "walk on the moon." Today, on one of the many hikes—most moderate to strenu-ous—you can traverse black sand and wild lava formations, follow the trail of blooming 'ahinahina (silverswords), watch for nēnē (Hawaiian geese) as they fly above you, and witness tremendous views of big sky and burned-red cliffs. If you're lucky enough to camp or stay in one of the cabins, you'll fall asleep under a wide screen of shooting stars. *For more information, see the Haleakalā National Park feature in this sec-tion.* ✉ *Haleakalā Crater Rd.* ☎ *808/572–4400* ⊕ *www.nps.gov/hale.*

A branch of Haleakalā National Park, **'Ohe'o Gulch** is famous for its pools (the area is sometimes called the "Seven Sacred Pools"). Truth is, there are more than seven pools, and there's nothing sacred about them. The former owner of the Hotel Hāna-Maui started calling the area "Seven Sacred Pools" to attract the masses to sleepy old Hāna. His plan worked and the name stuck, much to the chagrin of most Mauians.

The best time to visit the pools is in the morning, before the crowds and tour buses arrive. Start your day with a vigorous hike. 'Ohe'o has some fantastic trails to choose from, including our favorite, the Pipiwai Trail. When you're done, nothing could be better than going to the pools, lounging on the rocks, and cooling off in the freshwater reserves. (Keep in mind, however, that the park periodically closes the pools to swim-ming when the potential for flash flooding exists.)

You can find 'Ohe'o Gulch on Route 31, 10 mi past Hāna town. All visitors must pay a $10 national park fee (per car not per person), which is valid for three days and can be used at Haleakalā's summit as well. Be sure to visit Haleakalā National Park's Kipahulu Visitor Center, 10 mi past Hāna, for information about scheduled orientations and cultural demonstrations. Note that there is no drinking water here.

A much neglected hike in southwestern Maui is the 5.5-mi (allow four to six hours) coastal **Hoapili (King's) Trail** (✉ *Mākena Rd.*) beyond the 'Āhihi-Kīna'u Natural Area Reserve. Named after a bygone Hawaiian king, it follows the shoreline, threading through the remains of ancient Hawaiian villages. The once-thriving community was displaced by one of Maui's last lava flows. Later, King Hoapili was responsible for over-seeing the creation of an islandwide highway. This remaining section, a wide path of stacked lava rocks, is a marvel to look at and walk on, though it's not the easiest surface for the ankles. (It's rumored to have once been covered in grass.) You can wander over to the Hanamanioa

Continued on page 265

HALEAKALĀ NATIONAL PARK

HALEAKALA CRATER

From the Tropics to the Moon! Two hours, 38 mi, 10,023 feet—those are the unlikely numbers involved in reaching Maui's highest point, the summit of the volcano Haleakalā. Nowhere else on earth can you drive from sea level (Kahului) to 10,023 feet (the summit) in only 38 mi. And what's more shocking—in that short vertical ascent, you'll journey from lush, tropical-island landscape to the stark, moonlike basin of the volcano's enormous, otherworldly crater.

Established in 1916, Haleakalā National Park covers an astonishing 27,284 acres. Haleakalā "Crater" is the centerpiece of the park though it's not actually a crater. Technically, it's an erosional valley, flushed out by water pouring from the summit through two enormous gaps. The mountain has terrific camping and hiking, including a trail that loops through the crater, but the chance to witness this unearthly landscape is reason enough for a visit.

THE CLIMB TO THE SUMMIT

To reach Haleakalā National Park and the mountain's breathtaking summit, take Route 36 east of Kahului to the Haleakalā Highway (Route 37). Head east, up the mountain to the unlikely intersection of Haleakalā Highway and Haleakalā Highway. If you continue straight the road's name changes to Kula Highway (still Route 37). Instead, turn left onto Haleakalā Highway—this is now Route 377. After about 6 mi, make a left onto

Map Labels

378

Hosmer Grove
(6,800 ft)

Visitor Center
(7,000 ft)

Halemau'u Trailhead

KE'ANAE VALLEY

Leleiwi Overlook
(8,800 ft)

Hōlua Cabin

KO'OLAU GAP

Kalahaku Overlook

Halemau'u Trail

Pu'u Kumu

Hanakauhi
8,907 ft

Mauna Hina

Haleakalā National Park

Halali'i

Pu'u Naue

Halemau'u Trail

Kaluaiki

Visitor Center
(9,740 ft)

Ka Lu'u o ka'O'o

Pu'u o Maui

Kamoali'i

Ka Moa o Pele

Na Mana o ke Akua

'O'ilipu'u

Keonehe'ehe'e (Sliding Sands) Trailhead

Pu'u 'Ula'ula
10,023 ft

Pu'u 'Ula'ula Overlook

Magnetic Peak
10,008 ft

Pu'u o Pele

Pu'u Maile

Science City

Haupa'akea
9,159 ft

Keonehe'ehe'e Trail (aka Sliding Sands Trail)

Kapala'oa Cabin

KAUPŌ VALLEY

Hosmer Grove
0.5 mi loop trail

▶ At entrance to park

Ten minutes down the trail you can spy honeycreepers, some of the world's rarest birds, hopping from branch to branch.

Keonehe'ehe'e (a.k.a. Sliding Sands) Trail
5.0 mi round-trip

▶ Haleakalā Visitor Center parking lot

This trail descends 2,500 feet to the crater floor. Allow twice the time to hike out as it takes to hike in.

Halemau'u Trail
2.25 mi round-trip

▶ Parking lot 3.5 mi above Park Headquarters at mile marker 14.

The cliffside, snaking switchbacks of this trail offer views stretching across the crater's floors to its far walls.

Crater Road (Route 378). After several long switchbacks (look out for downhill bikers!) you'll come to the park entrance.

■ TIP→ Before you head up Haleakalā, call for the latest park weather conditions (☎ 866/944–5025). Extreme gusty winds, heavy rain, and even snow in winter are not uncommon. Because of the high altitude, the mountaintop temperature is often as much as 30 degrees cooler than that at sea level. Be sure to bring a jacket. Also make sure you have a full tank of gas. No service stations exist beyond Kula.

There's a $10 per car fee to enter the park; but it's good for three days and can be used at 'Ohe'o Gulch (Seven Sacred Pools), so save your receipt.

6,800 feet, Hosmer Grove. Just as you enter the park, Hosmer Grove has campsites and interpretive trails (*see* Hiking & Camping *on the following pages*). Park rangers maintain a changing schedule of talks and hikes both here and at the top of the mountain. Call the park for current schedules.

7,000 feet, Park Headquarters/Visitor Center. Not far from Hosmer Grove, the Park Headquarters/Visitor Center (open daily from 6:30 AM to 4) has trail maps and displays about the volcano's origins

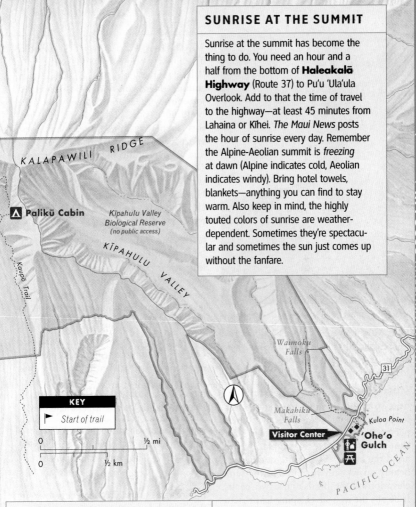

SUNRISE AT THE SUMMIT

Sunrise at the summit has become the thing to do. You need an hour and a half from the bottom of **Haleakalā Highway** (Route 37) to Puʻu ʻUlaʻula Overlook. Add to that the time of travel to the highway—at least 45 minutes from Lahaina or Kīhei. *The Maui News* posts the hour of sunrise every day. Remember the Alpine-Aeolian summit is *freezing* at dawn (Alpine indicates cold, Aeolian indicates windy). Bring hotel towels, blankets—anything you can find to stay warm. Also keep in mind, the highly touted colors of sunrise are weather-dependent. Sometimes they're spectacular and sometimes the sun just comes up without the fanfare.

KALAPAWILI RIDGE

△ **Palikū Cabin**

Kīpahulu Valley Biological Reserve (no public access)

KĪPAHULU VALLEY

Kaupō Trail

Waimoku Falls

31

KEY

▶ Start of trail

Makahiku Falls

Kuloa Point

Visitor Center

ʻOheʻo Gulch

0 ————— ½ mi

0 ————— ½ km

PACIFIC OCEAN

---

and eruption history. Hikers and campers should check-in here before heading up the mountain. Maps, posters, and other memorabilia are available at the gift shop.

8,800 feet, Leleiwi Overlook. Continuing up the mountain, you come to Leleiwi Overlook. A short walk to the end of the parking lot reveals your first awe-inspiring view of the crater. The small hills in the basin are volcanic cinder cones (called *puʻu* in Hawaiian), each with a small crater at its top, and each the site of a former eruption.

WHERE TO EAT

KULA LODGE (✉ Haleakalā Hwy., Kula ☎ 808/878–2517) serves hearty breakfasts from 7 to 11 AM, a favorite with hikers coming down from a sunrise visit to Haleakalā's summit, as well as those on their way up for a late-morning tramp in the crater. Spectacular ocean views fill the windows of this mountainside lodge.

If you're here in the late afternoon, it's possible you'll experience a phenomenon called the Brocken Specter. Named after a similar occurrence in East Germany's

Harz Mountains, the "specter" allows you to see yourself reflected on the clouds and encircled by a rainbow. Don't wait all day for this because it's not a daily occurrence.

9,000 feet, Kalahaku Overlook. The next stopping point is Kalahaku Overlook. The view here offers a different perspective of the crater, and at this elevation the famous silversword plant grows amid the cinders. This odd, endangered beauty grows only here and at the same elevation on the Big Island's two peaks. It begins life as a silver, spiny-leaf rosette and is the sole home of a variety of native insects (it's the only shelter around). The silversword reaches maturity between 7 and 17 years, when it sends forth a 3- to 8-foot-tall stalk with several hundred tiny sunflowers. It blooms once, then dies.

9,740 feet, Haleakalā Visitor Center. Another mile up is the Haleakalā Visitor Center, open daily from sunrise to 3 PM except Christmas and New Year's. There are exhibits inside, and a trail from here leads to White Hill—a short easy walk that will give you an even better view of the valley.

10,023 feet, Pu'u 'Ula'ula Overlook. The highest point on Maui is the Pu'u 'Ula'ula Overlook, at the 10,023-foot summit. Here you find a glass-enclosed lookout with a 360-degree view. The building is open 24 hours a day, and this is where visitors gather for the best sunrise view. Dawn begins between 5:45 and 7, depending on the time of year. On a clear day you can see the islands of Moloka'i, Lāna'i, Kaho'olawe, and Hawai'i (the Big Island). On a *really* clear day you can even spot O'ahu glimmering in the distance.

■TIP➔ The air is very thin at 10,000 feet. Don't be surprised if you feel a little breathless while walking around the summit. Take it easy and drink lots of water. Anyone who has been scuba diving within the last 24 hours should not make the trip up Haleakalā.

On a small hill nearby, you can see **Science City,** an off-limits research and communications center straight out of an espionage thriller. The University of Hawai'i maintains an observatory here, and the Department of Defense tracks satellites.

For more information about Haleakalā National Park, contact the **National Park Service** (☎ 808/572–4400,⊕ www.nps.gov/hale).

HIKING AND CAMPING

Exploring Haleakalā Crater is one of the best hiking experiences on Maui. The volcanic terrain offers an impressive diversity of colors, textures, and shapes—almost as if the lava has been artfully sculpted. The barren landscape is home to many plants, insects, and birds that exist nowhere else on earth and have developed intriguing survival mechanisms, such as the sun-reflecting, hairy leaves of the silversword, which allow it to survive the intense climate.

Stop at park headquarters to register and pick up trail maps on your way into the park.

1-Hour Hike. Just as you enter Haleakalā National Park, **Hosmer Grove** offers a short 10-minute hike, and an hour-long, $1/_2$-mi loop trail into the Waikamoi Cloud Forest that will give you insight into Hawai'i's fragile ecology. Anyone can go on the short hike, whereas the longer trail through the cloud forest is accessible only with park ranger–guided hikes. Call park headquarters for the schedule. Facilities here include six campsites (no permit needed, available on a first-come, first-served basis), pit toilets, drinking water, and cooking shelters.

4-Hour Hikes. Two half-day hikes involve descending into the crater and returning the way you came. The first, **Halemau'u Trail** (trailhead is between mile markers 14 and 15), is 2.25 mi round-trip. The cliffside, snaking switchbacks of this trail offer views stretching across the crater's pu'u-speckled floor to its far walls. On clear days you can peer through the Ko'olau Gap to Hāna. Native flowers and shrubs grow along the trail, which is typically misty and cool (though still exposed to the sun). When you reach the gate at the bottom, head back up.

The other hike, which is 5 mi round-trip, descends down **Keonehe'ehe'e (a.k.a. Sliding Sands) Trail** (trailhead is at the Haleakalā Visitor Center) into an alien landscape of reddish black cinders, lava bombs, and silverswords. It's easy to imagine life before humans in the solitude and silence of this place. Turn back when you hit the crater floor.

■ TIP➔ Bring water, sunscreen, and a reliable jacket. These are demanding hikes. Take it slowly to acclimate, and allow additional time for the uphill return trip.

8-Hour Hike. The recommended way to explore the crater in a single, but full day is to go in two cars and ferry yourselves back and forth between the head of **Halemau'u Trail** and the summit. This way, you can hike from the summit down **Keonehe'ehe'e Trail**, cross the crater's floor, investigate the **Bottomless Pit** and **Pele's Paint Pot**, then climb out on the **switchback trail (Halemau'u)**. When you emerge, the shelter of your waiting car will be very welcome (this is an 11.2-mi hike). If you don't have two cars, hitching a ride from Halemau'u back to the summit should be relatively safe and easy.

■TIP➜ Take a backpack with lunch, water, sunscreen, and a reliable jacket for the beginning and end of the 8-hour hike. This is a demanding trip, but you will never regret or forget it.

Overnight Hike. Staying overnight in one of Haleakalā's three cabins or two wilderness campgrounds is an experience like no other. You'll feel like the only person on earth when you wake up inside this enchanted, strange landscape. The cabins, each tucked in a different corner of the crater's floor, are equipped with 12 bunk beds, wood-burning stoves, fake logs, and kitchen gear.

Hōlua cabin is the shortest hike, less than 4 hours (3.7 mi) from Halemau'u Trail. **Kapala'oa** is about 5 hours (5.5 mi) down Keonehe'ehe'e Trail. The most cherished cabin is **Palikū**, an eight-hour (9.3-mi) hike starting from either trail. It's nestled against the cliffs above Kaupō Gap. Cabin reservations can be made up to 90 days in advance through the Friends of Haleakalā National Park's Web site (⊕ http:/fhnp.org/wcr) or by calling the National Park Service (☎ 808/572-4400) between 1 and 3 PM HST. Tent campsites at Hōlua

and Palikū are free and easy to reserve on a first-come, first-served basis.

■TIP➜ Toilets and nonpotable water are available—bring iodine tablets to purify the water. Open fires are not allowed and packing out your trash is mandatory.

For more information on hiking or camping, contact the National Park Service (✉ Box 369, Makawao 96768 ☎ 808/572-4459 ⊕ www.nps.gov/hale).

OPTIONS FOR EXPLORING

If you're short on time you can drive to the summit, take a peek inside, and drive back down. But the "House of the Sun" is really worth a day, whether you explore by foot, horseback, or helicopter.

BIKING
At this writing, all guided bike tours inside park boundaries were suspended indefinitely. However, the tours continue but now start outside the boundary of the park. These can provide a speedy, satisfying downhill trip. The park is still open to individual bikes for a $5 fee. There are no bike paths, however—just the same road that is used by vehicular traffic. Whether you're on your own or with a tour, be careful!

HELICOPTER TOURS
Viewing Haleakalā from above can be a mind-altering experience, if you don't mind dropping $200+ per person for a few blissful moments above the crater. Most tours buzz Haleakalā, where airspace is regulated, then head over to Hanā in search of waterfalls.

HORSEBACK RIDING
Several companies offer half-day, full-day, and even overnight rides into the crater. On one half-day ride you descend into the crater on Keonehe'ehe'e Trail and have lunch before you head back.

For complete information on any of these activities, ⇨ see Golf, Hiking and Outdoor Activities.

DID YOU KNOW?

You can get good views from lookouts at Haleakalā National Park, or try a hiking trail to get up close to the dramatic, eerie formations in the volcanic crater. Resembling small, steep hills, cinder cones made of volcanic rock mark the sites of past eruptions.

lighthouse, or quietly ponder the rough life of the ancients.

Wear sturdy shoes and bring extra water. This is brutal territory with little shade and no facilities. Beautiful, yes. Accommodating, no. To get here, follow Mākena Alanui to end of paved road at La Pérouse Bay, walk through parking lot along dirt road; follow signs.

★ In Hawaiian, 'Īao means "supreme cloud." When you enter the mystical valley of the **'Īao Valley State Monument,** in the middle of an unexpected rain forest near Wailuku in West Maui, you'll know why. At 750 feet above sea level, the 10-mi valley clings to the clouds as if it's trying to cover its naked beauty. One of Maui's great wonders, the valley is the site of a famous battle to unite the Hawaiian Islands. Out of the clouds, the **'Īao Needle,** a tall chunk of volcanic rock, stands as a monument to the long-ago lookout for Maui warriors.

Anyone (including your grandparents) can take the easy, short walk from the parking lot at 'Īao Valley State Monument. On your choice of two paved walkways, you can cross the 'Īao Stream and explore the junglelike area. Ascend the stairs up to the 'Īao Needle for spectacular views of Central Maui, or pause in the garden of Hawaiian heritage plants. To get to 'Īao Valley State Monument, go through Wailuku and continue to the western end of Route 32. The road dead-ends into the parking lot ($5 per car fee; honor system). The park is open daily 7 am to 7 pm. Facilities are available, but there is no drinking water. (For park information call ☎ 808/984–8109.) ✉ *Trailhead: Rte. 32, 'Īao Valley parking lot, Wailuku ⏱ 30 min, 0.5 mi round-trip.*

GOING WITH A GUIDE

Fodor's Choice ★ **Friends of Haleakalā National Park.** This nonprofit offers day and overnight service/learning trips into the volcanic crater. The purpose of your trip, the service work itself, isn't too much—mostly native planting, removing invasive plants, and light cabin maintenance. An interpretive park ranger accompanies each trip, taking you to places you'd never otherwise see and teaching you about the native flora and birds along the way. Visit the Web site to learn more about the trips and to certify your readiness before calling to make a reservation. Admission is free. ☎ 808/876–1673 ⊕ *www.fhnp.org.*

Fodor's Choice ★ **Hike Maui.** Started in 1983, the Islands' oldest hiking company remains extremely well regarded for waterfall and rain forest, Haleakalā Crater, and combination hikes led by enthusiastic, highly trained guides who weave botany, geology, ethnobotany, culture, and history into the outdoor experience. Prices range from $75 to $160 for excursions of 3 to 11 hours (discounts are available for advance, online bookings). Private and custom tours are also available. Hike Maui supplies day packs, rain gear, water shoes, mosquito repellent, first-aid supplies, bottled water, snacks, lunch for the longer trips, and transportation to and from the site. ☎ 808/879–5270 or 866/324–6284 ⊕ www. hikemaui.com.

★ **Sierra Club.** One great avenue into the island's untrammeled wilderness is Maui's chapter of the Sierra Club. Join one of the club's hikes into pristine forests, along ancient coastal paths, to historic sites, and to Haleakalā Crater. Several hikes a month are led by informative leaders who carry first-aid kits. Some outings require volunteer service, but most are just for fun. Bring your own food and water, rain gear, sunscreen, sturdy shoes, and a suggested donation of $5 for hikers over age 14 ($3 for Sierra Club members); this is a true bargain. ✉ Box 791180, Pā'ia 96779 ☎ 808/579–9802 ⊕ www.hi.sierraclub.org/maui.

HORSEBACK RIDING

Several companies on Maui offer horseback riding that's far more appealing than the typical hour-long trudge over a dull trail with 50 other horses.

GOING WITH A GUIDE

Fodor'sChoice **Maui Stables.** Hawaiian-owned and run, this company provides a trip
★ back in time, to an era when life moved more slowly and reverently. Tours begin at the stable in remote Kipahulu (near Hāna) and pass through several historic Hawaiian sites. Before heading up into the forest, your guide intones the words to a traditional *oli*, or chant, asking for permission to enter. Along the way, you can learn about the principles of Hawaiian culture, including a deep respect for the 'aina (land). By the time you reach the mountain pasture overlooking several waterfalls, including the 400-foot Waimoku Falls, you'll feel lucky to have been a part of the tradition. Rides begin at 10 am daily and cost $150 per rider—definitely well worth it. Maui Stables provides refreshments and bottled water only; bring a picnic lunch if you're a hearty eater. ✉ Hwy. 37, between mile markers 40 and 41, Hāna ☎ 808/248–7799 ⊕ www.mauistables.com.

Mendes Ranch. Family-owned and run, Mendes operates out of the beautiful ranchland of Kahakuloa on the windward slopes of the West Maui Mountains. Two-hour morning and afternoon trail rides ($110) are available. Cowboys will take you cantering up rolling pastures into the lush rain forest, and then you'll descend all the way down to the ocean for a photo op with a dramatic backdrop. Don't expect a cultural experience here—it's all about the horses and the ride. Skip the optional barbecue lunch ($20); you'll do better in town. Mendes caters to weddings and parties and offers private trail rides on request. ⊠ *Hwy. 340, Wailuku* ☎ *808/244–7320 or 808/871–8222* ⊕ *www.mendesranch.com.*

Pi'iholo Ranch. The local wranglers here will lead you on a rousing ride through family ranchlands—up hillside pastures, beneath a eucalyptus canopy, and past many native trees. One-hour rides ($75) and two-hour rides ($120) are offered twice daily; the three-hour ride ($180) is offered once per day. Their well-kept horses navigate the challenging terrain easily, but hold on when axis deer pass by! You must be at least eight years old and in good physical condition to participate. Small groups (no more than six riders) make it a more personal experience. Private rides and lessons are also available. ⊠ *End of Waiahiwi Rd., Makawao* ☎ *808/357–5544* ⊕ *www.piiholo.com.*

TENNIS

Most courts charge by the hour but will let players continue after their initial hour for free, provided no one is waiting. In addition to the facilities listed below, many hotels and condos have courts open to nonguests for a fee. The best free courts are the five at the **Lahaina Civic Center** (⊠ *1840 Honoapi'ilani Hwy., Lahaina* ☎ *808/661–4685*), near Wahikuli State Park. They're available on a first-come, first-served basis.

Kapalua Tennis Garden. Home to the Kapalua Tennis Club, this complex serves the Kapalua Resort with 10 courts, four lighted for night play, and a pro shop. You'll pay $14 per day if you're a guest, $16 if you're not. Each month the Kapalua Tennis Garden plays host to a special theme tournament for resort guests and residents. ⊠ *100 Kapalua Dr., Kapalua* ☎ *808/665–9112* ⊕ *www.kapalua.com.*

Wailea Tennis Club. The club has 11 Plexipave courts (its famed grass courts are, sadly, a thing of the past), lessons, rentals, and ball machines. On weekday mornings clinics are given to help you improve ground strokes, serve, volley, or doubles strategy. Rates are $15 per hour, per person, with three lighted courts available for night play. ⊠ *131 Wailea Ike Pl., Kihei* ☎ *808/879–1958 or 800/332–1614.*

ZIPLINE TOURS

Ziplining lets you satisfy your inner Tarzan by soaring high above deep gulches and canyons—for a price that can seem steep. A harness keeps you fully supported on each ride. There are now multiple zipline courses on Maui to choose from. Each has its own age minimums and weight restrictions but, generally, you must be at least 10 years old and weigh a minimum of 60–80 pounds and a maximum of 250–275 pounds. You should wear closed-toe athletic-type shoes and expect to get dirty.

■ TIP→ Although zipline tours are completely safe, you may want to reconsider this activity if you are pregnant, uncomfortable with heights, or have serious back or joint problems.

Flyin' Hawaiian Zipline. The newest entry into Maui's zipline scene, Flyin' Hawaiian has the longest line in the state of Hawai'i (a staggering 3,600 feet) as well as the most unique course layout. You build confidence on the first line, which is 250 feet long and only a few feet off the ground. Then you board a four-wheel-drive vehicle that takes you 1,500 feet above the town of Waikapū to 7 more lines that allow you to zip your way over 11 ridges and 9 valleys. The total distance covered is more than 2.5 mi, and the tour culminates in Mā'alaea—the next town over. The views are astonishing and you'll be impressed by the athleticism of the guides. The price of $185 includes water and snacks. You must be able to hike over steep and sometimes slippery terrain while carrying a 10-pound metal trolley. ☎ 808/463–5786 ⊕ *www.flyinhawaiianzipline.com.*

Kapalua Adventures Mountain Outpost. The zipline course here has almost 2 mi of parallel lines, enabling two riders to zip side by side. Line 3 is the longest at 2,300 feet. A "zipper lifter" (like a chair lift) takes you to the upper lines, but you must still be able to hike approximately 1 mi over sometimes-steep terrain while carrying a 15-pound trolley. Prices range from $49 to $249. The Mountain Outpost also has a high-ropes challenge course and a 35-foot pole from which you can leap to catch a trapeze. Don't miss the Giant Swing—an exhilarating 40-foot-high tandem experience that's as thrilling as any amusement park ride. ⊠ *2000 Village Rd., Kapalua* ☎ *808/665–4386 or 877/665– 4386* ⊕ *www.kapalua.com.*

Fodor'sChoice
★
Pi'iholo Ranch Zipline. This complex, on a gorgeous 900-acre family ranch in Upcountry, has six ziplines—five parallel lines and one quadruple— plus a 12-person climbing tower. Ziplines range from 480 to 2,800 feet, and prices are $140 for four lines and $190 for five. Access to the fifth and longest line is via a four-wheel-drive vehicle to the top of Pi'iholo Hill, where you are treated to stunning bicoastal views. Guides do a commendable job of weaving Hawaiian culture into the adventure. You must be able to climb three steep suspension bridges while hefting a 12-pound trolley over your shoulder. It can get chilly and misty in Makawao, so bring a lightweight jacket. ⊠ *Pi'iholo Rd., Makawao* ☎ *808/572–1717* ⊕ *www.piiholozipline.com.*

SHOPPING

Updated by
Eliza Escaño-
Vasquez

Whether you're searching for a dashboard hula dancer or an original Curtis Wilson Cost painting, you can find it on Front Street in Lahaina or at the Shops at Wailea. Art sales are huge in the resort areas, where artists regularly show up to promote their work. Alongside the flashy galleries are standards like Quicksilver and ABC store, where you can stock up on swim trunks, sunscreen, and flip-flops.

Don't miss the great boutiques lining the streets of small towns like Pā'ia and Makawao. You can purchase boutique fashions and art while strolling through these charming, quieter communities. Notably, several local designers—Tamara Catz, Letarte, and Maui Girl—all produce top-quality island fashions. In the neighboring galleries, local artisans turn out gorgeous work in a range of prices. Special souvenirs include rare hardwood bowls and boxes, prints of sea life, Hawaiian quilts, and blown glass.

Specialty food products—pineapples, coconuts, or Maui onions—and "Made in Maui" jams and jellies make great, less-expensive souvenirs. Cook Kwee's Maui Cookies have gained a following, as have Maui Potato Chips. Coffee sellers now offer Maui-grown-and-roasted beans alongside the better-known Kona varieties. Remember that fresh fruit must be inspected by the U.S. Department of Agriculture before it can leave the state, so it's safest to buy a box that has already passed inspection.

Business hours for individual shops on the island are usually 9 to 5, seven days a week. Shops on Front Street and in shopping centers tend to stay open later (until 9 or 10 on weekends).

BEST MADE-ON-MAUI GIFTS

■ *Koa* jewelry boxes from **Maui Hands.**

■ Sushi platters and bamboo chopsticks from the **Maui Crafts Guild.**

■ Black-pearl pendant from **Maui Divers.**

■ Handmade Hawaiian quilt from **Hāna Coast Gallery.**

■ Jellyfish paperweight from **Hot Island Glass.**

■ 'Ukulele from **Mele Ukulele.**

■ Plumeria lei, made by you!

WEST MAUI

SHOPPING CENTERS

Lahaina Cannery Mall. In a building reminiscent of an old pineapple cannery are 50 shops and an active stage. The mall hosts fabulous free events year-round, such as the Keiki Hula Festival and an annual ice-sculpting competition. Recommended stops include Na Hoku, purveyor of striking Hawaiian heirloom-quality jewelry and pearls; Banana Wind, which carries Island-inspired home decor; and Maui Toy Works, one of the best kite shops on Maui. Check the Web site for events. ⊠ *1221 Honoapi'ilani Hwy., Lahaina* ☎ *808/661–5304* ⊕ *www. lahainacannerymall.com.*

Lahaina Center. Island department store Hilo Hattie Fashion Center anchors the complex and puts on a free hula show at 2:30 pm every Wednesday. In addition to Hard Rock Cafe, Warren & Annabelle's Magic Show, and a four-screen cinema, you can find a replica of an ancient Hawaiian village complete with three full-size thatch huts built with 10,000 feet of Big Island *'ōhi'a* wood, 20 tons of *pili* grass, and more than 4 mi of handwoven coconut *senit* (twine). There's all that *and* validated parking. ⊠ *900 Front St., Lahaina* ☎ *808/667–9216.*

Whalers Village. Chic Whalers Village has a whaling museum and more than 50 restaurants and shops. Upscale haunts include Louis Vuitton and Coach. The complex also offers some interesting diversions: Hawaiian artisans display their crafts daily; hula dancers perform on an outdoor stage some weeknights from 7 to 8; sunset jazz is featured every first Sunday of the month; and Polynesian rhythms beat on Saturday. ⊠ *2435 Kā'anapali Pkwy., Kā'anapali* ☎ *808/661–4567* ⊕ *www. whalersvillage.com.*

BOOKSTORES

Fodor's Choice **Old Lahaina Book Emporium.** Down a narrow alley you will find this
★ bookstore stacked from floor to ceiling with new and antique finds.
Spend a few moments (or hours) browsing the maze of shelves filled
with mystery, sci-fi, nature guides, art, military history, and more. Col-
lectors can scoop up rare Hawaiian memorabilia: playing cards, coasters, rare editions, and out-of-print books chronicling Hawai'i's colorful
past. ⊠ *In the alley next door, 834 Front St., Lahaina* ☎ *808/661–1399*
⊕ *www.oldlahainabookemporium.com.*

CLOTHING

Hilo Hattie Fashion Center. Hawai'i's largest manufacturer of aloha shirts
and *mu'umu'u* also carries brightly colored blouses, skirts, and children's
clothing. ⊠ *Lahaina Center, 900 Front St., Lahaina* ☎ *808/667–7911.*

Honolua Surf Company. If you're not in the mood for a matching aloha
shirt and *mu'umu'u* ensemble, check out this surf shop—popular with
young men and women for surf trunks, casual clothing, and accessories.
⊠ *845 Front St., Lahaina* ☎ *808/661–8848.*

FOOD

Lahaina Square Shopping Center Foodland. This Foodland serves West
Maui and is open daily from 6 am to midnight. ⊠ *840 Waine'e St.,
Lahaina* ☎ *808/661–0975.*

Safeway. Safeway has three stores on the island open 24 hours daily.
⊠ *Lahaina Cannery Mall, 1221 Honoapi'ilani Hwy., Lahaina* ☎ *808/
667–4392.*

GALLERIES

Lahaina Galleries. Works of both national and international artists are
displayed at the gallery's two locations in West Maui. ⊠ *828 Front
St., Lahaina* ☎ *808/667–2152* ⊠ *In the Shops at Wailea, 3750 Wailea
Alanui Dr., Wailea* ☎ *808/874–8583* ⊕ *www.lahainagalleries.com.*

Lahaina Printsellers Ltd. Hawai'i's largest selection of original antique
maps and prints pertaining to Hawai'i and the Pacific is available here.
You can also buy museum-quality reproductions and original oil paintings from the Pacific Artists Guild. A second, smaller shop is at 505
Front Street. ⊠ *Whalers Village, 2435 Kā'anapali Pkwy., Kā'anapali*
☎ *808/667–7617* ⊕ *www.printsellers.com.*

Village Gallery. At its two locations in West Maui, this gallery showcases
the works of such popular local artists as Betty Hay Freeland, Carleton
Kinkade, George Allan, Joseph Fletcher, Pamela Andelin, Stephen Burr,
and Macario Pascual. ⊠ *120 Dickenson St., Lahaina* ☎ *808/661–4402*
⊠ *Ritz-Carlton, 1 Ritz-Carlton Dr., Kapalua* ☎ *808/669–1800* ⊕ *www.
villagegalleriesmaui.com.*

HOME FURNISHINGS

Hale Zen. If you're shopping for gifts in West Maui, do not miss this store
teeming with beautiful Island-inspired pieces for the home. Most of the
teak furniture is imported from Bali, but local purveyors supply the
inventory of clothing, accessories, beauty products, food items, kitch-
enware, and home accents. ⊠ *180 Dickenson St., Suite 111, Lahaina*
☎ *808/661–4802* ⊕ *www.halezen.com.*

JEWELRY

Jessica's Gems. Jessica's has a good selection of Hawaiian heirloom jewelry, and its Lahaina store specializes in black pearls. ⊠ *Whalers Village, 2435 Kā'anapali Pkwy., Kā'anapali* ☎ *808/661–4223* ⊠ *858 Front St., Lahaina* ☎ *808/661–9200.*

Lahaina Scrimshaw. Here you can buy brooches, rings, pendants, cuff links, tie tacks, and collector's items adorned with intricately carved sailors' art. The store sells a few antiques, but most pieces are modern creations. ⊠ *845A Front St., Lahaina* ☎ *808/661–8820* ⊠ *Whalers Village, 2435 Kā'anapali Pkwy., Kā'anapali* ☎ *808/661–4034.*

Maui Divers. This company has been crafting gold and coral into jewelry for more than 50 years. ⊠ *640 Front St., Lahaina* ☎ *808/661–0988* ⊕ *www.lahainascrimshaw.net.*

CENTRAL MAUI

SHOPPING CENTERS

Maui Marketplace. On the busy stretch of Dairy Road, just outside the Kahului Airport, this behemoth marketplace couldn't be more conveniently located. The 20-acre complex houses several outlet stores and big retailers, such as Pier One Imports, Sports Authority, and Borders Books & Music. Sample local food at the Kau Kau Corner food court. ⊠ *270 Dairy Rd., Kahului* ☎ *808/873–0400.*

Queen Ka'ahumanu Center. Maui's largest mall has 75 stores, a movie theater, an active stage, and a food court. The mall's interesting rooftop, composed of a series of manta ray–like umbrella shades, is easily spotted. Stop at Camellia Seeds for what the locals call "crack seed," a snack made from dried fruits, nuts, and lots of sugar. Other stops here include mall standards such as Macy's, Pacific Sunwear, and American Eagle Outfitters. ⊠ *275 W. Ka'ahumanu Ave., Kahului* ☎ *808/877–3369* ⊕ *www.queenkaahumanucenter.com.*

ARTS AND CRAFTS

Mele Ukulele. For those looking for a professional quality, authentically Maui 'ukulele, skip the souvenir shops. Mele's crafted beauties are made of koa or mahogany, and strung by hand by the store's owner, Michael Rock. ⊠ *1750 Ka'ahumanu Ave., Wailuku* ☎ *808/244–3938* ⊕ *www.meleukulele.com.*

CLOTHING

Bohemia. Find vintage Hawaiiana, upscale designer resale, *and* new pieces by local designers, all at affordable prices. ⊠ *105 N. Market St., Wailuku* ☎ *808/244–9995.*

Hi-Tech. Stop here immediately after deplaning to stock up on surf trunks, windsurfing gear, bikinis, and sundresses. ⊠ *425 Koloa Rd., Kahului* ☎ *808/877–2111.*

FOOD

Maui Coffee Roasters. This café and roasting house near Kahului Airport is the best stop for Kona and Island coffees. The salespeople give good advice and will ship items. You even get a free cup of joe in a signature to-go cup when you buy a pound of coffee. ⊠ *444 Hāna Hwy., Unit B,*

Kahului ☎ *808/877–2877* ⊕ *www.*
mauicoffeeroasters.com.

Safeway. Safeway has three stores
on the island open 24 hours daily.
⊠ *170 E. Kamehameha Ave., Kahu-*
lui ☎ *808/877–3377.*

THE SOUTH SHORE

SHOPPING CENTERS

Azeka Place Shopping Center. Azeka
II, on the *mauka* (toward the mountains) side of South Kīhei Road,
has the Coffee Store (the place for
iced mochas), Who Cut the Cheese
(the place for aged gouda), and the
Nail Shop (the place for shaping,
waxing, and tweezing). Azeka I,
the older half on the *makai* side
of the street, has a decent Vietnamese restaurant and Kīhei's post
office. ⊠ *1280 S. Kīhei Rd., Kīhei*
☎ *808/879–5000.*

FLEA MARKETS

Lahaina Civic Center Craft Fair.
An eclectic mix of vendors and
artists set up shop here, offering
the whole gamut of souvenir
shopping, from towels to aloha
prints. ⊠ *1840 Honoapi'ilani Hwy.,*
Lahaina 🏷 *$1 suggested donation*
⊙ *Most Sun. 9–4.*

Maui Swap Meet. Crafts, souvenirs, fruit, shells, and more make
this flea market in a college
parking lot the island's biggest
bargain. ⊠ *Off Kahului Beach Rd.,*
Kahului ☎ *808/244-3100* 🏷 *50¢*
⊙ *Sat. 7 am-1 pm.*

■TIP→ Check out
⊕ www.mauimarkets.com for
information.

Kīhei Kalama Village Marketplace. Head to this fun place to investigate.
Shaded outdoor stalls sell everything from printed and hand-painted
T-shirts and sundresses to jewelry, pottery, wood carvings, fruit, and
gaudily painted coconut husks—some, but not all, made by local crafts-
people. ⊠ *1941 S. Kīhei Rd., Kīhei* ☎ *808/879–6610.*

Shops at Wailea. Stylish, upscale, and close to most of the resorts, this
mall brings high fashion to Wailea. Luxury boutiques such as Gucci,
Fendi, Cos Bar, and Tiffany & Co. have shops, as do less-expensive
chains like Gap, Guess, and Tommy Bahama. Several good restaurants
face the ocean, and regular Wednesday-night events include live entertainment, art exhibits, and fashion shows. ⊠ *3750 Wailea Alanui Dr.,*
Wailea ☎ *808/891–6770* ⊕ *www.shopsatwailea.com.*

CLOTHING

Cruise. This upscale resort boutique has sundresses, swimwear, sandals, bright beach towels, and a few nice pieces of resort wear. ⊠ *In*
the Grand Wailea, 3850 Wailea Alanui Dr., Wailea ☎ *808/875–1234.*

Hilo Hattie Fashion Center. Hawai'i's largest manufacturer of aloha shirts
and *mu'umu'u* also carries brightly colored blouses, skirts, and children's clothing. ⊠ *297 Pi'ikea Ave., Kīhei* ☎ *808/875–4545* ⊕ *www.*
hilohattie.com.

Sisters & Company. Opened by four sisters, this little shop has a lot to
offer—current brand-name clothing such as True Religion and Love
Tan Jane, locally made jewelry, beach sandals, and gifts. Sister No. 3,
Rhonda, runs a tiny, ultrahip hair salon in back while Caroline, Sister
No. 2, offers mani-pedis. ⊠ *1913 S. Kīhei Rd., Kīhei* ☎ *808/875–9888*
⊕ *www.sistersandco.com.*

Tommy Bahama's. It's hard to find a man on Maui who *isn't* wearing a TB-logo aloha shirt. For better or worse, here's where you can get yours. Make sure to grab a Barbados Brownie on the way out at the restaurant attached to the shop. ⊠ *Shops at Wailea, 3750 Wailea Alanui Dr., Wailea* ☎ *808/879–7828* ⊕ *www.tommybahamas.com.*

FOOD

Foodland. In Kīhei town center, this is the most convenient supermarket for those staying in Wailea. It's open round-the-clock. ⊠ *1881 S. Kīhei Rd., Kīhei* ☎ *808/879–9350.*

Safeway. Safeway has three stores on the island open 24 hours daily. ⊠ *277 Piikea Ave., Kīhei* ☎ *808/891–9120.*

UPCOUNTRY, THE NORTH SHORE, AND HĀNA

CLOTHING

Alice in Hulaland. While the store is famous for its vintage-inspired Ts that pay homage to *Pā'ia*, it also carries a lovely mix of gift items and casual wear for the whole family. ⊠ *19 Baldwin Ave., Pā'ia* ☎ *808/579–9922* ⊕ *www.aliceinhulaland.com.*

Fodor'sChoice
★

Maui Girl. This is *the* place on Maui for swimwear, cover-ups, beach hats, and sandals. Maui Girl designs its own suits, which have been spotted in *Sports Illustrated* fashion features, and imports teenier versions from Brazil as well. Tops and bottoms can be purchased separately, greatly increasing your chances of finding a suit that actually fits. ⊠ *12 Baldwin Ave., Pā'ia* ☎ *808/579–9266* ⊕ *www.maui-girl.com.*

Moonbow Tropics. If you're looking for an aloha shirt that won't look out of place on the mainland, make a stop at this store, which sells the best-quality shirts on the island. There are separate stores for their men's and women's boutiques. ⊠ *20 Baldwin Rd., Pā'ia* ☎ *808/579–8775.* ⊠ *27 Baldwin Rd., Pā'ia* ☎ *808/579–3131.*

Pink By Nature. Owner Desiree Martinez's penchant for easy wearability keeps this rustic store stocked with select pieces from Indah, Riller and Fount, and LA Made. ⊠ *3663 Baldwin Ave., Makawao* ☎ *808/572–9576.*

Fodor'sChoice
★

Tamara Catz. This Maui designer already has a worldwide following, and her sarongs and superstylish beachwear have been featured in many fashion magazines. If you're looking for a sequined bikini or a delicately embroidered sundress, this is the place. And for the blushing beach bride, Catz also has a bridal line that is superhaute. Her pieces can cost a pretty penny; if you are visiting in December, you might just catch the annual sample sale. ⊠ *83 Hāna Hwy., Pā'ia* ☎ *808/579–9184.*

FOOD

Mana Foods. Stock up on local fish and grass-fed beef for your barbecue here. You can find the best selection of organic produce on the island, as well as a great bakery and deli at this typically crowded health-food store. ⊠ *49 Baldwin Ave., Pā'ia* ☎ *808/579–8078.*

Continued on page 278

ALL ABOUT LEI

Lei brighten every occasion in Hawai'i, from birthdays to bar mitzvahs to baptisms. Creative artisans weave nature's bounty—flowers, ferns, vines, and seeds—into gorgeous creations that convey an array of heartfelt messages: "Welcome," "Congratulations," "Good luck," "Farewell," "Thank you," "I love you." When it's difficult to find the right words, a lei expresses exactly the right sentiments.

WHERE TO BUY THE BEST LEI

These florists carry a nice variety of lei: **A Special Touch** (Emerald Plaza, 142 Kupuohi St., Ste. F-1, Lahaina, 808/661—3455); **Kahului Florist** (Maui Mall, 70 E. Ka'ahumanu Ave., Kahului, 808/877-3951 or 800/711—8881); **Nāpili Florist** (5059 Nāpilihau St., Lahaina, 808/669-4861); and **Kīhei-Wailea Flowers by Cora** (1280 S. Kīhei Rd., Ste. 126, Kīhei, 808/879-7249 or 800/339—0419). **Costco**, **Kmart**, **Wal-Mart**, and **Safeway** sell basic lei, such as orchid and plumeria.

LEI ETIQUETTE

■To wear a closed lei, drape it over your shoulders, half in front and half in back. Open lei are worn around the neck, with the ends draped over the front in equal lengths.

■ Pīkake, ginger, and other sweet, delicate blossoms are "feminine" lei. Men opt for cigar, crown flower, and ti leaf, which are sturdier and don't emit as much fragrance.

■ Lei are always presented with a kiss, a custom that supposedly dates back to World War II when a hula dancer fancied an officer at a U.S.O. show. Taking a dare from members of her troupe, she took off her lei, placed it around his neck, and kissed him on the cheek.

■ You shouldn't wear a lei before you give it to someone else. Hawaiians believe the lei absorbs your *mana* (spirit); if you give your lei away, you'll be giving away part of your essence.

ORCHID

Growing wild on every continent except Antarctica, orchids—which range in color from yellow to green to purple—comprise the largest family of plants in the world. There are more than 20,000 species of orchids, but only three are native to Hawai'i—and they are very rare. The pretty lavender vanda you see hanging by the dozens at local lei stands has probably been imported from Thailand.

MAILE

Maile, an endemic twining vine with a heady aroma, is sacred to Laka, goddess of the hula. In ancient times, dancers wore maile and decorated hula altars with it to honor Laka. Today, "open" maile lei usually are given to men. Instead of ribbon, interwoven lengths of maile are used at dedications of new businesses. The maile is untied, never snipped, for doing so would symbolically "cut" the company's success.

'ILIMA

Designated by Hawai'i's Territorial Legislature in 1923 as the official flower of the island of O'ahu, the golden 'ilima is so delicate it lasts for just a day. Five to seven hundred blossoms are needed to make one garland. Queen Emma, wife of King Kamehameha IV, preferred 'ilima over all other leis, which may have led to the incorrect belief that they were reserved only for royalty.

PLUMERIA

This ubiquitous flower is named after Charles Plumier, the noted French botanist who discovered it in Central America in the late 1600s. Plumeria ranks among the most popular leis in Hawai'i because it's fragrant, hardy, plentiful, inexpensive, and requires very little care. Although yellow is the most common color, you'll also find plumeria lei in shades of pink, red, orange, and "rainbow" blends.

PĪKAKE

Favored for its fragile beauty and sweet scent, pīkake was introduced from India. In lieu of pearls, many brides in Hawai'i adorn themselves with long, multiple strands of white pīkake. Princess Kaiulani enjoyed showing guests her beloved pīkake and peacocks at Āinahau, her Waikīkī home. Interestingly, pīkake is the Hawaiian word for both the bird and the blossom.

KUKUI

The kukui (candlenut) is Hawai'i's state tree. Early Hawaiians strung kukui nuts (which are quite oily) together and burned them for light; mixed burned nuts with oil to make an indelible dye; and mashed roasted nuts to consume as a laxative. Kukui nut lei may not have been made until after Western contact, when the Hawaiians saw black beads from Europe and wanted to imitate them.

GALLERIES

★ **Hāna Coast Gallery.** One of the best places to shop on the island, this 3,000-square-foot gallery has fine art, handcrafted furniture and jewelry on consignment from local artists. ✉ *Hotel Hāna-Maui, Hāna Hwy., Hāna* ☎ *808/248–8636 or 800/637–0188.*

Fodor'sChoice **Maui Crafts Guild.** This is one of the more interesting galleries on Maui.
★ Set in a two-story wooden building alongside the highway, the guild is crammed with treasures. Resident artists craft everything in the store—from *raku* (Japanese lead-glazed) pottery to original sculpture. The prices are surprisingly low. ✉ *43 Hāna Hwy., Pā'ia* ☎ *808/579–9697.* ⊕ *www.mauicraftsguild.com.*

JEWELRY

Maui Master Jewelers. The exterior of this shop is as rustic as all the old buildings of Makawao, so there's no way to prepare yourself for the elegance of the handcrafted jewelry displayed within. The store has recently added a diamond collection to its designs. ✉ *3655 Baldwin Ave., Makawao* ☎ *808/573–5400* ⊕ *www.mauimasterjewelers.com.*

SPAS

Updated by
Eliza Escaño-
Vasquez

Traditional Swedish massage and European facials anchor most spa menus, though you'll also find Shiatsu, Ayurveda, aromatherapy, and other body treatments drawn from cultures across the globe. *Lomilomi,* traditional Hawaiian massage involving powerful strokes down the length of the body, is a regional specialty passed down through generations. Many treatments incorporate local plants and flowers. *Awapuhi,* or Hawaiian ginger, and *noni,* a pungent-smelling fruit, are regularly used for their therapeutic benefits. *Limu,* or seaweed, and even coffee is employed in rousing salt scrubs and soaks. And this is just the beginning.

Fodor'sChoice **Heavenly Spa by Westin at the Westin Maui.** Pamper yourself with the
★ exquisite 80-minute Island Indulgence treatment that combines a body scrub and a warm coconut milk bath in a hydrotherapy tub. Other options include cabana massage (for couples, too) and sunburn relief with a lavender-aloe blend. The facility is flawless, and it's worth getting a treatment just to sip lavender lemonade in the posh, serene, ocean-view waiting room. The open-air yoga studio and the gym offer energizing workouts, and the hair salon has braiding services. ✉ *Westin Kā'anapali, 2365 Kā'anapali Pkwy., Kā'anapali* ☎ *808/661–2588* ⊕ *www.westinmaui.com* ☞ *$135 50-min massage, $255 day spa packages. Hair salon, hot tub, sauna, steam room, nail salon. Gym with: Cardiovascular machines, free weights, weight-training equipment. Services: Aromatherapy, body wraps, facials, hydrotherapy, massage, Vichy shower. Classes and programs: Aquaerobics, Pilates, spinning, yoga.*

★ **Honua Spa at Hotel Hāna-Maui.** A bamboo gate opens into an outdoor sanctuary with a lava-rock basking pool and hot tub; at first glimpse this spa seems to have been organically grown, not built. The decor here can hardly be called decor—it's an abundant, living garden. Ferns still wet from Hāna's frequent downpours nourish the spirit as you rest with a cup of Hawaiian herbal tea. Take an invigorating dip in the cold plunge pool or have a therapist stretch your limbs while soaking in the warm waters of the resort's aquatic therapy pool. The Malama Kino package is a blissful eight hours of treatments, which can be shared between the family, or enjoyed solo. ⊠ *Hotel Hāna-Maui, 5031 Hāna Hwy., Hāna* ☎ *808/270–5290* ⊕ *www.hotelhanamaui.com* ☞ *$120 50-min massage, $210 spa packages. Outdoor hot tub, steam room. Gym with: Cardiovascular machines, free weights, weight-training equipment. Services: Aromatherapy, body wraps, facials, hydrotherapy, massage. Classes and programs: Meditation, Pilates, yoga.*

Kapalua Spa. The spa's humble entrance opens to a majestic panoramic view of Kapalua Bay. While the space is designed like a modern beach house, treatments incorporate ancient Hawaiian healing practices. The *'awa* and cacao *lomi* wrap, designed by Big Island resident and healer Darrell Lapulapu, begins with a special cava tea for instant relaxation, is followed by a body wrap of *'awa*, cacao, ginger, sandalwood, and oats, and finishes with *lomilomi* (traditional Hawaiian massage involving strokes down the length of the body). Other interesting treatments include the Hawaiian *spirulina* wrap, *pōhaku* brown seaweed facial, and the dual-therapist massage, because four hands are always better than two. A juice bar serves health potions that combine pure fruits and juiced veggies with natural additives like yogurt, cocoa powder, agave nectar, vanilla extract, or honey. ⊠ *100 Bay Dr., Kapalua* ☎ *808/665–8282* ⊕ *www.kapalua.com* ☞ *$140 50-min massage, $375 half-day spa packages. Hair salon, hot tubs, sauna, steam room, whirlpool, juice bar, sunning deck, saline lap pool. Gym with: Cardiovascular machines, free weights, weight-training equipment. Services: Aromatherapy, body wraps, facials, massage. Classes and programs: Aquaerobics, cycling, nutrition, Pilates, yoga, Zumba.*

Fodor's Choice
★ **The Spa at Four Seasons Resort Maui.** The resort's hawklike attention to detail is reflected here. Thoughtful gestures like fresh flowers beneath the massage table (to give you something to stare at), organic herbal tea in the "relaxation room," and your choice of music begin to ease your mind and muscles before your treatment even begins. The spa is stylish and serene, and the therapists are among the best. Warm up for your treatment with a hot ginger blast before hopping into the steam room. Thanks to an exclusive partnership, the spa offers treatments created by celebrity skin-care specialist Kate Somerville. The spa also features ISUN Organic Skincare, an eco-friendly beauty line that infuses gemstones and crystal energy into its products. For the ultimate indulgence, reserve one of the seaside open-air *hale hau* (traditional thatch-roof houses). You can have not just one, but two therapists realign your body and spirit with a *lomilomi* massage (traditional Hawaiian massage involving powerful strokes down the length of the body). ⊠ *3900 Wailea Alanui Dr., Wailea* ☎ *808/874–8000 or 800/334–6284* ⊕ *www. fourseasons.com/maui* ☞ *$155 50-min massage, $370 3-treatment packages. Hair salon, steam room, seaside cabanas. Gym with: cardiovascular machines, free weights, weight-training equipment. Services: aromatherapy, body wraps, facials, massage. Classes and programs:*

aquaerobics, meditation, personal training, Pilates, spinning, tai chi, yoga, Zumba.

Fodor's Choice ★ **Spa Grande, Grand Wailea Resort.** Built to satisfy an indulgent Japanese billionaire, this 50,000-square-foot spa makes others seem like well-appointed closets. Slathered in honey and wrapped up in the steam room (if you go for the Ali'i honey steam wrap), you'll feel like royalty. All treatments include a loofah scrub and a trip to the *termé*, a hydrotherapy circuit including a Roman Jacuzzi, furo bath, plunge pool, powerful waterfall and Swiss jet showers, and five therapeutic baths. (Soak for 10 minutes in the moor mud to relieve sunburn or jellyfish stings.) To fully enjoy the baths, plan to arrive an hour before your treatment. Free with treatments, the *termé* is also available separately for $55 for two hours. At times—especially during the holidays—this wonderland can be crowded. When it isn't, it is quite difficult to pry yourself away. ✉ *3850 Wailea Alanui Dr., Wailea* ☎ *808/875–1234 or 800/888–6100* ⊕ *www.grandwailea.com* ☞ *$140 50-min massage, $263 half-day spa packages. Hair salon, hot tub, sauna, steam room. Gym with: Cardiovascular machines, free weights, racquetball, weight-training equipment. Services: Aromatherapy, body wraps, facials, hydrotherapy, massage, Vichy shower. Classes and programs: Aquaerobics, cycling, Pilates, spinning, aquayoga, yoga.*

Fodor's Choice ★ **Waihua Spa, Ritz-Carlton, Kapalua.** At this gorgeous 17,500-square-foot spa, you enter a blissful maze where floor-to-ceiling riverbed stones lead to serene treatment rooms, couples' *hales* (cabanas), and a rain forest–like grotto with a Jacuzzi, dry sauna, and steam rooms. With cucumber water in hand, hang out in the co-ed waiting area, where sliding glass doors open to a whirlpool overlooking a taro patch garden. Get any rough skin exfoliated with a pineapple papaya scrub; then wash it off in a private outdoor shower garden before indulging in a *lomilomi* massage (traditional Hawaiian massage involving powerful strokes down the length of the body). Some high-end beauty treatments uses advanced oxygen technology to tighten mature skin. Attention fitness junkies: personal TVs are attached to the cardiovascular machines in the ocean-view fitness center. ✉ *1 Ritz-Carlton Dr., Kapalua* ☎ *808/669–6200 or 800/262–8440* ⊕ *www.ritzcarlton.com* ☞ *$155 50-min massage, $375 half-day spa packages. Hair salon, hot tubs (outdoor and indoor), sauna, steam room. Gym with: Cardiovascular machines, free weights, weight-training equipment. Services: Aromatherapy, body wraps, facials, massage. Classes and programs: Aquaerobics, cycling, nutrition, Pilates, yoga.*

ENTERTAINMENT AND NIGHTLIFE

Updated by
Eliza Escaño-
Vasquez

Looking for wild island nightlife? We can't promise you'll always find it here. This quiet island has little of Waikīkī's after-hours decadence, and the club scene (if you want to call it that) can be quirky, depending on the season and the day of the week. But sometimes Maui will surprise you with a big-name concert, outdoor festival, or world-class DJ. Lahaina and Kīhei are your best bets for action. Outside those towns, you might be able to hit an "on" night in Pā'ia (North Shore) or

Makawao (Upcountry), mostly on weekend nights. Your best bet? Pick up the free *MauiTime Weekly,* or Thursday's edition of the *Maui News,* where you'll find a listing of all your after-dark options, islandwide.

ENTERTAINMENT

Before 10 pm, there's a lot to offer by way of lūʻau shows, dinner cruises, and tiki-lighted cocktail hours. Aside from that, you should at least be able to find some down-home DJ spinning or the strum of acoustic guitars at your nearest watering hole or restaurant.

ARTS CENTER

★ **Maui Arts & Cultural Center.** The hub of all highbrow arts and quality performances has an events calendar that features everything from rock to reggae to Hawaiian slack-key guitar, international dance and circus troupes, political and literary lectures, art films, cult classics—you name it. Each Wednesday (and occasionally Friday) evening, the MACC hosts movie selections from the Maui Film Festival. The complex includes the 1,200-seat Castle Theater, a 4,000-seat amphitheater for large outdoor concerts, the 350-seat McCoy Theater for plays and recitals, and a courtyard café offering preshow dining and drinks. For information on current events, check the Events Box Office (☎ *808/242–7469* ⊕ *www. mauiarts.org*) or *Maui News* (✉ *1 Cameron Way, above harbor on Kahului Beach Rd., Kahului* ☎ *808/242–2787*).

DINNER CRUISES AND SHOWS

There's no better place to see the sun set on the Pacific than from one of Maui's many boat tours. You can find a tour to fit your mood, anything from a quiet, sit-down dinner to a festive, beer-swigging booze cruise. Note, however, that many cocktail cruises have recently put a cap on the number of free drinks offered with open bars, instead including a limited number of drinks per ticket.

Dinner cruises typically feature music and are generally packed—which is great if you're feeling social, but you might have to fight for a good seat. You can usually get a much better meal at one of the local restaurants. Most nondinner cruises offer *pūpū* and an open bar. Winds are consistent in summer, but variable in winter—sometimes making for a rocky ride. If you're worried about seasickness, you might consider a catamaran, which is much more stable than a monohull. Take Dramamine before the trip, and if you feel sick, sit in the shade (but not inside the cabin), place a cold rag or ice on the back of your neck, and *breathe* as you look at the horizon. In the worst-case scenario, aim downwind—and shoot for distance. Tours leave from Māʻalaea or Lahaina harbors. Be sure to arrive at least 15 minutes early.

Paragon Champagne Sunset Sail. This 47-foot catamaran brings you a performance sail within a personal setting. Limited to groups of 24 (with private charters available), you can spread out on deck and enjoy the gentle trade winds. An easygoing, attentive crew will serve you hot and cold *pūpū*, such as grilled chicken skewers, spring rolls, and a fruit platter, along with beer, wine, mai tais, and champagne at sunset. ✉ *Loading Dock, Lahaina Harbor* ☎ *808/244–2087* ⊕ *www.sailmaui.*

com 🖃 *$47.60 adult, $33.15 child 4–12, free for children 3 and under*
⊘ *Mon., Wed., Fri. evenings only; call for check-in times.*

Pride Charters. A 65-foot catamaran built specifically for Maui's waters,
the *Pride of Maui* has a spacious cabin, dance floor, and large upper
deck for unobstructed viewing. Evening cruises include premium, top-
shelf cocktails and an impressive spread of baby back ribs, grilled
chicken, roasted veggies, warm artichoke dip, garlic fettuccine, and
peach cobbler for dessert. ✉ *Māʻalaea Harbor, Māʻalaea* 🕾 *877/867–
7433* ⊕ *www.prideofmaui.com* 🖃 *$69.95* ⊘ *Tues., Thurs., and Sat.
5–7:30 pm.*

Ⓢ **Spirit of Lahaina Dinner Cruise.** A family-style dinner cruise is the specialty
of this double-deck, 65-foot catamaran, with a meal that includes appetizers, warm taro rolls, freshly grilled steak, *huli-huli* chicken (barbecued
with flavors like brown sugarcane, ginger, and soy), shrimp skewered
on sugarcane, and fabulous desserts. The trip also has contemporary
Hawaiian music and a hula show that will definitely cure you of any
motion sickness. ✉ *Lahaina Harbor, Slip 4, Lahaina* 🕾 *808/662–4477*
⊕ *www.spiritoflahaina.com* 🖃 *$82 adult, $49 child 3–11* ⊘ *Tues.–Sat.
5–7:15 pm.*

Teralani Sailing Charters. Teralani catamarans are modern, spotless, and
laid out comfortably for dining. Check-in for this trip is at 3 and the
boat heads back shortly after sunset, which means plenty of light to
enjoy the food and view. During whale-watching season the best seats
are the corner booths at the front of the boat. The buffet is a few
notches up from other dinner-cruise spreads, featuring vegetable cru-
dités, ratatouille, chipotle citrus rotisserie chicken, and grilled ono fish
with pesto and sun-dried tomatoes. The trip departs from the shore
of Kāʻanapali's Dig Me Beach in front of Leilani's at Whalers Village. ✉ *2435 Kāʻanapali Pkwy., Kāʻanapali* 🕾 *808/661–1230* ⊕ *www.
teralani.net* 🖃 *$89.66 adult, $78.94 teen 13–19, $68.23 child 3–12.*

LŪʻAU

Locals still hold lūʻau to mark milestones or as informal, family-style
gatherings. For tourists, they are a major attraction and, for that reason, have become big business. Keep in mind—some are watered-down
tourist traps just trying to make a buck, others offer a night you'll never
forget. As the saying goes, you get what you pay for. ∎**TIP**→ Many of
the best lūʻau book weeks, sometimes months, in advance, so reserve early.
Plan your lūʻau night early on in your trip to help you get into the Hawaiian spirit.

The Feast at Lele. "Lele" is an older, more traditional name for Lahaina.
This feast redefines the lūʻau by crossing it with island-style fine dining
in an intimate beach setting. Each course of this succulent sit-down
meal expresses the spirit of specific island cultures—Hawaiian, Samoan,
Aotearoan, Tahitian—and don't forget dessert. Dramatic Polynesian
entertainment accompanies the dinner, along with excellent wine and
liquor selections. Tables are arranged to fit the size of your group. ✉ *505
Front St., Lahaina* 🕾 *808/667–5353* ⊕ *www.feastatlele.com* ⌖ *Reservations essential* 🖃 *$112 adult, $82 child 2–12* ⊘ *Nightly at sunset; 5:30
pm in winter, 6 pm in summer.*

The popular Old Lahaina Lū'au surveys Hawai'i's history through music, hula, chanting, and more.

★ **Hyatt Regency Maui Drums of the Pacific Lū'au.** Located by Kā'anapali beach, this lū'au excels in every category—breathtaking location, well-made food, smooth-flowing buffet lines, and a wonderfully authentic program that covers the Hawaiian, Samoan, Tahitian, Fijian, Tongan, and Maori cultures. You witness a colorfully festive show that includes arguably the best solo fire-knife dancer on the island. An open bar features beer, wine and the usual tropical concoctions. ✉ *200 Nohea Kai Dr., Kā'anapali* ☎ *808/667–4727* ⊕ *www.maui.hyatt.com* ⌨ *$96 adult ($119 for premium seating), $61 teen 13–20 ($86 for premium seating), $49 child 6–12 ($75 for premium seating), free for children 5 and under ($30 for premium seating)* ⊘ *Tues., Wed., Fri., and Sat., 5–8 pm.*

Fodor'sChoice
★ **Old Lahaina Lū'au.** Many consider this the best lū'au on Maui; it's certainly the most traditional. Located right on the water, at the northern end of town, the Old Lahaina Lū'au is small, personal, and as authentic as it gets. Sitting either at a table or on a *lauhala* mat, you'll dine on all-you-can-eat Hawaiian cuisine: pork *laulau* (wrapped with taro sprouts in tī leaves), 'ahi *poke* (pickled raw tuna, tossed with herbs and seasonings), *lomilomi* salmon (rubbed with onions and herbs), Maui-style mahimahi, *haupia* (coconut pudding), and more. At sunset the show begins a historical journey that relays key periods in Hawai'i's history, from the arrival of the Polynesians to the influence of the missionaries and, later, tourism. The tanned, talented performers will charm you with their music, chanting, and variety of hula styles (modern and *kahiko*, the ancient way of communicating with the gods). But if it's fire dancers you want to see, you won't find them here, as they aren't considered traditional. Although it's performed nightly,

this lūʻau sells out regularly. Make your reservations when planning your trip to Maui. You can cancel up until 10 am the day of the scheduled show. ✉ *1251 Front St., makai of Lahaina Cannery Mall, Lahaina* ☎ *808/667–1998* ⚓ *Reservations essential* ⊕ *www.oldlahainaluau. com* ✎ *$92 adult, $62 child 2–12* ⊙ *Nightly at 5:15 pm in winter, 5:45 pm in summer.*

WORD OF MOUTH

"Old Lahaina Lūʻau is great for all ages. It's expensive, but I consider the price as much for the setting, the show, the entire experience, and not just the buffet dinner (although I thought it was surprisingly nice, but then I love Hawaiian food)." –suze

Wailea Beach Marriott Te Au Moana.
This lūʻau offers an open bar, a tasty buffet, and a sunset backdrop that can't be beat. The stage is placed right next to the water, and the show features lei making and games stations, an *imu* (underground oven) ceremony to start, traditional hula, and Polynesian dancers featuring an impressive fire-knife dance. ✉ *3700 Wailea Alanui Dr., Wailea* ☎ *808/879–1922* ⊕ *www.marriotthawaii.com* ⚓ *Reservations essential* ✎ *$98 adult ($108 for premium seating), $53 child 6–12 ($63 for premium seating), free for child 5 and under ($10 for premium seating)* ⊙ *Mon. and Thurs.–Sat. 4:30–8 pm.*

FILM
In the heat of the afternoon, a theater may feel like paradise. There are megaplexes showing first-run movies in Kukui Mall (Kīhei), Lahaina Center, and Maui Mall and Kaʻahumanu Shopping Center (Kahului).

★ **Maui Film Festival.** In this ongoing program, the Maui Arts & Cultural Center presents art-house films on selected evenings at 5 and 7:30 pm, accompanied by live music, dining, and poetry in the Candlelight Café & Cinema. In summer, an international weeklong festival attracts big-name celebrities to Maui for cinema under the stars. ☎ *808/579–9244 recorded program information* ⊕ *www.mauifilmfestival.com.*

THEATER
For live theater, check local papers for events and showtimes.

Ⓒ ★ **Cirque Polynesia.** The island's only Cirque du Soleil–style show (at the Hyatt Regency Maui) might not have the grandeur of mainland productions, but it still packs a wow factor with its international cast of aerialists, contortionists, live musicians, and other acts such as the dynamic mother-daughter duo from the world-famous Wallenda circus family. VIP seating is the first five rows from the stage; the rest is open seating. If you have little ones, try to grab the first row of the elevated seats so that your vertically challenged party can watch with ease. Dinner packages are available with the hotel's poolside ʻUmalu and Sonʻz Restaurant. ✉ *200 Nohea Kai Dr., Kāʻanapali* ☎ *808/667–4540* ⊕ *www. cirquepolynesia.com* ⚓ *Reservations essential* ✎ *$67.71 adults ($78.13 for VIP seating), $30.21 child 12 and under ($40.63 for VIP seating)* ⊙ *Nightly except Sun. 7–8:15 pm.*

Ⓒ ★ **"ʻUlalena" at Maui Theatre.** One of Maui's hottest tickets, "ʻUlalena" is a 75-minute musical extravaganza that is well received by audiences and Hawaiian-culture experts alike. Cirque de Soleil–inspired, the ensemble cast (20 singer-dancers and a five-musician orchestra) mixes native rhythms and stories with acrobatic performance. High-tech stage wizardry gives an inspiring introduction to island culture. It has auditorium seating, and beer and wine are for sale at the concession stand. There are dinner-theater packages in conjunction with top Lahaina restaurants. ✉ *878 Front St., Lahaina* ☎ *808/661–9913 or 877/688–4800* ⊕ *www.mauitheatre.com* ⚲ *Reservations essential* 🖃 *$59.50–$129.50 for a dinner package* ☽ *Mon.–Sat. at 6:30 pm.*

Warren & Annabelle's. This is one show not to miss—it's serious comedy with amazing sleight of hand. Magician Warren Gibson entices guests into his swank nightclub with red carpets and a gleaming mahogany bar, and plies them with à la carte appetizers (coconut shrimp, crab cakes), desserts (chocolate pots de crème, assorted pies and cheesecakes, crème brûlée), and "smoking cocktails." Then, he performs tableside magic while his ghostly assistant, Annabelle, tickles the ivories. This is a nightclub, so no one under 21 is allowed. ✉ *Lahaina Center, 900 Front St., Lahaina* ☎ *808/667–6244* ⊕ *www.hawaiimagic.com* ⚲ *Reservations essential* 🖃 *$56 or $94.50, including food and drinks* ☽ *Mon.–Sat. 5 and 7:30 pm.*

NIGHTLIFE

Your best bet when it comes to bars on Maui? If you walk by and it sounds like it's happening, go in. If you want to scope out your options in advance, be sure to check the free *Maui Time Weekly,* found at most stores and restaurants, to find out who's playing where. The *Maui News* also publishes an entertainment schedule in its Thursday edition of the "Maui Scene." With an open mind (and a little luck), you can usually find a good scene for fun.

WEST MAUI

Cool Cat Café. One could easily miss this casual 1950s-style diner while strolling through Lahaina. Tucked in the second floor of the Wharf Cinema Center, its semi-outdoor area plays host to rockin' local music nightly. The entertainment lineup covers jazz, contemporary Hawaiian, and traditional Island rhythms. It doesn't hurt that the kitchen dishes out specialty burgers, fish that's fresh from the harbor, and delicious homemade sauces from the owner's family recipes. ✉ *658 Front St., Lahaina* ☎ *808/667–0908* ⊕ *www.coolcatcafe.com.*

Fodor's Choice
★ **Timba.** A fairly new venue at Lahaina's 505 Plaza, this place has raised Maui nightlife standards more than a few notches. The space combines a charming oceanfront setting with the island's most progressive musicians. Sleek and cozy white leather couches are perfect for sipping and conversing, while the elevated dance floor will have you dancing the night away. The upscale club attracts the bigger names in the electronic music scene and gives locals a reason to leave the slippahs at home and get dolled up. Co-owner Quinn Ross hosts a Friday weekly with rotating sax players, keyboardists, and vocalists to spice up the set. You might call it Maui's own Miami. ✉ *505 Front St., Suite 212., Lahaina* ☎ *808/661–9873* ⊕ *www.timbamaui.com.*

Performers in colorful costumes help make lū'au appealing to all ages.

THE SOUTH SHORE

Ambrosia Blues and Jazz Club. A South Maui favorite, Ambrosia is a cozy hangout for blues, jazz, funk, and folk music, as well as the occasional absinthe drink. The crowd is more sophisticated—less rowdy, but a lot of fun. ⊠ *1913 S. Kīhei Rd., Kīhei* ☎ *808/891–1011* ⊕ *www.ambrosiamaui.com* ☯ *5 pm–2 am.*

Lulu's. It could be your favorite bar in any beach town. Lulu's is a second-story, open-air tiki and sports bar, with a pool table, small stage, and dance floor to boot. The most popular night is Salsa Thursday, with dancing and lessons until 11. Friday starts off with Hawaiian music and hula from 5 pm to 7 pm, and a live band from 8 pm to 11 pm. Hawaiian music and hula also kick off Saturday from 6 pm to 8 pm, while pop and electronic DJs wrap up the evening. Wednesday and Sunday are karaoke nights. ⊠ *1945 S. Kīhei Rd., Kīhei* ☎ *808/879–9944.*

★ **Mulligan's on the Blue.** Frothy pints of Guinness and late-night fish-and-chips—who could ask for more? Sunday nights feature foot-stomping Irish jams that will have you dancing a jig, and singing something about "a whiskey for me Johnny." Local favorite Willie K performs every Wednesday. Other nights bring in various local bands. ⊠ *Blue Golf Course, 100 Kaukahi St., Wailea* ☎ *808/874–1131.*

South Shore Tiki Lounge. Good eats are paired with the island's most progressive DJs in this breezy, tropical tavern. Local DJs are featured every day of the week; if you're craving some old-school hip-hop, Thursday is your night. ⊠ *1913-J S. Kihei Rd., Kihei* ☎ *808/874–6444* ⊕ *www.southshoretikilounge.com.*

UPCOUNTRY AND THE NORTH SHORE

Casanova Italian Restaurant and Deli. Casanova can bring in some big acts, which in the past have included Kool and the Gang, Los Lobos, and Taj Majal. Most Friday and Saturday nights, though, it attracts a hip, local scene with live bands and eclectic DJs spinning house, funk, and world music. Don't miss the costume theme nights. Wednesday is for Wild Wahines (code for ladies drink half price), which can be more on the smarmy side. Cover is \$5 to \$25. ⊠ *1188 Makawao Ave., Makawao* ☎ *808/572–0220.*

Charley's. The closest thing to country Maui has to offer, Charley's is a down-home, divey bar in the heart of Pā'ia. It also hosts reggae, house, Latin soul, and jazz nights. Live bands are featured on Friday and Saturday. ⊠ *142 Hāna Hwy., Pā'ia* ☎ *808/579–9453.*

Stopwatch Sportsbar & Grill. This friendly dive bar books favorite local bands on Friday and charges only \$3. ⊠ *1127 Makawao Ave., Makawao* ☎ *808/572–1380.*

WHAT'S A LAVA FLOW?

Can't decide between a piña colada or strawberry daiquiri? Go with a lava flow—a mix of light rum, coconut and pineapple juice, and a banana, with a swirl of strawberry puree. Add a wedge of fresh pineapple and a paper umbrella, and mmm . . . good. Try one at Lulu's in Kīhei.

WHERE TO EAT

By Bonnie Friedman

From ethnic holes-in-the-wall to stunningly appointed fine dining rooms, and from seafood trucks to oceanfront fish houses with sweeping panoramic views. Much of it is excellent, but some of it is overpriced and touristy. If you're coming from a "food destination" city, you may have to adjust your expectations.

At fine and casual fine dining restaurants, choose menu items made with products that are abundant on the island, including local fish, onions, avocados, cabbage, broccoli, asparagus, hydroponic tomatoes, a myriad herbs, salad greens, *kalo* (taro), bananas, papaya, guava, *liliko'i* (passionfruit), coconut, mangoes, strawberries, and Maui gold pineapple. And items grown on neighboring islands like mushrooms, purple sweet potatoes, and watermelon.

Local cuisine is an amalgam of foods brought by the ethnic groups that have come here since the late 1700s blended, too, with the foods Native Hawaiians have enjoyed for centuries: *lomilomi* salmon, *laulau,* poi, Portuguese bean soup, kalbi ribs, chicken katsu, chow fun, hamburger steak, macaroni salad, the original "fusion" cuisine, and "everyman's" food. Always inexpensive—and always satisfying. For a food adventure, take a drive into Central Maui. Have lunch or dinner at one of the "local" spots recommended here. Or get even more adventurous. Take a drive around Wailuku or Kahului and find your own hidden gem. There are plenty out there.

WHAT IT COSTS				
¢	$	$$	$$$	$$$$
RESTAURANTS	under $10	$10–$17	$18–$26	$27–$35	over $35

Restaurant prices are for a main course at dinner.

WEST MAUI

LAHAINA

$ ✕ **Aloha Mixed Plate.** From the wonderful folks who bring you Maui's best
HAWAIIAN lū'au—the Old Lahaina Lū'au—comes this extremely casual, oceanfront
eatery, which is now open for breakfast. If you've yet to indulge in a
local-style "plate lunch," this is a good place to try it. A consistent award-
winner in local magazine and newspaper polls, each plate combines foods
representative of Hawai'i's ethnic mix. Take a plate of your Chinese chow
mein noodles, marinated and grilled Korean kalbi ribs, Japanese teriyaki
beef, and, of course, the requisite macaroni salad and two scoops of rice
to a table so close to the ocean you just might get wet. Wanna go whole
hog? We recommend the Ali'i Plate of traditional Hawaiian foods: *laulau*
(taro-leaf-wrapped bundles of meats and fish), *lomilomi* salmon (a cold
salad of raw salmon, tomatoes, onions), poi, rice, and *haupia* (luscious
coconut pudding). Oh, and don't forget the mai tai! ⊠ *1285 Front St.,
Lahaina* ☎ *808/661–3322* ⊕ *www.AlohaMixedPlate.com* ▤ *MC, V.*

$ ✕ **Cilantro.** The flavors of Old Mexico are given new life here, where no
MEXICAN fewer than nine chilis are used to create the salsas. The owner, a former
high-end food and beverage pro, spent three years visiting authentic eateries in 40 Mexican cities before opening this place. The restaurant is
tucked into an older mall, which is not fancy and requires you to order at
the counter and fill your own disposable beverage cup at the soda fountain. But as soon as you bite into a chipotle-citrus rotisserie chicken plate
or, really, anything on the menu, you'll forget all about the plastic cutlery . . . and the fact that the only view is of a parking lot. The brilliantly
colored, clever decor—a collection of worn-from-duty tortilla presses,
now hand-painted—coupled with consistently excellent food makes up
for the lack of view. ⊠ *Old Lahaina Center, 170 Papalaua Ave., Lahaina*
☎ *808/667–5444* ⊕ *www.cilantrogrill.com* ▤ *AE, MC, V.*

$$$$ ✕ **David Paul's Island Grill.** For years, he was one of Maui's most celebrated
NEW AMERICAN and determined chefs winning every possible award and rave review for his
original David Paul's Lahaina Grill. After an almost decade-long "hiatus"
on Hawai'i Island, he returned to his Maui culinary roots—Lahaina—and
opened a beautiful new restaurant in spring 2009. He cooks his own
distinctive style of New American Cuisine (think butter lettuce and bleu
cheese salad, bistro chicken, Princess and the Pea diver scallops), access-
ing local products and adding Island flavors. There's an unobstructed
ocean view from the front patio; the comfy seating out back is perfect
for a cocktail and late-night bites. The service can be spotty, but it's still
worth a visit. ⊠ *Lahaina Center, 900 Front St., Lahaina* ☎ *808/662–3000*
⊕ *www.davidpaulsislandgrill.com* ▤ *AE, D, DC, MC, V.*

BEST BETS FOR MAUI DINING

Fodor's Choice ★

Ba-Le Sandwiches & Plate Lunch, ¢, p. 300

Café des Amis, $, p. 301

Colleen's at the Cannery, $$, p. 302

Mala Ocean Tavern, $$$, p. 292

Pā'ia Fishmarket, $$, p. 302

Roy's Kahana Bar & Grill, $$$$, p. 295

Sam Sato's, ¢, p. 300

Star Noodle, $$, p. 292

Tokyo Tei, $, p. 301

Tommy Bahama, $$$, p. 298

Tropica Bar & Restaurant, $$$$, p. 294

By Price

¢

Ba-Le Sandwiches & Plate Lunch, p. 300

Kīhei Caffe, p. 296

Sam Sato's, p. 300

$

A.K.'s Café, p. 300

Café des Amis, p. 301

Cilantro, p. 288

Da Kitchen, p. 298

Tokyo Tei, p. 301

$$

Asian Star, p. 300

Colleen's at the Cannery, p. 302

Pā'ia Fishmarket, p. 302

Sansei Seafood Restaurant & Sushi Bar, p. 296

Star Noodle, p. 292

Tiki Terrace, p. 293

$$$

Mala Ocean Tavern, p. 292

Market Fresh Bistro, p. 301

Pineapple Grill, p. 295

Tommy Bahama, p. 298

$$$$

Banyan Tree, p. 294

Roy's Kahana Bar & Grill, p. 295

Spago, p. 298

Tropica Bar & Restaurant, p. 294

$$$$ ✕ **Gerard's.** For more than 25 years, classically trained French chef
FRENCH Gerard Reversade has remained true to his roots and kept his charming restaurant classically French. A native of Gascony, Reversade came up through the ranks in the traditional way, starting as an apprentice in acclaimed Paris restaurants when he was just 14. His exacting standards—in the dining room as well as in the kitchen—have been the hallmarks of his eponymous restaurant year in and year out. He cooks *his* way, utilizing Island ingredients in such classics as mushrooms in puff pastry, escargot Forestière, French onion soup, terrine of Foie Gras Maison, confit of duck, and scallops and shrimp au gratin. The wine list is first-class. ⊠ *Plantation Inn, 174 Lahainaluna Rd., Lahaina* ☎ *808/661–8939* ⊕ *www.gerardsmaui.com* ▤ *AE, D, DC, MC, V* ⊘ *No lunch.*

$$$$ ✕ **Lahaina Grill.** At the top of many best restaurants lists, this upscale
AMERICAN bistro is about as fashionably chic as it gets on Maui. It's gone through some "changes" over its 20-plus year history—it lost the "David Paul's" part of its name in late 2007—but internal politics aside, the food and service are consistently excellent and the place is abuzz with beautiful people every night of the week. The Cake Walk (little samples of Kona lobster crab cake, sweet Louisiana rock shrimp cake and seared 'ahi cake), toy-box tomato salad, and Kona coffee-roasted rack of lamb, are a few of the classics customers demand. Newer items include Maine lobsters flown in daily and seared California lion paw scallops. The full menu—including dessert—is available at the bar. The interior is as

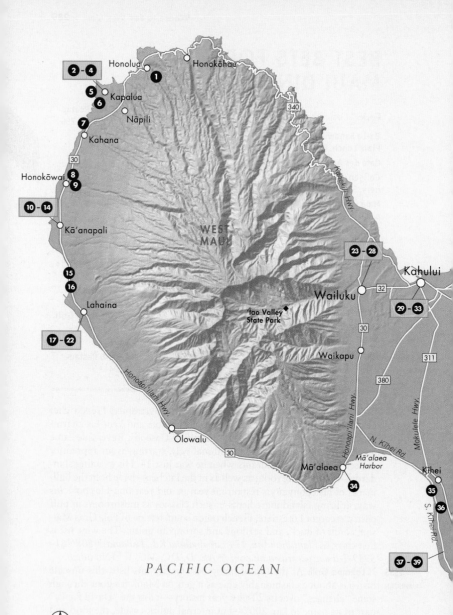

Honolua

Honokōhau

2 - 4

1

5

Kapalua

6

Nāpili

7

Kahana

340

30

Honokōwai

8

9

WEST
MAUI

10 - 14

Kāʻanapali

23 - 28

Kahului

Kahekili Hwy.

Wailuku

32

15

16

ʻĪao Valley
State Park

29 - 33

Lahaina

17 - 22

30

Waikapu

311

Honoāpiʻilani Hwy.

Olowalu

380

30

Honoāpiʻilani Hwy.

N. Kīhei Rd.

Mokulele Hwy.

Māʻalaea

Māʻalaea
Harbor

Kīhei

34

35

36

37 - 39

S. Kīhei Rd.

PACIFIC OCEAN

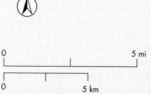

0 _____ 5 mi

0 _____ 5 km

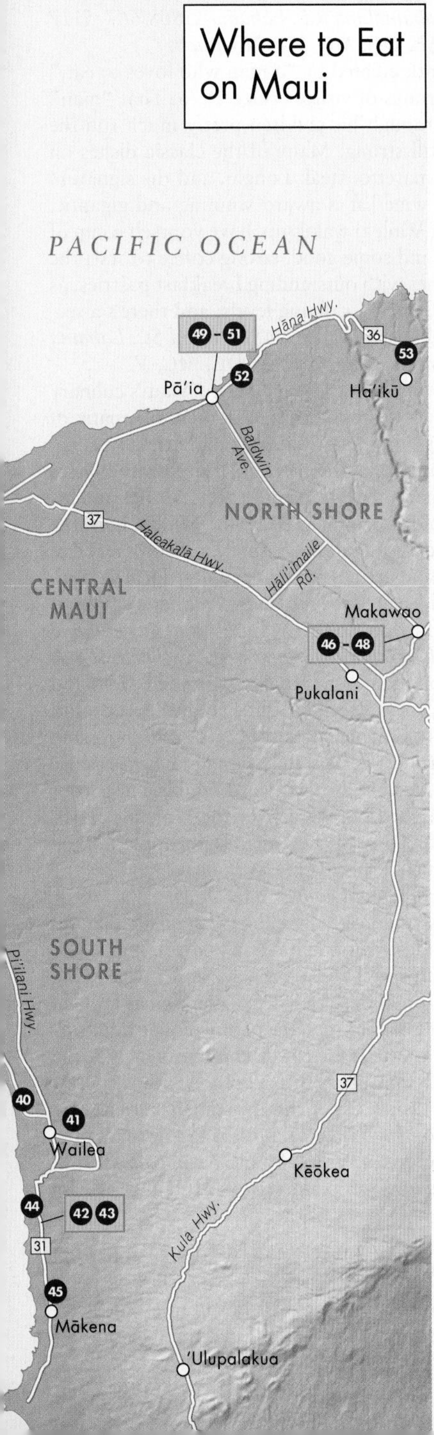

Where to Eat on Maui
PACIFIC OCEAN
Hāna Hwy.
49 - 51
52
53
36
Pā'ia
Ha'ikū
Baldwin Ave.
NORTH SHORE
37
Haleakalā Hwy.
Hāli'imaile Rd.
CENTRAL MAUI
Makawao
46 - 48
Pukalani
SOUTH SHORE
Pi'ilani Hwy.
37
40
41
Wailea
Kēōkea
44
42 43
31
Kula Hwy.
45
Mākena
'Ulupalakua

West Maui

- Aloha Mixed Plate 15
- The Banyan Tree 2
- Cilantro 17
- David Paul's Island Grill ... 22
- The Gazebo Restaurant 5
- Gerard's 19
- Honokowai Okazuya 8
- Hula Grill 10
- Kai Sushi 3
- Lahaina Grill 18
- Longhi's 20
- Mala Ocean Tavern 15
- 'OnO Bar & Grill 12
- Pacific'O 21
- Pineapple Grill 6
- Pizza Paradiso 9
- Plantation House Restaurant 1
- Roy's Kahana Bar & Grill 7
- Sansei Seafood Restaurant & Sushi Bar 4
- Son'z at Swan Court 11
- Tiki Terrace 13
- Tropica Restaurant and Bar 14

Central Maui

- A.K.'s Café 25
- Asian Star 24
- Ba Le 27
- Da Kitchen 30
- Dragon Dragon 31
- Marco's Grill & Deli 32
- Ramen Ya 33
- Saeng's Thai Cuisine 23
- Sam Sato 26
- Tokyo Tei 28
- Zippy's 29

The South Shore

- Ferraro's Bar e Ristorante 42
- Gannon's 45
- Kihei Caffe 39
- Matteo's 41
- Monsoon India 35
- Sarento's on the Beach ... 40
- Seascape Mā'alaea 34
- South Shore Tiki Lounge .. 38
- Spago 43
- Thailand Cuisine 37
- Tommy Bahama 44
- Wokstar International Noodle Café 36

Upcountry

- Casanova Italian Restaurant & Deli 46
- Hāli'imaile General Store 48
- Market Fresh Bistro 47

The North Shore

- Café Des Amis 51
- Colleen's at Cannery 53
- Flatbread Company 49
- Mama's Fish House 52
- Pā'ia Fishmarket Restaurant 50

3

pretty as its patrons. ✉ *127 Lahainaluna Rd., Lahaina* ☎ *808/667–5117* ⊕ *www.lahainagrill.com* ▭ *AE, DC, MC, V* ☺ *No lunch.*

$$$$
ITALIAN
✕ **Longhi's.** A Lahaina landmark created by "a man who loves to eat," Longhi's has been serving throngs of visitors since 1976. That "man" is owner Bob Longhi and although his children pretty much run the place now, his influence is still strong. Many of the classic dishes on the menu are his—prawns Amaretto, steak Longhi, and the signature lobster Longhi for two. The wine list is award winning and gigantic. Before the rest of Lahaina (or Wailea) wakes up, have yourself a cup of orange juice, a fluffy frittata and some good, strong coffee to start the day. The in-house bakery shines with outstanding breakfast pastries, as well. There are two spacious, open-air dining levels; and there's a second Maui restaurant at the Shops at Wailea. ✉ *888 Front St., Lahaina* ☎ *808/667–2288* ⊕ *www.longhis.com* ▭ *AE, D, DC, MC, V.*

$$$
MODERN
HAWAIIAN
Fodor's Choice
★
✕ **Mala Ocean Tavern.** Chef-owner Mark Ellman started Maui's culinary revolution of the late '80s with his restaurant Avalon. While many of us still mourn that landmark's "passing," Mala is a more than satisfactory successor. The place is adorable; the best tables are on the lānai, which actually juts out over the water. The menu reflects Mark's and his wife Judy's world travels with dishes influenced by the Middle East, the Mediterranean, Italy, Bali, and Thailand. Every single item on the menu is delicious, and there's a focus on ingredients that promote local sustainability. The cocktails and wine list are great, to boot. Another location of Mala is at the Wailea Beach Marriott Resort. ✉ *1307 Front St., Lahaina* ☎ *808/667–9394* ⊕ *www.malaoceantavern.com* ▭ *AE, D, DC, MC, V.*

$$$
PACIFIC RIM
✕ **Pacific'O.** Outdoor dining on the beach (no, really *on* the beach) and creative Island cuisine using local, fresh-caught fish and greens and veggies grown in the restaurant's own Upcountry O'o Farm (and, quite possibly, picked that very morning)—this is the Maui dining experience you've been dreaming about. Start with the award-winning appetizer of prawn and basil wontons, move on to any of the fantastic fresh-fish dishes, and for dessert, finish with the banana pineapple *lumpia* served hot with homemade banana ice cream. ✉ *505 Front St., Lahaina* ☎ *808/667–4341* ⊕ *www.pacificomaui.com* ▭ *AE, D, MC, V.*

$$
ASIAN
Fodor's Choice
★
✕ **Star Noodle.** This is Maui's brightest new culinary star. It's way up above the highway in a light industrial park, but don't be discouraged by the location. Take the drive and you'll find a hip place and a welcoming staff that knows the meaning of "aloha." There's a communal table in the center of the room, smaller tables around the perimeter and comfortable stools for those who like to eat at the bar. Menu musts include the 'Ahi Avo, pan-roasted brussels sprouts with bacon and kimchi purée, and really any of the noodle dishes, especially the Lahaina fried soup (fat chow fun, pork, bean sprouts). The cocktail list is fabulous and the lychee martinis served here may be the best on Maui. ✉ *286 Kupuohi St., Lahaina* ☎ *808/667–4500* ⊕ *www.starnoodle.com* ▭ *MC, V.*

KĀ'ANAPALI

$$$
MODERN
HAWAIIAN
✕ **Hula Grill.** This bustling, family-oriented restaurant designed to look like a sprawling '30s beach house, represents a partnership between TS Restaurants group and Hawai'i Regional Cuisine pioneer chef Peter Merriman. They serve up large dinner portions of everything from fresh

Pineapple and shrimp add local flavors to tasty grilled skewers.

local fish and Maui Cattle Company beef to Hula Grill "traditions" like rosemary- and wood-roasted rack of lamb to Kabocha squash ravioli. Just in the mood for an umbrella-adorned cocktail and some pūpū? Go to the Barefoot Bar where you can wiggle your toes in the sand while you sip. The beach is called "Dig Me"—you'll understand why after just a few moments. ⊠ Whalers Village, 2435 Kāʻanapali Pkwy., Kāʻanapali ☎ 808/667–6636 ▭ AE, D, DC, MC, V.

$$$$
MEDITERRANEAN

✕ Son'z at Swan Court. If you're celebrating a special occasion and want to splurge, this just might be the place for you. You'll descend a grand staircase into an amber-lighted dining room with soaring ceilings and a massive artificial lagoon complete with swans, waterfalls, and tropical gardens. Must-haves on chef Geno Sarmiento's contemporary, Mediterranean-influenced menu include the seared scallops "BLT," goat-cheese ravioli with Kula corn, edamame, and Hāmākua mushrooms, and grilled beef tenderloin marinated in coffee and served with Parmesan-garlic fries. The restaurant claims the largest wine cellar in Hawai'i with 3,000 bottles. ⊠ Hyatt Regency Maui, Kā'anapali Beach Resort, 200 Nohea Kai Dr., Kā'anapali ☎ 808/667–4506 ⊕ www.tristarrestaurants.com ▭ AE, D, DC, MC, V ☉ No lunch.

$$
MODERN
HAWAIIAN

✕ Tiki Terrace. Executive chef Tom Muromoto is a local boy who loves to cook modern, upscale Hawaiian food. He augments the various fresh fish dishes on his menu with items influenced by Hawai'i's ethnic mix. This restaurant is the only place on Maui—maybe in Hawai'i—where you can have a Native Hawaiian combination plate that is as healthful as it is authentic. Sunday brunch is renowned here, and if you're around for a holiday, chow down at the amazing holiday brunch buffets. Kā'anapali Beach Hotel, *Kā'anapali Beach Resort,* ⊠ 2525 Kā'anapali

Pkwy., *Kā'anapali* ☎ 808/667–0124 ⊕ *www.kbhmaui.com* ☰ *AE, D, DC, MC, V* ⊘ *No lunch.*

$$$$
MODERN
HAWAIIAN
Fodor's Choice
★

✕ **Tropica Restaurant & Bar.** As far as hotel restaurants go, this beautifully appointed, oceanfront restaurant is as cool, calm, comfortable and delicious as it gets. Start with an exceptionally creative cocktail—the martinis are award winning—or a glass of wine from a long, excellent list. You then must indulge in the golden potato gnocchi with Meyer-lemon cream, parsley, and pistachio, which is positively dreamy, or the coconut steamed mussels and clams. Tropica also offers lots of specially priced cocktail and dining options that will save you some bucks. And for the dining experience of a lifetime, reserve far in advance to get one of six tables on the beach. Yes, *on* the beach. *The Westin Maui Resort & Spa, Kā'anapali Beach Resort* ⊠ *2365 Kā'anapali Pkwy., Kā'anapali* ☎ 808/667–2525 ☰ *AE, D, DC, MC, V* ⊘ *Closed Mon. and Tues. No lunch.*

KAPALUA AND VICINITY

$$$$
PACIFIC RIM

✕ **The Banyan Tree.** The setting is sublime, the atmosphere serene, and the service elegant at this signature restaurant of the Ritz-Carlton Kapalua. Drink in views of the Pailolo Channel and the Island of Moloka'i while enjoying perfectly prepared Island cuisine full of worldly influences. The *dukka* (Middle Eastern spice mixture) delivered with your bread is just a hint of the delights to come. Chef JoJo Vasquez's recent seasonal offerings have included raw hamachi in Vietnamese marinade, grilled Colorado lamb with eggplant puree, and Maui-made Surfing Goat feta cheese and garlic confit. ⊠ *Ritz-Carlton, Kapalua, 1 Ritz-Carlton Dr., Kapalua* ☎ 808/669–6200 ⊕ *www.ritzcarlton.com/kapalua* ☰ *AE, D, DC, MC, V* ⊘ *Closed Sun. and Mon. No lunch.*

$
DINER

✕ **The Gazebo Restaurant.** Breakfast is the reason to seek out this restaurant located poolside at the Nāpili Shores resort. The ambience is a little funky but the oceanfront setting and views are spectacular—including the turtle, spinner dolphin, and, in winter, humpback-whale sightings. The food is standard diner fare and portions are big. Many folks think the Gazebo serves the best pancakes on West Maui. Have them with pineapple, bananas, macadamia nuts, chocolate chips, or make up your own combination. You will almost certainly have to wait for a table, sometimes for quite a while, but at least it's a pleasant place to do so. ⊠ *Nāpili Shores Resort, 5315 Lower Honoapi'ilani Hwy., Nāpili* ☎ 808/669–5621 ☰ *D, MC, V* ⊘ *No dinner.*

$
ECLECTIC

✕ **Honokōwai Okazuya.** Sandwiched between a dive shop and a salon in a nondescript mini strip mall, this small place only has a few stools and a couple of tables outside, but it's fast and the food is consistently good—all it takes to keep the place filled with locals. The mahimahi with lemon capers, and beef black bean chow fun are the top-selling favorites. There's plenty more including vegetarian and lighter fare like Grandma's spicy tofu, egg fu young, and even a veggie burger. The fresh *chow fun* noodles sell out quickly. ⊠ *3600-D Lower Honoapi'ilani Hwy., Honokōwai* ☎ 808/665–0512 ☰ *No credit cards* ⊘ *Closed Sun; closed between 2:30 and 4:30 pm every day.*

$$$
JAPANESE

✕ **Kai Sushi.** For a quiet, light dinner, or to meet friends for a cocktail and some ultrafresh sushi, head to this handsome restaurant on the lobby level of the Ritz-Carlton Kapalua. You have your choice of sushi, sashimi, and a list of rolls. The especially good Kai special roll combines spicy tuna, yellowtail, and green onion. In keeping with the hotel's commitment to the culture, the restaurant's design was inspired by the story of Native Hawaiians' arrival by sea; the hand-carved ceiling beams resemble outrigger canoes. ✉ *Ritz-Carlton, Kapalua, 1 Ritz-Carlton Dr., Kapalua* ☎ *808/669–6200* ⊕ *www.ritzcarlton.com/kapalua* ▭ *AE, D, DC, MC, V* ☺ *Closed Tues. and Wed. No lunch.*

$$$
MODERN
HAWAIIAN

✗ **Pineapple Grill.** High on the hill overlooking the Kapalua resorts, this restaurant exudes casual elegance. Young, Lahaina-born chef Ryan Luckey makes good use of the island's bounty, with dishes featuring Maui gold pineapple, Roselani ice cream, Maui Cattle Company beef, greens and vegetables from Waipoli and Nalo farms, and local, sustainable fish. If you've had enough of the gorgeous ocean, mountain, or resort views, you can watch the chef and his crew in the shiny exhibition kitchen as they assemble their specialties like pistachio-wasabi crusted rare 'ahi tuna, Maui farmers chopped salad, and the Maui gold pineapple-glazed 14-ounce pork chop. ✉ *200 Kapalua Dr., Kapalua* ☎ *808/669–9600* ⊕ *www.pineapplekapalua.com* ▭ *AE, D, DC, MC, V.*

$
ITALIAN

✗ **Pizza Paradiso.** When it opened in 1995, it was an over-the-counter pizza place. It has evolved over the years into a local favorite serving pasta, Mediterranean comfort food and still, of course, pizza. The pies are so popular because of the top ingredients—100% pure Italian olive oil, Maui produce whenever possible, and Maui Cattle Company beef. The menu also features gyros, falafel, grilled fish, rotisserie chicken, and tiramisu. ✉ *Honokōwai Marketplace, 3350 Lower Honoapi'ilani Rd., Honokōwai* ☎ *808/667–2929* ⊕ *www.pizzaparadiso.com* ▭ *AE, MC, V.*

$$$
MODERN
HAWAIIAN

✗ **Plantation House Restaurant.** It's a bit of a drive to the restaurant, but chef–partner Alex Stanislaw's skills—especially with fresh fish—make it worth the trip. Here you'll find a beautiful and comfortable restaurant with expansive views of the ocean below and the majestic mountains above. Chef Alex sources the best of the Islands' bounty; much of the produce he uses is grown within a few miles of the kitchen. And the fish preparations commonly reflect his Mediterranean heritage (think pistachio-crusted Hawaiian catch served on herbed couscous with extra virgin olive oil). Breakfast is glorious here, too. ✉ *Plantation Course Clubhouse, 2000 Plantation Club Dr., past Kapalua* ☎ *808/669–6299* ⊕ *www.theplantationhouse.com* ▭ *AE, MC, V.*

$$$$
MODERN
HAWAIIAN
Fodor's Choice
★

✗ **Roy's Kahana Bar & Grill.** Roy Yamaguchi is a James Beard Award–winning chef and the "granddaddy" of East meets West cuisine. He has restaurants all over the world but his eponymous Maui restaurant was one of the first and still one of the best. It's loud and brassy with a young vibe. And if that doesn't appeal to you, then overlook it because the food is so good. Signatures like fire-grilled, Szechuan-spiced baby back pork ribs, Roy's original blackened 'ahi tuna, hibachi-style grilled salmon, and the to-die-for hot chocolate soufflé have been on the menu from the beginning—with good reason. Roy's wine list was one of the first to be exceptionally user-friendly and, thankfully, remains so. The service here is welcoming and professional. ✉ *Kahana Gateway Shopping Center, 4405 Honoapi'ilani Hwy., Kahana* ☎ *808/669–6999* ⊕ *www.roysrestaurant.com* ▭ *AE, D, DC, MC, V* ☺ *No lunch.*

$$ ✕ **Sansei Seafood Restaurant & Sushi Bar.** If you are fish or shellfish lover
PACIFIC RIM then this is the place for you. One of the most wildly popular restaurants
in Hawai'i with locations on three Islands, Sansei takes sushi, sashimi,
and contemporary Japanese food to a new level. Favorite dishes include
the mango and crab salad handroll, panko-crusted 'ahi sashimi roll, Asian
shrimp cake, Japanese calamari salad, and Dungeness crab ramen with
Asian truffle broth. There are great deals on sushi and small plates for the
early birds and night owls. ⊠ *600 Office Rd., Kapalua* ☎ *808/669–6286*
⊕ *www.sanseihawaii.com* ▭ *AE, D, MC, V* ⊘ *No lunch.*

THE SOUTH SHORE

KĪHEI AND MĀ'ALAEA

¢ ✕ **Kīhei Caffe.** This small, unassuming place across the street from
AMERICAN Kalama Beach Park has a breakfast menu that runs the gamut from
healthy yogurt-filled papaya to the local classic, *loco moco*—two eggs,
ground beef patty, rice, and brown gravy—and everything in between.
And the best thing about it is that the breakfast menu is served all day
long. Prices are extremely reasonable and it's a good spot for people-
watching. This is a popular place with locals so, depending on the time
and day, you may have to wait for a table. ⊠ *1945 S. Kīhei Rd., Kīhei*
☎ *808/879–2230* ⊕ *www.kiheicaffe.com* ▭ *MC, V* ⊘ *No dinner.*

$$ ✕ **Monsoon India.** Here, enjoy a lovely ocean view while feasting on
INDIAN authentic Indian cuisine. Appetizers like *papadum* chips and *samosas*
are served with homemade chutneys. There are 10 breads—naan and
more—that come hot from the tandoori oven, along with six mix-
and-match curries, lots of vegetarian selections, kebabs, and biriyanis.
Live music on Tuesday and Saturday evenings is a big draw, as is their
Sunday brunch buffet. ⊠ *At Menehune Shores, 760 S. Kīhei Rd., Kīhei*
☎ *808/875–6666* ⊕ *www.monsoonindiamaui.com* ▭ *MC, V.*

$$$$ ✕ **Sarento's on the Beach.** This upscale Italian restaurant's setting
ITALIAN right on spectacular Keawakapu Beach, with views of Molokini and
Kaho'olawe, is irresistible. And, to be honest, the spectacular setting is
the best thing about Sarento's. The menu has a decidedly Italian bent,
with offerings like linguine with clam sauce, seafood *fra diavolo* (in a
tomato sauce spiced with chilis), and portobello napoleon with local
eggplant, mozzarella, tomatoes, and arugula pesto. The food is good,
if a bit old-fashioned, and the portions may be a bit too big for some.
⊠ *2980 S. Kīhei Rd., Kīhei* ☎ *808/875–7555* ⊕ *www.tristarrestaurants.
com* ▭ *AE, D, DC, MC, V* ⊘ *No lunch.*

$ ✕ **Seascape Mā'alaea.** A good choice for a seafood lunch, the Maui
SEAFOOD Ocean Center's signature restaurant (aquarium admission is not
ⓒ required to dine here) offers harbor views from its open-air perch. The
restaurant promotes heart-healthy cuisine, using sustainable seafood
and trans-fat-free items. Lunch-size salads, sandwiches, burgers, fish
tacos, teriyaki tofu, fish-and-chips, chicken, ribs, and a full kids' menu
is on offer. There's something for everyone here, and the view isn't
bad either. ⊠ *192 Mā'alaea Rd., Mā'alaea* ☎ *808/270–7000* ⊕ *www.
mauioceancenter.com* ▭ *AE, D, DC, MC, V* ⊘ *No dinner.*

3

$ **✗ South Shore Tiki Lounge.** Come on, how can you come to Hawaiʻi and
AMERICAN *not* go to a tiki bar? And this one—tucked into Kīhei KalamaVillage—is
consistently voted "Best Bar" by the readers of *Maui Time Weekly*. During the day, sit on the shaded lānai to enjoy a burger, sandwich, or, better yet, one of their delicious specialty pizzas, crafted from scratch with
sauces made from fresh Roma tomatoes and Maui herbs. Seven nights a
week, the tiny bar area lights up with a lively crowd, as DJs spin dance
tunes under the glowing red eyes of the lounge's namesake tiki. ⊠ *1913
S. Kīhei Rd., Kīhei* ☎ *808/874–6444* ⊕ *www.southshoretikilounge.com*
⊟ *AE, MC, V.*

$ **✗ Thailand Cuisine.** Fragrant tea and coconut-ginger chicken soup begin
THAI a satisfying meal at this excellent Thai restaurant, set unassumingly in
the middle of a shopping mall. The care and expense that goes into the
decor—glittering Buddhist shrines, elaborate hardwood facades, fancy
napkin folds, and matching blue china—also applies to the cuisine. Take
an exotic journey with the fantastic pad thai, special house noodles, curries, and crispy fried chicken. Can't decide? Try the family dinners for
two or four. The fried bananas with ice cream are wonderful. There's a
second location in Kahului's Maui Mall, a perfect choice before or after
a movie at the megaplex. ⊠ *In Kukui Mall, 1819 S. Kīhei Rd., Kīhei*
☎ *808/875–0839* ⊕ *www.thailandcuisinemaui.com* ⊟ *AE, D, DC, MC,
V* ⊗ *No lunch on Sun.*

$ **✗ WokStar International Noodle Café.** This fun, easy-on-the-budget eatery
PACIFIC RIM across from the beach, serves fresh food influenced by local products
and Asian flavors. You can't go wrong with any of the starters, like the
crispy spring rolls, chicken satay, and potstickers. But it's the bowls
of veggies with rice or noodles, topped with your choice of protein
(beef, pork, chicken, mahimahi, or tofu) that have customers coming
back for more. The place is open until midnight seven days a week to
accommodate the hungry "pub crawlers" in the neighborhood. ⊠ *Kīhei
Kalama Village, 1913-D S. Kihei Rd., Kīhei* ☎ *808/495–0066* ⊕ *www.
wokstarcafe.com* ⊟ *AE, D, DC, MC, V.*

WAILEA AND SOUTH SHORE (MĀKENA)

$$$$ **✗ Ferraro's Bar e Ristorante.** Overlooking the ocean from a bluff above
ITALIAN Wailea Beach, this outdoor Italian restaurant at the Four Seasons Resort
Maui is beautiful both day and night. For lunch, indulge in a lobster sandwich or a quinoa salad topped with teriyaki-glaze tofu. At
dinner try the arugula and endive salad and house-made pasta or the
osso buco veal Milanese. If chef Michael Cantin is offering one of
his tasting menus, you should order it. Not surprisingly, the wine list
includes excellent Italian choices. Live classical music often adds to
the atmosphere, and occasionally you can spot celebrities at the bar.
⊠ *Four Seasons Resort Maui at Wailea, 3900 Wailea Alanui Dr., Wailea*
☎ *808/874–8000* ⊕ *www.fourseasons.com/maui* ⊟ *AE, D, DC, MC, V.*

$$$$ **✗ Gannon's.** Acclaimed chef Beverly Gannon took over the former Sea-
CONTEMPORARY Watch, renovated it with the splashy new Red Bar, and reopened it in
AMERICAN 2009 as her eponymous "Gannon's." You'll love the amazing ocean and
mountain views. Here you'll find Beverly's style of food, which consists
of lots of local products mixed with international flavors. Breakfast is
especially nice here. The outdoor lānai seating is cool in the morning

and overlooks the parade of boats heading out to Molokini. ✉ *100 Golf Club Dr., Wailea* 🕾 *808/875–8080* ⊕ *www.gannonsrestaurant. com* ▭ *AE, D, DC, MC, V.*

$$
ITALIAN

✗ **Matteo's.** Listen closely and you might hear chef Matteo Mitsura singing as he pounds dough in the kitchen of his pizzeria. Originally from Liguria—and formerly the chef of Ferraro's at the Four Seasons—Mitsura can definitely cook. Traditional pies share menu space with such unconventional choices as "The Cowboy" topped with barbecue sauce, chicken, and Fontina cheese. The handmade pappardelle pasta is loaded with luxurious braised lamb. Located on the Wailea Blue golf course, this casual, open-air restaurant enjoys gentle trade winds in the afternoon and a sky full of stars at night. A voluptuous wine list and desserts such as tiramisu top it off. ✉ *100 Wailea Ike Dr., Wailea* 🕾 *808/874–1234* ⊕ *www.matteospizzeria.com* ▭ *D, MC, V* ☺ *No lunch weekends.*

$$$$
PACIFIC RIM

✗ **Spago.** It's a marriage made in Hawai'i heaven. The California cuisine of the original celebrity chef, Wolfgang Puck is combined with Maui flavors and served lobby level and oceanfront at the luxurious Four Seasons Resort. Try the spicy 'ahi tuna poke in sesame-miso cones to start. Then see what the chefs-in-residence can do with some of Maui's fantastic local fishes. Finish with a little wild liliko'i crème brûlée with white chocolate—macadamia-nut biscotti. Oh, it'll cost you. But the service is spot-on and the smooth Asian-inspired decor allows the food to claim the spotlight. ✉ *Four Seasons Resort Maui at Wailea, 3900 Wailea Alanui Dr., Wailea* 🕾 *808/879–2999* ▭ *AE, D, DC, MC, V* ☺ *No lunch.*

$$$
PACIFIC RIM
Fodor's Choice
★

✗ **Tommy Bahama.** It's more "island-style" than Hawai'i and yes, it's a chain, but the food is consistently great, the service is filled with aloha, and the ambience is just so island refined. Try the Loki-Loki tuna poke (fresh 'ahi napoleon with guacamole, capers, soy sauce, and sesame oil), The Island Cowboy (a grilled 8-ounce tenderloin fillet with red wine demi-glace, roasted garlic, Maytag bleu cheese served with grilled lemon garlic asparagus and roasted fingerling potatoes), or any of the local fish preparations, equally well-accompanied. The Copper Island crab bisque is worthy of a cross-island drive, as are the desserts. ✉ *The Shops at Wailea, 3750 Wailea Alanui Dr., Wailea* 🕾 *808/879–7828* ⊕ *www.tommybahama.com* ▭ *AE, D, MC, V.*

CENTRAL MAUI

KAHULUI

$
ECLECTIC
☺

✗ **Da Kitchen.** There's an "express" location in Kīhei, but we recommend that you come to the always-crowded Kahului location for the mahimahi tempura, the loco moco, Hawaiian plate, and chicken katsu. Everything on the menu is great and the portions are gigantic. It's a happy place and the upbeat ambience is reflected in the service as well as the food. ✉ *425 Koloa St., Kahului* 🕾 *808/871–7782* ⊕ *www. da-kitchen.com* ☺ *Lunch only on Sat. Closed Sun.*

$$
CHINESE

✗ **Dragon Dragon.** Whether you're a party of 10 or 2, this is the place to stop for a quality meal of Chinese food staples. Dim sum is available only during lunch, but for a real treat, try some of the house specialties like the honey walnut prawns, spicy crab Singapore-style, and the sizzling platter of fish with basil leaves. Top it all off with Maui's

Dig into pūpū—Hawaiian appetizers—such as seaweed salad and 'ahi (yellowfin tuna).

own Roselani lychee sherbet. ⊠ *In Maui Mall, 70 E. Ka'ahumanu Ave., Kahului* ☎ *808/893–1628* ▭ *AE, D, MC, V.*

$$
ITALIAN
✕ **Marco's Grill & Deli.** One of the go-to places for airport comers and goers, this popular Italian restaurant also draws a steady crowd of local residents. Meatballs, sausages, and sauces are all made fresh in-house; the owner was a butcher in his former life. There's a long list of sandwiches that is available all day; the salads are definitely big enough to share. Note that food substitutions or special requests are not appreciated here. ⊠ *444 Hāna Hwy., Kahului* ☎ *808/877–4446* ▭ *AE, D, DC, MC, V.*

$
JAPANESE
✕ **Ramen Ya.** Part of a Japanese chain, this outpost is the first and only location in Maui. All the ramen dishes are slurp-worthy, and the *gyoza* (dumplings) are reason enough to dine here. If you're not that hungry or just have a small appetite, you can order kid-size portions. The service is quick and friendly, and the prices are right. ⊠ *Queen Ka'ahumanu Center, 275 W. Ka'ahumanu Ave., Kahului* ☎ *808/873–9688* ▭ *MC, V.*

$
ECLECTIC
🅲
✕ **Zippy's.** Zippy's is Hawai'i's favorite casual, eat-in, or take-out restaurant. It was founded more than 40 years ago; today O'ahu has more than two-dozen locations from which to choose. Maui's version with its architecture, cushy booths, and local art make it quite posh for a 24-hour-a-day, Denny's-type establishment. Spaghetti with chili, oxtail soup, Korean chicken, chicken katsu, noodles, burgers, and burritos are just a few of the tasty menu options. Napolean's Bakery counter up front serves its only-in-Hawai'i-style turnovers, pies, cakes, and pastries. ⊠ *15 Ho'okele St., Kahului* ☎ *808/856–7599* ⊕ *www.zippys.com* ▭ *AE, D, MC, V.*

WAILUKU

$ ✕ A.K.'s Café. Nearly hidden between auto-body shops and karaoke
ECLECTIC bars is this wonderful, bright café serving good island fare. Chef-owner
Elaine Nakashima not only knows how to make everything taste delicious, she knows how to make local flavors more healthful, too. Her
Thai chicken, baked chicken, local fish preparations, roast turkey plate,
even her sweet potatoes—either steamed or fried—are excellent. And
her crab cakes are so good—some say the best on Maui—that retail
markets around the island stock them in their freezers and their prepared food sections. The place takes on a lovely warm glow at dinnertime and impromptu contemporary Hawaiian music is not uncommon.
✉ 1237 Lower Main, Wailuku 🕾 808/244–8774 ⊕ www.akscafe.com
🗖 D, MC, V ☺ Closed weekends.

$$ ✕ Asian Star. This restaurant in Wailuku's Millyard is the best choice for
VIETNAMESE Vietnamese food on Maui. Owner Jason Chau grows his own Hawaiian
chili peppers, mint, basil, chives, lemongrass, green onion around the
perimeter of the parking lot, which adds robust and concentrated fla-
vors to his dishes. Try the lemongrass chicken or tofu, the garlic beef or
green papaya salad, the crispy sesame or orange beef, the clay pots with
crunchy, charred rice bits on the bottom, and the *bun,* bowls brimming
with cold vermicelli noodles and topped with chicken. ✉ The Millyard,
1764 Wili Pa Loop, Wailuku 🕾 808/244–1833 🗖 MC, V.

¢ ✕ Ba-Le Sandwiches & Plate Lunch. It began as a French-Vietnamese bakery
VIETNAMESE on Oʻahu, and has branched into popular small restaurants sprinkled
FodorśChoice throughout the Islands—some are kiosks in malls; others are stand-
★ alones with some picnic tables out front, as is the case at this location.
Vietnamese *pho* (the famous soups laden with seafood or rare beef, fresh
basil, bean sprouts, and lime) share menu space with local-style *saimin,*
plates of barbecue or spicy chicken, beef, or pork with jasmine rice,
and sandwiches. There are a slew of tapioca flavors for dessert. ✉ 1824
Oihana St., Wailuku 🕾 808/249–8833 ⊕ www.ba-le.com 🗖 AE, MC, V.

$$ ✕ Saeng's Thai Cuisine. The satays, Panang curry, and crispy mahimahi
THAI are all reason to make your way to Saeng's. Other reliable menu choices
include the angel wings (chicken wings stuffed with carrots and bean-
thread noodles), fresh summer rolls, and any of the chicken entrées. The
dining room is a bit dark but there's a courtyard with a pond and foliage, and open-air tables. Take note: service can be slow. But it's Maui,
so who's in a hurry? ✉ 2119 Vineyard St., Wailuku 🕾 808/244–1567
🗖 MC, V ☺ No lunch on weekends.

¢ ✕ Sam Sato's. Every island has its noodle shrine, and this is Maui's.
ASIAN Dry mein, saimin, chow fun—they all come in different size portions
FodorśChoice and with add-ins to satisfy every noodle-craving. While you wait for
★ your bowl, chow down on a teriyaki beef-stick, or two, or six. Save
room for the turnovers—pineapple, coconut, apple, or peach. At busy
times—which are most of the opening hours—you will likely have to
wait for a table or a stool at the counter. Be sure to write your name
on the little yellow pad or you'll miss your "next." ✉ The Millyard,
1750 Wili Pa Loop, Wailuku 🕾 808/244–7124 🗖 No credit cards ☺ No
dinner. Closed Sun.

$ ✕ **Tokyo Tei.** Getting there is half . . . well, maybe a quarter, of the fun.
JAPANESE   Tucked in the back corner of a covered parking garage, Tokyo Tei is a
Fodor'sChoice   gem worth seeking out. At lunch, you'll rub elbows with bankers and
★   construction workers; at dinner, three generations might be celebrating
Tūtū's (grandma's) birthday at the next table. This is a bona fide local
institution where, for more than six decades, people have come for the
food and the comfort of familiarity. The freshest sashimi, feather-light
yet crisp shrimp and vegetable tempura piled high, are all the items that
locals love. ⊠ *1063 Lower Main St., Wailuku* ☎ *808/242–9630* ▭ *MC,
V* ☟ *No lunch Sun.*

UPCOUNTRY

$$$ ✕ **Casanova Italian Restaurant & Deli.** An authentic Italian dinner house
ITALIAN   and nightclub, this place is smack in the middle of Casanova's *paniolo*
(cowboy) country. The brick wood-burning oven, imported from Italy,
has been turning out perfect pies and steaming hot focaccia for more
than 20 years. You can pair a pie with a salad (they're all big enough to
share), and a couple of glasses of wine without breaking the bank. The
daytime deli is good for cappuccino, croissant, and people-watching.
The place turns positively raucous—in a good way—on Wednesday,
Friday, and Saturday nights. ⊠ *1188 Makawao Ave., Makawao* ☎ *808/
572–0220* ⊕ *www.casanovamaui.com* ▭ *D, DC, MC, V.*

$$$$ ✕ **Hāli'imaile General Store.** Chef-restaurateur Beverly Gannon's first res-
MODERN   taurant remains a culinary destination after more than two decades.
HAWAIIAN   The big, rambling former plantation store has two dining rooms. Sit
in the front to be seen and heard; head on back for some quiet and
privacy. Classic dishes like crab pizza, Asian duck tostada, grilled
lamb chops, and many more are complemented with daily and nightly
specials. ⊠ *900 Hāli'imaile Rd., take left exit halfway up Haleakalā
Hwy., Hāli'imaile* ☎ *808/572–2666* ⊕ *www.bevgannonrestaurants.com*
▭ *AE, D, MC, V.*

$$$ ✕ **Market Fresh Bistro.** This hidden jewel of a restaurant serves some seri-
MODERN   ously fabulous food by chef Justin Pardo, formerly of Union Square
HAWAIIAN   Café in New York City. The chef uses locally grown and produced ingredients, and in a nod to more healthful eating, prefers reductions and
infused-oils rather than butter. Representative dishes include the cold
curried watermelon gazpacho (in season) with either seared scallops or a
lump crab cake, and the slow-cooked Maui Cattle Company short ribs,
which are dreamy. ⊠ *3620 Baldwin Ave., Makawao* ☎ *808/572–4877*
⊕ *www.marketfreshbistromaui.com* ▭ *AE, D, MC, V.*

THE NORTH SHORE

$ ✕ **Café des Amis.** The menu is all over the place, featuring Mediterranean
ECLECTIC   and Indian dishes, but the food is fresh and tasty. The budget-friendly
Fodor'sChoice   cafe serves up a nice selection of savory crepes, sweet crepes, Indian
★   wraps, and salads; it's inexpensive, to boot. The umbrella-shaded tables
outside offer great people-watching opportunity. ⊠ *42 Baldwin Ave.,
Pā'ia* ☎ *808/579–6323* ▭ *No credit cards.*

$$ **✕ Colleen's at the Cannery.** From
AMERICAN the nondescript exterior, and the
Fodor'sChoice location in an old pineapple can-
★ nery-cum-strip-mall, you'd never
anticipate the delights inside. Col-
leen's is the most overlooked and
best all-around restaurants on
Maui. It's popular with locals for
breakfast and lunch, but we love
it most at dinner when the candles
come out and it's time for marti-
nis and filet mignon. The food is
consistently good, in particular the standout burger and fries, huge
salads made with Upcountry's best produce, and the simple, yet stellar
roast chicken. When eating here, you'll feel like you're at a hip, urban
eatery. ⊠ *In Haʻikū Cannery Marketplace, 810 Haʻikū Rd., Haʻikū*
☎ *808/575–9211* ⊟ *AE, D, MC, V.*

$$ **✕ Flatbread Company.** Vermont-based Flatbread Company marched right
PIZZA in to Pāʻia in 2007 and instantly became a popular restaurant and a
☾ valued addition to the community. As part of the company's mission,
they started "giving back" to local nonprofits immediately. Happily,
along with the altruism, the food is fantastic. There's a big, primitive-
looking, earthen, wood-fired oven from which emerge utterly delicious
flatbread pies. They use organic, local, sustainable products, including
100% organically grown wheat for the made-fresh-daily products. The
place is a good spot to take the kids. There's a no reservations policy
but they do have "call ahead seating"—you can put your name on the
wait list before you arrive. ⊠ *375 Hāna Hwy., Pāʻia* ☎ *808/579–8989*
⊕ *www.flatbreadcompany.com* ⊟ *MC, V.*

$$$$ **✕ Mama's Fish House.** For almost four decades, Mama's has been *the*
SEAFOOD Maui destination for special occasions. A path of gecko-shape stones
leads through the coconut grove past the giant clamshell and under
the banyan arch to an ever-changing fantasyland of Hawaiiana kitsch.
True, the setting couldn't be more spectacular, and yes, the menu even
names the angler that reeled in your fresh catch, but the dishes are decidedly dated in terms of preparation and presentation and the prices are
off the charts. But if you're looking for an overall experience, make a
reservation and celebrate your special occasion here. ⊠ *799 Poho Pl.,
Kūʻau* ☎ *808/579–8488* ⊕ *www.mamasfishhouse.com* ⚮ *Reservations
essential* ⊟ *AE, D, DC, MC, V.*

$$ **✕ Pāʻia Fishmarket Restaurant.** If you're okay with communal picnic
SEAFOOD tables, or taking your meal to a nearby beach, this place in funky Pāʻia
Fodor'sChoice town serves, arguably, the best fresh fish for the best prices on this side
★ of the island. Four preparations are offered and, on any given day, there
are at least four fresh fishes from which to choose. For the nonfish fans,
there are burgers, chicken, and pasta. The side dishes—Cajun rice, home
fries, and the amazing hand-cut crunchy cole slaw—are all as delectable
as the main event. You can have a beer or a glass of wine, too, as long
as you stay inside, of course. ⊠ *100 Hāna Hwy., Pāʻia* ☎ *808/579–8030*
⊕ *www.paiafishmarket.com* ⊟ *D, MC, V.*

WHERE TO STAY

Updated
by Bonnie
Friedman

Maui's accommodations run the gamut from rural bed-and-breakfasts to superopulent megaresorts. In between the extremes, there's something for every vacation style and budget.

If the latest and greatest is your style, be prepared to spend a small fortune. Properties like the Ritz-Carlton Kapalua, the Four Seasons Resort Maui at Wailea, and newer condo complexes such as the Wailea Beach Villas may set you back at least $600 a night, though the weaker economy has brought more discounts.

Although there aren't many of them, small bed-and-breakfasts are charming. They tend to be in residential or rural neighborhoods around the island, sometimes beyond the resort areas of West Maui and the South Shore. The B&Bs offer both a personalized experience and a window onto authentic local life. The prices tend to be the lowest available on Maui, often less than $200 per night.

Apartment and condo rentals are perfect for modest budgets, for two or more couples traveling together, and for families. Not only are the nightly rates lower than hotel rooms, but "eating in" (all have kitchens of some description) is substantially less expensive than dining out.

There are literally hundreds of these units, ranging in size from studios to luxurious four-bedrooms with multiple baths, all over the island. The vast majority is along the sunny coasts—from Mākena to Kīhei on the South Shore and Lahaina up to Kapalua on West Maui. Prices depend on the size of the unit and its proximity to the beach, as well as the amenities and services offered. For about $250 a night, you can get a lovely one-bedroom apartment without many frills or flourishes, close to but probably not on the beach. Many rentals have minimum stays (usually three to five nights).

Most of Maui's resorts—several are megaresorts—have opulent gardens, fantasy swimming pools, championship golf courses, and full-service fitness centers and spas. Expect to spend at least $350 a night at the resort hotels; they are all in the Wailea and Mākena resort area on the South Shore and Kā'anapali and Kapalua on West Maui. At all lodgings properties, ask about discounts and deals (free nights with longer stays, for example), which have proliferated.

WHAT IT COSTS					
	¢	$	$$	$$$	$$$$
HOTELS	under $100	$100–$180	$181–$260	$261–$340	over $340

Hotel prices are for two people in a double room in high season. Condo price categories reflect studio and one-bedroom rates. Prices do not include 13.42% tax.

LAHAINA

$$$–$$$$
B&B/INN
Fodor's Choice
★

Ho'oilo House. If you want to treat yourself to a luxurious but intimate getaway and don't require resort facilities, spend a few nights at this Bali-inspired B&B. In the foothills of the West Maui Mountains, just south of Lahaina town, the stunning property exemplifies quiet perfection. As you enter the house your eye is immediately drawn to the immense glass doors that open onto a small but sparkling pool and a breathtaking view of the Pacific. Almost all of the furnishings and the materials used to build the house were imported from Bali. Two "conversation tables" in the common area are filled with Balinese cushions, providing great spots to snack, chat, or just relax. Each uniquely decorated room features traditional Balinese doors with mother-of-pearl inlay, a custom bed, a private lānai, a huge bathroom with a giant bathtub, an iPod docking station, and, best of all, a private outdoor shower. **Pros:** friendly on-site hosts Amy and Dan Martin are an asset; beautiful furnishings. **Cons:** not good for families with younger children; no kitchen facilities; beaches are a short drive away. **TripAdvisor:** "the best B&B we've stayed in," "would go back in a heartbeat," "romantic peaceful setting." ✉ *138 Awaiku St., Lahaina* ☎ *808/667–6669* ⊕ *www.hooilohouse.com* ⟿ *6 rooms* ♻ *In-room: a/c, safe, Internet, Wi-Fi. In-hotel: pool, Wi-Fi hotspot, no kids under 16* ▤ *AE, MC, V.*

$
B&B/INN

Lahaina Inn. An antique jewel in the heart of town, this two-story wooden building is classic Lahaina and will transport romantics back to the turn of the 20th century. The small rooms shine with authentic period furnishings, including antique bureaus and headboards. You can while away the hours in a wooden rocking chair on your balcony, sipping coffee and watching Old Lahaina Town come to life. Guests may also take a free shuttle to the inn's sister property, the Royal Lahaina Resort in Ka'anapali, and enjoy the amenities such as the pool and tennis courts there. The Lahaina Grill restaurant is downstairs. **Pros:** a half block off Front Street, the location is within easy walking distance to shops, restaurants, and historical attractions; lovely antiques. **Cons:** rooms are really small, bathrooms particularly so; some street noise; the two-story property has no elevator. **TripAdvisor:** "very laid-back and friendly," "can be noisy," "great location for things happening downtown." ✉ *127 Lahainaluna Rd., Lahaina* ☎ *808/661–0577 or 806/222–5642* ⊕ *www.lahainainn.com* ⟿ *9 rooms, 3 suites* ♻ *In-room: a/c, Wi-Fi. In-hotel: restaurant, Wi-Fi hotspot* ▤ *AE, D, MC, V.*

$$–$$$
RENTAL

Lahaina Shores Beach Resort. You really can't get any closer to the beach than this. A local landmark, this lofty (by Lahaina standards), seven-story property offers panoramic ocean and mountain views. Most of the units are studios, but there are deluxe one-bedroom suites on the first floor that open right onto a beachfront lawn and penthouses on the top floors that have a dining area and an extra bathroom. All have fully equipped kitchens and large, private lānai. A 2010 enhancement refurbished the building's historic plantation-style exterior and new ceramic tile floor treatments on each condo's outdoor lānai. The units are individually owned and many of them have been refreshed with new furniture and upgraded kitchens. You can enter the shopping village next door through a private entrance for access to a spa,

Ho'oilo House

WHERE TO STAY IN WEST MAUI

Hotels and Resorts

	Property Name	Worth Noting	Cost $	Pools	Beach	Golf Course	Tennis Courts	Gym	Spa	Children's Programs	Rooms	Restaurants	Other	Location
2	Hyatt Regency Maui	130-foot water slide	$$$$	2	yes	priv.	4	yes	yes	3–12	806	3	Cirque Polynesia dinner show	Kā'anapali
5	Kā'anapali Beach Hotel	Hula and lei-making classes	$$$–$$$$	1	yes	priv.					432	3	Kupanaha dinner show	Kā'anapali
13	Nāpili Kai Beach Resort	Outstanding beach	$$$–$$$$	4	yes	priv.		yes		6–10	163	1	Hula and Hawaiian slack key guitar shows	Nāpili
14	Ritz-Carlton, Kapalua	Environmental education center	$$$$	2	yes	priv.	4	yes	yes	5–12	463	6	Shop; basketball court	Kapalua
8	Royal Lahaina Resort	Tennis stadium	$$$–$$$$	3	yes	priv.	11		yes	5–12	350	2	Nightly luau	Kā'anapali
6	Sheraton Maui Resort & Spa	Nightly torch-lighting ritual	$$$$	1	yes	priv.	3	yes	yes	5–12	538	2		Kā'anapali
4	The Westin Maui Resort	The Heavenly Spa	$$$$	5	yes	priv.		yes	yes	5–12	759	2		Kā'anapali

Condos and Vacation Rentals

	Property Name	Worth Noting	Cost $	Pools	Beach	Golf Course	Tennis Courts	Gym	Spa	Children's Programs	Rooms	Restaurants	Other	Location
9	Aston at Papakea Resort	Large rooms	$$$–$$$$	2	yes		3			5–12	364		Kitchens	Honokōwai
3	Kā'anapali Ali'i	Great location	$$$$	3	yes	Yes	3	yes			264		Clay tennis courts	Kā'anapali
1	Lahaina Shores Beach Resort	Oceanfront	$$–$$$	1	yes						199		Kitchens	Lahaina
10	Mahina Surf Oceanfront Resort	Free parking and phone	$$	1							56		All ocean view units	Mahinahina
12	The Mauian Boutique Beach Studios	On Nāpili Bay	$$–$$$	1	yes						44		No TVs	Nāpili
7	Outrigger Maui Eldorado	On golf course	$$$	3	yes	yes					204		Kitchens	Kā'anapali
11	Sands of Kahana	Kids' putting green	$–$$	2	yes		3				162	1	Kitchens	Kahana

For B&B and Inn options, please see reviews in the chapter

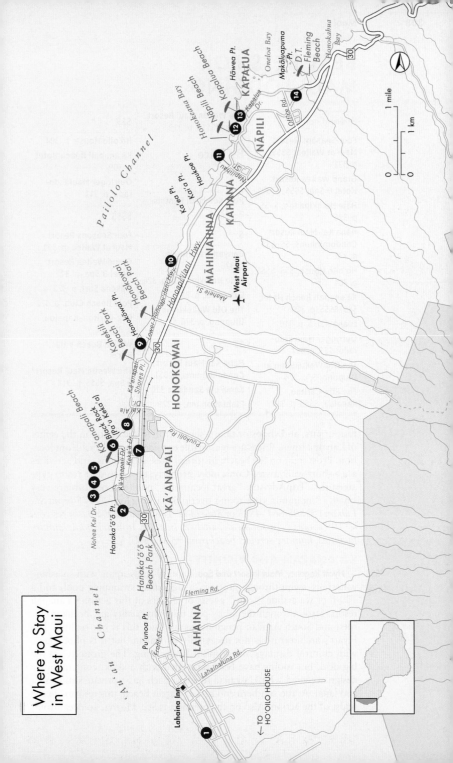

Where to Stay in West Maui

Pailolo Channel

'Au'au Channel

LAHAINA

KĀ'ANAPALI

HONOKŌWAI

MĀHINAHANA

KAHANA

NĀPILI

KAPALUA

West Maui Airport

Pu'unoa Pt.
Front St.
Lahainaluna Rd.
Lahaina Inn
HO'OILO HOUSE
Fleming Rd.
Hanaka'ō'ō Beach Park
Hanaka'ō'ō Pt.
Nohea Kai Dr.
Kā'anapali Beach
Black Rock ('ol
(Pu'u Keka'a)
Ka'anapali Dr.
Keka'a Dr.
Kai Ala Dr.
Ka'anapali Shores Pl.
Puukolii Rd.
Kahekili Beach Park
Honokōwai Pt.
Honokōwai Beach Park
Lower Honoapi'ilani Hwy.
Honoapi'ilani Hwy.
Akahele St.
Nāpilihau 'St.
Kō'eo Pt.
Kai'a Pt.
Haukoe Pt.
Honokeana Bay
Nāpili Beach
Nāpili Pt.
Kapalua Dr.
Office Rd.
Hāwea Pt.
Kapalua Beach
Makāluapuma Pt.
D.T. Fleming Beach
Honokahua Bay
Onelua Bay

TO HO'OILO HOUSE

30

0   1 km
0   1 mile

BEST BETS FOR MAUI LODGING

Fodor's Choice ★

Four Seasons Resort Maui at Wailea, $$$$, p. 321

Grand Wailea Resort Hotel & Spa, $$$, p. 321

Hale Ho'okipa Inn, $–$$, p. 326

Hāna Kai-Maui Resort Condominiums, $$–$$$, p. 331

Ho'oilo House, $$$–$$$$, p. 304

Kā'anapali Beach Hotel, $$$–$$$$, p. 309

Luana Kai, $, p. 316

Outrigger Maui Eldorado, $$$, p. 311

The Old Wailuku Inn at Ulupono, $, p. 326

The Ritz-Carlton, Kapalua, $$$$, p. 314

The Westin Maui Resort & Spa, $$$$, p. 312

By Price

¢

Pu'u Koa Maui Rentals, p. 331

$

Banyan Tree House, p. 326

Hale Ho'okipa Inn, p. 326

Luana Kai, p. 316

The Old Wailuku Inn at Ulupono, p. 326

$$

Hāna Kai-Maui Resort Condominiums, p. 331

Kama'ole Sands, p. 316

Plantation Inn, p. 329

$$$

Ho'oilo House, p. 304

Kā'anapali Beach Hotel, p. 309

Outrigger Maui Eldorado, p. 311

$$$$

Four Seasons Resort Maui at Wailea, p. 321

Grand Wailea Resort Hotel & Spa, p. 321

Mākena Surf, p. 322

Polo Beach Club, p. 322

Ritz-Carlton, Kapalua, p. 314

Wailea Beach Villas, p. 324

The Westin Maui Resort & Spa, $$$$, p. 312

restaurants, and shops or take a short stroll to the action in the center of Lahaina town. Prices are reasonable considering the beachfront location. **Pros:** right on the beach; historical sites, attractions, and activities are a short walk away. **Cons:** older property; no up-to-date resort-type amenities. **TripAdvisor:** "great location," "pool and hot tub are very small," "mountain view rooms overlook parking lot." ⊠ *475 Front St., Lahaina* ☎ *808/661–4835 or 866/934–9176* ⊕ *www.lahainashores.com* ➭ *199 rooms* ♿ *In-room: a/c, kitchen, Internet. In-hotel: pool, laundry facilities, laundry service, beachfront* ═ *AE, MC, V.*

KĀ'ANAPALI AND VICINITY

$$$$

RESORT

⊡ **Hyatt Regency Maui Resort and Spa.** Fantasy landscaping with splashing waterfalls, swim-through grottoes, a lagoonlike swimming pool, and a 130-foot waterslide "wow" guests of all ages at this active Kā'anapali resort. Stroll through the lobby past museum-quality art, brilliant parrots, and South African penguins (as we said, this is not reality). The Hyatt's architecture is not necessarily Hawaiian, but it is photogenic, with cultural displays and tropical landscaping. The grounds are the big deal, but rooms have been renovated with a sleek, contemporary design accented with Hawaiian touches. Each has a private sitting area and lānai. At the southern end of Kā'anapali Beach, this resort is in the midst of the action. Also on the premises is Spa Moana, an oceanfront, full-service facility. The redesigned restaurant has been renamed Japengo and features Pacific Rim cuisine served in an outdoor setting, a new Moon Bar and sushi lounge. There are nightly lūʻau shows and Cirque Polynesia is a musical acrobatic show staged in an outdoor theater. The rooftop Astronomy Tour of the Stars, where guests gaze at the heavens through digital telescopes,

is a unique, popular, and often thrilling activity offered at no other Maui resort. **Pros:** nightly lūʻau show on-site; home of new musical acrobatics show, Cirque Polynesia, and Astronomy Tour of the Stars; new restaurant and bar. **Cons:** it can be difficult to find a space in self-parking; service can be uneven. **TripAdvisor:** "separate pool areas for children," "ideally located," "best bed I've ever slept on." ⊠ *200 Nohea Kai Dr., Kāʻanapali* ☎ *808/661–1234 or 800/233–1234* ⊕ *www.maui.hyatt.com* ⟿ *806 rooms ⌂ In-room: a/c, safe, refrigerator, DVD, Internet, Wi-Fi. In-hotel: 3 restaurants, bars, golf courses, tennis courts, pools, gym, spa, beachfront, water sports, children's programs (ages 3–12), laundry facilities, laundry service, parking (free)* ☰ *AE, D, DC, MC, V.*

$$$$
RENTAL
⌂ Kāʻanapali Aliʻi. Four 11-story buildings are laid out so well that the feeling of seclusion you enjoy can make you forget you're in a condo complex. Instead of tiny units, you'll be installed in an ample (1,500–1,900 square feet) one- or two-bedroom apartment. Many of the units have been upgraded with new furnishings and appliances; all have a sunken living room and a separate dining room. It's the best of both worlds: homelike condo living with hotel amenities—daily maid service, an activities desk, small store with complimentary DVDs for guests to borrow, and 24-hour front-desk service. Amenities include: a state-of-the-art fitness center; three clay tennis courts; upgraded pool area with flat-screen TVs, cabanas, and barbecue grills (plastic utensils and paper plates are always in stock for guests' use); spa treatments and room service supplied by the nearby Westin hotel; and signing privileges at the Westin, Marriott, and Sheraton hotels within the Kaʻanapali Resort. **Pros:** large, comfortable units on the beach; good location in heart of the action in Kāʻanapali Resort. **Cons:** elevators are notoriously slow; crowded parking; no on-site restaurant. **TripAdvisor:** "the staff were so friendly," "parking was free," "clean, comfortable, modern accommodations." ⊠ *50 Nohea Kai Dr., Kāʻanapali* ☎ *808/667–1400 or 800/642–6284* ⊕ *www.kaanapalialii.com* ⟿ *264 units ⌂ In-room: a/c, safe, kitchen, DVD, Internet. In-hotel: room service, golf course, tennis courts, pools, gym, beachfront, children's programs, laundry facilities, laundry service, parking* ☰ *AE, D, MC, V.*

$$$–$$$$
HOTEL
Fodor's Choice
★
⌂ Kāʻanapali Beach Hotel. Older but still attractive, this charming hotel is full of aloha. Locals say that it's one of the few resorts on the island where you can get a true Hawaiian experience. The entire staff takes part in the hotel's ongoing Poʻokela program to learn about the history, traditions, and values of Hawaiian culture, and shares its knowledge

WHERE TO STAY IN MAUI

	LOCAL VIBE	PROS	CONS
West Maui	Popular and busy, the West Side includes the picturesque, touristy town of Lahaina and the upscale resort areas of Kāʻanapali and Kapalua.	A wide variety of shopping, water sports, and historic sites provide plenty to do. To relax, there are great beaches and brilliant sunsets.	Traffic is usually congested; parking is hard to find; beaches can be crowded.
South Shore	The protected South Shore of Maui offers diverse experiences, and accommodations, from comfortable condos to luxurious resorts—and golf, golf, golf.	Many beautiful beaches; sunny weather; great snorkeling.	Numerous strip malls; crowded with condos; there can be lots of traffic.
Upcountry	Country and chic come together in farms, ranches, and trendy towns on the cool, green slopes of Haleakalā.	Cooler weather at higher elevations; panoramic views of nearby Islands; distinctive shops, boutiques, galleries, and restaurants.	Fewer restaurants; no nightlife; can be very dark at night and difficult to drive for those unfamiliar with roads and conditions.
North Shore	The North Shore is a mecca for surfing, windsurfing, and kite sailing. When the surf's not up, the focus is on shopping: Pāʻia is full of galleries, shops, and hip eateries.	Wind and waves are terrific for water sports; colorful small towns to explore without the intrusion of big resorts.	Weather may not be as sunny as other parts of the island; no nightlife; most stores in Pāʻia close early.
Hāna	Remote and rural, laid-back and tropical Hāna is a special place.	Natural experience; rugged coastline and lush tropical scenery; lots of waterfalls.	Accessed by a long and winding road; no nightlife; few places to eat or shop.

and stories with guests. You can participate by taking complimentary classes in authentic hula dancing, lei making, *lauhala* weaving, ʻukulele playing, and other Hawaiian activities. The spacious rooms are decorated with Hawaiian motifs, wicker, and rattan; each has a lānai and faces either the beach beyond the courtyard or the lush mountains. The departure ceremony makes you want to come back. **Pros:** exceptional Hawaiian culture program; friendly staff; Tiki Terrace restaurant serves delicious dinners and one of the most bountiful Sunday brunches on the island. **Cons:** a bit run-down; fewer amenities than other places along this beach. **TripAdvisor:** "we enjoyed the hula show," "the room was a great size," "right on a beautiful beach." ⊠ *2525 Kāʻanapali Pkwy., Kāʻanapali* ☎ *808/661–0011 or 800/262–8450* ⊕ *www.kbhmaui.com* ⬦ *432 rooms* ⚒ *In-room: a/c, safe, refrigerator, Internet, Wi-Fi. In-hotel: 3 restaurants, bar, golf courses, pool, beachfront, laundry facilities, laundry service, parking* ▭ *AE, D, DC, MC, V.*

$$$
RENTAL
Fodor's Choice
★

Outrigger Maui Eldorado. The Kāʻanapali Golf Course's fairways wrap around this fine condo complex that offers several perks, most notably access to a fully outfitted beach cabana on a semiprivate beach. The complex itself isn't exactly *on* the beach—it's a quick golf-cart trip away. Although guests at other resorts get scolded for dragging lounge chairs onto neighboring resort beaches, here you can relax in luxury. Not only will you have beach chairs at your disposal, but a full kitchen and lounge area at the cabana, too. The privately owned units are tastefully decorated with modern appliances and have spacious bathrooms. These condos are a good value for pricey Kāʻanapali. **Pros:** privileges at five resort golf courses; daily maid service. **Cons:** not right on beach; some distance from attractions of the Kāʻanapali Resort; some units are privately owned so condition of units may vary. **TripAdvisor:** "we would definitely stay here again," "short walk to an almost private beach," "unit was extremely spacious and open." ⊠ *2661 Kekaʻa Dr., Kāʻanapali* ☎ *808/661–0021* ⊕ *www.mauieldorado.com* ⇒ *204 units* ⚘ *In-room: a/c, safe, kitchen, DVD, Internet, Wi-Fi. In-hotel: golf course, pools, laundry facilities, laundry service, parking* ⊟ *AE, D, DC, MC, V.*

$$$–$$$$
RESORT

Royal Lahaina Resort. Built in 1962 as the first hotel in the Kāʻanapali Resort, this grand property has hosted millionaires and Hollywood stars. In the 21st century, major upgrades have taken place including renovation of the 333 rooms in the 12-story Lahaina Kai Tower, which now feature dark-teak furnishings set against light-color walls, plush beds with 300-count Egyptian cotton linens, sound systems with an iPod and MP3 docking station, and 32-inch, high-definition flat-screen TVs. The resort's quaint low-rise cottages were scheduled to be replaced with individually owned luxury villas but those plans are on hold. So, you can still stay in one of the 27 plantation-style cottages that have been updated with new bedding, furnishings, and amenities. Another option at the Royal Lahaina Resort is the Kāʻanapali Ocean Inn where you can stay for less money and a little less comfort (it's a three-story building with no elevator), but enjoy the services and amenities of the resort. To experience the spirit of the hotel's early days, head to the poolside Don the Beachcomber bar, billed as "the Home of the Original Mai Tai," where the retro-Tiki style of Hawaiʻi's early days as a vacation paradise lives on. **Pros:** on-site lūʻau nightly; variety of accommodation types; tennis ranch with 11 courts and pro shop. **Cons:** older property still in need of updating. **TripAdvisor:** "great value," "Breakfast buffet was excellent," "beautiful snorkeling site within walking distance." ⊠ *2780 Kekaʻa Dr., Kāʻanapali* ☎ *808/661–3611 or 800/447–6925* ⊕ *www.hawaiihotels.com* ⇒ *350 rooms* ⚘ *In-room: a/c, safe, refrigerator, Wi-Fi. In-hotel: 2 restaurants, tennis courts, pools, beachfront, Internet terminal* ⊟ *AE, D, DC, MC, V.*

$$$$
RESORT

Sheraton Maui Resort & Spa. Set among dense gardens on Kāʻanapali's best stretch of beach, the Sheraton offers a quieter, more low-key atmosphere than its neighboring resorts. The open-air lobby has a crisp, cool look with understated furnishings and decor, and sweeping views of the pool area and beach. The majority of the spacious rooms come with ocean views; only one of the six buildings has rooms with mountain or garden views. All rooms have plenty of amenities, including 32-inch flat-screen TVs with video games and on-command movies; all suites also have Bose stereo systems. The huge swimming pool looks like a natural lagoon, with rock waterways and wooden bridges; and the Spa at Black Rock has been renovated and expanded. Best of all, the hotel sits next to and on top of the 80-foot-high Pu'u Keka'a (Black Rock), from which divers leap in a nightly torch-lighting and cliff-diving ritual. **Pros:** luxury resort with terrific beach location; great snorkeling right off the beach. **Cons:** extensive property can mean a long walk from your room to the lobby, restaurants, and beach; staff not overly helpful. **TripAdvisor:** "the grounds are beautiful," "location is excellent," "pool area is fantastic." ⊠ *2605 Kā'anapali Pkwy., Kā'anapali* ☎ *808/661–0031 or 888/488–3535* ⊕ *www.sheraton-maui.com* ➲ *508 rooms, 30 suites* ♿ *In-room: safe, refrigerator, Internet. In-hotel: 2 restaurants, bar, tennis courts, pool, gym, spa, beachfront, children's programs (ages 5–12), laundry service, Wi-Fi hotspot* ☰ *AE, D, DC, MC, V.*

$$$$
RESORT
Fodor's Choice
★

The Westin Maui Resort & Spa. The cascading waterfall in the lobby of this hotel gives way to an "aquatic playground" with five heated swimming pools, abundant waterfalls (15 at last count), lagoons complete with pink flamingos and swans, and a premier beach. The water features combined with a spa and fitness center and privileges at two 18-hole golf courses make this an active resort—great for families. Relaxation is by no means forgotten, though. The 15,000-square-foot Heavenly Spa has 16 treatment rooms and a yoga studio. Elegant dark-wood furnishings in the rooms accentuate the crisp linens of the chain's "Heavenly Beds." Rooms in the Beach Tower are newer and slightly larger than those in the Ocean Tower, and all rooms now include a sofa bed. The resort's Wailele Polynesian Lū'au features family-style dinner and colorful performances, including Maui's only "extreme" fire-knife dance finale. **Pros:** complimentary shuttle to Westin Kā'anapali Ocean Resort Villas and to Lahaina, where parking can be difficult; activity programs for all ages; one pool just for adults. **Cons:** you could end up with fantasy overload; can seem a bit stuffy at times. **TripAdvisor:** "staff was nothing but helpful," "rooms were small and tired," "pool area does get very crowded." ⊠ *2365 Kā'anapali Pkwy., Kā'anapali* ☎ *808/667–2525 or 888/716–8112* ⊕ *www.westinmaui.com* ➲ *731 rooms, 28 suites* ♿ *In-room: a/c, safe, refrigerator, DVD, Internet. In-hotel: 2 restaurants, bar, golf courses, pools, gym, spa, beachfront, children's programs (ages 5–12), laundry service, Wi-Fi hotspot, parking* ☰ *AE, D, DC, MC, V.*

KAPALUA AND VICINITY

$$$
RENTAL
☾

Aston at Papakea Resort. Although this casual, oceanfront condominium complex with studios and one- and two-bedroom units has no beach, there are several close by. Papakea has built-in privacy because its units are spread out among 11 low-rise buildings on about 13 acres of land; bamboo-lined walkways between buildings and fish-stocked ponds add to the serenity. Fully equipped kitchens and laundry facilities make longer stays easy here. **Pros:** units have large rooms; lovely garden landscaping. **Cons:** no beach in front of property; pool can get crowded; no on-site shops or restaurants. **TripAdvisor:** "grounds are beautiful," "cheaper than other hotels," "view was lovely." ✉ *3543 Lower Honoapi'ilani Hwy., Honokōwai* ☎ *808/669–4848 or 866/774–2924* ⊕ *www.astonhotels.com* ⤳ *364 units* ⚒ *In-room: a/c, safe, kitchen, DVD, Wi-Fi. In-hotel: tennis courts, pools, children's programs (ages 5–12), laundry facilities, Internet, parking* ☐ *AE, MC, V.*

$$
RENTAL

🛏 **Mahina Surf Oceanfront Resort.** Mahina Surf stands out from the many condo complexes lining the ocean-side stretch of Honoapi'ilani Highway by being both well managed and affordable. You won't be charged fees for parking or local phone use, and discount car rentals are available. The individually owned units are typically overdecorated (lots of rattan furniture, silk flowers, and decorative items), but each one has a well-equipped kitchen and, because they are all oceanfront, an excellent ocean view. The quiet complex is a short amble away from Honokōwai's grocery shopping, beaches, and restaurants. **Pros:** oceanfront barbecues; no "hidden" fees. **Cons:** set among a row of relatively nondescript condo complexes; oceanfront but with rocky shoreline rather than a beach. **TripAdvisor:** "pool is gorgeous," "property pretty and well maintained," "nice, simple condo resort." ✉ *4057 Lower Honoapi'ilani Hwy., Mahinahina* ☎ *808/669–6068 or 800/367–6068* ⊕ *www.mahinasurf.com* ⤳ *56 units* ⚒ *In-room: no a/c, safe, kitchen, Internet, Wi-Fi (some). In-hotel: pool, laundry facilities* ☐ *MC, V.*

$–$$
RENTAL

🛏 **The Mauian Boutique Beach Studios.** If you're looking for a quiet place to stay, the former Mauian Hotel way out in Nāpili may be for you. The rooms have neither TVs nor phones—such noisy devices are relegated to the 'Ohana Room, where a Continental breakfast is served daily. There's a new name and a new look for the simple two-story buildings dating from 1959; renovations have added new flooring, new island-style furnishings, and new appliances in the well-equipped kitchens. Best of all, the 2-acre property opens out onto lovely Nāpili Bay. **Pros:** reasonable rates; friendly staff. **Cons:** older building; few amenities. ✉ *5441 Lower Honoapi'ilani Hwy., Nāpili* ☎ *808/669–6205 or 800/367–5034* ⊕ *www.mauian.com* ⤳ *44 rooms* ⚒ *In-room: no a/c, no phone, kitchen (some), no TV. In-hotel: pool, beachfront, laundry facilities, Wi-Fi hotspot* ☐ *AE, D, MC, V.*

$$$$
RESORT
☾

🛏 **Nāpili Kai Beach Resort.** On 10 beautiful beachfront acres—the beach here is one of the best on West Maui for swimming and snorkeling—the Nāpili Kai draws a loyal following. The Hawaiian-style rooms open onto private lānai. The rooms closest to the beach have no air-conditioning, but ceiling fans usually suffice. "Hotel" rooms have only mini-refrigerators and coffeemakers, whereas studios and suites have fully equipped kitchenettes; many have recently been refreshed with new paint, furnishings, and accessories, and upgraded with modern granite countertops and stainless steel appliances. Services on property include an indoor/outdoor massage center offering a range of body treatments, and a boutique where you can find resort wear and estate jewelry. This is a family-friendly place, with children's programs and free classes in hula dancing and lei making. **Pros:** kids' hula performance and a Hawaiian slack-key guitar concert every week; fantastic swimming and sunning beach; old Hawaiian feel. **Cons:** older property; some might call it "unhip." **TripAdvisor:** "beautiful grounds," "many people of all ages there," "restaurant had good food." ✉ *5900 Lower Honoapi'ilani Hwy., Nāpili* ☎ *808/669–6271 or 800/367–5030* ⊕ *www.napilikai.com* ⇌ *163 units* ♿ *In-room: a/c (some), kitchen (some), Internet. In-hotel: restaurant, children's programs (ages 6–10), pools, gym, spa, beachfront, laundry facilities, laundry service, parking* ☰ *AE, D, MC, V.*

$$$$
RESORT
Fodor's Choice
★

🍽 **The Ritz-Carlton, Kapalua.** This elegant hillside property features luxurious service, upscale accommodations, spa, restaurants, and pool, along with an education center and an enhanced Hawaiian sense of place. In other words, this is one of Maui's most notable resorts. The guest rooms and 107 one- and two-bedroom condominium residential suites (some of which are available for rent) are decorated in themes incorporating the rich colors of the ocean, mountains, and rain forests that surround the resort. The residential suites are located in a separate wing but not on a separate property so all the amenities of the hotel are easily accessible—no shuttling between facilities is necessary. The elegant spa facility includes a fitness center, yoga studio, 15 treatment rooms, private outdoor shower gardens, and Hawaiian design elements. Set amid the lush grounds of the resort, the multilevel pool and hot tubs are open 24 hours, and children have their own pool area. The Environmental Education Center features Jean-Michel Cousteau's "Ambassadors of the Environment" program and the hotel also has a full-time cultural advisor who instructs employees and guests in Hawaiian traditions. Although not set directly on the sand, the Ritz does front D.T. Fleming Beach, recognized as one of Hawaii's best. **Pros:** luxury and service you'd expect from a Ritz; many cultural and recreational programs. **Cons:** expensive; can be windy on the grounds and at the pool; the hotel is not on the beach and not very close to major attractions such as Lahaina and Haleakalā. **TripAdvisor:** "the service was top notch," "dining at this hotel is pricey," "pool area was amazing." ✉ *1 Ritz-Carlton Dr., Kapalua* ☎ *808/669–6200 or 800/262–8440* ⊕ *www. ritzcarlton.com/en/properties/kapaluamaui* ⇌ *463 rooms* ♿ *In-room: a/c, safe, refrigerator, DVD, Internet, Wi-Fi. In-hotel: 6 restaurants, bar, tennis courts, children's programs (ages 5–12), pool, gym, laundry service, spa* ☰ *AE, D, MC, V.*

$$$
RENTAL

🍽 **Sands of Kahana.** Meandering gardens, spacious rooms, and an on-site restaurant distinguish this large condominium complex. Primarily a time-share property, a few units are available as vacation rentals and are managed by Sullivan Properties. The upper floors benefit from their height—matchless ocean views stretch away from private lānai. The oceanfront penthouse, which accommodates up to eight, is a bargain at $495 per night during peak season. One-, two-, and three-bedroom units are also available in the rental pool. Kids can enjoy their own swimming pool area near a putting green and ponds filled with giant koi. **Pros:** spacious units at reasonable prices; restaurant on the premises. **Cons:** you may be approached about buying a unit; street-facing units may get a bit noisy. **TripAdvisor:** "nice beach right in front," complex very clean and well kept," "a great place for families." ✉ *4299 Lower Honoapi'ilani Hwy., Kahana* ☎ *808/669–0400* ⊕ *www. mauiresorts.com* ⇌ *162 units* ♿ *In-room: a/c (some), kitchen, Internet. In-hotel: restaurant, tennis courts, pools, beachfront* ☰ *AE, D, MC, V.*

Ritz-Carlton, Kapalua

THE SOUTH SHORE

KĪHEI

$$–$$$
RENTAL

☒ **Hale Hui Kai.** Bargain hunters who stumble across this small three-story condo complex of two-bedroom units will think they've died and gone to heaven. The beachfront units are older, but most of them have been renovated. Some have granite countertops in the kitchens and all have outstanding views. But never mind the interior; you'll want to spend all your time outdoors—in the shady lava-rock lobby that overlooks a small pool perfect for kids, or on gorgeous Keawakapu Beach just steps away. Light sleepers should avoid the rooms just above the neighboring restaurant. **Pros:** far enough from the noise and tumult of "central" Kīhei; close enough to all the conveniences; it's only 40 steps from the farthest unit to the beach. **Cons:** nondescript 1970s architecture; a private home next door blocks the ocean view from some units. **TripAdvisor:** "just a few steps to the sand," "best on-beach value on Maui," "small and cozy complex, very private." ☒ *2994 S. Kīhei Rd., Kīhei* ☎ *808/879–1219 or 800/809–6284* ⊕ *www.halehuikaimaui.com* ☞ *40 units* ⌂ *In-room: a/c (some), safe, kitchen, DVD, Internet (some), Wi-Fi. In-hotel: pool, laundry facilities, beachfront, parking* ═ *MC, V.*

$$
☾
RENTAL

☒ **Kamaʻole Sands.** At this South Kīhei property, a good choice for active families, there are tennis courts for a friendly game, and the ideal family beach (Kamaʻole III) is just across the street. Ten four-story buildings wrap around 15 acres of grassy slopes with swimming pools, a small waterfall, and barbecues. Condos with one to three bedrooms are equipped with modern conveniences, but there's a relaxed, almost retro feel to the place. All units have two bathrooms, kitchens, laundry facilities, and private lānai. The property has a 24-hour front desk and an activities desk. **Pros:** in the seemingly endless strip of Kīhei condos, this stands out for its pleasant grounds and well-cared-for units. **Cons:** the complex of buildings may seem a bit too "citylike"; all buildings look the same, so remember a landmark to help you find your unit. **TripAdvisor:** "pool area was big and clean," "noise was our biggest complaint," "the condo is great for families." ☒ *2695 S. Kīhei Rd., Kīhei* ☎ *808/270–1200 or 800/367–5004* ⊕ *www.castleresorts.com* ☞ *205 units managed by Castle Resorts* ⌂ *In-room: a/c, safe, kitchen, DVD (some), Internet (some). In-hotel: tennis courts, pool, gym, laundry facilities, Wi-Fi hotspot* ═ *AE, D, MC, V.*

$
RENTAL
Fodor'sChoice
★

☒ **Luana Kai.** If you don't need everything to be totally modern, consider setting up house at this North Kīhei condominium-by-the-sea. Units are individually owned and are offered in two categories: standard and deluxe. Some are older and some have slightly dated furnishings, but the deluxe units have benefited from upgrades. Each one comes with everything you need to make yourself at home: a fully equipped kitchen with dishwasher; laundry facilities; TV; DVD; and stereo equipment. There are three different room plans suited for couples, families, or friends traveling together. The pool area and its deck is a social place, with five gas grills, a full outdoor kitchen, hot tub, men's and women's sauna rooms, and a shuffleboard court. The property adjoins a grassy county park with tennis courts, and the beach is a short way down the road. **Pros:** great value; meticulously landscaped grounds; excellent

CONDO COMFORTS

When you stay in a condo, you'll want to find the best places for food shopping, takeout, and other comforts. Here's a rundown of the best spors around Maui.

WEST MAUI
Foodland. This large grocery store should have everything you need, including video rentals and a Starbucks. ⊠ *Old Lahaina Center, 845 Waine'e St., Lahaina* ☎ *808/661–0975.*

Gaby's Pizzeria and Deli. The friendly folks here will toss a pie for takeout. ⊠ *505 Front St., Lahaina* ☎ *808/661–8112.*

The Maui Fish Market. It's worth stopping by this little fish market for an oyster or a cup of fresh-fish chowder. You can also get live lobsters and fillets marinated for your barbecue. ⊠ *4405 Lower Honoapi'ilani Hwy., Honokowai* ☎ *808/665–9895.*

SOUTH SHORE
Eskimo Candy. Stop here for fresh fish or fish-and-chips. ⊠ *2665 Wai Wai Pl., Kīhei* ☎ *808/879–5686.*

Safeway. Find every variety of grocery at this giant superstore. ⊠ *277 Pi'ikea Ave., Kīhei* ☎ *808/891–9120.*

Who Cut the Cheese. This shop has great party foods. ⊠ *Azeka Marketplace, 1279 S. Kīhei Rd., Suite 309, Kīhei* ☎ *808/874–3930.*

CENTRAL MAUI
Safeway. Newly renovated to look more like a gourmet grocery than a supermarket, this store has a deli, prepared foods section, and bakery that are all fantastic. There's a great wine selection, tons of produce, and a flower shop where you can treat yourself to a fresh lei. ⊠ *170 E. Ka'ahumanu Ave., Kahului* ☎ *808/877–3377.*

UPCOUNTRY
Pukalani Terrace Center. Stop by for pizza, a bank, post office, hardware store, and Starbucks. There's also a **Foodland** (☎ *808/572–0674*), which has fresh sushi and a good seafood section in addition to the usual grocery store fare. ⊠ *55 Pukalani St., Pukalani.*

NORTH SHORE
Ha'ikū Cannery. This marketplace is home to **Ha'ikū Grocery** (☎ *808/575–9291*), a somewhat limited grocery store where you can find the basics: veggies, meats, wine, snacks, and ice cream. Also part of the cannery are a few restaurants, along with a laundromat, pharmacy, and yoga studio. The post office is across the street. ⊠ *810 Ha'ikū Rd., Ha'ikū.*

management team. **Cons:** it's not right on the beach; three stories with no elevator; no maid service. **TripAdvisor:** "fabulous office staff, easy access into Kīhei," "for the budget-conscious traveler who wants quiet oceanfront," "pool and barbecue area were great." ⊠ *940 S. Kīhei Rd., Kīhei* ☎ *808/879–1268 or 800/669–1127* ⊕ *www.luanakai.com* ⤳ *113 units* ♿ *In-room: a/c (some), kitchen, DVD, Internet (some). In-hotel: tennis courts, pool, laundry facilities, parking* ⊟ *MC, V.*

$$–$$$ 🏨 **Mana Kai Maui.** An unsung hero of South Shore hotels, this place
HOTEL may be older than its competitors, but you simply cannot get any
☾ closer to gorgeous Keawakapu Beach than this. Hotel rooms with

WHERE TO STAY ON THE SOUTH SHORE

Hotels and Resorts

	Property Name	Worth Noting	Cost $	Pools	Beach	Golf Course	Tennis Courts	Gym	Spa	Children's Programs	Rooms	Restaurants	Other	Location
3	Fairmont Kea Lani	Villas available	$$$$	3	yes	yes		yes	yes	5–13	450	4	shops	Wailea
4	Four Seasons Resort	Luxurious	$$$$	3	yes	yes	2	yes	yes	5–12	380	3	poolside cabanas	Wailea
5	Grand Wailea Resort	Spa Grande	$$$$	9	yes	yes		yes	yes	5–12	780	6	Wedding Chapel	Wailea
11	Mana Kai Maui	Fabulous beach	$$–$$$	1	yes						158	1		Kīhei
13	Maui Coast Hotel	Beach across the street	$$$–$$$$	1				yes			265	2		Kīhei
6	Wailea Beach Marriott Resort & Spa	Mandara Spa	$$$$	3	yes	yes	2	yes	yes		544	2	Serenity pool for adults; separate children's pool	Wailea

Condos and Vacation Rentals

	Property Name	Worth Noting	Cost $	Pools	Beach	Golf Course	Tennis Courts	Gym	Spa	Children's Programs	Rooms	Restaurants	Other	Location
10	Hale Hui Kai	Oceanfront	$$–$$$	1	yes						40		kitchens	Kīhei
12	Kama'ole Sands	Beach across the street	$$	1			4	yes			205		kitchens	Kīhei
14	Luana Kai	Poolside BBQs	$	1			4				113		kitchens	Kīhei
1	Makena Surf	Secluded gated community	$$$$	2	yes	priv.	4				107		kitchens	Wailea
15	Maui Sunseeker Resort	Beach across the street	$								17		kitchens	Kīhei
2	Polo Beach Club	Location, location, location	$$$$	1	yes	yes					71		kitchens	Wailea
8	Wailea 'Ekahi	Studios available	$$$–$$$$	4	yes	priv.					300		kitchens	Wailea
7	Wailea 'Elua	Gated community	$$$–$$$$	2	yes	priv.					150		kitchens	Wailea
9	Wailea 'Ekolu	Hillside view	$$$–$$$$	2	no	priv.					160		kitchens	Wailea

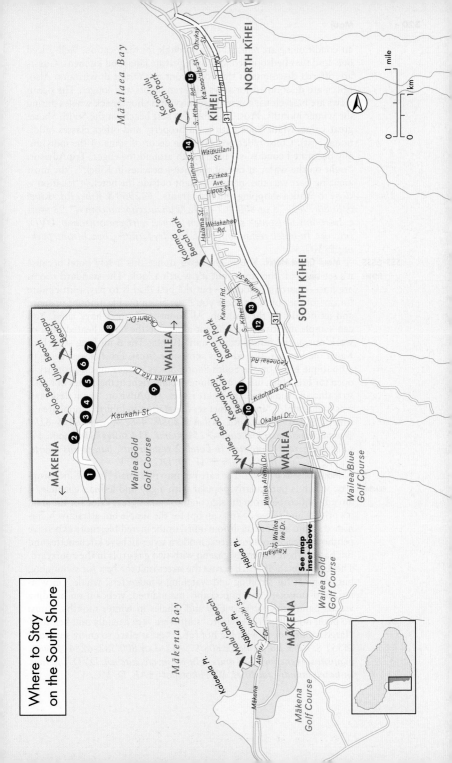

Where to Stay
on the South Shore

Mā'alaea Bay

NORTH KĪHEI

Piʻilani Hwy

15
Kaʻonoʻulu
Beach Park
Kaʻono-ʻulu St.
Ohukai St.
S. Kīhei Rd.

KĪHEI

14
Waipuilani
St.
Uluniu St.

Piʻikea
Ave.
Lipoa St.

Halama St.

Welakahao Rd.

Kalama Beach Park

SOUTH KĪHEI

Auhana St.

Kanani Rd. **13**

Kamaʻole
Beach Park
12
S. Kīhei Rd.
31

Keonekai Rd.

Kilohana Dr.
11

10
Okalani Dr.

Wailea Beach
Keawakapu Beach Park

WAILEA

Wailea Alanui Dr.

Wailea/Blue
Golf Course

Wailea Gold
Golf Course

See map
insert above

Kaukahi
St.
Wailea
Ike Dr.

Hāloa Pt.

MĀKENA

Mākena Bay

Kōleola Pt.

Maluʻaka Beach

Nāhuna Pt.
Honoiki St.
Alanui Dr.

Mākena

Mākena
Golf Course

MĀKENA
Polo Beach
Ulua Beach
Mokapu
Beach

2
3 **4** **5** **6** **7**
1
8
Kaukahi St.
9
Wailea Ike Dr.
Oʻolani Dr.
WAILEA
Wailea Gold
Golf Course

0   1 mile
0   1 km

air-conditioning are remarkably affordable for the location. Well-priced one- and two-bedroom condos have private lānai and kitchens. Guests are offered discounts at the oceanfront restaurant downstairs. Also, prices are discounted for stays of seven nights and longer. The ocean views are marvelous; you may see the visiting humpback whales during the winter months. **Pros:** arguably the best beach on the South Shore; great value; Maui Yoga Path is on property and offers classes (additional cost). **Cons:** older property; the decor of some of the individually decorated condos is a little rough around the edges. **TripAdvisor:** "right on the water at one of the nicest beaches in Kīhei," "the most amazing part was the snorkeling right outside the hotel," "location is close to Wailea shopping and restaurants." ⊠ *2960 S. Kīhei Rd., Kīhei* ☎ *808/879–2778 or 800/367–5242* ⊕ *www.crhmaui.com* ⤷ *98 units* ⚏ *In-room: a/c (some), safe, kitchen (some), refrigerator (some), DVD, Internet. In-hotel: restaurant, pool, laundry facilities, beachfront, parking* ⊟ *MC, V.*

\$\$\$–\$\$\$\$
HOTEL

🏨 **Maui Coast Hotel.** You might never notice this lovely hotel because it's set back off the street, but it's worth a look. The standard rooms are fine—clean and modern—but the best deal is to pay a little more for one of the suites. In these you'll get an enjoyable amount of space and jet nozzles in the bathtub. All rooms and suites have lānai. You can sample nightly entertainment alongside the large, heated pool or work out in the fitness center until 10 pm. The 6-mi-long stretch of Kama'ole Beach I, II, and III is across the street. **Pros:** closest thing to a boutique hotel on the South Shore; Spices restaurant on property is open for breakfast, lunch, and dinner. **Cons:** right in the center of Kīhei, so traffic and some street noise are issues. **TripAdvisor:** "front desk staff was wonderful," "free Internet service station in lobby," "pool area is small." ⊠ *2259 S. Kīhei Rd., Kīhei* ☎ *808/874–6284 or 800/895–6284* ⊕ *www.mauicoasthotel.com* ⤷ *151 rooms, 114 suites* ⚏ *In-room: a/c, safe, refrigerator, Internet. In-hotel: 2 restaurants, bar, tennis courts, pool, gym, laundry facilities* ⊟ *AE, D, DC, MC, V.*

\$
RENTAL

🏨 **Maui Sunseeker Resort.** The care put into this small North Kīhei property, which is particularly popular with a gay and lesbian clientele, is already noticeable from the sign on the road. A great value for the area, it's private and relaxed. You can opt for the simple but attractively furnished studio and one-bedroom units, or the incredible, more expensive penthouse decked out in a sleek, modern style; all have kitchenettes and full baths. There's a lovely gazebo with two gas grills in the courtyard. The 4-mi stretch of beach across the street isn't the best for swimming, but it's great for strolling and watching windsurfers, whales (in winter), and sunsets. **Pros:** impeccably maintained; webcam on building videos panoramic ocean views and whales in winter months. **Cons:** no pool; no frills. **TripAdvisor:** "staff were very friendly and helpful," "large rooftop deck with big hot tub," "great place to enjoy sunsets." ⊠ *551 S. Kīhei Rd., Kīhei* ☎ *808/879–1261 or 800/532–6284* ⊕ *www. mauisunseeker.com* ⤷ *17 units* ⚏ *In-room: a/c, kitchen, DVD, Internet. In-hotel: laundry facilities, Wi-Fi hotspot* ⊟ *AE, D, MC, V.*

WAILEA

$$$$
RESORT

🏨 **Fairmont Kea Lani Maui.** Gleaming white spires and tiled archways are the hallmark of this stunning resort that's particularly good for families. Spacious suites have microwaves, stereos, and marble bathrooms. The villas are the real lure, though. Each is a two-story structure with a private plunge pool, two (or three) large bedrooms, a laundry room, and a fully equipped kitchen—barbecue and margarita blender included. Best of all, maid service does the dishes. A fantastic haven for families, the villas are side by side, creating a sort of miniature neighborhood. Request one on the end, with an upstairs sundeck. The resort also boasts a new restaurant, Kō, and offers a small, almost private beach. **Pros:** for families, this is the best of the South Shore luxury resorts; excellent restaurant; on-site deli good for picnic fare. **Cons:** some feel the architecture and design scream anything *but* Hawai'i; great villas but price puts them out of range for many. **TripAdvisor:** "oceanfront suite was fabulous," "loved the place and would highly recommend," "my children enjoyed the water slide." ⌧ *4100 Wailea Alanui Dr., Wailea* ☎ *808/875–4100 or 800/659–4100* ⊕ *www.Fairmont.com/kealani* 🛏 *413 suites, 37 villas* ⚒ *In-room: a/c, kitchen (some), refrigerator, DVD, Internet. In-hotel: 4 restaurants, bar, pools, gym, spa, beachfront, water sports, children's programs (ages 5–13), laundry facilities* ▬ *AE, D, DC, MC, V.*

$$$$
RESORT
Fodor's Choice
★

🏨 **Four Seasons Resort Maui at Wailea.** Impeccably stylish, subdued, and relaxing describe most Four Seasons properties; this one fronting award-winning Wailea Beach is no exception. Thoughtful luxuries—like Evian spritzers poolside and twice-daily housekeeping—earned this Maui favorite its reputation. The property has an understated elegance, with beautiful floral arrangements, courtyards, and private cabanas. Most rooms have an ocean view (avoid those over the parking lot in the North Tower), and terry robes and a mini-refrigerator (stocked with your favorites on request) are among the amenities. Choose among three restaurants, including Wolfgang Puck's Spago and DUO. The spa is small but expertly staffed and impeccably appointed, or you can opt for poolside spa minitreatments. Families: request Suite 301, with its round tub and private lawn. **Pros:** the most low-key elegance on Maui; known for exceptional service. **Cons:** extremely expensive; a bit too pretentious for some. **TripAdvisor:** "well worth the price," "top-notch service," "got amazing oceanside massages." ⌧ *3900 Wailea Alanui Dr., Wailea* ☎ *808/874–8000 or 800/332–3442* ⊕ *www.fourseasons. com/maui* 🛏 *305 rooms, 75 suites* ⚒ *In-room: a/c, safe, refrigerator, DVD, Internet. In-hotel: 3 restaurants, bars, tennis courts, pools, gym, spa, beachfront, children's programs (ages 5–12)* ▬ *AE, D, DC, MC, V.*

$$$$
RESORT
Fodor's Choice
★

🏨 **Grand Wailea Resort Hotel & Spa.** "Grand" is no exaggeration for this opulent, sunny, 40-acre resort with elaborate water features such as a "canyon riverpool" with slides, caves, a Tarzan swing, and a water elevator. Tropical garden paths meander past artwork by Léger, Warhol, Picasso, Botero, and noted Hawaiian artists—sculptures even hide in waterfalls. Spacious ocean-view rooms are outfitted with stuffed chaises, comfortable desks, and oversize marble bathrooms. Spa Grande is the island's most comprehensive spa facility, offering everything from mineral baths to massage. For kids, Camp Grande has a full-size soda fountain, game room, and movie theater. Definitely not the place to go for a quiet retreat or for attentive service, the resort is astounding or way over the top, depending on your point of view. **Pros:** you can meet every vacation need without ever leaving the property; many shops. **Cons:** at these prices, service should be extraordinary, and it isn't; sometimes too much is too much. **TripAdvisor:** "breakfast buffet is awesome," "view is always outstanding," "resort grounds are beautiful." ⊠ *3850 Wailea Alanui Dr., Wailea* ☎ *808/875–1234 or 800/888–6100* ⊕ *www.grandwailea.com* ⌁ *728 rooms, 52 suites* ⌂ *In-room: a/c, safe, Internet, Wi-Fi. In-hotel: 6 restaurants, bars, golf courses, water sports, pools, gym, spa, beachfront, children's programs (ages 5 and up), laundry service, parking* ⊟ *AE, D, MC, V.*

$$$$ ⊡ **Mākena Surf.** For travelers who've done all there is to do on Maui
RENTAL   and just want simple but luxurious relaxation, this is the spot. The security-gate entrance gives way to manicured landscaping dotted with palm trees. The secluded complex is designed to belie its size—from the road it's hard to tell that the units are actually three-story buildings. "B" building is oceanfront; "A," "C," and "G" are the best value, just a bit farther from the shore. Water aerobics and tennis clinics are regularly offered. Privacy envelops the grounds—which makes the place a favorite with visiting celebrities. **Pros:** away from it all, yet still close enough to "civilization"; laundry facilities in every unit. **Cons:** too secluded and "locked-up" for some; Hawaiian legend has it that spirits may have been disturbed here. **TripAdvisor:** "comfortable condo," "short walk to beach," "complex is very quiet." ⊠ *3750 Wailea Alanui Dr., Wailea* ☎ *808/879–1595 or 800/367–5246* ⊕ *www.drhmaui.com* ⌁ *107 units* ⌂ *In-room: a/c, safe, kitchen, DVD, laundry facilities, Wi-Fi. In-hotel: tennis courts, pools, beachfront* ⊟ *AE, MC, V.*

$$$$ ⊡ **Polo Beach Club.** Lording over a hidden section of Polo Beach, this
RENTAL   wonderful old eight-story property somehow manages to stay under the radar. From your giant corner window, you can look down at the Fairmont Kea Lani villas and know you've scored the same great locale at a fraction of the price (and daily housekeeping service is included). Individually owned one- and two-bedroom apartments are well cared for and feature top-of-the-line amenities, such as stainless-steel kitchens, marble floors, and valuable artwork. An underground parking garage keeps vehicles out of the blazing Maui sun. **Pros:** you can pick fresh herbs for dinner out of the garden; beach fronting the building is a beautiful, private crescent of sand. **Cons:** some may feel isolated. **TripAdvisor:** "beach is fantastic," "clean and well-kept," "great location." ⊠ *3750 Wailea Alanui Dr., Wailea* ☎ *808/879–1595 or 800/367–5246* ⊕ *www.drhmaui.com* ⌁ *71 units* ⌂ *In-room: a/c, kitchen, DVD, Wi-Fi. In-hotel: pool, beachfront, laundry facilities* ⊟ *AE, MC, V.*

Four Seasons Resort Maui at Wailea

VACATION RENTAL COMPANIES

There are many real-estate companies that specialize in short-term vacation rentals. They may represent an entire resort property, most of the units at one property, or even individually owned units. The companies listed here have a long history of excellent service to Maui visitors.

AA Oceanfront Condominium Rentals. As the name suggests, the specialty is "oceanfront." With rental units in more than 25 condominium complexes on the South Shore from the northernmost reaches of Kīhei all the way to Wailea, there's something for everyone at prices that range from $130 to $435 a night. ⊠ 1279 S. Kīhei Rd., Kīhei ☎ 808/879-7288 or 800/488-6004 ⊕ www.aaoceanfront.com.

Aston Hotels & Resorts. Formerly ResortQuest Hawai'i, the company manages hotels and condos throughout the Islands, including nine properties on Maui. Most are on or near the beach, concentrated in the resort areas of Kā'anapali, Kīhei, and Wailea. Studios to three-bedroom units range in price from $120 to $695 per night. The company offers some interesting value-added programs like "Kids Stay, Play, and Eat Free." ⊠ 1819 S. Kīhei Rd., Suite D103, Kīhei ☎ 808/879-5445 or 800/822-4409 ⊕ www.astonhotels.com.

Bello Maui Vacations. The Bellos are Maui real-estate experts and have a full range of vacation rentals in 20 South Shore condominium complexes. They also have gorgeous houses for rent. Condos start at right around $100 per night (most are $200 or less); a seven-bedroom oceanfront estate rents for $1,500 per night. ⊠ 115 E. Lipoa, No. 101, Kīhei ☎ 808/879-3328 or 800/541-3060 ⊕ www.bellomauivacations.com.

Chase 'n Rainbows. Family-owned and -operated, this is the largest property management company on West Maui, with the largest selection of rentals from studios to three bedrooms. Rentals are everywhere from Lahaina town up to Kahana. Prices range from about $100 to $525 per night. The company has been in business since 1980, and it's good. ⊠ 118 Kupuohi St., Lahaina ☎ 808/667-7088 or 800/367-6092 ⊕ www.chasenrainbows.com.

Destination Resorts Hawai'i. If it's the South Shore luxury of Wailea and Mākena you seek, look no farther. This company has dozens of condominiums and villas ranging in size from studios to four bedrooms, and in price from $240 a night for a studio at Wailea 'Ekahi, an older property, to more than $3,500 for the new Wailea Beach Villas. The company offers excellent personalized service and is known for particularly fine housekeeping services. ⊠ 3750 Wailea Alanui Dr., Wailea ☎ 808/879-1595 or 866/384-1365 ⊕ www.drhmaui.com.

Mā'alaea Bay Realty and Rentals. Mā'alaea, a little strip of condominiums within the isthmus that links Central and West Maui, is often overlooked, but it shouldn't be. This company has 140 one-, two-, and three-bedroom units from $100 to $235 per night. The wind is usually strong here, but there's a nice beach, a harbor, and some good shopping and decent restaurants. ⊠ 280 Hau'oli St., Mā'alaea ☎ 808/244-5627 or 800/367-6084 ⊕ www.maalaeabay.com.

$$$$
RESORT

Wailea Beach Marriott Resort & Spa. The Marriott was built before current construction laws, so rooms sit much closer to the crashing surf than at most resorts. If you like to be lulled to sleep by the sound of the ocean, this is the place. Wailea Beach is a few steps away, as are the Shops at Wailea. Guest rooms are large and have been updated with sleek contemporary furnishings. Relaxation is luxurious here: the 10,000-square-foot Mandara Spa is elegant, peaceful, and rejuvenating; and, the gorgeous, adults-only serenity pool has an unobstructed panoramic ocean view from almost

> **LĀNAI**
>
> Islanders love their porches, balconies, and verandas, all wrapped up in the single Hawaiian word *lānai*. When booking your lodging, ask about the lānai and be sure to specify the view (understanding that top views command top dollars). Also, check that the lānai is not merely a step-out or Juliet balcony, with just enough room to lean against a railing. You want a lānai that is big enough for patio seating.

every lounge chair. Maui celebrity chef Mark Ellman's tony restaurant, Mala Wailea, also enjoys an ocean view. All rooms have private lānai and have been restyled with a contemporary residential feel; the new mattresses, quilts, and bed linens make for a great night's sleep. You have golf privileges at three nearby courses, as well as tennis privileges at the Wailea Tennis Club. **Pros:** spa is one of the best in Hawai'i; near good shopping. **Cons:** it's not quite beachfront and has a rocky shore, so you must walk left or right to sit on the sand; there can be a lot of foot traffic on the beachwalk along the coast. **TripAdvisor:** "service by infinity pool was slow," "great location right on the beach," "kiddie pool is awesome." ✉ *3700 Wailea Alanui Dr., Wailea* ☎ *808/879–1922 or 800/292–45326* ⊕ *www.waileamarriott.com* ⤵ *497 rooms, 47 suites* ⌂ *In-room: a/c, safe, Internet, Wi-Fi. In-hotel: 2 restaurants, pools, gym, spa, beachfront, laundry service* ▭ *AE, D, DC, MC, V.*

$$$–$$$$
RENTAL

Wailea 'Ekahi, 'Elua, and 'Ekolu. The Wailea Resort started out with three upscale condominium complexes named, appropriately, 'Ekahi, 'Elua, and 'Ekolu (One, Two, and Three). The individually owned units, managed by Destination Resorts Hawai'i, represent some of the best values in this high-class neighborhood; there's a wide range of prices. All benefit from air-conditioning, high-speed Internet, free long distance, lush landscaping, and preferential play at the neighboring world-class golf courses and tennis courts. You're likely to find custom appliances and sleek furnishings befitting the million-dollar locale. ■ **TIP**→ The concierges here will stock your fridge with groceries—even hard-to-find dietary items—for a nominal fee. 'Ekolu, farthest from the water, is the most affordable and benefits from a hillside view; 'Ekahi is a large V-shape property focusing on Keawakapu Beach; 'Elua has 24-hour security and overlooks Ulua Beach. **Pros:** probably the best value in this high-rent district; close to good shopping and dining. **Cons:** the oldest complexes in the neighborhood; it can be tricky to find your way around the buildings. **TripAdvisor:** "property is beautifully maintained," "fantastic beach," "location is superb." ✉ *3750 Wailea Alanui Dr., Wailea* ☎ *808/879–1595 or 800/367–5246* ⊕ *www.drhmaui.com*

⤵ *594 units* ☆ *In-room: a/c, kitchen, DVD, Wi-Fi (some). In-hotel: pools, beachfront, laundry facilities* ═ *AE, MC, V.*

CENTRAL MAUI

$

B&B/INN

Fodor'sChoice

★

☷ **The Old Wailuku Inn at Ulupono.** Built in 1924 and listed on the State of Hawai'i Register of Historic Places, this home may be the ultimate Hawaiian bed-and-breakfast. Each room is decorated with the theme of a Hawaiian flower, and the flower motif appears in the heirloom Hawaiian quilt on each bed. Other features include 10-foot ceilings and floors of native hardwoods; some rooms have delightful whirlpool tubs. The first-floor rooms have private gardens. A newer addition has three gorgeous rooms, each with a standing spa shower and bed coverings designed by Hawai'i's premier fabric designer, Sig Zane. A hearty and delicious gourmet breakfast is included. **Pros:** the charm of old Hawai'i; knowledgeable innkeepers; walking distance to Maui's best ethnic restaurants. **Cons:** closest beach is a 20-minute drive away; you may hear some traffic at certain times. **TripAdvisor:** "innkeepers are friendly," "we enjoyed having a gourmet breakfast," "the room is inviting and charming." ⊠ *2199 Kaho'okele St., Wailuku* ☎ *808/244–5897 or 800/305–4899* ⊕ *www.mauiinn.com* ⤵ *10 rooms* ☆ *In-room: a/c, Internet* ═ *AE, D, DC, MC, V.*

UPCOUNTRY

$–$$

B&B/INN

☾

☷ **The Banyan Tree House.** If a taste of rural Hawai'i life in plantation days is what you crave, you can find it here. The setting is pastoral—the 2-acre property is lush with tropical foliage, has an expansive lawn, and is fringed with huge monkeypod and banyan trees. The cottages (bedrooms, really, with updated baths and kitchenettes) are simple and functional. The gem, though, is the 1927 plantation house with its sprawling living and dining rooms, a kitchen any cook will adore, and a lānai that will take you back in time. The configuration of the property allows for lots of combinations; you can rent one, two, or all three bedrooms in the house or even add the adjoining one-bedroom cottage. And you can rent the entire property for a family reunion or a retreat and have access to a large yoga and meditation space complete with audio and video capabilities. **Pros:** one cottage and the pool are outfitted for travelers with disabilities; you can walk to Makawao town for dining and shopping. **Cons:** the furniture in the cottages is pretty basic; few amenities. **TripAdvisor:** "beautiful and comfortable," "quiet retreat," "delightful place to stay." ⊠ *3265 Baldwin Ave., Makawao* ☎ *808/572–9021* ⊕ *www.bed-breakfast-maui.com* ⤵ *7 rooms* ☆ *In-room: a/c (some), kitchen (some), Wi-Fi. In-hotel: pool, laundry facilities, Internet terminal* ═ *AE, D, MC, V.*

$–$$

B&B/INN

Fodor'sChoice

★

☷ **Hale Ho'okipa Inn.** A handsome 1924 Craftsman-style house in the heart of Makawao town, this inn on both the Hawai'i and the National Historic Registers provides a great base for excursions to Haleakalā or to Hāna. Owner Cherie Attix has furnished it with antiques and fine art, and she allows you to peruse her voluminous library of Hawai'i-related books. She's also a fountain of local knowledge. The house

The Old Wailuku Inn at Ulupono

Hale Ho'okipa Inn

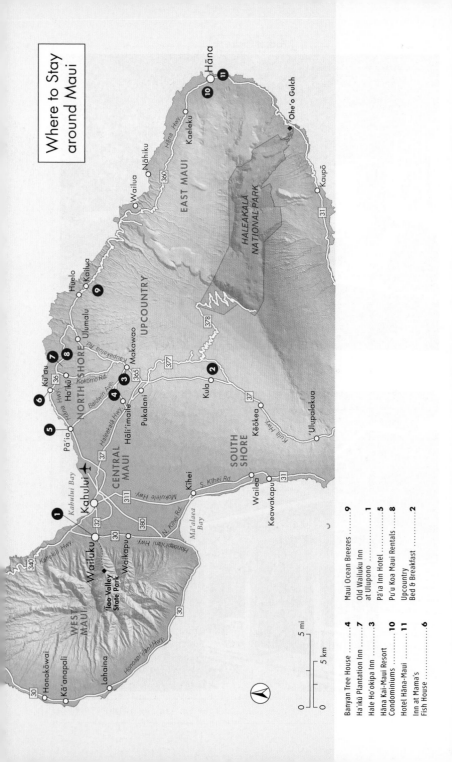

Where to Stay around Maui

Banyan Tree House **4**
Ha'ikū Plantation Inn **7**
Hale Ho'okipa Inn **3**
Hāna Kai-Maui Resort
Condominiums **10**
Hotel Hāna-Maui **11**
Inn at Mama's
Fish House **6**

Maui Ocean Breezes **9**
Old Wailuku Inn
at Ulupono **1**
Pā'ia Inn Hotel **5**
Pu'u Koa Maui Rentals **8**
Upcountry
Bed & Breakfast **2**

is divided into three single rooms, each prettier than the next, and the South Wing, which sleeps four and includes the kitchen. Two rooms have wonderful claw-foot tubs. The lush, serene grounds have a koi pond and the biggest Norfolk pine tree you've ever seen. Discounts are offered to guests who participate in volunteer projects through Cherie's site ⊕ *www.volunteers-on-vacation.com*. **Pros:** genteel rural setting; price includes buffet breakfast with organic fruit from the garden. **Cons:** a 20-minute drive to the nearest beach; this is not the sun, sand, and surf surroundings of travel posters. **TripAdvisor:** "breakfasts very well stocked," "lovely gardens," "fantastic place to stay." ⊠ *32 Pakani Pl., Makawao* ☎ *808/572–6698* ⊕ *www.maui-bed-and-breakfast.com* ⊐ *3 rooms, 1 suite* △ *In-room: a/c, Wi-Fi. In-hotel: no kids under 9* ▭ *MC, V.*

> ### B&BS
>
> Additional bed-and-breakfasts on Maui can be found by contacting **Bed & Breakfast Hawai'i** (☎ *808/822–7771 or 800/733–1632* ⊕ *www.bandb-hawaii.com*). **Bed and Breakfast Honolulu** (☎ *808/595–7533 or 800/288–4666* ⊕ *www.hawaiibnb.com*) is another good source. It's always a good idea to ask specifically if a property is licensed by the County of Maui.

$ | B&B/INN | **Upcountry Bed & Breakfast.** Spacious rooms and unobstructed views are two reasons to experience Upcountry Maui at this bed-and-breakfast. Owner Michael Sullivan has put a lot of heart and soul into it. He designed his house to take advantage of natural cooling and heating techniques, based on the principles of noted Hawai'i architect C. W. Dickey; he makes the tiles and light fixtures in his own ceramics studio on the property and he built comfortable, easy-to-get-around rooms for handicapped guests. Every room has a private bath, gas fireplace, wet bar, mini-refrigerator, and coffeemaker. Outside, the hot tub, shower, and swinging hammock make good places for watching the sunset or stargazing (astronomy guides are provided). Guests must be at least 21 years old. **Pros:** at 3,000 feet above sea level, it's closer to Haleakalā than most accommodations; two rooms are ADA accessible; local store and restaurant nearby. **Cons:** can be cool in Kula; far from beach; not everyone may enjoy the mellow and friendly resident dog. **TripAdvisor:** "nice and quiet," "rooms are very spacious," "great find." ⊠ *4925 Lower Kula Rd., Kula* ☎ *808/878–8083* ⊕ *www. upcountrybandb.com* ⊐ *4* △ *In-room: a/c (some), safe, refrigerator, DVD, Internet. In-hotel: laundry facilities, parking (free), no children.* ▭ *D, MC, V.*

THE NORTH SHORE

$ | B&B/INN | **Ha'ikū Plantation Inn.** Water lilies and a shade tree bedecked in orchids greet you at this forested bend in the road. A remnant of Ha'ikū's plantation history, this gracious estate was built in 1870 for the company doctor. The house has been restored with vintage pine floors, 12-foot ceilings, and the original windows. A feeling of wellness persists—revered Hawaiian healer Kahu Lyons Na'one teaches traditional medicine and *ho'oponopono*, literally "making right," on-site. A small massage *hale* stands beside a thatched-roof gazebo in a lush garden of *ulu* (breadfruit), *liliko'i* (passion fruit), sugarcane, bananas, and pineapple. Rooms are uncluttered and charming, with private baths; the Plumeria room has a claw-foot tub. Continetal breakfast is served on Granny's vintage dishes. **Pros:** quiet setting; close to restaurants, gas station, and post office; opportunities to experience authentic Hawaiian culture. **Cons:** no resort amenities; ten-minute drive from closest beach. **TripAdvisor:** "relaxing and rejuvenating," "noisy location," "wonderful breakfast." ⊠ *555 Ha'ikū Rd., Ha'ikū* ☎ *808/575-7500* ⊕ *www. haikuleana.net* ↪ *4 rooms* ♻ *In-room: no a/c, kitchen. In-hotel: parking (free).* ⊟ *AE, MC, V.*

$-$$

B&B/INN

▣ **The Inn at Mama's Fish House.** Nestled in gardens adjacent to one of Maui's most popular dining spots, Mama's Fish House, these well-maintained one- and two-bedroom cottages have a retro-Hawaiian style with rattan furnishings and local artwork. Each has a kitchen and a private garden patio. New junior suites for couples only feature a private courtyard, king bed, and kitchenette. There is a small beach in front of the property known as Kū'au Cove. It's best to make reservations for the restaurant when you book your accommodations or you may not get a table (inn guests get a discount). **Pros:** daily maid service; free parking; next to Ho'okipa Beach. **Cons:** three-night minimum stay; Mama's Fish House is popular, so there can be many people around in the evenings (it's more mellow during the day). **TripAdvisor:** "romantic getaway," "very reasonable," "quiet and peaceful." ⊠ *799 Poho Pl., Kū'au* ☎ *808/579-9764 or 800/860-4852* ⊕ *www.mamasfishhouse. com* ↪ *12 units* ♻ *In-room: a/c, safe, kitchen, DVD, Wi-Fi. In-hotel: restaurant, laundry facilities* ⊟ *AE, D, DC, MC, V.*

$

RENTAL

▣ **Maui Ocean Breezes.** The warm ocean breeze rolls through these pretty rentals and shoos the mosquitoes away, making this a perfect spot if you want quiet, gorgeous scenery. The decor is both whimsical and calming—expect colorfully painted walls and sheer curtains. The saltwater pool is fed by a waterfall. Fully equipped kitchens and Wi-Fi make these studios an ideal home away from home. Allergy-prone travelers can relax here—no chemicals or pesticides are used on the property. Although it seems far from civilization, you are only 5 minutes from Ha'ikū and 10 from Pā'ia. **Pros:** good for people sensitive to harsh chemicals; one of few licensed rentals in area; expansive lawn with ocean views. **Cons:** 15 minutes from closest beach; the owner prefers stays of seven nights or longer, though will negotiate depending on availability. **TripAdvisor:** "we loved the peaceful atmosphere," "good starting point for several Maui adventures," "salt water pool is great." ⊠ *240 N. Holokai Rd., Ha'ikū* ☎ *808/572-2775* ⊕ *www. mauivacationhideaway.com* ↪ *3 units* ♻ *In-room: no a/c, kitchen, Wi-Fi. In-hotel: pool, laundry facilities* ⊟ *MC, V.*

$$

B&B/INN

▣ **Pā'ia Inn Hotel.** Built in 1927 as a boarding house when Pā'ia was a bustling plantation town, this building was completely renovated and reopened as an inn in 2008. Set right in the heart of Pā'ia on busy Hāna Highway, it is amazingly quiet inside the lobby and guest rooms. The rooms are air-conditioned and each has a phone, flat-screen television, iPod clock/radio, and fully stocked minibar. All have private bathrooms with travertine tile and spa-quality amenities. Guests enter through a pleasant courtyard where complimentary coffee and tea, along with muffins and scones, are served daily. The guest rooms are up a set of stairs on the second floor; there is no elevator. If you want room service, a coffeehouse across the street will deliver. Access to secluded and sandy Pā'ia Bay is along a pathway between two private residences behind the inn. **Pros:** friendly and knowledgeable staff; no minimum-night stay required; guests receive a complimentary membership at Upcountry Fitness in Ha'ikū. **Cons:** no elevator; guest rooms are small and have no closets. **TripAdvisor:** "paradise away from the resorts," "secret path to the beach," "genuine friendly staff." ⊠ 93 *Hāna Hwy., Pā'ia* ☎ *808/579–6000 or 800/721–4000* ⊕ *www.paiainn. com* 🛏 *5 rooms* ⚐ *In-room: a/c, Wi-Fi. In-hotel: laundry facilities, parking* ▤ *AE, MC, V.*

¢ 🏠 **Pu'u Koa Maui Rentals.** Off a peaceful cul-de-sac in a residential area,
RENTAL these two well-maintained and immaculately clean homes offer studio and one-bedroom accommodations. Studios have an efficiency-style kitchen with a small refrigerator, hot plate, microwave, toaster oven, and coffeemaker. One-bedroom apartments have fully equipped kitchens, a separate bedroom, and a large living area. All units have private bathrooms and a lānai or patio, some with ocean views. The large yard with tropical flowers and fruit trees is great for a sunset barbecue or just relaxing. **Pros:** very clean; reasonable rates; good spot for a group. **Cons:** 10-minute drive to the beach; set in quiet residential area. ⊠ 66 *Pu'u Koa Pl., Ha'ikū* ☎ *808/573–2884* ⊕ *www.puukoa.com* 🛏 *7 rooms* ⚐ *In-room: no a/c, kitchen, DVD, Wi-Fi. In-hotel: laundry facilities* ▤ *AE, MC, V.*

HĀNA

$$–$$$ 🏠 **Hāna Kai-Maui Resort Condominiums.** Perfectly situated on Hāna Bay,
RENTAL this resort complex has a long history (it opened in 1970) and an excel-
Fodor'sChoice lent reputation for visitor hospitality. All you have to do is take your
★ morning coffee out onto the lānai of any of these lovely units to know why Hāna is often referred to as "heavenly." The units are tastefully and comfortably furnished with stylish furniture and tropical touches, and have well-equipped kitchens with all the appliances, table settings, and tools you need to prepare meals. They even have Egyptian cotton sheets on the beds and all-natural soaps and shampoos. **Pros:** it's a stone's throw to Hāna Bay, where you can take a swim or have a Rose-lani mac-nut ice-cream cone at Tutu's; one-night rentals are accepted. **Cons:** early to bed and early to rise—no nightlife or excitement here. **TripAdvisor:** "units very clean and fully furnished," "everyone was really friendly and helpful," "the view was great." ⊠ *1533 Uakea Rd., Hāna* ☎ *808/248–8426 or 800/346–2772* ⊕ *www.hanakaimaui.com* 🛏 *17 units* ⚐ *In-room: no a/c, kitchen, no TV, Wi-Fi. In-hotel: laundry facilities* ▤ *MC, V.*

$$$$ 🏠 **Hotel Hāna-Maui.** Small, secluded, and quietly luxurious, with unob-
HOTEL structed views of the Pacific, this tranquil property is a departure from the usual resort destinations on Maui. Here, horses nibble wild grass on the sea cliff nearby. Spacious rooms (680 to 830 square feet) have

bleached-wood floors, authentic kapa-print fabric furnishings, and sumptuously stocked minibars at no extra cost. Spa suites and a heated *watsu* (massage performed in warm water) pool complement a state-of-the-art spa-and-fitness center. The Sea Ranch Cottages with individual hot tubs are the best value. A shuttle takes you to beautiful Hāmoa Beach. At this writing, the hotel was due to have a new owner. **Pros:** if you want to get away from it all, there's no better or more beautiful place; spa is incredibly relaxing. **Cons:** everything moves slowly; if you can't live without your Blackberry, this is not the place for you; it's oceanfront but does not have a sandy beach (red- and black-sand beaches are nearby). **TripAdvisor:** "a lot of complimentary amenities," "cottage was well appointed and comfortable," "yoga classes were a delight." ⌧ *5031 Hāna Hwy.* ✆ *Box 9, Hāna 96713* ☎ *808/248–8211 or 800/321–4262* ⊕ *www.hotelhanamaui.com* ⤳ *69 rooms, 47 cottages, 1 house* ♿ *In-room: a/c, refrigerator, no TV, Internet. In-hotel: 2 restaurants, bar, tennis courts, pools, gym, spa, public Wi-Fi* ⊟ *AE, D, DC, MC, V.*

SHOPPING IN HĀNA

Hasegawa General Store.
Hāna's one-stop shopping option is charming, filled-to-the-rafters Hasegawa's. Buy fishing tackle, hot dogs, ice cream, and eggs here. You can rent videos and buy the newspaper, which isn't always delivered on time. Check out the bulletin board for local events. ⌧ *5165 Hāna Hwy.* ☎ *808/248–8231.*

The Big Island

WORD OF MOUTH

"The Big Island is fantastic and very diverse in its landscapes. Well worth exploring. . . . We spent 10 days there last year, and it is now in the top three places in the world for us."

—peterSale

WELCOME TO THE BIG ISLAND

TOP REASONS TO GO

★ **Hawai'i Volcanoes National Park:** Catch the lava fireworks at night and explore newly made land, lava tubes, steam vents, and giant craters.

★ **Waipi'o Valley:** Experience a real-life secret garden, the remote spot known as the Valley of the Kings.

★ **Kealakekua Bay Double Feature:** Kayak past spinner dolphins to the Captain Cook Monument, then go snorkeling along the fabulous coral reef.

★ **The Heavens:** Stargaze through gigantic telescopes on snow-topped Mauna Kea.

★ **Hidden Beaches:** Discover one of the Kohala Coast's lesser-known gems.

1 Kailua-Kona. A busy seaside town filled with quirky shops and dozens of restaurants along the main drag, Ali'i Drive.

2 The Kona Coast. An area that stretches a bit north of Kailua-Kona and much farther south, including the gorgeous Kealakekua Bay. This is the place to come for world famous Kona Coffee.

3 The Kohala Coast and Waimea. The sparkling coast is where all those long, white-sand beaches are found, and the expensive resorts that go with them. Ranches sprawl across the cool, upland meadows of Waimea (Kamuela), known as *paniolo* (cowboy) country.

4 Mauna Kea. Climb (or drive) this 13,796-foot mountain for what's considered the world's best stargazing, with 13 telescopes perched on top.

5 Hāmākua Coast. Waterfalls, dramatic cliffs, ocean views, ancient hidden valleys, rain forests, and the stunning Waipi'o Valley are just a few of the treats that await you here.

6 Hilo. Known as the City of Rainbows for all its rain, Hilo is often skipped by tourists in favor of the sunny Kohala Coast. But for what many

consider the "real" Hawai'i, as well as incredible rain forests, waterfalls, and the best farmers' market on the island, Hilo can't be beat.

7 Puna. This part of the island was recently covered by lava, so it has brand-new, jet-black beaches with volcanic hot springs.

8 Hawai'i Volcanoes National Park and Vicinity. The land around the park is continually expanding, as the active Kilauea Volcano sends lava spilling into the ocean. The nearby town of Volcano provides a great base for exploring the park.

9 Ka'ū and Ka Lae (South Point). Round the southernmost part of the island for two of Big Island's most famous beaches: Green Beach and Black Beach.

GETTING ORIENTED

You could fit all the other Hawaiian Islands into the Big Island and still have some room left over—hence the name. Locals refer to the island by side: Kona to the west and Hilo to the east. Most of the resorts, condos, and restaurants are crammed into 30 mi of the sunny Kona side, while rainy, tropical Hilo is much more residential.

4

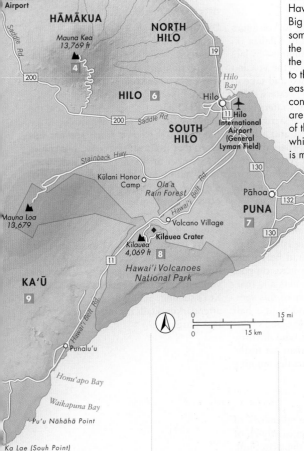

Waimea (Kamuela)
Kamuela Airport
240
19 (Māmalahoa Hwy.) Honoka'a
5
HĀMĀKUA COAST
Hawai'i Belt Rd.
HĀMĀKUA
Mauna Kea 13,769 ft
4
NORTH HILO
19
Saddle Rd.
200
Hilo Bay
HILO 6
Hilo
200 Saddle Rd.
SOUTH HILO
11 Hilo International Airport (General Lyman Field)
Stainback Hwy.
Kūlani Honor Camp
Ola'a Rain Forest
Hawai'i Belt Rd.
130
Pāhoa
132
PUNA 7
Mauna Loa 13,679
Volcano Village
Kilauea Crater
130
11 Kilauea 4,069 ft 8
Hawai'i Volcanoes National Park
KA'Ū 9
Hawai'i Belt Rd.
0   15 mi
0   15 km
Punalu'u
Honu'apo Bay
Waikapuna Bay
Pu'u Nāhāhā Point
Ka Lae (Souh Point)

GREAT ITINERARIES

If you'd prefer to spend your last few days sleeping on the beach, explore the island from east to west; if you'd rather end with rain-forest hikes and showers in water-falls, move from west to east. If you're short on time, head straight for Hawai'i Volcanoes National Park and briefly visit Hilo before traveling the Hāmākua Coast route and making your new base in Kailua-Kona.

Hike Volcanoes

Devote a full day (at least) to Volcanoes National Park. Head out to Kīlauea Iki trail—a 4-mi loop at the summit—by late morning. Grab a sandwich at the Volcano House when you're finished and take in their fantastic views of the craters. After lunch, head down Chain of Craters Road to the coast and potential active lava flows. Bring water, snacks, and a flash-light if you intend to hike where the lava flows into the ocean. Start your hike dur-ing the day (by 4 pm or earlier) to ensure that you're as close as you can safely be when night falls.

Black and Green Sand

Check out some of the unusual beaches you'll only find on the Big Island. Start with a hike into Green Sand Beach and plan to spend some time here, dipping into the bay's turquoise waters and mar-veling at the surreal beauty of this spot. Then hop into the car and head a half hour south to Punalu'u, the island's best-known black-sand beach and favorite resting place of the Hawaiian sea turtle. There are usually a few turtles sunning happily on the beach.

Majestic Waterfalls and Valley of the Kings

Take a day to enjoy the splendors of the Hāmākua Coast, a jagged stretch of coastline that embodies all things tropical.

Any gorge you see on the road indicates a waterfall waiting to be explored. For a sure bet, head to the beautiful Waipi'o Valley. Book a horseback, hiking, or 4WD tour or walk on in yourself (just keep in mind that it's an arduous hike back up). Once in the valley, take your first right to get to the black-sand beach. Take a moment to sit here—the ancient Hawai-ians believed this was where souls crossed over to the afterlife.

Underwater Day

Explore the colorful reefs off the Big Island's coast for one day and we dare you to stop thinking about the world beneath the waves when you're back on land. Our favorite spots include Two Step (near the Place of Refuge), Kealakekua Bay, and the Kapoho Tide Pools. Early morning is the best time to see the Hawaiian spinner dol-phins that frolic off this coast, but you're likely to see turtles any time of day, along with yellow and white angelfish, spot-ted moray eels, trumpet fish, and myriad other tropical varieties.

Sun and Stars

Spend the day lounging on a Kohala Coast beach (Hāpuna, Kauna'oa—also known as Mauna Kea—or Kua Bay), but throw jackets and boots in the car because you'll be catching the sunset from Mauna Kea's summit. Bundle up and stick around after darkness falls for some of the world's best stargazing.

Updated by
Katie Young
Yamanaka

4

Nicknamed "The Big Island," Hawaiʻi the island is a micro-cosm of Hawaiʻi the state. From long white-sand beaches and crystal clear bays to rain forests, waterfalls, lūʻau, exotic flowers, and birds, all things quintessentially Hawaiian are well represented here. But an assortment of happy surprises also distinguishes the Big Island from the rest of Hawaiʻi—an active volcano (Kīlauea) oozing red lava and creating new earth every day, the clearest place in the world to view stars in the night sky (Mauna Kea), and some seriously good coffee from the famous Kona district, and also from neighboring Kaʻū.

GEOLOGY
Home to 11 climate zones, this is the land of fire (thanks to active Kīlauea Volcano) and ice (compliments of not-so-active Mauna Kea, topped with snow and expensive telescopes). At just under a million years old, Hawaiʻi is the youngest of the Hawaiian Islands. The east rift zone on Kīlauea has been spewing lava intermittently since January 3, 1983; and an eruption began at Kīlauea's summit caldera in March 2008 (for the first time since 1982). Mauna Loa's explosions caused some changes back in 1984, and it could blow again any minute—or not for years. The third of the island's five volcanoes still considered active is Hualālai. It last erupted in 1801, but geologists say it will probably erupt again within 100 years. Mauna Kea is currently considered dormant. Kohala, which last erupted some 120,000 years ago, is likely extinct.

FLORA AND FAUNA
Sugar was the main agricultural and economic staple of all the Islands, but especially the Big Island. The drive along the Hāmākua Coast from Hilo illustrates recent agricultural developments on the island. Sugarcane stalks have been replaced by orchards of macadamia-nut

The Big Island of Hawai'i

THE KOHALA COAST AND WAIMEA

TO MAUI

'UPOLU PT.

'Upolu Airport
Kapa'a Beach Park
Māhukona Beach Park
Lapakahi State Historical Park

Hāwī
Kapa'au
250
Māhukona
Akoni Pule Hwy.

NORTH KOHALA

Pololū Valley
Pololū Beach

KOHALA FOREST RESERVE

KOHALA MOUNTAINS

Kawaihae
270
Pu'ukoholā Heiau National Historic Site, Mailekini Heiau
Spencer Beach Park
Kauna'oa Beach
Hāpuna Beach State Park
Puakō

Kohala Mountain Rd.
Kawaihae Rd.
Waiaka
Waimea (Kamuela)
Kamuela Airport

SOUTH KOHALA
Waikoloa

Hawai'i Belt Rd.

KOHALA COAST

Kiholo Bay

'Anaeho'omalu Bay
'Anaeho'omalu
19

Kaloko-Honokōhau National Historical Park
Kona International Airport
19
Honokōhau

Queen Ka'ahumanu Hwy.
Hu'ehu'e Ranch
Kalaoa
190
Pu'uanahulu

NORTH KONA

▲ Mount Hualalai 8,271 ft

Māmalahoa Hwy.

KAILUA-KONA
Kailua Bay

Hōlualoa
11
Kahalu'u
Kahalu'u Beach
Kealakekua

MAUNA KEA AND THE HĀMĀKUA COAST

HĀMĀKUA COAST

WAIPI'O VALLEY OVERLOOK

Waipi'o Valley
240
Honoka'a
19 (Māmalahoa Hwy.)
Kalōpā State Rec. Area

Pa'auilo
Kuka'iau
O'ōkala
Hawai'i Belt Rd.
Laupāhoehoe
Pāpa'aloa
Wailea
Ninole
Honohina
Hakalau
Honomū
Kolekole Beach Park

HĀMĀKUA

Hilo Forest Reserve

Akaka Falls State Park

▲ Mauna Kea 13,796 ft

Saddle Rd.
200
Saddle Rd.
Waiki'i
Hawai'i Belt Rd.

Mauna Loa Observatory ▲

Stainback Hwy.
Kūlani Honor Camp

Kawainui
Pāpa'ikou
Wainaku

NORTH HILO

Hilo Bay
LELEIWI POINT
Onekahakaha Beach Park
Hilo International Airport (General Lyman Field)

HILO

SOUTH HILO

11
Kea'au
Kurtistown
130
Mountain View
Kukui

Cape Kumukahi

Ahalanui

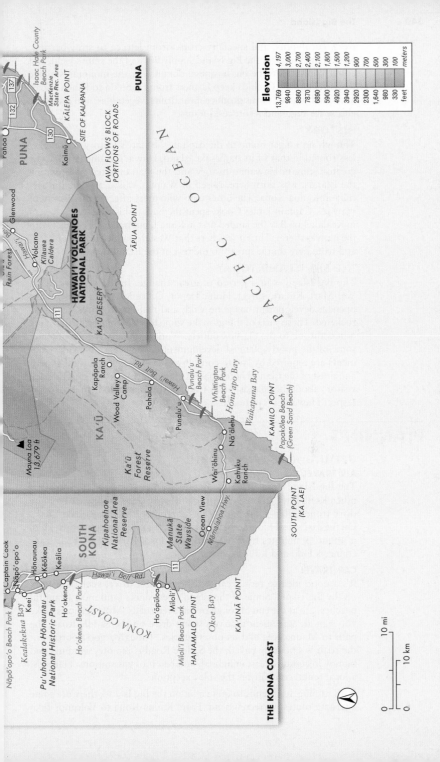

THE KONA COAST

Elevation

feet	meters
13,769	4,197
9840	3,000
8860	2,700
7870	2,400
6890	2,100
5900	1,800
4920	1,500
3940	1,200
2920	900
2300	700
1640	500
980	300
330	100

PACIFIC OCEAN

PUNA

Isaac Hale County Beach Park
MacKenzie State Rec. Area
KĀLEPA POINT
SITE OF KALAPANA
Pāhoa
132
137
130
Kaimū

LAVA FLOWS BLOCK PORTIONS OF ROADS.

'ĀPUA POINT

Rain Forest
Glenwood
Volcano
Kīlauea Caldera
HAWAI'I VOLCANOES NATIONAL PARK
KA'Ū DESERT
11

Mauna Loa 13,679 ft

Kapāpala Ranch
Wood Valley Camp
Pāhala
Punalu'u
Hawai'i Belt Rd.
Punalu'u Beach Park
Whittington Beach Park
Honu'apo Bay
Waikapuna Bay
KAMILO POINT
Papakōlea Beach (Green Sand Beach)

KA'Ū
Ka'ū Forest Reserve

Nā'ālehu
Wai'ōhinu
Kahuku Ranch
SOUTH POINT (KA LAE)

SOUTH KONA
Kīpāhoehoe Natural Area Reserve
Manukā State Wayside
Ocean View
Māmalahoa Hwy.
11

Captain Cook
Nāpō'opo'o
Keei
Hōnaunau
Kealakekua Bay
Kēōkea
Kealia
Pu'uhonua o Hōnaunau National Historic Park
Ho'okena
Ho'okena Beach Park
KONA COAST
Hawai'i Belt Rd.
Ho'ōpūloa
Miloli'i
Miloli'i Beach Park
HANAMALO POINT
Okoe Bay
KA'ŪNĀ POINT

0   10 mi
0   10 km

trees, eucalyptus, and specialty crops (from lettuce to strawberries). Macadamia nuts on the Big Island supply 90% of the state's yield, and coffee continues to be big business, dominating the mountains above Kealakekua Bay. Orchids keep farmers from Honok'a to Pāhoa afloat, and small organic farms produce meat, fruits, vegetables, and even goat cheese for high-end resort restaurants.

HISTORY

Though no longer home to the capital, the state's history is nonetheless rooted in that of its namesake island, Hawai'i. Kamehameha, the greatest king in Hawaiian history and the man credited with uniting the Islands, was born here, raised in Waipi'o Valley, and died peacefully in Kailua-Kona. The other man who most affected the history of Hawai'i, Captain James Cook, spent the bulk of his time here, docked in Kealakekua Bay (he landed first in Kaua'i, but had little contact with the natives there). Thus it was here that Western influence was first felt, and from here that it spread to the rest of the Islands.

THE BIG ISLAND TODAY

The Big Island is in a period of great change. In the last few years, Wal-Mart, Kmart, Target, Home Depot, Office Max and Costco have opened; development has gone wild; and real estate prices have skyrocketed. These sorts of things make some locals unhappy, while many others throng to the big-box outlets. Work is underway to counteract some of the poorly planned development of the island. New developments are required by law to consult with a Hawaiian cultural expert, and most of the island's hotels have a Hawaiian expert on staff to teach visitors about the Islands' history and customs, and to help developers respect Hawaiian traditions.

PLANNING

GETTING HERE AND AROUND

AIR TRAVEL

The Big Island's two airports are directly across the island from each other. Kona International Airport on the west side is about a 10-minute drive from Kailua-Kona and 30 to 45 minutes from the Kohala Coast. On the east side, Hilo International Airport, 2 mi from downtown Hilo, is about 40 minutes from Volcanoes National Park. A 2½-hour drive connects Hilo and Kailua-Kona.

CAR TRAVEL

It's a good idea to rent a car with four-wheel drive, such as a Jeep, on the Big Island. Some of the island's best sights (and most beautiful beaches) are at the end of rough or unpaved roads. Most agencies make you sign an agreement that you won't drive on the Saddle Road, the path to Mauna Kea and its observatories. Though a good portion of the road is smoothly paved, the Saddle Road is remote, winding, and bumpy in certain areas, unlighted, and bereft of gas stations. Harper's, a local rental company, is the sole exception.

If it's raining, as it tends to quite a bit on the Big Island, there are some alternate routes we recommend. From Kailua-Kona to Volcano: Take the southern route, following Highway 11 through South Kona and Ka'ū around South Point to Volcano (125 mi, just under three hours); Between Kailua-Kona and Hilo: Starting in Kailua-Kona, take Highway 190 east to Highway 19. Follow 19 through Waimea to Hilo (96 mi, two hours or less); From Kohala to Waimea: Take Highway 11 to Waikoloa Road (9 mi south of Hāpuna Beach) and follow it 10 mi to Highway 190. Turn left on 190 and follow it another 11 mi to Waimea (30 mi, 40 minutes).

See "Travel Smart Hawai'i" for more information on renting a car and driving.

ISLAND
DRIVING TIMES

Due to the Big Island's size, it can take quite a bit of time to get from one region of the island to another. Added to that, the island's increasing traffic problems are making driving times even longer, particularly between Kona and the Kohala Coast, and Kona to Kealakekua Bay and Ka'ū.

The state is working on widening Highway 19, which circles the island, and the hope is that the wider highway will cut down on traffic. In the meantime, the following are average driving times between some of the Big Island's most popular sights.

ISLAND DRIVING TIMES	
Kailua-Kona to Kealakekua Bay	14 mi/25 mins
Kailua-Kona to Kohala Coast	32 mi/50 mins
Kailua-Kona to Waimea	40 mi/1 hr 15 mins
Kailua-Kona to Hāmākua Coast	53 mi/1 hr 40 mins
Kailua-Kona to Hilo	75 mi/2 hrs
Kohala Coast to Waimea	16 mi/33 mins
Kohala Coast to Hāmākua Coast	29 mi/55 mins
Hilo to Volcano	30 mi/48 mins

RESTAURANTS

The same "buy local" trend that is spreading through the rest of the country is really taking hold on the Big Island. This is a giant shift from years past, in which most goods were imported, and it's a happy trend for visitors, who get to taste juicy, flavorful Waimea tomatoes and creamy handmade Hāmākua goat cheese. The fare here is as varied as the climates, with everything from fine dining to hole-in-the-wall joints to century-old family-run establishments. Chefs are serving up dishes from all parts of the globe as well as typical Hawai'i Pacific Rim or fusion cuisine that blends the best of the Islands' culture into some spectacular offerings.

HOTELS

Consider spending part of your vacation at a resort and part of it at bed-and-breakfasts. The big resorts sit squarely on some of the best beaches on the Big Island, and they have a lot to offer—spas, golf, and great restaurants for starters. The bed-and-breakfasts, on the other hand, provide a more intimate experience in settings as diverse as an

WILL I SEE FLOWING LAVA?

The best time to see lava is at night. However, you may or may not see flowing lava. Anyone who tries to tell you they can guarantee it or predict it is lying or trying to sell you something. Your best bet is to call the visitor center at the national park before you head out; even at that you could be pleasantly surprised or utterly disappointed. Keep in mind that the volcano is a pretty amazing sight even if it's not spewing fire.

The hike out to the closest viewing station to the flowing lava requires roughly three to four hours each way—the best way to handle it is to head out in the late afternoon, arrive at the viewing station by

nightfall, and then start the trek back when you've had your fill of Pele's fireworks. ■TIP→ Bring a flashlight and be prepared for some rough going over the lava fields at night.

There are viewing stations along the way as well, so you don't necessarily have to make an eight-hour round-trip journey. In fact, depending on how the lava is flowing, a viewing station farther from the lava could actually afford better views.

For more information about visiting Volcanoes National Park, see the Hawai'i National Park feature later in this chapter.

Upcountry ranch, a jungle tree house, and a Victorian mansion perched on sea cliffs. Several romantic bed-and-breakfasts are nestled in the rain forest surrounding Volcanoes National Park—very convenient after a nighttime lava hike.

WHAT IT COSTS					
	¢	$	$$	$$$	$$$$
Restaurants	under $10	$10–$17	$18–$26	$27–$35	over $35
Hotels	under $100	$100–$180	$181–$260	$261–$340	over $340

Restaurant prices are for a main course at dinner. Hotel prices are for two people in a standard double room in high season. Condo price categories reflect studio and one-bedroom rates.

VISITOR INFORMATION

Before you go, contact the Big Island Visitors Bureau to request a free official vacation planner with information on accommodations, transportation, sports and activities, dining, arts and entertainment, and culture. The Hawai'i Island Chamber of Commerce has links to dozens of museums, attractions, bed-and-breakfasts, and parks on its Web site as well.

Contacts Big Island Visitors Bureau (☎ 808/961–5797 *East Hawai'i, 808/885–1655 West Hawai'i, 800/648–2441 for vacation planner and brochures* ⊕ *www.bigisland.org*). **Hawai'i Island Chamber of Commerce** (☎ *808/935–7178* ⊕ *www.hicc.biz*).

EXPLORING

The first secret to enjoying the Big Island: rent a car, ideally one with four-wheel drive. The second: stay more than three days or return again and again to really explore this fascinating place. With 266 mi of coastline made up of white coral, black lava, and a dusting of green-olivine beaches, interspersed with lava cliffs, emerald gorges, and splashing waterfalls, the Big Island can be overwhelming. Depending on the number of days you have available, it would be best to divide your time between the Hilo and Kona sides of the island in order to take in the attractions of each.

KAILUA-KONA

Kailua-Kona is about 7 mi south of the Kona airport.

A fun and bustling seaside town, Kailua-Kona has the souvenir shops and open-air restaurants you'd expect in a major tourist hub, with the added bonus of a surprising number of historic sites. The main drag is Ali'i Drive, which runs parallel to the shoreline. Except for the rare deluge, the sun shines year-round. Though there are better beaches north of the town on the Kohala Coast, Kailua-Kona is still home to quite a few gems.

If you want to know more about the village's fascinating past, arrange for a 75-minute guided walking tour with the **Kona Historical Society** (✉ 81-6551 *Māmalahoa Hwy.* ☎ 808/323–3222 ⊕ *www.konahistorical.org*).

GETTING HERE AND AROUND

Half a day is plenty of time to explore Kailua-Kona; most of the town's sights are located in or near the downtown area. Still, if you add in a beach trip (Kahalu'u Beach has some of the best and easiest snorkeling on the island), it's easy to while away the bulk of a day. Another option for making a day of it is to tack on a short trip to the charming artists' village of Hōlualoa or to the coffee farms in the mountains just above Kealakekua Bay. There are a few great restaurants here that are far more affordable than those on the Kohala Coast and in Waimea. The town closest to the Kona International Airport (it's about 7 mi away), Kailua-Kona is a convenient home base from which to explore the island.

The easiest place to park your car is at King Kamehameha's Kona Beach Hotel ($15 per day). Some free parking is also available: When you enter Kailua via Palani Road (Hwy. 190), turn left onto Kuakini Highway, drive for a half block, and turn right into the small marked parking lot. Walk *makai* (toward the ocean) on Likana Lane a half block to Ali'i Drive, and you'll be in the heart of Kailua-Kona.

EXPLORING

★ **Hulihe'e Palace.** A lovely rambling old stone home surrounded by jewel green grass and sweeping ocean views and fronted by an elaborate wrought-iron gate, Hulihe'e Palace is one of only three royal palaces in America (the other two are in Honolulu on O'ahu). The two-story residence was built by Governor John Adams Kuakini in 1838, a year after he completed Moku'aikaua Church. During the 1880s it served

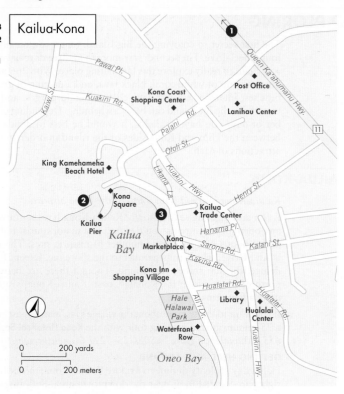

as King David Kalākaua's summer palace. It's constructed of local materials, including lava, coral, koa wood, and 'ōhi'a timber. Though severely damaged by the 2006 earthquakes, Hulihe'e Palace underwent a $1.5-million renovation and reopened in September 2009. The palace is operated by the Daughters of Hawai'i, a nonprofit organization focused on maintaining the heritage of the Islands, and its entrance fees, together with donations, are helping to repair the damage. ⊠ 75-5718 Ali'i Dr. ☎ 808/329–1877 ⊕ www.daughtersofhawaii.org ☞ $6 for adults, $4 for seniors, $1 for children under 18 ⊙ Wed.–Sat. 10–3.

Kamakahonu. King Kamehameha I spent his last years, from 1812 to 1819, near what is now King Kamehameha's Kona Beach Hotel. Part of what was once a 4-acre homestead, complete with several houses and religious sites, has been swallowed by Kailua Pier, but a replica of the temple, **Ahu'ena Heiau**, keeps history alive. ⊠ 75-5660 Palani Rd. ☎ 808/327–0123.

Natural Energy Lab of Hawai'i. Driving south from the Kona International Airport towards Kailua-Kona, you'll spot a large mysterious group of buildings with an equally large and mysterious photovoltaic (solar) panel installation just inside its gate. Although it looks like some sort of top-secret military station, this is the site of the Natural Energy Lab of Hawai'i, NELHA for short, where scientists, researchers, and entrepreneurs are developing and marketing everything from new uses for solar power to energy-efficient air-conditioning systems and environmentally friendly aquaculture techniques. Visitors are welcome at the lab, and there are 1½-hour tours for those interested in learning more about the experiments being conducted. ✉ *73-4460 Queen Kaʻahumanu Hwy., #101* ☎ *808/329–8073* ⊕ *www.friendsofnelha.org* ✆ *Free* ☉ *Tours Mon.–Thurs. at 10 am.*

THE KONA COAST

South of Kailua-Kona, Highway 11 hugs splendid coastlines, leaving busy streets behind. A detour along the winding narrow roads in the mountains above takes you straight to the heart of coffee country, where lush plantations and jaw-dropping views offer a taste of what Hawaiʻi was like before the resorts took over.

SOUTH KONA AND KEALAKEKUA BAY
Kealakekua Bay is 14 mi south of Kailua-Kona.

The winding road above Kealakekua Bay is home to a quaint little painted church, as well as several reasonably priced bed-and-breakfasts with great views. The communities surrounding the bay (Kainaliu and Captain Cook) are brimming with local and transplanted artists, making them great places to stop for a meal, some unique gifts, or an afternoon stroll.

GETTING HERE AND AROUND
Between the coffee plantations, artsy towns, and Kealakekua Bay, South Kona has plenty of activities to keep you occupied for a day. Bring a swimsuit and snorkel gear, and hit Kealakekua Bay first thing in the morning. You'll have a better chance of a dolphin sighting, and you'll beat the large snorkel cruise groups. Follow the signs off Highway 11 to the bay, then park at Nāpōʻopoʻo Beach (not much of a beach, but it provides easy access into the water).

TOP ATTRACTIONS
★ **Captain Cook Monument.** No one knows for sure what happened on February 14, 1779, when English explorer Captain James Cook was killed on this spot. He had chosen Kealakekua Bay as a landing place in November 1778. Cook, arriving during the celebration of Makahiki the harvest season, was welcomed at first. Some Hawaiians saw him as an incarnation of the god Lono. Cook's party sailed away in February 1779, but a freak storm forced his damaged ship back to Kealakekua Bay. Believing that no god could be thwarted by a mere rainstorm, the Hawaiians were not so welcoming this time, and various confrontations arose between them and Cook's sailors. The theft of a longboat brought Cook and an armed party ashore to reclaim it. One thing led to another: shots were fired, daggers and spears were thrown, and Captain Cook fell, mortally wounded. A 27-foot-high obelisk marks the spot where Captain Cook died on the shore of Kealakekua Bay. It wasn't long before other Westerners arrived on Hawaiʻi's shores: whalers, sailors, traders, missionaries, and others, bringing with them crime, debauchery, alcohol, disease, and a world unknown to the Hawaiians.

Kealakekua Bay is one of the most beautiful spots on the Big Island.

★ **Kealakekua Bay.** This is one of the most beautiful spots on the island. Dramatic cliffs surround crystal clear, turquoise water chock-full of stunning coral and tropical fish. The term "beach" is used a bit liberally for **Nāpōʻopoʻo Beach,** on the south side of the bay. There's no real beach to speak of, but there are easy ways to enter the water. This is a nice place to swim as it's well protected from weather or currents, so the water is almost always calm and clear. Excellent snorkel cruises can be booked through Fair Wind Cruises, the only company allowed to moor in Kealakekua. ⊠ *Bottom of Nāpōʻopoʻo Rd.*

★ **Puʻuhonua O Hōnaunau** *(City of Refuge).* This 180-acre National Historic Park was once a safe haven for women in times of war as well as for *kapu* (taboo) breakers, criminals, and prisoners of war—anyone who could get inside the 1,000-foot-long wall, which was 10 feet high and 17 feet thick, could avoid punishment. **Hale-o-Keawe Heiau,** built in 1650 as the burial place of King Kamehameha I's ancestor Keawe, has been restored. ⊠ *Rte. 160 ✛ About 20 mi south of Kailua-Kona* ☎ *808/328–2288* ⊕ *www.nps.gov/puho* ⊠ *$3 per person, $5 per vehicle* ☉ *Park daily 7 am–8 pm; visitor center daily 8 am–5:30 pm.*

WORTH NOTING

Hōlualoa. Hugging the hillside along the Kona Coast, the tiny village of Hōlualoa is just up winding Hualālai Road from Kailua-Kona. It's comprised almost entirely of galleries in which all types of artists, from woodworkers to jewelry makers and more traditional painters, work in their studios in back and sell the finished product up front. Formerly the exclusive domain of coffee plantations, it still has quite a few coffee farms offering free tours and cups of joe. Duck into the cleverly named

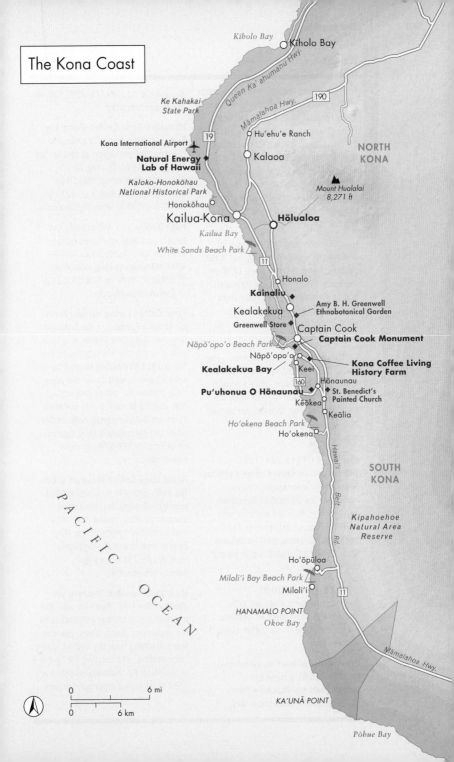

The Kona Coast

Kīholo Bay

● Kīholo Bay

Queen Kaʻahumanu Hwy.

Māmalahoa Hwy.

190

Ke Kahakai
State Park

NORTH
KONA

○ Huʻehuʻe Ranch

Kona International Airport ✈ 19

**Natural Energy
Lab of Hawaii** ◆

○ Kalaoa

▲ Mount Hualalai
8,271 ft

Kaloko-Honokōhau
National Historical Park

Honokōhau ○

Kailua-Kona

○ **Hōlualoa**

Kailua Bay

White Sands Beach Park

11

○ Honalo

Kainaliu

◆ Amy B. H. Greenwell
Ethnobotanical Garden

Kealakekua ○

Greenwell Store ○

Captain Cook ○

Captain Cook Monument

Nāpōʻopoʻo Beach Park

Nāpōʻopoʻo ○

Kealakekua Bay

○ Keʻei

**Kona Coffee Living
History Farm**

Hōnaunau ◆

Puʻuhonua O Hōnaunau

Kēōkea ◆ ● St. Benedict's
Painted Church

○ Keālia

Hoʻokena Beach Park

Hoʻokena ○

SOUTH
KONA

Hawaiʻi Belt Rd.

Kipahoehoe
Natural Area
Reserve

Hoʻōpuloa ○

Miloliʻi Bay Beach Park

Miloliʻi ○

11

HANAMALO POINT

Okoe Bay

Māmalahoa Hwy.

PACIFIC OCEAN

0 ———— 6 mi
0 ———— 6 km

KAʻŪNĀ POINT

Pōhue Bay

348 <   **The Big Island**

Kona Coffee

CLOSE UP

From the cafés, stores, and restaurants selling Kona coffee, to the farm tours, to the annual Kona Coffee Cultural Festival, coffee is a major part of life on this side of the Big Island. More than 600 farms, most from just 3 to 7 acres in size, grow the delicious—and luxurious, at generally more than $25 per pound—beans. Only coffee from the North and South Kona Districts can be called Kona.

Hawai'i is the only U.S. producer of commercially grown coffee, and it has been growing in Kona since 1828. In the early 1900s, the large Hawaiian coffee plantations subdivided their lots and began leasing parcels to local tenant farmers, a practice that continues today.

Coffee is harvested as "cherries"—the beans are encased in a hard red shell. Kona beans are hand-picked several times each season to guarantee the best product. The cherries are shelled and the beans roasted to a dark brown.

KONA'S COFFEE FESTIVAL
The fun annual **Kona Coffee Cultural Festival** (⊕ www.konacoffeefest. com) runs for 10 days in November and includes parades and concerts, special tours, an art stroll and coffee tasting in Hōlualoa, and the Gevalia Kona Cupping Competition (a judged tasting).

COFFEE-FARM TOURS
Some coffee-farm tours are self-guided, and most are free, with the exception of the Kona Coffee Living History Farm.

Greenwell Farms. This 20-minute tour of a working Hawaiian farm is great for the entire family. ⊠ 81-6581 Māmalahoa Hwy.,

Kealakekua ☎ 808/323–2295 ⊕ www. greenwellfarms.com.

Hōlualoa-Kona Coffee Company. See everything from dry milling to roasting and packaging at this facility. Tours are weekdays only. ⊠ 77-6261 Old Māmalahoa Hwy., Hwy. 180, Hōlualoa ☎ 808/322–9937 or 800/334–0348 ⊕ www.konalea.com.

Hula Daddy. You will actually get to pick and pulp your own coffee bean on Hula Daddy's tour. ⊠ 74-4944 Māmalahoa Hwy. Hōlualoa ☎ 808/327–9744 or 888/553–2339 ⊕ www.huladaddy.com.

Kona Coffee Living History Farm (D. Uchida Farm). On the National Register of Historic Places, this farm tour is worth the $20 admission fee. See a 1913 farmhouse shaded by coffee trees as well as an old Japanese bathhouse, coffee processing mill, and traditional drying platform. Tours are by reservation only. ⊠ 82-6199 Old Māmalahoa Hwy. Captain Cook ☎ 808/323–2006 ⊕ www. konahistorical.org.

Royal Kona Coffee Museum & Coffee Mill. Take this easy self-guided tour by following the descriptive plaques located around the coffee mill. ⊠ 83-5427 Māmalahoa Hwy., next to tree house in Hōnaunau ☎ 808/328–2511 ⊕ www. hawaiicoffeeco.com.

Mountain Thunder. Teaching you about coffee from "bean to cup," this tour includes a tasting and access to the processing plant, where you can see everything from dry milling, sizing, color, sorting, and roasting. ⊠ 79-7469 Hawai'i Belt Rd., Kainaliu ☎ 888/414–5662 ⊕ www.mountainthunder.com.

Take a tour of one of the many Kona coffee farms on the Big Island.

Hōluakoa Cafe (✉ *76-5900 Mamalahoa Hwy.* ☎ *808/322–2233*)—it refers to the *holua* (traditional Hawaiian grass sled) made of native koa wood—and grab a cup to sip while you stroll through town.

Kainaliu. Like many of the Big Island's old plantation towns, Kainaliu is experiencing a bit of a renaissance. In addition to a ribbon of funky old stores, a handful of new galleries and shops have sprung up in the last few years. Browse around Oshima's, established in 1926, and Kimura's, established in 1927, to find authentic Japanese goods beyond tourist trinkets, then pop into one of the local cafés for a tasty vegetarian snack. Cross the street to peek into the 1932 Aloha Theatre, where community-theater actors might be practicing a Broadway revue. ✉ *Hwy. 11, mile markers 112–114.*

Kona Coffee Living History Farm. Known as the D. Uchida Farm, this site is on the National Register of Historic Places. Completely restored by the Kona Historical Society, it includes a 1913 farmhouse surrounded by coffee trees, a Japanese bathhouse, *kuriba* (coffee-processing mill), and *hoshidana* (traditional drying platform). Farm tours take place Monday to Thursday from 10 until 2. ✉ *82-6199 Māmalahoa Hwy., Kealakekua* ☎ *808/323–2006* ⊕ *www.konahistorical.org* ✑ *$20.*

THE KOHALA COAST AND WAIMEA

The resorts on the Kohala Coast lay claim to some of the island's finest restaurants and its only destination spas. But the real attraction here is the island's best beaches. On a clear day, you can see Maui from them, and during the winter months, glistening humpback whales cleave the waters just offshore.

Rounding the northern tip of the island, the arid coast shifts rather suddenly to green villages and hillsides, leading to lush Pololū Valley in North Kohala, and the hot sunshine along the coast gives way to cooler temperatures. As you drive north into the mountains, you'll find the quaint towns of Hāwī and Kapa'au.

Just up the hill from Kohala, past Saddle Road (the route to Mauna Kea), Waimea offers a completely different experience from the rest of the island. Rolling green hills, large open pastures, cool evening breezes and morning mists, cattle everywhere, and regular rodeos are just a few of the surprises you'll stumble upon here in *paniolo* (Hawaiian for "cowboy") country.

THE KOHALA COAST
The Kohala Coast is about 32 mi north of Kailua-Kona.

If you had only a weekend to spend on the Big Island, this is probably where you'd want to go. The Kohala Coast is a mix of the island's best beaches and swankiest hotels just minutes from ancient valleys and temples, waterfalls, and funky artist enclaves.

In the sugar-plantations-turned-artsy enclaves of Hāwī and Kapa'au, new galleries are interspersed with charming reminders of old Hawai'i—wooden boardwalks, quaint local stores, delicious neighborhood restaurants, friendly locals, and a delightfully slow pace. There's great shopping for everything from designer beachwear to authentic Hawaiian crafts.

GETTING HERE AND AROUND
Two days is sufficient time for experiencing each unique side of Kohala—one day for the resort perks: the beach, the spa, the golf, the restaurants; one day for hiking and admiring the waterfalls and valleys of North Kohala, coupled with a wander around Hāwī and Kapa'au.

Diving and snorkeling are great along this coast, so bring or rent equipment. If you're staying at one of the resorts, they will usually have any equipment you could possibly want. If you're feeling adventurous, get your hands on a four-wheel-drive vehicle and head to one of the unmarked beaches along the Kohala Coast—you may end up with a beach to yourself.

The best way to explore the valleys of North Kohala is with a hiking tour. Look for one that includes lunch and a dip in one of the area's waterfall pools. There are a number of casual lunch options in Hāwī and Kapa'au (sandwiches, sushi, seafood, local-style "plate lunch"), and a few good dinner spots.

EXPLORING
Hāwī and Kapa'au. These neighboring villages thrived during plantation days. There were hotels, saloons, and theaters—even a railroad. They took a hit when "Big Sugar" left the island, but both towns are blossoming once again today, thanks to strong local communities and an influx of artists keen on honoring the towns' past. Old historic buildings have been restored and now hold shops, galleries, and eateries.

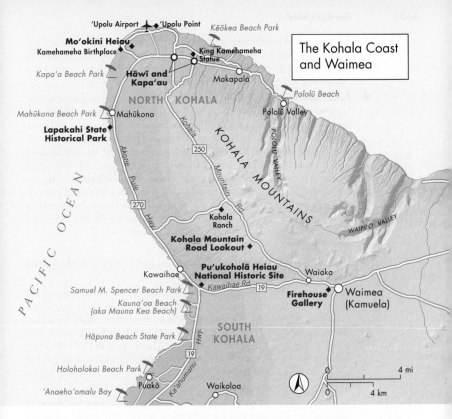

In Kapaʻau, browse through the extensive Hawaiian collection of the **Ackerman Gift Gallery** (✉ *54-3897 Akoni Pule Hwy. [Hwy. 270], North Kohala* ☎ *808/889–5971* ⊕ *www.ackermangalleries.com*).

★ **Lapakahi State Historical Park.** A self-guided, 1-mi walking tour leads through the ruins of the once-prosperous fishing village Koaiʻe, which dates as far back as the 15th century. Displays illustrate early Hawaiian fishing and farming techniques, salt gathering, games, and legends. Since the shoreline near the state park is an officially designated Marine Life Conservation District, and part of the site itself is considered sacred, swimming is discouraged. For some reason a distinction is made between swimming and snorkeling; the latter is allowed and superb. ✉ *Hwy. 270, mile marker 14 between Kawaihae and Māhukona, North Kohala* ☎ *808/974–6200 or 808/327–4958* ⊕ *www.hawaiistateparks. org* ⌦ *Free* ☉ *Daily 8–4.*

★ **Moʻokini Heiau.** This National Historic Landmark, an isolated *heiau* (an ancient place of worship), is so impressive in size it may give you what locals call "chicken skin" (goose bumps)—especially after you learn its history. The heiau's foundations date to about AD 480, but the high priest Paʻao from Tahiti expanded it several centuries later to offer sacrifices to please his gods. You can still see the lava slab where hundreds of people were sacrificed, which gives this place a truly haunted feel.

Be careful making the trek if there have been heavy rains recently. Even with four-wheel-drive, you could easily get stuck in the mud. ✛ *Turn off Hwy. 270 at sign for 'Upolu Airport, near Hāwī, and hike or drive in a four-wheel-drive vehicle 1½ mi southwest* ☎ 808/974–6200.

★ **Pu'ukoholā Heiau National Historic Site.** In 1790 a prophet told King Kamehameha to build a *heiau* on top of Pu'ukoholā (Hill of the Whale) and dedicate it to the war god Kūkā'ilimoku by sacrificing his principal rival, Keōua Kūahu'ula. By doing so the king would achieve his goal of conquering the Hawaiian Islands. The prophecy came true in 1810. A short walk over arid landscape leads from the impressive, recently renovated visitor center to temples **Pu'ukoholā Heiau** and **Mailekini Heiau.** An even older temple, dedicated to the shark gods, lies submerged just offshore. Bring along your cellular phone to listen to a free audio tour while you visit the site. ✉ *62-3601 Kawaihae Rd., Kawaihae* ☎ 808/882–7218 ⊕ *www.nps.gov/puhe/index.htm* ⊠ *Free* ☉ *Daily 7:45–5.*

WAIMEA

Waimea is 40 mi northeast of Kailua-Kona and 10 mi east of the Kohala Coast.

In addition to the horses and cattle, Waimea is also where some of the island's top Hawaiian regional cuisine chefs practice their art, which makes it an ideal place to find yourself at dinnertime. With its galleries, restaurants, and museums, as well as Parker Ranch, Waimea is well worth a stop if you're heading to Hilo or Mauna Kea. ■ TIP➔ The short highway that connects Waimea to North Kohala (Hwy. 170) affords some of our favorite Big Island views.

GETTING HERE AND AROUND

You can see most of what Waimea has to offer in one day, but if you're heading up to Mauna Kea for stargazing (which you should), it could easily be stretched to two. If you stay in Waimea overnight (there are a few bed-and-breakfast options), or just get up really early, you could go for a morning horseback (or ATV) ride around the Parker Ranch, spend the afternoon browsing through town or touring some of the area's fantastic farms and ranches, then indulge in a gourmet dinner— all before heading up Saddle Road for world-renowned stargazing atop Mauna Kea.

A word to the wise—there are no services or gas stations on Saddle Road, the only way to reach the summit of Mauna Kea. Fill up on gas and bring water, snacks and warm clothes with you (there are plenty of gas stations, cafés, and shops in Waimea).

EXPLORING

Firehouse Gallery. Walk across the Parker Ranch Shopping Center parking lot to a historic 79-year-old fire station, now a gallery, to glimpse what the artists in Hāmākua and Kohala are up to. The Waimea Arts Council sponsors free *kaha ki'is* (one-person shows). ✉ *67-1201 Māmalahoa Hwy., Waimea* ☎ 808/887–1052 ⊕ *www.waimeaartscouncil.org.*

Kohala Mountain Road Lookout. The lookout here provides a splendid view of the Kohala Coast and Kawaihae Harbor far below. On clear days, you can see well beyond the resorts. It's one of the most scenic spots on the island and great for a picnic. ✉ *Kohala Mountain Rd. (Hwy. 250).*

MAUNA KEA

Mauna Kea's summit is 18 mi southeast of Waimea and 34 mi northwest of Hilo.

Mauna Kea's summit—at 13,796 feet—is reputedly the best place in the world for viewing the night sky. For this reason, the summit is home to the world's largest astronomical observatory. Research teams from 11 different countries operate 13 telescopes on Mauna Kea, several of which are record holders: the world's largest optical/infrared telescopes (the dual Keck telescopes), the world's largest dedicated infrared telescope (UKIRT), and the largest submillimeter telescope (the JCMT). A still larger 30-meter telescope has just been cleared for construction, and is slated to open its record-breaking eye to the heavens in 2018.

GETTING HERE AND AROUND

Thanks to the steep drive, it takes about an hour and a half to get here from Hilo and an hour from Waimea. Between the ride there, sunset on the summit, and stargazing, we recommend allotting at least four hours for your Mauna Kea visit.

To reach the summit, you must drive on Saddle Road, which used to be a narrow, rough, winding highway, but has recently been rerouted and repaved, and is now a beautiful shortcut across the middle of the island (except for that stretch near Waimea). The road to the Visitor Center at Mauna Kea is fine, but the road from there to the summit is a bit more precarious—unpaved and very steep—although most cars can make it up slowly and four-wheel-drive vehicles won't have any trouble at all. If you're worried about your rental making the drive, you can still head for the summit with one of a handful of tour operators who will take care of everything. If you plan to drive yourself, fill up on gas and bring water and snacks and warm clothes with you, as there is nowhere along the way to stock up.

The second thing, which is extremely important to remember, is the altitude. ■ TIP➔ Take the change in altitude seriously—stop at the Visitor Center for at least half an hour, and don't overexert yourself, especially at the top. Scuba divers must wait at least 24 hours before attempting a trip to the summit to avoid getting the bends. The observatory recommends that children under 16, pregnant women, and those with heart, respiratory, or weight problems not go higher than the Visitor Center.

The last potential obstacle: it's cold, as in *freezing*. The military personnel stationed in Hawai'i do their cold-weather training atop Mauna Kea. It's difficult to find cold-weather clothing in Hawai'i, so, if you plan to visit Mauna Kea, pack your favorite warm things from home.

ONIZUKA VISITOR CENTER

★ **Onizuka Center for International Astronomy Visitor Information Station.** At a 9,300-foot elevation, this is an excellent amateur observation site, with a handful of telescopes and a knowledgeable staff. It hosts nightly stargazing sessions from 6 to 10. This is also where you should stop for a while to acclimate to the altitude if you're heading for the summit. This is a pleasure to do as you drink hot chocolate and peruse the exhibits on ancient Hawaiian celestial navigation, the ancient history

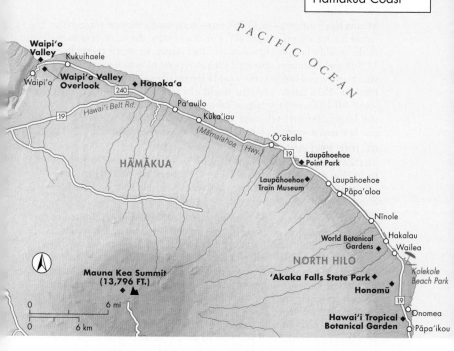

PACIFIC OCEAN

**Waipi'o
Valley** ◆ ○ Kukuihaele

○ Waipi'o   ◆ **Waipi'o Valley
Overlook**   ◆ **Honoka'a**

|240|

Hawai'i Belt Rd. |19| ○ Pa'auilo
   ○ Kūka'iau
(*Māmalahoa   Hwy.*)   ○ 'Ō'ōkala

HĀMĀKUA |19| ◆ **Laupāhoehoe
Point Park**

**Laupāhoehoe ◆
Train Museum**   ○ Laupāhoehoe
   ○ **Pāpa'aloa**

○ Nīnole

**World Botanical   ○ Hakalau
Gardens** ◆   ○ Wailea

NORTH HILO   Kolekole
Beach Park

**Mauna Kea Summit
(13,796 FT.)**   **'Akaka Falls State Park** ◆

▲   **Honomū** ◆ |19|

0 ——— 6 mi   **Hawai'i Tropical ◆   ○ Onomea
Botanical Garden**
0 ——— 6 km   ○ Pāpa'ikou

of the mountain as not only a quarry for the best basalt in the Hawaiian Islands, but also as one of its most revered spiritual retreats, and other exhibits on modern astronomy and the unique natural history of the summit. The gift shop is full of great books, posters, and other mementos. On weekends the Onizuka Center offers free escorted summit tours, heading up the mountain in a caravan. Participants must arrive at 1 pm, in your own all-wheel or four-wheel-drive vehicle. After watching a one-hour video, the caravan begins. To get here from Hilo, which is about 34 mi away, take Highway 200 (Saddle Road), and turn right at mile marker 28 onto John A. Burns Way, which is the only access road to the summit. ☎ *808/961–2180* ⊕ *www.ifa.hawaii.edu/info/vis* ☉ *Daily 9 am–9:30 pm.*

THE SUMMIT

Head to the summit before sunset so you're already there to witness the stunning sunset and emerging star show. Only the astronomers are allowed to use the telescopes and equipment up here, but the scenery is free for everybody. So, watch the sun sink into the horizon and then head down to the Visitor Center to warm up and stargaze some more. Or do your stargazing first and then head up here to get a different perspective—if you were blown away by the number of stars crowding the sky over the Visitor Center, this vantage point will really make you speechless. Just take it easy if you're driving back down in the dark—*slow and cautious* is the name of the game on this steep road.

If you haven't rented a four-wheel-drive vehicle, don't want to deal with driving to the summit, or don't want to wait in line to use the handful of telescopes at the Visitor Center, consider booking a tour. Operators provide transportation to and from the summit, and expert guides; some also provide parkas, gloves, telescopes, dinner, hot beverages, and snacks. Excursion fees range from $90 to $185.

GOING WITH A GUIDE

Arnott's Lodge & Hiking Adventures. A bit cheaper than the others at $125 per person, Arnott's tours leave from Hilo; their tour does not include dinner, they do not bring warm clothing for guests, and they do not have their own telescope. Focusing more on the experience of the mountain than astronomy, Arnott's brings binoculars for each guest and provides an informative lesson on major celestial objects and Polynesian navigational stars. ☎ 808/969–7097 ⊕ www.arnottslodge.com.

Hawai'i Forest & Trail. This outfitter stops for dinner along the way at a historic ranch, and brings parkas, gloves, and their own telescope along. Cookies and hot chocolate make cold stargazing more pleasant. The price is $189 per person. ☎ 808/331–8505 or 800/464–1993 ⊕ www.hawaii-forest.com.

Jack's Tours. Jack's follows the same itinerary as the other tours—sunset on the summit, followed by stargazing from the Visitor Center. They take larger groups than the other outfitters, and their guides speak English and Japanese. Boxed dinner, hot tea, bottled water, light snack, telescopes, and use of jackets and gloves are included. The price is $160 per person. ☎ 808/969–9507 or 800/442–5557 ⊕ www.jackstours.com.

Mauna Kea Summit Adventures. As the first company to specialize in tours to the mountain and the only company to offer only Mauna Kea tours, Mauna Kea Summit Adventures has a bit more cred than the rest of the pack. They use cushy new van coaches for their tours, bring along parkas and gloves, and serve dinner at the Visitor Center before heading up to sunset on the summit. They also bring along their own powerful telescope. The price is $200 per person, including tax. ☎ 808/322–2366 ⊕ www.maunakea.com.

Onizuka Visitor Center Tours. If you want to charge the summit with a group but don't fancy paying for one of the tours above, consider joining the Visitor Center's free summit tour. It begins at 1 pm every

WAIPI'O VALLEY TOURS

Na'alapa Stables (☎ 808/775–0419 ⊕ www.naalapastables.com) features friendly horses and friendly guides for tours of the valley floor.

Waipi'o on Horseback (☎ 808/775-7291, 877/775-7291 ⊕ www.waipioonhorseback.com) is a great outfit offering guided horseback riding trips on the valley floor.

Hawaiian Walkways (☎ 808/775-0372, 800/457-7759 ⊕ www.hawaiianwalkways.com) leads a Waipi'o Waterfall Hike along the rim above the valley, with stunning views of the vista below.

4

CLOSE UP

Ground Graffiti?

You will no doubt notice that the black-lava fields lining Highway 19 from Kona International Airport into Kailua-Kona or out to the Kohala resorts are littered with white-coral graffiti. This has been going on for decades, and locals still get a kick out of it, as do tourists. The first thing everyone asks is "where do the white rocks come from?" and the answer is this: they're bits of coral and they come from the ocean. Now that we've figured out that coral isn't totally expendable, no one starts from scratch anymore. If you want to write a message in the lava, you've got to use the coral that's already out there. This means that no one's message lasts for long, but that's all part of the fun. Some local couples even have a tradition of writing their names in the same spot on the lava fields every year on their anniversary.

Saturday and Sunday. Reservations are not required, but a four-wheel-drive vehicle is—you'll follow the center's staff up the summit in your own car after watching an informational video at the Visitor Center. ☎ 808/961–2180 ⊕ www.ifa.hawaii.edu/info/vis.

THE HĀMĀKUA COAST

The Hāmākua Coast is about 25 mi east of Waimea.

The spectacular waterfalls, mysterious jungles, emerald fields, and stunning ocean vistas along Highway 19 northwest of Hilo are collectively referred to as the Hilo–Hāmākua Heritage Coast. Brown signs featuring a sugarcane tassel reflect the area's history: thousands of acres of sugarcane are now idle, with no industry to support since "King Sugar" left the island in the early 1990s.

The 45-mi drive winds through little plantation towns, Pāpa'ikou, Laupāhoehoe, and Pa'auilo among them. It's a great place to wander off the main road and see "real" Hawai'i—untouched valleys, overgrown banyan trees, tiny coastal villages. ■ TIP→ The "Heritage Drive," a 4-mi loop just off the main highway, is well worth the detour. Signs mark various sites of historical interest, as well as scenic views along the 40-mi stretch of coastline. Keep an eye out for them and try to stop at the sights mentioned—you won't be disappointed.

Once back on Highway 19, you'll pass the road to Honoka'a, which leads to the end of the road bordering Waipi'o Valley, ancient home to Hawaiian royalty. The isolated valley floor has maintained the ways of old Hawai'i, with taro patches, wild horses, and a handful of houses.

GETTING HERE AND AROUND

Any turnoff along this coast could lead to an incredible view, so take your time and go exploring up and down the side roads. You'll find small communities still hanging on quite nicely, well after the demise of the big sugar plantations that first engendered them. There are homey cafés, gift shops, and galleries—and a way of life from a time gone by. If you're driving from Kailua-Kona, rather than driving around the northern tip of the island, cut across on the Māmalahoa Highway (190) to Waimea and then catch the 19 to the coast.

If you've stopped to explore the quiet little villages with wooden boardwalks and dogs dozing in backyards, or if you've spent several hours in Waipiʻo Valley, night will undoubtedly be falling by the time you've had your fill of the Hāmākua Coast. Don't worry: the return to Hilo via Highway 19 only takes about an hour, or you can go the other direction on

SEE THE SIGN

In addition to looking cool and hearkening back to the days when sugar was king, the brown-and-white Hilo–Hāmākua Heritage Coast signs mark various sites of historical interest, as well as scenic views along the 40-mi stretch of coastline. Keep an eye out for these signs and try to stop at the sights mentioned—you won't be disappointed.

the same road to stop for dinner in Waimea before heading back to the Kohala Coast resorts (another 25 to 45 minutes). Although you shouldn't have any trouble exploring the Hāmākua Coast in a day, a handful of romantic bed-and-breakfasts are available along the coast if you want to spend more time.

EXPLORING

★ **ʻAkaka Falls State Park.** A meandering 10-minute loop trail takes you to the best spots to see the two cascades, **ʻAkaka** and **Kahuna.** The 400-foot Kahuna Falls is on the lower end of the trail. The majestic upper ʻAkaka Falls drops more than 442 feet, tumbling far below into a pool drained by Kolekole Stream amid a profusion of fragrant white, yellow, and red torch ginger. ✉ *4 mi inland off Hwy. 19, near Honomū* ☎ *808/974–6200* 💰 *$5 per vehicle (non-residents); $1 for walk-ins* ⏱ *Daily 7–7.*

★ **Hawaiʻi Tropical Botanical Garden.** Eight miles north of Hilo, stunning coastline views appear around each curve of the 4-mi scenic jungle drive that accesses the privately owned nature preserve beside Onomea Bay. Paved pathways in the 17-acre botanical garden lead past ponds, waterfalls, and more than 2,000 species of plants and flowers, including palms, bromeliads, ginger, heliconia, orchids, and ornamentals. ✉ *27-717 Old Māmalahoa Hwy., Pāpaʻikou* ☎ *808/964–5233* ⊕ *www.hawaiigarden.com* 💰 *$15* ⏱ *Daily 9–4.*

Honokaʻa. In 1881 Australian William Purvis planted the first macadamia-nut trees in Hawaiʻi near what is now a very friendly, funky little town with a great antique shop, a few interesting galleries, and good cafés. But Honokaʻa's true heyday came when sugar was king in the early part of the 20th century. During World War II, this was the place for soldiers stationed around Waimea to cut loose. Today, it's still worth a look at its historic buildings, and a chat with its friendly residents. ✉ *Mamane St., Hwy. 240.*

Honomū. Its sugar-plantation past is reflected in the wooden boardwalks and tin-roof buildings of this small community. It's fun to poke through old dusty shops such as Glass from the Past, where you'll find an assortment of old bottles. The Woodshop Gallery/Café showcases

local artists. ⊠ *2 mi inland from Hwy. 19 en route to 'Akaka Falls State Park.*

Fodor's Choice **Waipi'o Valley.** Bounded by 2,000-foot cliffs, the "Valley of the Kings"
★ was once a favorite retreat of Hawaiian royalty. Waterfalls drop 1,200 feet from the Kohala Mountains to the valley floor, and the sheer cliff faces make access difficult. Though completely off the grid today, Waipi'o was once a center of Hawaiian life; somewhere between 4,000 and 20,000 people made it their home between the 13th and 17th centuries. To preserve this pristine part of the island, commercial transportation permits are limited—only four outfits offer organized valley trips—and Sunday the valley rests. A road leads down from the **Waipi'o Valley Overlook** (⊠ *Follow Hwy. 240 8 mi northwest of Honoka'a*), but only four-wheel-drive vehicles should attempt the steep road. The walk down into the valley is less than a mile from here—but keep in mind, the climb back up is strenuous in the hot sun. A crescent of black sand makes it a popular spot for experienced local surfers. ■TIP→ Continued overuse of the beach area and lack of sanitary facilities have caused serious unhealthy conditions to persist since 2003. Until it's cleaned up we don't recommend getting into the water. Even then, swimmers need to watch out for rip currents.

HILO

Hilo is 55 mi southeast of Waimea, 95 mi northeast of Kailua-Kona, and just North of the Hilo Airport.

When compared to Kailua-Kona, Hilo is often described as "the real Hawai'i." With significantly fewer tourists than residents, more historic buildings, and a much stronger identity as a long-established community, life does seem more authentic on this side of the island.

GETTING HERE AND AROUND

Hilo is a great base for exploring the eastern and southern parts of the island—just be sure to bring an umbrella for sporadic showers. If you're just passing through town or making a day trip, make the first right turn into the town off Highway 19 (it comes up fast) and grab a parking spot in the lot on your left or on any of the surrounding streets. Downtown Hilo is best experienced on foot. The **Hilo Downtown Improvement Association** (⊠ *329 Kamehameha Ave.* ☎ *808/935–8850* ⊕ *www. downtownhilo.com* ⊗ *Mon.–Fri. 8–4:30*) provides an excellent and free self-guided walking tour to downtown Hilo. The tour includes historical information, a map, and directions to 18 historic sites. You can download it from their Web site or pick it up in person at their downtown Hilo office.

There are plenty of gas stations and restaurants in the area. Hilo is a good spot to load up on food and supplies—just south of downtown there are several large budget chains. The Merrie Monarch Hula Festival takes place in Hilo every year during the second week of April, and dancers and admirers flock to the city from all over the world. If you're planning a stay in Hilo during this time, be sure to book your room well in advance.

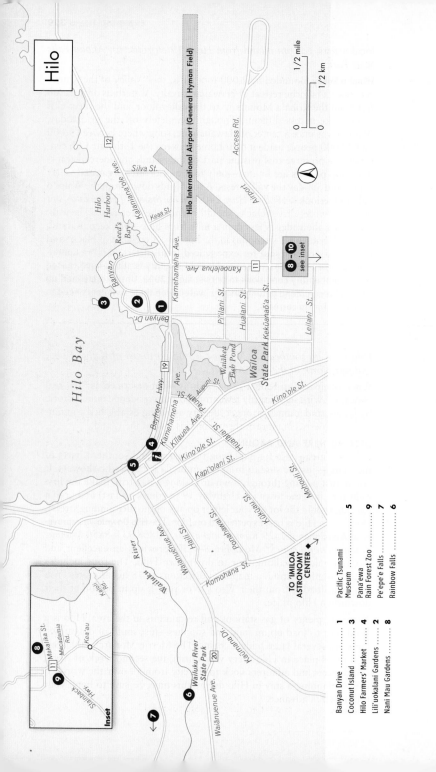

Hilo

Hilo International Airport (General Hyman Field)

Hilo Bay

Hilo Harbor

Reed's Bay

Banyan Dr.

Kalanianaʻole Ave.

Silva St.

Keaa St.

Kamehameha Ave.

Kanoelehua Ave.

Bayfront Hwy.

Kamehameha Ave.

Access Rd.

Airport

Piʻilani St.

Hualani St.

Kekūanaōʻa St.

Leilani St.

Wailoa State Park

Waiākea Fish Pond

Auani St.

Kinoʻole St.

Piʻopiʻo St.

Kamehameha Ave.

Kilauea Ave.

Kinoʻole St.

Kapiʻolani St.

Haʻili St.

Hualalai St.

Kilauea St.

Mohouli St.

Ponahawai St.

Komohana St.

Waiānuenue Ave.

Halaʻi St.

Wailuku River

Kaumana Dr.

Wailuku River State Park

TO ʻIMILOA ASTRONOMY CENTER ♦

12

19

11

1

2

3

1

4

5

8–10 see inset

8 – 10

0   1/2 mile
0   1/2 km

Inset

Kaʻū Rd.

Keaʻau

Macadamia Rd.

Makālika St.

Stainback Hwy.

20

8

9

7

6

Banyan Drive **1**
Coconut Island **3**
Hilo Farmers' Market **4**
Liliʻuokalani Gardens **2**
Nani Mau Gardens **8**

Pacific Tsunami
  Museum **5**
Panaʻewa
  Rain Forest Zoo **9**
Peʻepeʻe Falls **7**
Rainbow Falls **6**

TOP ATTRACTIONS

★ **Hilo Farmers' Market.** This abundant
and colorful market draws farmers and shoppers from all over the
island. Bright orchids, anthuriums,
and birds-of-paradise create a feast
for the eyes, while exotic vegetables, tropical fruits, and baked
goods satisfy the stomach. Craft

WORD OF MOUTH

"I would pick Hilo, definitely, every
time. When I go to Hawai'i, I want
it to be green and kind of away
from it all. Hilo defines that for
me." —Holly

and jewelry makers and clothing vendors round out the market. Don't
dawdle, as it closes in the early afternoon. ⊠ *Mamo and Kamehameha
Sts.* ⊕ *www.hilofarmersmarket.com* ☉ *Wed. and Sat. "from dawn till
it's gone."*

'Imiloa Astronomy Center. Part Hawaiian cultural center, part astronomy
museum, the 'Imiloa Astronomy Center provides an educational and
cultural complement to the research being conducted atop Mauna Kea.
Although visitors are welcome at Mauna Kea, its primary function is as
a research center—not observatory, museum, or education center. Those
roles have been taken on by 'Imiloa in a big way. With its exhibits, full-
dome planetarium shows, and regularly scheduled talks and events, the
center is a must-see for anyone interested in the stars, the planets, or
Hawaiian culture and history. The center, five minutes from downtown
Hilo, also provides an important link between the scientific research
being conducted at Mauna Kea and its history as a sacred mountain for
the Hawaiian people. ⊠ *600 'Imiloa Pl., at the UH Hilo Science & Technology Park, off Nowelo and Komohana* ☎ *808/969–9700* ⊕ *www.
imiloahawaii.org* ⊠ *$17.50* ☉ *Tues.–Sun. 9–4.*

★ **Lili'uokalani Gardens.** Designed to honor Hawai'i's first Japanese immigrants, Lili'uokalani's 30 acres of fish-filled ponds, stone lanterns, half-
moon bridges, elegant pagodas, and ceremonial teahouse make it a
favorite Sunday destination. The surrounding area used to be a busy
residential neighborhood until a tsunami in 1960 swept the buildings
away, taking the lives of 60 people in the process. ⊠ *Banyan Dr. at
Lihiwai St.* ☎ *808/961–8311.*

Pe'epe'e Falls *(Boiling Pots).* Four separate streams fall into a series
of circular pools, forming the Pe'epe'e Falls. The resulting turbulent
action—best seen after a good rain—has earned this stretch of the Wailuku River the name Boiling Pots. ■**TIP→** There's no swimming allowed at
Pe'epe'e Falls or anywhere in the Wailuku river, due to dangerous currents
and undertows. ✣ *3 mi northwest of Hilo on Waiānuenue Ave; keep to
right when road splits and look for a green sign for Boiling Pots.*

★ **Rainbow Falls.** After a hard rain, these falls thunder into the Wailuku
River gorge, often creating magical rainbows in the mist. ✣ *Take
Waiānuenue Ave. west of town 1 mi; when the road forks, stay right
and look for the Hawaiian warrior sign.*

WORTH NOTING

Banyan Drive. The more than 50 leafy banyan trees with aerial roots
dangling from their limbs were planted some 60 to 70 years ago by visiting celebrities. You'll find such names as Amelia Earhart and Franklin

Delano Roosevelt on plaques affixed to the trees. ⊠ *Begin at Hawai'i Naniloa Resort, 93 Banyan Dr.*

Coconut Island. This small island, just offshore from Lili'uokalani Gardens, is accessible via a footbridge. It was considered a place of healing in ancient times. Today children play in the tide pools while fisherfolk try their luck. ⊠ *Lili'uokalani Gardens, Banyan Dr.*

Nani Mau Gardens. The name means "forever beautiful" in Hawaiian, and that's a good description of this 20-acre botanical garden filled with several varieties of fruit trees and hundreds of varieties of ginger, orchids, anthuriums, and other exotic plants. Guided tours by tram are also available. There is one restaurant with a lunch buffet. ⊠ *421 Makalika St., off Hwy. 11* ☎ *808/959–3500* ⊕ *www.nanimau.com* ⊠ *$10, tram tour an additional $7* ☉ *Daily 10–3.*

☾ **Pacific Tsunami Museum.** A memorial to all those who lost their lives in tsunamis that have struck the Big Island, Hawai'i and the world, this small but informative museum offers a poignant history of the devastating waves. In a 1931 C. W. Dickey–designed building—the former home of the First Hawaiian Bank—you'll find an interactive computer center, a science room, a theater, a replica of Old Hilo Town, a children's corner, and a knowledgeable, friendly staff. In the background, a striking quilt tells a silent story. ⊠ *130 Kamehameha Ave.* ☎ *808/935–0926* ⊕ *www.tsunami.org* ⊠ *$8* ☉ *Mon.–Sat. 9–4.*

☾ **Pana'ewa Rain Forest Zoo.** Advertised as "the only natural tropical rain forest zoo in the United States," this is the home of white Bengal tiger, Namaste. There is a variety of native Hawaiian species, such as the state bird, the *nēnē* (Hawaiian goose), as well as a small petting zoo every Saturday 1:30–2:30. Come in the afternoon and watch Namaste's feeding at 3:30 daily. ⊠ *Left on Mamaki off Hwy. 11, just past the "Kulani 19, Stainback Hwy" sign* ☎ *808/959–7224* ⊕ *www.hilozoo. com* ⊠ *Free* ☉ *Daily 9–4.*

PUNA

Puna is about 6 mi south of Hilo.

The Puna District is wild in every sense of the word. The jagged black coastline is changing all the time; the trees are growing out of control, forming canopies over the few paved roads; the land is dirt cheap; and the people, well, there's something about living in an area that could be destroyed by lava at any moment (as Kalapana was in 1990) that makes the laws of modern society seem silly. So it is that Puna has its well-deserved reputation as the "outlaw" region of the Big Island. That said, it's a unique place that's well worth a detour, especially if you're in this part of the island anyway.

GETTING HERE AND AROUND

The sprawling Puna District includes part of the Volcano area and stretches northeast down to the coast. If you're staying in Hilo for the night, driving around wild lower Puna is a great way to spend a morning.

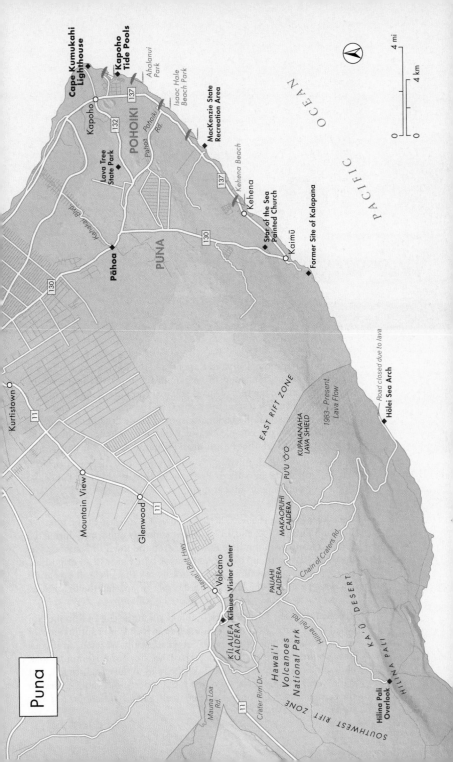

Puma

PACIFIC OCEAN

Cape Kumukahi Lighthouse
Kapoho Tide Pools
Kapoho
Ahalanui Park
Isaac Hale Beach Park
MacKenzie State Recreation Area
POHOIKI
Pāhoā Pohoiki Rd.
Lava Tree State Park
137
132
Keahou Blvd.
Kehena Beach
Kehena
137
PUNA
130
Star of the Sea Painted Church
Kaimū
Pāhoā
Former Site of Kalapana
PUNA
130

Kurtistown
11

Mountain View

Glenwood
11

Hawai'i Belt Hwy.

EAST RIFT ZONE

PU'U 'Ō'Ō

KUPAIANAHA LAVA SHIELD

1983–Present Lava Flow

Road closed due to lava

Hōlei Sea Arch

MAKAOPUHI CALDERA

Chain of Craters Rd.

Volcano
Kīlauea Visitor Center

PAUAHI CALDERA

KĪLAUEA CALDERA

Hawai'i Volcanoes National Park

Mauna Loa Rd.

Crater Rim Dr.

Hilina Pali Rd.

KA'Ū DESERT

HILINA PALI

Hilina Pali Overlook

SOUTHWEST RIFT ZONE

11

4 mi
4 km

"I learned that the best viewing area was at the end of the Pāhoa Kalapana Road past the Keauohana Forest Reserve." —NickiGgert, Fodors.com photo contest participant

The roads connecting Pāhoa to Kapoho and the Kalapana coast form a loop that's about 25 mi long; driving times are from two to three hours, depending on the number of stops you make and the length of time at each stop. There are restaurants, stores, and gas stations in Pāhoa, but services elsewhere in the region are spotty. There are long stretches of the road that may be completely isolated at any given point; this can be a little scary at night but beautiful and tranquil during the day.

Compared to big-city living, it's pretty tame, but there is a bit of a "locals only" vibe in parts of Puna, and a drug problem in Pāhoa, so don't go wandering around at night.

EXPLORING

Cape Kumukahi Lighthouse. The lighthouse, 1½ mi east of the intersection of highways 132 and 137, was miraculously unharmed during the 1960 volcano eruption here that destroyed the town of Kapoho. The lava flowed directly up to the lighthouse's base but instead of pushing it over, actually flowed around it. Locals say that, Pele, the volcano goddess, protected the Hawaiian fisherfolk by sparing the lighthouse. ⊠ *Past intersection of Hwys. 132 and 137, Kapoho.*

Kapoho Tide Pools. This network of tide pools at the end of Kapoho-Kai Road is great for a swim or a snorkel, or even just a beautiful view of new coastline. Some of the pools are volcanically warmed, so if your back's a little sore from exploring the island, stop for a 10-minute soak and you'll probably feel better. Take the road to the end, turn left, and park. A few of the pools are on private property, but those closest to the ocean, Wai'ōpae Ponds, are open to all. ⊠ *End of Kapoho-Kai Rd., off Hwy. 137, Puna District.*

Pāhoa. Sort of like a town from the Wild West, this little town even has some wooden boardwalks and rickety buildings—not to mention a reputation as a wild and woolly place where pot growers make up a significant part of the community. Now things are more civilized in town, but there are still plenty of hippies and other colorful characters pursuing alternative lifestyles. The secondhand stores, tie-dye clothing boutiques, and art galleries in quaint old buildings are fun to wander through during the day. Pāhoa's main street boasts a handful of island eateries, the best of which is **Luquin's Mexican Restaurant.** ⊠ *Turn southeast onto Hwy. 130 at Kea'au, drive 11 mi to a right turn marked Pāhoa.*

HAWAI'I VOLCANOES NATIONAL PARK AND VICINITY

4

Hawai'i Volcanoes National Park is about 22 mi southwest from the start of the Puna district, and about 27 mi southwest of Hilo.

Few visitors realize that in addition to "the volcano"(Kīlauea)—that mountain oozing new layers of lava onto its flanks—there's also Volcano, the village. Conveniently located next to Hawai'i Volcanoes National Park, Volcano village is a charming little hamlet in the woods that offers a dozen or so excellent inns and bed-and-breakfasts, a decent (although strangely expensive) Thai restaurant, some killer (although also strangely expensive) pizza, and a handful of things to see and do that don't include the village's namesake.

GETTING HERE AND AROUND

There are a handful of dining options, a couple of stores, and gas stations available in Volcano, so most of your needs should be covered. If you can't find what you're looking for, Hilo is about a 35-minute drive away, and the Ke'eau grocery store and fast-food joints are 25 minutes away.

Bring a fleece or a sweater if you plan to stay the night in Volcano; temperatures drop at night and mornings are usually cool and misty. One of the main reasons people choose to stay the night in Volcano is to see the dramatic glow at the summit vent and to drive to the coast to see the lava flow into the sea. ■TIP➔ Make sure you have enough gas to get down to the flow and back up. The entrance to Volcanoes National Park is about one minute from Volcano village, but the drive down is a good 30 minutes. Remember that you'll be coming back around midnight, long after the rangers have gone home.

EXPLORING

Kīlauea Caverns of Fire. Strap on a miner's hat and gloves and get ready to explore the underbelly of the world's largest active volcano. Tours through these fascinating caves and lava tubes underneath the volcano must be arranged in advance, but are well worth a little extra planning. Located off Highway 11 between Hilo and Volcanoes National Park, the caverns are comprised of four main tubes, each 500–700 years old and full of stalactites, stalagmites, and a variety of different-colored flowstone. The largest lava tube in the world is here—40 mi long, it has 80-foot ceilings and is 80 feet wide. Tours can range from safe and easy (safe enough for children five years old and up) to long

Continued on page 372

HAWAI'I VOLCANOES NATIONAL PARK

Exploring the surface of the world's most active volcano—from the moonscape craters at the summit to the red-hot lava flows on the coast to the kīpuka, pockets of vegetation miraculously left untouched—is the ultimate ecotour and one of Hawai'i's must-dos.

The park sprawls over 520 square miles and encompasses Kīlauea and Mauna Loa, two of the five volcanoes that formed the Big Island nearly half a million years ago. Kīlauea, youngest and most rambunctious of the Hawaiian volcanoes, erupted at its summit from the 19th century through 1982. Since then, the top of the volcano had been more or less quiet, frequently shrouded in mist; an eruption in the Halema'uma'u Crater in 2008 ended this period of relative inactivity.

Kīlauea's eastern side sprang to life on January 3, 1983, shooting molten lava four stories high. This eruption has been ongoing, and lava flows are generally steady and slow, appearing and disappearing from view. Over 500 acres have been added to Hawai'i's eastern coast since the activity began, and scientists say this eruptive phase is not likely to end anytime soon.

If you're lucky, you'll be able to catch creation at its most elemental—when molten lava meets the ocean, cools, and solidifies into brand-new stretches of coastline. Even if lava-viewing conditions aren't ideal, you can hike 150 miles of trails; camp amid wide expanses of 'a'ā (rough) and pahoehoe (smooth) lava; or sip cocktails at Volcano House, a hotel perched on the rim of Kīlauea Caldera. There's nothing quite like it.

- P.O. Box 52, Hawai'i Volcanoes National Park, HI 96718
- 808/985-6000
- www.nps.gov/havo
- $10 per vehicle; $5 for pedestrians and bicyclists. Ask about passes. Admission is good for seven consecutive days.
- The park is open daily, 24 hours. Kīlauea Visitor Center: 7:45 am–5 pm. Thomas A. Jaggar Museum: 8:30–5. Volcano Art Center Gallery: 9–5.

(top) Kīlauea Iki Trail
(left) Fuming rim of Pu'u' Ō'ō, source of the current eruption

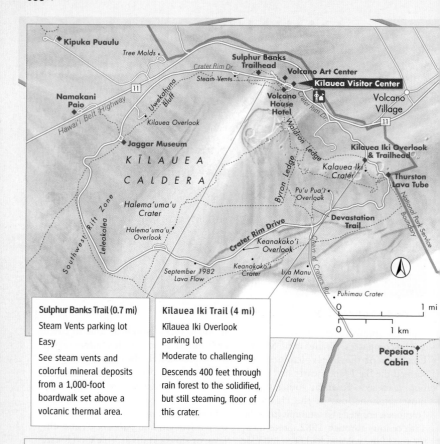

Sulphur Banks Trail (0.7 mi)

Steam Vents parking lot

Easy

See steam vents and colorful mineral deposits from a 1,000-foot boardwalk set above a volcanic thermal area.

Kīlauea Iki Trail (4 mi)

Kīlauea Iki Overlook parking lot

Moderate to challenging

Descends 400 feet through rain forest to the solidified, but still steaming, floor of this crater.

SEEING THE SUMMIT

The best way to explore the summit of Kīlauea is to cruise 11-mile Crater Rim Drive, which encircles the volcano's massive caldera. Volcano House's dining room offers front-row views of this eerie, awe-inspiring spot, which bears an uncanny resemblance to those old Apollo moon photos.

Depending on the number of stops you make, it'll take one to three hours to complete the circuit. Highlights include sulfur and steam vents, a walk-through lava tube, and the southwest rift zone—deep fissures, fractures, and gullies along Kīlauea's flanks.

There's also Halema'uma'u Crater, an awesome depression in Kīlauea Caldera measuring 3,000 feet across and nearly 300 feet deep. When skies are clear, this is a good place to see Mauna Loa and Mauna Kea.

The Thomas A. Jaggar Museum offers breathtaking looks at Halema'uma'u and Kīlauea Caldera, geologic displays, video presentations of volcanic eruptions, and exhibits of seismographs once used by volcanologists at the adjacent Hawaiian Volcano Observatory (not open to the public).

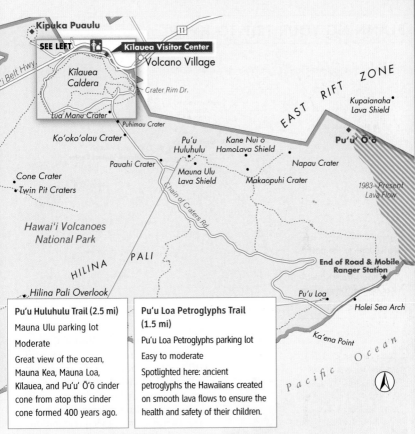

Kipuka Puaulu

SEE LEFT | Kīlauea Visitor Center

Volcano Village

Kīlauea Caldera

'Ewai'i Belt Hwy.

Crater Rim Dr.

Lua Manu Crater

Puhimau Crater

Ko'oko'olau Crater

Pu'u Huluhulu

Kane Nui o HamoLava Shield

Pauahi Crater

Pu'u 'Ō'ō

Cone Crater

Mauna Ulu Lava Shield

Napau Crater

Twin Pit Craters

Makaopuhi Crater

1983–Present Lava Flow

EAST RIFT ZONE

Kupaianaha Lava Shield

Hawai'i Volcanoes National Park

HILINA PALI

Chain of Craters Rd.

End of Road & Mobile Ranger Station

Hilina Pali Overlook

Pu'u Loa

Holei Sea Arch

Ka'ena Point

Pacific Ocean

Pu'u Huluhulu Trail (2.5 mi)

Moderate

Great view of the ocean, Mauna Kea, Mauna Loa, Kīlauea, and Pu'u' Ō'ō cinder cone from atop this cinder cone formed 400 years ago.

Pu'u Loa Petroglyphs Trail (1.5 mi)

Pu'u Loa Petroglyphs parking lot

Easy to moderate

Spotlighted here: ancient petroglyphs the Hawaiians created on smooth lava flows to ensure the health and safety of their children.

SEEING LAVA

Before you head out to find flowing lava, pinpoint the safe viewing spots at the Visitor Center. One of the best places usually is at the end of 19-mile Chain of Craters Road. Magnificent plumes of steam rise where the rivers of liquid fire meet the sea.

There are three guarantees about lava flows in HVNP. First: They constantly change. Second: Because of that, you can't predict when and where you'll be able to see them. Third: New land formed when lava meets the sea is highly unstable and can collapse at any time. Never go into areas that have been closed.

■TIP➜ The view of brilliant red-orange lava flowing from Kīlauea's east rift zone is most dramatic at night.

People watching lava flow at HVNP

PLANNING YOUR TRIP TO HVNP

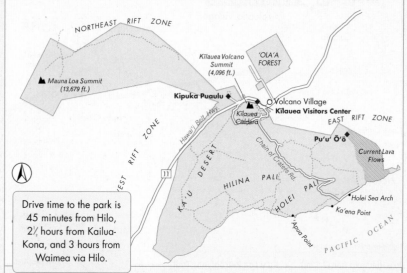

NORTHEAST RIFT ZONE

Mauna Loa Summit
(13,679 ft.)

Kīlauea Volcano
Summit
(4,096 ft.)

'OLA'A
FOREST

Kipuka Puaulu ◆

Volcano Village

Kīlauea Visitors Center

Kīlauea
Caldera

EAST RIFT ZONE

Pu'u' Ō'ō ◆

Current Lava
Flows

Hawaii Belt Hwy.

Chain of Craters Rd.

KAU DESERT

HILINA PALI

HOLEI PALI

11

Holei Sea Arch

Ka'ena Point

'Apua Point

PACIFIC OCEAN

Drive time to the park is 45 minutes from Hilo, 2½ hours from Kailua-Kona, and 3 hours from Waimea via Hilo.

Lava entering the ocean

WHERE TO START

Begin your visit at the Visitor Center, where you'll find maps, books, and DVDs; information on trails, ranger-led walks, and special events; and current weather, road, and lava-viewing conditions. Free volcano-related film showings, lectures, and other presentations are regularly scheduled.

WEATHER

Weather conditions fluctuate daily, sometimes hourly. It can be rainy and chilly even during the summer; the temperature usually is 14° cooler at the 4,000-foot-high summit of Kīlauea than at sea level.

Expect hot, dry, and windy coastal conditions at the end of Chain of Craters Road. Bring rain gear, and wear layered clothing, sturdy shoes, sunglasses, a hat, and sunscreen.

Photographer on lava table filming lava flow into ocean

FOOD

It's a good idea to bring your own favorite snacks and beverages. Stock up on provisions in Volcano Village, 1½ miles away.

PARK PROGRAMS

Rangers lead daily walks into different areas; check with the Visitor Center for details as times and destinations depend on weather conditions.

Over 60 companies hold permits to lead hikes at HVNP. Good choices are Hawai'i Forest & Trail (www.hawaii-forest.com), Hawaiian Walkways (www.hawaiianwalkways.com), and Native Guide Hawai'i (www.nativeguidehawaii.com).

CAUTION

"Vog" (volcanic smog) can cause headaches; breathing difficulties; lethargy; irritations of the skin, eyes, nose, and throat; and other health problems. Pregnant women, young children, and people with asthma and heart conditions are most susceptible, and should avoid areas such as Halema'uma'u Crater where fumes are thick.

Wear long pants and boots or closed-toe shoes with good tread for hikes on lava. Stay on marked trails and step carefully. Lava is composed of 50% silica (glass) and can cause serious injury if you fall.

Carry at least 2 quarts of water on hikes. Temperatures near lava flows can rise above 100°F, and dehydration, heat exhaustion, and sunstroke are common consequences of extended exposure to intense sunlight and high temperatures.

Remember that these are active volcanoes, and eruptions can cause parts of the park to close at any time. Check the park's Web site or call ahead for last-minute updates before your visit.

Volcanologists inspecting a vent in the East Rift Zone

and adventurous. ✉ *16-1953 7th Rd., Hawaiian Acres, Off Hwy. 11, between Kurtistown and Mountain View* ☎ *808/217–2363* ⊕ *www. kilaueacavernsoffire.com* 🖃 *$29 for walking tour, $79 for adventure tour* ⊙ *By appointment only.*

Volcano Farmers' Market. Local produce, flowers, and food products are on offer every Sunday morning at one of the better farmers' markets on the island. It's best to get there early, before 8 am, as vendors tend to sell out of the best stuff quickly. There's also a great bookstore (paperbacks 25¢, hardbacks 50¢, and magazines 10¢), and a thrift store with clothes and knickknacks. ■ TIP➔ There are also more prepared-food vendors at the Volcano market than Hilo, with such temptations as fresh baked breads and pastries, vegetarian lunch items, and homemade Thai food. ✉ *Cooper Center, 19-4030 Wright Rd.* ☎ *808/936–9705* ⊕ *www.thecoopercenter. org* ⊙ *Sun. 6–10 am.*

BEACHES

Don't believe anyone who tells you that the Big Island lacks beaches. It's just one of the myths about Hawai'i's largest island that has no basis in fact.

It's not so much that the Big Island has fewer than the other Islands, just that there's more island so getting to the beaches can be slightly less convenient. That said, there are plenty of those perfect white-sand stretches you think of when you hear "Hawai'i," and the added bonus of black- and green-sand beaches, thanks to the age of the island and its active volcanoes. New beaches appear—and disappear—regularly. In 1989 a black-sand beach, Kamoamoa, formed when molten lava shattered as it hit cold ocean waters; it was closed by new lava flows in 1992. It's part of the ongoing process of the volcano's creation and change dynamic.

The bulk of the island's beaches are on the northwest part of the island, along the Kohala Coast. Black-sand beaches and green-sand beaches are in the southern region, along the coast nearest the volcano. On the eastern side of the island, beaches tend to be of the rocky-coast–surging-surf variety, but there are still a few worth visiting, and this is where the Hawaiian shoreline is at its most picturesque.

KAILUA-KONA

There are a few good sandy beaches in the area near Kailua-Kona town. However, the coastline is generally rugged black lava rock, so don't expect long stretches of wide golden sand. The beaches near Kailua-Kona get lots of use by local residents and visitors will enjoy them, too. Excellent opportunities for snorkeling, scuba diving, swimming, kayaking, and other water sports are easy to find.

The beaches here are listed from north to south.

Kaloko–Honokōhau National Historical Park. There are few beaches with as many old Hawaiian archaeological ruins as these two, sheltered in a 1,160-acre park near Honokōhau Harbor, just north of Kailua-Kona

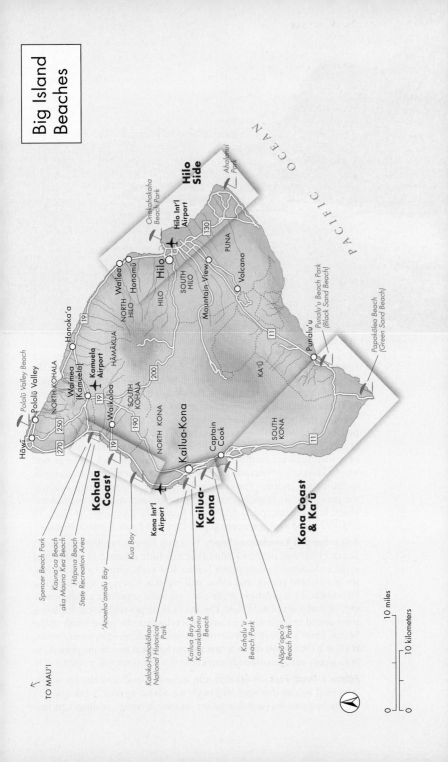

Big Island Beaches

TO MAUI

Hāwī

Pololū Valley
Pololū Valley Beach

270
250

NORTH KOHALA

Waimea (Kamuela)
19
Kamuela Airport

Honoka'a
19

Spencer Beach Park
Kauna'oa Beach aka Mauna Kea Beach
Hāpuna Beach State Recreation Area

HĀMĀKUA

Waikoloa

200

SOUTH KOHALA

NORTH HILO

Wailea
Honomū

Kohala Coast

'Anaeho'omalu Bay

Kua Bay

Kona Int'l Airport
19

190

NORTH KONA

HILO

SOUTH HILO

Hilo Int'l Airport
Hilo

Onekahakaha Beach Park

Hilo Side

130

PUNA

Mountain-View

Volcano
Volcano

Kailua-Kona
Kailua-Kona

Captain Cook

SOUTH KONA

111

KA'Ū

Punalu'u
Punalu'u Beach Park (Black Sand Beach)

Ahalanui Park

PACIFIC OCEAN

Papakōlea Beach (Green Sand Beach)

Kona Coast & Ka'ū

Kaloko-Honokōhau National Historical Park

Kailua Bay & Kamakahonu Beach

Kahalu'u Beach Park

Nāpō'opo'o Beach Park

0   10 miles

0   10 kilometers

Green Sand Beach is located near the tip of the southernmost point of Big Island, Ka Lae.

town. Both are good for swimming. ʻAiʻopio, a few yards north of the harbor, is a small beach with calm, protected swimming areas (good for kids) and great snorkeling in the water near the archaeological site of Hale o Mono. There are toilets at this beach. **Honokōhau Beach**, a ¾-mi stretch with ruins of ancient fishponds, is also north of the harbor and has no facilities. The park seeks to preserve early Hawaiian archaeological resources including *heiau* (an ancient Hawaiian place of worship), house platforms, fishponds, petroglyph rock etchings, and more. The park's wetlands provide refuge to a number of waterbirds, including the endemic Hawaiian stilt and coot. For information about the park, visit its headquarters, a five- to 10-minute drive away. **Amenities:** Parking lot, toilets. ⌂ *74-425 Kealakehe Pkwy.* ✛ *Off Hwy. 19* ☎ *808/329–6881* ⊕ *www.nps.gov* ⊗ *Park road gate 8 am–3:30 pm.*

Kailua Bay and Kamakahonu Beach. Fronting King Kamehameha's Kona Beach Hotel and next to Kailua Pier, this little crescent of white sand is the only beach in downtown Kailua-Kona. Protected by the harbor, the water here is nice and calm, making this a perfect spot for kids. For adults it's a great place for a swim, some stand-up paddleboarding, or just a lazy beach day. The water is surprisingly clear for being surrounded by an active pier and snorkeling can be good north of the beach. There's a kiosk with snorkeling and kayaking equipment rentals. ■ TIP➔ A little family of sea turtles likes to hang out next to the seawall, so keep an eye out. **Amenities:** Beach umbrellas, showers, toilets. ⌂ *Aliʻi Dr.*

Kahaluʻu Beach Park. Snorkelers can actually hand-feed the unusually tame reef fish at this spot, although we advise against it because fish fed by humans become dependent on easy feedings and start to lose

their survival instincts. Kahalu'u was a favorite of King Kalākaua, whose summer cottage is on the grounds of the neighboring Outrigger Keauhou Beach Resort. The salt-and-pepper beach is a combination of white and black sand mixed with lava and coral pebbles. This is one of the Big Island's most popular swimming and snorkeling sites, thanks to the fringing reef that helps keep the waters calm. But outside the reef there are very strong rip currents, so caution is advised. ■TIP→ Experienced surfers find good waves to ride beyond the reef, and scuba divers like the shore dives—shallow ones inside the breakwater, deeper ones outside. **Amenities:** Lifeguard, grills, parking lot, picnic tables, shower, toilets. ⊠ *Ali'i Dr.* ✛ *5½ mi south of Kailua-Kona* ☎ *808/961–8311.*

BEACHES KEY

🚻	*Restroom*
🚿	*Showers*
🏄	*Surfing*
🤿	*Snorkel/Scuba*
👪	*Good for kids*
🅿	*Parking*

THE KONA COAST AND KA'Ū

Don't expect to find sparkling white-sand beaches on the rugged and rocky coasts of South Kona and Ka'ū. What you will find is something a bit more rare and well worth the visit: black- and green-sand beaches. And there's the chance to see the endangered Hawaiian green sea turtles close up.

Beaches are listed from north to south.

Nāpō'opo'o Beach Park. There's no real beach here, but don't let that deter you—this is a great spot and a historically significant one. It's where Captain James Cook landed in late 1778 to refurbish his ships. When he returned in 1779 he was killed in a skirmish with Hawaiians; a monument marks the spot on the north end of the bay. Kealakekua Bay is surrounded by high green cliffs, so the water's usually fairly calm and clear, making it ideal for swimming. Bring a mask along, as the snorkeling in the Kealakekua Bay Underwater Marine Reserve is superb. It's a great place to spot varied marine life, schools of colorful reef fish, corals, and more. This is also a great kayaking spot. You can also take a snorkel, scuba, or glass-bottom boat tour from Keauhou Bay. ⚠ Be aware of the off-limits area (in case of rockfalls) marked by orange buoys. **Amenities:** Parking lot. ⊠ *Kealakekua Bay* ✛ *End of Nāpō'opo'o Rd., off Hwy. 11* ☎ *808/961–8311.*

★ **Papakōlea Beach** *(Green Sand Beach)*. Tired of the same old gold-, white-, or black-sand beach? Then how about a green-sand beach?

The calm Kailua Bay is an excellent spot for rowing, snorkeling, and swimming.

You'll need good hiking shoes or sneakers at the very least to get to this olive green crescent, one of the most unusual beaches on the island. It lies at the base of Pu'u o Mahana, at Mahana Bay, where a cinder cone formed during an early eruption of Mauna Loa. The greenish tint is caused by an accumulation of olivine crystals that form in volcanic eruptions. The dry barren landscape is totally surreal. The surf is often rough, and swimming is hazardous due to strong currents, so caution is advised. Take the road toward the left at the end of the paved road to Ka Lae (South Point) about 12 mi off Highway 11. Park at the end of the road. ⚠ Anyone trying to charge you for parking is running a scam. To reach the beach, follow the 2-mi coastal trail, which will end in a steep and dangerous descent down the cliff side on an unimproved trail. The hike will take about two hours each way so make sure to bring lots of drinking water. (4WD vehicles are no longer permitted on the trail). **Amenities:** None. ✉ *Off Hwy. 11 ✛ 2½ mi northeast of South Point.*

★ **Punalu'u Beach Park** *(Black Sand Beach).* Endangered Hawaiian green sea turtles nest in the black sand of this beautiful and easily accessible

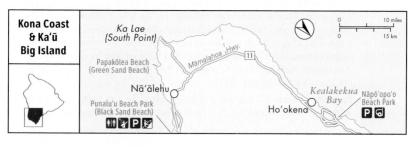

beach. You can see them feeding on the seaweed along the surf break or napping on the sand. You can even swim with the turtles; they're used to people and will swim along right next to you. (Resist the urge to touch them, though.) However, strong shoreward currents make being in the water here a hazard. Don't venture far out, and avoid going out past the boat ramp as very strong rip currents are active. ■ TIP→ It's quite rocky in the water, even close to shore—you might want to bring a pair of reef shoes if you plan to swim. The beach is a long black-sand crescent backed by low dunes with some rocky outcroppings at the shoreline. **Amenities:** Camping facilities (permit required), grills, parking lot, picnic tables, showers, toilets across the road. ⊠ *Hwy. 11 ✛ 27 mi south of Hawai'i Volcanoes National Park* ☎ 808/961–8311.

THE KOHALA COAST

Most of the white sandy beaches are found on the Kohala Coast, which is, understandably, home to the majority of the island's first-class resorts. Hawai'i's beaches are public property. The resorts are required to provide public access to the beach, so don't be frightened off by a guard shack and a fancy sign. There is some limited public parking as well. The resort beaches aside, there are some real hidden gems on the Kohala Coast accessible only by boat, four-wheel drive, or a 15- to 20-minute hike. It's well worth the effort to get to at least one of these. ■ TIP→ The west side tends to be calmer, but the surf still gets rough in winter.

The beaches here are listed in order from north (farthest from Kona) to south.

Pololū Valley Beach. On the North Kohala peninsula, this is one of the Big Island's most scenic black-sand beaches. About 8 mi past Hāwī town, Highway 270 terminates at the overlook of remote Pololū Valley. Beach access is gained by a 15-minute hike down (twice as long back up) a generally steep and rocky trail that can be muddy and slippery. Caution is advised. The beach itself is a nice wide expanse of fine black sand surrounded by sheer green cliffs and backed by high dunes dotted with pine trees. A gurgling stream leads from the beach to the back of the valley. ⚠ **This is not a particularly safe swimming beach even though locals do swim, body board, and surf here. Dangerous rip currents and usually rough surf pose a real hazard.** And because this is a remote, isolated area far from emergency help, extreme caution is advised. **Amenities:** None. ⊠ *End of Hwy. 270.*

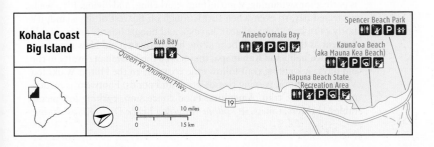

🕏 **Spencer Beach Park.** This smaller beach, gently sloping with white sand and a few pebbles, is popular with local families because of its reef-protected waters. ■ TIP→ **It's probably the safest beach in west Hawai'i for young children.** It's also safe for swimming year-round, which makes it an excellent spot for a lazy day at the beach. Unfortunately, it does tend to get crowded on weekends, and the beach is often dotted with litter, but the water is crystal clear, although there aren't loads of fish here. The beach park lies just below Pu'ukoholā Heiau National Historic Park, site of the historic temple built by King Kamehameha the Great in 1795. **Amenities:** Lifeguard on weekends and holidays only, grills, parking lot, picnic tables, showers, toilets. ⊠ *Off Hwy. 270* ⊹ *Uphill from Kawaihae Harbor* ☎ 808/961–8311.

Fodor'sChoice **Kauna'oa Beach** *(Mauna Kea Beach).* Hands-down one of the most beau-
★   tiful beaches on the island, Kauna'oa is a long white crescent of sand. The beach, which fronts the Mauna Kea Beach Hotel, slopes very gradually. It's a great place for snorkeling. When conditions permit, there are good body- and board surfing also. Currents can be strong, and power-ful winter waves can be dangerous, so be careful. ■ TIP→ **Public parking is limited to only 40 spaces, so it's best to arrive before 10 am. If the lot is full, head to nearby Hāpuna Beach, where a huge parking lot is never full, and try this spot again a different morning. It's worth it!** **Amenities:** Life-guard, parking lot, showers, toilets. ⊠ *Hwy. 19* ⊹ *Entry through gate to Mauna Kea Beach Resort.*

Fodor'sChoice **Hāpuna Beach State Recreation Area.** By any measurement, this is one
★   fine beach. Guidebooks usually say it's a toss-up between Hāpuna and Kauna'oa for "best beach" on the island, but most locals give the prize to Hāpuna. There is ample parking so you don't have to get here at dawn, although the lot can fill up by midday. And while the north end of the beach fronts the Hāpuna Beach Prince Hotel, rest assured that this is a public beach. The beach itself is a long (½-mi), white, perfect crescent, one of the Big Island's largest. The turquoise water is very calm in summer, with just enough rolling waves to make bodysurfing or boogie-boarding fun, but it can be rough in winter. There's some excellent snorkeling around the jagged rocks that border the beach on either side, but a strong current means it's only for experienced swim-mers. **Amenities:** Lifeguard, food concession, grills/firepits, parking lot, picnic tables, showers, toilets. ⊠ *Hwy. 19* ⊹ *Near mile marker 69, at Hāpuna Beach Prince Hotel* ☎ 808/974–6200.

★   **'Anaeho'omalu Beach** *(A-Bay).* This expansive beach of golden sand mixed with black lava grains fronts the Waikoloa Beach Marriott and is perfect for swimming, windsurfing, snorkeling, and diving. It's a well-protected bay, so even when surf is rough on the rest of the island, it's fairly calm here. Snorkel gear, kayaks, and boogie boards are available for rent at the north end. Behind the beach are two old Hawaiian fish-ponds, **Ku'uali'i** and **Kahapapa**, that served the Hawaiian royalty in the old days. A walking trail follows the coastline to the Hilton Waikoloa Village next door, passing by tide pools and ponds. Footwear is recom-mended for the trail. **Amenities:** Food concession, parking lot, picnic tables, showers, toilets. ⊹ *Follow Waikoloa Beach Dr. to Kings' Shops,* *then turn left; parking lot and beach right-of-way south of Waikoloa Beach Marriott.*

Kua Bay. Remoteness does have its merits at this lovely beach, the northernmost beach in the stretch of coast that comprises Kekaha Kai State Park. At one time you had to hike over a few miles of unmarked, rocky trail to get here, which kept many people out. Today, there is a separate entrance and a parking lot, making this bay much more accessible. It's easy to understand why area residents would be so protective. This is one of the most beautiful bays you will ever see—the water is crystal clear, deep aquamarine, and peaceful in summer. Rocky shores on either side keep the beach from getting too windy in the afternoon. ⚠ The surf here can get very rough in winter. **Amenities:** Picnic tables, showers, toilets, parking lot. ☒ *Hwy. 19* ✛ *North of mile marker 88.*

4

HILO

There are no real beaches along the jagged cliffs of the Hāmākua Coast, but there are a few surf spots and swimming holes worth an afternoon stop. Hilo isn't exactly known for its beautiful white beaches, but there are some in the area that provide good swimming and snorkeling opportunities, and most are surrounded by lush rain forest.

Beaches are listed from north to south.

🐚 **Onekahakaha Beach Park.** A white-sand beach with shallow, enclosed tide pools makes this a favorite for Hilo families with small children. The protected pools are great places to look for Hawaiian marine life. The water is usually rough beyond the line of large boulders protecting the inner tide pools. Caution is advised in times of heavy surf. **Amenities:** Lifeguard on weekends and holidays only, parking lot, picnic tables, showers, toilets. ☒ *Kalaniana'ole Ave.* ✛ *3 mi east of Hilo* ☎ *808/961–8311.*

Ahalanui Park. This 3-acre beach park has a ½-acre pond—fresh spring water mixed with seawater—heated by volcanic steam. There's nothing like swimming in this geothermal pool, especially when the nearby ocean is rough. ■ TIP➔ The pool has had ongoing bacterial contamination problems that are typical of some ocean tidal pools in Hawai'i. Those with skin-lesion problems, or chronic conditions like psoriasis may want to avoid the water here. Others should have no problem. Check with the lifeguard on duty, and heed all posted signs. **Amenities:** Lifeguard, grills, picnic tables, showers, toilets. ☒ *Hwy. 137* ✛ *2½ mi south of junction of Hwy. 132* ☎ *808/961–8311.*

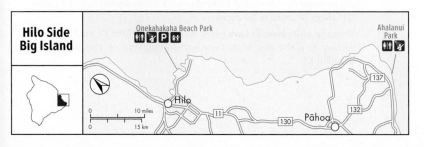

WATER SPORTS AND TOURS

All the Hawaiian Islands are surrounded by the Pacific Ocean, making them some of the world's greatest natural playgrounds. But certain experiences are even better on the Big Island: nighttime scuba-diving trips to see manta rays; deep-sea fishing in Kona's fabled waters, where dozens of Pacific blue marlin of 1,000 pounds or more have been caught; kayaking among the dolphins in Kealakekua Bay; and sighting humpback whales on a whale-watching cruise.

> **WORD OF MOUTH**
>
> "[Mauna Kea Beach] is possibly the best beach on the Big Island if you can get to it. It is long, white, and beautiful. When I was last there, the waves were small to nil, making it an excellent beach to swim and play. [Hāpuna Beach] is another beautiful white beach. The water is clear and picturesque. There is a large parking lot and tons of people. The waves were moderate—good for boogie boarding or playing in the surf."
> —wbpiii

BODY BOARDING AND BODYSURFING

Often the body boarders stay closer to shore and leave the outside breaks to the board surfers. Or the board surfers may stick to one side of the beach and the body boarders to the other. Sure, there's some good-natured trash talking between the groups, but nothing more. The truth is, body boarding (often called "boogie boarding" in homage to the first commercial manufacturer of this slick little flexible foam board) is a blast. ■TIP→ **Novice body boarders should catch shore-break waves only. Ask lifeguards or locals for the best spots.**

BEST SPOTS

When conditions are right, **Hāpuna Beach State Recreation Area** (⊠ *Hwy. 19* ✛ *Near mile marker 69*), north of Kailua-Kona, is fabulous. The water is very calm in summer, with just enough rolling waves for body-surfing or body boarding. But this beach isn't known as the "broken-neck capital" for nothing. Ask the lifeguards about conditions before heading into the water, and remember that if almost no one is in the water, there's a good reason for it.

Much of the sand at **White Sands, Magic Sands, or Disappearing Sands Beach Park** (⊠ *Ali'i Dr.* ✛ *4½ mi south of Kailua-Kona*) washes out to sea and forms a sandbar just offshore. This causes the waves to break in a way that's great for intermediate or advanced body boarding. There can be nasty rip currents at high tide. ■TIP→ **If you're not using fins, wear reef shoes because of the rocks.**

North of Hilo, **Honoli'i Cove** (✛ *Access road off Hwy. 19, just past mile marker 4*) is the best body boarding–surfing spot on the east side of the island.

EQUIPMENT

Equipment rental shacks are located at many beaches and boat harbors, along the highway, and at most resorts. Body board rental rates are anywhere from $5–$15 per day and around $60 per week. Ask the vendor if he'll throw in a pair of fins—some will for no extra charge.

Orchid Land Surf Shop. This shop has a wide variety of water sports and surf equipment for sale or rent. They stock professional custom surfboards, body boards, and surf apparel, and do repairs. You can rent your body board here for $12 a day. ⊠ *262 Kamehameha Ave., Hilo* ☎ *808/935–1533* ⊕ *www.orchidlandsurf.com.*

Pacific Vibrations. This surf shop sells it all, from clothing to surf gear. You can rent a Morey or LMNOP body board for $5 a day, but you have to buy or bring your own fins. If you keep your board for more than five days, the rental rate drops down to $3 a day. They rent surfboards, too. ⊠ *75-5702 Likana La., at Ali'i Dr., Kailua-Kona* ☎ *808/329–4140.*

DEEP-SEA FISHING

Along the Kona Coast you can find some of the world's most exciting "blue-water" fishing. Although July, August, and September are peak months, with the best fishing and a number of tournaments, charter fishing goes on year-round. You don't have to compete to experience the thrill of landing a Pacific blue marlin or other big-game fish. Some 60 charter boats, averaging 26 to 58 feet, are available for hire, most of them out of **Honokōhau Harbor,** north of Kailua-Kona.

For an exclusive charter, prices generally range from $400 to $750 for a half-day trip (about four hours) and $600 to $1,300 for a full day at sea (about eight hours). For share charters, rates range from $100 to $140 per person for a half day and $200 for a full day. If fuel prices continue increasing, expect charter costs to rise. Most boats are licensed to take up to six passengers, in addition to the crew. Tackle, bait, and ice are furnished, but you'll usually have to bring your own lunch. You won't be able to keep your catch, although if you ask, many captains will send you home with a few fillets.

Big fish are weighed in daily at **Honokōhau Harbor's Fuel Dock.** Show up at 11 am to watch the weigh-in of the day's catch from the morning charters, or 3:30 pm for the afternoon charters. If you're lucky, you'll get to see a "grander" weighing in at 1,000-plus pounds. A surprising number of these are caught just outside Kona Harbor. ■ **TIP→ On Kona's Waterfront Row look for the "Grander's Wall" of anglers with their prizes.**

BOATS AND CHARTERS

Charter Locker. This company can provide information on various charter boat fishing trips and make all the arrangements—they can even book you on the luxurious *Blue Hawai'i,* which has air-conditioned staterooms for overnight trips. ☎ *808/326–2553* ⊕ *www.charterlocker.com.*

Honokōhau Harbor Charter Desk. With about 60 boats on the books, this place can take care of almost anyone. You can make arrangements through your hotel activity desk, but we suggest you go down to the desk at the harbor and look things over for yourself. ⊠ *74-381*

Kealakehe Pkwy., Kailua-Kona ☎ *808/329–5735 or 888/566–2487* ⊕ *www.charterdesk.com.*

Humdinger Sportfishing. This game fisher guide has more than three decades of fishing experience in Kona waters. The experienced crew are marlin specialists. The 37-foot *Humdinger* has the latest in electronics and top-line rods and reels. Half-day exclusive charters begin at $600, full-day exclusives at $950. ☎ *808/936–3034 or 800/926–2374* ⊕ *www.humdinger-online.com.*

Illusions Sportfishing. Captain Steve Sahines is one of Kona's top fishing tourney producers with several years of experience. The 39-foot *Illusions* is fully equipped with galley, restrooms, an air-conditioned cabin for guest comfort, plus the latest in fishing equipment. Half-day exclusive charters begin at $500, full-day exclusives at $800. ☎ *808/960–7371* ⊕ *www.illusionssportfishing.com.*

Pamela Big Game Fishing. This family-operated company has been in the business since 1967. The 38-foot *Pamela* is captained by either Peter Hoogs or his son. They've also got an informative Web site with information on sportfishing. Half-day exclusive charters begin at $550, full-day exclusives at $950. ☎ *808/329–3600 or 800/762–7546* ⊕ *www. konabiggamefishing.com.*

KAYAKING

The leeward west coast areas of the Big Island are protected for the most part from the northeast trade winds, making for ideal near-shore kayaking conditions. There are miles and miles of uncrowded Kona and Kohala coastline to explore, presenting close-up views of stark raw lava rock shores and cliffs, lava tube sea caves, pristine secluded coves, and deserted beaches.

BEST SPOTS

Hilo Bay (⊕ *at the intersection of Banyan Way and Banyan Dr., about 1 mi from downtown Hilo*) is a favorite kayak spot. The best place to put in is at **Reeds Bay Beach Park.** Most afternoons you can share the bay with local paddling clubs. Stay inside the breakwater unless the ocean is calm (or you're feeling unusually adventurous). Conditions range from extremely calm to quite choppy.

Kailua Bay and Kamakahonu Beach (⊠ *Ali'i Dr.* ⊕ *next to Kailua Pier, south of Kailua-Kona*) The small, sandy beach that fronts the King Kamehameha Kona Beach Hotel is a perfect place to launch your kayak. Because the bay is protected by the harbor, the water here is especially calm and teeming with ocean life. It's easy to get to and great for all skill levels.

The excellent snorkeling and the likelihood of seeing dolphins makes **Kealakekua Bay** (⊠ *Bottom of Nāpō'opo'o Rd., south of Kailua-Kona*) one of the most popular kayak spots on the Big Island. The bay is usually calm, and the kayaking is not difficult—except during high surf. If you're there in the morning, you may very well see spinner dolphins. Depending on your strength and enthusiasm, you'll cross the bay in 30–45 minutes. Recent changes to state rules have made it illegal to land kayaks without a permit at the ancient canoe landing about 50 yards to the left of the **Captain Cook Monument,** however, you are allowed to snorkel from your kayak over to the monument. You can also download an application for a free permit to put in at the canoe landing before you go at ⊕ *www.hawaiistateparks.org/announcements* or call ☎ *808/974-6200.* (The state limits landing permits to 10 per day and it can take three to five days to get a permit, so plan ahead). The monument marks the landfall of Captain James Cook in 1778, the first European to visit Hawai'i. The coral around the monument itself is too fragile to land a kayak, but it makes for fabulous snorkeling.

EQUIPMENT, LESSONS, AND TOURS

There are several rental outfitters on Highway 11 between mile markers 110 and 113.

Aloha Kayak Co. This Honalo outfitter offers guided Wet-N-Wild Kayak Snorkel/Cave Tours out of Keauhou Bay—a four-hour morning tour ($89 per person) and a 2½-hour afternoon version ($69 per person). The morning tour includes sandwich lunch, snacks, and cold drinks; the afternoon tour includes snacks and drinks. Tours depart from Keauhou Bay. There's also an evening one-hour manta kayak snorkel tour ($99 per person). Daily kayak rental rates: single $35, double $60, triple $85. ⊠ *79-7248 Māmalahoa Hwy., Honalo* ☎ *808/322–2868 or 877/322–1444* ⊕ *www.alohakayak.com.*

Kona Boys. On the highway above Kealakekua Bay, this full-service outfitter handles kayaks, body boards, stand-up paddleboards, snorkeling gear, and related equipment. Single-seat kayaks are $47 daily (doubles $67), weekly rates are $150 (single) and $275 (double). The Boys also lead two different half-day guided trips that include kayaking and snorkeling ($125 per person, includes lunch, snacks, and drinks). One excursion goes along the Kona coastline, while the other trip explores Kamakahonu Cove and Pawai Bay. There's also a Sunset Kayak & Snorkel Tour for $125 per person. The Kona Boys recently set up a new beach shack location next to Kailua Pier, behind the King Kamehameha Kona Beach Hotel, that offers the same rental equipment as well as Hawaiian outrigger canoe rides and charters. ⊠ *79-7539 Mamalahoa Hwy., Kealakekua* ⊠ *75–5660 Palani Rd., Kailua-Kona* ☎ *808/328–1234* ⊕ *www.konaboys.com.*

Ocean Safari's Kayak Adventures. On the guided 3½-hour morning Sea Cave Tour that begins in Keauhou Bay, you can visit lava tube sea caves along the coast, then swim ashore for a snack. The kayaks are on the beach so you don't have to hassle with transporting them. The cost is $64 per person. A two-hour Early Riser Dolphin Quest Tour leaves at 7 am on Tuesdays. It's $35 per person. Kayak daily rental rates are $25 for singles and $40 for doubles. ⊠ *End of Kamehameha III Rd., Kailua-Kona* ☎ *808/326–4699* ⊕ *www.oceansafariskayaks.com.*

Pineapple Park. Pineapple Park is actually a hostel with locations in Hilo, Kona, and Mountain View, but they are also one of the only outfitters for kayak rentals in Hilo. Single kayaks are $35, doubles are $55, and triples are $65 per day (good for 24 hours) and the rental price also includes safety equipment such as life jackets, oars, a bag to keep all your gear dry, and a harness kit to strap your kayak to your car. There's a 10% discount if you book your rental a day in advance. Pineapple Park does not offer guided tours. Reeds Bay, where many people put in, is about a three-minute drive away. ✉ *860 Piilani Street, Hilo* ☎ *808/323–2224 or 877/800–3800* ⊕ *pineapple-park.com.*

SAILING

For old salts and novice sailors alike, there's nothing like a cruise on the Kona or Kohala coasts of the Big Island. Calm waters, serene shores, and the superb scenery of Mauna Kea, Mauna Loa, and Hualālai, the Big Island's primary volcanic peaks, make for a great sailing adventure.

Maile Charters. Maile Charters offers unique around-the-Islands sailing adventures on the 50-foot GulfStar sloop, *Maile.* Sails range from half-day excursions to five-day journeys to Maui, Moloka'i, or Lāna'i. Fees start at $979 for six passengers for a sunset charter, and go up to $6,797 for five days with a maximum of four adult passengers. Trips are also available for full-day and one, two, or three nights. ✉ *Kawaihae Harbor, Kawaihae* ☎ *808/960–9744* ⊕ *www.adventuresailing.com.*

SCUBA DIVING

The Big Island's underwater world is the setting for a dramatic diving experience. With generally calm waters, vibrant coral reefs and rock formations, and plunging underwater drop-offs, the Kona and Kohala coasts provide some great scuba diving. There are also some good dive locations in east Hawai'i, not far from the Hilo area. On special night dives to see manta rays, divers descend with bright underwater lights that attract plankton, which in turn attracts these otherworldly creatures.

The best spots to dive are listed in order from north to south; all are on the west coast.

BEST SPOTS

Just south of Hapuna Beach State Recreation Area is **Puakō** (✉ *Puakō Rd.* ✉ *off Hwy. 19*), which offers easy entry to some fine reef diving. Deep chasms, sea caves, rock arches, and more abound with varied marine life.

The water is usually very clear at **Pawai Bay Marine Reserve** (✉ *At beginning of Kuakini Hwy.* ✢ *Just north of Old Kona Airport Beach Park*). This bay near Kailua-Kona has numerous underwater sea caves, arches, and rock formations, plus lots of marine life. It can be busy with snorkel boats but is an easy dive spot.

One of Kona's best night dive spots is **Manta Village** (✉ *Off Sheraton Keauhou Bay Resort at Keauhou*). A booking with a scuba/snorkel night dive operator is required for the short boat ride to the area. If you're a diving or snorkeling fanatic, it's well worth it for the experience of seeing the manta rays.

A great spot to see manta rays is **Garden Eel Cove** (✉ *Off the Kona International Airport at Keahole*). At this site you're likely to spot hundreds

The Kona Coast's relatively calm waters and colorful coral reefs are excellent for scuba diving.

of tiny garden eels darting out from their sandy homes as well as manta rays somersaulting overhead as they feast on a plankton supper. There's also a steep drop-off and lots of marine life.

Come to **Pu'uhonua O Hōnaunau** *(Place of Refuge)* (⊠ *Rte. 160* ✛ *About 20 mi south of Kailua-Kona* ⊕ *www.nps.gov/puho*) for the steep drop-offs and dramatic views. A few dive boats come here but because boats can't drop anchor in this spot, most divers get in the water from the shore on the north end.

EQUIPMENT, LESSONS, AND TOURS

There are quite a few good dive shops on the Kona Coast. Most are happy to take on all customers, but a few focus on specific types of trips. Most instructors rent out dive equipment and snorkel gear, as well as underwater cameras. A few organize otherworldly manta-ray dives at night or whale-watching cruises in season.

★ **Aloha Dive Company.** Native-born Hawaiian and PADI master dive instructor Mike Nakachi, together with wife Buffy (a registered nurse and PADI dive instructor) and Earl Kam (a videographer and PADI dive master) have been instructing since 1990. Although they'll take anybody, they're biased in favor of experienced divers who want unique locations and know how to take care of themselves in deep water. Their boat is fast enough to take you places other companies can't reach. They're fun people with great attitudes. Rates begin at $140 for a two-tank boat dive and go up to $250 for a three-tank remote boat dive. ⊠ *Kailua-Kona* ☎ *808/325–5560.*

Jack's Diving Locker. The best place for novice and intermediate divers (certified to 60 feet), Jack's Diving Locker has trained and certified tens of thousands of divers since opening in 1981. The company has four boats that can each take between 10 to 18 divers. With more than 80 established dive sites along the Kona coast, Jack's has plenty to offer whether you want to see turtles, manta rays, garden eels, or schools of barracuda. It does a good job looking out for customers and protecting the coral reef. Before each charter the dive master briefs divers on various options and then everyone votes on where to go. Jack's also runs the biggest dive shop on the island, and has classrooms and a dive pool for beginning instruction. ■TIP→ Kona's best dive bargain for newbies is the introductory shore dive from Kailua Pier for $55. ⊠ 75-5813 Ali'i Dr., Kailua-Kona ☎ 808/329-7585 ⊕ www.jacksdivinglocker.com.

★ **Torpedo Tours.** Mike and Nikki Milligan specialize in small groups, which means you'll spend more time diving and less time hanging out on the boat waiting to dive. Two-tank morning dives run $110, one-tank manta ray dives are $89, or you can combine the two and do a late-afternoon dive plus a manta-ray dive for a very reasonable $130. Torpedo Tours will take snorkelers along with divers, and provides its namesake torpedo scooters to both for $30. The scooters allow both divers and snorkelers to cover more ground with less kicking and are a fun novelty to test out. ⊠ Honokōhau Harbor, Nā Pali Kai II boat, 74-425 Kealakehe Pkwy., Kailua-Kona ☎ 808/938–0405 ⊕ www.torpedotours.com.

SNORKELING

A favorite pastime on the Big Island, snorkeling is perhaps one of the easiest and most enjoyable water activities for visitors. By floating on the surface, looking through your mask, and breathing through your snorkel, you can see lava rock formations, sea arches, sea caves, and coral reefs teeming with colorful tropical fish. While the Kona and Kohala coasts have more beaches, bays, and quiet coves to snorkel, the east side around Hilo and at Kapoho are also great places to get in the water.

If you don't bring your own equipment, you can easily rent all the gear needed from a beach activities vendor, who will happily provide directions to the best sites for snorkeling in the area. For access to deeper water and assistance from an experienced crew, you can opt for a snorkel cruise.

BEST SPOTS

Since ancient times, the waters around **Kahalu'u Beach Park** (⊠ Ali'i Dr. ✛ 5½ mi south of Kailua-Kona) have been a traditional net-fishing area (the water is shallower here than at Kealakekua). The swimming is good, and the snorkeling is even better. You'll see angelfish, parrot fish, needlefish, puffer fish, and a lot more. ■TIP→ Stay inside the breakwater and don't stray too far, as dangerous and unpredictable currents swirl outside the bay.

Kapoho Tide Pools (⊠ End of Kapoho-Kai Road ✛ Off Hwy. 137) has the best snorkeling on the Hilo side. Fingers of lava from the 1960 flow that destroyed the town of Kapoho jut into the sea to form a network of tide pools. Conditions near the shore are excellent for beginners and challenging enough farther out for experienced snorkelers.

Fodor's Choice
★ **Kealakekua Bay** (⊠ *Bottom of Nāpō'opo'o Rd.* ✛ *South of Kailua-Kona*) is, hands-down, the best snorkel spot on the island, with fabulous coral reefs around the Captain Cook monument and generally calm waters. And with any luck, you'll probably get to swim with dolphins. Overland access is difficult, so opt for one of several guided snorkel cruises or kayak across the bay to get to the monument. ■ TIP→ Be on the lookout for kayakers who might not notice you swimming beneath them, and stay on the ocean side of the buoys near the cliffs.

The snorkeling just north of the boat launch at **Pu'uhonua O Hōnaunau** (*City of Refuge* ⊠ *Rte. 160* ✛ *about 20 mi south of Kailua-Kona* ⊕ *www. nps.gov/puho*) is almost as good as Kealakekua Bay, and it's much easier to reach. It's also a popular scuba diving spot.

EQUIPMENT, LESSONS, AND TOURS

★ **Body Glove Cruises.** This operator is a good choice for families, particularly if at least one member is a certified diver and the rest want to snorkel. Kids love the waterslide and the high-dive platform, and parents appreciate the reasonable prices. Snorkelers pay $78–$120 per adult. Ask about scuba prices. ⊠ *75-5629 Kuakini Hwy., Kailua-Kona* ☎ *808/326–7122 or 800/551–8911* ⊕ *www.bodyglovehawaii.com.*

Captain Zodiac Raft Expedition. This four-hour trip on an inflatable raft takes you along the Kona Coast to explore gaping lava tube caves, search for dolphins and turtles, and snorkel around Kealakekua Bay; the captain often throws in some Hawaiian folklore and Kona history, too. The morning trip departs at 8:15 am, the afternoon trip at 1 pm. The fee is $93 per adult. A seasonal (December–April) three-hour whale-watching cruise costs $49. ⊠ *Honokōhau Harbor, Kailua-Kona* ☎ *808/329–3199* ⊕ *www.captainzodiac.com.*

★ **Fair Wind Cruises.** This outfit offers both a 4½-hour morning snorkeling and a 3½-hour afternoon excursion to Kealakekua Bay, as well as a seasonal luxury cruise that sails into two different secret snorkeling spots a day. Snorkel gear is included (ask about prescription masks), but bring your own towel. On morning cruises you'll get a Continental breakfast and a barbecue lunch. These trips are great for families with small kids (lots of pint-size flotation equipment), and they provide underwater viewing devices for those who don't want to use a mask–snorkel setup. Morning cruises cost $129 for adults; afternoon cruises are cheaper, but you're less likely to see dolphins in the bay. The spring–summer afternoon deluxe cruise includes a late barbecue lunch and snorkel time; the trip is $109 for adults. ⊠ *78-7130 Kaleiopapa St., Keauhou Bay, Kailua-Kona* ☎ *808/322–2788 or 800/677–9461* ⊕ *www.fair-wind.com.*

Snorkel Bob's. You're likely to see his wacky ads in your airline in-flight magazine. The company actually delivers what it promises. Snorkel Bob's offers an assortment of snorkel cruises and manta ray night snorkels in the morning and afternoon. Adults cost $72–$125. ⊠ *75-5831 Kahakai St., Kailua-Kona* ☎ *808/329–0770 or 800/262–7725* ⊕ *www. snorkelbob.com.*

STAND-UP PADDLING

Stand-up paddling (or SUP for short), a sport with roots in the Hawaiian Islands, has grown popular worldwide over the past few years. It's available for all skill levels and ages, and even novice stand-up paddleboarders can get up, stay up, and have a great time paddling around a protected bay or exploring the gorgeous coastline. All you need is a large body of water, a board, and a paddle. The workout will test your core strength as well as your balance but truly offers a unique vantage point from which to enjoy the beauty of the island and the ocean.

BEST SPOTS

'Anaeho'omalu Beach *(A-Bay)*. This is a well-protected bay, so even when surf is rough on the rest of the island, it's fairly calm here. Boards are available for rent at the north end and the safe area for stand-up paddling is marked off by buoys. ✛ *Follow Waikoloa Beach Dr. to Kings' Shops, then turn left; parking lot and beach right-of-way south of Waikoloa Beach Marriott.*

Kailua Bay and Kamakahonu Beach. The small, sandy beach that fronts the King Kamehameha Kona Beach Hotel is protected by the harbor; the water here is especially calm and teeming with ocean life. If you're more daring, you can easily paddle out of the bay and along the coast for some great scenic views. ⊠ *Ali'i Dr., next to Kailua Pier, south of Kailua-Kona.*

Kealakekua Bay. The most protected deepwater bay in the islands, conditions at Kealakekua Bay are typically calm. You might see spinner dolphins (in the morning) or even the occasional whale in season. There aren't any shacks for rentals right at the bay, so you'll have to load up your board and transport it there yourself. ⊠ *Bottom of Nāpō'opo'o Rd. South of Kailua-Kona.*

EQUIPMENT AND LESSONS

Kona Boys. If you rent from the main location above Kealakekua Bay, your rental comes with the necessary gear to transport your board to the water on your car or visit their beach shack location and carry your board straight from the shack to the water. Board rentals at this outfitter are $25 per hour or $65 per day. Weekly rentals are $250. The Kona Boys also offer lessons: groups are $75 per person, private lessons are $125 per person. ⊠ *79-7539 Mamalahoa Hwy., Kealakekua* ⊠ *75–5660 Palani Rd., Kailua-Kona* ☎ *808/328–1234 or 808/329–2345* ⊕ *www.konaboys.com.*

Ocean Sports. This outfitter has the perfect location for easy access to A-Bay. Rentals are $30 per half hour or $50 per hour. Or go for the excursion rate: for $40 you'll get a 30-minute lesson from a guide who leads you around the bay. Ocean Sports also has rental shacks at Hilton Waikoloa Village and Mauna Kea Beach Hotel. The Hilton rentals are limited to paddling in the lagoon only, no open ocean adventuring. ✛ *Follow Waikoloa Beach Dr. to Kings' Shops, then turn left; parking lot and beach right-of-way south of Waikoloa Beach Marriott* ☎ *808/886–6666* ⊕ *www.hawaiioceansports.com.*

Continued on page 394

SNORKELING IN HAWAI'I

The waters surrounding the Hawaiian Islands are filled with life—from giant manta rays cruising off the Big Island's Kona Coast to humpback whales giving birth in Maui's Mā'alaea Bay. Dip your head beneath the surface to experience a spectacularly colorful world: pairs of milletseed butterflyfish dart back and forth, red-lipped parrotfish snack on coral algae, and spotted eagle rays flap past like silent spaceships. Sea turtles bask at the surface while tiny wrasses give them the equivalent of a shave and a haircut. The water quality is typically outstanding; many sites afford 30-foot-plus visibility. On snorkel cruises, you can often stare from the boat rail right down to the bottom.

Certainly few destinations are as accommodating to every level of snorkeler as Hawai'i. Beginners can tromp in from sandy beaches while more advanced divers descend to shipwrecks, reefs, craters, and sea arches just offshore. Because of Hawai'i's extreme isolation, the island chain has fewer fish species than Fiji or the Caribbean—but many of the fish that are here exist nowhere else. The Hawaiian waters are home to the highest percentage of endemic fish in the world.

The key to enjoying the underwater world is slowing down. Look carefully. Listen. You might hear the strange crackling sound of shrimp tunneling through coral, or you may hear whales singing to one another during winter. A shy octopus may drift along the ocean's floor beneath you. If you're hooked, pick up a waterproof fishkey from Long's Drugs. You can brag later that you've looked the Hawaiian turkeyfish in the eye.

Picasso Triggerfish

Milletseed Butterflyfish*

Yellow Tang

Moorish Idol

Hawaiian Whitespotted Toby*

Saddleback Wrasse*

Red-lipped Parrotfish

Hawaiian Turkeyfish*

Zebra Moray Eel

Stocky Hawkfish

Green Sea Turtle (Honu)

Spotted Eagle Ray

*endemic to Hawai'i

POLYNESIA'S FIRST CELESTIAL NAVIGATORS: HONU

Honu is the Hawaiian name for two native sea turtles, the hawksbill and the green sea turtle. Little is known about these dinosaur-age marine reptiles, though snorkelers regularly see them foraging for *limu* (seaweed) and the occasional jellyfish in Hawaiian waters. Most female honu nest in the uninhabited Northwestern Hawaiian Islands, but a few sociable ladies nest on Maui and Big Island beaches. Scientists suspect that they navigate the seas via magnetism—sensing the earth's poles. Amazingly, they will journey up to 800 miles to nest—it's believed that they return to their own birth sites. After about 60 days of incubation, nestlings emerge from the sand at night and find their way back to the sea by the light of the stars.

SNORKELING

Many of Hawai'i's reefs are accessible from shore.

The basics: Sure, you can take a deep breath, hold your nose, squint your eyes, and stick your face in the water in an attempt to view submerged habitats . . . but why not protect your eyes, retain your ability to breathe, and keep your hands free to paddle about when exploring underwater? That's what snorkeling is all about.

Equipment needed: A mask, snorkel (the tube attached to the mask), and fins. In deeper waters (any depth over your head), life jackets are advised.

Steps to success: If you've never snorkeled before, it's natural to feel a bit awkward at first, so don't sweat it. Breathing through a mask and tube, and wearing a pair of fins take getting used to. Like any activity, you build confidence and comfort through practice.

If you're new to snorkeling, begin by submerging your face in shallow water or a swimming pool and breathing calmly through the snorkel while gazing through the mask.

Next you need to learn how to clear water out of your mask and snorkel, an essential skill since splashes can send water into tube openings and masks can leak. Some snorkels have built-in drainage valves, but if a tube clogs, you can force water up and out by exhaling through your mouth. Clearing a mask is similar: lift your head from water while pulling forward on mask to drain. Some masks have built-in purge valves, but those without can be cleared underwater by pressing the top to the forehead and blowing out your nose (charming, isn't it?), allowing air to bubble into the mask, pushing water out the bottom. If it sounds hard, it really isn't. Just try it a few times and you'll soon feel like a pro.

Now your goal is to get friendly with fins—you want them to be snug but not too tight—and learn how to propel yourself with them. Fins won't help you float, but they will give you a leg up, so to speak, on smoothly moving through the water or treading water (even when upright) with less effort.

Flutter stroking is the most efficient underwater kick, and the farther your foot bends forward the more leg power you'll be able to transfer to the water and the farther you'll travel with each stroke. Flutter kicking movements involve alternately separating the legs and then drawing them back together. When your legs separate, the leg surface encounters drag from the water, slowing you down. When your legs are drawn back together, they produce a force pushing you forward. If your kick creates more forward force than it causes drag, you'll move ahead.

Submerge your fins to avoid fatigue rather than having them flailing above the water when you kick, and keep your arms at your side to reduce drag. You are in the water—stretched out, face down, and snorkeling happily away—but that doesn't mean you can't hold your breath and go deeper in the water for a closer look at some fish or whatever catches your attention. Just remember that when you do this, your snorkel will be submerged, too, so you won't be breathing (you'll be holding your breath). You can dive head-first, but going feet-first is easier and less scary for most folks, taking less momentum. Before full immersion, take several long, deep breaths to clear carbon dioxide from your lungs.

If your legs tire, flip onto your back and tread water with inverted fin motions while resting. If your mask fogs, wash condensation from lens and clear water from mask.

TIPS FOR SAFE SNORKELING

■ Snorkel with a buddy and stay together.

■ Plan your entry and exit points prior to getting in the water.

■ Swim into the current on entering and then ride the current back to your exit point.

■ Carry your flippers into the water and then put them on, as it's difficult to walk in them.

■ Make sure your mask fits properly and is not too loose.

■ Pop your head above the water periodically to ensure you aren't drifting too far out, or too close to rocks.

■ Think of the water as someone else's home—don't take anything that doesn't belong to you, or leave any trash behind.

■ Don't touch any sea creatures; they may sting.

■ Wear a T-shirt over your swimsuit to help protect you from being fried by the sun.

■ When in doubt, don't go without a snorkeling professional; try a guided tour.

Green sea turtle (Honu)

SUBMARINE TOURS

Atlantis VII Submarine. Want to stay dry while exploring the undersea world? Climb aboard the 48-foot *Atlantis VII* submarine anchored off Kailua Pier, across from King Kamehameha's Kona Beach Hotel in Kailua-Kona. A large glass dome in the bow and 13 viewing ports on the sides allow clear views of the aquatic world more than 100 feet down. This is a great trip for kids and nonswimmers. Each one-hour voyage costs $99 for adults. The company also operates on O'ahu and Maui. ☎ *808/326–7939 or 800/548–6262* ⊕ *www.atlantisadventures.com.*

Fodor's Choice
★

SURFING

The Big Island does not have the variety of great surfing spots found on O'ahu or Maui, but it does have decent waves and a thriving surf culture. Local kids and avid surfers frequent a number of places up and down the Kona and Kohala coasts of west Hawai'i. Expect high surf in winter and much calmer activity during summer. The surf scene is much more active on the Kona side.

Banyans (⊠ *Ali'i Dr.* ✛ *Near Kona Bali Kai condos*) is a popular spot with local and experienced surfers. There's no beach here—surfers need to wade in from the rocks and start paddling. On the east side near Hilo, try the waves at **Honoli'i Cove** (✛ *Access road off Hwy. 19, just past mile marker 4*). Slightly north of **Kahalu'u Beach Park** (⊠ *Ali'i Dr.* ✛ *5½ mi south of Kailua-Kona next to Sheraton Keauhou Beach Hotel*), intermediate surfers brave the rocks to get out to a popular break just past the beach's calm lagoons and snorkelers. Among the best places to catch the waves is **Pine Trees** (⊠ *Off Hwy. 11* ✛ *South of Kona Airport and Natural Energy Lab of Hawai'i on an unimproved beach road*). Keep in mind that this is a very popular local surf spot on an island where there aren't all that many surf spots, so be very respectful.

EQUIPMENT AND LESSONS

Hawai'i Lifeguard Surf Instructors. This certified school with experienced instructors helps novice surfers become wave riders and offers surf tours that take more experienced riders to Kona's top surfing spots. ⊠ *75-5909 Ali'i Dr., Kailua-Kona* ☎ *808/324–0442 or 808/936–7873* ⊕ *www.surflessonshawaii.com.*

Ocean Eco Tours Surf School. Kona's oldest surf school emphasizes the basics of safe surfing and specializes in beginners. All lessons are taught by certified CPR-trained lifeguard instructors, and they guarantee that you will surf! If you're hooked, you can sign up for a three-lesson package for $270. ⊠ *Honokōhau Harbor, 74-425 Kealakehe Pkwy., Kailua-Kona* ☎ *808/324–7873* ⊕ *www.oceanecotours.com.*

Orchid Land Surf Shop. The shop has a wide variety of water sports and surf equipment for sale or rent. They stock professional custom surfboards, body boards, and surf apparel, and do repairs. ⊠ *262 Kamehameha Ave., Hilo* ☎ *808/935–1533* ⊕ *www.orchidlandsurf.com.*

"Anaeho'omalu Beach Surf Shack—classic Hawai'i." —travel192, Fodors.com photo contest participant

WHALE-WATCHING

Each winter, some two-thirds of the North Pacific humpback whale population (about 4,000–5,000 animals) migrate more than 3,500 mi from icy Alaska to the warm waters of Hawai'i to give birth to and nurse their calves. Humpbacks are spotted here from early December through the end of April, but other species, like sperm, pilot, and beaked whales, can be seen year-round. Most ocean tour companies offer whale outings during the season, but two owner–operators (listed below) do it full time. They are much more familiar with whale behavior and you're more likely to have a quality whale-watching experience. ■TIP→ If you take the morning cruise, you're likely to see dolphins as well.

Blue Sea Cruises Inc. The *Makai* and the *Spirit of Kona*, a 46-foot and a 70-foot, respectively, double-deck catamaran, cruise along the Kona Coast once a day on two-and-a-half-hour tours. The boats have all the comforts, including a snack bar and restrooms. Sightings include spinner, spotted, and bottlenose dolphins, resident pilot whales, and seasonal humpbacks. They guarantee whale sightings or you can go again for free. Rates are $79 per adult. ✑ *Box 2429, Kailua-Kona* ☎ *808/331-8875* ⊕ *www.blueseacruisesinc.com.*

Captain Dan McSweeney's Year-Round Whale Watching Adventures. This is probably the most experienced small operation on the island. Captain Dan McSweeney offers three-hour trips on his 40-foot boat. In addition to humpbacks in the winter, he'll show you some of the six other whale species that live off the Kona Coast year-round. Three-hour tours cost $79.50 (snacks and juices included). McSweeney guarantees you'll see a whale or he'll take you out again free. ✉ *Honokōhau Harbor,*

Kailua-Kona ☎ *808/322–0028 or 888/942–5376* ⊕ *www.ilovewhales. com.*

GOLF, HIKING, AND OUTDOOR ACTIVITIES

With the Big Island's predictably mild year-round climate, it's no wonder the lifestyle emphasis is on outdoor activities. Whether you are an avid hiker or a beginning bicyclist, a casual golfer or a tennis buff, there are plenty of land-based activities to lure you away from the sun and surf.

AERIAL TOURS

There's nothing quite like the aerial view of a waterfall that drops a couple thousand feet into natural pools, or seeing lava flow to the ocean, where clouds of steam billow into the air. You can get this bird's-eye view from a helicopter or a small fixed-wing aircraft. Although there have been a few cases of pilots violating flight paths and altitudes over resident communities in recent years, most operators are reputable and fly with strict adherence to FAA safety rules. ■ TIP➔ Before you hire a company, be a savvy traveler and ask the right questions. What kind of aircraft do they fly? Do they have two-way headsets so you can talk with the pilot? What is their safety record?

go! Mokulele Airlines. In addition to regular interisland scheduled flights, this commuter line offers a 1½-hour Circle Island Tour in a nine-passenger Cessna Caravan. The air tour departs Kona Airport and goes over Hawai'i Volcanoes National Park, the Hilo-Hāmākua Coast, and the Kohala Coast. Rates are $349 per person. ☎ *808/326–7070 or 866/260–7070* ⊕ *www.iflygo.com.*

Paradise Helicopters. Paradise flies six-passenger Bell 407 and four-passenger Hughes 500 helicopters. Everyone has a window seat in the four-seaters, and most passengers get a window in the highly maneuverable six-passenger helicopters as well. The friendly and knowledgeable pilots communicate with passengers over two-way headsets. Paradise operates from Kona and Hilo, which are better for volcano viewing. The 50-minute Volcano & Waterfall "doors off" Adventure (from Hilo) is $226 per person; the top-of-the-line tour is a three-hour Volcanoes & Valley Adventure (from Kona) for $433 per person. For an additional thrill and an even better view, you can choose a Doors-Off Experience from Hilo. ⊠ *Hilo Airport, Kona Airport* ☎ *808/969–7392 or 866/876–7422* ⊕ *www.paradisecopters.com.*

Sunshine Helicopters. Ride the six-seater Astar *Black Beauty* on an exciting air tour that takes in the island's beauty and the formations and flows of the Kīlauea Volcano. Narrated tours range from 45 minutes ($169–$229 if you book online) to two hours ($405–$520); the longer tour covers both regions, while the shorter tour focuses on the volcano. Afterward, you can buy a DVD of your flight experience. ⊠ *Helipad at Hāpuna Beach Prince Hotel and Hilo Airport* ☎ *Hāpuna Beach Prince Hotel: 808/882–1223, Hilo: 808/969–7501 or 800/469–3000* ⊕ *www. sunshinehelicopters.com.*

Take an off-road ATV adventure to see remote areas of Big Island's wilderness.

ATV TOURS

A different way to experience the Big Island's rugged coastline and wild ranch lands is through an off-road adventure—a real backcountry experience. At higher elevations, weather can be nippy and rainy, but views can be awesome. Protective gear is provided. Generally, you have to be 16 or older to ride your own ATV, though some outfitters allow children seven and older to be passengers.

ATV Outfitters Hawai'i. These trips take in the scenic beauty of the rugged North Kohala Coast, traveling along coastal cliffs and into the forest in search of waterfalls. ATV Outfitters also offers double-seater ATVs for parents traveling with children or adults who don't feel comfortable operating their own ATV. ⊠ *Old Sakamoto Store, Hwy. 270, Kapa'au* ☎ *808/889–6000 or 888/288–7288* ⊕ *www.atvoutfittershawaii.com.*

Waipi'o Ride the Rim. On this Waipi'o Valley ride, you'll see expansive black-sand beaches, get to swim in the stream that feeds the 1,200-foot Hi'ilawe Falls, and travel through the lush rain forest surrounding the top edge of the valley. Rates for the three-hour rim tour begin at $159 per person. ⊠ *Waipi'o Valley Artworks Bldg., 48-5416 Kukuihaele Rd., Kukuihaele* ☎ *808/775–1450 or 877/775–1450* ⊕ *www.ridetherim.com.*

BIKING

The Big Island's biking trails and roads range from easy to moderate coastal rides to rugged backcountry wilderness treks that will challenge the most serious bikers.

The rainy Hilo side of the Big Island means lush hills and valleys and a ton of waterfalls.

Fodor's Choice ★ **Kulani Trails** has been called the best ride in the state—if you're an advanced rider who really wants to get gnarly. To reach the trailhead from the intersection of Highway 11 and Highway 19, take Highway 19 south about 4 mi, then turn right onto Stainback Highway and continue on 2½ mi, then turn right at the Waiakea Arboretum. Park near the gate. This technically demanding ride, which passes majestic eucalyptus trees, is for advanced cyclists.

The **Old Puna Trail** (⊹ *Trailhead: From Hwy. 130, take Kaloli Rd. to Beach Rd.*) is a 10½-mi ride through the subtropical jungle in Puna, one of the island's most isolated areas. You'll start out on a cinder road, which becomes a four-wheel-drive trail. If it's rained recently, you'll have to deal with some puddles—the first few of which you'll gingerly avoid until you give in and go barreling through the rest of them for the sheer fun of it. This is a great ride for all abilities that takes about 90 minutes.

EQUIPMENT

If you want to strike out on your own, there are several rental shops in Kailua-Kona and a couple in Waimea and Hilo. Many resorts rent bicycles that can be used around the properties. Most outfitters listed can provide a bicycle rack for your car. All offer reduced rates for rentals longer than one day.

Cycle Station. This shop, which has a variety of bikes to rent, from road sport to racing bikes, hybrids to tandems, will also deliver to and pick up at hotels. They have trailers for toddlers. Daily rentals range from $20 for a hybrid, to anywhere from $35 to $75 for road and triathlon bikes. ⊠ *Kamanu St., Kailua-Kona* ☎ *808/327–0087* ⊕ *www. cyclestationhawaii.com.*

Hawaiian Pedals. For those who prefer comfort over speed, Hawaiian Pedals rents seven-speed cruisers and hybrids starting at $15 for five hours. Full-day rental rates begin at $20. ⊠ *Kona Inn Shopping Village, 75-5744 Ali'i Dr., Kailua-Kona* ☎ *808/329–2294* ⊕ *www.hpbikeworks.com.*

TOURS

Orchid Isle Bicycling. Geared to cyclists of varying abilities, options range from challenging 3,500-foot climbs up Kohala Mountain to downhill-only rides. Tours, which last from two to five hours and cover 21 to 55 mi, start at $125 per person. ⊠ *73-5619 Kauhole St., Kailua-Kona* ☎ *808/327–0087 or 800/219–2324* ⊕ *www.cyclekona.com.*

Volcano Bike Tours. Volcano Bike Tours takes visitors on a three- or five-hour bike ride through the rain forests and past the craters of Volcanoes National Park on a mostly downhill route. After cruising through the volcanoes, the five-hour tour ($129) ends at the Volcano Winery for a tasting at one of the most unique wineries in the country. The three-hour tour costs $99. There's also a spectacular (and lengthy) seven-hour afternoon sunset tour that takes riders to the active lava flow ($129). ⊠ *2352 Kalanianaole St., Hilo* ☎ *808/934–9199 or 888/934–9199* ⊕ *www.bikevolcano.com.*

GOLF

For golfers, the Big Island is a big deal—starting with the Mauna Kea Golf Course, which opened in 1964 and remains one of the state's top courses.

Black lava and deep blue sea are the predominant themes on the island. In the roughly 40 mi from the Kona Country Club out to the Mauna Kea Resort, nine courses are carved into sunny seaside lava plains, with four more in the hills above.

Greens Fees: Greens fees listed here are the highest course rates per round on weekdays for U.S. residents. Courses with varying weekend rates are noted in the individual listings. (Some courses charge non-U.S. residents higher prices.) ■ TIP→ Discounts are often available for resort guests and for those who book tee times on the Web. Twilight fees are usually offered; call individual courses for information.

★ **Big Island Country Club.** Set 2,000 feet above sea level on the slopes of Mauna Kea, the Big Island Country Club is rather out of the way but well worth the drive. Pete and Perry Dye (1997) created a gem that plays through upland woodlands—more than 2,500 trees line the fairways. On the par-5 15th, a giant tree in the middle of the fairway must be avoided with the second shot. Five lakes and a meandering natural mountain stream mean water comes into play on nine holes. The most dramatic is on the par-3 17th, where Dye creates a knockoff of his infamous 17th at the TPC at Sawgrass. ⊠ *71-1420 Māmalahoa Hwy., Kailua-Kona* ☎ *808/325–5044* ⊕ *www.bigislandcountryclub.com* ⚑ *18 holes. 7075 yds. Par 72. Greens fee: $49.95* ⚐ *Facilities: Driving range, putting green, rental clubs, golf carts, pro shop, lessons.*

Hapuna Golf Course. Hapuna's challenging play and environmental sensitivity make it one of Hawai'i's most unique courses. Designed by Arnold Palmer and Ed Seay, the course is nestled into the natural contours of the land from the shoreline to about 700 feet above sea level. There are spectacular views of mountains and sea (Maui is often visible in the distance), and the holes wind through kiawe scrub, beds of jagged lava and tall grasses. Hole 11 at Hapuna is the favorite. ⊠ *62-100 Kanuna'oa Dr., Kohala* ☎ *808/880–3000* ⊕ *www.princeresortshawaii.com/hapuna-golf.php* ⟟ *18 holes 6875 yds. Par 72. Greens fee: $95, $65 after 11 am; $55 after 1:30 pm* ☞ *Facilities: Driving range, putting green, chipping green, golf carts, rental clubs, rental shoes, locker rooms, pro shop, lessons, restaurant.*

★ **Hualālai Resort.** Named for the volcanic peak that is the target off the first tee, the Nicklaus Course at Hualālai is semiprivate, open only to guests of the adjacent Four Seasons Resort Hualālai. From the forward and resort tees, this is perhaps Jack Nicklaus's most friendly course in Hawai'i, but the back tees play a full mile longer. The par-3 17th plays across convoluted lava to a seaside green, and the view from the tee is so lovely, you may be tempted to just relax on the koa bench and enjoy the scenery. ⊠ *100 Ka'ūpūlehu Dr., Kohala Coast* ☎ *808/325–8480* ⊕ *www.fourseasons.com/hualalai* ⟟ *18 holes. 7117 yds. Par 72. Greens fee: $250 for all-day access* ☞ *Facilities: Driving range, putting green, pull carts, golf carts, rental clubs, lessons, pro shop, restaurant, bar.*

★ **Kona Country Club.** This venerable country club offers two very different tests with the aptly named Ocean and Ali'i Mountain courses. The Ocean Course (William F. Bell, 1967) is a bit like playing through a coconut plantation, with a few remarkable lava features—such as the "blowhole" in front of the par-4 13th, where seawater propelled through a lava tube erupts like a geyser. The Ali'i Mountain Course (front nine, William F. Bell, 1983: back nine, Robin Nelson and Rodney Wright, 1992) plays a couple of strokes tougher than the Ocean and is the most delightful split personality you may ever encounter. Both nines share breathtaking views of Keauhou Bay, and elevation change is a factor in most shots. The most dramatic view on the front nine is from the tee of the par-3 5th hole, one of the best golf vistas in Hawai'i. The back nine is links style, with less elevation change—except for the par-3 14th, which drops 100 feet from tee to green, over a lake. The routing, the sight lines and framing of greens, and the risk-reward factors on each hole make this one of the single best nines in Hawai'i. ⊠ *78-7000 Ali'i Dr., Kailua-Kona* ☎ *808/322–2595* ⊕ *www.konagolf.com* ⟟ *Ocean Course: 18 holes. 6806 yds. Par 72. Greens fee: $165. Mountain*

Most of the Big Island's top golf courses are located on the sunny Kona Coast.

Course: 18 holes. 6673 yds. Par 72. Greens fee: $150; Twilight rates begin at noon: $107 ocean; $97 mountain ☞ Facilities: Driving range, putting green, golf carts, rental clubs, lessons, restaurant, bar.

Fodor's Choice **Mauna Lani Resort.** Black lava flows, lush green turf, white sand, and
★   the Pacific's multihues of blue define the 36 holes at Mauna Lani. The South Course includes the par-3 15th across a turquoise bay, one of the most photographed holes in Hawai'i. But it shares "signature hole" honors with the 7th. A long par 3, it plays downhill over convoluted patches of black lava, with the Pacific immediately to the left and a dune to the right. The North Course plays a couple of shots tougher. Its most distinctive hole is the 17th, a par 3 with the green set in a lava pit 50 feet deep. The shot from an elevated tee must carry a pillar of lava that rises from the pit and partially blocks your view of the green. ✉ *68-1310 Mauna Lani Dr., Kohala Coast* ☎ *808/885–6655* ⊕ *www. maunalani.com* ⚲ *North Course: 18 holes. 6601 yds. Par 72. Greens fee: $215. South Course: 18 holes. 6436 yds. Par 72. Greens fee: $215 ☞ Facilities: Driving range, putting green, golf carts, rental clubs, pro shop, lessons, restaurant, bar.*

★   **Mauna Kea Golf Course.** Originally opened in 1964, this golf course is one of the most revered in the state. It recently underwent a tee-to-green restoration guided by Rees Jones, son of the original architect, Robert Trent Jones, Sr. New hybrid grasses were planted, the number of bunkers increased, and the overall yardage was expanded. The par-3 3rd hole is one of the most famous holes in the world of golf (and one of the most photographed); you play from a cliff-side tee across a bay to a cliff-side green. Getting across the ocean is just half the battle because the third green is surrounded by seven bunkers, each one large and multi-undulated. The course is definitely a shot-maker's paradise and follows Jones' "easy bogey/tough par" philosophy. ⊠ *62-100 Mauna Kea Beach Dr., Kohala* ☎ *808/882–5400* ⊕ *www.maunakeagolf.com* ⅄ *18 holes 7360 yds. Par 72. Greens fee: $250; $175 after 11 am; $155 after 1:30 pm.* ☞ *Facilities: Driving range, putting green, chipping green, golf carts, rental clubs, locker rooms, pro shop, lessons, shoe shine service, restaurant.*

Volcano Golf & Country Club. Just outside Volcanoes National Park—and barely a stout drive from Halemaʻumaʻu Crater—Volcano is by far Hawaiʻi's highest course. At 4,200-feet elevation, shots tend to fly a bit farther than at sea level, even in the often cool, misty air. Because of the elevation and climate, Volcano is one of the few Hawaiʻi courses with bent-grass putting greens. The course is mostly flat and holes play through stands of Norfolk pines, flowering *lehua* trees, and multitrunk *hau* trees. The uphill par-4 15th doglegs through a tangle of *hau*. ⊠ *Piʻi Mauna Dr., off Hwy. 11, Volcanoes National Park* ☎ *808/967–7331* ⊕ *www.volcanogolfshop.com* ⅄ *18 holes. 6106 yds. Par 72. Greens fee: $55* ☞ *Facilities: Driving range, putting green, golf carts, rental clubs, restaurant, bar.*

Fodor'sChoice
★ **Waikoloa Beach Resort.** Robert Trent Jones Jr. built the Beach Course at Waikoloa (1981) on an old flow of crinkly *ʻaʻā* lava, which he used to create holes that are as artful as they are challenging. The third tee, for instance, is set at the base of a towering mound of lava. The par-5 12th plays through a chute of black lava to an ocean-side green, the blue sea on the right coming into play on the second and third shots. At the King's Course at Waikoloa (1990), Tom Weiskopf and Jay Morrish built a very links-esque track. It turns out lava's natural humps and declivities remarkably replicate the contours of seaside Scotland. But there are a few island twists—such as seven lakes. This is "option golf" as Weiskopf and Morrish provide different risk-reward tactics on each hole. Beach and King's have separate clubhouses. ⊠ *600 Waikoloa Beach Dr., Waikoloa* ☎ *808/886–7888* ⊕ *www.waikoloagolf.com* ⅄ *Beach Course: 18 holes. 6566 yds. Par 70. Greens fee: $135 for guests, $165 for nonguests. Kings' Course: 18 holes. 6594 yds. Par 72. Greens fee: $135 for guests, $165 for nonguests.* ☞ *Facilities: Driving range, putting green, golf carts, rental clubs, lessons, restaurant, bar.*

Waikoloa Village Golf Course. Robert Trent Jones Jr., the same designer who created some of the most expensive courses on the Kohala Coast, designed this little gem, which is 20 minutes from the coast, in 1972. Though not affiliated with the resorts, the Waikoloa Village course is the site of the annual Waikoloa Open, one of the most prestigious tournaments in Hawaiʻi. Holes run across rolling hills with sweeping mountain and ocean views. ⊠ *68-1792 Melia St., Waikoloa* ☎ *808/883–9621* ⊕ *www.waikoloa.org* ⅄ *18 holes. 6230 yds. Par 72. Greens fee: $83* ☞ *Facilities: Driving range, putting green, golf carts, rental clubs, lessons, restaurant, bar.*

Keep an eye out for flora and fauna unique to the Big Island while hiking through the island's varied microclimates.

HIKING

Meteorologists classify the world's weather into 13 climates. Eleven are here on the Big Island, and you can experience them all by foot on the many trails that lace the island. The ancient Hawaiians cut trails across the lava plains, through the rain forests, and up along the mountain heights. Many of these paths can still be used today. Part of the King's Trail at 'Anaeho'omalu winds through a field of lava rocks covered with prehistoric carvings called petroglyphs. Many other trails, historic and modern, crisscross the huge Hawai'i Volcanoes National Park and other parts of the island. Plus, the serenity of remote beaches, such as Papakōlea Beach (Green Sand Beach), is accessible only to hikers.

For information on all Big Island's state parks, contact the **Department of Land and Natural Resources, State Parks Division** (⊠ *75 Aupuni St., Hilo* ☎ *808/974–6200* ⊕ *www.hawaiistateparks.org*).

BEST SPOTS

Hawai'i Volcanoes National Park (⊠ *Hwy. 11 ✛ Near Volcano Village, 30 mi south of Hilo* ☎ *808/985–6000* ⊕ *www.hawaii.volcanoes.national-park.com*) is perhaps the Big Island's premier area for hikers. The 150 mi of trails provide close-up views of fern and rain-forest environments, cinder cones, steam vents, lava fields, rugged coastline, and current lava flow activity. Day hikes range from easy to moderately difficult, and from one or two hours to a full day. For a bigger challenge, consider an overnight or multiday backcountry hike with a stay in a park cabin (available by a remote coast, in a lush forest, or atop frigid Mauna Loa). To do so, you must first obtain a free permit at the Kīlauea Visitor

Center. There are also daily guided hikes led by knowledgeable and friendly park rangers.

At **Kekaha Kai (Kona Coast) State Park** (⊠ *Hwy. 19 ✛ Sign about 2 mi north of Keāhole–Kona International Airport marks rough road*), two 1½-mi-long unpaved roads lead to the Mahai'ula Beach and Kua Bay sections of the park. Connecting the two is the 4½-mi Ala Kahakai historic coastal trail. Midway, a hike to the summit of Pu'u Ku'ili, a 342-foot-high cinder cone, offers an excellent view of the coastline. It's dry and hot with no drinking water, so be sure to pack sunblock and water.

WORD OF MOUTH

" . . . We toured Volcanoes National Park. I enjoyed this and recommend the hike into the forest near the steam vents. I found this at least as enjoyable as the area around the lava tubes, as you will most likely have it all to yourself. The sound of the birds and the steam vents round every corner were wonderful. The view of the crater was spectacular all along the path." —cosmos

GUIDED HIKES

To get to some of the best trails and places, it's worth going with a skilled guide. Costs range from $95 to $185, and some hikes include picnic meals or refreshments, and gear such as binoculars, ponchos, and walking sticks. The outfitters mentioned here also offer customized adventure tours.

Hawai'i Forest & Trail. Expert naturalist guides take you to scenic Kohala waterfalls, the 4,000-year-old craters at Mount Hualālai, and on birdwatching expeditions throughout the island. In addition to its other expeditions, the company offers tours in Pinzgauers (Austrian all-terrain vehicles) that are perfect for groups, especially those that include off-road junkets. It also offers tours into lava tubes and through normally inaccessible areas of Hawai'i Volcanoes National Park. ☎ 808/331–8505 or 800/464–1993 ⊕ www.hawaii-forest.com.

Hawaiian Walkways. This company conducts several tours with knowledgeable guides—a Kona Cloud Forest botanical walk, a hike on Saddle Road between Mauna Kea and Mauna Loa, waterfall hikes, and jaunts through Hawai'i Volcanoes National Park—as well as custom-designed trips. ☎ 808/775–0372 or 800/457–7759 ⊕ www.hawaiianwalkways.com.

Kapoho Kine Adventures. This outfitter offers several interesting tours of Hawai'i Volcanoes National Park and surrounding areas, including a 14-hour tour that allows you to explore the region by day and see the lava at night. There is also a shorter day tour and a separate evening tour complete with a Hawaiian-style barbeque dinner. Prices range from $129 to $159 per person. ⊠ 28-1177 Old Railroad Way, Pepe'ekeo ☎ 808/964–1000 or 866/965–9552 ⊕ kapohokine.com.

Continued on page 408

BIRTH OF THE ISLANDS

How did the volcanoes of the Hawaiian Islands evolve here, in the middle of the Pacific Ocean? The ancient Hawaiians believed that the volcano goddess Pele's hot temper was the key to the mystery; modern scientists contend that it's all about plate tectonics and one very hot spot.

Plate Tectonics & the Hawaiian Question: The theory of plate tectonics says that the Earth's surface is comprised of plates that float around slowly over the planet's molten interior. The vast majority of earthquakes and volcanic eruptions occur near plate boundaries—the San Francisco earthquakes in 1906 and 1989, for example, were the result of activity along the nearby San Andreas Fault, where the Pacific and North American plates meet. Hawai'i, more than 1,988 miles from the nearest plate boundary, is a giant exception. For years scientists struggled to explain the island chain's existence—if not a fault line, what caused the earthquakes and volcanic eruptions that formed these islands?

What's a hotspot? In 1963, J. Tuzo Wilson, a Canadian geophysicist, argued that the Hawaiian volcanoes must have been created by small concentrated areas of extreme heat beneath the plates. Wilson hypothesized that there is a hotspot beneath the present-day position of the Big Island. Its heat produced a persistent source of magma by partly melting the Pacific Plate above it. The magma, lighter than the surrounding solid rock, rose through the mantle and crust to erupt onto the sea floor, forming an active seamount. Each flow caused the seamount to grow until it finally emerged above sea level as an island volcano. Plausible so far, but why then, is there not one giant Hawaiian island?

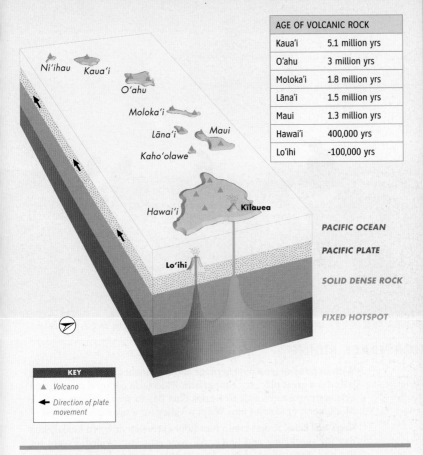

AGE OF VOLCANIC ROCK	
Kaua'i	5.1 million yrs
O'ahu	3 million yrs
Moloka'i	1.8 million yrs
Lāna'i	1.5 million yrs
Maui	1.3 million yrs
Hawai'i	400,000 yrs
Lo'ihi	-100,000 yrs

PACIFIC OCEAN

PACIFIC PLATE

SOLID DENSE ROCK

FIXED HOTSPOT

KEY
▲ Volcano
◄ Direction of plate movement

Volcanoes on the Move: Wilson further suggested that the movement of the Pacific Plate itself eventually carries the island volcano beyond the hotspot. Cut off from its magma source, the island volcano becomes dormant. As the plate slowly moved, one island volcano would become extinct just as another would develop over the hotspot. After several million years, there is a long volcanic trail of islands and seamounts across the ocean floor. The oldest islands are those farthest from the hotspot. The exposed rocks of Kaua'i, for example, are about 5.1 million years old, but those on the Big Island are less than .5 million years old, with new volcanic rock still being formed.

An Island on the Way: Off the coast of the Big Island, the volcano known as Lo'ihi is still submerged but erupting. Scientists long believed it to be a retired seamount volcano, but in the 1970s they discovered both old and new lava on its flanks, and in 1996 it erupted with a vengeance. It is believed that several thousand years from now, Lo'ihi will be the newest addition to the Hawaiian Islands.

The Kohala Coast along the east side of Big Island is known for its shimmering blue-water beaches and sunshine.

HORSEBACK RIDING

With its *paniolo* (cowboy) heritage and the ranches it spawned, the Big Island is a great place for equestrians. Riders can gallop through green Upcountry pastures, ride to Kealakekua Bay to see the Captain Cook Monument, or saunter into Waipi'o Valley for a taste of old Hawai'i.

King's Trail Rides. Riders take a four-hour excursion down to Kealakekua Bay for snorkeling and lunch. All your gear is provided, except for fins and reef walkers. Up to four people per trip. $135 per person. ✉ *Hwy. 11, mile marker 111, Kealakekua* ☎ *808/323–2388* ⊕ *www. konacowboy.com.*

Na'alapa Stables. This company is a good bet, especially for novice riders. The horses are well trained, and the stable is well run. Rides through the Waipi'o Valley cross freshwater streams and pass a black-sand beach. Na'alapa also offers open-range and horse-drawn wagon rides on the historic Kahua Ranch in North Kohala. ✛ *Off Hwy. 240, Kukuihaele* ☎ *808/775–0419* ⊕ *www.naalapastables.com.*

Waipi'o Ridge Stables. Two different rides around the rim of Waipi'o Valley are offered—a 2½-hour trek for $85 and a 5-hour hidden-waterfall adventure (with swimming) for $165. Riders meet at Waipi'o Valley Artworks. ✉ *Off Hwy. 240, Kukuihaele* ☎ *808/775–1007 or 877/757–1414* ⊕ *www.waipioridgestables.com.*

SKIING

Where else but Hawai'i can you surf, snorkel, and snow ski on the same day? In winter, the 13,796-foot Mauna Kea (Hawaiian for "white mountain") has snow at higher elevations—and along with that, skiing. No lifts, no manicured slopes, no faux-Alpine lodges, no après-ski nightlife—but the chance to ski some of the most remote (and let's face it, unlikely) runs on earth. Some people even have been known to use body boards as sleds, but we don't recommend it. As long as you're up there, fill your cooler with the white stuff for a snowball fight on the beach with local kids.

Ski Guides Hawai'i. Christopher Langan of Mauna Kea Ski Corporation is the only licensed outfitter providing transportation, guide services, and ski equipment on Mauna Kea. Snow can fall from Thanksgiving through June, but the most likely months are February and March. The runs are fairly short, and hidden lava rocks and other dangers abound. Langan charges $450 per person for a daylong experience that includes refreshments, lunch, ski or snowboard equipment, guide service, transportation from Waimea, and four-wheel-drive shuttle back up the mountain after each ski run. He also offers a $250 mountain ski service without the frills, and ski or snowboard rentals. ⌂ *Box 1954, Kamuela 96743* ☎ *808/885–4188* ⊕ *www.skihawaii.com.*

ZIPLINE TOURS

One of the few ways you can really see the untouched beauty of the Big Island is by flying over its lush forests, dense tree canopies, and glorious rushing waterfalls on a zipline course. You strap into a harness, get clipped to a cable and then zip, zip, zip your way through paradise. Most guide companies start you out easy on a slower, shorter line and by the end you graduate to faster, longer zips. It's an exhilarating adventure for all ages and has even been known to help some put aside their fear of heights (at least for a few minutes) to participate in the thrill ride. Check company credentials and specifics before you book to make sure your safety is their number one concern.

Big Island Eco Adventures. This company's four-hour tour takes you on eight ziplines through the oldest tropical rain forest on the island. You'll fly over tree canopies and three waterfalls, and get awesome views of the ocean, and, on clear days, Maui. This course is built for first timers who might be a bit timid. You build up to the climactic 1,050-foot zipline that dangles you 280 feet in the air. Adults ($169 per person) cannot weigh more than 270 pounds and children must be at least 80 pounds, 4-foot 6-inches and accompanied by an adult. Tours include snacks and beverages. Be aware that there is a very bumpy half-hour off-road ride in a Hummer or six-wheel-drive military vehicle to get to the start of the course. At this writing, an additional "extreme" course was expected to be ready sometime in 2011. ✉ *55-514 Hawi Rd., Hawi* ☎ *808/889–5111* ⊕ *bigislandecoadventures.com.*

Kapoho Kine Adventures. Boasting the longest zipline on the island at nearly a half-mile (2,040 feet), Kapoho Kine Adventure's three-hour tour ($189 per person) over the triple-tier Umauma Falls is spectacular. You soar over more than 14 waterfalls; have gorgeous views of the tropical river valley, sparkling ocean, and the summit of Mauna Kea; and can ride tandem on the island's longest dual-track run. There's a shorter course that runs an hour and a half ($149 per person). Children must be at least 10 years old; tours include light snacks and beverages. To cap off your adventure, opt for the giant swing ($15 for two people). You'll be hoisted up 50 feet in the air, and can control your own release to launch yourself out over the Umauma River. ⊠ *28-1177 Old Railroad Way, Pepeʻekeo* ☎ *808/964–1000 or 866/965–9552* ⊕ *kapohokine.com.*

SHOPPING

Residents like to complain that there isn't a lot of great shopping on the Big Island, but unless you're searching for winter coats or high-tech toys, you can find plenty to deplete your pocketbook. Dozens of shops in Kailua-Kona offer a range of souvenirs from far-flung corners of the globe and plenty of local coffee and foodstuffs to take home to everyone you left behind. Resorts along the Kohala Coast have high-quality clothing and accessories. Galleries and boutiques, many showcasing the work of local artists, fill historic buildings in Waimea and North Kohala.

In general, stores and shopping centers on the Big Island open at 9 or 10 am and close by 6 pm. Hilo's Prince Kūhiō Shopping Plaza stays open until 9 pm on weekdays. In Kona, most shops in shopping plazas that are geared to tourists remain open until 9 pm. Big outlets such as Wal-Mart are open until midnight.

KAILUA-KONA

SHOPPING CENTERS

Coconut Grove Marketplace. Just south of Kona Inn Shopping Village, this meandering labyrinth of airy buildings hides coffee shops, boutiques, ethnic restaurants, and an exquisite gallery. At night locals gather here to watch the outdoor sand volleyball games held in the middle of the marketplace or to grab a couple of beers at the sports bar. ⊠ *75-5795–75-5825 Aliʻi Dr.*

Kaloko Industrial Park. Developed for local consumers, this shopping plaza has outlets such as Costco Warehouse and Home Depot. It can be useful for practical purchases (food from Costco can be a good deal if you're staying in a condo for a week or more) and the occasional surprise gift item (you don't have to tell them you got it at the Hawaiʻi Costco). ⊠ *Off Hwy. 19 and Hina Lani St., near Keāhole-Kona International Airport.*

Kona Marketplace. On the *makai* (ocean) side of Aliʻi Drive, in the heart of Kailua-Kona and extending for an entire block along Kailua Bay, the village is crammed with boutiques selling bright beach wraps and knickknacks. ⊠ *75-5744 Aliʻi Dr.*

Makalapua Center. Just north of Kona, off Highway 19, this shopping center attracts islanders for the great bargains at Kmart and island-influenced clothing, jewelry, and housewares at the large Macy's. There's also one of the island's largest movie theaters here. ⊠ *Kamakaeha Ave. at Hwy. 19, Kailua-Kona.*

ARTS AND CRAFTS

★ **Antiques and Orchids.** Housed in a great old green building with white trim along Highway 11, this shop lives up to its name, offering shoppers a well-selected collection of antiques and Hawaiiana, interspersed with orchids of assorted colors and varieties. If you're on your way to Volcano, make a stop here (either drive through or walk in) to pick up a great cup of coffee, a yummy baked good, or a root beer float at the store's new coffee shop. ⊠ *81-6224 Māmalahoa Hwy., Captain Cook* ☎ *808/323–9851.*

Hōlualoa Gallery. In the little coffee town of Hōlualoa, this is one of several excellent galleries that crowd the narrow street. It carries stunning contemporary *raku* pottery, original paintings, sculptures, and other collectibles. ⊠ *76-5921 Māmalahoa Hwy., Hōlualoa* ☎ *808/322–8484* ⊕ *www.lovein.com.*

CLOTHING

★ **Hilo Hattie.** The well-known clothier matches his-and-her aloha wear and carries a huge selection of casual clothes, slippers, jewelry, and souvenirs. ■TIP➜ **Call for free transportation from nearby hotels.** ⊠ *75-5597 Palani Rd., across from Kopiko Plaza, Kailua-Kona* ☎ *808/329–7200* ⊕ *www.hilohattie.com.*

Honolua Surf Company. Surfer chic, compliments of Roxy, Volcom, and the like, is on offer here. This is a great place to look for a bikini or board shorts, or to pick up a cool, casual T-shirt. They have two additional locations in the Kings' Shops in Waikoloa: another branch like this one and one that focuses on women's clothing, with a large assortment of bathing suits and sundresses. ⊠ *Kona Inn Shopping Village* ☎ *808/329–1001* ⊠ *Kings' Shops, 250 Waikoloa Beach Dr., Waikoloa* ☎ *808/886-6422 (surf shop), 808/886–1019 (women's shop)* ⊕ *www. honoluasurf.com.*

Paradise Found. In the Upcountry town of Kainaliu, as well as in two of Kailua-Kona's shopping centers, this reputable spot carries contemporary silk and rayon clothing. ⊠ *Māmalahoa Hwy. 11, Kainaliu* ☎ *808/322–2111* ⊠ *Keauhou Shopping Center, 78-6831 Ali'i Dr., Kailua-Kona* ☎ *808/324–1177.*

FOOD

Kailua Candy Company. This chocolate company has been satisfying those with a sweet tooth for 34 years, with decadent desserts and sinful bites of pure chocolate heaven. Many truffles and candies incorporate local ingredients (passion-fruit truffles and chocolate-covered mango—yum). There are also a variety of cheesecakes and mousse cakes that will melt in your mouth. Of course, tasting is part of the fun. Through a glass wall you can watch the chocolate artists at work. ⊠ *In the Koloko Industrial Area, between Costco and Home Depot Kamanu and Kauholo Sts., Kailua-Kona* ☎ *808/329–2522* ⊕ *www.kailuacandy.com.*

Kona Coffee & Tea Company. A location 4 mi south of the airport and across from the Honokohau Marina makes this family-owned coffee company's retail outlet a good bet for some easy gourmet gift shopping—or just a coffee or tea stop. Try different roasts or a selection of flavored coffees from the coffee bar, and shop for other Hawaiian-made treats from honey and jams to chocolate-covered coffee beans. The shop is behind the Tesoro gas station. ⊠ *74-5035 Queen Ka'ahumanu Hwy., Kailua-Kona* ☎ *808/329–6577* ⊕ *www.konacoffeeandtea.com.*

Kona Wine Market. The new location of this popular wine market carries both local and imported varietals, other gourmet food items, Hawaiian gifts and products (macadamia nuts, coffee, etc.), and the best selection of cigars and tobacco products on the island. As an added bonus, they'll deliver wine and any of their gourmet food products to your hotel or condo. Their Mixx Bistro Bar, with live music and a happy hour, is still in operation at the store's old location on Kuakini Highway. ⊠ *Kona Commons, 74-5450 Makala Blvd.* ☎ *808/329–9400* ⊕ *www. konawinemarket.com.*

GALLERIES

Kona Art Gallery. Gallery owners Gary and Elizabeth Theriault showcase a variety of local art here, including Gary's Big Island life photos, Elizabeth's hand-painted drums and rattles. They also feature works from other artists, including Hawaiian *ipus* (gourds that are used as instruments in hula dancing), exotic wood items, paper sculptures, quilts, jewelry, and other local crafts. ⊠ *Māmalahoa Hwy., Hōlualoa* ☎ *808/322–5125.*

Pacific Fine Art. Both the oldest and largest gallery on the island, Pacific Fine Art represents 42 artists from across the globe. They have everything from original paintings to limited editions, sculptures, glass, and raku ceramic pieces. ⊠ *Kona Inn Shopping Village, 75-5744 Ali'i Dr., Kailua-Kona* ☎ *808/329–5009.*

MARKETS

★ **Ali'i Gardens Marketplace.** More a flea market than a farmers' market, this cluster of about 50 vendor stalls has beautiful tropical flowers, jewelry, clothing, produce, coffee, and even 'ukuleles. It's open Wednesday to Sunday, 9 am until 5 pm. ⊠ *75-6129 Ali'i Dr.* ⊹ *1½ mi south of Kona Inn Shopping Village, Kailua-Kona* ☎ *808/334–1381* ⊕ *www. aliigardens.com.*

Keauhou Farmers' Market. Less obvious than the others in its location 5 mi south of Kailua-Kona, this market is packed most Saturdays (8 am–noon) for good reason: live music, plus local produce (much of it organic, some of it experimental), honey, goat cheese, meat, seafood, flowers, coffee, macadamia nuts, and more. ⊠ *Keauhou Shopping Center, 78-6831 Ali'i Dr., Kailua-Kona* ⊕ *www.keauhoufarmersmarket.com.*

Kona Inn Farmers' Market. This low-key farmers' market is filled with produce, coffee, and macadamia nuts from around the region. It's held in the parking lot of the Kona Inn Shopping Village Wednesday through Sunday from 7 am until 3 pm. ⊠ *75-7544 Ali'i Dr.* ⊹ *Park at Kona Inn Shopping Village parking lot, Kailua-Kona.*

Kona International Market. The new kid on the block, housed in an open-air facility, has attracted vendors away from other island markets to sell flowers, local produce, Hawaiian crafts, clothes, and random collectibles. It's open Monday through Sunday, from 9 am to 5 pm, and includes both farmers' market vendor stalls and proper stores—it's great one-stop shopping for all your souvenirs. ⊠ *On Luhia St.* ✛ *In Kailua-Kona's Old Industrial Area* ⊕ *www.konainternationalmarket.com.*

THE KOHALA COAST

SHOPPING CENTERS

Kawaihae Harbor Center. This harborside shopping plaza houses a dive shop, several restaurants, and a few art galleries, including the Harbor Gallery. ⊠ *Hwy. 270, Kawaihae.*

Kings' Shops at Waikoloa Beach Resort. Here you can find fine stores such as Under the Koa Tree, with its upscale gift items crafted by artisans, along with high-end outlets including Coach, Tiffany & Co., and Louis Vuitton. There are also several specialty resort shops and boutiques and, at the other end of the spectrum, a couple of convenience stores, though the prices are stiff. ⊠ *250 Waikoloa Beach Dr., Waikoloa Beach Resort, Waikoloa* ☎ *808/886–8811* ⊕ *www.waikoloabeachresort.com.*

The Shops at Mauna Lani. This complex includes restaurants (Tommy Bahama's Tropical Café, Ruth's Chris Steakhouse, and Monstera), clothing (Tommy Bahama's and Jams World), high-end housewares (Oasis), galleries (Lahaina Galleries and the Third Dimension Gallery), jewelry stores, a lingerie shop, and a Foodland Farms market. ⊠ *68-1330 Mauna Lani Dr., Kohala Coast* ☎ *808/885–9501* ⊕ *www. shopsatmaunalani.com.*

Waikoloa Queens' Marketplace. Another large shopping complex on the Kohala Coast, this one houses several clothing shops, a jewelry store, a gallery, gift shops, a few restaurants, and a food court. Their newest anchor tenant is Island Gourmet Markets, a 20,000-square-foot gourmet grocery store. The marketplace butts up against a new performing arts center and a landscaped network of "Cultural Gardens." ⊠ *201 Waikoloa Beach Dr., Waikoloa Beach Resort, Waikoloa* ☎ *808/886– 8822* ⊕ *www.waikoloabeachresort.com.*

ARTS AND CRAFTS

Elements Jewelry & Fine Crafts. This shop recently moved out of its old home at Nanbu Hotel and is now located in artsy Hāwī. John Flynn no longer creates his jewelry in the front window for passersby, but he still owns the shop and showcases his exquisite jewelry pieces. Look for the delicate silver lei and gold waterfalls. The shop also carries carefully chosen gifts, including unusual ceramics, paintings, prints, and glass items. ⊠ *55-3413 Akoni Pule Hwy., Hāwī* ☎ *808/889–0760* ⊕ *www. elementsjewelryandcrafts.com.*

Island Pearls. This store carries a wide selection of fine pearl jewelry, including Tahitian black pearls, South Sea white and golden pearls, and chocolate Tahitian pearls. Prices are high but you're paying for quality and beauty. ⊠ *Waikoloa Queens' Marketplace, 201 Waikoloa Beach Dr., Waikoloa* ☎ *808/886–4817* ⊕ *www.waikoloabeachresort.com.*

Gallery at Bamboo. Inside the Bamboo Restaurant, one of the island's favorite eateries, this gallery seduces visitors with elegant koa-wood furniture pieces. It also has a wealth of gift items such as boxes, jewelry, and even aloha shirts. ⊠ *Hwy. 270, Hāwī* ☎ *808/889–1441* ⊕ *www. bamboorestaurant.info*

Hawaiian Quilt Collection. The Hawaiian quilt is a work of art that is prized and passed down through generations. At this store you find everything from hand-quilted purses and bags to wall hangings and blankets. You can even get a take-home kit and make your very own Hawaiian quilt, if you have the time. ⊠ *Waikoloa Queens' Marketplace, 201 Waikoloa Beach Dr., Waikoloa* ☎ *808/886–0494* ⊕ *www. hawaiianquilts.com.*

CLOTHING

As Hāwī Turns. This North Kohala shop, in the historic 1932 Toyama Building, adds a sophisticated touch to resort wear with items made of hand-painted silk. There are vintage and secondhand treasures, jewelry, and other gift items as well. ⊠ *Akoni Pule Hwy., Hāwī* ☎ *808/889–5023.*

Blue Ginger. The Waikoloa branch of this 25-year fashion veteran has really sweet matching aloha outfits for the entire family. ⊠ *Waikoloa Queens' Marketplace, 201 Waikoloa Beach Dr., Waikoloa* ☎ *808/886– 0022* ⊕ *www.blueginger.com.*

Cinnamon Girl. Famous for its original print dresses, skirts, and tops for women and girls, this store's feminine, flirty outfits are all designed in Hawai'i and offer a contemporary twist on traditional "aloha" wear. In addition to clothing, this boutique carries jewelry, hats, slippers, stuffed animals, and other trinkets and toys. ⊠ *Kings' Shops at Waikoloa Beach Resort, 250 Waikoloa Beach Dr., Waikoloa* ☎ *808/886–4201* ⊕ *www. cinnamongirl.com.*

Local Motion. This is one of Hawai'i's favorite local surf shops. Geared towards the younger surfer set, the store carries men's, women's, and children's clothing, plus everything you need for a laid-back day at the beach. Their locally designed license-plate frames, slippers, towels, and bags are a great reminder of your trip to the island. ⊠ *Waikoloa Queens' Marketplace, 201 Waikoloa Beach Dr., Waikoloa* ☎ *808/886– 7873* ⊕ *www.localmotionhawaii.com.*

Persimmon. This darling little boutique is stocked with trendy women's clothing from lines such as Three Dots, Trinity, Sky, Michael Stars, Hard Tail, and 7 Jeans. They also carry beautiful locally made jewelry. Other gift items include funky stationery and cards, and Island-themed bath and body products. ⊠ *Waikoloa Queens' Marketplace, 201 Waikoloa Beach Dr., Waikoloa* ☎ *808/886–0303* ⊕ *www.persimmonboutique.com.*

Reyn's. Reyn Spooner aloha shirts are well known throughout Hawai'i and have been since 1959. The store offers aloha shirts for both men and boys, men's shorts, and some dresses for women and girls. The aloha shirts, by the way, are high quality—and high price. ⊠ *Waiko-*

loa Queens' Marketplace, 201 Waikoloa Beach Dr., Waikoloa ☎ *808/ 886–1162* ⊕ *www.reyns.com.*

GALLERIES

Ackerman Fine Art Gallery. This gallery is truly a family affair. Painter Gary Ackerman's daughter, Alyssa, and her husband, Ronnie, run the gallery that showcases several family members' artworks. Don't miss the fine and varied collection of gifts for sale in their side-by-side gallery and gift shop near the King Kamehameha statue. ⊠ *54-3878 Akoni Pule Hwy., Kapaʻau* ☎ *808/889–5971* ⊕ *www.ackermangalleries.com and www.ackermanhawaii.com.*

Rankin Gallery. Watercolorist and oil painter Patrick Louis Rankin showcases his own work in his shop in a restored old plantation store (the Wo On Store), next to the Chinese community and social hall, the Tong Wo Society, on the way to Pololū Valley. ⊠ *53-4380 Akoni Pule Hwy., Kapaʻau* ☎ *808/889–6849* ⊕ *www.patricklouisrankin.net.*

WAIMEA

SHOPPING CENTERS

Parker Ranch Center. With a snazzy ranch-style motif, this shopping hub includes a supermarket, some great local eateries, a coffee shop, natural foods store, and some clothing boutiques. The Parker Ranch Store and Parker Ranch Visitor Center and Museum are also here, and the Kahilu Center next door hosts plays and musical entertainment most nights. ⊠ *67-1185 Māmalahoa Hwy., Waimea* ⊕ *www. parkerranchcenterads.com.*

Parker Square. Browse around boutiques here and in the adjacent **High Country Traders,** where you may find hand-stitched Hawaiian quilts, antiques, or local artworks. ⊠ *65-1279 Kawaihae Rd., Waimea* ☎ *808/331–1000.*

ARTS AND CRAFTS

Gallery of Great Things. At this Parker Square shop, you might fall in love with the Niʻihau shell lei ranging from $350 to $7,000. More affordable are koa mirrors and other high-quality artifacts from around the Pacific basin. ⊠ *65-1279 Kawaihae Rd., Waimea* ☎ *808/885–7706.*

Harbor Gallery. Though it carries some of the usual ocean-scene schlock, Harbor has one of the better and more unique selections of art on the island. Expect to find fine art, furniture, and decorative pieces made with koa and other native woods. The gallery is next to Café Pesto. ⊠ *Kawaihae Harbor Center, Hwy. 270, Kawaihae* ☎ *808/882–1510* ⊕ *www.harborgallery.biz.*

THE HĀMĀKUA COAST

ARTS AND CRAFTS

Glass from the Past. The best place to stop for a quirky gift or just to poke around, Glass from the Past is a truly unique store chock-full of antiques, vintage clothing, furniture, a colorful assortment of old

bottles, and ephemera. ⊠ *28-1672 Old Māmalahoa Hwy., #A, Honomū*
☎ *808/963–6449.*

GALLERIES

Waipi'o Valley Artworks. In this remote gallery you can find finely crafted
wooden bowls, koa furniture, paintings, and jewelry—all made by local
artists, plus a great little café where you can pick up a sandwich or ice
cream before descending into the valley. ⊠ *Off Hwy. 240, Kukuihaele*
☎ *808/775–0958* ⊕ *www.waipiovalleyartworks.com.*

Woodshop Gallery. This pleasant surprise in Honomū, run by local artists
Peter and Janette McLaren, showcases their woodwork and photography collections along with beautiful ceramics, woodwork, photography,
glass, and fine art from other Big Island artists. The McLarens also serve
up plate lunches, shave ice, homemade ice cream, and espresso to hungry tourists in their adjoining café. ⊠ *28-1692 Old Government Rd.,
Honomū* ☎ *808/963–6363* ⊕ *www.woodshopgallery.com.*

HILO

SHOPPING CENTERS

Hilo Shopping Center. This shopping plaza has blossomed with the addition of its newest tenant: Island Naturals Market & Deli. Also look for
several trendy boutiques, a store selling everything you need for baby, a
salon, a coffee shop, and a few other restaurants. Great cookies, cakes,
and baked goodies are at Lanky's Pastries. There's plenty of free parking. ⊠ *345 Kekuanaoa St. at Kīlauea Ave., Hilo.*

Prince Kūhiō Shopping Plaza. Hilo's most comprehensive mall, Prince
Kūhiō Shopping Plaza is where you can find Macy's for fashion, Blockbuster for entertainment, Safeway for food, and Longs Drugs for just
about everything else, along with several other shops and boutiques.
⊠ *111 E. Puainako St., at Hwy. 11, Hilo* ☎ *808/959–3555* ⊕ *www.
princekuhioplaza.com.*

Waiakea Center. Here you can find a Down to Earth vegetarian store,
Ross Dress for Less, Office Max, and a Wal-Mart. If all the shopping
makes you hungry, there's also a food court and one of the island's
best restaurants, Hilo Bay Café, tucked away in the corner. ⊠ *315-325
Maka'ala St. at Kanoelehua Ave., across from Prince Kūhiō Shopping
Plaza, at Hwy. 11, Hilo* ☎ *808/792–7225.*

ARTS AND CRAFTS

Dan DeLuz's Woods. Master bowl-turner Dan DeLuz creates works of art
from 50 types of exotic wood grown on the Big Island. The shop features a variety of items—from picture frames to jewelry boxes—made
from koa, monkeypod, mango, kiawe, and other fine local hardwoods.
Dan's wife, Mary Lou, operates the Koa Shop Kaffee restaurant next
door. ⊠ *Hwy. 19, Mountain View* ☎ *808/968–6607.*

Most Irresistible Shop. This place lives up to its name by stocking unique
gifts from around the Pacific, be it coconut-flavored butter or whimsical
wind chimes. ⊠ *256 Kamehameha Ave.* ☎ *808/935–9644.*

BOOKS AND MAGAZINES

Basically Books. This shop stocks one of Hawai'i's largest selections of maps and charts, including topographical and relief maps. It also has Hawaiiana books, with great choices for children. ✉ *160 Kamehameha Ave., Hilo* ☎ *808/961-0144 or 800/903-6277* ⊕ *www.basicallybooks.com.*

CLOTHING AND SHOES

★ **Hilo Hattie.** The east coast outlet of the well-known clothier is slightly smaller than its Kailua-Kona cousin, but still offers plenty of the same his-and-her aloha wear, casual clothes, slippers, jewelry, and souvenirs. ✉ *Prince Kūhiō Shopping Plaza, 111 E. Puainako St., Hilo* ☎ *808/961-3077* ⊕ *www.hilohattie.com.*

★ **Sig Zane Designs.** This acclaimed boutique sells distinctive island wearables with bold colors and motifs. ✉ *122 Kamehameha Ave., Hilo* ☎ *808/935-7077* ⊕ *www.sigzane.com.*

FLOWERS AND LEI

Fuku-Bonsai Cultural Center. In addition to selling and shipping dwarf schfflera plants, this place on the way to Volcano has interesting exhibits of different ethnic styles of pruning. ✉ *Ola'a Rd., Kurtistown* ☎ *808/982-9880.*

FOOD

★ **Big Island Candies.** This local legend in the cookie- and chocolate-making business is a must-see if you have a sweet tooth. Enjoy a free cookie sample and a cup of Kona coffee as you watch the sweets being made through a big glass window overlooking the factory. Big Island Candies has a long list of interesting and tasty products but they are best known for their chocolate-dipped shortbread cookies. Open 365 days a year, this is a great spot to look for tasty gifts to take home. ✉ *585 Hinano St., Hilo* ☎ *808/935-8890* ⊕ *www.bigislandcandies.com.*

Hilo Coffee Mill. In addition to a fantastic coffee-farm tour, the Hilo Coffee Mill sells coffee from a variety of local producers, along with locally made baked goods, candies, artwork, and gifts. ✉ *17-995 Volcano Rd., between mile markers 12 and 13, Mountain View* ☎ *808/968-1333* ⊕ *www.hilocoffeemill.com.*

Two Ladies Kitchen. This hole-in-the-wall confections shop in the heart of Hilo makes a variety of pillowy *mochi* (Japanese rice that is pounded into a sticky paste and molded into shape). They're best known for their fresh strawberry option: a huge ripe strawberry covered in creamy *adzuki* (sweet red) beans and wrapped in a white mochi covering. These won't last as long as a box of chocolates—most mochi items are only good for two or three days, and the fresh strawberry mochi can't be carried back to the mainland. To guarantee you get your fill, call ahead a few days out and place your order because these sweets go fast! ✉ *274 Kilauea Ave., Hilo* ☎ *808/961–4766* ⊘ *Closed Sun.–Tues.*

HOME DECOR

Dragon Mama. Step into this popular downtown Hilo spot to find authentic Japanese fabrics, futons, and antiques, along with a limited but elegant selection of clothing, sleepwear, and slippers for women. ✉ *266 Kamehameha Ave., Hilo* ☎ *808/934–9081* ⊕ *www.dragonmama. com.*

MARKETS

★ **Hilo Farmers' Market.** The farmers here sell a profusion of tropical flowers, high-quality produce, and macadamia nuts. This colorful, open-air market—the most popular in the state—opens for business Wednesday and Saturday from 6:30 am to 2:30 pm. ✉ *Kamehameha Ave. and Mamo St., Hilo* ☎ *808/933–1000* ⊕ *www.hilofarmersmarket.com.*

SPAS

The Big Island's spa directors have done their homework and produced menus full of "only in Hawai'i" treatments well worth a holiday splurge. Local specialties include *lomilomi* massages, hot lava stone massages, and scrubs and wraps that incorporate plenty of coconut, orchids, ginger, and macadamia nuts. The only full-service spas on the Big Island are associated with the resorts on the west coast; most of these are also open to nonguests.

Ho'ōla Spa at the Sheraton Keauhou Bay. The Sheraton Keauhou Bay occupies one of the prettier corners of the island, with an unbeatable view from most parts of the hotel. That said, it's too bad that the Ho'ōla Spa fails to truly take advantage of its location. Although there are plenty of windows with pretty views of the bay, the spa lacks the outdoor treatment areas other island spas are known for. Still, the spa menu includes a variety of locally influenced treatments, and the warm lava-rock massage is a little slice of heaven. The packages are an excellent deal, combining several services for far less than you would pay à la carte. For couples, the spa offers an ocean-side massage that takes place on a balcony overlooking the water, followed by a dip in a whirlpool bath. ✉ *78-128 Ehukai St., Kailua-Kona* ☎ *808/930–4848* ⊕ *www. sheratonkeauhou.com* ✐ *$120 50-min lomilomi massage; $225–$380 packages. Hair salon, hot tub, sauna, steam room. Services: aromatherapy, body scrubs and wraps, facials, massages, waxing.*

★ **Kohala Spa at the Hilton Waikoloa Village.** The orchids that run riot in the rain forests of the Big Island suffuse the signature treatments at the Kohala Spa. By the end of the Orchid Isle Wrap, you're completely immersed in the scent and in bone-deep relaxation. The island's volcanic character is also expressed in several treatments, as well as in the design of the lava-rock soaking tubs. Locker rooms are outfitted with a wealth of beauty and bath products. The extensive hair and nail salon could satisfy even Bridezilla with its updo consultations and luxe pedicure stations. The nearby ocean-side cabanas are the perfect venue for a massage on the beach. The fitness center is well-equipped and group classes are plentiful with everything from Zumba to water aerobics to yoga to gyrokinesis. ⊠ *Hilton Waikoloa Village, 69-425 Waikoloa Beach Dr., Waikoloa* ☎ *808/886–2828 or 800/445–8667* ⊕ *www.kohalaspa. com* ☞ *$145 50-min lomilomi massage, $489–$599 half-day packages. Hair salon, hot tubs (indoor and outdoor), sauna, steam room. Gym with: Cardiovascular machines, free weights, weight-training equipment. Services: Aromatherapy, body scrubs and wraps, facials, massage. Classes and programs: Personal training, Pilates, Spinning, water aerobics, yoga.*

★ **Mamalahoa Hot Tubs and Massage.** Tucked into a residential neighborhood above Kealekekua, this little gem is a welcome alternative to the large resort spas. Soaking tubs are made of the finest quality wood, tropical plants and flowers abound, and each tub is enclosed in its own little tiki hut, with portholes in the roof for your stargazing pleasure. Tastefully laid out and run, there's no seedy "hot tub party" vibe here, just a pleasant soak followed by, if you like, an hour-long massage. Mamalahoa offers *lomilomi,* Swedish, deep tissue, and a Hawaiian hot stone massage performed with lava rocks collected from around the island. Indulge in some romance with a twilight soak from 7:30 to 9 pm at $40 per couple. In addition to its secret hideaway ambience, Mamalahoa's prices are lower than any other spa on the island. ⊠ *81-1016 St. John's Rd., Kealekekua, south of Kailua-Kona* ☎ *808/323–2288* ⊕ *www.mamalahoa-hottubs.com* ☞ *$30 60-min soak; $95 30-min soak plus 60-min lomilomi, Swedish, or deep-tissue massage, $150 30-min soak plus 90-min hot stone massage.* ⊗ *By appointment only. Open Wed.–Sat. noon–8 pm.*

★ **Mandara Spa at the Waikoloa Beach Marriott Resort.** Overlooking the hotel's main pool with a distant view of the ocean, Mandara offers a very complete if not unique spa menu, with more available facial options than you'll find at the island's other spas. Mandara operates spas throughout the world and on a number of cruise lines, and they are managing this one for Marriott, using Elemis and La Therapie products in spa and salon treatments. The spa menu contains the usual suspects—*lomilomi,* a variety of facials, scrubs, and wraps—but they do incorporate local ingredients where appropriate (lime and ginger in the scrubs, warm coconut milk in the wraps), and the new facilities, designed in a style that combines 20th-century modern American with traditional Asian motifs, are beautiful. ⊠ *69-275 Waikoloa Beach Dr., Waikoloa* ☎ *808/886–8191* ⊕ *www.mandaraspa.com* ☞ *$145 50-min lomilomi massage; $450-$500 half-day packages. Hair salon, steam room. Gym with: Cardiovascular machines, free weights, weight-training equipment. Services: Aromatherapy, body scrubs and wraps, facials, massage, nail treatments, waxing.*

Mauna Kea Spa by Mandara. Mandara Spas blend one-third European, one-third Balinese, and one-third indigenous treatments to create the ultimate spa experience. Things are no different at this newly renovated spa at the Mauna Kea Beach Hotel. Though the facility is on the smaller side, the excellent treatments are up to Mandara Spa standards. Try the Elemis Tri-Enzyme Resurfacing Facial or, even better, the Mandara Four Hand Massage where two therapists work out the kinks simultaneously. The hotel operates a separate hair salon that offers manicures and pedicures in addition to standard salon services. ⊠ *69-100 Mauna Kea Beach Drive., Kohala Coast* ☎ *808/882–5630* ⊕ *www. mandaraspa.com* ☞ *$181 50-min lomilomi. Services: Body treatments, facials, massage, waxing. Gym with: Cardiovascular machines, weight-training equipment. Classes and programs: Yoga.*

Fodor'sChoice
★

Mauna Lani Spa. If you're looking for a one-of-a-kind experience, this is your destination. Most treatments take place in outdoor *hales* (houses) surrounded by lava rock. Incredible therapists offer a mix of the old standbys (*lomilomi* massage, moisturizing facials) and innovative treatments, many of which are heavily influenced by ancient traditions and incorporate local products. One exfoliating body treatment is self-administered in one of the outdoor saunas—a great choice for people who aren't too keen on therapists seeing them in their birthday suits. Watsu therapy takes place in an amazing pool filled and heated by the adjacent lava tube, with help from solar panels overhead. Meant to re-create the feeling of being in a womb, the hour-long therapy is essentially an underwater massage. You feel totally weightless, thanks to some artfully applied weights and the buoyancy of the warm saltwater. It's a great treatment for people with disabilities that keep them from enjoying a traditional massage. The aesthetic treatments on the menu incorporate high-end products from Epicuran and Emminence, so a facial will have a real and lasting therapeutic effect on your skin. The spa also offers a full regimen of fitness and yoga classes. ⊠ *Mauna Lani Resort, 68-1365 Pauoa Rd., Kohala Coast* ☎ *808/881–7922* ⊕ *www. maunalani.com* ☞ *$159 50-min lomilomi massage; $345–$799 packages. Hair salon, hot tubs (indoor and outdoor), sauna, steam room. Gym with: Cardiovascular machines, free weights, weight-training equipment. Services: Aquatic therapy, baths, body wraps, facials, massage, scrubs, waxing and tinting, nail treatment. Classes and programs: body sculpting, kickboxing, personal training, Pilates, Spinning, weight training, yoga.*

Paul Brown Salon & Spa at the Hāpuna Beach Prince Hotel. It's not unusual for locals to drive an hour each way to get their hair cut here. Paul Brown has been in the business for 30 years, and he now has three locations in Hawai'i. Hair is still the specialty, but it's not just a salon. The full-service spa—nicely designed to let in lots of light—has an extensive menu of massages, facials, and body treatments. The most popular massage is the *lomilomi* (traditional Hawaiian massage) but don't overlook the spa's unique body treatments including the seaweed wrap, the detoxifying volcanic clay treatment, and the Hawaiian salt and aloe exfoliation. This is also the best place for waxing. You can use the gym at the Hāpuna Golf Course's clubhouse, accessible via a free shuttle. ⊠ *62-100 Kauna'oa Dr., Kohala Coast* ☎ *808/880–3335* ⊕ *www. paulbrownhawaii.com* ☞ *$115 50-min lomilomi massage, $338–$410 half-day package; $575 full-day package. Hair salon, sauna, steam room. Services: Acupuncture, body wraps, facials, massage. Classes and programs: Aerobics, Pilates, Spinning, yoga.*

Fodor'sChoice
★

Spa Without Walls at the Fairmont Orchid Hawai'i. This is possibly the best massage on the island, partially due to having the best setting—massage tables face either the ocean or a waterfall. Though most people will probably opt for the ocean, both settings are absolutely peaceful. There are other great treatments as well, including caviar facials, fragrant herbal wraps, and coffee and vanilla scrubs, but the massages are the best things going. ⊠ *Fairmont Orchid Hawai'i, 1 N. Kanikū Dr., Kohala Coast* ☎ *808/887–7540 or 808/885–2000* ⊕ *www.fairmont.com/orchid* ☞ *$159–$179 50-min lomilomi massage. Sauna, steam room. Gym with: cardiovascular machines, free weights, weight-training equipment. Services: baths, body wraps, facials, massage, scrubs. Classes and programs: aquaerobics, guided walks, meditation, personal training, yoga.*

ENTERTAINMENT AND NIGHTLIFE

4

If you're the sort of person who doesn't come alive until after dark, you might be a little lonely on the Big Island. Blame it on the plantation heritage. People did their cane raising in the morning. Still, there are a few lively bars on the island, a handful of great local playhouses, half a dozen or so movie houses (including those that play foreign and independent films), and plenty of musical entertainment to keep you occupied. And let's not forget the lū'au. These fantastic dance and musical performances are combined with some of the best meals on the island and are plenty of fun for the whole family.

ENTERTAINMENT

DINNER CRUISES AND SHOWS

★ **Evening on the Reef Glass Bottom Dinner Cruise.** Blue Sea Cruises offers a classed-up alternative to the booze cruise, with soothing Hawaiian music, buffet dinner, and tropical juices and cocktails. It's focus is on the sunset and the scenery, with the chance to see spinner dolphins, manta rays (and whales from November to May). Guests also enjoy what's below the surface through the boat's glass bottom. ⊠ *Kailua Pier, Kailua-Kona* ☎ *808/331–8875* ⊕ *www.blueseacruisesinc.com* 🎫 *$98* ⊗ *Mon., Wed., Thurs., Fri. and Sat., times vary by season.*

LŪ'AU AND POLYNESIAN REVUES

KAILUA-KONA

King Kamehameha's Kona Beach Hotel. Witness the royal court procession at the Island Breeze Lū'au, a beachfront event, which includes a 22-item buffet, an open bar, and a show. ⊠ *75-5660 Palani Rd., Kailua-Kona* ☎ *808/326–4969 or 808/329–8111* ⊕ *www.islandbreezeluau.com* 🎫 *$78.80* ⊗ *Tues., Wed., Thurs., and Sun. 5–8.*

Royal Kona Resort. This resort lights lū'au torches for a full Polynesian show and a Hawaiian-style oceanfront buffet three times a week. ⊠ *75-5852 Ali'i Dr., Kailua-Kona* ☎ *808/329–3111, Ext. 4* ⊕ *www. royalkona.com* 🎫 *$65 if you book online, $78 if you book at the hotel* ⊗ *Mon., Wed., and Fri. at 5.*

Sheraton Keauhou Bay. A recent addition to the Big Island's lū'au scene, Island Breeze's production of "Firenesia," tells the story of a young man who journeys through Polynesia and embraces a greater understanding

of fire. Get ready for lots of mesmerizing fire dancing in addition to storytelling through traditional hula and Hawaiian language. The open bar doesn't hurt either. ⊠ *75-5852 Aliʻi Dr., Kailua-Kona* 🕾 *808/930–4900* ⊕ *www.sheratonkeauhou.com or www.firenesia.com* 🍴 *$83.28* 🕐 *Mon. at 5.*

KOHALA COAST

Fairmont Orchid. The Fairmont's "Gathering of the Kings Polynesian Feast" offers the most entertainment bang for your resort buck. The show is slickly produced and well choreographed, incorporating both traditional and modern dance and choreography as well as beautiful costumes. The meal offers more variety than most, with options representing all the early Hawaiian settlers, including those from New Zealand, Hawaii, Tahiti, and Samoa. ⊠ *1 N. Kaniku Dr., Kohala Coast* 🕾 *808/885–2000* ⊕ *www.fairmont.com/orchid* 🍴 *$103* 🕐 *Sat. at 6.*

Hilton Waikoloa Village. The Hilton seats 400 people outdoors at the Kamehameha Court, where the acclaimed Polynesian group Tihati performs a lively show. A buffet dinner provides samplings of Hawaiian food as well as fish, beef, and chicken to appeal to all tastes. **TripAdvisor:** "not the best location," "rooms are worn," "great place for kids." ⊠ *425 Waikoloa Beach Dr., Waikoloa* 🕾 *808/886–1234* ⊕ *www.hiltonwaikoloavillage.com* 🍴 *$99, includes two cocktails* 🕐 *Tues., Fri., Sun. at 6.*

★ **Kona Village Resort.** At this writing the Kona Village Resort was closed indefinitely due to tsunami damage in March 2011. In its utter isolation, the lūʻau here is one of the most authentic and traditional on the Islands. As in other lūʻau, activities include the steaming of a whole pig in the *imu* (ground oven). The Wednesday night show focuses solely on Hawaiian traditions and music, while Friday night incorporates Polynesian dancing, music, and traditions as well. The dancing, done on a stage over a lagoon, is magical. ⊠ *Queen Kaʻahumanu Hwy., 6 mi north of Kona International Airport, Kailua-Kona* 🕾 *808/325–5555 or 808/325–4273* ⊕ *www.konavillage.com* 🍴 *$98, includes one cocktail* 🕐 *Wed. and Fri. from 5:15, imu ceremony at 6, dinner at 6:30, show at 7:30; Tues. barbecue 6–8.*

Mauna Kea Beach Hotel Clambake. A departure from the normal outdoor Hawaiian lūʻau, the Mauna Kea Beach Hotel's weekly clambake is the perfect way to enjoy the bounty of the Pacific Ocean beachside under the stars. There isn't a pig cooked in an underground oven but you will get your fill of fine seafood with an extensive menu that includes oysters on the half shell, ʻahi sashimi, fresh island fish, Manila clams, mussels, Dungeness crab legs and steamed Keāhole lobster. There's even prime rib of beef for meat lovers. The best part of this clambake besides the food is the setting (which can't be beat), and the live Hawaiian music that is often accompanied by a graceful hula dancer. ⊠ *62-100 Mauna Kea Beach Dr., Kohala Coast* 🕾 *808/882–5810 or 808/882–7222* ⊕ *www.maunakeabeachhotel.com* 🍴 *$86* 🕐 *Sat. at 6.*

Waikoloa Beach Marriott. At this celebration, entertainment includes a Samoan fire dance as well as songs and dances of various Pacific cultures. Traditional Hawaiian dishes are served alongside more familiar fare. ✉ 69-275 *Waikoloa Beach Dr., Waikoloa* ☎ 808/886–6789 ⊕ *www.marriott.com* ✍ *$88, including open bar* ⊙ *Wed. and Sun. 5–8:30.*

FESTIVALS

There is a festival dedicated to just about everything on the Big Island. Some of them are small community affairs, but a handful of film, food, and music festivals provide quality entertainment for visitors and locals alike. *The following is a list of our favorites:*

Black & White Night. This lovely annual outdoor party is in downtown Hilo. The stores stay open late, the sidewalks are dotted with live jazz bands, and everyone dresses in black and white, some in shorts and tees and others in gowns and tuxes, to enter the "Best Dressed" contest. ☎ *808/935–8850* ⊕ *www.downtownhilo.com* ⊙ *First Friday in Nov.*

Chinese New Year. Hilo throws a big free party complete with live music, food, drums, and fireworks downtown to commemorate this holiday every year. There's a smaller celebration along Aliʻi Drive in Kona as well. ☎ *808/935–8850* ⊕ *www.downtownhilo.com* ⊙ *Feb.*

Kona Brewers Festival. At this great annual party, roughly 30 breweries and 25 restaurants offer samples and live music, fire dancers, and fashion shows. ☎ *808/331–3033* ⊕ *www.konabrewersfestival.com* ⊙ *Early Mar.*

Kona Coffee Cultural Festival. The oldest food festival in Hawaiʻi brings together a variety of events over a 10-day period, but our favorite is the coffee recipe cooking contest. Coffee chili is one of the best things you've never tasted. ⊕ *www.konacoffeefest.com* ⊙ *Early Nov.*

★ **Merrie Monarch Festival.** The mother of all Big Island festivals, the Merrie Monarch celebrates all things hula and completely overtakes Hilo for one fantastic weekend a year. The largest event of its kind in the world honors the legacy of King David Kalākaua, Hawaiʻi's last king and the man responsible for reviving a lot of the fading Hawaiian traditions including the hula (of which he was a big fan). The festival is staged at the spacious Edith Kanakaʻole Stadium during the first week following Easter Sunday. Hula *hālau* (schools) compete in various classes of ancient and modern dance styles. ■ TIP→ You need to reserve accommodations and tickets up to a year in advance. If you're planning on being in Hilo during this time of year but not attending the festival, know that most accommodations will be booked about a year out and plan accordingly. ☎ *808/935–9168* ⊕ *www.merriemonarchfestival.org* ⊙ *Apr.*

A Taste of the Hawaiian Range Food and Agricultural Festival. Since 1995, this culinary event has been giving locals and visitors a taste of what the Islands' best chefs and farms have to offer, from grass-fed beef and bison to organic produce, cheese, chocolates, and coffee. ☎ *808/981–5199* ⊕ *www.ctahr.hawaii.edu/taste* ⊙ *Sept. or Oct.*

Catch a Big Island sunset while hiking on mountaintops covered with lava fields.

THEATER

Aloha Theatre. Local talent stages musicals and Broadway plays at this charming old plantation center near Kailua-Kona. ✉ *79-7384 Māmalahoa Hwy., Kainaliu* ☎ *808/322–9924* ⊕ *www.alohatheatre. com.*

Kahilu Theater. For legitimate theater, the little town of Waimea is your best bet. The Kahilu Theater hosts regular internationally acclaimed performances, interspersed with a variety of top-notch music acts. In a recent season, Chick Corea, Laurie Anderson, and Pink Martini shared the calendar with modern dance performances, plays, and traditional Hawaiian dance shows. ✉ *Parker Ranch Center, 67-1185 Māmalahoa Hwy., Waimea* ☎ *808/885–6868* ⊕ *www.kahilutheatre.org.*

★ **Volcano Art Center.** Annual and special performances of Hawaiian music and dance, as well as theater performances, are hosted by this local art center. People drive here from all over the island for some of their Hawaiian music concerts. ✉ *P.O. Box 129* ☎ *808/967–8222* ⊕ *www. volcanoartcenter.org.*

NIGHTLIFE

KAILUA-KONA
BARS

Kona Brewing Company. Still very popular, the Kona Brewery has been a local favorite practically since it opened. Good food, good local beer (go for the sampler and try them all), and an outdoor patio with live

BEST SUNSET MAI TAIS

Crystal Blue at the Sheraton Keauhou (Kailua-Kona). Fantastic sunset views from plush lounge chairs, followed by spotlighted glimpses of nearby manta rays.

Huggo's on the Rocks (Kailua-Kona). Literally on the rocks with a sand-floored bar, strong drinks, and live music Friday and Saturday.

Kona Inn (Kailua-Kona). Wide, unobstructed view, in the middle of downtown, best mai tais on the island.

Wai'oli Lounge in the Hilo Hawaiian Hotel (Hilo). A nice view of Coconut Island, live music Friday and Saturday nights.

music on Sunday nights make sure it stays that way. ⊠ *75-5629 Kuakini Hwy.* ☎ *808/334–2739* ⊕ *www.konabrewingco.com.*

Mixx Bar & Bistro. Kailua-Kona's first and only wine bar, Mixx, is also the only air-conditioned bar in Kona, but it's got a few other things going for it as well—namely good food, stiff and inventive cocktails, and live music nightly on their outdoor patio. ⊠ *King Kamehameha Mall, 75-5626 Kuakini Hwy.* ☎ *808/329–7334* ⊕ *www.mixxbistro.com.*

Oceans Sports Bar & Grill. A popular gathering place, this sports bar in the back of the Coconut Grove Marketplace has a pool table and an outdoor patio, along with the dozens of TVs you'd expect at a sports bar. This place really gets hopping on the weekends and on karaoke nights (Tuesday and Thursday after 10). ⊠ *Coconut Grove Marketplace, 75-5811 Ali'i Dr., Kailua-Kona* ☎ *808/327–9494.*

CLUBS

Huggo's on the Rocks. Jazz, country, and even rock bands perform at this popular restaurant, so call ahead to find out what's on. Outside, people often dance in the sand to Hawaiian songs. The crowd skews to slightly older and better behaved than Lulu's across the street. ⊠ *75-5828 Kahakai Rd., at Ali'i Dr., Kailua-Kona* ☎ *808/329–1493* ⊕ *www.huggos.com.*

Lulu's. On weekends, the young crowd gyrates until late in the evening to hot dance music—hip-hop, R&B, and rock—spun by a professional DJ. ⊠ *Coconut Grove Marketplace 75-5819 Ali'i Dr., Kailua-Kona* ☎ *808/331–2633.*

THE KOHALA COAST

BARS

Luana Terrace. This wood-paneled watering hole in the Fairmont Orchid Hawai'i has a huge lānai and an impressive view. Bartenders are great, and service is impeccable. The crowd's not rowdy, so it's a nice place for an early evening cocktail or an after-dinner port. ⊠ *1 N. Kanikū Dr., Kohala Coast* ☎ *808/885–2000* ⊕ *www.fairmont.com/orchid.*

Malolo Lounge. A favorite after-work spot for employees from the surrounding hotels, this lounge in the Hilton Waikoloa Village offers decent music every night of the week (usually jazz), friendly bartenders, and a pool table. ⊠ *425 Waikoloa Beach Dr., Waikoloa* ☎ *808/886–1234* ⊕ *www.hiltonwaikoloavillage.com.*

HILO
BARS

Cronie's Bar & Grill. A sports bar and hamburger joint by day, Cronie's is a local favorite when the lights go down, with a packed bar. ⊠ *11 Waianuenue Ave, Hilo* ☎ *808/935–5158.*

Hilo BBQ Shack. This sports bar turns into a nightclub. Come for the game, stay for the late-night live music and drunken karaoke. ⊠ *121 Banyan Dr., Hilo* ☎ *808/969–7069.*

W.A.I. The Water and Ice Lounge. This may be Hilo's only true nightclub. It's a little hard to find, but if you're looking to party past 11 pm in this town then this is the place to go. Catering to a younger age group (20s to 30s), W.A.I.'s DJ plays mostly Top 40 music with the occasional break for Reggae and House tunes. All ages are welcome until 9:30 pm; the lounge serves a decent pūpūs and dinner menu. Wednesday through Friday W.A.I. is open from 4 pm until the wee hours; on Saturday it's open 9 pm until 3 am. ⊠ *124 Makaala Street, Hilo* ☎ *808/961–9190* ⊘ *Closed Sun. and Tues., open Mon. early evening during football season only.*

WHERE TO EAT

Between star chefs and an influx of quality local farms, the Big Island restaurant scene has been heating up in the past couple of years. In the past it used to be a pleasant surprise for visitors to discover a gourmet meal on the island; now food writers from national magazines are praising the chefs of the Big Island for their ability to turn the local bounty into inventive blends of the island's cultural heritage. Hotels along the Kohala Coast have long invested in celebrated chefs who know how to make a meal memorable, from inventive entrées to spot-on wine pairings. But great food on the Big Island doesn't begin and end with the resorts. A handful of cutting-edge chefs have retired from the fast-paced hotel world and opened up their own small bistros closer to the farms in Upcountry Waimea. And, as the old plantation towns transform into youthful arts communities, unique and wonderful restaurants have cropped up in Hāwī, Kainaliu, and on the east side of the island in Hilo. Though the larger, gourmet restaurants (especially those at the resorts) tend to be very pricey, there are still *ono grindz* (Hawaiian slang for tasty local food) to be found at budget prices throughout the island, from greasy plate lunch specials to reasonably priced organic fare at a number of cafés and health food markets.

WHAT IT COSTS					
	¢	$	$$	$$$	$$$$
Restaurants	under $10	$10–$17	$18–$26	$27–$35	over $35

Prices are for one main course at dinner.

KAILUA-KONA

¢ ✕ **Ba-Le.** Comparable to Kona Mix Plate in terms of prices, food qual-
HAWAIIAN ity, and street cred, Ba-Le serves a great plate lunch. It also has tasty
Vietnamese-influenced food, such as their popular sandwiches served on
freshly baked croissants or French baguettes, stuffed with pickled dai-
kon and carrots, cucumber, cilantro, homemade mayo, and your choice
from a variety of Vietnamese-style meats. ⊠ *Kona Coast Shopping Center, 74-5588 Palani Rd., Kailua-Kona* ☎ 808/327–1212 ▭ *MC, V.*

$ ✕ **Bangkok House Thai Restaurant.** It may not look like much, with its
THAI small, dark interior and tired carpets, but Bangkok House is the local
go-to for good Thai food. One of few Thai restaurants on the island
to add enough spice to their sauces, Bangkok serves up tasty curries,
satays, and soups, along with a random assortment of Chinese entrées.
The Rainbow salad, panang curry, and spring rolls are all standouts.
Make sure to save room for homemade lychee ice cream. ⊠ *75-5626
Kuakini Hwy., in King Kamehameha Mall* ☎ 808/329–7764 ▭ *D, DC,
MC, V* ⊗ *No lunch weekends.*

$ ✕ **Big Island Grill.** This typical, local Hawaiian restaurant looks like an
☺ old coffee shop or a Denny's—it's dark and nondescript inside, with
HAWAIIAN booths along the walls and basic tables with bingo hall chairs in the
middle of the room. Local families love it for the huge portions of
pork chops, chicken *katsu* (breaded, fried cutlet), and an assortment of
fish specialties at very reasonable prices. "Biggie's" also serves a great
breakfast—the prices and portions make this a good place to take large
groups or families. ⊠ *75-5702 Kuakini Hwy.* ☎ 808/326–1153 ▭ *AE,
MC, V* ⊗ *Closed Sun.*

$$ ✕ **Bubba Gump Shrimp Company.** Okay, it's a chain, and a chain that
☺ centers on a Tom Hanks movie, no less. However, it has one of the larg-
AMERICAN est oceanfront patios on the island, and the food's not bad, once you
get past the silly names. Anything with popcorn shrimp in it is good,
and the pear and berry salad (a combination of chicken, strawberries,
pears, and glazed pecans) is the perfect size for lunch. ⊠ *75-5776 Ali'i
Dr., Kailua-Kona* ☎ 808/331–8442 ⊕ *www.bubbagump.com* ▭ *AE,
D, DC, MC, V.*

$ ✕ **Chubby's Diner.** Bowling alley food has never been better. The recently
☺ renovated Chubby's Diner in the KB Xtreme family entertainment cen-
HAWAIIAN ter (it still says Kona Bowl on the outside of the building) offers a variety
of burgers, sandwiches, and "plate lunch" fare. Chubby's (whose own-
ers also run Big Island Grill) serves up a great teri beef that's cut more
like a steak; and their oxtail soup topped with sautéed watercress keeps
patrons coming back again and again. The portion size is big so you'll
be fueled up and ready to play; the facility has everything to keep the
whole family occupied, from bowling lanes to an arcade to karaoke to
live concerts. ⊠ *75-5591 Palani Road, Kailua-Kona* ☎ 808/329–2960
▭ *MC, V.*

$ ✕ **Harbor House.** This open-air restaurant on the docks at Kona's busy
AMERICAN harbor is one of the best spots on the island for fresh fish, and a fun
place to grab a beer and a bite after a long day fishing, surfing, or diving.
The fish is probably a few hours off the boat—if that. The place is noth-
ing fancy but Harbor House is a local favorite for fresh-fish sandwiches

BEST BETS FOR BIG ISLAND DINING

Fodor's Choice★

Bamboo, $$, p. 436
Brown's Beach House, $$$$, p. 437
Ke'ei Café, $$$, p. 435
Manta & Pavilion Wine Bar, $$$$, p. 438
Merriman's, $$$, p. 442
Pahui'a, $$$$, p. 439

By Price

¢

Ba-Le, p. 429
Lilikoi Café, p. 442
Village Burger, p. 442

$

Hilo Bay Café, p. 444
Kona Brewing Company & Brewpub, p. 431

Pau, p. 442

$$

Beach Tree at the Four Seasons Resort Hualālai, p. 436
Café Pesto, p. 443
Kīlauea Lodge, p. 445
Merriman's Market Café, p. 438

$$$–$$$$

KPC (Kamuela Provision Company), p. 438
Sansei Seafood Restaurant & Sushi Bar, p. 440

By Cuisine

PLATE LUNCH

Ba-Le, p. 429
Big Island Grill, $, p. 429

Café 100, p. 443

SUSHI

Norio's Sushi Bar, $$$$, p. 439
Sansei Seafood Restaurant & Sushi Bar, $$$, p. 440
Sushi Rock, $$, p. 440

By Experience

MOST ROMANTIC

Manta & Pavilion Wine Bar, $$$$, p. 438
Pahui'a, $$$$, p. 439

BEST VIEW

Brown's Beach House, $$$$, p. 437
Huggo's, $$$$, p. 430
Island Lava Java, $, p. 430

and a variety of fried fish-and-chip combos. The icy schooners of Kona Brewing Company ale don't hurt, either. ☒ *74-425 Kealakehe Pkwy., Suite 4, Honokohau Harbor* ☎ *808/326–4166* ☐ *AE, MC, V.*

$$$$
PACIFIC RIM
✕ **Huggo's.** This is the only restaurant in town with prices and atmosphere comparable to the splurge restaurants at the Kohala-coast resorts. Open windows extend out over the rocks at the ocean's edge, and at night you can almost touch the manta rays drawn to the spotlights. Relax with a cocktail for two and feast on fresh local seafood; the catch changes daily, and the nightly chef's special is always a good bet. If you're on a budget, try Huggo's happy hour: pūpūs are half price from 5:30 to 6 pm and drink specials abound from 4 to 6 pm daily. **Huggo's on the Rocks**, next door, is a great outdoor bar with a floor of sand; it's become Kailua-Kona's hot spot for drinks and live music on Friday nights. ☒ *75-5828 Kahakai Rd., off Ali'i Dr., Kailua-Kona* ☎ *808/329–1493* ⊕ *www.huggos.com* ☐ *AE, D, DC, MC, V.*

$
AMERICAN
✕ **Island Lava Java.** This place is packed to the gills, especially on weekends. Order your food at the counter then sit outside at one of the wooden, umbrella-shaded tables where you can sip 100% Kona coffee and take in the ocean view. The delicious eats on offer include island-style pancakes for breakfast, fresh-fish tacos for lunch, and butternut squash lasagna for dinner. There are also pizzas, salads, sandwiches,

and plenty of choices for both vegetarians and meat eaters. The giant cinnamon rolls are hugely popular. Portions are large and most everything on the menu is fresh, local, and organic. You get free Wi-Fi with purchase. ⊠ *75-5799 Ali'i Dr., Kailua-Kona* ☎ *808/327–2161* ⊕ *www. islandlavajava.com* ⊟ *AE, D, MC, V.*

$$ ✕**Jackie Rey's Ohana Grill.** Uphill from downtown Kailua-Kona, this
MODERN bright green open-air restaurant is a popular lunch destination, and
HAWAIIAN increasingly crowded for dinner as well, thanks to the chef's fantastic *poke* (raw fish salad), perfectly prepared local seafood dishes, and a few juicy meat standouts, including Korean-style short ribs. Be sure to wash your meal down with a selection from Jackie Rey's outstanding list of 100 different wines. At lunchtime, the fresh-fish sandwiches with wasabi mayo are excellent, and the fries are crisped to perfection. On the lighter side, inventive salads keep it healthy but flavorful. ⊠ *Pottery Terrace, 75-5995 Kuakini Hwy., Kailua-Kona* ☎ *808/327–0209* ⊕ *www.jackiereys.com* ⊟ *AE, D, MC, V* ⊗ *No lunch weekends.*

$ ✕**Kai at the Sheraton Keauhou Bay.** Facing Keauhou Bay, Kai has a primo
PACIFIC RIM view. The enormous windows are left open most of the time, making it almost feel like an outdoor restaurant. The menu is limited, but each entrée is good, from the sweet chili-glazed ono to the award-winning Kona coffee–crusted lamb chops. Everything is prepared with that fusion of Pacific Rim and Continental that makes up Hawaiian cuisine. The seared 'ahi appetizer is not to be missed. Breakfast is a good bet as well; very reasonable, great buffet, and the view during the daytime is just about perfect. ⊠ *78-128 Ehukai St., Kailua-Kona* ☎ *808/930–4900* ⊕ *www.sheratonkeauhou.com* ⊟ *AE, D, DC, MC, V.*

$ ✕**Kanaka Kava.** A popular local hangout, and not just because da kava
HAWAIIAN makes you mellow. Their *pūpū* (appetizers) rock! Fresh poke, smoky, tender bowls of pulled kālua pork, and healthy organic greens are available in fairly large portions for less than you'll pay anywhere else on the island. The restaurant also offers fresh-fish plates, vegetarian options, and even traditional Hawaiian *lau lau* (pork and butterfish wrapped in taro leaves and steamed). Seating is at a premium, but don't be afraid to share a table and make friends. ⊠ *75-5803 Ali'i Dr., Space B6, in Coconut Grove Marketplace* ☎ *808/883–6260* ⊕ *www.kanakakava. com* ⊟ *No credit cards.*

$$ ✕**Kenichi Pacific.** With its black-lacquer tables and lipstick red ban-
JAPANESE quettes, Kenichi's seems a little out of place in this small strip mall. The location keeps many tourists from finding it, even though it's been open for several years now. This is where everyone in Kailua-Kona goes when they feel like splurging on top-notch sushi. It's a little on the pricey side, but it's worth it. The sashimi is so fresh it melts in your mouth, and the signature rolls are inventive and tasty. If you're looking to save a buck or two, go early for happy hour (4:30 to 6:30 pm daily) when all sushi rolls are half off. ⊠ *Keauhou Shopping Center, 78-6831 Ali'i Dr., D-125, Kailua-Kona* ☎ *808/322–6400* ⊕ *www.kenichirestaurants. com* ⊟ *AE, D, DC, MC, V* ⊗ *Closed Mon.*

$ ✕**Kona Brewing Company & Brewpub.** This large and cheery spot with
AMERICAN a huge outdoor patio features an excellent and varied menu including pulled-pork quesadillas, gourmet pizzas, and a killer spinach salad with

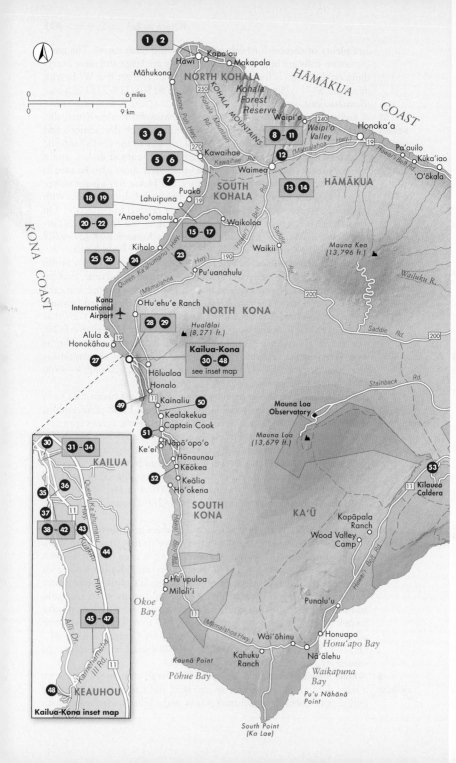

Hilo inset map

Hilo Bay

Waianuenue Ave. · 61 · 62 · 65 · 64 · 67 · Bayfront Hwy. · Kamehameha Ave. · 66 · 63 · 68 · Ponahawai St. · Kilauea Ave. · Kinoole St. · Kapiolani St. · Kanoelehua Ave. · Manono St.

19 · 19

Pāpa'aloa
Weleka
Ninole
Hakalau
Wailea
Honomū

NORTH HILO

19

Pāpa'ikou

Wainaku

Hilo Bay

Leleiwi Point

Hilo
61 – 68
see inset map

Hilo International Airport
(General Lyman Field)

59 · 60

SOUTH HILO

11
Kea'au
Kurtistown

Kukui

130

Mountain View

Belt Rd. · Hawaii Belt Rd.

Glenwood

Cape Kumakahi

Pāhoa

132

PUNA

58

57
Volcano

54 – 56

130

Kaimū

*Hawai'i Volcanoes
National Park*

Kalapana

PACIFIC OCEAN

Where to Eat
on the Big Island

Gorgonzola cheese, macadamia nuts, and strawberries. Go for the beer tasting menu—your choice of four of their eight available microbrews in miniature glasses that add up to about two regular-size mugs for the price of one. ⊠ *75-5629 Kuakini Hwy., off Kaiwi St. at end of Pawai Pl., Kailua-Kona* ☎ *808/329–2739* ⊕ *www.konabrewingco.com* ▭ *AE, MC, V.*

$$$
FRENCH

✕ **La Bourgogne.** A genial husband-and-wife team owns this relaxing, country-style bistro with dark-wood walls and private, romantic booths. The traditional French menu has classics such as escargots, beef with a Cabernet Sauvignon sauce, rack of lamb with roasted garlic and rosemary, and a less-traditional venison with a pomegranate glaze. Call well in advance for reservations. ⊠ *77-6400 Nālani St., Kailua-Kona* ☎ *808/329–6711* ⌖ *Reservations essential* ▭ *AE, MC, V* ⊗ *Closed Sun. and Mon. No lunch.*

¢
MEXICAN

✕ **Los Habaneros.** A surprising find in the corner of this shopping mall, next to the movie theater, Habaneros serves up tasty, fresh, and fast Mexican food for low, low prices. Our favorites are usually the day's specials, which can be anything from enchilada plates to homemade sopes and chiles rellenos. Their giant burritos are also a solid pick, stuffed with meat, beans, cheese, and all the fixings. ⊠ *78-631 Ali'i Dr., Keauhou Shopping Center, Keauhou* ☎ *808/324–4688* ▭ *MC, V* ⊗ *Closed Sun.*

¢
CAFÉ

✕ **Mixx Bar & Bistro.** Kona never knew it needed a wine bar until it got Mixx, but now the town would seem strange without it. In addition to their fantastic wine service, Mixx serves up a tasty menu of bistro-inspired *pūpū* (appetizers) ranging from super healthy plates of sautéed veggies and tofu to what they claim are "the island's best fries." They also offer a handful of entrée options, including salt and pepper fish, ribs, and roasted duck, all served family-style. And then of course there's the wine. *Sigh.* Live music keeps the patio lively most weekend evenings. On sweltering summer nights, head to Mixx to cool off—it's the only bar in Kona that has air conditioning. ⊠ *75-5626 Kuakini Hwy., in King Kamehameha Mall* ☎ *808/329–7334* ⊕ *www.mixxbistro.com* ▭ *D, MC, V* ⊗ *Closed Sun. and Mon.*

$
FRENCH

✕ **Peaberry & Galette.** This little creperie is a welcome addition to the neighborhood. It serves Illy espresso, excellent sweet and savory crepes, and rich desserts like lemon cheesecake and chocolate mousse that are made fresh daily. It's got a cool, urban-café vibe, and is a nice place to hang for a bit if you're waiting for a film at the theater next door, or just feel like taking a break from paradise to sip a decent espresso and flip through the latest *W.* ⊠ *Keauhou Shopping Center, 78-6831 Ali'i Dr., Kailua-Kona* ☎ *808/322–6020* ▭ *MC, V.*

$$
AMERICAN

✕ **Quinn's Almost by the Sea.** OK, Quinn's is a bit of a dive. That said, it does have a few things going for it—some of the best ono sandwiches on the island, for example. It's also open until 11 pm, later than almost every other restaurant in Kailua-Kona (except Denny's). If time gets away from you on a drive to South Point, Quinn's is awaiting your return with a cheap beer and a basket of excellent calamari. ⊠ *75-5655A Palani Rd., Kailua-Kona* ☎ *808/329–3822* ▭ *D, MC, V.*

¢ ✕ **Tacos El Unico.** An array of authen-
MEXICAN tic soft-taco choices (beef and
chicken, among others), burritos,
quesadillas, and great homemade
tamales. Order at the counter, take
a seat outside at one of a dozen yellow tables with blue umbrellas, and
enjoy all the good flavors served up
in those red plastic baskets. ⊠ *Kona
Marketplace, 75-5729 Ali'i Dr., Kailua-Kona* ☎ *808/326–4033* ▭ *No
credit cards.*

4

$ ✕ **Thai Rin Restaurant.** The Thai owner at this old-timer in Ali'i Sunset
THAI Plaza is likely to take your order, cook it, and bring it to your table himself. The menu includes five curries, a green-papaya salad, and a popular platter that combines spring rolls, satay, beef salad, and *tom yum*
(lemongrass soup). ⊠ *75-5799 Ali'i Dr., Kailua-Kona* ☎ *808/329–2929*
⊕ *www.aliisunsetplaza.com* ▭ *D, MC, V.*

$ ✕ **U-Top-It.** Tucked behind the shops and cafés of the Ali'i Sunset Plaza,
HAWAIIAN U-Top-It is a local favorite breakfast joint. Opened by a former Kona
☺ Village resort chef, all dishes at U-Top-It are built upon the restaurant's
terrific taro pan crepes, which guests can choose to top with any combination of over 100 different toppings ranging from straightforward
fruit or egg combinations to more unusual toppings. At lunchtime,
try pairing one of the crepes with beef or chicken teriyaki. ⊠ *75-5799
Ali'i Dr., Ali'i Sunset Plaza* ☎ *808/329–0092* ⊕ *www.utopitkona.com*
▭ *AE, D, DC, MC, V.*

$ ✕ **Wasabi's.** A tiny little place tucked into the back of the Coconut Plaza
JAPANESE on Ali'i, Wasabi's five little tables tend to be occupied by the west side's
Japanese population, here for some of the best sashimi on the island.
Prices may seem steep, but the fish is of the highest quality. Fans of
Americanized sushi rolls will find the familiar California and spicy tuna
rolls here, along with a few unique inventions. And for those who will
never be hip to the raw fish thing, teriyaki, udon, and sukiyaki options
abound. ⊠ *75-5803 Ali'i Dr., Coconut Grove Marketplace* ☎ *808/326–
2352* ⊕ *www.wasabishawaii.com* ▭ *AE, MC, V.*

THE KONA COAST

$ ✕ **The Coffee Shack.** There's really no flaw to this place. The view is
AMERICAN stunning, the service is excellent even when it's busy (which is most of
the time), and the eggs Benedict and hot Reuben sandwich are the best
on the island. Breads and pastries are all homemade, and the coffee is
strong and tasty. On your way to nowhere in particular, stop by for a
Hawaiian smoothie, an iced honey mocha latte, or homemade lū'au
bread—all worth a detour. In the afternoon, enjoy gourmet pizza and
an amazing sunset view. ⊠ *83-5799 Mamalahoa Hwy.* ☎ *808/328–9555*
▭ *D, MC, V* ☺ *No dinner.*

$$$ ✕ **Ke'ei Café.** This beautiful restaurant is in a plantation-style building
ECLECTIC 15 minutes south of Kona. Delicious dinners with Brazilian, Asian, and
Fodor'sChoice European flavors utilize fresh ingredients provided by local farmers. Try
★ the Thai red curry or wok-seared 'ahi accompanied by a selection from

the extensive wine list. The owners are Brazilian, so the caipirinhas are outstanding if you're tired of mai tais. ⊠ *79-7511 Māmalahoa Hwy., ½ mi south of Kainaliu, Kealakekua* ☎ *808/322–9992* ⌃ *Reservations essential* ⊟ *No credit cards* ⊙ *Closed Sun. and Mon. for dinner.*

$ ✕ **Manago Hotel.** About 20 minutes south of Kailua-Kona, Manago is
AMERICAN a time-warp experience. A vintage neon sign identifies the hotel, and Formica tables, ceiling fans, and venetian blinds add to the flavor of this film-noir spot. The T-shirts (which are great souvenirs for friends at home) brag that the hotel has the best pork chops in town, and it's not false advertising. The fresh fish is excellent as well, especially the ono and butterfish. Unless you request otherwise, the fish is all sautéed with a tasty house butter-soy sauce concoction. Meals come with rice for the table and an assortment of side dishes that changes from time to time, but usually includes a macaroni, potato, and tuna salad, and some sort of braised tofu and sautéed veggie dish. ⊠ *82-6155 Māmalahoa Hwy., Captain Cook* ☎ *808/323–2642* ⊕ *www.managohotel.com* ⊟ *D, MC, V* ⊙ *Closed Mon.*

$ ✕ **Teshima's.** Locals show up at this small, neighborhood restaurant 15
JAPANESE minutes south of Kailua-Kona whenever they're in the mood for fresh sashimi, puffy shrimp tempura, or *hekka* (beef and vegetables cooked in an iron pot) at a reasonable price. Teshima's doesn't look like much, inside or out, but it's been crowded since 1929 for a reason. You might also want to try a *teishoku* (tray) of assorted Japanese delicacies, or the popular bento box lunch. The service is laid-back and friendly. ⊠ *79-7251 Māmalahoa Hwy., Honalo* ☎ *808/322–9140* ⊟ *No credit cards.*

THE KOHALA COAST

$$ ✕ **Bamboo Restaurant.** It's out of the way, but the food at this spot in
PACIFIC RIM the heart of Hāwī is good and the service and ambience have a Hawai-
Fodor's Choice ian–country flair. Creative entrées feature fresh island fish prepared
★ several ways. The Thai-style fish, for example, combines lemongrass, Kaffir lime leaves, and coconut milk; it's best washed down with a passion-fruit margarita or passion-fruit iced tea. Bamboo accents, bold local artwork, and an old unfinished wooden floor make the restaurant cozy. Local musicians entertain on Friday or Saturday evenings. ⊠ *Hwy. 270, Hāwī* ☎ *808/889–5555* ⊕ *www.bamboorestaurant.info* ⊟ *MC, V* ⊙ *Closed Mon. No dinner Sun.*

$$ ✕ **Beach Tree at the Four Seasons Resort Hualālai.** True oceanside dining
AMERICAN is one of the main attractions at Beach Tree, the Four Seasons Resort
☾ Hualālai's newest restaurant that sits right on the sand. The beautifully designed restaurant with vaulted ceilings and custom wood furnishings has expansive outdoor seating and a casual, relaxed feel. Chef de Cuisine Nick Mastrascusa is a transplant from New York who brings California cuisine with Italian influence to Beach Tree's new menu. The braised short ribs with carrot puree literally slide off the bone and the gnocchi in oxtail ragout are fluffy little pillows that melt in your mouth. Dishes are elegant but not pretentious. There's also a great children's menu and activities to keep them busy, like a fun rotating pasta fork and ice-cream cone spinner. The entire family can enjoy the live Hawaiian music played nightly. ⊠ *72-100 Ka'ūpūlehu Dr.* ⌂ *Box 1269, Kailua-Kona*

96745 ☎ 808/325–8000 ⊕ www.
fourseasons.com/hualalai ⊟ AE,
D, DC, MC, V.

$$$$ | ✕ **Brown's Beach House at the Fair-**
MODERN | **mont Orchid Hawai'i.** This waterfront
HAWAIIAN | wonder is well worth the splurge—
Fodor's Choice | the menu is inventive (but not too
★ | inventive), and the wine list is excel-
lent. Though you can order steak
here, the seafood is really where
it's happening. Their crab-crusted
mahimahi is a little piece of heaven,
sitting on clouds of Waimea sweet

corn mashed potatoes. Leave room for dessert; the sweets change regularly, but they're always worth the indulgence. Local musicians play on the grassy knoll outside. ⊠ *Fairmont Orchid Hawai'i, 1 N. Kanikū Dr., Kohala Coast* ☎ *808/885–2000* ⊕ *www.fairmont.com/orchid* ⊟ *AE, D, DC, MC, V* ⊗ *No lunch.*

$$$$ ✕ **CanoeHouse at the Mauna Lani Bay Hotel & Bungalows.** This landmark
PACIFIC RIM restaurant has gotten a food face-lift recently with the addition of new head chef James Ortiaga, who offers his own approach to contemporary Hawai'i cuisine. Like many other nearby resort restaurants, Canoe-House's menu focuses on what's fresh and local. However, chef Ortiaga likes to mix up the traditional preparations with interesting items including Kona prawns with coconut polenta, Day Boat scallops with caviar and *wakame* (seaweed) butter, and *furikake*-crusted (a dried seaweed Japanese seasoning) 'ahi with green papaya. The wine list is great, and the open-air beachfront setting makes the hefty price tag worth it on clear evenings. ⊠ *Mauna Lani Bay Hotel & Bungalows, 68-1400 Mauna Lani Dr., Kohala Coast* ☎ *808/885–6622* ⊕ *www.maunalani. com* ⊟ *AE, D, DC, MC, V.*

$$$ ✕ **Coast Grille at Hāpuna Beach Prince Hotel.** This is a beautiful spot, with
MODERN high ceilings and a lānai overlooking the ocean. American Bistro-style
HAWAIIAN dishes showcase what the Big Island has to offer, using sustainable, organic, and wild ingredients whenever possible. Try the Kona lobster bisque, the grass-fed Big Island burger with Maui onion marmalade, or the pan-roasted mahimahi with Waipo'o warabi fern. ⊠ *Hāpuna Beach Prince Hotel, 62-100 Kauna'oa Dr., Kohala Coast* ☎ *808/880–3192* or ⊕ *www.princeresortshawaii.com* ⊟ *AE, D, DC, MC, V* ⊗ *No lunch.*

$$$$ ✕ **Hale Samoa at Kona Village Resort.** At this writing the Kona Village
MODERN Resort was closed indefinitely due to tsunami damage in March 2011.
HAWAIIAN Distinctive and romantic, this Kona Village restaurant has a magical atmosphere, especially at sunset. Sit beneath the stars and feast on five-course prix-fixe dinners that change nightly. The chef likes to showcase local ingredients and 70 percent of the food here comes fresh from the Big Island. Specialties may include sautéed abalone from a local aqua-farm, papaya-and-coconut bisque, *sous vide opakapaka* (Hawaiian snapper) with coconut *ogo* (seaweed) sauce, or wild boar porchetta. Don't overlook the unique à la carte side dishes as well, such as the truffled *ulu* (breadfruit) fries or *luau* (leaves of the taro plant) risotto

cakes. ⊠ *Kona Village Resort, Hwy. 19, 12 mi north of Kailua-Kona, North Kona Coast* ☎ *808/325–5555* ⊕ *www.konavillage.com* ⌁ *Reservations essential* ⊟ *AE, D, MC, V* ⊙ *Closed Tues. and Wed.*

$$$$
MODERN
HAWAIIAN

✕ **KPC (Kamuela Provision Company) at the Hilton Waikoloa Village.** Tables set along a breezy lānai and a sweeping view of the Kohala Coast are the perfect accompaniments to the elegant yet down-to-earth Hawai'i regional cuisine. The lānai offers the best seats in the house—get there by 5:30 if you want to score a seat for the sunset. Popular are the sesame-crusted 'ahi filet, the ginger-steamed monchong, and the "new wave mauka and makai" (a grilled beef tenderloin and tempura lobster). ⊠ *Hilton Waikoloa Village, 69-425 Waikoloa Beach Dr., Waikoloa* ☎ *808/886–1234* ⊕ *www.hiltonwaikoloavillage.com* ⊟ *AE, D, DC, MC, V* ⊙ *No lunch.*

$$
SEAFOOD

✕ **Kawaihae Seafood Bar.** Upstairs in a structure that dates from the 1850s, this seafood bar has been a hot spot since it opened in 2003, serving up a dynamite and well-priced bar menu with tasty *pūpū* (appetizers), and a newly expanded dinner menu that includes at least four fresh-fish specials daily. There's fare for landlubbers, too, including boneless braised short ribs, rib eye steak, specialty pizza and lots of salad options. Don't miss their escargot, oysters Rockefeller, and ginger steamed clams. At lunch, the menu is limited to a few sandwich items; breakfast is served only on weekends; and happy hour runs daily from 3 to 5:30 pm. If you've got the late-night munchies, this is a great spot—they serve food until midnight. ⊠ *61-3642 Kawaihae Harbor, Hwy. 270, Kawaihae* ☎ *808/880–9393* ⊕ *www.seafoodbargrill.com* ⊟ *MC, V.*

$$$$
MODERN
HAWAIIAN
Fodor'sChoice
★

✕ **Manta & Pavilion Wine Bar at the Mauna Kea Beach Hotel.** The Mauna Kea Beach Hotel has long been known for excellence in dining and the newly renovated Manta & Pavilion Wine Bar is no exception. Perched on the edge of a bluff overlooking the sparkling waters of Mauna Kea Beach, this is an amazing spot for a romantic meal at sunset, especially at one of the outside tables. The restaurant's Enomatic wine system (one of only two in the state) allows guests to sample 48 different wines by the glass in 1-, 2-, or 5-ounce pours. Dinner here is beyond fantastic. The crispy pork belly appetizer with Kona baby abalone is not to be missed. Main dishes include a macadamia nut–crusted lamb, a Big Island butterfish, Ka'ū coffee beef filet, a butter-poached Keāhole lobster, and a perfectly prepared seared 'ahi with Moloka'i sweet potato puree and foie gras spring roll. This is also the spot for a spectacular Sunday brunch with an impressive spread that includes an omelet station, prime rib, smoked salmon, tempura, lobster bisque, and a build-your-own-sundae bar. ⊠ *62-100 Mauna Kea Beach Dr. Kohala Coast* ☎ *808/882–5810* ⊕ *www.maunakeabeachhotel.com* ⊟ *AE, D, DC, MC, V* ⊙ *No lunch.*

$$
MEDITERRANEAN

✕ **Merriman's Market Café.** From Peter Merriman, one of Hawai'i's star chefs, comes a more affordable alternative to his upscale Waimea and Maui restaurants. The Mediterranean-influenced menu includes a variety of pasta dishes, tasty appetizers, and some of the island's best salads. Its huge patio has quickly become a favorite for locals and visitors alike, which means you could have a bit of a wait for a table. ⊠ *Kings'*

Shops at Waikoloa Beach Resort, 250 Waikoloa Beach Dr., Waikoloa 📞 *808/886–1700* 🞸 *AE, MC, V.*

$$
JAPANESE

✕ **Monstera.** It may not be beachfront with a view of the sunset, but the newest addition to the Shops at Mauna Lani is worth a visit for its casual Japanese pub food with a touch of local inspiration. Chef Norio Yamamotos tasty lunch and dinner menu includes his signature tuna tataki, crispy whole moi, *hamachi kama* (broiled Japanese yellowtail cheek) and seafood papaya (shrimp and scallops with veggies baked in a papaya). There are excellent sizzling plate items like short ribs and rib-eye steak, hot and cold noodle dishes, and, of course, the outstanding sushi. Most people make a meal out of sharing several small plate items so you can sample a bit of everything. Save room for the tempura banana drizzled with chocolate and caramel for dessert. It's best to make a reservation; you can also get some of the menu to go. ✉ *The Shops at Mauna Lani, 68-1330 Mauna Lani Dr., Waikoloa* 📞 *808/887–2711* 🌐 *www.monterasushi.com* 🞸 *AE, D, DC, MC, V.*

$$$$
JAPANESE

✕ **Norio's Sushi Bar & Restaurant.** Norio's is great, but it's pricey for sushi and there are sushi restaurants of equal or higher caliber down the road at The Shops at Mauna Lani (Monstera), or north of Kohala in Hawi (Sushi Rock). Still, Norio's is a solid choice. Sashimi and sushi are lovingly prepared with the freshest possible fish (both from the ocean and from the numerous aqua-farms on the island). The flounder, 'ahi, and abalone are not to be missed. Some equally delicious hot dishes include baked sea scallops and miso butterfish. The assortment of tropical drinks is tasty, as is the sinfully good chocolate fondue, served with an assortment of tropical fruits. ✉ *Fairmont Orchid Hawai'i, 1 N. Kaniku Dr., Kohala Coast* 📞 *808/885–2000* 🌐 *www.fairmont.com/orchid* 🞸 *AE, D, DC, MC, V* ⊘ *Closed Tues. and Wed. No lunch.*

$$
AMERICAN

✕ **Number 3 at the Mauna Kea Beach Hotel.** Though it sits right on the edge of the hotel's golf course, this is not just a restaurant for golf enthusiasts. A short walk from the main entrance to the hotel, the newly renovated, spacious dining room has seating both inside and out, and service is quick and on-point. Number 3 serves up a great lunch menu with dishes such as 'ahi sashimi, a kālua pig quesadilla, and beer-battered freshfish tacos. The best item has to be their signature #3 burger—a Kahuā Ranch American Wagyu beef burger with caramelized onion, Waimea tomatoes, Maytag blue aioli, and sweet onion fries. For the kids and kids-at-heart, order the "loaded" banana split (with banana bread, ice cream, sorbet, crème fraîche, and toasted macadamia nuts). Then lie down for a well-deserved nap. ✉ *62-100 Mauna Kea Beach Dr., Kohala Coast* 📞 *808/882–5810* 🌐 *www.maunakeabeachhotel.com* 🞸 *AE, D, DC, MC, V* ⊘ *No dinner.*

$$$$
MODERN
HAWAIIAN
Fodor's Choice
★

✕ **Pahui'a at the Four Seasons Resort Hualālai.** *Pahui'a* means aquarium, so it's fitting that a 9- by 4-foot aquarium in the entrance casts a dreamy light through this exquisite restaurant. Presentation is paramount, and the food tastes as good as it looks. Asian-influenced dishes stand out for their layers of flavor. Chef Jacob Anaya creates something spectacular with each plate. Opt for a tasting menu of up to seven small items or go for a full entrée—you'll be happy with whatever you choose. The chef changes the menu four times a year and focuses on showcasing local ingredients. You're likely to find unique preparations of your favorite dishes, such as baby abalone, white shrimp, Keahole lobster, Big Island moi, Hawaiian Snapper, lamb, and prime beef. Breakfasts are superb; the lemon ricotta pancakes are so good they should be illegal. Reserve a table on the patio and you may be able to spot whales while dining. ⊠ *Four Seasons Resort Hualālai, 100 Ka'ūpūlehu Dr., North Kona Coast* ☏ *808/325–8000* ⊕ *www.fourseasons.com/hualalai* ⊟ *AE, D, DC, MC, V* ⊗ *No lunch.*

$$$
MODERN
HAWAIIAN

✕ **Roy's Waikoloa Bar & Grill.** Roy's is part of a chain, and it's located in a strip mall. If either of those things turns you off immediately, skip it—there are as good or better meals to be had elsewhere on the island. If, however, you're looking for consistently decent food and you're staying nearby, you could do worse. And if you're looking for a light meal, you can easily fill up on the enormous selection of great appetizers, and the extensive wine-by-the-glass list offers good pairing options. Roy's changes its menu frequently based on what local items are in season but mainstays include Roy's signature short ribs and his macadamia nut-crusted fish. Both are quite tasty. ⊠ *Kings' Shops at Waikoloa Village, 250 Waikoloa Beach Dr., Kohala Coast* ☏ *808/886–4321* ⊕ *www. roysrestaurant.com* ⊟ *AE, D, DC, MC, V* ⊗ *No lunch.*

$$$
JAPANESE

✕ **Sansei Seafood Restaurant & Sushi Bar.** This restaurant serves heavenly interpretations of sushi and contemporary Asian cuisine. More than a few dishes have won awards including the shrimp dynamite in a creamy garlic masago aioli and unagi glaze, and the Dungeness crab ramen with Asian truffle broth. There are tried-and-true favorites that are mainstays, however, the menu is consistently updated to include new and exciting options such as the Hawaiian *moi* sashimi rolls and the Japanese yellowtail nori aioli poke. You can certainly make a meal out of the appetizers and sushi rolls, or try some of Sansei's great entrees from both land and sea. Go for an early dinner on Sunday or Monday when sushi and other food items are half off until 6 pm (limited seating; first come, first served). Or opt for a late-night meal on Friday or Saturday when a good section of the menu is half off from 10 pm until 1 am (you just have to put up with the karaoke singers). ⊠ *201 Waikoloa Beach Dr., 801 Queens' MarketPlace, Waikoloa* ☏ *808/886–6286* ⊕ *www.dkrestaurants.com* ⊟ *AE, D, MC, V* ⊗ *No lunch.*

$$
JAPANESE

✕ **Sushi Rock.** In Hāwī's funky Without Boundaries shop, Sushi Rock isn't big on ambience—its narrow dining room is brightly painted and casually decorated with various Hawaiian and Japanese knickknacks— but hungry locals and visiting couples flock here for some of the island's freshest raw fish. The restaurant prides itself on using fresh local ingredients like grass-fed beef tenderloin, goat cheese, macadamia nuts, and mango in their Island-inspired sushi rolls but also serves up a variety of cooked seafood, chicken, noodle dishes, and salads for lunch and dinner. Everything is plated beautifully and served either at the sushi bar, at one of the handful of indoor tables in the restaurant's narrow dining room, or on the covered front patio. There's also a full bar. ⊠ *55-3435 Akoni Pule Hwy., Hāwī* ☏ *808/889–5900* ⊕ *sushirockrestaurant.net* ⊟ *MC, V* ⊗ *Closed Wed.*

$$$
MODERN
HAWAIIAN

✕ **Tommy Bahama's Tropical Café.** It's funny that a chain known for its "Hawaiian-ness" would start in California and then one day end up in Hawaii, but that is Tommy Bahama's story. In an open-air space above the Tommy Bahama store in the shops at Mauna Lani, the restaurant does a good job of making guests forget they're in a shopping complex. And the food is decent, although derivative of other menus on the island. The macadamia-crusted *opakapaka* (Pacific red snapper) is a standout. Some of the best items, and best values, on the menu are actually in the appetizer section—the poke is outstanding—and on the salad list, which includes the "Bungalow" salad with macadamia nuts, Granny Smith apples, Big Island goat cheese, smoked bacon and sweet corn served over mixed greens with a honey lime vinaigrette. Desserts are decadent and meant for sharing. ✉ *68-1330 Mauna Lani Dr., #102* ☎ *808/881–8686* ⊕ *www.tommybahama.com* ⊟ *AE, D, DC, MC, V.*

4

WAIMEA

$
MEXICAN

✕ **Big Island Brewhaus/Tako Taco.** Everyone in Waimea and beyond has always loved Tako Taco as one of the best Mexican restaurants on the island. As it turns out, owner Tom Kerns is also a master brewer and is now churning out some decent ales, lagers, and specialty beers from his on-site brewery. Housed in a small, brightly painted hut, Tako Taco feels more like a mainland burrito joint than an island Mexican food restaurant. Its authentic food makes it hugely popular with both locals, who line up for to-go orders, and visitors who snag one of the plastic booths and eat in. With a focus on fresh ingredients, Tako Taco whips up awesome tacos, burritos, Mexican salads, enchiladas, rellenos, and seriously *ono* (Hawaiian slang for "tasty") quesadillas fresh to order. The tomatillo pineapple salsa is the bee's knees, and they also serve top-shelf margaritas, both classic and *liliko'i* (passion fruit). Of course, nothing beats a cold local brew to wash down that spicy enchilada. ✉ *64-1066A Mamalahoa Hwy.* ☎ *808/887–1717* ⊕ *www. bigislandbrewhaus.com* ⊟ *MC, V.*

$$
MODERN
HAWAIIAN

✕ **Daniel Thiebaut Restaurant.** This fine-dining restaurant features the creations of respected local chef Thiebaut in a quaint little yellow building that once housed the historic Chock In Store, which catered to the ranching community beginning in 1900. Collectibles abound, such as antique porcelain pieces. The French-Asian menu includes an amazing appetizer of sweet-corn crab cake with a lemongrass, coconut, and lobster sauce. Other signature dishes include Hunan-style rack of lamb served with eggplant compote and Big Island goat cheese. The restaurant has reopened for lunch during the week with a buffet on Sundays. Good lunch choices are the local grass-fed beef burger or the braised short ribs. ✉ *65-1259 Kawaihae Rd., Waimea* ☎ *808/887–2200* ⊕ *www.danielthiebaut.com* ⊟ *MC, V* ☺ *Closed Sun. dinner and Mon.*

$
MODERN
HAWAIIAN

✕ **Huli Sue's BBQ and Grill.** Huli Sue's serves large portions of updated Hawaiian classics in a casual little restaurant along the highway between Waimea and Honoka'a. The barbecue menu, which includes your choice of meat (classics like ribs, pork roast, brisket) with one of four sauces, is melt-in-your-mouth delicious. The menu includes many other options, including a baked potato stuffed with your choice of meat, cilantro sour cream, and Fontina cheese, a variety of curry dishes, and a handful of fantastic appetizers. ⊠ *64-957 Mamalahoa Hwy. (Hwy. 11)* ☎ *808/885–6268* ⊕ *www.hulisues.com* ⊟ *AE, D, DC, MC, V.*

¢

CONTINENTAL

✕**Lilikoi Café.** This gem of a café is tucked away in the back of the Parker Ranch Shopping Center. Locals love that it's hard to find because they want to keep Lilikoi Café's delicious breakfast crepes, freshly made soups, and croissants Waimea's best-kept secret. Owner and chef John Lorda puts out an impressive display of salad choices daily, including chicken curry, beet, fava bean, chicken pesto, and Mediterranean pasta. The Israeli couscous with tomato, red onion, cranberry, and basil is a hit, as is the half avocado stuffed with tuna salad. There are also sandwiches and hot entrées. The food is fresh, many of the ingredients are organic, and everything is homemade. ⊠ *67-1185 Māmalahoa Hwy. (Hwy. 11), Waimea* ☎ *808/887–1400* ⊟ *AE, D, MC, V* ⊗ *Closed Sun. No dinner.*

$$$

MODERN
HAWAIIAN

Fodor'sChoice

★

✕**Merriman's.** By far one of the best restaurants in Waimea, this is the signature restaurant of Peter Merriman, one of the pioneers of Hawaiian regional cuisine. Merriman's is the home of the original wok-charred 'ahi, usually served with buttery Wainaku corn. If you prefer meat, try the Kahuā Ranch lamb, raised to the restaurant's specifications, or the prime Kansas City Cut steak, grilled to order. The wine list includes 22 selections poured by the glass, and the staff is refreshingly knowledgeable. For true foodies, Merriman's now offers a local farm tour—four hours spent browsing around local ranches and food stands, culminating in a fantastic five-course meal using produce and meat bought throughout the day. ⊠ *'Opelo Plaza, 65-1227 'Opelo Rd., Waimea* ☎ *808/885–6822* ⊕ *www.merrimanshawaii.com* ⌲ *Reservations essential* ⊟ *AE, MC, V.*

$

ITALIAN

✕**Pau.** The name here is the Hawaiian word for "done," which we're guessing alludes to how eagerly you will gobble up their sensational pizzas. You order at the counter and find your own seat in the small but neat inside dining area. The big draw is the wide selection of appetizers, salads, sandwiches, pastas, and pizzas loaded with lots of local, fresh ingredients. Try the "Superfood" salad with quinoa, brown rice, edamame, grapes, and spiced nuts or the tangy vintner's salad with local organic greens, spiced pecans, apples, Gorgonzola, and Pau's champagne vinaigrette. All sauces and salad dressings are made in-house. When it comes to the pizzas, anything goes: order one of Pau's 16-inch signature pies or create your own. Lunch is a deal if you order the Slice of Italy: a quarter pizza cut into three slices plus a side salad for just $9. The restaurant is a little tricky to find, but it's right next to Merriman's in Waimea. ⊠ *65-1227 Opelo Rd., Waimea* ☎ *808/885–6325* ⊕ *www. paupizza.com* ⊟ *AE, MC, V* ⊗ *Closed Sun.*

¢

AMERICAN

✕**Village Burger.** You can't get a burger fresher than this. Village Burger is bringing a whole new meaning to the term "fast food" with Big Island pasture-raised, hormone-free beef that is ground fresh, hand-shaped daily at their restaurant, and grilled to perfection right before your eyes. Top your burger (be it 'ahi, veal, Kahua Ranch Wagyu beef, Hamakua mushroom, or Waipio Taro) with everything from local avocados, baby greens, and chipotle goat cheese to slow-cooked "60-minute onions," tomato marmalade, and a broken egg. Even though Village Burger is a newcomer to the area, they have already built a following, thanks to their commitment to local ingredients. Even the ice cream for their milk shakes is made right in Kamuela, and the delicious brioche buns that house these juicy burgers are baked fresh in nearby Hāwī. At this place, you really can taste the difference. ⊠ *Parker Ranch Center, 67-1185 Mamalahoa Highway, Waimea* ☎ *808/885–7319* ⊕ *villageburgerwaimea.com* ▭ *D, MC, V.*

HILO AND PUNA

$$
ITALIAN
✕ **Big Island Pizza.** If spending $20 on a large pizza is something you just can't come to grips with, steer clear of Big Island Pizza. If, on the other hand, you can rationalize paying more for a pie that's topped with things like shrimp and smoked salmon, then order up and get ready for a little slice of heaven. They also serve sandwiches, wraps, pastas, and salads. There are only a handful of tables for eating in, but they do a brisk take-out business and also deliver to the eastern side of the island. ⊠ *760 Kīlauea Ave.* ☎ *808/934–8000* ⊕ *www.bigislandpizza. com* ▭ *AE, D, MC, V.*

¢
HAWAIIAN
✕ **Blane's Drive-In.** With a vast menu second only to Ken's House of Pancakes, Blane's serves up everything from standard hamburgers to chicken *katsu.* There's a mean plate lunch with tons of fresh fish for only $8. At one point it was a real drive-in, with car service. Now, customers park, order at the window, and then eat at one of the few picnic tables provided or take their food to go. ⊠ *217 Wainuenue Ave., Hilo* ☎ *808/969–9494* ▭ *MC, V.*

¢
HAWAIIAN
✕ **Café 100.** This popular local restaurant is famous for its tasty loco moco, prepared in more than a dozen ways, and its dirt-cheap breakfast and lunch specials. (You can stuff yourself for $3 if you order right.) The word "restaurant," or even "café," is used liberally here—you order at a window and eat on one of the outdoor benches provided—but you come here for the food and prices, not the ambience. ⊠ *969 Kīlauea Ave., Hilo* ☎ *808/935–8683* ▭ *MC, V* ⊗ *Closed Sun.*

$$
ITALIAN
✕ **Café Pesto.** One of the better restaurants in Hilo for the price, Café Pesto offers exotic pizzas (with fresh Hāmākua mushrooms, artichokes, and rosemary Gorgonzola sauce, for example), Asian-inspired pastas and risottos, fresh seafood, delicious salads, and appetizers that you could make a meal of. Products from local farmers feature heavily on the menu here—everything from the Kulana free-range beef to the Kawamata Farms tomatoes to the Kapoho Farms lehua-blossom honey is made on the island. Live local musicians provide entertainment at dinner Thursday through Sunday. ⊠ *308 Kamehameha Ave., Hilo* ☎ *808/969–6640* ⊕ *www.cafepesto.com* ▭ *AE, D, DC, MC, V.*

$
THAI
✕ **Full Moon Cafe.** This cozy restaurant in a newly renovated downtown Hilo building offers a small American menu of burgers, fish, and steak, but where the eatery truly stands out is in its fresh and tasty traditional Thai fare. The owners grow their own spices, herbs, and papayas organically on their Puna farm. The chefs here also sauté with olive oil to keep things heart-healthy. Try the hot and sour Tom Yum soup that is loaded with fresh veggies, pineapple curry, and the Thai basil eggplant. Wash

it all down with a Thai iced tea or coffee as a musician strums relaxing Hawaiian music (nightly, from 6 to 8:30). Also look for outdoor seating on the lānai and a new coffee shop soon. ⊠ *51 Kalakaua Street, Hilo* ☎ *808/961–0599* ⊕ *www.fullmooncafe.net* ⊟ *D, MC, V.*

$ ✕**Hilo Bay Café.** What this eatery lacks in setting—it's in a strip mall

AMERICAN that contains Office Max and Wal-Mart—it makes up for with modern decor and fantastic food. It's a popular restaurant among locals for "special" occasions like birthdays and anniversaries due to the high quality of food, but truth be told, the prices are reasonable enough you can come just to celebrate a Tuesday. Highly recommended are the roasted eggplant-Parmesan custard and the peppered local beef carpaccio with horseradish cream. The vegan offerings, which range from coconut-crusted tofu with stir-fry veggies to potpie, are good enough to seduce meat eaters. Daily specials always include a vegetarian, meat, and fish choice, and the menu changes twice a year to keep things fresh. The chef tries to use organic and local products wherever possible. ⊠ *315 Maka'ala St., Hilo* ☎ *808/935–4939* ⊕ *www.hilobaycafe.com* ⊟ *AE, D, MC, V.*

$ ✕**Ken's House of Pancakes.** For years this 24-hour coffee shop between

AMERICAN the airport and the hotels along Banyan Drive has been a gathering place for Hilo residents. As its name implies, Ken's serves good pancakes, but there are about 180 other tasty local specialties and American diner–inspired items from which to choose. Sunday is all-you-can-eat spaghetti night, Tuesday is all-you-can-eat tacos, and Wednesday is prime rib night. ⊠ *1730 Kamehameha Ave., Hilo* ☎ *808/935–8711* ⊟ *D, MC, V.*

¢ ✕**Kūhiō Grille.** There's no ambience to speak of, and water is served in

HAWAIIAN unbreakable plastic, but if you're searching for local fare—that eclectic and undefinable fusion of ethnic cuisines—Kūhiō Grille is a must. Sam Araki serves a 1-pound *laulau* (a steamed bundle of taro leaves and pork) that is worth the trip. This diner at the edge of Hilo's largest mall opens at 6 am. ⊠ *Prince Kūhiō Shopping Plaza, 111 E. Puainako St., at Hwy. 11* ☎ *808/959–2336* ⊟ *AE, D, DC, MC, V.*

¢ ✕**Luquin's Mexican Restaurant.** Long an island favorite for tasty, albeit

MEXICAN greasy, Mexican grub, Luquin's is still going strong in the funky town of Pahoa. Tacos are great here (go for crispy), especially when stuffed with grilled, seasoned local fish. Chips are warm and salty, the salsa's got some kick, and the beans are thick with lard and topped with melted cheese. Not something you'd eat before a long swim, but perfect after a long day of exploring. ⊠ *15-2942 Pahoa Village Rd., Pahoa* ☎ *808/965–9990* ⊟ *MC, V.*

¢ ✕**Ocean Sushi.** What this restaurant lacks in ambience it certainly makes

JAPANESE up for in quality and price. We're talking about light and crispy tempura; tender, moist teriyaki chicken; and about 25 specialty sushi rolls that, on average, will cost you a mere $5 per roll. If you're a sushi lover, be sure to try the "hospital roll" with shrimp tempura, cream cheese, cucumber, and spicy 'ahi, or the "volcano roll," a California roll topped with flying fish eggs, dried fish shavings, green onions, and spicy mayo. Don't let the low price tag fool you—the service is friendly and the food here is fresh, filling, and delicious. ⊠ *250 Keawe Street, Hilo* ☎ *808/961–6625* ⊟ *MC, V* ☺ *Closed Sun.*

$$ ✕**The Seaside Restaurant & Aqua Farm.** The Nakagawa family has been
SEAFOOD running this eatery since the early 1920s. The latest son to manage the
☺ restaurant has transformed both the menu and the decor, and that,
paired with the setting (the restaurant sits on a 30-acre natural brackish
water fishpond) makes this one of the most romantic and interesting
places to eat in Hilo. You can't get fish fresher than this. Islanders travel
great distances for the fried *āholehole* (young Hawaiian flagtail) that's
raised on the aqua-farm. Other great dishes from the sea include the
steamed moi, furikake salmon, miso butterfish, and macadamia nut–
crusted mahimahi. The Pacific Rim menu includes plenty of selections
for landlubbers, too. Arrive before sunset and request a table by the
window for a view of the egrets roosting around the fishponds. ✉ *1790
Kalaniana'ole Ave., Hilo* ☎ *808/935–8825* ⊕ *www.seasiderestaurant.
com* ▭ *AE, DC, MC, V* ☺ *Closed Mon. No lunch.*

HAWAI'I VOLCANOES NATIONAL PARK AND VICINITY

$$ ✕**Kiawe Kitchen.** Everyone around here says the same thing: "Kiawe has
ITALIAN awesome pizza, but it's a little expensive." And it's true—the wood-fired
pizza at this warm and pretty Italian eatery, with red walls and wood
floors, has a perfect thin crust and an authentic Italian taste, but you
have to be prepared to spend around $15 on a typical pie. Food options
are limited in this area, though. Go for it. ✉ *19-4005 Old Volcano Rd.,
Volcano* ☎ *808/967–7711* ▭ *MC, V.*

$$ ✕**Kīlauea Lodge.** Chef Albert Jeyte combines contemporary trends with
CONTINENTAL traditional cooking styles from the mainland, France, and his native
Hamburg, Germany. The menu changes daily, and features such entrées
as venison, duck à l'orange with an apricot-mustard glaze, and authen-
tic *hasenpfeffer* (braised rabbit). The coconut-crusted Brie appetizer is
huge, melty, and absolutely delicious, as are Jeyte's made-from-scratch
soups and breads. Built in 1937 as a YMCA camp, the restaurant still
has the original "Friendship Fireplace" made from stones from around
the world. The roaring fire, koa-wood tables, and warm lighting make
the dining room feel like a cozy lodge. ✉ *19-3948 Old Volcano Hwy.,
Volcano Village* ☎ *808/967–7366* ⊕ *www.kilauealodge.com* ▭ *AE,
MC, V.*

$ ✕**Lava Rock Café.** This is a decent place to grab a sandwich or a coffee
AMERICAN and check your email before heading to the volcano. (Lava Rock also
serves dinner, but service tends to be less than stellar.). Though it's not
perfect, Lava Rock is a good place to stop if you want to take a picnic
into the park: once inside, the park's concessionaires sell bland, over-
priced food, and within Volcano Village there are no other fast and tasty
deli options. ✉ *19-3972 Old Volcano Hwy., behind Kīlauea General
Store, Volcano* ☎ *808/967–8526* ☺ *No dinner Sun. and Mon.* ▭ *MC, V.*

$ ✕**Thai Thai Restaurant.** The food is authentic, and the prices are reason-
THAI able at this little Volcano Village find. A steaming hot plate of curry is
the perfect antidote to a chilly day on the volcano. The chicken satay
is excellent—the peanut dipping sauce the perfect match of sweet and
spicy. Be careful when you order, as "medium" is more than spicy
enough even for hard-core chili addicts. The service is warm and
friendly and the dining room is pleasant, with white tablecloths, Thai

art, and a couple of silk wall hangings. Thai Thai recently expanded to include more space for diners and a small gift shop. ⊠ *19-4084 Old Volcano Rd., Volcano* ☎ *808/967–7969* ⊙ *No lunch Wed.* ⊟ *AE, D, MC, V.*

¢ ✕**Volcano Golf & Country Club.** This restaurant doesn't feel much like a
AMERICAN   country club—it's simple and not at all fancy, with oak tables filled with local old-timers talking story and chowing down on greasy local favorites. Locals love this spot for its large portions and classic breakfasts: ordering the breakfast burger (with fried egg, cheese, and your choice of meat) and a cup of local coffee is the way to go. If it's lunchtime, you can't beat the burgers. ⊠ *Pi'i Mauna Dr., off Hwy. 11, Volcano* ☎ *808/967–8228* ⊙ *No dinner* ⊟ *AE, D, MC, V.*

WHERE TO STAY

Even among locals, there is an ongoing debate about which side of the Big Island is "better," so don't worry if you're having a tough time deciding where to stay. Our recommendation? Do both. Each side of the island offers a totally different range of accommodations, restaurants, and activities.

Consider staying at one of the resorts along the Kohala Coast or in a condo in Kailua-Kona for half of your trip. Then, shift gears and check into a romantic bed-and-breakfast on the Hāmākua Coast or near the volcano. If you've got children in tow, opt for a vacation home or one of Hilo's family-friendly hotels. On the west coast, lounge on the pristine beaches and try some of the fine-dining restaurants; on the east, hike through rain forests, frolic in waterfalls, and go for a plate lunch.

Some locals like to say that the east is "more Hawaiian," but we argue that King Kamehameha himself made the west his last resting place, and Hawaiians have always loved the beach. Another reason to try a bit of both: your budget. While Kohala Coast and Kailua-Kona resorts and condos tend to be on the pricier side, the smaller bed-and-breakfasts and Hilo hotels on the east side are more affordably priced. You can see all the island has to offer and save a little money by opting not to spend your entire vacation at the more expensive resorts.

If you choose a bed-and-breakfast, inn, or an out-of-the-way hotel, explain your expectations fully and ask plenty of questions before booking. Be clear about your travel and location needs. Some places require stays of two or three days. When booking, ask about car-rental arrangements, as many bed-and-breakfast networks offer discounted rates. No matter where you stay, you'll want to rent a car—preferably one with four-wheel drive. This is imperative for getting to some of the best beaches and really seeing the island. However, some rental car companies do have restrictions about taking their vehicles to certain Big Island scenic spots, so make sure to ask about rules before you book.

Members of the Big Island–based **Hawai'i Island Bed & Breakfast Association** (⊕ *www.stayhawaii.com*) are listed with phone numbers and rates in a comprehensive online brochure. In order to join this network, bed-and-breakfasts must be evaluated and meet fairly stringent minimum requirements, including a yearly walk-through by association officers, to maintain their membership.

Other bed-and-breakfast associations include **Hawai'i's Best Bed & Breakfasts** (☎ *808/985–7488 or 800/262–9912* ⊕ *www.bestbnb.com*).

For information on camping at county parks, including Spencer Beach Park, contact the **Department of Parks and Recreation** (⊠ *25 Aupuni St., Hilo* ☎ *808/961–8311* ⊕ *www.hawaii-county.com*).

WHAT IT COSTS					
	¢	$	$$	$$$	$$$$
HOTELS	under $100	$100–$180	$181–$260	$261–$340	over $340

Hotel prices are for two people in a standard double room in high season. Condo price categories reflect studio and one-bedroom rates. Prices do not include 13.42% tax.

KAILUA-KONA

$$$–$$$$
RENTAL

🏠 **Aston Kona by the Sea.** Complete modern kitchens, tile lānai, and washer-dryer units can be found in every suite of this comfortable oceanfront condo complex. The nearest sandy beach is 2 mi away, but the pool is next to the ocean and many of the rooms have ocean views. **Pros:** oceanfront; quiet and peaceful. **Cons:** no beach; not many kid-friendly features. **TripAdvisor:** "maid service was provided daily," "peace and quiet," "great location." ⊠ *75-6106 Ali'i Dr., Kailua-Kona* ☎ *808/327–2300 or 877/997–6667* ⊕ *www.astonhotels.com* ⤶ *86 units* ⚄ *In-room: a/c, kitchen. In-hotel: pool, spa* ☐ *AE, D, DC, MC, V.*

$
RENTAL
☺

🏠 **Casa de Emdeko.** A large and pretty complex on the *makai* (oceanfront) side of Ali'i Drive, Casa de Emdeko offers a few more amenities than most condo complexes, including an on-site convenience store that makes great sandwiches, a sandy oceanfront area for sunbathing, and both fresh and saltwater pools. All units have lānai, with either garden or ocean views. Each unit is individually owned and managed by various property companies, so it's best to check the Web site if you want to make a reservation. **Pros:** oceanfront fresh- and saltwater pools; on-site convenience store. **Cons:** quality can be hit or miss depending on owner; some units are close to high-traffic road. **TripAdvisor:** "market and park nearby," "shaded sitting/picnic area," "condo was clean and tidy." ⊠ *75-6082 Ali'i Dr., Kailua-Kona* ☎ *808/329–2160* ⊕ *www.casadeemdeko.org* ⤶ *106 units* ⚄ *In-room: a/c, kitchen. In-hotel: pools, beachfront* ☐ *AE, MC, V.*

$
B&B/INN

🏠 **Hale Hualālai.** Perfect for couples, Hale Hualālai has two suites with exposed beams, whirlpool bathtubs, and private lānai. Perhaps the most memorable aspect of Hale Hualālai is the food—owner Lonn Armour was a professional chef for 20 years, and cooks up a breakfast that puts other bed-and-breakfast offerings to shame. His creations reflect individual guest preferences, and options include everything from blueberry coffee cake to frittatas to sweet bread French toast. Lonn even grows and serves his own Kona coffee. **Pros:** gourmet breakfast with Kona coffee; new and tastefully decorated house; whirlpool tubs. **Cons:** not

BEST BETS FOR BIG ISLAND LODGING

Fodor's Choice★

Ahu Pohaku Ho'omaluhia, $$$-$$$$, p. 457

Four Seasons Resort Hualālai, $$$$, p. 456

Mauna Kea Beach Hotel, $$$$, p. 462

Waianuhea, $$-$$$, p. 466

By Price

¢

Kona Tiki Hotel, p. 453
Manago Hotel, p. 455

$

Coconut Cottage B&B, p. 470
Hale Hualālai, p. 447

Hale Ohia Cottages, p. 471
Kona Pacific, p. 453
Waimea Gardens Cottage, p. 466

$$

Kīlauea Lodge, p. 473
Royal Kona Resort, p. 454
Shipman House B&B Inn, p. 470
Jacaranda Inn, p. 465

$$$

Vista Waikoloa, p. 463
Sheraton Keauhou Bay Resort & Spa, p. 454

$$$$

Aston Kona by the Sea, p. 447

Fairmont Orchid Hawai'i, p. 456
Hōlualoa Inn, p. 448
Mauna Kea Beach Hotel, p. 462
Mauna Lani Bay Hotel & Bungalows, p. 462
Waikoloa Beach Marriott, p. 464

By Experience

BEST BEACH

Four Seasons Resort Hualālai, $$$$, p. 456
Hāpuna Beach Prince Hotel, $$$$, p. 457
Kona Village Resort, $$$$, p. 458
Mauna Kea Beach Hotel, $$$$, p. 462
Waikoloa Beach Marriott, $$$$, p. 464

kid-friendly; removed from local beaches and restaurants. **TripAdvisor:** "best place we stayed," "cooler temperatures," "lots of space." ⌧ 74-4968 *Māmalahoa Hwy., Hōlualoa* ☎ *808/326–2909* ⊕ *www.hale-hualalai.com* ⟿ *2 suites* ⚲ *In-room: no a/c, no phone, refrigerator, Wi-Fi.* ⊟ *MC, V.*

$$$-$$$$
B&B/INN

Hōlualoa Inn. Six spacious rooms are available in this beautiful cedar home on a 30-acre coffee country estate, 4 mi above Kailua Bay and steps away from the artists' town of Hōlualoa. A lavish breakfast includes estate-grown coffee, fresh fruits, jams, and eggs straight from the inn's coop, as well as homemade breads and macadamia-nut butter. There are rooftop gazebos, a dedicated massage pavilion, a labyrinth, and an old donkey trail dotted with historic sites if you feel like taking a stroll. **Pros:** within walking distance to small village; well appointed with wood floors and lots of windows; panoramic views. **Cons:** a bit far away from beaches and restaurants; expensive for location; not kid-friendly. **TripAdvisor:** "grounds were well kept," "very relaxing," "wonderful view of Kona." ⌧ *76-5932 Māmalahoa Hwy., Box 222, Hōlualoa* ☎ *808/324–1121 or 800/392–1812* ⊕ *www.holualoainn.com* ⟿ *6 rooms* ⚲ *In-room: no a/c, no TV. In-hotel: pool* ⊟ *AE, D, DC, MC, V.*

$$$-$$$$
RESORT

Keauhou Beach Resort. Recent renovations at this resort have gone a long way in rejuvenating the property. The lobby and restaurant have

WHERE TO STAY ON THE BIG ISLAND

	LOCAL VIBE	PROS	CONS
Kailua-Kona	Kailua-Kona is a bustling little village. Ali'i Drive is crammed with hotels and condo complexes.	Plenty to do, day and night; main drag of shops and beaches within easy walking distance of most hotels; several grocery stores in the area.	More traffic than anywhere else on the island; parking can be challenging in beach areas when it's crowded.
The Kona Coast and Ka'ū	A nice place to stay if you want to be out of the fray, there are plenty of fantastic bed-and-breakfasts and inns around Kealakekua Bay.	Kealakekua Bay is one of the best places on the island to kayak and snorkel; excellent dining, shopping, and coffee-farm tours in Captain Cook and Kainaliu towns.	No resorts or resort amenities; no beaches in the area.
The Kohala Coast	The Kohala Coast is home to all of the Big Island's megaresorts.	Beautiful beaches; spectacular resorts; lots of activities for adults and children.	Pricey; with the exception of resort bars and luau events, not much nightlife.
Waimea	Though it seems a world away, Waimea is only about a 15- to 20-minute drive from the Kohala Coast.	Less expensive to stay here than at the Kohala resorts; home to some exceptional local restaurants.	Can be colder and rainy, depending on the season; have to drive 15 minutes to nearby beaches.
The Hāmākua Coast	The Hāmākua Coast is an ideal spot for those seeking peace, tranquillity, and beautiful views.	Oustanding views; plenty of peace and quiet; good spot for honeymooners.	Beaches are an hour's drive away (or more) and the nearest grocery store is 15 mi up the road; no resort amenities.
Hilo	Hilo is the wetter, more lush eastern side of the Big Island.	Proximity to waterfalls and rainforest hikes; good bed-and-breakfast options.	White-sand beaches are more than an hour's drive away; no high-end resorts.
Puna	Puna doesn't attract nearly as many visitors as other regions on the island, so you'll find great deals at rentals and B&Bs here.	A few black-sand beaches; off the beaten path with lots of outdoor wilderness to explore.	Few dining and entertainment options; no resorts or resort amenities.
Hawai'i Volcanoes National Park and Vicinity	If you are going to visit Volcanoes National Park, stay the night in Volcano Village so you can do the late-night lava hike without worrying about driving an hour or more back to your hotel.	Good location for watching lava at night; lots of great, reasonably priced places to stay; close to Hilo and Puna.	Not many dining options (just enough for a one-or two-night stay); not much nightlife.

4

Hotels and Resorts

#	Property Name	Worth Noting	Cost $	Pools	Beach	Golf Course	Tennis Courts	Gym	Spa	Children's Programs	Rooms	Restaurants	Other	Location
8	Keauhou Beach Resort	Close to Kahulu'u Beach	$$$-$$$$	1	yes		6	yes			309	1		Kailua-Kona
14	Kona Tiki Hotel	Oceanfront lānai	¢	1							15		no a/c	Kailua-Kona
3	Manago Hotel	Low price point	¢								64	1	no a/c	Captian Cook
15	Royal Kona Resort	Good rates for oceanfront	$$	1	yes		4	yes	yes		444	1		Kailua-Kona
6	Sheraton Keauhou Bay Resort & Spa	Cool pool with slide	$$-$$$	1			2	yes	yes		521	1		Kailua-Kona

Condos and Vacation Rentals

#	Property Name	Worth Noting	Cost $	Pools	Beach	Golf Course	Tennis Courts	Gym	Spa	Children's Programs	Rooms	Restaurants	Other	Location
10	Aston Kona by the Sea Resort	Oceanfront pool	$$$-$$$$	1					yes		86		kitchen	Kailua-Kona
11	Casa de Emdeko	Oceanfront saltwater pool	$	2							106		kitchen	Kailua-Kona
9	Kona Magic Sands	Ocean view from all units	$-$$	1							37	1	kitchen	Kailua-Kona
12	Kona Nalu	Huge lānai, ocean views	$$	1	yes						15		kitchen	Kailua-Kona
13	Kona Pacific	Ocean view from pool, BBQ	¢-$	1							25		kitchen	Kailua-Kona
7	Outrigger Kanaloa at Kona	Multiple pools	$$$	3			2				166		kitchen	Kailua-Kona

B&Bs and Inns

#	Property Name	Worth Noting	Cost $	Pools	Beach	Golf Course	Tennis Courts	Gym	Spa	Children's Programs	Rooms	Restaurants	Other	Location
2	Aloha Guesthouse	Eco-conscious	$								5		no a/c	South Kona
5	Hale Hualalai	Outstanding breakfast	$								2		no a/c	Hōlualoa
4	Hōlualoa Inn	Beautiful interior	$$$-$$$$	1							6		no a/c	Hōlualoa
1	Kalaekilohana	Hot breakfast, cozy linens	$$								4		no a/c	Ka'ū

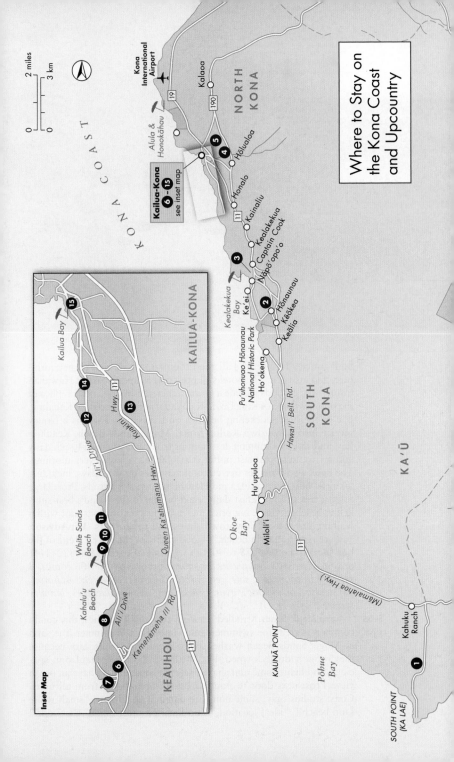

Where to Stay on
the Kona Coast
and Upcountry

Inset Map

KONA COAST

Kona International
Airport

Kalaoa

Kalaoa

NORTH
KONA

Alula &
Honokōhau

Kailua-Kona ⑥-⑮
see inset map

⑤
④
Hōlualoa

Honalo

Kainaliu

Kealakekua
Captain Cook
Nāpoʻopoʻo

③

Kealakekua
Bay
Keʻei

②
Hōnaunau
Keōkea
Keēlia

Puʻuhonuao Hōnaunau
National Historic Park
Hoʻokena

SOUTH
KONA

Hawaiʻi Belt Rd.

KAʻŪ

Huʻupuloa

Okoe
Bay

Miloliʻi

KAUNĀ POINT

Pōhue
Bay

(Mamalahoa Hwy.)

Kahuku
Ranch

①

SOUTH POINT
(KA LAE)

Inset Map

⑮

Kailua Bay

KAILUA-KONA

Hwy.

⑭

⑫

⑬

Aliʻi Drive

White Sands
Beach

⑨ ⑩ ⑪

Kuakini

Kahaluʻu Beach

⑧

Aliʻi Drive

Queen Kaʻahumanu Hwy.

Kamehameha III Rd.

⑦ ⑥

KEAUHOU

2 miles
3 km

"We saw lava flowing into the sea. The sun went down, the steam turned shades of red and orange. It was one of the most memorable moments in my life." —disneydan, Fodors.com photo contest participant

both gotten a face-lift and all guest rooms now have new carpet, furniture, and artwork. The hotel still preserves a unique part of Hawaiian history (the grounds include a *heiau*, a sacred fishpond, and a replica of the summer home of King David Kalākaua) and is adjacent to Kahalu'u, one of the best snorkeling beaches on the island. There is a trolley service into downtown Kailua-Kona, Magic Sands Beach, Keauhou Bay, and several shopping destinations from 9:15 am to 7:40 pm daily and a free, full breakfast buffet is available to guests every morning. The hotel also provides free cultural activities on weekdays, including 'ukulele, hula, lei making, and Hawaiian language lessons. **Pros:** large rooms; free full breakfast daily; next to one of the island's best snorkeling beaches. **Cons:** big price increase since renovations; not within walking distance of downtown shops and restaurants. **TripAdvisor:** "adjacent to Kahalu'u Beach," "good value for the price," "one of the best snorkel spots." ✉ 78-6740 Ali'i Dr., Kailua-Kona ☎ 808/322-3441 or 866/326-6803 ⊕ www.keauhoubeachresort.com ↝ 306 rooms, 3 suites ♿ In-room: a/c, safe, refrigerator, Internet. In-hotel: restaurant, bar, tennis courts, pool, gym, beachfront, laundry facilities, laundry service ⊟ AE, D, DC, MC, V.

$-$$

RENTAL

Kona Magic Sands. Cradled between two small beaches, this condo complex is great for swimmers and sunbathers in summer (the sand at Magic Sands Beach washes away in winter). Units vary because they're individually owned, but all the studios are oceanfront, spacious, and light. Some units have enclosed lānai, and all have an ocean view. **Pros:** next door to popular beach; ocean view from all units. **Cons:** studios only; some units are dated. **TripAdvisor:** "small white sand beach," "ideal location," "no lānai on most units." ✉ 77-6452

Ali'i Dr., Kailua-Kona ☎ 808/329–9393 or 800/622–5348 ⊕ *www. konahawaii.com/ms.htm* ⤵ 37 units ♿ *In-room: a/c (some), kitchen. In-hotel: restaurant, pool* ⊟ *D, MC, V.*

\$\$ 🍴 **Kona Nalu.** One of the nicest
RENTAL   complexes on the ocean side of Ali'i, Kona Nalu units are large and beautifully furnished with supersize lānai, and ocean views from all units. The pool is tiny, but they have a small sandy beach for lying in the sun, and the complex itself is small so you won't be fighting for pool room. **Pros:** extra-large units; ocean views. **Cons:** not within walking distance to stores or restaurants; sandy beach doesn't provide safe ocean entry. **TripAdvisor:** "pool is tiny," "sunsets cannot be beat," "view was really nice." ✉ *76-6212 Ali'i Dr., Kailua-Kona* ☎ *808/329–6438* ⊕ *www.sunquesthawaii.com* ⤵ *15 units* ♿ *In-room: a/c (some), kitchen. In-hotel: pool, beachfront, laundry facilities* ⊟ *D, MC, V.*

¢–\$ 🍴 **Kona Pacific.** Once a hotel, the Kona Pacific gives you plenty of space.
RENTAL   The one-bedroom units, which comfortably sleep four, are the size of two large hotel rooms, with a full kitchen and usually two bathrooms. There are ocean views from the lānai of most units and the pool. This large and well-maintained complex is just at the edge of Kailua-Kona, within walking distance of shops and restaurants. Note that the acceptance of credit cards varies with the unit owners. **Pros:** very large units; some with two lānai; ocean-view pool; well-maintained complex. **Cons:** some units in better shape than others; some units get noise from nearby highway. **TripAdvisor:** "everything was just right," "nice pool," "walking distance to Kona." ✉ *75-5865 Walua Rd., Kailua-Kona* ☎ *808/329–6140* ⊕ *www.konacoastvacations.com* ⤵ *25 units* ♿ *In-room: a/c (some), kitchen. In-hotel: pool.*

¢   🍴 **Kona Tiki Hotel.** The best thing about this three-story walk-up bud-
HOTEL   get hotel, about a mile south of Kailua-Kona, is that all the units have lānai right next to the ocean. The rooms are modest but pleasantly decorated. You can sunbathe by the seaside pool, where a complimentary Continental breakfast is served. Some would call this place old-fashioned; others would say it's local, has a certain kitschy charm, and is the best deal in town. **Pros:** very low price; oceanfront lānai and pool; convenient location; free parking. **Cons:** older hotel in need of update; no beach; doesn't accept credit cards. **TripAdvisor:** "check-in was quick," "close to town," "friendly, laid-back place." ✉ *75-5968 Ali'i Dr., Kailua-Kona* ☎ *808/329–1425* ⊕ *www.konatikihotel.com* ⤵ *15 rooms* ♿ *In-room: no a/c, no phone, refrigerator, no TV, Wi-Fi. In-hotel: pool, parking (free)* ⊟ *No credit cards.*

KAILUA-KONA CONDO COMFORTS

Crossroads Shopping Center. The **Safeway** here is the cleanest, largest, and best-stocked store on the island. It's right next to **Kona Natural Foods**, so you can supplement with local organic produce. ✉ *75-1000 Henry St., Kailua-Kona.*

Pizza-wise, **Kona Brewing Company** (✉ *75-5629 Kuakini Hwy.* ⊹ *Just past Palani intersection on right, Kailua-Kona* ☎ *808/329–2739*) is best if you're willing to go pick it up.

4

$$$
RENTAL

⬚ **Outrigger Kanaloa at Kona.** The 16-acre grounds provide a peaceful and verdant background for this low-rise condominium complex bordering the Keauhou-Kona Country Club. It's walking distance from the golf course and within a five-minute drive of the nearest beaches (Kahalu'u and White Sands). Large units have koa-wood cabinetwork and washer-dryers; some oceanfront villas have private hot tubs. **Pros:** across the street from acclaimed golf course; three pools with hot tubs. **Cons:** not within walking distance of grocery store or beach; no restaurant on property. **TripAdvisor:** "magnificent grounds," "would highly recommend for family stay," "next to a small cove." ✉ *78-261 Manukai St., Kailua-Kona* ☎ *808/322–9625, 808/322–2272, or 800/688–7444* ⊕ *www.outrigger.com* ⇘ *166 units* ⚲ *In-room: a/c (some), safe, kitchen. In-hotel: tennis courts, pools, laundry facilities* ▭ *AE, D, DC, MC, V.*

$$
RESORT

⬚ **Royal Kona Resort.** This is a great option if you're on a budget. The location is great, the lobby, pool, and restaurant are right on the water, and most of the hotel's large, lānai-front rooms have been recently updated from Hawaiian kitsch to a more toned-down modern take that includes neutral-tone walls, classic Hawaiian art, and bamboo headboards. The hotel is within walking distance of Kailua-Kona and across the street from numerous shops and restaurants. The weekly lū'au with Polynesian entertainment (on Monday, Wednesday, and Friday) is fun and quite popular. Make sure to book online, where the rates can be as much as 50% less than the rack rates, and select rooms in the Ali'i or Lagoon tower if you'd like a recently renovated room. **Pros:** convenient location; waterfront pool; low prices. **Cons:** oceanfront lagoon is often closed; staff are sometimes grumpy. **TripAdvisor:** "right by the water," "easy walking distance to the town," "older property." ✉ *75-5852 Ali'i Dr., Kailua-Kona* ☎ *808/329–3111 or 800/222–5642* ⊕ *www. royalkona.com* ⇘ *436 rooms, 8 suites* ⚲ *In-room: a/c, safe, refrigerator, Internet. In-hotel: restaurant, bar, tennis courts, pool, gym, spa, beachfront, laundry facilities, Internet terminal* ▭ *AE, D, DC, MC, V.*

$$–$$$
RESORT
☾

⬚ **Sheraton Keauhou Bay Resort & Spa.** For the big-resort style of the Kohala Coast at a less astronomical price, the Sheraton is a good bet. Longtime Big Island visitors might remember it as the old Kona Surf. Left empty for several years, the hotel still shows some of its wear and tear, but the new owners have gone to great lengths to restore it to its former glory. The lobby, with floor-to-ceiling windows and carved marble architectural elements, is particularly stunning. The only remnants of the old hotel in the bright and modern Sheraton rooms are the small and unimpressive bathrooms. On the upside, many of the rooms have great views of the bay, and all have the Sheraton's signature Sweet Sleeper beds, which ensure a good night's sleep. The big selling point for those traveling with kids is the pool, one of the coolest on the island, with a slide, waterfalls, and an ocean view. **Pros:** fantastic pool; manta rays on view nightly; resort style at lower price. **Cons:** no beach; only one restaurant. **TripAdvisor:** "staff was very pleasant and accommodating," "grounds are beautiful," "absence of a beach." ✉ *78-128 Ehukai St., Kailua-Kona* ☎ *808/930–4900* ⊕ *www.sheratonkeauhou.com* ⇘ *510 rooms, 11 suites* ⚲ *In-room: a/c, safe, refrigerator, Internet, Wi-Fi. In-hotel: restaurant, bar, tennis courts, pool, gym, spa, water sports* ▭ *AE, D, DC, MC, V.*

THE KONA COAST AND KA'Ū

$ ▣ **Aloha Guesthouse.** In the hills above Kealakekua Bay, Aloha Guest-
B&B/INN house offers quiet elegance, complete privacy, and ocean views from
every room. With a focus on nature, the house is furnished in earth
tones. The bath products are 100% organic, and the yummy full breakfasts are as close to organic as they can muster. Common areas include a
kitchenette, a high-definition television, a DVD library, and a computer
with high-speed Internet. **Pros:** eco-conscious; full breakfast; views of
Kealakekua Bay. **Cons:** remote location; no grocery stores or restaurants
within walking distance. **TripAdvisor:** "house is really nice," "room
was very clean," "great place to chat with other guests." ⊠ *Old Tobacco
Rd., off Hwy. 11 near mile marker 104, Honaunau* ☎ *808/328–8955*
⊕ *www.alohaguesthouse.com* ⇆ *5 rooms* ♿ *In-room: no a/c, refrigerator, DVD, Wi-Fi. In-hotel: Internet terminal* ⊟ *AE, MC, V.*

$$ ▣ **Kalaekilohana.** You wouldn't really expect to find a top-notch bed-and-
B&B/INN breakfast in Ka'ū, but just up the road from South Point, this charming
yellow house offers large, comfortable private suites with beautifully
restored hardwood floors, private lānai with ocean and mountain views,
and big, comfy beds decked out with high-thread-count sheets and fluffy
down comforters. Choose between a full hot breakfast or a Continental
breakfast of local fruits and baked goods—both come with plenty of
award-winning local Ka'ū estate coffee. For those who want to explore
the area's green- and black-sand beaches, or hike the south side of Vol-
canoes National Park (the newly opened south entrance is less than 2 mi
away), hosts Kenny Joyce and Kilohana Domingo are happy to share
their knowledge of the area. The bed-and-breakfast prides itself on its
programs and work surrounding Hawaiian cultural arts, and guests are
welcome to take part in lei-making workshops and other lessons in tra-
ditional Hawaiian handicrafts. **Pros:** luxurious beds; beautifully restored
house; delicious breakfast. **Cons:** not for children under 10; no pool. **Trip-
Advisor:** "house is brand new," "large comfortable and clean rooms,"
"balcony with French doors." ⊠ *94-2152 South Point Rd., Nā'ālehu*
☎ *808/939–8052* ⊕ *www.kau-hawaii.com* ⇆ *4 rooms* ♿ *In-room: no
a/c, Wi-Fi. In-hotel: laundry facilities* ⊟ *AE, D, MC, V.*

¢ ▣ **Manago Hotel.** This historic hotel is a good option if you want to
HOTEL escape the touristy thing but still be close to everything on the island.
Don't let the front TV room creep you out—you have not checked into
an old folks' home. The place has an authentic Hawai'i vibe, and the
restaurant is one of the best on the island. Dwight Manago—whose
grandparents, Kinzo and Osame Manago, built the main building in
1917—has maintained one Japanese-style room with tatami mats and
a *furo*, a traditional Japanese bath, and this is the room to book. The
other rooms are nothing special, but they're clean, and those in the
newer wing have great views high above the Kona Coast. **Pros:** local
color; rock-bottom prices; terrific on-site restaurant. **Cons:** a bit run-
down; not the best sound insulation between rooms. **TripAdvisor:**
"clean but definitely no-frills," "good value hotel," "low price." ⊠ *81-
6155 Māmalahoa Hwy., Box 145, Captain Cook* ☎ *808/323–2642*
⊕ *www.managohotel.com* ⇆ *64 rooms, 42 with bath* ♿ *In-room: no
a/c, no phone, no TV. In-hotel: restaurant* ⊟ *D, MC, V.*

4

THE KOHALA COAST

$$$–$$$$
RESORT

Fairmont Orchid Hawai'i. The Fairmont is a megaresort in every sense of the word—huge and crowded, with grand staircases, domed ceilings, chandeliers, and marble everywhere. If you're looking for a unique, intimate experience, this is not your hotel, but with its antiques and 32 acres of beachfront gardens the Orchid provides the perfect old-school hotel experience for some. Its restaurants are also among the best on the island, with a large variety of options ranging from sushi to modern Hawaiian cuisine to local style family-friendly fare. The "Gold Floor" of the hotel includes free breakfast and a daily hors d'oeuvres hour. **Pros:** oceanfront location; great restaurants, new 42-inch flat-screen TVs in every room. **Cons:** mammoth resort lacks personal feel; room decor needs updating. **TripAdvisor:** "staff is friendly," "spacious room," "beach was immaculately looked after." ⊠ *1 N. Kanikū Dr., Kohala Coast* ☎ *808/885–2000 or 800/845–9905* ⊕ *www.fairmont. com/orchid* ↺ *486 rooms, 54 suites* ♿ *In-room: a/c, safe, Wi-Fi. In-hotel: 4 restaurants, bars, golf courses, tennis courts, pool, gym, spa, beachfront, water sports, children's programs (ages 5–12)* ⊟ *AE, D, DC, MC, V.*

$$$$
RESORT
☾
Fodor'sChoice
★

Four Seasons Resort Hualālai. Beautiful views everywhere, polished wood floors, brand-new furnishings and linens in warm earth and cool white tones, and Hawaiian artwork make Hualālai a peaceful retreat. Ground-level rooms have outdoor garden showers. Bungalows are large and cozy, with down comforters and spacious slate-floor bathrooms. One of the five pools, called King's Pond, is a brackish pond with loads of fish and two manta rays that guests have the opportunity to feed daily. The main infinity pool looks like something out of an ad for an expensive liquor—it's long and peaceful, surrounded by cabanas and palm trees with a clear view to the ocean beyond. The on-site Hawaiian Cultural Center honors the grounds' spiritual heritage, and the sports club and spa offer top-rate health and fitness options. Hualālai's golf course hosts the Senior PGA Tournament of Champions. Despite its quiet luxury, the resort is also super kid-friendly, with a great activities program, and a few pool options for families. The property is beautiful, the restaurants are fantastic, the rooms are more than comfortable, and the service is definitely of Four Seasons quality. **Pros:** beautiful location; island's best restaurants. **Cons:** can be noisy poolside; pricey. **TripAdvisor:** "don't need a car," "rooms were spacious and clean," "absolute authentic Hawaiian beauty." ⊠ *72-100 Ka'ūpūlehu Dr.* ⏎ *Box 1269, Kailua-Kona 96745* ☎ *808/325–8000, 800/819–5053, or 888/340–5662* ⊕ *www.fourseasons.com/hualalai* ↺ *243 rooms, 51 suites* ♿ *In-room: a/c, safe, DVD, Internet, Wi-Fi. In-hotel: 3 restaurants, room service, bars, golf course, tennis courts, pools, gym, spa, beachfront, children's programs (ages 5–12), laundry service* ⊟ *AE, D, DC, MC, V.*

$
B&B/INN

Hale Ho'onanea. A comfortable home with three detached guest suites, this 3-acre property in the Kohala Estates lives up to the English translation of its name, "House of Relaxation." From its bluff above the ocean you can watch the sun rise over Mauna Kea and set over the Pacific, and view the sparkling beauty of Hawai'i's night sky. The rooms are comfortable and spacious and the price is a steal at less than half the nightly rate of the Kohala Resorts. Continental breakfast is included. There's a two-night minimum; a $25 fee applies to single-night bookings made within seven days of arrival. **Pros:** detached suites for maximum privacy; panoramic ocean views from private lānai; good price for the neighborhood. **Cons:** not within walking distance to restaurants; no pool. **TripAdvisor:** "nice place for stargazing," "off the beaten tourist path," "early morning noise." ✉ *Kohala Estates, 59-513 Ala Kahua Dr., Kawaihae* ☎ *808/882–1653 or 877/882–1653* ⊕ *www. houseofrelaxation.com* ⤳ *3 suites* ⅏ *In-room: no a/c* ▭ *AE, D, MC, V.*

$$$$
HOTEL
⅏

🖼 **Hāpuna Beach Prince Hotel.** Often more reasonably priced than its neighbors, thanks to a variety of ongoing discount options, the Hāpuna Beach Prince is no less luxurious and happens to be sitting on a corner of one of the best beaches on the island. Initially designed with business travelers in mind, rooms at the Hāpuna Prince are spacious, with large marble bathrooms and plenty of in-room amenities. However, the spacious rooms and beachfront location have turned the hotel into more of a family vacation destination than a business hotel, which means that couples seeking a romantic getaway might be disappointed by the number of kids playing Marco Polo at the pool. Still, the place is large enough to escape from other guests if you so desire, and the staff is exceedingly helpful. The golf course, designed by Arnold Palmer and Ed Seay, has topped many a "best courses" list. **Pros:** extra-large rooms; full or partial ocean views from most rooms; direct access to one of island's best beaches. **Cons:** no supermarkets or shopping centers within walking distance; no nightlife nearby. **TripAdvisor:** "restful and relaxing location," "restaurants are good," "almost all rooms are ocean view." ✉ *62-100 Kauna'oa Dr., Kohala Coast* ☎ *808/880–1111 or 800/882–6060* ⊕ *www.princeresortshawaii.com* ⤳ *350 rooms, 61 suites* ⅏ *In-room: a/c, refrigerator, Internet. In-hotel: 5 restaurants, bars, golf course, tennis courts, pool, gym, spa, beachfront, children's programs (ages 5–12)* ▭ *AE, D, DC, MC, V.*

$$$–$$$$
B&B/INN
Fodor'sChoice
★

🖼 **Hawai'i Island Retreat at Ahu Pohaku Ho'omaluhia.** Ahu Pohaku is set above the cliffs of North Kohala near Pololū Valley. The retreat generates its own solar power, uses water from its own well, and grows almost all its own food. Beautiful hardwood floors are built from sustainably harvested woods, and rooms take advantage of natural light and ventilation to keep energy usage low. Surrounded by 60 acres, 20 of which are a dedicated conservation area, the retreat feels both luxurious and completely hidden from the world. Rooms are large and bright, with ocean views and brightly colored walls. All have private balconies, and all are equipped with large bathrooms that include both soaking tubs and showers. Sustainability meets luxury here without sacrificing comfort. The owners added seven luxury yurts during a recent renovation, a full-service spa in 2008, and a saltwater infinity pool. Three meals a day are prepared from the retreat's garden supply, augmented by additions from local farms. **Pros:** stunning location; new and beautiful construction with no expense spared; eco-friendly. **Cons:** not within walking distance of restaurants; off the beaten path. **TripAdvisor:** "tastefully decorated," "daily yoga," "emphasis is on organic living." ✛ *Follow signs off Hwy. 270 in Kapa'au, North Kohala* ☎ *808/889–6336* ⊕ *www.*

4

hawaiiislandretreat.com ↩ *9 rooms* ⟐ *In-room: no a/c, no phone, no TV. In-hotel: pool, spa* ⊟ *D, MC, V.*

$$$–$$$$ ⊞ **Hilton Waikoloa Village.** Dolphins chirp in the lagoon; a pint-size
RESORT   daredevil zooms down the 175-foot waterslide; a bride poses on the
☺   grand staircase; a fire-bearing runner lights the torches along the sea-
side path at sunset—these are some of the scenes that may greet you
at this 62-acre megaresort. Shaded pathways lined with a multimil-
lion-dollar Pacific Island art collection connect the three tall buildings;
Swiss-made trams and canal boats shuttle those weary of the long hall-
ways and meandering paths. Though there's no ocean beach, there is
a seaside trail to 'Anaeho'omalu Bay, aka A-Bay, one of the island's
most pleasant beaches. An ocean-side saltwater lagoon is great for
families. Modern rooms in neutral tones have private lānai and are
large enough to accommodate the families that flock here. The stars
of **Dolphin Quest** (☎ *800/248–3316* ⊕ *www.dolphinquest.org*) are the
resort's pride and joy; reserve in advance for an interactive learning
session. ■ TIP➔ Brides-to-be, take note: this is one-stop shopping, as the
resort has a wedding-planning office, cakes, flowers, photography, and a
"Just Married" boat ride. **Pros:** a kid's idea of paradise; lots of restaurant
and activity options. **Cons:** gigantic, crowded, and often noisy; restau-
rants are pricey. **TripAdvisor:** "lagoon and pool are great," "activities
"cost you more"," "grounds were impeccably kept." ⊠ *69-425 Waiko-
loa Beach Dr., Waikoloa* ☎ *808/886–1234 or 800/445–8667* ⊕ *www.
hiltonwaikoloavillage.com* ↩ *1,240 rooms, 57 suites* ⟐ *In-room: a/c,
safe, refrigerator, Internet. In-hotel: 9 restaurants, room service, bars,
golf courses, tennis courts, pools, gym, spa, beachfront, water sports,
children's programs (ages 5-12), laundry facilities, laundry service*
⊟ *AE, D, DC, MC, V.*

$$$$ ⊞ **Kona Village Resort.** At this writing the Kona Village Resort was closed
RESORT   indefinitely due to tsunami damage in March 2011. Check the hotel's
☺   Web site for updates. The most Hawaiian of the Kohala Coast resorts,
Kona Village was one of the first, and it makes a real effort to keep
modern life at bay. Without phones, televisions, or radios, the Kona
Village is in a time warp—the perfect place for couples or families to get
away from it all in their own thatch-roof *hale* (house) near the resort's
sandy beach. Built on the grounds of an ancient Hawaiian village, the
bungalows reflect styles of South Seas cultures—Tahitian, Samoan,
Māori, Fijian, or Hawaiian. Some of the bungalows are oceanfront,
some nestled around the ancient Hawaiian fishing lagoon, and no mat-
ter where you hail from and how crowded the resort is, you'll feel like
this is your own little hideaway. There's really no place else like it in
the state. The beach here is small, but idyllic, with sea turtles nesting
in the sand around a calm, turquoise bay. Rates include all meals, an
authentic Polynesian Wednesday- or Friday-night lū'au, grounds tours,
tennis, and sports activities. **Pros:** detached bungalows afford ultimate
privacy; sea turtles nest on the resort's private beach; all meals and
many activities included. **Cons:** somewhat isolated location; no phones
or TVs in rooms. **TripAdvisor:** "a bit on the older side," "beautiful and
uncrowded," "completely unique experience." ⊠ *Queen Ka'ahumanu
Hwy., Box 1299, Kailua-Kona* ☎ *808/325–5555 or 800/367–5290*

Hawai'i Island Retreat at Ahu Pohaku Ho'omaluhia

WHERE TO STAY ON THE KOHALA COAST AND WAIMEA

	Property Name	Worth Noting	Cost $	Pools	Beach	Golf Course	Tennis Courts	Gym	Spa	Children's Programs	Rooms	Restaurants	Other	Location
Hotels and Resorts														
❼	Fairmont Orchid Hawaiʻi	Massages on the beach	$$$-$$$$	1	yes	priv.	10	yes	yes	5–12	540	4	shops	South Kohala
❶	Four Seasons Resort Hualālai	King's Pond snorkeling	$$$$	5	yes	yes	8	yes	yes	5–12	294	3		North Kona
❿	Hāpuna Beach Prince Hotel	Fantastic beach	$$$$	1	yes	yes	13	yes	yes	5–12	411	5		South Kohala
❸	Hilton Waikoloa Village	Dolphin Quest program	$$$-$$$$	3	yes	priv.	8	yes	yes	5–12	1297	9	shops	Waikoloa
❷	Kona Village Resort	2 lūʻau options	$$$$	2	yes		3	yes	yes	5–17	125	2	no a/c	North Kona
⓫	Mauna Kea Beach Hotel	Amazing design; fantastic beach	$$$$	1	yes	yes	11	yes	yes	5–12	268	4	shops	South Kohala
❽	Mauna Lani Bay Hotel & Bungalows	Renowned golf and spa	$$$$	1	yes	yes	16	yes	yes	5–12	343	3		South Kohala
❹	Waikoloa Beach Marriott	Great deal for location	$$$$	1	yes	yes	6	yes	yes		545	1		Waikoloa
⓱	Waimea Country Lodge	Quiet setting	$					yes	yes		21		no a/c	Waimea
Condos and Vacation Rentals														
⓮	Aloha Vacation Cottages	Private, grills	$								2		no a/c	Waimea
❾	Mauna Lani Point, Islands	Waterfall pool	$$$$	1		priv.					61		kitchen	South Kohala
❺	Outrigger Kolea at Waikoloa	Infinity pool, kids' pool	$$$$	2				yes			126		kitchen	Waikoloa
❻	Vista Waikoloa	2 lānai per unit	$$-$$$	1			1	yes			122		kitchen	Waikoloa
⓯	Waimea Gardens Cottage	Mountainside stream	$								3		kitchen	Waimea
B&Bs and Inns														
⓲	Aaah, The Views!	Stream-side, those views	$								3		no a/c	Waimea
⓬	Hale Hoʻonanea	Great deal	$								3		no a/c	Kawaihae
⓰	Jacaranda Inn	Big rooms	$-$$								9		no a/c	Waimea
⓭	Hawaii Island Retreat at Ahu Pohaku Hoʻomaluhia	Eco-resort	$$$-$$$$	1					yes		9		no a/c	North Kohala

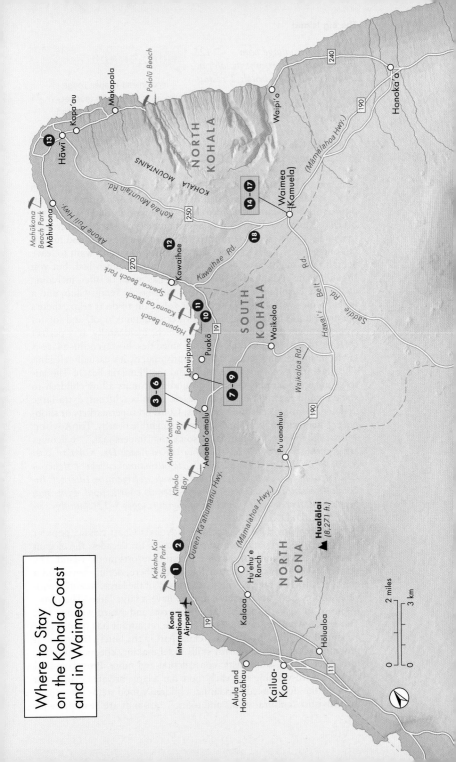

Where to Stay on the Kohala Coast and in Waimea

⊕ *www.konavillage.com* ⤴*125 bungalows* ⌖ *In-room: no a/c, no phone, no TV. In-hotel: 2 restaurants, bars, tennis courts, pools, gym, spa, beachfront, children's programs (ages 5–17), Internet terminal* ⊟ *AE, D, MC, V.*

$$$$ Fodor's Choice ★   ⊡ **Mauna Kea Beach Hotel.** The grande dame of Kohala Coast, the Mauna Kea Beach Hotel was designed by Laurance S. Rockefeller in the early 1960s and opened in 1965. It has long been regarded as one of the world's premier vacation resort hotels, and it borders one of the island's finest white-sand beaches, Kauna'oa. Renovations after an earthquake in 2006 increased the hotel's luxury status tenfold. The bathrooms are large and luxurious and come with L'Occitane bath amenities you won't want to leave behind. You might never want to rise from your plush bed, but you should because Mauna Kea Beach Hotel has much to offer, including an 18-hole championship golf course, the Seaside Tennis Club, and a fitness center with daily classes. If all you want to do is relax, there's the first-rate Mandara spa, a freshwater swimming pool, and lots of comfy lounge chairs on the beach, which, incidentally, is a perfect crescent of sand and sea. Despite the amenities, however, this place is far from formal and stuffy. More appropriately, it's casually elegant. The hotel has two wings: the Main and the Plumeria Beach. The latter is great for families because ground-floor units allow children to wake up and run right out to the beach. **Pros:** beachfront; extra-large updated rooms; excellent restaurants. **Cons:** no supermarkets or shopping centers within walking distance; no nightlife nearby. **TripAdvisor:** "very classy venue and setting," "somewhat impersonal," "balconies are generously sized." ✉ *62-100 Mauna Kea Beach Dr., Kohala Coast* ☎ *808/882–7222 or 800/882–6060* ⊕ *www.maunakeabeachhotel.com* ⤴*258 rooms, 10 suites* ⌖ *In-room: a/c, safe, refrigerator, Internet. In-hotel: 4 restaurants, bars, golf courses, tennis courts, pool, gym, spa, beachfront, water sports, children's programs (ages 5–12), laundry service* ⊟ *AE, D, DC, MC, V.*

$$$$ HOTEL   ⊡ **Mauna Lani Bay Hotel & Bungalows.** A Kohala Coast classic, popular with honeymooners and anniversary couples for decades, the elegant Mauna Lani is still one of the most beautiful resorts on the island. The open-air lobby has ceilings near the stratosphere, ocean views, and a constant, pleasant breeze. The vast majority of the large, recently renovated rooms have ocean views, and all have a large lānai. The resort is known for its two spectacular golf courses and award-winning spa. The award-winning, on-site CanoeHouse restaurant has been highly acclaimed for years. Make sure to take part in the hotel's free cultural programs where you can learn skills in lei making, coconut husking, throw net fishing, sand castle construction and more. **Pros:** beautiful design; award-winning spa; each room has a large private lānai. **Cons:** some of the decor needs updating; children's food items are pricey. **TripAdvisor:** "cultural walks and tours," "grounds are beautiful with

fish ponds," "friendly staff." ✉ 68-
1400 Mauna Lani Dr., Kohala
Coast ☎ 808/885–6622 or 800/
367–2323 ⊕ www.maunalani.com
⬅ 324 rooms, 14 suites, 5 bungalows ☐ In-room: a/c, safe, refrigerator, Wi-Fi. In-hotel: 3 restaurants,
bars, golf courses, tennis courts,
pool, gym, spa, beachfront, children's programs (ages 5–12) ▭ AE,
D, DC, MC, V.

$$$$
RENTAL
🏠 **Mauna Lani Point Villas and the
Islands of Mauna Lani Condominiums.**
Surrounded by the emerald greens
of a world-class ocean-side golf
course, spacious two-story suites
at Islands of Mauna Lani offer a
private, independent home away from home. The privately owned units,
individually decorated according to the owners' tastes, have European
cabinets and oversize soaking tubs in the main bedrooms. The Mauna
Lani Point villas are closer to the beach, which means they're priced
a little higher, but an ocean view from the lānai of most units may
be worth it. At both properties you're just a short distance from The
Shops at Mauna Lani where you can shop, dine, or stock up your
kitchen with gourmet groceries from Foodland Farms. **Pros:** privacy;
soaking tubs; extra-large units. **Cons:** can get very pricey; no access to
nearby resort amenities. **TripAdvisor:** "fantastic snorkeling right off the
beach," "access to the private beach club," "a hidden gem for families."
✉ 68-1050 Mauna Lani Point Dr., Kohala Coast ☎ 808/885–5022 or
800/642–6284 ⊕ www.classicresorts.com ⬅ 61 units ☐ In-room: a/c,
kitchen. In-hotel: pool ▭ AE, DC, MC, V.

$$$$
RENTAL
🏠 **Outrigger Kolea at Waikoloa.** One of the latest upscale condo developments to join the Waikoloa Beach Resort, Kolea is aiming to capture the
very high-end crowd typically associated with the Mauna Lani and Four
Seasons. These fairly new condos are impeccably furnished and turned
out, views from each unit's lānai are spectacular, and the complex is
closer to the beach than any of the others in this area. Kolea also offers
far more amenities than the average condo complex, with both an infinity pool and a kids' pool at their ocean-side Beach Club, a fitness center,
and a lava-rock hot tub. **Pros:** high design; close to beach and activities;
resort amenities. **Cons:** pricey; no on-property restaurants. ✉ Waikoloa
Beach Resort, 69-289 Waikoloa Beach Dr., Waikoloa ☎ 808/886–0036
⊕ www.outrigger.com ⬅ 126 units ☐ In-room: a/c, kitchen, DVD. In-
hotel: pools, gym ▭ AE, D, DC, MC, V.

$$–$$$
RENTAL
🏠 **Vista Waikoloa.** Older and more reasonably priced than most of the
condo complexes along the Kohala Coast, the two-bedroom, two-
bath Vista condos offer ocean views and a great value for this part of
the island. All are large and well-appointed, with two lānai per unit,
plus they are within walking distance to A-Bay, the Kings' Shops and
Queens' Marketplace at Waikoloa, and the restaurants and amenities of

the Hilton Waikoloa, and within short driving distance of the airport, other resorts, and a variety of Big Island sights. **Pros:** centrally located; reasonably priced; very large units; newly renovated 75-foot lap pool. **Cons:** hit or miss on decor because each unit is individually owned; some owners charge (refundable) security deposits. **TripAdvisor:** "truly a value," "excellent location," "short walk to access Anaeho'omalu Beach (A-Bay)." ⊠ *Waikoloa Beach Resort, 69-1010 Keana Pl., Waikoloa* ☎ *808/886–3594* ↪ *122 units* ⛵ *In-room: a/c, kitchen. In-hotel: pool, gym, laundry facilities, Internet terminal* ⊟ *AE, MC, V.*

$$$$
RESORT

⊡ **Waikoloa Beach Marriott.** The most affordable resort on the Kohala Coast, the Waikoloa Beach Marriott covers 15 acres and encompasses ancient fishponds, historic trails, and petroglyph fields. All of the Marriott's rooms have low-slung, sleek modern beds, bright white linens, Hawaiian art, and private lānai. The new pool area has three separate pools—a heated infinity pool, a pool with a partial sand bottom for kids, and one with a waterslide for the young and young-at-heart. Dining is not the hotel's strong suit but their Hawai'i Calls Restaurant & Lounge has weekly food specials including entrée discounts on specified nights. In addition, there are tons of restaurants within walking distance at the Kings' Shops and Queens' Marketplace. The hotel's Mandara Spa offers a full range of treatments in a spacious new wellness center. Bordering the white-sand beach of 'Anaeho'omalu Bay, the hotel offers a range of ocean activities through Ocean Sports Hawai'i, including stand-up paddleboards, hydro-bikes, kayaks, and wedding-vow renewals on a catamaran. **Pros:** great location at a great price; brand-new hotel; well-designed interiors. **Cons:** no standout restaurants; nothing particularly Hawaiian about it. **TripAdvisor:** "attractive looking hotel," "the food is pretty good," "stunning sunsets." ⊠ *69-275 Waikoloa Beach Dr., Waikoloa* ☎ *808/886–6789 or 800/228–9290* ⊕ *www.marriott.com* ↪ *523 rooms, 22 suites* ⛵ *In-room: a/c, refrigerator. In-hotel: restaurant, bars, golf courses, tennis courts, pool, gym, spa, beachfront, laundry facilities* ⊟ *AE, D, DC, MC, V.*

WAIMEA

$
B&B/INN

⊡ **Aaah, The Views!** This tranquil and pretty stream-side mountain home in Upcountry Waimea is lovingly tended by owners Erika and Derek Stuart. Rooms are clean and bright, with lots of windows to enjoy the views. The house has a sauna and an in-house massage therapist as well. This is a popular spot with couples and is not well suited for large families. **Pros:** away from it all; beautiful countryside views; on-site massage. **Cons:** not kid-friendly; no pool; must drive to area restaurants and attractions. **TripAdvisor:** "very clean and quiet," "semi-rural setting," "truly has some incredible views." ⊠ *66-1773 Alaneo St., off Akulani, just past mile marker 60 on Hwy. 19, Waimea* ☎ *808/885–3455* ⊕ *www.aaahtheviews.com* ↪ *3 rooms* ⛵ *In-room: no a/c, kitchen (some), refrigerator, Wi-Fi. In-hotel: Wi-Fi hotspot* ⊟ *MC, V.*

$
RENTAL

⊡ **Aloha Vacation Cottages.** Set on several acres of North Kohala property, these two rental cottages don't look like much from the outside, but inside they are clean, comfortable, and well stocked with beach toys, towels and mats, snorkel gear, body boards, kayaks, fishing gear,

KOHALA COAST CONDO COMFORTS

There are fewer stores and takeout options on the Kohala Coast than elsewhere on the island, but, as the condos are all associated with resorts, most of your needs will be met. If you require anything not provided by the management, both the **Kings' Shops** (✉ *250 Waikoloa Beach Dr., Waikoloa* ☎ *808/886–8811*) and the **Queens' Market-place** (✉ *201 Waikoloa Beach Dr., Waikoloa* ☎ *808/886–8822*) in the Waikoloa Beach Resort are good places to go. There is a small grocery store, a liquor store, and a couple of decent takeout options at the Kings' Shops. The newer Queens' Market-place also has restaurants willing to do takeout, as well as a gourmet market where you can order pizza with interesting toppings, baked to order. It's not exactly cheap, but you're paying for the convenience of not having to drive into town.

laptop computers, books, cable TV, videos, you name it. The price is right, and they are just a 10-minute drive from the Kohala Coast. There is a minimum stay of five nights, though this rule is sometimes waived, depending on availability. The owners give generous discounts for extended stays, so check the Web site. **Pros:** each cottage equipped with gas grill; free Wi-Fi; 10-minute drive from great beaches. **Cons:** somewhat remote location; can't walk to restaurants or stores; no pool. **TripAdvisor:** "hosts are wonderful people," "serene and quiet surroundings," "a home away from home." ⌂ *Box 1395, Waimea 96743* ☎ *877/875–1722 or 808/885–6535* ⊕ *www.alohacottages.net* ⌕ *2 units* ⌂ *In-room: no a/c, kitchen, DVD, Wi-Fi. In-hotel: laundry facilites, parking (free)* ▭ *AE, D, DC, MC, V.*

$–$$
B&B/INN

⌂ **Jacaranda Inn.** Charming inside and out, the lavender Jacaranda Inn can be spotted from miles away. Built in 1897, the sprawling estate was once the home of the manager of Parker Ranch; it's been redecorated in hues of raspberry and lavender, with lots of koa wood accents. Most of the rooms have hot tubs. A separate nearby cottage that sleeps six has been recently renovated with new hardwood floors, a stone fireplace, and large outdoor hot tub. **Pros:** country charm; hot tubs in most rooms; walking distance to Waimea restaurants. **Cons:** no pool; lots of purple. **TripAdvisor:** "historic and very interesting old ranch house," "walking distance from central Waimea," "quiet, romantic get-away." ✉ *65-1444 Kawaihae Rd., Waimea* ☎ *808/557–5068* ⊕ *www.jacarandainn.com* ⌕ *8 suites, 1 cottage* ⌂ *In-room: no a/c, no phone, no TV (some). In-hotel: Wi-Fi hotspot, parking (free)* ▭ *MC, V.*

$
HOTEL

⌂ **Waimea Country Lodge.** In the heart of cowboy country, this modest ranch house–style lodge offers views of the green, rolling slopes of Mauna Kea. It's so quiet you forget you're close to busy Waimea. The rooms are large and clean, with Hawaiian quilts lending an authentic touch. A handful of studios with kitchenettes are also available. **Pros:** affordable; large rooms equipped with kitchenettes. **Cons:** rooms could use some updating; no pool. **TripAdvisor:** "needs an overhaul," "try to request a 2nd floor room," "great view of a volcano cone." ✉ *65-1210 Lindsey Rd., Waimea* ☎ *808/885–4100 or 800/367–5004* ⊕ *www.castleresorts.com* ⌕ *21 rooms* ⌂ *In-room: no a/c, kitchen* *(some), Internet. In-hotel: laundry facilities, parking (free)* ☰AE, D, DC, MC, V.

$ ▦ **Waimea Gardens Cottage.** Charming country cottages surrounded by
RENTAL   flowering private gardens contain surprisingly luxe suites that look like they just leapt out of a glossy magazine. One (Kohala) includes a full kitchen and the others (Waimea and the Garden Studio) a kitchenette, and all are stocked with provisions (including fresh farm eggs) for a hearty self-serve Continental breakfast. All have their own private gardens and beautiful hardwood floors. The Kohala cottage has a luxury bath with whirlpool soaking tub and the Garden Studio is equipped with a rain-head shower. The grounds are full of birds and plant life that will make you want to move in for good. Inquire for seasonal specials. **Pros:** no detail left out; beautiful self-contained cottages; gardens; complete privacy. **Cons:** pricey for the area; requires payment in full six weeks prior to arrival. **TripAdvisor:** "bright and airy," "nice break from the pricey resorts," "for both couples and families." ⌂ *Box 563, Kamuela 96743* ☎ *808/885–8550* ⊕ *www.waimeagardens.com* ⤴ *2 cottages, 1 studio* ⌂ *In-room: no a/c, kitchen, DVD, Wi-Fi* ☰ *No credit cards.*

THE HĀMĀKUA COAST

$$$–$$$$ ▦ **The Palms Cliff House Inn.** This handsome Victorian-style mansion,
B&B/INN   15 minutes north of Hilo, is perched on the sea cliffs 100 feet above the crashing surf of the tropical coast. You can pick tropical fruit and macadamia nuts from the gardens of the 3½-acre estate. Individually decorated rooms have private lānai. Suites include double hot tubs (the one in Room 8 is by the window with a stunning view of the coast), but there's also a communal hot tub in the garden. A husband-and-wife team serves breakfast with pride on the veranda overlooking the cliffs; meals generally include fresh-baked muffins, locally grown fruit, a warm egg or meat dish (they always ask about food allergies or dietary restrictions ahead of time), and, of course, fantastic local coffee. They can help you plan activities, including hula lessons. **Pros:** stunning views; terrific breakfast; comfortable rooms with every amenity. **Cons:** no pool; no lunch or dinner on-site; remote location means you have to drive to Hilo town for restaurants and shopping. **TripAdvisor:** "great lodging experience," "grounds were immaculate," "really pricey." ⌂ *28-3514 Māmalahoa Hwy., Honomū* ☎ *866/963–6076 or 808/963–6076* ⊕ *www.palmscliffhouse.com* ⤴ *4 rooms, 4 suites* ⌂ *In-room: a/c (some), safe, DVD. In-hotel: Internet terminal, Wi-Fi hotspot* ☰ *AE, D, DC, MC, V.*

$$–$$$ ▦ **Waianuhea.** Waianuhea defines Hawaiian country elegance. Fully self-
B&B/INN   contained and run off solar power, this gorgeous country home sits in a
Fodor's Choice   forested area on the Hāmākua Coast. The four guest rooms and large
★   suite have tasteful color schemes and lavish furnishings, complete with extra pillows, fluffy down comforters, and soaking tubs, and there is contemporary artwork throughout. The large common room with its stunning ocean views and lava-rock fireplace is a big attraction, especially at the wine tasting and hors d'oeuvres hour each evening. **Pros:** eco-friendly hotel; hot and healthy breakfast; beautiful views. **Cons:**

very remote location; unreliable phone and Internet access. **TripAdvisor:** "a personal touch," "wine hour is a very nice touch," "wonderful staff." ✉ 45-3503 *Kahana Dr., Honoka'a* ✆ *Box 185, Honoka'a 96727* ☎ *888/775–2577 or 808/775–1118* ⊕ *www.waianuhea.com* ⟳ *4 rooms, 1 suite* ⌂ *In-room: no a/c, DVD. In-hotel: Internet terminal, Wi-Fi hotspot* ⊟ *AE, D, MC, V.*

$
B&B/INN
🏨 **Waipi'o Wayside.** Nestled amid the avocado, mango, orchid, and kukui trees of a plantation estate, this serene inn provides a retreat close to the Waipi'o Valley. Each room has its own character with, for example, rare Chinese antiques or patchwork quilts. A sprawling garden has an orchid-covered deck and a little gazebo has hammocks to help you indulge your lazy side. Many of the rooms have ocean views. A full organic breakfast is included. **Pros:** close to Waipi'o; authentic Hawaiian feel; hammocks with views. **Cons:** remote location; no lunch or dinner on property. **TripAdvisor:** "large deck with hammock," "good location for Waipi'o Valley," "great host." ✉ *Waipi'o Valley Rd., Hwy. 240, Honoka'a* ☎ *808/775–0275 or 800/833–8849* ⊕ *www.waipiowayside.com* ⟳ *5 rooms* ⌂ *In-room: no a/c, no phone, no TV, Wi-Fi* ⊟ *MC, V.*

HILO

$
HOTEL
☼
🏨 **Dolphin Bay Hotel.** A glowing lava flow sign marks the office and bespeaks owner John Alexander's passion for the volcano. Stunning lava pictures adorn the common area, and Alexander is a great source of information for visiting the park and for exploring the back roads of Hilo. Units in the 1950s-style motor lodge are modest, but clean and inexpensive. Coffee and fresh fruit are offered daily. Four blocks from downtown Hilo, in a residential area called Pu'ue'o, the hotel borders a verdant 2-acre Hawaiian garden with jungle trails and shady places to rest. Guests of the hotel return repeatedly, and it's ideal for families who seek a home base. **Pros:** great value; extremely helpful and pleasant staff; rates go down every night you stay. **Cons:** located along a busy road; basic; motel-style rooms. **TripAdvisor:** "staff were very friendly and helpful," "quiet neighborhood," "frogs are loud." ✉ *333 'Iliahi St., Hilo* ☎ *808/935–1466* ⊕ *www.dolphinbayhotel.com* ⟳ *18 rooms, 12 studios, 4 1-bedroom units, 1 2-bedroom unit* ⌂ *In-room: no a/c, no phone, kitchen, Wi-Fi* ⊟ *MC, V.*

$
B&B/INN
🏨 **Hale Kai.** On a bluff above Hilo Bay, this 5,400-square-foot modern home is 2 mi from downtown Hilo. Three impeccable rooms with patios have been freshly painted and spruced up by new owners Maria Macias and Ricardo Zepeda. All rooms have grand ocean views and are within earshot of lapping waves. Fresh flowers add a warm, European touch. Maria and Ricardo serve a full hot breakfast every morning on an outdoor deck or in the kitchen's bay-window dining area. **Pros:** delicious hot breakfast; panoramic views; privacy. **Cons:** removed from town; no kids under 13. **TripAdvisor:** "great for whale-watching," "beautiful view," "fantastic breakfast." ✉ *111 Honoli'i Place, Hilo* ☎ *808/935–6330* ⊕ *www.halekaihawaii.com* ⟳ *3 rooms, 1 suite* ⌂ *In-room: no a/c, no phone, Wi-Fi. In-hotel: pool, no kids under 13* ⊟ *MC, V.*

Waianuhea

$$ ⊞ **Hilo Hawaiian Hotel.** Though it does show its age and some of the
HOTEL rooms are in dire need of a refresh, this older hotel, with large bay-front
rooms offering spectacular views of Mauna Kea and Coconut Island,
is one of the most pleasant lodgings on Hilo Bay. Street-side rooms
overlook the golf course. Most accommodations have private lānai,
and kitchenettes are available in the banyan and ocean suites. Views of
the bay are showcased in the recently renovated Queen's Court dining
room, and the Wai'oli Lounge—where you can get a grab-and-go lunch
or cocktails and appetizers—has entertainment Friday and Saturday.
Pros: Hilo Bay views; private lānai in most rooms; large rooms. **Cons:**
not many options for lunch at the hotel; prices high for quality of rooms.
TripAdvisor: "rooms are a bit shopworn," "great location," "clean and
comfortable." ⊠ *71 Banyan Dr., Hilo* ☎ *808/935–9361; 800/367–5004
from mainland; 800/272–5275 interisland* ⊕ *www.castleresorts.com*
⇆ *264 rooms, 21 suites* ♿ *In-room: a/c, kitchen (some), refrigerator
(some), Internet, Wi-Fi (some). In-hotel: restaurant, bar, pool, laundry
facilities* ⊟ *AE, D, DC, MC, V.*

$–$$ ⊞ **Hilo Honu Inn.** A charming old Craftsman home lovingly restored by
B&B/INN a friendly and hospitable couple from North Carolina, the Hilo Honu
offers quite a bit of variety. The Honu's Nest provides fantastic views
of the sunrise over Hilo Bay from the comforts of a large, comfy bed.
The larger Bali Hai Suite has a sitting room and a window seat that
looks out on tree ferns, orchids, and anthuriums. Upstairs, the entire
second floor is the Samurai Suite, furnished with traditional tatami mats
and beautiful antiques imported from Japan. Breakfast is delicious and
usually includes a variety of homemade baked goods. **Pros:** beautifully
restored home; spectacular Hilo Bay views; delicious breakfast; free
Wi-Fi. **Cons:** only one room and two suites; not walking distance to
downtown Hilo. **TripAdvisor:** "very comfortable, especially the beds,"
"lovely section of town," "the showers will spoil you." ⊠ *465 Haili St.,
Hilo* ☎ *808/935–4325* ⊕ *www.hilohonu.com* ⇆ *3 rooms* ♿ *In-room:
a/c (some), no phone, refrigerator, DVD, Wi-Fi. In-hotel: no kids under
6* ⊟ *AE, DC, MC, V.*

$–$$ ⊞ **Naniloa Volcanoes Resort.** The Naniloa's newly renovated guest rooms
RESORT in the Mauna Kea tower are a vast improvement over the old ones. The
pool was recently redone, but renovations are ongoing in the hotel's
other two towers and lobby area. However, Naniloa is still a great
home base to explore the island's unspoiled east side. Remodeled rooms
feature new beds, a tile bathroom with imported fixtures from Spain
and Italy, flat-screen TVs, and original tropical oil paintings painted by
the owner's daughter. All ocean view rooms have small lānai and great
views of Hilo Bay. The hotel has one restaurant that currently only
serves breakfast. **Pros:** newly renovated rooms; great views of Hilo Bay,
Mauna Kea, and Mauna Loa volcanoes from some rooms. **Cons:** ongoing renovations; limited dining options. **TripAdvisor:** "stark but clean,"
"grounds appear to be very rundown," "not a luxury resort area." ⊠ *93
Banyan Drive, Hilo* ☎ *808/969–3333* ⊕ *www.volcanohousehotel.com/
naniloa_volcanoes_resort.htm* ⇆ *313 rooms, 7 suites.* ♿ *In-room: a/c,
refrigerator, Internet (some). In-hotel: restaurant, golf course, pool,
laundry facilities, Wi-Fi hotspot* ⊟ *AE, D, MC, V.*

$$ **Shipman House Bed & Breakfast Inn.** You'll have a choice between three
B&B/INN rooms in the mansion—the turreted main house dating from 1899—or
two rooms in a separate cottage. The bed-and-breakfast is on 5½ ver-
dant acres on Reed's Island; the house is furnished with antique koa
and period pieces, some dating from the days when Queen Lili'uokalani
came to tea. On Thursday night, a hula class practices Hawai'i's dances
out on the lānai. Guests are allowed to participate or just hang out and
watch. Barbara (part of the Shipman family) and her husband Gary
are friendly hosts with a vast knowledge of the area and the rest of the
island. Don't miss the tropical breakfast buffet with macadamia-nut
granola, special breads and muffins, and a variety of tropical fruits that
are grown right on property. Barbara will even teach you how to string
a lei with sweet-smelling flowers from the garden. Two-night minimum.
Pros: 10-minute walk to downtown Hilo; historic home; friendly and
knowledgeable local hosts. **Cons:** chock-full of antiques; not a great
spot for kids. **TripAdvisor:** "fabulous view," "beautifully furnished,"
"room was very comfortable." ⊠ *131 Ka'iulani St., Hilo* ☎ *808/934–
8002 or 800/627–8447* ⊕ *www.hilo-hawaii.com* ⟿ *3 rooms, 2 cottage
rooms* ⟁ *In-room: no a/c, no phone, refrigerator, no TV, Wi-Fi* ⊟ *AE,
MC, V.*

PUNA

¢–$ **Bed & Breakfast Mountain View.** This modern home is surrounded by
B&B/INN rolling forest and farmland. The secluded 4-acre estate has extensive
floral gardens and a fishpond. Owners Linus and Jane Chao are long-
time Big Island art educators and have an art studio on the lower level
where they teach classes. Some special packages include art lessons. The
house itself is a virtual art gallery with varied displays in oil, acrylic,
watercolor, and Oriental brush paintings. **Pros:** reasonable prices; local
artist hosts; beautiful landscaping. **Cons:** rooms could use some updat-
ing; location is remote. **TripAdvisor:** "perfect hosts," "wonderful gar-
dens with ponds," "the breakfast was awesome." ⊠ *South Kulani Rd.,
Kurtistown* ☎ *808/968–6868 or 888/698–9896* ⊕ *www.bbmtview.com*
⟿ *4 rooms, 2 with shared bath* ⟁ *In-room: no a/c. In-hotel: no kids
under 5* ⊟ *MC, V.*

$ **Coconut Cottage Bed & Breakfast.** New to the bed-and-breakfast scene,
B&B/INN Coconut Cottage has quickly become a favorite among visitors for
its beautiful grounds, hosts' attention to detail, and proximity to dif-
ferent island adventures. Owners Jerry and Todd refurbished the old
Jade Garden B& B in 2007 to include two additional rooms with vin-
tage, island-style furnishings. The Bali Spirit Suite is perhaps the most
romantic, with an antique Balinese four-poster bed and windows that
overlook the anthurium garden. The larger Garden Bungalow sleeps
four and is great for families. Guests enjoy a full breakfast with popular
dishes like coconut/macadamia-nut pancakes and quiche. This area of
the island has little in the way of nightlife, so Coconut Cottage boasts
a library of more than 500 DVDs that you can watch in the privacy of
your room, or you can reach ultimate relaxation by soaking for hours
in the outdoor hot tub. Inquire about special rates for extended stays.
Pros: great breakfast; centrally located between Hilo and Volcanoes

National Park. **Cons:** no nightlife nearby; some may have a hard time sleeping with the coqui frogs chirping. **TripAdvisor:** "grounds were beautiful," "spectacular lava trees," "peaceful and relaxing." ⊠ *13-1139 Leilani Ave., Pahoa* ☎ *808/965–0973 or 866/204–7444* ⊕ *www.coconutcottagehawaii.com* ⤳ *3 rooms, 1 bungalow* ⚭ *In-room: no a/c, refrigerator, DVD, Wi-Fi. In-hotel: laundry facilities, Wi-Fi hotspot* ⊟ *AE, D, MC, V.*

¢–$

B&B/INN

▦ **Yoga Oasis.** This center, on 26 tropical acres, has a bit of a commune feel. With its exposed redwood beams, Balinese doorways, and imported art, Yoga Oasis draws those who seek relaxation and rejuvenation, and perhaps a free yoga lesson or two. A 1,600-square-foot state-of-the-art yoga and gymnastics space, with 18-foot ceilings, crowns this friendly retreat. You're close to hot springs and black-sand beaches, and the volcano is a 45-minute drive away. Individual rooms share bathrooms; private cabins have private bathrooms. **Pros:** daily yoga; focus on relaxation; very low prices. **Cons:** remote location; shared bathrooms in the main building. **TripAdvisor:** "rainforest setting," "non-touristy side of Hawai'i," "the yoga was nice." ⊠ *Pohoiki Rd., Box 1935, Pāhoa* ☎ *808/965–8460 or 800/274–4446* ⊕ *www.yogaoasis.org* ⤳ *4 rooms with shared bath, 4 deluxe cabins, 1 Bali house* ⚭ *In-room: no a/c, no phone, no TV, Wi-Fi. In-hotel: laundry service, Wi-Fi hotspot* ⊟ *MC, V.*

HAWAI'I VOLCANOES NATIONAL PARK AND VICINITY

$–$$

HOTEL/RENTAL

▦ **Chalet Kīlauea Collection.** The Collection comprises three inns and lodges and five vacation houses in and around Volcano Village. The rooms, suites, and vacation homes range from a historic lodge with no-frills, basic bedrooms to a deluxe inn with themed rooms and its own six-person hot tub. The Collection's showpiece property, the **Inn at Volcano** ($116–$239), along with the rest of the properties were refurbished recently with new flooring, fixtures, paint, mounted flat-screen TVs, imported linens, and custom-made wooden bed frames. The **Lokahi Lodge** ($98–$128) provides cozy rooms in a country lodge with plenty of exposed beams and wood, and comfy beds. A large kitchen is available for guest use, as is an on-site hot tub. For those looking for a bit more privacy, the **Volcano Cottages** are dispersed vacation homes and cottage rentals around Volcano Village. The Collection's most reasonably priced offering is the **Volcano Hale** ($61–$70 double-occupancy room), which has a communal kitchen and fireplace. **Pros:** free afternoon tea at main office; large variety of lodging types to choose from; hot tub; fireplace. **Cons:** Wi-Fi only available at main office; office closes at 5 pm—late arrivals allowed but you need to formally check in the following morning. **TripAdvisor:** "many amenities," "very comfortable stay," "clean and spacious." ⊠ *Wright Rd., Volcano* ☎ *808/967–7786 or 800/937–7786* ⊕ *www.volcano-hawaii.com* ⤳ *14 rooms, 3 suites, 5 houses* ⚭ *In-room: no a/c, no phone (some). In-hotel: Wi-Fi hotspot* ⊟ *D, DC, MC, V.*

$

RENTAL

▦ **Hale Ohia Cottages.** A stately and comfortable Queen Anne–style mansion, Hale Ohia was built in the 1930s as a summer place for a wealthy Scotsman. The namesake Ohia cottage, large enough for a family, has a full kitchen. Cottage 44 is the cushiest of the group; built into an old

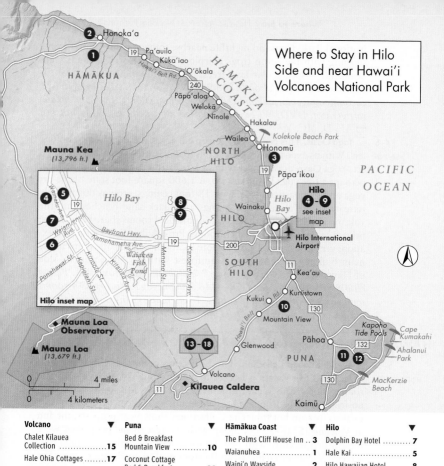

Where to Stay in Hilo
Side and near Hawai'i
Volcanoes National Park

HONOKA'A
Pa'auilo
Kūka'iao
'O'ōkala
Hawai'i Belt Rd.
HĀMĀKUA
Pāpa'alog
Weloka
Nīnole
Hakalau
HĀMĀKUA COAST
Wailea
Kolekole Beach Park
NORTH
HILO
Honomū
Pāpa'ikou
PACIFIC
OCEAN
Mauna Kea
(13,796 ft.)
Hilo
see inset
map
Wainaku
Hilo
Bay
HILO
Hilo International
Airport
SOUTH
HILO
Kea'au
Kurtistown
Kukui
Mountain View
Kapoho
Tide Pools
Cape
Kumakahi
Ahalanui
Park
Pāhoa
PUNA
MacKerzie
Beach
Glenwood
Volcano
Kīlauea Caldera
Kaimū
Mauna Loa
Observatory
Mauna Loa
(13,679 ft.)

Hilo inset map
Hilo Bay
Waiānuenue Ave.
Keawe St.
Wainaku Ave.
Bayfront Hwy.
Kamehameha Ave.
Ponahawai St.
Kino'ole St.
Kapiolani St.
Kīlauea Ave.
Waiākea
Fish
Pond
Mamo St.
Kanoelehua Ave.

0   4 miles
0   4 kilometers

water tank, it's naturally lighted, beautifully designed, and completely private. Continental breakfast is left in your refrigerator while you're away in the afternoon so that you can enjoy it at your leisure in the morning. **Pros:** unique architecture; plenty of props like umbrellas and flashlights for volcano excursions. **Cons:** no TVs; property cat roams around, which could be a problem for allergic guests. **TripAdvisor:** "very comfortable bed," "wonderful private cottage in lush property," "you'll hear it when it rains." ⊠ *Hale Ohia Rd., off Hwy. 11, Volcano* ☎ *808/967–7986 or 800/455–3803* ⊕ *www.haleohia.com* ↝ *4 rooms, 3 cottages, 1 suite* ⚑ *In-room: no a/c, no phone, no TV, kitchen (some), refrigerator, Wi-Fi* ⊟ *MC, V.*

$–$$
HOTEL
🏨 **Kīlauea Lodge.** A mile from the entrance of Hawai'i Volcanoes National Park, this lodge was initially built as a YMCA camp in the 1930s. Now it is a pleasant inn, tastefully furnished with European antiques. Rooms have rich quilts and Hawaiian photographs, and some have their own wood-burning or gas fireplace. A charming one-bedroom cottage with a gas fireplace and a porch is perfect for romance. Cottages off the main property include Pi'i Mauna House, on the fairway of the Volcano Golf Course. Rates include a full hot breakfast at the Lodge's restaurant, which has an excellent and unusual dinner menu that includes braised rabbit, medallions of venison, ostrich, and leg of antelope. The duck a l'orange is a customer favorite. The restaurant is open to the public for breakfast, lunch, and dinner. **Pros:** great restaurant; close to volcano; fireplaces. **Cons:** a little pricey for the area; no TV or phone in room. **TripAdvisor:** "evening volcano watch," "everything was spotless," "bed was very comfortable." ⊠ *19-3948 Old Volcano Rd., 1 mi northeast of Volcano Store* 🖃 *Box 116, Volcano 96785* ☎ *808/967–7366* ⊕ *www.kilauealodge.com* ↝ *12 rooms, 2 cottages (off property)* ⚑ *In-room: no a/c, no phone, no TV (some), Wi-Fi. In-hotel: restaurant* ⊟ *AE, MC, V.*

¢–$
B&B/INN
🏨 **My Island Bed & Breakfast Inn.** Gordon and Joann Morse, along with their daughter Ki'i, opened their historic home and 7-acre botanical estate to visitors in 1985. The oldest in Volcano, it was built in 1886 by the Lyman missionary family. Three rooms, one with a private bath, are in the main house. Also on property are three garden units with private entrances and bathrooms, and one guesthouse. You won't start the day hungry after an all-you-can-eat deluxe Continental breakfast. **Pros:** historic home; full breakfast. **Cons:** remote location; some shared bathrooms, cat on property can be an issue for those with allergies. **TripAdvisor:** "take the rain forest walk," "cute rooms," "room was tidy and had fresh flowers." ⊠ *19-3896 Old Volcano Hwy., Volcano Village* 🖃 *Box 100, Volcano 96785* ☎ *808/967–7216* ⊕ *www. myislandinnhawaii.com* ↝ *6 rooms, 4 with bath; 1 guesthouse* ⚑ *In-room: no a/c, no phone, no TV* ⊟ *D, MC, V.*

$–$$
RENTAL
🏨 **Volcano Places.** A collection of lovely vacation homes, the accommodations range from a simple cottage in the rain forest to a stunning Craftsman-style house with its own spa room. Many can accommodate up to six people comfortably. All come equipped with full kitchens. Recent renovations to the Kahi Malu cottage include revamped bathrooms, a completely redone kitchen, and a covered lānai from where

you can view the stars on a clear evening. **Pros:** unique architecture; rain-forest location; total privacy. **Cons:** not much nightlife nearby; prices of more expensive units are high for the area. **TripAdvisor:** "wonderful modern kitchen," "cottage was spic and span," "central for volcano exploration." ✉ *19-3951 Laukapua, Volcano* ☎ *808/967–7990 or 877/967–7990* ⊕ *www.volcanoplaces.com* ⤢ *4 cottages* ⚲ *In-room: no a/c, kitchen, DVD, Wi-Fi* ⊟ *MC, V.*

$$ 🏠 **Volcano Teapot Cottage.** A near-perfect spot for couples seeking a
RENTAL   romantic getaway, this cute two-bedroom red-and-white cottage is completely private. The claw-foot bathtub, hot tub, and fireplace add to the general coziness. Continental breakfast is included, and the restaurants in Volcano Village are nearby. **Pros:** claw-foot tub; hot tub; fireplace; laundry facilities. **Cons:** not much nightlife close by; single or double occupancy only. **TripAdvisor:** "owners are lovely people," "charmingly decorated," "great place in a great location." ✉ *19-4041 Kīlauea Rd., Volcano Village* ⌂ *Box 511, Volcano 96785* ☎ *808/967–7112* ⊕ *www. volcanoteapot.com* ⤢ *1 cottage* ⚲ *In-room: no a/c, kitchen, DVD, Wi-Fi* ⊟ *AE, MC, V.*

5

Kaua'i

WORD OF MOUTH

"My idea of a perfect day is: watching the sunrise over the 'Anini reef; sipping a homemade pineapple/banana/mango smoothie and eating breakfast while looking out over the ocean from my patio; going for a long morning walk at Kē'ē or 'Anini Beach.

—Songdoc

WELCOME TO KAUA'I

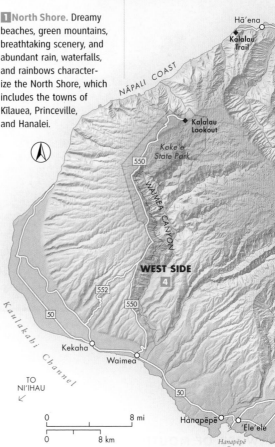

TOP REASONS TO GO

★ **Nāpali Coast:** On foot, by boat, or by air—explore what is unarguably one of the most beautiful stretches of coastline in all Hawai'i.

★ **Kalalau Trail:** Hawai'i's ultimate adventure hike will test your endurance but reward you with lush tropical vegetation, white-sand beaches, and unforgettable views.

★ **Kayaking:** Kaua'i is a mecca for kayakers, with four rivers plus the spectacular coastline to explore.

★ **Waimea Canyon:** Dramatic, colorful rock formations and frequent rainbows make this natural wonder one of Kaua'i's most stunning features.

★ **Birds:** Birds thrive on Kaua'i, especially at the Kīlauea Point National Wildlife Refuge.

1 **North Shore.** Dreamy beaches, green mountains, breathtaking scenery, and abundant rain, waterfalls, and rainbows characterize the North Shore, which includes the towns of Kīlauea, Princeville, and Hanalei.

2 **East Side.** This is Kaua'i's commercial and residential hub, dominated by the island's largest town, Kapa'a. The airport, harbor, and government offices are found in the county seat of Līhu'e.

3 **South Shore.** Peaceful landscapes, sunny weather, and beaches that rank among the best in the world make the South Shore the resort capital of Kaua'i. The Po'ipū resort area is here along with the main towns of Kōloa, Lāwa'i, and Kalāheo.

Princeville

Hanalei Bay

560

Kīlauea

Hanalei **1**

NORTH SHORE

Anahola

56

Wai'ale'ale
5,148ft

581

Kapa'a

580

Wailua
Bay

EAST SIDE **2**

56

Kilohana Crater
1,138ft

583

Hanama'ulu

Līhu'e

Līhu'e Airport

50

58

Nawiliwili Bay

520

Kaua'i Channel

alaheo

530

Kōloa

SOUTH SHORE

3

Po'ipū

GETTING ORIENTED

Despite its small size—550 square mi—Kaua'i has four distinct regions, each with its own unique characteristics. The windward coast, which catches the prevailing trade winds, consists of the North Shore and East Side, while the drier leeward coast encompasses the South Shore and West Side. One main road nearly encircles the island, except for a 15-mi stretch of sheer cliffs called Nāpali Coast. The center of the island—Mt. Wai'ale'ale, completely inaccessible by car and rarely viewable except from above due to nearly year-round cloud cover—is reported to be the wettest spot on Earth, getting about 450 inches of rain per year.

5

4 West Side. Dry, sunny, and sleepy, the West Side includes the historic towns of Hanapēpē, Waimea, and Kekaha. This area is ideal for outdoor adventurers because it's the entryway to the Waimea Canyon and Kōke'e State Park, and the departure point for most Nāpali Coast boat trips.

GREAT ITINERARIES

As small as Kaua'i may be, you still can't do it all in one day: hiking Kalalau Trail, kayaking Wailua River, showering in a waterfall, watching whales at Kīlauea Lighthouse, waking to the sunrise above Keālia, touring underwater lava tubes at Tunnels, and shopping for gifts at Kōloa Town shops. Rather than trying to check everything off your list in one fell swoop, we recommend choosing your absolute favorite and devoting a full day to the experience.

Adventure Galore

For big-time adventure, kayak Nāpali Coast or spend a day learning to fly a microlight. For those whose idea of adventure is a good walk, take the flat, coastal trail along the East Side—though incomplete, you can pick it up starting at the southern end of Lydgate Park, heading north. It'll eventually take you all the way to Anahola, if you desire. After it's all over, recuperate with a massage by the ocean—or in the comfort of your own room, so you can crash immediately afterward.

Shop 'Til You Drop

You could actually see a good many of the island's sights by browsing in our favorite island shops. Of course, you can't see the entire island, but this itinerary will take you through Kapa'a and north to Hanalei. Don't miss Marta's Boat—high-end clothing for mom and child—across from Foodland in Waipouli. Just a few blocks north, Kela's Glass has great art pieces. From there, a leisurely drive north will reveal the rural side of Kaua'i. If you enjoy tea, sake, or sushi, stop at Kīlauea's Kong Lung, where you can stock up on complete place settings for each. Then, head down the road to Hanalei. If you're inspired by surf, stop in Hanalei Surf

Company. Our favorite for one-of-a-kind keepsakes—actually antiques and authentic memorabilia—is Yellow Fish Trading Company, and we never head into Hanalei without stopping at On the Road to Hanalei.

Relax Kaua'i-Style

If you're headed to Kaua'i for some peace and quiet, you'll want to start your day with yoga at Yoga Hanalei or Studio Yoga Kaua'i (formerly Bikram Yoga Kaua'i) in Kapa'a. If you're staying on the South Shore, try yoga on the beach (actually a grassy spot just off the beach) with longtime yoga instructor Joy Zepeda (⊕ www.kauaioceanfrontyoga. com). If it happens to be the second or last Sunday of the month, you might then head to the Lāwa'i International Center (⊕ www.lawaicenter.org) for an afternoon stroll among 88 Buddhist shrines. On the North Shore, Limahuli Gardens is the perfect place to wander among native plants. Then watch the sun slip into the sea on any west-facing beach and call it a day with a glass of wine.

Have a Little Romance

We can't think of a better way to ensure a romantic vacation for two than to pop a bottle of champagne and walk the Māhā'ulepū shoreline at sunrise, hand in hand with a loved one. Make this a Sunday and follow your walk with brunch at the Grand Hyatt. Then spend the afternoon luxuriating with facials, body scrubs, and massage in the Hyatt ANARA Spa's Garden Treatment Village, in a private, thatched hut just for couples. That'll put you in the mood for a wedding ceremony or renewal of vows on the beach followed by a sunset dinner overlooking the ocean at the Beach House restaurant. Can it get any more romantic than this?

Updated
by Charles
Roessler and
Nathan Eagle

Even a nickname like "The Garden Island" fails to do justice to Kaua'i's beauty. Verdant trees grow canopies over the few roads, and brooding mountains are framed by long, sandy beaches, coral reefs, and sheer sea cliffs. Pristine trade winds moderate warm daily temperatures while offering comfort for deep, refreshing sleep through gentle nights.

5

For adventure seekers, Kaua'i offers everything from difficult hikes to helicopter tours. The island has top-notch spas and golf courses, and its beaches are known to be some of the most beautiful in the world. Even after you've spent days lazing around drinking mai tais or kayaking your way down a river, there's still plenty to do, as well as see: plantation villages, a historic lighthouse, wildlife refuges, a fern grotto, a colorful canyon, and deep rivers are all easily explored.

GEOLOGY

Kaua'i is the oldest and northernmost of the main Hawaiian Islands. Five million years of wind and rain have worked their magic, sculpting fluted sea cliffs and whittling away at the cinder cones and caldera that prove its volcanic origin. Foremost among these is Wai'ale'ale, one of the wettest spots on Earth. Its 450-inch annual rainfall feeds the mighty Wailua River, the only navigable waterway in Hawai'i. The vast Alaka'i Swamp soaks up rain like a sponge, releasing it slowly into the watershed that gives Kaua'i its emerald sheen.

FLORA AND FAUNA

Kaua'i offers some of the best birding in the state, due in part to the absence of the mongoose. Many *nēnē* (endangered Hawaiian state bird) reared in captivity have been successfully released here, along with an endangered forest bird called the *puai'ohi*. The island is also home to a large colony of migratory nesting seabirds and has two refuges protecting endangered Hawaiian water birds. Kaua'i's most noticeable fowl, however, is the wild chicken. A cross between jungle fowl (*moa*) brought by the Polynesians and domestic chickens and fighting cocks that escaped during the last two hurricanes, they are everywhere, and the roosters crow when they feel like it, not just at dawn. Consider yourself warned.

HISTORY

Kaua'i's residents have had a reputation for independence since ancient times. Called "the separate kingdom," Kaua'i alone resisted King Kamehameha's charge to unite the Hawaiian Islands. In fact, it was only by kidnapping Kaua'i's king, Kaumuali'i, and forcing him to marry Kamehameha's widow that the Garden Isle was joined to the rest of Hawai'i. That spirit lives on today as Kaua'i residents resist the lure of tourism dollars captivating the rest of the Islands. Local building rules maintain that no structure may be taller than a coconut tree, and Kaua'i's capital city, Līhu'e, is still more small town than city.

LEGENDS AND MYTHOLOGY: THE MENEHUNE

Although all the Islands have a few stories about the *Menehune*—magical little people who accomplished great feats—Kaua'i is believed to be their home base. The Menehune Fishpond, above Nāwiliwili Harbor, is a prime example of their work. The story goes that the large pond (initially 25 mi in diameter) was built in one night by thousands of Menehune passing stones from hand to hand. A spy disrupted their work in the middle of the night, leaving two gaps that are still visible today (drive to the pond on Hulemalu Road or kayak up Huleia Stream).

PLANNING

GETTING HERE AND AROUND

AIR TRAVEL

All commercial and cargo flights use the Līhu'e Airport, 2 mi east of the town of Līhu'e. It has just two baggage-claim areas, each with a visitor information center. The Princeville Airport is a tiny strip on the North Shore and is used sparingly by a tour helicopter company and a few private planes.

GROUND TRANSPORTATION
A rental car is the best way to get to your hotel, though taxis and some hotel shuttles are available. From the airport it will take you about 15 to 25 minutes to drive to Wailua or Kapa'a, 30 to 40 minutes to reach Po'ipū, and 45 minutes to an hour to get to Princeville or Hanalei.

CAR TRAVEL

Unless you plan to stay strictly at a resort or do all your sightseeing as part of guided tours, you'll need a rental car. There is bus service on the island, but the buses tend to be slow, run limited hours, and don't go everywhere.

You most likely won't need a four-wheel-drive vehicle anywhere on the island, so save yourself the money. And while convertibles look fun, the frequent, intermittent rain showers and intense tropical sun make hardtops a better (and cheaper) choice.

If possible, avoid the "rush" hours when the local workers go to and from their jobs. Some sections of the main highway are often particularly congested, specifically the Kapa'a–Wailua stretch, even on weekends.

Kaua'i has some of the highest gas prices in the country.

ISLAND DRIVING TIMES It might not seem as if driving from the North Shore to the West Side, say, would take very much time, as Kaua'i is smaller than O'ahu, Maui, and certainly the Big Island. But it will take longer than you'd expect, and Kaua'i roads are subject to some heavy traffic, especially going through Kapa'a and Līhu'e. *Here are average driving times that will help you plan your excursions accordingly.*

DRIVING TIMES	
Ha'ena to Hanalei	5 mi/15 mins
Hanalei to Princeville	4 mi/10 mins
Princeville to Kīlauea	5 mi/12 mins
Kīlauea to Anahola	8 mi/15 mins
Anahola to Kapa'a	5 mi/10 mins
Kapa'a to Līhu'e	10 mi/20 mins
Līhu'e to Po'ipū	13 mi/25 mins
Po'ipū to Kalaheo	8 mi/20 mins
Kalaheo to Hanapēpē	4 mi/10 mins
Hanapēpē to Waimea	7 mi/10 mins

RESTAURANTS

Kaua'i's cultural diversity is apparent in its restaurants, which offer authentic Vietnamese, Chinese, Korean, Japanese, Thai, Mexican, Italian, and Hawaiian specialties. Less specialized restaurants cater to the tourist crowd, serving standard American fare—burgers, pizza, sandwiches, surf-and-turf combos, and so on. Kapa'a offers the best selection of restaurants, with options for a variety of tastes and budgets; most fast-food joints are in Līhu'e.

Parents will be relieved to encounter a tolerant attitude toward children, even if they're noisy. Men can leave their jackets and ties at home; attire tends toward informal, but if you want to dress up, you can. Reservations are accepted in most places and required at some of the top restaurants.

HOTELS

If you want to golf, play tennis, or hang at a spa, stay at a resort. You'll also be more likely to find activities for children at resorts, including camps that allow parents a little time off. The island's hotels tend to be smaller and older, with fewer on-site amenities. Some of the swankiest places to stay on the island are the St. Regis Princeville Resort on the North Shore, where rooms run more than $900 per night in high season, and the Grand Hyatt Kaua'i on the South Shore for a bit less; of course, those with views of the ocean book faster than those without.

Condos and vacation rentals on Kaua'i tend to run the gamut from fabulous luxury estates to scruffy little dives. It's buyer-beware in this totally unregulated sector of the visitor industry, though the County of Kaua'i is in the process of developing new regulations for these types of properties, particularly those in agricultural and rural areas. If you're planning to stay at one of these, be sure to contact the operator prior to traveling to ensure it's still open.

Properties managed by individual owners can be found on online vacation-rental directories such as CyberRentals and Vacation Rentals By Owner, as well as on the Kaua'i Visitors Bureau's Web site. There are also several Kaua'i-based management companies with vacation rentals.

The island's bed-and-breakfasts allow you to meet local residents and more directly experience the aloha spirit. Many have oceanfront settings and breakfasts with everything from tropical fruits and juices, Kaua'i coffee, and macadamia-nut waffles to breads made with local bananas and mangoes. Some have pools, hot tubs, services such as *lomilomi* massage, and breakfasts delivered to your lānai. Some properties have stand-alone units on-site.

WHAT IT COSTS					
	¢	$	$$	$$$	$$$$
Restaurants	under $10	$10–$17	$18–$26	$27–$35	over $35
Hotels	under $100	$100–$180	$181–$260	$261–$340	over $340

Restaurant prices are for a main course at dinner. Hotel prices are for two people in a standard double room in high season. Condo price categories reflect studio and one-bedroom rates.

VISITOR INFORMATION

The Kaua'i Visitors Bureau has an office at 4334 Rice Street, Līhu'e's main thoroughfare, near the Kaua'i Museum.

Information Kaua'i Visitors Bureau (⊠ 4334 Rice St., Suite 101, Līhu'e ☎ 808/245–3971 or 800/262–1400 ⊕ www.kauaidiscovery.com). **Po'ipū Beach Resort Association** (✉ Box 730, Kōloa 96756 ☎ 808/742–7444 or 888/744–0888 ⊕ www.poipu-beach.org).

EXPLORING

The main road tracing Kaua'i's perimeter takes you past much more scenery than would seem possible on one small island. Chiseled mountains, thundering waterfalls, misty hillsides, dreamy beaches, lush vegetation, and small towns make up the physical landscape. Perhaps the most stunning piece of scenery is a place no road will take you—the breathtakingly beautiful NāpaliCoast, which runs along the northwest side of the island.

■ TIP➔ While exploring the island, try to take advantage of the many roadside scenic overlooks to pull off and take in the constantly changing view. And don't try to pack too much into one day. Kaua'i is small, but travel is slow. The island's sights are divided into four geographic areas, in clockwise order: the North Shore, the East Side, the South Shore, and the West Side.

DID YOU KNOW?

You'll find a welcome respite at gorgeous and secluded Kalalau Beach when you reach the end of the arduous 11-mile Kalalau Trail.

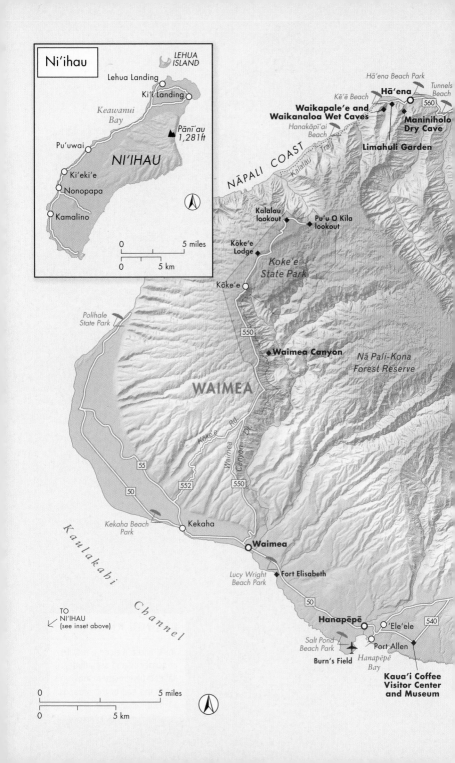

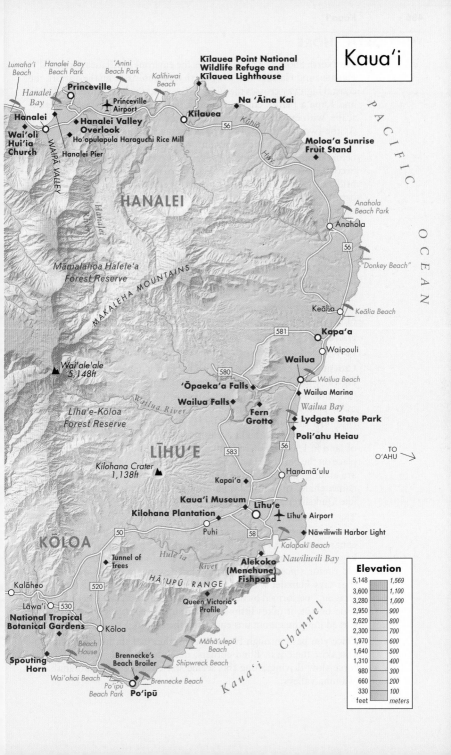

Kaua'i

Lumaha'i Beach
Hanalei Bay Beach Park
'Anini Beach Park
Kalihiwai Beach

Kīlauea Point National Wildlife Refuge and Kīlauea Lighthouse

Princeville
Princeville Airport

Na 'Āina Kai

Hanalei
Kīlauea

Hanalei Bay

Wai'oli Hui'ia Church

Hanalei Valley Overlook
Ho'opulapula Haraguchi Rice Mill

WAIPĀ VALLEY

Hanalei Pier

Moloa'a Sunrise Fruit Stand

56
Kūhiō Hwy

PACIFIC OCEAN

HANALEI

Hanalei

Anahola Beach Park

Anahola

56

"Donkey Beach"

Māmalahoa Halele'a Forest Reserve

MAKALEHA MOUNTAINS

Keālia

Keālia Beach

581

Kapa'a

Waipouli

Wai'ale'ale 5,148ft

580

Wailua

Wailua Beach

Līhu'e-Kōloa Forest Reserve

Wailua River

'Ōpaeka'a Falls

Wailua Falls

Fern Grotto

Wailua Marina

Wailua Bay

Lydgate State Park

Poli'ahu Heiau

LĪHU'E

Kilohana Crater 1,138ft

583

56

Kapai'a

Hanamā'ulu

TO O'AHU →

Kaua'i Museum

Kilohana Plantation

Puhi

Līhu'e
Līhu'e Airport

50

58

Nāwiliwili Harbor Light

KŌLOA

Kalapakī Beach

Nawiliwili Bay

Kalāheo

Tunnel of Trees

Hule'ia River

Alekoko (Menehune) Fishpond

HĀ'UPŪ RANGE

520

Lāwa'i
530

National Tropical Botanical Gardens

Kōloa

Queen Victoria's Profile

Māhā'ulepū Beach

Beach House

Shipwreck Beach

Spouting Horn

Brennecke's Beach Broiler

Wai'ohai Beach
Po'ipū Beach Park
Po'ipū
Brennecke Beach

Kaua'i Channel

Elevation

feet	meters
5,148	1,569
3,600	1,100
3,280	1,000
2,950	900
2,620	800
2,300	700
1,970	600
1,640	500
1,310	400
980	300
660	200
330	100
feet	meters

THE NORTH SHORE

The North Shore of Kaua'i includes the environs of Kīlauea, Princeville, Hanalei, and Hā'ena. Traveling north on Route 56 from the airport, the coastal highway crosses the Wailua River and the busy towns of Wailua and Kapa'a before emerging into a decidedly rural and scenic landscape, with expansive views of the island's rugged interior mountains. As the two-lane highway turns west and narrows, it winds through spectacular scenery and passes the posh resort community of Princeville before dropping down into Hanalei Valley. Here it narrows further and becomes a federally recognized scenic roadway, replete with one-lane bridges (the local etiquette is for six or seven cars to cross at a time, before yielding to those on the other side), hairpin turns, and heart-stopping coastal vistas. The road ends at ēēKē'ē, where the ethereal rain forests and fluted sea cliffs of Nāpali Coast Wilderness State Park begin.

In winter, Kaua'i's North Shore receives more rainfall than other areas of the island. Don't let this deter you from visiting. The clouds drift over the mountains of Nāmolokama, creating a mysterious mood and then, in a blink, disappear, rewarding you with mountains laced with a dozen waterfalls or more. The views of the mountains—as well as the sunsets over the ocean—from the St. Regis Bar, adjacent to the lobby of the St. Regis Princeville Resort, are fantastic.

HANALEI, HĀ'ENA, AND WEST

Hā'ena is 40 mi northwest of Līhu'e; Hanalei is 5 mi east of Hā'ena.

Crossing the historic one-lane bridge into Hanalei reveals old-world Hawai'i, including working taro farms, poi making, and evenings of throwing horseshoes at Black Pot Beach Park—found unmarked (as many places are on Kaua'i) at the east end of Hanalei Bay Beach Park. Although the current real-estate boom on Kaua'i has attracted mainland millionaires to build estate homes on the few remaining parcels of land in Hanalei, there's still plenty to see and do. It's *the* gathering place on the North Shore. Restaurants, shops, and people-watching here are among the best on the island, and you won't find a single brand name, chain, or big-box store around—unless you count surf brands like Quiksilver and Billabong.

The beach and river at Hanalei offer swimming, snorkeling, boogie boarding, surfing, and kayaking. Those hanging around at sunset often congregate at the Hanalei Pavilion, where a husband-and-wife slack-key-guitar-playing combo makes impromptu appearances. There's an old rumor, since quashed by the local newspaper, *The Garden Island,* that says Hanalei was the inspiration for the song "Puff the Magic Dragon," performed by the 1960s singing sensation Peter, Paul & Mary. True or not, it takes little imagination to see the shape of a dragon carved into the mountains encircling the town.

Once you pass through Hanalei town, the road shrinks even more as you skirt the coast. Blind corners, quick turns, and one-lane bridges force slow driving along this scenic stretch across the Lumaha'i and Wainiha valleys.

GETTING HERE AND AROUND

There is only one road leading beyond Princeville to ēēKē'ē Beach at the western end of the North Shore: Route 560. Hanalei's commercial stretch fronts this route, and you'll find parking at the shopping compounds on each side of the road. After Hanalei, parking is restricted to two main areas, Hā'ena Beach Park and a new lot at Hā'ena State Park, and there are very few pullover areas along Route 560. Traffic is usually light, though the route can become congested right after sunset.

EXPLORING

Hanalei Valley Overlook. Dramatic mountains and a patchwork of neat taro farms bisected by the wide Hanalei River make this one of Hawai'i's loveliest sights. The fertile Hanalei Valley has been planted in taro since perhaps AD 700, save for a century-long foray into rice that ended in 1960. (The historic Haraguchi Rice Mill is all that remains of the era.) Many taro farmers lease land within the 900-acre Hanalei National Wildlife Refuge, helping to provide wetland habitat for four species of endangered Hawaiian water birds. ☒ *Rte. 56 ⊹ Across from Foodland, Princeville.*

Limahuli Garden. Narrow Limahuli Valley, with its fluted mountain peaks and ancient stone taro terraces, creates an unparalleled setting for this botanical garden and nature preserve. Dedicated to protecting native plants and unusual varieties of taro, it represents the principles of conservation and stewardship held by its founder, Charles "Chipper" Wichman. Limahuli's priomordial beauty and strong *mana* (spiritual power) eclipse the extensive botanical collection. It's one of the most gorgeous spots on Kaua'i and the crown jewel of the National Tropical Botanical Garden, which Wichman now heads. Call ahead to reserve a guided tour, or tour on your own. Be sure to check out the quality gift shop and revolutionary compost toilet, and be prepared to walk a somewhat steep hillside. ☒ *Rte. 560, Hā'ena* ☎ *808/826–1053* ⊕ *www.ntbg.org* ☒ *Self-guided tour $15, guided tour $30 (reservations required)* ☉ *Tues.–Sat. 9:30–4.*

Maniniholo Dry Cave. According to legend, Maniniholo was the head fisherman of the Menehune—the possibly real, possibly mythical first inhabitants of the island. As they were preparing to leave Kaua'i and return home (wherever that was), Maniniholo called some of his workers to Hā'ena to collect food from the reef. They gathered so much that they couldn't carry it all, and left some near the ocean cliffs, with plans to retrieve it the following day. It all disappeared during the night, however, and Maniniholo realized that imps living in the rock fissures were the culprits. He and his men dug into the cliff to find and destroy the imps, leaving behind the cave that now bears his name. Across the highway from Maniniholo Dry Cave is **Hā'ena State Park.** ☒ *Rte. 560, Hā'ena.*

Waikapala'e and Waikanaloa Wet Caves. Said to have been dug by Pele, goddess of fire, these watering holes used to be clear, clean, and great for swimming. Now stagnant, they're nevertheless a photogenic example of the many haunting natural landmarks of Kaua'i's North Shore. Waikanaloa is visible right beside the highway, near the end of the road. Waikapala'e is back a few hundred yards and is accessed by a five-minute uphill walk. ⊹ *Western end of Rte. 560.*

Wai'oli Hui'ia Church. Designated a National Historic Landmark, this little church—affiliated with the United Church of Christ—doesn't go unnoticed right alongside Route 560 in downtown Hanalei, and its doors are usually wide open (from 9 to 5, give or take) inviting inquisitive visitors in for a look around. Like the Wai'oli Mission House next door, it's an exquisite representation of New England architecture crossed with Hawaiian thatched buildings. During Hurricane 'Iniki's visit in 1992, which brought sustained winds of 160 mph and wind gusts up to 220 mph, this little church was lifted off its foundation but, thankfully, lovingly restored. Services are held at 10 am on Sunday with many hymns sung in Hawaiian. ⊠ *5-5393A Kuhio Hwy.* ✛ *Located at mile marker 3 on Rte. 560* ☎ *808/826–6253.*

PRINCEVILLE, KĪLAUEA, AND AROUND

Princeville is 4 mi northeast of Hanalei; Kīlauea is 5 mi southeast of Princeville.

Built on a bluff offering gorgeous sea and mountain vistas, including Hanalei Bay, Princeville is the creation of a 1970s resort development. The area is anchored by a few large hotels, world-class golf courses, and lots of condos and time-shares.

A former plantation town, Kīlauea town itself maintains its rural flavor in the midst of unrelenting gentrification encroaching all around it. Especially noteworthy are its historic lava-rock buildings, including **Christ Memorial Episcopal Church** on Kolo Road and, on Keneke and Kīlauea Road (commonly known as Lighthouse Road), the Kong Lung Company, now an expensive shop.

GETTING HERE AND AROUND

There is only one main road through the Princeville resort area, so maneuvering a car here can be a nightmare. If you're trying to find a smaller lodging unit, be sure to get specific driving directions. Ample parking is available at the Princeville Shopping Center at the entrance to the resort. Kīlauea is about 5 mi east on Route 56. There's a public parking lot in the town center as well as parking at the end of Kīlauea Road for access to the lighthouse.

EXPLORING

Fodor's Choice ★ **Kīlauea Point National Wildlife Refuge and Kīlauea Lighthouse.** A beacon for sea traffic since it was built in 1913, this National Historic Landmark has the largest clamshell lens of any lighthouse in the world. It's within a national wildlife refuge, where thousands of seabirds soar on the trade winds and nest on the steep ocean cliffs. Endangered nēnē geese, red-footed boobies, Laysan albatross, wedge-tailed shearwaters, white- and red-tailed tropic birds, great frigate birds, Pacific golden plovers (all identifiable by educational signboards) along with native plants, dolphins, humpback whales, huge winter surf, and gorgeous views of the North Shore add to the drama of this special place, making it well worth the modest entry fee. The gift shop has a great selection of books about the island's natural history and an array of unique merchandise, with all proceeds benefiting education and preservation efforts. ⊠ *Kīlauea Lighthouse Rd., Kīlauea* ☎ *808/828–0168* ⊕ *www. fws.gov/kilaueapoint* 🖾 *$5* ☉ *Daily 10–4.*

Stop by the farmers' market in Kapa'a to pick up locally grown mangoes and other fruits.

Moloa'a Sunrise Fruit Stand. Don't let the name fool you; they don't open at sunrise (more like 7:30 am, so come here after you watch the sun rise elsewhere). And it's not just a fruit stand. Breakfast is light and includes bagels, granola, smoothies, coffee, espresso, cappuccino, latte, and, of course, tropical-style fresh juices (pineapple, carrot, watermelon, guava, even sugarcane, in season). This is also a great spot to get out and stretch, take in the mountain view, and pick up sandwiches to go. Select local produce is always available, although the variety may not be as good as at the island's farmers' markets. What makes this fruit stand different is the fresh, natural ingredients like multigrain breads and *nori* (seaweed) wraps as a wheat-free bread alternative. ✛ *Just past mile marker 16 makai on Rte. 56* ☎ *808/822–1441* ⏲ *Mon.–Sat. 7:30–5, Sun. 10–5.*

☾ **Na 'Āina Kai.** One small sign along the highway is all that promotes this
★ once-private garden gone big time. Joyce Doty's love for plants and art now spans 240 acres and includes 13 different gardens, a hardwood plantation, a canyon, lagoons, a Japanese teahouse, a Poinciana maze, a waterfall, and a sandy beach. Throughout are more than 100 bronze sculptures, reputedly one of the nation's largest collections. The latest project is a children's garden with a 16-foot-tall Jack and the Beanstalk bronze sculpture, gecko maze, tree house, kid-size train and, of course, a tropical jungle. Located in a residential neighborhood and hoping to maintain good neighborly relations, the garden, which is now a non-profit organization, limits tours (guided only). Tour lengths vary widely, from 1½ to 5 hours. Reservations are strongly recommended. ✉ *Rte. 56* ✛ *North of mile marker 21, turn makai on Wailapa Rd. and follow*

signs ☎ *808/828–0525* ⊕ *www.naainakai.org* ✉ *$35 for 1½-hr stroll to $85 for 5-hr hiking tour* ☉ *Tues.–Fri., call ahead for hrs.*

THE EAST SIDE

The East Side encompasses Līhu'e, Wailua, and Kapa'a; it's also known as the "Coconut Coast," as there was once a coconut plantation where today's aptly named Coconut Marketplace is located. A small grove still exists on both sides of the highway. *Mauka* (toward the mountain), a fenced herd of goats keep the grass tended; on the *makai* (toward the ocean) side, you can walk through the grove, although it's best not to walk directly under the trees—falling coconuts can be dangerous. Līhu'e is the county seat and the whole East Side is the island's center of commerce, so early-morning and late-afternoon drive times (or rush hour) can get congested. (Because there's only one main road, if there's a serious traffic accident the entire roadway may be closed, with no way around. Not to worry; it's a rarity.)

KAPA'A AND WAILUA
Kapa'a is 16 mi southeast of Kīlauea; Wailua is 3 mi south of Kapa'a.

Old Town Kapa'a was once a plantation town, which is no surprise—most of the larger towns on Kaua'i once were. Old Town Kapa'a is made up of a collection of wooden-front shops, some built by plantation workers and still run by their progeny today. Kapa'a houses the two biggest grocery stores on the island, side by side: Foodland and Safeway. It also offers plenty of dining options for breakfast, lunch, and dinner, and gift shopping. Wailua comprises a few restaurants and shops, a few midrange resorts along the coastline, and a housing community *mauka*.

GETTING HERE AND AROUND
Turn to the right out of the airport at Līhu'e for the road to Wailua. Two bridges—under which the very culturally significant Wailua River gently flows—mark the beginning of town. It quickly blends into Kapa'a; there's no real demarcation. Careful, though—the zone between Līhu'e and Wailua has been the site of many car accidents.

EXPLORING
Fern Grotto. The Fern Grotto has a long history on Kaua'i. For some reason, visitors seem to like it. It's really nothing more than a yawning lava tube swathed in lush fishtail ferns 3 mi up the Wailua River. Though it was significantly damaged after Hurricane 'Iniki and again after heavy rains in 2006, the greenery has completely recovered. Smith's Motor Boat Services is the only way to legally see the grotto. You can access the entrance with a kayak, but if boats are there, you may not be allowed to land. ✥ *Depart from Wailua Marina on mauka side of Rte. 56, just south of Wailua River* ✉ *$20* ☉ *Daily departures 9:30–3:30* ☎ *808/821–6892.*

Lydgate State Park. The park, named for the Reverend J.M. Lydgate, founder of the Līhu'e English Union Church, has a large children-designed and community-built playground, pavilion, and picnic area. It also houses the remains of an ancient site where commoners who broke a royal taboo could seek refuge from punishment. It's part of

Continued on page 494

HAWAI'I'S PLANTS 101

Hawai'i is a bounty of rainbow-colored flowers and plants. The evening air is scented with their fragrance. Just look at the front yard of almost any home, travel any road, or visit any local park and you'll see a spectacular array of colored blossoms and leaves. What most visitors don't know is that the plants they are seeing are not native to Hawai'i; rather, they were introduced during the last two centuries as ornamental plants, or for timber, shade, or fruit.

Hawai'i boasts nearly every climate on the planet, excluding the two most extreme: arctic tundra and arid desert. The Islands have wine-growing regions, cactus-speckled ranchlands, icy mountaintops, and the rainiest forests on earth.

Plants introduced from around the world thrive here. The lush lowland valleys along the windward coasts are predominantly populated by non-native trees including yellow- and red-fruited **guava**, silvery-leafed **kukui**, and orange-flowered **tulip trees**.

The colorful **plumeria flower**, very fragrant and commonly used in lei making, and

the giant multicolored **hibiscus flower** are both used by many women as hair adornments, and are two of the most common plants found around homes and hotels. The umbrella-like **monkeypod tree** from Central America provides shade in many of Hawai'i's parks including Kapiolani Park in Honolulu. Hawai'i's largest tree, found in Lahaina, Maui, is a giant **banyan tree**. Its canopy and massive support roots cover about two-thirds of an acre. The native **o'hia tree**, with its brilliant red brush-like flowers, and the **hapu'u**, a giant tree fern, are common in Hawai'i's forests and are also used ornamentally in gardens and around homes.

> **493**

Bougainvillea	Guava	Monkeypod
Banyan	Ohia Lehua*	Tulip Tree
Plumeria	Pandanus	Hibiscus
Anthurium	Kukui Tree	Hapu'u

*endemic to Hawai'i

5

IN FOCUS HAWAI'I'S PLANTS 101

DID YOU KNOW?

Over 2,200 plant species are found in the Hawaiian Islands, but only about 1,000 are native. Of these, 310 are so rare, they are endangered. Hawai'i's endemic plants evolved from ancestral seeds arriving on the islands over thousands of years as baggage on birds, floating on ocean currents, or drifting on winds from continents thousands of miles away. Once here, these plants evolved in isolation, creating many new species known nowhere else in the world.

an extensive complex of sacred archaeological sites that runs from Wai'ale'ale to the sea, underscoring the significance of this region to the ancient Hawaiians. In recent years the community expanded the playground to include a bridge of mazes, tunnels, and slides, as well as access to the new bike/walking path that hugs the ocean. It's located a short walk or drive south of the main park, off Nehe Drive. ⊠ *Nalu Rd.* ✥ *South of Wailua River turn makai off Rte. 56 onto Leho Dr. and makai onto Nalu Rd.* ⛱ *Free* ☉ *Daily dawn–dusk.*

★ **'Ōpaeka'a Falls.** The mighty Wailua River produces many dramatic waterfalls, and 'Ōpaeka'a (pronounced oh-pie-kah-ah) is one of the best. It plunges hundreds of feet to the pool below and can be easily viewed from a scenic overlook with ample parking. 'Ōpaeka'a means "rolling shrimp," which refers to tasty native crustaceans that were once so abundant they could be seen tumbling in the falls. ■ TIP→ Just before reaching the parking area for the waterfalls, turn left into a scenic pullout for great views of the Wailua River valley and its march to the sea. ⊠ *Kuamo'o Rd.* ✥ *From Rte. 56, turn mauka onto Kuamo'o Rd. and drive 1½ mi Wailua.*

Poli'ahu Heiau. Storyboards near this ancient *heiau* (sacred site) recount the significance of the many sacred structures found along the Wailua River. It's unknown exactly how the ancient Hawaiians used Poli'ahu Heiau—one of the largest pre-Christian temples on the island—but legend says it was built by the Menehune because of the unusual stonework found in its walled enclosures. From this site, drive downhill toward the ocean to *pōhaku hānau*, a two-piece birthing stone said to confer special blessings on all children born there, and *pōhaku piko*, whose crevices were a repository for umbilical cords left by parents seeking a clue to their child's destiny, which reportedly was foretold by how the cord fared in the rock. Some Hawaiians feel these sacred stones shouldn't be viewed as "tourist attractions," so always treat them with respect. Never stand or sit on the rocks or leave any offerings. ⊠ *Rte. 580, Kuamo'o Rd., Wailua.*

Wailua Falls. You may recognize this impressive cascade from the opening sequences of the *Fantasy Island* television series. Kaua'i has plenty of noteworthy waterfalls, but this one is especially gorgeous, easy to find, and easy to photograph. ⊠ *End of Rte. 583, Ma'alo Rd.* ✥ *In Kapai'a 4 mi from Rte. 56.*

LĪHU'E

7 mi southwest of Wailua.

The commercial and political center of Kaua'i County, which includes the Islands of Kaua'i and Ni'ihau, Līhu'e is home to the island's major airport, harbor, and hospital. This is where you can find the state and county offices that issue camping and hiking permits and the same fast-food eateries and big-box stores that blight the mainland. The avid golfer will like the three golf courses in Līhu'e—all within a mile or so of each other. The county is seeking help in reviving the downtown; for now, once your business is done, there's little reason to linger in lackluster Līhu'e.

GETTING HERE AND AROUND

Route 56 leads into Līhu'e from the north and Route 50 comes here from the south and west. The road from the airport (where Kaua'i's car rental agencies are) leads to the middle of Līhu'e. Many of the area's stores and restaurants are on and around Rice Street, which also leads to Kalapakī Bay and Nawiliwili Harbor.

EXPLORING

Alekoko (Menehune) Fishpond. No one knows just who built this intricate aquaculture structure in the Hule'ia River. Legend attributes it to the Menehune, a possibly real, possibly mythical ancient race of people known for their small stature, industrious nature, and superb stone-working skills. Volcanic rock was cut and fit together into massive walls 4 feet thick and 5 feet high, forming an enclosure for raising mullet and other freshwater fish that has endured for centuries. ⊠ *Hulemalu Rd., Niumalu.*

Kaua'i Museum. Maintaining a stately presence on Rice Street, the historic museum building is easy to find. It features a permanent display, "The Story of Kaua'i," which provides a competent overview of the Garden Island and Ni'ihau, tracing the Islands' geology, mythology, and cultural history. Local artists are represented in changing exhibits in the second-floor Mezzanine Gallery. The gift shop alone is worth a visit, with a fine collection of authentic Ni'ihau shell lei, feather hatband lei, hand-turned wooden bowls, reference books, and other quality arts, crafts, and gifts, many of them locally made. ⊠ *4428 Rice St., Līhu'e* ☎ *808/245–6931* 🖃 *$10* ☉ *Mon.–Sat. 9–5, closed Sun.*

Kilohana Plantation. This estate dates back to 1896, when plantation manager Albert Spencer Wilcox first developed it as a working cattle ranch. His nephew, Gaylord Parke Wilcox, took over in 1936, building Kaua'i's first mansion. Today the 16,000-square-foot, Tudor-style home houses specialty shops, art galleries, and Gaylord's, a pretty restaurant with courtyard seating. Nearly half the original furnishings remain, and the gardens and orchards were replanted according to the original plans. You can tour the grounds for free; children enjoy visiting the farm animals. A train runs 2½ mi through 104 acres of lands representing the agricultural story of Kauai—then and now. ⊠ *3-2087 Kaumuali'i Hwy., Rte. 50, Līhu'e* ☎ *808/245–5608* ☉ *Mon.–Sat. 9:30–9:30, Sun. 9:30–5:30.*

THE SOUTH SHORE

As you follow the main road south from Līhu'e, the landscape becomes lush and densely vegetated before giving way to drier conditions that characterize Po'ipū, the South Shore's major resort area. Po'ipū owes much of its popularity to a steady supply of sunshine and a string of sandy beaches, although the beaches are smaller and more covelike than those on the West Side. With its extensive selection of accommodations, services, and activities, the South Shore attracts more visitors than any other region on Kaua'i. It's also attracting developers with big plans for the onetime sugar fields that are nestled in this region and enveloped by mountains. There are few roads in and out, and local residents are

"Jungle fowl were all over some of the scenic stops in Kaua'i. They had beautiful colors and it was cool just to see them walking around." —jedivader

concerned about increased traffic and noise and dust pollution as a result of chronic construction. If you're planning to stay on the South Shore, be sure to ask if your hotel, condo, or vacation rental will be impacted by the ongoing development during your visit.

Both Po'ipū and nearby Kōloa (site of Kaua'i's first sugar mill) can be reached via Route 520 (Maluhia Road) from the Līhu'e area. Route 520 is known locally as "Tree Tunnel Road" due to the stand of eucalyptus trees lining the road that were planted at the turn of the 20th century by Walter Duncan McBryde, a Scotsman who began cattle ranching on Kaua'i's South Shore. The canopy of trees was ripped to literal shreds twice—in 1982 during Hurricane 'Iwa and again in 1992 during Hurricane 'Iniki. And, true to Kaua'i, both times the trees grew back into an impressive tunnel. It's a distinctive way to announce, "You are now on vacation," for there's a definite feel of leisure in the air here. There's still plenty to do—snorkel, bike, walk, horseback ride, take an ATV tour, surf, scuba dive, shop, and dine—everything you'd want on a tropical vacation. From the west, Route 530 (Kōloa Road) slips into downtown Kōloa, a string of fun shops and restaurants, at an intersection with the only gas station on the South Shore.

PO'IPŪ
13 mi southwest of Līhu'e.

Thanks to its generally sunny weather and a string of golden-sand beaches dotted with oceanfront lodgings, Po'ipū is a top choice for many visitors. Beaches are user-friendly, with protected waters for *keiki* (children) and novice snorkelers, lifeguards, clean restrooms, covered pavilions, and a sweet coastal promenade ideal for leisurely strolls.

Some experts have even ranked Po'ipū Beach Park number one in the nation. It depends on your preferences, of course, though it certainly does warrant high accolades. ■TIP→ In summertime, don't be surprised to see a monk-seal mom and her pup on the beach here; the seals seem to like this beach as much as the visitors.

GETTING HERE AND AROUND

Po'ipū is the one area on Kaua'i where you could get by without a car, though that could mean an expensive taxi ride from the airport and limited access to other parts of the island. To reach Po'ipū by car, follow Po'ipū Road south from Kōloa. After the traffic circle, the road curves to follow the coast, leading to some of the popular South Shore beaches.

EXPLORING

National Tropical Botanical Gardens *(NTBG).* Tucked away in Lāwa'i Valley, these gardens include lands and a cottage once used by Hawai'i's Queen Emma for a summer retreat. Visitors can take a self-guided tour of the rambling 252-acre **McBryde Gardens** to see and learn about plants collected throughout the tropics. It is known as a garden of "research and conservation." The 100-acre **Allerton Gardens,** which can be visited only on a guided tour, artfully display statues and water features that were originally developed as part of a private estate. Reservations are required for tours of Allerton Gardens, but not for the self-guided tours of McBryde Gardens. The visitor center has a high-quality gift shop with botany-theme merchandise.

Besides harboring and propagating rare and endangered plants from Hawai'i and elsewhere, NTBG functions as a scientific research and education center. The organization also operates gardens in Limahuli, on Kaua'i's North Shore, and in Hāna, on Maui's east shore. ⊠ *Lāwa'i Rd., across from Spouting Horn parking lot, Po'ipū* ☎ *808/742-2623* ⊕ *www.ntbg.org* 🏛 *McBryde self-guided tour $20, Allerton guided tour $45* ☉ *McBryde Gardens Mon.–Sat. 9:30–2:30, hourly; Sun. 11:30–2:30, hourly. Allerton Gardens tours (by reservation) Mon.–Sat. at 9, 10, 1, and 2; Sun. at 10 and 1.*

Spouting Horn. If the conditions are right, you can see a natural blowhole in the reef behaving like Old Faithful, shooting salt water high into the air and making a cool, echoing sound. It's most dramatic during big summer swells, which jam large quantities of water through an ancient lava tube with great force. ■TIP→ Stay on the paved walkways as rocks can be slippery and wave action unpredictable. Vendors hawk inexpensive souvenirs and collectibles in the parking lot. You may find good deals on shell jewelry, but ask for a certificate of authenticity to ensure it's a genuine Ni'ihau shell lei before paying the higher price that these intricate creations command. ⊠ *At end of Lāwa'i Rd., Po'ipū.*

QUICK BITES

Stop in at Brennecke's Beach Broiler (⊠ 2100 Ho'ōne Rd., Po'ipū ☎ 808/742-7588), a longtime fixture on the beach in Po'ipū. After a day of sun, this is a perfect spot to chill out with a mango margarita or "world famous" mai tai, paired with a yummy pūpū platter.

THE WEST SIDE

Exploring the West Side is akin to visiting an entirely different world. The landscape is dramatic and colorful: a patchwork of green, blue, black, and orange. The weather is hot and dry, the beaches are long, the sand is dark. Ni'ihau, a private island and the last remaining place in Hawai'i where Hawaiian is spoken exclusively, can be glimpsed offshore. This is rural Kaua'i, where sugar is making its last stand and taro is still cultivated in the fertile river valleys. The lifestyle is slow, easy, and traditional, with many folks fishing and hunting to supplement their diets. Here and there modern industry has intruded into this pastoral scene: huge generators turn oil into electricity at Port Allen; scientists cultivate experimental crops of genetically engineered plants in Kekaha; the navy launches rockets at Mānā to test the "Star Wars" missile defense system; and NASA mans a tracking station in the wilds of Koke'e. It's a region of contrasts that simply shouldn't be missed.

Heading west from Līhu'e or Po'ipū, you pass through a string of tiny towns, plantation camps, and historical sites, each with a story to tell of centuries past. There's Hanapēpē, whose coastal salt ponds have been harvested since ancient times; Kaumakani, where the sugar industry still clings to life; Fort Elisabeth, from which an enterprising Russian tried to take over the island in the early 1800s; and Waimea, where Captain Cook made his first landing in the Islands, forever changing the face of Hawai'i.

From Waimea town you can head up into the mountains, skirting the rim of magnificent Waimea Canyon and climbing higher still until you reach the cool, often-misty forests of Kōke'e State Park. From the vantage point at the top of this gemlike island, 3,200 to 4,200 feet above sea level, you can gaze into the deep verdant valleys of the North Shore and Nāpali Coast. This is where the "real" Kaua'i can still be found: the native plants, insects, and birds that are found nowhere else on Earth.

HANAPĒPĒ

15 mi northwest of Po'ipū.

In the 1980s Hanapēpē was fast becoming a ghost town, its farm-based economy mirroring the decline of agriculture. Today it's a burgeoning art colony, with galleries, crafts studios, and a lively art-theme street fair on Friday nights. The main street has a new vibrancy enhanced by the restoration of several historic buildings. The emergence of Kaua'i Coffee as a major West Side crop and expanded activities at Port Allen, now the main departure point for tour boats, also gave the town's economy a boost.

SUNSHINE MARKETS

If you want to rub elbows with the locals and purchase fresh produce and flowers at very reasonable prices, head for **Sunshine Markets** (☎ 808/241–6303 ⊕ www.kauai. gov), also known as Kaua'i's farmers' markets. These busy markets are held weekly, usually in the afternoon, at locations all around the island. They're good fun, and they support small, neighborhood farmers. Arrive a little early, bring dollar bills to speed up transactions and plastic shopping bags to carry your produce, and be prepared for some pushy shoppers. Farmers are usually happy to educate visitors about unfamiliar fruits and veggies, especially when the crowd thins.

North Shore Sunshine Markets. ✉ Waipa, mauka of Rte. 560 north of Hanalei after mile marker 3 ⊙ Tues.

2 PM ✉ Kīlauea Neighborhood Center, on Keneke St. in Kīlauea ⊙ Thurs. 4:30 PM ✉ Hanalei Community Center ⊙ Sat. 9:30 AM.

East Side Sunshine Markets. ✉ Vidinha Stadium, Līhu'e, ½ mi south of airport on Rte. 51 ⊙ Fri. 3 PM ✉ Kapa'a, turn mauka on Rte. 581/ Olohena Rd. for 1 block, ⊙ Wed. 3 PM.

South Shore Sunshine Markets. ✉ Ballpark, Kōloa, north of intersection of Kōloa Road and Rte. 520 ⊙ Mon. noon.

West Side Sunshine Markets. ✉ Kalāheo Community Center, Kalāheo, on Papalina Rd. just off Kaumuali'i Hwy. ⊙ Tues. 3 PM ✉ Hanapēpē Park ⊙ Thurs. 3 PM ✉ Kekaha Neighborhood Center, Kekaha, 'Elepaio Rd. ⊙ Sat. 9 AM.

5

GETTING HERE AND AROUND

Hanapēpē, locally known as Kaua'i's "biggest little town," is just past the 'Ele'ele Shopping Center on the main highway (Route 50). A sign leads you to the town center, where street parking is easy and there's an enjoyable walking tour.

EXPLORING

Kaua'i Coffee Visitor Center and Museum. Two restored camp houses, dating from the days when sugar was the main agricultural crop on the Islands, have been converted into a museum, visitor center, and gift shop. About 3,400 acres of McBryde sugar land have become Hawai'i's largest coffee plantation. You can walk among the trees, view old grinders and roasters, watch a video to learn how coffee is processed, sample various estate roasts, and check out the gift store. New to the grounds is a self-guided tour through a small coffee grove with informative signage; allow approximately 15 minutes to complete it. From 'Ele'ele, take Highway 50 in the direction of Waimea Canyon and veer right onto Highway 540, west of Kalāheo. The center is 2½ mi from the Highway 50 turnoff. ✉ 870 Halawili Rd., Kalāheo ☎ 808/335–0813 ⊕ www.kauaicoffee.com 💲 Free ⊙ Daily 9–5.

QUICK BITES

It's not ice cream on Kaua'i if it's not **Lappert's Ice Cream** (✉ On Hwy. 50 mauka, Hanapēpē ☎ 808/335–6121). Guava, mac nut, pineapple, mango, coconut, banana—Lappert's is the ice-cream capital of Kaua'i. Warning:

Waterfalls are often visible from the hiking trails in Waimea Canyon. "The views into the Grand Canyon of the Pacific were amazing on our hike." —koala

Even at the factory store in Hanapēpē, the prices are no bargain. But, hey, you gotta try it.

WAIMEA, WAIMEA CANYON, AND AROUND

Waimea is 7 mi northwest of Hanapēpē; Waimea Canyon is approximately 10 mi north of Waimea.

Waimea is a serene, pretty town that has the look of the Old West and the feel of Old Hawai'i, with a lifestyle that's decidedly laid-back. It's an ideal place for a refreshment break while sightseeing on the West Side. The town has played a major role in Hawaiian history since 1778, when Captain James Cook became the first European to set foot on the Hawaiian Islands. Waimea was also the place where Kaua'i's King Kaumuali'i acquiesced to King Kamehameha's unification drive in 1810, averting a bloody war. The town hosted the first Christian missionaries, who hauled in massive timbers and limestone blocks to build the sturdy Waimea Christian Hawaiian and Foreign Church in 1846. It's one of many lovely historic buildings preserved by residents who take great pride in their heritage and history.

North of Waimea town, via Route 550, you'll find the vast and gorgeous Waimea Canyon, also known as the Grand Canyon of the Pacific. The spectacular vistas from the lookouts along the road culminate with an overview of Kalalau Valley. There are various hiking trails leading to the inner heart of Kaua'i. A camera is a necessity in this region.

Waimea Canyon (right): You don't have to hike to see sweeping Waimea Canyon vistas. Many overlooks, like the one pictured above, are reachable by car, right off the main road.

GETTING HERE AND AROUND

Route 50 continues northwest to Waimea and Kekaha from Hanapēpē. You can reach Waimea Canyon and Kōke'e State Park from either town—the way is clearly marked. Some pull-off areas on Route 550 are fine for a quick view of the canyon, but the designated lookouts have bathrooms and parking.

EXPLORING

Fodor's Choice ★ **Waimea Canyon.** Carved over countless centuries by the Waimea River and the forces of wind and rain, Waimea Canyon is a dramatic gorge nicknamed the "Grand Canyon of the Pacific."

Hiking and hunting trails wind through the canyon, which is 3,600 feet deep, 2 mi wide, and 10 mi long. The cliff sides have been sharply eroded, exposing swatches of colorful soil. The deep red, brown, and green hues are constantly changing in the sun, and frequent rainbows and waterfalls enhance the natural beauty.

This is one of Kaua'i's prettiest spots, and it's worth stopping at both the **Pu'u ka Pele** and **Pu'u hinahina** lookouts. Clean public restrooms and parking are at both lookouts.

QUICK BITES

There's only one place to buy food and hot drinks in Kōke'e State Park, and that's the dining room of rustic Kōke'e Lodge (✉ *Kōke'e State Park, 3600 Kōke'e Rd., mile marker 15* ☎ *808/335–6061* ⊗ *No dinner*). It's known for its corn bread, of all things. Peruse the gift shop for T-shirts, postcards, or campy Kōke'e memorabilia.

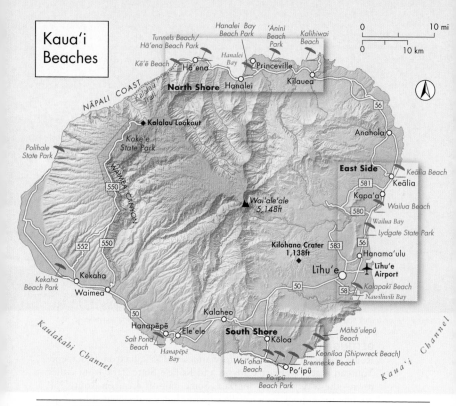

Kauaʻi
Beaches

Tunnels Beach/
Hāʻena Beach Park
Hanalei Bay
Beach Park
ʻAnini
Beach
Park
Kalihiwai
Beach

Kēʻē Beach
Hāʻena
Hanalei
Bay
Princeville

NĀPALI COAST
Kalalau Trail
North Shore
Hanalei
Kīlauea

0 ___ 10 mi
0 ___ 10 km

Kalalau Lookout
Kokeʻe
State Park
Anahola

Polihale
State Park
Wai'ale'ale
5,148ft
56
East Side
Keālia Beach
581
Keālia
Kapaʻa
580
Wailua Beach

WAIMEA CANYON
552
550
550
Kilohana Crater
1,138ft
583
56
Wailua Bay
Lydgate State Park
Hanamaʻulu

Kekaha
Beach Park
Kekaha
Waimea
50
Līhuʻe
Līhuʻe
Airport
58
50
Kalapakī Beach
Nawiliwili Bay

Kaulakahi Channel
Kalaheo
Hanapēpē
Salt Pond
Beach
ʻEleʻele
Hanapēpē
Bay
South Shore
Kōloa
Wai'ohai
Beach
Poʻipū
Poʻipū
Beach Park
Māhāʻulepū
Beach
Keoniloa (Shipwreck Beach)
Brennecke Beach
Kauaʻi Channel

BEACHES

With more sandy beaches per mile of coastline than any other Hawaiian Island, Kauaʻi could be nicknamed the Sandy Island just as easily as it's called the Garden Island. Totaling more than 50 mi, Kauaʻi's beaches make up 44% of the island's shoreline—almost twice that of Oʻahu, second on this list. It is, of course, because of Kauaʻi's age—it's the eldest sibling of the inhabited Hawaiian Islands, allowing more time for water and wind erosion to break down rock and coral into sand. But not all Kauaʻi's beaches are the same. If you've seen one, you certainly haven't seen them all. Each beach is unique unto itself, for that day, that hour. Conditions, scenery, and intrigue can change throughout the day and certainly throughout the year, transforming, say, a tranquil lakelike ocean setting in summer into monstrous waves drawing internationally ranked surfers from around the world in winter.

There are sandy beaches, rocky beaches, wide beaches, narrow beaches, skinny beaches, and alcoves. Generally speaking, surf kicks up on the North Shore in winter and the South Shore in summer, although summer's southern swells aren't nearly as frequent or big as the northern winter swells that attract those surfers. Kauaʻi's longest and widest beaches are found on the North Shore and West Side and are popular with beachgoers, although during winter's rains, everyone heads to the

KAUAʻI SIGHTSEEING TOURS

Aloha Kauaʻi Tours. You get *way* off the beaten track on these four-wheel-drive van excursions. Choose from several options, including the half-day Backroads Tour covering mostly haul-cane roads behind the locked gates of Grove Farm Plantation, and the half-day Rainforest Tour, which follows the Wailua River to its source, Mt. Waiʻaleʻale. The expert guides are some of the best on the island. Rates are $75 and $80, respectively. ⊠ *Check in at Kilohana Plantation on Rte. 50 in Puhi, Līhuʻe* ☎ *808/245-6400 or 800/452-1113* ⊕ *www.alohakauaitours.com.*

Roberts Hawaiʻi Tours. The Round-the-Island Tour, sometimes called the Wailua River–Waimea Canyon Tour, gives a good overview of half the island, including the Russian Fort Elisabeth and ʻŌpaekaʻa Falls. Guests are transported in air-conditioned, 25-passenger minibuses or larger coaches. The $79.50 trip includes a boat ride up the Wailua River to the Fern Grotto and a visit to the lookouts above Waimea Canyon. ☎ *808/245-9101 or 800/831-5541* ⊕ *www.robertshawaii.com.*

Waimea Historic Walking Tour. Led by a *kupuna*, a lifetime elder, this 2½- to 3-hour tour begins promptly at 9:30 am, every Monday at the West Kauaʻi Visitor Center. While sharing her personal remembrances, Aletha Kaohi leads an easy walk that explains Waimea's distinction as a recipient of the 2006 National Trust for Historic Preservation Award. The tour is free, but a reservation is required. ☎ *808/338-1332.*

dry West Side or usually sunny Poʻipū. The East Side beaches tend to be narrower and have onshore winds less popular with sunbathers, although fishers abound. Smaller coves are characteristic of the South Shore and attract all kinds of water lovers year-round, including the critically endangered Hawaiian monk seals.

In Hawaiʻi, all beaches are public, but their accessibility varies greatly. On Kauaʻi, some require an easy ½-mi stroll, some require a four-wheel-drive vehicle, others require boulder hopping, and one takes an entire day of serious hiking. And then there are those "drive-in" beaches onto which you can literally pull up and park your car. Kauaʻi is not Disneyland, so don't expect much signage to help you along the way. One of the top-ranked beaches in the whole world—Hanalei—doesn't have a single sign in town directing you to the beach. Furthermore, the majority of Kauaʻi's beaches are remote, offering no services. ■TIP→ If you want the convenience of restrooms, picnic tables, and the like, stick to county beach parks, but don't expect concessions.

THE NORTH SHORE

If you've ever dreamed of Hawaiʻi—and who hasn't—you've dreamed of Kauaʻi's North Shore. *Lush, tropical,* and *abundant* are just a few words to describe this rugged and dramatic area. And the views to the sea aren't the only attraction—the inland views of velvety-green valley folds and carved mountain peaks will take your breath away. Rain is the reason for all the greenery on the North Shore, and winter is the

Be sure to set aside time to catch a sunset over Nāpali Coast from Kēʻē Beach on Kauaʻi's North Shore.

rainy season. Not to worry, though; it rarely rains *everywhere* on the island at one time. ■TIP→ The rule of thumb is to head south or west when it rains in the north.

The waves on the North Shore can be big—and we mean huge—in winter, drawing crowds to witness nature's spectacle. By contrast, in summer the waters can be completely serene. The beaches below are listed in order—west to east—from ēēKēʻē to Kalihiwai. Try one-stop shopping at Ching Young Village in Hanalei, which has several stores that will fill your trunk with goodies such as snorkel gear, surf and body boards, beach chairs, umbrellas, snacks, and coolers.

The beaches in this section are listed in order from west to east.

Kēʻē Beach. Highway 560 on the North Shore literally dead-ends at this beach, which is also the trailhead for the famous Kalalau Trail and the site of an ancient *heiau* dedicated to hula. The beach is protected by a reef—except during high surf—creating a small sandy-bottom lagoon and making it a popular snorkeling destination. If there's a current, it's usually found on the western edge of the beach as the incoming tide ebbs back out to sea. Makana (a prominent peak also known as Bali Hai after the blockbuster musical *South Pacific*) is so artfully arranged, you'll definitely want to capture the memory, so don't forget your camera. The popularity of this beach makes parking difficult. Start extra early or, better yet, arrive at the end of the day, in time to witness otherworldly sunsets sidelighting Nāpali Coast. **Amenities:** Lifeguard, parking lot, showers, toilets. ⊠ *End of Rte. 560 ✛ 7 mi west of Hanalei.*

Fodor'sChoice
★

Hāʻena Beach Park *(Tunnels Beach).* This is a drive-up beach park popular with campers year-round. The wide bay here—named Mākua

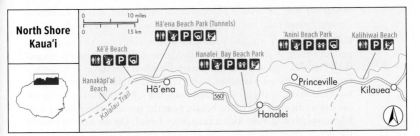

and commonly known as Tunnels—is bordered
by two large reef systems creating favorable waves
for surfing during peak winter conditions. In July
and August, waters at this same beach are as calm
as a lake, usually, and snorkelers enjoy the variety
of fish life found in a hook-shape reef made up of
underwater lava tubes, on the east end of the bay.
■ TIP➜ During the summer months only, this is the
premier snorkeling site on Kaua'i. It's not unusual to
find a food vendor parked here selling sandwiches
and drinks out of a converted bread van. **Amenities:** Lifeguard, camping, picnic tables, grills/fire pits, parking lot, showers, toilets. ⊠ *Rte.
560* ✛ *Near end of Rte. 560, across from lava-tube sea caves, after
stream crossing.*

BEACHES KEY

👫	*Restroom*
🚿	*Showers*
🏄	*Surfing*
🤿	*Snorkel/Scuba*
👫	*Good for kids*
P	*Parking*

Ⓒ **Hanalei Bay Beach Park.** This 2-mi, crescent beach surrounds a spacious
Fodor'sChoice bay that is quintessential Hawai'i. After gazing out to sea and realizing
★ you have truly arrived in paradise, look landward. The site of the mountains, ribboned with waterfalls, will take your breath away. All this
beauty accounts for why coastal expert "Dr. Beach" named Hanalei the
number one in the U.S. in 2009. In winter Hanalei Bay boasts some of
the biggest onshore surf breaks in the state, attracting world-class surfers. Luckily, the beach is wide enough to have safe real estate for your
beach towel even in winter. In summer the bay is transformed—calm
waters lap the beach, sailboats moor in the bay, and outrigger-canoe
paddlers ply the sea. Pack the cooler, haul out the beach umbrellas, and
don't forget the beach toys, because Hanalei Bay is worth scheduling
for an entire day, maybe two. **Amenities:** Lifeguard, camping, grills/fire
pits, parking lot, picnic tables, showers, toilets. ⊠ *Weli Weli Rd.* ✛ *In
Hanalei, turn makai at Aku Rd. and drive 1 block to Weli Weli Rd.
Parking areas are on makai side of Weli Weli Rd.*

Ⓒ **'Anini Beach Park.** A great family park, 'Anini is unique in that it features one of the longest and widest fringing reefs in all Hawai'i, creating a shallow lagoon that is good for snorkeling and quite safe in all
but the highest of winter surf. The reef follows the shoreline for some
2 mi and extends 1,600 feet offshore at its widest point. During times
of low tide—usually occurring around the full moon of the summer
months—much of the reef is exposed. 'Anini is inarguably the windsurfing mecca of Kaua'i, even for beginners, and it also attracts participants
in the growing sport of kiteboarding. **Amenities:** Camping, grills/fire
pits, parking lot, picnic tables, showers, toilets. ⊠ *'Anini Rd.* ✛ *Turn*

5

makai off Rte. 56 onto Kalihiwai Rd., on Hanalei side of Kalihiwai Bridge; follow road left at "Y" to reach 'Anini Rd. and beach.

Kalihiwai Beach. A winding road leads down a cliff face to this picture-perfect beach. A jewel of the North Shore, Kalihiwai Beach is on par with Hanalei, just without the waterfall-ribbon backdrop. It's another one of those drive-up beaches, so it's very accessible. Most people park on the sand under the grove of ironwood trees. Families set up camp for the day at the west end of the beach, near the stream, where young kids like to splash and older kids like to body board. On the eastern edge of the beach, from which the road descends, there's a locals' favorite surf spot during winter's high surf. The onshore break can be dangerous during this time. During the calmer months of summer, Kalihiwai Beach is a good choice for beginning board riders and swimmers. The toilets here are the portable kind. **Amenities:** Parking lot, toilets. ⊠ *Kalihiwai Rd.* ⊹ *Turn makai off Rte. 56 onto Kalihiwai Rd., on Kīlauea side of Kalihiwai Bridge.*

THE EAST SIDE

The East Side of the island is considered the *windward* side, a term you'll often hear in weather forecasts. It simply means the side of the island receiving onshore winds. The wind helps break down rock into sand, so there are plenty of beaches here. Unfortunately, only a few of those beaches are protected, so many are not ideal for beginning ocean-goers, though they are perfect for long sunrise ambles. On superwindy days, kiteboarders sail along the east shore, sometimes jumping waves and performing acrobatic maneuvers in the air.

The beaches below are listed in order from north to south.

Keālia Beach. A half-mile long and adjacent to the highway heading north out of Kapa'a, Keālia Beach attracts body boarders and surfers year-round (possibly because the local high school is just up the hill). Keālia is not generally a great beach for swimming or snorkeling. The waters are usually rough and the waves crumbly because of an onshore break (no protecting reef) and northeasterly trade winds. A scenic look-out on the southern end, accessed off the highway, is a superb location for saluting the morning sunrise or spotting whales during winter. A level, paved trail follows the coastline north and is one of the most scenic coastal trails on the island for walking, running, and biking. **Amenities:** Lifeguard, parking lot, picnic tables, showers, toilets. ⊠ *Rte. 56* ⊹ *At mile marker 10.*

Wailua Beach. Some say the first Polynesians to migrate to Hawai'i landed at Wailua Beach. At the river's mouth, petroglyphs carved on boulders are sometimes visible during low surf and tide conditions. Surfers, body boarders, and bodysurfers alike enjoy this beach year-round thanks to its dependable waves (usually on the north end); however, because of Hawai'i's northeast trade winds, these waves are not the "cleanest" for surf aficionados. Many families spend the day under the Wailua Bridge at the river mouth, even hauling out their portable grills and tables to go with their beach chairs. The great news about Wailua Beach is that it's almost impossible to miss; however, parking can be a

CLOSE UP

Best Beaches

He says "to-mah-toe," and she says "to-may-toe." When it comes to beaches on Kaua'i, the meaning behind that axiom holds true: People are different. What rocks one person's world wreaks havoc for another. Here are some additional tips on how to choose a beach that's right for you.

BEST FOR FAMILIES

Lydgate State Park, East Side. The kid-designed playground, the protected swimming pools, and Kamalani Bridge guarantee you will not hear these words from your child: "Mom, I'm bored."

Po'ipū Beach Park, Po'ipū, South Shore. The *keiki* (children's) pool and lifeguards make this a safe spot for kids. The near-perpetual sun isn't so bad, either.

BEST STAND-UP PADDLING

'Anini Beach Park, North Shore. The reef and long stretch of beach give beginners to stand-up paddling a calm place to give this new sport a try. You won't get pummeled by waves here.

Wailua Beach, East Side. On the East Side, the Wailua River bisects the beach and heads inland 2 mi, providing stand-up paddlers with a long and scenic stretch of water before they have to figure out how to turn around.

BEST SURFING

Hanalei Bay Beach Park, North Shore. In the winter, Hanalei Bay offers a range of breaks, from beginner to advanced. You may even see the Irons brothers—international surf champions—paddling out here. They grew up surfing these waters.

Wai'ohai Beach, South Shore. Surf instructors flock to this spot with their students for its gentle, near-shore break. Then, as students advance, they can paddle out a little farther to an intermediate break—if they dare.

BEST SUNSETS

Kē'ē Beach, North Shore. Even in the winter, when the sun sets in the south and out of view, you won't be disappointed here, because the "magic hour," as photographers call the time around sunset, paints Nāpali Coast with a warm gold light.

Polihale State Park, West Side. This due-west-facing beach may be tricky to get to, but it does offer the most unobstructed sunset views on the island. The fact that it's so remote means you won't have strangers in your photos, but you will want to depart right after sunset or risk getting lost in the dark.

BEST FOR SEEING AND BEING SEEN

Hā'ena Beach Park, North Shore. Behind those gated driveways and heavily foliaged yards that line this beach live—at least, part-time—some of the world's most celebrated music and movie moguls. Need we say more?

Hanalei Bay Beach Park, North Shore. We know we tout this beach often, but it deserves the praise. It's a mecca for everyone—regular joes, surfers, fishers, young, old, locals, visitors, and, especially, the famous. Could you recognize Jennifer Aniston and Courteney Cox? How about Pierce Brosnan and Ben Stiller? They—and more—have frequented this beach.

5

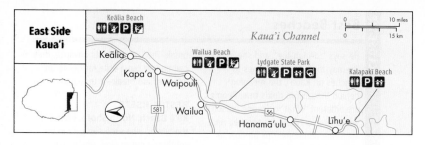

challenge. **Amenities:** Parking lot, showers, toilets. ⊹ *The best parking for the north end of the beach is on Papaloa Rd. behind the Shell station. For the southern end of the beach, the best parking is in the Wailua River State Park (where toilets—the portable kind—are also found). To get there, turn mauka on Kuamo'o Rd. and left into the park, then walk along the river and under the bridge.*

🝔 **Lydgate State Park.** This is hands-down the best family beach park on Kaua'i. The waters off the beach are protected by a hand-built breakwater creating two boulder-enclosed saltwater pools for safe swimming and snorkeling just about year-round (although after heavy rains, river debris collects here, contaminating the water). The smaller of the two is perfect for *keiki* (children). Behind the beach is Kamalani Playground, designed by the children of Kaua'i and built by the community. Children of all ages—that includes you—enjoy the swings, lava-tube slides, tree house, and more. Picnic tables abound in the park, and a large covered pavilion is available by permit for celebrations. The Kamalani Kai Bridge is a second playground—also built by the community —south of the original. (The two are united by a bike and pedestrian path that is part of the Nāwiliwili-to-Anahola multi-use path project currently under construction.) ■TIP→ **This park system is perennially popular; the quietest times to visit are early mornings and weekdays. If you want to witness a "baby lū'au," Lydgate State Park attracts them year-round, especially in summers. Amenities:** Lifeguard, grills/fire pits, parking lot, picnic tables, playground, showers, toilet. ✉ *Nalu Rd.* ⊹ *Just south of Wailua River, turn makai off Rte. 56 onto Lehu Dr. and left onto Nalu Rd.*

🝔 **Kalapakī Beach.** Five minutes south of the airport in Līhu'e, you'll find this wide, sandy-bottom beach fronting the Kaua'i Marriott. One of the big attractions is that this beach is almost always safe from rip currents and undertow because it's around the backside of a peninsula, in its own cove. There are tons of activities here, including all the usual water sports—beginning and intermediate surfing, body boarding, bodysurfing, and swimming—plus, there are two outrigger canoe clubs paddling in the bay and the Nāwiliwili Yacht Club's boats sailing around the harbor. Kalapakī is the only place on Kaua'i where sailboats—in this case Hobie Cats—are available for rent (at Kaua'i Beach Boys, which fronts the beach next to Duke's Canoe Club restaurant). Visitors can also rent snorkel gear, surfboards, body boards, and kayaks from Kaua'i Beach Boys. A volleyball court on the beach is often used by a loosely organized group of local players; visitors are always welcome.

■TIP→ Families prefer the stream end of the beach, whereas those seeking more solitude will prefer the cliff side of the beach. Duke's Canoe Club restaurant is one of only a couple of restaurants on the island actually on a beach; the restaurant's lower level is casual, even welcoming beach attire and sandy feet, perfect for lunch or an afternoon cocktail. **Amenities:** Grills/fire pits, parking lot, picnic tables, showers, toilets. ⊠ *Off Wapa'a Rd., which runs from Līhu'e to Nāwiliwili.*

THE SOUTH SHORE

The South Shore's primary access road is Highway 520, a tree-lined, two-lane, windy road. As you drive along it, there's a sense of tunneling down a rabbit hole into another world, à la Alice. And the South Shore is certainly a wonderland. On average, it rains only 30 inches per year, so if you're looking for fun in the sun, this is a good place to start. The beaches with their powdery-fine sand are consistently good year-round, except during high surf, which, if it hits at all, will be in summer. If you want solitude, this isn't it; if you want excitement—well, as much excitement as quiet Kaua'i offers—this is the place for you.

The beaches in this section are listed from east to west.

Fodor's Choice
★   **Māhā'ulepū Beach.** This 2-mi stretch of coast with its sand dunes, lime-stone hills, sinkholes, and caves is unlike any other on Kaua'i. Remains of a large, ancient settlement, evidence of great battles, and the discovery of a now-underwater petroglyph field indicate that Hawaiians lived in this area as early as 700 AD. Māhā'ulepū's coastline is unprotected and rocky, which makes venturing into the ocean hazardous. There are three beach areas with bits of sandy-bottom swimming; however, we think the best way to experience Māhā'ulepū is simply to roam, especially at sunrise. ■TIP→ Access to this beach is via private property. The owner allows access during daylight hours, but be sure to depart before sunset or risk getting locked in for the night. **Amenities:** Parking lot. ⊠ *Po'ipū Rd.* ⊹ *Continue on Po'ipū Rd. past Hyatt (it turns into dirt road) to a T-intersection and turn makai; road ends at beach parking area.*

Keoniloa Beach *(Shipwreck Beach).* Few—except the public relations specialists at the Grand Hyatt Kauai Resort and Spa, which backs the beach—refer to this beach by anything other than its common name: Shipwreck Beach. Its Hawaiian name means "long beach." Both make sense. It is a long stretch of crescent-shape beach punctuated by cliffs on both ends, and, yes, a ship once wrecked here. With its onshore break, the waters off Shipwreck are best for body boarding and bodysurfing; however, the beach itself is plenty big for sunbathing, sand-castle building, Frisbee, and other beach-related fun. Fishers pole fish from shore and off the cliff and sometimes pick *opihi* (limpets) off the rocks lining the foot of the cliffs. The eastern edge of the beach is the start of an interpretive dune walk (complimentary) held by the hotel staff; check with the concierge for dates and times. **Amenities:** Parking lot, showers, toilets. ⊠ *'Āinako Rd.* ⊹ *Continue on Po'ipū Rd. past Hyatt, turn makai on 'Āinako Rd.*

Brennecke Beach. There's little beach here on the eastern end of Po'ipū Beach Park, but Brennecke Beach is synonymous on the island with

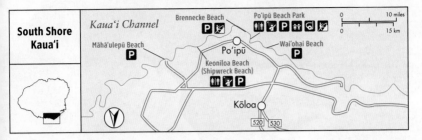

board surfing and bodysurfing, thanks to its shallow sandbar and reliable shore break. Because the beach is small and often congested, surfboards are prohibited near shore. The water on the rocky eastern edge of the beach is a good place to see the endangered green sea turtles noshing on plants growing on the rocks. **Amenities:** Parking lot, picnic tables. ⊠ *Hoʻone Rd.* ✛ *Turn makai off Poʻipū Rd. onto Hoʻowili Rd., then left onto Hoʻone Rd.; beach is at intersection with Kuai Rd.*

Poʻipū Beach Park. The most popular beach on the South Shore, and perhaps on all of Kauaʻi, is Poʻipū Beach Park. The snorkeling's good, the body boarding's good, the surfing's good, the swimming's good, and the fact that the sun is almost always shining is good, too. The beach can be crowded at times, especially on weekends and holidays, but that just makes people-watching that much more fun. You'll see *keiki* (children) experiencing the ocean for the first time, snorkelers trying to walk with their flippers on, ʻukulele players, birthday party revelers, young and old, visitors and locals. Even the endangered Hawaiian monk seal often makes an appearance. **Amenities:** Lifeguard, grills/fire pits, parking lot, picnic tables, playground, showers, toilets. ⊠ *Hoʻone Rd.* ✛ *From Poʻipū Rd., turn right on Hoʻone Rd.*

Waiʻohai Beach. The first hotel built in Poʻipū in 1962 overlooked this beach, adjacent to Poʻipū Beach Park. Actually, there's little to distinguish where one starts and the other begins other than a crescent reef at the eastern end of Waiʻohai Beach. That crescent, however, is important. It creates a small, protected bay—good for snorkeling and beginning surfers. If you're a beginner, this is the spot. However, when a summer swell kicks up, the near-shore conditions become dangerous; offshore, there's a splendid surf break for experienced surfers. The beach itself is narrow and, like its neighbor, gets very crowded in summer. **Amenities:** Parking lot. ⊠ *Hoʻone Rd.* ✛ *From Poʻipū Rd., turn right on Hoʻone Rd.*

THE WEST SIDE

Whereas Kauaʻi's North Shore is characterized by the color green, the West Side's coloring is red. When you look more closely, you'll see that the red is dirt that happens to have high iron content. With little vegetation on the West Side, the red dirt is everywhere—in the air, in a thin layer on the car, even in the river. In fact, the only river on the West Side is named Waimea, which means "reddish water." The West Side of the island receives hardly enough rainfall year-round to water a cactus,

Lydgate State Park is a great place for families. Kids love watching fish in the nearby koi ponds and blowing off steam on the two playgrounds designed by local *keiki* (children).

and because it's also the leeward side, there are few tropical breezes. That translates to sunny and hot with long, languorous, and practically deserted beaches. You'd think the leeward waters—untouched by wind—would be calm, but there's no reef system, so the waters are not as inviting as one would like.

Salt Pond Beach Park. A great family spot, Salt Pond Beach Park features a naturally made, shallow swimming pond behind a curling finger of rock where keiki splash and snorkel. This pool is generally safe except during a large south swell, which usually occurs in summer, if at all. The center and western edge of the beach is popular with body boarders and bodysurfers. On a cultural note, the flat stretch of land to the east of the beach is the last spot in Hawai'i where ponds are used to harvest salt in the dry heat of summer. The beach park is popular with locals and can get crowded on weekends and holidays. **Amenities:** Lifeguard, camping, grills/fire pits, parking lot, picnic tables, showers, toilets. ⊠ *Lolokai Rd.* ⊕ *From Rte. 50 in Hanapēpē, turn makai onto Lele Rd., then right onto Lolokai Rd. (Salt Pond Rd.).*

Kekaha Beach Park. This is one of the premier spots on Kaua'i for sunset walks and the start of the state's longest beach. We don't recommend much water activity here without first talking to a lifeguard: The beach is exposed to open ocean and has an onshore break that can be hazardous any time of year. However, there are some excellent surf breaks—for experienced surfers only. Or, if you would like to run on a beach, this is the one—the hard-packed sand goes on for miles, all the way to Nāpali Coast, but you won't get past the Pacific Missile Range Facility and its post-9/11 restrictions. Another bonus for this beach is

CLOSE UP

Seal-Spotting on the South Shore

When strolling on one of Kaua'i's lovely beaches, don't be surprised if you find yourself in the rare company of Hawaiian monk seals. These are among the most endangered of all marine mammals, with perhaps fewer than 1,200 remaining. They primarily inhabit the northwestern Hawaiian Islands, although more are showing their sweet faces on the main Hawaiian Islands, especially on Kaua'i. They're fond of hauling out on the beach for a long snooze in the sun, particularly after a night of gorging on fish. They need this time to rest and digest, safe from predators.

During the past several summers, female seals have birthed young on the beaches around Kaua'i, where they stay to nurse their pups for upward of six weeks. It seems the seals enjoy particular beaches for the same reasons we do: the shallow, protected waters.

If you're lucky enough to see a monk seal, keep your distance and let it be. Although they may haul out near people, they still want and need their space. Stay several hundred feet away, and forget photos unless you've got a zoom lens. It's illegal to do anything that causes a monk seal to change its behavior, with penalties that include big fines and even jail time. In the water, seals may appear to want to play. It's their curious nature. Don't try to play with them. They are wild animals—mammals, in fact, with teeth. If you have concerns about the health or safety of a seal, or just want more information, contact the **Hawaiian Monk Seal Conservation Hui** (☎ *808/651–7668* ⊕ *www.kauaiseals. com*).

5

its relatively dry weather year-round. If it's raining where you are, try Kekaha Beach Park. Toilets here are the portable kind. **Amenities:** Lifeguard, grills/fire pits, parking lot, picnic tables, showers, toilets. ⊠ *Rte. 50* ⊹ *From Rte. 50, drive to the west side of Kekaha and park across from the 27 mile marker.*

Fodor'sChoice
★ **Polihale State Park.** The longest stretch of beach in Hawai'i starts in Kekaha and ends about 15 mi away at the start of Nāpali Coast. At the Nāpali end of the beach is the 5-mi-long, 140-acre Polihale State Park. In addition to being long, this beach is 300 feet wide in places and backed by sand dunes 50 to 100 feet tall. Polihale is a remote beach accessed via a 5-mi haul cane road (four-wheel drive preferred but not required) at the end of Route 50 in Kekaha. ■TIP➔ Be sure to start the day with a full tank of gas and a cooler filled with food and drink. Many locals wheel their four-wheel-drive vehicles up and over the sand dunes right onto the beach, but don't try this in a rental car. You're sure to get stuck and found in violation of your rental car agreement.

On weekends and holidays Polihale is a popular locals' camping location, but even on "busy" days this beach is never crowded. On days of high surf, only experts surf the waves. In general, the water here is extremely rough and not recommended for recreation; however, there's one small fringing reef, called Queen's Pond, where swimming is usually safe. Neighboring Polihale Beach is the Pacific Missile Range Facility (PMRF), operated by the U.S. Navy. Since September 11, 2001, access to the beaches fronting PMRF has been restricted. **Amenities:** Camping, grills/fire pits, parking lot, picnic tables, showers, toilets. ⊠ *Rte. 50* ✛ *Drive to end of Rte. 50 and continue on dirt road; several access points along the way.*

WATER SPORTS AND TOURS

So, you've decided to vacation on an island. That means you're going to run into a little water at some time. Ancient Hawaiians were notorious water sports fanatics—they invented surfing, after all—and that proclivity hasn't strayed far from today's mindset. Even if you're not into water sports or sports in general, there's a slim chance that you'll leave this island without getting out on the ocean, as Kaua'i's top attraction—Nāpali Coast—is something not to be missed.

BOAT TOURS

Deciding to see Nāpali Coast by boat is the easy decision. Choosing the outfitter to go with is the tough decision. There are numerous boat tour operators to choose from, and, quite frankly, they all do a good job. Before you even think about this company or that, answer these three questions: What kind of boat do I prefer? Where am I staying? Do I want to go in the morning or afternoon? Once you settle on these three, you can easily zero in on the tour outfitter.

First, the boat. The most important thing is to match your personality and that of your group with the personality of the boat. If you like thrills and adventure, the rubber, inflatable rafts—often called Zodiacs, which Jacques Cousteau made famous and which the U.S. Coast Guard uses—will entice you. They're fast, sure to leave you drenched, and quite bouncy. If you prefer a smoother, more leisurely ride, then the large catamarans are the way to go. The next boat choice is size. Both the rafts and catamarans come in small and large. Again—think smaller, more adventurous; larger, more leisurely. ■ TIP→ Do not choose a smaller boat because you think there will be fewer people. There might be fewer people, but you'll be jammed together sitting atop strangers. If you prefer privacy over socializing, go with a larger boat, so you can have more room to spread out. One advantage to smaller boats, however, is that—depending on ocean conditions—some may slip into a sea cave or two. If that sounds interesting to you, call the outfitter and ask their policy on entering sea caves. Some won't no matter the conditions, because they consider the caves sacred or because they don't want to cause any environmental damage.

There are three points where boats leave from around the island (Hanalei, Port Allen, and Waimea), and all head to the same spot: Nāpali Coast. Here's the inside skinny on which is the best: If you're staying on the North Shore, choose to depart out of the North Shore. If you're staying anywhere else, depart out of the West Side. It's that easy. Sure, the North Shore is closer to Nāpali Coast; however, you'll pay more for less overall time. The West Side boat operators may spend more time getting to Nāpali Coast, but they'll spend about the same amount of time along Nāpali, plus you'll pay less. Finally, you'll also have to decide whether you want to go on the morning tour, which includes a deli lunch and a stop for snorkeling, or the afternoon tour, which does not stop to snorkel but does include a sunset over the ocean. The 5½-hour morning tour with snorkeling is more popular with families and those who love dolphins. You don't have to be an expert snorkeler or even have any prior experience, but if it is your first time, note that although there will be some snorkeling instruction, there might not be much. Hawaiian spinner dolphins are so plentiful in the mornings that some tour companies guarantee you'll see them, although you can't get in the water and swim with them. The 3½-hour afternoon tour is more popular with nonsnorklers—obviously—and photographers interested in capturing the setting sunlight on the coast.

CATAMARAN TOURS

Fodor's Choice
★
Blue Dolphin Charters. This company operates 63-foot and 65-foot sailing (rarely raised and always motoring) catamarans designed with three decks of spacious seating with great visibility. ■ TIP→ The lower deck is best for shade seekers. Upgrades from snorkeling to scuba diving—no need for certification—are available and run $35, but the diving is really best for beginners or people who need a refresher course. On Tuesday and Friday a tour of Nāpali Coast includes a detour across the channel to Ni'ihau for snorkeling and diving. Blue Dolphin likes to say they have the best mai tais "off the island," and truth is, they probably do. Morning snorkel tours of Nāpali include a deli lunch, and afternoon sunset sightseeing tours include a meal of kalua pork, teriyaki chicken, Caesar salad, and chocolate-chip cookies. Prices range from $105 to $196, depending on the tour. Two-hour whale-watching/sunset tours, offered during winter, run $63. ⊠ In Port Allen Marina Center ✛ Turn makai onto Rte. 541 off Rte. 50, at 'Ele'ele ☎ 808/335-5553 or 877/511-1311 ⊕ www.kauaiboats.com.

♺ **Capt. Andy's Sailing Adventures.** Departing from Port Allen and running two 55-foot sailing catamarans, Capt. Andy's runs the same five-hour snorkeling and four-hour sunset tours along Nāpali Coast as everyone else, though we're not crazy about the boat's layout, which has most of the seating inside the cabin. They also embark out of Kukui'ula Harbor in Po'ipū for a two-hour sunset sail along the South Shore—with live Hawaiian music—on select days (check Web site for particulars). ■ TIP→ If the winds and swells are up on the North Shore, this is usually a good choice—especially if you're prone to seasickness. This is the only tour boat operator that allows infants on board—but only on the two-hour trip. Note, if you have reservations for the shorter tour, you'll check in at their Kukui'ula Harbor office. Prices range from $69 to $139. ⊠ In Port Allen Marina Center ✛ Turn makai onto Rte. 541 off Rte. 50 at 'Ele'ele ☎ 808/335-6833 or 800/535-0830 ⊕ www.napali.com.

Captain Sundown. If you're staying on the North Shore, Captain Sundown is a worthy choice, especially for the nonadventurous. Get this: Captain Bob has been cruising Nāpali Coast for 35 years—six days a week, sometimes twice a day. (And right alongside Captain Bob is his son Captain Larry.) To say he knows the area is a bit of an understatement. Here's the other good thing about this tour: they take only

15 passengers. Now, you'll definitely pay more, but it's worth it. The breathtaking views of the waterfall-laced mountains behind Hanalei and Hā'ena start immediately, and then it's around Kē'ē Beach and the magic of Nāpali Coast unfolds before you. All the while, the captains are trolling for fish, and if they catch any, guests get to reel 'em in. Afternoon sunset sails (seasonal) run three hours and check in around 3 pm—these are BYOB. Prices range from $138 to $168. During the winter months, Captain Bob moves his operation to Nāwiliwili Harbor, where he runs four- to five-hour whale-watching tours. ⊠ *Meet in Hanalei at Tahiti Nui parking lot* ☎ *808/826–5585* ⊕ *www.captainsundown. com and www.whale-watching-kauai.com.*

Catamaran Kahanu. This Hawaiian-owned-and-operated company has been in business since 1985 and runs a 40-foot power catamaran with 18-passenger seating. The five-hour tour includes snorkeling at Nu'alolo Kai. The four-hour afternoon tour includes a hot dinner and sunset. The boat is smaller than most and may feel a tad crowded, but the tour feels more personal, with a laid-back, *'ohana* style. Salt water runs through the veins of Captain Lani. Guests can learn the ancient cultural practice of weaving on board. There's no alcohol allowed. Prices range from $95 to $135. ⊠ *Rte. 541* ⊹ *From Rte. 50, turn left on Rte. 541 at 'Ele'ele, proceed just past Port Allen Marina Center, turn right at sign; check-in booth on left* ☎ *808/645–6176 or 888/213–7711* ⊕ *www. catamarankahanu.com.*

HoloHolo Charters. Choose between a 50-foot sailing catamaran trip to Nāpali Coast, and a 65-foot powered catamaran trip to the island of Ni'ihau. Both boats have large cabins and little outside seating. Originators of the Ni'ihau tour, HoloHolo Charters built their 65-foot powered catamaran with a wide beam to reduce side-to-side motion, and twin 425 HP turbo diesel engines specifically for the 17-mi channel crossing to Ni'ihau. ■TIP➔ It's the only outfitter running daily Ni'ihau tours. Prices range from $99 to $179. ⊠ *Check in at Port Allen Marina Center* ⊠ *Rte. 541* ⊹ *Turn makai onto Rte. 541 off Rte. 50, at 'Ele'ele* ☎ *808/335– 0815 or 800/848–6130* ⊕ *www.holoholocharters.com.*

RAFT TOURS

Capt. Andy's Rafting Expeditions. This company used to be known as Captain Zodiac; however, the outfit has changed hands over the years. It first started running Nāpali in 1974, and currently, Capt. Andy's (as in the sailing catamaran Capt. Andy's) is operating the business. Departing out of Port Allen, this tour is much like the other raft tours, offering both snorkeling and beach-landing excursions. The rafts are on the smaller side—24 feet with a maximum of 15 passengers—and all seating is on the rubber hulls, so hang on. They operate three different rafts, so there's a good chance of availability. Price is $159 in summer; $139 in winter, including snorkeling at Nu'alolo Kai (ocean conditions permitting), sightseeing along Nāpali Coast, a hiking tour through an ancient Hawaiian fishing village, and a hot buffet lunch on the beach. In 2010 Capt. Andy's introduced a three-hour morning whale watch raft tour (winter only). You're closer to the water on the Zodiacs, so you'll have great views of humpbacks, spinner dolphins, sea turtles, and other wildlife. ⊠ *In Port Allen Marina Center* ⊹ *Turn makai onto*

Get out on the water and see Nāpali Coast in style on a luxe cruising yacht.

Rte. 541 off Rte. 50 at 'Ele'ele ☎ *808/335–6833 or 800/535–0830* ⊕ *www.napali.com.*

★

Nāpali Explorer. Owned by a couple of women, these tours operate out of two locations: Waimea, a tad closer to Nāpali Coast than most of the other West Side catamaran tours, and Hanalei in the summer. Departing out of the West Side, the company runs two different sizes of inflatable rubber raft: a 48-foot, 35-passenger craft with an onboard toilet, freshwater shower, shade canopy, and seating in the stern (which is surprisingly smooth and comfortable) and bow (which is where the fun is); and a 26-foot, 16-passenger craft for the all-out fun and thrills of a white-knuckle ride in the bow. Departing out of Hanalei, the *Ocean Adventurer* is a 38-foot, 25-passenger rigid-hull inflatable. The smaller vessel stops at Nu'alolo Kai and ties up onshore for a tour of the ancient fishing village. Rates are $105 to $149, including snorkeling. Charters are available. ⊠ *Follow Rte. 50 west to Waimea; office is mauka across from the Shrimp Station, Waimea* ⊠ *In Hanalei, meet at the river mouth, at the end of Weke Rd., Hanalei* ☎ *808/338–9999 or 877/335–9909* ⊕ *www.napaliexplorer.com.*

Z-Tourz. What we like about Z-Tourz is that it is the only boat company to make snorkeling its priority. As such, it focuses on the South Shore's abundant offshore reefs, stopping at two locations. If you want to see Nāpali, this boat is not for you; if you want to snorkel with the myriad of Hawai'i's tropical reef fish and turtles (pretty much guaranteed), this is your boat. Z-Tourz runs daily three-hour tours on a 26-foot rigid-hull inflatable (think Zodiac) with a maximum of 16 passengers. These snorkel tours are guided, so someone actually identifies what you're seeing.

Rate is $94. Check in at the business center then ride to Kukui'ula Harbor in Po'ipū. ✉ *3417 Poipu Rd., Suite 112* ☎ *808/742–7422 or 888/998–6879* ⊕ *www.ztourz.com.*

RIVER BOAT TOURS TO FERN GROTTO

This 2-mi, upriver trip culminates at a yawning lava tube that is covered with enormous fishtail ferns. During the boat ride, guitar and 'ukulele players regale you with Hawaiian melodies and tell the history of the river. It's a kitschy bit of Hawaiiana, worth the little money ($20) and short time required. Flat-bottom, 150-passenger riverboats (that rarely fill up) depart from Wailua Marina at the mouth of the Wailua River. ■ TIP→ **It's extremely rare, but occasionally after heavy rains the tour doesn't disembark at the grotto; if you're traveling in winter, ask beforehand.** Round-trip excursions take 1½ hours, including time to walk around the grotto and environs. Tours run at 9:30, 10, 11:30, 1:30, 2, and 3:30 daily. Reservations are not required. Contact **Smith's Motor Boat Services** (☎ *808/821–6892* ⊕ *www.smithskauai.com*) for more information.

BODY BOARDING AND BODYSURFING

The most natural form of wave riding is bodysurfing, a popular sport on Kaua'i because there are many shore breaks around the island. Wave riders of this style stand waist deep in the water, facing shore, and swim madly as a wave picks them up and breaks. It's great fun and requires no special skills and absolutely no equipment other than a swimsuit.

The next step up is body boarding, also called boogie boarding. In this case, wave riders lie with their upper body on a foam board about half the length of a traditional surfboard and kick as the wave propels them toward shore. Again, this is easy to pick up, and there are many places around Kaua'i to practice. The locals wear short-finned flippers to help them catch waves, although they are not necessary for and even hamper beginners. It's worth spending a few minutes watching these experts as they spin, twirl, and flip—that's right—while they slip down the face of the wave. Of course, all beach safety precautions apply, and just because you see wave riders of any kind in the water doesn't mean the water is safe for everyone. Any snorkeling gear outfitter also rents body boards.

BEST SPOTS

Some of our favorite bodysurfing and body boarding beaches are **Brennecke, Wailua, Keālia, Kalihiwai,** and **Hanalei.** *For directions, see Beaches, earlier in this chapter.*

DEEP-SEA FISHING

Simply step aboard and cast your line for mahimahi, 'ahi, ono, and marlin. That's about how quickly the fishing—mostly trolling with lures—begins on Kaua'i. The water gets deep quickly here, so there's less cruising time to fishing grounds. Of course, your captain may elect to cruise to a hot location where he's had good luck lately.

There are oodles of charter fishermen around; most depart from Nāwiliwili Harbor in Līhu'e, and most use lures instead of live bait. Inquire about each boat's "fish policy," that is, what happens to the fish if any are caught. Some boats keep all; others will give you enough for a meal or two. On shared charters, ask about the maximum passenger count and about the fishing rotation; you'll want to make sure everyone gets a fair shot at reeling in the big one. Another option is to book a private charter. Shared and private charters run four, six, and eight hours in length.

BOATS AND CHARTERS

Captain Don's Sport Fishing & Ocean Adventure. Captain Don is very flexible and treats everyone like family—he'll stop to snorkel or whale watch if that's what the group (four to six) wants. Saltwater fly-fishermen (bring your own gear) are welcome. He'll even fish for bait and let you keep part of whatever you catch. The *June Louise* is a 34-foot twin diesel. Rates start at $135 for shared, $575 for private charters. ⊠ *Nāwiliwili Small Boat Harbor* ☎ 808/639–3012 ⊕ *www.captaindonsfishing.com.*

Explore Kaua'i Sportfishing. If you're staying on the West Side, you'll be glad to know that Nāpali Explorer (of the longtime rafting tour business) is now running fishing trips out of Port Allen under the name Explore Kaua'i Sportfishing. It offers shared and exclusive charters of four, six, and eight hours in a 41-foot Concord called *Happy Times.* The shared tours max out at six fishermen, and a portion of the catch is shared with all. The boat is also used for specialty charters—that is, film crews, surveys, burials, and even Ni'ihau fishing. Rates range from $145 to $195 per person. ⊠ *Check in at Port Allen Small Boat Harbor* ☎ *808/338–9999 or 877/335–9909* ⊕ *www.napali-explorer.com.*

Hana Pa'a. The advantage with Hana Pa'a is that it takes fewer people (minimum two, maximum four for a nonprivate excursion), but you pay for it. Rates start at $310 for shared, $600 for private charters, which can accommodate up to six people. The company's fish policy is flexible, and the boat is roomy. The *Maka Hou II* is a 38-foot Bertram. ⊠ *Nāwiliwili Harbor* ☎ 808/823–6031 or 866/776–3474 ⊕ *www. fishkauai.com.*

KAYAKING

Kaua'i is the only Hawaiian Island with navigable rivers. As the oldest inhabited island in the chain, Kaua'i has had more time for wind and water erosion to deepen and widen cracks into streams and streams into rivers. Because this is a small island, the rivers aren't long, and there are no rapids; that makes them perfectly safe for kayakers of all levels, even beginners.

For more advanced paddlers, there aren't many places in the world more beautiful for sea kayaking than Nāpali Coast. If this is your draw to Kaua'i, plan your vacation for the summer months, when the seas are at their calmest. ■TIP→ Tour and kayak-rental reservations are recommended at least two weeks in advance during peak summer and holiday seasons. In general, tours and rentals are available year-round, Monday through Saturday. Pack a swimsuit, sunscreen, a hat, bug repellent, water shoes (sport sandals, aqua socks, old tennis shoes), and motion-sickness medication if you're planning on sea kayaking.

RIVER KAYAKING

Tour outfitters operate on the Hulē'ia, Wailua, and Hanalei rivers with guided tours that combine hiking to waterfalls, as in the case of the first two, and snorkeling, as is the case of the third. Another option is renting kayaks and heading out on your own. Each has its advantages and disadvantages, but it boils down as follows:

If you want to swim at the base of a remote 100-foot waterfall, sign up for a five-hour kayak (4 mi round-trip) and hiking (2 mi round-trip) tour of the **Wailua River.** It includes a dramatic waterfall that is best accessed with the aid of a guide, so you don't get lost. ■TIP→ Remember—it's dangerous to swim under waterfalls no matter how good a water massage may sound. Rocks and logs are known to plunge down, especially after heavy rains.

If you want to kayak on your own, choose the **Hanalei River.** It's most scenic from the kayak itself—there are no trails to hike to hidden waterfalls. And better yet, a rental company is right on the river—no hauling kayaks on top of your car.

If you're not sure of your kayaking abilities, head to the **Hulē'ia River;** 3½-hour tours include easy paddling upriver, a nature walk through a rain forest with a cascading waterfall, a rope swing for playing Tarzan and Jane, and a ride back downriver—into the wind—on a motorized, double-hull canoe.

As for the kayaks themselves, most companies use the two-person sit-on-top style that is quite buoyant—no Eskimo rolls required. The only possible danger comes in the form of communication. The kayaks seat two people, which means you can share the work (good) with a guide, or your spouse, child, parent, or friend (the potential danger part). On the river, the two-person kayaks are known as "divorce boats." Counseling is not included in the tour price.

SEA KAYAKING

Kayaking Nāpali Coast is the adventure of a lifetime. You can do the trip in one day, involving eight hours of paddling. Although it's good to have some kayaking experience, feel comfortable on the water, and be reasonably fit, it doesn't require the preparation, stamina, or fortitude of, say, climbing Mt. Everest. Tours run May through September, ocean conditions permitting. In the winter months sea-kayaking tours operate on the South Shore—beautiful, but not Nāpali.

EQUIPMENT AND TOURS

Kayak Kaua'i. Based in Hanalei, this company offers guided tours on the Hanalei and Wailua rivers, and along Nāpali Coast. It has a great shop right on the Hanalei River for kayak rentals and camping gear. The guided Hanalei River Kayak and Snorkel Tour starts at the shop and heads downriver, so there's not much to see of the scenic river valley. (For that, rent a kayak on your own.) Instead, this three-hour tour paddles down to the river mouth, where the river meets the sea. Then, it's a short paddle around a point to snorkel at either Pu'u Poa Beach or, ocean conditions permitting, a bit farther at Hideaways Beach. This is a great choice if you want to try your paddle at a bit of ocean kayaking.

A second location in Kapaʻa is the base for Wailua River guided tours and kayak rentals. It's not right on the river, however, so shuttling is involved. For rentals, the company provides the hauling gear necessary for your rental car. Guided tours range from $60 to $214. Kayak rentals range from $28 to $75, depending on the river, depending on kayak size (single or double). ⊠ *Hanalei: 1 mi past Hanalei bridge, on makai side* ⊠ *Kapaʻa: south end of Coconut Marketplace near movie theaters* ☎ *808/826–9844 or 800/437–3507* ⊕ *www.kayakkauai.com.*

Kayak Wailua. We can't quite figure out how this family-run business offers pretty much the same Wailua River kayaking tour as everyone else—except for lunch and beverages, which are BYO—for half the price, but it does. They say it's because they don't discount and don't offer commission to activities and concierge desks. Their 4½-hour kayak, hike, and waterfall swim costs $39.95, and their three-hour kayak-to-a-swimming-hole costs $34.95. We say fork over the extra $5 for the longer tour and hike to the beautiful 150-foot Secret Falls. ⊠ *In Wailua next to Wailua Shell Food Mart* ☎ *808/822–3388* ⊕ *www. kayakwailua.com.*

Fodor'sChoice
★

NāpaliKayak. A couple of longtime guides ventured out on their own a few years back to create this company, which focuses solely on sea kayaking—Nāpali Coast in summer, as the name implies, and the South Shore in winter (during peak times only). These guys are highly experienced and still highly enthusiastic about their livelihood. So much so, that REI Adventures hires them to run their multiday, multisport tours. Now, that's a feather in their cap, we'd say. Prices start at $200. You can also rent kayaks; price range from $25 to $75. If you want to try camping on your own at Kalalau (you'll need permits), NāpaliKayak will provide outfitted kayaks and transportation drop-off and pickup. ⊠ *5-575 Kūhiō Hwy., next to Postcards Café* ☎ *808/826–6900 or 866/977–6900* ⊕ *www.napalikayak.com.*

Outfitters Kauaʻi. This well-established tour outfitter operates year-round river-kayak tours on the Hulēʻia and Wailua rivers, as well as sea-kayaking tours along Nāpali Coast in summer and the South Shore in winter. Outfitters Kauaʻi's specialty, however, is the **Kipu Safari.** This all-day adventure starts with kayaking up the Hulēʻia River and includes a rope swing over a swimming hole, a wagon ride through a working cattle ranch, a picnic lunch by a private waterfall, hiking, and two "zips" across the rain-forest canopy (strap on a harness, clip into a cable, and zip over a quarter of a mile). It ends with a ride on a motorized double-hull canoe. It's a great tour for the family, because no one ever gets bored. The Kipu Safari costs $178; other guided tours range from $98 to $225. ⊠ *2827-A Poʻipū Rd., Poʻipū* ☎ *808/742–9667 or 888/742–9886* ⊕ *www.outfitterskauai.com.*

Wailua Kayak & Canoe. This is the only purveyor of kayak rentals on the Wailua River, which means no hauling your kayak on top of your car (a definite plus). Rates are $45 for a single, $75 for a double, for either a morning or afternoon. Guided tours are also available with rates ranging from $55 to $90. This outfitter promotes itself as "Native Hawaiian owned and operated." ⊠ *169 Wailua Rd., Kapaʻa* ✣ *Across*

In summer you can reach Kalalau Beach by sea kayaking along Nāpali Coast. "[We had a] great day at the river by Kalalau." —clitopower

from Wailua Beach, turn mauka at Kuamo'o Rd. and take first left ☎ 808/821–1188 ⊕ *www.wailuakayakandcanoe.net.*

KITEBOARDING

Several years ago, the latest wave-riding craze to hit the Islands was kiteboarding, and the sport is still going strong. As the name implies, there's a kite and a board involved. The board you strap on your feet; the kite is attached to a harness around your waist. Steering is accomplished with a rod that's attached to the harness and the kite. Depending on conditions and the desires of the kiteboarder, the kite is played out some 30 to 100 feet in the air. The result is a cross between waterskiing—without the boat—and windsurfing. Speeds are fast and aerobatic maneuvers are involved. Unfortunately, neither lessons nor rental gear are available for the sport on Kaua'i (Maui is a better bet), so if you aren't a seasoned kiteboarder already, you'll have to be content with watching the pros—who can put on a pretty spectacular show. The most popular year-round spots for kiteboarding are **Kapa'a Beach Park, 'Anini Beach Park,** and **Māhā'ulepū Beach.** ■TIP→ Many visitors come to Kaua'i dreaming of parasailing. If that's you, make a stop at Maui or the Big Island. There's no parasailing on Kaua'i.

SCUBA DIVING

The majority of scuba diving on Kaua'i occurs on the South Shore. Boat and shore dives are available, although boat sites surpass the shore sites for a couple of reasons. First, they're deeper and exhibit the complete symbiotic relationship of a reef system, and second, the visibility is better a little farther offshore.

The dive operators below offer a full range of services, including certification dives, referral dives, boat dives, shore dives, night dives, and drift dives. ■TIP→ As for certification, we recommend completing your confined-water training and classroom testing before arriving on the island. That way, you'll spend less time training and more time diving.

BEST SPOTS

The best and safest scuba-diving sites are accessed by boat on the South Shore of the island, right off the shores of Po'ipū. The captain selects the actual site based on ocean conditions of the day. Beginners may prefer shore dives, which are best at **Kōloa Landing** on the South Shore year-round and **Mākua (Tunnels) Beach** on the North Shore in the calm summer months. Keep in mind, though, that you'll have to haul your gear a ways down the beach.

For the advanced diver, the island of Ni'ihau—across an open ocean channel in deep and crystal clear waters—beckons and rewards, usually with some big fish. Seasport Divers, Fathom Five, and Bubbles Below venture the 17 mi across the channel in summer when the crossing is smoothest. Divers can expect deep dives, walls, and strong currents at Ni'ihau, where conditions can change rapidly. To make the long journey worthwhile, three dives and Nitrox are included.

EQUIPMENT, LESSONS, AND TOURS

Fodor's Choice ★ **Ocean Quest Watersports/Fathom Five.** A few years ago, Fathom Five, the South Shore boat-diving specialist, teamed up with Ocean Quest Watersports, a separate company specializing in shore dives at Tunnels on the North Shore. Today, they offer it all: boat dives, shore dives, night dives, certification dives. They're pretty much doing what everyone else is with a couple of twists. First, they offer a three-tank premium charter for those really serious about diving. Second, they operate a Nitrox continuous-flow mixing system, so you can decide the mix rate. Third, they tag on a twilight dive to the standard, one-tank night dive, making the outing worth the effort. Fourth, their shore diving isn't an afterthought. Finally, we think their dive masters are pretty darn good, too. They even dive Ni'ihau in the summer aboard their 35-foot Force. Prices start at $70 for a one-tank shore dive and top out at $495 for full certification. The standard two-tank boat dive runs $120 plus $35 for gear rental, if needed. ■TIP→ In summer, book way in advance. ⊠ *3450 Po'ipū Rd.* ✚ *Just south of Kōloa on Po'ipū Rd.* ☎ *808/742–6991 or 800/972–3078* ⊕ *www.fathomfive.com.*

Sacred Seas Scuba. This company specializes in shore diving only, typically at Kōloa Landing (year-round) and Tunnels (summers). They're not only geared toward beginning divers—for whom they provide a very thorough and gentle certification program as well as the Discover Scuba program—but also offer night dives and scooter (think James Bond) dives. Their main emphasis is a detailed review of marine biology, such as pointing out rare dragon eel and harlequin shrimp tucked away in pockets of coral. ■TIP→ Hands down, we recommend Sacred Seas Scuba for beginners, certification (all levels), and refresher dives. One reason is

If you get up close with a Hawaiian monk seal, consider yourself lucky—they're endangered. But look, don't touch—it's illegal.

that their instructor-to-student ratio never exceeds 1:4—that's true of all their dive groups. Rates range from $79 for a one-tank certified dive to $450 for certification—all dive gear included. ☎ *877/441–3483 or 808/742–9534* ⊕ *www.sacredseasscuba.com.*

Seasport Divers. Rated highly by readers of *Scuba Diving* magazine, Seasport Divers' 48-foot *Anela Kai* tops the chart for dive-boat luxury. But owner Marvin Otsuji didn't stop with that. In 2006, he added a second boat—a 32-foot catamaran—that's outfitted for diving, but we like it as an all-around charter. The company does a brisk business, which means it won't cancel at the last minute because of a lack of reservations, like some other companies, although they may book up to 18 people per boat. ■ TIP→ There are slightly more challenging trips in the morning; mellower dive sites are in the afternoon. The company also runs a good-size dive shop for purchases and rentals, as well as a classroom for certification. Ni'ihau trips are available in summer. All trips leave from Kukui'ula Harbor in Po'ipū. Rates start at $125 for a two-tank boat dive; rental gear is $25 extra. ⊠ *Check-in office on Po'ipū Rd.* ⊹ *Just north of Lāwa'i Rd. turnoff to Spouting Horn. Look for yellow submarine in parking lot, 2827 Po'ipū Rd., Po'ipū* ☎ *808/742–9303 or 800/685–5889* ⊕ *www.seasportdivers.com.*

SNORKELING

Generally speaking, the calmest water and best snorkeling can be found on Kaua'i's North Shore in summer and South Shore in winter. The East Side, known as the windward side, has year-round, prevalent northeast trade winds that make snorkeling unpredictable, although there are some good pockets. The best snorkeling on the West Side is accessible only by boat.

A word on feeding fish: Don't. As Captain Ted with HoloHolo Charters says, fish have survived and populated reefs for much longer than we have been donning goggles and staring at them. They will continue to do so without our intervention. Besides, fish food messes up the reef and—one thing always leads to another—can eliminate a once-pristine reef environment. As for gear, if you're snorkeling with one of the Nāpali boat tour outfitters, they'll provide it. However, depending on the company, it might not be the latest or greatest. If you have your own, bring it. On the other hand, if you're going out with SeaFun or Z-Tourz, not to worry. Their gear is top-notch. If you need to rent, hit one of the "snorkel-and-surf" shops such as Snorkel Bob's in Kōloa and Kapaʻa, Nukumoi in Poʻipū and Waimea, or Seasport in Pōipū and Kapaʻa, or shop Wal-Mart or Kmart if you want to drag it home. Typically, though, rental gear will be better quality than that found at Wal-Mart or Kmart. ■TIP➜ If you wear glasses, you can rent prescription masks at the rental shops—just don't expect them to match your prescription exactly.

BEST SPOTS

Just because we say these are good places to snorkel doesn't mean that the exact moment you arrive, the fish will flock—they are wild, after all. The beaches here are listed in clockwise fashion starting on the North Shore.

Although it can get quite crowded, **Kēʻē Beach** (⊠ *At end of Rte. 560*) is quite often a good snorkeling destination. Just be sure to come during the off-hours, say early in the morning or later in the afternoon. ■TIP➜ Snorkeling here in winter can be hazardous. Summer is the best and safest time, although you should never swim beyond the reef.

★ The search for **Tunnels (Mākua)** (⊠ *At Hāʻena Beach Park ✣ Near end of Rte. 560, across from lava-tube sea caves, after stream crossing*) is as tricky as the snorkeling. Park at Hāʻena Beach Park and walk east—away from Nāpali Coast—until you see a sand channel entrance in the water, almost at the point. Once you get here, the reward is fantastic. The name of this beach comes from the many underwater lava tubes, which always attract marine life. The shore is mostly beach rock interrupted by three sand channels. You'll want to enter and exit at one of these channels (or risk stepping on a sea urchin or scraping your stomach on the reef). Follow the sand channel to a drop-off; the snorkeling along here is always full of nice surprises. Expect a current running east to west. Snorkeling here in winter can be hazardous; summer is the best and safest time for snorkeling.

☺ **Lydgate Beach Park** (⊠ *Nalu Rd. ✣ Just south of Wailua River, turn makai off Rte. 56 onto Lehu Dr. and left onto Nalu Rd.*) is the absolute safest place to snorkel on Kauaʻi. With its lava-rock wall creating a protected swimming pool, this is the perfect spot for beginners, young and old. The fish are so tame here it's almost like swimming in a saltwater aquarium.

You'll generally find good year-round snorkeling at **Poʻipū Beach Park** (⊠ *Hoʻōne Rd. ✣ From Poʻipū Rd., turn right on Hoʻōne Rd.*), except during summer's south swells (which are not nearly as frequent as winter's north swells). The best snorkeling fronts the Marriott Waiohai Beach Club. Stay inside the crescent created by the sandbar and rocky point. The current runs east to west.

Don't pack the beach umbrella, beach mats, or cooler for snorkeling at **Beach House** (*Lāwaʻi Beach*) (⊠ *Makai side of Lāwaʻi Rd.* ✚ *park on road in front of Lāwaʻi Beach Resort*). Just bring your snorkeling gear. The beach—named after its neighbor the Beach House restaurant (yum)—is on the road to Spouting Horn. It's a small slip of sand during low tide and a rocky shoreline during high tide. However, it's right by the road's edge, and its rocky coastline and somewhat rocky bottom make it great for snorkeling. Enter and exit in the sand channel (not over the rocky reef) that lines up with the Lāwaʻi Beach Resort's center atrium. Stay within the rocky points anchoring each end of the beach. The current runs east to west.

With little river runoff and hardly any boat traffic, the waters off the island of **Niʻihau** are some of the clearest in all Hawaiʻi, and that's good for snorkeling. Like Nuʻalolo Kai, the only way to snorkel here is to sign on with one of the two tour boats venturing across a sometimes rough open ocean channel: Blue Dolphin Charters and HoloHolo (*see Boat Tours*).

★ **Nuʻalolo Kai** was once an ancient Hawaiian fishpond and is now home to the best snorkeling along Nāpali Coast (and perhaps on all of Kauaʻi). The only way to access it is by boat, and only a few Nāpali snorkeling tour operators are permitted to do so. We recommend **Nāpali Explorer** and **Kauaʻi Sea Tours**.

TOURS

☾ **SeaFun Kauaʻi.** This guided snorkeling tour, for beginners and intermediates alike, is led by a marine expert, so not only is there excellent how-to instruction, but the guide actually gets in the water with you and identifies marine life. You're guaranteed to spot tons of critters you'd never see on your own. This is a land-based operation and the only one of its kind on Kauaʻi. (Don't think those snorkeling cruises are guided snorkeling tours—they rarely are. A member of the boat's crew serves as lifeguard, not a marine life *guide*.) A half-day tour includes all your snorkeling gear—and a wet suit to keep you warm—and stops at two snorkeling locations, chosen based on ocean conditions. The cost is $80. ⊠ *Check in at Kilohana Plantation in Puhi, next to Kauaʻi Community College* ☎ *808/245–6400 or 800/452–1113* ⊕ *www.alohakauaitours. com.*

STAND-UP PADDLING

Unlike kiteboarding, this is a new sport that even a novice can pick up—*and* have fun doing. Technically, it's not really a new sport but a reinvigorated one from the 1950s. Beginners start with a heftier surfboard and a longer-than-normal canoe paddle. And, just like the name implies, stand-up paddlers stand on their surfboards and paddle out from the beach—no timing a wave and doing a push-up to stand. The perfect place to learn is a river (think **Hanalei** or **Wailua**) or a calm lagoon (try **'Anini** or **Kalapakī**). But this sport isn't just for beginners. Tried-and-true surfers turn to it when the waves are not quite right for their preferred sport, because it gives them another reason to be on the water. Stand-up paddlers catch waves earlier and ride them longer than longboard surfers. In the past couple years, professional stand-up paddling competitions have popped up.

EQUIPMENT

Not all surf instructors teach stand-up paddling, but more and more are, like Blue Seas Surf School and Titus Kinimaka Hawaiian School of Surfing *(see Surfing)*.

Hawaiian Surfing Adventures. This stand at Hanalei Beach Park rents stand-up paddle equipment ($20 for the first hour; $10 for each additional hour). Lessons are available on the scenic Hanalei River or in Hanalei Bay, and include one hour of instruction and two hours to practice with the board (lessons range from $55 to $75, depending on group size). The company also offers surfboard rentals and surfing lessons. ⊠ *Hanalei Beach Park, Hanalei* ☎ *808/482–0749* ⊕ *www. hawaiiansurfingadventures.com.*

Kaua'i Beach Boys. This outfitter is located right on the beach at Kalapakī, so there's no hauling your gear on your car. ⊠ *Kalapakī Beach, Līhu'e* ☎ *808/246–6333.*

SURFING

Good ol' surfing is alive and well on Kaua'i, especially in winter's high surf season on the North Shore. If you're new to the sport, we highly recommend taking a lesson. Not only will this ensure you're up and riding waves in no time, but instructors will provide the right board for your experience and size, help you time a wave, and give you a push to get your momentum going. ■TIP→ You don't need to be in top physical shape to take a lesson. Because your instructor helps push you into the wave, you won't wear yourself out paddling. If you're experienced and want to hit the waves on your own, most surf shops rent boards for all levels, from beginners to advanced.

BEST SPOTS

Perennial-favorite beginning surf spots include **Po'ipū Beach** (the area fronting the Marriott Waiohai Beach Club); **Hanalei Bay** (the area next to the Hanalei Pier); and the stream end of **Kalapakī Beach.** More advanced surfers move down the beach in Hanalei to an area fronting a grove of pine trees known as **Pine Trees.** When the trade winds die, the north ends of **Wailua** and **Keālia** beaches are teeming with surfers. Breaks off **Po'ipū** and **Beach House/Lāwa'i Beach** attract intermediates year-round. During high surf, the break on the cliff side of **Kalihiwai** is for experts only.

LESSONS

Blue Seas Surf School. Surfer and instructor Charlie Smith specializes in beginners (especially children) and will go anywhere on the island to find just the right surf. His soft-top longboards are very stable, making it easier to stand up. Rates start at $75 for a 1½-hour lesson. (Transportation

Winter brings big surf to Kaua'i's North Shore. You can see some of the sport's biggest celebrities catching waves at Hā'ena and Hanalei Bay.

provided, if needed.) ⊠ *Meet at beach; location varies depending on surf conditions* ☎ *808/634–6979* ⊕ *www.blueseassurfingschool.com.*

Margo Oberg Surfing School. Seven-time world surfing champion Margo Oberg runs a surf school that meets on the beach in front of the Sheraton Kaua'i in Po'ipū. Lessons are $68 for two hours, though Margo herself rarely teaches anymore. ⊠ *Po'ipū Beach* ☎ *808/332–6100* ⊕ *www. surfonkauai.com.*

Titus Kinimaka Hawaiian School of Surfing. Famed as a pioneer of big-wave surfing, this Hawaiian believes in giving back to his sport. Beginning, intermediate, and "extreme" lessons, including tow-in, are available. If you want to learn to surf from a living legend, this is the man. ∎ **TIP→** He employs other instructors, so if you want Titus, be sure to ask for him. (And good luck, because if the waves are going off, he'll be surfing, not teaching.) Rates are $55 for a 90-minute group lesson; $65 for a 90-minute group stand-up paddle lesson; $150 for a one-hour, tow-in lesson. ⊠ *Meets at Quicksilver shop in Hanalei* ☎ *808/652–1116.*

EQUIPMENT

Hanalei Surf Company. You can rent boards here and shop for rash guards, wet suits, and some hip surf-inspired apparel. ⊠ *Mauka at Hanalei Center, 5-5161 Kūhiō Hwy., Hanalei* ☎ *808/826–9000.*

Progressive Expressions. This full-service shop has a choice of rental boards and a whole lotta shopping. ⊠ *On Kōloa Rd. in Old Kōloa Town* ☎ *808/742–6041.*

Tamba Surf Company. This is your best bet for surf rentals on the East Side. ⊠ *Mauka on north end of Hwy. 56 in Kapa'a; across from Scotty's Beachside BBQ; 4-1543 Kūhiō Hwy., Kapa'a* ☎ *808/823–6942.*

WHALE-WATCHING

Every winter North Pacific humpback whales swim some 3,000 mi over 30 days, give or take a few, from Alaska to Hawai'i. Whales arrive as early as November and sometimes stay through April, though they seem to be most populous in February and March. They come to Hawai'i to breed, calve, and nurse their young.

Of course, nothing beats seeing a whale up close. During the season, any boat on the water is looking for whales; they're hard to avoid, whether the tour is labeled "whale-watching" or not. Several boat operators add two-hour afternoon whale-watching tours during the season that run on the South Shore (not Nāpali). Operators include **Blue Dolphin, Catamaran Kahanu, HoloHolo,** and **Nāpali Explorer** (*see Boat Tours*). **Capt. Andy's** now has a three-hour morning whale-watch tour along the West Side. Trying one of these excursions is a good option for those who have no interest in snorkeling or sightseeing along Nāpali Coast, although keep in mind, the longer you're on the water, the more likely you'll be to see the humpbacks.

WINDSURFING

Windsurfing on Kaua'i isn't nearly as popular as it is on Maui but 'Anini Beach Park is the place if you're going to windsurf or play the spectator. Rentals and lessons are available from **Windsurf Kaua'i** (☎ *808/828–6838*). Lessons run $100 for three hours, equipment included; rentals run $25 per hour. The instructor will meet you on 'Anini Beach.

GOLF, HIKING, AND OUTDOOR ACTIVITIES

For those of you who love ocean sports but need a little break from all that sun, sand, and salt, there are plenty of options on Kaua'i to keep you busy on the ground. You can hike the island's many trails, or consider taking your vacation into flight with a treetop zipline or a helicopter tour. You can have a backcountry adventure in a four-wheel drive, or relax in an inner tube floating down the cane-field irrigation canals.

AERIAL TOURS

If you only drive around Kaua'i in your rental car, you will not see *all* of Kaua'i. There is truly only one way to see it all, and that's by air. Helicopter tours are the favorite way to get a bird's-eye view of Kaua'i—they fly at lower altitudes, hover above waterfalls, and wiggle their way into areas that a fixed-wing aircraft cannot.

★ **Blue Hawaiian Helicopters.** This multi-island operator flies the latest in helicopter technology, the Eco-Star, costing $1.8 million. It has 23% more interior space for its six passengers, has unparalleled viewing, and

Humpback whales arrive at Kaua'i in December and stick around until early April. Head out on a boat tour for a chance to see these majestic creatures breach.

offers a few extra safety features. As the name implies, the helicopter is also a bit more environmentally friendly, with a 50% noise-reduction rate. Flights run a tad shorter than others (50 to 55 minutes instead of the 55 to 65 minutes that other companies tout), but the flight feels very complete. The rate is $225 and includes taxes and fuel surcharge. A DVD of your actual tour is available for an additional $25. ⊠ *Harbor Mall in Nāwiliwili, Līhu'e* ☎ *808/245–5800 or 800/745–2583* ⊕ *www. bluehawaiian.com.*

Inter-Island Helicopters. This company flies four-seater Hughes 500 helicopters *with the doors off.* It can get chilly at higher elevations, so bring a sweater and wear long pants. Tours depart from Hanapēpē's Port Allen Airport, so if you're staying on the West Side, this is a good bet. Prices range from $260 to $355 per person. ⊠ *From Rte. 50, turn makai onto Rte. 543 in Hanapēpē* ☎ *808/335–5009 or 800/656–5009* ⊕ *www.interislandhelicopters.com.*

Fodor's Choice
★
Jack Harter Helicopters. Jack Harter was the first company to offer helicopter tours on Kaua'i. The company flies the six-passenger ASTAR helicopter with floor-to-ceiling windows, and the four-person Hughes 500, which is flown with no doors. The doorless ride can get windy, but it's the best bet for taking reflection-free photos. Pilots provide information on the Garden Island's history and geography through two-way intercoms. The company flies out of Līhu'e and has a second office at the Kaua'i Marriott. Tours are 60 to 65 minutes and 90 to 95 minutes and cost $259 to $384, including taxes and fuel surcharge. ⊠ *4231 Ahukini Rd., Līhu'e* ☎ *808/245–3774 or 888/245–2001* ⊕ *www.helicopters-kauai.com.*

Safari Helicopters. This company flies the "Super" ASTAR helicopter, which offers floor-to-ceiling windows on its doors, four roof windows, and Bose X-Generation headphones. Two-way microphones allow passengers to converse with the pilot. The price is $224 and includes taxes and fuel surcharge; a DVD is $40 extra.

✉ *3225 Akahi St., Līhu'e* ☎ *808/246–0136 or 800/326–3356* ⊕ *www. safariair.com.*

Sunshine Helicopter Tours. If the name of this company sounds familiar, it may be because its pilots fly on all the main Hawaiian Islands. On Kaua'i, Sunshine Helicopters departs out of three different locations: Līhu'e, Port Allen, and limited service at Princeville. They fly the six-passenger FX STAR and super-roomy six-passenger WhisperSTAR birds. The standard 50-minute flight starts at $229 and includes taxes and fuel surcharge. ✉ *3-3222 Kūhiō Hwy., Līhu'e* ✉ *3441 Kuiloko Rd., Port Allen Airport, Hanapēpē Princeville Airport, Princeville* ☎ *808/245–8881 or 888/245–4354* ⊕ *www.helicopters-hawaii.com.*

ATV TOURS

Although all the beaches on the island are public, much of the interior land—once sugar and pineapple plantations—is privately owned. This is really a shame, because the valleys and mountains that make up the vast interior of the island easily rival the beaches in sheer beauty. The good news is some tour operators have agreements with landowners making exploration possible, albeit a bit bumpy, and unless you have back troubles, that's half the fun.

Kaua'i ATV Tours. This is *the* thing to do when it rains on Kaua'i. Consider it an extreme mud bath. Kaua'i ATV in Kōloa is the originator of the island's all-terrain-vehicle tours. Its $125 three-hour Kōloa tour takes you through a private sugar plantation and historic cane-haul tunnel. The $155 four-hour waterfall tour visits secluded waterfalls and includes a picnic lunch. This popular option includes a hike through a bamboo forest and a swim in a freshwater pool at the base of the falls—to rinse off all that mud. You must be 16 or older to operate your own ATV, but Kaua'i ATV also offers its four-passenger "Ohana Bug" and two-passenger "Mud Bugs" to accommodate families with kids ages five and older. ✉ *3477A Weliweli Rd., Kōloa* ☎ *808/742–2734 or 877/707–7088* ⊕ *www.kauaiatv.com.*

Kipu Ranch Adventures. This 3,000-acre property extends from the Hulē'ia River to the top of Mt. Haupu. *Jurassic Park, Indiana Jones,* and *Mighty Joe Young* were filmed here, and you'll see the locations for all of them on the $125 three-hour Ranch Tour. The $150 four-hour Waterfall Tour includes a visit to two waterfalls and a picnic lunch. Kipu Ranch was once a sugar plantation, but today it is a working cattle ranch, so you'll be in the company of bovines as well as pheasants, wild boars, and peacocks ⊠ *Kipu Rd.* ✛ *Take Puhi Bypass Rd. off Hwy. 50 and turn right on Kipu Rd.* ☏ *808/246–9288* ⊕ *www.kiputours.com.*

BIKING

Kaua'i is a labyrinth of cane-haul roads, which are fun for exploring on two wheels. The challenge is finding the roads where biking is allowed and then not getting lost in the maze. Maybe that explains why Kaua'i is not a hub for the sport . . . yet. Still, there are some epic rides for those who are interested—both the adrenaline-rush and the mellower beach-cruiser kind. If you want to crank out some mileage, much of the main highway that skirts the coastal areas is somewhat safe, though there are frequent narrow or nonexistent shoulders, only a few designated bike routes, and no bike lanes along the highways. But from Kalāheo going west via the alternate Halewili Road to 'Ele'ele and out to Kekaha there are consistent shoulders. Much of the island is hilly, but you'll find that keeping your eyes on the road and not the scenery is the biggest challenge. A new section of Ke Ala Hele Makalae, a multi-use path that runs along the East Side of Kaua'i, was completed in the summer of 2009, totaling 6½ mi of completed path in two unconnected sections: within Lydgate Beach Park and then along the coast from Kapa'a to Kealia. You can rent bikes (with helmets) from the activities desks of certain hotels, but these are not the best quality. You're better off renting from Kaua'i Cycle in Kapa'a, Outfitters Kaua'i in Po'ipū, or Pedal 'n' Paddle in Hanalei.

★ **Ke Ala Hele Makalae** *(Nāwiliwili to Anahola Bike/Pedestrian Path).* For the cruiser, this path follows the coastline on Kaua'i's East Side. Eventually, it will run some 20 mi and offer scenic views, picnic pavilions, and restroom facilities along the way—all in compliance with the Americans with Disabilities Act. For now, there are 2.5 mi of path in Lydgate Beach Park to secluded Kuna Bay (aka Donkey Beach). The easiest way to access the completed sections of the path is from Keālia Beach. Park here and head north into rural lands with spectacular coastline vistas or head south into Kapa'a for a more interactive experience. ⊠ *Trailhead: 1 mi north of Kapa'a; park at north end of Keālia Beach.*

Wailua Forest Management Road. For the novice mountain biker, this is an easy ride, and it's also easy to find. From Route 56 in Wailua, turn mauka on Kuamo'o Road and continue 6 mi to the picnic area, known as Keāhua Arboretum; park here. The potholed four-wheel-drive road includes some stream crossings—⚠ stay away during heavy rains, because the streams flood—and continues for 2 mi to a T-stop, where you should turn right. Stay on the road for about 3 mi until you reach a gate; this is the spot where the gates in the movie *Jurassic Park* were filmed, though it looks nothing like the movie. Go around the gate and down the road for another mile to a confluence of streams at the base of Mt. Wai'ale'ale. Be sure to bring your camera.

Waimea Canyon Road. For those wanting a very challenging road work-out, climb this road, also known as Route 550. After a 3,000-foot climb, the road tops out at mile 12 adjacent to Waimea Canyon, which will pop in and out of view on your right as you ascend. From here

One of the most visited sites on Kaua'i is Waimea Canyon. Make sure to stop at Pu'u ka Pele and Pu'u hinahina lookouts.

it continues several miles (mostly level) past the Kōke'e Museum and ends at the Kalalau Lookout. It's paved the entire way, uphill 100%, and curvy. ⚠ There's not much of a shoulder on either road—sometimes none—so be extra cautious. The road gets busier as the day wears on, so you may want to consider a sunrise ride. A slightly more moderate uphill climb is Kōke'e Road, Route 552, from Kekaha, which intersects with Route 550. By the way, bikes aren't allowed on the hiking trails in and around Waimea Canyon and Kōke'e State Park, but there are miles of wonderful 4WD roads perfect for mountain biking. Check at Kōke'e Lodge for a map and conditions. ⊹ *Road turns mauka off Rte. 50 just after grocery store in downtown Waimea.*

EQUIPMENT AND TOURS

Kaua'i Cycle. This reliable, full-service bike shop rents, sells, and repairs bikes. Cruisers, mountain bikes (front- and full-suspension), and road bikes are available for $20 to $45 per day and $110 to $250 per week with directions to trails. The Ke Ala Hele Makalae is right out their back door. ✉ *934 Kūhiō Hwy.* ⊹ *Across from Taco Bell, Kapa'a* ☎ *808/821–2115* ⊕ *www.kauaicycle.com.*

Outfitters Kaua'i. Hybrid "comfort" and mountain bikes (both full-suspension and hardtails), as well as road bikes, are available at this shop in Po'ipū. You can ride right out the door to tour Po'ipū, or get information on how to do a self-guided tour of Kōe'e State Park and Waimea Canyon. The company also leads sunrise coasting tours (under the name **Bicycle Downhill**) from Waimea Canyon to the island's West Side beaches. Rentals cost $25 to $45 per day. Tours cost $98. ✉ *2827-A Po'ipū Rd.* ⊹ *Follow Po'ipū Rd. south from Kōloa town;*

shop is on right before turnoff to Spouting Horn, Po'ipū ☎ *808/742–9667 or 888/742–9887* ⊕ *www.outfitterskauai.com.*

★ **Pedal 'n' Paddle.** This company rents old-fashioned, single-speed beach cruisers and hybrid road bikes for $15 to $20 per day; $60 to $80 per week. In the heart of Hanalei, this is a great way to cruise the town; the more ambitious cyclist can head to the end of the road. Be careful, though, because there are no bike lanes on the twisting and turning road to ēēKē'ē. ⊠ *Ching Young Village, Rte. 560, Hanalei* ☎ *808/826–9069* ⊕ *www.pedalnpaddle.com.*

GOLF

For golfers, the Garden Island might as well be known as the Robert Trent Jones Jr. Isle. Four of the island's nine courses, including Po'ipū Bay—home of the PGA Grand Slam of Golf—are the work of Jones, who maintains a home at Princeville. Combine these four courses with those from Jack Nicklaus, Robin Nelson, and local legend Toyo Shirai, and you'll see that golf sets Kaua'i apart from the other Islands as much as the Pacific Ocean does. ■TIP→ Afternoon tee times can save you big bucks.

Kaua'i Lagoons Golf Club. With the development of the Kaua'i Lagoons Resort, the golf club is getting a face-lift, albeit a slow one due to the economy. Yes, Jack is back. When Nicklaus is done with this course, 27 championship-style holes (the links-style course is gone) will await golfers. For now, 18 holes are playable including a half mile of ocean-hugging holes redesigned to take advantage of the obvious visual spender of Kalapakī Bay. Number 18 is the island green named "The Bear" for its challenging play into the trade winds. At this writing, construction was expected to be completed in May 2011. ⊠ *3351 Ho'olaulea Way, Līhu'e* ☎ *808/241–6000 or 800/634–6400* ⊕ *www.kauailagoonsgolf. com* ⚑ *18 holes. 6977 yds. Par 72. Greens fee: $140–195* ⚐ *Facilities: Driving range, putting green, golf carts, rental clubs, lessons.*

Kiahuna Plantation Golf Course. A meandering creek, lava outcrops, and thickets of trees give Kiahuna its character. Robert Trent Jones Jr. was given a smallish piece of land just inland at Po'ipū, and defends par with smaller targets, awkward stances, and optical illusions. In 2003 a group of homeowners bought the club and brought Jones back to renovate the course (it was originally built in 1983), adding tees and revamping bunkers. The pro here boasts his course has the best putting greens on the island. This is the only course on Kaua'i with a complete set of junior's tee boxes. ⊠ *2545 Kiahuna Plantation Dr., Kōloa* ☎ *808/742–9595* ⊕ *www.kiahunagolf.com* ⚑ *18 holes. 6214 yds. Par 70. Greens fee: $103* ⚐ *Facilities: Driving range, putting green, rental clubs, lessons, pro shop, restaurant, bar.*

Kukuiolono Golf Course. Local legend Toyo Shirai designed this fun, funky 9-holer where holes play across rolling, forested hills that afford views of the distant Pacific. Though Shirai has an eye for a good golf hole, Kukuiolono is out of the way and a bit rough, and so probably not for everyone. But at $9 for the day, it's a deal—bring cash, though, as they don't accept credit cards. No tee times. ⊠ *854 Pu'u Rd., Kalāheo*

☏ 808/332–9151 ⚑ 9 holes. 3173 yds. Par 36. Greens fee: $9 ☞ Facilities: Driving range, putting green, golf carts, pull carts, rental clubs.

Po'ipū Bay Golf Course. Po'ipū Bay has been called the Pebble Beach of Hawai'i, and the comparison is apt. Like Pebble Beach, Po'ipū is a links course built on headlands, not true links land. And as at Monterey Bay, there's wildlife galore—except that the animals are not quite as intrusive to play. It's not unusual for golfers to see monk seals sunning on the beach below, sea turtles bobbing outside the shore break, and humpback whales leaping offshore. From 1994 to 2006, the course (designed by Robert Trent Jones Jr.) hosted the annual PGA Grand Slam of Golf. That means Tiger was a frequent visitor—and winner—here. Call ahead to take advantage of varying prices for tee times. ⊠ 2250 Ainako St., Kōloa ☏ 808/742–8711 ⊕ www.poipubaygolf.com ⚑ 18 holes. 6612 yds. Par 72. Greens fee: $145 to $240 ☞ Facilities: Driving range, putting green, rental clubs, golf carts, golf academy/lessons, restaurant, bar.

Fodor's Choice **Princeville Resort.** Robert Trent Jones Jr. built two memorable courses
★ overlooking Hanalei Bay, the 27-hole Princeville Makai Course (1971) and the 18-hole Prince Course (1990). The Makai Course underwent extensive renovations in 2009, including new turf throughout, reshaped greens and bunkers, refurbished cart paths and comfort stations, and the creation of an extensive practice facility. The Prince, which was closed for renovations at this writing, is certifiably rated Hawai'i's second toughest (behind O'ahu's Ko'olau). This is jungle golf, with holes running through dense forest and over tangled ravines, out onto headlands for breathtaking ocean views, then back into the jungle. The course was expected to reopen in October 2011; visit the Web site for updates. **Makai Golf Course:** ⊠ 4080 Lei O Papa Rd., Princeville ☏ 808/826–3580 ⊕ www.princeville.com ⚑ 27 holes. 6886 yds. Par 72. Greens fee: $210 ☞ Facilities: Driving range, putting green, rental clubs, golf carts, pro shop, golf academy/lessons, snack bar. **Prince Golf Course:** ⊠ 5-3900 Kūhiō Hwy., Princeville ☏ 808/826–5001 ⊕ www.princeville.com ⚑ 18 holes. 6960 yds. Par 72. Greens fee: $125 to $200 ☞ Facilities: Driving range, putting green, rental clubs, golf carts, pro shop, golf academy/lessons, restaurant, bar.

Wailua Municipal Golf Course. Voted by Golf Digest as one of Hawaii's 15-best golf courses, this seaside course was first built as a 9-hole golf course in the 1930s. The second 9 holes were added in 1961. Course designer Toyo Shirai created a course that is fun but not punishing. Not only is this an affordable game with minimal water hazards, but it is challenging enough to have been chosen to host three USGA Amateur Public Links Championships. The trade winds blow steadily on the East Side of the island and make the game all the more challenging. An ocean view and affordability make this one of the most popular courses on the island. Tee times are accepted up to seven days in advance. ⊠ 5350 Kūhiō Hwy., five mins north of airport, Līhu'e ☏ 808/241–6666 ⚑ 18 holes. 6585 yds. Par 72. Greens fee: $48 weekdays, $60 weekends. Half price after 3 pm. Cart rental: $18. Cash or traveler's checks only. ☞ Facilities: Driving range, rental clubs, golf carts, pro shop, lessons, snack bar.

HIKING

The best way to experience the *'aina*—the land—on Kaua'i is to step off the beach and hike into the remote interior. You can find waterfalls so tall you'll strain your neck looking, pools of crystal-cool water for swimming, tropical forests teeming with plant life, and ocean vistas that will make you wish you could stay forever. ■TIP➔ For your safety wear sturdy shoes—preferably water-resistant ones. Keep in mind that the island rock is lava, not granite. Even experienced hikers have gone missing, most likely as a result of crumbling or dislodged rock and fern-hidden crevices. All hiking trails on Kaua'i are free, so far. There's a development plan in the works that will turn the Waimea Canyon and Kōke'e state parks into admission-charging destinations. Whatever it may be, it will be worth it.

Kalalau Trail. Of all the hikes on the island, Kalalau Trail is by far the most famous and in many regards the most strenuous. A moderate hiker can handle the 2-mi trek to Hanakapi'ai Beach, and for the seasoned outdoorsman, the additional 2 mi up to the falls is manageable. But be prepared to rock-hop along a creek and ford waters that can get waist high during the rain. Round-trip to Hanakapi'ai Falls is 8 mi. This steep and often muddy trail is best approached with a walking stick. The narrow trail will deliver one startling ocean view after another along a path that is alternately shady and sunny. Wear hiking shoes or sandals, and bring drinking water since the creeks on the trail are not potable. Plenty of food is always encouraged on a strenuous hike such as this one. If your plan is to venture the full 11 mi into Kalalau, you need to acquire a camping permit. ✛ *Drive north past Hanalei to end of road. Trailhead is directly across from Ke'e Beach.*

Māhā'ulepū Heritage Trail. This trail offers the novice hiker an accessible way to appreciate the rugged southern coast of Kaua'i. A cross-country course wends its way along the water, high above the ocean, through a lava field and past a sacred *heiau* (stone structure). Walk all the way to Māhā'ulepū, 2 mi north for a two-hour round-trip. ✛ *Drive north on Po'ipū Rd., turn right at Po'ipū Bay Golf Course sign. The street name is Ainako, but the sign is hard to see. Drive down to beach and park in lot* ⊕ *www.hikemahaulepu.org.*

Sleeping Giant Trail. An easy and easily accessible trail practically in the heart of Kapa'a, the Sleeping Giant Trail—or simply Sleeping Giant—gains 1,000 feet over 2 mi. We prefer an early-morning—say, sunrise—hike, with sparkling blue-water vistas, up the east-side trailhead. At the top you can see a grassy grove with a picnic table. Experienced hikers may want to go a step farther, all the way to the giant's nose and chin. From here there are 360-degree views of the island. ⊠ *Haleilio Rd.* ✛ *In Wailua, turn mauka off Rte. 56 onto Haleilio Rd.; proceed 1 mi to small parking area on right.*

Waimea Canyon and Kōke'e State Parks. This park contains a 50-mi network of hiking trails of varying difficulty that take you through acres of native forests, across the highest-elevation swamp in the world, to the river at the base of the canyon, and onto pinnacles of land sticking their necks out over Nāpali Coast. All hikers should register at Kōke'e

Natural History Museum, where you can find trail maps, current trail information, and specific directions.

All mileage mentioned below is one-way.

The **Kukui Trail** descends 2½ mi and 2,200 feet into Waimea Canyon to the edge of the Waimea River—it's a steep climb. The **Awa'awapuhi Trail,** with 1,600 feet of elevation gains and losses over 3¼ mi, feels more gentle than the Kukui Trail, but it offers its own huffing-and-puffing sections in its descent along a spiny ridge to a perch overlooking the ocean.

The 3½-mi **Alaka'i Swamp Trail** is accessed via the **Pihea Trail** or a four-wheel-drive road. There's one strenuous valley section, but otherwise it's a pretty level trail—once you access it. This trail is a bird-watcher's delight and includes a painterly view of Wainiha and Hanalei valleys at the trail's end. The trail traverses the purported highest-elevation swamp in the world on a boardwalk so as not to disturb the fragile plant- and wildlife.

The **Canyon Trail** offers much in its short trek: spectacular vistas of the canyon and the only dependable waterfall in Waimea Canyon. The easy 2-mi hike can be cut in half if you have a four-wheel-drive vehicle. If you were outfitted with a headlamp, this would be a great hike at sunset as the sun's light sets the canyon walls ablaze in color. ✉ *Kōke'e Natural History Museum: Kōke'e Rd., Rte. 550* ☎ *808/335–9975 for trail conditions.*

EQUIPMENT AND TOURS

Fodor's Choice
★

Kaua'i Nature Tours. Father and son scientists started this hiking tour business. As such, their emphasis is on education and the environment. If you're interested in flora, fauna, volcanology, geology, oceanography, and the like, this is the company for you. They offer daylong hikes along coastal areas, beaches, and in the mountains. Hikes range from easy to strenuous and rates range from $110 to $140. Transportation is often provided from hotel. ✉ *Meets at designated spots around island* ☎ *808/742–8305 or 888/233–8365* ⊕ *www.kauainaturetours.com.*

HORSEBACK RIDING

Most of the horseback riding tours on Kaua'i are primarily walking tours with very little trotting and no cantering or galloping, so no experience is required. Zip. Zilch. Nada. If you're interested, most of the stables offer private lessons. The most popular tours are the ones including a picnic lunch by the water. Your only dilemma may be deciding what kind of water you want—waterfalls or ocean. You may want to make your decision based on where you're staying. The "waterfall picnic" tours are on the wetter North Shore, and the "beach picnic" tours take place on the South Shore.

CJM Country Stables. Just past the Hyatt in Po'ipū, CJM Stables offers a three-hour picnic ride with noshing on the beach, as well as their more popular two-hour trail ride. The landscape here is rugged and beautiful, featuring sand dunes and limestone bluffs. CJM sponsors seasonal rodeo events that are free and open to the public. Prices range from

Continued on page 546

NĀPALI COAST: EMERALD QUEEN OF KAUA'I

If you're coming to Kaua'i, Nāpali ("cliffs" in Hawaiian) is a major must-see. More than 5 million years old, these sea cliffs rise thousands of feet above the Pacific, and every shade of green is represented in the vegetation that blankets their lush peaks and folds. At their base, there are caves, secluded beaches, and waterfalls to explore.

The big question is how to explore this gorgeous stretch of coastline. You can't drive to it, through it, or around it. You can't see Nāpali from a scenic lookout. You can't even take a mule ride to it. The only way to experience its magic is from the sky, the ocean, or the trail.

FROM THE SKY

If you've booked a helicopter tour of Nāpali, you might start wondering what you've gotten yourself into on the way to the airport. Will it feel like being on a small airplane? Will there be turbulence? Will it be worth all the money you just plunked down?

Your concerns will be assuaged on the helipad, once you see the faces of those who have just returned from their journey: Everyone looks totally blissed out. And now it's your turn.

Climb on board, strap on your headphones, and the next thing you know the helicopter gently lifts up, hovers for a moment, and floats away like a spider on the wind—no roaring engines, no rumbling down a runway. If you've chosen a flight with music, you'll feel as if you're inside your very own IMAX movie.

Pinch yourself if you must, because this is the real thing. Your pilot shares history, legend, and lore. If you miss something, speak up: pilots love to show off their island knowledge. You may snap a few pictures (not too many or you'll miss the eyes-on experience!), nudge a friend or spouse, and point at a whale breeching in the ocean, but mostly you stare, mouth agape. There is simply no other way to take in the immensity and greatness of Nāpali but from the air.

Helicopter flight over Nāpali Coast

GOOD TO KNOW	WHAT YOU MIGHT SEE
Helicopter companies depart from the north, east, and west side of the island. Most are based in Līhue, near the airport.	■ Nu'alolo Kai (an ancient Hawaiian fishing village) with its fringed reef
If you want more adventure—and air—choose one of the helicopter companies that flies with the doors off.	■ The 300-foot Hanakāpī'ai Falls
Some companies offer flights without music. Know the experience you want ahead of time. Some even sell a DVD of your flight, so you don't have to worry about taking pictures.	■ A massive sea arch formed in the rock by erosion
Wintertime rain grounds some flights; plan your trip early in your stay in case the flight gets rescheduled.	■ The 11-mile Kalalau Trail threading its way along the coast

IS THIS FOR ME?

Taking a helicopter trip is the most expensive way to see Nāpali—as much as $280 for an hour-long tour.

Claustrophobic? Choose a boat tour or hike. It's a tight squeeze in the helicopter, especially in one of the middle seats.

Short on time? Taking a helicopter tour is a great way to see the island.

■ The amazing striations of a'a and pāhoehoe lava flows that helped push Kaua'i above the sea

FROM THE OCEAN

Nāpali from the ocean is two treats in one: spend a good part of the day on (or in) the water, and gaze up at majestic green sea cliffs rising thousands of feet above your head.

There are three ways to see it: a mellow pleasure-cruise catamaran allows you to kick back and sip a mai tai; an adventurous raft (Zodiac) tour will take you inside sea caves under waterfalls, and give you the option of snorkeling; and a daylong outing in a kayak is a real workout, but then you can say you paddled 16 miles of coastline.

Any way you travel, you'll breathe ocean air, feel spray on your face, and see pods of spinner dolphins, green sea turtles, flying fish, and, if you're lucky, a rare Hawaiian monk seal.

Nāpali stretches from Kē'ē Beach in the north to Polihale beach on the West Side. If your departure point is Kē'ē, you are already headed toward the lush Hanakāpī'ai Valley. Within a few minutes, you'll see caves and waterfalls galore. About halfway down the coast just after the Kalalau Trail ends, you'll come to an immense arch—formed where the sea eroded the less dense basaltic rock—and a thundering 50-foot waterfall. And as the island curves near Nu'alolo State Park, you'll begin to notice less vegetation and more rocky outcroppings.

(left and top right) Kayaking on Nāpali Coast
(bottom right) Dolphin on Nāpali Coast

5

GOOD TO KNOW

If you want to snorkel, choose a morning rather than an afternoon tour—preferably during a summer visit—when seas are calmer.

If you're on a budget, choose a non-snorkeling tour.

If you want to see whales, take any tour, but be sure to plan your vacation for December through March.

If you're staying on the North Shore or East Side, embark from the North Shore. If you're staying on the South Shore, it might not be worth your time to drive to the north, so head to the West Side.

IS THIS FOR ME?

Boat tours are several hours long, so if you have only a short time on Kaua'i, a helicopter tour is a better alternative.

Even on a small boat, you won't get the individual attention and exclusivity of a helicopter tour.

Prone to seasickness? A large boat can be surprisingly rocky, so be prepared.

WHAT YOU MIGHT SEE

■ Hawai'i's state fish—the humuhumunukunukuapuaa—otherwise known as the reef triggerfish

■ Waiahuakua Sea Cave, with a waterfall coming through its roof

■ Tons of marine life, including dolphins, green sea turtles, flying fish, and humpback whales, especially in February and March

■ Waterfalls—especially if your trip is after a heavy rain

FROM THE TRAIL

If you want to be one with Nāpali—feeling the soft red earth beneath your feet, picnicking on the beaches, and touching the lush vegetation—hiking the Kalalau Trail is the way to do it.

Most people hike only the first 2 miles of the 11-mile trail and turn around at Hanakāpī'ai. This 4-mile round-trip hike takes three to four hours. It starts at sea level and doesn't waste any time gaining elevation. (Take heart—the uphill lasts only a mile and tops out at 400 feet; then it's downhill all the way.) At the half-mile point, the trail curves west and the folds of Nāpali Coast unfurl.

Along the way you might share the trail with feral goats and wild pigs. Some of the vegetation is native; much is introduced.

After the 1-mile mark the trail begins its drop into Hanakāpī'ai. You'll pass a couple of streams of water trickling across the trail, and maybe some banana, ginger, the native uluhe fern, and the Hawaiian ti plant. Finally the trail swings around the eastern ridge of Hanakāpī'ai for your first glimpse of the valley and then switchbacks down the mountain. You'll have to boulder-hop across the stream to reach the beach. If you like, you can take a 4-mile, round-trip fairly strenuous side trip from this point to the gorgeous Hanakāpī'ai Falls.

(left) Awaawapuhi mountain biker on razor-edge ridge
(top right) Feral goats in Kalalau Valley
(bottom right) Nāpali Coast

GOOD TO KNOW

Wear comfortable, amphibious shoes. Unless your feet require extra support, wear a self-bailing sort of shoe (for stream crossings) that doesn't mind mud. Don't wear heavy, waterproof hiking boots.

During winter the trail is often muddy, so be extra careful; sometimes it's completely inaccessible.

Don't hike after heavy rain—flash floods are common.

If you plan to hike the entire 11-mile trail (most people do the shorter hike described at left) you'll need a permit to go past Hanakāpī'ai.

IS THIS FOR ME?

Of all the ways to see Nāpali (with the exception of kayaking the coast), this is the most active. You need to be in decent shape to hit the trail.

If you're vacationing in winter, this hike might not be an option due to flooding—whereas you can take a helicopter or boat trip year-round.

WHAT YOU MIGHT SEE

- Big dramatic surf right below your feet

- Amazing vistas of the cool blue Pacific

- The spectacular Hanakāpī'ai Falls; if you have a permit don't miss Hanakoa Falls, less than ½ mile off the trail

- Wildlife, including goats and pigs

- Zany-looking ōhi'a trees, with aerial roots and long, skinny serrated leaves known as hala. Early Hawaiians used them to make mats, baskets, and canoe sails.

$98 to $125. ⊠ *Po'ipū Rd.* ✛ *1½ mi from Grand Hyatt Kaua'i Kōloa* ☎ *808/742–6096* ⊕ *www.cjmstables.com.*

Esprit de Corps. If you ride, this is the company for you. Esprit de Corps has three- to eight-hour rides and allows some trotting and cantering based on the rider's experience and comfort with the horse. What's also nice is the maximum group size: six. Weddings on horseback can be arranged (in fact, Dale, the owner, is a wedding officiant, specializing in Jewish and interfaith marriages), and custom rides for less experienced and younger riders (as young as two) are available, as well as private lessons (starting at age six). Rates range from $130 to $390. ⊠ *End of Kualapa Pl., Kapa'a* ☎ *808/822–4688* ⊕ *www.kauaihorses.com.*

Fodor's Choice

★

Princeville Ranch Stables. A longtime *kama'āina* (resident) family operates Princeville Ranch. They originated the waterfall picnic tours, which run three or four hours and include a short but steep hike down to Kalihi-wai Falls, a dramatic three-tier waterfall, for swimming and picnicking. Princeville also has shorter, straight riding tours and private rides, and if they're moving cattle while you're visiting, you can sign up for a cattle drive. Prices range from $125 up to $245 for some private tours. ⊠ *Kūhiō Hwy.* ✛ *West of Princeville Airport mauka between mile markers 27 and 28, Princeville* ☎ *808/826–6777* ⊕ *www.princevilleranch.com.*

MOUNTAIN TUBING

Ⓢ **Kaua'i Backcountry Adventures.** Very popular with all ages, this laid-back adventure can book up two weeks in advance in busy summer months. Here's how it works: you recline in an inner tube and float down fern-lined irrigation ditches that were built more than a century ago—the engineering is impressive—to divert water from Mt. Wai'ale'ale to sugar and pineapple fields around the island. Simple as that. They'll even give you a headlamp so you can see as you float through five covered tunnels. The scenery from the island's interior at the base of Mt. Wai'ale'ale on Līhu'e Plantation land is superb. Ages five and up are welcome. The tour takes about three hours and includes a picnic lunch and a swim in a swimming hole. You'll definitely want to pack water-friendly shoes (or rent some from the outfitter), sunscreen, a hat, bug repellent, and a beach towel. Tours cost $100 per person and are offered morning and afternoon, daily. ⊠ *3-4131 Kūhiō Hwy.* ✛ *Across from gas station, Hanamā'ulu* ☎ *808/245–2506 or 888/270–0555* ⊕ *www. kauaibackcountry.com.*

SKYDIVING

Skydive Kauai. Ten thousand feet over Kaua'i and falling at a rate of 120 mph is probably as thrilling as it gets while airborne. First, there's the 25-minute plane ride to altitude in a Cessna 182, then the exhilaration of the first step into sky, the sensation of sailing weightless in the air over Kaua'i, and finally the peaceful buoyancy beneath the canopy of your parachute. A tandem free-fall rates among the most unforgettable experiences of a lifetime. Wed that to the aerial view over Kaua'i

LEPTOSPIROSIS

The sparkling waters of those babbling brooks trickling around the island can be life threatening, and we're not talking about the dangers of drowning, although they, too, exist. Leptospirosis is a bacterial disease that is transmitted from animals to humans. It can survive for long periods of time in freshwater and mud contaminated by the urine of infected animals, such as mice, rats, and goats. The bacteria enter the body through the eyes, ears, nose, mouth, and broken skin. To avoid infection, do not drink untreated water from the island's streams; do not wade in waters above the chest or submerge skin with cuts and abrasions in island streams or rivers. Symptoms are often mild and resemble the flu—fever, diarrhea, chills, nausea, headache, vomiting, and body pains—and may occur two to 20 days after exposure. If you think you have these symptoms, see a doctor right away.

and you've got a winning marriage. Tandem dive: $229. ⊠ *Salt Pond Beach Park, Port Allen Airport* ☎ *808/335–5859* ⊕ *skydivekauai.com.*

TENNIS

If you're interested in booking some court time on Kaua'i, there are public tennis courts in Waimea, Kekaha, Hanapēpē, Kōloa, Kalaheo, Līhu'e, Wailua Homesteads, Wailua Houselots, and Kapa'a New Park. For specific directions or more information, call the **County of Kaua'i Parks and Recreation Office** (☎ *808/241–4463*).

Many hotels and resorts have tennis courts on property; even if you're not staying there, you can still rent court time. Rates range from $10 to $15 per person per hour. On the South Shore, try the **Grand Hyatt Kaua'i** (☎ *808/742–1234*) and **Kiahuna Swim and Tennis Club** (☎ *808/742–9533*). On the North Shore try the **Hanalei Bay Resort** (☎ *808/826–6522 Ext. 8225*).

ZIPLINE TOURS

The latest adventure on Kaua'i is "zipping" or "ziplining." It's so new that the vernacular is still catching up with it, but regardless of what you call it, chances are you'll scream like a rock-star fan while trying it. Strap on a harness, clip onto a cable running from one side of a river or valley to the other, and zip across. The step off is the scariest part. ■ TIP→ Pack knee-length shorts or pants, athletic shoes, and courage for this adventure.

Fodor'sChoice   **Just Live.** When Nichol Baier and Julie Lester started Just Live in 2003,
★   their market was exclusively school-age children, but soon they added visitor tours. Experiential education through adventure is how they describe it. Whatever you call it, sailing 70 feet above the ground for 3½ hours will take your vacation to another level. This is the only treetop zipline in the state where your feet never touch ground once you're in the air: Seven zips and four canopy bridges make the Tree Top Tour ($120) their most popular one. For the heroic at heart, there's

the Zipline Eco Adventure ($125), which includes three ziplines, two canopy bridges, a climbing wall, a 100-foot rappelling tower, and a "Monster Swing." If you're short on time—or courage—you can opt for the Wikiwiki Zipline Tour ($79), which includes three ziplines and two canopy bridges in under two hours. They still incorporate team building in the visitor tours, although their primary focus remains community programming. Enjoy knowing that money spent here serves Kaua'i's children. ⊠ *Kōloa* ☎ *808/482–1295* ⊕ *www.justlive.org.*

Princeville Ranch Adventures. The North Shore's answer to ziplining is a nine-zipline course with a bit of hiking, and suspension bridge crossing thrown in for a half-day adventure. The 4½-hour Zip N' Dip tour includes lunch and swimming at a waterfall pool, while the Zip Express whizzes you through the entire course in three hours. Both excursions conclude with a 1,200-foot tandem zip across a valley. Guides are energetic and fun and can offer good dining and nightlife recommendations. This is as close as it gets to flying; just watch out for the albatross. Prices start at $125 for the Zip Express and $145 for the Zip N' Dip. ⊠ *West of Princeville Airport on Rte. 56, between mile markers 27 and 28, Princeville* ☎ *808/826–7669 or 888/955–7669* ⊕ *www.adventureskauai.com.*

SHOPPING

There aren't a lot of shops and spas on Kaua'i, but what you will find here are a handful of places very much worth checking out for the quality of their selection of items sold and services rendered. Many shops now make an effort to sell as many locally made products as possible. When buying an item, ask where it was made, or even who made it. Often you will find that a product handcrafted on the island may not be that much more expensive than a similar product made overseas. You can also look for the purple "Kaua'i Made" sticker many merchants display.

Along with one major shopping mall, a few shopping centers, and a growing number of big-box retailers, Kaua'i has some delightful mom-and-pop shops and specialty boutiques with lots of character.

The Garden Island also has a large and talented community of artisans and fine artists, with galleries all around the island showcasing their creations. You can find many island-made arts and crafts in the small shops, and it's worthwhile to stop at crafts fairs and outdoor markets to look for bargains and mingle with island residents.

If you're looking for a special memento of your trip that is unique to Kaua'i County, check out the distinctive Ni'ihau shell lei. The tiny shells are collected from beaches on Kaua'i and Ni'ihau, pierced, and strung into beautiful necklaces, chokers, and earrings. It's a time-consuming and exacting craft, and these items are much in demand, so don't be taken aback by the high price tags. Those made by Ni'ihau residents will have certificates of authenticity and are worth collecting. You often can find cheaper versions made by non-Hawaiians at crafts fairs.

Stores are typically open daily from 9 or 10 am to 5 pm, although some stay open until 9 pm, especially those near resorts. Don't be surprised if the posted hours don't match the actual hours of operation at the smaller shops, where owners may be fairly casual about keeping to a regular schedule.

THE NORTH SHORE

The North Shore has three main shopping areas, all conveniently located in towns off the highway. Hanalei has two shopping centers directly across from each other, which offer more than you would expect in a remote, relaxed town. Princeville Shopping Center is a bustling little mix of businesses, necessities, and some unique shops, often pricey. Kīlauea is a bit more sprawled out and offers a charming, laid-back shopping scene with a neighborhood feel.

SHOPPING CENTERS

Ching Young Village. Despite a face-lift, this popular shopping center looks a bit worn, but that doesn't deter business. Hanalei's only grocery store, **Big Save,** is here along with a number of other shops useful to locals and visitors. These include **Hanalei Music's Strings and Things,** where you can buy Hawaiian sheet music, compact discs, handmade instruments, and knitting supplies, as well as rent DVDs; **Village Variety,** which has a bit of everything; **Savage Pearls,** a fine jewelry store that specializes in Tahitian pearls and gifts; **Hot Rocket,** a teen-oriented surf-wear shop; **Hanalei Surf Company Back Door,** for beachwear and gear; **Hula Moon Gifts of Kaua'i,** which offers an assortment of island-themed treasures; **Divine Planet,** for exotic clothing, jewelry, and home furnishings (also in Kapa'a); **Village Snack & Bakery,** which sells excellent chocolate cake and coconut-cream pie; and several restaurants. A few steps away are **Evolve Love Artists Gallery,** a good place to find high-quality work by local artisans, and **On the Road to Hanalei,** a neat boutique with gifts, clothing, jewelry, housewares, and collectibles from Indonesia. ⊠ *5-5190 Kūhiō Hwy. ⊹ Makai, after mile marker 2, Hanalei* ☎ *808/826–7222* ⊕ *www.chingyoungvillage.com.*

Hanalei Center. Listed on the Historic Register, the old Hanalei school has been refurbished and rented out to boutiques and restaurants. You can dig through '40s and '50s vintage memorabilia in the **Yellow Fish Trading Company,** find Polynesian artifacts at **Hawa'iki,** or search for that unusual gift at **Sand People.** Buy beach gear at the classic **Hanalei Surf Company and Hanalei Paddler,** as well as island wear at **Hula Beach Clothing,** or women's clothing at **Tropical Tantrum.** Find a range of fine jewelry and paper art jewelry from Uganda at **Jewel of Paradise.** For the kids, pick up something at **Rainbow Ducks Toys & Clothing.** For a little exercise, catch a class at the **Yoga Hanalei** studio in the two-story modern addition to the center, which also houses **Harvest Market** (formerly Papaya's), a well-stocked health-food store. ⊠ *5-5161 Kūhiō Hwy., ⊹ Mauka, after mile marker 2, Hanalei* ☎ *808/826–7677.*

Princeville Shopping Center. The big draws at this small center are **Foodland,** a full-service grocery store, and **Island Ace Hardware.** This is the last stop for gas and banking on the North Shore. You'll also find five restaurants and live music on Friday afternoon, a sandal shop, a mail service center, a post office, an ice-cream shop, a kiosk with a good collection of Hawaiian and contemporary artists called **Paradise Music,** and **Magic Dragon Toy & Art Supply Co.,** a tiny but interesting toy-and-hobby shop. ⊠ *5-4280 Kūhiō Hwy.* ⊹ *Makai, mile marker 28, Princeville* ☎ *808/826–9497.*

SHOPS

Kong Lung Co. Sometimes called the Gump's of Kaua'i, this gift store sells elegant clothing, exotic glassware, ethnic books, gifts, and artwork—all very lovely and expensive. The shop is housed in a beautiful 1892 stone structure right in the heart of Kīlauea. It's the showpiece of the pretty little Kong Lung Center, whose shops feature distinctive jewelry, handmade soaps and candles, hammocks, plants, excellent pizza and baked goods, artwork, and consignment clothing, among other items. Next door is the farmers' market, a good place to buy natural and gourmet foods, wines, and sandwiches. ⊠ *2484 Keneke St., Kīlauea* ☎ *808/828–1822.*

THE EAST SIDE

KAPA'A AND WAILUA

Kapa'a is the most heavily populated area on Kaua'i, so it's not surprising that it has the most diverse shopping opportunities on the island. Unlike the North Shore's retail scene, shops here are not neatly situated in centers; they are spread out along a long stretch of road, with many local retail gems tucked away that you may not find if you're in a rush.

SHOPPING CENTERS

Coconut Marketplace. This visitor-oriented complex is on the busy Coconut Coast near resort hotels and condominiums. A variety of shops sell everything from snacks and slippers (as locals call flip-flop sandals) to scrimshaw. There are also restaurants open from breakfast to evening and a free Wednesday evening Polynesian show at 5 and Saturday at noon. The marketplace parking lot now also hosts a farmers' market Tuesdays from 9 am to 1 pm. ⊠ *4-484 Kūhiō Hwy., Kapa'a* ☎ *808/245–4700.*

Kaua'i Village Shopping Center. The buildings of this Kapa'a shopping village are in the style of a 19th-century plantation town. **ABC Discount Store** sells sundries; **Safeway** carries groceries and alcoholic beverages; **Longs Drugs** has a pharmacy, health and beauty products, and a good selection of Hawaiian merchandise; **Papaya's** has health foods. There's also a **Vitamin World** and a **UPS store.** Other shops sell jewelry, art, gift items, children's clothes and toys. Restaurants include Chinese, vegetarian, and Vietnamese options, and there's also a **Starbucks** and an ice-cream parlor. ⊠ *4-831 Kūhiō Hwy., Kapa'a* ☎ *808/822–3777.*

Kinipopo Shopping Village. Kinipopo is a tiny little center on Kūhiō Highway. **Korean Barbeque** fronts the highway, as does **Goldsmith's Kaua'i Gallery,** which sells handcrafted Hawaiian-style gold jewelry. **Monaco's** has authentic Mexican food, and **Icing on the Cake** is a new pastry shop specializing in cakes. ⊠ *4-356 Kūhiō Hwy., Kapa'a.*

Waipouli Town Center. Foodland is the focus of this small retail plaza, one of three shopping centers anchored by grocery stores in Kapaʻa. You can also find a **Blockbuster** video outlet, **McDonald's, Pizza Hut, Fun Factory** video arcade, and **The Coffee Bean & Tea Leaf,** along with a local-style restaurant. ⊠ *4-901 Kūhiō Hwy., Kapaʻa.*

SHOPS AND GALLERIES

★ **Bambulei.** Two 1930s-style plantation homes have been transformed into a boutique featuring vintage and contemporary clothing, antiques, jewelry, and accessories. Also featured are rare Hawaiian collectibles and furniture. ⊠ *4-369 Kūhiō Hwy., Wailua* ☎ *808/823–8641.*

Deja Vu Surf Outlet. This mom-and-pop operation has a great assortment of surfwear and clothes for outdoor fanatics, including tank tops, visors, swimwear, and Kauaʻi-style T-shirts. Good deals can be found at sidewalk sales. ⊠ *4-1419 Kūhiō Hwy., Kapaʻa* ☎ *808/822–4401.*

Jim Saylor Jewelers. Jim Saylor has been designing beautiful keepsakes for over 30 years on Kauaʻi. Gems from around the world, including black pearls and diamonds, appear in his unusual settings. ⊠ *1318 Kūhiō Hwy., Kapaʻa* ☎ *808/822–3591.*

Kauaʻi Products Fair. Open daily, this outdoor market features fresh produce, tropical plants and flowers, aloha wear, jewelry, gifts, a Thai food eatery, and shave ice stand. ⊠ *Outside on north side of Kapaʻa* ✚ *Across from Otsuka's Furniture* ☎ *808/246–0988.*

Kela's Glass Gallery. The colorful vases, bowls, and other fragile items sold in this distinctive gallery are definitely worth viewing if you appreciate quality handmade glass art. It's expensive, but if something catches your eye, they'll happily pack it for safe transport home. ⊠ *4-1354 Kūhiō Hwy., Kapaʻa* ☎ *808/822–4527.*

Vicky's Fabric Shop. This small shop is packed full of tropical prints, silks, slinky rayons, soft cottons, and other fine fabrics. A variety of sewing patterns and notions are featured, making it a must-stop for any seamstress. If you're seeking something that's truly one-of-a-kind, check out the selection of purses, aloha wear, and other quality hand-sewn items. ⊠ *4-1326 Kūhiō Hwy., Kapaʻa* ☎ *808/822–1746.*

LĪHUʻE

Līhuʻe is the business area on Kauaʻi, as well as home to all the big-box stores and the only real mall. Do not mistake this town as lacking in rare finds, however. Līhuʻe is steeped in history and diversity while simultaneously welcoming new trends and establishments.

SHOPPING CENTERS

Kilohana Plantation. This 16,000-square-foot Tudor mansion contains art galleries, a jewelry store, and the new farm-to-table restaurant 22 North. The house itself is filled with antiques from its original owner and the restored outbuildings house a craft shop and a Hawaiian-style clothing shop. Train rides on a restored railroad are available, with knowledgeable guides reciting the history of sugar on Kauaʻi. The site is also now the home of Lūʻau Kālamakū (*see Entertainment*) and Kōloa Rum Company. ⊠ *3-2087 Kaumualiʻi Hwy.* ✚ *1 mi west of Līhuʻe* ☎ *808/245–5608.*

Kukui Grove Center. This is Kaua'i's only true mall. Besides **Sears Roebuck** and **Kmart**, anchor tenants are **Longs Drugs, Macy's,** and **Times Supermarket. Borders Books & Music,** with its **Seattle's Best Coffee** shop, is one of the island's most popular stores. The mall's stores offer women's clothing, surf wear, art, toys, athletic shoes, jewelry, and locally made crafts. Restaurants range from fast food and sandwiches to Mexican and Korean. The center stage often has entertainment. ⊠ *3-2600 Kaumuali'i Hwy.* ✛ *West of Līhu'e* ☎ *808/245–7784.*

SHOPS AND GALLERIES

Hilo Hattie, The Store of Hawai'i, Fashion Factory. This is the big name in aloha wear for tourists throughout the Islands. You can visit the only store on Kaua'i, a mile from Līhu'e Airport, to pick up cool, comfortable aloha shirts and mu'umu'u in bright floral prints, as well as other souvenirs. While here, check out the line of Hawai'i-inspired home furnishings. ⊠ *3252 Kūhiō Hwy., Līhu'e* ☎ *808/245–3404* ⊕ *www. hilohattie.com.*

Fodor's Choice
★　**Kapaia Stitchery.** Hawaiian quilts made by hand and machine, a beautiful selection of fabrics, quilting kits, and fabric arts fill this cute little red plantation-style structure. There are also many locally made gifts for sale. The staff is friendly and helpful, even though a steady stream of customers keeps them busy. ⊠ *3-3551 Kūhiō Hwy., ½ mi north of Līhu'e* ☎ *808/245–2281.*

Kaua'i Fruit and Flower Company. At this shop near Līhu'e and five minutes away from the airport, you can buy fresh Hawai'i-grown sugarloaf pineapple, sugarcane, ginger, tropical flowers, coconuts, local jams, jellies, and honey, plus Kaua'i-grown papayas, bananas, and mangoes. The fruit has been inspected and approved for shipment to take home out of Hawai'i; airlines do not charge for the fruit carry-ons. ⊠ *3-4684 Kūhiō Hwy., Kapa'a* ☎ *808/245–1814.*

★　**Kaua'i Museum.** The gift shop at the museum sells some fascinating books, maps, and prints, as well as lovely feather lei hatbands, Ni'ihau shell jewelry, handwoven *lau hala* hats, and koa wood bowls. Also featured are tapa cloth, authentic *tikis* (hand-carved wooden figurines), and other good-quality local crafts at reasonable prices. ⊠ *4428 Rice St., Līhu'e* ☎ *808/246–2470.*

Kaua'i Products Store. Seed lei, finely crafted koa-wood boxes, tropical-flower earrings, and Ni'ihau leis are on hand in this boutique. Ninety percent of the products are handcrafted on Kaua'i. Other gift options include a collection of local Hawaiian music CDs, koa-oil lamps, pottery, sculpture, paintings, and homemade fudge. ⊠ *Kukui Grove Center, 3-2600 Kaumuali'i Hwy., Līhu'e* ☎ *808/246–6753.*

THE SOUTH SHORE AND WEST SIDE

The South Shore, like the North Shore, has convenient shopping clusters, including Po'ipu Shopping Village and the new Kukui'ula Shopping Village. There are many high-priced shops but some unique clothing and gift selections. By comparison, the West Side is years behind in development, offering charming, simple shops with authentic local flavor.

SHOPPING CENTERS

'Ele'ele Shopping Center. Kaua'i's West Side has a scattering of stores, including those at this no-frills strip-mall shopping center. It's a good place to rub elbows with local folk at **Big Save** grocery store or to grab a quick bite to eat at the casual **Grinds Cafe** or **Tois Thai Kitchen.** ⊠ *Rte. 50 near Hanapēpē, 'Ele'ele.*

Kukui'ula Shopping Village. This is the South Shore's newest shopping center, with shops, exclusive galleries, restaurants, and cafés. Check out the Kaua'i Culinary Market on Wednesday from 4 to 6, to see cooking demonstrations, listen to live Hawaiian music, and browse wares from local vendors. While the complex debuted in late 2009, at this writing 90 percent of its establishments were expected to be open by Summer 2011. This attractive open-air, plantation-style center is just beyond the roundabout as you enter Po'ipū. ⊠ *2829 Kalanikaumaka, Po'ipū* ☎ *808/742-0234* ⊕ *www.kukuiula.com* ⊙ *Daily 10–9.*

Po'ipū Shopping Village. Convenient to nearby hotels and condos on the South Shore, the two-dozen shops here sell resort wear, gifts, souvenirs, and art. The upscale **Black Pearl Kaua'i** and **Na Hoku** shops are particularly appealing jewelry stores. There's a couple of art galleries and several fun clothing stores, including **Bamboo Lace, Making Waves** and **Blue Ginger.** Also worth a visit are **Sand Kids** and **Whaler's General Store.** Restaurants include **Keoki's Paradise, Roy's, Po'ipū Tropical Burgers,** and **Puka Dog Hawaiian Style Hot Dogs,** along with **Papalani Gelato.** A Tahitian dance troupe performs in the open-air courtyard Tuesday and Thursday at 5 pm. ⊠ *2360 Kiahuna Plantation Dr., Po'ipū Beach* ☎ *808/742-2831.*

Waimea Canyon Plaza. As Kekaha's retail hub and the last stop for supplies before heading up to Waimea Canyon, this tiny, tidy complex of shops is surprisingly busy. Look for local foods, souvenirs, and island-made gifts for all ages. ⊠ *Kōke'e Rd. at Rte. 50, Kekaha.*

SHOPS AND GALLERIES

Kaua'i Coffee Visitor Center and Museum. Kaua'i produces more coffee than any other island in the state. The local product can be purchased from grocery stores or here at the source, where a sampling of the nearly one-dozen coffees is available. Be sure to try some of the estate-roasted varieties. ⊠ *870 Halawili Rd.* ⊹ *Off Rte. 50, west of Kalāheo* ☎ *808/335-0813 or 800/545-8605.*

Kaua'i Tropicals. You can have this company ship heliconia, anthuriums, ginger, and other tropicals in 5-foot-long boxes directly from its flower farm in Kalāheo. It accepts phone-in orders only. ⊠ *Kalāheo* ☎ *800/303-4385.*

Paradise Sportswear. This is the retail outlet of the folks who invented Kaua'i's popular "red dirt" shirts, which are dyed and printed with the characteristic local soil. Ask the salesperson to tell you the charming story behind these shirts. Sizes from infants up to 5X are available. ⊠ *4350 Waialo Rd., Port Allen* ☎ *808/335-5670.*

SPAS

Though most spas on Kaua'i are associated with resorts, none are restricted to guests only. And there's much by way of healing and wellness to be found on Kaua'i beyond the traditional spa—or even the day spa. More and more retreat facilities are offering what some would call alternative healing therapies. Others would say there's nothing alternative about them; you can decide for yourself.

Alexander Day Spa & Salon at the Kaua'i Marriott. This sister spa of Alexander Simson's Beverly Hills spa focuses on body care rather than exercise, so don't expect any fitness equipment or exercise classes. Tucked away in the back corner of the Marriott, the spa has the same ambience of stilted formality as the rest of the resort, but it is otherwise a sunny, pleasant facility. Massages are available in treatment rooms and on the beach, although the beach locale isn't as private as you might imagine. Wedding-day and custom spa packages can be arranged. ⊠ *Kaua'i Marriott Resort & Beach Club, 3610 Rice St. Suite 9A, Līhu'e* ☎ *808/246–4918* ⊕ *www.alexanderspa.com* ☞ *$65–$190 massage. Facilities: Hair salon, steam room. Services: Body treatments—including masks, scrubs, and wraps—facials, hair styling, makeup, manicures, massages, pedicures, waxing.*

Fodor's Choice
★ **ANARA Spa.** This luxurious facility is far and away the best on Kaua'i, setting a standard that no other spa has been able to meet. It has all the equipment and services you expect from a top resort spa, along with a pleasant, professional staff. Best of all, it has indoor and outdoor areas that capitalize on the tropical locale and balmy weather, further distinguishing it from the Marriott and Princeville spas. Its 46,500 square feet of space includes the new Garden Treatment Village, an open-air courtyard with private thatched-roof huts, each featuring a relaxation area, misters, and open-air shower in a tropical setting. Ancient Hawaiian remedies and local ingredients are featured in many of the treatments, such as a red-dirt clay wrap, coconut-mango facial, and a body brush scrub that polishes your skin with a mix of ground coffee, orange peel, and vanilla bean. The open-air lava-rock showers are wonderful, introducing many guests to the delightful island practice of showering outdoors. The spa, which includes a full-service salon, adjoins the Hyatt's legendary swimming pool. ⊠ *Hyatt Regency Kaua'i Resort and Spa, 1571 Po'ipū Rd., Po'ipū* ☎ *808/240–6440* ⊕ *www.anaraspa.com* ☞ *Massages start at $160. Facilities: Hair salon, outdoor hot tubs, sauna, steam room. Gym with: Cardiovascular machines, free weights, weight-training equipment. Services: Body scrubs and wraps, facials, manicures, massage, pedicures. Classes and programs: Aerobics, aquaerobics, body sculpting, fitness analysis, flexibility training, personal training, Pilates, step aerobics, weight training, yoga.*

Angeline's Mu'olaulani Wellness Center. It doesn't get more authentic than this. In the mid-1980s Aunty Angeline Locey opened her Anahola home to offer traditional Hawaiian healing practices. Now her son and granddaughter carry on the tradition. There's a two-hour treatment ($150) that starts with a steam, followed by a sea-salt-and-clay body scrub and a two-person massage. The real treat, however, is relaxing on Aunty's open-air garden deck. Hot-stone lomi is also available. Aunty's mission is to promote a healthy body image; as such, au naturel is the accepted way here, so if you're nudity-shy, this may not be the place for you. On second thought, Aunty would say it most definitely is; *Mu'olaulani* translates to "a place for young buds to bloom." ⊠ *Directions provided upon reservation, Anahola* ☎ *808/822–3235* ⊕ *www. angelineslomikauai.com* ☞ *Facilities: Steam room. Services: Body scrubs and massage.*

Fodor's Choice
★

Halele'a Spa. This superb spa at The St. Regis Princeville Resort is indeed a House of Joy, as its Hawaiian name translates. Opened in 2009, this 11,000-square-foot space transports users to a place of utter tranquillity. The spa's 12 luxurious treatment rooms afford a subdued indoor setting only outmatched by the professional service. Take advantage of the dedicated couples' room and enjoy a taro butter pohaku hot stone massage. Follow that with a few hours sipping tea in the relaxation lounge, sweating in the sauna, and rinsing in an overhead rain shower. There is a qualified wellness consultant and spa programs are inspired by Native Hawaiian healing rituals. You can find health, beauty, and inner peace at this spa, but expect to pay for it. ⊠ *The St. Regis Princeville Resort, 5520 Ka Haku Rd., Princeville* ☎ *877/787–3447 or 808/826–9644* ⊕ *www.stregisprinceville.com* ☞ *Massage $170–$245. Services: Body scrubs and wraps, facials, massage, waxing.*

Hanalei Day Spa. As you travel beyond tony Princeville, life slows down. The single-lane bridges may be one reason. Another is the Hanalei Day Spa (opened in 2004), an open-air, thatched-roof, Hawaiian-style hut nestled just off the beach on the grounds of Hanalei Colony Resort in Hā'ena. Though this no-frills day spa offers facials, waxing, wraps, scrubs, and the like, its specialty is massage: Ayurveda, Zen Shiatsu, Swedish, and even a baby massage (and lesson for Mom, to boot). Owner Darci Frankel teaches yoga, a discipline she started as a young child living in south Florida. That practice led her to start the Ayurveda Center of Hawaii, which operates out of the spa and offers an ancient Indian cleansing and rejuvenation program known as Pancha Karma. Think multiday wellness retreat. ⊠ *Hanalei Colony Resort, Rte. 560, 6 mi past Hanalei* ☎ *808/826–6621* ⊕ *www.hanaleidayspa. com* ☞ *Massage $95–$210. Services: Body scrubs and wraps, facials, massage, waxing. Classes and programs: Yoga.*

★ **A Hideaway Spa.** This is the only full-service day spa on the laid-back West Side. It's in one of the restored plantation cottages that make up the guest quarters at Waimea Plantation Cottages, creating a cozy and comfortable setting you won't find elsewhere. The overall feel is relaxed, casual, and friendly, as you'd expect in this quiet country town. The staff is informal, yet thoroughly professional. Beach yoga and massages are available, as well as a full-service salon with hair, nails, and makeup services. Try the kava kava ginger wrap followed by the lomi *'ili'ili*—hot stone massage. Ooh la la! ⊠ *Waimea Plantation Cottages, 9400 Kaumuali'i Hwy., Cottage No. 30, Waimea* ☎ *808/338–0005* ⊕ *www. ahideawayspa.com* ☞ *Massage $50–$170. Facilities: Outdoor hot tub, steam room. Services: Acupuncture, body scrubs and wraps, facials, hydrotherapy, massage. Classes and programs: Yoga.*

5

Qi Center. Technically, the Qi Center of Kaua'i is not a spa. It does, however, concern itself with healing, and because its technique is so gentle, it is, in a sense, pampering. More than that, it can be life changing—even life saving. Hong Liu, a qigong grand master of the highest degree opened the center in 2005 as part of his lifelong goal to share qigong with the West. The essence of qigong centers on building, increasing, and directing energy: physical, mental, and spiritual. Master Liu does not suggest qigong as an alternative to Western medicine but as an adjunct. The center in Līhu'e conducts all levels of qigong training as well as "humanitarian" (i.e., free) events for the community on such topics as the immune system, asthma, allergies, and heart and senior health. ⊠ *3343 Kanakolu St., Līhu'e* ☎ *808/639–4300 Services: Quigong.*

Tri Health Ayurveda Spa. The goal of this spa isn't a one-time massage for momentary bliss, although relaxation is a key ingredient. Rather, this spa's focus is a multiweek, multitreatment, intensive program designed to eliminate toxins stored in the body and increase the flow and energy of all systems. Treatments are designed around the ancient Ayurvedic tradition of heat to open the pores, oil to deliver nutrients to tissues and nerve endings, and massage (by two therapists working in synchronized movement) to accelerate circulation. Note: Because the massage strokes are long and can run the length of the body, there is no draping involved. Ayurvedic doctors, food, and treatments are available, as is lodging in the 10-bedroom retreat facility, on 25 acres hidden by design for privacy—hence, no glaring signs. Single sessions are available. ☎ *808/828–2104* ⊕ *www.trihealthayurvedaspa.com* ☞ *Massage $130–$275. Facilities: Steam room. Services: Herbal body scrubs, massage.*

ENTERTAINMENT AND NIGHTLIFE

Kaua'i has never been known for its nightlife. It's a rural island, where folks tend to retire early, and the streets are dark and deserted well before midnight. While the after-dark entertainment scene may not be expanding, it is present in areas frequented by tourists.

Most of the island's dinner and lū'au shows are held at hotels and resorts. Hotel lounges are a good source of live music, often with no cover charge, as are a few bars and restaurants around the island.

Check the local newspaper, *The Garden Island,* for listings of weekly happenings as well as entertainment features in its Sunday *Kaua'i Times* insert, or tune in to community radio station KKCR—found at 90.9, 91.9, and 92.7 on the FM dial, depending on where you are—at 5:30 pm for the arts and entertainment calendar. Free publications such as *Kaua'i Gold, This Week on Kaua'i,* and *Essential Kaua'i* also list entertainment events. You can pick them up at Līhu'e Airport near the baggage claim area, as well as at numerous retail areas on the island.

ENTERTAINMENT

Although lū'au remain a primary source of evening fun for families on vacation, there are a handful of other possibilities. There are no traditional dinner cruises, but some boat tours do offer an evening buffet with music along Nāpali Coast. A few times a year, Women in Theater (WIT), a local women's theater group, performs dinner shows at the Hukilau Lānai in Wailua. You can always count on a performance of *South Pacific* at the Kaua'i Beach Resort, and the Kaua'i Community College Performing Arts Center draws well-known artists.

Kaua'i Community College Performing Arts Center. This is the main venue for island entertainment, hosting a concert music series, visiting musicians, dramatic productions, and special events such as the International Film Festival. ✉ *3-1901 Kaumuali'i Hwy., Līhu'e* ☎ *808/245–8270* ⊕ *kauai. hawaii.edu/pac.*

DINNER SHOW

South Pacific Dinner Show. It seems a fitting tribute to see the play that put Kaua'i on the map. Rodgers and Hammerstein's original *South Pacific* has been playing at the Kaua'i Beach Resort to rave reviews since 2002. The full musical production, accompanied by a buffet dinner, features local talent. ✉ *Jasmine Ballroom, Kaua'i Beach Resort, 4331 Kaua'i Beach Dr., Līhu'e* ☎ *808/346–6500* ⊕ *www.southpacifickauai. com* ✆ *$85* ⊙ *Wed., doors open at 5:30 pm, show at 6:45.*

LŪ'AU

Although the commercial lū'au experience is a far cry from the backyard lū'au thrown by local residents to celebrate a wedding, graduation, or baby's first birthday, they're nonetheless entertaining and a good introduction to the Hawaiian food that isn't widely sold in restaurants. Besides the feast, there's often an exciting dinner show with Polynesian-style music and dancing. It all makes for a fun evening that's suitable for couples, families, and groups, and the informal setting is conducive to meeting other people. Every lū'au is different, reflecting the cuisine and tenor of the host facility, so compare prices, menus, and entertainment before making your reservation. Most lū'au on Kaua'i are offered only on a limited number of nights each week, so plan ahead to get the lū'au you want. We tend to prefer those *not* held on resort properties, because they feel a bit more authentic. The lū'au shows listed below are our favorites.

Grand Hyatt Kaua'i Lū'au. What used to be called Drums of Paradise has a new name and a new dance troupe but still offers a traditional lū'au buffet and an exceptional performance. This oceanfront lū'au comes with a view of the majestic Keoneloa Bay. ✉ *Grand Hyatt Kaua'i Resort and Spa, 1571 Po'ipū Rd., Po'ipū* ☎ *808/240–6456* ⊕ *www.hyatt.com/ gallery/kauailuau* ✆ *$94* ⊙ *Thurs. and Sun. at 5:30.*

★ **Lū'au Kālamakū.** Set on historic sugar-plantation land, this new lū'au bills itself as the only "theatrical" lū'au on Kaua'i. The lū'au feast is served buffet-style, there's an open bar, and the performers aim to both entertain and educate about Hawaiian culture. Guests sit at tables around a circular stage; tables farther from the stage are elevated, providing unobstructed views. Additional packages offer visitors the opportunity to tour the 35-acre plantation via train or special romantic perks like a lei greeting and champagne. ✉ *3-2087 Kaumuali'i St., Līhu'e* ☎ *877/622–1780* ⊕ *www.luaukalamaku.com* ✆ *$99* ⊙ *Tues. and Fri. check-in begins at 5, dinner at 6:30, show at 7:30.*

Continued on page 564

MORE THAN A FOLK DANCE

Hula has been called "the heartbeat of the Hawaiian people" and also "the world's best-known, most misunderstood dance." Both are true. Hula isn't just dance. It is storytelling. No words, no hula.

Chanter Edith McKinzie calls it "an extension of a piece of poetry." In its adornments, implements, and customs, hula integrates every important Hawaiian cultural practice: poetry, history, genealogy, craft, plant cultivation, martial arts, religion, protocol. So when 19th century Christian missionaries sought to eradicate a practice they considered depraved, they threatened more than just a folk dance.

With public performance outlawed and private hula practice discouraged, hula went underground for a generation, to rural villages. The fragile verbal link by which culture was transmitted from teacher to student hung by a thread. Even increasing literacy did not help because hula's practitioners were a secretive and protected circle.

As if that weren't bad enough, vaudeville, Broadway, and Hollywood got hold of

the hula, giving it the glitz treatment in an unbroken line from "Oh, How She Could Wicky Wacky Woo" to "Rock-A-Hula Baby." Hula became shorthand for paradise: fragrant flowers, lazy hours. Ironically, this development assured that hundreds of Hawaiians could make a living performing and teaching hula. Many danced *'auana* (modern form) in performance; but taught *kahiko* (traditional), quietly, at home or in hula schools.

Today, 30 years after the cultural revival known as the Hawaiian Renaissance, language immersion programs have assured a new generation of proficient—and even eloquent—chanters, songwriters, and translators. Visitors can see more, and more authentic, traditional hula than at any other time in the last 200 years.

Like the culture of which it is the beating heart, hula has survived.

Lei *po'o*. Head lei. In kahiko, greenery only. In 'auana, flowers.

Face emotes appropriate expression. Dancer should not be a smiling automaton.

Shoulders remain relaxed and still, never hunched, even with arms raised. No bouncing.

Eyes always follow leading hand.

Lei. Hula is rarely performed without a shoulder lei.

Traditional hula skirt is loose fabric, smocked and gathered at the waist.

Arms and hands remain loose, relaxed, below shoulder level—except as required by interpretive movements.

Hip is canted over weight-bearing foot.

Knees are always slightly bent, accentuating hip sway.

Kupe'e. Ankle bracelet of flowers, shells, or—traditionally—noise-making dog teeth.

In kahiko, feet are flat. In 'auana, they may be more arched, but not tiptoes or bouncing.

BASIC MOTIONS

Speak or Sing

Moon or Sun

Grass Shack or House

Mountains or Heights

Love or Caress

At backyard parties, hula is performed in bare feet and street clothes, but in performance, adornments play a key role, as do rhythm-keeping implements.

In hula kahiko (traditional style), the usual dress is multiple layers of stiff fabric (often with a pellom lining, which most closely resembles *kapa*, the paperlike bark cloth of the Hawaiians). These wrap tightly around the bosom but flare below the waist to form a skirt. In pre-contact times, dancers wore only kapa skirts. Monarchy-period hula is performed in voluminous Mother Hubbard muʻumuʻu or high-necked muslin blouses and gathered skirts. Men wear loincloths or, for monarchy period, white or gingham shirts and black pants—sometimes with red sashes.

In hula ʻauana (modern), dress for women can range from grass skirts and strapless tops to contemporary tea-length dresses. Men generally wear aloha shirts, but sometimes grass skirts over pants or even everyday gear. (One group at a recent competition wore wetsuits to do a surfing song!)

SURPRISING HULA FACTS

■ Grass skirts are not traditional; workers from Kiribati (the Gilbert Islands) brought this custom to Hawaiʻi.

■ In olden-day Hawaiʻi, *mele* (songs) for hula were composed for every occasion—name songs for babies, dirges for funerals, welcome songs for visitors, celebrations of favorite pursuits.

■ Hula *maʻi* is a traditional hula form in praise of a noble's genitals; the power of the *aliʻi* (royalty) to procreate gave *mana* (spiritual power) to the entire culture.

■ Hula students in old Hawaiʻi adhered to high standards: scrupulous cleanliness, no sex, daily cleansing rituals, certain food prohibitions, and no contact with the dead. They were fined if they broke the rules.

WHERE TO WATCH

■ Coconut Marketplace, ⊠ 4-484 Kūhiō Hwy., Kapaʻa, ⊙ Show also at 5 PM Wed. and Sat. 1 PM.

■ Poʻipū Shopping Village, ⊠ 2360 Kiahuna Plantation Dr., Poʻipū Beach, ☎ 808/742-7444 ⊙ Tues. and Thurs. 5 pm.

■ Smith's Tropical Paradise, ⊠ 174 Wailua Rd., Kapaʻa, ☎ 808/821-6895, ⊙ Mon., Wed., and Fri. 5–9:15. Dinner included.

■ Festivals: There are many festivals on the island year-round where you can see hula performed. For more information visit *www.kauaifestivals.com*.

Fodor'sChoice   **Smith's Tropical Paradise Lū'au.** A 30-acre tropical garden provides the
★   lovely setting for this popular lū'au, which begins with the traditional
blowing of the conch shell and *imu* (pig roast) ceremony, followed
by cocktails, an island feast, and an international show in the amphitheater overlooking a torch-lighted lagoon. It's fairly authentic and a
better deal than the pricier resort events. ⊠ *174 Wailua Rd., Kapa'a*
☎ *808/821–6895* ⊠ *$78* ⊗ *Sept.–May, Mon., Wed., and Fri. 5–9:15;
June–Aug., weekdays 5–9:15.*

MUSIC

Check the local papers for outdoor reggae and Hawaiian-music shows,
or one of the numbers listed below for more formal performances.

Hanalei Slack Key Concerts. Relax to the instrumental music form created
by Hawaiian *paniolo* (cowboys) in the early 1800s. Shows are at Hale
Halawai 'Ohana 'O Hanalei, which is *mauka* down a dirt access road
across from St. William's Catholic Church (Malolo Road) and then left
down another dirt road. Look for a thatched-roof *hale* (house), several
little green plantation-style buildings, and the brown double-yurt community center around the gravel parking lot. ⊠ *Hanalei Family Community Center, 5-5299 Kūhiō Hwy., Hanalei* ☎ *808/826–1469* ⊕ *www.
hawaiianslackkeyguitar.com* ⊠ *$20* ⊗ *Fri. at 4, Sun. at 3.*

Kaua'i Concert Association. This group offers a seasonal program at the
Kaua'i Community College Performing Arts Center. A range of big-
name artists, from Ricky Lee Jones to Taj Mahal, have been known to
show up on Kaua'i for planned or impromptu performances. ⊠ *3-1901
Kaumuali'i Hwy., Līhu'e* ☎ *808/245–7464* ⊕ *www.kauai-concert.org.*

BARS AND CLUBS

Nightclubs that stay open until the wee hours are rare on Kaua'i,
and the bar scene is pretty limited. The major resorts generally host
their own live entertainment and happy hours. All bars and clubs that
serve alcohol must close by 2 am, except those with a cabaret license,
which allows them to close at 4 am. For information on events or specials, check out the local newspaper's nightlife section, *Kaua'i Times*
(⊕ *kauaitimes.net*).

THE NORTH SHORE

Hanalei Gourmet. The sleepy North Shore stays awake—until 10:30,
that is—each evening in this small, convivial setting inside Hanalei's
restored old school building. The emphasis here is on local live jazz,
rock, and folk music. ⊠ *5-5161 Kūhiō Hwy., Hanalei Center, Hanalei*
☎ *808/826–2524.* ⊕ *www.hanaleigourmet.com.*

★   **St. Regis Bar.** This spacious lounge overlooking Hanalei Bay offers
drinks daily from 3 to 10:30. Stop by between 5 and 10 for *pūpū*
(hors d'oeuvres), acoustic guitar or piano music, and an ocean view.
⊠ *Princeville Resort, 5520 Ka Haku Rd., Princeville* ☎ *808/826–9644.*

Tahiti Nui. This venerable and decidedly funky institution in sleepy Hanalei no longer offers its famous lū'au, ever since owner and founder Auntie Louise Marston died. Its fun-loving new owner, a Kiwi from New
Zealand, is doing his best to keep the place hopping with live nightly

entertainment, including Hawaiian music earlier in the evening and rock and roll starting around 9. Don't miss the new wine bar, Tahiti Iti, around back. ⊠ *5-5134 Kūhiō Hwy., Hanalei* ☎ *808/826–6277* ⊕ *www. thenui.com.*

THE EAST SIDE

Duke's Barefoot Bar. This is one of the liveliest bars in Nawiliwili. Contemporary Hawaiian music is performed at this beachside bar on Wednesday, Thursday, and Saturday from 4 to 6 pm, Friday from 9 to 11 pm, and sometimes on Sunday evening. The bar closes at 11 most nights. ⊠ *3610 Rice St., Kalapakī Beach, Līhu'e* ☎ *808/246–9599* ⊕ *www.dukeskauai.com.*

Hukilau Lānai. This open-air bar and restaurant is on the property of the Kaua'i Coast Resort but operates independently. Trade winds trickle through the modest little bar, which looks out into a coconut grove. If the mood takes you, go on a short walk to the sea, or recline in big, comfortable chairs while listening to mellow jazz or Hawaiian slack-key guitar. Live music plays Sunday, Tuesday, and Friday, though the bar is open every day but Monday. Freshly infused tropical martinis—perhaps locally grown lychee and pineapple or a Big Island vanilla bean infusion—are house favorites. ⊠ *520 Aleka Loop Kūhiō Hwy., Wailua* ☎ *808/822–0600* ⊕ *www.hukilaukauai.com.*

Rob's Good Times Grill. Let loose at this popular sports bar, which features DJs spinning Thursday through Saturday from 9 pm to 2 am with the occasional live band. Wednesday you can kick up your heels with country line dancing from 7:30 to 11 pm. Sunday, Monday, and Tuesday evenings are karaoke nights. ⊠ *4303 Rice St., Līhu'e* ☎ *808/246–0311* ⊕ *www.robsgoodtimesgrill.com.*

Tradewinds—A South Seas Bar. This salty mariner's den is surprisingly located within the cliché confines of a cheesy mall. Tradewinds has a tattered palm-frond roof and a tropical theme reminiscent of Jimmy Buffett, but you aren't likely to hear Buffett tunes here. In fact, you're more likely to meet Ernest Hemingway types. From karaoke to dart league competitions to live music, this little bar busts at the seams with local flavor. It's open daily from 10 am to 2 am but opens early (7 am) on Sunday mornings, serving as a home away from home to displaced NFL fans. ⊠ *Coconut Marketplace, 484 Kūhiō Hwy., Kapa'a* ☎ *808/822–1621* ⊕ *www.tradewinds-kauai.com.*

THE SOUTH SHORE AND WEST SIDE

Keoki's Paradise. A young, energetic crowd makes this a lively spot on Friday and Saturday nights. There's live music from 7 to 9 on Friday and Saturday, at 6:30 on Wednesday, and 6 on Thursday. After 9 pm, when the dining room clears out, there's a bit of a bar scene for singles. The bar closes at 10:30 pm. ⊠ *Po'ipū Shopping Village, 2360 Kiahuna Plantation Dr., Po'ipū* ☎ *808/742–7534* ⊕ *www.keokisparadise.com.*

The Point at Sheraton Kaua'i. This is *the* place to be on the South Shore to celebrate sunset with a drink; the ocean view is unsurpassed. Starting at 8 pm on Friday, Saturday, and Monday, there's live entertainment until 12:30 or 1 am. The lineup isn't set in stone, so call before you arrive to see who's playing that night. ⊠ *Sheraton Kaua'i Resort, 2440*

5

Kaua'i: Undercover Movie Star

Though Kaua'i has played itself in the movies (you may remember Nicolas Cage frantically shouting "Is it Kapa'a or Kapa'a-a?" into a pay phone in *Honeymoon in Vegas* (1992), most of its screen time has been as a stunt double for a number of tropical paradises. The island's remote valleys and waterfalls portrayed Venezuelan jungle in Kevin Costner's *Dragonfly* (2002) and a Costa Rican dinosaur preserve in Steven Spielberg's *Jurassic Park* (1993). Spielberg was no stranger to Kaua'i, having filmed Harrison Ford's escape via seaplane from Menehune Fishpond in *Raiders of the Lost Ark* (1981). The fluted cliffs and gorges of Kaua'i's rugged Nāpali Coast play the misunderstood beast's island home in *King Kong* (1976), and a jungle dweller of another sort, in *George of the Jungle* (1997), frolicked on Kaua'i. Harrison Ford returned to the island for 10 weeks during the filming of *Six Days, Seven Nights* (1998), a romantic adventure set in French Polynesia. Part-time Kaua'i resident Ben Stiller used the island as a stand-in for the jungles of Vietnam in *Tropic Thunder* (2008) and Johnny Depp came here to film some of *Pirates of the Caribbean: On Stranger Tides* (2011). But these are all relatively contemporary movies. What's truly remarkable is that Hollywood discovered Kaua'i in 1933 with the making of *White Heat*, which was set on a sugar plantation and—like another more memorable movie filmed on Kaua'i—dealt with interracial love stories. In 1950, Esther Williams and Rita Moreno arrived to film *Pagan Love Song*, a forgettable musical. Then, it was off to the races, as Kaua'i saw no fewer than a dozen movies filmed on island in the 1950s, not all of them Oscar contenders. Rita Hayworth starred in *Miss Sadie Thompson* (1953) and no one you'd recognize starred in the tantalizing *She Gods of Shark Reef* (1956).

The movie that is still immortalized on the island in the names of restaurants, real estate offices, a hotel, and even a sushi item is *South Pacific* (1957). (You guessed it, right?) That mythical place called Bali Hai is never far away on Kaua'i. There's even an Off-Off-Off-Broadway musical version performed at the Kaua'i Beach Resort in Līhu'e.

In the 1960s Elvis Presley filmed *Blue Hawaii* (1961) and *Girls! Girls! Girls!* (1962) on the island. A local movie tour likes to point out the stain on a hotel carpet where Elvis's jelly doughnut fell.

Kaua'i has welcomed a long list of Hollywood's A-List: John Wayne in *Donovan's Reef* (1963); Jack Lemmon in *The Wackiest Ship in the Army* (1961); Richard Chamberlain in *The Thorn Birds* (1983); Gene Hackman in *Uncommon Valor* (1983); Danny DeVito and Billy Crystal in *Throw Momma from the Train* (1987); and Dustin Hoffman, Morgan Freeman, Renee Russo, and Cuba Gooding Jr. in *Outbreak* (1995).

Yet the movie scene isn't the only screen on which Kaua'i has starred. A long list of TV shows, TV pilots, and made-for-TV movies make the list as well, including *Gilligan's Island, Fantasy Island, Starsky & Hutch, Baywatch-Hawai'i*—even reality TV shows *The Bachelor* and *The Amazing Race 3*.

Ho'onani Rd., Po'ipū ☎ *808/742–1661* ⊕ *www.sheraton-kauai.com/ dining/thepoint.*

Waimea Brewing Company. Sip one of several home-brewed beers in an airy plantation-style house on the grounds of Waimea Plantation Cottages, which in late 2009 added a new moniker—the Grove Cafe. Outdoor seating and a wraparound lānai make this brewery/eatery a worthwhile West Side experience. Expect slow service and mediocre fare. There is live music most evenings, or grab a growler to go, take a stroll out back to the beach, and enjoy views of Ni'ihau while the sun sets. ⊠ *9400 Kaumuali'i Hwy., Waimea* ☎ *808/338–9733.*

WHERE TO EAT

In Kaua'i, if you're lucky enough to win an invitation to a potluck, baby lū'au, or beach party, don't think twice—just accept. The best *grinds* (food) are homemade, and so you'll eat until you're full, then rest, eat some more, and make a plate to take home, too.

But even if you can't score a spot at one of these parties, don't despair. Great local-style food is easy to come by at countless low-key places around the island, and as an extra bonus these eats are often inexpensive, and portions are generous. Expect plenty of meat—usually deep-fried or marinated in a teriyaki sauce and grilled *pulehu*-style (over an open fire) and starches. Rice is standard, even for breakfast, and often served alongside potato-macaroni salad, another island specialty. Another local favorite is *poke,* made from chunks of raw tuna or octopus seasoned with sesame oil, soy sauce, onions, and pickled seaweed. It's a great *pūpū* (appetizer) when paired with a cold beer.

■TIP→ One cautionary note: most restaurants stop serving dinner at 8 or 9 pm, so plan to eat early.

WHAT IT COSTS					
	¢	$	$$	$$$	$$$$
RESTAURANTS	under $10	$10–$17	$18–$26	$27–$35	over $35

Prices are for one main course at dinner.

THE NORTH SHORE

Because of the North Shore's isolation, restaurants have enjoyed a captive audience of visitors who don't want to make the long, dark trek into town for dinner. As a result, dining in this region has been characterized by expensive fare that isn't especially tasty, either. Fortunately, the situation is slowly improving as new restaurants open and others change hands or menus.

Still, dining on the North Shore can be pricier than other parts of the island, and not especially family-friendly. Most of the restaurants are found either in Hanalei town or the Princeville resorts. Consequently,

BEST BETS FOR KAUA'I DINING

Fodor's Choice★	$$	Hamura Saimin ¢, p. 576
Bar Acuda $, p. 568	The Eastside, p. 573	PLATE LUNCH
Beach House $$$, p. 577	Plantation Gardens, p. 583	Dani's Restaurant ¢, p. 576
Dondero's $$$, p. 578	Pomodoro Ristorante	Hanamā'ulu Restaurant
Hukilau Lana'i $$, p. 573	Italiano, p. 583	$, p. 576
Restaurant Kintaro $$–$$$, p. 574	$$$	By Experience
By Price	Tidepools, p. 583	MOST ROMANTIC
	Wrangler's Steakhouse, p. 584	Beach House $$$, p. 577
¢	$$$$	Café Portofino $$–$$$, p. 576
Hamura Saimin, p. 576	Kaua'i Grill, p. 569	Dondero's $$$, p. 578
Joe's on the Green, p. 578	Roy's Po'ipū Bar & Grill, p. 583	BEST VIEW
Mermaid's Café, p. 574	By Cuisine	Beach House $$$, p. 577
$		Brennecke's Beach Broiler $$, p. 578
Caffé Coco, p. 573	HAWAIIAN	Café Portofino $$–$$$, p. 576
Mema Thai Chinese Cuisine, p. 574	Dani's Restaurant ¢, p. 576	

you'll encounter delightful mountain and ocean views, but just one restaurant with oceanfront dining.

$ ✕ **Bar Acuda.** This tapas bar is a very welcome addition to the Hanalei
MEDITERRANEAN dining scene, rocketing right to top place in the categories of tastiness,
Fodor's Choice creativity, and pizzazz. Owner-chef Jim Moffat's brief menu changes
★ regularly: You might find banderillas (grilled flank steak skewers with
honey and chipotle chili oil), polenta, Gorgonzola endive salad, grilled
veggies, a diverse cheese and fruit plate, and sausages with onions, all
served with fresh bread. The small servings are intended to be shared,
tapas-style. The food is consistently remarkable, with subtly intense
sauces that further elevate the outstanding cuisine. It's super casual, but
chic, with a nice porch for outdoor dining and the service is discreet, but
thorough. ☒ *Hanalei Center, 5-5161 Kūhiō Hwy., Hanalei* ☎ *808/826–
7081* ⊕ *www.restaurantbaracuda.com* ▬ *MC, V* ☾ *Closed Mon.*

$ ✕ **Bouchon's.** This second-story restaurant and sushi bar, known until
JAPANESE recently as Sushi Blues, has a nice ambience, with copper tabletops,
lovely views of mountains streaked with waterfalls, and photos of international jazz greats lining the staircase. Regular entertainment, a full
bar, and a sake menu add to its appeal. Choose from steaks, seafood
dishes, and specialty sushi items such as the Osaka 2 Me Roll, which

is filled with tuna, snow crab, masago, and avocado, wrapped in seaweed and tempura-fried. ⊠ *Ching Young Village, 5-5190 Kūhiō Hwy., Hanalei* ☎ *808/826–9701* ⊟ *AE, D, DC, MC, V.*

$$ **✕ Hanalei Gourmet.** This spot in Hanalei's restored old schoolhouse
AMERICAN offers dolphin-safe tuna, low-sodium meats, fresh-baked breads, and homemade desserts as well as a casual atmosphere where both families and the sports-watching crowds can feel equally comfortable. Early birds can order coffee and toast or a hearty breakfast. Lunch and dinner menus feature sandwiches, burgers, filling salads, and nightly specials of fresh local fish. They also will prepare a picnic and give it to you in an insulated backpack. A full bar and frequent live entertainment keep things hopping even after the kitchen closes. Thursday evenings fill up for fish taco night. ⊠ *5-5161 Kūhiō Hwy., Hanalei* ☎ *808/826–2524* ⊕ *www.hanaleigourmet.com* ⊟ *D, DC, MC, V.*

$$$$ **✕ Kaua'i Grill.** Savor an artful meal created by world-renowned chef
ECLECTIC Jean-Gorges Vongerichten, surrounded by a dramatic Hanalei Bay scene. Located at the recently renovated St. Regis Princeville Resort, Kaua'i Grill has dark wood decor and an ornate red chandelier, the centerpiece of the room. The attention here is on the flavors of robust meat and local, fresh seafood. Most dishes are plainly grilled, accompanied by exotic sauces and condiments. The specials change frequently and use as many Hawaiian-grown ingredients as possible. Expect attentive service with the somewhat stiff feel of an exclusive hotel, and an expertly created meal. ⊠ *St. Regis Princeville, 5520 Ka Haku Rd., Princeville* ☎ *808/826–9644* ⚄ *Reservations essential* ⊟ *AE, D, DC, MC, V* ☉ *No lunch. Closed Sun.–Mon.*

$ **✕ Kīlauea Bakery and Pau Hana Pizza.** This bakery has garnered tons of
AMERICAN well-deserved good press for its starter of Hawaiian sourdough made with guava as well as its specialty pizzas topped with such yummy ingredients as smoked *ono* (a Hawaiian fish), Gorgonzola-rosemary sauce, barbecued chicken, goat cheese, and roasted onions. Open from 6:30 am, the bakery serves coffee drinks, delicious fresh pastries, bagels, and breads in the morning. Late risers beware: breads and pastries sell out quickly on weekends. Pizza, soup, and salads can be ordered for lunch or dinner. If you want to hang out or do the coffee shop bit in Kīlauea, this is the place. A cute courtyard with covered tables is a pleasant place to linger. ⊠ *Kong Lung Center, 2484 Keneke St., Kīlauea* ☎ *808/828–2020* ⊟ *MC, V.*

$$$$ **✕ Makana Terrace.** Enjoy breakfast, lunch, or dinner in front of one of
MODERN the most exquisite views of Hanalei Bay. There's no doubt it's pricey,
HAWAIIAN but you're paying for the view—sit on the terrace if you can—and for an attentive staff. There is a focus on local, Hawaiian-grown foods here, including the fish plate of a fresh Pacific catch, which is your best bet for lunch. Feast at the extensive breakfast buffet for $34 per person from 6:30 to 11:00 am, but it's traditional fare: nothing spectacular or exotic. For a special evening, splurge on the surf and turf (around $45) and time your dinner around sunset for an unforgettable Hawaiian vista. ⊠ *5520 Ka Haku Rd., Princeville* ☎ *808/826–9644* ⊟ *AE, D, DC, MC, V.*

$$ **✕ Postcards Café.** With its postcard artwork, beamed ceilings, and light
AMERICAN interiors, this plantation-cottage restaurant has a menu consisting

Where to Eat on Kaua'i

Hāʻena Beach Park
Tunnels Beach
Kēʻē Beach
Hāʻena
560
Hanakāpīʻai Beach
Kalalau Trail
NĀPALI COAST

Princeville
31 **32**
Hanalei Bay
33
Hanalei
34
Hanalei Bay Beach Park
36 **35**
WAIPĀ VALLEY

Kalalau Lookout
Puʻu O Kila Lookout
Kōkeʻe State Park
Kōkeʻe Lodge

Kōkeʻe

550

WAIMEA CANYON

NāPali-Kona Forest Reserve

Wai'ale'ale
5,148ft ▲

WAIMEA

Kōke'e Rd.
Waimea Canyon Dr.

55

552

550

KŌLOA

Kekaha Beach Park
Kekaha
1
Menehune Ditch ◆
Waimea

Kaulakahi Channel

Lucy Wright Beach Park

50

2
Kalāheo

Lāwaʻi
530

Hanapēpē
'Eleʻele
540

Burn's Field ✈
Port Allen
Hanapēpē Bay

Spouting Horn

Beach House

| 0 | | 5 miles |
| 0 | | 5 km |

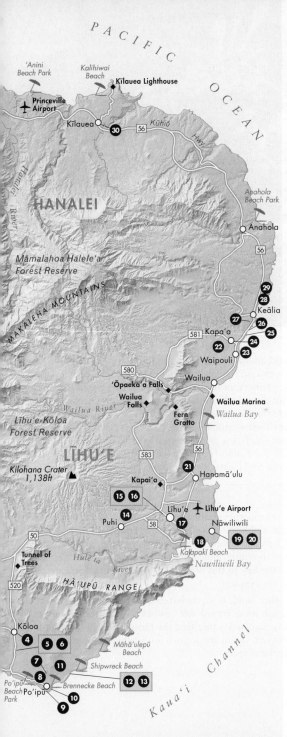

5

Mahimahi is a popular fish dish on Kaua'i. The Beach House adds a macadamia-nut crust for local flavor.

mostly of organic, additive-free vegetarian foods and fish. But don't get the wrong idea—this isn't simple cooking: specials might include carrot-ginger soup, taro fritters, or fresh fish served with peppered pineapple-sage sauce, or blackened 'ahi. Desserts are made without refined sugar. Try the chocolate silk pie made with barley malt chocolate, pure vanilla, and creamy tofu with a crust of graham crackers, sun-dried cherries, and crushed cashews. This is probably your best bet for dinner in Hanalei town. ⊠ *5-5075A Kūhiō Hwy., Hanalei* ☎ *808/826–1191* ⊕ *www.postcardscafe.com* ⊟ *AE, MC, V* ☉ *No lunch.*

THE EAST SIDE

In recent years, the most affordable, hip new eateries on the island have opened in Kapa'a. Unlike the resort-dominated South and North shores, Kapa'a is local, fun, and eclectic, with steakburger stands on the side of the road, vegetarian venues, and swanky bars serving up artful appetizers. Diversity is the key to this area; there is something for everyone, especially those on a budget.

Līhu'e, on the other hand, is somewhat extreme when it comes to restaurants. There are some remarkable (and expensive) restaurants and some great low-cost eateries that feed the business lunch crowd—but not much in between. If you are in town for lunch, don't pass up some of the authentic, local spots.

The Beach House on the South Shore is a prime spot to watch the sun set.

KAPA'A AND WAILUA

$
CAFÉ

✕ **Caffé Coco.** A restored plantation cottage set back off the highway and surrounded by tropical foliage is the setting for this island café. You'll know it by its bright lime green storefront. An attached black-light art gallery and an apparel shop called Bambulei make this a fun stop for any meal. Outdoor seating in the vine-covered garden is pleasant during nice weather, although on calm nights, it can get buggy. Acoustic music is offered regularly, attracting a laid-back local crowd. Potstickers filled with tofu and chutney, 'ahi wraps, Greek and organic salads, fresh fish and soups, and a daily list of specials are complemented by a full espresso bar and wonderful desserts. Allow plenty of time, because the tiny kitchen can't turn out meals quickly. ⊠ *4-369 Kūhiō Hwy., Wailua* ☎ *808/822–7990* ▤ *MC, V* ☺ *Closed Mon.*

$$–$$$
PACIFIC RIM

✕ **The Eastside.** Excellent service, an open-air casual atmosphere, and live music are great perks of this new hot spot. The reason people flock here is the food. The Cuban sandwich and rib eye tickle the taste buds, and you can't go wrong with the mahimahi served in a plantain and pistachio crust with a tropical fruit curry sauce. Fresh strawberry and grapefruit martinis are staples on the menu. The Eastside is run by brothers John Pfleuger and Dylan Scott; both have extensive restaurant experience and run a seamless operation in the central spot in Kapa'a town that used to serve ice cream. ⊠ *4-1380 Kūhiō Hwy., Kapa'a* ☎ *808/823–9500* ⊕ *www.theeastsidekauai.com* ▤ *MC, V* ☺ *Closed Sun.–Mon.*

$$
AMERICAN
Fodor'sChoice
★

✕ **Hukilau Lana'i.** Relying heavily on super-fresh island fish and locally grown vegetables, this restaurant offers quality food that is competently and creatively prepared. The fish—grilled, steamed, or sautéed and served with succulent sauces—shines here. Other sound choices are the savory meat loaf and prime rib. Chicken and a few pasta dishes round out the menu. The 'ahi nachos appetizer is not to be missed, nor is the warm chocolate dessert soufflé. The spacious dining room looks out to the ocean, and it's lovely to eat at the outdoor tables when the weather is nice. Overall, it's a solid choice on the East Side. ⊠ *Kaua'i Coast Resort, Coconut Marketplace, 520 Aleka Loop, Kapa'a* ☎ *808/822–0600* ⊕ *www.hukilaukauai.com* ▤ *AE, D, DC, MC, V* ⊘ *No lunch. Closed Mon.*

$ ✕**Kaua'i Pasta.** If you don't mind a no-frills atmosphere for affordable

ITALIAN   food, this is the place. The husband of the husband-and-wife team that runs the restaurant left his executive-chef position at Roy's to open a catering business. He leased a kitchen that happened to have a small dining area, and rather than let it go to waste, they open for dinner every evening except Monday. Specials, written on the whiteboard at the entrance, are satisfying and delicious. The locals have this place figured out; they show up in droves. The chic KP Lounge stays open late, offering a handsome hideout for tasty nighttime grinds and cocktails. There's a branch in Līhu'e that also serves lunch. ⊠ *4-939B Kūhiō Hwy., Kapa'a* ☎ *808/822–7447* ⊕ *www.kauaipastarestaurants.com* ▤ *MC, V.*

$ ✕**Kountry Kitchen.** If you're big on breakfasts, try Kountry Kitchen,

AMERICAN   which serves breakfast and lunch items until 1:30 pm daily. Across the

☺   street from the library in Kapa'a, this family-friendly restaurant has a sunny interior, and a cozy, greasy-spoon atmosphere with friendly service. It is a great spot for omelets, banana pancakes, and eggs Benedict in two sizes. Lunch selections include sandwiches, burgers, and *loco mocos* (a popular local rice, beef, gravy, and eggs concoction). Take-out orders are also available. ⊠ *1485 Kūhiō Hwy., Kapa'a* ☎ *808/822–3511* ▤ *MC, V* ⊘ *No dinner.*

$ ✕**Mema Thai Chinese Cuisine.** Refined and intimate, Mema Thai serves its

THAI   dishes on crisp white linens accented by tabletop orchid sprays. Menu items such as broccoli with oyster sauce and cashew chicken reveal Chinese origins, but the emphasis is on Thai dishes. A host of curries— red, green, yellow, and house—made with coconut milk and kaffir-lime leaves run from mild to mouth searing. The traditional green-papaya salad adds a cool touch for the palate. ⊠ *Wailua Shopping Plaza, 369 Kūhiō Hwy., Kapa'a* ☎ *808/823–0899* ▤ *AE, D, DC, MC, V* ⊘ *No lunch weekends.*

¢   ✕**Mermaid's Café.** Sit and watch as your meal is prepared at this café

ECLECTIC   in Kapa'a. The small yet diverse menu of sophisticated dishes features homemade sauces and local ingredients. Try the 'ahi nori wrap with fresh seared tuna, rice, cucumber, and wasabi cream sauce with pickled ginger and soy sauce—their most popular pick. Other dishes include rice, fresh vegetables, and either tofu or chicken served with a peanut sauce or coconut curry sauce. Everything can be made either vegetarian or vegan. The fish is caught daily by local fisherman, and produce is grown on the island. ⊠ *1384 Kūhiō Hwy., Kapa'a* ☎ *808/821–2026* ▤ *MC, V.*

$$–$$$ ✕**Restaurant Kintaro.** If you want to eat someplace that's a favorite with

JAPANESE   locals, visit Kintaro's. But be prepared to wait on weekends, because the

Fodor's Choice   dining room and sushi bar are always busy. Try the unbeatable Bali Hai

★

Some of the best eats on Kaua'i come from the sea. Ask what the local catch of the day is for the freshest option.

Bomb, a roll of eel and smoked salmon, baked and topped with wasabi mayonnaise. For an "all-in-one-dish" meal, consider the *Nabemono*, a single pot filled with a healthful variety of seafood and vegetables. *Teppanyaki* dinners are meat, seafood, and vegetables flash-cooked on tabletop grills in an entertaining display. Tatami-mat seating is available behind shoji screens that provide privacy for groups. Like many long-time restaurants, it's an enduring favorite. ⊠ *4-370 Kūhiō Hwy., Wailua* ☎ *808/822–3341* ⊟ *AE, D, DC, MC, V* ⊙ *No lunch. Closed Sun.*

LĪHU'E

$$$
ECLECTIC

✕ **22 North.** The former Gaylord's restaurant received a welcome overhaul when it became 22 North. Located in what was at one time Kaua'i's most expensive plantation estate, 22 North pays tribute to the elegant dining rooms of 1930s high society. Tables with candlelight sit on a cobblestone patio surrounding a fountain and overlooking a wide lawn. The sustainability-minded menu features classic American cooking with a focus on locally produced ingredients. Try the spiced samosas for starters, followed with a Wailua lamb chop, stuffed eggplant or A'akukui Ranch beef tenderloin with gorgonzola-stuffed potato cake. Lunches feature the tasty (grilled eggplant and peppers with pickled vegetables, rouille, and smoked provolone) and the daily burger, the chef's "whimsical preparation" of ground local meat. The lavish Sunday brunch includes a variety of eggs Benedict offerings in addition to standard omelets with farm-fresh eggs and a pancake station. Before or after dining you can wander around the estate grounds. ⊠ *Kilohana Plantation, 3-2087 Kaumuali'i Rd., Līhu'e* ☎ *808/245–9593* ⊕ *22northkauai. com* ⊟ *AE, D, DC, MC, V.*

$$–$$$ ✕ **Café Portofino.** The menu at this mostly authentic northern Italian
ITALIAN restaurant is as impressive as the views of Kalapakī Bay and the Hā'upu
range. Owner Giuseppe Avocadi's better-sounding-than-tasting dishes
have managed to garner a host of culinary awards and raves from
dining critics. The fresh 'ahi carpaccio is a signature dish, and pasta,
scampi, and veal are enhanced by sauces. Linger over coffee and ice
cream–filled profiteroles or traditional tiramisu while enjoying romantic
harp music. Solid service and a soothing, dignified ambience complete
the dining experience, making this a great place for a date if only the
food was better and wine less overpriced. ⊠ *Kaua'i Marriott Resort &
Beach Club, 3610 Rice St., Līhu'e* ☎ *808/245–2121* ⊕ *cafeportofino.
com* ▭ *AE, D, DC, MC, V* ☺ *No lunch.*

¢ ✕ **Dani's Restaurant.** Kaua'i residents frequent this big, sparsely furnished
HAWAIIAN eatery near the Līhu'e Fire Station for hearty, local-style food at breakfast and lunch. Dani's is a good place to try lū'au food without commercial lū'au prices. You can order Hawaiian-style *laulau* (pork and
taro leaves wrapped in tī leaves and steamed) or kālua pig, slow roasted
in an underground oven. Other island-style dishes include Japanese-
prepared *tonkatsu* (pork cutlet) and teriyaki beef, and there's always the
all-American New York steak. Omelets are whipped up with fish cake,
kālua pig, or seafood; everything is served with rice. ⊠ *4201 Rice St.,
Līhu'e* ☎ *808/245–4991* ▭ *MC, V* ☺ *Closed Sun. No dinner.*

$$ ✕ **Duke's Canoe Club.** Surfing legend Duke Kahanamoku is immortal-
SEAFOOD ized at this casual bi-level restaurant set on Kalapakī Bay. Guests can
admire surfboards, photos, and other memorabilia marking the Duke's
long tenure as a waterman. It's an interesting collection, and an indoor
garden and waterfall add to the pleasing sights. You'll find simple fare
ranging from fish tacos and stir-fried cashew chicken to hamburgers,
served 11 am to 11 pm. At dinner, fresh fish prepared in a variety of
styles is the best choice. Duke's claims to have the biggest salad bar on
the island, though given the lack of competition, that isn't saying much.
A happy-hour drink and appetizer is a less expensive way to enjoy the
moonrises and ocean views here—though it can get pretty crowded.
The Barefoot Bar is a hot spot for after-dinner drinks, too. ⊠ *Kaua'i
Marriott Resort & Beach Club, 3610 Rice St., Līhu'e* ☎ *808/246–9599*
⊕ *www.dukeskauai.com* ▭ *AE, D, DC, MC, V.*

¢ ✕ **Hamura Saimin.** Folks just love this funky old plantation-style diner.
HAWAIIAN Locals and tourists stream in and out all day long, and Neighbor Island-
ers stop in on their way to the airport to pick up take-out orders for
friends and family back home. *Saimin* is the big draw, and each day
the Hiraoka family dishes up about 1,000 bowls of steaming broth
and homemade noodles, topped with a variety of garnishes. The bar-
becued chicken and meat sticks adopt a smoky flavor during grilling.
The landmark eatery is also famous for its *liliko'i* (passion fruit) chiffon
pie. ■TIP➔ **As one of the few island eateries open late, until 8:30 pm on
weeknights and midnight on Friday and Saturday, it's favored by night owls.**
⊠ *2956 Kress St., Līhu'e* ☎ *808/245–3271* ▭ *No credit cards.*

$ ✕ **Hanamā'ulu Restaurant, Tea House, Sushi Bar, and Robatayaki.** Business is
JAPANESE brisk at this landmark Kaua'i eatery. The food is a mix of Japanese, Chi-
nese, and local-style cooking, served up in hearty portions. The ginger

chicken and fried shrimp are wildly popular, as are the fresh sashimi and sushi. Other choices include tempura, chicken *katsu* (Japanese-style fried chicken), beef broccoli, and *robatayaki* (grilled seafood and meat). The main dining room is rather unattractive, but the private rooms in back look out on the Japanese garden and fishponds and feature traditional seating on tatami mats at low tables. These tearooms can be reserved and are favored for family events and celebrations. ⊠ *1-4291 Kūhiō Hwy., Rte. 56, Hanamāʻulu* ☎ *808/245–2511* ▤ *MC, V* ⊘ *Closed Mon.*

$$
AMERICAN

✕**JJ's Broiler.** This spacious, low-key restaurant serves hearty fare, with dinner specials such as lobster and Slavonic steak, a broiled sliced tenderloin dipped in buttery wine sauce. On sunny afternoons, ask for a table on the lānai overlooking Kalapakī Bay and try one of the generous salads. The upstairs section is currently only available for private events, but you can still eat at the restaurant's lower level, which is open-air and casual. JJ's is a relaxed place to enjoy lunch, dinner, or just sit at the bar for a drink, with one of the best ocean views in Līhu'e. ⊠ *Anchor Cove, 3416 Rice St., Nāwiliwili* ☎ *808/246–4422* ⊕ *www. jjsbroiler.com* ▤ *D, MC, V.*

$
AMERICAN

✕**Līhu'e Barbecue Inn.** Few Kaua'i restaurants are more beloved than this family-owned eatery, a mainstay of island dining since 1940. The menu runs from traditional American to Asian. The dishes are decent but nothing to send a postcard home about. Try the baby back ribs, or fried loco moco, or choose a full Japanese dinner from the other side of the menu. If you can't make up your mind, strike a compromise with the inn's tri-sampler. Opt for the fruit cup—fresh, not canned—instead of soup or salad, and save room for a hefty slice of homemade cream pie, available in all sorts of flavors. ⊠ *2982 Kress St., Līhu'e* ☎ *808/245–2921* ▤ *MC, V* ⊘ *Closed Sun.*

THE SOUTH SHORE AND WEST SIDE

The South Shore and West Side are two different worlds when it comes to dining. Most South Shore restaurants are more upscale and located within the Po'ipū resorts, whereas West Side eateries tend to be more local style and are generally found along Kaumuali'i Highway.

$$$
AMERICAN
Fodor'sChoice
★

✕**Beach House.** This restaurant partners a dreamy ocean view with impressive cuisine. Few Kaua'i experiences are more delightful than sitting at one of the outside tables and savoring a delectable meal while the sun sinks into the glassy blue Pacific. It's the epitome of tropical dining, and no other restaurant on Kaua'i can offer anything quite like it. Chef Todd Barrett's menu changes often, but the food is consistently creative and delicious. A few trademark dishes appear regularly, such as Chinese-style roast duck, mint-coriander lamb rack, fire-roasted 'ahi, and lemongrass and kaffir-lime sea scallops. Seared macadamia-nut-crusted mahimahi, a dish ubiquitous on island menus, gets a refreshing new twist when served with a *liliko'i* (passion fruit)–lemongrass beurre blanc. Save room for the signature molten chocolate desire, a decadent finale at this pleasing and deservedly popular restaurant. ⊠ *5022 Lāwa'i Rd., Kōloa* ☎ *808/742–1424* ⊕ *www.the-beach-house.com* ⊰ *Reservations essential* ▤ *AE, DC, MC, V* ⊘ *No lunch.*

$$ ✕ **Brennecke's Beach Broiler.** Brennecke's is decidedly casual and fun, with
STEAKHOUSE   a busy bar, windows overlooking the beach, and a cheery blue-and-
white interior. It specializes in big portions in a wide range of offerings
including New York steaks, crab legs, shrimp, and the fresh catch of
the day. Can't decide? Then, create your own combination meal. This
place is especially good for happy hour (3 pm to 5 pm), as the drink
and pūpū menus bring the prices closer to reality. The fare is fair, but
the ocean view and convenient location compensate for the food's short-
comings. There's a take-out deli downstairs. ✉ *2100 Ho'ōne Rd., Po'ipū*
☎ *808/742–7588* ⊕ *www.brenneckes.com* ▭ *AE, D, DC, MC, V.*

$$ ✕ **Casa di Amici.** Tucked away in a quiet neighborhood above Po'ipū
ITALIAN   Beach, this "House of Friends" has live classical piano music on Satur-
day nights and an outside deck open to sweeping ocean views. Entrées
from the internationally eclectic menu include a saffron-vanilla paella
risotto made with black tiger prawns, fresh fish, chicken breast, and
homemade Italian sausage. For dessert, take the plunge with a baked
Hawai'i: a chocolate-macadamia-nut brownie topped with coconut and
passion-fruit sorbet and flambéed Italian meringue. The food and setting are pleasant, but the knowledgeable servers can be slow, especially
when you're really hungry ✉ *2301 Nalo Rd., Po'ipū* ☎ *808/742–1555*
⊕ *www.casadiamicipoipu.com* ▭ *D, DC, MC, V* ⊘ *No lunch.*

$$$ ✕ **Dondero's.** The inlaid marble floors, ornate tile work, and Italianate
ITALIAN   murals that compose the elegant interior at this restaurant compete
Fodor'sChoice   with a stunning ocean view. In addition to the beautiful setting, Don-
★   dero's offers outstanding food, a remarkable wine list, and impeccable
service, making this one of Kaua'i's best restaurants. Chef Patrick Shi-
mada's elegant tasting menu features Italian dishes, including home-
made pastas, risotto, and flatbread pizza. Try the four-cheese risotto
with Kaua'i cherry tomatoes, or the grilled Pacific swordfish filet, served
with oregeno, lemon, olive oil, and baby bell pepper relish. The wait-
staff deserves special praise for its thoughtful, discrete service. ✉ *Grand
Hyatt Kaua'i Resort and Spa, 1571 Po'ipū Rd., Kōloa* ☎ *808/240–6456*
▭ *AE, D, DC, MC, V* ⊘ *No lunch.*

¢   ✕ **Joe's on the Green.** Eat an open-air breakfast or lunch with an expan-
AMERICAN   sive vista of Po'ipū. Located on the Kiahuna Golf Course, this res-
taurant boasts such favorites as eggs Benedict, tofu scramble, and
banana-macadamia-nut pancakes. For lunch, try the Reuben sandwich
or ribs, or build your own salad. The "small plates" menu and happy-
hour drink specials are available from 3 to 5:30, including favorites such
as herb and garlic chicken skewers, seared 'ahi tacos, and homemade
chili nachos, all accompanied by live Hawaiian music. With a casual
atmosphere and generous portions, Joe's is a refreshing alternative to
the pricier hotel brunch venues in this area. ✉ *2545 Kiahuna Plantation
Dr. Po'ipū* ☎ *808/742–9696* ▭ *MC, V* ⊘ *No dinner.*

$$ ✕ **Keoki's Paradise.** Built to resemble a dockside boathouse, this active,
SEAFOOD   boisterous place fills up quickly at night thanks to the live music. Sea-
food appetizers span the tide from sashimi to Thai shrimp sticks, crab
cakes, and scallops crusted in *panko* (Japanese-style bread crumbs).
The day's fresh catch is available in half a dozen styles and sauces.
And there's a sampling of beef, chicken, and pork-rib entrées for the

Continued on page 583

LŪ'AU: A TASTE OF HAWAI'I

The best place to sample Hawaiian food is at a backyard lū'au. Aunties and uncles are cooking, the pig is from a cousin's farm, and the fish is from a brother's boat.

But invitations to those occasions are rare. So your choice is most likely between a commercial lū'au and a restaurant that serves Hawaiian food.

Most commercial lū'au will offer you some of the authentic diet; they're also about umbrella drinks, laughs, spectacle, and fun. Expect to spend a leisurely evening and no small amount of cash.

For greater authenticity, folksy experiences, and rock-bottom prices, visit a Hawaiian restaurant (most are in simple, anonymous storefronts in residential neighborhoods). Locals will be happy to help you negotiate the menu.

In either case, much of what is known today as Hawaiian food would be as foreign to a 16th-century Hawaiian as risotto or chow mein. The pre-contact diet was simple and healthy–mainly raw and steamed seafood and vegetables. Early Hawaiians used earth ovens and heated stones to cook seafood, taro, sweet potatoes, and breadfruit and seasoned their food with sea salt and ground kukui nuts. Seaweed, fern shoots, sweet potato vines, coconut, banana, sugarcane, and select greens and roots rounded out the diet.

Successive waves of immigrants added their favorites to the ti leaf–lined table. So it is that foods as disparate as salt salmon and chicken long rice are now Hawaiian— even though there is no salmon in Hawaiian waters and long rice (cellophane noodles) is Chinese.

AT THE LŪʻAU: KĀLUA PORK

The heart of any lūʻau is the *imu*, the earth oven in which a whole pig is roasted. The preparation of an imu is a bonding affair for most families, who tackle it only once a year or so, for a baby's first birthday or at Thanksgiving, when many Islanders prefer to imu their turkeys. Commercial lūʻau operations have it down to a science, however.

THE ART OF THE STONE

The key to a proper imu is the *pohaku*, the stones. Imu cook by means of long, slow, moist heat released by special stones that can withstand a hot fire without exploding. Many Hawaiian families treasure their imu stones, keeping them in a pile in the backyard and passing them on through generations.

PIT COOKING

The imu makers first dig a pit about the size of a refrigerator, then lay down *kiawe* (mesquite) wood and stones, and build a white-hot fire that is allowed to burn itself out. The ashes are raked away, and the hot stones covered with banana and ti leaves. Well-wrapped in ti or banana leaves and a net of chicken wire, the pig is lowered onto the leaf-covered stones. *Laulau* (leaf-wrapped bundles of meats, fish, and taro leaves) may also be placed inside. Leaves—ti, banana, even ginger—cover the pig followed by wet burlap sacks (to create steam). The whole is topped with a canvas tarp and left to steam overnight.

OPENING THE IMU

This is the moment everyone waits for: The imu is unwrapped like a giant present and the imu keepers gingerly wrestle out the steaming pig. When it's unwrapped, the meat falls moist and smoky-flavored from the bone, looking and tasting just like Southern-style pulled pork, but without the barbecue sauce.

WHICH LŪʻAU?

Grand Hyatt Kauaʻi Lūʻau. Choose this oceanfront lūʻau if it's a romantic evening you're after.

Lūʻau Kālamakū. This lūʻau is on a former sugar plantation and has a more theatrical style than the resort type.

Paʻina o Hanalei. Lavish, with upscale Pacific Rim cuisine.

Smith's Tropical Paradise. Our top pick, set on a lovely 30-acre tropical garden.

MEA 'AI 'ONO.
GOOD THINGS TO EAT.

LAULAU
Steamed meats, fish, and taro leaf in ti-leaf bundles: fork-tender, a medley of flavors; the taro resembles spinach.

LOMILOMI SALMON
Salt salmon in a piquant salad or relish with onions, tomatoes.

POI (DON'T CALL IT LIBRARY PASTE.)
Poi, a paste made of pounded taro root, is an acquired taste, but give it a try.

Consider: The Hawaiian Adam is descended from *kalo* (taro). Young taro plants are called "keiki"–children. Poi is the first food after mother's milk for many Islanders. 'Ai, the word for food, is synonymous with poi in many contexts.

Not only that, we like it. "There is no meat that doesn't taste good with poi," the old Hawaiians said.

But you have to know how to eat it: with something rich or powerfully flavored. "It is salt that makes the poi go in," is another adage. When you're served poi, try it with a mouthful of smoky kālua pork or salty lomilomi salmon. Its slightly sour blandness cleanses the palate. And if you don't like it, smile and say something polite. (And slide that bowl over to a local.)

Laulau

Lomilomi Salmon

Poi

5

IN FOCUS LŪ'AU: A TASTE OF HAWAI'I

E HELE MAI 'AI! COME AND EAT!

Hawaiian restaurants tend to be inconveniently located in well-worn storefronts with little or no parking, outfitted with battered tables and clattering Melmac dishes, open odd (and usually limited) hours and days, and often so crowded you have to wait. But they personify aloha, invariably run by local families who welcome tourists who take the trouble to find them.

Many are cash-only operations and combination plates are a standard feature: one or two entrées, a side such as chicken long rice, choice of poi or steamed rice and—if the place is really old-style—a tiny portion of coarse Hawaiian salt and some raw onions for relish.

Most serve some foods that aren't, strictly speaking, Hawaiian, but are beloved of kama'āina, such as salt meat with watercress (preserved meat in a tasty broth), or *akubone* (skipjack tuna fried in a tangy vinegar sauce).

Our favorite: **Dani's Restaurant** (✉ 4201 Rice St., Līhu'e, ☎ 808/245–4991).

MENU GUIDE

Much of the Hawaiian language encountered during a stay in the Islands will appear on restaurant menus and lists of lūʻau fare. Here's a quick primer.

ʻahi: *yellowfin tuna.*

aku: *skipjack, bonito tuna.*

ʻamaʻama: *mullet; it's hard to get but tasty.*

bento: *a box lunch.*

chicken lūʻau: *a stew made from chicken, taro leaves, and coconut milk.*

haupia: *a light, pudding-like sweet made from coconut.*

imu: *the underground ovens in which pigs are roasted for lūʻau.*

kālua: *to bake underground.*

kaukau: *food. The word comes from Chinese but is used in the Islands.*

kimchee: *Korean dish of pickled cabbage made with garlic and hot peppers.*

Kona coffee: *coffee grown in the Kona district of the Big Island.*

laulau: *literally, a bundle. Laulau are morsels of pork, chicken, butterfish, or other ingredients wrapped with young taro leaves and then bundled in ti leaves for steaming.*

lilikoʻi: *passion fruit, a tart, seedy yellow fruit that makes delicious desserts, juice, and jellies.*

lomilomi: *to rub or massage; also a massage. Lomilomi salmon is fish that has been rubbed with onions and herbs; commonly served with minced onions and tomatoes.*

lūʻau: *a Hawaiian feast; also the leaf of the taro plant used in preparing such a feast.*

lūʻau leaves: *cooked taro tops with a taste similar to spinach.*

mahimahi: *mild-flavored dolphinfish, not the marine mammal.*

mai tai: *potent rum drink with orange and lime juice, from the Tahitian word for "good."*

malasada: *a Portuguese deep-fried doughnut without a hole, dipped in sugar.*

manapua: *dough wrapped around diced pork or other fillings.*

manō: *shark.*

niu: *coconut.*

ʻōkolehao: *a liqueur distilled from the ti root.*

onaga: *pink or red snapper.*

ono: *a long, slender mackerel-like fish; also called wahoo.*

ʻono: *delicious; also hungry.*

ʻopihi: *a tiny shellfish, or mollusk, found on rocks; also called limpets.*

pāpio: *a young ulua or jack fish.*

pohā: *Cape gooseberry. Tasting a bit like honey, the pohā berry is often used in jams and desserts.*

poi: *a paste made from pounded taro root, a staple of the Hawaiian diet.*

poke: *chopped, pickled raw tuna or other fish, tossed with herbs and seasonings.*

pūpū: *Hawaiian hors d'oeuvre.*

saimin: *long thin noodles and vegetables in broth, often garnished with small pieces of fish cake, scrambled egg, luncheon meat, and green onion.*

sashimi: *raw fish thinly sliced and usually eaten with soy sauce.*

tī leaves: *a member of the agave family. The fragrant leaves are used to wrap food while cooking and removed before eating.*

uku: *deep-sea snapper.*

ulua: *a member of the jack family that also includes pompano and amberjack. Also called crevalle, jack fish, and jack crevalle.*

committed carnivore. A lighter menu is available at the bar for lunch and dinner. ⊠ *Po'ipū Shopping Village, 2360 Kiahuna Plantation Dr., Kōloa* ☎ *808/742-7534* ⊕ *www.keokisparadise.com* ▭ *AE, D, DC, MC, V.*

$$ ✕**Plantation Gardens.** A historic plantation manager's home has been
ITALIAN converted to a restaurant that serves seafood and kiawe-grilled meats with a Pacific Rim and Italian influence. You'll walk through a tropical setting of torch-lighted orchid gardens and lotus-studded koi ponds to a cozy, European-style dining room with cherry wood floors and a veranda. The menu is based on fresh, local foods: fish right off the boat, herbs and produce picked from the plantation's gardens, fruit delivered by neighborhood farmers. The result is cuisine with an island flair— seafood *laulau* (seafood wrapped in tī leaves and steamed) served with mango chutney—served alongside traditional classics such as sugarcane-skewered pork tenderloin. Definitely save room for dessert: The warm pineapple upside-down cake is a dream. In short, the food is excellent and the setting charming. ⊠ *Kiahuna Plantation, 2253 Po'ipū Rd., Kōloa* ☎ *808/742–2121* ⊕ *www.pgrestaurant.com* ▭ *AE, DC, MC, V* ⊙ *No lunch.*

$$ ✕**Pomodoro Ristorante Italiano.** Two walls of windows brighten this
ITALIAN intimate second-story restaurant in the heart of Kalāheo, where you'll find good food at reasonable prices. Begin with prosciutto and melon, then proceed directly to the multilayer meat lasagna, a favorite of the chefs—two Italian-born brothers. Other highlights include eggplant or veal parmigiana, chicken saltimbocca, and scampi in a garlic, caper, and white wine sauce. ⊠ *Upstairs at Rainbow Plaza, Kaumuali'i Hwy., Rte. 50, Kalāheo* ☎ *808/332–5945* ▭ *MC, V* ⊙ *Closed Sun. No lunch.*

$$$$ ✕**Roy's Po'ipū Bar & Grill.** Hawai'i's culinary superstar, Roy Yamaguchi,
MODERN is fond of sharing his signature Hawaiian fusion cuisine by cloning the
HAWAIIAN successful Honolulu restaurant where he got his start. You'll find one of these copycat eateries on Kaua'i's South Side in a shopping-center locale that feels too small and ordinary for the exotic food. The menu changes daily, and the hardworking kitchen staff dreams up 15 to 20 (or more) specials each night—an impressive feat. Though the food reflects the imaginative pairings and high-quality ingredients of the original Roy's and the presentation is spectacular, the atmosphere is a little different. As with most restaurant branches, it just doesn't have the heart and soul of the original. ⊠ *Po'ipū Shopping Village, 2360 Kiahuna Plantation Dr., Kōloa* ☎ *808/742–5000* ⊕ *www.roysrestaurant.com* ▭ *AE, D, DC, MC, V* ⊙ *No lunch.*

$$$ ✕**Shells Steak and Seafood.** Chandeliers made from shells light the dining
SEAFOOD room and give this restaurant its name. The menu is upscale surf and turf, with prime cuts of steak and fresh fish enhanced by tropical spices and sauces. Shells is one of three signature restaurants in the Sheraton's Oceanfront Galleria. Each of these restaurants has been designed to embrace the view of the Pacific Ocean from sunrise to starlight. ⊠ *Sheraton Kaua'i Resort, 2440 Ho'onani Rd., Po'ipū Beach, Kōloa* ☎ *808/742–1661* ▭ *AE, D, DC, MC, V* ⊙ *No lunch.*

$$$ ✕**Tidepools.** The Grand Hyatt Kaua'i is notable for its excellent res-
SEAFOOD taurants, which differ widely in their settings and cuisine. This one is

5

definitely the most tropical and campy, sure to appeal to folks seeking a bit of island-style romance and adventure. Private grass-thatch huts seem to float on a koi-filled pond beneath starry skies while torches flicker in the lushly landscaped grounds nearby. The equally distinctive food has an island flavor that comes from the chef's advocacy of Hawai'i Regional Cuisine and extensive use of Kaua'i-grown products including fresh herbs from the resort's organic garden. You won't go wrong ordering one of the signature dishes, such as wok-seared soy-, sake-, and ginger-marinated 'ahi; grilled mahimahi; or pan-seared beef tenderloin. Start with Tidepools' pūpū platter for two—with a lobster cake, peppered beef fillet, and 'ahi sashimi—to wake up your taste buds. If you're still hungry at the end of the meal, the ginger crème brūlée is sure to satisfy. ⊠ *Grand Hyatt Kaua'i Resort and Spa, 1571 Po'ipū Rd., Kōloa* ☎ *808/240–6456 Ext. 4260* ▭ *AE, D, DC, MC, V* ☉ *No lunch.*

$ ✕**Tomkats Grille.** Tropical ponds, a waterfall, a large bar area, and a
AMERICAN porch overlooking an inner courtyard give this grill a casual island vibe. Try the macadamia-nut-crusted "katch of the day" with a passion-fruit butter glaze or the homemade chili and burger. Wash it down with a glass of wine or one of 15 ales, stouts, ports, and lagers. Plenty of Tomkats' Nibblers—such as buffalo wings and sautéed shrimp—enliven happy hour from 3 to 6 pm. ⊠ *Old Kōloa Town, 5402 Kōloa Rd., Kōloa* ☎ *808/742–8887* ▭ *MC, V.*

$$$ ✕**Wrangler's Steakhouse.** Denim-covered seating, decorative saddles, and
STEAKHOUSE a stagecoach in a loft helped to transform the historic Ako General Store in Waimea into a West Side steak house. You can eat under the stars on the deck out back or inside the old-fashioned, wood-panel dining room. The 16-ounce New York steak comes sizzling, and the rib eye is served with capers. A tasty salad is part of each meal. Those with smaller appetites might consider the vegetable tempura or the 'ahi served on penne pasta. Local folks love the special lunch: soup, rice, beef teriyaki, and shrimp tempura served in a three-tier *kaukau* tin, or lunch pail, just like the ones sugar-plantation workers once carried. A gift shop has local crafts (and sometimes a craftsperson doing demonstrations). ⊠ *9852 Kaumuali'i Hwy., Waimea* ☎ *808/338–1218* ▭ *AE, MC, V* ☉ *Closed Sun.*

WHERE TO STAY

The Garden Island has lodgings for every taste, from swanky resorts to rustic cabins, and from family-friendly condos to romantic bed-and-breakfasts. The savvy traveler can also find inexpensive places that are convenient, safe, and accessible to Kaua'i's special places and activities. When choosing a place to stay, location is an important consideration. Kaua'i may seem small on a map, but because it's circular with no through roads, it can take more time than you think to get from place to place. If at all possible, stay close to your desired activities. This way, you'll save time to squeeze in all the things you'll want to do. Prices are highest near the ocean and in resort communities such as Princeville and Po'ipū.

WHAT IT COSTS					
	¢	$	$$	$$$	$$$$
HOTELS	under $100	$100–$180	$181–$260	$261–$340	over $340

Hotel prices are for two people in a standard double room in high season. Condo price categories reflect studio and one-bedroom rates. Prices do not include 13.42% hotel tax.

THE NORTH SHORE

$$–$$$
RESORT
Fodor'sChoice
★

Hanalei Bay Resort. This time-share condominium resort has a lovely location overlooking Hanalei Bay and Nāpali Coast. Three-story buildings angle down the cliffs, making for some steep walking paths. Units are extremely spacious, with high, sloping ceilings and large private lānai. Rattan furniture and island art add a casual feeling to rooms. Studios have small kitchenettes not meant for serious cooking. The larger units have full kitchens. The resort's upper-level pool is one of the nicest on the island, with authentic lava-rock waterfalls, an open-air hot tub, and a kid-friendly sand "beach." The tennis courts are on-site. **Pros:** beautiful views; tennis courts on property; tropical pool. **Cons:** steep walkways; long walk to beach. **TripAdvisor:** "large rolling property," "no parking near many of the units," "view of Hanalei Bay." ✉ 5380 Honoiki Rd., Princeville ☎ 808/826–6522 or 866/507–1428 ⊕ www.hanaleibayresort.com ➫ 134 units ⌂ In-room: a/c, safe, kitchen, refrigerator. In-hotel: tennis courts, pools, beachfront, children's programs (ages 5–12), laundry facilities ⊟ AE, D, DC, MC, V.

$$$–$$$$
HOTEL

Hanalei Colony Resort. This 5-acre property, the only true beachfront resort on Kaua'i's North Shore, is a laid-back, go-barefoot kind of place sandwiched between towering mountains and the sea. Its charm is in its simplicity. There are no phones, TVs, or stereos in the rooms, but you can get complimentary wireless Internet access in the resort's oceanfront common room. Each of the two-bedroom units can sleep a family of four, although these units are popular with the honeymoon crowd. The units are well maintained, with Hawaiian-style furnishings, full kitchens, and lānai. Amenities, such as cocktail receptions and cultural activities, vary from season to season. There's an art gallery, spa and restaurant on-site. **Pros:** oceanfront setting; private, quiet; seventh night free. **Cons:** remote location; damp in winter. **TripAdvisor:** "well decorated," "nice, caring staff," "beautiful hiking to secluded beaches." ✉ 5-7130 Kūhiō Hwy., Hā'ena ☎ 808/826–6235 or 800/628–3004 ⊕ www.hcr.com ➫ 48 units ⌂ In-room: no a/c, no phone, kitchen, no TV. In-hotel: restaurant, bar, pool, spa, beachfront, laundry facilities, Wi-Fi ⊟ AE, MC, V.

$$$$
RESORT
Fodor'sChoice
★

St. Regis Princeville Resort. Built into the cliffs above Hanalei Bay, this unbeatable Starwood resort offers expansive views of the sea and mountains, including Makana, the landmark peak immortalized as the mysterious Bali Ha'i island in the film *South Pacific*. Reopened in October 2009 with the upgraded St. Regis brand, the spacious guest rooms reflect an ocean ambience with subtle earth tones in signature hues. The butler service (included with some rooms) is top-notch. Little details

5

make a difference, such as lighted closets, original artwork, and a wine cellar. Bathrooms are all elegant marble with a privacy window—flip a switch and it goes from clear to opaque so you can see the sights outside without becoming an attraction yourself. The restaurants serve excellent food with priceless views, and the rebuilt pool is lavish with extremely comfortable lounge furniture. The St. Regis Bar hosts nightly entertainment and the huge windows showcase gorgeous sunsets and a breathtaking view of Hanalei Bay. The new in-house spa connotes a Zen-like atmosphere with traditional Hawaiian healing and Western techniques. There's shuttle service to the resort's two top-ranked golf courses and tennis center. **Pros:** great views; excellent restaurants; attractive lobby; professional staff. **Cons:** minimal grounds; reefy beach for swimming. **TripAdvisor:** "warm welcome in the lobby," "ultimate in luxury accommodations," "most beautiful spot on Earth." ⊠ *5520 Ka Haku Rd., Princeville* ☎ *877/787–3447 or 808/826–9644* ⊕ *www. stregisprinceville.com* ⟿ *201 rooms, 51 suites* ⚑ *In-room: a/c, safe, DVD, Wi-Fi. In-hotel: 4 restaurants, room service, bars, 2 golf courses, 4 tennis courts, pool, gym, spa, beachfront, water sports, children's programs (ages 5–12), laundry service, Internet terminal, Wi-Fi hotspot, parking (paid)* ▭ *AE, D, DC, MC, V.*

THE EAST SIDE

KAPA'A AND WAILUA

$$–$$$

RENTAL

Aloha Cottages. Owners Charlie and Susan Hoerner restored a three-bedroom plantation home on Kapa'a's Baby Beach to reflect the charm of yesteryear with the conveniences of today. Think plank flooring, gingerbread, and stained glass alongside a Wolf stove, Bosch dishwasher, and granite countertops. The orientation is due east; you won't have to leave your bed—or living room or lānai—to watch the sunrise, the whales breach, or the full moon rise. In addition to the main house, there's a cozy bungalow called Moonrise Cottage in back that's perfect for honeymooners. Rent both (weekly rentals only) to sleep a total of eight. Credit cards are accepted via PayPal only. **Pros:** comfortable, homelike ambience; good for large groups; safe children's beach. **Cons:** can be windy in winter; not great for swimming. **TripAdvisor:** "private and comfortable," "mountain views," "reminiscent of "old" Hawai'i." ⊠ *1041 Moana Kai Rd., Kapa'a* ☎ *808/823–0933 or 877/915–1015* ⊕ *www.alohacottages.com* ⟿ *2 cottages* ⚑ *In-room: no a/c, kitchen. In-hotel: beachfront* ▭ *MC, V.*

$$$

RESORT

Aston Aloha Beach Hotel. Nestled between Wailua Bay and the Wailua River, this low-key, low-rise resort is an easy, convenient place to stay. Families will enjoy being within walking distance of Lydgate Beach Park. It's also close to shops and low-cost restaurants. Rooms are in two wings and have beach, mountain, or ocean views. The resort also offers one-bedroom beach cottages with kitchenettes. **Pros:** excellent cultural program; walk to beach and park; convenient locale. **Cons:** exiting hotel parking lot onto highway can be difficult; restaurant meals are average. **TripAdvisor:** "very quiet place," "rooms are older," "next to a good snorkeling lagoon." ⊠ *3-5920 Kūhiō Hwy., Kapa'a* ☎ *808/823–6000 or 888/823–5111* ⊕ *www.astonhotels.com* ⟿ *216 rooms, 10 suites, 24*

BEST BETS FOR
KAUA'I LODGING

Fodor'sChoice★

Grand Hyatt Kaua'i Resort and Spa $$$$, p. 593

Hanalei Bay Resort $$–$$$, p. 585

Sheraton Kaua'i Resort $$$–$$$$, p. 596

St. Regis Princeville Resort $$$$, p. 585

Waimea Plantation Cottages $$–$$$, p. 597

By Price

¢–$

Best Western Plantation Hale Suites, p. 587

Garden Island Inn, p. 593

Kōke'e Lodge, p. 597

Rosewood Bed and Breakfast, p. 589

$$

Hotel Coral Reef, p. 587

Po'ipū Shores, p. 596

$$$

Hanalei Colony Resort, p. 585

Po'ipū Kapili, p. 594

$$$$

Kaua'i Marriott Resort & Beach Club, p. 593

Whalers Cove, p. 597

By Experience

BEST BEACH

Kaua'i Marriott Resort & Beach Club $$$–$$$$, p. 593

Outrigger at Lae Nani $$–$$$, p. 588

BEST B&BS AND INNS

Po'ipū Plantation Resort $-$$, p. 596

Rosewood Bed and Breakfast ¢–$, p. 589

MOST KID-FRIENDLY

Grand Hyatt Kaua'i Resort and Spa $$$$, p. 593

Kaua'i Marriott Resort & Beach Club $$$–$$$$, p. 593

5

---

beach cottages ⚐ *In-room: a/c, safe, Internet, kitchen (some). In-hotel: restaurant, tennis court, pools, gym* ⊟ *AE, D, DC, MC, V.*

$ ▦ **Best Western Plantation Hale Suites.** These attractive plantation-style
RENTAL   one-bedroom units have well-equipped kitchenettes and garden lānai.
Rooms are clean and pretty, with white-rattan furnishings and pastel
colors. You couldn't ask for a more convenient location for dining,
shopping, and sightseeing: It's across from Waipouli Beach and near
Coconut Marketplace. Request a unit away from noisy Kūhiō Highway.
Pros: bright, spacious units; three pools; walking distance to shops,
restaurant, beach. **Cons:** traffic noise in mountain-view units; coral
reef makes ocean swimming challenging. **TripAdvisor:** "comfortable
and spacious," "great value," "Coconut Marketplace in walking dis-
tance." ⊠ *484 Kūhiō Hwy., Kapa'a* ☎ *808/822–4941 or 800/775–4253*
⊕ *www.plantation-hale.com* ⊅ *110 units* ⚐ *In-room: a/c, safe, kitchen,
Internet. In-hotel: pools, laundry facilities, Wi-Fi hotspot* ⊟ *AE, D,
DC, MC, V.*

$–$$ ▦ **Hotel Coral Reef.** Coral Reef has been in business since the 1960s and
HOTEL   is something of a beachfront landmark. It went through a major reno-
☾   vation in 2006, and now the accommodations are on a par with the
prime location. Besides remodeling the rooms, the owners added a large
pool that looks onto the ocean. The two two-room units are good for
families. **Pros:** nice pool; sauna; oceanfront setting; convenient location.

Cons: located in a busy section of Kapa'a; ocean swimming is marginal; few resort amenities. **TripAdvisor:** "staff was very friendly," "very comfortable bed," "ocean breeze through room was lovely." ✉ *4-1516 Kūhiō Hwy., Kapa'a* ☎ *808/822–4481 or 800/843–4659* ⊕ *www.hotelcoralreefresort.com* ⟳ *19 rooms, 2 suites ⊘ In-room: a/c, safe, refrigerator (some). In-hotel: pool, beachfront, laundry facilities, parking (free)* ⊟ *AE, D, MC, V.*

$
RENTAL

⛺ **Kapa'a Sands.** An old rock etched with *kanji*, Japanese characters, reminds you that the site of this condominium gem was formerly occupied by a Shinto temple. Two-bedroom rentals—equipped with full kitchens and private lānai—are a fair deal. Studios feature pull-down Murphy beds to create more daytime space. Ask for an oceanfront room to get the breeze. **Pros:** discounts for extended stays; walking distance to shops, restaurants, and beach; turtle and monk seal sightings common. **Cons:** no-frills lodging; traffic noise in mountain-facing units. **TripAdvisor:** "unit was meticulously cleaned every day," "very relaxing," "beach isn't swimmable." ✉ *380 Papaloa Rd., Kapa'a* ☎ *808/822–4901 or 800/222–4901* ⊕ *www.kapaasands.com* ⟳ *21 units ⊘ In-room: no a/c, kitchen. In-hotel: pool, beachfront* ⊟ *MC, V.*

$$$
RENTAL

⛺ **Kaua'i Coast Resort.** Fronting an uncrowded stretch of beach, this three-story primarily time-share resort is convenient and a bit more upscale than nearby properties. The fully furnished one- and two-bedroom condo units, each with a private lānai and well-equipped kitchen, are housed in three buildings. They are decorated in rich woods, tropical prints, and Hawaiian-quilt designs. The 8-acre property looks out on the ocean and offers a heated pool with waterscapes, a day spa, a children's pool, a good restaurant, and an ocean-side hot tub. It's in the Coconut Marketplace, so it's within walking distance of shops and restaurants. **Pros:** lovely pool; excellent restaurant; convenient. **Cons:** area is a bit touristy. **TripAdvisor:** "staff is courteous and attentive," "full maid service once a week," "great ocean view." ✉ *520 Aleka Loop, Kapa'a* ☎ *808/822–3441 or 866/678–3289* ⊕ *www.shellhospitality.com* ⟳ *108 units ⊘ In-room: a/c, safe, kitchen, refrigerator, Internet. In-hotel: restaurant, tennis court, pool, gym, spa, beachfront* ⊟ *AE, D, DC, MC, V.*

$$-$$$
RENTAL

⛺ **Outrigger at Lae Nani.** Ruling Hawaiian chiefs once returned from ocean voyages to this spot, now host to condominiums comfortable enough for minor royalty. Hotel-sponsored Hawaiiana programs and a booklet for self-guided historical tours are nice extras. Units are all uniquely decorated, with bright, full kitchens and expansive lānai. Your view of landscaped grounds is interrupted only by a large pool before ending at a sandy, swimmable beach. You can find plenty of dining and shopping at the nearby Coconut Marketplace. **Pros:** nice swimming

WHERE TO STAY IN KAUA'I

	Local Vibe	Pros	Cons
The North Shore	Properties here have the "wow" factor with ocean and mountain beauty; laid-back Hanalei and Princeville set the high-end pace.	When the weather is good (summer) this side has it all. Epic winter surf, gorgeous waterfalls, and verdant vistas create some of the best scenery in Hawai'i.	Lots of rain (being green has a cost) means you may have to travel south to find the sun; expensive restaurants and shopping offer few deals.
The East Side	The most reasonably priced area to stay for the practical traveler; lacks the pizzazz of expensive resorts on North and South shores; more traditional Hawaiian hotels.	The best travel deals show up here; more direct access to the local population; plenty of decent restaurants with good variety, along with delis in food stores.	Beaches aren't the greatest (rocky, reefy) at many of the lodging spots; bad traffic at times; some crime issues in parks.
The South Shore	Resort central; plenty of choices where the consistent sunshine is perfect for those who want to do nothing but play golf or tennis and read a book by the pool.	Beautiful in its own right; many enchanted evenings with stellar sunsets; summer surf easier for beginners to handle.	Some areas are deserty with scrub brush; construction can be brutal on piece of mind.
The West Side	There are few options for lodging in this mostly untouristlike setting with contrasts such as the extreme heat of a July day in Waimea to a frozen winter night up in Kōke'e.	A gateway area for exploration into the wilds of Kōke'e or for boating trips on NāpaliCoast; main hub for boat and helicopter trips; outstanding sunsets.	Least convenient side for most visitors; daytime is languid and dry; river runoff can ruin ocean's clarity.

beach; walking distance to playground; attractively furnished. **Cons:** occasional odors from nearby sewage-treatment plant. **TripAdvisor:** "all the comforts of home," "beautiful grounds and pool," "ocean view also means highway view." ⊠ *410 Papaloa Rd., Kapa'a* ☎ *808/822–4938 or 800/688–7444* ⊕ *www.outrigger.com* ⤴ *84 units* ⌂ *In-room: no a/c, safe, kitchen. In-hotel: tennis court, pool, beachfront, laundry facilities* ⊟ *AE, D, DC, MC, V.*

¢–$ 🏠 **Rosewood Bed and Breakfast.** This charming bed-and-breakfast on a
B&B/INN   macadamia-nut plantation estate offers five separate styles of accommodations, including a two-bedroom Victorian cottage; a three-bedroom, two-bath home; a little one-bedroom grass-thatch cottage; a bunkhouse with three rooms and a shared bath; and the traditional main plantation home with two rooms, each with private bath. The bunkhouse and thatched cottage feature outside hot-cold private shower areas hidden from view by a riot of tropically scented foliage and a fence. The entire property has Wi-Fi. **Pros:** varied accommodations; good breakfast; attractive grounds. **Cons:** some traffic noise; no beach. ⊠ *872 Kamalu Rd., Kapa'a* ☎ *808/822–5216* ⊕ *www.rosewoodkauai.com* ⤴ *One 3-bedroom home, one 2-bedroom cottage, one 1-bedroom cottage, 3*

WHERE TO STAY ON THE KOHALA COAST AND WAIMEA

	Property Name	Worth Noting	Cost	Pools	Beach	Golf Course	Tennis Courts	Gym	Spa	Children's Programs	Rooms	Restaurants	Other	Location
	Hotels and Resorts													
15	Aston Aloha Beach Hotel	Beach cottages available	$$$	2			1	yes		3–12	250	1		Kapa'a
3	Grand Hyatt Kaua'i Resort and Spa	5 acres of swimming lagoons	$$$$	1	yes	yes	4	yes	yes		639	6	shops	Kōloa
22	Hanalei Bay Resort	Great views	$$–$$$	2	yes	priv.	8			5–12	134		kitchen	North Shore
24	Hanalei Colony Resort	Go-barefoot kind of place	$$$–$$$$	1	yes						48	1	no a/c	North Shore
21	Hotel Coral Reef	Good location, low price	$–$$	1	yes						21			Kapa'a
13	Kaua'i Marriott Resort & Beach Club	26,000-sq-ft pool	$$$–$$$$	1	yes	yes	7	yes	yes	5–12	599	5	shops	Lihu'e
8	Sheraton Kaua'i Resort	Ocean wing right on water	$$$–$$$$	2	yes		3	yes	yes	5–12	402	4		Kōloa
23	St. Regis Princeville Resort	Extravagant	$$$$	1	yes	yes	4	yes	yes	5–12	252	4	shops	North Shore
	Condos and Vacation Rentals													
20	Aloha Cottages	Oceanfront	$$–$$$		yes						2		no a/c	Kapa'a
19	Best Western Plantation Hale Suites	Beach across the street	$	3							110		kitchen	Kapa'a
11	Hideaway Cove	Quiet	$$								7		kitchen	South Shore
16	Kapa'a Sands	Hawai'i-owned and operated	$	1	yes						21		no a/c	Kapa'a
18	Kaua'i Coast Resort	Uncrowded beach	$$$	1	yes		1	yes	yes		108	1	kitchen	Kapa'a
17	Outrigger at Lae Nani	Cultural programs	$$–$$$	1	yes		1				84		no a/c	Kapa'a

#	Name	Description	Price								Region
6	Outrigger Kiahuna Plantation	Popular with families	$$$–$$$$	1	yes	6		333	1	no a/c	South Shore
5	Poʻipū Kapili	Delux PH suites available	$$–$$$	1		2		60		no a/c	South Shore
9	Poʻipū Plantation Resort	Full breakfast	$–$$					13		3-night minimum	South Shore
10	Poʻipū Shores	Excellent whale-watching	$$$	1				39		no a/c	South Shore
7	Suite Paradise Poʻipū Kai	Short walk to beach	$$–$$$	6		9		130	1	2-night minimum	South Shore
4	Whalers Cove	Rocky beach	$$$–$$$$	1	yes			39		no a/c	South Shore
2	Waimea Plantation Cottages	Good for large groups	$$–$$$	1	yes		yes	48	1	no a/c	West Side

B&Bs and Inns

#	Name	Description	Price								Region
12	Garden Island Inn	Beach across the street	$–$$					26		kitchen	Lihuʻe
1	Kōkeʻe Lodge	Rustic wilderness cabins	¢					12	1	no a/c	West Side
14	Rosewood Bed and Breakfast	Located on a plantation	¢–$					11			Kapaʻa

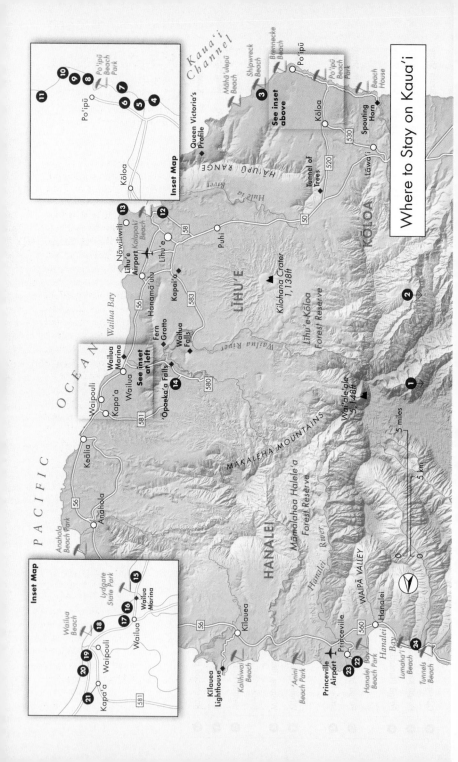

Where to Stay on Kaua'i

Inset Map (top left)

10 9 8 7 6 5 4

Po'ipū Beach Park
Po'ipū
Kōloa

Inset Map (bottom left)

Kīlauea Lighthouse
Kalihiwai Beach
'Anini Beach Park

Lydgate State Park
Wailua Marina
Wailua Beach
15 16 17 18
19 20 21
Wailua
Waipouli
Kapa'a
581

Kaua'i Channel

Māhā'ulepū Beach
Shipwreck Beach
Brennecke Beach
Po'ipū
3
Queen Victoria's Profile
See inset above
Kōloa
Po'ipū Beach Park
Beach House
Spouting Horn
Lāwa'i
HĀ'UPŪ RANGE
Tunnel of Trees
Huleʻia River
520
530
50
KŌLOA

13 Nāwiliwili
12
Līhu'e
Līhu'e Airport
Hanamā'ulu
Kapa'a
583
58
Puhi
LĪHU'E
Kilohana Crater 1,138ft
Līhu'e-Kōloa Forest Reserve
2

Wailua Bay
Wailua Marina
See inset at left
Waipouli
Kapa'a
Wailua
Fern Grotto
Wailua Falls
14 'Ōpeka'a Falls
580
581
Wailua River
Wai'ale'ale 5,148ft
1

PACIFIC OCEAN
Kealia
Anahola
Anahola Beach Park
56
MAKALEHA MOUNTAINS

Māmalahoa Halele'a Forest Reserve
Hanalei River
HANALEI
WAIPĀ VALLEY

Kīlauea
56
Princeville
Princeville Airport
560
Hanalei
Hanalei Bay
Hanalei Bay Beach Park
22
23
24
Lumaha'i Beach
Tunnels Beach

5 miles
5 km

rooms in bunkhouse, 2 rooms in main house & In-room: no a/c, no phone, kitchen ▭ No credit cards.

LĪHU'E

$–$$
B&B/INN

Garden Island Inn. Bargain hunters love this three-story inn near Kalapakī Bay and Anchor Cove shopping center. You can walk across the street and enjoy the majesty of Kalapakī Beach or check out the facilities and restaurants of the Marriott. It's clean and contemporary, and the innkeepers are friendly, sharing fruit and beach gear. **Pros:** walk to beach, restaurants, and shops; good for families, extended stays, and budget travel. **Cons:** some traffic noise; near a busy harbor; limited grounds; no pool. **TripAdvisor:** "rooms are clean and cute," "centrally located," "light traffic noise." ✉ *3445 Wilcox Rd., Kalapakī Beach, Līhu'e* ☎ *808/245–7227 or 800/648–0154* ⊕ *www.gardenislandinn. com* ⤢ *22 rooms, 2 suites, 2 condos & In-room: a/c, kitchen, refrigerator, Wi-Fi. In-hotel: Wi-Fi hotspot ▭ AE, DC, MC, V.*

WORD OF MOUTH

"We checked out the St. Regis. Great views from their balcony… Hanalei Bay and the mountains are absolutely beautiful!" —kureiff

$$$–$$$$
RESORT
☼

Kaua'i Marriott Resort & Beach Club. An elaborate tropical garden, waterfalls right off the lobby, Greek statues and columns, and an enormous 26,000-square-foot swimming pool characterize the grand—and grandiose—scale of this resort on Kalapakī Bay, which looks out at the dramatic Hā'upu Mountains. This resort has it all—fine dining, shopping, a spa, golf, tennis, and water activities of all kinds. Rooms have tropical decor, and most have expansive ocean views. It's comfortable and convenient with free airport shuttle service. Many of the rooms have been converted to time-shares, too. **Pros:** oceanfront setting; good restaurants; convenient location; airport shuttle. **Cons:** distant airport noise; inconvenient parking. **TripAdvisor:** "staff was very friendly and helpful," "restaurants very expensive, but good food," "pool is awesome." ✉ *3610 Rice St., Kalapakī Beach, Līhu'e* ☎ *808/245–5050 or 800/220–2925* ⊕ *www.kauaimarriott.com* ⤢ *356 rooms, 11 suites, 232 time-share units & In-room: a/c, refrigerator. In-hotel: 5 restaurants, room service, golf courses, tennis courts, pool, gym, spa, beachfront, children's programs (ages 5–12) ▭ AE, D, DC, MC, V.*

THE SOUTH SHORE

$$$$
RESORT
☼
Fodor's Choice
★

Grand Hyatt Kaua'i Resort and Spa. Dramatically handsome, this classic Hawaiian low-rise is built into the cliffs overlooking an unspoiled coastline. It's open, elegant, and very island-style, making it one of our favorite megaresorts. It has mouth-watering restaurants, including Dondero's and Tidepools. Spacious rooms, two-thirds with ocean views, have a plantation theme. Five acres of meandering fresh- and saltwater-swimming lagoons—a big hit with kids—are beautifully set amid landscaped grounds. While adults enjoy treatments at the recently renovated ANARA Spa, kids can check out Camp Hyatt. The resort has taken strides in reducing its carbon footprint by installing photovoltaic panels, renting hybrid vehicles, establishing a waste-diversion

5

program, and planting an organic garden. **Pros:** fabulous pool; excellent restaurants; Hawaiian ambience. **Cons:** poor swimming beach during summer swells; small balconies. **TripAdvisor:** "caring Aloha Spirit," "you will not be disappointed," "amazing pool." ⊠ *1571 Po'ipū Rd., Kōloa* ☎ *808/742–1234 or 800/633–7313* ⊕ *www.grandhyattkauai. com* ⇨ *602 rooms, 37 suites* ⚭ *In-room: a/c, safe, refrigerator, Wi-Fi (some). In-hotel: 6 restaurants, room service, bars, golf course, tennis courts, pool, gym, spa, beachfront, children's programs (ages 3–12)* ▤ *AE, D, DC, MC, V.*

$$
RENTAL ⛱ **Hideaway Cove.** On a quiet street ending in a cul-de-sac, Hideaway Cove is very quiet, even though it's one block from the ocean's edge in the heart of Po'ipū. What were once two homes have been converted to seven complete vacation homes. Owner Herb Lee appointed each with resort-quality furniture and furnishings—even original artwork. The two-bedroom Seabreeze villa comes with a hot tub on the lānai. The three-bedroom Oceanview villa connects via an internal staircase with the two-bedroom Aloha villa to provide a large five-bedroom home with two complete living areas—perfect for two families traveling together. Rates drop with a seven-night stay, effectively making the seventh night free. **Pros:** high-quality furnishings; private lānai; hot tub or Jacuzzi in each unit. **Cons:** not on the ocean; high cleaning fee. **TripAdvisor:** "all the basic necessities," "romantic getaway," "condo is very clean." ⊠ *2307 Nalo Rd., Po'ipū* ☎ *808/635–8785 or 866/849–2426* ⊕ *www. hideawaycove.com* ⇨ *7 units* ⚭ *In-room: a/c, kitchen. In-hotel: laundry facilities* ▤ *AE, D, MC, V.*

$$$–$$$$
RENTAL ⛱ **Outrigger Kiahuna Plantation.** Kaua'i's largest condo project is lackluster, though the location is excellent. Forty-two plantation-style, low-rise buildings arc around a large, grassy field leading to the beach. The individually decorated one- and two-bedroom units vary in style, but all are clean, have lānai, and get lots of ocean breezes. This is a popular destination for families who take advantage of the swimmable beach and lawn for picnics and games. **Pros:** great sunset and ocean views are bonuses in some units. **Cons:** not the best place to stay if you're looking for a romantic getaway. **TripAdvisor:** "exceptionally friendly and efficient," "grounds are beautiful," "don't expect luxury." ⊠ *2253 Po'ipū Rd., Kōloa* ☎ *808/742–6411 or 800/688–7444* ⊕ *www.outrigger.com* ⇨ *333 units* ⚭ *In-room: no a/c, kitchen, Internet. In-hotel: restaurant, golf course, tennis courts, pool, beachfront* ▤ *AE, DC, MC, V.*

$$–$$$
RENTAL ⛱ **Po'ipū Kapili.** Spacious one- and two-bedroom condo units are minutes from Po'ipū's restaurants and beaches. White-frame exteriors and double-pitched roofs complement the tropical landscaping. Interiors include full kitchens and entertainment centers. Choose from garden and across-the-street ocean views. Three deluxe 2,600-square-foot penthouse suites have enormous lānai, private elevators, and cathedral ceilings. You can mingle at a weekly coffee hour held beside the ocean-view pool or grab a good read from the resort library. Fresh seasonings are ready to be picked from the herb garden, and there's a barbecue poolside. In winter you can whale-watch as you cook. A five-night minimum stay is required. **Pros:** units are roomy; good guest services;

Grand Hyatt Kaua'i Resort and Spa

Grand Hyatt Kaua'i Resort and Spa

Waimea Plantation Cottages

property is small. **Cons:** units are ocean-view but not oceanfront. **Trip-Advisor:** "office staff is very helpful," "perfect for a family," "ocean view." ✉ *2221 Kapili Rd., Kōloa* ☎ *808/742–6449 or 800/443–7714* ⊕ *www.poipukapili.com* ⇥ *60 units* ⚮ *In-room: no a/c, kitchen, Internet. In-hotel: tennis courts, pool, laundry facilities* ⊟ *MC, V.*

$–$$
RENTAL

🏠 **Po'ipū Plantation Resort.** Plumeria, ti, and other tropical foliage create a lush landscape for this resort, which has one bed-and-breakfast–style plantation home and nine one- and two-bedroom cottage apartments. All cottage units have wood floors and full kitchens and are decorated in light, airy shades. The 1930s plantation home has two rooms with private baths and two suites. A full complimentary breakfast is served daily for those staying in the main house. A minimum three-night stay is required, but rates decrease with the length of stay. **Pros:** attractively furnished; full breakfast at B&B. **Cons:** three-night minimum; no Internet in room. **TripAdvisor:** "price, location, and hospitality are perfect," "tropical flowers and huge lush trees," "scenic view." ✉ *1792 Pe'e Rd., Po'ipū* ☎ *808/742–6757 or 800/634–0263* ⊕ *www.poipubeach.com* ⇥ *4 suites, 9 cottages* ⚮ *In-room: a/c, kitchen (some). In-hotel: laundry facilities, Wi-Fi* ⊟ *D, MC, V.*

$$$
RENTAL

🏠 **Po'ipū Shores.** Sitting on a rocky point above pounding surf, this is a perfect spot for whale- or turtle-watching. Weddings are staged on a little lawn beside the ocean, and a sandy swimming beach is a 10-minute walk away. There are three low-rise buildings, with a pool in front of the middle one. Condo units are individually owned and decorated. All have large windows, and many of them have bedrooms on the ocean side; each unit either shares a sundeck or has a lānai. **Pros:** every unit faces the water; oceanfront pool; wildlife viewing. **Cons:** units vary widely in style; no resort amenities. **TripAdvisor:** "condo was outdated," "pool is great," "beautiful ocean view." ✉ *1775 Pe'e Rd., Kōloa* ☎ *808/742–7700 or 800/367–5004* ⊕ *www.castleresorts.com* ⇥ *39 units* ⚮ *In-room: no a/c, kitchen, Internet. In-hotel: pool, laundry facilities* ⊟ *AE, MC, V.*

$$$–$$$$
RESORT
Fodor's Choice
★

🏠 **Sheraton Kaua'i Resort.** The resort's ocean-wing accommodations here are so close to the water you can practically feel the spray of the surf as it hits the rocks below. Beachfront rooms have muted sand and eggshell colors, which complement the soothing atmosphere of this quiet, calm resort. Brighter palettes enliven the garden rooms. Dining rooms, king beds, and balconies differentiate the suites. Hawaiian artisans stage crafts demonstrations under a banyan tree in the central courtyard. The dining Galleria was designed so that all restaurants take advantage of the endless ocean horizon. **Pros:** ocean-view pool; quiet; nice dining views. **Cons:** no swimming beach; rather staid ambience. **TripAdvisor:** "staff was extremely friendly," "nice resort in a great location," "free seminars and activities." ✉ *2440 Ho'onani Rd., Po'ipū Beach, Kōloa* ☎ *808/742–1661 or 888/488–3535* ⊕ *www.sheraton-kauai.com* ⇥ *394 rooms, 8 suites* ⚮ *In-room: a/c, safe, refrigerator, Wi-Fi. In-hotel: 4 restaurants, room service, bar, tennis courts, pools, gym, beachfront, children's programs (ages 5–12), laundry facilities, Internet terminal* ⊟ *AE, D, DC, MC, V.*

$$–$$$
RENTAL

Suite Paradise Po'ipū Kai. Condominiums, many with cathedral ceilings and all with big windows overlooking the lawns, give this property the feeling of a spacious, quiet retreat inside and out. Large furnished lānai have views to the ocean and across the 110-acre grounds. All the condos are furnished with modern kitchens. Some units are two-level; some have sleeping lofts. One- to four-bedroom units are also available. A two-night minimum stay is required. Walking paths connect to both Brennecke and Shipwreck beaches. **Pros:** close to nice beaches; full kitchens; good rates for the location. **Cons:** units aren't especially spacious; beaches not ideal for swimming. **TripAdvisor:** "buildings were clearly well kept," "close to golf," "great location." ✉ *1941 Po'ipū Rd., Kōloa* ☎ *808/742–6464 or 800/367–8020* ⊕ *www.suite-paradise.com* ⏎ *130 units* ♿ *In-room: a/c (some), safe, kitchen, Internet. In-hotel: restaurant, tennis courts, pools* ▭ *AE, D, DC, MC, V.*

$$$–$$$$
RENTAL

Whalers Cove. Perched about as close to the water's edge as they can get, these two-bedroom condos are the most luxurious on the South Shore. The rocky beach is good for snorkeling, and a short drive or brisk walk will get you to a sandy stretch. A handsome koa-bedecked reception area offers services for the plush units. Two barbecue areas, big picture windows, spacious living rooms, lānai, and modern kitchens with washer-dryers make this a home away from home. **Pros:** daily service; on-site staff; extremely luxurious; outstanding setting; fully equipped units (1,400–2,000 square feet). **Cons:** rocky beach not ideal for swimming. **TripAdvisor:** "very spacious," "well equipped," "nice comfortable furniture." ✉ *2640 Pu'uholo Rd., Kōloa* ☎ *808/742–7571 or 800/225–2683* ⊕ *www.whalerscoveresort.com* ⏎ *39 units* ♿ *In-room: no a/c, kitchen (some), Internet. In-hotel: pool, beachfront, laundry facilities* ▭ *AE, MC, V.*

5

THE WEST SIDE

¢
B&B/INN

Kōke'e Lodge. If you're an outdoors enthusiast, you can appreciate Kaua'i's mountain wilderness from the 12 rustic cabins that make up this lodge. They are austere, to say the least, but more comfortable than a tent, and the mountain setting is grand. Wood-burning stoves ward off the chill and dampness (wood is a few dollars extra). If you aren't partial to dormitory-style sleeping, request the cabins with two bedrooms; both styles sleep six and have kitchenettes. The lodge restaurant serves a light breakfast and lunch between 9 and 5 daily. **Pros:** outstanding setting; more refined than camping; cooking facilities. **Cons:** very austere; no restaurants for dinner; remote. **TripAdvisor:** "don't forget the firewood," "cabins are old and dirty," "huge picnic area." ✉ *3600 Kōke'e Rd.* ✢ *At mile marker 15, Waimea* ✉ *Box 819, Waimea 96796* ☎ *808/335–6061* ⊕ *www.thelodgeatkokee.net* ⏎ *12 cabins* ♿ *In-room: no a/c, no phone, kitchen (some), no TV. In-hotel: restaurant* ▭ *D, DC, MC, V.*

$$–$$$
RENTAL
Fodor'sChoice
★

Waimea Plantation Cottages. History buffs will adore these reconstructed sugar-plantation cottages, which were originally built in the early 1900s. The one- to five-bedroom cottages are tucked among coconut trees along a lovely stretch of coastline on the sunny West Side. (Note that swimming waters here are sometimes murky, depending on weather conditions.) ■TIP→ It's a great property for family reunions or other large gatherings. These cozy little homes, replete with porches, feature plantation-era furnishings, modern kitchens, and cable TV. Barbecues, hammocks, porch swings, a gift shop, a spa, and a museum are on the property. **Pros:** unique, homey lodging; quiet and low-key. **Cons:** not a white-sand beach; rooms are not luxurious. **TripAdvisor:** "like staying in a very clean museum," "beach here is not great," "great beer brewed on site." ⊠ *9400 Kaumuali'i Hwy., Box 367, Waimea* ☎ *808/338–1625 or 800/992–4632* ⊕ *www.waimea-plantation.com* ⤳ *48 cottages* ⚄ *In-room: no a/c, kitchen (some), Internet. In-hotel: restaurant, bar, pool, spa, beachfront, Internet terminal* ▭ *AE, D, DC, MC, V.*

Moloka'i

WORD OF MOUTH

"I took the ferry and rented a car on Moloka'i for one day and LOVED the drive to the Hālawa Valley. The winding little drive east—with virtually no traffic, then the drive down into the valley— is truly breathtaking. I'd call it a don't-miss, especially if you are going to Moloka'i at all."

—NeoPatrick

WELCOME TO MOLOKA'I

TOP REASONS TO GO

★ **Kalaupapa Peninsula:** Hike or take a mule ride down the world's tallest sea cliffs to a fascinating, historic community that still houses a few patients suffering from leprosy.

★ **A waterfall hike in Hālawa:** A fascinating guided hike through private property takes you past ancient ruins, restored taro patches, and a sparkling cascade.

★ **Deep-sea fishing:** Sport fish are plentiful in these waters, as are gorgeous views of several Islands. Fishing is one of the island's great adventures.

★ **Closeness to nature:** Deep valleys, sheer cliffs, and the untamed ocean are the main attractions on Moloka'i.

★ **Pāpōhaku Beach:** This 3-mi stretch of golden sand is one of the most sensational beaches in all of Hawai'i. Sunsets and barbecues are perfect here.

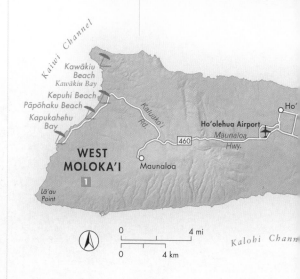

1 West Moloka'i. The most arid part of the island, known as the west end, has two inhabited areas: the coastal stretch includes a few condos and luxury homes and the largest beaches on the island. Nearby is the fading hilltop hamlet of Maunaloa.

2 Central Moloka'i. The island's only true town, Kaunakakai, with its mile-long wharf, is here. Nearly all of the island's eateries and stores are in or close to Kaunakakai. Highway 470 crosses the center of the island, rising to the top of the sea cliffs and the Kalaupapa overlook. At the base of the cliffs is Kalaupapa National Historic Park, a top attraction.

PACIFIC OCEAN

Kalaupapa
Airfield
KALAUPAPA
PENINSULA
Kalaupapa
Kalaupapa National
Historic Park
'olehua
Kualapu'u
470
**CENTRAL
MOLOKA'I**
2
450
Kaunakakai
Kamiloloa
Heights
Kawela
One Ali'i
Beach Park
Kamehameha V Hwy.
'Ualapu'e
Kalua'aha
Pūko'o
Pauwalu
Waialua
Waialua
Beach Park
450
Moa'ula Falls ◆
Kamakou
Preserve
Wailau Trail
3 **EAST
MOLOKA'I**
Hālawa
Hālawa
Beach
Pailolo Channel

6

3 **East Moloka'i.** The scenic drive on Route 450 around this undeveloped area, also called the east end, passes through the green pastures of Pu'u O Hoku Ranch and climaxes with a descent into Hālawa Valley. As you continue east, the road becomes increasingly narrow and the island ever more lush.

GETTING ORIENTED

Shaped like a long bone, Moloka'i is about 10 mi wide on average, and four times that long. The north shore thrusts up from the sea to form the tallest sea-cliffs on Earth, while the south shore slides almost flat into the water, then fans out to form the largest shallow-water reef system in the United States. Kaunakaki, the island's main town, has most of the stores and restaurants. Surprisingly, the highest point on Moloka'i rises only to 4,970 feet.

Updated by
Heidi Pool

Moloka'i is generally thought of as the last bit of "real" Hawai'i. Tourism has been held at bay by the island's unique history and the pride of the island's predominantly native Hawaiian population, despite the fact that the longest white-sand beach in Hawai'i can be found along its western shore. Exploring the great outdoors and visiting the historic Kalaupapa Peninsula, where St. Damien helped people with leprosy, are attractions for visitors.

With sandy beaches to the west, sheer sea cliffs to the north, and a rainy, lush eastern coast, Moloka'i offers a bit of everything, including a peek at what the Islands were like 50 years ago. Large tracts of land from Hawaiian Homeland grants have allowed the people to retain much of their traditional lifestyle. A favorite expression is "Slow down, you're on Moloka'i." Although Moloka'i Ranch, the island's biggest land-owner and employer, is closed and up for sale, residents are adapting and welcoming visitors. If you are friendly, they are friendly.

Only 38 mi long and 10 mi wide at its widest point, Moloka'i is the fifth-largest island in the Hawaiian archipelago. Eight thousand residents call Moloka'i home, nearly 60% of whom are Hawaiian.

Moloka'i is a great place to be outdoors. There are no tall buildings, no traffic lights, no streetlights, no stores bearing the names of national chains, and nothing at all like a resort. You will, however, find 15 parks, and more than 100 mi of shoreline to play on. At night the whole island grows dark, creating a velvety blackness and a wonderful, rare thing called silence.

GEOLOGY

Roughly 1½ million years ago two large volcanoes—Kamakou in the east and Mauna Loa in the west—broke the surface of the Pacific Ocean and created the island of Moloka'i. Shortly thereafter a third and much smaller caldera, Kauhako, popped up to form the Makanalua Peninsula on the north side. After hundreds of thousands of years of rain, surf, and wind, an enormous landslide on the north end sent much of the mountain into the sea, leaving behind the sheer sea cliffs that make Moloka'i's north shore so spectacularly beautiful.

HISTORY

Moloka'i is named in chants as the child of the moon goddess Hina. For centuries, the island was occupied by native people who took advantage of the reef fishing and ideal conditions for growing taro. When leprosy broke out in the Hawaiian Islands in the 1840s, the Makanalua Peninsula, surrounded on three sides by the Pacific and accessible only by a steep trail, was selected as the place to exile people suffering from the disease. The first patients were thrown into the sea to swim ashore as best they could, and left with no facilities, shelter, or supplies. In 1873 a missionary named Father Damien arrived and began to serve the peninsula's suffering inhabitants. He died in 1889 from leprosy and was canonized as a saint by the Catholic Church in 2009. Though leprosy, now known as Hansen's disease, is no longer contagious and can be remitted, the buildings and infrastructure created by those who were exiled here still exist, and some longtime residents have chosen to stay in their homes. Today the area is Kalaupapa National Historic Park. Visitors are welcome but must prebook a tour operated by Damien Tours of Kalaupapa. You can reach the park by plane or by hiking or taking a mule ride down the steep Kalaupapa Trail.

THE BIRTHPLACE OF HULA

Tradition has it that centuries ago La'ila'i came to Moloka'i and lived on Pu'u Nana at Ka'ana. She brought the art of hula and taught it to the people, who kept it secret for her descendants, making sure the sacred dances were performed only at Ka'ana. Five generations later Laka was born into the family and learned hula from an older sister. She chose to share the art and traveled throughout the Islands teaching the dance, though she did so without her family's consent. The yearly Ka Hula Piko Festival, held on Moloka'i in May, celebrates the birth of hula at Ka'ana.

PLANNING

WHEN TO GO

If you're keen to explore Moloka'i's beaches, coral beds, or fishponds, summer is your best bet for nonstop calm seas and sunny skies. The weather mimics that of the other Islands: low to mid-80s year-round, slightly rainier in winter. As you travel up the mountainside, the weather changes with bursts of downpours. The strongest storms occur in winter when winds and rain shift to come in from the south.

For a taste of Hawaiian culture, plan your visit around a festival. In January, islanders and visitors compete in ancient Hawaiian games at the Ka Moloka'i Makahiki Festival. The Moloka'i Ka Hula Piko, an annual daylong event in May, draws premier hula troupes, musicians, and storytellers. Long-distance canoe races from Moloka'i to O'ahu are in late September and early October. Although never crowded, the island is busier during these events—book accommodations and transportation six months in advance.

GETTING HERE AND AROUND

AIR TRAVEL

If you're flying in from the mainland United States or one of the neighbor islands, you must first make a stop in Honolulu. From there, it's a 25-minute trip to Moloka'i. Moloka'i's transportation hub is Ho'olehua Airport, a tiny airstrip 8 mi west of Kaunakakai and about 18 mi east of Maunaloa. An even smaller airstrip serves the little community of Kalaupapa on the north shore.

From Ho'olehua Airport, it takes about 10 minutes to reach Kaunakakai and 25 minutes to reach the west end of the island by car. There's no public bus. A taxi will cost about $28 from the airport to Kaunakakai with Hele Mai Taxi. Shuttle service costs about $28 per person from Ho'olehua Airport to Kaunakakai. For shuttle service, call Moloka'i Outdoors. Keep in mind, however, that it's difficult to visit the island without a rental car.

Contacts Hele Mai Taxi (☎ 808/336–0967 or 808/553–5700). **Moloka'i Outdoors** (☎ 808/553–4477 or 877/553–4477 ⊕ www.molokai-outdoors.com).

CAR TRAVEL

If you want to explore Moloka'i from one end to the other, you must rent a car. With just a few main roads to choose from, it's a snap to drive around here. The gas stations are in Kaunakakai. Ask your rental agent for a free *Moloka'i Drive Guide.*

Alamo maintains a counter at Ho'olehua Airport. Make arrangements in advance because cars may not be available when you walk in. Locally owned Island Kine Rent-a-Car offers airport or hotel pickup. Be sure to check the vehicle to make sure the four-wheel-drive is working before departing the agency. There is a $75 surcharge for taking a four-wheel-drive vehicle off-road. *See Travel Smart Maui for more information on renting a car and driving.*

Major Agency Alamo (☎ 877/222–9075 ⊕ www.alamo.com).

Local Agency Island Kine Rent-a-Car (☎ 808/553–5242 or 877/553–5242 ⊕ www.molokai-car-rental.com).

FERRY TRAVEL

The Moloka'i Ferry crosses the channel every day between Lahaina (Maui) and Kaunakakai. Boats depart from Lahaina daily at 6 pm and Monday to Saturday at 7:15 am, and from Kauanakakai daily at 4 pm and Monday to Saturday at 5:15 am. The 1½-hour trip takes passengers but not cars, so arrange ahead of time for a car rental or tour at the arrival point.

Contact Moloka'i Ferry (☎ 808/661–3392 or 866/307–6524 ⊕ www.molokaiferry.com).

RESTAURANTS

Dining on Moloka'i is more a matter of eating. There are no fancy restaurants, just pleasant low-key places to eat out. Try Hula Shores at the Hotel Moloka'i for a selection of fresh, local-style food. Other options include plate lunch, pizza, coffee shop–style sandwiches, and make-it-yourself health-food fixings.

HOTELS

Moloka'i appeals most to travelers who appreciate genuine Hawaiian ambience rather than swanky digs. Most hotel and condominium properties range from adequate to funky. Visitors who want to lollygag on the beach should choose one of the condos or home rentals in West Moloka'i. Locals tend to choose Hotel Moloka'i, located seaside just 2 mi from Kaunakakai. Travelers who want to immerse themselves in the spirit of the island should seek out a condo or cottage, the closer to East Moloka'i the better.

WHAT IT COSTS					
	¢	$	$$	$$$	$$$$
Restaurants	under $10	$10–$17	$18–$26	$27–$35	over $35
Hotels	under $100	$100–$180	$181–$260	$261–$340	over $340

Restaurant prices are for a main course at dinner. Hotel prices are for two people in a standard double room in high season. Condo price categories reflect studio and one-bedroom rates.

6

COMMUNICATIONS

There are many locations on the island where cell phone reception is difficult, if not impossible, to obtain. Your best bet for finding service is in Kaunakakai. There is in-room Internet access at the Hotel Moloka'i.

VISITOR INFORMATION

Contacts Maui Visitors Bureau (☎ *808/244–3530 or 800/525–6284* ⊕ *www.visitmaui.com*). **Moloka'i Visitors Association** (✉ *12 Kamo'i St., Suite 200, Kaunakakai* ☎ *808/553–3876 or 800/800–6367* ⊕ *www. molokai-hawaii.com*).

EXPLORING MOLOKA'I

The first thing to do on Moloka'i is to drive everywhere. It's a feat you can accomplish comfortably in two days. Depending on where you stay, spend one day exploring the west end and the other day exploring the east end. Basically you have one 40-mi west–east highway (two lanes, no stoplights) with three side trips: the little west-end town of Maunaloa; the Highway 470 drive (just a few miles) to the top of the north shore and the overlook of Kalaupapa Peninsula; and the short stretch of shops in Kaunakakai town. After you learn the general lay of the land, you can return to the places that interest you most. ■TIP➔ **Directions on the island are often given as mauka (toward the mountains) and makai (toward the ocean).**

Kapuāiwa Coconut Grove in central Moloka'i is a survivor of royal plantings from the 19th century.

WEST MOLOKA'I

Pāpōhaku Beach is 17 mi west of the airport; Maunaloa is 10 mi west of the airport.

The remote beaches and rolling pastures on Moloka'i's west end are presided over by Mauna Loa, a dormant volcano, and a sleepy little former plantation town of the same name. Pāpōhaku, the Hawaiian Islands' second-longest white sand beach, is here, as is the 53,000-acre Moloka'i Ranch, which has closed its resort property, shut down ranch operations, and is up for sale.

GETTING HERE AND AROUND

The sometimes winding paved road through West Moloka'i begins as Highway 460 and ends at Kapukahehu Bay. The drive from Kaunakakai to Maunaloa is about 30 minutes.

EXPLORING

Kaluako'i. Although the late-1960s Kaluako'i Hotel and Golf Club is closed and forlorn, some nice condos and a gift shop are operating nearby. The white-sand beach along the coast (Kepuhi Beach) is still worth a visit. ⊠ *Kaluako'i Rd., Maunaloa.*

Maunaloa. Built in 1923, this quiet small town at the western end of the highway housed the workers on the island's pineapple plantation. Although the fields of golden fruit are long gone, some of the old plantation houses have been torn down and reproduced. You'll find a kite shop, a gallery with local and imported art and jewelry, and an eclectic general store on the short main street. This is the last place to buy

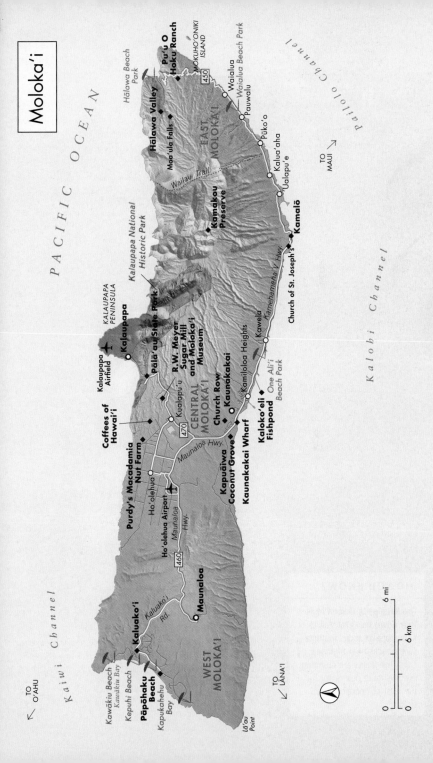

Moloka'i

PACIFIC OCEAN

Kaiwi Channel

TO O'AHU

TO LĀNA'I

MOKUHO'ONIKI ISLAND

Pailolo Channel

Kalohi Channel

TO MAUI

Pu'u O Hoku Ranch

Hālawa Beach Park

Hālawa Valley

Waialua
Waialua Beach Park
Pauwalu

Mo'oula Falls

Pūko'o

Kalua'aha
Kalua'e
Ualapu'e

EAST MOLOKA'I

Wailau Trail

Kamakou Preserve

Kamalō

Church of St. Joseph's

Kamiloloa Heights
Kawela

Kalaupapa National Historic Park

KALAUPAPA PENINSULA

Kalaupapa

Kalaupapa Airfield

Pālā'au State Park

R.W. Meyer Sugar Mill and Moloka'i Museum

Kualapu'u

CENTRAL MOLOKA'I

Church Row
Kaunakakai

One Ali'i Beach Park

Koloko'eli Fishpond

Kaunakakai Wharf
Kapuāiwa Coconut Grove

470
Maunaloa Hwy.

Kamehameha V. Hwy.

Coffees of Hawai'i

Purdy's Macadamia Nut Farm

Ho'olehua

Ho'olehua Airport

Maunaloa Hwy.

460

Kaluako'i Rd.

Maunaloa

WEST MOLOKA'I

Kaluako'i Beach
Kawākiu Beach
Kawākiu Bay
Kepuhi Beach
Kapukahehu Bay
Lā'au Point

Pāpōhaku Beach

450

0   6 mi
0   6 km

N

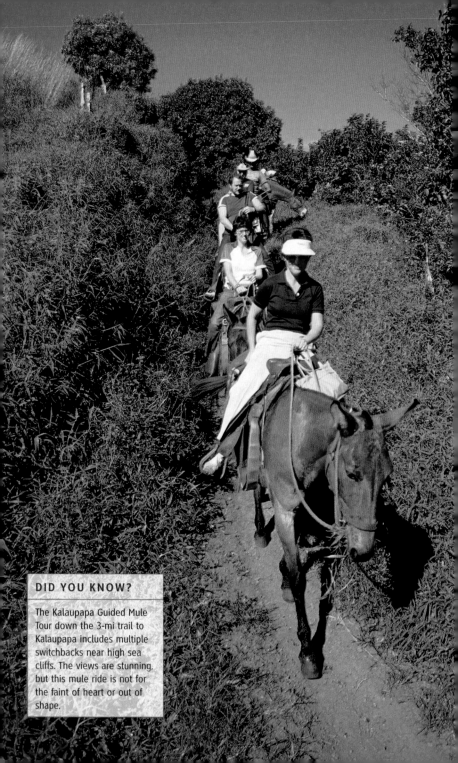

DID YOU KNOW?

The Kalaupapa Guided Mule Tour down the 3-mi trail to Kalaupapa includes multiple switchbacks near high sea cliffs. The views are stunning, but this mule ride is not for the faint of heart or out of shape.

supplies before heading out to explore the beaches of the west end. ✉ *Maunaloa Hwy., Rte. 460.*

Fodor's Choice ★ **Pāpōhaku Beach.** The most splendid stretch of golden-white sand on Moloka'i, Pāpōhaku is also the island's largest beach—it stretches 3 mi along the western shore. Even on busier days you're likely to see only a handful of other people. If the waves are high, swimming is dangerous. The beach is 2 mi beyond the closed Kaluako'i Hotel and Golf Club. ✉ *Kaluako'i Rd.*

CENTRAL MOLOKA'I

Kaunakakai is 8 mi southeast of the airport.

Most residents live centrally, near the island's one and only true town, Kaunakakai. It's just about the only place on the island to get food and supplies. It *is* Moloka'i. Go into the shops along and around Ala Mālama Street. Buy stuff. Talk with people. Take your time and you'll really enjoy being a visitor. Also in this area, on the north side, are Coffees of Hawai'i, a 500-acre coffee plantation, and the Kalaupapa National Historic Park, one of the island's most notable sights.

GETTING HERE AND AROUND

Central Moloka'i is the hub of the island's road system, and Kaunakakai is the commercial center. Watch for kids, dogs, and people crossing the street in downtown Kaunakakai.

EXPLORING

TOP ATTRACTIONS

Coffees of Hawai'i. Visit the headquarters of a 500-acre Moloka'i coffee plantation, where the espresso bar serves freshly made sandwiches, *liliko'i* (passion fruit) cheesecake, and java in artful ways. The "Mocha Mama" is a special Moloka'i treat. This is the place to pick up additions to your picnic lunch if you're headed to Kalaupapa. The gift shop offers a wide range of Moloka'i handicrafts, memorabilia, and, of course, coffee. Call in advance to ask about various tours (fee) of the plantation. ✉ *1630 Farrington Hwy., off Rte. 470, Kualapu'u* ☎ *877/322–3276 or 808/567–9490* ⊕ *www.coffeesofhawaii.com* ☉ *Café and gift shop weekdays 6 am–5 pm, Sat. 8–8, Sun. 8–5.*

Fodor's Choice ★ **Kalaupapa.** *See photo feature, Kalaupapa Peninsula: A Tale of Tragedy and Triumph.*

Fodor's Choice ★ **Kalaupapa Guided Mule Tour.** Mount a friendly, well-trained mule and wind along a thrilling 3-mi, 26-switchback trail to reach the town of Kalaupapa, which was once home to patients with leprosy who were

---

HAWAI'I'S FIRST SAINT

A long-revered figure on Moloka'i and in Hawai'i, Father Damien, who cared for the desperate patients at Kalaupapa, was elevated to sainthood in 2009. Plans call for a small museum and bookstore in his honor in Kaunakakai, and the refurbishment of the three churches in the Catholic parish. Visitors who cannot visit Kalaupapa can find information on St. Damien at the Damien Center in Kaunakakai, and may worship at St. Sophia's in Kaunakakai; Our Lady of Seven Sorrows, just west of Kaunakakai; or St. Vincent Ferrer in Maunaloa. For more information call ☎ *808/553–5220.*

6

exiled to this remote spot. The path was built in 1886 as a supply route for the settlement below. Once in Kalaupapa, you take a guided tour of the town. A light picnic lunch is provided. The trail is steep, down (and up, on the way back) some of the highest sea cliffs in the world, and views are spectacular. ■TIP➔ Only those in good shape should attempt the ride, as two hours each way on a mule can take its toll. You must be at least 16 years old and weigh no more than 249

pounds; pregnant women are not allowed on the ride. The entire event takes seven hours. Make reservations ahead of time, as spots are limited and the tour is especially popular since the canonization of Saint Damien. The same outfit can arrange for you to hike down or fly in, or some combination of a hike in and fly out. No one is allowed in the park or on the trail without booking a tour; hikers must be down in the park by 10 am. *See Kalaupapa Peninsula: A Tale of Tragedy and Triumph photo feature, below, for more information.* ⊠ *100 Kala'e Hwy., Rte. 470, Kualapu'u* ☎ *808/567–6088 or 800/567–7550* ⊕ *www.muleride. com* ⊠ *$189* ⊗ *Mon.–Sat. 8–2:40.*

★ **Kaunakakai.** Central Moloka'i's main town looks like a classic 1940s movie set. Along the one-block main drag is a cultural grab bag of restaurants and shops. Many people are friendly and willing to supply directions. The preferred dress is shorts and a tank top, and no one wears anything fancier than a cotton skirt or aloha shirt. ⊠ *Rte. 460, about 3 blocks north of Kaunakakai Wharf.*

QUICK BITES

Stop for some of Dave's Hawaiian Ice Cream at the Kamo'i Snack-n-Go (⊠ 28 Kamo'i St., Kaunakakai ☎ 808/553–3742). Sit on one of the benches in front for a Moloka'i rest stop. Snacks, crack seed, cold drinks, and water are also available.

★ **Pālā'au State Park.** One of the island's few formal recreation areas, this cool retreat covers 233 acres at a 1,000-foot elevation. A short path through an ironwood forest leads to **Kalaupapa Lookout,** a magnificent overlook with views of the town of Kalaupapa and the 1,664-foot-high sea cliffs protecting it. Informative plaques have facts about leprosy, Saint Damien, and the colony. The park is also the site of **Kauleonānāhoa** (the phallus of Nānāhoa)—where women in old Hawai'i would come to the rock to enhance their fertility, and it is said some still do. It is a sacred site, so be respectful and don't deface the boulders. The park is well maintained, with trails, camping facilities, restrooms, and picnic tables. To get here, take Highway 460 west from Kaunakakai and then head mauka (toward the mountains) on Highway 470, which ends at the park. ⊠ *Rte. 470* ☎ *No phone* ⊠ *Free* ⊗ *Daily dawn–dusk.*

DID YOU KNOW?

Taro, grown in engineered ponds called loʻi, is a Hawaiian food staple; the pounded root is used to make poi. The taro plant is revered as an ancestor of the Hawaiian people.

Purdy's Macadamia Nut Farm. Moloka'i's only working macadamia-nut farm is open for educational tours hosted by the knowledgeable and entertaining owner. A family business on Hawaiian homestead land in Ho'olehua, the farm takes up 1½ acres with a flourishing grove of some 50 trees more than 70 years old. Taste a delicious nut right out of its shell or home roasted, and dip it into macadamia-blossom honey; then buy some at the shop. Look for Purdy's sign behind Moloka'i High School. ✉ *Lihipali Ave., Ho'olehua* ☎ *808/567–6601* ⊕ *www.molokai-aloha.com/macnuts* ☞ *Free* ⊙ *Tues.–Fri. 9:30–3:30, Sat. 10–2.*

> **BE PREPARED**
>
> Because Moloka'i is not oriented to the visitor industry, you won't find much around to cater to your needs. Pick up a disposable cooler in Kaunakakai town, then visit the local markets and fill it with road supplies. Don't forget water, sunscreen, and mosquito repellent.

R.W. Meyer Sugar Mill and Moloka'i Museum. Built in 1877, this three-room mill has been reconstructed as a testament to Moloka'i's agricultural history. Some of the equipment may still be in working order, including a mule-driven cane crusher, redwood evaporating pans, some copper clarifiers, and a steam engine. A small museum with changing exhibits on the island's early history, information on Kalaupapa, and a gift shop are on-site as well. ✉ *Rte. 470, 2 mi southwest of Pālā'au State Park, Kala'e* ☎ *808/567–6436* ☞ *$5 for adults and $1 for students ages 5–18* ⊙ *Mon.–Sat. 10–2.*

WORTH NOTING

Church Row. Standing together along the highway are several houses of worship with primarily native-Hawaiian congregations. Notice the unadorned, boxlike architecture so similar to missionary homes. ✉ *Rte. 460, mauka (toward the mountains) side, 5½ mi south of airport.*

Kapuāiwa Coconut Grove. At first glance this looks like a sea of coconut trees. Closer up you can see that the tall, stately palms are planted in long rows leading down to the sea. This is a remnant of one of the last surviving royal groves planted for Prince Lot, who ruled Hawai'i as King Kamehameha V from 1863 until his death in 1872. The park, which once boasted more than 1,000 trees, is now closed for renovations, but you can park on the side of the road and walk in to the beach. Watch for falling coconuts. ✉ *Rte. 460, makai (toward the ocean) side, 5½ mi south of airport.*

Kaunakakai Wharf. Docks, once bustling with barges exporting pineapples, now host visiting boats, the ferry from Lahaina, and the weekly barge from O'ahu. The wharf is also the starting point for excursions, including fishing, sailing, snorkeling, whale-watching, and scuba diving. It's a nice place at sunset to watch fish rippling on the water. To get here, drive makai (toward the ocean) on Kaunakakai Place, which dead-ends at wharf. ✉ *Rte. 450 at Ala Mālama St.*

Continued on page 617

Father Damien's Church, St. Philomena

KALAUPAPA PENINSULA: TRAGEDY & TRIUMPH

For those who crave drama, there is no better destination than Moloka'i's Kalaupapa Peninsula—but it wasn't always so. For 100 years this remote strip of land was "the loneliest place on earth," a feared place of exile for those suffering from leprosy (now known as Hansen's Disease).

The world's tallest sea cliffs, rain-chiseled valleys, and tiny islets dropped like exclamation points along the coast emphasize the passionate history of the Kalaupapa Peninsula. Today, it's impossible to visit this stunning National Historic Park and view the evidence of human ignorance and heroism with-out responding. You'll be tugged by emotions—awe and disbelief for starters. But you'll also glimpse humorous facets of everyday life in a small town. Whatever your experience here may be, chances are you'll return home feeling that the journey to present-day Kalaupapa is one you'll never forget.

THE SETTLEMENT'S EARLY DAYS

Father Damien with patients outside St. Philomena church.

IN 1865, PRESSURED BY FOREIGN RESIDENTS, the Hawaiian Kingdom passed "An Act to Prevent the Spread of Leprosy." Anyone showing symptoms of the disease was to be permanently exiled to Kalawao, the north end of Kalaupapa Peninsula—a spot walled in on three sides by nearly impassable cliffs. The peninsula had been home to a fishing community for 900 years, but those inhabitants were evicted and the entire peninsula declared settlement land.

The first 12 patients were arrested and sent to Kalawao in 1866. People of all ages and many nationalities followed, taken from their homes and dumped on the isolated shore. Officials thought the patients could become self-sufficient, fishing and farming sweet potatoes in the stream-fed valleys. That was not the case. Settlement conditions were deplorable.

Belgian missionary Father Damien was one of four priests who volunteered to serve the leprosy settlement at Kalawao on a rotating basis. There were 600 patients at the time. His turn came in 1873; when it was up, he refused to leave. Father Damien is

credited with turning the settlement from a merciless exile to a place where hope could be heard in the voices of his recruited choir. He organized the building of the St. Philomena church (and other churches on the island), nearly 300 houses, and a home for boys. A vocal advocate for his adopted community, he pestered the church for supplies, administered medicine, and oversaw the nearly daily funerals. Sixteen years after his arrival, in 1889, he died from the effects of leprosy, having contracted the disease during his service. Known around the world for his sacrifice, Father Damien was beatified by the Catholic Church in 1995, and canonized in 2009.

Mother Marianne heard of the mission while working at a hospital in Syracuse, New York. Along with six other Franciscan Sisters, she volunteered to work with those with leprosy in the Islands. They sailed to the Kalaupapa Peninsula in 1888. Like the Father, the Sisters were considered saints for their work. Mother Marianne stayed at Kalaupapa until her death in 1918; she was beatified by the Catholic Church in 2005.

VISITING KALAUPAPA TODAY

Kalaupapa Peninsula

FROZEN IN TIME, Kalaupapa's one-horse town has bittersweet charm. Signs posted here and there remind residents when the bankers will be there (once monthly), where to pick up lost sunglasses, and what's happening around town. It has the nostalgic, almost naive ambience expected from a place almost wholly segregated from modern life.

About 19 former patients remain at Kalaupapa (by choice, as the disease is controlled by drugs and the patients are no longer carriers), but many have traveled to other parts of the world and all are over the age of 70. They never lost their chutzpah, however. Having survived a lifetime of prejudice and misunderstanding, Kalaupapa's residents haven't been willing to be pushed around any longer—in past years, several made the journey to Honolulu from time to time to testify before the state legislature about matters concerning them.

To get a feel for what residents' lives were like, visit the National Park Ser-

vice Web site (⊕ www.nps.gov/kala/historyculture/) or buy one of several heartbreaking memoirs at the park's library-turned-bookstore.

THE TRUTH ABOUT HANSEN'S DISEASE

■ A cure for leprosy has been available since 1941. Multi-drug therapy, a rapid cure, has been available since 1981.

■ With treatment, none of the disabilities traditionally associated with leprosy need occur.

■ Most people have a natural immunity to leprosy. Only 5% of the world's population is even susceptible to the disease.

■ There are still about 500,000 new cases of leprosy each year; at least two-thirds are in India.

■ All new cases of leprosy are treated on an outpatient basis.

■ The term "leper" is offensive and should not be used. It is appropriate to say "a person is affected by leprosy" or "by Hansen's Disease."

GETTING HERE

The Kalaupapa Trail and Peninsula are all part of Kalaupapa National Historic Park (☎ 808/567–6802 ⊕ www.nps. gov/kala/), which is open every day but Sunday for tours only. Keep in mind, there are no public facilities (except an occasional restroom) anywhere in the park. Pack your own food and water, as well as light rain gear, sunscreen, and bug repellent.

TO HIKE OR TO RIDE?

There are two ways to get down the Kalaupapa Trail: in your hiking boots, or on a mule.

Hiking: Hiking allows you to travel at your own pace and stop frequently for photos—not an option on the mule ride. The hike takes about 1 hour down and 1½ hours up. You must book a tour in order to access the trail. **Damien Tours** ☎ 808/567–6171.

Kalaupapa Beach & Peninsula

THE KALAUPAPA TRAIL

Unless you fly (flights are available through Pacific Wings [☎ 808/873–0877 or 888/575–4546 ⊕ www.pacificwings. com]), the only way into Kalaupapa National Historic Park is on a dizzying switchback trail. The switchbacks are numbered—26 in all—and descend 1,700 feet to sea level in just under 3 mi. The steep trail is more of a staircase, and most of the trail is shaded. Keep in mind, however, that footing is uneven and there is little to keep you from pitching over the side. If you don't mind heights, you can stare straight down to the ocean for most of the way. *Access Kalaupapa Trail off Hwy. 470 near the Kalaupapa Overlook. There is ample parking near end of Hwy. 470.*

Mule-Skinning: You'll be amazed as your mule trots up to the edge of the switchback, swivels on two legs, and completes a sharp-angled turn—26 times. The guides tell you the mules can do this in their sleep, but that doesn't take the fear out of the first few switchbacks. Make reservations well in advance. **Kalaupapa Guided Mule Tour** ☎ 808/567–6088 or 808/567–7550 ⊕ *www.muleride.com.*

IMPORTANT INFORMATION

Daily tours are offered Monday through Saturday through Damien Tours or Moloka'i Mule Ride. Be sure to reserve in advance. Visitors ages 16 and under are not allowed at Kalaupapa, and photographing patients without their written permission is forbidden.

EAST MOLOKA'I

Hālawa Valley is 36 mi northeast of the airport.

On the beautifully undeveloped east end of Moloka'i, you can find ancient fishponds, a magnificent coastline, splendid ocean views, and a fertile valley that's been inhabited for 14 centuries. The eastern uplands are flanked by Mt. Kamakou, the island's highest point at 4,961 feet and home to the Nature Conservancy's Kamakou Preserve. Mist hangs over waterfall-filled valleys, and ancient lava cliffs jut out into the sea.

GETTING HERE AND AROUND

Driving the east end is a scenic adventure, but the road narrows and becomes curvy after the 20-mile marker. Take your time, especially in the seaside lane, and watch for oncoming traffic. Driving at night is not recommended.

EXPLORING

Fodor's Choice
★

Hālawa Valley. As far back as AD 650 a busy community lived in this valley, the oldest recorded habitation on Moloka'i. Hawaiians lived in a sustainable relationship with the valley's resources, growing taro and fishing until the 1960s, when cultural changes plus an enormous flood wiped out the taro patches and forced the old-timers to abandon their traditional lifestyle. Now a new generation of Hawaiians has returned and begun the challenging task of restoring the taro fields. Much of this work involves rerouting stream water to flow through carefully engineered level ponds called *lo'i*. The taro plants with their big dancing leaves grow in the submerged mud of the lo'i, where the water is always cool and flowing. Hawaiians believe that the taro plant is their ancestor and revere it both as sustenance and as a spiritual necessity. The Hālawa Valley Cooperative leads hikes through the valley, which is home to two sacrificial temples, many historic sites, and the trail to **Moa'ula Falls**, a 250-foot cascade. The $69 fee ($45 for children 7–12) goes to support the restoration efforts. The 4.2-mi round-trip hike is rated intermediate to advanced and includes two moderate river crossings. ⊠ *Rte. 450, eastern end* ☎ *808/553–5926* ⊕ *www.molokaifishanddive.com.*

★

Kaloko'eli Fishpond. With its narrow rock walls arching out from the shoreline, Kaloko'eli is typical of the numerous fishponds that define southern Moloka'i. Many of them were built around the 13th century under the direction of powerful chiefs. This early type of aquaculture, particular to Hawai'i, exemplifies the ingenuity of native Hawaiians. One or more openings were left in the wall, where gates called *makaha* were installed. These gates allowed seawater and tiny fish to enter the enclosed pond but kept larger predators out. The tiny fish would then grow too big to get out. At one time there were 62 fishponds around Moloka'i's coast. ⊠ *Rte. 450, 6 mi east of Kaunakakai.*

OFF THE
BEATEN
PATH

Kamakou Preserve. Tucked away on the slopes of Mt. Kamakou, Moloka'i's highest peak, the 2,774-acre rain-forest preserve is a dazzling wonderland full of wet 'ōhi'a (hardwood trees of the myrtle family, with red blossoms called *lehua* flowers) forests, rare bogs, and native trees and wildlife. Guided hikes, limited to eight people, are held one Saturday each month; reserve well in advance. You can visit the park without a tour, but you need a good four-wheel-drive vehicle (which is hard to find on the island), and the Nature Conservancy requests that you sign in at the office and get directions first. The office is at Moloka'i Industrial Park, about 3 mi west of Kaunakakai. ⊠ *The Nature Conservancy, 23 Pueo Pl., Kualapu'u* ☎ *808/553–5236* ⊕ *www.nature.org* ⚲ *Free. $25 guided hike.*

Kamalō. A natural harbor used by small cargo ships during the 19th century and a favorite fishing spot for locals, this is also the location of the **Church of St. Joseph's,** a tiny white church built by Saint Damien of the Kalaupapa colony in the 1880s. It's a state historic site and place of pilgrimage. The door is often open; if it is, slip inside and sign the guest book. The congregation keeps the church in beautiful condition. ⊠ *Rte. 450, about 11 mi east of Kaunakakai, makai (toward the ocean).*

> **BEACH SAFETY**
>
> Unlike protected shorelines such as Kā'anapali on Maui, the coasts of Moloka'i are exposed to rough sea channels and dangerous rip currents. The ocean tends to be calmer in the morning and in summer. No matter what the time, however, always study the sea before entering. Unless the water is placid and the wave action minimal, it's best to stay on shore, even though locals may be in the water. Don't underestimate the power of the ocean. Protect yourself with sunblock. Cool breezes make it easy to underestimate the power of the sun as well.

QUICK BITES

The best place to grab a snack or picnic supplies is **Mana'e Goods & Grinds** (⊠ *Rte. 450, Puko'o* ☎ *808/558–8498 or 808/558–8186*), 16 mi east of Kaunakakai. It's the only place on the east end where you can find essentials such as ice and bread, and not-so-essentials such as seafood plate lunches, bentos, burgers, and shakes. Try a refreshing smoothie while here.

Pu'u O Hoku Ranch. A 14,000-acre private spread in the highlands of East Moloka'i, Pu'u O Hoku was developed in the 1930s by wealthy industrialist Paul Fagan. Route 450 ambles right through this rural treasure with its pastures and grazing horses and cattle. As you drive slowly along, enjoy the splendid views of Maui and Lāna'i. The small island off the coast is Mokuho'oniki, a favorite spot among visiting humpback whales, and a nesting seabird sanctuary. The ranch has limited accommodations, too. ⊠ *Rte. 450 about 25 mi east of Kaunakakai* ☎ *808/558–8109* ⊕ *www.puuohoku.com.*

BEACHES

Moloka'i's unique geography gives the island plenty of drama and spectacle along the shorelines but not so many places for seaside basking and bathing. The long north shore consists mostly of towering cliffs that plunge directly into the sea and is inaccessible except by boat, and even then only in summer. Much of the south shore is enclosed by a huge reef that stands as far as a mile offshore and blunts the action of the waves. Within this reef you can find a thin strip of sand, but the water

Lava ridges make Kepuhi Beach beautiful, but swimming is hard unless the water is calm.

here is flat, shallow, and at times clouded with silt. This reef area is best suited to wading, pole fishing, kayaking, or learning how to windsurf.

The big, fat, sandy beaches lie along the west end. The largest of these—one of the largest in the Islands—is Pāpōhaku Beach, which fronts a grassy park shaded by a grove of *keawe* (mesquite) trees. These stretches of west-end sand are generally unpopulated. At the east end, where the road hugs the sinuous shoreline, you encounter a number of pocket-size beaches in rocky coves, good for snorkeling. Don't venture too far out, however, or you can find yourself caught in dangerous currents. The island's east end road ends at Hālawa Valley with its unique double bay, which is not recommended for swimming.

If you need beach gear, head to Molokaʻi Fish and Dive at the west end of Kaunakakai's only commercial strip or rent kayaks from Molokaʻi Outdoors at Kaunakakai Wharf.

All of Hawaiʻi's beaches are free and public. None of the beaches on Molokaʻi have telephones or lifeguards, and they're all under the jurisdiction of the **Department of Parks, Land and Natural Resources** (☎ 808/553–3204 ⊕ *www.hawaiistateparks.org*).

WEST MOLOKAʻI

Molokaʻi's west end looks across a wide channel to the island of Oʻahu. Crescent shape, this cup of coastline holds the island's best sandy beaches as well as the most arid and sunny weather. Remember: all beaches are public property, even those that front developments, and

most have public access roads. *Beaches below are listed from north to south.*

Kawākiu Beach. Seclusion is the reason to come to this remote beach, accessible only through a gate (that is sometimes locked) by four-wheel drive or a 45-minute walk. The white-sand beach is beautiful. To get here, drive past Ke Nani Kai condos on Kaluako'i Road and look for a dirt road off to the right. Park here and hike in or, with four-wheel drive, drive along the dirt road to beach. ⚠ Rocks and undertow make swimming extremely dangerous at times, so use caution. **Amenities:** None. ⊠ *Off Kaluako'i Rd.*

Kepuhi Beach. Kaluako'i Hotel is closed, but it does have this half mile of ivory white sand. The beach shines beautifully against the turquoise sea, black outcroppings of lava, and magenta bougainvillea flowers of the resort's landscaping. When the sea is perfectly calm, lava ridges in the water make good snorkeling spots. With any surf at all, however, the water around these rocky places churns and foams, wiping out visibility and making it difficult to avoid being slammed into the jagged rocks. **Amenities:** Toilets, showers. ⊠ *Kaluako'i Rd.*

Fodor's Choice ★ **Pāpōhaku Beach.** One of the most sensational beaches in Hawai'i, Pāpōhaku is a 3-mi-long strip of light golden sand, the longest of its kind on the island. ■TIP→ Swimming is not recommended; there is a dangerous undertow except on exceptionally calm summer days. There's so much sand here that Honolulu once purchased barge loads in order to replenish Waīkīkī Beach. A shady beach park just inland is the site of the Ka Hula Piko Festival of Hawaiian Music and Dance, held each year in May. The park is also a great sunset-facing spot for a rustic afternoon barbecue. A park ranger patrols the area at random to check on campers. The beach is 2 mi south of the Kaluako'i Hotel and Golf Club (now closed). **Amenities:** Toilets, showers, picnic tables, grills/firepits. ⊠ *Kaluako'i Rd.*

Kapukahehu Bay. Locals like to surf just out from this bay in a break called Dixie's or Dixie Maru. The sandy protected cove is usually completely deserted on weekdays but can fill up when the surf is up. The water in the cove is clear and shallow with plenty of well-worn rocky areas. These conditions make for excellent snorkeling, swimming, and boogie boarding on calm days. The beach is 3½ mi south of Pāpōhaku Beach; beach access signs point to parking. **Amenities:** None. ⊠ *End of Kaluako'i Rd.*

CENTRAL MOLOKA'I

The south shore is mostly a huge, reef-walled expanse of flat saltwater edged with a thin strip of gritty sand and stones, mangrove swamps, and the amazing system of fishponds constructed by the chiefs of ancient Moloka'i. From this shore you can look out across glassy water to see people standing on top of the sea—actually, way out on top of the reef—casting fishing lines into the distant waves. This is not a great area for beaches, but is a good place to snorkel or wade in the shallows.

One Ali'i Beach Park. Clear, close views of Maui and Lāna'i across the Pailolo Channel dominate One Ali'i Beach Park (*One* is pronounced *o-nay*, not *won*), the only well-maintained beach park on the island's south-central shore. Moloka'i folks gather here for family reunions and community celebrations; the park's tightly trimmed expanse of lawn could almost accommodate the entire island population. Swimming within the reef is perfectly safe, but don't expect to catch any waves. Nearby is the restored One Ali'i fishpond. **Amenities:** Toilets, showers, picnic tables. ⊠ *Rte. 450, east of Hotel Moloka'i.*

EAST MOLOKA'I

The east end unfolds as a coastal drive with turnouts for tiny cove beaches—good places for snorkeling, shore fishing, or scuba exploring. Rocky little Mokuho'oniki Island marks the eastern point of the island and serves as a nursery for humpback whales in winter and nesting seabirds in spring. The road loops around the east end, then descends and ends at Hālawa Valley.

Waialua Beach Park. This arched strip of golden sand, a roadside pull-off near mile marker 20, also goes by the name Twenty Mile Beach. The water here, protected by the flanks of the little bay, is often so clear and shallow (sometimes too shallow) that even from land you can watch fish swimming among the coral heads. Watch out for traffic when you enter the highway. ■ TIP➜ This is the most popular snorkeling spot on the island, a pleasant place to stop on the drive around the east end. **Amenities:** None. ⊠ *Rte. 450, near mile marker 20.*

Hālawa Beach Park. The vigorous water that gouged the steep, spectacular Hālawa Valley also carved out two bays side by side. Coarse sand and river rock has built up against the sea along the wide valley mouth, creating some protected pool areas that are good for wading or floating around. Most people come here just to hang out and absorb the beauty of this remote valley. All the property in the valley is private, so do not wander without a guide. Sometimes you'll see people surfing, but it's not wise to entrust your safety to the turbulent open sea along this coast. **Amenities:** Toilets. ⊠ *End of Rte. 450.*

WATER SPORTS AND TOURS

Moloka'i's shoreline topography limits opportunities for water sports. The north shore is all sea cliffs; the south shore is largely encased by a huge, taming reef. ⚠ Open-sea access at west-end and east-end beaches should be used only by experienced ocean swimmers, and then with caution because seas are rough, especially in winter. Generally speaking, there's no one around—certainly not lifeguards—if you get into trouble. For this reason alone, guided excursions are recommended. At least be sure to ask for advice from outfitters or residents. Two kinds of water activities predominate: kayaking within the reef area, and open-sea excursions on charter boats, most of which tie up at Kaunakakai Wharf.

BODY BOARDING AND BODY SURFING

You rarely see people body boarding or body surfing on Moloka'i, and the only surfing is for advanced wave riders. The best spots for body boarding, when conditions are safe (occasional summer mornings), are the west-end beaches. Another option is to seek out waves at the east end around mile marker 20.

DEEP-SEA FISHING

For Moloka'i people, as in days of yore, the ocean is more of a larder than a playground. It's common to see residents fishing along the shoreline or atop South Shore Reef, using poles or lines. Deep-sea fishing by charter boat is a great Moloka'i adventure. The sea channels here, though often rough and windy, provide gorgeous views of several islands. Big fish are plentiful in these waters, especially mahimahi, small marlin, and various kinds of tuna. Generally speaking, boat captains will customize the outing to your interests, share a lot of information about the island, and let you keep some or all of your catch.

EQUIPMENT

If you'd like to try your hand, you can rent or buy fishing equipment and ask for advice at **Moloka'i Fish and Dive** (⊠ *61 Ala Mālama St., Kaunakakai* ☎ *808/553–5926* ⊕ *molokaifishanddive.com*).

BOATS AND CHARTERS

Alyce C. The six-passenger, 31-foot cruiser runs excellent sportfishing excursions in the capable hands of Captain Joe. The cost for the boat is $550 for a full-day trip, $500 for six to seven hours, and $450 for four to five hours. Shared charters are available for six passengers maximum. Gear is provided. It's a rare day when you don't snag at least one memorable fish. ⊠ *Kaunakakai Wharf, Kaunakakai* ☎ *808/558–8377* ⊕ *www.alycecsportfishing.com*.

Fun Hogs Sportfishing. Trim and speedy, the 27-foot flybridge sportfishing boat named *Ahi* offers half-day ($428), six-hour ($535), and full-day ($642) sportfishing excursions. Skipper Mike Holmes also provides one-way or round-trip fishing expeditions to Lāna'i, as well as (in winter only) sunset cruises. ⊠ *Kaunakakai Wharf, Kaunakakai* ☎ *808/567–6789* ⊕ *www.molokaifishing.com*.

Moloka'i Action Adventures. Walter Naki's Moloka'i roots go back forever. What's more, he has traveled (and fished) all over the globe. He will create customized fishing expeditions and gladly share his wealth of experience. He will also take you to remote beaches for a day of swimming. If you want to explore the north side under the great sea cliffs, this is the way to go. His 21-foot *Boston Whaler* is usually seen at the mouth of Hālawa Valley, in the east end. ☎ *808/558–8184*.

KAYAKING

Moloka'i's south shore is enclosed by the largest reef system in the United States—an area of shallow, protected sea that stretches over 30 mi. This reef gives inexperienced kayakers an unusually safe, calm environment for shoreline exploring. ⚠ Outside the reef, Moloka'i waters are often rough, and strong winds can blow you out to sea. Kayakers out here should be strong, experienced, and cautious.

BEST SPOTS

Inside the **South Shore Reef** area is superb for flat-water kayaking any day of the year. It's best to rent a kayak from Moloka'i Outdoors in Kaunakakai and slide into the water from Kaunakakai Wharf, on either side. Get out in the morning before the wind picks up and paddle east, exploring the ancient Hawaiian fishponds. When you turn around to return, you'll usually get a push home by the wind.

Independent experienced kayakers who are confident about testing their skills in rougher seas can launch at the west end of the island from **Hale O Lono Harbor** (at the end of a long, bumpy, often closed, private dirt road from Maunaloa town). At the east end of the island, enter the water near mile marker 20 or beyond and explore in the direction of Mokuho'oniki Island.

EQUIPMENT, LESSONS, AND TOURS

Moloka'i Fish and Dive. At the west end of Kaunakakai's commercial strip, this all-around outfitter provides guided kayak excursions inside the South Shore Reef. One excursion paddles through a mangrove forest and explores a huge, hidden ancient fishpond. A bonus of going with guides: if the wind starts blowing hard, they tow you back with their boat. The fee is $69 for the half-day trip, which includes sodas and water. Check at the store for other outdoor activities. ⊠ *61 Ala Mālama St., Kaunakakai* ☎ *808/553–5926* ⊕ *molokaifishanddive.com.*

Moloka'i Outdoors. This is the place to rent a kayak for exploring on your own. Kayaks rent for $26–$39 per day or $130–$195 per week, and extra paddles are available. ⊠ *Kaunakakai Wharf, Kaunakakai* ☎ *808/553–4477 or 877/553–4477* ⊕ *www.molokai-outdoors.com.*

SAILING

Moloka'i is a place of strong, usually predictable winds that make for good and sometimes rowdy sailing. The island views in every direction are stunning. Kaunakakai Wharf is the home base for all of the island's charter sailboats.

SCUBA DIVING

Moloka'i Fish and Dive is the only PADI-certified purveyor of scuba gear, training, and dive trips on Moloka'i. Shoreline access for divers is extremely limited, even nonexistent in winter. Boat diving is the way to go. Without guidance, visiting divers can easily find themselves in risky situations with wicked currents. Proper guidance, though, opens an undersea world rarely seen.

Moloka'i Fish and Dive. Owners Tim and Susan Forsberg can fill you in on how to find dive sites, rent you the gear, or hook you up with one of their PADI-certified dive guides to take you to the island's best underwater spots. Their 32-foot dive boat, the *Ama Lua*, is certified for 18 passengers and can take eight divers and gear. Two tank dives lasting about five hours cost $155 with gear, $135 if you bring your own. Three tank dives cost $275, take six hours round-trip, and depend on the weather. They know the best blue holes and underwater-cave systems, and they can take you swimming with hammerhead sharks. ⊠ *61 Ala Mālama St., Kaunakakai* ☎ *808/553–5926* ⊕ *molokaifishanddive.com.*

SNORKELING

During the times when swimming is safe—mainly in summer—just about every beach on Moloka'i offers good snorkeling along the lava outcroppings in the island's clean and pristine waters. Certain spots inside the South Shore Reef are also worth checking out.

BEST SPOTS

Kepuhi Beach. In winter, the sea here is rough and deadly. But in summer, this ½-mi-long west-end beach offers plenty of rocky nooks that swirl with sea life. The presence of outdoor showers is a bonus. Take Kaluako'i Road all the way to the west end. Park at Kaluako'i Resort (it's closed) and walk to the beach. ⊠ *Kaluako'i Rd.*

Waialua Beach Park. A thin curve of sand rims a sheltered little bay loaded with coral heads and aquatic life. The water here is shallow—sometimes so shallow that you bump into the underwater landscape—and it's crystal clear. Head to the east end on Route 450, and pull off near mile marker 20. When the sea is calm, you can find several other good snorkeling spots along this stretch of road. ⊠ *Rte. 450.*

EQUIPMENT AND TOURS

Rent snorkel sets from either Moloka'i Outdoors or Moloka'i Fish and Dive in Kaunakakai. Rental fees are nominal—$6 to $10 a day. All the charter boats carry snorkel gear and include dive stops.

Fun Hog Sportfishing. Mike Holmes, captain of the 27-foot powerboat *Ahi*, knows the island waters intimately, likes to have fun, and is willing to arrange any type of excursion—for example, one dedicated entirely to snorkeling. His two-hour snorkel trips leave early in the morning and explore rarely seen fish and turtle sites outside the reef west of the wharf. Bring your own food and drinks; the trips cost $70 per person. ⊠ *Kaunakakai Wharf, Kaunakakai* ☎ *808/567–6789* ⊕ *www.molokaifishing.com.*

Moloka'i Fish and Dive. Climb aboard a 27-foot cabin cruiser or 31-foot twin-hull Power Cat for a snorkel trip to Moloka'i's pristine barrier reef. Trips cost $69 per person and include equipment, water, and soft drinks. ⊠ *61 Ala Mālama St., Kaunakakai* ☎ *808/553–5926* ⊕ *www.molokaifishanddive.com.*

WHALE-WATCHING

Maui gets all the credit for the local wintering humpback-whale population. Most people don't realize that the big cetaceans also come to Moloka'i from December to April. Mokuho'oniki Island at the east end serves as a whale nursery and courting ground, and the whales pass back and forth along the south shore. This being Moloka'i, whale-watching here will never involve floating amid a group of boats all ogling the same whale.

BOATS AND CHARTERS

Alyce C. Although this six-passenger sportfishing boat is usually busy hooking mahimahi and marlin, the captain gladly takes three-hour excursions to admire the hump-back whales in season. The price varies from $75 per person, and is based on the number of passengers in the group. ⊠ *Kaunakakai Wharf, Kaunakakai* ☎ *808/558–8377* ⊕ *www.alycecsportfishing.com.*

Ama Lua. This 32-foot dive boat, certified for up to 18 passengers, is respectful of whales' privacy and the laws that protect them. A 2½-hour whale-watching trip is $69 per person; it departs from Kaunakakai Wharf at 7 am during whale season, roughly from December to April. Call Moloka'i Fish and Dive for reservations or information. ⊠ *61 Ala Mālama St., Kaunakakai* ☎ *808/553–5926 or 808/552–0184* ⊕ *molokaifishanddive.com.*

Fun Hogs Sportfishing. The *Ahi*, a flybridge sportfishing boat, takes 2½-hour whale-watching trips in the morning from December to April. The cost is $69 per person. Bring your own snacks and drinks. You can print your ticket online ahead of time and arrive ready to go. ⊠ *Kaunakakai Wharf, Kaunakakai* ☎ *808/567–6789* ⊕ *www.molokaifishing.com.*

GOLF, HIKING, AND OUTDOOR ACTIVITIES

Activity vendors in Kauanakakai are a good source of information on outdoor adventures on Moloka'i. For a mellow round of golf head to the island's only golf course, Ironwood Hills, where you'll likely share the green with local residents. Moloka'i's steep and uncultivated terrain offers excellent hikes and some stellar views. Although the island is largely wild, all land is owned, so get permission before hiking.

BIKING

Street biking is a dream for pedalers who like to eat up the miles, since Moloka'i's few roads are long, straight, and extremely rural. You can really stretch out and go for it—no traffic lights and most of the time no traffic. You can rent a bike from **Moloka'i Bicycle** (⊠ *80 Mohala St., Kaunakakai* ☎ *808/553-3931 or 800/709-2453*) in Kaunakakai.

Bikers on Moloka'i can explore the north-shore sea cliffs overlooking the Kalaupapa Peninsula.

GOLF

Moloka'i is not a prime golf destination, but the single 9-hole course makes for a pleasant afternoon.

Ironwood Hills Golf Course. Like other 9-hole plantation-era courses, Ironwood Hills in central Moloka'i is in a prime spot, with basic fairways and not always manicured greens. It helps if you like to play laid-back golf with locals and can handle occasionally rugged conditions. On the plus side, most holes offer ocean views. Fairways are *kukuya* grass and run through pine, ironwood, and eucalyptus trees. Carts and clubs are rented on the honor system; there's not always someone there to assist you. Bring your own water. ⊠ *Kala'e Hwy., Kualapu'u* ☎ *808/567–6000* ⚑ *9 holes. 3088 yds. Par 34. Greens Fee: $18 for 9 holes; $24 for 18 holes* ☞ *Facilities: golf carts, pull carts, rental clubs.*

HIKING

Rural and rugged, Moloka'i is an excellent place for hiking. Roads and developments are few. The island is steep, so hikes often combine spectacular views with hearty physical exertion. Because the island is small, you can come away with the feeling of really knowing the place. And you won't see many other people around. Much of what may look like deserted land is private property, so be careful not to trespass without permission or an authorized guide.

BEST SPOTS

Kalaupapa Trail. You can make a day of hiking down to Kalaupapa Peninsula and back by means of a 3-mi, 26-switchback trail. The trail is nearly vertical, traversing the face of high sea cliffs. Only those in excellent condition should attempt this hike. You can arrange a guided hike with Moloka'i Outdoors, who will book you with Damien Tours (☎ 808/567–6171) to access the trail and see the peninsula; if you hike on your own you must make your own reservation with Damien Tours. *See A Tale of Tragedy and Triumph in this chapter.*

★ **Kamakou Preserve.** Four-wheel drive is essential for this half-day (minimum) journey into the Moloka'i highlands. The Nature Conservancy of Hawai'i manages the 2,774-acre Kamakou Preserve, one of the last stands of Hawai'i's native plants and birds. A long rough dirt road, which begins not far from Kaunakakai town, leads to the preserve. The road is not marked, so you must check in with the **Nature Conservancy's Moloka'i office** (✉ *23 Pueo Pl.* ☎ *808/553–5236* ⊕ *www.nature.org*) for directions. The office is at Moloka'i Industrial Park, about 3 mi west of Kaunakakai. Let them know that you plan to visit the preserve, and pick up the informative 24-page brochure with trail maps.

On your way up to the preserve, be sure to stop at Waikolu Overlook, which gives a view into a precipitous north-shore canyon. Once inside the preserve, various trails are clearly marked. The trail of choice—and you can drive right to it—is the 1.5-mi boardwalk trail through Pēpē'ōpae Bog, an ecological treasure. Organic deposits here date back at least 10,000 years, and the plants are undisturbed natives. Be aware that incoming fog can blot out your trail and obscure markers. This is the landscape of prediscovery Hawai'i and can be a mean trek.

Kawela Cul-de-Sacs. Just east of Kaunakakai, three streets—Kawela One, Two, and Three—jut up the mountainside from the Kamehameha V Highway. These roads end in cul-de-sacs that are also informal trailheads. Rough dirt roads work their way from here to the top of the mountain. The lower slopes are dry, rocky, steep, and austere. (It's good to start in the cool of the early morning.) A hiker in good condition can get all the way up into the high forest in two or three hours. There's no park ranger and no water fountain. These are not for the casual stroller, but you will be well rewarded.

GOING WITH A GUIDE

Fodor's Choice ★ **Hālawa Valley Cultural Waterfall Hike.** Hālawa is a gorgeous, steep-walled valley carved by two rivers and rich in history. Site of the earliest Polynesian settlement on Moloka'i, Hālawa is a sustained island culture with its ingeniously designed *lo'i*, or taro fields. Because of a tsunami in 1948 and changing cultural conditions in the 1960s, the valley became largely abandoned. Now Hawaiian families are restoring the lo'i and taking visitors on guided hikes through the valley, which includes two of Moloka'i's *luakini heiau* (sacred temples), many historic sites, and the trail to **Moa'ula Falls,** a 250-foot cascade. Call ahead to book your visit; the fee supports restoration work. Bring water, food, and insect repellent, and wear shoes that are stable and can get wet. The hike is rated intermediate to advanced, is 4.2 mi round-trip, and includes two moderate river crossings. ☎ 808/553–5926 ⊕ *www.molokaifishanddive. com* ✉ $69.

Moloka'i Outdoors. The company can arrange guided hiking options to fit your time frame and physical condition. They will take you down into Kalaupapa and arrange for a plane to pick you up. ✉ *Kaunakakai Wharf, Kaunakakai* ☎ 808/553–4477 or 877/553–4477 ⊕ *www. molokai-outdoors.com.*

SHOPPING

Moloka'i has one main commercial area: Ala Mālama Street in Kaunakakai. There are no department stores or shopping malls, and the clothing available is typical island wear. Local shopping is friendly and you may find hidden treasures. A few family-run businesses define the main drag of Maunaloa, a rural former plantation town. Most stores in Kaunakakai are open Monday through Saturday between 9 and 6. In Maunaloa shops close by 4 in the afternoon.

ARTS AND CRAFTS

Moloka'i Art From the Heart. A small shop downtown, the artists and crafters' co-op has locally made folk art like dolls, clay flowers, hula skirts, aloha-print visors, and children's wear. They also carry original art by Moloka'i artists and Giclée prints, jewelry, locally produced music, and Saint Damien keepsakes. Store hours are Monday to Friday 10 to 4:30 and Saturday 9:30 to 2. ✉ *64 Ala Mālama St., Kaunakakai* ☎ 808/553–8018.

CLOTHING AND SHOES

Imports Gift Shop. Across from Kanemitsu Bakery, this one-stop shop offers fancy and casual island-style wear, including Roxy and Quicksilver for men, women, and children, and footwear. The store is open Monday to Saturday 9 to 6 and Sunday 9 to 1. ✉ *82 Ala Mālama St., Kaunakakai* ☎ 808/553–5734.

FOOD

Friendly Market Center. The best-stocked supermarket on the island has a slogan—"Your family store on Moloka'i"—that is truly credible. Hats, T-shirts, and sun-and-surf essentials keep company with fresh produce, meat, groceries, liquor, and sundries. Locals say the food is fresher here than at the other major supermarket. It's open weekdays 8:30 am to 8:30 pm and Saturday 8:30 am to 6:30 pm. ✉ *90 Ala Mālama St., Kaunakakai* ☎ 808/553–5595.

Maunaloa General Store. Victuals and travel essentials, like meat, produce, dry goods, drinks, sandwiches, and boxed meals are available here. It's convenient for guests staying at the nearby condos and for those wishing to picnic at one of the west-end beaches. It's open Monday through Saturday 9 am to 6 pm and Sunday 9 am to noon. ✉ *200 Maunaloa Hwy., Maunaloa* ☎ 808/552–2346.

Misaki's Inc. In business since 1922, Misaki's has authentic island allure. Pick up housewares and beverages here, as well as your food staples,

Monday through Saturday 8:30 am to 8:30 pm, and Sunday 9 am to noon. ⊠ *78 Ala Mālama St., Kaunakakai* ☎ *808/553–5505.*

JEWELRY

Imports Gift Shop. You'll find gifts, soaps, and lotions, a small collection of 14-karat-gold chains, rings, earrings, and bracelets, plus a jumble of Hawaiian quilts, pillows, books, and postcards here. The shop also carries stunning Hawaiian heirloom jewelry, a unique style of gold jewelry inspired by popular Victorian pieces, that has been crafted in Hawai'i since the late 1800s. It's made to order. ⊠ *82 Ala Mālama St., Kaunakakai* ☎ *808/553–5734.*

Moloka'i Island Creations. Stop here to see the store's own unique line of jewelry, including sea opal, coral, and silver, as well as other gifts and resort wear. ⊠ *61 Ala Mālama St., Kaunakakai* ☎ *808/553–5926.*

ENTERTAINMENT AND NIGHTLIFE

Local nightlife consists mainly of gathering with friends and family, sipping a few cold ones, strumming 'ukuleles and guitars, singing old songs, and talking story. Still, there are a few ways to kick up your heels. Pick up a copy of the weekly Moloka'i *Dispatch* and see if there's a concert, church supper, or dance.

The bar at the Hotel Moloka'i is always a good place to drink. It has live music by island performers every night, and Moloka'i may be the best place to hear authentic, old-time, nonprofessional Hawaiian music. Don't be afraid to get up and dance. The "Aloha Friday" weekly gathering here, from 4 to 6 pm, features Na Kapuna, a group of accomplished *kūpuna* (old-timers) with guitars and 'ukuleles.

For something truly casual, stop in at Kanimitsu Bakery on Ala Mālama Street in Kaunakakai for their nightly hot bread sale (Tuesday through Sunday, until 10 pm, or until they sell out of bread); it's fresh from the ovens. You'll meet everyone in town, and you can take some hot bread home to your condo for a late-night treat.

WHERE TO EAT

During a week's stay, you might easily hit all the dining spots worth a visit and then return to your favorites for a second round. The dining scene is fun because it's a microcosm of Hawai'i's diverse cultures. You can find locally grown vegetarian foods, spicy Filipino cuisine, and Hawaiian fish with a Japanese influence—such as 'ahi or aku (types of tuna), mullet, and moonfish grilled, sautéed, or mixed with seaweed and eaten raw as *poke* (salted and seasoned raw fish). Most eating establishments are on Ala Mālama Street in Kaunakakai, with pizza, pasta, and ribs all within a block or two. If you're heading to West Moloka'i for the day, be sure to stock up on provisions before you go as there is no place to eat here. If you are on the east end stop by Mana'e Goods and Grinds (☎ *808/558–8186*) near mile marker 16 for good local seafood plates, burgers, and ice cream.

WHAT IT COSTS					
	¢	$	$$	$$$	$$$$
AT DINNER	under $10	$10–$17	$18–$26	$27–$35	over $35

Restaurant prices are for a main course at dinner.

CENTRAL MOLOKA'I

Central Moloka'i offers most of the island's dining options, from local plate lunch take-out joints, to the dining room (Hula Shores) at the Hotel Moloka'i.

$$
HAWAIIAN

✕ **Hula Shores.** The Hotel Molokai's restaurant is *the* place to hang out on Moloka'i. Service is brisk and friendly, the food is good, and the atmosphere casual. Prime-rib specials on Friday and Saturday nights draw a crowd. Every Friday from 4 to 6 pm Moloka'i's *kūpuna* (old-timers) bring their instruments here for a lively Hawaiian jam session, a wonderful experience of grassroots aloha spirit, followed by dance music until 10:30. ⊠ *Hotel Moloka'i, 1300 Kamehameha V Hwy., Kaunakakai* ☎ *808/660–3408* ▭ *AE, DC, MC, V.*

¢
CAFÉ
Fodor'sChoice
★

✕ **Kanemitsu Bakery and Restaurant.** Stop at this Moloka'i institution for morning coffee with fresh-baked bread or a taste of *lavosh*, a pricey flat bread flavored with sesame, taro, Maui onion, Parmesan cheese, or jala-peño. Or try the round Moloka'i bread—a sweet, pan-style white loaf that makes excellent cinnamon toast. Take a few loaves with you for a picnic or a condo breakfast. You can slow down here and settle into Moloka'i time. ⊠ *79 Ala Mālama St., Kaunakakai* ☎ *808/553–5855* ▭ *No credit cards* ☉ *Open Mon. and Wed.–Sat. 5:30 am–6:30 pm, Sun. 5:30 am–4 pm. Closed Tues.*

$
HAWAIIAN

✕ **Kualapu'u Cookhouse.** The only restaurant in rural Kualapu'u and a local favorite, this laid-back diner is a classic refurbished green-and-white plantation house. Inside, paintings of hula dancers and island scenes enhance the simple furnishings. Typical fare is a plate of chicken or pork *katsu* served with rice, but they do also offer a nice, more expensive sautéed opakapaka at dinner. It's across the street from the Kualapu'u Market. ⊠ *Farrington Hwy., 1 block west of Rte. 470, Kualapu'u* ☎ *808/567–9655* ▭ *No credit cards* ☉ *Open Tues.–Sat. 7 am–8 pm. No dinner Sun. and Mon.*

¢
HAWAIIAN

✕ **Moloka'i Drive Inn.** Fast food Moloka'i-style is served at a walk-up counter. Hot dogs, fries, and sundaes are on the menu, but residents usually choose the foods they grew up on, such as *saimin* (thin noodles and vegetables in broth), plate lunches, shave ice, and the beloved *loco moco* (rice topped with a hamburger and a fried egg, covered in gravy). ⊠ *15 Kamoi St., Kaunakakai* ☎ *808/553–5655* ▭ *No credit cards.*

$
AMERICAN

✕ **Moloka'i Pizza Cafe.** Cheerful and busy, Moloka'i Pizza is a popular gathering spot for families and a good place to pick up food for a picnic. Pizza, sandwiches, salads, pasta, and fresh fish are simply prepared and served without fuss. Eat in or take out. Kids keep busy at the nearby arcade, and art by local artists decorates the lavender walls. ⊠ *Kaunaka-kai Pl. at Wharf Rd., Kaunakakai* ☎ *808/553–3288* ▭ *No credit cards.*

$ ✕ **Oviedo's.** Don't let the sagging front door fool you. This modest and
PHILIPPINE   spotless lunch counter, a Moloka'i tradition, specializes in delicious
adobos (stews) with traditional Filipino spices and sauces. Try the tripe,
pork, or beef adobo for a taste of tradition. Locals say that Oviedo's
makes the best crispy roast pork in the state. You can eat in at one of the
four tables or take out. ⊠ *145 Puali St., Kaunakakai* ☎ *808/553–5014*
⊟ *No credit cards* ⊙ *Closed Sun.*

¢   ✕ **Sundown Deli.** Small and clean, this rose-color deli focuses on freshly
DELI   made take-out food. Sandwiches come on a half dozen types of bread,
and the Portuguese bean soup and chowders are rich and filling. It's
open weekdays from 7:30 to 3:30. ⊠ *145 Ala Mālama St., Kaunakakai*
☎ *808/553–3713* ⊟ *No credit cards* ⊙ *Closed weekends. No dinner.*

WHERE TO STAY

The coastline along Moloka'i's west end has ocean-view condominium
units and luxury homes available as vacation rentals. If you are familiar
with the high-end Lodge at Moloka'i Ranch, please note that the resort
and ranch operations are closed and up for sale. Central Moloka'i offers
seaside condominiums and the icon of the island—Hotel Moloka'i. The
only lodgings on the east end are some guest cottages in magical settings
and the ranch house at Pu'u O Hoku. The **Moloka'i Visitors Association**
(☎ *800/800–6367*) has a brochure with an up-to-date listing of vacation
rentals operated by their members.

Moloka'i Vacation Properties (☎ *800/367–2984 or 808/553–8334* ⊕ *www.
molokai-vacation-rental.net*) handles upgraded condo rentals that
include initial bathroom amenities, cleaning supplies, maps, and complimentary coffee. The company can act as an informal concierge during
your stay. There is a three-night minimum on all properties. They also
handle private rental properties from beach cottages to large estates.

Note: Maui County has regulations concerning vacation rentals; to
avoid disappointment, always contact the property manager or the
owner and ask if the accommodation has the proper permits and is in
compliance with local ordinances.

WHAT IT COSTS				
¢	$	$$	$$$	$$$$
FOR TWO PEOPLE	under $100	$100–$180	$181–$260	$261–$340	over $340

Hotel prices are for two people in a double room in high season, including tax
and service. Condo price categories reflect studio and one-bedroom rates. Prices
do not include 13.42% tax.

WEST MOLOKA'I

If you want to stay in West Moloka'i and have access to unspoiled
beaches, your only choices are condos or vacation homes. Keep in mind
that units fronting the abandoned Kaula Koi golf course present a bit
of a dismal view.

No traffic lights here: Moloka'i's rural, uncrowded roads have wide-open views.

$ 🏠 Ke Nani Kai. These pleasant spacious one- and two-bedroom condo
RENTAL units have ocean views and nicely maintained tropical landscaping.
Furnished lānai have flower-laden trellises and the spacious interiors are
decorated with rattans and pastels. Each unit has a washer-dryer and a
fully equipped kitchen. The beach is across the road. **Pros:** located on
island's secluded west end; Internet; uncrowded pool. **Cons:** amenities
vary as each unit is individually owned; far from commercial center; golf
course units overlook abandoned course. **TripAdvisor:** "very quiet,"
"best-kept secret," "large, clean pool and hot tub." ✉ *50 Keuphi Beach
Rd., Maunaloa* ☎ *808/553–8334 or 800/367–2984* ⊕ *www.molokai-
vacation-rental.net* ⤶ *120 units* ♿ *In-room: no a/c, kitchen, Internet.
In-hotel: tennis courts, pool, laundry facilities* 🖃 *AE, MC, V.*

$–$$ 🏠 Paniolo Hale. Perched high on a ridge overlooking a favored local
RENTAL surfing spot, this is Moloka'i's best condominium property. Architec-
turally elegant studios and one- or two-bedroom units all have beautiful screened lānai, well-equipped kitchens, and washers and dryers;
some have spectacular ocean views. The property boasts mature tropical landscaping and a private serene setting. **Pros:** close to beach; quiet
surroundings; perfect if you are an expert surfer. **Cons:** amenities vary
in units; far from shopping; golf course units front abandoned course;
three-night minimum. **TripAdvisor:** "complex is well-maintained,"
low-key, restful place," "groceries 25 minutes away." ✉ *100 Lio Pl.,
Kaunakakai* ☎ *808/553–8334 or 800/367–2984* ⊕ *www.molokai-
vacation-rental.net* ⤶ *77 units* ♿ *In-room: a/c (some), kitchen, Internet
(some). In-hotel: pool, laundry facilities* 🖃 *AE, MC, V.*

CENTRAL MOLOKA'I

Aside from the popular Hotel Moloka'i, there are two condo properties in this area, one close to shopping and dining in Kaunakakai, and the other on the way to the east end.

$–$$
HOTEL
🏨 **Hotel Moloka'i.** Staff members are helpful and friendly at this local favorite, where the two-story, semi-A-frame buildings are arranged in a landscaped tropical setting. Part of the Aqua Hotels and Resorts group, the hotel benefits from its

reservations system. Prime units overlook the reef and distant Lana'i. The pool area and the rooms are bright and comfortably furnished. A popular hangout, the airy Hula Shores restaurant is on the ocean and serves breakfast, lunch, dinner, and libations—with local entertainment nightly. Ask about deals in conjunction with airlines and rental-car companies when you make your reservation. The full-service activities desk in the lobby will book any island adventure. **Pros:** five minutes to shopping and town; some kitchenettes; authentic Hawaiian entertainment. **Cons:** not many frills; can be difficult to secure weekend reservations; lower-priced rooms are small and plain; late-night live music and bar activities can be loud. **TripAdvisor:** "rooms were small but cozy," "noisy at night," "best place for the sunset." ✉ *1300 Kamehameha V Hwy., Kaunakakai* ☎ *808/553–5347 or 877/553–5347* ⊕ *www.hotelmolokai.com* ➳ *40 rooms* ⌂ *In-room: no a/c, Internet. In-hotel: restaurant, room service, pool, spa, laundry facilities, Internet terminal* ▤ *AE, D, MC, V.*

$
RENTAL
🏨 **Moloka'i Shores.** Some of the units in this oceanfront, three-story condominium complex have a view of the water. One-bedroom, one-bath units or two-bedroom, two-bath units all have full kitchens and furnished lānai, which look out on 4 acres of lawn. There's a great view of Lāna'i in the distance and a chance to see whales in season. **Pros:** convenient location; some units upgraded; near water. **Cons:** uninspiring basic accommodations; fussy cancellation policy. **TripAdvisor:** "doesn't feel crowded," pool is great," "great base for exploring the island." ✉ *1000 Kamehameha V Hwy., Kaunakakai* ☎ *808/553–5954 or 800/535–0085* ⊕ *www.molokai-vacation-rental.net* ➳ *100 units* ⌂ *In-room: no a/c, kitchen. In-hotel: pool, laundry facilities* ▤ *AE, D, MC, V.*

$
RENTAL
🏨 **Wavecrest.** This oceanfront condominium complex is convenient if you want to explore the east side of the island—it's 13 mi east of Kaunakakai. Individually decorated one- and two-bedroom units have full kitchens. Each has a furnished lānai, some with views of Maui and Lāna'i. Be sure to ask for an updated unit when you reserve. The 5-acre oceanfront property has access to a beautiful reef, excellent snorkeling and kayaking, and an oceanfront pool with covered barbecue. **Pros:** convenient location for divers; good value; nicely maintained grounds. **Cons:** amenities vary as each unit is individually owned; far

from shopping; overlooks channel and sometimes gets windy. **TripAdvisor:** "does not have a swimmable beach," "right by the ocean," "be careful which condo you choose." ⊠ *Rte. 450, near mile marker 13* ⚲ *Moloka'i Vacation Properties, HC 01 Box 28, Kaunakakai 96748* ☎ *800/367–2984 or 808/553–8334* ⊕ *www.molokai-vacation-rental. net* ⤴ *126 units* ⚘ *In-room: no a/c, kitchen, Internet. In-hotel: tennis courts, pool, laundry facilities, beachfront* ⊟ *AE, MC, V.*

EAST MOLOKA'I

Pu'u O Hoku Ranch, a rental facility on East Moloka'i, is the main lodging option on this side of the island. The ranch is quite far from the center of the island.

$ ▦ **Pu'u O Hoku Ranch.** At the east end of Moloka'i, near mile marker 25,

RENTAL   lie these three ocean-view accommodations, on 14,000 isolated acres of pastures and forest. This is a remote and serene location for people who want to get away or meet in a retreat atmosphere. One country cottage ($140 per night) has two bedrooms, basic wicker furnishings, and *lauhala* (natural fiber) woven matting on the floors. An airy four-bedroom cottage ($160 per night) has a small deck and a somewhat Balinese air. For large groups—family reunions, for example—the ranch has a lodge with 11 bedrooms, 9 bathrooms, and a large kitchen. The full lodge goes for $1,250 nightly (rooms are not available on an individual basis). **Pros:** ideal for large groups; authentic working organic ranch; great hiking. **Cons:** on remote east end of island; rooms in the main lodge cannot be individually rented; road to property is narrow and winding. **TripAdvisor:** "wonderful upcountry retreat," "close to beaches," "great views." ⊠ *Rte. 450, Kaunakakai* ☎ *808/558–8109* ⊕ *www.puuohoku.com* ⤴ *1 2-bedroom cottage, 1 4-bedroom cottage, 11 rooms in lodge* ⚘ *In-room: no a/c, kitchen. In-hotel: pool* ⊟ *MC, V.*

Lāna'i

WORD OF MOUTH

"If you're just looking to play on the beach on Lāna'i, go to Mānele
Bay. If you want to see a different kind of terrain for a day, take
the bus up to Kō'ele. Both Four Seasons resorts are fabulous, with
different activities. You can catch the bus from the landing to either
destination, and you can ride back and forth between the two."
                                                            —ErinK09

WELCOME TO LĀNAʻI

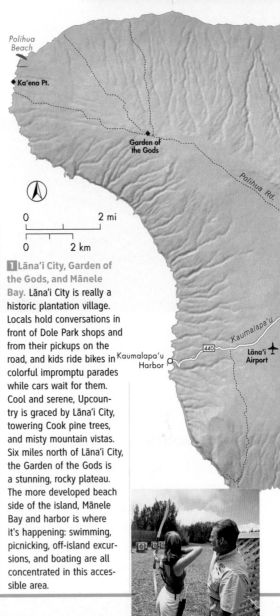

TOP REASONS TO GO

★ **Seclusion and serenity:** Lānaʻi is small: local motion is slow motion. Get into the spirit and go home rested instead of exhausted.

★ **Garden of the Gods:** Walk amid the eerie red-rock spires that Hawaiians believe to be a sacred spot. The ocean views are magnificent, too; sunset is a good time to visit.

★ **A dive at Cathedrals:** Explore underwater pinnacle formations and mysterious caverns lighted by shimmering rays of light.

★ **Dole Park:** Hang out in the shade of the Cook pines in Lānaʻi City and talk story with the locals for a taste of old-time Hawaiʻi.

★ **Hit the water at Hulopoʻe Beach:** This beach may have it all: good swimming, a shady park for perfect picnicking, great reefs for snorkeling, and sometimes plenty of spinner dolphins.

Polihua Beach

◆ Kaʻena Pt.

Garden of the Gods

Polihua Rd.

0   2 mi

0   2 km

Kaumalapaʻu

440

Lānaʻi Airport

Kaumalapaʻu Harbor

1 Lānaʻi City, Garden of the Gods, and Mānele Bay. Lānaʻi City is really a historic plantation village. Locals hold conversations in front of Dole Park shops and from their pickups on the road, and kids ride bikes in colorful impromptu parades while cars wait for them. Cool and serene, Upcountry is graced by Lānaʻi City, towering Cook pine trees, and misty mountain vistas. Six miles north of Lānaʻi City, the Garden of the Gods is a stunning, rocky plateau. The more developed beach side of the island, Mānele Bay and harbor is where it's happening: swimming, picnicking, off-island excursions, and boating are all concentrated in this accessible area.

GETTING ORIENTED

Unlike the other Hawaiian Islands with their tropical splendors, Lānaʻi looks like a desert: kiawe trees right out of Africa, red-dirt roads, and a deep blue sea. Lānaʻihale (house of Lānaʻi), the mountain that bisects the island, is carved into deep canyons by rain and wind on the windward side, and the drier leeward side slopes gently to the sea, where waves pound against surf-carved cliffs. The town of Lānaʻi City is in the center of the island, Upcountry. Mānele Bay, on the south side of the island, is popular for swimming and boating.

7

2 Windward Lānaʻi. This area is the long white-sand beach at the base of Lānaʻihale. Now uninhabited, it was once occupied by thriving Hawaiian fishing villages and a sugarcane plantation.

By Joana Varawa

With no traffic or traffic lights and miles of open space, Lāna'i seems lost in time, and that can be a good thing. Small (141 square mi) and sparsely populated, it is the smallest inhabited Hawaiian Island and has just 3,500 residents, most of them living Upcountry.

Though it may seem a world away, Lāna'i is separated from Maui and Moloka'i by two narrow channels, and is easily accessed by boat from either island. The two resorts on the island are run by the Four Seasons. If you yearn for a beach with amenities, a luxury resort, and golf course, the Four Seasons Resort Lāna'i at Mānele Bay beckons from the shoreline. Upcountry, the luxurious Four Seasons Resort Lodge at Kō'ele provides cooler pleasures. This leaves the rest of the 100,000-acre island open to explore. An afternoon strolling around Dole Park in historic Lāna'i City offers shopping and the opportunity to mingle with locals.

FLORA AND FAUNA

Lāna'i bucks the "tropical" trend of the other Hawaiian Islands with African kiawe trees, Cook pines, and eucalyptus in place of palm trees, and deep blue sea where you might expect shallow turquoise bays. Abandoned pineapple fields are overgrown with drought-resistant grasses, Christmas berry, and lantana; native plants, a'ali'i and 'ilima, are found in uncultivated areas. Axis deer from India dominate the ridges, and wild turkeys lumber around the resorts. Whales can be seen December through April, and a family of resident spinner dolphins drops in regularly at Hulopo'e Bay.

ON LĀNA'I TODAY

Despite its fancy resorts, Lāna'i still has that sleepy old Hawai'i feel. The island is 98% owned by billionaire David Murdock. Residents are a mix of just about everything—Hawaiian/Chinese/German/Portuguese/Filipino/Japanese/French/Puerto Rican/English/Norwegian—you name it. When Dole owned the island in the earlier part of the 20th century and grew pineapples, the plantation was divided into ethnic camps, which helped retain cultural cuisines. Potluck dinners feature sashimi, Portuguese bean soup, *laulau* (morsels of pork, chicken, butterfish, or other ingredients wrapped with young taro shoots in tī leaves), potato salad, teriyaki steak, chicken *hekka* (a gingery Japanese chicken stir-fry), and Jell-O. The local language is pidgin, a mix of words as complicated and rich as the food.

PLANNING

WHEN TO GO

Lāna'i has an ideal climate year-round, hot and sunny at the sea and a few delicious degrees cooler Upcountry. In Lāna'i City and Upcountry, the nights and mornings can be almost chilly when a fog or harsh trade winds settle in. Winter months are known for *slightly* rougher weather—periodic rain showers and higher surf.

As higher mountains on Maui capture the trade-wind clouds, Lāna'i receives little rainfall and has a near-desert ecology. Consider the wind direction when planning your day. If it's blowing a gale on the windward beaches, head for the beach at Hulopo'e or check out Garden of the Gods. Overcast days, when the wind stops or comes lightly from the southwest, are common in whale season. At that time, try a whale-watching trip or the windward beaches.

Whales are seen off Lāna'i's shores from December through April. A Pineapple Festival on the July 4 Saturday in Dole Park features local food, Hawaiian entertainment, a pineapple-eating and -cooking contest, and fireworks. Buddhists hold their annual outdoor Obon Festival, honoring departed ancestors with joyous dancing, food booths, and taiko drumming, in early July. During hunting season weekends, from mid-February through mid-May, and mid-July through mid-October, it's best to watch out for hunters on dirt roads even though there are designated safety zones.

GETTING HERE AND AROUND

AIR TRAVEL

Island Air and go! are the only commercial airlines serving Lāna'i City. All flights to the island depart from O'ahu's Honolulu International Airport.

If you're staying at the Hotel Lāna'i or either Four Seasons hotel, you'll be met at the airport or ferry dock by a shuttle, which serves as transportation between the resorts and Lāna'i City. If you're not taking a shuttle, bus drivers at the ferry docks will herd you onto the appropriate bus and take you into town for $10 per person. Advance reservations aren't necessary (or even possible), but be prepared for a little confusion on the dock.

Dollar Rent A Car will arrange to pick you up if you're renting a Jeep or minivan. Cost is $5 per person round-trip, and one person in your party rides for free.

Information go! (☎ 888/435–9462 ⊕ *www.iflygo.com*). **Island Air** (☎ 800/ 652–6541 ⊕ *www.islandair.com*).

CAR TRAVEL

Lāna'i has no traffic, no traffic lights, and only 30 mi of paved roads. Keōmuku Highway starts just past the Lodge at Kō'ele and runs northeast to the dirt road that goes to Shipwreck Beach and Lōpā Beach. Mānele Road (Highway 440) runs south down to Mānele Bay and Hulopo'e Beach. Kaumalapau Highway (also Highway 440) heads west to Kaumalapau Harbor. The rest of your driving takes place on bumpy, dusty, secondary roads that aren't marked. Driving in thick mud is not recommended, and the car rental agency will charge for Jeep cleaning fees.

Renting a four-wheel-drive vehicle is expensive but almost essential if you'd like to explore beyond the resorts and Lāna'i City. Make reservations far in advance of your trip, because Lāna'i's fleet of vehicles is limited. Lāna'i City Service, a subsidiary of Dollar Rent A Car, is open daily 7 to 7.

Bring along a good topographical map, and keep in mind your directions. Stop from time to time and refind landmarks and gauge your progress. Never drive or walk to the edge of lava cliffs, as rock can give way under you. ■ TIP→ **Directions on the island are often given as mauka (toward the mountains) and makai (toward the ocean).**

Information **Lāna'i City Service** (✉ *Lāna'i Ave. at 11th St.* ☎ *808/565–7227 or 800/533–7808*).

FERRY TRAVEL

Expeditions' ferries cross the channel seven times daily, departing from Lahaina and Mā'alaea on Maui, to Mānele Bay Harbor on Lāna'i. The crossing takes 45 minutes from Lahaina, and 75 minutes from Mā`alaea, and costs $30 each way for adults and $20 for kids age 2 to 11. Be warned: Passage can be rough, especially in winter.

Contact **Expeditions** (☎ *808/661–3756 or 800/695–2624* ⊕ *www.go-lanai.com*).

SHUTTLE TRAVEL

A shuttle transports hotel guests between the Hotel Lāna'i, the Four Seasons Resort Lodge at Kō'ele, the Four Seasons Resort Lāna'i at Mānele Bay, and the airport. A $45 fee for adults, $22.50 for children, added to the room fee covers all transportation during the length of stay.

RESTAURANTS

Although Lāna'i has a somewhat wide range of choices for dining, from simple plate-lunch local eateries to fancy upscale gourmet resort restaurants, the range of lodgings is limited. Essentially there are only three resort options: the two Four Seasons Resorts Lāna'i (at Mānele Bay and Upcountry at the Lodge at Kō'ele) and the venerable Hotel Lāna'i.

HOTELS

House rentals give you a feel for everyday life on the island; ⊕ *www.gohawaii.com* has information. In hunting seasons, from mid-February through mid-May, and from mid-July through mid-October, most private properties are booked way in advance. **Note:** Maui County has regulations concerning vacation rentals; to avoid disappointment, always contact the property manager or owner and ask if the accommodation has the proper permits and is in compliance with local laws.

WHAT IT COSTS					
	¢	$	$$	$$$	$$$$
Restaurants	under $10	$10–$17	$18–$26	$27–$35	over $35
Hotels	under $100	$100–$180	$181–$260	$261–$340	over $340

Restaurant prices are for a main course at dinner. Hotel prices are for two people in a standard double room in high season. Condo price categories reflect studio and one-bedroom rates.

VISITOR INFORMATION

The Lāna'i Culture & Heritage Center, in the old Dole Administration Building at 730 Lāna'i Avenue in Lāna'i City, has information and maps.

Contact Lāna'i Visitor's Bureau (☎ *808/563-0484* ⊕ *www.visitlanai.net*).

EXPLORING LĀNA'I

You can easily explore Lāna'i City and the island's two resorts without a car; just hop on the hourly shuttle. A small fee applies. To access the rest of this untamed island, rent a four-wheel-drive vehicle. Take a map, be sure you have a full tank, and bring a snack and plenty of water. Ask the rental agency or your hotel's concierge about road conditions before you set out. It's always good to carry a cell phone. The main road on Lāna'i, Route 440, refers to both Kaumalapau Highway and Mānele Road.

LĀNA'I CITY, GARDEN OF THE GODS, AND MĀNELE BAY

Lānai'i City is 3 mi northeast of the airport; Mānele Bay is 9 mi southeast of Lāna'i City; Garden of the Gods is 6 mi northwest of Lāna'i City.

Pineapples once blanketed the Pālāwai, the great basin south of Lāna'i City. Before that it was a vast dryland forest; now most of it is fenced-in pasture or a game-hunting reserve, and can only be viewed from the Mānele Road. Although it looks like a volcanic crater, it isn't. Some say that the name Pālāwai is descriptive of the mist that sometimes fills the basin at dawn and looks like a huge shining lake.

The area northwest of Lāna'i City is wild; the Garden of the Gods is one of its highlights.

GETTING HERE AND AROUND

Lāna'i City serves as the island's hub, with roads leading to Mānele Bay, Kaumalapau Harbor, and Windward Lāna'i. Garden of the Gods is usually possible to visit by car, but beyond that you will need four-wheel drive.

EXPLORING
TOP ATTRACTIONS

Fodor's Choice **Garden of the Gods.** This preternatural plateau is scattered with boulders
★ of different sizes, shapes, and colors, the products of a million years of wind erosion. Time your visit for sunset, when the rocks begin to

Ocean views provide a backdrop to the eroded rocks at Garden of the Gods.

glow—from rich red to purple—and the fiery globe sinks to the horizon. Magnificent views of the Pacific Ocean, Moloka'i, and, on clear days, O'ahu provide the perfect backdrop for photographs. Lāna'i landowner David Murdock has proposed a development plan that would transform this area into a large wind farm, but local and visitor opposition has delayed the plan's approval.

The ancient Hawaiians shunned Lāna'i for hundreds of years, believing the island was the inviolable home of spirits. Standing beside the oxide-red rock spires of this strange, raw landscape, you might be tempted to believe the same. This lunar savanna still has a decidedly eerie edge, but the shadows disappearing on the horizon are those of mouflon sheep and axis deer, not the fearsome spirits of lore. According to tradition, Kawelo, a Hawaiian priest, kept a perpetual fire burning on an altar at the Garden of the Gods, in sight of the island of Moloka'i. As long as the fire burned, prosperity was assured for the people of Lāna'i. Kawelo was killed by a rival priest on Moloka'i and the fire went out. The Hawaiian name for this area is Keahiakawelo, meaning the "fire of Kawelo." The site is 6 mi north of Lāna'i City. From Stables at Kō'ele, follow dirt road through pasture, turn right at crossroad marked by carved boulder, head through abandoned fields and ironwood forest to open red-dirt area marked by a carved boulder. ⊠ *Off Polihua Rd.*

Ka Lokahi o Ka Mālamalama Church. Built in 1938, this picturesque painted, wooden church provided services for Lāna'i's growing population—for many people, the only other Hawaiian church, in coastal Keōmuku, was too far away. A classic structure of ranching days, the church had to be moved from its original Lāna'i Ranch site when the

Lodge at Kō'ele was built. It's open all day and Sunday services are still held, in Hawaiian and English; visitors are welcome but are requested to attend quietly. The church is north of the entrance to the Four Seasons Resort Lodge at Kō'ele. ⊠ *Keōmuku Hwy.*

Kānepu'u Preserve. Hawaiian sandalwood, olive, and ebony trees characterize the largest example in Hawai'i of a rare native dryland forest. Thanks to the combined efforts of the Nature Conservancy and Castle & Cooke Resorts, the 590-acre remnant forest is protected from the axis deer and mouflon sheep that graze on the land beyond its fence. More than 45 native plant species, including *na'u*, the endangered Hawaiian gardenia, can be seen here. A short self-guided loop trail, with eight signs illustrated by local artist Wendell Kaho'ohalahala, reveals this ecosystem's beauty and the challenges it faces. ⊠ *Polihua Rd., 4.8 mi north of Lāna'i City.*

Kaumalapau Harbor. Built in 1926 by the Hawaiian Pineapple Company, which later became Dole, this is Lāna'i's principal commercial seaport. The cliffs that flank the western shore are as much as 1,000 feet tall. Water activities aren't allowed here, but it's a dramatic sunset spot. The harbor is closed to visitors on barge days: Tuesday, Wednesday, and Thursday. From Lāna'i City, follow Highway 440 (Kaumalapau Highway) 6 mi west as far as it goes. ⊠ *Hwy. 440.*

★ **Lāna'i City.** A tidy plantation town, built in 1924 by Jim Dole for the needs of the growing pineapple business that dominated the island, is home to old-time residents, recently arrived resort workers, and second-home owners, and is slowly changing from a quiet rural village to a busier little town. A simple grid of roads is lined with stately Cook pines and basic services; the pace is calm and the people are friendly. **Dole Park,** in the center of Lāna'i City, is surrounded by small shops and restaurants and is a favorite spot among locals for sitting, strolling, and talking story. Visit the **Lāna'i Culture and Heritage Center** to get a glimpse of this island's rich past, purchase historical publications and maps, and get directions to anywhere on the island.

QUICK BITES

The Sweetest Days (⊠ *338 8th St., Lāna'i City* ☎ *808/559–6253* ☉ *Closed Sun.*) sells premium Roselani ice cream made in Maui and local treats like crack seed and traditional candies. Choose from scoops, splits, floats, sundaes, smoothies, and slush puppies. You can sit on benches shaded by umbrellas and watch the slow world of Lāna'i pass by.

Lu'ahiwa Petroglyphs. On a steep slope overlooking the Pālāwai Basin are 34 boulders with carvings. Drawn in a mixture of styles dating to the late 1700s and early 1800s, the simple stick figures depict animals, people, and mythical beings. A nearby *heiau*, or temple, no longer visible, was used to summon the rains and was dedicated to the god Kāne. Do not draw on or deface the carvings, and do not add to the collection. From Lāna'i City turn south on Highway 440 (Mānele Road) and continue to the first dirt road on your left. Follow the dirt road along fields 1.2 mi; do not go left uphill but continue straight, and when you see boulders on hillside, park and walk up to petroglyphs. ⊠ *Off Hwy. 440 (Mānele Rd.).*

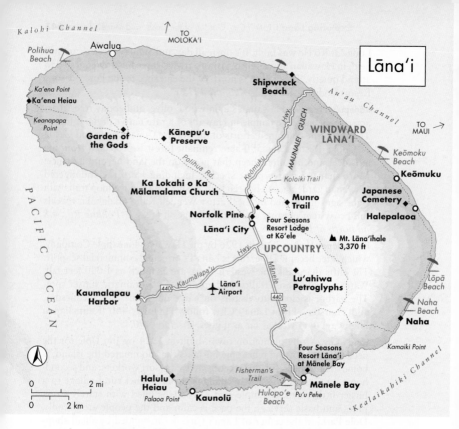

Lāna'i

Kalohi Channel
TO MOLOKA'I
Polihua Beach
Awalua
Ka'ena Point
Ka'ena Heiau
Keanapapa Point
Garden of the Gods
Kānepu'u Preserve
Polihua Rd.
Shipwreck Beach
Au'au Channel
WINDWARD LĀNA'I
TO MAUI
Keōmuku Beach
Keōmuku
Ka Lokahi o Ka Mālamalama Church
Koloiki Trail
Munro Trail
Japanese Cemetery
Halepalaoa
Norfolk Pine
Lāna'i City
Four Seasons Resort Lodge at Kō'ele
UPCOUNTRY
Mt. Lāna'ihale 3,370 ft
PACIFIC OCEAN
Kaumālapa'u Hwy.
440
Lāna'i Airport
Manele Rd.
440
Lu'ahiwa Petroglyphs
Lōpā Beach
Naha Beach
Naha
Kaumalapau Harbor
Kamaiki Point
Kealaikahiki Channel
Halulu Heiau
Fisherman's Trail
Four Seasons Resort Lāna'i at Mānele Bay
Mānele Bay
Kaunolū
Palaoa Point
Hulopo'e Beach
Pu'u Pehe

0   2 mi
0   2 km

Mānele Bay. The ferries to and from Maui and Ma'alea pull in here. Public restrooms, a small café, water, and picnic tables make it a busy pit stop—you can watch the boating activity as you rest and refuel. The site of a Hawaiian village dating from AD 900, Mānele Bay is flanked by lava cliffs hundreds of feet high. Though included in a Marine Life Conservation District, the completely rebuilt harbor is the island's only small boat harbor and was the location of most postcontact shipping until Kaumalapau Harbor was built in 1926. To get here from Lāna'i City, follow Highway 440 (Mānele Road) 9 mi south to bottom of hill and look for a sign marking the harbor on your left. Just offshore to the west is **Pu'u Pehe.** Often called Sweetheart Rock, the isolated 80-foot-high islet carries a romantic Hawaiian legend that is probably not true. The rock is said to be named after Pehe, a woman so beautiful that her husband kept her hidden in a sea cave. One day, the surf surged into the cave and she drowned. Her grief-stricken husband buried her on the summit of this rock and then jumped to his own death. A more authentic story is that the enclosure on the summit is a shrine to birds, built by bird-catchers. Archaeological investigation has revealed that the enclosure was not a burial place. Protected shearwaters nest in the nearby sea cliffs from July through November. ⊠ *Hwy. 440 (Mānele Rd.).*

WORTH NOTING

Halulu Heiau. The well-preserved remains of an impressive *heiau* (temple) at Kaunolū village, which was actively used by Lāna'i's earliest residents, attest to this spot's sacred history. As late as 1810, this hilltop temple was considered a place of refuge, where those who had broken *kapu* (taboos) were forgiven and where women and children could find safety in times of war. If you explore the area, be respectful; take nothing with you and leave nothing behind. This place is hard to find, so get someone to mark a map for you. The road is alternately rocky, sandy, and soft at the bottom. From Lāna'i City, follow Highway 440 (Kaumalapau Highway) west toward Kaumalapau Harbor. Pass the airport, then look for the carved boulder on the hill on your left. Turn left on the dirt road and follow it 3 mi to another carved boulder; turn right and head downhill. ⊠ *On dirt road off Hwy. 440 (Kaumalapau Hwy.).*

Kaunolū. Close to the island's highest cliffs, Kaunolū was once a prosperous fishing village. This important archaeological site includes a major *heiau* (temple), terraces, stone floors, and house platforms. The impressive 90-foot drop to the ocean through a gap in the lava rock is called **Kahekili's Leap.** Warriors would make the dangerous jump into the shallow 12 feet of water below to show their courage. King Kamehameha came here for the superb fishing and to collect taxes. The road is rocky, then gets soft and sandy at the bottom. From Lāna'i City, follow Highway 440 (Kaumalapau Highway) west past the airport turnoff; at carved boulder on your left on the hill, turn left onto an unmarked dirt road; continue 3 mi until you reach the second carved boulder, and then go right (makai [toward the ocean]) 3 mi to village. ⊠ *On dirt road off Hwy. 440 (Kaumalapau Hwy.).*

Lāna'i Culture and Heritage Center. Small and carefully arranged, this historical museum features artifacts and photographs from Lāna'i's varied and rich history. Plantation-era clothing and tools, precious feather lei, stone adzes and poi pounders, ranch memorabilia, old maps, and family portraits combine to give you a good idea of the history of the island and its people. Postcards, maps, books, and pamphlets are for sale. The friendly staff can orient you to the island's historical sites and provide directions. ⊠ *730 Lana'i Ave., Lāna'i City* ☎ *808/565-7177* ⊕ *www. lanaichc.org* ☞ *Free* ☉ *Weekdays 8:30-3:30, Sat. 9-1.*

Norfolk pine. Considered the "Mother" of all the pines on the island, and more than 160 feet high, this majestic tree was planted here, at the former site of the ranch manager's house, in 1875. Almost 30 years later, George Munro, then the manager, would observe how, in foggy weather, water collected on its foliage, forming a natural rain. This fog drip led Munro to supervise the planting of Cook pines along the ridge of Lāna'ihale and throughout the town in order to add to the island's water supply. The tree is at the entrance of the Four Seasons Resort Lodge at Kō'ele. ⊠ *1 Keōmuku Hwy., Lāna'i City.*

7

The calm crescent of Hulopo'e Beach is perfect for swimming, snorkeling, or just relaxing.

WINDWARD LĀNA'I

9 mi northeast of Lodge at Kō'ele to end of paved road.

The eastern section of Lāna'i is wild and untouched. An inaccessible *heiau*, or *temple*, is the only trace of human habitation, with the exception of rocks and boulders marking old shrines, and trails. Four-wheel drive is a must to explore this side of the isle, and be prepared for hot, rough conditions. Hawaiians request that you not stack or disturb rocks. Pack a picnic lunch, a hat and sunscreen, and drinking water.

GETTING HERE AND AROUND

Once you leave paved Keōmuku Highway and turn left toward Shipwreck Beach or right to Naha, the roads are dirt and sand; conditions vary with the seasons. Mileage doesn't matter much here, but figure on 20 minutes from the end of the paved road to Shipwreck Beach, and about 45 minutes to Lōpā Beach. Don't get stuck in the sand!

EXPLORING

TOP ATTRACTIONS

★ **Munro Trail.** This 12.8-mi Jeep trail along a fern- and pine-clad narrow ridge was named after George Munro, manager of the Lāna'i Ranch Co., who began a reforestation program in the 1950s to restore the island's much-needed watershed. The trail climbs **Lāna'ihale** (House of Lāna'i), which, at 3,370 feet, is the island's highest point; on clear days you'll be treated to a panorama of canyons and almost all the Hawaiian Islands. ■ TIP→ **The one-way road gets very muddy, and trade winds can be strong. A sheer drop-off in some sections requires an attentive driver. Keep an eye out for hikers along the way.** You can also hike the Munro Trail *(see Golf, Hiking, and Outdoor Activities later in this chapter)*, though it's a long trek: it's steep, the ground is uneven, and there's no water. From the Four Seasons Resort Lodge at Kō'ele, head north on Highway 440 (Keōmuku Highway) for 1¼ mi, then turn right onto Cemetery Rd. and continue straight, passing cemetery on right. ⊠ *Cemetery Rd.*

★ **Shipwreck Beach.** The rusting World War II tanker off this 8-mi stretch of sand adds just the right touch to an already photogenic beach. Maui is visible in the distance, and Moloka'i lies just across beautiful but unrelenting Kalohi Channel. Strong trade winds have propelled vessels onto the reef since at least 1824, when the first shipwreck was recorded. The unnamed Navy oiler you see stranded today, however, was intentionally scuttled. To see petroglyphs of warriors and dogs decorating dark red boulders, follow the painted rocks and signs at the end of the road south about 200 yards. ■TIP➔ The water is unsafe for swimming. There are no lifeguards, so kids should play only in the shallows, and adults should stick to beachcombing. Take Highway 440 (Keōmuku Highway) to its eastern terminus, and then turn left on dirt road and continue north for 2 mi. ⊠ *Dirt road off Hwy. 440 (Keōmuku Hwy.).*

WORTH NOTING

Halepalaoa. Named for the whales that once washed ashore here, Halepalaoa, or house of whale ivory, was the site of the wharf used by the short-lived Maunalei Sugar Company to ship cane in 1899. Some say the sugar company failed because the sacred stones of nearby **Kahe'a Heiau** were used for the construction of the cane railroad. Angry gods turned the drinking water salty, forcing the sugar company to close after just two years in 1901. The remains of the *heiau* (temple), once an important place of worship for the people of Lāna'i, are now difficult to find through the *kiawe* (mesquite) overgrowth. There's good public beach access here and clear shallow water for swimming, but no other facilities. Take Highway 440 (Keōmuku Highway) to its eastern terminus; then turn right on dirt road and continue south for 5½ mi. ⊠ *On dirt road off Hwy. 440 (Keōmuku Hwy.).*

Japanese Cemetery. In 1899 sugar came to this side of Lāna'i. A plantation took up about 2,400 acres and seemed a profitable proposition, but that same year, disease wiped out the labor force. This authentic Buddhist shrine commemorates the Japanese workers who died, and the local Buddhist congregation comes down to clean the area each year. Take Highway 440 (Keōmuku Highway) to its eastern terminus; then turn right on dirt road and continue south for 6½ mi. ⊠ *On dirt road off Hwy. 440 (Keōmuku Hwy.).*

Keōmuku. There's an eerie beauty about Keōmuku, with its faded memories and forgotten homesteads. During the late 19th century, this busy Lāna'i community of some 900 to 2,000 residents served as the headquarters of Maunalei Sugar Company. After the company failed, the land was used for ranching, but by 1954 the area lay abandoned. Its church, **Ka Lanakila O Ka Mālamalama**, was built in 1903. It has been partially restored by volunteers, and visitors often leave some small token, a shell or faded lei, as an offering. Take Highway 440 (Keōmuku Highway) to its eastern terminus; then turn right on dirt road and continue south for 5 mi. ✉ *On dirt road off Hwy. 440 (Keōmuku Hwy.).*

Naha. An ancient rock-walled fish-pond—visible at low tide—lies here, where the sandy shoreline ends and the cliffs begin their rise along the island's shores. The beach is a fre-quent resource for local fisherfolk. ⚠ Treacherous currents make this a dangerous place for swimming. Take Highway 440 (Keōmuku Highway) to its eastern terminus; then turn right on the dirt road and continue south for 11 mi. The shoreline dirt road ends here. ✉ *On dirt road off Hwy. 440 (Keōmuku Hwy.).*

THE COASTAL ROAD

Road conditions can change over-night and become impassable due to rain in the uplands. Car-rental agencies should be able to give you updates before you hit the road. Many of the spur roads lead-ing to the windward beaches from the coastal dirt road cross private property and are closed off by chains. Look for open spur roads with recent tire marks (a fairly good sign that they are safe to drive on). It's best to park on firm ground and walk in to avoid get-ting your car mired in the sand.

BEACHES

Lāna'i offers miles of secluded white-sand beaches on its windward side, plus the moderately developed Hulopo'e Beach, which is adjacent to the Four Seasons Resort Lāna'i at Mānele Bay. Hulopo'e is accessible by car or hotel shuttle bus; to reach the windward beaches you need a four-wheel-drive vehicle. Reef, rocks, and coral make swimming on the windward side problematic, but it's fun to splash around in the shallow water. Expect debris on the windward beaches due to the Pacific con-vergence ocean currents. Driving on the beach itself is illegal and can be dangerous. *Beaches in this chapter are listed alphabetically.*

Fodor's Choice
★

Hulopo'e Beach. A short stroll from the Four Seasons Resort Lāna'i at Mānele Bay, Hulopo'e is considered one of the best beaches in Hawai'i. The sparkling crescent of this Marine Life Conservation District beck-ons with calm waters safe for swimming almost year-round, great snor-keling reefs, tide pools, and, sometimes, spinner dolphins. A shady, grassy beach park is perfect for picnics. If the shore break is pounding, or if you see surfers riding big waves, stay out of the water. In the after-noon, watch Lāna'i High School students heave outrigger canoes down the steep shore break and race one another just offshore. From Lāna'i City, turn left on Highway 440 (Mānele Road) and go 9 mi south to bottom of hill; turn right, and the road dead-ends at the beach's parking lot. **Amenities:** Toilets, showers, picnic tables, grills, parking. ✉ *From Lāna'i City, off Hwy. 440 (Mānele Rd.).*

Lōpā Beach. A popular surfing spot for locals, Lōpā is also an ancient fishpond. With majestic views of West Maui and Kaho'olawe, this remote, white-sand beach is a great place for a picnic. ⚠ Don't let the sight of surfers fool you: the channel's currents are too strong for swimming. The beach is on the east side of Lāna'i; take Highway 440 (Keōmuku Highway) to its eastern terminus. Turn right on the dirt road and continue south for 7 mi. **Amenities:** None. ⊠ *On dirt road off Hwy. 440 (Keōmuku Hwy.)* ☞ *No facilities.*

★ **Polihua Beach.** Often deserted, this beach gets a star for beauty with its long wide stretch of white sand and clear views of Moloka'i. However, the dirt road to get here can be bad with deep sandy places (when it rains it's impassable), and frequent high winds whip up sand and waves. In addition, strong currents and a sudden drop in the ocean floor make swimming dangerous. On the more positive side, the northern end of the beach ends at a rocky lava cliff with some interesting tide pools. Polihua is named after the sea turtles that lay their eggs in the sand. (Do not drive on the beach and endanger their nests.) Curiously, wild bees sometimes gather around your car for water at this beach. To get rid of them, put out water some place away from the car and wait a bit. The beach is in windward Lāna'i, 11 mi north of Lāna'i City. Turn right on the marked dirt road past Garden of the Gods. **Amenities:** None. ⊠ *On marked dirt road off Polihua Rd.*

Shipwreck Beach. Beachcombers come to this fairly accessible beach for shells and washed-up treasures; photographers for great shots of Moloka'i, just across the 9-mi-wide Kalohi Channel; and walkers for the long stretch of sand. It may still be possible to find glass-ball fishing floats but more common are waterborne debris from the Moloka'i channel. Kaiolohia, its Hawaiian name, is a favorite local diving spot. ■ TIP➜ An offshore reef and rocks in the water mean that it's not for swimmers, though you can play in the shallow water on the shoreline. To get to this north shore beach, take Highway 440 (Keōmuku Highway) to its eastern terminus; then turn left on the dirt road and continue north for 3 mi. **Amenities:** None. ⊠ *On dirt road off Hwy. 440 (Keōmuku Hwy.).*

WATER SPORTS AND TOURS

The easiest way to enjoy the water on Lāna'i is to wade in at Hulopo'e Beach and swim or snorkel. If you prefer an organized excursion, a fishing trip is a good bet (you keep some of the fish). Snorkel sails are a great way to see the island—above and below the surface, and scuba divers can marvel at one of the top cave dive spots in the Pacific.

DEEP-SEA FISHING

Some of the best sportfishing grounds in Maui County are off the southwest shoreline of Lāna'i. Pry your eyes open and go deep-sea fishing in the early morning, with departures at 6 or 6:30 am from Mānele Harbor. Console yourself with the knowledge that Maui fishers have to leave an hour earlier to get to the same prime locations. Peak seasons are spring and summer, although good catches have been landed year-round. Mahimahi, *ono* (a mackerel-like fish; the word means "delicious" in Hawaiian), *'ahi* (yellowfin tuna), and marlin are prized catches and preferred eating.

Lānai has miles of good coast for kayaking; the water is calmer in the morning.

BOATS AND CHARTERS

Fish-N-Chips. This roomy new 36-foot Twin-Vee with tuna tower will get you and your family to the fishing grounds in comfort, and Captain Jason will do everything except reel in the big one for you. Plan on trolling along the south coast for ono and around the point at Kaunolū for mahimahi or marlin. A trip to the offshore buoy often yields skipjack tuna or big 'ahi, and the captain and crew are always open to a bit of bottom fishing. Fishing gear, sodas, and water are included. A four-hour charter (six-passenger maximum) is $700; each additional hour costs $110. Guests can keep up to a third of all fish caught. Shared charters on Sunday are $150 per person. ☎ 808/565–7676 ⊕ *www. sportfishinglanai.com.*

KAYAKING

Lāna'i's windward coast offers leisurely paddling and miles of scenic coastline with deserted beaches to haul up on inside the reef. Curious sea turtles and friendly manta rays may tag along your kayak for company. When the wind comes from the southwest, this area is tranquil. Kayaking along the leeward cliffs is more demanding with rougher seas and strong currents. No kayaking is permitted in the Marine Conservation District at Hulopo'e Bay.

Early mornings tend to be calmer. The wind picks up as the day advances. Expect strong currents along all the coasts. Experience on the water is advised, and knowing how to swim is essential. There is one other glitch: there are no kayak rentals on the island, so you need to book a tour or bring your own.

TOURS

Trilogy Oceansports Lāna'i. Join Trilogy's experienced ocean kayak guide for a full morning of kayaking inside the reef of Lāna'i's unspoiled north shore coastline. This six-hour adventure costs $170 for adults, $125 for youth, and $88 for *keiki*, or kids (ages 3 to 5). Lunch, sodas, bottled water, and snacks are served. Reservations are required at least 24 hours in advance. Book with your hotel concierge or online. ☎ *888/628–4800* ⊕ *www.sailtrilogy.com.*

RAFTING

If you're looking to get out on the water without fishing, Trilogy Oceansports Lāna'i offers comfortable marine mammal tours on a 32-foot, hard-bottom inflatable raft.

TOURS

Trilogy Oceansports Lāna'i. Trilogy offers a 1½-hour marine mammal watch on the *Manele Kai*, a 32-foot, jet-drive, hard-bottom inflatable raft. Cruise the coast and search for protected whales, dolphins, and monk seals. Sodas and bottled water provided. Cost is $80 for adults, $60 for youth, and $40 for *keiki* (kids) under 12. You can book trips through your hotel concierge, but try online first, where discounts are often available. ☎ *888/628–4800* ⊕ *www.scubalanai.com.*

SCUBA DIVING

When you have a dive site such as Cathedrals—with eerie pinnacle formations and luminous caverns—it's no wonder that scuba-diving buffs consider exploring the waters off Lāna'i akin to having a religious experience.

BEST SPOTS

Just outside of Hulopo'e Bay, the boat dive site **Cathedrals** was named the best cavern dive site in the Pacific by *Skin Diver* magazine. Shimmering light makes the many openings in the caves look like stained-glass windows. A current generally keeps the water crystal clear, even if it's turbid outside. In these unearthly chambers, large *ulua* and small reef shark add to the adventure.

Sergeant Major Reef, off Kamaiki Point, is named for big schools of yellow- and black-striped *manini* (sergeant major fish) that turn the rocks silvery as they feed. The site is made up of three parallel lava ridges, a cave, and an archway, with rippled sand valleys between the ridges. Depths range 15 to 50 feet.

EQUIPMENT, LESSONS, AND TOURS

Trilogy Oceansports Lāna'i. Serious divers should go for Trilogy's four-hour, two-tank dive; location depends on the weather, and duration includes sailing time. You must be certified, so don't forget your documentation. The $175 fee includes a light breakfast of cinnamon rolls and coffee. Equipment, wet suits, and accessories are included. Non-certified beginners (minimum age 12) can try a one-tank introductory dive for $99. You can wade into Hulopo'e Bay with an instructor at your side; actual dive time is 20 to 30 minutes. Certified divers can choose a 35- to 40-minute wade-in dive at Hulopo'e, also for $101. ☎ *888/628–4800* ⊕ *www.scubalanai.com.*

SNORKELING

Snorkeling is the easiest ocean sport available on the island, requiring nothing but a snorkel, mask, fins, and good sense. Borrow equipment from your hotel or purchase some in Lāna'i City if you didn't bring your own. Wait to enter the water until you are sure no big sets of waves are coming; and observe the activity of locals on the beach. If little kids are playing in the shore break, it's usually safe to enter. ■ TIP→ To get into the water safely, always swim in past the breakers, and in the comparative calm put on your fins, then mask and snorkel.

BEST SPOTS

Hulopo'e Beach is an outstanding snorkeling destination. The bay is a State of Hawai'i Marine Conservation District, and no spearfishing or diving is allowed. Schools of *manini* (seargent major fish) feeding on the coral coat the rocks with flashing silver, and you can view *kala* (unicorn fish), *uhu* (parrot fish), and *papio* (small trevally) in all their rainbow colors. As you wade in from the sandy beach, the best snorkeling is toward the left. Beware of rocks and surging waves. When the resident spinner dolphins are in the bay, watch them from the shore. If swimmers and snorkelers go out, the dolphins may leave and be deprived of their necessary resting place. A wade-in snorkel spot is just beyond the break wall at **Mānele Small Boat Harbor**. Enter over the rocks, just past the boat ramp. ■ TIP→ It's dangerous to enter if waves are breaking.

EQUIPMENT, LESSONS, AND TOURS

Trilogy Oceansports Lāna'i. A 4½-hour blue-water snorkeling and adventure catamaran trip explores Lāna'i's pristine coastline with Trilogy's experienced captain and crew. The trip includes lessons, equipment, and deluxe lunch served onboard. Tours are offered Monday, Wednesday, Friday, and Saturday; cost is $176 for adults, $132 for youth, and $88 for kids ages 3 to 12. You can book trips through your hotel concierge, but try online first for possible discounts. ☎ *888/628–4800* ⊕ *www. sailtrilogy.com.*

SURFING

Surfing on Lāna'i can be truly enjoyable. Quality, not quantity, characterizes this isle's few breaks. Be considerate of the locals and they will be considerate of you—surfing takes the place of megaplex theaters and pool halls here, serving as one of the island's few recreational luxuries.

BEST SPOTS

Don't try to hang 10 at **Hulopo'e Bay** without watching the conditions for a while. When it "goes off," it's a tricky left-handed shore break that requires some skill. Huge summer south swells are for experts only. The southeast-facing breaks at **Lōpā Beach** on the east side are inviting for beginners. Give them a try in summer, when the swells roll in nice and easy.

EQUIPMENT AND LESSONS

Lāna'i Surf School. Nick and his wife, Alex, offer the only surf instruction on the island. Sign up for their "4x4 Safari"—a four-hour adventure that includes hard- or soft-top boards, snacks, and transportation to "secret spots." Nick, who was born on Lāna'i, is a former Hawai'i State Surfing Champion. Group lessons are $175 per person (minimum of three); private lessons are $200 (minimum of two). Experienced riders can rent short- or longboards overnight for $58 with a $125 deposit; stand-up paddles are available for an additional $25. ☎ 808/306–9837 ⊕ *www.lanaisurfsafari.com.*

GOLF, HIKING, AND OUTDOOR ACTIVITIES

Lāna'i is privately owned, and land-based activities are at the owner's discretion, though permission is not necessary on a day-to-day basis. Not all areas of the island are open, however. The island's two world-class championship golf courses will certainly test your skill on the green. Experienced hikers can choose from miles of dirt roads and trails, but note that you're on your own—there's no water or support.

BIKING

Many of the same red-dirt roads that invite hikers are excellent for biking, offering easy flat terrain and long clear views. There's only one hitch: you may have to bring your own bike, as there are no rentals or tours available for nonresort guests.

BEST SPOTS

A favorite biking route is along the fairly flat red-dirt road northward from Lāna'i City through the old pineapple fields to Garden of the Gods. Start your trip on Keōmuku Highway in town. Take a left just before the Lodge at Kō'ele's tennis courts, and then a right where the road ends at the fenced pasture, and continue on to the north end and the start of Polihua and Awalua dirt roads. If you're really hardy you could bike down to Polihua Beach and back, but it would be a serious all-day trip. In wet weather these roads turn to mud and are not advisable. Go in the early morning or late afternoon because the sun gets hot in the middle of the day. Take plenty of water, spare parts, and snacks.

For the exceptionally fit, it's possible to bike from town down the Keōmuku Highway to the windward beaches and back, or to bike the Munro Trail *(see Hiking).* Experienced bikers also bike up and down the Mānele Highway from Mānele Bay to town.

GOLF

Lāna'i has two gorgeous resort courses that offer very different environments and challenges. They are so diverse that it's hard to believe they're on the same island, let alone just 20 minutes apart by resort shuttle.

The Challenge at Mānele. Designed by Jack Nicklaus (1993), this course sits right over the water of Hulopo'e Bay. Built on lava outcroppings, it features three holes on cliffs that use the Pacific Ocean as a water

Some holes at the Challenge at Mānele use the Pacific Ocean as a water hazard.

hazard. The five-tee concept challenges the best golfers—tee shots over natural gorges and ravines must be precise. This unspoiled natural terrain is a stunning backdrop, and every hole offers ocean views. Early morning tee times are recommended to avoid the midday heat. ⊠ *Four Seasons Resort Lāna'i at Mānele Bay, Challenge Dr., Lāna'i City* 🕾 *808/565–2222* ⊕ *www.fourseasons.com/manelebay/golf* ♿ *18 holes. 6310 yds. Par 72, slope 126. Green Fee: hotel guests $210, nonguests $225* ☞ *Facilities: driving range, putting green, golf carts, rental clubs, pro shop, lessons, restaurant, bar.*

The Experience at Kō'ele. This challenging Greg Norman (1991) layout begins at an elevation of 2,000 feet. The front 9 move dramatically through ravines wooded with pine, koa, and eucalyptus trees; seven lakes and streams with cascading waterfalls dot the course. No other course in Hawai'i offers a more incredible combination of highland terrain, inspired landscape architecture, and range of play challenges. Beware of the superfast greens. The course is currently closed Monday and Tuesday. ⊠ *Four Seasons Resort Lodge at Kō'ele, 1 Keōmuku Hwy., Lāna'i City* 🕾 *808/565–4653* ⊕ *www.fourseasons.com/koele/golf* ♿ *18 holes. 6310 yds. Par 72, slope 134. Green Fee: hotel guests $210, nonguests $225* ☞ *Facilities: driving range, putting green, golf carts, rental clubs, pro shop, lessons.*

HIKING

Only 30 mi of Lāna'i's roads are paved, but red-dirt roads and trails, ideal for hiking, will take you to sweeping overlooks, isolated beaches, and shady forests. Don't be afraid to leave the road to follow deer trails;

just make sure to keep your landmarks in clear sight so you can retrace your steps. Or take a self-guided walk through Kāne Puʻu, Hawaiʻi's largest native dryland forest. You can explore the Munro Trail over Lānaʻihale with views of plunging canyons, or hike along an old, coastal fisherman trail or across Koloiki Ridge. Wear hiking shoes, a hat, and sunscreen, and carry plenty of water.

BEST SPOTS

Koloiki Ridge. This marked, moderate trail starts behind the Lodge at Kōʻele and takes you along the cool and shady Munro Trail to overlook the windward side, with impressive views of Maui, Molokaʻi, Maunalei Valley, and Naio Gulch. The average time for the 5-mi round-trip is two hours. Bring snacks and water, and take your time. A map is available at Four Seasons Resort Lodge at Kōʻele; tell the concierge you are taking the hike.

Lānaʻi Fisherman Trail. Local fishermen still use this trail to get to their favorite fishing spots. The trail takes about 1½ hours to hike and follows the rocky shoreline below the Four Seasons Resort at Lānaʻi Mānele Bay, along cliffs bordering the golf course. Caves and tide pools beckon beneath you, but be careful climbing down. The marked trail entrance begins at the west end of Hulopoʻe Beach. Keep your eyes open for spinner dolphins cavorting offshore and the silvery flash of fish feeding in the pools below you. The condition of the trail varies with weather and frequency of maintenance; it can be slippery and rocky. Take your time, wear shoes, not flip-flops, and carry water.

Munro Trail. This is the real thing: a strenuous 12.8-mi trek that begins behind the Four Seasons Resort Lodge at Kōʻele and follows the ridge of Lānaʻihale through the rain forest. The island's most demanding hike, it has an elevation gain of 1,400 feet and leads to a lookout at the island's highest point, Lānaʻihale. It's also a narrow dirt road; watch out for careening Jeeps. The trail is named after George Munro, who supervised the planting of Cook pine trees and eucalyptus windbreaks. Mules used to wend their way up the mountain carrying the pine seedlings. Unless you arrange for someone to pick you up at the trail's end, you have a 3-mi hike back through the Pālāwai Basin to return to your starting point. The summit is often cloud-shrouded and can be windy and muddy, so check conditions before you start.

Puʻu Pehe Trail. Beginning to the left (facing the ocean) of Hulopoʻe Beach, this trail travels a short distance around the coastline, and then climbs up a sharp, rocky rise. At the top, you're level with the offshore stack of Puʻu Pehe and can overlook miles of coastline in both directions. The trail is not difficult, but it's hot and steep. Be aware of nesting protected seabirds and don't approach their nests. ⚠ **Never approach the edge, as the cliff can easily give way.** The hiking is best in the early morning or late afternoon, and it's a perfect place to look for whales in season (December–April). Wear shoes; this is not a hike for sandals or slip-ons, and take water so you can spend some time at the top admiring the view.

HORSEBACK RIDING

A horseback ride can be a memorable experience on the island.

Stables at Kō'ele. The subtle beauty of the high country slowly reveals itself to horseback riders on the backcountry Paniolo rides. Two-hour adventures traverse leafy trails with scenic overlooks. Well-trained horses take riders (must be under 225 pounds; 9 years and older) of all skill levels. Prices start at $105 for a two-hour group ride and go to $170 for a two-hour private ride. Lessons are also available. Another option is a carriage ride in the uplands for up to four people, $65 per person per hour. Book rides at the Four Seasons Resort Lodge at Kō'ele. ⊠ *1 Keōmuku Hwy., Lāna'i City* ☎ *808/563–0717.*

SPORTING CLAYS AND ARCHERY

For something different, you can try your hand at shooting or archery.

★ **Lāna'i Pine Sporting Clays and Archery Range.** Outstanding rustic terrain, challenging targets, and a well-stocked pro shop make this sporting-clays course top-flight in the expert's eyes. Sharpshooters can complete the meandering 14-station course, with the help of a golf cart, in 1½ hours. There are group tournaments, and even kids can enjoy skilled instruction at the archery range and compressed-air rifle gallery. The $60 archery introduction includes an amusing "pineapple challenge"— contestants are given five arrows with which to hit a paper pineapple target. The winner takes home a crystal pineapple as a nostalgic souvenir of the old Dole Plantation days. Guns and ammunition are provided with the lessons. Prices range from $90 to $170 depending on amount of ammunition and activity. The range is just past Cemetery Road on the windward side of island; take the first left at the sign on Highway 440 (Keōmuku Highway). ⊠ *Off Hwy. 440 (Keōmuku Hwy)* ☎ *808/559–4600.*

SHOPPING

A miniforest of Cook pine trees in the center of Lāna'i City surrounded by small shops and restaurants, Dole Park is the closest thing to a mall on Lāna'i. Except for the high-end resort boutiques and pro shops, it provides the island's only shopping. A morning or afternoon stroll around the park offers an eclectic selection of gifts and clothing, plus a chance to chat with friendly shopkeepers. Well-stocked general stores are reminiscent of the 1920s, and galleries and a boutique have original art and fashions for men, women, and children. The shops close Sunday and after 5 pm, except for the general stores, which are open a bit later.

CLOTHING

Lāna'i Beach Walk. The shop may be small, but it's crammed with many styles and colors of the now indispensable "crocs," as well as colorful resort clothing, logo tee shirts, swimwear, and classy skirts and dresses. Tropical knickknacks, souvenirs, and jewelry complete the whimsical inventory, and Gail, the owner, is always up for a bit of local conversation and advice. ⊠ *850 Fraser Ave., Lāna'i City* ☎ *808/565–9249.*

Local Gentry. Spacious and classy, this store has clothing for every need, from casual men's and women's beachwear to evening resort wear, shoes, jewelry, and hats. A selection of original Lāna'i logo-wear is also available, including their signature "What happens on Lāna'i everybody knows" T-shirts. Proprietor Jenna Gentry Majkus will mail your purchases. ⊠ *363 7th St., Lāna'i City* ☎ *808/565–9130.*

FOOD

Pine Isle Market. One of Lāna'i City's two all-purpose markets stocks everything from beach toys to cosmetics, canned goods, meat, fresh vegetables, and even electronics. Staff is friendly, and it's the best place to buy fresh fish. The market is closed Sunday and during lunch hours from noon to 1:30 pm, Monday through Thursday. ⊠ *356 8th St., Lāna'i City* ☎ *808/565–6488.*

Richard's. Castle & Cooke Resorts took over this store from Richard Tamashiro, who founded it in 1946. Along with fresh meat, vegetables, and groceries, Richard's has camping gear, common household items, a good array of fine wines, and a few gourmet food items. ⊠ *434 8th St., Lāna'i City* ☎ *808/565–3780.*

GALLERIES

Lāna'i Art Center. Local artists practice and display their work at this dynamic center staffed by volunteers. Workshops in the pottery, photography, woodworking, and painting studios welcome visitors, and individual instruction may be arranged. The gift shop sells original art and Lāna'i handicrafts. Check with the center about occasional concerts or cultural events held here, or visit the Web site. It's closed Sunday. ⊠ *339 7th St., Lāna'i City* ☎ *808/565–7503* ⊕ *www.lanaiart.org.*

Mike Carroll Gallery. The dreamy, soft-focus oil paintings of award-winning resident painter Mike Carroll feature island scenes and are showcased along with crafts from other local artists. ⊠ *443 7th St., Lāna'i City* ☎ *808/565–7122* ⊕ *www.mikecarrollgallery.com.*

GENERAL STORES

International Food and Clothing Center. You may not find everything the name implies, but this old-fashioned emporium does stock items for your everyday needs, from fishing gear to beer. It's a good place for last-minute camping supplies and picking up something on Sunday when other stores are closed. Hours are weekdays 10 am to 9 pm and Sunday 8 am to 4 pm; closed Saturday. ⊠ *833 'Ilima Ave., Lāna'i City* ☎ *808/565–6433.*

Lāna'i City Service. In addition to being Lāna'i's only gas station, auto-parts store, and car-rental operation, this outfit sells Hawaiian gift items, sundries, hot dogs and *manapua* (steamed buns with pork filling), T-shirts, beer, sodas, snacks, and bottled water in the Plantation Store. It's open 6:30 am to 8:30 pm daily for gas and sundries; the auto-parts store is open weekdays 7 am to 4 pm, but closes from noon to 1 pm. ⊠ *1036 Lāna'i Ave., Lāna'i City* ☎ *808/565–7227.*

SPAS

If you're looking for rejuvenation, the whole island could be considered a spa, though the only spa facilities are at the Mānele Bay hotel or the Lodge at Kō'ele. You can get a quick polish in Lāna'i City at a couple of spots, though.

Lodge at Kō'ele's Banyan Suite Spa. On the mezzanine of the Great Hall, this simple, serene spa offers a varied menu of massage treatments, including a hot-shell treatment, Hawaiian *lomilomi*, sports massage, and the Hehi Lani Royal Foot Treatment. Relax after your massage with herbal tea on the adjacent balcony, which has great sunset views, or return to your room in a fluffy spa robe. Two tables accommodate couples, and all massages are private. The spa is open to non–resort guests with advance reservations. Massage services can also be enjoyed in the privacy of your room for an extra charge. ⊠ *Four Seasons Resort Lodge at Kō'ele, 1 Keōmuku Hwy., Lāna'i City* ☎ *808/565–4555* ⊕ *www. fourseasons.com/koele/spa* ☞ *$165–$175 50-min massage. Gym with: cardiovascular machines, free weights. Services: aromatherapy, hot-rock massage, guided stretching, reflexology.*

The Spa at Mānele. A tropical fantasy mural, granite stone floors, eucalyptus steam rooms, and private cabanas set the scene for indulgence. State-of-the-art pampering enlists a panoply of oils and unguents that would have pleased Cleopatra. The Spa After Hours Experience relaxes you with private services including a neck and shoulder massage and a 50-minute treatment of your choice. You can further unwind in the sauna or steam room, finish off with a scalp massage and light *pūpū* (snacks), and ooze out to your room. The *Ali'i* banana-coconut scrub and pineapple-citrus polish treatments have inspired their own cosmetic line. Massages in private *hale* (houses) in the courtyard gardens are available for singles or couples. ⊠ *Four Seasons Resort Lāna'i at Mānele Bay, 1 Mānele Rd., Lāna'i City* ☎ *808/565–2000* ⊕ *www.fourseasons. com/manelebay/spa* ☞ *$165–$175 50-min massage; $360 per person 2-hr Spa After Hours Experience (2-person minimum). Gym with: cardiovascular equipment, free weights. Services: aromatherapy, body wraps, facials, hair salon, hair care, mani/pedicures, reflexology, waxing. Classes and programs: aquaerobics, guided hikes, hula classes, personal training, tai chi, yoga.*

ENTERTAINMENT AND NIGHTLIFE

Lāna'i is certainly not known for its nightlife. Fewer than a handful of places stay open past 9 pm. At the resorts, excellent piano music or light live entertainment makes for a quiet, romantic evening. Another alternative is star watching from the beaches or watching the full moon rise in all its glory.

Four Seasons Resort Lāna'i at Mānele Bay. Hale Aheahe (House of Gentle Breezes), the classy open-air lounge with upscale *pūpū* (snacks) and complete bar, offers musical entertainment nightly from 5:30 to 9:30. Local musicians invite you to try your hula skills; darts, pool, and shuffleboard are riotous fun. ⊠ *1 Mānele Rd., Lāna'i City* ☎ *808/565–2000.*

Four Seasons Resort Lodge at Kō'ele. The cozy cocktail bar stays open until 11 pm. The lodge also features quiet piano music in its Great Hall every evening from 7 to 10, as well as special performances by well-known Hawaiian entertainers and local hula dancers. Sit fireside and enjoy a late-night cocktail and plan your next day's activities. ⊠ *1 Keōmuku Hwy., Lāna'i City* ☎ *808/565–4000.*

Hotel Lāna'i. A visit to the small, lively bar here is an opportunity to visit with locals and find out more about the island. Enjoy entertainment by Lāna'i musicians in the big green tent on Friday nights. Last call is at 9:30. ⊠ *828 Lāna'i Ave., Lāna'i City* ☎ *808/565–7211.*

Trilogy Oceansports Lāna'i. On Tuesday, Thursday, and Saturday, Trilogy offers a Sunset Sail on a large catamaran, departing at either 3:45 (April–September), or 4:45 (October–March). This trip is perfect if you want to get out on the ocean and experience a relaxing time on the water. The two-hour sail includes hot and cold appetizers, soft drinks, and filtered water. Bring your own beer and wine, and the crew will keep it cold for you. The sunset sail costs $84 for adults; $63 for youth, and $42 for children 12 and under. You can book trips through your hotel concierge, but try online first, where discounts are often available. ☎ *888/628–4800* ⊕ *www.scubalanai.com.*

WHERE TO EAT

7

Lāna'i's own version of Hawai'i regional cuisine (modern Hawaiian food) draws on the fresh bounty provided by local farmers and fishermen, combined with the skills of well-trained chefs. The upscale menus at the Lodge at Kō'ele and the Four Seasons Resort at Lāna'i Mānele Bay encompass European-inspired cuisine as well as innovative preparations of international favorites and vegetarian delights. All Four Seasons Resort restaurants offer a children's menu. Lāna'i City's eclectic ethnic fare runs from construction-worker-size local plate lunches to *poke* (raw fish), pizza, and pesto pasta. ■ TIP→ **Lāna'i "City" is really a small town; restaurants sometimes choose to close the kitchen early, and only a few are open on Sunday.**

WHAT IT COSTS				
	¢	$	$$	$$$	$$$$
RESTAURANTS	under $10	$10–$17	$18–$26	$27–$35	over $35

Prices are for a main course at dinner.

MĀNELE BAY

Dining at Mānele Bay offers the range of options provided by Four Seasons Lāna'i resorts, from informal poolside meals to relaxed, eclectic dining.

$$
AMERICAN
✕ **The Challenge at Mānele Clubhouse.** A stunning view of the legendary Pu'u Pehe offshore island only enhances the imaginative fare of this terraced restaurant. Tuck into a Hulopo'e Bay prawn BLT, or the

crispy battered fish-and-chips with Meyer lemon tartar sauce. The fish tacos are splendid, and specialty drinks add to the informal fun. ⊠ *Four Seasons Resort Lāna'i at Mānele Bay, 1 Mānele Bay Rd., Lāna'i City* ☎ *808/565–2230* ⊕ *www.fourseasons.com/manelebay* ⊟ *AE, DC, MC, V* ☽ *No dinner.*

$$$$ ╳ **Four Seasons Hulopo'e Court.** Dinner and an extensive breakfast buffet
PACIFIC RIM   are served in airy comfort on the hotel terrace, which overlooks the wide sweep of the bay; retractable awnings provide shade. Inside, comfy upholstered chairs, cream walls, wood paneling, and modern Hawaiian decor create an almost equally inviting backdrop. At breakfast, fresh-baked pastries and made-to-order omelets ensure that your day starts well. For dinner, the menu is divided into Pacific Island, Chinese, Japanese, and Portuguese sections with dishes and sides from each cuisine. This is eclectic dining at its best. ⊠ *Four Seasons Resort Lāna'i at Mānele Bay, 1 Mānele Bay Rd., Lāna'i City* ☎ *808/565–2290* ⊕ *www. fourseasons.com/manelebay* ⚲ *Reservations essential* ⊟ *AE, DC, MC, V* ☽ *No lunch.*

$$$$ ╳ **The Ocean Grill Bar & Restaurant.** Poolside at the Four Seasons Resort
SEAFOOD   Lāna'i at Mānele Bay, the Ocean Grill offers informal lunch and dinner in a setting with a stunning view of Hulopo'e Bay. The big umbrellas are cool and cheerful, and bamboo-inspired upholstered chairs in yellow and green are deliciously comfortable. If you're a coffee drinker, a Kona Cappuccino Freeze by the pool is a must. Favorite lunch items include the *kālua* (pit-roasted) pork and cheese quesadilla, or the 'ahi tuna salad Niçoise with fresh island greens. The dinner menu includes a combination of small and large plates that lean toward the healthy side. Service is the Four Seasons' brand of cool aloha. ⊠ *Four Seasons Resort Lāna'i at Mānele Bay, 1 Mānele Bay Rd., Lāna'i City* ☎ *808/565–2092* ⊕ *www.fourseasons.com/manelebay* ⊟ *AE, DC, MC, V.*

LĀNA'I CITY AND UPCOUNTRY

All the dining options on the island are Upcountry in Lāna'i City, except for those at the Four Seasons Lāna'i Resorts. Choose from an array of local-style plate lunches, bistro Italian, or upscale gourmet. For a small area there are a number of good places to eat and drink, but remember that Lāna'i City closes down on Sunday; call in advance.

¢   ╳ **565 Café.** Named after the oldest telephone prefix on Lāna'i, this is
HAWAIIAN   a convenient stop for anything from pizza to a Pālāwai chicken-breast sandwich on fresh-baked focaccia. Make a quick stop for plate lunches or try a picnic *pūpū* (appetizer) platter of chicken *katsu* (Japanese-style breaded and fried chicken) to take along for the ride. You may bring your own beer or wine for lunch or dinner. The patio and outdoor tables are kid-friendly, and an outdoor Saturday afternoon flea market adds to the quirkiness. ⊠ *408 8th St., Lāna'i City* ☎ *808/565–6622* ⊟ *D, MC, V* ☽ *Closed Sun.*

$ ╳ **Blue Ginger Café.** Owners Joe and Georgia Abilay have made this
HAWAIIAN   cheery place into a Lāna'i City institution with consistent, albeit simple, food. Locally inspired paintings and photos line the walls inside, while the town passes the outdoor tables in parade. For breakfast, try the

Portuguese sausage omelet with rice or fresh pastries. Lunch selections range from burgers and pizza to Hawaiian staples such as saimin noodles or *musubi* (fried Spam wrapped in rice and seaweed). Try a shrimp stir-fry for dinner. The café sometimes closes early on slow days. ⊠ *409 7th St., Lānaʻi City* ☎ *808/565–6363* ⊕ *www.bluegingercafelanai.com* ⊟ *No credit cards.*

$$$$ ✕ **The Dining Room.** Reflecting the lodge's country-manor elegance, this
HAWAIIAN   peaceful and romantic octagonal restaurant is fine dining at its best.
Fodor's Choice   Terra-cotta walls and soft peach lighting flatter everyone, and intimate
★   tables are well spaced to allow for private conversations. Expanding on Hawaiian regional cuisine, the changing menu includes lava rock–seared venison prepared table-side and succulent crispy *onaga* (red snapper) with Kona crab and leek fondue. Finish with a warm raspberry soufflé (ordered in advance). A master sommelier provides exclusive wine pairings, and the service is flawless. ⊠ *Four Seasons Resort Lodge at Kōʻele, 1 Keōmuku Hwy., Lānaʻi City* ☎ *808/565–4580* ⊕ *www.fourseasons. com/koele* ⌲ *Reservations essential* ⊟ *AE, DC, MC, V* ⊗ *No lunch.*

$$$–$$$$ ✕ **Lānaʻi City Grille.** Simple white walls, local art, ceiling fans, and unob-
AMERICAN   trusive service provide the setting for a menu designed and supervised by celebrity chef Beverly Gannon. Oysters on the half shell, blackened ʻahi or steamed Manila clams are a great way to start the evening. The entrée menu is on the meaty side for Hawaiʻi, and should satisfy serious appetites. The Grille is a friendly and comfortable alternative to the Four Seasons, and a convenient gathering place for large parties. ⊠ *Hotel Lānaʻi, 828 Lānaʻi Ave., Lānaʻi City* ☎ *808/565–4700* ⊕ *www. hotellanai.com* ⌲ *Reservations essential* ⊟ *AE, MC, V* ⊗ *Closed Mon. and Tues.*

¢ ✕ **Lānaʻi Coffee.** A block off Dole Park, this northern California–style
CAFÉ   café offers a nice covered deck where you can sit outside, sip cappuccinos, and watch the slow-pace life of the town slip by. Bagels with lox, deli sandwiches, and pastries add to the caloric content, while blended espresso shakes and gourmet ice cream complete the barista vibe. Caffeine-inspired specialty items make good gifts and souvenirs. ⊠ *604 ʻIlima St., Lānaʻi City* ☎ *808/565–6962* ⊗ *Closed Sun. No dinner.*

¢–$ ✕ **Lānaʻi ʻOhana Poke Market.** This is the closest you can come to dining
HAWAIIAN   on traditional cuisine in a Hawaiian setting on Lānaʻi. Enjoy fresh food prepared by a Hawaiian family and served in a cool and shaded garden. The emphasis is on *poke*, which is raw ʻahi, flavored with Hawaiian salt and seaweed. Hawaiian plate lunches and take-out kim chee shrimp, mussel poke, and ʻahi and aku tuna steaks complete the menu. They also cater picnics and parties. ⊠ *834 A Gay St., Lānaʻi City* ☎ *808/559–6265* ⌲ *Reservations not accepted* ⊟ *No credit cards* ⊗ *Closed Sun.*

$$ ✕ **Pele's Other Garden.** Colorful and small, Pele's is a deli and bistro all
ITALIAN   in one. For lunch, deli sandwiches or daily hot specials satisfy hearty appetites. At night the restaurant turns into a busy tablecloth-dining bistro, complete with soft jazz music. A nice wine list enhances an Italian-inspired menu. Start with bruschetta, then choose from a selection of pasta dishes or pizzas. Designer beers and an intimate backroom bar add to the liveliness, and sometimes impromptu entertainers

drop in. ⊠ *811 Houston St., at 8th St., Lāna'i City* ☎ *808/565–9628
or 888/764–3354* ⊕ *www.pelesothergarden.com* ⊟ *AE, DC, MC, V.*

$$$ ✕ **The Terrace.** Floor-to-ceiling glass doors open onto formal gardens and
AMERICAN lovely vistas of the mist-clad mountains at this informal spot serving
breakfast, lunch, and dinner. Try poached eggs on crab cakes to start the
day and grilled mahimahi with charred lime to finish it. A "design your
entrée" menu lets you choose sauces for your meat, poultry, or seafood
entrée as well as an appropriate side dish. The soothing sounds of the
grand piano in the Great Hall in the evening complete the ambience.
⊠ *Four Seasons Resort Lodge at Kō'ele, 1 Keōmuku Hwy., Lāna'i City*
☎ *808/565–4580* ⊕ *www.fourseasons.com/koele* ⊟ *AE, DC, MC, V.*

WHERE TO STAY

Though Lāna'i has few properties, it does have a range of price options.
Four Seasons manages both the Lodge at Kō'ele and Four Seasons
Resort Lāna'i at Mānele Bay. Although the room rates are different,
guests can partake of all the resort amenities at both properties. If you're
on a budget, consider the Hotel Lāna'i.

WHAT IT COSTS					
	¢	$	$$	$$$	$$$$
FOR TWO PEOPLE	under $100	$100–$180	$181–$260	$261–$340	over $340

Hotel prices are for two people in a double room in high season, including tax
and service. Condo price categories reflect studio and one-bedroom rates. Prices
do not include 13.42% tax.

$$$$ ⊡ **Four Seasons Resort Lāna'i at Mānele Bay.** Overlooking Hulopo'e Bay,
RESORT this elegantly decorated retreat combines Mediterranean and Asian
☾ architectural elements: elaborate life-size paintings of Chinese court
Fodor'sChoice officials, gold brocade warrior robes, and artifacts decorate the open-air
★ lobbies. Courtyard gardens separate the two-story guest-room buildings
with cool, shaded arcades. Ground-floor rooms are best—many open
right up onto a lawn overlooking Hulopo'e Beach. Though coastline
views enhance many rooms, others overlook rather dismal brushland.
Adults can indulge in Evian spritzers and massage by the pool while
keiki (children) hunt for crabs and play 'ukulele. At night, everyone
can meet for shuffleboard and darts in Hale Ahe Ahe, the swank game
room. A shuttle runs from the resort to the Lodge at Kō'ele and the
Hotel Lāna'i every half hour during high season and every hour dur-
ing low season. **Pros:** fitness center with ocean views and daily classes;
teens have their own center; friendly pool bar. **Cons:** 20 minutes to
town for shopping and restaurants; need shuttle or rental car to leave
beach area; ambience may seem formal to some. **TripAdvisor:** "secluded
and very romantic resort," "a great beach just minutes away," "dining
options are a bit limited." ⌂ *Box 631380, 1 Mānele Bay Rd., Lāna'i
City 96763* ☎ *808/565–2000 or 800/321–4666* ⊕ *www.fourseasons.
com/manelebay* ⇨ *215 rooms, 21 suites* ♿ *In-room: a/c, safe, refrigera-
tor, DVD, Internet. In-hotel: golf course, 3 restaurants, room service,*

Four Seasons Resort Lāna'i at Mānele Bay

Four Seasons Resort Lodge at Kō'ele

tennis courts, bars, children's programs (ages 5–12), pool, gym, laundry service, spa, Internet terminal ⊟ *AE, DC, MC, V.*

$$$–$$$$

RESORT

Fodor's Choice

★

🔲 **Four Seasons Resort Lodge at Kō'ele.** In the highlands edging Lāna'i City, this grand country estate exudes luxury and quiet romance. Secluded by old pines, 1½ mi of paths meander through formal gardens with a huge reflecting pond, a wedding gazebo, and an orchid greenhouse. Afternoon tea ($21 and up) is served privately beneath the high-beamed ceilings of the magnificent Great Hall. The music-room lounge is a relaxing haven after a day on the lodge's golf course or sporting-clays range. A long veranda, furnished with wicker lounge chairs, looks out over rolling green pastures toward spectacular sunsets. **Pros:** beautiful surroundings; impeccable service; walking distance to shops and restaurants in Lāna'i City. **Cons:** doesn't seem much like Hawai'i; can get chilly at 1,700-foot elevation (especially in winter); not much to do in rainy weather. **TripAdvisor:** "the most peaceful place on Earth," interesting alternative to the typical beach experience," "golf course very beautiful and challenging." ⌂ *Box 631380, 1 Keōmuku Hwy., Lāna'i City 96763* ☎ *808/565–4000 or 800/321–4666* ⊕ *www.fourseasons. com/koele* ↠ *94 rooms, 8 suites* ♿ *In-room: a/c, safe, refrigerator, Internet. In-hotel: golf course, 3 restaurants, room service, tennis courts, bar, children's programs (ages 5–12), pool, gym, laundry service, spa, bicycles* ⊟ *AE, DC, MC, V.*

$–$$

HOTEL

🔲 **Hotel Lāna'i.** Built in 1923 to house visiting pineapple executives, this inn, now part of Aqua Hotels and Resorts, was once the only accommodation on the island. The South Pacific–style rooms, with country quilts, white walls, ceiling fans, and bamboo shades, make it seem like you're staying in someone's plantation guest room. Two end rooms offer views with porches overlooking the pine trees and Lāna'i City. The restaurant, Lāna'i City Grille, has an intimate and well-stocked bar. A self-serve Continental breakfast with fresh-baked breads, offered in the foyer, is included in the rate. **Pros:** historic atmosphere; walking distance to town. **Cons:** rooms are a bit stark; noisy at times; no room phones. **TripAdvisor:** "still has the charm of Hawaiian days gone by," "friendly, accommodating staff," "walking distance to everything." ✉ *828 Lāna'i Ave., Lāna'i City* ☎ *808/565–7211 or 800/795–7211* ⊕ *www.hotellanai.com* ↠ *10 rooms, 1 cottage* ♿ *In-room: no a/c, no phone, no TV (some), Wi-Fi. In-hotel: restaurant* ⊟ *AE, MC, V.*

HAWAIIAN VOCABULARY

Although an understanding of Hawaiian is by no means required on a trip to the Aloha State, a *malihini,* or newcomer, will find plenty of opportunities to pick up a few of the local words and phrases. Traditional names and expressions are widely used in the Islands. You're likely to read or hear at least a few words each day of your stay.

With a basic understanding and some uninhibited practice, anyone can have enough command of the local tongue to ask for directions and to order from a restaurant menu. One visitor announced she would not leave until she could pronounce the name of the state fish, the *humuhumunukunukuāpua'a.*

Simplifying the learning process is the fact that the Hawaiian language contains only eight consonants—*H, K, L, M, N, P, W,* and the silent *'okina,* or glottal stop, written '—plus one or more of the five vowels. All syllables, and therefore all words, end in a vowel. Each vowel, with the exception of a few diphthongized double vowels such as *au* (pronounced "ow") or *ai* (pronounced "eye"), is pronounced separately. Thus *'Iolani* is four syllables (ee-oh-la-nee), not three (yo-la-nee). Although some Hawaiian words have only vowels, most also contain some consonants, but consonants are never doubled.

Pronunciation is simple. Pronounce *A* "ah" as father; *E* "ay" as in weigh; *I* "ee" as in marine; *O* "oh" as in no; *U* "oo" as in true.

Consonants mirror their English equivalents, with the exception of *W.* When the letter begins any syllable other than the first one in a word, it is usually pronounced as a *V. 'Awa,* the Polynesian drink, is pronounced "ava," *'ewa* is pronounced "eva."

Almost all long Hawaiian words are combinations of shorter words; they are not difficult to pronounce if you segment them. *Kalaniana'ole,* the highway running east from Honolulu, is easily understood as *Kalani ana 'ole.* Apply the standard pronunciation rules—the stress falls on the next-to-last syllable of most two- or three-syllable Hawaiian words—and Kalaniana'ole Highway is as easy to say as Main Street.

Now about that fish. Try *humu-humu nuku-nuku āpu a'a.*

The other unusual element in Hawaiian language is the *kahakō,* or macron, written as a short line (¯) placed over a vowel. Like the accent (´) in Spanish, the kahakō puts emphasis on a syllable that would normally not be stressed. The most familiar example is probably *Waikīkī.* With no macrons, the stress would fall on the middle syllable; with only one macron, on the last syllable, the stress would fall on the first and last syllables. Some words become plural with the addition of a macron, often on a syllable that would have been stressed anyway. No Hawaiian word becomes plural with the addition of an *S,* since that letter does not exist in the language.

What follows is a glossary of some of the most commonly used Hawaiian words. Hawaiian residents appreciate visitors who at least try to pick up the local language.

'a'ā: rough, crumbling lava, contrasting with *pāhoehoe,* which is smooth.

'ae: yes.

aikane: friend.

āina: land.

akamai: smart, clever, possessing savoir faire.

akua: god.

ala: a road, path, or trail.

ali'i: a Hawaiian chief, a member of the chiefly class.

aloha: love, affection, kindness; also a salutation meaning both greetings and farewell.

'ānuenue: rainbow.

'a'ole: no.

'apōpō: tomorrow.

'auwai: a ditch.

auwē: alas, woe is me!

'ehu: a red-haired Hawaiian.

'ewa: in the direction of 'Ewa plantation, west of Honolulu.

hala: the pandanus tree, whose leaves (*lau hala*) are used to make baskets and plaited mats.

hālau: school.

hale: a house.

hale pule: church, house of worship.

ha mea iki or **ha mea 'ole:** you're welcome.

hana: to work.

haole: ghost. Since the first foreigners were Caucasian, *haole* now means a Caucasian person.

hapa: a part, sometimes a half; often used as a short form of *hapa haole*, to mean a person who is part-Caucasian.

hau'oli: to rejoice. *Hau'oli Makahiki Hou* means Happy New Year. *Hau'oli lā hānau* means Happy Birthday.

heiau: an outdoor stone platform; an ancient Hawaiian place of worship.

holo: to run.

holoholo: to go for a walk, ride, or sail.

holokū: a long Hawaiian dress, somewhat fitted, with a yoke and a train. Influenced by European fashion, it was worn at court, and at least one local translates the word as "expensive mu'umu'u."

holomū: a post–World War II cross between a *holokū* and a mu'umu'u, less fitted than the former but less voluminous than the latter, and having no train.

honi: to kiss; a kiss. A phrase that some tourists may find useful, quoted from a popular hula, is *Honi Ka'ua Wikiwiki:* Kiss me quick!

honu: turtle.

ho'omalimali: flattery, a deceptive "line," bunk, baloney, hooey.

huhū: angry.

hui: a group, club, or assembly. A church may refer to its congregation as a *hui* and a social club may be called a *hui.*

hukilau: a seine; a communal fishing party in which everyone helps to drive the fish into a huge net, pull it in, and divide the catch.

hula: the dance of Hawai'i.

iki: little.

ipo: sweetheart.

ka: the. This is the definite article for most singular words; for plural nouns, the definite article is usually *nā.* Since there is no S in Hawaiian, the article may be your only clue that a noun is plural.

kahuna: a priest, doctor, or other trained person of old Hawai'i, endowed with special professional skills that often included prophecy or other supernatural powers; the plural form is kāhuna.

kai: the sea, saltwater.

kalo: the taro plant from whose root *poi* (paste) is made.

kamā'aina: literally, a child of the soil; it refers to people who were born in the Islands or have lived there for a long time.

kanaka: originally a man or humanity, it is now used to denote a male Hawaiian or part-Hawaiian, but is occasionally taken as a slur when used by non-Hawaiians. *Kanaka maoli,* originally a full-blooded Hawaiian person, is used by some native Hawaiian rights activists to embrace part-Hawaiians as well.

kāne: a man, a husband. If you see this word on a door, it's the men's room. If you see *kane* on a door, it's probably a misspelling; that is the Hawaiian name for the skin fungus tinea.

kapa: also called by its Tahitian name, *tapa,* a cloth made of beaten bark and usually dyed and stamped with a repeat design.

kapakahi: crooked, cockeyed, uneven. You've got your hat on *kapakahi.*

kapu: keep out, prohibited. This is the Hawaiian version of the more widely known Tongan word *tabu* (taboo).

kapuna: grandparent; elder.

kēia lā: today.

keiki: a child; *keikikāne* is a boy, *keikiwahine* a girl.

kona: the leeward side of the Islands, the direction (south) from which the *kona* wind and *kona* rain come.

kula: upland.

kuleana: a homestead or small plot of ground on which a family has been installed for some generations without necessarily owning it. By extension, *kuleana* is used to denote any area or department in which one has a special interest or prerogative. You'll hear it used this way: If you want to hire a surfboard, see Moki; that's his *kuleana*.

lā: sun.

lamalama: to fish with a torch.

lānai: a porch, a balcony, an outdoor living room. Almost every house in Hawai'i has one. Don't confuse this two-syllable word with the three-syllable name of the island, Lāna'i.

lani: heaven, the sky.

lau hala: the leaf of the *hala*, or pandanus tree, widely used in handicrafts.

lei: a garland of flowers.

limu: sun.

lolo: stupid.

luna: a plantation overseer or foreman.

mahalo: thank you.

makai: toward the ocean.

malihini: a newcomer to the Islands.

mana: the spiritual power that the Hawaiians believe inhabit all things and creatures.

manō: shark.

manuwahi: free, gratis.

mauka: toward the mountains.

mauna: mountain.

mele: a Hawaiian song or chant, often of epic proportions.

Mele Kalikimaka: Merry Christmas (a transliteration from the English phrase).

Menehune: a Hawaiian pixie. The *Menehune* were a legendary race of little people who accomplished prodigious work, such as building fishponds and temples in the course of a single night.

moana: the ocean.

mu'umu'u: the voluminous dress in which the missionaries enveloped Hawaiian women. Now made in bright printed cottons and silks, it is an indispensable garment. Culturally sensitive locals have embraced the Hawaiian spelling but often shorten the spoken word to "mu'u." Most English dictionaries include the spelling "muumuu."

nani: beautiful.

nui: big.

ohana: family.

'ono: delicious.

pāhoehoe: smooth, unbroken, satiny lava.

Pākē: Chinese. This *Pākē* carver makes beautiful things.

palapala: document, printed matter.

pali: a cliff, precipice.

pānini: prickly pear cactus.

paniolo: a Hawaiian cowboy, a rough transliteration of *español,* the language of the Islands' earliest cowboys.

pau: finished, done.

pilikia: trouble. The Hawaiian word is much more widely used here than its English equivalent.

puka: a hole.

pupule: crazy, like the celebrated Princess Pupule. This word has replaced its English equivalent in local usage.

pu'u: volcanic cinder cone.

waha: mouth.

wahine: a female, a woman, a wife, and a sign on the ladies' room door; the plural form is *wāhine.*

wai: freshwater, as opposed to saltwater, which is *kai.*

wailele: waterfall.

wikiwiki: to hurry, hurry up (since this is a reduplication of *wiki,* quick, neither W is pronounced as a V).

Note: Pidgin is the unofficial language of Hawai'i. It is a Creole language, with its own grammar, evolved from the mixture of English, Hawaiian, Japanese, Portuguese, and other languages spoken in 19th-century Hawai'i, and it is heard everywhere.

Travel Smart Hawai'i

GETTING HERE AND AROUND

▌ AIR TRAVEL

Flying time to Hawai'i is about 10 hours from New York, 8 hours from Chicago, and 5 hours from Los Angeles.

Hawai'i is a major destination link for flights traveling between the U.S. mainland and Asia, Australia, New Zealand, and the South Pacific. Although the Neighbor Island airports are smaller and more casual than Honolulu International, during peak times they can also be quite busy. Allot extra travel time to all airports during morning and afternoon rush-hour traffic periods.

Plan to arrive at the airport at least 60 minutes before departure for interisland flights.

Plants and plant products are subject to regulation by the Department of Agriculture, both on entering and leaving Hawai'i. Upon leaving the Islands, you'll have to have your bags X-rayed and tagged at one of the airport's agricultural inspection stations before you proceed to check-in. Pineapples and coconuts with the packer's agricultural inspection stamp pass freely; papayas must be treated, inspected, and stamped. All other fruits are banned for export to the U.S. mainland. Flowers pass except for gardenia, rose leaves, jade vine, and mauna loa. Also banned are insects, snails, soil, cotton, cacti, sugarcane, and all berry plants.

You'll have to leave dogs and other pets at home. A 120-day quarantine is imposed to keep out rabies, which is nonexistent in Hawai'i. If specific pre- and post-arrival requirements are met, animals may qualify for a 30-day or five-day-or-less quarantine.

Airline Security Issues Transportation Security Administration (⊕ www.tsa.gov).

Air Travel Resources in Hawai'i State of Hawaii Airports Division Offices

(☎ 808/836–6413 ⊕ www.hawaii.gov/dot/airports).

AIRPORTS

All of Hawai'i's major islands have their own airports, but Honolulu's International Airport is the main stopover for most domestic and international flights. From Honolulu, there are flights to the Neighbor Islands almost every half-hour from early morning until evening. In addition, some carriers now offer non-stop service directly from the mainland to Maui, Kaua'i, and the Big Island on a limited basis. No matter the island, all of Hawai'i's airports are "open-air," meaning you can enjoy those trade-wind breezes up until the moment you step on the plane.

HONOLULU/O'AHU AIRPORT

Hawai'i's major airport is Honolulu International, on O'ahu, 20 minutes (9 mi) west of Waikīkī. When traveling interisland from Honolulu, you will depart from either the interisland terminal or the commuter-airline terminal, located in two separate structures adjacent to the main overseas terminal building. The airport operates a free shuttle system between the terminals from 6 am to 10 pm every day.

Information Honolulu International Airport (HNL) (☎ 808/836–6413 ⊕ www.hawaii.gov/dot/airports).

MAUI AIRPORTS

Maui has two major airports. Kahului Airport handles major airlines and interisland flights; it's the only airport on Maui that has direct service from the mainland. If you're arriving from another island and you're staying in West Maui, you can avoid the hour drive from the Kahului Airport by flying into Kapalua–West Maui Airport, which is served by Hawaiian Air and Island Air. The tiny town of Hāna in East Maui also has an airstrip, served by Pacific

Wings and charter flights from Kahului and Kapalua. Flying here from one of the other airports is a great option if you want to avoid the long and winding drive to Hāna.

Information Kahului Airport (OGG)
(☎ 808/872-3893 ⊕ hawaii.gov/ogg).
Kapalua–West Maui Airport (JHM)
(☎ 808/669-0623 ⊕ hawaii.gov/jhm). **Hāna Airport (HNM)** (☎ 808/248-8208 ⊕ hawaii. gov/hnm).

BIG ISLAND AIRPORTS

Those flying to the Big Island of Hawai'i regularly land at one of two fields. Kona International Airport at Keāhole, on the west side, best serves Kailua-Kona, Keauhou, and the Kohala Coast. Hilo International Airport is more appropriate for those going to the east side. Waimea-Kohala Airport, called Kamuela Airport by residents, is used primarily for commuting among the Islands.

Information Hilo International Airport (ITO) (☎ 808/961-9373 ⊕ hawaii.gov/ito).
Kona International Airport at Keāhole (KOA) (☎ 808/329-3423 ⊕ hawaii.gov/koa).
Waimea-Kohala Airport (MUE) (☎ 808/887-8126 ⊕ hawaii.gov/mue).

KAUA'I AIRPORT

On Kaua'i, visitors fly into Līhu'e Airport, on the east side of the island.

Information Līhu'e Airport (LIH)
(☎ 808/274-3800 ⊕ hawaii.gov/lih).

MOLOKA'I AND LĀNA'I AIRPORTS

Moloka'i's Ho'olehua Airport is small and centrally located, as is Lāna'i Airport. Both rural airports handle a limited number of flights per day. Visitors coming from the mainland to these Islands must first stop in Maui or O'ahu and change to an interisland flight.

Information Lāna'i: Lāna'i Airport (LNY)
(☎ 808/565-7942 ⊕ hawaii.gov/lny). Moloka'i:
Ho'olehua Airport (MKK) (☎ 808/567-6361
⊕ hawaii.gov/mkk).

FLIGHTS

US Airways, American, and United fly into O'ahu, Maui, Kaua'i, and the Big Island. Alaska flies into O'ahu, Maui, Kaua'i, and the Big Island. Delta serves O'ahu (Honolulu), Maui, and the Big Island. Continental flies into Honolulu and Maui.

Hawaiian Airlines, go! Mokulele Airlines, Island Air, and Pacific Wings offer regular service between the Islands. In addition to offering very competitive rates and online specials, all have frequent-flier programs, which will entitle you to rewards and upgrades the more you fly. Be sure to compare prices offered by all the interisland carriers. If you are somewhat flexible with your dates and times for island hopping, you should have no problem getting a very affordable round-trip ticket.

There are three companies that provide charter flights between the Islands. go! Mokulele Airlines services O'ahu, Maui, and Moloka'i. Pacific Wings serves O'ahu, Lāna'i, Maui, Moloka'i, and the Big Island. Services include premiere (same-day departures on short notice), premium (24-hour notice), group, and cargo/courier. The company also has a frequent-flier program. Paragon Air offers 24-hour private charter service from any airport in Hawai'i. In business since 1980, the company prides itself on its perfect safety record. Should you want to explore Kaluapapa or other sites on Moloka'i and Maui from the air and ground, you can book tours through Paragon that depart from either the Kahului or Kapalua–West Maui airport.

Airline Contacts Alaska Airlines
(☎ 800/252-7522 ⊕ www.alaskaair.com).
American Airlines (☎ 800/433-7300
⊕ www.aa.com). **Continental Airlines**
(☎ 800/523-3273 ⊕ www.continental.com).
Delta Airlines (☎ 800/221-1212 ⊕ www.
delta.com). **United Airlines** (☎ 800/864-8331
⊕ www.united.com). **US Airways** (☎ 800/428-
4322 ⊕ www.usairways.com).

Interisland Flights go! Mokulele Airlines (☎ 888/435-9462 or ☎ 866/260-7070 ⊕ www.iflygo.com or www.mokuleleairlines.com). Hawaiian Airlines (☎ 800/367-5320 ⊕ www.hawaiianair.com). Pacific Wings (☎ 888/866-5022 ⊕ www.pacificwings.com).

BOAT TRAVEL

There is daily ferry service between Lahaina or Ma'alaea Harbor, Maui, and Mānele Bay, Lāna'i, with Expeditions Lāna'i Ferry. The 9-mi crossing costs $60 round-trip, per person, and takes 45 minutes or so, depending on ocean conditions (which can make this trip a rough one). Moloka'i Ferry offers twice daily ferry service between Lahaina, Maui, and Kaunakakai, Moloka'i. Travel time is about 90 minutes each way and the one-way fare is $56.40 per person (including taxes and fees); a book of six one-way tickets costs $260.85 (including taxes and fees). Reservations are recommended for both ferries.

Information Expeditions Lāna'i Ferry (☎ 800/695-2624 ⊕ www.go-lanai.com). Molokai Ferry (☎ 866/307-6524 ⊕ www.molokaiferry.com).

CRUISES
For more information on cruises to and around Hawai'i, see Cruising the Hawaiian Islands in Chapter 1, Experience.

BUS TRAVEL

OAHU
While bus service is not as practical on some of the Neighbor Islands, getting around by bus is a convenient and affordable option on O'ahu.

You can go all around the island or just down Kalākaua Avenue for $2.50 on Honolulu's municipal transportation system, affectionately known as TheBus. It's one of the island's best bargains. Taking TheBus in the Waikīkī and downtown Honolulu areas is especially easy, with buses making stops in Waikīkī every 15

minutes to take passengers to nearby shopping areas, such as Ala Moana Center.

You're entitled to one free transfer per fare if you ask for it when boarding. Exact change is required, and dollar bills are accepted. A four-day pass for visitors costs $25 and is available at ABC convenience stores in Waikīkī and in the Ala Moana Shopping Center. Monthly passes cost $60.

You can find privately published route booklets at most drugstores and other convenience outlets. The important route numbers for Waikīkī are 2, 4, 8, 19, 20, 58, and City Express Route B. If you venture farther afield, you can always get back on one of these.

The Waikiki Trolley has four lines and dozens of stops that allow you to design your own itinerary while riding on brass-trimmed, open-air trolleys. The Honolulu City Line (Red Line) travels between Waikīkī and the Bishop Museum and includes stops at Aloha Tower, Ala Moana, and downtown Honolulu, among others. The Ocean Coast Line (Blue Line) provides a tour of O'ahu's southeastern coastline, including Diamond Head Crater, Hanauma Bay, and Sea Life Park. The Blue Line also has an express trolley to Diamond Head that runs twice daily. The Ala Moana Shuttle Line (Pink Line) stops at Ward Warehouse, Ward Centers, and Ala Moana Shopping Center. These trolley lines depart from the DFS Galleria Waikīkī or Hilton Hawaiian Village. The Local Shopping & Dining Line (Yellow Line) starts at Ala Moana Center and stops at Ward Farmers' Market, Ward Warehouse, Ward Centers, and other shops and restaurants. A one-day, four-line ticket costs $30. Four-day tickets, also good for any of the four lines, are $52. There are discounts when ordering online, and there are often online specials including a "buy one adult 4-day pass and get a second for free."

In Waikīkī, in addition to TheBus and the Waikīkī Trolley, there also are a number of brightly painted private buses, many of which are free, that will take you to such commercial attractions as dinner cruises, garment factories, and the like.

Bus Information TheBus (📞 808/848–5555 🌐 www.thebus.org). **Waikīkī Waikiki Trolley** (📞 808/591–2561 or 800/824–8804 🌐 www.waikikitrolley.com).

MAUI

Maui Bus, operated by Roberts Hawai'i, offers 10 routes in and between various Central, South, and West Maui communities, seven days a week, including all holidays. Passengers can travel in and around Wailuku, Kahului, Lahaina, Kā'anapali, Kapalua, Kīhei, Wailea, Mā'alaea, the North Shore (Pā'ia), and Upcountry (including Pukalani, Makawao, Hāli'imaile, and Ha'ikū). The Upcountry and Ha'ikū Islander routes include a stop at Kahului Airport. The Kahului and Wailuku loops and Lahaina Villager are free; other routes are $1. Infants under two years of age, riding on the lap of an accompanying adult, travel for free.

For travelers who prefer not to rent a car, Maui Bus is a great way to go. It runs from early morning to late evening daily, and stops at most of the major towns and sightseeing destinations. And, you can't beat the price. Bus maps and schedules may be viewed online.

Bus Contact Roberts Hawai'i (📞 808/871–4838 🌐 mauicounty.gov/bus).

KAUA'I

The Kaua'i Bus operates a route from Hanalei (on the North Shore) to Kekaha (on the West Side) daily except Sunday. It runs once each hour from early morning until the evening, and provides a lunchtime shuttle around Līhu'e. The fare for adults is $2 per ride. Children six and under travel free.

Bus Contact The Kaua'i Bus (📞 808/241–6410 🌐 kauai.gov/oca/transportation).

BIG ISLAND

In Hawai'i County, the Hele-On Bus provides public transportation around the island, including a four-hour trip from

Kona to Hilo (each way) three times each day. The service is free on all routes islandwide. The county Transit Agency offers a shared-ride taxi program that provides door-to-door service. Participating companies charge as little as $2 per person for trips between one and four miles and as little as $4 per person for trips between four and nine miles (the longest trip covered by the program). Fares are paid with prepurchased vouchers. Maps, schedules, and taxi details are available online.

Bus Contact Hele-On Bus (📞 808/961–8744 🌐 www.heleonbus.org).

∎ CAR TRAVEL

Technically, the Big Island of Hawai'i is the only island you can completely circle by car, but each island offers plenty of sightseeing from its miles of roadways.

O'ahu can be circled except for the roadless west-shore area around Ka'ena Point. Elsewhere, major highways follow the shoreline and traverse the island at two points. Rush-hour traffic (6:30 to 8:30 am and 3:30 to 6 pm) can be frustrating around Honolulu and the outlying areas, as many thoroughfares allow no left turns due to contraflow lanes.

Traffic on Maui can be very bad branching out from Kahului to and from Pā'ia, Kīhei, and Lahaina. Drive here during peak hours and you'll know why local residents are calling for restrictions on development. Parking along many streets is curtailed during these times, and towing is strictly practiced. Read curbside parking signs before leaving your vehicle, even at a meter.

On Kaua'i, the 15-mi stretch of the Nāpali Coast is the only part of the island that's not accessible by car. Otherwise, one main road can get you from Barking Sands Beach on the West Side to Ha'ena on the North Shore.

Although Moloka'i and Lāna'i have fewer roadways, car rental is still worthwhile and will allow plenty of interesting sightseeing. A four-wheel-drive vehicle is best on these islands.

Asking for directions will almost always produce a helpful explanation from the locals, but you should be prepared for an Island term or two. Instead of using compass directions, remember that Hawai'i residents refer to places as being either *mauka* (toward the mountains) or *makai* (toward the ocean) from one another. Other directions depend on your location: in Honolulu, for example, people say to "go Diamond Head," which means toward that famous landmark to your East, or to "go *'ewa*," meaning in the opposite direction, toward a town in leeward (West) O'ahu. A shop on the mauka–Diamond Head corner of a street is on the mountain side of the street on the corner closest to Diamond Head. It all makes perfect sense once you get the lay of the land.

GASOLINE

Gasoline is widely available everywhere but the farthest corners of the main Islands. National chains like 76, Chevron, 7-Eleven, and Shell are ubiquitous, and accept all major credit cards right at the pump or inside the station. Prices can range from $3 to $4 for one gallon of "regular" fuel, which is sufficient for all models of rental cars. Gasoline is generally more expensive closer to the airports, where you'll need to refuel before returning your car. Neighbor Islands have higher gasoline prices than O'ahu.

Information Hawai'i Gas Prices (⊕ *www. hawaiigasprices.com*).

ROAD CONDITIONS

It's difficult to get lost in most of Hawai'i. Roads and streets, although they may challenge the visitor's tongue, are well marked; just watch out for the many one-way streets in Waikīkī. Keep an eye open for the Hawai'i Visitors and Convention Bureau's red-caped King Kamehameha signs, which mark attractions and scenic spots. Ask for a map at the car-rental counter. Free publications containing high-quality road maps can be found on all Islands.

Many of Hawai'i's roads are two-lane highways with limited shoulders—and yes, even in paradise, there is traffic, especially during the morning and afternoon rush hour. In rural areas, it's not unusual for gas stations to close early. If you see that your tank is getting low, don't take any chances; fill up when you see a station. In Hawai'i, turning right on a red light is legal, except where noted. Use caution during heavy downpours, especially if you see signs warning of falling rocks. If you're enjoying views from the road or need to study a map, pull over to the side. Remember the aloha spirit when you are driving; allow other cars to merge, don't honk (it's considered extremely rude in the Islands), leave a comfortable distance between your car and the car ahead of you; use your headlights, especially during sunrise and sunset, and use your turn signals.

ROADSIDE EMERGENCIES

If you find yourself in an emergency or accident while driving on any of the Islands, pull over if you can. If you have a cell phone with you, call the roadside assistance number on your rental car contract or AAA Help. If you find that your car has been broken into or stolen, report it immediately to your rental car company and they can assist you. If it's an emergency and someone is hurt, call 911 immediately and stay there until medical personnel arrive.

Emergency Services AAA Help (☎ *800/222–4357*).

RULES OF THE ROAD

Be sure to buckle up. Hawai'i has a strictly enforced seat-belt law for front-seat passengers. Always strap children under age four into approved child-safety seats. Children 18 and under, riding in the backseat, are also required by state law to use seat belts. The highway speed limit is usually 55 mph. In-town traffic moves from 25 to 40 mph. Jaywalking is very common, so be particularly watchful for pedestrians, especially in congested areas such as Waikīkī. Unauthorized use of a parking space reserved for persons with disabilities can net you a $150 fine. All four Hawaiian counties have implemented bans on hand-held cell phone use by drivers. If you must use the phone, pull to the side of the road to avoid a costly ticket.

CAR RENTAL

If you plan to do lots of sightseeing, it's best to rent a car. Even if all you want to do is relax at your resort, you may want to hop in the car to check out a popular restaurant. All the big national rental car agencies have locations throughout Hawai'i, but Dollar is the only company that has offices on all of the major Hawaiian Islands. There also are several local rental car companies so be sure to compare prices before you book. While in the Islands, you can rent anything from an econobox to a Ferrari. On the Big Island, Lāna'i, and Moloka'i, four-wheel-drive vehicles are recommended for exploring off the beaten path. Rates are usually better if you reserve through a rental agency's Web site. It's wise to make reservations far in advance and make sure that a confirmed reservation guarantees you a car, especially if visiting during peak seasons or for major conventions or sporting events. It's not uncommon to find several car categories sold out during major events on some of the smaller Islands.

Rates begin at about $25 to $35 a day for an economy car with air-conditioning, automatic transmission, and unlimited mileage, depending on your pickup location. This does not include the airport concession fee, general excise tax, rental vehicle surcharge, or vehicle license fee. When you reserve a car, ask about cancellation penalties and drop-off charges should you plan to pick up the car in one location and return it to another.

In Hawai'i you must be 21 years of age to rent a car and you must have a valid driver's license and a major credit card. Those under 25 will pay a daily surcharge of $15 to $25. Your unexpired mainland driver's license is valid for rental for up to 90 days. Request car seats and extras such as GPS when you make your reservation. Hawai'i's Child Restraint Law requires that all children three years and younger be in an approved child-safety seat in the backseat of a vehicle. Children ages four to seven must be seated in a rear booster seat or child restraint such as a lap and shoulder belt. Car seats and boosters range from $5 to $8 per day. Since many Island roads are two lanes, be sure to allow plenty of time to return your vehicle so that you can make your flight. Traffic can be bad during morning and afternoon rush hour. Give yourself about 2½ hours before departure time to return your vehicle.

Car Rental Resources

Automobile Associations		
U.S.: American Automobile Association	☎ 315/797–5000	⊕ www.aaa.com
	most contact with the organization is through state and regional members	
National Automobile Club	☎ 650/294–7000	⊕ www.thenac.com
	membership is open to California residents only	
Local Agencies		
AA Aloha Cars-R-Us	☎ 800/655–7989	⊕ www.hawaiicarrental.com
Advantage Rent-A-Car (O'ahu)	☎ 800/777–5500	⊕ www.advantage.com
Adventure Lâna'i EcoCentre (Lâna'i)	☎ 808/565–7373	⊕ www.adventurelanai.com
Aloha Campers (Maui)	☎ 808/281–8020	⊕ www.alohacampers.com
Discount Hawaii Car Rentals	☎ 800/292–1930	⊕ www.discounthawaiicarrental.com
Happy Campers Hawai'i (Big Island)	☎ 888/550–3918	⊕ www.happycampershawaii.com
Harper Car and Truck Rental (Big Island)	☎ 800/852–9993	⊕ www.harpershawaii.com
Hawaiian Discount Car Rentals	☎ 800/591–8605	⊕ www.hawaiidrive-o.com
Island Kine Auto Rental (Moloka'i)	☎ 877/553–5242	⊕ www.molokai-car-rental.com
JN Car and Truck Rentals (O'ahu)	☎ 800/475–7522, 808/831–2724	⊕ www.jnautomotive.com
Major Agencies		
Alamo	☎ 800/462–5266	⊕ www.alamo.com
Avis	☎ 800/331–1212	⊕ www.avis.com
Budget	☎ 800/527–0700	⊕ www.budget.com
Dollar	☎ 800/800–4000	⊕ www.dollar.com
Enterprise	☎ 800/261–7331	⊕ www.enterprise.com
Hertz	☎ 800/654–3131	⊕ www.hertz.com
National Car Rental	☎ 800/227–7368	⊕ www.nationalcar.com
Thrifty	☎ 800/847–4389	⊕ www.thrifty.com

ESSENTIALS

▮ ACCOMMODATIONS

Hawai'i truly offers something for everyone. Are you looking for a luxurious ocean-front resort loaded with amenities, an intimate two-room bed-and-breakfast tucked away in a lush rain forest, a house with a pool and incredible views for your extended family, a condominium just steps from the 18th hole, or even a campsite at a national park? You can find all these and more throughout the Islands.

Most hotels and other lodgings require you to give your credit-card details before they will confirm your reservation. If you don't feel comfortable e-mailing this information, ask if you can fax it (some places even prefer faxes). However you book, get confirmation in writing and have a copy of it handy when you check in. Be sure you understand the hotel's cancellation policy. Some places allow you to cancel without any kind of penalty—even if you prepaid to secure a discounted rate—if you cancel at least 24 hours in advance. Others require you to cancel a week in advance or penalize you the cost of one night. Small inns and bed-and-breakfasts are most likely to require you to cancel far in advance. Most hotels allow children under a certain age to stay in their parents' room at no extra charge, but others charge for them as extra adults; find out the cutoff age for discounts.

▮TIP→ Assume that hotels operate on the European Plan (EP, no meals) unless we specify that they use the Breakfast Plan (BP, with full breakfast), Continental Plan (CP, Continental breakfast), Full American Plan (FAP, all meals), Modified American Plan (MAP, breakfast and dinner) or are all-inclusive (AI, all meals and most activities).

BED-AND-BREAKFASTS

For many travelers, nothing compares to the personal service and guest interaction offered at bed-and-breakfasts. There are hundreds of bed-and-breakfasts throughout the Islands; many even invite their guests to enjoy complimentary wine tastings and activities such as lei making and basket weaving. Each island's Web site also features a listing of member B&Bs that are individually owned.

Contacts Bed and Breakfast.com (☎ 512/322–2710 or 800/462–2632 ⊕ www.bedandbreakfast.com) also sends out an online newsletter. **Bed & Breakfast Inns Online** (☎ 310/280–4363 or 800/215–7365 ⊕ www.bbonline.com). **Better Bed and Breakfasts** (⊕ www.betterbedandbreakfasts.com). **BnB Finder.com** (☎ 888/547–8226 ⊕ www.bnbfinder.com). **Hawai'i's Best Bed & Breakfasts** (☎ 808/263–3100 or 800/262–9912 ⊕ www.bestbnb.com).

CONDOMINIUM AND HOUSE RENTALS

Vacation rentals are perfect for couples, families, and friends traveling together who like the convenience of staying at a home away from home. Properties managed by individual owners can be found on online vacation rental listing directories such as CyberRentals and Vacation Rentals By Owners, as well as on the visitors bureau Web site for each island. There also are several Island-based management companies with vacation rentals.

Compare companies, as some offer Internet specials and free night stays when booking. Policies vary, but most require a minimum stay, usually greater during peak travel seasons.

Contacts CyberRentals (⊕ www.cyberrentals.com). **Vacation Rentals By Owner** (⊕ www.vrbo.com).

HOME EXCHANGES

With a direct home exchange you stay in someone else's home while they stay in yours. The exchange clubs listed below feature dozens of Hawai'i homes available for exchange. Many of the homes are on the beach or have ocean views.

Exchange Clubs **HomeExchange.com** (📧 *800/ 877–8723* ∰ *www.homeexchange.com*); $119.40 for a one-year online listing. **HomeLink International** (📧 *800/638–3841* ∰ *www.homelink.org*); $119 annual membership fee. **Intervac** (📧 *800/ 756–4663* ∰ *www.intervac-homeexchange.com*); $99.99 for one-year membership.

HOTELS
All hotels listed have private bath unless otherwise noted.

▮ COMMUNICATIONS

INTERNET
If you've brought your laptop with you to the Islands, you should have no problem connecting to the Internet. Most of the major hotels and resorts offer high-speed access in rooms and/or lobbies. You should check with your hotel in advance to confirm that access is wireless; if not, ask whether in-room cables are provided. In some cases there will be an hourly or daily charge billed to your room. If you're staying at a small inn or bed-and-breakfast without Internet access, ask the proprietor for the nearest café or coffee shop with wireless access.

Visitors can also access the Internet at any Hawai'i State Public Library. You can reserve a computer for 60 minutes once a week, via phone or walk-in. You'll need to sign up for a library card, which costs $10 for a three-month period.

Contacts Cybercafes (∰ *www.cybercafes. com*) lists more than 4,000 Internet cafés worldwide. **Hawai'i State Public Library System** (∰ *www.librarieshawaii.org*).

▮ EATING OUT

Whether it's a romantic candlelit dinner for two along the ocean or a hole-in-the-wall serving traditional Hawaiian fare like *kālua* pig, poi, *lomilomi* salmon, chicken long rice, and *pipikaula,* you'll find this and more throughout the Islands. When it comes to eating, Hawai'i has something for every taste bud and every budget. With chefs using abundant locally grown fruits and vegetables, vegetarians often have many exciting choices for their meals. And because Hawai'i is a popular destination for families, restaurants almost always have a kids' menu. When you're booking your accommodations or making a reservation at a hotel dining establishment, ask if they have free or reduced-price meals for children.

MEALS AND MEALTIMES
Breakfast is usually served from 6 or 7 am to 9:30 or 10 am.

Lunch typically runs from 11:30 am to around 1:30 or 2 pm, and will include salads, sandwiches, and lighter fare. The "plate lunch" is a favorite of many local residents, and usually consists of grilled teriyaki chicken, beef, or fish, served with two scoops of white rice and two side salads, with a big ladle of gravy over the meat and rice. The phrase "broke da mouth," often used to describe these plates, refers not only to their size, but also their tastiness.

Dinner is usually served from 5 to 9 pm and, depending on the restaurant, can be a simple or lavish affair. Stick to the chef specials if you can because they usually represent the best of the season. *Poke* (marinated raw tuna) is a local hallmark and can often be found on *pūpū* (appetizer) menus.

Meals in resort areas are pricey but often excellent. The restaurants we list are the cream of the crop in each price category.

Unless otherwise noted, the restaurants listed in this guide are open daily for lunch and dinner.

For guidelines on tipping see Tipping below.

RESERVATIONS AND DRESS
Hawai'i is decidedly casual. Aloha shirts and shorts or long pants for men and island-style dresses or casual resort wear for women are standard attire for evenings in most hotel restaurants and local

eateries. T-shirts and shorts will do the trick for breakfast and lunch.

Regardless of where you are, it's a good idea to make a reservation if you can. In some places, it's expected. We only mention reservations specifically when they are essential (there's no other way you'll ever get a table) or when they are not accepted. For popular restaurants, book as far ahead as you can (often 30 days), and reconfirm as soon as you arrive. (Large parties should always call ahead to check the reservations policy.) We mention dress only when men are required to wear a jacket or a jacket and tie.

WINES, BEER, AND SPIRITS

Hawai'i has a new generation of micro-breweries, including on-site microbreweries at many restaurants. The drinking age in Hawai'i is 21 years of age, and a photo ID must be presented to purchase alcoholic beverages. Bars are open until 2 am; venues with a cabaret license can stay open until 4 am. No matter what you might see in the local parks, drinking alcohol in public parks or on the beaches is illegal. It's also illegal to have open containers of alcohol in motor vehicles.

▮ HEALTH

Hawai'i is known as the Health State. The life expectancy here is 79 years, the longest in the nation. Balmy weather makes it easy to remain active year-round, and the low-stress aloha attitude certainly contributes to general well-being. When visiting the Islands, however, there are a few health issues to keep in mind.

The Hawai'i State Department of Health recommends that you drink 16 ounces of water per hour to avoid dehydration when hiking or spending time in the sun. Use sunblock, wear UV-reflective sunglasses, and protect your head with a visor or hat for shade. If you're not acclimated to warm, humid weather, you should allow plenty of time for rest stops and refreshments. When visiting freshwater streams, be aware of the tropical bacterial infection leptospirosis, which is spread by animal urine and carried into streams and mud. Symptoms include fever, headache, nausea, and red eyes. If left untreated, it can cause liver and kidney damage, respiratory failure, internal bleeding, and even death. To avoid this, don't swim or wade in freshwater streams or ponds if you have open sores and don't drink from any freshwater streams or ponds, especially after it has rained.

On the Islands, fog is a rare occurrence, but there can often be "vog," an airborne haze of gases released from volcanic vents on the Big Island. During certain weather conditions such as "Kona Winds," the vog can settle over the Islands and wreak havoc with respiratory and other health conditions, especially asthma or emphysema. If susceptible, stay indoors and get emergency assistance if needed.

The Islands have their share of bugs and insects that enjoy the tropical climate as much as visitors do. Most are harmless but annoying. When planning to spend time outdoors in hiking areas, wear long-sleeve clothing and pants and use mosquito repellent containing deet. In very damp places you may encounter the dreaded local centipede. On the Islands they usually come in two colors, brown and blue, and they range from the size of a worm to an 8-inch cigar. Their sting is very painful, and the reaction is similar to bee- and wasp-sting reactions. When camping, shake out your sleeping bag before climbing in, and check your shoes in the morning, as the centipedes like cozy places. If planning on hiking or traveling in remote areas, always carry a first-aid kit and appropriate medications for sting reactions.

▮ HOURS OF OPERATION

Even people in paradise have to work. Local business hours are generally weekdays 8 to 5. Banks are usually open Monday through Thursday 8:30 to 3 and until 6 on Friday. Some banks have Saturday-morning hours. Grocery and department stores, as well as shopping malls and boutiques, are open seven days a week.

Many self-serve gas stations stay open around the clock, with full-service stations usually open from around 7 am until 9 pm. U.S. post offices are open weekdays 8:30 am to 4:30 pm and Saturday 8:30 to noon. On Oʻahu, the Ala Moana post office branch is the only branch, other than the main Honolulu International Airport facility, that stays open until 4 pm on Saturday.

Most museums generally open their doors between 9 am and 10 am and stay open until 5 pm Tuesday through Saturday. Many museums operate with afternoon hours only on Sunday and close on Monday. Visitor-attraction hours vary throughout the state, but most sights are open daily with the exception of major holidays such as Christmas. Check local newspapers upon arrival for attraction hours and schedules if visiting over holiday periods. The local dailies carry a listing of "What's Open/What's Not" for those time periods.

Stores in resort areas sometimes open as early as 8, while shopping centers open at 9:30 or 10 on weekdays and Saturday, a bit later on Sunday. Bigger malls stay open until 9 pm weekdays and Saturday and close between 5 and 6 pm on Sunday. Boutiques in resort areas may stay open as late as 11.

▌ MONEY

Prices throughout this guide are given for adults. Substantially reduced fees are almost always available for children, students, and senior citizens.

ATMS AND BANKS

Automatic teller machines for easy access to cash are everywhere on the Islands. ATMs can be found in shopping centers, small convenience and grocery stores, and inside hotels and resorts, as well as outside most bank branches.

CREDIT CARDS

Throughout this guide, the following abbreviations are used: **AE**, American Express; **D**, Discover; **DC**, Diners Club; **MC**, MasterCard; and **V**, Visa.

▌ PACKING

Hawaiʻi is casual: sandals, bathing suits, and comfortable, informal clothing are the norm. In summer, synthetic slacks and shirts, although easy to care for, can be uncomfortably warm. Only a few upscale restaurants require a jacket for dinner. The aloha shirt is accepted dress in Hawaiʻi for business and most social occasions. Shorts are standard daytime attire, along with a T-shirt or polo shirt. There's no need to buy expensive sandals on the mainland—here you can get flip-flops for a couple of dollars and off-brand sandals for $20. Golfers should remember that many courses have dress codes requiring a collared shirt; call courses you're interested in for details. If you're not prepared, you can pick up appropriate clothing at resort pro shops. If you're visiting in winter or planning to visit a high-altitude area, bring a sweater or light- to medium-weight jacket. A polar fleece pullover is ideal.

One of the most important things to tuck into your suitcase is sunscreen. Hats and sunglasses offer important sun protection, too. All major hotels in Hawaiʻi provide beach towels.

You might also want to pack a light raincoat or folding umbrella, as morning rain showers are not uncommon. And on each of the island's windward coasts, it can be rainy, especially during the winter months. If you're planning on doing any exploration in rain forests or national parks, bring along a sturdy pair of hiking boots.

▌ SAFETY

Hawaiʻi is generally a safe tourist destination, but it's still wise to follow common sense safety precautions. Hotel and visitor-center staff can provide information should you decide to head out on your own to more remote areas. Rental cars are magnets for break-ins, so don't leave any valuables in the car, not even in a locked trunk. Avoid poorly lighted areas, beach parks, and isolated areas after dark as a precaution.

When hiking, stay on marked trails, no matter how alluring the temptation might be to stray. Weather conditions can cause landscapes to become muddy, slippery, and tenuous, so staying on marked trails will lessen the possibility of a fall or getting lost.

Ocean safety is of the utmost importance when visiting an island destination. Don't swim alone, and follow the international signage posted at beaches that alerts swimmers to strong currents, man-of-war jellyfish, sharp coral, high surf, sharks, and dangerous shore breaks. At coastal lookouts along cliff tops, heed the signs indicating that waves can climb over the ledges. Check with lifeguards at each beach for current conditions, and if the red flags are up, indicating swimming and surfing are not allowed, don't go in. Waters that look calm on the surface can harbor strong currents and undertows, and not a few people who were just wading have been dragged out to sea.

Be wary of those hawking "too good to be true" prices on everything from car rentals to attractions. Many of these offers are just a lure to get you in the door for time-share presentations. When handed a flier, read the fine print before you make your decision to participate.

Women traveling alone are generally safe on the Islands, but always follow the safety precautions you would use in any major destination. When booking hotels, request rooms closest to the elevator, and always keep your hotel-room door and balcony doors locked. Stay away from isolated areas after dark; camping and hiking solo are not advised. If you stay out late visiting nightclubs and bars,

use caution when exiting nightspots and returning to your lodging.

▌ TAXES

There's a 4.16% statewide sales tax on all purchases, including food (it's actually half a percent higher on O'ahu to pay for a proposed rail project). An additional hotel room tax, combined with the sales tax, equals a 13.42% rate added onto your hotel bill on most Islands, and a 13.96% rate on O'ahu. A $3-per-day road tax is also assessed on each rental vehicle.

▌ TIME

Hawai'i is on Hawaiian Standard Time, five hours behind New York, two hours behind Los Angeles, and 10 hours behind London.

When the U.S. mainland is on daylight saving time, Hawai'i is not, so add an extra hour of time difference between the Islands and U.S. mainland destinations. You may also find that things generally move more slowly here. That has nothing to do with your watch—it's just the laid-back way called Hawaiian time.

▌ TIPPING

As this is a major vacation destination and many of the people who work in the service industry rely on tips to supplement their wages, tipping is not only common, but expected.

▌ TOURS

Globus has seven Hawai'i itineraries ranging from 7 to 13 days, including an escorted cruise on Norwegian Cruise Lines' *Pride of America*. Perillo Tours offers a 7-day two-islander tour to O'ahu and Maui and a 10-day three-islander tour to O'ahu, Maui and Kaua'i. Tauck Travel and Trafalgar offer several land-based Hawai'i itineraries with plenty of free time to explore the Islands. Tauck offers an 11-night, four-island tour.

Bartender	$1 to $5 per round of drinks, depending on the number of drinks
Bellhop	$1 to $5 per bag, depending on the level of the hotel and whether you have bulky items like golf clubs, surfboards, etc.
Hotel Concierge	$5 or more, depending on the service
Hotel Doorman	$1 to $5 if s/he helps you get a cab or helps with bags, golf clubs, etc.
Hotel Maid	$2 to $5 a day, depending on the level of the hotel (either daily or at the end of your stay, in cash)
Hotel Room-Service Waiter	$1 to $2 per delivery, even if a service charge has been added
Porter/Skycap at Airport	$1 to $3 per bag
Spa Personnel	15% to 20% of the cost of your service
Taxi Driver	15% to 20%, but round up the fare to the next dollar amount
Tour Guide	10% of the cost of the tour
Valet Parking Attendant	$2 to $5, each time your car is brought to you
Waiter	15% to 20%, with 20% being the norm at high-end restaurants; nothing additional if a service charge is added to the bill

Trafalgar has 7-, 9-, 10-, and 12-night multi-island tours. If you want to stay in the Islands longer, YMT Vacations has a 15-day, four-island (O'ahu, Maui, Kaua'i, and the Big Island) tour.

EscortedHawaiiTours.com, owned and operated by Atlas Cruises & Tours, sells more than a dozen Hawai'i trips ranging from 7 to 12 nights, operated by various guided-tour companies including Globus, Tauck, and Trafalgar.

Recommended Companies Atlas Cruises & Tours (☎ 800/942–3301

⊕ www.escortedhawaiitours.com). **Globus** (☎ 866/755–8581 ⊕ www.globusjourneys. com). **Perillo Tours** (☎ 800/431–1515 ⊕ www.perillotours.com). **Tauck Travel** (☎ 800/788–7885 ⊕ www.tauck.com). **Trafalgar** (☎ 866/544–4434 ⊕ www.trafalgar.com). **YMT Vacations** (☎ 800/922–9000 ⊕ www. ymtvacations.com).

SPECIAL-INTEREST TOURS
BIRD-WATCHING

There are more than 150 species of birds that live in the Hawaiian Islands. Field Guides has a three-island (O'ahu, Kaua'i, and the Big Island), 11-day guided bird-watching trip that focuses on endemic land birds and specialty seabirds. The trip is held in the spring when bird activity is at its peak. The trip costs about $4,475 per person and includes accommodations, meals, ground transportation, interisland air, an eight-hour pelagic boat trip, and guided bird-watching excursions. Travelers must make their own travel arrangements to and from their gateway city.

Victor Emanuel Nature Tours offers two eight-night birding trips to the Islands: *Kaua'i and Hawai'i in March* and *Fall Hawai'i* to O'ahu, Kaua'i, and the Big Island. The guide for both tours is Bob Sundstrom, a skilled birder with a special interest in birdsong, who has been leading birding tours in Hawai'i and other destinations since 1989. The tour costs between $3,000 and $4,000 per person, including accommodations, meals, interisland air, ground transportation, and guided excursions. Travelers must purchase their own tickets to and from their gateway city.

Contacts Field Guides (☎ 800/728–4953 ⊕ www.fieldguides.com). **Victor Emanuel Nature Tours** (☎ 800/328–8368 ⊕ www. ventbird.com).

CULTURE
Road Scholar—formerly Elderhostel—offers several guided Hawai'i tours for older adults that provide fascinating in-depth looks into the culture, history, and beauty of the Islands. The nonprofit

educational travel organization has been leading all-inclusive learning adventures around the world since 1975. For all Road Scholar programs, travelers must purchase their own airfare if coming from outside of Hawai'i. Below are a few typical trips; the Web site shows more options.

Presented in association with Volcano Arts Center, Moloka'i Museum & Cultural Center, and Hawai'i Pacific University, *Islands of Life in the Pacific* is a 15-night, five-island, Road Scholar tour. Travelers start their tour on the Big Island where they explore Hawai'i Volcanoes National Park, Pu'uhonua O Hōnaunau, and Kaloko-Honokōhau National Historic Park. While on Maui, visitors will explore 'Īao Valley and Hāna, hike into the crater of Haleakala, discover the charms of Upcountry Maui and the towns of Olinda, Makawao, and Pā'ia, and enjoy lectures on the geology, history, and culture of the island. Following a ferry ride to Moloka'i, participants will get a tour of the Moloka'i Museum and Sugar Mill and journey into the awe-inspiring Kalaupapa National Historic Park. They'll enjoy two nights on Kaua'i with visits to Waimea Canyon and Kōke'e State Park; Kīlauea Point National Wildlife Refuge and Kīlauea Lighthouse, where thousands of endangered birds make their home; and the charming town of Hanalei, the setting for the movie *South Pacific*. The trip ends on O'ahu with visits to the USS *Arizona* and the National Memorial Cemetery of the Pacific at Punchbowl Crater. Prices for the tour start at around $4,500 per person and include accommodations, meals, ground transportation, interisland air, and ferry transportation between the Islands and all activities.

Road Scholar offers a number of other multi-island tours, including: *Tall Ship Sail Training: Sailing the Hawaiian Islands,* a six-night sailing adventure through the Hawaiian Islands aboard a 96-foot three-masted schooner; the 11-night *Paradise Adventure from Mountains to Sea* tour,

whose participants will do everything from river kayaking and hiking to surfing; the nine-night *Snorkeling Hawaii's Spectacular Marine Environments* tour, on which travelers can immerse themselves in Hawai'i's fascinating marine life; and the Oahu and Big Island *Hawaiian Water Adventure: An Intergenerational Marine Exploration* tour for children ages 10 to 14 accompanied by an adult.

Contact Road Scholar (☎ 800/454–5768 ⊕ *www.roadscholar.org*).

HIKING

Hawaii Three Island Hiker is a seven-night hiking tour to Kaua'i, the Big Island, and Maui offered by The World Outdoors. Included in the price of about $3,700 per person are accommodations, meals, interisland air between the three islands, shuttle transportation, support vehicle, professional guides, T-shirt, and water bottle. The trip is rated moderately easy to moderate. The World Outdoors has been organizing and leading adventure trips around the world for more than 20 years.

Contacts The World Outdoors (☎ 800/488–8483 ⊕ *www.theworldoutdoors.com*).

❚ TRIP INSURANCE

Comprehensive trip insurance is valuable if you're booking a very expensive or complicated trip (particularly to an isolated region like Hawai'i) or if you're booking far in advance. Comprehensive policies typically cover trip cancellation and interruption, letting you cancel or cut your trip short because of illness, or, in some cases, acts of terrorism in your destination. Such policies might also cover evacuation and medical care. Some also cover you for trip delays because of bad weather or mechanical problems as well as for lost or delayed luggage.

Another type of coverage to consider is financial default—that is, when your trip is disrupted because a tour operator, airline, or cruise line goes out of business.

Generally you must buy this when you book your trip or shortly thereafter, and it's available to you only if your operator isn't on a list of excluded companies.

Always read the fine print of your policy to make sure that you're covered for the risks that most concern you. Compare several policies to be sure you're getting the best price and range of coverage available.

Insurance Comparison Info Insure My Trip (☎ 800/487–4722 ⊕ www.insuremytrip.com). **Square Mouth** (☎ 800/240–0369 ⊕ www. squaremouth.com).

Comprehensive Insurers Access America (☎ 800/284–8300 ⊕ www.accessamerica.com). **AIG Travel Guard** (☎ 800/826–4919 ⊕ www. travelguard.com). **CSA Travel Protection** (☎ 800/873–9855 ⊕ www.csatravelprotection. com). **Travelex Insurance** (☎ 888/228–9792 ⊕ www.travelex-insurance.com). **Travel Insured International** (☎ 800/243–3174 ⊕ www.travelinsured.com).

▎VISITOR INFORMATION

Before you go, contact the Hawai'i Visitors & Convention Bureau (HVCB), ⊕ www.gohawaii.com, for general information on each island. You can request via phone or online, "Islands of Aloha," a free visitors guide with information on accommodations, transportation, sports and activities, dining, arts and entertainment, and culture. The HVCB Web site has a calendar section that allows you to see what local events are in place during the time of your stay.

You might also want to check out ⊕ www. ehawaii.gov, the state's official Web site, for information on camping, fishing licenses, and other visitor services. Each island has its own Web site as well: ⊕ www.bigisland. org (Big Island Visitors Bureau); ⊕ www. visitmaui.com (Maui County Visitors Bureau); ⊕ www.visit-oahu.com (O'ahu Visitors Bureau); ⊕ www.kauaidiscovery. com (Kaua'i Visitors Bureau); ⊕ www. visitlanai.net (Lāna'i Visitors Bureau); and

FODORS.COM CONNECTION

Before your trip, be sure to check out what other travelers are saying in Talk on ⊕ www.fodors.com.

⊕ www.molokai-hawaii.com (Moloka'i Visitors Association).

Visit ⊕ www.honoluluweekly.com for a weekly guide to the arts, entertainment, and dining in Honolulu; ⊕ www. honolulu.gov, from the City and County of Honolulu with calendar of events for Blaisdell arena and concert hall and the Royal Hawaiian Band; ⊕ www. hawaiimuseums.org, the Web site from the Hawai'i Museums Association. Be sure to check out ⊕ www.nps.gov for information on the eight parks managed by the National Park Service.

The Hawai'i Ecotourism Site, ⊕ www. alternative-hawaii.com, provides listings of everything from eco-culture events on the Islands to Hawai'i Heritage tour guides, and the Hawai'i Ecotourism Association, ⊕ www.hawaiiecotourism. org, has an online directory of more than 100 member companies offering tours and activities. The Hawai'i Department of Land and Natural Resources, ⊕ www. hawaii.gov/dlnr, has information on hiking, fishing and camping permits and licenses; on-line brochures on hiking safety and mountain and ocean preservation; as well as details on volunteer programs.

Contact Hawai'i Visitors & Convention Bureau (☎ 808/923–1811, 800/464–2924 for brochures ⊕ www.gohawaii.com).

INDEX

PHOTO CREDITS

1-2, Douglas Peebles / eStock Photo. 5, J.D.Heaton/Picture Finders/age fotostock. **Chapter 1: Experience:** 8-9, SuperStock/age fotostock. 10, J.D.Heaton/Picture Finders/age fotostock. 11 (left), Super-Stock/age fotostock. 11 (right), Big Island Visitors Bureau. 14, Kaua'i Visitors Bureau. 15, (left) Hawaii Tourism Japan (HTJ). 15 (right), Hawaii Tourism Japan (HTJ). 16, (left) Danita Delimont/Alamy. 16 (top center), Oahu Visitors Bureau. 16 (bottom center), David Schrichre/Photo Resource Hawaii. 16 (top right), Andre Nantel/Shutterstock. 16 (bottom right), Deborah Davis/Alamy. 17 (top left), Stephen Frink Collection/Alamy. 17 (bottom left), Polynesian Cultural Center. 17 (bottom center), Lee Foster/Alamy. 17 (top center), Photo Resource Hawaii/Alamy. 17 (right), Robert Coello/Kauai Visitors Bureau. 18, Skip ODonnell/iStockphoto. 19 (left), Jarvis grey/Shutterstock. 19 (right), Jess Moss. 20, James Michael Kruger/Stockphoto. 21 (left), Mark Pinkerton/iStockphoto. 21 (right), chris driscoll/Stockphoto. 22, Amy Kuck/Stockphoto. 25 (left), Luca Tettoni/viestiphoto.com. 25 (right), SuperStock/age fotostock. 26, iStockphoto. 27, James Michael Kruger/iStockphoto. 28, Ray Kachatorian/Starwood Hotels & Resorts. 29 (left), iStockphoto. 29 (right), muhawi001/Flickr. 30, Dwight Smith/iStockphoto. 31, Kauai Visitors Bureau. 32, Jose Gil/Shutterstock. 33 (left), Cheryl Casey/Shutterstock. 33 (right), Katja Govorushchenko/iStockphoto. 34, iStockphoto. 35 (left), nicole waring/iStockphoto. 35 (right), iStockphoto. 37 (left), Kuai Visitors Bureau. 37 (right), Hawaii Tourism Authority (HTA)/ Ron Dahlquist. 38, Jess Moss. 39, Jay Spooner/iStockphoto. 40, Patrick Roherty/iStockphoto. 41 (left), Jay Spooner/iStockphoto. 41 (right), Amanda Ostrom-Eckelbarger, Fodors.com member. 42, Michael Brake/iStockphoto. **Chapter 2: Oahu:** 43, Polynesian Cultural Center. 44 (center), Michael S. Nolan/age fotostock. 44 (bottom), SuperStock/age fotostock. 44 (top), Ken Ross/viestiphoto.com. 45, Oahu Visitors Bureau. 47, Rory Hanrahan. 48, Drazen Vukelic/Shutterstock. 59, J.D.Heaton/Picture Finders/age fotostock. 60, Oahu Visitors Bureau. 61 (left and center), Walter Bibikow/viestiphoto.com. 61 (right), Douglas Peebles/age fotostock. 62, Stuart Westmorland/age fotostock. 63 (left), The Royal Hawaiian. 63 (center), Atlantide S.N.C./age fotostock. 63 (right), Liane Cary/age fotostock. 69, U.S. National Archives. 71 (top), Corbis. 71 (bottom), NPS/ USS Arizona Memorial Photo Collection. 72 (left), Army Signal Corps Collection in the U.S. National Archives. 72 (right), USS Missouri Memorial Association. 73, USS Bowfin Submarine Museum & Park. 82, Polynesian Cultural Center. 80 and 85, Rory Hanrahan. 99 (left and right), Pierre Tostee. 100 and 101, ASP Tostee. 91, Val Bakhtin/iStockphoto, 92, Hawaii Tourism Authority (HTA)/Tor Johnson. 95, SuperStock/age fotostock. 102, cunninghamphotos. com. 102, cunninghamphotos.com.106, Photo Resource Hawaii/Alamy. 111, Hawaii Tourism Authority (HTA)/Tor Johnson. 113, Hawaii Tourism Authority (HTA)/Tor Johnson. 117, Hawaii Tourism Japan (HTJ). 122, Photo Resource Hawaii/Alamy. 133, Ann Cecil/Photo Resource Hawaii/Alamy. 137, Polynesian Cultural Center. 140, Robert Cravens/iStockphoto. 145 and 151, Rory Hanrahan. 167 (top and bottom), Kahala. 169 (top and bottom), Halekulani. 178 (top and bottom), Turtle Bay Resort. **Chapter 3: Maui:** 181, Michael S. Nolan/age fotostock. 182 (top), Chris Hammond/viestiphoto.com. 182 (bottom) and 183 (top), Walter Bibikow/viestiphoto.com. 183 (bottom), Douglas Peebles/age fotostock. 185, The_seeker, Fodors.com member. 189, tmdave, Fodors.com member. 198, Jay Spooner/istock. 206, kjkltz, Fodors.com member. 211, Chris Hammond/viestiphoto.com. 213, Ron Dahlquist/Maui Visitors Bureau. 214, Chris Hammond/viestiphoto.com. 217, Richard Genova/viestiphoto.com. 218, SuperStock/age fotostock. 219, Chris Hammond/viestiphoto.com. 223, Aurora Photos. 228, Robert Plotz/iStockphoto. 232, SuperStock/age fotostock. 241, SUNNYphotography.com/Alamy. 247, Michael S. Nolan/age fotostock. 250, Max Earey/Shutterstock. 254, Bart Everett/Shutterstock. 259, National Park Service. 262, Maui Visitors Bureau. 263, Photodisc. 264, Maui Visitors Bureau. 265, Brent Wong/iStockphoto. 275 (top), Linda Ching/HVCB. 275 (bottom), Sri Maiava Rusden/HVCB. 276, Michael Soo/Alamy. 277 (top), leisofhawaii.com. 277 (second from top), kellyalexanderphotography. com. 277 (third, fourth, and fifth from top), leisofhawaii.com. 277 (bottom), kellyalexanderphotography. com. 283, Hiroyuki Saita/Shutterstock. 286, LukeGordon1/Flickr. 293, RoJo Images/Shutterstock. 299, tomas del amo/Shutterstock. 305 (all), Ho'oilo House. 315 (top and bottom), Ritz Carlton Kapalua. 323 (top and bottom), Four Seasons Maui at Wailea/ Vitale, Peter. 327 (top), Old Wailuku Inn at Ulupono. 327 (bottom), Rough Guides/Alamy. **Chapter 4: The Big Island:** 333, Walter Bibikow/viestiphoto. com. 334 (top left), PhotoDisc. 334 (top right and bottom), Big Island Visitors Bureau. 337 (left and right), Hawaii's Big Island Visitor Bureau (BIVB). 346, BVIB..349, Hawaii Tourism Authority (HTA)/ Kirk Lee Aeder. 358, Russ Bishop/Alamy. 364, Nicki Geigert, Fodors.com member. 366, Big Island Visitors Bureau. 367, Russ Bishop/age fotostock. 369, Photo Resource Hawaii/Alamy. 370, Cornforth Images/Alamy. 371 (top), Big Island Visitors Bureau. 371 (bottom), Linda Robshaw/Alamy. 374, James M. House/Shutterstock. 376, Luis Castañeda/age fotostock. 385, Andre Seale/Alamy. 389, Ron Dahlquist/HVCB. 390, Pacific Stock/SuperStock. 392 (top), SPrada/iStockphoto. 392 (bottom), Gert Very/Stockphoto. 393, sweetlifephotos/Stockphoto. 395, Holly McKee, Fodors.com member. 397 and

398, Hawaii Tourism Authority HTA)/Kirk Lee Aeder. 401, Pacific Stock/SuperStock. 403, Hawaii Tourism Authority (HTA)/Kirk Lee Aeder. 405, Greg Vaughn/Alamy. 406, Pacific Stock/SuperStock. 408, Hawaii Tourism Authority (HTA)/Kirk Lee Aeder. 422-23, Kushch Dmitry/Shutterstock. 426, Hawaii Tourism Authority (HTA)/Kirk Lee Aeder. 452, Daniel Valiukas, Fodors.com member. 459 (top), Ahu Pohaku Ho'omaluhia, hawaii-island-retreat.com. 459 (bottom), Lia Watkins. 468 (all), Waianuhea. **Chapter 5: Kauai:** 475, Karl Weatherly/age fotostock. 476 (top and bottom) and 477 (left and right), Kaua'i Visitors Bureau. 479, Tor Johnson/HVCB. 483, Douglas Peebles/Aurora Photos. 489, John Sigler/iStockphoto. 491, Luca Tettoni/viestiphoto.com. 492, Kauai Visitors Bureau. 493 (bottom), Jack Jeffrey. 496, jedivader, Fodors.com member. 500-01, Hawaii Tourism Authority/Ron Dahlquist. 504, Cornforth Images/Alamy. 509, Junko Kubota/iStockphoto. 512, Fire Horse Leo/Flickr. 517, Photo Resource Hawaii/Alamy. 522, Clinton Cornell, Fodors.com member. 524, David Fleetham/Alamy. 528, jarvis gray/Shutterstock. 530, Robert Plotz/iStockphoto. 533, Mark A. Johnson/Alamy. 538-40, Douglas Peebles Photography. 541 (top right), Douglas Peebles Photography. 541 (bottom right), iStockphoto. 542 and 543 (top right), Photo Resource Hawaii/ Alamy. 543 (bottom right), SuperStock/age fotostock. 544, Mark A. Johnson / Alamy. 545 (top right), Photo Resource Hawaii/ Alamy. 545 (bottom right), Dallas & John Heaton/age fotostock. 547, Kelli Glaser, Fodors.com member. 550, Princeville Ranch Adventures. 560, HVCB. 561, Thinkstock LLC. 563, Hawaii Visitors & Convention Bureau. 572, Beach House Restaurant. 573, Beach House Restaurant. 575, Ray Kachatorian/Starwood Hotels & Resorts. 579, Polynesian Cultural Center. 580 (top and second from top), Douglas Peebles Photography. 580 (third from top), Dana Edmunds/Polynesian Cultural Center. 580 (fourth from top), Douglas Peebles Photography/Alamy. 580 (bottom), Purcell Team/Alamy. 581 (top, second from top, and third from top), HTJ/HVCB. 581 (bottom), Oahu Visitors Bureau. 595 (top and bottom left), Grand Hyatt Kauai Resort and Spa. 595 (bottom right), Douglas Peebles Photography/Alamy. **Chapter 6: Molokai:** 599, Molokai Visitors Association. 600 (top), Walter Bibikow. 600 (bottom), Michael Brake/ Stockphoto. 601 (top), Douglas Peebles/aee fotostock. 601 (bottom), Molokai Visitor Association. 602, Michael Brake/Stockphoto. 606, JS Callahan/tropicalpix/aStockphoto. 608, R. Frazier Photolibrary, Inc./Alamy. 611, Aurora Photos. 613, Walter Bibikow/viestiphoto.com. 614, IDEA. 615 and 616, Walter Bibikow/viestiphoto.com. 619, Michael Brake/iStockphoto. 620, Tony Reed/Alamy. 627, Molokai Visitors Association. 628, Greg Vaughn/Alamy. 634, JS Callahan/tropicalpix/iStockphoto. **Chapter 7: Lanai:** 637, Lanai Image Library. 638 (top), Walter Bibikow/viestiphoto.com. 638 (bottom), Lanai Image Library. 639 (top left), Michael S. Nolan/age fotostock. 639 (top right), Walter Bibikow/ viestiphoto.com. 639 (bottom), Lanai Visitors Bureau. 640, Sheldon Kralstein/iStockphoto. 644, iStockphoto. 648, Pacific Stock/SuperStock. 652, Hawaii Tourism Authority/Tor Johnson. 656, Hawaii Tourism Japan (HTJ). 665 (top and bottom), Four Seasons Lanai at Manele Bay/ Vitale, Peter.

ABOUT OUR WRITERS

Melissa Chang is a lifelong Honolulu resident and has worked in public relations for more than 20 years, representing a range of travel, retail, and restaurant clients. She is also a food reviewer for Honolulu's NonstopHonolulu.com and is a regular contributor to the *InsideOut Hawaii* magazine. For this edition she updated the Shopping, Spas, Nightlife and Entertainment, and Dining sections of the O'ahu chapter.

Nathan Eagle lives, works, and plays on Kaua'i, where he is managing editor of *The Garden Island* daily newspaper. For this edition, he updated the Lodging, Shopping, Spas, Nightlife and Entertainment, and Dining sections of the Kaua'i chapter.

Eliza Escaño-Vasquez was raised in Manila, Philippines, lived in California, and fell deeply in aloha with Maui in 2005. She is a contributing writer for the *Maui Concierge* and *Modern Luxury* Hawaii. For this edition, she updated the Water Sports and Tours, Shops and Spas, and Entertainment and Nightlife sections of the Maui chapter. Eliza currently resides on Maui with her family.

Bonnie Friedman, a native New Yorker, has made her home on Maui for almost 30 years. A well-published freelance writer, she also owns and operates Grapevine Productions. She traveled around Maui to get the latest news for the Exploring, Beaches, Where to Eat, and Where to Stay sections of the Maui chapter, adding some of her favorite places.

Trina Kudlacek splits her time between her home in Hawai'i, where she is a faculty member at the University of Hawai'i, and Italy, where she is a tour guide. For this edition she updated the Experience chapter.

Michael Levine is a reporter-host for Civil-Beat.com, a Honolulu-based local, investigative news service. He covers land use, energy policy, environmental news, and state and city government. He updated the Travel Smart chapter.

Chad Pata is a freelance writer who has spent the past 18 years falling in love with Hawai'i. Originally hailing from Georgia, he has gladly traded in Southern hospitality for the aloha spirit. He updated the Exploring, Beaches, Water Sports, Hiking, Golf, Outdoor Activities, and Lodging sections of the O'ahu chapter.

Heidi Pool is a freelance writer and personal fitness trainer who moved to Maui in 2003 after having been a frequent visitor for the previous two decades. She updated the Golf, Hiking, and Outdoor Activities section of the Maui chapter, and also the Moloka'i chapter.

Charles E. Roessler is a long-time Kaua'i resident who was an editor for the *Japan Times* and the *Buffalo News* after teaching English and journalism for 10 years. He regularly contributes to the *New York Times* as a stringer/freelancer. Charles updated the Exploring; Beaches; Water Sports and Tours; and Golf, Hiking, and Outdoor Activities sections of the Kaua'i chapter.

Joana Varawa has lived on Lāna'i for more than 30 years and is editor of the *Lāna'i Times Community Email*, an online newspaper. She has authored three books and many magazine and newspaper stories, and continues to explore her island. Her Fodor's beat for this edition was—no surprise—Lāna'i.

Katie Young Yamanaka now writes about Hawai'i for a variety of print media from her home base on the Big Island after six years prior as an editor, columnist, and writer for *MidWeek* newspaper in Honolulu, where she covered everything from arts and entertainment to island living. Her articles have also been published in the *Honolulu Star-Bulletin*, Hawaiian Airlines' *Hana Hou!* magazine, and the *Hawaii Tribune-Herald*. Katie updated the Big Island chapter.